*Handbook of Human
Performance Technology*

Handbook of Human Performance Technology

Second Edition

Improving Individual and Organizational Performance Worldwide

Harold D. Stolovitch
Erica J. Keeps
Editors

Foreword by Robert F. Mager

Jossey-Bass
Pfeiffer

San Francisco

Copyright © 1999 by the International Society for Performance Improvement
ISBN: 0-7879-1108-9

Library of Congress Cataloging-in-Publication Data
Handbook of human performance technology: improving individual and
organizational performance worldwide/Harold D. Stolovitch, Erica
J. Keeps, editors; foreword by Robert F. Mager.—2nd ed.
p.   cm.
Includes bibliographical references and indexes.
ISBN 0-7879-1108-9
1. Performance technology—Handbooks, manuals, etc.
I. Stolovitch, Harold D.   II. Keeps, Erica J.
HF5549.5.P37H36   1999
658.3'14—dc21   99-10862

Printed in the United States of America

Published by

350 Sansome Street, 5th Floor
San Francisco, California 94104–1342
(415) 433–1740; Fax (415) 433–0499
(800) 274–4434; Fax (800) 569–0443

Visit our website at: www.pfeiffer.com

Acquiring Editor: Matthew Holt
Director of Development: Kathleen Dolan Davies
Senior Production Editor: Pam Berkman
Manufacturing Supervisor: Becky Carreño
Cover Design: Lynn Knipe

Printing 10   9   8   7   6   5   4   3   2

CONTENTS

v

FOREWORD TO
THE SECOND EDITION

"Good grief!" you might exclaim as you note the number of pages in this volume. True, there are a lot of pages, but then there is an incredible amount of worthy information at your fingertips. Fortunately, you don't have to read all the pages at once—or ever.

Were you to read this entire volume at a single sitting (prudence forbid!), it might be easy to feel overwhelmed by the sheer magnitude of the information, assertions, techniques, and procedures described herein. It would be easy to be awed by the seemingly boundless domain under discussion. And, although such an impression might have merit, it would be improper to conclude that learning one's way to the level of a competent practitioner in the performance craft would represent an insurmountable task. After all, just as it can easily be verified that the world of music is huge, one need learn only a minuscule fraction of what is knowable to become a very competent musician. And, though the domain of medical knowledge is beyond the ability of any single person to master, many practitioners provide useful services to their clients. Similarly, that there is much one *could* know about Human Performance Technology (HPT) should not deter one from an effort to become worthy in the field.

One also need not conclude that a lifetime of academic preparation is required to acquire the necessary skills. Many of the useful contributors to the field developed their expertise from the experience and coaching they received from mentors more professionally senior to themselves.

Thus it would be a mistake to conclude that formal training is the only door through which to enter the exciting and personally rewarding field of HPT, or even that the HPT classroom is where one will surely observe state-of-the-art HPT practices being modeled. Unfortunately, although there are now many graduate programs teaching aspects of HPT in our universities, few of their faculty members appear as yet to be applying much if any of that technology to their own instruction. It is as if they were still operating on the belief that telling is the same as teaching, as your own academic experience may confirm. Even so, there are many competent HPT practitioners who ply their profession from inside the walls of academe, and from whom you could learn a great deal.

WHAT IS HPT?

That is the question this volume will attempt to answer. In the chapters that follow, you will read about the nature of HPT, about the breadth of human performance problems being addressed, about the techniques and procedures used to solve these problems, about some of the research from which these techniques and procedures have been derived, and about some of the results achieved. This content will provide you with a solid foundation on which to build your own expertise in the field of human performance. (Note: though this volume is called a handbook, it isn't intended to serve as a how-to-do-it manual; it is left largely for you to decide which components and techniques will be applicable to your own world.)

Because this volume does not tell a story that must be read from beginning to end, you should feel comfortable reading the chapters in any order you find interesting. To provide a framework, however, a few words about the purpose and scope of the field may be helpful.

The term *HPT* refers to a powerful collection of techniques, procedures, and approaches intended to solve problems involving human performance. What kinds of problems? All kinds of problems, in all kinds of locations, for all kinds of people. Here is just a short sampling of the types of events that might trigger application of one or more HPT interventions, much as a leaky faucet or a decision to build a new house might trigger the need for a master plumber.

"These students have a bad attitude toward school."

"Production is down in the shipping department."

"These managers aren't motivated."

"My team doesn't believe that they've been empowered."

"It's taking too long to get these people up to speed."

"We're having way too many accidents."

"These people aren't taking charge of their own health and safety."

"Our Little League coach is a bully."

"My dog piddles on the carpet."

Each of these statements describes a symptom of a problem in need of attention, and each could benefit from the magic touch of HPT. That touch might involve any number of interventions (remedies), some involving instruction, and many not. But, regardless of the solutions applied, all are intended to improve the lives of their targets. There seems to be no limit to the types of human performance problems that can be profitably addressed, or the types of human situations that can be improved.

IT WASN'T ALWAYS THUS

It wasn't always thus. In earlier days, for example, every problem (or nonproblem) was treated with a single pill—instruction. Wrong attitude? Not motivated? Not authorized to do what they already know how to do? Not to worry; instruction will solve all. Instruction was seen as the remedy for almost every problem of human performance. The mantra seemed to be "If it moves, instruct it—and hang the cost, or the time required." This was hardly surprising, since there were as yet no techniques to facilitate systematic analysis for divining the cause(s) of a problem, nor was there an array of remedies (other than instruction) with which those problems might be solved.

The analysis issue became critical for me while working out of Paris during the 1960s. Though our company intended to solve performance problems mainly through development of programmed instruction solutions, it became clear that those who alleged to have "training problems" seldom presented problems that could be solved through instruction. In more than 80 percent of these client contacts, the appropriate remedy was something other than instruction. It was this reality that forced me to begin development of a performance analysis procedure that would quickly sort through the symptoms, identify the underlying problems, and point to relevant solutions.

Two years later, while I was managing a behavioral research laboratory for a large corporation, the same reality presented itself. My research program was designed to discover how close we could come to instantaneous development of instruction. The focus, in other words, was on severely shortening development time rather than on having an impact on delivery time. But it wasn't easy to complete the experiments. No sooner would we begin a speed run intended to quickly extract relevant information from a subject matter specialist (in a closed environment especially designed for the purpose) than we would discover that we were again faced with a problem that could (and should) be solved without instruction. Again and again we were asked to solve problems allegedly requiring instruction for their solutions, and again and again we discovered that something else would work better—and faster. This exasperation intensified the development not only of a performance analysis procedure but of nontraining solutions as well.

Other common practices of the day underline how far we have progressed in just three short decades. For example, until recently there was little or no concern with assessment of the results or outcomes of the treatments (interventions, solutions, remedies) being applied. Practitioners seemed far more concerned with the processes they were promoting than with their effects on the lives of their clients and their organizations. Evaluation tools were hardly thought to be needed when it was common knowledge that if students performed poorly or not at all, it was *their* fault—not the fault of the interventionists (for example, instructors), or of the materials, or of the procedures. Whatever the source of a failure, the finger was pointed squarely at the performers—it was always the student who got the grade. And what a diabolical grading system it was. Evaluation, such as it was, consisted of a comparison of the performance of one student (usually measured by a multiple-choice test) with that of another, rather than with an objective standard. (In the industrial arena, evaluation consisted mainly in end-of-course distribution of a "happiness sheet" intended to sample the warmth of the glow left behind by the instructors.) Thus it was that faulty measuring instruments were mated with faulty evaluation practices. The mantra "70 percent is passing" permeated the entirety of our educational system as though this magical number had been handed down from the gods themselves. Thus the conspiracy required that no matter how well students performed, at least some of them would be required to consider themselves inferior.

Instructors were often "selected" through a primitive incantation such as "You've been doing such a great job in your present assignment that now you are an instructor." And presto! With that incantation, a good artist or cabinet-maker or medical technician or salesperson was instantly transformed into an untrained, inexperienced instructor. University professors were similarly selected. Those with rich or promising publication track records and a willingness to work tirelessly on committees were judged qualified to teach—and ripe for promotion. It didn't matter much whether the teaching led to learning; after all, the Holy Grail of academe was the pursuit of publication, seldom the pursuit of academic excellence. And besides, if students didn't learn, it was their own fault. These outdated and mostly ineffective practices still exist, of course, but because of professionals such as those contributing to this volume, these practices are no longer the only option, nor are they in vogue.

BRIGHT WITH PROMISE

Currently available interventions present a much wider array of possibilities, from problem analysis to the selection, creation, and application of effective remedies. And the effectiveness of correct application of the technology is truly wondrous to behold. For example, not only can learning be guaranteed to take place and production problems to be solved, but health can be improved, self-efficacy can be made to soar, lifelong phobias can permanently be cured in less than half a day, public school students can be helped to grow two full grade levels in but a few weeks, and failure-oriented lives can firmly be put onto a path toward success. These are outcomes well worth the effort and, needless to say, they provide a great source of satisfaction to those who produce them.

Not only do currently available interventions present far more available solutions than the solution of instruction, but these interventions are also available from a broadening array of sources (which is especially gratifying when you know that instruction is often contraindicated as the primary intervention for improving performance). Human performance can be improved through proper design of buildings as well as of workstations; through improvement of mental and physical health; through redesign of tools and controls; through restructuring of the physical work environment as well as through redesign of the missions, policies, and structure of the organization; and through proper design and implementation of performance aids and incentive and feedback systems, to mention only some interventions. Today, when we think of performance improvement specialists, we no longer think only of instructors but also of health professionals, human factors engineers, tool and job aid designers, and architects. All these and more can have a profound effect on the successful performance of the wide array of clients with whom one might work (for example, students, workers, managers, marriage partners, parishioners, and so forth).

Interestingly, successful application of HPT often causes difficulties for HPT practitioners when their solutions prove too powerful (read: work "too well") for the establishment or client to tolerate—when, for example, those commissioning a project aimed at improving their instructional program discover that the best solution would be to abandon existing instruction in its entirety, or when it is discovered that unacceptable worker performance is caused not by deficiencies in the workers themselves but instead by the incompetence of their managers or by obstacles imposed by organizational policies and practices (for example, "Sorry, I'm not authorized to solve your problem"). And, all too often, the very livelihood of large numbers of people—in and out of government—depends on problems *not* being solved (for example, the drug "problem").

SCIENCE-BASED

That performance technology works as well as it does is no surprise, nor is it accidental. Just as medical practice is based on medical science, HPT prides itself on being science-based, on the derivation of its basic methodology from the best available research. Though there is no shortage of pseudoscience masquerading as sound practice, or of fads notable more for the dazzle of their processes and trappings than for the results they achieve, the field of HPT is moving rapidly toward the acceptance of science as the primary guide for the creation and perfection of its techniques. Research from the field of neuroscience, for example, not only has verified that the brain is not like a computer (when was the last time you deliberately moved information from one side of your brain to the other?) but also has provided us with a growing knowledge base from which to devise even more effective ways to accomplish our mission. It is this reliance on science as one of the arbiters of our success or failure that will expand the integrity of HPT as well as the power of its techniques.

But HPT is about a great deal more than just the prudent application of scientific research to the design of HPT interventions, for what good is the science-based design of an intervention if it is brutishly applied? What good is the application of a science-based procedure if the effectiveness of the treatment is impeded by unnecessary obstacles, or if the objects of the treatments are insulted, humiliated, or robbed of their self-esteem? What good is the application of a well-researched procedure if its best effect is too small to be easily noticeable? And how much should we value science-based practices applied more for evil than for good?

As you proceed through these pages, and then through your quest to become an exemplary HPT practitioner, it might be well to remember that accomplishment of your mission begins and ends with a concern for those human beings who will be the objects of your attention—with those who are the intended targets of your interventions. It begins with a deep respect for the lives and the agendas of those people, and with a profound concern that you not only do no harm but also do not impose (inflict?) yourself and your interventions on their lives when doing nothing would work just as well.

Nonetheless, keeping one's eye firmly on the ball is essential if we are to be perceived as effective and caring professionals. This is a mission that requires a focus on the well-being, existing abilities, and agendas of those with whom we interact rather than on the satisfaction of an urge to brandish the latest technique or hardware iteration as a glittering sword with which to skewer the objects of our attention. Among other things, this means attention to the wants and needs of clients—to the "business case" underlying our activities, to the refinement of our ability to interact tactfully, to the strengthening of our ability to function with discretion, and especially to our habit of acting reliably.

Those striving to become competent practitioners of the performance craft would do well, therefore, to remember that most of those who lose their jobs do so not because of an inability to perform their jobs but because of an absence of those critical social skills that lead to their performing reliably, politely, tactfully, discreetly, and responsibly. Those who lack these skill sets will always lose out against those who possess them.

THERE'S STILL WORK TO BE DONE

As you study the material contained herein, you might begin to think that the technology is now mature, that everything has been invented, that all the techniques have been honed to perfection, and that they have been applied to all applicable areas where they might conceivably improve performance. Nothing could be further from the truth. HPT is an evolving technology, and there's still much to learn, especially about how to disseminate the fruits of the technology to those who might benefit. For example, we have yet to make much of a dent in the bureaucracy that passes the laws and makes the rules. We have yet to attract the attention of those who create the rules that make it "illegal" to teach efficiently in our schools (for example, "70 percent is passing"), who pass the laws that require us to revere process over results, and who make the rules that confine the measurement of competence to the straitjacket of the multiple-choice test. We have yet to attract the attention of those institutions that package their wisdom into time-based chunks called "credit hours" and that have yet to require anything much in the way of instructional literacy on the part of the faculty members they employ. And we have yet to make a significant impact on those government agencies whose primary criterion for certification (and recertification) of competence in critical skills consists mainly of assessing the knowledge that may be necessary for supporting desired performances (rather than the performances themselves) and of counting the number of hours the student posteriors have been glued to classroom chairs.

It is clear that opportunities stretch as far as the eye can see, and not only for development of "new and improved" components of the technology itself. Opportunities exist for the improvement of the environments where people work and the places where they live. Opportunities exist for improvement in the performance of large systems as well as for improvement in the health, well-being, and performance of a single individual, a marriage, a family, or the family dog. And if you can but contribute to the elimination of a single obstacle to effective performance, you will have made a significant contribution to the betterment of the lives you touch. Happily, the contents of this volume will help you to do exactly that.

THE REWARD IS WORTH THE EFFORT

HPT provides a set of powerful tools with which we can and do perform humane acts of value for individuals and organizations alike. As long as we remember that these tools are intended to serve as means rather than as ends in themselves—as long as we remember to measure our success by the results we achieve rather than by the glitter of our processes—we will continue to grow in value to our mission, and HPT will justifiably be perceived as an enterprise worthy of acclaim. This volume will introduce you to the practitioners and the practices through which that accomplishment can indeed be achieved.

Carefree, Arizona　　　　　　　　　　　　　　　　　　　ROBERT F. MAGER
January 1999

PREFACE

Plus ça change, plus c'est la même chose. Since the first edition of this handbook was published, in 1992, much apparently has changed. The world is far more interconnected. Communication at very low cost is at almost everyone's fingertips via the Internet and the World Wide Web. Information circles the globe at lightning speed. The economies of nations are increasingly—some would say irrevocably—interlocked. The expansion of deregulation has eliminated many barriers to international trade and cooperation.

Since 1992 we have also seen unprecedented expansion in business, record economic growth, and unnerving volatility in the marketplace. There is greater pressure to produce, in ever faster cycles and with high-quality output. Distinctions among technologies blur as communication and media become more intimately enmeshed, intertwined, and integrated. In seven short years, the world of work has shifted dramatically. Workers' loyalty has declined. New industries—in switches, routers, Web browsers, and multimedia—have emerged into the limelight. Even manufacturing, long in decline, has gone through a kind of renaissance.

And yet . . . Despite these changes, stable themes remain. The expanding presence of technology, miracles of innovation in telecommunications, the growing presence of virtual work environments—all are continuing to draw attention, but fundamental issues related to people and performance persist unresolved.

Overall, according to a national study by the Families and Work Institute, people in the United States in 1999 are working longer hours now (47.1 hrs. per week) than they were in 1992 (when the total was 43.8 per week), but until recently, and despite a sixfold increase since 1978 in technology investments, the average productivity increase per worker was steadily on the decline (an average of 2.6 percent in 1969–1973 versus an average of 0.98 percent in 1990–1996). Quality is supposed to have risen, and yet consumers' dissatisfaction is at an all-time high: more books and articles than ever before emphasize customer service as the key to business success, but customers increasingly complain of reductions in the quality of service (see, for example, the July 1998 issue of *Training* and its lead article, by Rebecca Ganzel, which focuses on this issue). Indeed, who has not been held hostage by an automated customer service system, forced to jump through endless electronic hoops while seeking, often in vain, a live person who can lend a hand?

If much has changed since the first edition of this handbook was published, many of the human performance problems that it discussed are still with us today. The topography is greatly changed; not so the basic terrain.

HUMAN PERFORMANCE TECHNOLOGY AT THE THRESHOLD OF THE NEW MILLENNIUM

The purpose of the first edition of this handbook was very specific and direct, as expressed in the Preface (p. xx): to be a "solid cornerstone" for the field of Human Performance Technology (HPT) that "clearly articulate[d], to the world and to HPT professionals, that we ha[d] arrived"—"to announce the existence of an emerging, highly relevant field, and to express what this field is about, where it comes from, what it does, and how its principles and practices can significantly benefit organizations that seek outstanding results." In large measure, this purpose still has relevance seven years later.

The emphases have shifted, however. The first edition did its job of creating a foundational document for HPT. Its numerous printings, record sales, and multiple uses, in addition to the high frequency with which the volume has been cited, attest to its success in this respect. Since its appearance, many other books about HPT have been published, virtually all of them making reference to the original handbook, a level of recognition that gratifies our initial desire to announce HPT's existence. Now, at the dawn of the twenty-first century, it can be affirmed with confidence that HPT has indeed arrived. Therefore, the second edition has been conceived with a new purpose: to bring HPT to every corner of the world. Thus the volume has a new subtitle in this edition, "Improving Individual and Organizational Performance Worldwide."

HPT has mostly developed and matured in North America and, to a somewhat lesser extent, in western Europe, but over the past several years there have been signs that HPT is beginning to take hold in Asia and Africa as well. The phenomenon of globalization has relevance beyond economics, encompassing ideas and practices that benefit all of humanity. As one example, cooperative HPT projects linking diverse countries and cultures have grown in number. As another, the International Society for Performance Improvement (ISPI), which is the professional association of HPT practitioners and scholars, has seen its membership figures soar throughout the world. It is now the professional home of more than ten thousand HPT professionals from some forty countries and sixty chapters around the globe, with its membership (comprising practitioners and academics alike) dedicated to advancing the science, technology, and professional practice of improving human performance. It is also meaningful that the publication of this edition of the handbook coincides with the convening of the first joint international conference of ISPI and the International Federation of Training and Development Organizations. At the gateway to the twenty-first century, new possibilities are opening up for HPT to assume a significant role on the world stage.

INTENDED AUDIENCES

The *Handbook of Human Performance Technology,* sponsored by ISPI and designed for a broad variety of readers and users, is first and foremost a major reference work for practicing HPT professionals. (Thus, although the handbook could be read from cover to cover, having this portion of the book's audience do so is not our primary intent.) It provides the latest thoughts of carefully selected experts on a variety of topics that, when not of core importance to HPT, are at the very least completely germane. For this major audience, the second edition of the handbook includes solid, documented material on performance improvement issues, strategies, tactics, and interventions that are immediately applicable to current projects. It also offers sage advice and perspectives on the future from experienced practitioners and reputable researchers in the field.

A second important audience is the growing number of HPT students. In the seven years between the publication of this volume's two editions, many universities have introduced HPT programs at the master's and doctoral levels, in addition to individual HPT courses that are integrated into curricula for human resources development, educational technology, and master's degree programs in business administration. Not only can this volume serve as a textbook, it provides a wealth of suggestions for research. Faculty members intrigued by HPT will also discover thought-provoking material to stimulate their own investigative activities.

This handbook has relevance to many professionals who work outside the field of HPT but who are engaged in activities relevant to the field. This group includes specialists in organizational design and development, sociotechnical experts, consultants in the area of human resources management and development, and others whose purpose is to improve human performance in the workplace. HPT processes, models, interventions, points of view, and even the very foundations of HPT should evoke a sense of both familiarity and novelty for these diverse specialists, who can expect to discover in these pages the many concerns that they share with HPT practitioners. To this group HPT offers a data-based, systemic, rigorous approach to solving human performance problems and taking advantage of opportunities for improving human performance. In other words, HPT offers these specialists a set of tools, techniques, and perspectives that can greatly enhance their professional repertoires.

Because the second edition of this handbook focuses so much on human performance, not only at work but also in a global context, managers and professionals in general should find it a rich source of information and inspiration. Most organizations depend on their human capital to produce desired results; therefore, the issues raised in this volume will have universal pertinence. Like any other field, HPT has its necessary jargon, but the editors have made a concerted effort to respect the fact that the improvement of human performance, as a universal issue, should be discussed in language with which all organizational players can feel at ease.

Finally, the handbook raises issues of importance to educators, professionals operating in social agencies, and those involved in volunteer or community work. Through their goals, all these groups express the results they desire, and all will find guidance in this volume, whether they are working in schools, hospitals, or community settings to achieve, with limited resources, ambitious objectives and the improvement of human performance.

Like the first edition, this handbook is divided into parts and chapters with appeal for specific audiences. The first two parts on foundations and on the HPT process model should be of particular interest to organizational development specialists, whose own bases reflect both similarities and dramatic differences. The writings on noninstructional interventions should provide solid material for change management specialists, as well as for sociotechnical and ergonomics professionals. Trainers and educators will find the part on instructional interventions—with its persistent theme of performance improvement—both informative and enlightening from a practical application perspective. Although the part on professional practice is directed at HPT practitioners, it deals with issues that affect all business consultants. Particularly relevant to this group are the chapters on survival tactics and return on investment. The final part of the book, which looks to the future, is highly informative for many audiences.

OVERVIEW OF THE CONTENTS

The second edition of this handbook bears a strong resemblance to the first but is also markedly different. As before, the contributors are cutting-edge thinkers and doers in the areas for which they were invited to contribute. The book itself is divided into the same six parts. The original foreword, by the late Thomas F. Gilbert, has been preserved here in memory of this prominent pioneer, but the second edition also features a second foreword, this one by the well-known and universally respected Robert F. Mager, key luminary and major foundational figure of HPT. There is a new afterword as well, by Roger Kaufman, a figure of equal importance in the development of the field.

As with the first edition, readers may wish to interact with the contents in diverse ways. Some may start at the beginning and read through to the end in order to obtain a complete and panoramic view of HPT. Others may be interested in specific parts (for example, professional practice) and may begin with all the chapters related to this specific theme. Most will probably pick and choose specific chapters of interest. The handbook has been crafted to accommodate all of these approaches. What follows is a brief overview of the part contents.

Part One, "The Fundamentals of Human Performance Technology," presents HPT as a field of both practice and academic interest. Its seven chapters take the reader from a phenomenological perspective, describing what the field is and is not, to an epistemological journey of the origins and evolution of HPT. Part One also clearly articulates why and how HPT is relevant to organizations seeking to transform themselves so that they can achieve their goals. It links professional practices to the key foundational principles embedded in general systems theory and in the behavioral and cognitive sciences. The final two chapters of this introductory part provide guidelines for planning and managing HPT projects and for dealing with the omnipresent and inevitable politics of performance improvement.

Part Two, "The General Process of Human Performance Technology," introduces the overall HPT process model and then details the major phases of its application. Its first five chapters take the reader through analysis, design, and development of high-impact interventions and then through evaluation, performance tracking (a unique approach to measurement), and implementation of performance improvement systems. The remaining three chapters lead the reader to explore a model for applying the HPT process (the Language of Work model), offer strategies and tactics for transforming training groups to performance organizations, and provide numerous examples to illustrate HPT in action.

Part Three, "Human Performance Interventions of a Noninstructional Nature," contains nine chapters, each focused on a particular way of achieving desired performance results. Major themes include a comparison of organization design; organization development and HPT; methods of analyzing and aligning corporate cultures with their missions and goals; human resource selection; motivational, feedback, and compensation systems; job aids; performance support systems; and workplace design. Together, this unique set of chapters clearly describes major approaches to improving performance without recourse to instructional interventions.

Part Four, "Human Performance Interventions of an Instructional Nature," turns its attention to the matter of learning to meet performance goals. The seven chapters take the reader from the live classroom, small-group activities, and mentoring to multimedia, structured on-the-job training, and distributed learning systems. As a group, these chapters make a clear statement about the potential and the limitations of instruction as a tool for achieving significant changes in performance.

Part Five, "The Professional Practice of Human Performance Technology," focuses on issues of HPT application in real-world settings. The eight chapters explore the skills, characteristics, and value requirements of HPT practitioners, for both the present and the future. They also discuss standards and ethics for professional practice, what the job of performance consultant means, how HPT professionals can survive and prosper in the chaos of HPT projects, and how HPT consultants can influence their clients' actions and outcomes. The final three chapters of Part Five take a hard-nosed stance with respect to HPT practice: the business side, the legal implications of what HPT practitioners and their clients do, and the necessity and means of demonstrating return on investment in performance improvement projects.

Part Six, "The Future of Human Performance Technology," looks ahead. Its five chapters explore emerging trends in HPT interventions, current and future research issues, the practice of HPT in an ever-expanding global business environment, and new frontiers for HPT.

Although the organization of this edition is similar to that of the first edition, they have marked differences in content. Fifteen of the original chapters have been replaced by new chapters on current topics of interest. Ten chapters from the first edition have been retained with respect to their content but now have new or additional authors. In fact, this edition features twenty-seven new contributors. Every chapter that was retained from the first edition has been updated and revised to include the latest changes affecting the field. Moreover, references reflecting a broader and more international range of sources have been added to each chapter. There is also a completely new team of editors, who have brought fresh viewpoints to the volume's six parts.

The most significant difference is that the current edition emphasizes the global nature of HPT, as is reflected in the new subtitle, "Improving Individual and Organizational Performance Worldwide." Given the expanding global role of HPT, this theme is a natural fit.

The *Handbook of Human Performance Technology* is sponsored by ISPI.

ACKNOWLEDGMENTS

To our associates and colleagues whose contributions appear in this handbook, we offer our sincere appreciation. Their cooperation, which in some cases involved their extensive reorganization and rewriting of their chapters in response to reviewers' comments and our own editorial suggestions, helped us produce an integrated volume. We hope that the final product measures up to their vision and expectations.

We also thank our six part editors—Peter J. Dean, Marc J. Rosenberg, Dale M. Brethower, Sharon A. Shrock, Miki M. Lane, and Diane M. Gayeski—who comprise an editorial advisory board of distinguished scholars and practitioners. They all helped at many stages of this project by commenting on the draft table of contents, offering advice about prospective authors, and reviewing draft chapters. Our appreciation goes to all of them for their conscientious dedication to making this volume both informative and enlightening.

We thank ISPI for its interest and support in sponsoring this volume. Special thanks go to Charline (Seyfer) Wells, 1997–1998 ISPI president, who initiated the project of producing a second edition and encouraged the editors to adopt an international focus; to Ann Parkman, 1998–1999 ISPI president, who continued the society's support; and to Matthew Davis, ISPI's director of publications, and Rick Baitaglia, ISPI's executive director, for the resources they organized and the autonomy they granted us to produce the handbook as we saw fit.

Great appreciation goes to Mariangela Vincenzi for the critical role she played in coordinating this project while continuing her work as manager of support services at Harold D. Stolovitch & Associates (HSA) Ltd. Special thanks to Erica Groschler, Michael J. Peters, and Gina Walker, members of the HSA management team, and to Arlene Reed, who handled many of our own business responsibilities and made it possible for us to invest the time and effort that were needed to bring this handbook to fruition.

Our thanks to Xavier Callahan, the copyeditor, for her careful, thoughtful, and efficient editing of the handbook manuscript. To Mary Garrett, who managed the production of the handbook, we offer our appreciation for her constant guidance, support, and outstanding counsel. It was a pleasure working with such fine professionals on both the first and second editions of the handbook. We were also very fortunate in working with Kathleen Dolan Davies, director of development at Jossey-Bass/Pfeiffer. She worked with us every step of the way, from the second edition's conception through to its birth.

Creating and producing a work of this magnitude is a major undertaking, one that requires constant and mutual support from one's coeditor. It is our extraordinary good fortune to be partners in marriage, business, and professional work. We are thankful for the passion that we share for our field and for the love that we have for each other. Therefore, each of us offers our heartfelt thanks for the contributions that the other has made.

Montreal, Quebec,　　　　　　　　　　　　　　　Harold D. Stolovitch
and Los Angeles, California　　　　　　　　　　　Erica J. Keeps
January 1999

THE EDITORS AND
EDITORIAL ADVISORY BOARD

THE EDITORS

Harold D. Stolovitch
President
Harold D. Stolovitch & Associates Ltd.
Montreal, Quebec, and Los Angeles, California

Erica J. Keeps
Executive Vice President
Harold D. Stolovitch & Associates Ltd.
Montreal, Quebec, and Los Angeles, California

EDITORIAL ADVISORY BOARD

Part One:
The Fundamentals of Human Performance Technology

Peter J. Dean
Senior Fellow
Wharton Ethics Program, Department of Legal Studies
The Wharton School of the University of Pennsylvania
Philadelphia, Pennsylvania

FOREWORD TO
THE FIRST EDITION

In Memoriam

Thomas F. Gilbert

1927–1995

I offer my foreword in the hope that it can help readers focus the lenses they use to look at the *Handbook of Human Performance Technology,* which promises to offer a technology—a science, really—of human performance. At least I have had a lot of time to look at this subject in many different ways.

It has been almost thirty years now since I advertised my first workshop in "performance technology." At that time, I thought I had developed a sort of scientific way to improve human performance in the workplace. And what did I think I meant by that? A philosophy professor who is a friend of mine warned me, "You have a lot of jargon and excitement—but is it really a science, or just an urge?"

"Well, I can get results in the workplace," I huffed.

"Can you ever!" he said. "You get enough people to share your excitement, and they will improve something!"

He did not know how good a point he had made. Since then, I have discovered that job performance and job management are still so primitive that almost anyone can go into the workplace and find ways to improve performance, to a noticeable extent. An urge and some common sense will do quite well as a start. And why should the "modern" workplace not be primitive? It has been around only a hundred years or so. At Ford Motors, they are still using Henry Ford's original metal-stamping machines on the assembly lines, and there were no training development departments when I was born.

According to my dictionary, a *technology* is a system that applies the best techniques and sciences to a subject matter. Theoretically, we could have a technology of just about anything—a "cosmohirsutology," for example: how the heavens determine hair growth. Or perhaps we would prefer "hirsutocosmology": the way hair growth affects the movements of the stars. No bandwagons of this nature have come along recently, simply because they do not offer much opportunity to make a difference.

Does Human Performance Technology (HPT) pose a greater opportunity? Some economists claim that the best we can do is improve human productivity by no more than 4 or 5 percent, so why waste our precious days with Human Performance Technology? But economists look at large variables that few of us have any control over, like the weather, the aging of capital plants, government regulations, and foreign competition. A technology of human performance, however, focuses on those doing and managing the jobs, and here we find much greater potential for improving performance—the PIP, or the ratio of exemplary performance to the average. I have often discussed this elsewhere, but the rule-of-thumb PIP in the workplace runs about double: the top clerks perform 50 to 75 percent better than the average, and the spread in performance grows as jobs become more complicated. The top performers can usually be emulated because they typically do things more logically and systematically than others. That is why I call them *exemplary performers*—we can make examples of them. Obviously, then, there is a great opportunity to make huge differences in human performance, and not just the 10 or 20 percent improvement that almost any enthusiastic person walking in from outside might bring.

The opportunity is there, but it cannot be seized by our just saying that we have a technology. We must really have one and practice it systematically. If we can all agree that science is at the base of a technology, what are the characteristics of science, and does our effort here share them? I will use the characteristics of science to help polish the lenses through which you will be viewing this book.

SCIENCE HAS A CLEAR SUBJECT MATTER

Every science must be clear about its subject matter, and the science of human performance has not always been. From the start, there was an easy assumption that the focal part of our subject is human behavior, and this has caused a lot of confusion.

A subject matter has two parts: a focus (the philosophers call this the *dependent variable*) and the controls (they call these the *independent variables*). A little thought must lead us to abandon human behavior as our focal, dependent variable, since we have no interest in changing human behavior for its own sake alone. In fact, the more we think about it, the more we see that our focus is on human accomplishment, the valuable output of behavior, and that behavior itself is our independent variable. This may be very obvious when we talk about it, but it is not so obvious when we set out to practice our technology. I believe that the most difficult thing we as performance technologists have to do—or have our clients do—is focus on *accomplishments* rather than on human *behavior*.

Get a group of managers or HRD specialists together and ask them to identify the accomplishments expected in some rather simple jobs. You will find that this is not an easy task. Even bus drivers are often expected to move their buses quickly from one point to another (behavior), rather than deposit customers on time at their destinations (accomplishment). Cities that measure the *behavior* of their bus drivers tend to have too many customers complaining that buses did not stop for them. The following memory aid is about the most useful device I have found to help us distinguish accomplishment from behavior:

Behavior, you take with you;
accomplishments, you leave behind.

SCIENCE SIMPLIFIES

In getting us to focus clearly on improving human accomplishments, the contributors to this book are also making an effort to contribute to Human Performance Technology. The old philosophers of science insisted that scientific contributions be evaluated using a three-edged ruler: *parsimony, elegance,* and *utility.*

Parsimony, simply put, means *stinginess.* A good scientific concept should be relieved of any unnecessary baggage. It should never use three ideas to explain something if one idea will do as well. *Elegance* means that the pieces and parts of a scientific theory fit together coherently and that the science is not a messy jumble of eclectic ideas. *Utility* simply refers to the scientific contribution's usefulness—if not in the marketplace today, then at least in the development of the science.

If we look at the early development of Newtonian physics, we see how closely it adhered to these characteristics. The same is true of Skinner's rules of reinforcement: they explain the development of behavior patterns with great parsimony, elegance, and utility.

SCIENCE IS GROUNDED IN MEASUREMENT

Acceptable evidence about performance must rely on measurement. If science does nothing else, it measures, and we must become very good at measuring human performance. As a general rule, our clients in the workplace are not good at it, and here is where we can be of especially great help. We can have our greatest effects on human performance just by measuring performance correctly and making the information available.

There are three kinds of measurement, and we need them all. *Direct measures* are measures of quality, quantity, and costs (QQC). Quality measures concern such things as accuracy, class (quality beyond mere accuracy), and novelty. Quantity measures concern rate (speed of productivity), volume (where time is not critical), and timeliness. Cost measures concern labor costs, management time, and material costs. *Comparative measures,* once we know the critical QQC dimensions, can enlighten us by showing variance on performance. True exemplary performers can begin to suggest the PIP to us—roughly, the ratio of exemplary to average performance. Where exemplary performers are not available to give us estimates of the PIP, we must use our heads and our experience and begin to estimate what is possible. *Economic measures* are also necessary; direct and comparative measures of performance are not enough. We need to translate these measures into dollar values, or stakes. What is at stake for us in improving human performance? Performance engineers should acquire basic financial skills to become adequate at estimating financial worth. For example, they should know what a load factor is. (This is the number by which we multiply a person's wage in order to obtain a rough estimate of what it costs an organization to employ the person. If a maintenance specialist in a power company earns $15 an hour, for example, it actually costs the company about three times that hourly amount to employ him—in insurance, benefits, work space, utilities, supervision, training, and so on.)

One device that performance technologists should not use in measuring performance is the instrument called the *performance appraisal.* Look closely at one, and you will see that it is largely concerned with people's estimates of such vague behavioral traits as initiative, creativity, and attitude. Even if we could estimate those traits reliably, they would be poor correlatives of actual job performance. It is much easier to measure job performance directly than it is to rate such presumed correlatives.

SCIENCE IS CAREFUL OF ITS LANGUAGE

Physicists are careful when they use words like *velocity* and *speed,* because those words mean something slightly different. In the Human Performance Technology business, we need to be careful about some of our basic terms, and we can do this without creating jargon. For example, I use the term *exemplary performer,* since *top* or *peak performers* may have come to be known as such for reasons other than their performance. (Perhaps they buttered up the boss, cheated, worked eighty hours a day, or possessed some sort of genius, but we need not try to make examples of them.) To take another example, I use the word *accomplishment* because it connotes value. (*Outputs* can be malodorous and *results* disastrous.) It would be nice if we could settle on some basic terminology that really says what we want it to say.

ENGINEERING SCIENCE FOCUSES ON ITS MOST PROMISING INDEPENDENT VARIABLES

How many kinds of things could influence our achieving exemplary standards of performance? The literature is full of suggestions, from leadership to motivation, from management sensitivity to self-esteem. I have concluded that if we make people's pay contingent on their performance, tell them clearly what we expect of them and whether they have delivered it, and give them excellent instruction when they need it, then they will mostly rise to exemplary levels of performance, no matter what else we do. If we get the three I's right—information, incentives, and instructional design—we will have done 95 percent of the job.

I am proud to have written the foreword to the *Handbook of Human Performance Technology.* As you read the book, I hope you will stay alert to how well these characteristics of a science have been considered.

Hampton, New Jersey
January 1992

THOMAS F. GILBERT

*Handbook of Human
Performance Technology*

THE FUNDAMENTALS OF HUMAN PERFORMANCE TECHNOLOGY

A field of professional practice that offers a vision of how human performance can be improved does not spring into existence instantaneously mature, as did the goddess Pallas Athena in ancient Greek mythology. Human Performance Technology (IIPT) has taken some thirty to forty years to evolve to its current state. To have matured into its present form required it to possess certain fundamental characteristics. It needed a firm foundation on which to rest. It had to be committed to a set of clear, basic principles and tenets that the majority of its scholars and professional practitioners could accept. It had to possess a vision and character that gave focus to those who called themselves HP technologists. All these fundamentals, in addition to what the field stands for, what common agreements exist concerning the goals of HPT, where the field has emerged from, and how it has evolved collectively, form the content of Part One of this handbook.

A key purpose of the chapters in Part One is to explain in unambiguous terms what HPT is, to present its origins and ancestry, and to describe significant conceptual milestones it has achieved. Another equally important purpose is to present, through clear explanations and examples, what is meant by an HPT approach to helping organizations function more productively. The chapters in Part One also have another mission: to describe the significant concepts and influences that have shaped HPT into its current form. In particular, these concepts and influences include general systems theory, behavioral psychology, and the cognitive sciences.

HPT is a professional field of practice. It is project-based in its activities, and it integrates teams of people with disparate talents for the purpose of improving human performance. This first part of the handbook acknowledges the fundamental character of HPT. The two chapters that conclude Part One deal with how HPT projects must be structured, organized, and monitored for the attainment of optimal results and with the extent to which HPT must account for the political realities of the organizations where it is applied.

The authors of the chapters included in Part One have four characteristics in common. All possess solid academic backgrounds in the behavioral and cognitive sciences. All have acted in a senior capacity as HP consultants to a variety of organizations in business and industry, government, and the public sector. All are professionally active in promoting the principles of HPT, both inside and outside of the profession. Finally, all have had international professional experience in teaching and applying HPT in work settings. The chapters in Part One make a strong statement about what is meant by HPT conceptually, philosophically, and operationally. Together, these first seven chapters create the base from which the remainder of the handbook builds.

CHAPTER ONE

What Is Human Performance Technology?

Harold D. Stolovitch
Erica J. Keeps

Human Performance Technology (HPT) is a field of practice that has evolved largely as a result of the experience, reflection, and conceptualization of professional practitioners striving to improve human performance in the workplace. It is a relatively new field that has emerged from the coalescing of principles derived from the carefully documented practice of thoughtful behavioral and cognitive psychologists, instructional technologists, training designers, organizational developers, and various human resource specialists. HPT possesses a base of research and theory but, as a rapidly evolving professional field, its practice frequently outpaces its research and theoretical foundations.

The major purpose of this chapter is to introduce HPT as a significant applied field whose aim is the achievement of valued human performance in the workplace. It presents the field as an evolving one actively seeking to define itself. It also positions HPT as a field with growing international impact. The chapter is divided into six sections. The first presents *HPT* as a term, exploring the meanings of the words that serve to identify it. The second examines HPT more epistemologically, ultimately focusing on it as a concept with a specific and unique set of critical attributes. The third explores the relevance of HPT for persons concerned with organizational effectiveness and productivity improvement around the world. The fourth presents a human performance system model and lays out key elements of human performance systems within organizational contexts. The fifth describes an operational-procedural model for engineering effective performance. The sixth raises some questions and concerns about the field and provides answers to each of these. The chapter concludes with an invitation to those whose professional interests and practices encompass organizational development, personnel management, human factors engineering, training, and human resource development to explore this emerging technology aimed at improving human performance.

HPT: THE TERM

Generally, HPT is referred to and spoken of without the word *human*. It is understood that the focus of this field of application is on human performers in organizational and work settings, although recently there have been successful efforts to apply HPT principles to societal issues. *Human* is emphasized here, and throughout the handbook, to clearly underscore this focus. For the most part, HP technologists deal with the performance of people operating within results-oriented systems.

With the world firmly embarked upon the knowledge era, there is a growing emphasis on human capital and its essential role in contributing to organizational success. The pioneer work performed by Nobel laureates Schultz (1981) and Becker (1993) has laid the foundation for other writers, such as Crawford (1991), Stewart (1997), and Edvinsson and Malone (1997), to demonstrate that it is people, with their ability to learn, who offer the greatest potential for organizational success. The value of human performance has been empirically demonstrated to yield higher rates of return than physical capital (see, for example, Lickert and Pyle, 1971; Stewart, 1994; Bradley, 1996). HPT, as a field, focuses on maximizing the valued achievements of people within work settings.

The word *performance* is one that tends to disquiet persons who first encounter it in the serious setting of the workplace. At first glance, it appears to suggest something theatrical rather than substantive, and yet *performance* is an appropriate term for this technology. The word also denotes a quantified result or a set of obtained results, just as it refers to the accomplishment, execution, or carrying out of anything ordered or undertaken, to something performed or done, to a deed, achievement, or exploit, and to the execution or accomplishment of work.

Nickols (1977, p. 14) defines performance as "the outcomes of behavior. Behavior is individual activity whereas the outcomes of behavior are the ways in which the behaving individual's environment is somehow different as a result of his or her behavior." Gilbert (1974), in the same vein, equates performance with "accomplishments" that we value. We may even link the term to Ryle's (1949) use of the term *achievements*, which he employs to describe the effects of behavior related to the term *performance*. Outcomes, accomplishments valued by the system, achievements—these are the concerns of HPT.

Recently, the word *performance, linked with the word improvement,* has gained considerable attention and respectability. *Performance improvement* has become a catchphrase connoting increased productivity, as well as greater effectiveness and efficiency from work groups. Various recent books (for example, Robinson and Robinson, 1995; Dean and Ripley, 1997; Kaufman, Thiagarajan, and MacGillis, 1997; Fuller, 1997) have made performance improvement their central focus. Improved performance is the goal, but HPT offers a scientific and systematic means for its successful attainment.

The word *technology* also often rings discordant in the ears of human resource professionals, for whom the term conjures up mechanistic images. But technology is not simply machinery; in its origins, it is essentially referred to as the scientific study of practical matters. Recently, the term has been used increasingly to denote the application of procedures derived from scientific research and professional experience to the solution of practical problems (Clark and Sugrue, 1990; Hawkridge, 1976; Stolovitch and Maurice, 1998). Joined with the word *performance* and introduced into the workplace, it suggests objectivity and systematic procedure. It implies the application of what is known about human and organizational behavior to the enhancement of accomplishments, economically and effectively, in ways that are valued within the work setting. Thus HPT is a field of endeavor that seeks to bring about changes to a system, and in such a way that the system is improved in terms of the achievements it values.

THE ORIGINS OF HPT

HPT is one of the many offspring of general systems theory as applied to organizations. It conceives of a system as "a complex grouping of human beings and machines for which there is an overall objective" (Checkland, 1972, p. 91). HP technologists take a systemic (total system) approach to performance analysis and change, as opposed to making piecemeal interventions. HP technologists adopt a holistic viewpoint with respect to performance problems. This means that they examine any given problem (defined as the gap between desired and actual states) within the broader context of the subsystem in which it is situated, within other interacting subsystems, and, ultimately, within the overall system where it occurs. This is not to suggest that, for every problem, HP technologists endlessly examine all systems, in an exercise that lasts forever. It does mean, however, that each performance problem is studied in relation to the more global aims of the setting within which it is identified. Study will extend to settings beyond the immediate site of a problem's occurrence if performance in these other settings is (or eventually will be) significantly affected by the problem or by its solution.

Although HPT is concerned with systems, it is not generally conceived of as applying to all systems. It is a technology that has application to results-driven, productivity-oriented systems (as opposed, for example, to pure social systems). This makes HPT particularly valuable to business and industry, where organizational purposes and goals are generally clearly defined. HPT need not be limited to the workplace, however. At recent conferences of the International Society for Performance Improvement (ISPI), a number of sessions have focused on HPT in the community. Roy (1998), for example, in a research study, used HPT to improve the quality of life of chronically ill elderly persons while decreasing their medical emergency and rehospitalization rates. HPT has also been applied to such social issues as workplace equity (Stolovitch, 1995). In summary, HPT is applicable to all systems in which improved performance is sought (Dean and Ripley, 1997).

HPT also has roots in behaviorism and is often seen as an offshoot of the programmed instruction movement. Ainsworth (1979, p. 3) has critically suggested that "what theory does propel performance technology is still closely allied to programmed instruction theory." HPT is concerned with measurable performance and the structuring of elements within the system to improve performance. The HP technologist must identify and analyze stimuli within the system that may affect performance, responses that are emitted, and the consequences of those responses (rewards and punishments) in order to uncover root causes of performance inadequacy. Once this is done, he or she can go on to define observable and measurable performance objectives. According to Ainsworth (p. 5), "A cornerstone of performance technology is outcome signification, discovering valid, useful performance objectives and stating them in terms that are easily understood." Suitable interventions are designed to effect change, and these are monitored and modified until the system attains the required level of measurable performance. (In Chapter Four of this volume, Dale M. Brethower discusses behaviorism's contributions to HPT at length.)

More recently, the cognitive sciences have come to have a strong influence on HPT. Work during the Industrial Age was largely manual; the current Information Age demands more mental tasks and activities from workers. If work in the twenty-first century will be primarily knowledge generation, and if knowledge processing is a mental task, then HPT must become increasingly attuned to cognitive operations and enriched by findings from the biological and neural sciences.

In the motivational arena, the trend in research is away from a focus on external rewards. Research now centers on the internal beliefs and expectations of individuals and groups with respect to external events and rewards (Solso, 1995): flattened organizations encourage the empowerment of individuals and work groups, and empowerment in turn implies a need to understand how people perceive their environment and make choices. Similarly, HPT in the past was mostly concerned with external events; today it is equally interested in the internal consequences of those events. Research evidence suggests that examination of both provides HPT with more powerful means of influencing human performance. Thus, although HPT's roots extend deep into behaviorist soil, they are currently nourished by the cognitive sciences. (See Chapter Five, by Richard E. Clark.)

An emerging influence on HPT is the field of neuroscience. Along with discoveries in the cognitive sciences, neuroscientific discoveries about humans' physiological handling of information, and about how they store and retrieve it, offer insights hidden until now from professionals seeking to influence people's performance. Alkon (1992) and other neuroscientists have delved into how memory is actually formed and what it takes to alter deeply entrenched behavior. Discoveries about brain chemistry, information-load limitations, and memory facilitators and inhibitors are just some of those that have implications for how HPT practitioners can set performance expectations and engineer change.

Economics, particularly those aspects dealing with human and intellectual capital, is also becoming a major contributory foundation of HPT. Emergence of the awareness that human capital is the key commodity for organizational (and even national) success (see, for example, Becker, 1993; Crawford, 1991), has stimulated the demand to find ways of "refining the value extraction of idle intellectual property" (Edvinsson and Malone, 1997, p. 18). Skandia, the largest insurance and financial services company in Scandinavia, has pioneered the effort to measure and report the value of corporate intellectual capital and has done so in ways that speak credibly to financial experts and shareholders. Skandia's success has attracted worldwide attention and laid a foundation from which HPT specialists can demonstrate the value-added features of human accomplishment. Stolovitch and Maurice (1998), for example, have built on the work at Skandia and created a model for calculating return on investment in training and performance. This work has resulted in the ability to report increases in the value of human capital. Moreover, Phillips (1997) has produced a comprehensive set of tools for calculating financial return on investment in programs for training and performance improvement. As further refining work is done, the relationships between HPT and economic theory and practice will naturally be enhanced.

HPT also carries with it a number of underlying assumptions. Well articulated by Geis (1986), they remain largely true today. What follows is an adaptation and updating of key points noted by Geis:

1. Human performance follows specific laws and can often be predicted and controlled.

2. Knowledge of human behavior is limited, and so HPT must rely on practical experience as well as scientific research.

3. HPT draws from many research bases while generating its own.

4. HPT is the product of a number of knowledge sources: cybernetics, behavioral psychology, communications theory, information theory, systems theory, management science, and, more recently, the cognitive sciences and neuroscience.

5. HPT is neither committed to any particular delivery system nor confined to any specific population and subject matter area. It can address any human performance, but it is most commonly applied within organizational, work, and social improvement settings.

6. HPT is empirical. It requires systematic verification of the results of both its analysis and intervention efforts.

7. HPT is evolving. Based on guiding principles, it nevertheless allows enormous scope for innovation and creativity.

8. Although HPT cannot yet pretend to have generated a firm theoretical foundation of its own, the theory- and experience-based principles that guide it are molded by empirical data that have accumulated as a result of documented, systematic practice. In many ways, HPT shares attributes with other applied fields (for example, management, organizational development, medicine, and psychiatry).

A number of authors have attempted to define HPT. Some have emphasized process and methods: "Human performance technology is a set of methods and processes for solving problems or realizing opportunities related to the performance of people. It may be applied to individuals, small groups, or large organizations" (National Society for Performance and Instruction, cited in Rosenberg, 1990, p. 46). For Benefit and Tate (1990), "[Human] Performance Technology is the systematic process of identifying opportunities for performance improvement, setting performance standards, identifying performance improvement strategies, performing cost/benefit analysis, selecting performance improvement strategies, ensuring integration with existing systems, evaluating the effectiveness of performance improvement strategies, [and] monitoring performance improvement strategies."

For Jacobs (1988, p. 67), "Human performance technology represents the use of the systems approach in a number of different forms, depending upon the problem of interest and professional activity required."

Other authors have focused on end results: "The purpose of [human] performance [technology] . . . is to increase human capital, which can be defined as the product of time and opportunity . . . technology is an orderly and sensible set of procedures for converting potential into capital" (Gilbert, 1996, pp. 11–12). For Harless (cited in Geis, 1986, p. 1), "Human performance technology is the process of selection, analysis, design, development, implementation, and evaluation of programs to most cost effectively influence human behavior and accomplishment." Rosenberg (1990, p. 46) has been more concerned with positioning: "The total performance improvement system is actually a merger of systematic performance analysis with comprehensive human resource interventions. And the science of linking the total system together is known as human performance technology." Foshay and Moller (1992) stress relevance and range in their definition of HPT, seeing it as structured primarily by the problem of human performance in the workplace and as drawing from any discipline with prescriptive power for solving human performance problems, as well as from other applied fields. For them, this range constitutes the field's uniqueness.

Dick and Wager (1995, p. 35) offer a more conceptual view of HPT as being "a fundamental commitment to the identification of organizational performance problems and the development of the most appropriate solutions." This view corresponds to Carr's definition of the field as one whose goal is "diagnosing organizational ills and improving human performance within organizations" (1995, p. 59). Perhaps Harless (1995, p. 75) best sums up the various definitions by adapting one proposed by Stolovitch and Keeps (1992). He defines HPT as "an engineering approach to attaining desired accomplishment from human performers by determining gaps in performance and designing cost-effective and efficient interventions."

No single definition is likely to elicit universal agreement, but a consensus on its critical attributes appears to have formed:

HPT is systematic. It is organized, rigorous, and applied in a methodical manner. Procedures exist that permit practitioners to identify performance gaps (problems or opportunities), characterize these in measurable or observable ways, analyze them, select suitable interventions, and apply these in a controlled and monitored manner.

HPT is systemic. It perceives identified human performance gaps as elements of systems, which in turn interface with other systems. It rejects the acceptance of apparent causes and solutions without an examination of other facets of the system. Performance is seen as the result of a number of influencing variables (selection, training, feedback, resources, management support, incentives, task interference), all of which must be analyzed before appropriate, cost-effective interventions are selected and deployed.

HPT is grounded in scientifically derived theories and the best available empirical evidence. It seeks to achieve desired human performance through means that have been derived from scientific research, when possible, or from documented evidence, when not. It rejects enthusiastic, unsubstantiated interventions that cannot demonstrate firm theoretical foundations or valid performance results. HPT is open to new ideas and potentially valuable methods or interventions. It requires, however, that these offer systematically organized evidence to support their potential value.

HPT is open to all means, methods, and media. It is not limited by a set of resources or technologies that it must apply. On the contrary, HPT is constantly searching for the most effective and efficient ways to obtain results at the least cost.

HPT is focused on achievements that human performers and the system value. It seeks bottom-line results or, as Gilbert (1996, p. 17) characterizes these valuable accomplishments, "worthy performance." The focus is not on behavior or on one-sided victories. HPT's aim is worthy performance as perceived by both the performer and the organization in which she or he performs.

HPT, therefore, is an engineering approach to attaining desired accomplishments from human performers. HP technologists are those who adopt a systems view of performance gaps, systematically analyze both gaps and systems, and design cost-effective and cost-efficient interventions that are based on analysis of data, scientific knowledge, and documented precedents, in order to close these gaps in the most desirable manner.

HPT is also a field that has attracted global attention. Thirty-seven nations are represented in ISPI's 1998 membership directory. In Italy, Germany, France, the United Kingdom, Australia, and New Zealand, the number of HPT practitioners more than doubled between 1994 and 1999, as evidenced by the growth in ISPI membership. The application of HPT is also on the rise in Latin America, the Middle East, and Asia. Two recent studies from Africa attest to the relevance of HPT in developing countries. The first, carried out in Benin (Sohoudji-Agbossou, 1997), was concerned with facilitating the adoption of innovations in the workplace. The second, conducted in Cameroon (Ngoa Nguele, 1998), was focused on structuring existing human resources to improve performance. (See also Chapter Forty-Three, by Alicia M. Rojas and Dawn E. Zintel.)

HPT'S RELEVANCE TO ORGANIZATIONS

Because HPT adopts a systems view of organizations rather than operating piecemeal, it seeks to link the actions and interventions of all the organizational elements that affect overall performance (Rummler and Brache, 1996). In this way, selection, training, feedback systems, incentives, and organizational design can all be woven into the performance fabric. The movement toward the systems approach, although still in its early stages, has accelerated over the past five years, and several authors have been influential in encouraging its growth (see, for example, Fuller, 1997; Robinson and Robinson, 1995, 1998). Thus training departments, for example, which are frequently viewed as creating costly interventions that eat into profits and remove personnel from their posts (where they are, to some degree, productive), now show up as playing a critical role in improving organizational productivity. One result is that many organizations have renamed their training departments to include the words *performance, per-*

formance support, or *performance consulting,* but the systems approach to performance improvement also offers benefits to the organization as a whole. The orderliness of the HP technology, the objectivity and care with which analysis, design, and evaluation procedures are conducted, and the linking of training, environmental redesign, feedback systems, and incentive systems to measurable performance—all these elements build credibility and buy-in for the interventions that are applied.

Because HPT has a solid scientific, theoretical, and empirical base, it approaches the solution of performance problems with a coherence that is in contrast to the more eclectic stances and procedures still adopted by most departments of training and human resource development. The foundations of the field permit proponents of HPT to undertake interventions with a uniformity of purpose, but with no sacrifice of flexibility (see Chapter Two, by Marc J. Rosenberg, William C. Coscarelli, and Cathleen Smith Hutchison). HPT seeks optimal solutions, regardless of how they look.

The HP technologist's usual first step in approaching a performance problem, before attempting any kind of solution, is to conduct a performance analysis in which discrepancies between actual and desired performance are brought to light. Therefore, HP technologists are more cause-conscious than solution-oriented. In the alternatives that they propose, rather than attempting to overcome a performance discrepancy as such, they seek primarily to eliminate the cause of the discrepancy (it generally costs less and takes less time to eliminate the cause than to construct an intervention).

The bottom-line orientation of HPT makes it particularly credible to money-conscious decision makers. Performance analysis, fundamental to HPT, includes as a basic element the assessment of the costs for alternative means of overcoming a gap between actual and desired performance—and this assessment includes the cost of *not* overcoming the gap. Gilbert (1996), the founder and, in his lifetime, probably the leading thinker of HPT, devised what he called the "performance audit" as a procedure for conducting a performance analysis. This audit is conducted in seven stages:

1. Identify accomplishments (what the system is currently accomplishing)

2. Identify requirements (what the system needs to have done)

3. Identify exemplary performance (what the realistic potential is)

4. Measure exemplary performance

5. Measure typical performance

6. Compute the potential for improving performance (the discrepancy between exemplary and typical performance)

7. Translate this potential into *stakes,* a measure of economic potential (the savings or improvement that can be expected from the attainment of exemplary performance)

What is interesting in Gilbert's approach is that poor performance is cast in a positive light, as offering great potential for economic gains. What is also noteworthy is that, if the stakes are too low, a performance discrepancy can be left unaddressed until reducing it becomes economically viable. Others (Rummler and Brache, 1988; Swanson and Gradous, 1988) have also devised procedures that address organizational concerns for cost containment; see Chapter Thirty-Nine, by Richard A. Swanson, for more on this topic.

In this vein, Langdon (1995) has introduced a new language of work that addresses human performance improvement in direct, verifiable ways (see also Chapter Thirteen of this volume, where he elaborates on this theme). Works on reengineering (for example, Hammer and Champy, 1993) and intellectual capital (for example, Stewart, 1997; Edvinsson and Malone, 1997; Organization for Economic Cooperation and Development, 1996) also focus on economic means of maximizing performance through efficient processes and appropriate investments in people.

HPT adopts a rational and logical approach to performance improvement. With its systems orientation, it requires that thorough performance analyses be conducted to identify all factors contributing to the current level of performance. It requires a precise statement of the mission(s) of the system in which improved performance is being sought. If there are incompatibilities at the level of the mission—if, for example, the organization says it wants healthy and highly productive workers but has put them to work in a poorly ventilated asbestos-fiber plant—then the performance technologist will focus first on that incompatibility. If the organization's stated mission is accepted by all, then alternative solutions to the incompatibility are elaborated and objectively analyzed for costs and benefits. The process is reasoned and data-driven. In fact, because all relevant factors must be taken into account, it is highly participative: data are collected directly and indirectly from everyone who is involved. It is an honest and transparent approach to improving performance.

HPT has a close kinship with instructional technology (see, for example, Dean and Ripley, 1998); and, in many ways, as Rosenberg (1982) has pointed out, HPT evolved from instructional technologists' realization that organizational instruction and training systems were ineffective or inappropriate if other organizational factors were not also attended to. Thus, over time, HPT has moved toward taking the general position of seeking to avoid training solutions. This position may appear disconcerting at first, but closer examination reveals the reasoning behind this stance.

Training, as already mentioned, is generally expensive. This is true because of what it costs to develop and deliver training and, even more important, because those undergoing the training must take time away from their jobs. In addition, recent studies and literature reviews (for example Baldwin and Ford, 1988; Broad and Newstrom, 1992; Ford and Weissbein, 1997) suggest that, unless many other performance interventions have also been initiated, the lasting effects of training on job performance (that is, effects that can still be observed a year after the training has occurred) will be minimal (that is, only 10 to 20 percent of what was learned will have been retained). If performance can be improved by less costly means—for example, through the elimination of incompatible tasks, the introduction of feedback systems, the designing of job aids—then a higher cost-benefit ratio can be derived. Similarly, if there are more fundamental problems (counterproductive organizational structures, for example, or incompatible organizational processes), then they must be attended to through organizational redesign or strategic realignment before investments in training can achieve the desired results. This kind of thinking, characteristic of the HPT approach, tends to elicit greater confidence from decision makers (see Chapter Three, by Geary A. Rummler). It can also more readily bring about the acquisition of adequate training funds when training actually is the optimal solution.

The language of HP technologists is highly compatible with the language of many organizational decision makers (Langdon, 1995). The approach taken by the professional using HPT is not unlike that taken by the prudent investor or company director. Systems thinking and a concern about measurable benefits are common in many industrial and economic arenas (see, for example, Stolovitch and Maurice, 1998). The professional who considers investments for solving human performance problems in terms of payback periods, costs and benefits, and return on investment is likely to find that organizational decision makers are more open to the proposed interventions.

A HUMAN PERFORMANCE SYSTEM

As mentioned several times before in this chapter, HPT seeks to improve the performance of organizations and the people responsible for achieving desired results. It is useful, therefore, to conceptualize organizations from the perspective of a human performance system. Figure 1.1 presents a human performance system model. In brief, as shown in the figure, the *external environment* presents organizations with *opportunities, pressures, events,* and *resources.* These stimulate the organization to generate *goals and objectives* (its responses to the environment) and *internal requirements* (a set of actions that will allow it to use the opportunities and meet the pressures from the external environment). One set of internal requirements is specifically related to *human performance.* These requirements, once articulated, trigger a number of *behaviors* that result in *accomplishments.* Behaviors and accomplishments are strongly *influenced* by both the external environment (what is happening "out there" and how the organization has decided to respond) and the internal *organizational environment* (composed of many elements). Accomplishments may or may not suffice; therefore, they must be subject to *verification* and either accepted as being *aligned* with the business requirements (a criterion relevant even for nonbusiness-oriented systems) or judged as not being so aligned and as needing modification, in which case the result is usually some alteration in behaviors, which in turn will result in a change in the organization's accomplishments. Analysis of the system, along with a diagnosis of the changes required and the design of suitable interventions, drives the HPT practitioner to engineer the solution that will entail the lowest cost, the fastest turnaround, and the greatest payback.

Figure 1.1. A Conceptual Model for a Human Performance System.

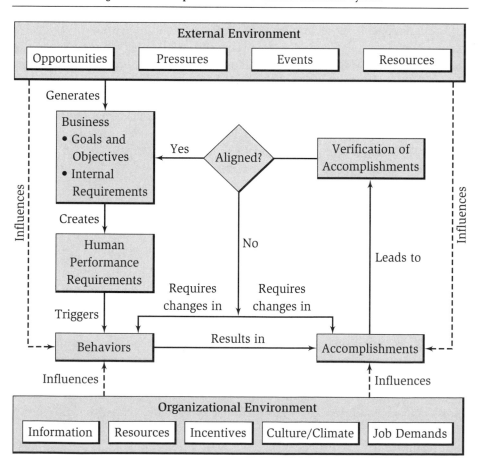

ENGINEERING EFFECTIVE PERFORMANCE

A second, more operational model for engineering effective performance on the basis of HPT principles is represented in Figure 1.2. Taken together, the two models—the first conceptual, and the second operational—sum up the terrain and the tasks of the HP technologist.

In the model depicted in Figure 1.2, the first step toward the achievement of the desired results is to *identify the business requirements* clearly. The HPT practitioner can accomplish this step by being *proactive* in seeking out and probing for opportunities to improve business performance, anticipating the performance requirements that have been created by business initiatives (sometimes even before management has fully articulated them) or surveying business units for changed responses to the external environment. More commonly, however, the requirements come seeking the practitioner, who responds in a *reactive* but systematic way. In either case, the practitioner is led, in the second step, to *identify performance requirements.* These requirements may be of a *legal/regulatory* nature, or they may be related to *new skills and knowledge* or to some *performance improvement* that has already taken place (Rossett, 1987). The third step requires the practitioner to precisely *specify current performance,* which will include not only *exemplary* performance but also *deficient* and *related* behaviors and accomplishments. The identified requirements and the specification of current performance allow the practitioner, in the fourth step, *to define performance gaps* in terms of their *magnitude* (size, pervasiveness), *value* to the system, and/or degree of *urgency.* The fifth step is one that demands considerable investigative capability and experience, as well as the tools and techniques that can be used to *specify performance-gap factors* that have (as listed in the figure) direct effects, as causes, or indirect effects, as constraints. These first five steps bring the practitioner to the point of being able, in the sixth step, to *identify potential interventions,* which may be *environmental* in nature, may involve *skills and knowledge,* and may involve *incentives and motivation.* The seventh step is to *select the performance interventions,* keeping in mind their *appropriateness* (in terms of both the *internal* and the *external* environment), their *economics,* their *feasibility* (where the given system's resources and constraints are concerned), and their *acceptability* to the organization and its human performers. The eighth step is to *develop the performance interventions* in terms of their *design,* their actual *creation,* and the *verification* of their effectiveness. In step nine, the practitioner will *implement the performance interventions* that have been selected and, in the tenth and final step, will *monitor and maintain the performance interventions.*

Figure 1.2. An Operational Model for Engineering Effective Human Performance.

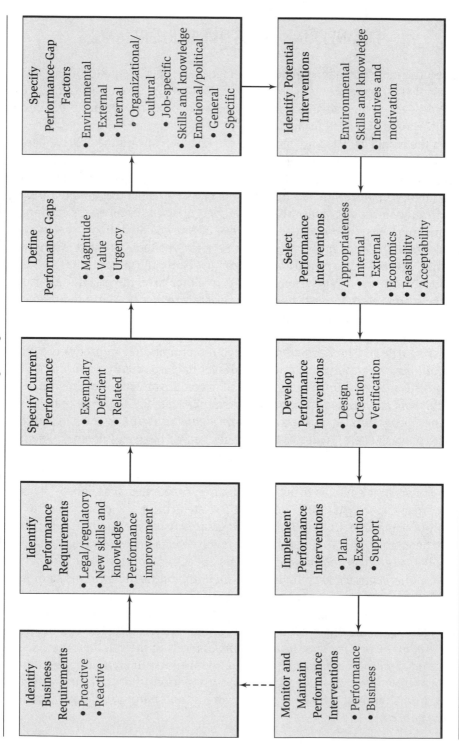

QUESTIONS AND CONCERNS ABOUT HPT

As a field, HPT is still relatively unknown to the majority of human resource professionals, organizational developers, and corporate senior managers. When they are introduced to HPT, they are bound to have questions and concerns raised by its nature and approach. What follows is an attempt to respond to these issues.

Why does HPT appear to employ a specialized and somewhat mysterious jargon? It is true that some HP technologists have created specialized terms to refer to specific concepts or procedures that they have invented, but the general vocabulary of HPT has mostly been drawn from other fields: economics, behavioral and cognitive psychology, management science, education, engineering, and ergonomics. Given HPT's close relationship to instructional technology, many of the terms and tools utilized by professionals in this field and in the others just mentioned have also become part of HP technologists' verbal repertoire, and, certainly in recent years, systems analysis, computer technology, and human factors engineering have had strong effects on the HPT field and consequently on its vocabulary. The growing interest in the tools and techniques of measurement and evaluation, quantitative business analysis, artificial intelligence, telecommunications, and information-systems technology has also left its imprint. HPT is not so much a jargon-generating field as one that is perpetually going through a process of assimilating other fields' technical vocabularies as it seeks richer resources for helping to improve human (and hence system) performance.

As a "technology," is HPT mechanistic and dehumanizing? HPT is essentially concerned with the kinds of human performance that are valued by individual performers and organizations. It is not a field of social engineering. Its practice is rational, not ideological. HP technologists are very aware of the individual nature of human motivation, goal orientation, and value systems. Where these are defined as essential to the mission or missions of a system, they are treated with great care. Where they are not so defined, they nevertheless remain of critical importance when changes are prescribed for a system. If they are to be effective, efforts to improve any system that relies on human performance must maintain the strongest respect for the human being. Organizations in which productivity is high and quality is maintained are those where morale, employees' self-esteem, and workers' satisfaction are also at a high level. It is not axiomatic that what is good for the company is necessarily evil for employees. Excellent performance is often translated into greater job security, higher salaries, and employees' overall high level of interest and satisfaction in their work. Pride of performance in the workplace is still an important value for most workers, although its value has been lessened as a result of the poorly conceived downsizing initiatives undertaken by many companies during the 1990s. HPT, far from being mechanistic and dehumanizing, attempts to affect systems in ways that foster both worthy performance and individual self-worth.

Is HPT intolerant of other approaches to achieving desired human performance? HPT requires (1) clear definition of a system's mission and its strategic plan, (2) measurable indicators of actual and desired outcomes, and (3) consideration of the relationship between costs and projected benefits for each intervention (see, for example, Stolovitch and Keeps, 1997). Therefore, HPT practitioners manifest intolerance only toward those who disregard the results that a system must produce, or who make arbitrary decisions that cannot be supported by a clear base of data. Similarly, HP technologists become uncomfortable when they are faced with interventions that appear to spring more from the ideologies and interests of their proponents than from the documented needs of those performers whom the workplace has also designated as relevant to the organization's overall mission. Nevertheless, HPT is far from being closed or intolerant or from considering itself complete. It has consistently remained open to new technologies and theory bases. Many HP technologists follow, with interest, the developments in brain research, electronic performance-support systems (EPSS), and knowledge management, to name only a few such areas (see Chapter Twenty-Three, by Steven W. Villachica and Deborah L. Stone, and Chapter Forty, by Dale C. Brandenburg and Carl Binder). HPT remains cautious, however, about accepting approaches or innovations that are still lacking in well-documented empirical evidence of their effectiveness.

Is HPT too enamored of new information and new communication technologies, or is it too ignorant of their capabilities? As the twenty-first century opens, virtually every facet of every organization will be affected by an ever-growing array of increasingly sophisticated technologies. The HP technologist cannot ignore the proliferation of electronic communication devices, performance-support tools, and work-enhancing systems. There is perpetual enthusiasm for exploiting technology, which requires deep knowledge of electronic hardware and software advances. How can HP technologists keep up? How can they separate valid potential for performance improvement from expensive but unproductive ventures? The answer is simple yet difficult to apply: HPT is committed to systemic thinking, to data-based analysis, and to rational decision making. Its goal is worthy performance, in which value is compared to costs before an intervention is selected. The HP technologist's role is to hone analytical and evaluative capabilities while staying informed about advances in technology. Therefore, the experienced HP technologist characteristically avoids becoming enamored of any solution and constantly remains aware of all potential prospects for performance enhancement. This form of equilibrium is an essential commitment of the HP technologist and is a major form of the value added by HPT.

Is HPT too management-biased because it is driven by results? It is usually management that brings the HP technologist into contact with a performance gap. Therefore, the HP technologist must report back to management. But data on performance (or lack of performance) are collected from the actual performers for whom interventions are designed. Job aids, feedback systems, training courses, and incentive systems cannot possibly be effective if the characteristics and value systems of these performers are not taken fully into account (see Tosti and O'Brien, 1979; Stolovitch and Lane, 1989). In the workplace, the performance valued by the employer must be the prime consideration, but this does not exclude careful analysis of employees' goals and motivations. The ideal intervention, which often results in increased freedom and initiative for the performer, as well as in greater sensitivity to personal style, is one that equally favors management and the individual employee or performer. Recently, HP technologists have turned their attention to the community at large. For example, as cited earlier, Roy (1998) applied an HPT model to improving the quality of life for the elderly. Other HP technologists have used HPT to improve the performance of volunteers in charitable mission–related work or the nature of human interactions in a mental health facility. HPT is driven by results, but this does not imply a bias in favor of management; rather, the overall goal of HPT is to achieve accomplishments that are valued by everyone in the targeted system.

Is HPT essentially an American and western European phenomenon? Much of HPT has roots in Western science, but the field is not narrowly focused on any one particular culture or ideology. It is true that HPT does seek to improve performance, and this implies a commitment to continuous progress, but this value is not limited to the United States and Europe. Globalization has opened almost all cultures and countries to international scrutiny. The Internet creates a world of instantaneous communication. HPT is open to all means of helping to achieve the ends that individual systems value; it imposes no restrictions on what constitutes a valued end within the dictates of ethical practice (see Chapter Thirty-Three, by Peter J. Dean). In this respect, HPT accepts influences from any quarter, so long as whatever claims are made for those influences can be substantiated to the global community.

Can only those who have had extensive formal training in HPT employ its principles? HPT, like any other field, requires careful study, practice, and feedback—the same characteristics of most other kinds of formal training programs. The purpose of this chapter, however, is not to create and develop professional HP technologists; rather, its intent is to encourage a wide range of professionals to explore the viewpoints and tools of HPT. Doing so should help them improve their own performance and, ultimately, should have a positive effect on organizational performance as relevant concepts and practices are applied from this growing field. Articles about HPT abound, particularly in such journals as

Performance Improvement and *Performance Improvement Quarterly,* the official publications of ISPI. (The remaining chapters of this handbook will certainly also aid the reader in gaining greater knowledge of and insights into the field.) Seminars and workshops by many of the authors featured in this volume are generally well structured and informative and provide ready-to-use skills. Conferences on HPT, such as those held annually by ISPI, or the HPT Institutes that are run by ISPI worldwide, are also useful for learning about the field and its applications, and, more important, for sharing experiences in informal, after-session conversations. Reading, formal workshops, conferences, institutes, and sharing of information and experience can all make HPT readily accessible to the interested person. With respect to specific skill sets for the HP technologist, Chapter Thirty-Two, by Harold D. Stolovitch, Erica J. Keeps, and Daniel Rodrigue, also provides considerable information.

CONCLUSION

There is little doubt that HPT adopts a hard-nosed, highly objective approach to improving human performance. HPT takes into consideration the cost of any intervention aimed at improving human performance. It views this cost as an investment that must yield those returns that are valued by the investing system. It is the system rather than the HP technologist that defines what these returns should be. Once the purpose of the system has been defined and the desired returns have been overtly specified, however, HPT demands systematic and objective study of performance problems and opportunities. Its point of reference is worthy performance, as determined by the system. If HP technologists, human resource specialists, organizational developers, and other professionals and managers cannot demonstrate effectiveness in terms of what is valued by the system in which they operate, then they must not be surprised when their departments experience heavy budget cuts, are maligned, or become dumping grounds for persons whose contributions to the system are no longer judged useful.

HPT is a powerful, emerging field that has the potential to offer organizations astonishing benefits. Almost twenty years ago, Blount (1980, p. 16) wrote that "the untapped and unapplied proven potential for improvement in our business, in our people, in our products, in our service, [and] in our customer relations" that could be realized through HPT was "absolutely awesome." This affirmation still rings true today as we embark on a new millennium. The results of improved human performance can be dramatic increases in productivity, greater satisfaction among workers, and an enhanced world community—and that is what HPT is all about.

References

Ainsworth, D. (1979). Performance technology: A view from the Fo'c'sle. *NSPI Journal* 18:4, 3–7.

Alkon, D. L. (1992). *Memory's voice: Deciphering the mind-brain code.* New York: HarperCollins.

Baldwin, T. T., and Ford, K. J. (1988). Transfer of training: A review and directions for future research. *Personnel Psychology* 41:1, 63–105.

Becker, G. S. (1993). *Human capital: A theoretical and empirical analysis with special reference to education* (3rd ed.). Chicago: University of Chicago Press.

Benefit, A., and Tate, D. L. (1990, Mar.). *Building your credibility as a performance technologist.* Paper presented at annual conference of the National Society for Performance and Instruction, Toronto.

Blount, W. F. (1980). A system in search of a system. *NSPI Journal* 19:5, 14–17, 26.

Bradley, K. (1996, Oct.). Intellectual capital and the new wealth of nations. Lecture delivered to the Royal Society of Arts, London.

Broad, M. L., and Newstrom, J. W. (1992). *Transfer of training: Action-packed strategies to ensure high payoff from training investments.* Reading, MA: Addison-Wesley.

Carr, A. (1995). Performance technologist preparation: The role of leadership theory. *Performance Improvement Quarterly* 8:4, 59–74.

Checkland, P. B. (1972). Towards a system-based methodology for real-world problem solving. *Journal of Systems Engineering* 3:2, 87–116.

Clark, R. E., and Sugrue, B. M. (1990). *New techniques for effective training management.* Los Angeles: University of Southern California Press.

Crawford, R. C. (1991). *In the era of human capital.* New York: HarperBusiness.

Dean, P. J., and Ripley, D. E. (1997). *Performance improvement pathfinders: Models for organizational learning systems.* Washington, DC: International Society for Performance Improvement.

Dean, P. J., and Ripley, D. E. (1998). *Performance improvement interventions.* Vol. 2: *Methods for organizational learning—instructional design and training.* Washington, DC: International Society for Performance Improvement.

Dick, W., and Wager, W. (1995). Preparing performance technologists: The role of the university. *Performance Improvement Quarterly* 8:4, 34–42.

Edvinsson, L., and Malone, M. S. (1997). *Intellectual capital.* New York: HarperBusiness.

Ford, J. K., and Weissbein, D. A. (1997). Transfer of training: An updated review and analysis. *Performance Improvement Quarterly* 10:2, 22–41.

Foshay, W. R., and Moller, L. (1992). Advancing the field through research. In H. D. Stolovitch and E. J. Keeps (eds.), *Handbook of human performance technology: A comprehensive guide for analyzing and solving performance problems in organizations.* San Francisco: Jossey-Bass.

Fuller, J. (1997). *Managing performance improvement projects.* San Francisco: Jossey-Bass/Pfeiffer.

Geis, G. L. (1986). Human Performance Technology: An overview. In M. E. Smith (ed.), *Introduction to performance technology.* Vol. 1. Washington, DC: National Society for Performance and Instruction.

Gilbert, T. F. (1974). *Levels and structure of performance analysis.* Morristown, NJ: Praxis Corporation.

Gilbert, T. F. (1996). *Human competence: Engineering worthy performance.* Amherst, MA, and Washington, DC: Human Resources Development Press and International Society for Performance Improvement.

Hammer, M., and Champy, J. (1993). *Reengineering the corporation: A manifesto for business revolution.* New York: HarperCollins.

Harless, J. (1995). Performance technology skills in business: Implications for preparation. *Performance Improvement Quarterly* 8:4, 75–88.

Hawkridge, D. (1976). Next year, Jerusalem! The rise of educational technology. *British Journal of Educational Technology* 1:7, 7–30.

Instructional design, Human Performance Technologies, EPSS, and systems design [Tenth-year anniversary edition]. (1998). *Performance Improvement Quarterly* 10:1.

Jacobs, R. L. (1988). A proposed domain of Human Performance Technology: Implications for theory and practice. *Performance Improvement Quarterly* 1:2, 2–12.

Kaufman, R., Thiagarajan, S., and MacGillis, P. (1997). *The guidebook for performance improvement: Working with individuals and organizations.* San Francisco: Jossey-Bass/Pfeiffer.

Langdon, D. G. (1995). *The new language of work.* Amherst, MA: Human Resources Development Press.

Lickert, R., and Pyle, W. C. (1971). Human resource accounting: A human organizational measurement approach. *Financial Analysts Journal* 101–102, 75–84.

Ngoa Nguele, D. (1998). *La rentabilité des systèmes de formation structurée sur le lieu du travail pour les pays en développement.* Preliminary report of a study conducted in Cameroon and presented to the Department of Educational Studies and Administration, Université de Montréal.

Nickols, F. W. (1977). Concerning performance and performance standards: An opinion. *NSPI Journal* 16:1, 14–17.

Organization for Economic Cooperation and Development. (1996). *Measuring what people know: Human capital accounting for the knowledge economy.* Paris: Organization for Economic Cooperation and Development.

Phillips, J. J. (1997). *Return on investment in training and performance improvement programs.* Houston, TX: Gulf.

Robinson, D. G., and Robinson, J. C. (1995). *Performance consulting: Moving beyond training.* San Francisco: Berrett-Koehler.

Robinson, D. G., and Robinson, J. C. (1998). *Moving from training to performance: A practical guidebook.* San Francisco: Berrett-Koehler.

Rosenberg, M. J. (1982). Our instructional media roots. *Performance & Instruction* 21:3, 12–15, 33.

Rosenberg, M. J. (1990). Performance technology: Working the system. *Training* 27:2, 42–48.

Rossett, A. (1987). *Training needs assessment.* Englewood Cliffs, NJ: Educational Technology Publications.

Roy, O. (1998). *Impacte des interventions éducatives et non éducatives sur l'assidüité au traitement, la qualité de vie et les nouvelles hospitalisations des personnes âgées.* Doctoral dissertation, Université de Montréal.

Rummler, G. A., and Brache, A. P. (1988). The systems view of human performance. *Training* 25:9, 45–53.

Rummler, G. A., and Brache, A. P. (1996). *Improving performance: How to manage the white space on the organization chart* (2nd ed.). San Francisco: Jossey-Bass.

Ryle, G. (1949). *The concept of mind.* London: Hutchison.

Schultz, T. W. (1981). *Investing in people: The economics of population quality.* Berkeley: University of California Press.

Sohoudji-Agbossou, B. (1997). *Nouvelles technologies et innovations: Elaboration d'un modèle d'implantation de nouveaux programmes de formation professionnelle, le cas des techniciens de gestion de bureau au Bénin.* Doctoral dissertation, Université de Montréal.

Solso, R. L. (1995). *Cognitive psychology* (4th ed.). New York: Simon & Schuster.

Stewart, T. A. (1994, Mar. 10). Your company's most valuable capital: Intellectual capital. *Fortune,* pp. 68–74.

Stewart, T. A. (1997). *Intellectual capital: The new wealth of organizations.* New York: Doubleday.

Stolovitch, H. D. (1995). *A study of workplace equity at Canadian Pacific Railway.* Final report to the executive committee, Canadian Pacific Railway, Montreal.

Stolovitch, H. D., and Keeps, E. J. (1992). *Handbook of human performance technology: A comprehensive guide for analyzing and solving performance problems in organizations.* San Francisco: Jossey-Bass.

Stolovitch, H. D., and Keeps, E. J. (1997). *Front-end analysis.* Montreal: HSA Publications.

Stolovitch, H. D., and Lane, M. (1989). Multicultural training: Designing for affective results. *Performance & Instruction* 28:6, 10–15.

Stolovitch, H. D., and Maurice, J.-G. (1998). Calculating the return on investment: A critical analysis and case study. *Performance Improvement* 37:9, 9–20.

Swanson, R. A., and Gradous, D. B. (1988). *Forecasting financial benefits of human resource development.* San Francisco: Jossey-Bass.

Tosti, D. T., and O'Brien, A. T. (1979). Ten types of on-the-job reinforcers: A taxonomy. *NSPI Journal* 17:6, 7, 19.

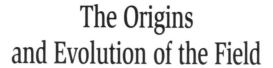

CHAPTER TWO

The Origins
and Evolution of the Field

Marc J. Rosenberg
William C. Coscarelli
Cathleen Smith Hutchison

The term *performance technology* (HPT) has slowly evolved to define an emerging field of practice in organizations. The adjective *human*, however, is often used in front of this term in an effort to make it refer more specifically to the study of people than to the study of machines. With its roots in what was then the National Society for Programmed Instruction (now known as the International Society for Performance Improvement, or ISPI), the field of HPT is now finding additional professional support and discussion in such professional societies as the American Society for Training and Development and the International Federation of Training and Development Organizations, as well as in such professional journals as *Training.*

In defining any new field, theorists and practitioners alike struggle to decide exactly what the new ideas mean and how concepts and practices from one field can aid in describing another. Moreover, in studying the framework on which any new field is built, it is essential to look at new and creative ideas, as well as at the disciplines of science.

Why is it important to review the foundations of HPT? One reason is that HPT is consistently being described as using the science and techniques of other disciplines. Thus, to apply HPT successfully, it is necessary to understand the foundation on which the practice is built. Another reason is that by understanding the origins and conceptual milestones of HPT, researchers and practitioners can better communicate HPT's role to peers in more established fields, as well as to managers and colleagues in work settings where HPT is a new resource. Because the HPT field is still in an emerging and changing state, a grounding in its foundation and history will be crucial to any future attempts to define and set the parameters of HPT itself. Finally, as HPT is implemented globally, an understanding of its conceptual and historical origins provides common ground for practitioners as they apply HPT across borders, cultures, and economic systems.

In this chapter, the emerging field of HPT will be described from both a process and a management point of view. Specifically, this chapter will examine the significant contributions and viewpoints of the discipline's pioneering practitioners, as well as the more established scientific fields from which they came. This chapter will also note the significant contributions of learning psychology, instructional systems, analytical systems, information technology, cognitive engineering, ergonomics and human factors, feedback systems, organizational development, and change. The importance of model building (a clarifying technique used successfully by other, related fields during their evolution) and the relevance of this process for HPT will be discussed. Finally, this chapter will take a look at how the field may evolve over the next ten years as it gains acceptance in organizations around the world.

SIGNIFICANT CONTRIBUTIONS TO THE PROCESS OF HPT

According to Brethower (1995, p. 17), "HPT has enjoyed a 30-year record of achievement," but just where did it come from? A definitive answer is probably some years away, but several major influences can be clearly identified.

Systems

A *system* is a group of interrelated elements forming an entity and usually operating toward a purpose or goal. The use of systems, or the systems approach, is essential to HPT. Without a systemic framework, it would be extremely difficult to achieve improved performance. In fact, it may be impossible to engage in any form of engineering or technology outside a systemic context.

Banathy (1968) provides an excellent overview of the relationship among systems. A system can be either a subsystem or a suprasystem; which one it is depends on the perspective adopted. For example, the internal combustion engine is a subsystem to the suprasystem of the automobile, which in turn is a subsystem to the transportation suprasystem. In the HPT suprasystem, instructional technology is a subsystem, and HPT is a subsystem in the overall management suprasystem (Mager, 1988, p. 10).

According to Jacobs (1988, p. 7), "No one use of the systems approach defines the field," but the relationship among systems allow HPT to be placed in its proper perspective. This paradigm is helpful in understanding the components of HPT and how the field fits into the larger world. Because HPT is composed of and uses the concepts and techniques of many disciplines—for example, Svenson and Wallace (1989) suggest that HPT uses an engineering-science metaphor—a systemic framework is crucial to fitting its components together, developing models of how they will work and interact, and implementing HPT in practice.

Learning Psychology

For most of recorded history, learning occurred in the mode of apprenticeship. Until about five hundred years ago, all the knowledge and skill of one person could be passed on individually to another. When, through discovery and invention, the amount of available knowledge increased substantially, and when the number of people who knew it all correspondingly decreased, a way had to be found to make learning more efficient. The newly invented medium of writing helped for a while, but soon classroom-based or group instruction was born. Thus information could be imparted to many learners at one time.

In the twentieth century, the pace of discovery and invention, coupled with the population explosion, soon made it necessary that learners spend more and more years acquiring an ever-growing body of skills and knowledge. The classroom teaching model had to be made more efficient. In response to this need, learning psychologists began to merge new techniques of instruction with audiovisual technology (media) (Rosenberg, 1982).

There appears to be general agreement that HPT ultimately stems from the work of a number of behavioral psychologists who began, in the 1950s, to experiment with innovative methods of enhancing learning. This research also led to new perspectives on how people learn. To learning psychologists concerned with prescriptive theory, instructional efficiency and effectiveness were functions of how information is structured, presented, and received by the learner.

Most of the pioneers in the field point to the work of Skinner (1954, 1958), who proposed the revolutionary idea that small-step instruction, coupled with extensive feedback, could significantly enhance learning. Skinner's ideas led directly to the development of the first teaching machines, which made use of a format known as *programmed instruction* (Crowder, 1960). Programmed instruction is one example of the early attempt to marry the principles of learning psychology to audiovisually based instruction. Research and practice in this area led to the important concepts of *instructional feedback* and *reinforcement*.

Out of this work came two important events. First, in 1961 and 1962, Thomas F. Gilbert, a former student of Skinner's, published the *Journal of Mathetics* (the term *mathetics* comes from Greek and refers to learning). In the only two volumes of this journal that were ever published, Gilbert laid the foundation for what was later to develop into the field of instructional technology. In 1962, many of the researchers who had contributed to the *Journal of Mathetics* came together to form the National Society for Programmed Instruction (NSPI). In the development of any discipline, an important milestone is the point where ideas begin to be shared, especially through publications and meetings of professional societies. Hence the second event to come out of the early research and practice in this new field: NSPI's first meeting. As the 1960s moved into the 1970s, the new discipline began to emerge in the literature, and the use of a systematic approach to creating and delivering instruction has now come to be known as *instructional technology* or *instructional systems design* (ISD).

There were also significant contributions from cognitive psychologists in identifying the nature of skills and knowledge. It was Bloom (1956) who first organized objectives along a taxonomy related to what the learner was supposed to do. Glaser (1966), Bruner (1969) and Gagné (1970) provided seminal work to link the learning process to instructional events.

Instructional Systems Design

The concepts, theories, and practices of ISD are among the most significant underpinnings of HPT, especially when it is viewed from a historical perspective. Reiser (1987) points to the work of Skinner, and to the work of others from the orientation of behavioral psychology, as being a significant contribution to the systematic process that includes programmed instruction (already discussed), task analysis, behavioral objectives, and criterion-referenced evaluation.

Task analysis became critical as instructional technologists realized the need to identify, before instruction was designed, what they intended to teach people to do. Behavioral objectives, popularized most notably by the work of Mager (1975), infused the designers with the realization that the outcomes of instruction must be identifiable, observable, and measurable. Criterion-referenced evaluation was adopted as a way of providing practitioners with techniques for proving that learning had taken place.

ISD, the systems approach applied to learning, directly attacked the problem of inefficient and ineffective instruction. As the demands of society and the exponential growth in knowledge continued to require new approaches to teaching and learning, especially during the two world wars, the need to train large numbers of people in short periods of time had led to the advent of audiovisually based instruction, of which film was a primary example. Research consistently showed that audiovisual media could teach as well as people could, and this finding was a significant breakthrough.

Researchers and practitioners in the field of ISD have been able to use these important concepts in describing a generalized systematic model for their field. First, the instructional requirements of both the learner and the task or job are analyzed, to determine the precise instructional need. Next, an instructional program is designed, with objectives and testing that are linked to the preceding analysis. Instructional materials are then produced and delivered according to the design. In each phase, evaluation data are collected and revisions are made so that the outcome of the process meets the identified need as closely as possible. One such systematic model has come to be known simply as ADDIE: analysis, design, development, implementation, and evaluation. Today many operational ISD models exist in practice, but most either can trace their roots to ADDIE or accept the ADDIE concept as a foundation.

The development of ADDIE-like models for ISD was crucial to the establishment of the HPT field. As instructional programs depended more and more on the analysis of a need, and as instructional evaluation became more refined, in order to reflect the degree to which the instruction had met that need, it became apparent that a variety of needs could not be met through instructional programs alone. No matter how well the programs were designed, learning did not always result in improved performance. As practitioners became better and better at identifying problems, they soon discovered that their repertoire of instructional solutions could solve only a small set of those problems. A broader paradigm was required.

As practitioners and theorists worked to describe and use this newly expanded paradigm, they relied in part on their extensive experience with the ADDIE model. Because they recognized the limitations of ISD, most notably in the phases of analysis and evaluation (Richey, 1995), important questions surfaced: Analysis of what? Design, development, and implementation of what? Evaluation of what? A new and more analytical paradigm was needed.

Analytical Systems

While working on a variety of government-sponsored training and education projects in the 1960s, many of the earliest learning psychologists and instructional technologists, such as Harless, Gilbert, and Mager, began to develop strategies that dealt with an important realization: if training and education did not accomplish what was expected, then there must be other strategies that might be more effective. They worked on describing ways to analyze problems as a means of determining appropriate solutions.

Harless (1970) coined the term *front-end analysis* when he realized that analysis of an instructional problem often comes too late in the process. When analysis is pushed forward, ahead of an instructional program's design, it becomes possible to look at a particular performance problem in isolation from any perceived solution. Harless and other researchers began to realize that instructional technology was not, after all, the superordinate concept; thus they brought the relationship between instructional and performance systems into proper perspective.

Gilbert (1996) reached several conceptual milestones in describing performance and how it is analyzed. He articulated a process of assigning value to performance by measuring its accomplishments, thus providing a framework for assessing impacts of HPT beyond changes in behavior. Gilbert's behavior-engineering model also identified six general aspects of behavior that can be manipulated to improve performance: data, instruments, incentives, knowledge, capacity, and motives. Gilbert's model, in one form or another, plays a critical role in the analysis and evaluation of performance.

Rummler and Brache (1988b), using systematic analysis techniques to examine organizational structures, found that individual performance is influenced by organizational performance, and vice versa. They describe organizations partly as collections of integrated systems (for example, the finance, manufacturing, and marketing systems). To this list they add a performance system and suggest that all these systems (and their subsystems) are influenced by a complex and ever-changing variety of outside forces. These systems dynamics require organizational analysis, and the analysis of performance problems requires the analysis of the organization in which those problems occur; thus the "analysis tree" grows larger.

Collectively, the work of Gilbert, Mager, Harless, and Rummler forms a large part of the foundation on which performance analysis and HPT are built. Mager and Pipe (1984), Kaufman and English (1979), Rossett (1987), and many other practitioners have used this work to develop practical suggestions for analyzing performance problems (or opportunities) and their causes.

Cognitive Engineering

The field of cognitive engineering is an interesting example of how multiple fields combine to form a new discipline for dealing with new challenges. Woods and Roth (1988, p. 415) define cognitive engineering as "an applied cognitive science that draws on the knowledge and techniques of cognitive psychology and related disciplines to provide the foundation for principle-driven design of person-machine systems." This new field shows how adaptable learning psychology is when it is confronted with new vehicles (machines or computers) of knowledge delivery. When the old models no longer fit, they can be adapted, borrowed from, or redesigned to create a new approach. This is how cognitive engineering was born.

Cognitive engineering's domain is more limited than that of HPT, but its goals are quite similar. The cognitive engineer links the world of learning with that of computer technology and measures success in terms of the human-machine interface and the resulting productivity. Woods and Roth (1988) stress that their field deals with improved performance. These authors advocate analysis as the first and most important step in achieving this goal. They are emphatic in their argument that knowing how to use a new machine or technology is far less important than accomplishing something with the new tool. They also see their field as systemic. The critical system here, however, is the human-machine system (that is, the interface between humans and machines) rather than the machine and its electronic and mechanical components.

Information Technology

The concepts embraced by cognitive engineering have profoundly influenced the relatively new field of information technology. In addition, the advances made in information technology have had a significant impact on HPT. Gilbert (1996) notes that the effects of a good information system can be staggering. The overwhelming amount of complex information required to perform work at a competent level has placed considerable strain on traditional education and training systems. This situation has led to the development of job aids, computer databases, and electronic training systems as well as of structured text design (Horn, 1982). It has also had a significant impact on work design and organizational structures.

Electronic performance-support systems (EPSS)—linking training, information systems, computer applications, and so on (Gery, 1989)—will have a significant impact on the design and operation of an organization, and on human performance. According to Rosenberg (1995), HPT and EPSS will have essentially the same future; he predicts that "they will be integrated directly into the key processes of an organization" (p. 98). This prediction has been borne out in the growing use of these tools to support increased productivity and quality in a variety of jobs, such as customer care, sales, manufacturing, project management, and even in the HPT field itself.

Eucker (1989) notes that "our assumptions regarding information systems in traditional organizations are out of date" (p. 87) and that "the potential influence of information technology on human performance is likewise limited by inadequate organizational strategies and structures" (p. 89). In his analysis of the influence of information technology on human performance, Foshay (1989) also sees such systems as potentially having a profound impact on organizations. New work routines, changed career orientations, redesigned job environments, and, perhaps, new missions for training and education require a new approach to managing and evaluating such changes. Foshay suggests that HPT may be that new approach, and these developments are already affecting the field. Foshay notes that the traditional view of HPT, in which particular jobs are a given and interventions for improving performance in the jobs are developed, may give way to the design of "organizational structures and information architectures" (p. 125). In other words, it may be necessary to redesign the jobs themselves.

The explosion of information available through the World Wide Web has drastically changed the role and impact of information technology. New fields of knowledge management and information design radically expand the HPT practitioner's toolkit. Having access to just-in-time information and knowledge databases is a capability essential to the modern organization. Access to information clearly has an impact on performance, and the power of the Internet and of company intranets has profoundly increased capabilities in this area (Hinrichs, 1997).

Ergonomics and Human Factors

Ergonomics and human factors are disciplines that developed in response to the world's increasingly complex technology. They can be seen as companion disciplines to information technology and cognitive engineering. According to Phillips (1989, pp. 44–45), "ergonomics and human factors link our quantitative skills to the integrated systems of people, machines, and materials." The fields of ergonomics and human factors help in ensuring that the design of systems complies with the requirements of users. From desk chairs to computer systems to automobiles, the most successful products—those used to their fullest potential—are those that are easily operated, maintained, and understood.

There is an important implication for HPT here. Ergonomics and human factors are concerned with the design of machines, but their primary goal is to improve human performance. According to Shephard (1974, pp. 8–9), "Systems are examined to see (1) how their purpose can be achieved with minimum damage to either operator or machine, and (2) how their design may be improved to facilitate transfer of energy, materials, or information across the man-machine interface." It is clear that in a complex, technological world, human performance is enhanced through the proper application of ergonomics and human factors. For the HP technologist, then, the field encompasses more than the role of human beings; it includes their interactions with their tools.

Psychometrics

Psychometrics is the measurement of human achievement and capabilities. In the past, it was used primarily to measure learning and general ability. Many standardized tests are administered each year to millions of public school and college-bound students. These normative tests were designed to predict performance in learning environments. More recently, valid and reliable tests have been developed to predict performance in task accomplishment or in the demonstration of sets of behaviors. It was only natural that these techniques would be found useful in the development of methods for selecting people to fill jobs or for certifying competence in a job.

Leibler and Parkman (1986) and Ross (1986) provide a good overview of the use of assessment techniques in personnel selection and staffing. Techniques for accurately predicting performance have become important HPT tools. Ross notes that the preliminary purpose of selection is cost-effectiveness, and the implication for HPT is that it may be more cost-effective to select people who are already classified as high performers than to train or motivate mediocre performers. The development of more accurate assessment devices (such as paper-and-pencil tests, expert or peer evaluation, assessment centers, and so on) relies in part on the advances made by psychometricians.

Feedback Systems

In an extensive review of the literature on feedback systems, Ilgren, Fisher, and Taylor (1979, p. 349) note that "feedback about the effectiveness of an individual's behavior has long been recognized as essential for learning and for motivation in performance-oriented organizations." These researchers see feedback as an essential feature of interpersonal relations and as an appropriate tool for improving performance.

Feedback is a unique type of information. It is reflected in praise, criticism, corrective instruction, nonverbal communication (smiling, anger), and so on. It can be informal, as in a supervisor's daily behavior with subordinates, or formalized, as in a system for performance appraisal. Feedback is directly related to motivation, incentives, and rewards. According to Donald Tosti and Stephanie F. Jackson (see Chapter Twenty of this volume), the critical characteristics of feedback are tied to who gives it, what the content the feedback is, and when and where the feedback is given (see also Tosti, 1986). The literature on supervision devotes considerable space to feedback as a management tool, and HPT embraces performance feedback as an effective and efficient strategy for improving performance.

Recognition of the substantial impact that feedback systems have on overall performance improvement has had a tremendous effect on HPT. Feedback is an essential ingredient of the new performance management systems, which incorporate many other HPT interventions. These include interventions concerned with training, participative decision making, teamwork, quality, incentives, and rewards, among other elements.

Organizational Development and Change

Much of this chapter has considered new approaches to instruction, information, and management as having a significant impact on the organization. Organizational development (OD) is a large field that seeks to deal with this impact. It encompasses many interventions, including organizational design, team building, culture change, leadership, strategy development, management systems, and a variety of techniques designed to transform an organization's beliefs, values, operations, or interrelationships. OD practitioners are extremely people-oriented. They consistently look for opportunities to make the human part of a system work better and thus focus on humanistic rather than behavioristic strategies. The field draws its theory from psychology and organizational behavior.

In an extensive review of the literature, Beer and Walton (1987) look at organizational development from several perspectives. Each perspective has its own implications for HPT. From the first perspective, where the view is of *OD as general management,* attention centers on the operation and general management of an organization. Of specific concern is the culture of the organization, especially the issues of how to manage it and change it. Sometimes an organization's culture can enhance performance by espousing the ideal of a supportive environment. At other times the culture may inhibit performance by inhibiting risk, change, or growth. The performance technologist must understand the culture of the organization in order to implement the interventions most likely to succeed. Another concern is leadership. Research shows that true leadership can be an effective vehicle for change, including change in performance. The HP technologist can use leaders to set a vision, model behaviors, and challenge others.

From the second perspective, OD is seen as *creation of an adaptive organization.* Here we find the component of organizational redesign. Innovative, responsive, and flexible organizational structures can enhance workers' performance; in turn, workers' enhanced performance can help create adaptive organizations. Organizations that are more flexible and more adaptive are more likely to respond to HPT-related changes. Inflexible or rigid organizations, by contrast, make it difficult for new performance improvement strategies to succeed, especially if they involve changes in work patterns, the introduction of new tools or methods, or realignment of jobs.

The third perspective, from which OD is viewed as *human resource management,* gives insight into the effort to "develop high commitment work systems that will attract, motivate and retain superior employees" (Beer and Walton, 1987, p. 353). Such issues as compensation, benefits, and labor relations are important here. For HPT, the challenge is to use these human resource functions appropriately in an integrated approach to improving performance.

OD as implementation of change, as it is viewed from the fourth perspective, embodies much of the research on change and how to make it happen. Change theory and processes are at the very heart of HPT. Lasting, positive change in the workforce's productivity and competence is the goal of any performance improvement system. Change-oriented strategies have been instrumental in enabling the HPT field to expand its goals from individual to organizational results.

Nevertheless, the influence of organizational development and change on HPT has been hampered by the conflict between the imprecise, solution-oriented focus of the OD field and the more rigid, systematic, and measurement-oriented focus of many of the other disciplines. Beer and Walton (1987, p. 363) note that "tension has always existed in the [OD] field between a concern for effectiveness and a concern for the well-being of employees." In the conclusion to their review of the literature (such as it was more than a decade ago), they suggest that the OD field look at a broader array of interventions, moving away from structured, preprogrammed, consultant-centered interventions; and, similarly, that HP technologists with roots in training obtain more exposure to the OD field. In the future, perhaps, integration between HPT and OD will help achieve these ends.

Intervention Systems

From the intervention side, "human performance technology represents the use of the systems approach in a number of different forms, depending upon the problem of interest and professional activity required" (Jacobs, 1988, pp. 6–7). Interventions are responses to identified causes of human performance problems or to opportunities for improving performance. They are often referred to as *solutions,* although it is difficult to determine whether the problem is "solved" before the intervention is developed. Some practitioners refer to interventions as *strategies, tactics,* or *human resource functions.*

The conventional wisdom holds that if some form of individual or organizational change can be designed, implemented, and evaluated with respect to a performance analysis, then it can be considered an intervention. Examples (taken from the preceding discussion) of areas in which interventions can be used are training and education, job design, feedback systems, incentives and rewards, selection and staffing, and environmental engineering. Many practitioners use some type of derivative of Gilbert's behavior-engineering model as an organizational framework.

How many interventions are there? No boundary or categorization scheme has yet been established for determining what is and what is not an intervention. Rosenberg (1990) elaborates on the ISPI model as a strategic overview of HPT. Rothwell and Kazanas (1997), Hutchison and Stein (1997), and Rothwell (1996) provide the most recent attempts to identify and categorize interventions at both the strategic and the tactical level.

HPT is emerging as a two-sided coin. On one side, analysis is concerned with identifying specific problems and opportunities. On the other side, interventions seek to fulfill the recommendations of the analysis. Many contributions from established disciplines have been expansions of intervention options. By looking at the field of HPT, it is possible to identify the initial set of skills necessary for conducting a performance analysis. Determining appropriate interventions is not so simple, however. For example, expertise in instructional systems design is adequate knowledge if training or education is the only intervention used. If, however, performance analysis indicates the possible applicability of dozens or hundreds of different interventions, it quickly becomes apparent that no one person will possess the expertise needed to design, implement, and evaluate them all.

This is a dilemma in HPT: although it is now possible to identify myriad performance problems (or opportunities) and their causes, it is also true that the number of options at a practitioner's disposal has significantly increased. What can be done? Is the practitioner limited to analyzing a performance problem or an opportunity but not recommending an intervention? If an intervention is recommended, can the HP technologist design, implement, and evaluate it? Is the practitioner essentially a manager or a designer of interventions? Does the practitioner belong to a larger team of experts beyond the still undefined boundaries of the profession? Is HPT not also a superordinate concept? These questions and others are causing the management of HPT to emerge as an important area for study.

MANAGEMENT OF HPT

Where the process of HPT is concerned, much has been contributed by more established fields, but there has been little discussion of the management of that process. It is generally agreed that managing a performance improvement system that is based on HPT is more complex than managing a single intervention, but the information is sparse on how to do this more complex kind of management.

Bullock (1973, p. 3) suggests that HP technologists may not offer a "unique total capability for solving human performance problems" but that the field "brings together a variety of individuals whose combined skills offer a total capability." Hutchison (1990) recognizes this concern by distinguishing between the practice of HPT and the design of specific interventions. She identifies two types of HPT practitioners: the *HP technologist,* concerned primarily with analysis, management, and evaluation, and the *intervention specialist,* concerned primarily with the design and implementation of specific interventions. These roles may be performed by one or more individuals, according to the expertise of the individual and the parameters of the performance gap.

Hutchison stresses the importance of the interrelationships between HPT and other specialist strategies, and she points to the significance of process management in the role of the HP technologist, especially as process management involves the phased and integrated implementation and evaluation of combined interventions. According to Hutchison, it is crucial to distinguish between the practices of HP technologists and those of intervention specialists.

What makes HPT unique is that it is emerging as a field characterized by the integration of the disciplines on which it is built. The usefulness of this integration lies in the assumption that combinations of interventions, taken from a variety of fields, provide greater value when applied to a performance problem or opportunity than does any specific intervention when used alone. This necessary integration will be a cornerstone of how human resources, training, and other such departments are restructured in the future (Robinson and Robinson, 1998).

Gilley (1989) notes that career development in an organization is enhanced when strategies are linked to training and organizational development processes.

With respect to staffing issues, as a result of integrated selection, training, and performance evaluation processes, test subjects have been able to attain higher levels of measurable performance than was previously possible (Pucel, Cerrito, and Noe, 1989). These researchers conclude (p. 28) that "the linkage between selection, training and performance appraisal can result in a legally defensible human resource system that can contribute to management's ability to improve productivity." These two studies are examples of how HPT applications can demonstrate the strategic results of integrated responses, and this emerging orientation of HPT allows the field to be more strategic than the individual fields that compose it. HPT's strategic ability to achieve not just enhanced individual performance but also organizational results is another important foundation of the field.

CONCEPTUAL MODELS OF HPT

While the ISD field was emerging from the established disciplines of learning psychology (behavioral and cognitive), education, and communications, practitioners relied on modeling to help define it. Modeling is a useful technique for describing a new concept, idea, or process. Models like ADDIE helped researchers and practitioners communicate and apply the concepts of the new field. As more people were able to talk about and use ISD, it became more accepted as a legitimate discipline in its own right.

HPT continues the struggle to define itself and understand its roots and boundaries. Meanwhile, new models of the field are emerging. This is to be expected. Any science or technology moves through the following four phases as it attempts to define itself:

1. Observation of phenomena: the realization that there is something new "out there"

2. Classification of phenomena: the description of the new field's components

3. Generalization of phenomena: the identification of consistencies across the components

4. Manipulation and control of phenomena: the application of the new field to some purpose

The pioneers of HPT were reporting observed phenomena, especially in behavioral psychology. They knew that improved performance was a result of a combination of interventions that corresponded to the findings of a valid and reliable analysis of a problem or an opportunity. Furthermore, they realized that no single discipline, whether it involved training, organizational development, or feedback systems, was now adequate to address situations effectively and efficiently. Models were then built to classify and generalize this new reality and help communicate these conclusions. Once general agreement on models has been reached, it will be possible to move with assurance toward the manipulation and control of phenomena, and applications of HPT will be more likely to succeed. It might be expected that, over time (as was the case with ISD), HPT practitioners will move beyond models, internalizing the systematic process in the ways they think and act. In the meantime, two general types of models have been developed: *diagnostic* and *prescriptive* models. Each type has an important role to play in describing the field of HPT.

Diagnostic Models

Diagnostic models classify the areas where HPT can be applied and can have an impact on performance. Different theorists and practitioners divide the HPT world in different ways. Some focus on types of performance, whereas others focus on aspects of an organization in which various types of performance occur. The four diagnostic models discussed here present the HPT field from three perspectives: the individual, the individual as a member of an organization, and the organization as a whole.

Gilbert (1996) has proposed a diagnostic model that classifies six major elements on two levels: those elements at the level of an individual's repertoire, and those at the level of the environment that supports the individual's performance. Using a behavioral model of stimulus-response-consequences, Gilbert identifies the six elements as data, instrumentation, incentives, knowledge, response capacity, and motives. These six elements can be altered in some way to affect the performance of the individual or a group. A major feature of this model is its movement beyond the narrower focus of instructional interventions and its having begun to broaden the perspective of ISD practitioners. Gilbert's model has been recognized for several important strengths. It identifies and classifies specific areas for performance impact, and each area can be altered to influence behavior. Thus there is a framework for identifying appropriate interventions into each area. It also builds on the contributions of behavioral psychology by tying HPT directly to one of its strongest roots.

Harless (1979) has another perspective on the HPT universe. He places the focus of HPT within the context of the organization and directs it toward human performance on the job. Rather than carving performance into six areas, as Gilbert does, Harless identifies three categories that influence human performance on the job: skill or knowledge, the environment, and motivation. Harless's diagnostic model, by placing human performance in an organizational context, indicates that performance should be in alignment with the organization's goals. His model also implies that it is important for us, in addition to analyzing influences on performance, to consider who the performers are, what the specific performance is, and how well it is being carried out. Harless's model presents generic areas of intervention that are relevant to the three categories that influence performance, and it depicts interrelationships among the three categories.

Mager and Pipe (1984), adding more structure to a similar assumption, expand yet again the notion of an integrated performance perspective.

Whereas the focus of the Gilbert, Harless, and Mager and Pipe diagnostic models is individual performance, Rummler and Brache (1988a) turn to organizational analysis to provide a framework for enhancing human performance. The realization that organizational performance is as important as individual performance has proved to be a significant contribution to the development of HPT. The belief of Rummler and Brache, in part, is that organizational and individual performance are so different that unique strategies must be developed for each.

Process Models

Diagnostic models help classify areas where HPT *can* be applied; prescriptive models attempt to describe how HPT *could* be applied. Because HPT is partly an outgrowth of ISD, it is natural for practitioners to attempt to use linear systems models (like ADDIE) to describe HPT processes. After all, such models represent a systematic approach and are familiar to the wide range of people engaged in HPT. Although sophisticated practitioners have never assumed that the linear systematic process is adequate for describing multifaceted projects, they have often found it useful in highlighting common stages of problem solving. (This fact is apparent in Bullock's description of an early model for HPT, a model in which the major emphasis is on performance diagnosis; see Bullock, 1973.) Nevertheless, as practitioners attempted to integrate the myriad potential interventions that could be applied to solving performance problems or realizing opportunities for performance improvement, the linear systematic process began to break down.

Mager and Pipe (1984) relate specific interventions to the outcomes of performance analysis. Their model uses a decision-tree format whereby specific interventions are tied to corresponding yes-or-no questions. Mager and Pipe's model is primarily a tool for determining the best intervention to use in removing a discrepancy between actual and desired performance.

Rosenberg (1990), building on the work of Rossett (1987), provides a more detailed view of a performance analysis process. He categorizes a list of potential interventions into four major human resource functions: human resource development, organizational development, human resource management, and environmental engineering. The model shows interrelationships among interventions, and, through the application of the HPT process, the interventions are brought to bear on the performance problems or opportunities identified in the performance analysis.

As previously noted, Hutchison's HPT model (1990) adds a layer of management to the process. In a sense, Hutchison sees HPT practice as two distinct processes: managing HPT and designing interventions.

The HPT field has not developed its own widely accepted model, but the building of models, both diagnostic and prescriptive, still stands as one of the best methods available for continuing to define the field. New models will enable researchers and practitioners to integrate new disciplines, concepts, and interventions more successfully into the expanding practice of HPT.

HPT AT THE MILLENNIUM

Historically, HPT has been in the domain of scientific inquiry and research into specific areas (learning psychology, systems, instruction, and the like). Currently and in the future, however, HPT seems much more likely to evolve from its practical application in organizations. Of particular interest for the field will be the continuing study of how HPT will be used in differing organizations, as well as how HPT will be applied in different cultures and in global corporations.

Corporations, as well as some academic and governmental institutions, can be categorized by several means, and the characteristics of any particular organization's category will affect the nature of HPT development, practices, and emphases within that organization. For example, in what industry does the organization exist? Is it a high-tech organization, a durable-goods manufacturer, or a nonprofit? Is it young or mature? Some start-up organizations are locked in fierce competitive battles over market share; others, more well established in mature industries, are looking for ways to move into other markets as business opportunities become limited in current ones. The nature of the organization's products or services will also affect the nature of its HPT needs; thus, in various categories, successful interventions in recruitment, training, motivation, feedback, the work environment, and so forth may be significantly different, and interventions that work well in one organization may be totally inappropriate to another, even if the performance problems are similar. In fact, HPT itself, born of the merger of many fields, is likely to be practiced quite differently in disparate organizational environments (Coscarelli, 1996). How is the practice of HPT, as well as the fundamental understanding of the field, influenced by the environment in which it is applied? A few examples may shed some light.

A premier consumer products organization in a competitive market knows that, once it introduces a new product, it has about nine months to establish its new product before competitors can respond with a similar product. Thus, for some start-up products, the organization will invest millions of dollars in an assembly line that may fold in less than a year. Given the prospect of such a short life for some products, the organization's heavy investment in training and other technologies seems risky, at least initially. Its first goal is to keep the new-product assembly line running at the lowest possible cost until it can be determined whether the marketplace will support continued investment in and refinement of the new product. Therefore, the organization is relying on EPSS to provide instant advice, at relatively low cost, about repairing or maintaining of the assembly line.

A large international consulting firm is in a competitive service industry that is heavily driven by the need to understand people in organizations and the systems they use to achieve goals. There is a strong emphasis on the ability to think clearly, creatively, and systematically about organizations' problems and the solutions for them. The firm is very selective in its hiring, and it places a premium on both technical and consulting skills; the firm believes that hiring smart, motivated people is the most important step in ensuring high performance from the workforce. The firm also relies on apprenticeships (conducted in person or via electronic media) to develop people's skills, in the belief that people will learn by making mistakes and having experts share their knowledge and experiences with them. Multimedia systems founded on a constructivist philosophy now form the basis of the firm's entry-level course in business practices.

A major manufacturer of large appliances finds itself in a mature industry. Very few refrigerators wear out these days, and washers and dryers last a long time, too. The market has settled down to a few suppliers competing for a relatively small market. The pace of change is not brutal, and heavy emphasis on the more traditional manufacturing processes creates a need for performance solutions that work on the shop floor. The company uses a great deal of on-the-job training and little formal or systematically designed instruction; given the relatively stable workforce, HPT selection strategies are unlikely to pay off significantly for this organization.

A computer company is in a fast-paced, fiercely competitive market, but certain aspects of its manufacturing process cannot be left to informal training. Job performance in the company's "clean room," for example, relies on exceedingly high standards to be successful. Therefore, performance in the clean room begins with formal training that has been systematically designed, developed, and evaluated.

A start-up company that makes electronically based training-and-information systems for physicians has the feel of a high-tech "garage" business and only recently moved to a state-subsidized small-business incubator. Performance at the company depends on the talent pool that can be recruited and on the need to get the next demo done. No formal training or performance-support systems exist, and they are unlikely to be created until a critical mass of staff and income is reached.

A large telecommunications firm has characteristics of both a mature and a fledgling organization, of both a high-tech and a consumer-oriented company, and of both a product and a service orientation. The practice of HPT in this firm is quite complex. In the somewhat mature and highly competitive consumer long-distance market, the company uses EPSS and highly structured on-line training to keep its customer care representatives up to speed on new products and new service offerings. The company's data networking and Internet businesses are closer to high-tech services in this industry that is constantly redefining itself, but the technical and account specialists in this area tend to be more experienced. For them, the use of knowledge and information systems (that is, knowledge management) is appropriate as a performance improvement strategy.

A global industrial corporation is moving its manufacturing operations to countries outside its home base. Its emphasis on quality is posing challenges as it recruits and trains workers from new countries and cultures. In one country, where the workforce is highly skilled, the firm is not putting an initial focus on extensive training but is concentrating instead on the stiff competition in attracting and retaining talent. If employees jump from job to job, the firm may have to give its workers incentives not only to perform to expectations but also to stay with the company. Given the prospect of high turnover, the company, through EPSS, embeds some of its knowledge in processes and systems rather than in people. In another country, this one less developed, recruitment and retention are less of an issue; here, unskilled workers do require extensive training before they can be productive. In a third, highly unionized country with a culture of lifetime employment, the firm must motivate and maintain high performance in a stable and perhaps aging workforce.

Thus, in a global environment, the diversity of cultures, governmental regulations, and economic systems clearly influences how HPT will be used. Many global firms are finding that a mix of HPT interventions (for example, involving training, compensation, motivation, and performance support) must be applied differently, and often delicately, from one country to another.

At any rate, these cases illustrate a quickly emerging, fundamental characteristic of HPT practice: its diversity. "One size fits all" is less likely to be the catchphrase when organizations differ on such fundamental factors as markets, products (and products' life cycles), maturity of the industry, and region of the world where operations are conducted. Although HPT's roots in science and engineering still define its components, especially in the areas of performance analysis and evaluation, these roots will increasingly be intertwined with new ones that are growing from HPT's awareness of business realities, the nature of today's organizations, and the increasingly global nature of work. Therefore, practice rather than research is likely to have the greater impact on continued evolution of the field.

HPT UNTIL 2010

HPT is directly descended from systems theory and behavioral psychology. Most of its practitioners and theorists have their roots in the training profession, but these people have borrowed extensively from related disciplines (for example, information and feedback systems, ergonomics and human factors, organizational development and change theory, and human resource management). As more work is done to define the multidimensional nature of HPT and performance interventions, practitioners and theorists will have to address more fully the issue of who designs, implements, and manages the performance improvement process. Tosti alludes to the resolution of these issues:

> HPT practitioners have emphasized prescription; the goal is to clearly specify results and to define the performance factors required to produce those results. OD practitioners have emphasized description, with the goal of creating understanding so that people can take action to produce the needed outcomes. For example, if we are measuring individual performance, then task analysis, performance analysis, and skill/knowledge development are key tools. If we are measuring team performance, then interpersonal working relationships are likely to become important factors. If we are measuring departmental performance, then process mapping, information systems, and a host of other factors enter the equation as well. If we are measuring organizational performance, then the importance of organizational culture, strategy, and cross-functional working relationships increases. As we move out from the level of the individual performer to the level of the organization two things happen: (1) the variety of influences on performance increases, and (2) our ability to precisely define and control those influences decreases [Tosti, 1998, pp. 2–3].

Simultaneously, as HPT is applied in more diverse and global settings, not only HPT practitioners but also general managers, employees, and business leaders will begin to shape it in the ways that will be of most benefit to individual organizations. Future HPT concepts, systems, and models will no doubt reflect this complexity and diversity. Moreover, as organizations implement new management techniques, these techniques will increasingly incorporate an HPT perspective. Indeed, as Rosenberg (1996) points out, the processes used by the quality movement are in many respects the same as those used in HPT. In fact, integrating HPT into already established and accepted processes (performance management, reengineering, and the like) may ease the transition to a performance-centered environment and lower resistance to what some may perceive as uncomfortable or even unnecessary change.

We expect that by the year 2010 the competition among several structures currently framing HPT practice will have resolved itself in particular organizations, if not in the field as a whole. From a macro perspective, "ownership" of HPT will reflect an organization's philosophy of empowerment. Some philosophies argue for the placement of HPT processes within the purview of an HRD department (McLagan, 1989); others seek holographic skill development and empowerment in learning organizations (Senge, 1990). In the first situation, the training and interdisciplinary teams offered by existing ID or OD programs may suffice; in the second, context may be so important to success (as in a high-tech organization) that HPT skills will begin to be integrated into the in-house training of subject matter experts.

And this brings us back to the beginning—to systems theory and systems management. Referring to industrial engineering, Phillips (1989, p. 45) notes, "Without this integrated perspective, we will relegate ourselves to the position of overpaid, useless technicians looking for individual problems to shoehorn into individual methodologies." The same challenge may confront HPT.

No one model or conceptual approach addresses all a practitioner's needs or totally defines the field of HPT. There are, however, five cornerstones that form a basis for describing the discipline:

1. HPT operates within a systemic framework.

2. HPT depends on a comprehensive analytical process.

3. The application of interventions to solve performance problems, or to realize opportunities for performance improvement, requires a nonlinear perspective.

4. HPT will most probably involve expertise that resides not in individuals but in diverse teams.

5. Future HPT practice will depend in many ways on organizational settings and on the requirements of practitioners and sponsors.

Given these five cornerstones, HPT will involve a substantial amount of sophisticated project management and contextually sensitive solutions.

Taken together, the conceptual underpinnings and models of the field can provide a framework to help define both where HPT is relevant and how it can be used. Over time, the field of HPT will develop a more solid base on which researchers and practitioners will be able to build while developing a more diverse set of applications. From these developments will emerge others. They will include a curriculum for teaching the HPT profession, a body of replicable research that builds on previous work, sets of standards and competencies that define HPT practice, and a more definitive set of boundaries and parameters for the field.

While HPT is becoming more mature as a unique field of study and practice, it is also becoming more accepted in the workplace—and acceptance in the business arena, especially in global companies, means that HPT is generating worldwide interest. Indeed, the language of HPT, its processes, and its fundamental pillars are universal, transcending geography and culture and truly beginning to have an impact on the world economy. As this development proceeds, HPT practitioners will become more valued and respected for the specific and organizationally beneficial contributions they can make, and the field will develop even more. It is essential that study and discussion of the foundations, origins, and conceptual milestones of HPT, as well as our envisioning of the next stages of HPT's evolution, continue in a robust way. As this chapter has shown, an understanding of HPT's roots can be an essential instrument in the evolution of its future.

References

Banathy, B. H. (1968). *Instructional systems.* Belmont, CA: Fearon.

Beer, M., and Walton, A. E. (1987). Organizational change and development. *Annual Review of Psychology* 38, 339–367.

Bloom, B. S. (1956). *Taxonomy of educational objectives.* Vol. 1: *Cognitive domain.* New York: McKay.

Brethower, D. M. (1995). Specifying a Human Performance Technology knowledgebase. *Performance Improvement Quarterly* 8:2, 17–39.

Bruner, J. S. (1969). *On knowing.* New York: Atheneum.

Bullock, D. H. (1973). The president reports. *NSPI Newsletter* 12:4, 3.

Coscarelli, W. C. (1966). *The future of ID models in corporate training.* Presentation at the annual meeting of the Association for Educational Communications and Technology, Indianapolis.

Crowder, N. A. (1960). Automatic tutoring by intrinsic programming. In A. Lumsdaine and R. Glaser (eds.), *Teaching machines and programmed learning.* Washington, DC: National Education Association.

Eucker, T. R. (1989). Information technology and the emerging organization. *Performance Improvement Quarterly* 2:3, 87–105.

Foshay, W. R. (1989). Information technology as performance technology. *Performance Improvement Quarterly* 2:3, 115–125.

Gagné, R. M. (1970). *The conditions of learning* (2nd ed.). Austin, TX: Holt, Rinehart and Winston.

Gery, G. J. (1989). Training versus performance support: Inadequate training is now insufficient. *Performance Improvement Quarterly* 2:3, 51–71.

Gilbert, T. F. (1996). *Human competence: Engineering worthy performance.* Amherst, MA, and Washington, DC: Human Resources Development Press and International Society for Performance Improvement.

Gilley, J. W. (1989). Career development: The linkage between training and organizational development. *Performance Improvement Quarterly* 2:1, 43–54.

Glaser, R. (1966). Psychological bases for instructional design. *Audiovisual Communication Review* 14:4, 433–449.

Harless, J. H. (1970). *An ounce of analysis is worth a pound of objectives.* Newnan, GA: Harless Performance Guild.

Harless, J. H. (1979). *Front-end analysis of soft skills training (FEASST).* Newnan, GA: Harless Performance Guild.

Hinrichs, R. J. (1997). *Intranets: What's the bottom line?* San Jose, CA: Sun Microsystems Press.

Horn, R. E. (1982). Structured writing in text design. In D. H. Jonassen (ed.), *The technology of text.* Englewood Cliffs, NJ: Educational Technology.

Hutchison, C. S. (1990). A process model for performance technology. *Performance & Instruction* 29:3, 1–5.

Hutchison, C. S., and Stein, F. S. (1997). A whole new world of interventions: The performance technologist as integrating generalist. *Performance Improvement* 36:10, 28–35.

Ilgren, D. R., Fisher, C. D., and Taylor, S. M. (1979). Consequences of feedback on behavior in organizations. *Journal of Applied Psychology* 64:4, 349–371.

Jacobs, R. L. (1988). A proposed domain of Human Performance Technology: Implications for theory and practice. *Performance Improvement Quarterly* 1:2, 2–12.

Kaufman, R., and English, F. W. (1979). *Needs assessment: Concept and application.* Englewood Cliffs, NJ: Educational Technology.

Leibler, S., and Parkman, A. (1986). Selection of personnel. In M. E. Smith (ed.), *Introduction to performance technology.* Washington, DC: National Society for Performance and Instruction.

Mager, R. F. (1975). *Preparing instructional objectives* (2nd ed.). Belmont, CA: Fearon.

Mager, R. F. (1988). *Making instruction work.* Belmont, CA: Lake.

Mager, R. F., and Pipe, P. (1984). *Analyzing performance problems.* Belmont, CA: Lake.

McLagan, P. (1989). *Models for HRD practice.* Alexandria, VA: American Society for Training and Development.

Phillips, D. T. (1989). Operations research and ergonomics/human factors form scientific roots of IE. *Industrial Engineering* 21, 42–45.

Pucel, D. J., Cerrito, J. C., and Noe, R. (1989). Integrating selection, training, and performance evaluation. *Performance Improvement Quarterly* 2:4, 21–29.

Reiser, R. A. (1987). Instructional technology: A history. In R. M. Gagné (ed.), *Instructional technology: Foundations.* Hillsdale, NJ: Erlbaum.

Richey, R. C. (1995). Trends in instructional design: Emerging theory-based models. *Performance Improvement Quarterly* 8:3, 96–110.

Robinson, D. C., and Robinson, J. C. (eds.). (1998). *Moving from training to performance.* Alexandria, VA: American Society for Training and Development.

Rosenberg, M. J. (1982). Our instructional media roots. *Performance & Instruction* 21:3, 12–15, 33.

Rosenberg, M. J. (1990). Performance technology: Working the system. *Training* 27:2, 42–48.

Rosenberg, M. J. (1995). Performance technology, performance support and the future of training. *Performance Improvement Quarterly* 8:1, 94–99.

Rosenberg, M. J. (1996). Human Performance Technology. In R. L. Craig (ed.), *The ASTD training and development handbook.* New York: McGraw-Hill.

Ross, P. C. (1986). Commentary: Behavioral technology in personnel selection. In M. E. Smith (ed.), *Introduction to performance technology.* Washington, DC: National Society for Performance and Instruction.

Rossett, A. (1987). *Training needs assessment.* Englewood Cliffs, NJ: Educational Technology.

Rothwell, W. (ed.). (1996). *ASTD models for human performance improvement: Roles, competencies, and outputs.* Alexandria, VA: American Society for Training and Development.

Rothwell, W., and Kazanas, H. C. (1997). *Mastering the instructional design process: A systematic approach* (2nd ed.). San Francisco: Jossey-Bass.

Rummler, G. A., and Brache, A. P. (1988a). *Improving performance: How to manage the white space on the organization chart.* San Francisco: Jossey-Bass.

Rummler, G. A., and Brache, A. P. (1988b). The systems view of human performance. *Training* 25:9, 45–53.

Senge, P. (1990). *The fifth discipline.* New York: Doubleday.

Shephard, R. J. (1974). *Men at work: Applications of ergonomics to performance and design.* Springfield, IL: Thomas.

Skinner, B. F. (1954). The science of learning and the art of teaching. *Harvard Educational Review* 24, 86–97.

Skinner, B. F. (1958). Teaching machines. *Science* 128, 969–977.

Svenson, R., and Wallace, K. (1989). Performance technology: A strategic management tool. *Performance & Instruction* 28:8, 1–7.

Tosti, D. F. (1986). Feedback systems. In M. E. Smith (ed.), *Introduction to performance technology.* Washington, DC: International Society for Performance Improvement.

Tosti, D. F. (1998, Feb.). Performance technology and organizational development. *News & Notes* (publication of the International Society for Performance Improvement), pp. 2–3.

Woods, D. D., and Roth, E. M. (1988). Cognitive engineering: Human problem solving with tools. *Human Factors* 30:4, 415–430.

CHAPTER THREE

Transforming Organizations Through Human Performance Technology

Geary A. Rummler

The term *transforming* means a lot of different things these days. In the context of this chapter, we will be talking about transforming an organization from one that performs at a particular level of output to one that performs at a higher level. Such a transformation may include a change in what is called the organization's *culture,* but the organization will certainly undergo a change in its performance infrastructure, or *performance system.* To complete such a transformation, two things are required:

1. A method for designing the necessary performance system to achieve the new levels of performance

2. Organizational leadership that can recognize the need for the higher levels of performance and make the changes and sacrifices necessary to achieve them

This chapter will focus on the first requirement, the method; the critical issue of leadership is addressed elsewhere in this handbook.

Underlying the method is Human Performance Technology (HPT), which is distinctly different from other approaches to change and performance improvement. Unfortunately, this distinction is not obvious to the casual observer. This chapter deals with the two ways in which the HPT approach differs from other approaches to improving performance and solving problems. The first way concerns the unique worldview or vantage point held by the HP technologist;

his or her conceptual framework is key to the identification of what is causing problems and to the specification of appropriate solutions. The second way concerns the systematic process that the HP technologist follows in applying this conceptual framework to the identification of problems or opportunities and to the determination and implementation of the changes necessary to improve performance.

THE NEED

The president of a midsized international company has just returned from a disastrous sales trip around the world, during which six major customers said they were not going to do any more business with the company until it "cleaned up its quality act." In an effort to get to the bottom of this quality problem, the president assembles the top managers and demands their views of the problem and recommendations for action. The group of subordinate managers quickly generates the following list of problems they see contributing to poor quality:

1. Poor attitude—the workers just do not care.
2. Communication is lacking between departments.
3. Suppliers are doing sloppy work.
4. The manufacturing processes require automating.
5. Engineering doesn't give a damn and just throws product designs over the wall.
6. The company cannot get and keep skilled inspectors.

The president is more frustrated than ever by this lack of consensus and direction from the staff and turns to outside consultants for their professional view of the situation. The first consultant says that the fundamental problem is strategy and that the strategy for the organization needs to be rethought. The second consultant says the problem is the antiquated work processes; they should be updated and automated. The third consultant says the problem is employee involvement: if only management were more participative and the employees more involved, they would be more motivated and quality would improve.

Stop! What is happening to our president? Actually, nothing different from what happens hundreds of times every day in organizations. The president *is* participative and asks the staff for help. Unfortunately (but predictably), each subordinate manager's view reflects his or her function's unique perspective on the organization and the problem. It is a classic "six blind men and an elephant" situation. Furthermore, each subordinate manager has a predictable, experience-based, discipline-bound set of solutions for addressing the problem as he or she sees it. Moreover, professional consultants tend to view the world from inside an even narrower set of blinders. They have designed approaches and trained staff to deliver a proposed solution (reorganization, performance appraisal, quality circles); clearly, they are purveyors of solutions in search of a problem.

What our president is missing, and what is missing from most situations in which management currently finds itself, is a framework that allows him to understand the variables that affect performance, to diagnose which of these variables are not operating as expected, and to determine the precise set of actions required to address the deficient variables. What is required is an *anatomy of human and organizational performance* equivalent to the framework of human anatomy that a physician uses when interpreting symptoms, identifying the cause of an illness, and prescribing a comprehensive set of treatments. Compare, on the one hand, how the members of an indigenous, preindustrial tribe traditionally deal with illness and, on the other, the approach of a modern medical team when it is asked to help. The medical team collects data, runs tests, identifies causes, and takes action, both to cure those with the disease and to prevent the disease from spreading or recurring. The determination of exactly what data are collected, which tests are run, and which actions are prescribed will start with team members' understanding of human anatomy—their framework.

What is required in the situation that our president faces is in fact very much what the HP technologist possesses: a view of the world, or a framework, that is the equivalent of an anatomy of performance, an anatomy that not only will help him cure current performance problems but also will allow him to design work environments that promote good performance at the outset by providing a healthy environment. Among all the disciplines and areas whose work addresses some aspect of human performance (psychology, industrial engineering, training and development, ergonomics and human factors engineering, compensation and benefits, to mention just a few), only HP technology endeavors to bring such a holistic framework or anatomy to issues of human performance. And, just as HP technologists can cure, they can also address the organizational and human performance equivalents of public health and wellness.

AN HP TECHNOLOGIST'S VIEW

If the president were to ask a group of HP technologists for help with the quality problem, each of them would respond differently because each would see the situation in a different way. All HP technologists have fundamentally different views of what is going on (or, as the case may be, *not* going on) in organizations. What HP technologists see—their framework—is shown in Figures 3.1 through 3.5.

First (see Figure 3.1), the HP technologist understands that an organization is an adaptive system, taking in various inputs and producing valued products and services for its customers. It exists in a larger environment or system that consists of competitors, who are competing for the organization's markets and resources; the general economy; legislation; government policy; and culture. The organization must continuously and successfully adapt to feedback from the environment, most notably the market (sales, customer complaints, market trends) and changes in resource availability and public sentiment, or it will soon fail to exist. This systems view of the organization and the "supersystem" in which it operates is particularly helpful to the HP technologist who must sort through the complexity of global markets and competition, where competitors are also customers and partners (see Chapter One). In the larger context of the organization as an adaptive system, the HP technologist focuses on three levels of performance variables that ultimately determine the performance of organizations and individuals: the levels of the *organization,* of *process,* and of the *job/performer.*

Figure 3.1. Organizations as Adaptive Systems.

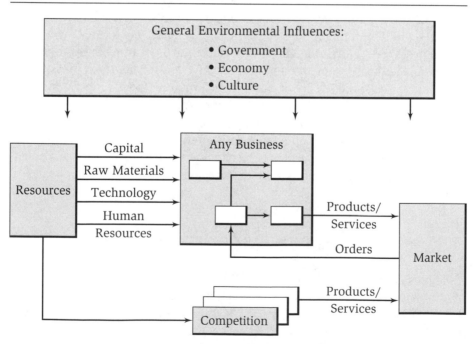

Level 1: The Organizational Level

At this level (see Figure 3.2), the HP technologist knows that the key performance variables are the organization's strategy and goals (What market does it intend to serve, with which products and services, at what levels of price and quality?); its structure (Is the organization structured to effectively and efficiently provide and support those products and services for that market, at that price, and with that level of quality?); measurement (Is organizational performance being measured in a way that supports the strategy?); and management (How is performance being tracked and corrective action taken?).

Level 2: The Process Level

Figure 3.2 displays a basic "skeleton" of the organization, showing its relationship with its environment and its basic internal structure. Figure 3.3 illustrates another level of what our HP technologist sees. As we look inside an organization, we see myriad cross-functional and cross-organizational processes by which work gets done and gets managed. Furthermore, organizations produce their outputs through these processes. Examples of such cross-functional processes include the new-product design process, the merchandising process, the production process, the sales process, the billing process, and the recruiting process. It is important to understand that these processes can span organizations and countries

Figure 3.2. The Organizational Level of Performance.

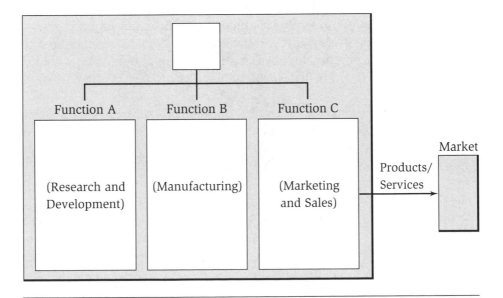

Figure 3.3. The Process Level of Performance.

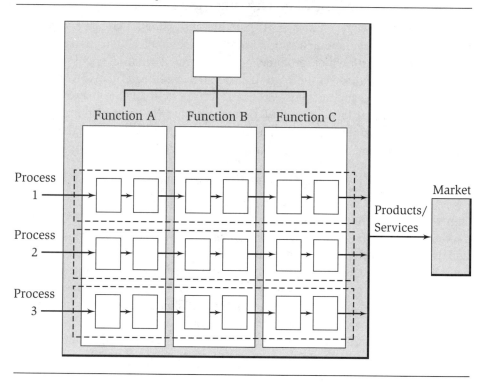

as well as functions. For example, one prominent electronics firm has a new-product development process that is capable of identifying a customer need in Europe, having the product designed in a Hong Kong design facility, having the prototype developed in Texas, and getting the product manufactured in Malaysia.

Figure 3.3 shows both the "skeleton" of the organizational level and the "musculature" of the cross-functional processes. The HP technologist understands the following about processes:

1. An organization is only as good as its internal processes.

2. The cross-functional processes are the flywheel that drives the organization. There will be no permanent change in an organization until the processes are changed (Rummler and Brache, 1995; Hammer and Champy, 1993).

3. Processes are the link between individual performance and organizational performance.

4. Organizations tend to manage according to function (the engineering function, the production function, the sales function), a practice that seriously inhibits effective cross-functional process flow.

5. Cross-functional processes are largely invisible, hard to fix (there is no mechanism in most organizations for improving cross-functional processes), and seldom managed.

6. The performance variables that determine the effectiveness of a process are parallel to those at the organizational level and include process goals, process design or structure, process measurement, and process management.

Level 3: The Job/Performer Level

As already mentioned, organizational outputs are produced through processes. Processes in turn are ultimately performed and managed by individuals and teams doing various jobs. If we increase the power of our X ray, as in Figure 3.4,

Figure 3.4. The Job/Performer Level of Performance.

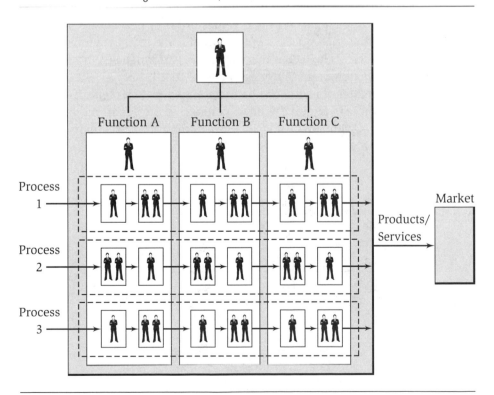

we can see this third level of performance, which might be equivalent to the cellular portion of the human anatomy.

The HP technologist has a framework for viewing the factors that affect the performance of an individual at the job level (regardless of whether that individual is a machine operator in Germany, a production supervisor in China, a CEO in France, or a vice president of sales in Mexico). What the HP technologist knows is that every performer exists in what we call the *Human Performance System* (HPS) (see Figure 3.5). Whether the desired job output will be produced is determined by the five components of the HPS: The *performer* (component 1) is required to process a variety of *inputs* (component 2), such as forms, sales opportunities, or phone calls. For each input there is a desired *output* (component 3), such as an inquiry answered or a form processed, and for every output (as well as for the action required to produce the output) there is a resulting set of *consequences* (component 4), or events that affect the performer. In general, these events are interpreted (uniquely) by the performer as being either positive or negative. We believe in a behavioral law that dictates how people's behavior will be influenced by consequences: regardless of the culture in which they live, people ultimately will do things that lead to positive consequences and will avoid things that lead to negative consequences. It is important to understand, however, that an individual's interpretation of what is positive or negative will be strongly influenced by the customs and values of his or her culture. *Feedback* (component 5) on the consequences of the output is the final component of the HPS. The significance of the HPS is that individual performance in an organization is always a function of these five components.

As a practical matter, the HPS can be transformed into the template shown in Figure 3.6. (Whereas Figure 3.4 does summarize the "anatomy of performance" perspective guiding the HP technologist, implicit but not shown in that figure is the idea that every performer exists within an HPS; Figure 3.6 repre-

Figure 3.5. The HPS.

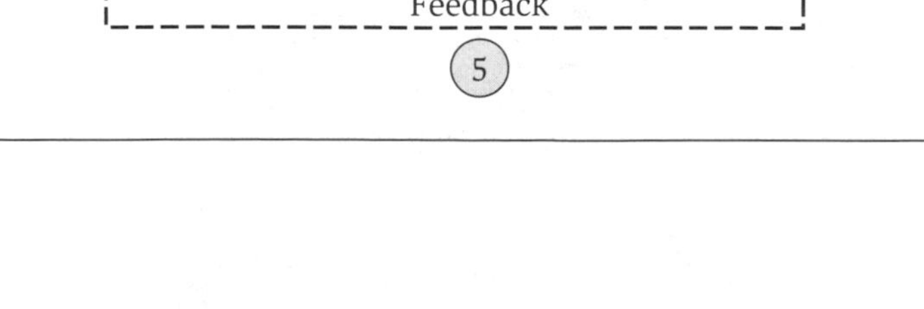

sents this final piece of the HPT framework.) Thus individual performance is a function of (1) *performance specifications* (Have we adequately specified and communicated the desired performance?), (2) *task interference* (Have we removed the barriers to performing the job by offering good design and by providing necessary resources?), (3) *consequences* (Do the consequences for the performer support his or her producing the desired output?), (4) *feedback* (Does the performer know if the output is on target and, if not, how to get it on target?), (5) *knowledge and skill* (Does the performer have the necessary knowledge or skill to produce the desired output?), and (6) *individual capacity* (Does the performer have the capacity to produce the output, given that the other five factors are adequate?). The HP technologist understands the following four principles concerning the performer/job level of performance and the HPS:

1. Consistent performance is a function of all six of the factors shown in Figure 3.6, not just of five out of six. For example, the performer may know what is expected, may have minimal interference, may get regular feedback, may know how to do the job, and may have the capacity to perform. If he or she experiences negative consequences after having performed as desired, however, the output will not be forthcoming on a regular basis

2. In a large majority of cases of poor job performance, the cause is a breakdown in one or more elements of the nonperformer components of the HPS.

3. If you pit a good performer against a bad HPS, the system will win every time.

4. The preceding three principles apply to all levels of an organization and all cultures.

To return to our frustrated president, as he discusses the quality problems with the HP technologist, certain questions will be guided by this framework:

What is meant by quality?

How is quality measured by the organization?

How is the organization structured?

What processes affect quality?

What is expected of those processes, and how are they measured?

What jobs are critical to those processes, and what are the measures for those jobs?

What jobs are not meeting quality standards?

What are the feedback, resources, and consequences relative to those key jobs?

Figure 3.6. Variables Affecting Job Performance.

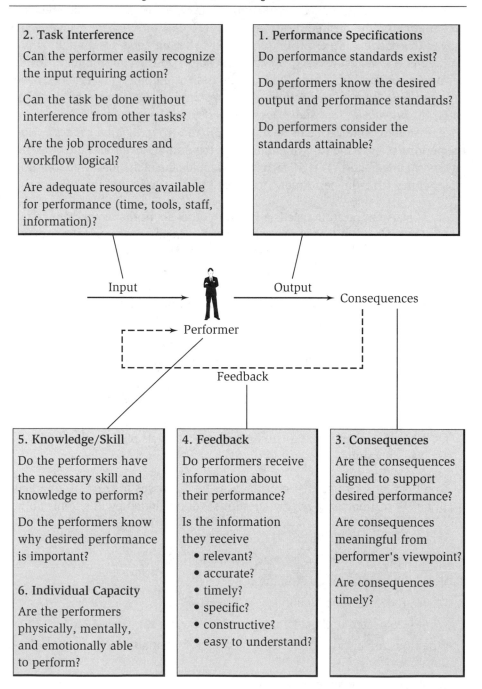

This framework or "anatomy" for viewing the performance world brings a number of benefits. A major benefit to the HP technologist is the ability, regardless of country or organization, to quickly and accurately identify and understand the issues affecting performance. When HP technologists first sit down with the president, they will not know the problem or the likely solution. They will know, however, that the problem is likely to involve all three levels of performance (organization, process, and job/performer) and that there is not likely to be one quick, simple solution. The major benefit to the president and his organization is that a correct and complete solution will be prescribed and will lead to long-term, permanent improvement.

The framework shows what the HP technologist must learn about the problem, and this learning is one part—the fundamental part—of the HPT approach. The second part is the process, that is, the steps that the HP technologist will follow to conduct a diagnosis and identify and implement the appropriate treatment.

THE HPT APPROACH

The HP technologist has a view of the world that provides insight into complex performance situations. But how is this view converted to action—that is, to accurate diagnosis and implemented solutions?

What is required is an approach that can address the range of performance improvement situations. *Problems* are indicated by a clear gap between desired and actual performance. (For example, Canadian bank tellers do not exhibit the desired behavior in the area of customer service. The productivity of a French sales force is lagging. A Spanish manufacturing plant is missing its cost, delivery, and quality standards. The members of a Mexican sales and service team will not work together.) *Opportunities* occur when current performance standards are being met but there is a chance to improve by 20 percent and thereby create a significant competitive edge. A *new situation* may be created by the introduction of new services or by the design of a new organization. The HPT approach has evolved over twenty-five years of international application and has demonstrated the ability to address this range of situations. Although there are limitless variations on the basic approach, it is always a systemic (reflecting the holistic view just described), performance-focused, and data-driven approach. The steps in the process can be summarized as follows:

Step 1: Problem/Opportunity Definition

The objective of this step is to identify and reach agreement on the performance desired by the client or organization. This definition is the starting point of the process. (It is also the ending point because, ultimately, it will be the basis for evaluating the effectiveness of the project.) In addition to a definition of desired performance, this step usually includes a statement of the project's scope and a plan for the project.

For example, in the case of the HP technologists attempting to help our president with his quality problem, it is important that the HP technologists identify the level of quality that the president and customers expect, how quality will be measured, and the time frame in which it will be measured. The scope of the project is another crucial piece of information: the HP technologists will not be effective if they cannot investigate and make changes at all three levels of the framework.

Step 2: Analysis

This is the step where the HP technologists apply the HPT framework to diagnose the problem, determine its cause, and specify or prescribe the treatment. A complete analysis requires an examination of each of the three levels—ideally, but not necessarily, in the macro-to-micro sequence described in the passages that follow.

The Organizational Level. The objectives of this step are to determine what changes will be required in the organization-level variables in order to attain the desired level of performance and identify the cross-functional processes that, because they are having a negative effect on the desired performance, should be examined further. The substeps usually include developing a systems picture of the organization (to depict how the various functions and processes are related to and affect the desired performance) and analyzing performance data to identify gaps in performance and name the critical processes.

For example, when HP technologists use the HPT framework to examine the organizational level of our president's company, they determine that quality is not considered a serious element of the company's strategy. As a result, the organization is not structured, nor are resources allocated, to support high quality, and quality is not consistently measured, tracked, or managed. From an operational standpoint, quality is considered important twenty-seven days of the month; in the last three days of the month, the priority shifts to meeting the monthly shipping goals. Obviously, changes must be made at the organizational level if quality is to be improved in this company. The HP technologists make these observations and offer possible solutions.

The Process Level. The objectives here are to determine the changes that will be required at the process level in order to improve performance and identify the jobs that, because they are key to the effective operation of these processes, should be examined further. The substeps include determining the operation of key processes (in terms of the desired performance goals); identifying which process steps are not being performed properly and are leading to the poor operation of those processes; determining the actions required to improve the operation of the processes; and identifying the jobs that are crucial to the successful operation of the processes and that need to be analyzed further for performance improvement.

For example, the HP technologists working with our president identify and subsequently analyze three work processes critical to the quality problems that have been identified. First, the production/assembly process itself is inappropriate to the current product line. The assembly process was designed when the company sold only ten different products. Now the company sells over one hundred different products, all of which are assembled on the line designed for ten, with substantially the same tooling and procedures. Second, in the process for product design there is a classic problem: strong functional goals that inhibit effective product design. Thus the design engineers develop products without considering what will be required in the production portion of the process. The result is that new products get designed on time and within the engineering budget, but the assembly function is never able to put the products together correctly, and so products that do not work are shipped to customers. Third, the company's process for forecasting sales is so inaccurate that the production area cannot rely on the forecasts. As a result, those in production must wait to see what orders are actually received each day and then schedule assembly accordingly. The error rate is high, largely because different products are assembled each day. Thus a substantial number of the changes required to improve quality in this company will revolve around the process level.

The Job/Performer Level. The objectives at this step in the analysis are (1) to determine what job outputs of which critical jobs need to be improved in order for the key processes to work effectively and produce the desired quality and (2) to identify the actions required to improve job outputs. This step consists primarily of identifying the gaps between desired and actual job outputs and using the HPS framework to determine the cause of poor job performance and the appropriate corrective action.

For example, our HP technologists in search of quality learn the following things about the assembly job. First, the printed assembly specifications for most parts are outdated and covered with handwritten modifications. This situation, along with the need to produce different parts each day, contributes significantly to assembly errors. Second, the emphasis is on "making shipments," not on achieving high quality: as long as the production area meets its shipping goals, nothing is said about quality. Third, because there is a shortage of tools that work, assemblers frequently "borrow" tools from one another to get the job done. The HP technologists also learn that for years the assemblers have been raising questions about the specifications and tools, but management's response has been "Quit griping." The HP technologists summarize their observations of factors at the job/performer level of performance that are affecting quality, and they note the changes that will be necessary at this level.

Step 3: Design and Development

At the conclusion of the analysis steps, the HP technologists have made a thorough diagnosis and identified a comprehensive, multilevel set of treatments that will address the company's quality problem. The objective of the next step is to design and develop those recommended changes, or treatments, that were specified in the analysis step. Design and development may include a broad range of actions, from modifying organizational strategy to redesigning processes and jobs to designing a new measurement system, a performance management system, and training. HP technologists could propose many of these actions to address a problem with quality. What also must be developed in this step is the process that will be used to evaluate the effectiveness of the treatment.

An HP technologist is not likely to be an expert in the design of all the treatments necessary to bring about a complete "cure." To expand our medical metaphor, the HP technologist may function as a general practitioner, conducting the critical diagnosis and bringing in a team of specialists to design and implement a broad set of treatments.

Step 4: Implementation and Maintenance

The objective of this step is to successfully implement and maintain the various solutions. Key to success at this step are not only planning of the sequence for introducing the various treatments but also top management's support, which should be forthcoming if a significant organizational performance problem is being effectively addressed through identification of problems and opportunities.

Step 5: Evaluation

The objective of this step is to gather data on performance and to assess whether the treatments are producing the desired results—and, if not, to determine how the treatments must be modified to achieve the desired outcome. In lists of process steps like this one, evaluation always comes last. It is important to note, however, that evaluation for the HP technologist starts in step 1, where the problem or opportunity is identified along with the performance to be improved. Evaluation procedures are developed along with solutions. The tracking of performance starts at the implementation stage and should continue as an aspect of the ongoing management of the performance in question. As the data are gathered and analyzed, the loop is closed: either the treatment is effective and the problem is eradicated (or significantly mitigated) or the performance/evaluation data provide more insight into the changes that are required at one or more levels, at which point the treatment is altered or a new one is prescribed.

THE CASE OF THE DEFECTIVE "PERFORMANCE GENE"

A young, fast-growing international telecommunications organization was experiencing slipping profits and customer defections. The business consisted of selling and designing complex communications network services. Three types of services were sold by the company: basic, advanced, and custom.

One symptom of trouble was that 30 percent of the company's new customers were dropping out before they actually got hooked up. Another was that the selling organization was offering services that the operations organization could not profitably design and deliver. Still another was that management was in constant "scramble" mode, and the firm's continued rapid growth was threatened by the inability of management to get its arms around the problem. Senior executives began to seriously consider that salvation might lie in a reorganization of the company into three divisions centered on the three types of service.

At this point, HP technologists got involved and quickly took the following actions, using the "anatomical" view already discussed:

1. They learned about the organization itself, including its strategy, goals, structure, key processes, and management system.
2. They examined the processes for selling and for filling customers' orders, noting how work was done and managed.
3. They examined key sales and design jobs, using the HPS template.

Their two-week analysis uncovered the fundamental cause of sick organization performance (the defective "performance gene"): lack of feedback on performance. Individual salespersons never received any feedback on the consequences of their having sold particular services, on the specifications that had been developed for the services, or on what was being charged for the services. Without feedback, there was no learning on the part of these individuals or the organization. The solution to this problem was a process management system that included development and distribution of cost data linking the downstream operations process with the upstream sales process. With the data distribution and the management system in place, the firm was able to learn which customer engagements were profitable, which types of service meant profitable business and should be emphasized, who was making profitable sales, and what needed to be done for engagements to become even more profitable.

And the reorganization? Not only was it unnecessary, but, had it been implemented, it would have obscured the real cause of the problems, prolonged and exacerbated the problems, and led to disaster in the areas of finance and customer service. The HP technologists' understanding of the "anatomy" of performance made it possible for them to quickly isolate the root cause (or the defective "performance gene") and make the appropriate microscopic corrections rather than amputate.

VARIATIONS ON THE HPT APPROACH

This chapter has already shown how the basic five-step HPT approach can be used to solve a performance problem—that is, a gap between a desired level of performance (a performance involving quality, in the example we have been using) and the actual level of performance. To date, most applications of HPT have addressed performance problems, but there are also variations on this approach, which ultimately prove even more beneficial because they deal less with cures and more with prevention. Here are two examples of such variations.

Example A: Realizing an Opportunity Through Implementation of a New Strategy

Situation. A large chain of retail stores that sold paint and supplies for home decorating concluded that it needed to expand into the wholesale business (selling to commercial painters, maintenance people in large apartment complexes, and so on) in order to maintain the necessary level of growth.

Problem/Opportunity Definition. The strategic goal was to penetrate the wholesale market. The specific opportunity was to increase wholesale sales by a given dollar amount and increase the chain's share of the wholesale market by a certain percentage while maintaining the chain's position in the retail market.

Analysis. The HPT team members looked at all three levels of performance to determine what would be required in order for the chain to operate effectively in the wholesale market. At the *organization*al level, they viewed the chain as a system and identified the structures, measures, and processes that would have to be modified or invented (as well as how this would have to be done) in order to support the new strategy. At the *process* level, critical work and management processes (such as billing and sales management) were analyzed and redesigned, and several new processes (such as sales planning and forecasting) were developed to address this new market. Process measures were specified and process goals were established, in keeping with the strategic goals. At the *job* level, new goals, measures, feedback systems, job aids, and training were specified for those jobs (comprising hourly employees and employees in sales and management) that were crucial to the chain's effective operation in the wholesale market. Three new jobs were specified, and one management job was significantly altered.

Design and Development. The procedures, measures, job aids, and training for supporting the new processes and jobs were all developed.

Implementation and Maintenance. All the components of the new performance system necessary to the support of the new strategic direction were implemented over a six-month period.

Evaluation. The organization achieved its goals for sales and market share over the next three years. Because it had successfully expanded into the wholesale market, it withstood a major industry recession.

Example B: Designing a New Organization

Situation. An international electronics manufacturer decided to build a "factory of the future." The objectives included the ability to produce products at a fraction of their current cost and to design an innovative work environment. A team of functional specialists from around the world began working with an HP technologist. At the outset, the team received training in the HPT framework.

Analysis. The HP technologist and the international team of specialists began with a macro-to-micro effort of designing the organization. They started at the organizational level, where decisions were made about global markets, products, structure, locations, performance parameters, and goals. Next, they determined what processes would be required for producing the products and meeting the goals established at the organizational level. Process specification started with the basic production processes, moved on to all the necessary support processes, and ended with the management processes necessary to make the new organization work. Finally, jobs were identified (with the job of operator as the starting point), and the team then moved on to jobs in support functions and in management. Jobs were specified and measures were identified. At both the process and the job levels, objectives in keeping with an innovative work environment were considered, and the result in many instances was the design of self-directed work teams. Analysis and a general design process were accomplished over a two-week period.

Design and Development/Implementation and Maintenance. Over the next two years, the project team specifically designed all the components of the system and built and started up the new facility. This work went substantially as planned.

Evaluation. The bottom-line evaluation was recently summed up by a vice president who said, "Given the current level of competition, we wouldn't be in that business today if we hadn't built that plant the way we did." This firm not only achieved its economic objective but also designed an organization that should provide a sound performance environment at all three levels.

BENEFITS OF THE APPROACH

The benefits of the approach are an extension of the benefits of the framework. For the HP technologist, the process provides a map for working through complex performance situations in complicated organizational settings. Each situation dictates the disciplines, techniques, and tools that should be used (Rummler, 1983). The process ensures that the HP technologist, like the physician, asks the proper questions and reviews all relevant data before reaching important conclusions. This approach has moved human performance–related "art" toward HPT and a human performance profession (Dean and Ripley, 1997).

Clients of HP technologists feel the same reassurance that we all feel when we go to a skilled physician, for whom questioning, diagnosis, and treatment are not random or based on the latest article. Like the physician, the HP technologist is following a bona fide, systematic process proved to accurately identify causes and lead to the prescription of effective treatments. And the results support the confidence of the clients.

"IF YOU'RE SO DAMNED SMART, WHY AREN'T YOU RICH?"

Good question. If the HPT approach is so great and so effective, why is it not *the* way organizations go about approaching performance problems and opportunities? Part of the problem, no doubt, has been the relatively slight exposure that this approach has enjoyed, despite some publications (Gilbert, 1978; Harless, 1970; Jones, Standke, and Zemke, 1981; Mager, 1970; Stolovitch and Keeps, 1992; Kaufman, Thiagarajan, and MacGillis, 1997). Another part of the problem is that, on the part of clients, there certainly has been no perceived need for a better approach. In the past, many of the performance problems faced by organizations have been transitory and elusive, and the problems eventually went away independently (or in spite of) the actions taken.

The problems that many organizations face today are not trivial or transitory, however. The need to compete successfully in the global market will require major, fundamental changes. The increasingly complex situation in which organizations find themselves is a natural for the application of HPT.

Unfortunately, two factors pose major challenges to the broader use of the HPT approach in the future. The first is the continuing search by management for the quick fix ("Just give me a shot, Doc—I'll be all right"). It seems that organizations have to try all the quick, simple solutions first, resorting to thorough analysis and comprehensive treatment only after all the "easy" alternatives have been exhausted. Organizations want simple answers, and so they tend to define problems in terms of readily available solutions. HP technologists, with their view of the world, suspect (and are usually proved correct) that problems are not quite that simple, and that quick shots in the arm may bring only short-term relief of symptoms. Permanent cures often require severe changes. HP technologists frequently bring news that organizations do not want to—and will not—hear.

The second factor is the apparent need for every change or improvement effort in an organization (initiatives involving empowerment, teams, reengineering, and "the learning organization," to name only a few) to be conceived, packaged, and conveyed as a "program." The comprehensive range of treatments likely to be prescribed by an HP technologist seldom fits neatly into a program, and programs quickly become "things"—entities unto themselves, with their own implementation objectives, champions, teams, and slogans. The emphasis becomes "Have we conducted the program?" rather than "Have we effectively addressed the issues?"

The classic example of both these factors is the way the vast majority of U.S. firms have addressed the issue of quality over the past fifteen years. Only after having tried every conceivable quick fix, with no quick results, have some companies come to realize the depth and breadth of the problem (the HP technologist, of course, would say that there are three levels of depth and breadth) and begun to make significant changes in how they manage.

Likewise, there is no quick solution or easy answer for the HP technologist facing these organizational obstacles. The first factor will probably be affected to some degree by better "patient education" on the need for long-term approaches rather than quick fixes, but HP technologists also will have to conduct their diagnoses and administer their treatments faster, fully appreciating the reality of their clients' environmental pressure for results. Programs, moreover, are probably here to stay. They seem to be a necessary way for organizations to gain focus on a problem and muster resources. But programs can certainly be conceived and administered better than most have been in the past, and HP technologists will have to learn either to integrate their treatments into existing programs or to package their treatments into soundly conceived and effectively administered programs (Rummler and Brache, 1995, chap. 8).

CONCLUSION

The HPT approach described in this chapter is unique, powerful, and proved. At the heart of its uniqueness and effectiveness is the holistic view or "anatomy of performance" that guides HP technologists as they thoroughly and systematically gather data, analyze and identify causes of performance problems, and prescribe comprehensive treatments to improve performance. If their clients are willing to invest beyond the quick fix, they will be the beneficiaries of long-term performance improvement. The value of the HPT approach goes beyond closing performance gaps, however. It also has the potential to serve as a blueprint for building an overall high-performance environment within an organization, an environment in which the traditional HP issues never arise. Realizing this potential for HPT will be the challenge of the new millennium.

References

Dean, J. P., and Ripley, D. E. (1997). *Performance improvement pathfinders: Models for organizational learning systems.* Washington, DC: International Society for Performance Improvement.

Gilbert, T. F. (1978). *Human competence: Engineering worthy performance.* New York: McGraw-Hill.

Hammer, M., and Champy, J. (1993). *Reengineering the corporation: A manifesto for business revolution.* New York: HarperBusiness.

Harless, J. (1970). *An ounce of analysis is worth a pound of objectives.* Newnan, GA: Harless Performance Guild.

Jones, P., Standke, L., and Zemke, R. (1981). *Designing and delivering cost-effective training—and measuring the results.* Minneapolis: Lakewood.

Kaufman, R., Thiagarajan, S., and MacGillis, P. (1997). *The guidebook for performance improvement: Working with individuals and organizations.* San Francisco: Pfeiffer.

Mager, R. F. (1970). *Analyzing performance problems.* Belmont, CA: Fearon.

Rummler, G. A. (1983). Technology domains and NSPI. *Performance & Instruction 9,* 32–36.

Rummler, G. A., and Brache, A. P. (1995). *Improving performance: How to manage the white space on the organization chart* (2nd ed.). San Francisco: Jossey-Bass.

Stolovitch, H. D., and Keeps, E. J. (1992). *Handbook of Human Performance Technology: A comprehensive guide for analyzing and solving performance problems in organizations.* San Francisco: Jossey-Bass.

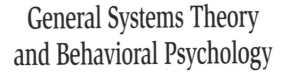

CHAPTER FOUR

General Systems Theory and Behavioral Psychology

Dale M. Brethower

General systems theory and behavioral psychology provide a knowledge base for Human Performance Technology (HPT). The knowledge base supports powerful methods for constructing instructional systems and performance management systems that improve individual and organizational performance; enable people to learn effectively both on and off the job; connect the interests of individuals, groups, and organizations; and support the achievement of results that benefit the individual, the organization, and the customer.

HPT helps individuals and organizations achieve better results. HPT helps people both to learn how to perform competently and to perform competently once they do know how. Today, over thirty-five years into the development of the field, it is becoming clear that HP technologists fundamentally do only two things: they work with others to build *instructional systems* (which help people learn how to perform well) and to build *performance systems* (which help people perform well once they do know how).

When an organization embarks on a major initiative, HPT can help design or build the instructional systems and performance systems that are needed for successful implementation. The instructional systems might include classroom training, on-the-job training, job aids, and on-the-job coaching. The performance systems might include feedback systems, incentive systems, and systems for work processes. Some of the systems might be built from the ground up in their entirety; others might be built from components already in place.

HPT is not restricted to classroom training in which the instructor "knows the answers" at the beginning. Performance-based instructional systems can support real learning, in real organizations, in real time. For example, facilitating the work of a strategic planning group is powerful real-time instruction. When HPT practitioners facilitate strategic planning, they help people learn the answers to such questions as "How can Ecotech prosper in the future?" Once the group learns or creates answers to questions involving strategic planning, HPT practitioners can help establish the performance systems that will be required in implementing the given strategy.

THE KNOWLEDGE BASE OF HPT

HPT grew from a foundation in general systems theory and behavioral psychology. General systems theory provides basic concepts that integrate ideas from many different disciplines and subdisciplines that are relevant to HPT. These include not only behavioral psychology (which contributes to an understanding of human beings and the many complex variables affecting individual performance) but also economics, psychology, sociology, accounting, the cognitive sciences, finance, management, compensation practice, and benefits administration.

A major irony of the Information Age is that ignorance grows more rapidly than knowledge. Collectively, more is known than ever before; at the same time, people individually are falling farther behind the knowledge curve. For example, a manager in a high-technology corporation must learn more and more to keep up with the industry, but knowledge is still growing too rapidly for personal mastery to keep up; similarly, a professional in a health maintenance organization will fall behind even while learning a great deal. The old solution to this problem—greater specialization—can work only if specialists communicate with other specialists, but specialists all speak in the languages of their specializations and often cannot communicate effectively with others. The HP technologist who knows general systems theory can help.

General Systems Theory

General systems theory was created in response to practical problems emerging from the knowledge explosion. General systems theory enables people with different sets of specialized knowledge to work together toward common goals. The driving force among early general systems theorists was the quest for important similarities across specialized disciplines (see Bertalanffy, 1968; Laszlo, 1972; and Mesarovic, 1964).

One similarity is illustrated by the concept of the *system*. There are (among many other kinds) physical, biological, electronic, governmental, heating, communication, family, social, sociotechnical, and ecosystems. General systems theory is about figuring out what they all have in common.

General Systems Principles. There are many common points that are useful to know about. Seven principles based on system commonalities are described in the passages that follow.

1. *The principle of open systems.* All systems, from the simple amoeba to the human being and the commercial organization, are open systems (see Miller, 1978). This means that they must import energy to survive. For example, biological systems must acquire food and convert it to energy. Commercial systems must acquire economic resources and put them to useful purposes. Electronic systems must have electrical energy. Families, as systems, must acquire economic resources, converting them to food and shelter and to opportunities for learning. No matter what the type of system, there is an energy "overhead" that must be paid to keep the system going. Thus systems are open, not hermetically sealed, perpetual-motion machines.

2. *The principle of information processing.* Every biological system has specific mechanisms for processing information as well as for absorbing matter and converting it to life-giving energy (Miller, 1978). Flowcharts can be used to describe information processing systems and matter/energy processing systems, to help promote an understanding of how they work, repair them when they are defective, and redesign them when external conditions change. A description of how work, information, and money flow through an organization is a very important aspect of any major organizational change effort.

3. *The principle of guided systems.* Many open systems are also guided systems; that is, their energies can be redirected toward the achievement of specific goals. For example, families can spend less on recreation and more on education, or less on food and more on medicine. Commercial enterprises can spend more on advertising and less on production, or they can put more into the profit margin for shareholders and less into employee development.

4. *The principle of adaptive systems.* Many open systems are also adaptive systems; that is, they can change their goals and redirect their energies from the old goals to the new ones. For example, commercial organizations can move from emphasizing their products to emphasizing their services, or from increasing shareholder value to increasing market share.

5. *The principle of energy channeling.* All open systems must have mechanisms for channeling energy. For example, electronic systems can be designed to power down in a crisis so as to preserve specific functions. Energy channeling is a fundamental motivational process. Commercial organizations, like individual human beings, cannot be all things to all people; they must set priorities: With whom will they align? Whom will they serve? To whom will

they go to for help should the need arise? Individuals must have mechanisms for setting the priorities that are related to their personal and professional lives. Setting and following through on priorities are the cognitive and behavioral components of motivation.

6. *The principle of environmental intelligence.* An open system functions most effectively when it has and can process good information about its environments because it is then more likely to survive if the environment changes. For example, commercial organizations do well to have information about market trends, international economic trends, local political trends, and social trends. Successful individuals require good information about the social, economic, and workplace trends that affect their lives. This principle has strong implications for the practice of HPT: poor information interferes with good performance and supports poor performance. Successful projects for performance improvement involve improving information processing, whether by establishing feedback systems, performance-support systems, or systems for tracking quality.

7. *The principle of subsystem maximization.* An open system operates within the constraints imposed by the external environment and, therefore, by the available resources. These constraints give rise to the principle of subsystem maximization, which concerns the impossibility of maximizing the functioning of both a subsystem and the total system at the same time. This principle represents the basis in systems theory of many vexing practical problems in organizations. It describes why priority setting is essential, and why internal competition can be extremely harmful. It also describes why vaguely insisting on "high standards" of performance can be counterproductive; a much better performance standard is one that says, "Keep your performance within this range, and help others keep their performances within specified ranges." This principle has major implications for efforts to align individual and organizational goals, reduce internal conflict, set operational and strategic goals, and develop high-performance teams. Indeed, this extremely important principle comes into play in any major organizational design or development initiative.

How the Systems Principles Can Be Used. HP technologists can use these seven principles to quickly learn fundamental things about an organization. The most straightforward way is to use them as an interviewing guide. With a little practice, interview questions can be tailored to specific types of organizations or to specific industries. The questions can be asked in structured interviews or in casual conversations. (In fact, a good way to practice is to ask such questions informally, in conversations with the stranger in the adjacent seat on a plane or with people at receptions, business lunches, or social events.)

Validation of the Systems Principles. Brethower (1970) has demonstrated that real public school classrooms can be described as adaptive systems and that student performance can be improved through a systems approach to self-management of teacher and student performance. Brethower's research validates the Total Performance System model shown in Figure 4.1, which depicts a performance system as an adaptive system. The Receiving System and the external feedback loop symbolize an adaptive interdependence with a larger environment (performance system with Receiving System). The internal feedback loop symbolizes all the many internal guidance systems that enable the system to produce the outputs (goods and services) required by the Receiving System. If any of the seven components of an adaptive system (mission, inputs, processing system, outputs, internal feedback, receiving system, external feedback) are defective, an adaptive system will not function properly (Brethower, 1970, 1995; Brethower and Smalley, 1998).

The validation research was part of a comprehensive effort that took a systems approach to running a reading clinic at the University of Michigan. Staff members analyzed the clinic in systems terms, defining the mission, establishing goals and measuring them, clarifying the primary service processes, and providing feedback to staff members as part of staff development and process improvement.

The principle of subsystem maximization guided the work. This principle, as already discussed, involves the realization that no one can do everything well, all at once, all the time, and with limited resources. For example, had staff attempted to maximize the staff training function, that would have interfered with service delivery and with research. Similarly, an attempt to provide the best possible service to the largest number of clients would have interfered with the goal of providing the best possible service to special categories of clients. Thus, because most of the clients were university students who were relatively easy to serve, putting most of the clinic's resources into serving them would have meant

Figure 4.1. An Adaptive System Model.

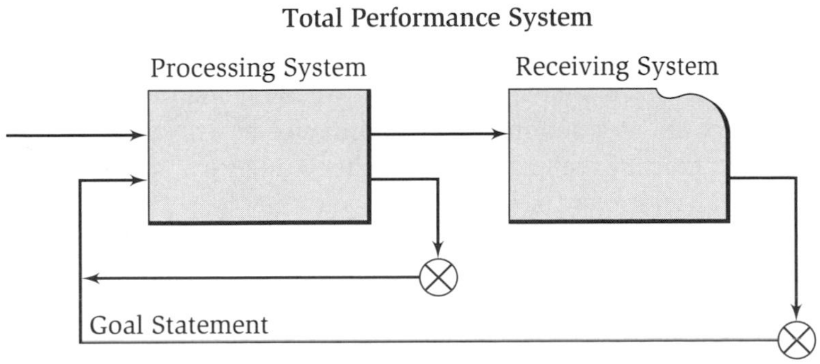

Total Performance System

reducing services to university students who were experiencing difficult problems, to elementary school students who could not be served by local schools, to institutionalized young adults, and to adults whose reading performance was limited by their lack of basic literacy. Moreover, leaving out any of these populations would have seriously harmed staff development programs because one important goal was to train staff to serve these special populations. It would also have harmed the research programs.

The clinic staff established goals that were balanced across several subsystems and over short- and long-term considerations. For example, staff scheduled peak levels of service to children at times when there was a lower demand for services to university students. There were also priorities established to balance the subsystems. For example, one summer the major priority was to achieve high gains in services to children, and that summer the average gain was six months' worth of increased reading skill for each month of instruction. The next summer, because of different external demands, the major priority was for key staff members to complete their graduate degree requirements, and so more progress was made toward degrees than had been made the previous summer, and the average gain for clients fell to three months' worth of increased reading skill for each month of instruction. (Staff considered this gain acceptable because the "industry standard" for improvement in the population served was less than one month's worth of improvement per month of instruction.) The systems issue in this case was not "Should we sacrifice staff development to support client development?" but rather "How can we balance staff development and client development over time so that both are achieved at a high level?" Both goals were attained over a two-year period, and unsatisfactory compromises were avoided.

Behavioral Psychology

Behavioral psychology, like general systems theory, is an important source of the knowledge base of HPT (Brethower, 1995; Dean and Ripley, 1997). Like other psychologists, behavioral psychologists study behavior; what makes behaviorists unique is that they seek to identify the variables that can be used to improve the performance of specific persons in specific settings at specific times. Behaviorists do research to identify essential variables, and they use that knowledge to modify variables and improve performance in real settings.

Behavioral clinical psychologists help clients identify functional and dysfunctional behaviors relevant to life tasks, and they help clients increase the functional behaviors and decrease the dysfunctional ones. The research literature demonstrating the effectiveness of behavioral approaches to clinical issues is enormous, and it grows significantly every year (Azrin, McMahon, Donohue, and Besalel, 1994; Franks and Wilson, 1973–1996; Lovaas, Freitag, Gold, and Kassorla, 1965). Behavioral psychologists also help clients improve their performance in educational settings. There is a very large and rapidly expanding research literature demonstrating the effectiveness of behavioral approaches in schools (Binder and Watkins, 1990; Gardner and others, 1994; Heiman and Slomianko, 1992; Johnson and Layng, 1994; Lindsley, 1991). Behavioral psychologists help clients improve their performance in the workplace as well, and a large and growing research literature demonstrates the effectiveness of behavioral approaches in public and private organizations (Abernathy, Duffy, and O'Brien, 1982; Bennett, 1988; Brethower and Rummler, 1966; Daniels, 1989; Eickhoff, 1991; Fellner and Sulzer-Azaroff, 1984; Fox, Hopkins, and Anger, 1987; Frederiksen, 1982; Gilbert, 1996; Gordon, 1992; Komaki, 1986; Komaki, Barwick, and Scott, 1978; Kopelman, 1986; Marr and Roessler, 1994; McNally and Abernathy, 1989; McSween, 1995; O'Brien, Dickinson, and Rosow, 1982; Rummler and Brache, 1995).

Its focus on improving the specific performance of specific individuals in specific situations sets behavioral psychology apart, as does the range of validated applications across settings and populations. No other approach can match the breadth and depth of the behaviorist approach.

In other approaches, experiments are conducted that yield probability statements about how a typical person might perform in a typical environment. These approaches use research designs in which two groups of people are studied under two different treatment conditions, and results are stated in terms of statistical differences pertaining to one or two of the data points collected from each group. Thus the research methodology yields results that simply do not tell anyone very much about how a specific person will perform in a specific environment.

By contrast, behavioral psychologists use time-series research designs in which many data points are collected with respect to each person's performance. Collecting many data points before, during, and after an intervention allows a researcher to make specific statements about specific instances of performance in specific environments.

Behavioral psychology contributes specific principles about the interaction of individual and environment. For example, the *law of effect* states that actions leading to immediate positive consequences are likely to be repeated (conversely, actions leading to immediate negative consequences are less likely to be repeated). This law is important in the design of systems for motivation, recognition, supervision, and compensation. Immediacy is an important but often neglected aspect of the law of effect: most formal systems for rewards and recognition systems set up rewards or recognition that may occur days, weeks, or months after the successful performance in question, but delayed recognition is much less powerful than immediate positive consequences. (Everyone has experienced this phenomenon, perhaps in struggling to align long-term goals with daily urgencies or to balance the delayed gratification of weight loss with the immediate gratification of a delicious dessert.)

Another contribution of the behaviorist approach is the *principle of conceptual learning,* which states that conceptual learning "requires direct interactions with multiple examples and non-examples" (Brethower, 1995, p. 30). This principle, also adopted by cognitive psychologists, is violated by most textbooks and most training materials; there are too few examples and far too few nonexamples. For example, this failure in instructional design contributes to outcomes in which people can recite the words they have been taught but do not understand them well enough to apply what they have learned or transfer their learning to other settings.

A Link Between Behavioral Psychology and General Systems Theory

The link is very close: just as organizations are systems, so too are individuals (Ford, 1987). Information processing (as a foundation for intelligence) and matter/energy processing (as a foundation for health) are both important to individuals. People who are better able to learn and process information are better suited to survive and prosper in the modern world. Much of education and training is intended to enable people to acquire and process information intelligently. The principle of subsystem maximization holds true for individuals, as everyone knows who has attempted to balance family matters, health, friendships, and a career over long periods of time.

Behaviorists know a lot about how to change behavior. But how does anyone know what behavior to change? Which behaviors are functional, and which are dysfunctional? It is surprisingly difficult to tell them apart. Experienced practitioners can guess what is functional with reasonable accuracy, but the only real test is to look and see what the behaviors are accomplishing in a larger system. Behaviors that get good results over long periods of time are functional; those that interfere or get bad results are dysfunctional. Whether a behavior is functional or dysfunctional depends on the larger social system. For example, if making eye contact improves communication with clients, perhaps by making it easier to get issues into the open, improve the quality of solutions to problems, or close sales, then making eye contact is functional. In some cultures, however, making eye contact would be dysfunctional. Similarly, praising people in public is functional in some cultures and dysfunctional in others, as is voicing criticism of someone's ideas. The point is that, in any culture, whether a behavior is functional or dysfunctional is determined by the results or consequences of the behavior within a larger system, not by the behavior per se. That is one reason why skills (behaviors) should be taught and learned in context, not in isolated classroom exercises that provide no support for transfer of the skills.

Taken together, general systems theory and behavioral psychology provide a firm foundation for HPT. People and organizations are systems, and they function as systems. Knowing and using the principles that underlie the performance of individuals and organizations can help HPT add value.

GENERAL SYSTEMS THEORY AND OTHER APPROACHES

General systems theory is designed to show what a variety of "special" systems theories have in common. It is not an approach that says that a special systems theory is wrong but rather an approach that seeks to identify essential elements that systems have in common. That, indeed, is what management theories try to do. For example, Peters and Waterman (1982) attempt to show what excellent organizations have in common, and their book rather brilliantly identifies key characteristics of excellent organizations; unfortunately, many of the excellent organizations have not survived into the 1990s, which shows that the search for excellence has not concluded. Collins and Porras (1994), by looking backward, circumvent the embarrassment of having their putative excellent companies fail. They attempt to sort out the essential characteristics of organizations that last by pairing enduring organizations with organizations that did not endure over the same time period. By seeking to discover key differences between the organizations that survived and those that did not, the authors attempt to tease out the characteristics that help organizations thrive and prosper.

A strength of both books is that they are not theoretical. They both try to analyze real organizations—and to do so without the blinders and biases of a specific theory. But that strength is also a weakness: it derives from a method that required the authors of these two books to begin with as blank a slate as possible, looking at all possible similarities and differences between exemplary organizations and those that fail. That is an arduous task, and one that sets aside prior knowledge; it does not build on what has gone before, at least not in a planned way.

General systems theory takes a different approach. General systems theorists seek to avoid specific blinders by using concepts that have stood the test of time across many different situations, and across many different disciplines. General systems research is about the discovery of the systemic similarities among all forms of systems, especially biological systems. HPT professionals can and should analyze organizations to determine whether a few key systemic functions are being performed adequately. The systemic similarities can be thought of as the deep structure of organizations, and the deep structure can be found only if one knows where to look and what to look for—only, that is, through analysis. For example, consider a sports event, whose surface structure is composed of many unique features that can be captured with video cameras or audio recorders. They are what a play-by-play *announcer* would see and report, and they are important, but they are not fundamental. The deep structure of a sports event is what a good sports *analyst* would see and report.

Management books, in the main, are consistent with general systems theory. The notion of managing an organization as a system is almost explicit in some management books; for example, see Kaplan and Norton (1996). Nevertheless, management practices are shaped by variables of the surface structure—and therein lies an opportunity for HPT. The variables of the surface structure obscure the deep structure, and so it is easier for harmful practices to creep in: "empire building" (subsystem maximization), rewarding what looks good more than what works, benchmarking against inappropriate practices, rewarding hard but ineffectual work, or rewarding loyalty more than contributions. These practices distract attention from important organizational variables and generate confusion, political infighting, and poor communication. The HPT practitioner who can cut through the confusion to focus attention on the basic organizational variables can perform an enormous service.

BEHAVIORAL PSYCHOLOGY AND OTHER APPROACHES

Behavioral psychology, like cognitive, humanistic, or psychodynamic psychology, seeks answers to this question: "Why do people act the way they do?" Why do some succeed in a task, whereas others fail? Why are some people cheerful and others grumpy? Why does Aunt Maude hate cats, whereas her twin sister loves them? Psychologists agree on the broad-brush answer to such questions: what a person does and who the person is are functions of inherited characteristics and environmental experiences.

Psychologists also agree that what is known about a person is learned through observation of that person's behavior, or of the results or products of that behavior. The products of behavior might be the artifacts left behind by a prehistoric culture, or the products might be paintings or symphonies or novels or scholarly treatises or widgets. The behavior might be measured by direct observation or by standardized tests or clinical interviews. In any case, psychologists agree that behavior is what is being measured.

Psychologists differ in what they want to know about the behavior they study. Some are interested in current behavior for what it can tell them about the person. For example, a clinical psychologist might look at how a person responds to items in a battery of psychological tests to learn more about the person's current state of emotional development. A school psychologist might look at a different set of tests to learn more about a person's intellectual development.

Introductory textbooks and pop-psychology books make much of the differences in surface structure among psychological approaches. These differences, however, like differences between brand names of dishwashers, are overblown in the marketplace in an effort to attain market share. (Market share in academia is measured by numbers of research grants, faculty positions, job opportunities, textbook sales, consulting fees, and the like. If market share drops, so do faculty incomes.) HPT professionals can look beyond the differences of the surface structure and let themselves be guided by the similarities of the deep structure.

HPT'S APPLICATION IN MULTIPLE CULTURES

General systems theory is part of HPT. General systems theory is also used and understood in many of the physical, biological, social, and behavioral sciences, which encompass such areas as economics, computer science, engineering, and management. HPT has much to gain by adopting both the language and the concepts of general systems theory. Many of HPT's intellectual leaders already do so (see, for example, Dean and Ripley, 1997).

General systems theory's language and concepts are translatable not only among disciplines and theories but also, and readily, into French, German, Spanish, and so forth. Describing HPT in systems language (see Langdon, 1995) has the advantage of making HPT easy to translate into languages all around the world. But only the concepts and principles of the deep structure are translatable; specific tactics of the surface structure are not. Cookie-cutter approaches do not work very well anywhere, but the basic principles of HPT work well everywhere. For example, the people in two different U.S. companies might all benefit from better incentives, clearer goals, and better feedback, but the best tactics for improving incentives, goals, and feedback will not be the same in the two companies. One may have a history of punitive management, so that "improvement" attempts will be viewed with suspicion; the other may have a history of "programs of the month," so that improvement attempts will be viewed as random acts of managerial ineptitude. Similarly, the tactics that work in the U.S. division will not roll out to the Argentine or Hong Kong divisions. The same concepts and principles will work in all cultures, but the specific tactics will have to evolve from within the specific culture of each division. Thus HPT can provide useful tools for organizations as they move into international markets and toward globalization of their operations. HPT can contribute in emerging nations, in a world economy, and across cultures, if practitioners focus on the principles of the deep structure and avoid the trap of confusing those principles with manifestations of the surface structure.

A LOOK TOWARD THE FUTURE

HPT is about performance. Behavioral psychology and general systems theory interrelate to provide guidance that HPT practitioners can use to ensure that instructional systems are connected to performance, and that performance is supported by performance systems. General systems theory helps identify the key performances on which energies for improvement should be focused. Behavioral psychology helps identify the performance supports that will be necessary if people are to be able to learn and, having learned, to perform. Business sense (and general systems theory) will help answer, at the organizational level, these two questions:

1. What are we doing now to add value to (or that harms) customers and the world in general?

2. What could or should we be doing in the future to add value (and reduce harm)?

These two questions are at the heart of formulating strategy, identifying current business issues, and identifying current and future performance gaps. Harm is not a trivial business issue; business sense helps identify economic value and economic costs, but general systems theory should also be used to identify other types of impact. Environmental impact studies are becoming a necessity in some areas of business, but that is not enough. For example, businesses are concerned with the impact on communities of opening a new plant or closing an old one. Businesses must be concerned about product liability. HPT practitioners and organizational leaders should learn from sociology, political science, economics, environmental studies, and other disciplines to ensure that what gets done contributes as much value and as little harm as possible. HPT can help organizations learn in the classroom and proactively so that they are less often focused on learning reactively in the school of hard knocks.

THE RESPONSIBILITY OF ADDING VALUE

A key leadership responsibility is to ensure that the organization adds value. Adding value is also a key responsibility of every person in the organization; it is everyone's primary job. Therefore, two questions should be asked by every individual, from the CEO to the custodian:

1. What am *I* doing now to add value to (or that harms) customers and the organization?

2. What could or should *I* do in the future to add value (and to reduce harm)?

Helping individuals answer these questions is an important task for human resource development. The questions are key to the development of each person and are a prime element of the implementation of strategic plans. It is no secret that the strategic development of human resources (see Odiorne, 1984) is a constraint and an enabler of organizational success. Once human resource development is viewed strategically, the two central tasks of HPT come into focus: establishing instructional systems that enable people to learn how to perform to high standards, and establishing performance systems that enable people actually to perform to those high standards. Each is a never-ending task, for the characteristics of desired performance and the standards for performance change rapidly. Each person must repeatedly acquire new knowledge, skills, and attitudes, and workplaces must be repeatedly reengineered to support performance.

The research base and the theory base exist for effective team development, effective learning of knowledge-skill-attitude complexes, and establishment of effective motivational systems. HPT practitioners can use it to develop the instructional systems and the performance systems necessary to meet the demands of the global economy, the business community, and society.

References

Abernathy, W. B., Duffy, E. M., and O'Brien, R. M. (1982). Multi-branch, multi-system programs in banking: An organization-wide intervention. In R. M. O'Brien, A. M. Dickinson, and M. P. Rosow (eds.), *Industrial behavior modification.* New York: Pergamon Press.

Azrin, N. H., McMahon, P. T., Donohue, B. C., and Besalel, V. A. (1994). Behavior therapy for drug abuse: A controlled treatment outcome study. *Behaviour Research & Therapy* 32, 857–866.

Bennett, R. D. (1988). Improving performance without training: A three-step approach. *Performance Improvement Quarterly* 1:1, 58–68.

Bertalanffy, L. (1968). *General systems theory.* New York: Braziller.

Binder, C., and Watkins, C. L. (1990). Precision teaching and direct instruction: Measurably superior instruction techniques in schools. *Performance Improvement Quarterly* 3:4, 74–96.

Brethower, D. M. (1970). *The classroom as a self-modifying system.* Ann Arbor: Doctoral dissertation, University of Michigan.

Brethower, D. M. (1995). Specifying a Human Performance Technology knowledge-base. *Performance Improvement Quarterly* 8:2, 17–39.

Brethower, D. M., and Rummler, G. A. (1966). For better work performance: Accentuate the positive. *Personnel* 43:5, 40–49.

Brethower, D. M., and Smalley, K. A. (1998). *Performance-based instruction: Linking training to business results.* San Francisco: Jossey-Bass/Pfeiffer.

Collins, J. C., and Porras, J. I. (1994). *Built to last: Successful habits of visionary companies.* New York: HarperBusiness.

Daniels, A. C. (1989). *Performance management: Improving quality productivity through positive reinforcement* (3rd ed.). Tucker, GA: Performance Management Publications.

Dean, P. J., and Ripley, D. E. (1997). *Performance improvement pathfinders: Models for organizational learning systems.* Washington, DC: International Society for Performance Improvement.

Eickhoff, S. M. (1991). *Organizational development through the implementation of strategic plans.* Doctoral dissertation, Western Michigan University.

Fellner, D. J., and Sulzer-Azaroff, B. (1984). A behavioral analysis of goal setting. *Journal of Organizational Behavior Management* 6, 33–51.

Ford, D. H. (1987). *Humans as self-constructing living systems: A developmental perspective on behavior and personality.* Hillsdale, NJ: Erlbaum.

Fox, D. K., Hopkins, B. L., and Anger, W. K. (1987). The long-term effects of a token economy on safety performance in open-pit mining. *Journal of Applied Behavior Analysis* 20, 215–234.

Franks, D. M., and Wilson, G. T. (1973–1996). *Annual review of behavior therapy: Theory and practice.* New York: Brunner/Mazel.

Frederiksen, L. W. (ed.). (1982). *Handbook of organizational behavior management.* New York: Wiley.

Gardner, R., and others (eds.). (1994). *Behavior analysis in education: Focus on measurably superior instruction.* Pacific Grove, CA: Brooks/Cole.

Gilbert, T. (1996). *Human competence: Engineering worthy performance.* Amherst, MA, and Washington, DC: Human Resources Development Press and International Society for Performance Improvement.

Gordon, J. (1992). Performance technology: Blueprint for the learning organization? *Training* 29, 27–36.

Heiman, M., and Slomianko, J. (1992). *Success in college and beyond.* Allston, MA: Learning to Learn.

Johnson, K. R., and Layng, T.V.J. (1994). Morningside model of generative instruction. In R. Gardner and others (eds.), *Behavior analysis in education: Focus on measurably superior instruction.* Pacific Grove, CA: Brooks/Cole.

Kaplan, R. S., and Norton, D. P. (1996). *The balanced scorecard: Translating strategy into action.* Boston: Harvard Business School Press.

Komaki, J. (1986). Toward effective supervision: An operant analysis and comparison of managers at work. *Journal of Applied Psychology* 71:2, 270–279.

Komaki, J., Barwick, K. D., and Scott, L. R. (1978). A behavioral approach to occupational safety: Pinpointing and reinforcing safe performance in a food manufacturing plant. *Journal of Applied Psychology* 63, 434–435.

Kopelman, R. E. (1986). *Managing productivity in organizations: A practical, people oriented approach.* New York: McGraw-Hill.

Langdon, D. (1995). *The new language of work.* Amherst, MA: Human Resources Development Press.

Laszlo, E. (1972). *The systems view of the world.* New York: Braziller.

Lindsley, O. R. (1991). Precision teaching's unique legacy from B. F. Skinner. *Journal of Behavioural Education* 1:2, 253–266.

Lovaas, O. I., Freitag, G., Gold, J. J., and Kassorla, I. C. (1965). Experimental studies in childhood schizophrenia: Analysis of self-destructive behavior. *Journal of Experimental Child Psychology* 2, 67–84.

Marr, J. N., and Roessler, R. T. (1994). *Supervision and management: A guide to modifying work behavior.* Fayetteville: University of Arkansas Press.

McNally, K., and Abernathy, W. B. (1989). Effects of monetary incentives on customer behavior: Use of automatic teller machines (ATMs) by low frequency users. *Journal of Organizational Behavior Management* 10:1, 79–91.

McSween, T. E. (1995). *The values-based safety process: Improving your safety culture with a behavioral approach.* New York: Van Nostrand Reinhold.

Mesarovic, M. D. (ed.). (1964). *Views on general systems theory: Proceedings of the second systems symposium at Case Institute.* New York: Wiley.

Miller, J. G. (1978). *Living systems.* New York: McGraw-Hill.

O'Brien, R. M., Dickinson, A. M., and Rosow, M. R. (1982). *Industrial behavior modification: A management handbook.* New York: Pergamon Press.

Odiorne, G. S. (1984). *Strategic management of human resources.* San Francisco: Jossey-Bass.

Peters, T. J., and Waterman, R. H. (1982). *In search of excellence.* New York: Harper-Collins.

Rummler, G. A., and Brache, A. P. (1995). *Improving performance: How to manage the white space on the organization chart* (2nd ed.). San Francisco: Jossey-Bass.

CHAPTER FIVE

The Cognitive Sciences and Human Performance Technology

Richard E. Clark

The impact of global competition has included many sweeping changes:

1. A shift from the manufacturing and distribution of products to services

2. A gradual movement from vertically integrated management hierarchies in organizations to relatively flat networks of workers with multiple specialties

3 The tying of pay to market value and not to a worker's position within the organization

4. A dramatic increase in the cultural diversity of workers who interact on a daily basis

5. The redefinition of work from executing a stable set of tasks to satisfying the dynamic, novel, and shifting requirements of the customer

In this climate, the knowledge and motivation required to support the continued success of organizations will change quickly over short periods of time. These changes will continue to place new and ever more complex demands on the organizational specialists charged with providing ways to diagnose and solve performance problems and spot opportunities. Are Human Performance (HP) specialists prepared to meet the challenge?

COGNITIVE PROCESSES THAT SUPPORT HP AT WORK

HP support requires that we understand what influences people's achievement of organizational goals in a shifting and novel business environment. Can we make the most accurate predictions about how people will perform in our complex Information Age without knowing how and what they think about the goals and conditions of the performance context? Is it possible to make the most successful enhancement of human performance without a grasp of people's beliefs, values, emotions, thoughts, expectations, and information processing strategies and tactics? When you read and think about these and other questions, you are engaged in cognition.

This chapter is about cognition and the cognitive sciences. Cognitive science attempts to understand the way our thoughts and our perceptions of information influence our understanding (you read and search for the meaning of the questions above). It tries to understand understanding (you interpret the questions and the reasons the questions are asked). It endeavors to describe our motivational processes (perhaps you ask yourself whether the questions are important to you or whether you are curious about the answers or about their implications for your personal success). It seeks to describe what happens when we solve problems (you may search for past examples and find your own answers to some of the questions).

WHAT THE COGNITIVE SCIENCES ARE

The cognitive sciences encompass many different subspecialties that study the impact of thinking and other mental events on performance. Some cognitive scientists study the mental structures and processes that we use to manipulate the information that supports performance. Nearly all performance in the workplace is now mental or cognitive and no longer physical or manual. Thus understanding the mental aspects of performance is vital. Yet, in my view, our field now functions without incorporating the insights offered by the cognitive sciences.

Why? Part of the reason is that many of the developers and leaders of the field were educated when all North American and many European universities based learning and performance sciences almost exclusively on external events and processes. This group of developers and leaders includes training and media specialists, learning and organizational psychologists, and organizational development specialists. Their established specialties had more or less adequate solutions to performance problems when work was primarily physical. Thus HP technologists now have clear ideas about how such external enhancements as systems for organizational policy and procedures, training design and presentation, media for delivering solutions, job aids, and incentives may influence performance. Yet this is only half of the performance picture: in any given context, these enhancements help some people but not others; any incentive may be motivating for a few people but neutral for some and discouraging to others; a performance system that works in one organization may fail in another. The other half of the picture involves knowing something about the many different ways in which diverse individuals, teams, and cultures think about external events. Research and practice in many of the cognitive sciences began only in the 1970s, however. Moreover, research in some areas (such as the study of biological processes in the brain) began in earnest only within the past decade, and it takes a great deal of time for information to move from research to practice.

The goal of this chapter is to present some of the important contributions of the new cognitive sciences to a better understanding of Human Performance Technology (HPT). It will focus on how the cognitive sciences provide knowledge about the interaction between internal cognitive thinking processes and external environmental conditions. In order to fully understand HPT, we must examine both the work environment and the way people at work think about their environment (see, for example, Anderson, 1993; Locke and Latham, 1990; Solso, 1995). Because the environment is important to cognitive scientists, they incorporate many of the behavioral principles and build on them.

The goal of this chapter, then, is to introduce and briefly explain the contributions of cognitive science to two areas that are relevant to performance systems—the *knowledge* and *motivation* aspects of performance—with the purpose of stimulating interest in cognitive principles among those who design and manage HPT systems.

KNOWLEDGE AND PERFORMANCE

All performance requires knowledge, and yet all information about any performance goal is understood in many different ways by different people. Cognitive scientists suggest that meaning is actively constructed by individuals, who create their own interpretations of incoming information, interpretations based in part on their past experience and expectations.

Construction of Knowledge

Cognitive scientists suggest that new knowledge is not received and understood in the same way in which it is sent and intended. Meaning and understanding are dynamic processes. Knowledge is constructed in a slightly (and sometimes significantly) different way by everyone who receives the same message. The difference between receiving and constructing may seem slight, but the impact of this insight can be profound. Our active knowledge-fabrication process involves a number of thinking mechanisms that are more or less under the control of the receiver but not always under the control of the sender. As individuals or groups, we strive to attain understanding and solve problems. During this active process of constructing meaning and editing our understanding of problems, we exercise and strengthen our capacity to learn and solve future problems. This insight from cognitive science suggests that organizations should encourage individuals to interpret, restructure, practice, and revise new knowledge rather than simply master, memorize, and reproduce it. This insight also implies that successful communication requires an attempt to understand the current experience and expectations of the receiver and to ensure that we are using shared meanings for all important information.

Because information is also knowledge, we must also ensure that people acquire the type of knowledge that will support organizational goals. In the past, HP technologists were able to draw on knowledge descriptions such as those suggested by the task analysis systems developed in the 1920s (Clark and Estes, 1996). The result was a very effective system for making observations of work and describing the knowledge required for others to do the work. Thus our understanding of knowledge is largely based on our external observations of work. These task analyses are incorporated into training and job aid design systems, and yet cognitive scientists have invested considerable effort in understanding the way that the brain uses information during thinking and problem solving. The result is a relatively new system for describing how different types of knowledge produce different types of performance.

Two Types of Knowledge

Our mental architecture for thinking has severe limits. One of the most important constraints on performance stems from the limit on the number of thoughts we can consider at any one time. Cognitive science has estimated that we can actively think about only five to nine "chunks" of knowledge at once. This limitation on thinking requires that a great deal of the knowledge we use for complex thinking be automated so that it does not take up precious thinking space. Therefore, every human being uses two types of knowledge for many thinking tasks: automated *procedural* knowledge, and conscious *declarative* knowledge. Each type is learned and used in a very different way during problem solving and during the development and exercise of expertise. Procedural knowledge tells us how to do something; declarative knowledge tells us why things work the way they do, or that something has a particular name, appearance, definition, or location. We can learn either or both types of knowledge about anything. For example, we can learn a procedure for boiling water to make coffee or tea, and we can automate the task so that we can talk to a friend in the kitchen while we perform the procedure. But we can also learn declarative knowledge about why water boils, and we can use this knowledge to understand why water never boils in an open container when we are at high altitudes.

Procedural Knowledge. We all use procedural knowledge to master job-related tasks that can be accomplished in discrete steps or stages, or to decide between predetermined alternatives (Anderson, 1993). We use procedural knowledge when, for example, we log on to a computer, make diagnostic decisions about when to order preventive maintenance on equipment, or drive a car. We also use procedural knowledge whenever we mentally analyze a problem that falls within our established areas of expertise, no matter how complex the problem. A critical advantage of procedural knowledge is that it becomes automatic with practice and can be used without our conscious attention while we think about something else. The surprising element of procedural knowledge is that it can automate mental analysis as well as manual tasks. Its purpose is to help us accomplish all routine mental tasks without using up our precious thinking space. Thus we can often perform many procedures at once without thinking about any one of them. For example, we can drive a car and talk to a friend in the passenger seat without giving conscious thought to how we are operating the car or pronouncing our words; our conscious mind is reserved for novel tasks, such as what we will say to our passenger. Most of the knowledge that develops over long experience in a job is procedural. A large part of the problem-solving knowledge acquired by advanced experts is also procedural. For that reason, cognitive psychologists generally equate expertise with the development of elaborately composed and effective procedures for performing all aspects of a job. One of the problems with procedural knowledge, however, is precisely that it *is* no longer conscious, and so experts are often wrong when they attempt to tell us how they perform very complex diagnostic and problem-solving tasks within their areas of expertise. As a result, cognitive scientists advise caution in the use of subject matter experts to determine the information content required for training or job aids intended to support performance.

Declarative Knowledge. When we need to know *why* things are the way they are, or *that* something is in a particular place or has a particular name and definition, or *what* causes things to go bad or get better in a specific situation, we acquire declarative knowledge. Declarative knowledge has the advantages of being more flexible than procedural knowledge. Therefore, it allows for more creative applications. Declarative knowledge also allows us to explain why things happen and to make predictions about the future. There are varieties of declarative knowledge, such as principles (the laws of a science, or the informal rules of thumb that characterize long experience with a problem), concepts ("hard drive," "resistance," "assertiveness"), and facts (the name of a specific brand of computer, or the location of the on/off switch). It takes a great deal of intelligence to master and make effective use of complex principles and concepts. The main disadvantage of declarative knowledge is that it can be used only consciously (that is, we must be actively thinking about declarative knowledge to use it). Moreover, by contrast with our use of procedural knowledge, we cannot use very much of our declarative knowledge at once; each bit of declarative knowledge takes up space in our thoughts and precludes other thoughts.

Both declarative and procedural knowledge are used together as people perform mental and physical tasks. These active cognitive arrangements of different types of knowledge are often called *schemas* or *scripts.* In mental scripts, models of work processes are developed, and plans are tested and revised. Declarative knowledge seems to help us form procedures and decide when to employ them. As we use and revise a procedure that we invent or learn from training, it gradually becomes automatic and unconscious. Procedural knowledge cannot be changed after it has become automatic, and the gradual process of its becoming automatic ensures that the resulting automated procedure will be very consistent. Yet the down side is that it is also rigid and difficult to replace. This is why the QWERTY keyboard has never been modified, even though we now have research that suggests a more efficient layout of keys: all expert typists would become novices if a new keyboard were introduced. Declarative knowledge, however, is constantly and easily changed with use; its strength is its flexibility, but its weakness is that, unlike automated procedural knowledge, it can be very wrong or inefficient. It is likely that in the future we will find out much more about these mental schemas or scripts and how they influence our learning and problem solving.

Why Distinctions Between
Types of Knowledge Are Important

If the categories we use to define job or task knowledge ignore or are incompatible with the way our minds process information, it will be very difficult for us to perform, to teach someone else to perform effectively, or to judge performance. For example, many organizations make a distinction between skills and knowledge. The use of skills characterizes such tasks as typing or routine maintenance of equipment. Knowledge is presumed to support such tasks as delegating authority and predicting future trends in the financial markets. Training specialists tend to recommend that skills be taught and supported with different methods from those that support knowledge. According to evidence from cognitive research (for example, Anderson, 1993), both skill- and knowledge-based tasks require both procedural and declarative knowledge for the support of successful performance. In more direct terms, our minds seem not to care whether something to be learned or performed is an instance of skill or of knowledge; our minds take account only of the procedural or declarative aspects of the job. Therefore, the skills/knowledge distinction (and many other distinctions, such as most of those found in the Bloom taxonomy; see Bloom, 1956) will not support the most productive performance systems or the most productive activities for training design and development.

Evaluation of Performance Knowledge

Training and testing for memory do not ensure that people will be able to apply what they know on the job, or vice versa. Our mental processes recognize at least two different and more or less independent performances of knowledge: *remembering* or recalling of declarative knowledge, and *using* or applying of both declarative and procedural knowledge. Adding performance-level requirements to the task-analysis aspects of performance systems is very important because training for memory does not improve application performance, nor does knowing how to apply a procedure ensure that we will be able to remember the steps of the procedure. For example, people who use the same procedure for logging on to a computer day after day are often not able to remember the log-on steps even though they successfully perform the procedure; the memory for the steps will begin to form when one imagines oneself performing the initial steps. In similar fashion, many people are taught to memorize the steps in a job procedure but are completely unable to use or perform the procedure in an acceptable fashion. The bottom-line behavior evaluated by many performance systems is the ability to recall steps in a procedure. If the job requires only that a person be able to recite a list of facts (for example, the performance capacity of a product) or the steps in a procedure, then recall is adequate. If, however, a person must perform a procedure or use a principle to make a forecast or construct a plan, then recall of facts or steps in a procedure is insufficient. Before it can be established that a person is able to use a procedure, he or she must actually be able to perform the procedure. The evidence from cognitive research suggests that declarative memory for a procedure is more or less independent of the ability to use or apply the procedure. For example, we can talk fluently without being able to recall the exact positions of our lips, teeth, and tongue that were required for us to produce the component sounds of our words, and an expert typist does not have to consciously remember the positions of the keys on the keyboard. Even consciously used declarative knowledge does not depend on memory. Knowing the definition of a concept used on the job does not necessarily enable most employees to adequately identify examples of the concept as they work. We have all met managers who might be able to define the terms *empathy* or *active listening* without being at all able to use those concepts in interaction with others.

Transfer of Knowledge from Training to Work

The transfer of training to the job is currently a hot topic in cognitive science research (for example, see Stolovitch, 1997). Studies now focus on conditions that produce "far" transfer (creative uses of knowledge) and "near" transfer (routine uses of knowledge). An example of near transfer of a skill would be using a new banking software package on the job when one has been trained on a different computer at a different location. We have a fairly thorough understanding of near transfer as a result of behavioral research conducted in the 1950s and 1960s. Far transfer, however, was not understood until cognitive theories were developed. Far transfer occurs when knowledge is successfully applied to a highly novel problem. Managers who learn principles of economics in classes and then apply them to the understanding of interpersonal and social interaction are most likely engaging in far transfer. Cognitive models have a way to conceptualize both the mental operations and the performance interventions that produce both near and far transfer of learning. Recent research on far transfer of learning and problem solving (Clark and Blake, 1997) has brought about an important extension of the behavioral research on transfer of learned skills from training to the job. Managers, for example, who must constantly edit their performance to fit very novel problems, sometimes require far transfer of learning. When people face more predictable aspects of their jobs, they need more routine applications of their knowledge, and therefore near transfer of learning.

The behaviorists have taught us that near transfer is acquired through the use of procedural knowledge over time, along with adequate incentives and corrective feedback. The more that the training setting and problems mirror the application setting and problems, the more likely that near transfer will occur. The nearest transfer is presumed to occur with procedural learning. The most recent evidence is that creative performance is a result of acquiring important declarative knowledge (concepts and principles) and being able to create and use analogies that connect declarative knowledge in more than one domain of understanding. For example, a child's distressing first encounter with fractions may be smoothed by a teacher's use of a far-transfer analogy: the concept of "less than one" can be very difficult to grasp, and so many teachers use an analogy that likens fractions to slices of pie or cake, thereby connecting information in a familiar domain (the dividing of a pie or a cake among many people) to an unfamiliar domain (the adding and subtraction of fractions). There is evidence that most creative insights in science and mathematics have occurred when people with great amounts of relevant declarative knowledge used analogies to solve problems. The more that people who need far-transfer use of knowledge can think of previously unrelated events that are similar to the new problems they face, the more they are able to develop creative solutions.

Transfer Problems

The down side is that when we train for near transfer (job-specific performance), the people who have been trained are less able to make creative adjustments in their performance to solve novel problems or accommodate unanticipated changes: constant practice of a skill on similar types of problems apparently inhibits creativity. Conversely, when we encourage very creative use of knowledge by assigning people to constantly changing problems and settings, we inhibit their development of performance related to any specific problem or setting.

The Knowledge Solution

The task is to set up the conditions that enhance creative problem solving and far transfer but also promote the development of practical skill. Cognitive performance technology suggests that, for this kind of task, we need to suggest practice that is appropriate to both types of performance. Near transfer requires considerable opportunity to work on the type of problem for which one wishes to achieve practical skill. Far transfer requires practice on the greatest possible variety of problems, even on the most novel problems that we can imagine.

COGNITIVE APPROACHES TO PERFORMANCE MOTIVATION

The cognitive processes that produce learning and those that produce motivation are as different as the mechanical system and the fuel system of a car. Nevertheless, both systems must function at an optimal level and must collaborate for solid performance to occur. If we have ample motivation but lack learning or problem-solving skills, performance will be less than adequate. Likewise, intelligence and expertise will not overcome inadequate motivation. Motivation is governed by our values and expectations about the job goals we face and by our feelings about our own aptitude.

Cognitive Performance Motivation and Problems It Solves

Recent cognitive research (for example, Ford, 1992; Clark, 1998) on work motivation has identified two different types of problems that can be solved by a cognitive motivation system. First, motivation influences the strength and persistence of the commitment we make to all of our performance goals. Therefore, it concerns itself with our active pursuit of goals and tasks (as opposed to our intention to work). This element of motivation also influences how easily we are distracted by new or competing goals. Because tasks can be handled by both conscious declarative knowledge and by automated procedural knowledge, the effort required to complete tasks varies; we can be totally committed to a task and yet not invest enough effort to succeed. Thus the second performance problem solved by a cognitive motivation system involves the mental effort invested in a task. Mental effort is higher when the work task or goal is novel to a person or team. Novel tasks require more effortful, conscious problem solving, whereas routine, familiar tasks can be performed with less effort because the knowledge that supports them is partly automated.

What Supports Commitment to Work Goals

According to the last ten years of cognitive motivation research, there is one key reason people fail to make or strengthen their commitment to a work task or goal: the belief that performing the task or accomplishing the goal will make them less effective, reduce their perceived control, or make them appear less effective in other people's eyes. This reason is paramount in all human commitments, regardless of culture or individual differences. For some people, incentives in the form of money or praise give them immediate indications of effectiveness. Nevertheless, the problem with focusing on external incentives divorced from knowledge about perceptions of those incentives is that individuals have very different ideas about what makes them effective.

An increase (or a decrease) in our confidence about our effectiveness will increase (or decrease) our commitment to a performance goal. Three factors have been found, in research and practice, to increase (or decrease) people's confidence in their effectiveness, and therefore their commitment to work goals (for a review of the research on this theory, see Ford, 1992; Clark, 1998).

1. *Task assessment.* All of us analyze any task we are assigned, to determine whether we can successfully complete it. We all tend to ask ourselves two questions about a new task: Can I do it? Will I be permitted to do it? If we think we have the ability to accomplish the task, and that we will be permitted to accomplish it, our commitment will increase. If we doubt our ability or the organization's willingness to let us use our skills, commitment will decrease.

2. *Emotion or mood.* All positive emotions facilitate commitment, and all powerful negative emotions discourage commitment. This may seem like a minor issue. For temperamental people, however, or in organizations where pressure is high and/or change is constant, negative emotional undercurrents can be strong. Angry or depressed people find it nearly impossible to make a commitment to new work goals.

3. *Values.* It is my experience that values are the most important element in increasing or decreasing the strength of our commitments. Psychologists now have good evidence that the most important value at work concerns our beliefs about whether the achievement of a work goal

will increase our personal control or effectiveness. The more we believe that achievement of a work goal will make us more successful, the higher our level of commitment to the goal. The reverse is also true. Few of us will give a high priority to tasks that we sincerely believe will lead us to fail or to be perceived as incompetent.

Utility, Interest, and Importance Value

Three varieties of value have been found to be important in research and practice concerning effectiveness: utility value, interest (curiosity) value, and importance value.

Utility value comes into play when we do not value the task at hand but do value the consequences of successfully completing the task. In this case, we may perform a task that we do not like or value if we believe that the result of completing the task will be positive.

Interest value is active when we are curious or simply like the pursuit of a particular goal. We do not have to believe that completing the task will make us successful or more effective. Instead, the opportunity to pursue our curiosity or interests is enough to increase our commitment (and, presumably, is also enough to make us feel more effective because we are able to pursue something personally interesting).

Importance value comes from the recognition that our commitment to a specific task represents our strengths and personal goals.

What Enhances Motivated Commitment at Work

The critical element in solving a problem that concerns commitment to a goal is to view the goal from the standpoint of the person whose commitment we want to influence. The HP specialist must be fully able to empathize with the person and see the problem through his or her eyes and his or her beliefs (which may be very different from the HP specialist's beliefs). When we are solving commitment problems, we must think of solutions that will be meaningful to the person whose commitment we want to influence so that we can provide effective enhancements where task assessment, mood, or value are concerned.

Enhancements Regarding Task Assessment. Problems in this area require us to convince people that they can do a job and that existing barriers to their performance will be removed. We can do this by pointing out aspects of past performance that are similar to what is required by the new task. The HP specialist's job is to increase the person's confidence in his or her ability to perform the task or reach the goal. It helps to break big goals into smaller, specific tasks with short time lines and clear criteria. In addition, job aids can bolster confidence. Involving staff in the elimination of any procedural or policy barriers to performance reduces resistance that is based on environmental or organizational barriers that may be involved in a negative task assessment. The key element here is to persuade or empower people to believe that they can succeed at the tasks they are avoiding.

Enhancements Regarding Mood. Research evidence suggests a number of ways in which we can foster more positive emotions about problematic work tasks. Solutions that have been found to change moods include listening to positive mood music, writing or telling about a positive mood-related experience, watching a movie or listening to stories that emphasize positive mood, and using positive self-talk to control emotions. Negative emotions derive in part from beliefs that we have lost control of work situations. The HP specialist should try to convince people that the system is flexible. There are also indications that trusted, enthusiastic, positive, energetic managers and positive, coping, but not perfect work mentors and coaches encourage positive emotions in others and support committed choices about work goals. I have found that positive, optimistic, and confident line managers can improve the mood of many of the people who report to them. Keep in mind that some moods in some individuals are caused by biological events and are less controllable with external solutions. In most work settings, except for a few employees, mood tends not to be a major barrier to task commitment. The exception occurs when rapid and difficult changes occur in jobs and in organizational culture.

Enhancements Regarding Value. Solving value problems is often the major issue where most commitment problems and opportunities are concerned. People simply will not do what they believe will make them less effective or less successful. Many people are suspicious of change simply because they feel that they will be perceived as less effective in new, novel, negative, or uncertain conditions. They must be convinced that if they commit themselves to the avoided task(s), they will become significantly more effective or successful. The specific solution that accomplishes this goal may be quite different for different individuals and work cultures. Some organizations have adopted various empowerment solutions for value problems. In many such settings, staff are asked to choose their own work goals as a way of getting them to value their work. There is good research evidence that this is not necessary, however. Solid evidence exists that employees do not have to participate in goal setting at work in order to make a strong commitment to the goals they have been assigned. Value for the goal is enhanced if people (1) perceive that the goal has been assigned by a legitimate, trusted authority with an inspiring vision, one who (2) reflects a convincing rationale for the goal (importance value) and who holds out the expectation of outstanding performance (importance value) and (3) gives ownership to individuals and teams for specific tasks (interest value) while (4) expressing confidence in individual and team abilities (interest value) and (5) providing feedback that includes recognition for success and corrective but supportive suggestions for mistakes (utility value).

Cognitive Systems: The Third Generation

The training strategies in use today evolved, in the first generation, from the old experience-based craft approach (that is, learning a job through observation and apprenticeship). In the second generation, there was a dramatic shift to the more systematic, behavioral and experience-based "technology" systems (Heinich, 1984). Now the training function itself is in question. The third and next evolutionary step may be to exchange the training function for a comprehensive, cognitively based performance management technology. The goal of this technology would be to incorporate the best of the previous environmentally focused performance improvements and add what we know about internal, cognitive processes that yield enhanced performance at work. The resulting system must support a more diverse and cost-effective achievement of organizational goals than in the past. Two key elements of a cognitively based performance management system are *knowledge* solutions and *motivation* solutions. Cognitively based knowledge systems will make it more likely for workers to acquire the thinking strategies that will be useful in a rapidly changing, high-pressure work environment. Cognitive motivational systems will ensure maximum commitment to work goals and an appropriate quantity and quality of effort from workers. A system that combines goal-relevant knowledge with maximum motivation is one of our most important professional goals, and studies of our mental processes and structures, when added to our current knowledge about environmental events, can provide the next generation of HPT.

References

Anderson, J. R. (1993). *Rules of the mind.* Hillsdale, NJ: Erlbaum.

Bloom, B. S. (1956). *Taxonomy of educational objectives.* Vol. 1: *Cognitive domain.* New York: McKay.

Clark, R. E. (1998). The CANE model of motivation to learn and to work: A two-stage process of goal commitment and effort. In J. Lowzck (ed.), *Trends in corporate training.* Louvain, Belgium: University of Louvain Press.

Clark, R. E., and Blake, S. B. (1997). Designing training for novel problem solving transfer. In R. D. Tennyson, F. Schott, N. Seel, and S. Dijkstra (eds.), *Instructional design: International perspectives.* Vol. 1: *Theory, research and models.*

Clark, R. E., and Estes, F. (1996). Cognitive task analysis. *International Journal of Educational Research* 25:5, 403–417.

Ford, M. E. (1992). *Motivating humans: Goals, emotions and personal agency beliefs.* Thousand Oaks, CA: Sage.

Heinich, R. (1984). The proper study of instructional technology. *Educational Communication and Technology Journal* 32:2, 67–87.

Locke, E. A., and Latham, G. P. (1990). *A theory of goal setting and task performance.* Englewood Cliffs, NJ: Prentice-Hall.

Solso, R. L. (1995). *Cognitive psychology* (4th ed.). New York: Simon & Schuster.

Stolovitch, H. D. (1997). Introduction [Special issue on transfer of training and transfer of learning]. *Performance Improvement Quarterly* 10:2, 5–7.

CHAPTER SIX

Planning and Managing Human Performance Technology Projects

Michael Greer

Human Performance Technology (HPT) projects may be as complicated as the worldwide rollout of a performance improvement initiative or as straightforward as the creation of a simple set of performance aids. But projects, no matter how simple or complex, should be planned and managed carefully if they are to achieve high-quality results on time and within budget. The good news is that, in recent years, project management (PM) has emerged as a distinct profession that has consolidated a set of recommended standards and practices, which can be learned by anyone and implemented with any kind of project, in any industry, and in any culture. By applying these standards and practices to your projects, you can get high-quality results while avoiding delays and cost overruns.

This chapter provides some basic definitions and a brief discussion of the forces that are universal to the PM process. In addition, the chapter offers the model of the Generic Project Life Cycle, which can be applied to any project for the purpose of helping to organize its activities into logical phases. The chapter then reviews the essential PM processes that project managers can use to ensure that each phase—and, in turn, the entire project life cycle—will be successfully completed. With this foundation established, the chapter examines the typical deliverables (work output) of HPT projects, as well as some project life cycles that are appropriate to attaining these deliverables. Finally, the chapter reviews the specific actions and broad general practices that HPT project managers should be implementing to ensure successful completion of projects.

PM BASICS

This section provides basic PM definitions as set forth by the Project Management Institute (PMI) Standards Committee (1996). Representing thousands of PM professionals from around the world, PMI has spent considerable effort defining and standardizing PM terms and procedures. In addition, this section draws on the present author's previous work (see Greer, 1996).

Fundamental Definitions

A project is defined as *a temporary endeavor undertaken to create a unique product or service.* Let us note the critical elements of this definition.

That a project is by definition *temporary* means that it has a definite ending point. In this way, a project is different from an ongoing operation or program. A project team cannot endlessly rework project outputs; the project will eventually come to an end. A particular project may take a few weeks or several years to complete, but the key is that the project is finite; it is not an ongoing effort.

That the product or service created is *unique* means that it is different from similar products or services. In other words, the completion of the project results in something new, even if that something is simply an enhancement of what already exists. Because the product or service is unique, it must be built in a series of steps that evolve progressively from broad idea to refined design to preliminary deliverable or prototype to final deliverable.

To continue with our basic definitions, a *deliverable* is any measurable, tangible, verifiable item that must be produced before the project can be considered complete. Deliverables include things that must be produced as interim outputs (such as a video script, a floor plan, or a marketing analysis) as well as whatever is finally associated with these interim outputs (the completed video presentation, the finished building, the completed marketing plan). Because deliverables are *measurable, tangible,* and *verifiable,* the project manager can focus on the completion of these deliverables' production as important events in the life of the project. As each deliverable is produced, it becomes clear that progress is being made toward completion of the project as a whole.

It is easier to plan the project, discuss project events with team members, and analyze and track the project when project activities are gathered together into a few major phases. A *project phase* is a collection of logically related project activities that usually culminate in the completion of a major deliverable. For example, the planning phase of a project involves such related activities as estimating the time that will be required, estimating the project's costs, and identifying the necessary project team members. These activities, with their associated planning, culminate in a comprehensive plan for the project.

Completion of this comprehensive plan is typically considered a *milestone.* A milestone is a significant event in the project, usually the completion of a major deliverable. In a motion picture project, for example, completion of the script is a milestone. Milestones differ from project to project according to the type of deliverables the project is designed to create.

The *project life cycle* is a collection of project phases, the number and names of which are determined by the control needs of the organization involved in the project. Thus the life cycle of a motion picture project would include such phases as casting, scripting, shooting, and editing, whereas the life cycle for a home building project might include such phases as creating the blueprint, building the foundation, framing the walls, and installing wallboard. In each case, the project phases are unique to the industry and designed to achieve specific deliverables. Moreover, the project phases in each case allow the deliverables to evolve gradually and systematically, one step at a time. In this way, the project manager and the professionals on the project team can more effectively exercise control over the quality, timing, and cost of the deliverables. By using industry-standard project life cycles, project managers can help ensure that deliverables will conform to recognized quality standards and best practices.

It is important to identify and involve all a project's *stakeholders* so that everyone's expectations can be met; the last thing a project manager wants is to complete a project and discover only at that point that a major stakeholder has been overlooked and is now demanding that the project deliverables be changed. Project stakeholders are individuals and organizations who are actively involved in the project, or whose interests may be affected by it. The following individuals, groups, and organizations are examples of project stakeholders:

- The sponsor of the project (sometimes called the *client,* the *customer,* the *owner,* or the *funder*)
- Subject matter experts (SMEs)
- Suppliers, contractors, or vendors
- Professionals, craftspeople, and other specialists who serve on the project team
- The project manager
- Government agencies that regulate the project's processes or deliverables
- The public, which will use or be affected by project outputs

Project *resources* are defined as the people, equipment, and materials needed to execute the project. Resources may take many forms, which will depend on the project and the industry. For example, human resources include suppliers, contractors, or vendors, as well as all manner of professionals, craftspeople, and other specialists. Equipment resources can include such things as construction cranes, computers, copying machines, media production equipment, and all manner of devices used by project team members. Materials can take forms as divergent as lumber, office supplies, computer disks, or photographic film. Resources may be salaried, rented by the hour, or purchased outright. The bottom line is that the project manager must identify, plan for, and manage all the resources needed to get the project done.

Project *scope* is defined as the sum of the products (deliverables) and services to be provided by the project. Thus a statement of project scope includes a list of deliverables, a list of project objectives, a description of the criteria for success (involving costs, schedules, and quality measures, for example), and a list of all the activities that team members will perform to complete the project.

In the context of the preceding definitions, then, *PM* can be defined as *the application of knowledge, skills, tools, and techniques to the project's activities for the purpose of meeting or exceeding stakeholders' needs and expectations.*

Key Distinctions

One important distinction is that PM is not the same as general management. General management encompasses planning, organizing, staffing, executing, and controlling an enterprise's ongoing operations (such as manufacturing, marketing, product delivery, and customer support), which require different management strategies from those used in the management of finite, unique projects.

Another important distinction is that PM is not the same as practice within an application area or job specialty. The latter involve those activities typically undertaken by professionals who work in a particular field or industry sector. For example, there are "best practices" or standard operating procedures for developing instructional materials, conducting a performance analysis, or producing a video. Nevertheless, the specialists undertaking these activities as part of a project not only must conform to the standards and practices of their profession but also must work within the context of good PM practices.

Another key distinction is that projects are not the same as ongoing operations. Ongoing operations are those activities undertaken by an organization to routinely and repetitively generate the goods or services it has been set up to generate. For example, a trucking company's ongoing operations typically include picking up freight, making deliveries, handling paperwork, and servicing trucks. In contrast, projects are temporary endeavors undertaken to create unique products or services. When the trucking company decides to build a new warehouse, it is engaged in a project. This project (a temporary endeavor) will eventually come to an end, culminating in a new warehouse that will become part of the company's ongoing operations.

Projects are not the same as programs. A program is a group of related projects managed together. Programs usually include an element of ongoing activity.

To extend our example, imagine that the trucking company has set the long-term goal of expanding its operations from handling regional, East Coast freight to handling continentwide deliveries. It will need to build several more warehouses to achieve this goal. The building of each new warehouse is a project; the overall expansion effort is a program consisting of many projects.

If you are a new or part-time project manager who also has general management responsibilities in your organization, it is easy to become confused about whether you are managing an ongoing operation, a program, or a project. In particular, a project (a temporary, finite endeavor) demands that you closely monitor the project budget and schedule, take steps to keep things moving, obtain timely approval of deliverables, and attain closure of project phases. Therefore, the actions required to manage a project are sometimes different from those required to manage an ongoing operation or program.

Note also that the concept of a project is relative. For example, if you decided to move your family from one house to another, you would probably view the move as a project. For a company in the moving business, however, your move would simply be another part of its ongoing operations.

A project manager may decide to divide a large or complicated project into more manageable components, called *subprojects,* which can then be contracted out to vendors or assigned to smaller teams. Hence another important distinction: projects are not the same as subprojects. Imagine, for example, that you have decided to take on the project of remodeling your kitchen. Because you are familiar with painting and enjoy it, you decide to paint the walls yourself. But because you do not know how to install all the tile that will be required for the floor and the countertops, you decide to hire a tiling contractor to do that portion of the work. Thus you have divided your overall project (remodeling your kitchen) into two subprojects—painting and tiling.

In decisions about when and how to organize a project into subprojects, project managers must rely on their knowledge of their industries, their available resources, and other considerations. Note, for example, that a subproject may require a separate tracking system by which the "owner" or manager of the subproject keeps detailed records of her subproject's activities. This separate tracking makes it particularly important to establish clear lines of communication between the subproject team and those involved in the larger project to which the subproject belongs.

Finally, deliverables are not the same as project goals, although it is easy to confuse the two. Recall, however, that a deliverable is any measurable, tangible, verifiable item that must be produced to complete the project. In other words, deliverables can be planned, observed, inspected, shaped, and, ultimately, described in the project's contract specifications. Goals, by contrast, although they may be worth the effort of pursuing them, are less tangible and therefore less easy to measure and track. For example, imagine that your goal is to build a sailboat fast enough to win the America's Cup. This is a worthy goal, but it is not the sort of thing that you could promise as a project deliverable. Instead, the project would more appropriately focus on such deliverables as a boat with certain hull specifications, sail designs, and other specific, observable characteristics that would help it win the race. With luck, such a boat would beat the competition; win or lose, however, the project would be judged a success if it produced, within the schedule and budget allotted, a boat with the stated specifications.

Project Life Cycles

Recall that we defined a project life cycle as a collection of project phases, the number and names of which are determined by the control needs of the organization involved in the project. Project life cycles and their phases are industry-specific and driven by the deliverables to be created. In every industry, a unique project life cycle encourages the gradual evolution of that industry's unique deliverables. Thus the project life cycle provides control through the application of the industry's best practices and through successive approximation of its deliverables, both of which help to reduce the need for rework.

In the film industry, for example, the scriptwriting phase typically precedes the production phase, and so the script can be used as a set of guidelines for planning the production and for casting the actors. In addition, a rehearsal or read through phase typically precedes the shooting of scenes. This phase allows the actors to prepare their roles without consuming the time and salaries of the entire production crew.

Consider another example: In the pharmaceutical industry, a "clinical trials" phase is undertaken before a new product is distributed to the public. The government requires the manufacturer to prove that the new product is safe and effective before it can be approved for sale. This phase allows the government to protect citizens from the dangers of untested pharmaceutical products.

Finally, in the defense industry it is common practice for funding agencies to impose a "proof of concept" phase in the development of a new defense system. Vendors must include this phase, typically involving the building of a scaled-down or prototype version, in their project plans. Only after the prototype is approved will full-scale production and spending begin.

In each of these examples, the control needs of the stakeholders determine the industry-specific project life cycle. Each of the life cycle's phases encourages the gradual and controlled evolution of the deliverables. By incorporating several points for review and approval, project planners can help reduce the need for costly and time-consuming rework.

The Generic Project Life Cycle

What if you have no idea what your ideal project phases might be? If you find yourself in search of a project life cycle, consider the Generic Project Life Cycle (see Figure 6.1). It incorporates phases and activities that are nearly universal to all projects.

Figure 6.1. Generic Project Life Cycle.

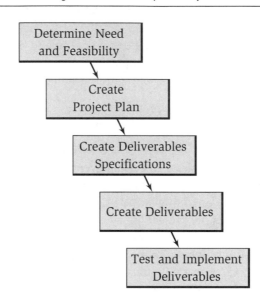

The five phases of the Generic Project Life Cycle are illustrated by the figure. Descriptions of each phase follow.

Phase 1: Determine Need and Feasibility. In this phase, the project manager and application specialists attempt to confirm that there is a need for the project deliverables. In addition, they try to decide whether the project is "doable"—that is, whether it is possible to plan and execute a project to create these deliverables. Activities that should be undertaken at this phase include those listed here:

- Goal definition
- Concept definition
- Needs analysis
- Market analysis
- Strategy definition
- Preliminary cost-benefit analysis

This phase culminates in formal approval of the project concept, or a "go/no go" decision.

Phase 2: Create Project Plan. Because projects are of finite duration and sometimes use unique work processes, the planning of a project is particularly important. In this phase, the project manager and/or application specialists create a formal document to guide project team members as they execute the project. Two major activities should be undertaken at this phase. The first activity is to *create a formal planning document,* which may be used in the following ways:

- To link project activities with expressed needs and feasibility studies (that is, to tie the plan in with the outputs of phase 1)
- To provide a written record of assumptions (regarding deliverables, work processes, resources required) and other perspectives shared by the planning team
- To help in fostering clear communication among the stakeholders
- To provide a written record of agreed-upon scope, costs, and schedule
- To facilitate stakeholders' critique of project assumptions

The second major activity at this phase is to *secure sponsors' and other stakeholders' approval of the project plan* before project work begins.

Phase 3: Create Deliverables Specifications. In this phase, application specialists, such as human performance (HP) technologists or video producers, create a formal document that describes in detail the deliverables to be created. Examples of such detailed specifications would be software design documents, instructional design specifications, or a detailed media treatment for a videotape production.

It is important to distinguish these extensive phase 3 deliverables specifications from the preliminary specifications created as part of the phase 2 planning process. In the phase 2 planning process, the project team describes the deliverables in just enough detail to create a project plan. Once the plan is approved, the project team may begin spending resources (including time and money) on the project. Thus it is simply good business to wait until phase 3 to extend the preliminary specifications. At this time, they should be fleshed out substantially so that project stakeholders can evaluate them at length. This allows the project team to make modifications on paper instead of reworking the deliverables. Note that these detailed specifications sometimes identify unanticipated deliverables. Therefore, this phase often includes descriptions of ways in which project schedules or budgets must be refined, and it may also include new project assumptions. Activities that should be undertaken at this phase include the following:

- Creating one or more documents describing deliverables specifications in substantial detail
- Obtaining approval of the deliverables specifications from sponsors and other stakeholders

Phase 4: Create Deliverables. This is typically the most time-consuming and resource-intensive phase of the project. In this phase the project deliverables are created according to the approved deliverables specifications. In other words, to extend the examples from phase 3, the software is created from the software design documents, the training materials are developed from the instructional design specifications, and the videotape is produced from the detailed media treatment for a videotape production.

The specific activities involved in this phase differ dramatically from one industry or application to another. For example, the software developer will likely create and test small units of code before programming and integrating all software modules. The training developer may conduct several internal reviews of draft materials, followed by revisions, before finalizing the materials for testing. A video producer would likely create scripts, conduct casting sessions and rehearsals, and produce other interim deliverables prior to full-blown production activities. Activities that should be undertaken at this phase include the following:

- Creating prototypes of deliverables
- Creating portions or pieces of deliverables
- Providing services as promised in the project plan
- Completing fully integrated deliverables
- Obtaining sponsors' and other stakeholders' approval of each deliverable or service provided

Phase 5: Test and Implement Deliverables. In this phase, the project deliverables are shown to work as planned and are turned over to the sponsor for use. As in phase 4, the specific activities involved in this phase differ dramatically from one industry or application to another. The software producer is likely to run user tests and make revisions prior to delivery to the customer. The training developer may conduct developmental and pilot tests, followed by revisions, prior to implementation. The video producer may conduct audience tests of rough cuts prior to final editing and delivery to the client. Activities that should be undertaken at this phase include the following:

- Testing of deliverables, all together or in parts
- Refinement of deliverables on the basis of test results
- Implementation of deliverables on a limited basis (such as a field trial)
- Further refinement of deliverables on the basis of preliminary implementation
- Full production of final deliverables
- Obtaining of sponsors' or other stakeholders' approval of the test results, of the resulting plans for modification of the deliverables, and of the final deliverables

Essential PM Processes

The Generic Project Life Cycle presented in Figure 6.1 is linear; that is, each phase results in work products, which are passed on to the next phase. Throughout the life cycle, the project deliverables evolve gradually, culminating in the finished product or service. This is in keeping with the finite nature of projects, which should always move inevitably toward completion. In contrast, there are five essential processes that recur throughout the project. These are processes in which the project manager must engage in order to keep things moving and bring the project to a successful conclusion. In other words, these processes describe the behaviors of project managers. Figure 6.2 illustrates these processes.

Students of general management theory will immediately recognize three of these processes—*planning, executing,* and *controlling*—but the remaining two processes are unique to PM and distinguish PM from the management of ongoing operations. These two unique processes are *initiating* (getting activities or phases started) and *closing* (formally concluding activities or phases), and they, too, are essential if a project is to start and finish within its scheduling and cost limitations. All these processes eventually come to constitute unconscious habits of effective project managers. Through practicing them in a conscious way at first, managers can eventually internalize them and begin to move among them fluently, thus helping to ensure their projects' success. The following passages take a closer look at each of these essential processes.

Initiating. *Initiating* means getting the project started. It involves obtaining the organization's commitment to the project as a whole or to a particular project phase. Typically, the sponsor, customer, or person providing the funds gives the authorization to begin work.

Planning. Planning is of major importance to a project because, by definition, the project involves creating something unique. Planning includes, among many

Figure 6.2. Essential PM Processes.

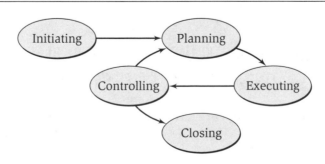

other activities, defining the project's scope (all the products and services to be provided by the project); determining the required activities, resources, and schedule; and creating detailed cost estimates and budgets.

Executing. Executing is the process by which project plans are carried out. Executing involves carrying out the project plan as written. In addition, executing can involve such activities as developing team members' skills to enhance project performance, making needed information available to project stakeholders in a timely manner, obtaining bids from contractors, selecting contractors, and managing relationships with contractors.

Controlling. Controlling involves comparing actual performance with planned performance. In other words, are you doing exactly what you planned to do? If you discover deviations from the plan (often called *variances*), you must analyze them and figure out alternative actions that will get the project back on track. You can then decide which alternative is best and take appropriate corrective action. Progress reporting, change control, cost control, and quality control are all part of project controlling.

Closing. Because projects are temporary endeavors, projects and project phases must eventually come to an end. But who is to say when a project or phase is "done," and the expenditure of time and money must stop? To help prevent disputes among stakeholders, it is necessary to set up a formal process by which the project or project phase can be declared officially completed. This formal process is called *closing* and involves scope verification (ensuring that all identified project deliverables are completed as specified), obtaining formal approval, and settlement of vendor contracts. Note that clear-cut and effective closing is based on the formal project plan, which should spell out exactly what the deliverables will look like and how and by whom the deliverables will be approved. By formally agreeing to the plan, the stakeholders have agreed in advance to specific deliverables that will be created by specific methods. Through comparison of actual results with planned results, the project team can minimize disputes over whether the deliverables are suitable.

HPT PROJECTS: UNIQUE DELIVERABLES, UNIQUE PROJECT LIFE CYCLES

This section identifies common deliverables (work outputs) of HPT projects and examines some project life cycles that are appropriate to attaining these deliverables.

Typical HPT Project Deliverables

The deliverables resulting from HPT projects typically fall into three broad categories: analyses, reports, and recommendations; workplace enhancements; and training materials and performance-support tools. The category of *analyses, reports, and recommendations* includes efforts such as these:

- Front-end analysis
- Performance analysis
- Job analysis
- Workplace or organization analysis
- Training needs analysis

The category of *workplace enhancements* includes interventions such as these:

- Modifications to the physical environment (affecting noise, light, temperature, room layout, and so forth)
- Enhancement of tools (computers, software, job-specific equipment)
- Modification of incentives (compensation, feedback, reinforcement, interesting or meaningful work)
- Modification of work processes or business operations
- Enhancement of organizational systems, leading to clearer goals, better job designs, improved policies, a balance between authority and responsibility, appropriate workloads, access to appropriate people, and so forth (see Chapter Sixteen)

The category of *training materials and performance-support tools* includes deliverables such as these:

- Formal training, including materials for instructors and students
- On-the-job training materials
- Programs for testing performance
- Job aids and documentation
- Follow-up coaching materials
- Supervisory training materials

Typical HPT Project Life Cycles

The following passages discuss typical project life cycles that can be employed to achieve the kinds of HPT deliverables just identified. The purpose of listing these phases here is to illustrate the typical project stages from a PM perspective, not to provide detailed recommendations for executing the phases. There are many texts whose purpose is to guide practitioners in successful completion of the tasks identified here (see, for example, Rossett, 1987; Zemke and Kramlinger, 1982; Greer, 1992; Smith and Kearny, 1994). The reader is urged to consult these texts, as well as other chapters in this volume, for detailed professional guidance.

Analysis Projects. These type of project typically results in some kind of report or set of recommendations. The following project phases may be included:

- *Identify project variables.* This phase should involve meeting with stakeholders in order to clearly identify the questions to be answered by the analysis. Afterward, the project manager should develop and obtain approval of a brief statement describing the scope of the project.

- *Create project plan.* On the basis of the variables identified in the previous step, the project team should create a specific plan for conducting the analysis and developing answers to the questions to be asked. This plan should include samples of data-gathering instruments (observation forms, questionnaires, and so forth) and a clear description of how each instrument will be used. A schedule and a project budget (if appropriate) should also be created.

- *Confirm assumptions and approach.* At this point the plan, the data-gathering tools, and strategies should be reviewed, revised as necessary, and approved by the sponsor and other key stakeholders.

- *Conduct analyses.* In this phase the strategies and tools approved in the preceding phase are put to use. Focus groups are assembled, interviews are conducted, observations are made, and other appropriate research is undertaken.

- *Synthesize preliminary results.* In this phase the raw data that have been gathered are examined, and notes are made regarding potential recommendations. No formal reports are created at this point.

- *Conduct a "yellow pad" review of findings.* In this phase the rough notes made by the project team (often simply compiled on a pad of yellow paper) are discussed with key stakeholders and with the sponsor. On the basis of their feedback, the team is able to determine where further research or analysis may be needed, or which findings need more or less emphasis. This important interim discussion can save a lot of time that otherwise might go to the rewriting of a formal report created without the sponsors' or the stakeholders' input.

- *Develop final report.* At this point the team should be ready to write up a formal report that describes findings and recommendations. As appropriate, the team may develop a supporting presentation of the results.

- *Present report.* The project concludes with a formal presentation of the findings and recommendations, as well as with a discussion of how the recommendations can be implemented. Future action items and project approval are typically obtained.

Workplace Enhancement Projects. This type of project typically involves the implementation of new tools, facilities, processes, or other enhancements to the workplace. (The following discussion assumes that, before this project begins, an analysis project like the one just described will have identified one or more necessary workplace enhancements.) The following project phases may be included:

- *Confirm need and feasibility.* In this phase the project team meets with stakeholders and with the project sponsor to make sure that the project is still needed and feasible. This step is essential because considerable time may have passed between the completion of the analysis (which identified the need) and the actual approval to begin work. In the interim, changes in circumstances may have rendered the project unnecessary or infeasible.

- *Create project plan.* Once it is clear that the project is needed and feasible, the project team must identify a specific set of steps for developing and implementing the enhancement. Specific team members, person-hours, resource requirements, and costs of completing each step have to be determined and documented. This plan must be approved by the project sponsor before the next phase can begin.

- *Create deliverables specifications for the enhancement.* This phase is similar in function to the blueprint for a house or a motion picture script. A detailed written description (sometimes supported by models, prototypes, or blueprints) is created and reviewed by stakeholders—including key SMEs—and the sponsor. On the basis of their feedback, the deliverables specifications are either revised or approved.

- *Develop the prototype enhancement.* In this phase a first version of the enhancement is created for testing. This version should include all the features and functions of the system to be implemented.

- *Test and adjust the enhancement.* At this point the first version of the enhancement is put to work in as realistic a setting as possible. Observers gather data about the enhancement's effectiveness, and test subjects provide feedback. On the basis of the test results, revisions are identified and made. Further rounds of testing and adjustment may be required.

- *Implement the enhancement.* In this phase, the enhancement is put to work by most or all of the intended users.

- *Evaluate effectiveness and cost of the enhancement.* Finally, long-term follow-up data are gathered on how well the enhancement works. In addition, cost information should be obtained in order to determine the enhancement's cost-effectiveness.

Projects Resulting in Training and Performance-Support Tools. Sometimes called *instructional development (ID) projects,* these are focused on the building of specific instructional materials and performance aids. The model described here is elaborated by Greer (1992) and includes the phases common to most ID models. (The following discussion assumes that an analysis project like the one already described has identified training and/or performance-support tools as an appropriate intervention.) The following project phases may be included:

- *Determine project scope.* This phase involves creating preliminary materials specifications (estimates of such deliverables as videotapes, workbooks, instructor notes, and computer-based training, or CBT, frames), project time and cost estimates, and a description of sponsor/stakeholder involvement. The scope statement should be formally approved before the next phase begins.

- *Organize the project.* Once the team has been given the green light to execute the project as described in the scope statement, the project manager can pull together the project team and describe roles and responsibilities, organize a project diary to control project documentation (budgets, contracts, status reports, and the like) and conduct a formal kickoff meeting to get the project started. As appropriate, vendors' bids are solicited, vendors are chosen, and the vendor team is integrated into the in-house project team.

- *Gather information.* In this phase the project team gathers detailed information (content) that will comprise the training or reference materials, as well as details about the work environment and target audience. The broad performance objectives identified in the initial analysis are refined and expanded.

- *Develop the blueprint or specification.* At this point the team develops a set of design specifications. This activity allows reviewers to clearly visualize the training and performance-support tools before large amounts of labor are expended on their creation. The document should outline performance objectives, instructional strategies, content details (in bulleted lists, for example), and the media treatments to be employed. The sponsor, SMEs, and other key stakeholders should review and approve the blueprint before the next phase begins.

- *Create draft materials.* This phase involves the creation of preliminary or first-draft versions of the final materials. Drafts should contain all the detail and much of the polish of the finished materials. Review and approval by sponsors, SMEs, and other stakeholders will be essential. Time should be included for revisions, as specified by reviewers.

- *Test draft materials.* This phase involves one or more test runs of all materials, with members of the target audience using them as intended. Each round of testing should conclude with debriefing and with specification of the required revisions. Sponsors' and stakeholders' approval should be obtained.

- *Produce master materials.* In this phase, the master version of the finished product is created in preparation for its reproduction. Videotapes are produced, CBT files are created, printed documents are finalized, and sponsors' and stakeholders' approval should be obtained.

- *Reproduce the master materials.* After the masters have been created, copies can be made and packaged for distribution.

- *Distribute the materials.* At this point, some means is determined and implemented for storing (warehousing) the materials and disseminating them as the need arises.

- *Evaluate.* This final phase involves follow-up evaluation of how effective the training and materials are in supporting job performance. A systematic evaluation strategy should be employed, and the results should be formally reported and should serve as the basis for enhancements.

Although they may differ in their specific phases, all these HPT project life cycles have one thing in common: they are designed to support the gradual and systematic evolution of the project deliverables in small increments that can be reviewed, revised, and approved by sponsors and stakeholders. In this way, the life cycles help HPT project managers attain control of their projects and avoid costly, time-consuming rework.

STEP BY STEP:
WHAT HPT PROJECT MANAGERS SHOULD BE DOING

After the project team identifies the appropriate project life cycle and phases for completing the project, the project manager must take action to get the project under way and keep things moving toward a successful conclusion. What actions should the project manager take? Recall that the essential PM processes are initiating, planning, executing, controlling, and closing, and that these processes must be put to work by the project manager at each phase of a project's life cycle. Table 6.1 summarizes the specific actions that the project manager should take as part of the PM processes and lists specific results that these actions should produce.

Table 6.1. Summary of Key PM Actions and Results.

Action	Results of Successful Performance
	Initiating
1. Demonstrate project need and feasibility	A document that confirms a need for the project deliverables and describes, in broad terms, the deliverables, means of creating the deliverables, costs of creating and implementing the deliverables, and benefits to be obtained by implementing the deliverables.
2. Obtain project authorization	A "go/no go" decision is made by the sponsor. A project manager is assigned. A "project charter" is created that • Formally recognizes the project. • Is issued by a manager external to the project and at a high enough organizational level so that project needs can be met. • Authorizes the project manager to apply resources to project activities.
3. Obtain authorization for the phase	A "go/no go" decision is made by the sponsor and authorizes the project manager to apply organizational resources to the activities of a particular phase. Written approval of the phase is created that • Formally recognizes the existence of the phase. • Is issued by a manager external to the project and at a high enough organizational level so that project needs can be met.
	Planning
4. Describe project scope	Statement of project scope Scope-management plan Work-breakdown structure (WBS)
5. Define and sequence project activities	An activity list (list of all activities that will be performed on the project) Updates to the WBS A project-network diagram

6. Estimate duration of activities and re- sources required

Estimate of duration (time required) for each activity, and assumptions related to each estimate
Statement of resource requirements
Updates to activity list

7. Develop a project schedule

Project schedule in the form of Gantt charts, network diagrams, milestone charts, or text tables
Supporting details, such as resource use over time, cash flow projections, and order/delivery schedules

8. Estimate costs

Cost estimates for completing each activity
Supporting detail, including assumptions and constraints
Cost-management plan describing how cost variances will be handled

9. Build a budget and spending plan

A cost baseline or time-phased budget for measuring/monitoring costs
A spending plan, telling how much will be spent on what resources at what time

10. Create a formal quality plan (optional)

Quality-management plan, including operational definitions
Quality-verification checklists

11. (Optional) Create a formal project communications plan

A communication management plan, including
- Collection structure
- Distribution structure
- Description of information to be disseminated
- Schedules listing when information will be produced
- A method for updating the communication plan

12. Organize and acquire staff

Role and responsibility assignments
Staffing plan
Organizational chart with detail, as appropriate
Project staff
Project team directory

13. Identify risks and plan to respond (optional)

A document describing potential risks, including their sources, symptoms, and ways to address them

Table 6.1. Summary of Key PM Actions and Results, cont'd.

Action	Results of Successful Performance
	Planning
14. Plan for and acquire outside resources (optional)	Procurement-management plan describing how contractors will be obtained Statement of work or statement of requirements describing the item (product or service) to be procured Bid documents, such as requests for proposals, invitations for bids, and so on Evaluation criteria (means of scoring contractors' proposals) Contract with one or more suppliers of goods or services
15. Organize the project plan	A comprehensive project plan that pulls together all the outputs of the preceding planning activities
16. Close out the project planning phase	A project plan that has been approved, in writing, by the sponsor A "green light" to begin work on the project
17. Revisit the project plan and replan as necessary	Confidence that the detailed plans for executing a particular phase are still accurate and will effectively achieve results as planned
	Executing
18. Execute project activities	Work results (deliverables) are created. Change requests (based on expanded or contracted project) are identified. Periodic progress reports are created. Team performance is assessed, guided, and improved, as necessary. Bids/proposals for deliverables are solicited, contractors (suppliers) are chosen, and contracts are established. Contracts are administered to achieve desired work results.

Controlling

19. Control project activities

Decision to accept inspected deliverables
Corrective actions (rework of deliverables, adjustments to work process, and so on)
Updates to project plan and scope
List of lessons learned
Improved quality
Completed evaluation checklists (if applicable)

Closing

20. Close out project activities

Formal acceptance, documented in writing, that the sponsor has accepted the product of this phase or activity
Formal acceptance of contractors' work products and updates to the contractors' files
Updated project records prepared for archiving
A plan for follow-up and/or handoff of work products

Source: Adapted from Greer, 1996.

CRITICAL SUCCESS PRACTICES:
WHAT WORKS WELL IN HPT PROJECTS

So far we have outlined the basics of HPT PM and identified many of the formal processes and procedures that a project manager should consider implementing. This section provides an informal and somewhat idiosyncratic list of PM principles and practices that are crucial to the success of HPT projects.

Project managers must focus on three dimensions of project success. To put this idea simply, we can say that project success means completing all project deliverables on time, within budget, and at a level of quality acceptable to sponsors and stakeholders. The project manager must keep the team's attention focused on achieving these broad goals.

Planning is everything—and ongoing. On one thing all PM texts and authorities agree: the single most important activity that project managers engage in is planning. Detailed, systematic, team-involved plans are the only foundation for project success. When real-world events conspire to change the plan, the project manager must make a new one to reflect the changes. Planning and replanning, therefore, are a way of life for project managers.

Project managers must feel, and transmit to their team members, a sense of urgency. Because projects are finite endeavors with limited available time, money, and other resources, projects must be kept moving toward completion. Most team members have many other priorities, and so it is up to the project manager to keep team members' attention on project deliverables and deadlines. Regular status checks, meetings, and reminders are essential.

Successful projects use a time-tested, proven project life cycle. We know what works. Models like those described in this chapter can help ensure that professional standards and best practices are built into project plans. Typically, these models not only support quality but also help to minimize rework. When time or budget pressures seem to encourage shortcuts, it is up to the project manager to identify and defend the best project life cycle for the job.

All project deliverables and all project activities must be visualized and communicated in vivid detail. In short, the project manager and the project team must create, early on, a tangible picture of the finished deliverables in the minds of all who are involved so that all effort is moving in the same direction. Vague descriptions must be avoided at all costs; deliverables and activities must be spelled out, pictured, and prototyped, and the project manager must make sure that everyone involved agrees to them.

Deliverables must evolve gradually, in successive approximations. It simply costs too much and risks too much rework to jump in with both feet and begin building all the project deliverables. Build a little at a time. Obtain incremental reviews and approvals. Maintain a controlled evolution.

Projects require clear approval by sponsors. Clear approval, accompanied by the formal sign-off of sponsors, SMEs, and other key stakeholders, should be a demarcation point in the evolution of project deliverables. It is this simple: anyone who has the power to reject the deliverables, or to demand revisions after they are complete, must be required to examine and approve them as they are being built.

Project success is correlated with thorough analysis of the need for project deliverables. Research by Halprin and Greer (1993) shows that when a project results in deliverables that are designed to meet a thoroughly documented need, there is greater likelihood of the project's success. Managers should insist that there be a documented business need for the project before they agree to consume organizational resources in completing it.

Project managers must fight for time to do things right. The following complaint is a common one among project managers: "We always seem to have time to do the project over. I just wish we had taken the time to do it right in the first place!" Projects must have enough time available for the work to be done right the first time. Project managers must fight for this time by demonstrating to sponsors and top managers why the time is necessary, and how spending it will result in high-quality deliverables.

Project managers' responsibility must be matched by an equivalent amount of authority. It is not enough to be held responsible for project outcomes; project managers must ask for and obtain enough authority to carry out their responsibilities. Specifically, managers must have the authority to acquire and coordinate resources, request and receive cooperation from SMEs, and make appropriate and binding decisions that have an impact on the success of their projects.

Project sponsors and stakeholders must be active participants, not passive customers. Most project sponsors and stakeholders rightfully demand the authority to approve project deliverables, either wholly or in part. Along with this authority comes the responsibility to be an active participant in the early stages of the project (helping to define deliverables), to complete reviews of interim deliverables in a timely fashion (keeping the project moving), and to help expedite the project manager's access to SMEs, members of the target audience, and essential documentation.

Projects typically must be sold, and resold. There are times when the project manager must function as a salesperson to maintain the commitment of stakeholders and sponsors. With project plans in hand, the project manager may need to periodically remind people of the business need that is being met and of the fact that their own contributions are essential in meeting this need.

Project managers should acquire the best people they can and then do whatever it takes to clear the garbage out of their way. By acquiring the best people— the most skilled, the most experienced, the best qualified—a project manager can often compensate for too little time or money or other project constraints.

The project manager should serve as an advocate for these valuable team members, helping to protect them from outside interruptions and helping them acquire the tools and working conditions they need in order to apply their talents.

Top managers must actively set priorities. In today's leaner, self-managing organizations, project team members are not uncommonly expected to play active roles on many project teams at the same time. Ultimately, there comes a time when team members are stretched to the limit and have more projects than they can successfully complete. In response, an organization may establish a project office, composed of top managers from all departments, to act as a clearinghouse for projects and project requests. The project office reviews the organization's overall mission and strategies, establishes criteria for project selection and funding, monitors workloads, and determines which projects are of high enough priority to be approved. In this way, top management provides the leadership necessary to prevent multiproject logjams.

BEYOND THE FUNDAMENTALS

This discussion of HPT PM has been necessarily limited. The following topics bear further investigation by serious project managers:

- *PM software.* Powerful software packages allow project managers to create detailed, easily edited plans for the most complex projects. In addition, they allow presentation, communication, and "selling" of the project plan in highly graphic and professional form, including Gantt charts, PERT charts, and tabular data. Finally, they allow the project manager to keep track of and easily report a project's progress in terms of variances in schedule, costs, and resource use.

- *Internet and intranet PM sites.* Both public Internet and private intranet sites provide enormous potential for posting project plans, gathering project data, and communicating with fellow project team members in a geography-free fashion. Because some PM software packages allow output of project reports as Web-postable files, the creation and maintenance of project Web sites is becoming increasingly simple for project managers and teams.

- *Virtual project teams.* The geographically dispersed project team is rapidly becoming the norm. Project managers must learn all they can about such effective team-oriented communication technologies as e-mail, teleconferencing, and voice messaging. They should explore the special problems and opportunities of working with virtual teams.

MANAGING INTERNATIONAL PROJECTS

Project managers working with international project teams must overcome, in addition to the challenges just identified, unique hurdles brought about by team members' cultural and political differences, their dispersal across geographic and time zones, and their access to appropriate communication mechanisms.

As Radosevich (1996) observes in an informative on-line article describing the difficulties faced by managers of intercontinental software development projects,

> cultural differences can cause tense moments. Indian programmers, for instance, are known for keeping quiet, even when they notice problems . . . and subtle differences in gestures can cause confusion. In the United States, shaking your head from side to side means no. In the south of India, it means yes. . . . [A U.S. manager] once asked programmers whether they had finished a TCP/IP port. They shook their heads, which he took to mean no. "My blood pressure went up 10 points," he says. After 10 minutes of befuddlement, he figured it out. "One has to learn these things," he says with resignation.

Here, distilled and extrapolated from Radosevich's article, are some tips for managing multinational HPT projects:

1. Make sure that technical people (media developers, instructional developers, and programmers, for example) speak the same language and understand one another's technical jargon.

2. Make sure that those directly managing task specialists are fully proficient in the specialists' native language. Better yet, hire managers who live near and work with local team members.

3. Make sure that the telecommunications resources devoted to the project are first-rate and dependable. Asynchronous communication methods, such as e-mail and voice mail, are especially important because they allow some team members to create and send messages while other team members are off duty or sleeping.

4. Start with a small project or subproject, and take on a larger and more complex project only if the small one proves manageable across international borders.

5. For special working models and advice, turn to someone who has a good track record internationally.

6. Make sure that team leaders and key stakeholders, especially SMEs, make meaningful contact with off-site team members by visiting them regularly to establish strong relationships.

7. Consider developing and implementing the following mechanisms:

- A formal quality-assurance, work-flow review process that has been published and discussed before work begins on deliverables
- A project-specific dictionary of terms and technical jargon
- The hiring of local, on-site, culturally attuned project managers
- A formal process for defining, in advance, the structure and content of deliverables, and for establishing agreement among all team members on the deliverables that have been defined
- Budgeting and cost-control mechanisms that take account of the differences among international currencies

8. In decisions about whether to pursue an international project, consider these factors:

- Team members' expertise (Is the level of expertise appropriate to the job? Are team members who are performing similar jobs also at similar levels of expertise?)
- Local copyright, patent, and intellectual property laws (Are your deliverables adequately protected?)
- Political instability that could impede communications or disrupt project work
- Stability and financial status of potential international vendor partners
- Firmness of deliverables specifications (If the definition of the deliverables is shifting rapidly, then it may make sense to avoid a project design that seeks to create them through a large international effort.)
- Your organization's experience and track record in working with local project teams that are dispersed across international borders

CONCLUSION

PM is detailed and demanding work. It involves continual planning, simultaneously pushing and begging team members to keep things moving, making heroes of SMEs, sponsors, or stakeholders who may not always deserve that status, and paying attention to a thousand details and early warning signs. By taking a systematic approach and one step at a time, and by enlisting the support of good people, the HPT project manager can achieve high-quality results on time and within budget.

References

Greer, M. (1992). *ID project management: Tools and techniques for instructional designers and developers.* Englewood Cliffs, NJ: Educational Technology Publications.

Greer, M. (1996). *The project manager's partner: A step-by-step guide to project management.* Amherst, MA, and Washington, DC: Human Resources Development Press and International Society for Performance Improvement.

Halprin, M., and Greer, M. (1993). Critical attributes of ID project success: Part II—the survey results. *Performance & Instruction* 31:6, 15–21.

Project Management Institute Standards Committee. (1996). *A guide to the project management body of knowledge (PMBOK).* Upper Darby, PA: Project Management Institute.

Radosevich, L. (1996, Sept.). Offshore development: Shipping out. *CIO Magazine.* < www.cio.com/archive/090196_offshore_content.html >

Rossett, A. (1987). *Training needs assessment.* Englewood Cliffs, NJ: Educational Technology Publications.

Smith, P., and Kearny, L. (1994). *Creating workplaces where people can think.* San Francisco: Jossey-Bass.

Zemke, R., and Kramlinger, T. (1982). *Figuring things out: A trainer's guide to needs and task analysis.* Reading, MA: Addison-Wesley.

CHAPTER SEVEN

The Dynamics of Politics in Organizational Change

Esther Safir Powers

T he purpose of this chapter is to help Human Performance (HP) consultants use knowledge about politics to make their individual and organizational interventions more successful. The chapter first explores the context for the HP consultant's role in the politics of organizations and defines the terms *power* and *politics*. The chapter then presents a process model for intervention and discusses how politics are involved at each phase of the intervention.

ROLE OF THE HP CONSULTANT

The role of the HP consultant is constantly evolving. The HP consultant must be skilled in diagnosing and analyzing performance problems and prescribing solutions to deliver both individual and organizational results. This requires an understanding that learning, teamwork, process design, and culture influence an organization's ability to get things done. Whereas many HP consultants focus on activities, the *effective* HP consultant focuses on outcomes (Ulrich, 1997).

HP consultants must facilitate organizational outcomes, from planning to execution. This includes partnering with senior and line managers and assuming

---

Portions of this chapter are excerpted from "The Politics of Intervening in Organizations," by John B. Duncan and Esther S. Powers, which appeared as Chapter Six of this volume's first edition.

the role of their champion, vigorously representing their concerns while increasing their commitment. By applying the methodology and interacting with clients, the HP consultant enhances people's ability to produce results. Ultimately, the most important role of the HP consultant in the delivery of outcomes is to be an agent of continuous transformation, shaping processes and a culture that together improve an organization's capacity for change (Ulrich, 1997).

Political savvy is essential in understanding the dynamics of fostering organizational results among the various constituents encountered in the organization. From the shop floor to the boardroom, the HP consultant must be concerned with others' power bases, motivations, cultural expectations, and attitudes—in a word, with their politics. These can either encourage or inhibit the effort to achieve organizational objectives.

POWER AND POLITICS

According to Bennis and Nanus (1985, pp. 15, 18), power is "the basic energy to initiate and sustain action translating intention into reality, the quality without which leaders cannot lead. . . . Vision is the commodity of leaders, and power is their currency." Power is the ability to influence or even control behavior; politics are the behaviors that powerful people use to make the changes they want in organizations. In other words, to possess influence is to have power, and politics is the use of power. By comparison with other behavioral topics, the topic of politics—the use of power—is sparsely covered in the literature, and yet politics are a daily phenomenon in our lives.

The meaning and impact of a power resource may differ according to how the power is used and according to the relationship between the power holder and the power user. For example, the effects of a manager's performance rating would seem to depend in part on "whether the employee experienced the rating as a reward or punishment and whether the employee believed the relationship was cooperative or competitive" (Tjosvold, 1995, p. 730). In an intervention, power used to reward within a cooperative context will have a more positive impact on the objective than will power used to punish within a competitive context.

Organizations as Political Arenas

Traditional theory views the ideal organization as rational, objective, efficient, and fair, but this perspective has been expanded to include a view of the organization as a political arena where games are played by rules that often are not explicit. When we recognize the presence of politics in organizations, we realize that politics can take different forms. Politics are more implicit than explicit and are not widely communicated in a formal sense, and yet they are critical to an organization's success.

Acquiring the skill to play political games is easier for the dominant group, or insiders, in an organization (Ferris and others, 1996). The term *insiders* suggests the existence of another group, the outsiders, who are effectively shut out of the political network. Typically, these outsiders are women and racial or ethnic minorities, who are denied membership as "insiders" because the "rules, boundaries, and intricacies of the game are kept quiet, and doled out selectively" (Ferris and others, 1996, p. 26). The HP consultant should be aware of the potential challenges of being outside the political power games and should help the outsiders become insiders, thus promoting diversity and expanding the organization's intellectual capital.

The HP consultant needs to learn the cultural context of the organization in order to be fully prepared to deal with the organization's politics. The international and multinational companies and workforces that proliferate today offer a rich and varied cultural environment, one that may be fraught with unsuspected political land mines. The HP consultant working in this environment must look beyond obvious gender or race differences and explore how people's cultural backgrounds may be influencing their expectations of others' behavior. The HP consultant who is sensitive to cultural implications is better equipped to deal with organizational politics.

The Importance of Acquiring Power

Innovators must reach beyond the limits of their formal positions to acquire the resources, information, and support they need. They require power—the capacity to mobilize resources and people to get things done. Innovative managers know how to put themselves in arenas where power circulates, grab it, and invest it in their projects. Acquiring power can be the most time-consuming and difficult part of the process (Kanter, 1997).

Power Bases

Schein (1985) has identified a number of power bases from which HP consultants operate and suggests various strategies for using them in powerful ways so as to implement projects successfully. These power bases included the following:

- *Expertise* is the knowledge, education, skill, and prior on-the-job experience that the consultant is perceived as possessing.

- *Informational power* comes from having access to functional groups and from maintaining contact with sources of information about the organization.

- *Political access* is an expression of the consultant's ability to call on, gain audience with, and influence powerful people in the organization.

- *Staff support* depends on the consultant's own work group and is the trust that the consultant's colleagues have in his or her leadership, as well as their resulting willingness to contribute to shared responsibilities. It is also evident in the consultant's ability to develop liaisons with peers in other groups, thereby increasing the amount of knowledge—and thus power—flowing into the consultant's own unit.

- *Tradition* is involved in longtime service to and affiliation with an organization, whereby the consultant acquires unique organizational knowledge and uses it to influence others.

- *Credibility* (or *mobility*) is derived from ties outside the organizational unit or outside the organization as a whole.

- *Assured stature* comes from organization members' positive feelings about the consultant's bases of expertise. It reflects the total degree of respect that the consultant enjoys because of all his or her other power bases and includes perceptions about the consultant's compassion for and understanding of others.

Dysfunctional Versus Healthy Politics

The pinnacle of organizational effectiveness is reached when the healthy use of political power allows organization members to achieve clarity about changes and develop consensus to support decisions. To get there is to manage a journey out of chaos. The HP consultant must purge personal concerns and expectations, listen to and acknowledge the needs of others, and then seek genuine consensus within the constituent group(s).

What is meant by the "healthy" use of political power or politics? Healthy organizational politics involve initiating and implementing change for the purpose of business results and organizational growth and learning. Dysfunctional politics, by contrast, result in the aggrandizement of individuals or special interests to the detriment of the organizational body as a whole. Business results may occur on a short-term basis, but eventually the organization runs out of fuel.

Healthy politics will give rise to debate, argument, and conflict. Dysfunctional politics tend to repress dissension and to force decision making behind the scenes. The difference can be seen in the effects on participants' self-esteem.

Individual empowerment depends on people's having power bases, but HP consultants may encounter the opposite situation in organizations where layoffs and downsizing have been the results of restructuring. The survivors may be exhibiting symptoms of organizational codependency. People who are organizationally codependent have enabled the system to control their sense of worth and self-esteem at the same time that they have been investing tremendous energy in attempts to control the system (Noer, 1993). Sometimes the HP consultant's support, by helping these employees maintain internal control and keep their personal power, offers a way for them to begin breaking the co-dependent relationship.

Dysfunctional political power, when it is wielded by people who are motivated by self-interest, makes others feel powerless. When political power is shared by those who respect others and whose motivation is for the good of the organization, it promotes empowerment, trust, and productivity. Dysfunctional organizational politics thrive on unfocused chaos. Chaos in and of itself is neither good nor bad. When it is expected, as in the midst of a change effort, it can kindle creativity and progress. The opposite is true when people exploit chaos to increase their own power at the expense of others.

The dysfunctional system feeds on rumor and innuendo. To promote the healthy use of politics, the HP consultant should help clients generate valid information as well as free, informed choice and internal commitment. These are the basic requirements for any intervention activity (Argyris, 1973).

Political Myths

HP consultants frequently feel powerless and beleaguered by the persistent myths that undermine their self-confidence and ability to influence. The following list of myths is offered in the spirit of helping to dispel them.

Myth 1. *Consensus requires total or unanimous agreement.* This is not true. Consensus is achieved when the people involved believe the group's selected option is the best of all possible alternatives for a given course of action. It may not be each member's preferred option, but each member must be able to support it.

Myth 2. *Support functions are rarely genuinely helpful and tend to consume resources rather than generate them.* The HP consultant is usually associated with the less powerful support staff in the organization and is perceived as fairly ignorant about the business and the day-to-day issues facing the company. As soon as executives and line managers see the value that HP consultants add to the essential functions of the organization, they come to rely on HP consultants' services. This change comes about when the consultants have business acumen, believe themselves to possess power, and act accordingly.

Myth 3. *Only a few people can be powerful.* Not so. Power is like human energy: the supply is unlimited. Like leadership, power can be shared.

Myth 4. *A participative or power-sharing organization is founded on consensus.* Organizations will always require some hierarchy. They cannot be run primarily by consensus; there is still a very strong need for directive and consultative decision making. Nevertheless, of one hundred decisions of approximately equal importance, 40 percent will be directive (the manager decides alone), 40 percent will be consultative (the manager decides after seeking advice), and at best 20 percent will be genuine consensus decisions (the manager is an equal on the team, and the team decides as a unit).

Myth 5. *Managers are bad if they take charge and give direction.* This is true only if managers should consult more with others. Many situations demand that managers take charge, and directive decision making is very useful in implementing performance interventions. The error lies not in being directive but rather in being *inappropriately* directive.

Consensus as a Power Strategy

HP consultants must be aware of and vigilant about others' attempts to leverage chaos for personal gain. One effective technique is for HP consultants to build consensus by using their own power bases. Building consensus in the organization drives true alignment for results and is the hallmark of a successful consultant.

Consensus cannot be forced on a group or team through outside influence; rather, it surfaces from within the group. The HP consultant can facilitate this process by ensuring sufficient time and opportunity for all relevant opinions to be raised and evaluated. Consensus does not require everyone involved to participate in all discussions; representatives from various functions and hierarchical levels may act as subject matter experts and peer group advocates. This is a more efficient way of giving the total population an opportunity to influence decision making. Without a healthy participation process that ensures recourse, consensus is rarely achieved.

Interaction Model

Taking a systems view (Figure 7.1) will illustrate how to bring about healthy interactions and thus healthy politics in an organization. An organization's *people* (individuals, groups, and teams), *structure,* and *communication* are inputs into the interaction system. These inputs are essential in producing the desired

Figure 7.1. Organizational Interaction System.

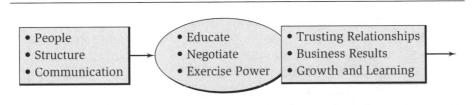

trusting relationships, business results, and organizational *growth and learning.* (For a full picture of the organization as a system, see Chapter Sixteen.)

People as individuals, groups, and teams are the entities of an organization that perform the work necessary to achieve the desired outcomes. They operate within a structure, which includes a vision and charter, or an understanding of their responsibilities. Communicating in order to generate results with others, among groups, and within teams is crucial to the organization's ability to reach its desired outcomes.

Insufficient communication causes people to distrust prospective interventions. The HP consultant must encourage open communication and accurate information about the intervention to help build trust and avoid unhealthy politics. To build trusting relationships, people must trust information and the channels of information.

People interact and influence each other in order to achieve results. People interact to *educate, negotiate,* and *exercise power* (see Figure 7.1). The successful HP consultant is able to use each of these methods to influence others and is able to help others do the same. Each method is appropriate to a particular situation. The first approach to influence is to educate. This means sharing information and discussing areas of opportunity. The next approach involves negotiating, exploring the pros and cons and looking for a win-win solution. Exercising power is the method of last resort and is sometimes the only way to make progress in an intervention.

THE ESSENCE OF ACTING POLITICALLY: MANAGING THE INTERVENTION AND FACILITATING CHANGE

This section provides an overview of understanding the change process—the key to intervening politically in organizations. (For a more detailed examination of this topic, see Chapter Twelve.)

The HP consultant's role in facilitating change is to help people move through the stages of change. The stages are *awareness, acceptance, preparation, implementation,* and *adoption.*

The notion of awareness implies that people have had some contact with the impending change; they know about it generally, without much detail. To get to acceptance, they must understand the details: people must have the opportunity to ask questions and understand what the change will mean to them. In the preparation stage, people are actively involved in deciding on and designing the change and the new behaviors that will be required. Change is actualized in the implementation stage, and, after experiencing the change, people adopt it. At the adoption stage, people are skilled enough in the new behaviors not to need coaching for routine functions.

The Nature of Resistance

Between awareness and acceptance there is usually resistance, although resistance may actually occur at any point during the change process and may be present whether people have formed positive or negative perceptions of the change. Resistance occurs only after people know enough about the impending change (through data or rumors) to be in the process of deciding whether or not it will be in their best interests. Before reaching the point of resistance, however, people ask questions and search for understanding, and this search need not be interpreted as resistance.

Resistance based on a positive perception of the change may provoke a number of emotions—hope, for example, as people enter a kind of honeymoon period. When they begin to see more of reality, however, they begin to form doubts. They may even become anxious and try to withdraw. Withdrawal is a natural and not uncommon part of the change process, but if it is handled correctly it will be thwarted, and hope will be renewed.

When people resist change on the basis of a negative perception, they react as they would to any other trauma in their lives. First they are immobilized by shock and cannot function at all. They then deny that the change will occur. Anger, depression, and bargaining follow as a part of the process.

The key to dealing with resistance is listening and allowing people to vent their anger, or their complaints about the change, without taking their points personally. It involves keeping the vision of the change in front of people while respecting their points of view. Encouraging people to be open about their resistance helps in avoiding unhealthy political behavior. Only then can the HP consultant understand the underlying causes of resistance. The consultant can then position the change in a way that reduces the perceived negative forces and helps leaders positively influence their followers and gain their commitment.

Who the Players Are

Another way to look at gaining commitment is to categorize people as supporting, opposing, or maintaining neutrality toward organizational change. These categories represent, respectively, the *go-getters,* the *opponents,* and the *fence-sitters.*

The go-getters see a proposed change as beneficial to the organization or to themselves. They are typically cooperative and helpful toward others. They promote the change plan, contribute suggestions, and display a positive attitude toward the work involved in implementing the change.

Those who fear that the change initiative may in some way threaten their position or power oppose the change and take an actively skeptical approach toward it. They discourage others from participating in the change process, hinder its implementation, and generally exhibit negative attitudes toward the change and those who support it.

The fence-sitters adopt a wait-and-see approach to the change initiative. They neither intentionally undermine nor actively encourage the change effort. They will not support the change until it appears to benefit them or the organization.

Go-getters and opponents each vie for the fence-sitters' allegiance. Go-getters emphasize the positive aspects of the change and encourage fence-sitters to become involved. Opponents, obviously, are negative and discourage involvement (Collins, 1995).

The long-term stability of the change intervention depends on whether these three constituent groups believe that the intervention fulfills their perceived interests. The HP consultant needs to understand what motivates different types of people and to discuss the intervention in terms that will remove the negative aspects of the change and appeal to the self-interest of the involved parties. The focus should be less on the opponents than on the fence-sitters and on gaining their commitment to the change, since they are the group more likely to be swayed. In this way, the HP consultant can maximize the influence of the go-getters while positively influencing the fence-sitters.

THE PERFORMANCE IMPROVEMENT PROCESS

The intervention process is dynamic and consists of phases that may be concurrent or consecutive. The phases are *launch, assessment, design, implementation,* and *monitoring/adjusting.* This section describes a typical intervention model and offers some cautions about each phase.

Launch Phase

The launch phase is the most important one on the political playing field. It is here that the foundation of the change is laid. This is also where the change's integration with other projects in the organization is examined, as well as where there is an exploration of what other processes must be changed because of it. An intervention may fail because efforts are directed at only one component of the system (workflow, for example) and "don't address the need to modify the other elements, the jobs, incentives, management system, etc., necessary to get and maintain real change" (Rummler, 1996, p. 31).

During the launch phase, the HP consultant's constituents talk and establish a contract that embodies their understanding of the change's scope and its desired results. This contract, sometimes called the *charter,* includes the key concepts relevant to the change and spells out the key functional areas of management that will be affected by the change. Establishing all these agreements at the start prevents endless battles later on. The HP consultant must also assess the capabilities and willingness of those involved in the change. Uncovering hidden agendas is essential in the launch phase; the success of the change initiative depends on it.

Visualizing the future is another important activity during the launch phase. The personal visions of the participants and the combined visions of the teams that will carry out the change are crucial to the establishment of the project plan. The HP consultant's role is to see that the visions are shared and developed as the change process is carried forward.

Several roles must be filled in the process of managing a major change. These are the roles of the *executive sponsor* (the person at the top who provides the resources), the *implementing sponsors* (those who are closer to the target audience and who will help implement the change), the *change facilitators* (those who help in making the change), the *target audience* (comprising those who will actually make the change), and the *champion* (someone who lobbies for the change).

The importance of defining and filling these roles cannot be overemphasized. For example, consider a process improvement effort in an insurance company. The two implementing sponsors (the vice presidents of marketing and operations) disagreed on the scope of the intervention, and the executive sponsor would take no action to help them settle their conflict, insisting that the project go forward despite the two implementing sponsors' differences. As a result, the implementing sponsors continued to be at odds with each other, publicly and privately, and ultimately they destroyed the entire effort. For a change agenda to be realized, cosponsors must agree on the scope of the change and must engage in healthy political behaviors.

Assessment Phase

The assessment phase involves examination of the organization's internal and external environments, the processes in place at the time of the change initiative, and the measures of those processes. This phase is rife with political battles. In times of fear and limited resources, people may withhold data and true numbers. In a pharmaceuticals company, for example, members of a steering team (vice presidents in the organization) were asked to determine improvement targets for the redesign of a core business process. Their mutual mistrust and their political posturing outside the meetings delayed the project for an entire quarter as they worked on their hidden agendas. Like the launch phase, the assessment phase requires healthy politics and an environment of trust.

Design Phase

The design phase is the heart of the change initiative. The blueprint for improvement is created at the assessment phase; the design phase provides the architecture for achieving the change's vision.

Consider the example of a manufacturing plant that was undergoing an organizational redesign effort. The design team (a representative sample of organization members) created a structure that involved nontraditional participative roles and corresponding human resource systems. Because the union was reluctant to embrace a compensation system based on anything but seniority, team members were subjected to much pressure from their peers to change the design. The design team used a combination of education and open dialogue to demonstrate the benefits of the change to the union and to the rest of the business while removing the pressures against it. Ultimately, the union reversed its position and agreed to move toward a pay-for-performance and gainsharing program. Union members adopted the motto "Seniority only where it makes sense for the business" (and for themselves, because they shared in the gains).

Implementation Phase

In this phase, a matrix is developed that lists all the constituents who must implement the change. It also lists their current stages in the process and specifies a strategy for helping them move ahead. This is the phase where many projects fail, but usually because a previous phase (most likely the launch) was inadequately executed.

A successful implementation was undertaken by a financial institution. The presenting opportunity involved employees' inability to fill the roles required of them in a competitive environment. An external HP consultant was engaged to help remedy the situation. She worked first with the company's partners, to develop a charter. The charter was then taken to the next level down, and employees at that level developed a plan for themselves. Finally, a cross-functional, multilevel design team worked on the charter, which was then communicated to the entire organization, along with a request for input. All the while, the HP consultant worked with the partners to uncover and confront hidden agendas. The HP consultant made powerful allies, and they guided her in dealing with the organizational politics, principally through a strategy of consensus and participation. The desired business results were what drove the process, and the project progressed in a totally participative way. As the project proceeded and people in the organization became involved in the change, they became more open to it, more energized by it, and ready to implement the recommendations of the design team. Thus, as people planned and implemented the change, their participation and empowerment increased. Therefore, the HP consultant must know how and when to involve others.

Monitoring/Adjusting Phase

The last phase of an intervention is the phase of monitoring and adjusting. This is an ongoing process in which constituents assess the results of the intervention, as well as the new behaviors and new knowledge that have accompanied it. Here gains and losses are summarized, and the causes of any losses are determined; people take action, communicate about their progress, and, it is to be hoped, celebrate their success.

This phase is often neglected: people are afraid of not having met their goals, or they lack the time needed to monitor results. But monitoring and adjusting are crucial, not only to business results but also to the likelihood of the organization's willingness to undertake future projects. This phase also adds to the power of the HP consultants who have been involved.

Keys to Successful Interventions

This section reviews the critical elements of a successful intervention:

- Executive leadership, as well as management's commitment to seeing the project through to successful implementation
- A clear statement of why the change is necessary
- A clear vision of how the organization will be different after the changes
- Sound, comprehensive recommendations
- A sound implementation strategy and plan
- Adequate resources and time
- Communication
- Willingness of affected functions and individuals to support the proposed changes
- Effective management and execution of the implementation

If the HP consultant understands and cultivates his or her political power as it can be brought to bear on incorporating these crucial elements, the intervention is more likely to be successful and its effects to be sustained.

The HP consultant functions in a political environment, and healthy political power must be used to effect change in an organization. The advice given in the paragraphs that follow has helped many HP consultants undertake and implement successful change initiatives.

1. *Make the most of power.* Thoroughly read and understand this chapter. Prepare yourself. Become aware of the power bases in the target organization.

2. *Present an unthreatening image.* Use your power quietly; no one wants to work with a consultant who is seen as pushy or political. The HP consultant should present the change in increments, always focusing on the client's needs.

3. *Defuse opposition.* In a change initiative, HP consultants bring out conflict as they hold legitimate and open discussion. To defuse opposition, they need to acknowledge the pain of the change, answer objections clearly and boldly, allay fear with facts, and keep innovation within parameters that are as safe and familiar as possible.

4. *Align with a powerful other.* Operating or line managers directly affected by the change make the most effective allies. They can help HP consultants maneuver around the mines.

5. *Make trade-offs.* The HP consultant can build up credit by attending to projects that the client perceives as having high priority. This credit can then be used to start projects in which the HP consultant has a particular interest.

6. *Strike while the iron is hot.* Upon successful implementation of a change initiative, the HP consultant should follow up immediately with a somewhat less popular or less understood program.

7. *Conduct research.* This strategy is especially useful in emotionally charged areas. Data can help defuse the power of someone who resists by creating an awareness of the need to change.

8. *Use a neutral cover.* Pilot programs are usually unthreatening and neutral. The client feels in control of both the intervention and the decision to continue. Be careful, however, because pilot programs are also easy targets for opponents; those who feel threatened will sometimes try to sabotage a pilot.

9. *Inch along.* By focusing on a client's immediate needs and, within professional standards, serving those needs well, the HP consultant can allay management's fears. Growing acceptance eases the introduction of larger changes.

10. *Nurture the key players in a change.* The HP consultant must be constantly aware of how the key people feel and must share information with them regularly (Schein, 1985).

The HP Consultant's Competence

The HP consultant must have certain attributes and particular kinds of competence in order to achieve power in organizations. Business knowledge is essential. To become effective in leading interventions, the HP consultant must have an understanding of the economic and operational dimensions of the organization's business.

Respect from top management, supervisors, and operating members comes from building credibility and using power. The HP consultant should be perceived as (1) being a good listener who understands the various needs of people and groups and appreciates individual differences, (2) working in the best interests of the whole organization, and (3) helping people arrive at workable solutions and develop the consensus to support them.

The HP consultant must be able to orchestrate effective and efficient meetings. Behind-the-scenes influence is a key part of the successful facilitation of group dynamics, both before and after meetings.

Individuals often require coaching in behavioral change. The HP consultant should provide counsel and be a role model for people who are making behavioral changes. He or she should help people formulate political strategies to make interventions work. Communication and leadership skills are vital.

The HP consultant must be an early adopter of change. He or she must be open to innovation and creativity and thoroughly committed to the idea that adults can learn from one another as peers, regardless of the formal or informal power structure. What the HP consultant must be able to foster in people is great respect for others' experience and thorough curiosity about their knowledge; respect and curiosity should be apparent, with all the parties to an interaction always striving for improvement. Such fostering, however, depends on a variety of skills that take considerable time to develop in oneself and to nurture in others.

Challenges

Internal and external HP consultants both have a role in implementing interventions. For example, an internal consultant may advocate change for quite some time in his or her own organizations but get no results until an external consultant is hired.

The external consultant is important in recommending interventions; the internal consultant is important in fostering their implementation through change agentry. If the external consultant is the only change agent, then the intervention may be too easily viewed as belonging to the consultant instead of to the organization (and if this happens, the project is at risk for slowing down or even coming to a complete stop when the consultant leaves).

The nurturing of the relationship between internal and external consultants is crucial to successful implementation. Internal consultants often become frustrated and feel abused by their organizations. They are the ones who deal constantly with resistance to change, and there is often little glory in their role. External consultants, by contrast, arrive, suggest, bless, and depart, leaving internal consultants to follow up and make things happen.

The internal/external consultant relationship can be a very fruitful and fulfilling one if it is properly nurtured. The consultants should clarify their roles with each other at the outset, and again at regular intervals throughout the project. They should confide in each another and give feedback on how they are fulfilling expectations. Each should keep the other constantly informed of schedules, processes, and outcomes. Together, they should closely monitor the political arena and analyze its dynamics.

Building relationships with members of the target audience is an extremely important part of the change agent's role, and the more that consultants fit in with the group and are visible in the organization, the more quickly they will be accepted by the target audience, which includes sponsors and other players. The playing field may be the meeting room, the boardroom, or the front line; full equipment for the game includes one's knowledge, one's preparation, and the application of one's skills.

A special challenge is presented when multiple consultants are working together on a single project. The consultants may be from the same consulting organization or from several different organizations, but the external consultants themselves must form a healthy organization or risk contributing to the failure of a project. Clients who are resistant to an intervention may attempt to divide and conquer by trying to pit the HP consultants against one another, thereby hoping to interfere with the change, or a resistant client may try, subversively, to gain ammunition against a powerful consultant, attempting to get him or her reassigned or fired. Whenever they can, external HP consultants should stay out of organizational politics and, above all, present a united front.

CONCLUSION

Just as change is a reality of life, so is evolution a natural part of the HP consultant's role. While working with clients, HP consultants must dedicate their energy and awareness to adding value to the organization. They should stay focused on business results instead of getting stuck in activities.

HP consultants who feel powerless are actually often wasting their power defending themselves and convincing others of their abilities; thus their focus is on themselves. But, armed with true power from within, with subject matter expertise, and with knowledge of politics, HP consultants can observe the forces at work in the organization. Then and only then will they be able to intervene effectively and provide the kind of service that accomplishes valued results.

References

Argyris, C. (1973). *Intervention theory and method: A behavioral science view.* Reading, MA: Addison-Wesley.

Bennis, W., and Nanus, B. (1995). *Leaders: The strategies for taking charge.* New York: HarperCollins.

Collins, D. (1995). Death of a gainsharing plan: Power politics and participatory management. *Organizational Dynamics* 24, 23–39.

Ferris, G., and others. (1996). Reactions of diverse groups to politics in the workplace. *Journal of Management* 3, 23.

Kanter, R. (1997). *On the frontiers of management.* Boston: Harvard Business School Press.

Rummler, G. (1996). Redesigning the organization and making it work. *CMA Magazine* 70, 29–32.

Schein, V.E. (1985). Organizational realities: The politics of change. *Training and Developmental Journal* 39, 37–41.

Tjosvold, D. (1995). Effects of power to reward and punish in cooperative and competitive contexts. *Journal of Social Psychology* 135, 723–737.

Ulrich, D. (1997). *Human resource champions.* Boston: Harvard Business School Press.

PART TWO

THE GENERAL PROCESS OF HUMAN PERFORMANCE TECHNOLOGY

Human Performance Technology (HPT), as an offspring of general systems theory applied to organizations, very much adheres to principles familiar to systems analysts and engineers. The "systems approach" requires a total-system perspective in examining organizations and creating interventions aimed at improving results. This approach is also imbued with a heavy emphasis on empirical tryout and testing and involves a fundamental commitment to the recycling of intervention efforts until satisfactory results are obtained. The systems approach is the foundation on which what is loosely termed the *general process model* of HPT was created. It is important to underline, however, that there is no one model to which all HP technologists adhere; far from it. The literature is replete with endless variants on the general systems process model, which is sometimes affectionately labeled by the acronym *ADDIE:* analyze, design, develop, implement, and evaluate. (The final two elements, *implement* and *evaluate,* are frequently reversed in many of the published models).

Part Two presents eight chapters that deal with the various major components of the general process model. The first of these, Chapter Eight, presents a global view of analysis, laying out some of the fundamental issues related to this phase of HPT activities and the essential role it plays in any HPT project. It also describes key analyses that characterize HPT. Chapter Nine describes the two critical phases of design and development. It is during design and development that the HP technologist demonstrates creative abilities to transform analysis-derived data into concrete structures for performance intervention. Essential to the success of any HP intervention design is the evaluation of its components, individually and in combination, and yet this is frequently the most neglected phase of HPT projects. Chapter Ten deals with issues of evaluation from both conceptual and operational perspectives. It provides readers with a basis for making evaluation decisions that can ensure the generation of appropriate data, as well as the reporting of these data in ways that will be meaningful to decision makers. In Chapter Eleven, the issue of performance tracking is uniquely presented, with concrete examples and a method for consistently reporting improvement results. Chapter Twelve, on implementation, stresses how important it is for HP projects to consider implementation factors even before interventions are designed. Because HP projects generally bring about changes in organizations, this chapter also considers how change variables can be factored into implementation plans. Chapter Thirteen lays out the "Language of Work" model, a tight conceptual and operational model for applying the complete HPT process. In Chapter Fourteen, the emphasis is on making the transformation from a traditional training department to an organization for performance design and performance consulting. This transformation represents a major shift, which requires careful planning and evolutionary execution. Chapter Fifteen brings all the components of the general process model together through a series of concrete examples that demonstrate how a well-executed HPT intervention, systematically designed and implemented, generates valued results.

Part Two makes a statement about the tools and conduct of HPT. It demonstrates the commitment of HPT to systems thinking and to systematic planning, execution, and implementation of performance improvement projects. It unequivocally shows its adherence to the critical role that evaluation plays in creating effective HP interventions. It also illustrates through varied examples how HPT, as a process and a field of professional practice, has powerful applicability across cultures, countries, and continents.

The chapter authors are specialists who possess strong academic backgrounds and international, transcultural consulting experience. All of them have already made significant contributions to the HPT literature. Their chapters, taken together, set the stage for Parts Three and Four of this handbook, where the general process model is operationalized into HPT interventions.

CHAPTER EIGHT

Analysis for Human Performance Technology

Allison Rossett

Without analysis, there is no Human Performance Technology (HPT). Analysis provides the foundation for HPT, a profession and a perspective that demands study before recommendations, data before decisions, and involvement before actions.

This chapter is about analysis. Analysis, whether it is called that, or whether it is called *assessment* or *needs assessment* or *training needs assessment* or *performance analysis* or *front-end analysis,* is important because it helps professionals make better plans for serving customers. It provides professionals with insight into the organization, job, workplace, and individual. HPT, like the other professions to which it is compared, derives success from the fact that analysis is the fresh look that defines and directs our efforts. Analysis enables professionals to do better than merely salute the requests that they receive from customers and clients.

For doctors, architects, engineers, urban planners, and performance professionals, analysis is the process that ensures movement from ambiguity to what Mager (1970) has dubbed "the heart of the matter." In analysis, professionals scan for opportunities, find and describe problems, ask questions, establish hypotheses, eliminate possibilities, parse elements, separate facts from fiction, involve colleagues, and render recommendations. The architect who seeks the work and play patterns of a family, the doctor figuring out why the new mother is fatigued, the urban planner casting about for mixed land and property uses, and the HP technologist investigating what it will take to move employees from an analog to a digital environment—all share a need to know so that decisions can be predicated on more than habit and special interests. This chapter concentrates on the ways in which HP technologists gain their knowledge.

THE EXPANDING DEFINITION OF *ANALYSIS*

Before answering questions about what analysis is, it is useful to take on the question of *when*: When do we do analyses? Many would answer with a single word: "First." But is that the best way to play a strategic role in the organization? Should we wait to swing into action until after a request is made for a class about a software package or negotiating skills or numerical control lathes, or for some help in reducing error rates or improving customer service? If we wait for impetus from others, we are often too late. Sponsors acting in haste rarely support anything but a tactical response that matches the initial framing of a matter. They want to see a half-day class or a jazzy Web site—not analysis—and they want what they want when they want it.

To provide appropriate services, however, analysis must be both responsive and anticipatory, immediate and perpetual. Some of the information necessary for responding to requests for assistance should already reside in files that are just a few keystrokes away, and this will be the case when the performance professional has been in a state of virtual analysis.

It all sounds very modern, but analysis actually has deep roots in America. Dewey (1933), the most famous American philosopher of education, deserves credit as the parent of analysis. He turned away from the European and manufacturing traditions and urged a distinctively American approach to education, one that responded to the needs of the learner. As obvious as that concern seems now, it was revolutionary for educators to be interested in anything other than the subject matter, the content, or the job.

Tyler (1949), generally recognized as the father of behavioral objectives, contributed the focus on tangible intentions for curriculum planning and provided an early raison d'être for analysis. Tyler emphasized the questioning process as a means of determining objectives. Two decades later, Mager (1970) made Tyler's work accessible by providing tools to find and write useful instructional objectives.

Instructional objectives are dear to HP professionals only if they are the right objectives—that is, if they support the planning process and lead to better performance. This is a key purpose of analysis. Linking analysis to the bottom line, Gilbert (1978) offers strategies for assessing, in dollars and cents, the potential for improved performance.

As professionals stretched to evaluate cost benefits, the shift from instructional to performance technology was ensured. Kaufman and English (1979) highlight the gap between the desired and the current state, not just in terms of the learner's skill and knowledge but also in terms of the organization and the means it uses to support performance. Gilbert (1978), Mager and Pipe (1984), and Harless (1975), as leaders of an evolution that is still in progress (see Robinson and Robinson, 1995; Rossett, 1997), rivet analysis to HPT by emphasizing five related notions:

1. Instruction is not the answer to every challenge in the workplace.

2. There is a wide array of interventions that can be used to enhance performance. These include but are not limited to instruction. Examples of interventions are job aids, selection strategies, compensation and incentive programs, reengineered processes, and job redesign. A combination of these interventions is called a *performance system* or *solution system.*

3. Matching appropriate interventions to the challenge, opportunity, or problem is a process that is based on analysis of a cause or causes. The HP technologist cannot be expected to be an expert in every intervention, but he or she must be an expert in analysis. That kind of expertise will enable identification of an appropriate intervention or performance system, collaboration with appropriate colleagues, and marketing of the approach to the organization.

4. One good way to influence the organization is with analysis, a process that brings the HP technologist out of the cubicle and into the field and yields compelling data about the individual, the work environment, and the organization.

5. The move to a global environment increases the need for a fresh look at the various and richly diverse settings involved in an effort. Analysis provides that new, data-driven view.

PERFORMANCE ANALYSIS
AND TRAINING NEEDS ASSESSMENT

The foregoing statements are becoming reality in some organizations; SBC Center for Learning and IBM Education and Training worldwide offer two examples from among many possibilities. Their commitment to analysis, consultation, and solution systems can be seen in what they say and in the ways they define jobs and parse their organizations. In both situations, some professionals are formally and informally bonded to customers and clients, with a focus on defining requirements, business needs, and tailored solutions. These professionals act as performance consultants. They do performance analysis (PA). They scan for requirements, thinking of themselves as early-warning systems, as relationship managers. Their job is to broker effective handoffs, sometimes to education and training specialists and sometimes to colleagues, internal and external, whose bailiwicks are organizational effectiveness, technology, or compensation.

PA is what they do. It is predicated on relationships that enable continuous, up-front study to identify needs and define solutions that go beyond the automatic to fresh, data-driven, coordinated approaches. They use PA to figure out what to do and to make the case for the resources inherent in collaboration with solution partners. Once PA has determined that skill, knowledge, and motivation are part of the mix, more explicit and focused needs assessment is carried out.

Needs assessment, or training needs assessment (TNA) (Rossett, 1987), is then conducted in order to design and develop instructional and informational programs and materials. TNA may involve in-depth study of subject matter, extensive audience analysis, determination of prerequisite skills and attitudes, resolution of disagreements between experts, establishment of consensus approaches and standards, and determination of the details that underpin learning and information programs.

There are, of course, similarities between TNA and PA. They both represent methods for figuring out what to do, although at different levels of detail, and with varying proximity to the solution. They are also both efforts to understand and serve customers, and they are based on asking questions of sources (Rossett, 1987, forthcoming; Swanson, 1994). Their difference has to do with where they are in the "food chain," and how much is known before their use begins. PA is what is done first and fast, or virtually, as professionals take the pulse of the people and the organizations they serve. PA ensures that we find the right thing or things to do for customers; TNA is the study that helps us do the right things in the right way.

Elsewhere (Rossett, 1987, 1997, forthcoming) I contend that the nature of the initiating situation provides direction for planning. Analysis aimed at supporting the introduction of a new product is different from analysis aimed at solving a chronic problem. In the first situation, the challenge is to capture the essence of the new product and *anticipate* barriers to its successful rollout; in the second, the question that dominates the analysis is "Why?" The combined results of work by Mager and Pipe (1984), Harless (1975), Gilbert (1978), and Rossett (1987, forthcoming) can serve as a template for determining the causes of performance problems and deriving solutions based on those causes. Gilbert, for example, elegantly distinguishes between two kinds of deficient performers: those who cannot do what is expected of them, and those who, for some other reason, *can* do what is expected but *do not* do it. Obviously, a primary role for the analyst during PA is to find out why people in the latter group are not performing, to propose a performance or solution system that fits the situation, and then work to put in place.

Benjamin (1989), Rodriguez (1988), Rosenberg (1990), and Rossett (1997) herald expanding views of analysis that respect a holistic vision of how organizations work, and Kaufman in particular presses the profession to consider how performance gaps and interventions affect the group, the organization, and society, not just the individual performer. Rosenberg (1990), Rossett (1996), and Rummler (1986) point out that analysis must occur throughout the system and must result in scrutiny of and involvement in human resources development, product development, organizational development, human resources management, and environmental engineering.

It is one kind of task to design a course or a lesson; it is quite another to take responsibility for human performance and for the interdependent organizational systems that impinge on it. Finding an apt mix of interventions, selling the system to customers who have a smaller or functional view, and brokering the system with cross-functional colleagues are not minor challenges. Where to turn for help? The answer: to analysis. Through analysis we figure out where to go and why, gathering opinions, data, sponsors, and friends. That is what the remainder of this chapter is about.

ANALYSIS: GOALS AND TOOLS

This section is about the goals for conducting analysis and about the tools that are used to achieve those goals. Three broad goals for both kinds of analysis (PA and TNA) are discussed in this section:

1. Gathering and disseminating information, perspectives, and recommendations regarding optimal performance, actual performance, feelings, causes of performance problems, and solutions
2. Involving key people and bringing in the appropriate data
3. Modeling and employing a systematic process for improving human performance

This discussion is followed by a brief review of tools and technologies, including the interview, observation, surveys, and focus groups.

GOALS FOR ANALYSIS

Finding Out What Is Going On

The first goal for analysis is to find out what is going on and to disseminate and verify those perceptions. "What is going on" is a phrase that demands explication. There are five substantive purposes for analysis efforts.

Finding and Disseminating Information About Optimal Performance. What would the organization be doing if it were functioning splendidly? What does the exemplary performer know and do that exemplifies success? What is an effective line manager thinking about when operating from a market-driven perspective? How are french fries kept crisp? How are better loan decisions made? How is computerized equipment sold? Answers to these questions provide the basis for any intervention that is enacted.

Finding and Disseminating Information About Actual Performance. Now that information regarding optimal performance is in hand, it can serve as a template for examining the current status of the organization. What are employees doing now? What are the criteria by which loan officers are currently making loans, and what verification procedures are they using? Some analysts begin by looking for the criteria of optimal performance, but in some circumstances it is appropriate to begin with a picture of what is actually going on. If we know in general what good performance is and can tell when it is not present, we can begin with the errors, accidents, and complaints. Those obvious instances of actual performance obviate the need to engage at the beginning in a resource-depleting quest for detailed criteria of optimal performance. These instances of the actual also enable the swift narrowing of the practitioner's focus. If there is any uncertainty, however, about what constitutes a good loan document or a good engineering report, then the practitioner will need first to capture a picture of optimal performance to serve as a benchmark.

Finding and Disseminating Information About How Key Sources Feel. People's feelings matter; feelings influence the outcome of any endeavor. When we ignore the feelings of job incumbents, we imperil our efforts at performance improvement. HP technologists derive useful information when they seek information about whether employees and related others value a skill, a kind of knowledge, a program, or an initiative. The extent to which employees feel competent to meet a challenge, problem, or opportunity is also valuable information, as is information about the strength of the feelings that are aroused by any particular approach to a problem or opportunity.

Finding and Disseminating Information About the Causes of Problems. Gilbert (1978), Mager and Pipe (1984), Harless (1975), and Senge (1990) are credited with focusing attention on the factors that drive or cause performance. Why are managers not turning in performance appraisals? Why are the ones they turn in incorrectly completed? Why are french fries limp or sales down? When poor performance is continuous, the focus typically is on why. (This is what propelled Mager and Pipe to write in 1984, "They really shoulda oughta wanna.")

Questions about causes are equally important for rollouts. What might get in the way? Where are employees with respect to the shift from analog to digital, or from the Rambo approach to teaming? Analysts must ask about the causes of current glitches and anticipate future impediments.

Whereas work in the past has highlighted three causes of performance problems (skill/knowledge, motivational, environmental dynamics), the cognitively oriented work of Bandura (1977) and Keller (1983) calls for an expansion of our thinking, to encompass the four kinds of causes (Rossett, 1987, 1997, forthcoming) presented in Table 8.1.

1. *Employees lack skill or knowledge.* Even if they wanted to—even if Robert Mager and Peter Pipe put a gun to their heads—they could not do what is required of them. The knowledge essential to writing, say, behavioral statements on performance appraisals, or to explaining digitized equipment, is not in their repertoire.

2. *The environment is in the way.* Employees do not have the tools, forms, or work space necessary to perform. For example, the computer keeps going down, or job aids are either not updated or not available.

3. *There are no, few, or improper incentives.* What are the consequences of doing the job badly, or not doing it at all? Are supervisors paying

Table 8.1. Causes of Performance Problems.

Causes	Examples
Lack of skill and/or knowledge	Employees don't know product features. Employees have forgotten how equipment works. Employees can't find the documentation.
Lack of motivation	Workers don't see what's good about this system or product. Workers have doubts about their abilities to do the job. Employees don't see how this is a good change.
Flawed incentives	The best workers are burdened with more work. Salary increases are automatic. There is no pay for performance. There are no incentives. Supervisors ignore or fail to value workers' efforts.
Flawed environment	The computer keeps going down. Forms are overly complex or ambiguous. The environment is characterized by poor lighting, excessive noise, and cramped quarters.

attention to desired outcomes? Does the compensation program recognize excellence and extraordinary effort? Perhaps the production of crisp french fries has been ignored in the past, or the failure to submit performance appraisals has likewise been ignored. Do star performers get loaded down with additional work? If managers are expected to implement a program, will the performance appraisals that they write be reflections of that priority?

4. *Employees are unmotivated.* Traditionally, during the analysis phase of an intervention, HP professionals have sought externally oriented information about employees' motivation. But what about the internal state of the individuals involved? What is going on inside employees as they contemplate a new system, mandate, or product? The work of Keller (1983) and Bandura (1977) has influenced my suggestions (Rossett, 1987, 1997, forthcoming) about the role of motivation in analysis. What I recommend is a quest for information about two areas: first, about whether and how much an element of the job (customer service, or computerized management functions) is valued by job incumbents; and, second, about the amount of confidence each employee has in his or her ability to master particular skills or knowledge ("Am I the kind of person who is going to be able to learn how to use a computer?").

Finding and Disseminating Information About Solutions. The quest for the causes of performance problems is urgent because recommendations about solutions are based on identified causes. Here is where the performance analyst defines who must sit at the table to collaborate in solving the customer's problem, or in realizing the customer's opportunity.

When problems of incentive and of motivation are seen as separate causes of performance problems, as shown in Table 8.1 and again in Table 8.2, the ken of the HP technologist is enlarged. Table 8.2 also shows training and job aids, interventions traditionally associated with the HP technologist, extended to the enhancing of motivation, as well as to the increasing of skills and knowledge. Problems caused by an improper environment and improper incentives must be handled through a broader array of strategies, which will often involve redesign of management and the organization. Table 8.2 pairs four causes of performance problems with a variety of interventions.

Involving Key Figures and Data

The second goal for analysis is to involve key figures and data in the effort. This is not a casual concern. The need for extensive participation is great because analysis, consultation, and HPT represent new perspectives for most organiza-

Table 8.2. Causes and Interventions.

Causes	Interventions
Lack of skill and/or knowledge	Training Documentation, job aids Coaching Knowledge management tools and databases
Lack of motivation (including lack of appreciation for value and lack of confidence)	Information, so workers can see benefits, impact, and value Links to work challenges Use of role models Early successes to instill confidence Participatory roles in selecting goals
Flawed incentives	Revised policies Revised contracts Training for supervisors and managers Incentive, recognition, and bonus plans
Flawed environment	Work and process redesign New and/or better tools and technologies Better selection and job-person matches

tions. Exposure is needed to these perspectives, as well as to their benefits, and exposure is better achieved through a real effort on behalf of the organization than through exhortations. Every project and request for assistance must be seen not only as an occasion for collecting the data and perspectives that will enlighten the particular task but also as an opportunity to sell and inform.

Different sources and stages of analysis are appropriate to different projects. For example, a customer says, "I think we need some advanced teaming workshops. We've been trying to get our engineers out of Rambo mode for two years now, and I don't see much progress. Let's schedule another class or something." Exhibit 8.1 presents one possible tool for analyzing this situation. Before handing the problem off to colleagues—to the education manager, say, for more detailed assessment targeted at training needs in areas where the engineers lack skills, knowledge, or information—the analyst will first take the steps outlined in Exhibit 8.1.

If, however, the analyst is responsible for developing a program to support the introduction of automation into back-office operations for seven thousand real estate offices, he or she would focus the analysis effort on different sources from those listed in Exhibit 8.1. These sources might include the following people and documents:

- Executives
- Back-office employees
- Office managers
- Sales managers
- Salespeople
- Vendors
- Vendors' materials
- Contracts between the company and vendors

During any kind of analysis, the professional grapples with the question of how broadly to cast a net for information and perspectives. During PA, brevity is fa-

Exhibit 8.1. Analysis Tool for a Teaming Initiative.

Stages and Sources	Sample Questions
Meet with the customer who has expressed dissatisfaction with the current teaming situation	Why did you establish the teaming initiative to begin with?
	Why are you distressed with your progress? What is missing? What is happening?
	Do the engineers share your enthusiasm for teaming? Do their managers?
Review the literature on teaming in technical environments	What is the range of ways in which teaming can be accomplished in engineering environments? What are the roles and goals?
	What happened in efforts that have succeeded? What happened in ones that have failed? What were the causes of these successes and failures?
Review policies, communications, and any training that has accompanied the teaming effort	What clear message has been given to engineers?
	Have they been told *why?* Do they have examples of positive benefits for individuals and the organization? Are there any related policies? Is there recognition?
Conduct interviews and/or focus groups with randomly pulled engineers and engineering managers	Is it a defining force in the way they work? Should it be? Do they think it is yielding better engineering deliverables?
	What must the organization do to make it a part of the way that engineers work and think?

vored. Later on, after it has been determined that there is a need for a class or a performance-support system (perhaps including what I have been calling TNA), a larger effort is justified.

The nature of the sources consulted will influence the nature and richness of the proposed solutions. Given the incentive structure of most organizations, if the inquiry is limited to any one unit, the solution is most likely to highlight that unit. If collaboration is extended, however, to colleagues from data processing, organizational development, personnel, and career and strategic planning, as well as to colleagues in the training unit, then performance systems will emerge that are more dynamic and more integrated.

HP technologists are doing two important things by extending themselves into the organization. First, they are gathering essential information to design the performance system. Second, they are winning friends, influencing people, and making certain that the proposed solutions belong to more than the department to which the HP technologist belongs.

Modeling and Employing a Systematic Process

The third goal for analysis is to model and employ a systematic process for improving human performance. What is meant by a systematic approach to analysis? A systematic analysis has defined purposes and components. It is orderly and consistent. Most important, the output of each of its activities serves as input for subsequent efforts and decisions. What the HP technologist learns through each contact influences the next series of questions and actions, as illustrated by Exhibit 8.1. Once the professional has identified the cause or causes of a problem, as he or she might do at every one of the stages represented in the exhibit, some prospective interventions will be eliminated, whereas concentration on others will be ensured.

As another example of a systematic approach to analysis, consider the structure offered when an initiating situation is used to direct and focus front-end efforts (Rossett, 1987, 1990, forthcoming). Initiating situations present themselves in many ways, but here we will focus on those that arise from the following three sets of circumstances:

1. The rollout of a new policy, program, initiative, or technology

2. A need for the organization to deal with performance problems

3. A need for the organization to develop its people

Each of these initiating situations will influence the analysis in a different way.

Rollout of a New Policy, Program, Initiative, or Technology. This situation arises when the organization is making a change and the HP technologist is expected to facilitate it. For example, the company decides to automate sales activities, or to move its lending practices from a conservative to a risk-oriented stance, or to encourage managers to adopt a participative approach.

In the introduction of a major change, PA efforts should focus on swiftly defining the effort and then anticipating the barriers to it. This task is accomplished through quick but critical attention to optimal performance, to job incumbents and their supervisors, and to literature. Do employees like the idea of moving to automation? Are they familiar with its benefits? Do they believe they will be able to become successful in an automated sales organization? What are they concerned about? What, in their opinion, can the organization do to support the change?

Subsequent needs assessments will unearth and operationalize the details of what the sources envision as optimal perspectives, skills, and knowledge. For example, what does upper management want the automated system to provide to job incumbents at all levels of the organization? How does the system work, in detail? How does it facilitate the functions that salespeople care about?

Need for the Organization to Deal with Performance Problems. Performance problems occur in situations where there is good reason to assume that employees have the capacity to do what is expected of them but do not get it done. In other words, results do not fulfill performance expectations. This is the situation made famous by Harless (1975), Mager and Pipe (1984), and Robinson and Robinson (1995): employees ought to be able to fill out performance appraisals or maintain a certain level of sales or continue to produce award-winning french fries, but they do not.

In the face of a performance problem, analysis focuses on finding the gap between desired performance and current performance and then identifying causes of the discrepancies. For example, consider the case of a company that is concerned about weak performance appraisals. In the words of the personnel director, "They're lousy. They're useless. They aren't helping anybody." Analysis for that challenge must focus on the broad outlines of the problem. What, exactly, is it that is lousy? Is the problem with written appraisals or with interviews? The focus then shifts to determining causes: Can managers and supervisors, when they try hard, fill out appraisal forms in a meaningful way? Are the forms understandable to them? Do they perceive the reasons for the different lines on the form? Do they believe that performance appraisals have the potential to contribute to the work of their units?

Need for the Organization to Develop Its People. This situation arises in an organization that is focusing its attention on particular jobs, roles, or positions. Usually there is a strategic intention, and organizational leaders are looking ahead and thinking about how to ensure that one or all segments of the workforce will be ready for the future. Requests for assistance might sound like these:

"Our salespeople are going to be expected to sell a whole new line of digital products, and we must prepare them to be fluent in this new world."

"How can we develop our nurses to play the team leadership roles that new medical care and reimbursement policies demand?"

"We want to be the best financial services professionals serving the automotive industry. How can we make certain that our training and development will parallel the company's commitment to continuous improvement?"

The analyst in this situation will cast a wide net in efforts to collect sources' views of where the particular field and practice within it are headed. It will be helpful for the analyst to take the following steps:

- Review the efforts of writers, leaders within and outside the organization, professional associations, and benchmark organizations.

- Scrutinize customer feedback, as well as error and success data (such as sales figures and number of callbacks). From this array of information about optimal performance and data about current performance, construct scenarios and queries that enable executives and employees to weigh in with their priorities.

- Use these priorities to hand the initiative off to another HP professional, who will then conduct more detailed TNAs that are focused on the highest priorities.

TOOLS AND TECHNOLOGY FOR ANALYSIS

Tools

This section describes the four tools most frequently used for gathering information and perspectives during analysis. These tools are *interviews, observation, surveys,* and *focus groups.* (For a more detailed approach to this topic, see Rossett, 1987.)

Interviews. The interview is the most popular tool for analysis. An interview conducted in person or by phone can be used to gather information about optimal and actual performance, feelings, causes, and solutions. When the information is technical, detailed, or emotionally charged, an interview is appropriate. The interview, especially when conducted in person, is also an effective device for establishing rapport. Another advantage of the interview is that the analyst is able to generate follow-up questions. For example, when an employee says, "We can't sell this product because it isn't as good as our competitor's," the analyst can seek specific information about the product's problems and assess the salesperson's familiarity with its particular strengths. Three kinds of queries are used during interviews:

1. *Open-ended questions and probes:* "When you envision a 'quality' approach to wafer fabrication, what do you see going on?"

2. *Structured or forced-choice questions:* "Would you describe yourselves as enthusiastic or unenthusiastic about the introduction of portable computers?"

3. *Mirror-statement questions:* "You've indicated that the drop in sales has more to do with salespeople's time management than with any doubts they have about product features. Is that an accurate statement of what you see as the cause of the problem?"

Observation. Observation is used to determine what is going on in the workplace. It is a powerful tool for capturing information about current skills and knowledge, as well as for examining the context surrounding the individual performer.

Observation enables the analyst to make inferences about the work climate, supervision, tools, accessibility of job aids, workflow, and employees' habits and patterns. The word *inferences* is important: the analyst must be cognizant of the impact that an observer tends to have on the people and the workplace, an influence that has the potential to tamper with reality.

There are two major levels of observation (Zemke and Kramlinger, 1982). At the first level, the observer has a general "take" on the situation—an "establishing shot" of what is going on, say, at the teller window. At the second level, it is possible to capture the details of a teller's interactions with customers around the promotion of a particular product, with the observer's attention focused, for example, on how the teller counters the customer's objections. Because observation often raises as many questions as it answers, analysts often choose to conduct interviews or distribute surveys after having engaged in observation of a workplace.

Surveys. Written surveys are excellent tools for soliciting the thoughts and concerns of large numbers of people. Surveys effectively seek controversial and emotionally loaded information, such as sources' feelings about the topic at hand, their perceptions of their own and other employees' confidence with respect to that topic, and the perceived reasons for a particular problem. Because surveys are completed anonymously, the analyst can be hopeful that people will report honestly.

The key is clarity about what one is trying to accomplish. Successful survey construction requires the devising of items that are obviously linked to the information being sought. For example, there must be no confusion about whether the quest is for information on what employees currently know, or for information on what managers want their people to know, or for information on why employees are not getting a job done. Professionals rarely begin an effort with a survey: surveys rely primarily on forced-choice questions, and so a survey should be constructed only after the analyst knows enough to devise credible, plausible, realistic options. The survey can then be used to help the analyst cast a wider and larger net in search of information.

Another element of a successfully constructed survey is an effective cover letter. A good letter does the following things:

- Explains why the survey has been distributed
- Clarifies the purposes of the survey
- Provides information about how the results will be used
- States whether the results will be shared with all respondents
- Gives prospective respondents reasons to participate
- Provides directions for how and when to respond
- Explains what has already been done to analyze the situation in question
- Expresses sincere appreciation for the respondents' participation

Surveys have a role to play in both PA and TNA. In PA, a survey can be used to seek priorities for optimal performance. HP professionals regularly reach out, and not always in connection with requests for assistance, to see what is on the minds of constituents. What are they concerned about? Where would they like to see development resources concentrated? In TNA, once a topic or domain has been identified, a survey can establish different levels of skill, confidence, or interest.

It is generally useful to put a survey through pilot testing. A survey that is tried out on colleagues, and on selected members of the target population, will benefit from its exposure to additional eyes.

Focus Groups. Structured meetings provide an effective means of obtaining and dispensing information and of generating relationships among people and across units. When the analyst wants to involve many groups, or people from different geographical locations, and wants people's ideas to build on each other, focus groups are appropriate.

A focus group is difficult to lead, however. One would think that working with a group would be a guaranteed way to promote synergy and produce an abundance of useful ideas. Unfortunately, it does not always work that way; people and politics often interfere.

The answer is planning. It is essential to carefully construct an agenda and anticipate differences in opinion. The analyst must know ahead of time, for example, whether there are major areas of disagreement among the experts who have been drawn together from across the globe to talk about the maintenance of turbine engines in desert climates. If so, it will be better initially to work with them alone, put them in smaller work groups, and ask upper management to designate the expert who is "first among equals." Participants should be thoroughly briefed before they appear for the focus group.

Being clear about roles during the meeting is also an important part of planning. Will there be a group leader? Who will it be? Who will be the recorder? How will disagreements be handled? The establishment of roles and rules, and of communication about both, will be important to the success of any event that involves a focus group.

Technology

Technology is revolutionizing the way we gather data for analysis. More and more tools, both quantitative and qualitative, also permit us to deal with the continually growing fund of HPT-related information. What else does technology allow us to do?

1. *Quickly reach out to a few, or to many.* For example, one HP professional wanted to position herself out ahead of the development needs of the employees she served. After reviewing the literature regarding trends in teaming and team leadership, she distributed an e-mail survey to determine priorities and perceptions regarding barriers to successful teaming. Another professional used e-mail to make certain that she had a clear picture of what the organization wanted to accomplish with some new software that had been purchased. After interviews with internal leaders and contact with the vendor, she distributed e-mail to key people to confirm that she had a sturdy handle on their intentions.

2. *Use the World Wide Web and mailing-list manager programs like LIST-SERV.* For example, a graduate student was given the task of assisting a manufacturing company in its attempts to strengthen its adult literacy efforts. She immediately turned for advice to the Web and LISTSERV. Another associate was asked about the new kinds of competence required for management development. Again, the Web and LISTSERV were rich resources.

3. *Engage in continuous collaboration in organizations.* As more organizations struggle to becoming learning organizations (Senge, 1990; Stewart, 1997), interest in on-line chats, discussions, and collaboration

increases. For example, educators at San Diego State University (Fulop, Loop-Bartick, and Rossett, 1997) established a moderated on-line discussion group to flesh out technology-based information-seeking strategies for university health educators. As another example, an initiative at a pharmaceuticals company involves chemists and others from related disciplines in on-line meetings to ponder problems and identify cross-functional solutions. A course is one aspect of this rich on-line mix, but it is not the essence of the effort; far more crucial are the examples and "war stories" shared by the participants themselves.

OBSTACLES TO ANALYSIS

If analysis is such a good idea, and if HP technologists possess robust conceptual models, tools, and technologies, then why do so many HP technologists fail to do analysis? The answer is that there are obstacles in the path of successful analysis. This section examines three in particular: lack of support for analysis, lack of fit between analysis and the organization, and "analysis paralysis."

Lack of Support for Analysis

"Analysis is very important. It's my priority, but it's not my management's. Managers provide no support for it and no time to do it. Analysis is not on their agenda."

Does this sound familiar? It should. It is a typical complaint, according to a study by Rossett and Czech (1996). Although analysis sounds crucial, most who study it and believe in it do not get to do as much of it as they deem necessary. There are three strategies that can increase support for analysis (Rossett, 1990, 1997):

1. Conduct effective analyses, and then document what has been done and how it has contributed to the bottom line. Are there instances where analysis has contributed to whittling a four-week course down to three weeks, or where the effort has pinpointed necessary changes in policies, thereby diminishing the need for training? Can you document performance improvements derived from cross-functional solutions? It is important to find and collect examples of how analysis has unearthed information and opinions that have made a difference in subsequent decisions and effectiveness.

2. Make the case for analysis through analogies to other professions. Would an engineer launch a project without serious "scoping" activities? Would a physician prescribe treatment without cautious diagnosis? Would an urban planner develop low-income housing without

constant interaction with community leaders? If not, then why would an HP technologist select and build an intervention without careful field study?

3. Avoid our peculiar professional jargon ("performance analysis," "needs assessment," "front-end analysis") if management does not respond well to it. Until there is clarity and a successful history behind these phrases, consider using others that are more familiar to the customer. Think about using the terms *planning* or *auditing* or *study* or, if you are associated with an engineering company, *scoping*. Focus management's attention on the substantive information that is needed, such as information about why sales are plummeting, how much the salespeople know about different products, or whether the sales staff is confident about those products that reflect the shift from analog to digital equipment.

Lack of Fit Between Analysis and the Organization

For professionals associated with traditional training units (and they are still in the majority), there are special barriers to successful practice. Often an organization's training unit is funded on the basis of the number of student days. This economic reality has two major effects: first, there is limited budgetary support for analysis; and, second, there are few or no incentives to build job aids or involve colleagues from career planning or organizational development. The existing measurement system points the professional toward more and longer courses, not toward analysis that might result in a multidisciplinary performance system.

For obstacles related to lack of fit between analysis and the organization, there are two solutions:

1. Confront the lack of fit. This solution is the more direct of the two and the more difficult to bring about. Explain why the organization is focusing its attention on the wrong goal—on courses and student days rather than on performance. Explain the cost of this misdirected attention, and explain the alternatives, using material from the International Society for Performance Improvement (ISPI) literature and conferences. Frame your examples so that you can easily communicate them to people in your organization.

2. Use a speedy PA that identifies the causes of targeted problems, and then report that information to executives. Show them where training actually is needed and, referring to the data that have been gathered, where other, sibling interventions will be more potent. Make the case for subsequent needs assessment and solution systems. Be willing to shine light on the organization's history of wasted training resources.

"Analysis Paralysis"

Analysis is fascinating. It takes the HP technologist into the organization, into meetings with subject matter experts and job incumbents and customers, into files and records, into the bank or the lab, onto the plant floor or the battlefield. Analysis provides the opportunity to be a problem finder and solver. But the appeal of analysis, an appeal heightened by many HP technologists' tendency toward perfectionism, can also lead to excessive analyzing rather than to speedy and appropriate consultation.

One cure for "analysis paralysis" is planning. What are the goals for analysis? What kinds of questions will achieve those goals? Where are the sources of information? Where are the areas of disagreement or potential problems? What are the resource limits? Professionals must be ready to add interviews or schedule extra observations, but they must be even readier to call off a survey (for example, because a clear picture of the feelings surrounding a new product has already been obtained).

Another useful strategy for curing "analysis paralysis" is to constantly bounce the findings of analysis off experienced people in the organization. If professionals are new to banking or sales or the computer industry, for example, they will need more data before they can feel confident about what analysis is unearthing. Experienced job incumbents, managers, and subject matter experts can help in differentiating useful results from those that are odd or surprising. Those deemed odd or surprising will require confirmation through additional contacts with sources. The other findings—those confirmed by experienced colleagues and other sources—enable an analyst to move forward with the effort.

A final strategy is to move toward two-part analysis. In this approach, the first part is a flyby PA that seeks a quick picture of the challenge and the factors that drive it. The second part is a more rigorous needs assessment that focuses on aspects related to skills, knowledge, and motivation (if one is certain that those are critical considerations).

TRENDS IN ANALYSIS

As the world changes, so does analysis. This section presents information about four trends—performance consulting, cognitive science, centralization and decentralization in organizations, and knowledge management—and shows how they are influencing what analysts think about and do.

Performance Consulting

Three publications are influencing the profession and the practices associated with analysis. One recent influence has been the first edition of this book. Another is Dana and Jim Robinson's 1995 book, *Performance Consulting*. Still another is ISPI's *Performance Improvement Quarterly,* a journal devoted to articles about analysis, human performance interventions, and solution systems. The role of the performance consultant is predicated on analysis. If every interaction with clients and customers involves tailoring solutions to particular needs and circumstances, then analysis provides the defining energy and direction.

Cognitive Science

Professionals, whether they call themselves *trainers, instructional designers, educational specialists, knowledge engineers,* or *HP technologists,* are increasingly influenced by cognitive psychology (Keller, 1983; Richey, 1986; Merrill, 1987; Clark, 1989; Jonassen, 1996). All practitioners can name the behaviorist B. F. Skinner as an influence, but it is much harder to get a handle on the cognitivists because they are a more diverse group. As Richey (1986, p. 65) points out, cognitivists focus on many areas:

- Readiness of the learner
- Organization of knowledge, most particularly the mental models, or schemata, that people construct to represent what they know
- Insight
- The relationship between computers and intelligence
- Short-term memory, as well as strategies for ensuring storage in and retrieval from long-term memory
- Individual perspectives on materials or jobs
- The creation of meaning through the attachment of new material to what is already familiar and useful

For an analyst, what are the implications of cognitive science? First, the analyst finds himself or herself asking about what is going on inside the learner— about the learner's eagerness, readiness, and enthusiasm. Observation is insufficient; now that employees are no longer considered to be impenetrable "black boxes," front-end inquiry must expand to include employees' perspectives on a change, an opportunity, or a problem. Second, the analyst must determine a natural and meaningful structure for the subject matter that is related to a job. In addition to a task analysis that captures what a star performer *does,* the analyst must conduct a subject matter or cognitive task analysis that unearths what the star performer *knows and thinks about* during performance. Finally, the analyst must attend to employees' cognitive and metacognitive strategies, thus expanding the analysis to questions about the professional development and learning history of employees and about their ability to manage their own growth and development. This concern grows in importance as a part of analysis because of the increased presence of technology-based options (Bassi, Cheney, and Van Buren, 1997).

Centralization and Decentralization in Organizations

Organizations tend to struggle with where decisions will be made, and so do human resource and training units. As Tovar, Rossett, and Carter (1989) have explained, centralization of the training function was common in the 1970s. In the 1980s there was a move to decentralization, with organizations shifting decisions and delivery to line units. The 1990s, however, are characterized by debate on the topic of centralization and decentralization and by the development of mixed patterns. In this decade, selected efforts have been handled by the decentralized line organization, whereas such common and controversial arenas as automation, affirmative action, and leadership development have had centralized oversight. The shift to performance consulting and analysis complicates this area because the effectiveness of performance consultants and performance analysts must be judged by the quality of their bonds with the business units.

Analysts walk the line between centralization and decentralization. They are expected to solicit, understand, and respond to the particular—to the needs and special requirements of the unit. At the same time, they are pressed to develop cost-effective solutions that are palatable, consistent, and applicable to many settings across the larger organization.

The best response to this trend is to be ready for it. HP technologists must increase the amount of outreach that is a natural and virtual part of the analysis process. They must make certain that their sources reflect many viewpoints, and that their inquiries seek commonalities as well as differences. They have to consider modular solutions that are readily customized. They must also rely on contemporary technologies to support interactions between units, and between the centralized unit and the line organizations. They can establish reporting mechanisms that present results and programs of general interest, and they can highlight unique departmental efforts. Finally, HP technologists must acknowledge the challenge of the centralization/decentralization issue in discussions with colleagues and management. Doing so will bring about recognition of this issue on the part of upper management, often in the establishment of advisory and collaborative committees. An emerging trend is the one in which analysts have both "solid line" reporting relationships to business units and dynamic "dotted line" ties to central human resources and performance organizations.

Knowledge Management

Senge (1990) and Stewart (1997) have established knowledge management as a key goal for human performance professionals. How does that goal influence analysis?

Knowledge management focuses attention on strategies for increasing value and accessibility, as well as on the information that resides in the organization and its people. How do we capture that information? How do we find what it is that savvy salespeople or responsive customer service reps or effective school counselors know? How do we make certain that this information reflects not just the obvious but also the more subtle, cultural aspects that are essential to success? How do we make this information available to more people, and how do we make it available in more ways? How do we begin to take advantage of technology so that, as Evans and Wurster (1997) suggest, we can "unbundle information from its physical carrier?" How do we ensure that the information is kept current? How do we define jobs, roles, processes, and systems in ways that "informate," "automate," "outsource," and "capitalize" effectively and flexibly (Stewart, 1997)? Analysts will find themselves expanding both their questions and their solutions to reflect the emergence of knowledge management as an organizational priority.

CONCLUSION

Analysis is the leading edge of HPT. It defines the effort, establishes the parameters, and prepares the organization for new and better ways of doing business. An effective analysis generates both sponsorship and answers to hard questions.

After a long and complicated project, an executive vice president of sales for a large company said, "I just assumed that we would be training our people. It never occurred to me that we could rearrange other aspects of our effort, like the job descriptions in the offices and the incentive system, to achieve even bigger results. Where did you get that idea?" The answer, of course, is "from analysis." What the vice president appreciated so much was that analysis and HPT resulted in a solution tailored to his organization; what he appreciated even more was that it resulted in performance improvement (Strayer and Rossett, 1994).

The movement to HPT represents a paradigm shift. Such shifts do not come easily, or from decisions made by holding one's finger up to the wind. They are born of data and compelling examples of the success that flows from the data. They succeed because of relationships and policies that enable collaboration across the organization. Analysis is and will continue to be the foundation for the emergence of the performance professional.

References

Bandura, A. (1977). Self-efficacy: Toward a unifying theory of behavioral change. *Psychological Review* 84, 191–215.

Bassi, L. J., Cheney, S., and Van Buren, M. (1997, Nov.). Training industry trends 1997. *Training and Development* 51:11, 46–59.

Benjamin, S. (1989). A closer look at needs analysis and needs assessment: Whatever happened to the systems approach? *Performance & Instruction* 28:9, 12–16.

Clark, R. C. (1989). *Developing technical training*. Phoenix, AZ: Performance Technology Press.

Dewey, J. (1933). *How we think*. Lexington, MA: Heath.

Evans, P. B., and Wurster, T. S. (1997, Sept.–Oct.). Strategy and the new economics of information. *Harvard Business Review* 75:5, 71–82.

Fulop, M., Loop-Bartick, K., and Rossett, A. (1997, July). Using the World Wide Web to conduct a needs assessment. *Performance Improvement* 36:6, 22–27.

Gilbert, T. (1978). *Human competence: Engineering worthy performance*. New York: McGraw-Hill.

Harless, J. H. (1975). *An ounce of analysis is worth a pound of objectives*. Newnan, GA: Harless Performance Guild.

Jonassen, D. H. (ed.). (1996). *Handbook of research for educational communications and technology*. New York: Simon & Schuster.

Kaufman, R., and English, F. W. (1979). *Needs assessment*. Englewood Cliffs, NJ: Educational Technology Publications.

Keller, J. M. (1983). Motivation design of instruction: A theoretical perspective. In C. M. Reigeluth (ed.), *Instructional design theories and models: An overview of their current status*. Hillsdale, NJ: Erlbaum.

Mager, R. M. (1970). *Goal analysis*. Belmont, CA: Pitman Learning.

Mager, R. M., and Pipe, P. (1984). *Analyzing performance problems*. Belmont, CA: Pitman Learning.

Merrill, M. D. (1987). A lesson based on component display theory. In C. M. Reigeluth (ed.), *Instructional design theories in action*. Hillsdale, NJ: Erlbaum.

Richey, R. C. (1986). *The theoretical and conceptual bases of instructional design*. London: Kogan Page.

Robinson, D. G., and Robinson, J. C. (1995). *Performance consulting*. San Francisco: Berrett-Koehler.

Rodriguez, S. R. (1988). Needs assessment and analysis: Tools for change. *Journal of Instructional Development* 11:1, 23–28.

Rosenberg, M. J. (1990, Feb.). Performance technology working the system. *Training* 27:2, 42–48.

Rossett, A. (1987). *Training needs assessment*. Englewood Cliffs, NJ: Educational Technology.

Rossett, A. (1990, Mar.). Overcoming obstacles to needs assessment. *Training* 27:3, 36–41.

Rossett, A. (1996, Mar.). Training and organizational development: Siblings separated at birth. *Training* 33:4, 53–59.

Rossett, A. (1997, July). That was a great class, but. . . . *Training and Development* 51:7, 18–24.

Rossett, A. (forthcoming). *First things fast: A handbook for performance analysis.* San Francisco: Jossey-Bass.

Rossett, C., and Czech, C. (1996). They really wanna but . . . : The aftermath of professional preparation in performance technology. *Performance Improvement Quarterly* 8:4, 114–132.

Rummler, G. A. (1986). Organization redesign. In National Society for Performance and Instruction, *Introduction to performance technology.* Vol. 1. Washington, DC: National Society for Performance and Instruction.

Senge, P. M. (1990). *The fifth discipline: The art and practice of the learning organization.* New York: Doubleday.

Stewart, T. A. (1997). *Intellectual capital: The new wealth of organizations.* New York: Doubleday.

Strayer, J., and Rossett, A. (1994). Coaching sales performance: A case study. *Performance Improvement Quarterly* 7:4, 39–53.

Swanson, R. A. (1994). *Analysis for improving performance: Tools for diagnosing organizations and documenting workplace expertise.* San Francisco: Berrett-Koehler.

Tyler, R. L. (1949). *Basic principles of curriculum and instruction.* Chicago: University of Chicago Press.

Zemke, R., and Kramlinger, T. (1982). *Figuring things out: A trainer's guide to needs and task analysis.* Reading, MA: Addison-Wesley.

CHAPTER NINE

The Design and Development of High-Impact Interventions

Dean R. Spitzer

uman performance (HP) technologists are in the business of improving employee performance in organizations. They do this through creating performance improvement *interventions* that reduce the gaps between current performance and desired performance. Like so many other consultants who have no direct authority over organizational change, HP technologists must use indirect influence. However, unlike other types of consultants, HP technologists generally target their interventions at improving the particular constellation of factors—the *human performance system*—that directly affect the person doing the work (see Figure 9.1).

Human performance systems include the factors (both internal and external to the performer) that affect human performance. Although there are many versions of human performance systems, they typically include knowledge, skill, attitudes, and other personal attributes, or *internal factors,* and environmental variables such as expectations, work methods and procedures, tools, resources and constraints, measurement, consequences, and feedback, or *external factors*. (A number of Human Performance System models, including the present author's, are discussed in Wile, 1996.)

Human performance improvement interventions (which will be abbreviated *performance improvement interventions* in this chapter) can take virtually any form, ranging from a job aid that helps employees perform a specific task to the development of a completely new organizational system or structure. However, as we will see, the success of any intervention is not determined by how large

Figure 9.1. The Human Performance System.

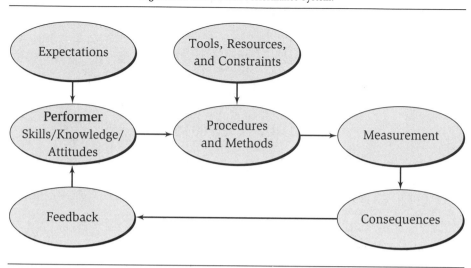

it is, but rather by the extent of its positive impact on human performance. For that reason, the focus of this chapter will be on how to design and develop *high-impact performance improvement interventions*.

DESIGN AND DEVELOPMENT IN THE SYSTEMS APPROACH

Performance improvement interventions are created with what is typically called the *systems approach*, which is traditionally depicted as a process with five discrete, sequential phases—analysis, design, development, implementation, and evaluation—as shown in Figure 9.2.

All five phases of the traditional systems approach are crucial to high-impact interventions, but the design phase is where all interventions are actually created. Design can thus be considered the heart of the systems approach. Whereas analysis is the process of taking a performance problem apart in order to understand it, design is the process of putting together (synthesizing) an intervention to solve it. Development is really just an extension of design. It prepares the design for implementation. Development typically involves the production of any methods, instrumentation, or materials (such as a training guide) that might be required to support the intervention.

In the real world, however, interventions are rarely created through the following of a linear path involving mutually exclusive phases. For example, although analysis typically precedes design, it is also true that analysis should, more often than not, continue well into the design phase. This is true as well

Figure 9.2. The Traditional Systems Approach.

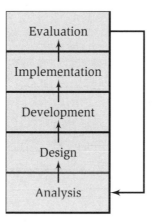

about development and implementation, which should both be proactively considered during the design phase because effective intervention designs must always take account of implementation requirements. Moreover, evaluation should be ubiquitous and thought of as an *ongoing* activity, not as a final process step. That is why, although this chapter focuses on design—and, to a lesser extent, on development—neither phase can be separated from the other or from the remaining phases of the systems approach to which they belong. In fact, the real-world version of the systems approach probably looks more like the one depicted in Figure 9.3.

Perhaps the importance of design can best be grasped by way of some examples from outside the arena of Human Performance Technology (HPT). Everyone can appreciate the importance of the blueprint for a house: no matter how outstanding the construction work may be, a poorly designed house is not very likely to satisfy the customer. Likewise, no matter how well constructed a bridge or a road may be, if there are inherent design flaws, neither bridge nor road will be very safe. In the same way, a good HPT design will probably lead to a good intervention, whereas any shortcuts in the design may lead to a flawed intervention.

There is no doubt that good design can be a time-consuming activity, but poor design (and its consequences) can be even more costly. As Bailey (1982, p. 26) explains, "Designing systems for people is serious business." In fact, in ancient times (around 2150 BC), a law called the Code of Hammurabi stated, in part, "If a builder has built a house for a man and his work is not strong and the house falls in and kills the householder, that builder shall be slain." Fortunately, HPT interventions are rarely a matter of life or death. However, it would

Figure 9.3. The Systems Approach in the Real World.

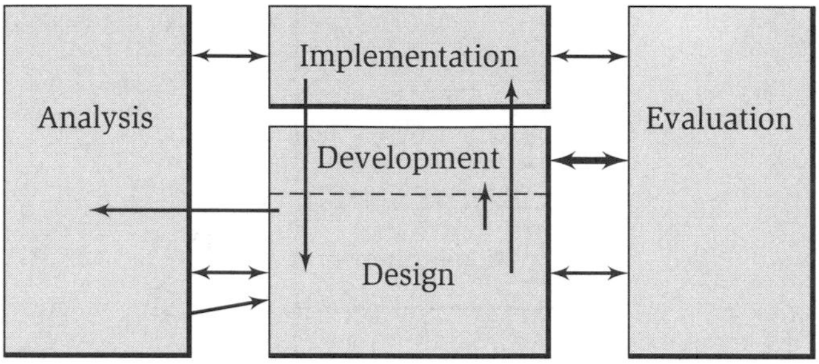

be interesting to ponder how well HP technologists would sleep at night if such a code applied to the design of their interventions!

Certainly the design of high-impact interventions is no easy task. However, the suggestions offered in this chapter dramatically increase the chances of achieving a major organizational impact while greatly reducing the possibility of failure.

THE DESIGN PROCESS

Successful design usually proceeds, in a disciplined fashion, through a series of steps like the ones shown in Figure 9.4. Although there are many possible variants on the design process, the design process for a high-impact intervention should probably include the following six steps:

1. Review and expand the analysis
2. Identify intervention objectives
3. Identify and prioritize requirements
4. Select the intervention components
5. Prepare a high-level intervention design
6. Complete the detailed intervention plan

Step 1: Review and Expand the Analysis

Most HP technologists are well aware of the importance of doing a thorough analysis prior to designing an intervention. However, it is important that the analysis be reviewed before the actual design is embarked on. There are many reasons for this, including the possibility that the analysis might have been per-

Figure 9.4. The Intervention Design Process.

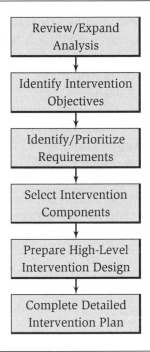

formed by someone else, or that a time lag has occurred between the original analysis and the start of the intervention design.

No matter what the circumstances, high-impact intervention design should always begin with a review of the analysis findings. Presumably, these findings will have identified a high-priority performance gap (the gap between the current level of performance and a more desirable level) and the causes of the gap. (Incidentally, the terms *performance gap, performance problem,* and *performance improvement opportunity* are, for all intents and purposes, synonymous.)

Most initial analysis does not go far enough. The problem and its causes may be clear, but too often the context of the situation is not adequately investigated. Understanding the causes of performance problems might not be sufficient to ensure a successful intervention without additional "context analysis" (Spitzer, 1982). Furthermore, the organizational context should be continually monitored for potential changes throughout the design process.

Most intervention design does not occur under ideal circumstances. Just as roads, bridges, and houses must be constructed with limited resources and many constraints, so also are most performance improvement interventions. For instance, too many interventions are designed without adequate appreciation for the political complexity of organizations. As a result, some HP technologists who design otherwise excellent interventions find them being sabotaged by contextual factors that they never even considered (such as a single influential detractor or an incompatible cultural norm). This is because HP technologists tend to focus on the issue of immediate concern and ignore the larger systems of which it is a part (Oshry, 1996). In HPT, understanding the political, economic, and cultural factors in an organization is often as crucial as understanding the causes of the specific problem we are trying to solve.

No intervention should be designed in a vacuum. Organizations are composed of a large number of complex, multilevel systems, each in some way affecting the others. Rummler and Brache (1995) have identified three levels of systems in organizations (see also Chapter Three):

1. The level of *organizational systems* (where we find the influences that affect the organization as a whole: business goals, strategy, structure, culture, and the like)

2. The level of *process systems* (where we find all the horizontal, cross-functional processes by which organizations accomplish their goals)

3. The job/performer level, or the level of the *Human Performance System* (where we find the work environment, which most immediately affects employees)

This way of looking at organizational systems is depicted in Figure 9.5. The key point to remember is that, although HPT interventions are most often focused

Figure 9.5. Three Levels of Organizational Systems.

at the level of the job and the performer, the impact of organizational systems at the other two levels must always be considered.

Step 2: Identify the Intervention Objectives

An old adage says, "If you don't know where you're going, any road will take you there." Two prominent contemporary design experts have put this idea in the following way: "Unless you know what you want, you'll never be very sure of what you'll get" (Gause and Weinberg, 1989, p. 1). The obvious antidote to such problems is to clearly specify the objectives of the intervention (the destination) before one begins thinking about the means (the road to get there).

Covey (1990) notes that highly effective people "begin with the end in mind." In other words, instead of asking about means, HP technologists should begin by asking questions like "What performance is desired? How much improvement is needed? Is the focus of the performance improvement the organization? the unit? the team? the individual? Precisely who comprises the target audience?" In short, interventions should be driven by *ends*, not by means.

Nevertheless, in too many cases, unfortunately, preferred methods (whether or not they are appropriate) drive intervention design. In fact, the advent of HPT was largely a response to the tendency of trainers to view training as the method of choice for solving virtually any human performance problem. That is why it is important that we resist any temptation to predetermine an intervention before the necessary analysis has been done.

Bailey (1982) offers a very useful rule of thumb for formulating intervention objectives: they should be general enough to allow designers considerable freedom in finding a really good solution, but specific enough to convey to the designers what the intervention ought to accomplish.

Step 3: Identify and Prioritize Requirements

Interventions are driven by objectives but designed according to requirements. Requirements define the attributes that the intervention should possess in order to be successful. More than any other consideration, requirements will dictate the design of the intervention. Correctly specified requirements will virtually ensure a high-quality intervention design, whereas faulty requirements will generally result in faulty interventions.

Unfortunately, the term *requirements* can be somewhat misleading because it implies that the intervention, to be effective, requires all the characteristics listed. As Emery (1987, p. 145) explains, "In most cases a 'requirement' is entirely discretionary, and depends only on the trade-off between the value and cost of satisfying it." Nevertheless, designers must also avoid the possibility that requirements become nothing more than a "wish list."

Requirements are usually generated through interviews and focus groups with key stakeholder groups (such as managers, system owners, and users) and subject matter experts. Even if many of the intervention requirements appear to have already been identified through previous analysis, requirements should still be reviewed and revised early in the design phase.

There are two categories of requirements that HP technologists should be concerned with: technical requirements and human requirements. The technical requirements basically focus on the characteristics that the intervention should have if it is going to accomplish its ultimate objectives (especially from a managerial perspective). The human requirements pertain to how the intervention should be designed in order to be acceptable to the people who will be expected to use it. It is sadly true that too many intervention designers (even those who purport to be HP technologists) focus almost entirely on the technical aspects of the project and ignore the human aspects. What they fail to realize is that such issues as user involvement, user-friendliness, and cultural compatibility are often just as crucial to the intervention's success as its technical functionality and cost-effectiveness are.

This technical bias is a serious threat to the success of any performance improvement intervention (Spitzer, 1998). The authors of one major study of hundreds of failed information technology projects concluded that "for the overwhelming majority of bankrupt projects we studied, there was not a single technological issue to explain the failure" (DeMarco and Lister, 1987, p. 4). In other words, most problems were caused by user resistance. Why, then, do intervention designers focus so much attention on technical issues? DeMarco and Lister respond in this way: "The main reason we tend to focus on the technical rather than the human side of work is not because it's more crucial, but because it's easier to do" (p. 5).

Not only should requirements be identified, they should also be prioritized. All requirements are not created equal. It is particularly crucial to distinguish between mandatory requirements (features the intervention *must* possess) and desirable requirements (features that stakeholders *want*).

The first pass at prioritization involves distinguishing the requirements that are "musts" from those that are "wants." Because all the "must" requirements are essential, there is no reason to prioritize them further. However, the "want" requirements should be further prioritized in the order of their desirability—from most to least desired—typically with the use of a "10" to "1" rating scale. Often, cost or time constraints make it difficult to build all of the "want" requirements into an intervention.

If an essential ("must") feature of the intervention is not considered, the results can be very serious indeed. That is why it is so important to specify all the "must" requirements. For example, in an experiment comparing five program design teams, each team was given the same set of customer requirements except for one single crucial sentence (Gause and Weinberg, 1989). This subtle difference produced software applications with dramatically different levels of performance and customer satisfaction.

Step 4: Select the Intervention Components

Components are the building blocks of any intervention. The most successful interventions usually have more than one component (methodology) and often a great many; Stolovitch and Keeps (1998) make a similar point with their "basket of solutions" concept. Figure 9.6 shows how a job design intervention can involve numerous components.

When intervention components are being chosen, it is vitally important that an objective search be done for the most effective methods. Too often, HP technologists fixate on a very limited set of tools with which they are most comfortable, and there is rarely more than a cursory search for "outside the box" options and alternatives. Although there are literally thousands of tools at the disposal of HP technologists, very few ever get used. However, the ultimate criterion for component selection should be a component's contribution to meeting the mandatory ("must") requirements and the highest-priority desirable ("want") requirements.

Of course, it is impossible for HP technologists to know everything about everything. In fact, it is detrimental for any HP technologist to have too much specific tool knowledge because this can cause a bias toward one approach. As already mentioned, it is important for designers to consider a wide range of options and not to focus on predetermined or obvious ones. This is why HP technologists should serve more as facilitators and integrators than as sources of

Figure 9.6. Intervention Components.

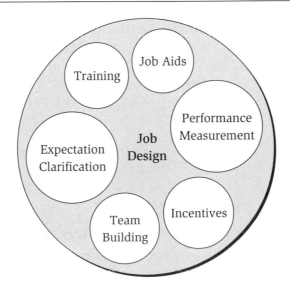

specific knowledge about tools or technology. This is also why a network of experts in particular tools and technologies should be available to supply tool-specific expertise.

It is inadvisable to reinvent the wheel. Designers should be aware that there are many intervention components that already exist. Myriad excellent "off the shelf" products and services are available. These existing intervention components can be used as they are or customized. However, no intervention component should be selected just because it is available. It must be appropriate and cost-effective. On the one hand, some HP technologists may be too eager to use existing intervention components. On the other hand, HP technologists are sometimes reluctant to use ready-designed interventions, or intervention components, because of the NIH ("Not Invented Here") mind-set. There should never be prejudgment one way or the other. The key is to build the most cost-effective solution that meets the intervention requirements, no matter where the components come from.

Step 5: Prepare a High-Level Intervention Design

Once the best intervention components have been identified, a conceptual or high-level intervention design should be prepared. This visual and/or verbal description outlines the proposed intervention and all its elements.

The term *high-level* refers to the fact that this version of the design is like the sight of the earth from an airplane that is flying at thirty thousand feet. From that altitude, one can discern only the most general topographical features. Similarly, at this stage in the design process, the concern is with identifying only the "topography" of the components that will lead to a successful intervention, and their relationships, not the fine-grained details. This is a point where creativity plays a large role. Like an architect, the HP technologist takes all the previously acquired information and transforms it, through a combination of research, previous experience, and creativity, into a blueprint of the solution.

It is most important for designers to realize that there is no one right way to design an intervention. The greatest danger at this step in intervention design (as in the previous one) is the failure to consider alternatives. It is incumbent upon those who seek to have a high impact to explore options rather than accepting the most obvious approach. Designers become locked in to a particular solution and seldom take time to systematically compare alternatives. As one expert explains, "It is usually best to develop several alternative designs before selecting one to use" (Bailey, 1982, p. 197).

Step 6: Complete the Detailed Intervention Plan

Once a high-level design is created, the final step in the design process involves specifying the intervention in more detail. At this point, specific events, activities, tasks, schedules, and resource requirements must be identified. It is important to add all the detail that will be necessary to develop and implement the intervention. Although good design usually involves obtaining feedback and preliminary approvals at each step in the process, it is this sixth step that generates the final plan, or proposal, that must be approved by organizational decision makers. Documentation is often a weak link in intervention design because it tends to be viewed as an onerous, and unnecessary, task. However, it is important to provide an appropriate level of description and supporting information so that expectations will be clear and decision makers will be able to make an informed decision.

If any concerns are expressed by decision makers about the design, modifications may have to be made. Compromise is an inherent aspect of design, but the integrity of the intervention should never be compromised. In some cases, the intervention may be rejected altogether. This often occurs because of political circumstances that were not anticipated—another reason why the "context analysis" suggested in step 1 is so important. Understanding the political context of the intervention, and being flexible enough to adapt without compromising it, are essential.

Once the design is finally approved, the project generally moves into development. The development phase will be discussed toward the end of this chapter.

PRINCIPLES OF DESIGNING HIGH-IMPACT INTERVENTIONS

It seems as if every field of endeavor has its own principles, which tend to guide those involved in design and help them maximize the probability of success. In HPT, there are two types of principles. The first type includes tool- or technology-specific principles (such as principles for designing instruction, job aids, measurement systems, motivational systems, and the like); many of these intervention-specific principles are covered in other chapters of this handbook. The second type includes general design principles that are relevant to all HP technology interventions, regardless of the tools used; it is the latter type that are discussed in this section. The HP technologist can use the following ten principles to guide the design of any intervention and dramatically improve its impact.

1. *High-impact interventions should aim at high-leverage performance improvement opportunities.* There is no lack of performance improvement opportunities (PIOs) in organizations. In fact, there is usually an overabundance of them (Spitzer, 1996). Because a great many performance improvement needs compete for increasingly scarce resources in today's organizations, prioritization is essential. That is why performance improvement interventions must be targeted at needs that will give "the most bang for the buck."

The key is to find the ones that have the greatest leverage, or the greatest potential for achieving valuable results at the least cost. The most promising PIOs generally exist when there is a large performance gap among employees in the same job or task (there is high variance in performance); when closing this gap can mean significant benefits for the organization (there is a strategic need); and when the resources available to the HP technologist are adequate to bridge the gap (there is a high probability of success).

It is not enough to establish the need for an intervention from a training or HPT perspective. In order to have a high impact, the intervention must occur in an area that is strategic to the organization's success. Tactical interventions rarely have much of an impact. Unfortunately, organizational resources are too often squandered on low-impact (or no-impact) interventions while high-priority needs go unaddressed. That is why HP technologists should make sure that any intervention is aligned with strategic organizational goals.

The HP technologist who wants to design high-impact interventions must search for the right opportunities for impact from a large number of alternatives (see Figure 9.7). Doing so requires considerable analytical ability. Unfortunately, the wrong choice of a target PIO can doom even an otherwise well-designed intervention to fail to deliver high impact.

2. *High-impact interventions should be powerful.* One of the major reasons why performance improvement interventions fail is that they are too weak to make a significant difference in performance. Human performance is notoriously prone to inertia (a concept borrowed from physics, stating that a body at rest tends to remain at rest). Social systems, like physical systems, tend to resist change. Because all interventions represent change, they are often resisted.

Figure 9.7. Targeting a High-Impact PIO.

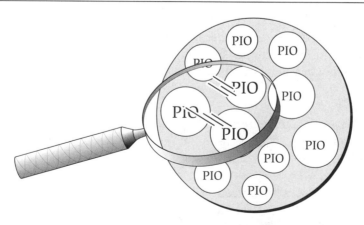

Organizations are inclined to stay just as they are because the people and groups who compose them have a vested interest in the status quo. It takes quite a lot of effort (energy) to get most individuals and organizations to change. Only powerful interventions can do it (see Figure 9.8).

Performance improvement interventions must be powerful enough to overcome all the forces in the performance system that resist change (Spitzer, 1986). That is why the best interventions are generally designed with some redundancy, even overkill, to ensure that goals are met. It is almost always better to design an intervention that is too strong than one that is too weak.

However, one cannot just throw isolated tools at performance problems and expect high-impact results. The highest-impact interventions are composed of multiple components, but these components should not just be haphazardly combined. High-impact interventions should represent synergistic solutions. When the components of an intervention build on and reinforce one another, a synergy effect can be obtained.

Another way to achieve synergy is to link a new intervention with a successful existing one. This piggybacking of a new intervention on an older one can cause a number of positive results. This was done when an employee motivation initiative was linked to one organization's Total Quality Management (TQM) effort. Unlike previous efforts to energize employees, the resulting "Total Quality Motivation" process was enormously successful (Spitzer, 1995). In addition to providing for improvement synergy, this gave the new intervention instant credibility. It also leveraged scarce resources, avoided the need for creating a new management structure, and reduced the learning curve.

3. *High-impact interventions should be sustainable.* Unfortunately, too many organizations just tinker with problems rather than solving them. It is common for organizations to exhibit a "quick fix" mentality: build it now, build it cheap, and worry later about fixing it. These interventions may be quick, and they may be inexpensive, but they rarely work; simplistic "solutions" are almost never effective (Spitzer, 1985).

Figure 9.8. Designing Powerful Interventions.

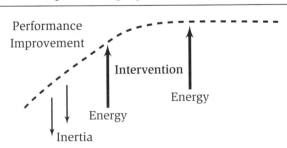

Performance improvement takes time. It is sad how many performance improvement interventions have failed because they were not sustained. What good is an intervention if the positive impact does not last? Performance improvement does not occur overnight. Unfortunately, many interventions lack the staying power to have the impact they were designed to have.

The major problem is entropy—another concept borrowed from the physical sciences (Spitzer, 1985). Entropy is the tendency of all things over time to deteriorate. What happens when people fail to maintain their cars or homes? No matter how outstanding the initial quality might be, they will eventually deteriorate. The same is true of interventions (see Figure 9.9). Interventions deteriorate for a variety of reasons. Some die as soon as the driving force (the champion) leaves the scene, or when management becomes distracted by other priorities. There is rarely any energizing force to fill the void. Without ongoing attention, even when short-term performance improvement has been realized, the improvement rarely lasts. The well-known Hawthorne effect was a dramatic demonstration of this phenomenon, when factory workers' performance, which had greatly improved, returned to preintervention levels as soon as the experimenters left.

It should never be assumed that interventions will be self-perpetuating or that sponsorship will be perpetual. Just as the human body eventually rejects an organ transplant unless preventive action is taken, so too do organizations often reject interventions that are perceived as "foreign entities"—especially after the initial enthusiasm wears off—unless the interventions become integrated into the mainstream of the organization and the way work is done.

Whether the intervention involves a minor change or a major one, there must be some provision for ongoing maintenance built into the design (consider it the intervention's "service contract"). A good example of this can be found in the area of transfer of training, where multiple transfer methods (such as job aids, on-the-job support systems, follow-up evaluation, review sessions, and so on) are often used to ensure that on-the-job performance occurs and is sus-

Figure 9.9. Sustainable Interventions.

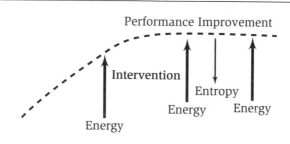

tainable (Broad, 1997). Incorporating an ongoing employee-involvement team, follow-up training, reinforcement meetings, continual ongoing communication, or any of a number of other options will also help sustain an intervention when others have fizzled out (Spitzer, 1995).

4. *High-impact interventions should be enhanced interventions.* One of the best ways to increase the power and longevity of interventions is through designing enhanced interventions. The components of an intervention that address the specific performance gap represent the core intervention. However, most large interventions must also include components for change management. This is what is being referred to as the "enhanced" part of the intervention, as depicted in Figure 9.10.

As discussed earlier in this chapter, most performance improvement interventions tend to be technical in nature and often neglect some human and organizational issues. Therefore, it is useful to think of interventions in a broader context because this helps the HP technologist remember the importance of issues related to change management, which might otherwise be neglected or receive inadequate attention.

Obviously, larger and more complex interventions will be most in need of enhancement. If an intervention is small and does not require a great deal of change, the technical (or core) intervention alone might be sufficient. A lot has to do with how invested in the status quo the various stakeholders are. The

Figure 9.10. Enhanced Interventions.

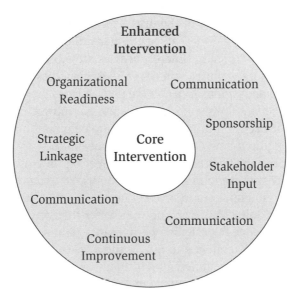

larger the change, the more important an expanded intervention is. According to Carr, Hard, and Trahant (1996), it is particularly important to address such issues as intervention leadership, accountability, team building, training, communication, measurement, and rewards in constructing the framework for successful organizational change. Many of the remaining five principles are relevant to enhanced intervention design.

5. *A high-impact intervention often starts with a small, focused intervention.* The saying "You only have one chance to make a good first impression" is a principle of interpersonal behavior, but it is just as relevant to intervention design. It is much easier to make a good first impression by designing a highly successful small intervention than by designing a large one. Once the small intervention's success has been realized, it is usually easier to gain support for a larger intervention. As Mager (1992, p. 746) explains, "If you contribute to the elimination of a single obstacle to effective performance, you will have made an enormous contribution"—and whetted the appetite for more.

Furthermore, Schaffer (1997) has found that when interventions are too large, there is a much greater chance of failure. This is because of a combination of resource constraints and lack of long-term commitment. At the beginning of projects, there is usually great enthusiasm. Unfortunately, the attention span of most managers is relatively short, and this initial enthusiasm often diminishes as managers are distracted by other priorities.

It is better to break large projects down into a series of smaller interventions. This reduces the "cycle time" and generates modest successes that can ultimately be leveraged into greater accomplishments. Success is more likely when the intervention is relatively small, and when the length of time required is consistent with the attention span of the organization. To summarize this principle, "scope" interventions so that, at least initially, the probability of success is high and the cycle time is short. Small successes are more likely to become big successes, whereas large failures will never lead to success.

6. *High-impact interventions focus on the users.* Just as product design should be user-focused, so should intervention design. No intervention is any better than how well it is used. Unfortunately, it is quite common for interventions to meet the initial requirements of management but not the ongoing operational requirements of users. The greatest performance improvement system in the world will fail unless those who are expected to use it actually do use it.

That is why it is so important to involve the users in high-impact intervention design. The person doing the work knows it better than anyone else. It is folly not to tap that knowledge in designing performance improvement interventions.

The all-too-common tendency to ignore the user is further exacerbated by the threat and inconvenience inherent in virtually any change. Threatened users have been known to reject interventions in a wide variety of ways, ranging from disuse to sabotage. It has been said that people do not resist change; they resist *being* changed. On the positive side of the ledger, people tend to support those systems that they help to create. That is why the employees who are most affected by an intervention should be involved in its design. This kind of involvement in design is particularly important in organizations' increasingly international and cross-cultural contexts.

7. *High-impact interventions should involve the right people in the design process.* Intervention design should seldom be done in isolation. Multifaceted performance improvement interventions are often very complex. They require input from a variety of areas. Most HP technologists are unlikely to have sufficient depth of knowledge in all the fields involved—nor should they. Interventions frequently span employee selection, training, documentation, communication, compensation, information systems, evaluation and measurement, management, work design, and quality improvement, to name but a few.

There is a huge body of research that supports the efficacy of employee involvement. Writers in many different fields have emphasized the importance of interdisciplinary design teams. The most successful design projects require synthesis, or cross-pollination, of ideas (Lorenz, 1986). According to Stolovitch and Keeps (1992), the ideal intervention integrates both managers' and employees' perspectives during its design. This involvement is no longer limited to face-to-face collaboration; virtual teamwork through electronic communication has made employee involvement much easier.

Considerations of change management offer additional compelling reasons for involving others in intervention design. There are many social and political, as well as functional, reasons for doing so.

One possible format for involvement is the use of an advisory team consisting of managers, supervisors, and employees from the areas most affected (Spitzer, 1995). When included in the design process, these people can contribute valuable insights. They are also much more likely to support the intervention. The involvement of these stakeholders can have a profound effect on how the intervention is perceived: "The best . . . design intentions are helpless in achieving their ends if people throughout the organization are disinterested in, or distracted from, participation" (Taylor and Felton, 1993, p. 3).

However, one caveat is in order: it is vital that the right people be involved and that meetings be well facilitated. One should never forget that a camel is a horse designed by a committee!

8. *High-impact interventions should have a strong evaluation component.* Too often, we think of evaluation as an add-on, an afterthought, or something that is forced on us. Evaluation is an integral part of any high-impact intervention, however. It is virtually impossible to design a perfect intervention on the first attempt. Formative evaluation provides an early-warning system to identify and correct problems and to fine-tune an intervention.

Unfortunately, in most performance improvement interventions, there is little or no feedback. This oversight often exists, consciously or unconsciously, as a way of reducing the chance that poor results might become visible. The trouble with failing to perform this kind of evaluation is that problems may not be corrected in a timely fashion, and no one ultimately will know if the intervention has succeeded. Furthermore, because of the inevitability of changing circumstances, any sustainable intervention must have a prominent feedback/adaptation mechanism.

9. *High-impact interventions should be designed with development and implementation in mind.* Everything that is designed eventually must be developed and implemented. Design may be the most creative part of the systems approach, but it is not usually the major cost. In designing interventions, it is important to consider the feasibility and cost of subsequent phases. Development and implementation requirements are particularly important to consider during the design phase. The costs, complexity, and difficulty of implementation typically pose the greatest challenge.

Spitzer (1986) and many others have stressed the importance of considering implementation issues as early as possible in the design process. In their model for engineering effective performance, Stolovitch and Keeps (1998) suggest that the most important factors to consider in planning for implementation are appropriateness, economics, feasibility, and acceptability.

Intervention implementation also often includes the involvement and coordination of a large number of people. That is why implementation planning should be a key aspect of every high-impact intervention design, although it rarely is. Fortunately, many of the ideas and principles presented in this chapter will contribute to more effective implementation.

10. *High-impact interventions should be designed with an iterative approach.* Very few interventions are perfect from the start. According to Wilson and Wilson (1970, p. 10), "Progress in design depends on revising, revising, revising!" Using the iterative approach when designing an intervention means getting as much feedback as possible from as many different perspectives as possible, preferably early in the design process. Intervention designers operate too often as closed-loop systems and are reluctant to solicit feedback until it is too late. Too often, iteration is viewed as a sign of weakness or indecision. Nothing could be farther from the truth, however. The best HP technologists constantly seek input from managers, employees, and subject matter experts during the design of performance improvement projects, rather than waiting for implementation. The earlier the formative data are collected, the easier and less costly the revisions are. Continuous improvement is a key concept in organizations today, and it is one of the most critical features of successful intervention design.

INTERVENTION DEVELOPMENT

Once an intervention design has been approved, the project generally proceeds to the development phase. However, as discussed earlier in this chapter, there is not always a well-defined distinction between design and development. It is common for development to overlap design.

During the development phase, the detailed intervention plan is converted into a form that can be implemented. Some interventions require extensive development, whereas others require very little. Common products of the development phase include manuals, training materials, assessment instruments, videotapes, and job aids. Development usually requires skills that are different from those used in design, and it sometimes involves different people. The increasing use of technology-based intervention components requires further specialized development skills. It is interesting to note that design is more conceptual, whereas development generally involves the production of materials (Spitzer, 1990). That is one reason why designers do not always make the best developers—nor do developers make the best designers.

The extent and difficulty of development depend largely on how clearly the design plans have been specified, on whether existing materials are available, and on the types of materials being developed. If the design specifications are very precise, development can usually be delegated to production people. However, many intervention designs are quite sketchy and require designers to be more involved in the development process.

The magnitude of development depends on the type of intervention being designed. Some interventions (for example, a new sales incentive system) may require little more than descriptions of the methods to be used to allocate rewards. Other interventions (for example, a distance training program) may require extensive audiovisual and computer-based courseware development.

When there is large-scale development to be done, one of the most important decisions is whether to build or buy the intervention materials. It is sometimes more cost-effective to buy "off the shelf" products or to outsource development.

Although the intervention development process (like the design process) can take many different forms, the following steps are common in most intervention development efforts.

Step 1: Select the Development Team

Although it is possible for designers to develop the intervention, it is more common for development to be assigned to those with more specialized production skills. Often, when intervention development involves extensive production of materials, it is wise to contract it to an outside vendor.

In the staffing of a development effort, people with the right skills need to be identified and assembled. As in design, a team approach to development is often preferable, since it is rarely possible for one person to do all the work effectively. Also, as in any other kind of team effort, the interpersonal skills possessed by team members are usually as important as the technical skills.

Step 2: Prepare the Development Plan

Development sometimes involves a major effort and requires extensive resources. If this is the case, it is important to prepare a detailed plan that identifies development tasks, responsibilities, schedules, and resources required. This plan generally has to be approved by the client and/or other organizational decision makers.

Step 3: Develop and Test the Prototype

Just as with design, it is always desirable to do formative evaluation before implementation. The extent of formative evaluation will usually depend on the stakes involved. If the stakes are high, or if there will be a major production effort involved, it is usually desirable to produce and test prototypes of the intervention materials before final production and implementation. (A prototype is an incomplete version, or rough draft, of the intervention materials, which may include procedures, scripts, storyboards, or even a sample of final materials.) The purpose of prototype development and testing is to obtain preliminary feedback and make revisions prior to final production. Prototype testing, or pilot testing, may involve reviews by the client, by subject matter experts, or by members of the target audience in actual field trials.

Step 4: Revise the Development Plan

On the basis of formative evaluation and feedback, modifications are made in the development plan. Formative evaluation often identifies major weaknesses in the intervention. It is only prudent to correct them before final production and full-scale implementation.

Step 5: Produce the Final Intervention Materials

After the development plan has been revised, the implementation materials are ready for final production. These final materials are produced, packaged, and prepared for implementation.

CONCLUSION

This chapter has discussed the design and development of high-impact performance improvement interventions. The intent has been to help HP technologists increase their success rate and organizational impact.

This chapter has clearly presented design as the major value-adding activity in the systems approach, and development as a continuation of the design process. Although the emphasis has been on intervention design and, to a lesser extent, on development, readers should note the close interrelationships among all the phases in the systems approach. Other themes of this chapter have been the value of continuing analysis well beyond the end of the officially designated analysis phase; the need for ongoing evaluation (especially formative evaluation); and the importance of considering implementation requirements as early as possible.

The major points of the chapter can be summarized as follows:

1. Performance improvement interventions should be designed in a disciplined manner that uses an appropriate design process and is based on thorough and continuing analysis.

2. Whenever possible, interventions should be targeted at areas in which they will have the greatest organizational impact.

3. Interventions can and should be designed for the purpose of maximizing positive organizational impact.

4. Intervention impact can be enhanced through the incorporation of multiple, synergistic components; through the involvement of key stakeholders in the design process; and through the iterative design of the intervention.

5. High-impact interventions should be sustainable. There is an implicit warning in this chapter to avoid simplistic and "quick fix" interventions that may respond to immediate pressures and address superficial symptoms but that do not solve the underlying performance problems.

6. A well-designed intervention is the best assurance of a well-developed, successful intervention.

Performance improvement interventions are created through design, on the basis of analysis. They are completed through development and refined through formative evaluation. But implementation is where the effectiveness of any design is really tested. Discussions of how to optimize intervention design and development are all very well, but in HPT, when all is said and done, it is really only results that count. It is hoped that this chapter will help all HP technologists to produce better results by designing higher-impact interventions and, ultimately, to improve human performance at work.

References

Bailey, R. W. (1982). *Human performance engineering.* Englewood Cliffs, NJ: Prentice-Hall.

Broad, M. L. (1997). Overview of transfer of training: From learning to performance. *Performance Improvement Quarterly* 10:2, 7–21.

Carr, D. K., Hard, K. J., and Trahant, W. J. (1996). *Managing the change process.* New York: McGraw-Hill.

Covey, S. (1990). *The seven habits of highly effective people.* New York: Fireside.

DeMarco, T., and Lister, T. (1987). *Peopleware.* New York: Dorsett House.

Emery, J. C. (1987). *Management information systems.* New York: Oxford University Press.

Gause, D. C., and Weinberg, G. M. (1989). *Exploring requirements: Quality before design.* New York: Dorsett House.

Lorenz, C. (1986). *The design dimension.* Oxford, England: Blackwell.

Mager, R. F. (1992). Afterword. In H. D. Stolovitch and E. J. Keeps (eds.), *Handbook of Human Performance Technology: A comprehensive guide for analyzing and solving performance problems in organizations.* San Francisco: Jossey-Bass.

Oshry, B. (1996). *Seeing systems.* San Francisco: Berrett-Koehler.

Rummler, G. A., and Brache, A. P. (1995). *Improving performance.* San Francisco: Jossey-Bass.

Schaffer, R. H. (1997). *High-impact consulting.* San Francisco: Jossey-Bass.

Spitzer, D. R. (1981). Analyzing training needs. *Educational Technology* 21:11, 36–37.

Spitzer, D. R. (1982). Context/learner analysis. *Educational Technology* 22:2, 37–38.

Spitzer, D. R. (1985). Twenty ways to energize your training. *Training* 22:5, 37–40.

Spitzer, D. R. (1986). *Improving individual performance.* Englewood Cliffs, NJ: Educational Technology.

Spitzer, D. R. (1990). *Introduction to instructional technology.* Boise, ID: Boise State University.

Spitzer, D. R. (1995). *SuperMotivation: A blueprint for energizing your organization from top to bottom.* New York: AMACOM.

Spitzer, D. R. (1996). Ensuring successful performance improvement interventions. *Performance Improvement* 35:9, 26–27.

Spitzer, D. R. (1998). *Rediscovering the social context of distance learning.* Englewood Cliffs, NJ: Educational Technology.

Stolovitch, H. D., and Keeps, E. J. (1998). Performance improvement interventions: Selection-design/development-implementation phase. In D. G. Robinson and J. C. Robinson (eds.), *From training to performance: A practical guidebook.* Alexandria, VA: American Society for Training and Development.

Stolovitch, H. D., and Keeps, E. J. (eds.). (1992). *Handbook of Human Performance Technology.* San Francisco: Jossey-Bass.

Taylor, J. C., and Felton, D. F. (1993). *Performance by design.* Englewood Cliffs, NJ: Prentice-Hall.

Wile, D. (1996, Feb.). Why doers do. *Performance & Instruction,* pp. 30–35.

Wilson, I. G., and Wilson, M. E. (1970). *From idea to working model.* New York: Wiley.

CHAPTER TEN

Evaluation

Sharon A. Shrock
George L. Geis

Evaluation is that part of Human Performance Technology (HPT) that provides information about worth or value or meaning (Reynolds, 1993) in order to guide decision making. The object of an evaluation (the *evaluand*) can be almost anything   for example, an instructional program, a performance improvement intervention, or an individual's competence. HPT is often characterized as a systems approach to organizational and individual performance improvement. All systems have a feedback and revision loop—a mechanism for determining if the output of the system meets the intended objectives. In its most general sense, then, evaluation is the process of collecting information and feeding it back to those who need the information so that the system can succeed.

The foregoing description of evaluation is, however, misleadingly simple and contributes to underuse of evaluation. When this description is taken literally, evaluation is viewed merely as the last box in the HPT algorithmic model, a step to be undertaken after everything else has been finished. Worse, evaluation is thought to be impossible unless all the earlier steps in the model have been completed. In fact, when well conducted, evaluation is nested within each box or step of these models, pumping information, like blood, into the body of an organization. And, to push this analogy farther, the organization needs evaluation as long as the organization exists; that is, evaluation is not a one-time event (Geis and Smith, 1992) but rather a continual process.

In spite of its essential function, evaluation may well be the most widely misunderstood, avoided, and feared activity in the practice of HPT. Let us start with the misunderstanding of evaluation and then move on to avoidance and fear of evaluation.

The word *evaluation* is used to describe many different kinds of activities undertaken for many different purposes. A trip to the physician's office can be used to illustrate many evaluations. To begin with, the physician's credentials displayed on the wall reflect several individual, summative evaluations of her. She has graduated from an accredited medical school, and the accreditation process itself has required extensive summative, program evaluations. She takes the patient's temperature (collects quantitative evaluation data) and asks questions (collects qualitative evaluation data) to assess his condition. She will monitor his treatment, ordering tests that give her formative evaluation data about how he is doing and revising his regimen until he is well. When the patient leaves the office, the receptionist asks him to complete a survey that asks his opinions of the physician's services (a level 1 evaluation; see Kirkpatrick, 1994), as well as a test that covers what the physician has told him to do about his condition, to see if he understands (a level 2 evaluation). Just when the patient thinks he has seen enough of evaluation, a nurse calls two weeks after his visit to the physician, to determine if he has transferred what the physician told him to do into his daily routine (a level 3 evaluation). And, later that day, he gets the bill for all of this and asks (a level 4 evaluation), "How much healthier and more productive am I after all of this medical treatment? What am I getting as a return on my investment [ROI] in this medical treatment?" Evaluation comprises all these purposes and activities and more. But notice that, in every case, information is being gathered that will allow a judgment about value.

The avoidance of evaluation and the fear of it stem partly from the confusion surrounding what it is and how to do it "right." (Does doing it "right" mean one has to have a control group? a hundred subjects? that one must hire a statistician? go back to school for a master's degree in psychometrics?) But confusion is not the only reason why evaluation is underused. The term *evaluation* is associated with negative scrutiny and failure to meet a standard. Evaluation evokes the fear of being unfairly judged, and the negative affect surrounding evaluation is probably enough to keep this powerful technology from being used to its fullest potential. But evaluation is critical to the practice of HPT; without it, the success of any HPT intervention is unknown, and decisions are left to hearsay, politics, egos, impressions, personal connections, and other enemies of sound thinking. The productive use of evaluation will be encouraged by improvement in its quality.

This chapter is designed to provide information about current conceptualizations of evaluation. It begins with a brief history of the evolution of evaluation and then describes the integral role that evaluation plays in HPT. The chapter provides an overview of the major steps in conducting an evaluation, along with general principles and caveats. The chapter ends with a characterization of successful evaluation in HPT.

A QUICK HISTORY: FROM MEASUREMENT TO EVALUATION

Although evaluation has changed over the decades, it has retained every function it has ever served. Its evolution has been like that of a snowball rolling down a hill: over time, it has come to address larger issues and to encompass more and different methods. These changes have been described by Guba and Lincoln (1989) and by Geis (1989).

Evaluation has its roots in measurement. Initially, the focus was on measurement of individual differences, starting with physical differences (such as reaction times) and moving on to individual differences in cognitive abilities (such as IQ). Therefore, evaluation historically has been allied with psychology and education. Before the 1930s, the terms *evaluation* and *measurement* were synonymous. One still sees this view in the titles of the many texts in this area that include both terms, and in the preference among many evaluators for statistical data (so-called hard data).

During the 1930s, Tyler's work on behavioral objectives ushered in a focus on the extent to which prespecified outcomes had been attained by learners. Thus was born program evaluation—the placing of value on a complex, coordinated, and goal-driven human activity—although its focus was very narrow. Evaluators at the time saw their job as the description of instructional programs in terms of how well the intended objectives had been met. Objectives dominated these evaluations, and measurement of their attainment kept intact evaluation's earlier technical, psychometric character. It is from these early days that we have the view of evaluation as equivalent to a scientific, experimental study. Like good scientists, evaluators were exhorted to remain at an objective distance from the persons and programs they evaluated, lest they introduce bias into the data.

The 1960s saw evaluation's focus broaden to include other factors besides the achievement of prespecified outcomes. Other process and context factors, including the value of the objectives themselves, fell under the evaluator's purview. And, as Guba and Lincoln (1989) emphasize, evaluators were encouraged to go beyond the description of programs and to serve as the judges of program quality. During this time, evaluation developed its identity as a distinct profession in its own right. In the United States, the large government-sponsored educational projects of the day required evaluation, and the field experienced rapid development as evaluators came to grips with real-world demands. As a result, many models of evaluation were written during this era, and these models still characterize many evaluations performed today. These various models are nicely summarized and critically compared by Worthen and Sanders (1987).

The late 1970s brought heavy criticism of these evaluation models. The critics were unhappy with the lack of use of evaluation results and with the dominance of quantification and experimentalism in the prevailing approaches to evaluation. They preferred a more involved, naturalistic approach that allowed significant issues to emerge from an evaluation, rather than an approach requiring that important questions be specified in advance. Just as notably, these critics thought that evaluators too often served the interests of managers or decision makers—those who decided what questions the evaluation would answer—at the expense of the interests of other stakeholders, such as learners in an instructional program or clients of a service program. The naturalists wanted to include in evaluation data the perspectives of all parties holding a stake in the evaluand.

By the 1980s, a large debate had opened up within the field of evaluation between those who advocated traditional, quantitative, preordinate evaluation designs and those who favored more participative, narrative, emergent evaluation strategies. This debate forced examination of the political side of evaluation and the misuse or nonuse of evaluation findings. As the naturalists gained legitimacy, their arguments encouraged the field to accept such qualitative methods as observation and interviews, along with traditional surveys and other instruments that had long been the evaluator's tools. By the 1990s, this naturalistic paradigm of evaluation had gained the respect of most evaluators, and the field had been enriched by another major perspective and its accompanying methods.

EVALUATION TODAY: FOCUS ON UTILIZATION

Evaluation today reflects all the perspectives just described and comprises an arsenal of generally accepted methods from which a well-informed evaluation specialist may choose. Many experienced evaluators warn that it is a mistake to assume that one model or approach to evaluation is the best one for all circumstances (Worthen and Sanders, 1987), even though the evaluation literature is replete with impassioned advocates of the different perspectives.

Although formal evaluation was first practiced in education projects and schools, today evaluation has grown well beyond those boundaries. There are academic programs offering advanced degrees in evaluation, and evaluators can be found working in hospitals, social service agencies, government offices, museums, and corporations, as well as in educational institutions around the globe. It is also important to note that many, perhaps most, evaluations are performed by nonspecialists: the critical need for evaluation feedback early in and throughout a project often means that those on the scene must act as evaluators. Evaluation skills are an important asset that an HP technologist should bring to an organization.

Although evaluation is indeed a powerful performance technology, evaluators still often see their reports ignored by the organizations that have commissioned them. Discussion of how to increase the use of evaluation results has been an aspect of the field for decades. There are many ways in which evaluation can go wrong apart from the numerous technical and/or methodological mistakes that an evaluator may make. Political schemes, career enhancement, cover-ups, scapegoating, public relations scams, and other forms of illegitimate activity frequently seek to use evaluation as a front. When this happens, it is no wonder that evaluators feel as if their attempts to find meaningful conclusions about the strengths and weaknesses of the evaluand are futile. However, use of evaluation results is enhanced by broad participation in the evaluation, starting at the design phase, and by a sense of shared ownership of the process. This chapter will return later to this theme; the importance of using the results of evaluation cannot be ignored.

LOCATION OF EVALUATION IN THE HPT MODEL

Given the multiple purposes that evaluation can serve, it is difficult to portray its location in the HPT model in a static way. As already mentioned, when evaluation is being used well in an organization, it is a continual process. However, there are three points where evaluation tends most often to occur in the application of HPT:

1. The point where a prototype of an intervention has been created, and formative evaluation data are needed so that any required revisions can be made before the intervention proceeds

2. After an intervention has been implemented, and evaluation data are required to determine whether the intervention has been successful

3. During front-end analysis, when performance problems and their possible causes and solutions are being defined

It may seem that these three locations can be roughly translated as the middle, end, and beginning in the HPT model being used—a sequence that appears to be out of chronological order. Where typical practice is concerned, however, evaluation is most often begun when there is at least a draft, mock-up, or prototype to be examined. Evaluation is frequently continued as the intervention is piloted and/or implemented in the larger organization. How, then, does evaluation figure into the early stages of HPT? There are at least two ways:

1. Some enlightened organizations begin the evaluation function with what Stufflebeam and Shinkfield (1985) have called *context* and *input* evaluations. The purpose of context evaluation is essentially what HPT refers to as *needs assessment*; input evaluations determine the ability of the organization to undertake alternative proposed solutions to the identified needs.

2. In a good evaluation, the functioning of the intervention as implemented is studied comprehensively. Therefore, evaluation near the end of the HPT model often leads either to the identification of other performance problems or of problems with the front-end analysis phases. Moreover, formative evaluation of an intervention can turn up problems with any of the initial analysis phases of HPT—the performance analysis, the job/task analysis, or the context analysis. This discovery pushes the evaluation function to the front of the HPT model more frequently than early renderings of the model anticipated.

Thus it becomes difficult to depict the evaluation function as fitting inside a box in an algorithmic model; in practice, it may look more like a spiderweb.

Even though evaluation is often nonlinear in practice, it is totally compatible with—and, in fact, is essential to—a systems model like the one that characterizes HPT. Most steps in the HPT model do not occur in a linear, mechanistic fashion, and evaluation is no exception. Because evaluation potentially informs every other step in the process, it should be integral to HPT practice, and HP technologists have an excellent perspective from which to do evaluation work. In spite of the difficulty of rendering an image that truly captures the iterative nature of HPT, the systems model is extremely useful as a way of thinking about solving performance problems. Its power for the evaluator, as for any other performance technologist, is not that it serves the function of a road map on paper but rather that it serves the function of a cognitive organizer and cueing schema in the brain. The HPT systems model helps the evaluator see where problems with the evaluand may originate.

DIFFERENT CONCEPTS OF EVALUATION

As mentioned earlier, for different people the word *evaluation* brings to mind different purposes and activities. The various concepts make communication about evaluation difficult. To one person, the word may suggest small-group testing of individuals; to another, large-scale program evaluation involving the sampling of hundreds of subjects; and to still another, in-depth interviewing and observation of a carefully selected group of performers. This section seeks to clarify the alternative subordinate meanings that the general term *evaluation* connotes and will discuss the following four concepts:

1. Formative and summative evaluation
2. The methodological continuum from controlled experiments to qualitative evaluations
3. Kirkpatrick's four levels of evaluation (1994)
4. Evaluation as certification

Formative and Summative Evaluation

Scriven (1967) is credited with making the fundamental distinction, now widely accepted among practitioners, between *formative* and *summative* evaluation. The two forms of evaluation differ in purpose and often in technique as well. Formative evaluation seeks to provide information regarding the evaluand while the intervention is still under development and can be revised before additional investments are made. Summative evaluation is conducted to determine whether the evaluand is worthy of adoption or continuance and leads to a "go/no go" decision.

Because much of formative evaluation is performed on prototype materials or solutions, it is typically smaller in scale and less formal than summative evaluation. Worthen and Sanders (1987) argue that formative evaluation is probably best done by an internal evaluator, one who works closely with the development team, because the insider is likely to have the intimate familiarity with the evaluand that best guides revision of the intervention. HP technologists are often asked to perform this type of evaluation.

There are several different strategies used to conduct formative evaluation. The most common are tryouts of the intervention with individuals or with small groups drawn from the target population (the population for whom the intervention is ultimately intended) and expert review of prototype materials. Thiagarajan (1991) lists six different kinds of experts who should be considered for this type of formative evaluation. The purpose of the expert review is typically to ascertain the accuracy or validity of the information or approach contained in the intervention; the target-audience tryout is conducted to see if the intervention is likely to meet its objectives (which involve performance data) and prove satisfactory to users (a determination involving preference data). Several formative evaluations using different strategies may be conducted on a single intervention at different stages of its development (Thiagarajan, 1991), and for different purposes. The terms *alpha testing* (formative evaluation within the development team) and *beta testing* (formative evaluation with a select group of target users) are now often used to distinguish two levels of formative evaluation (see Chapter Twenty-Nine).

The advancing technology of performance interventions and their associated costs, the increasing globalization of HPT interventions, and changes in learning theory have increased the need for formative evaluation and altered its methods. Thus the importance of formative evaluation increases as the cost of making revisions to the evaluand increases, and today's expensive technologies demand greater certainty of the proposed solution's effectiveness. Moreover, the growing likelihood that HPT interventions will have to be effective with and acceptable to those in other lands argues strongly for cross-cultural formative evaluation; the target audience used in a field test must reflect the international composition of the ultimate users, and expert review may need to include experts in the languages, customs, and cultures of the international audience. Further, as Tessmer (1994) argues, changes in learning theory have suggested new ways to conduct formative evaluations of instruction; the ascendance of cognitive learning theories has focused attention on the processes of learning, as well as on the outcomes that were the focus of behaviorist theories, and so Tessmer's suggestions focus on qualitative strategies for encouraging discussion of possible problems with the evaluand. For example, Tessmer proposes think-aloud protocols and computer interviewing as alternatives to the traditional one-evaluator-to-one-student tryout and debriefing; formal review by the development team ("self-evaluation," p. 10) and expert panel reviews as alternatives to the traditional expert review process; and evaluation meetings with target learners, computer journals, and rapid prototyping as alternatives to the traditional field test.

Perhaps the most important point about formative evaluation is that years of research substantiate its contribution to improved products and processes. Trying out a proposed intervention with even one target subject usually yields important formative feedback well worth the time and effort. Formative evaluation is not a step in the HPT model that a practitioner should skip; doing so will not save time or money in the long run.

Many evaluators would agree that most evaluation is in fact formative rather than summative, although it is not necessarily done when the evaluand is under development. In other words, much of the feedback used to make revisions to an intervention is collected after the intervention is implemented. After all, strategies for continual improvement are an important outcome of the Total Quality Management (TQM) movement, and continual development and improvement are the expectation in many organizations. The methods of formative evaluation can be used in these efforts as well.

Stake (1969) distinguishes between formative evaluation and summative evaluation on the basis of the different audiences to which each is responsive rather than on the basis of when evaluations occur with respect to the development of the evaluand. Stake thinks that summative evaluation—unlike formative evaluation, which is conducted for development people on the inside—answers questions of interest to outsiders, questions about what the evaluand is and what it can do. Worthen and Sanders (1987) recommend that summative evaluations be conducted by external evaluators because it is difficult for those who are close to an instructional program or other intervention to remain objective.

It is summative evaluation that is most apt to look like a discrete study with five distinct phases. Briefly, these phases are *planning, materials development, data collection, analysis,* and *reporting* (Smith and Brandenburg, 1991). Summative evaluations must be very carefully planned and conducted. They are often costly and time-consuming. An evaluability assessment (discussed later in this chapter) should precede the orchestration of a summative evaluation.

Before moving on from the topics of formative and summative evaluation, it is important for us to note that the two kinds of evaluation apply to individuals as well as to programs or interventions. Formative evaluation of an individual usually takes the form of diagnostic testing to see where the performer is having difficulty. Summative evaluation of an individual may take the form of an end-of-course assessment, a placement test to determine whether instruction is needed, or a certification test.

The Methodological Continuum
from Controlled Experiments to Qualitative Studies

As mentioned earlier, in the section on the history of evaluation, the accepted methods for conducting evaluations have broadened over the decades. All these methods cause evaluation to look very different at different times and in different organizations, a circumstance that contributes to the overall confusion surrounding the process. Numerous books treat, in great detail, the topic of how to plan and conduct these different types of studies (see, for example, Kerlinger, 1986; Patton, 1990). Here, we can only illustrate this breadth. The extremes of the methodological continuum are marked by experimental evaluations, at one pole, and naturalistic evaluations, at the other.

At one time, all "good" evaluations were controlled experiments—tightly focused statistical comparisons of the outcomes of a control group and a treatment group, with all confounding (interfering) variables controlled. The design of such an evaluation must be clearly specified in advance: the independent (treatment) and dependent (outcome) variables must be operationalized (clearly defined), and measurements of the dependent variable must be selected or created.

Control is the hallmark of an experimental study. Subjects for the study are typically chosen at random in fairly large numbers from well-defined populations, in order to control for possible differences that are due to the two comparison groups' composition. Once the study is designed and begun, it cannot be modified without risk to its validity. The attribution of measured differences between the two groups to the treatment is entirely dependent on the amount of control the evaluator can exert over conditions of the study. Data for this type of evaluation are almost always numbers. This design (or any of its close cousins) is the only way that social scientists have devised for determining causation. (This characteristic of experiments has implications for level 4 evaluations, which will be discussed a bit later.)

At the other end of the continuum are the qualitative (or naturalistic, or constructivist) studies, which rely primarily on observation, interviews, and document analysis. These studies must also be carefully planned and conducted, but their strength is in their so-called emergent design—that is, evaluators decide what data they need and where to get it as the evaluation progresses. Sampling is usually not random; instead "initial choices of informants lead [the evaluator] to similar and different ones; observing one class of events invites comparison with another. . . . This is conceptually-driven sequential sampling" (Miles and Huberman, 1994, p. 27).

The presumption with this type of evaluation is that it is impossible to know in advance of data collection all the outcomes that are important. Unlike the situation in an experimental study, in a naturalistic evaluation the work of conducting the study cannot be delegated across a number of data collectors without risk to the evaluation's validity. The data for this type of evaluation are primarily words. Analysis of qualitative data is a search for patterns and themes in what is heard and seen. This process is extremely demanding and can be very time-consuming, as are the data-collection procedures themselves; data collection and analysis are done at the same time. The results are those themes and issues that are supported by triangulation of data sources.

Between these two extremes are evaluations with some characteristics of both experimentalism and naturalism—surveys, for example, with both closed and open-ended questions. Today's evaluator has a number of choices to make in designing an evaluation that will meet the information needs of an organization. In terms of subjects sampled, the experimental, quantitative studies tend to be broad but shallow; they include data on a great number of subjects, but the data are reduced to what can be measured. Naturalistic, qualitative studies tend to be narrow but deep; they include data from fewer subjects but also great depth of information. Causation is the province of the controlled experiment; fluidity to pursue unanticipated outcomes and issues is the strength of the naturalistic investigation.

Kirkpatrick's Four Levels of Evaluation

Decades ago, Kirkpatrick (1959) introduced a classification scheme for training evaluations that depicted four levels:

1. Reaction to training
2. Learning from training
3. Transfer of learned skills to the job
4. Impact of training on organizational results.

This scheme is widely known among HPT and human resources development practitioners, who simply refer to these different evaluations as "level 1, level 2" and so on. Reynolds (1993) refers to the Kirkpatrick scheme as a summative evaluation model; however, Robinson and Robinson (1989) point out that level 1 is typically used for formative purposes, level 2 can be either formative or summative (that depends on how the data are used), and levels 3 and 4 are truly summative in nature.

Level 1 data are usually collected via a questionnaire that asks course participants to rate the course materials, course instructor, support visuals, and so on. As one might expect, level 1, because of its relative ease of use, is by far the most commonly conducted of the four levels of evaluation (Robinson and Robinson, 1989), even though it is frequently disparaged as "Smile-O-Meter" data. Robinson and Robinson (1989) make some useful suggestions for how to get the most out of level 1 assessment.

Level 2 is typically synonymous with criterion-referenced, end-of-course testing. The goal of level 2 evaluations is to determine whether participants have met the course objectives. Measuring the attainment of objectives is all that evaluation means to some practitioners. Clearly, this type of evaluation is mandated by instructional design and development models, where the evaluation of the attainment of instructional objectives, and the consequent feedback for purposes of revision, give these models their systems property. Even so, many organizations do no level 2 measurement at all, or they measure competence at levels well below what is required on the job. Level 2 measures usually take the form of performance or cognitive tests that are thoroughly grounded in course objectives. These measures must be very carefully constructed to protect their validity, especially if results will be used not just to evaluate the instructional program but also to make decisions regarding individual test takers. Shrock and Coscarelli (1989) provide guidance for creating these instruments.

Level 3 and level 4 evaluations are frequently written and talked about but not frequently done. Level 3 evaluations are generally considered more feasible than those at level 4. Because level 3 addresses transfer of skills to the job, data collection usually involves either on-site observations of performance or the questioning of those who are in a position to observe the on-the-job performance of the trainees. In the latter case, level 3 assessments are strengthened when data from more than one observer are included (for example, data from a trainee's supervisor, subordinates, and/or colleagues). This kind of evaluation must be handled with great care, particularly in an international context. For example, questions regarding the competence of colleagues may be considered rude, and, in some countries, union rules backed by law may severely restrict who may obtain data from an individual's supervisor.

Level 4 evaluation is usually extremely difficult to do (Dionne, 1996), although case studies using return-on-investment analyses of training are increasingly appearing (see, for example, see Lachenmaier and Moor, 1997). Such accounts need to be read very carefully, however; many of them do not isolate effects that are due to training alone, and others rely on perceptions rather than on data (Torraco, 1995), whereas still others are grounded in assumptions and estimates that lack credibility for anyone except those who are already true believers. If establishing the effects that are due to training is the goal, then the best methods to use are either a controlled experiment or a multiple-regression analysis. Both methods require control and/or measurements that most organizations would find an interference, at the very least. Therefore, level 4 return-on-investment evaluations are typically approximations of training's effect on the bottom line.

Kirkpatrick's four levels of evaluation seem to have stood the test of time, but the scheme has been criticized (Newstrom, 1995) and improvements have been suggested. Kaufman, Keller, and Watkins (1996) and Dick and King (1994) suggest modifying the four levels if they are applied to HPT interventions that involve anything other than training. Kaufman, Keller, and Watkins (1996) also advocate adding a fifth level, to assess contributions that the organization makes to society's welfare.

Evaluation as Certification

The literature regarding evaluation has been dominated by program evaluation for many years. However, recently the focus of much professional discussion has turned to individual assessment, and it is now not unusual for an HPT practitioner to be asked to create tests. This change in focus is a result of the demand for assessment of competence and, sometimes, for certification of employees.

There are many possible reasons for this increased interest in evaluation of individual employees. For one thing, global competition has forced renewed interest in competence in the workforce. For another, technology changes so rapidly that employers need to be certain that workers' knowledge is current. For yet another, technology has become so sophisticated and complex that buyers of technology are demanding that certification of their employees' competence to operate and maintain equipment be included in purchase agreements.

Until recently, summative evaluations of individuals (level 2 assessment) were used only to evaluate training efforts. Gradually, however, some organizations have been coming to feel pressure from line managers to use data from these evaluations to make substantive decisions about employees. Certification of individuals represents a step beyond, for it can arouse the expectation that individuals will have more than the minimum necessary skill or competence (Eyres, 1998); thus this latest trend—marketing not just a product but also the certification of a buyer's employees—puts evaluation in a new light, as itself a product to be sold to a client.

These latest uses of individual evaluation have raised the stakes and risks associated with evaluation. As long as data on individuals were averaged or otherwise grouped, and as long as the scores of individuals were not released to managers, there was not much concern about litigation, but certification of individuals has changed all that. Therefore, it is absolutely essential that certification tests be validated for job-relatedness and fairness in administration and scoring (Eyres, 1998; Shrock and Coscarelli, 1989). Documentation of the test-creation process, and especially of the test's validation, is very important. The technology of individual assessment is powerful and totally consistent with other aspects of HPT, relying as it does on careful and thorough job and task analysis. However, the term *certification* has referred recently to a variety of procedures, some of which involve no assessment and clearly yield no defensible evidence of competence (Coscarelli, Robins, Shrock, and Herbst, forthcoming). This haphazard use of evaluation language presents ethical and legal risks that should not be underestimated.

STEPS IN CONDUCTING AN EVALUATION

Although every evaluation is different because of its unique context, and because procedures differ by method chosen, there are discernible steps that characterize every well-conducted evaluation. These steps are grouped into four stages—early, middle, concluding, and follow-up—as discussed in the passages that follow.

Early Stage: Determining Evaluability

Many of the evaluations that are done every year should not have been undertaken, either because they are inappropriate at the time they are done or because they have serious technical flaws. Nevertheless, just as it is very difficult for a training department to say that a request for training is inappropriate (because the so-called solution has been prematurely determined), so it is tough for an HPT practitioner to turn down a request for an evaluation. The key principle to keep in mind is this: front-end analysis applies just as much to evaluation as it does to the generation of solutions to performance problems. The steps in determining evaluability are very similar to the elements of needs assessment and front-end analysis. And the good news is that what is done in order to determine evaluability is what should be done anyway in planning an evaluation. We will call these early planning steps the process of determining evaluability, as a reminder that deciding to do a different evaluation, or not to do an evaluation at all, should remain a valid option during the planning stage. (The phrase *evaluability assessment* is often used in describing the process outlined here; see Rutman, 1980; Smith, 1989; Wholey, 1975.)

Identifying Key Players. In thinking about whether and how to proceed with an evaluation, the first step is to recognize that something or someone will be evaluated, for somebody (the client), and for a reason. Each of the people involved must cooperate and be informed if the evaluation is to be successful. The evaluator should make every effort to ensure that all the proposed participants in the evaluation will be accessible, will cooperate, and will have the same perceptions of the evaluation as the evaluator, the client, and the other participants do. Building this consensus is an even greater challenge when the evaluation is international in scope.

The evaluator should reflect on who is being evaluated. For example, the evaluator may think he is evaluating a training program rather than a person, but, at least to some extent, the learners are being evaluated—they will think so, anyway. The designers of the training program are being evaluated, and many others may see the evaluation as being directed toward them as well, including the human resources (HR) staff members who bought the program, those who adapted it, the vice president who ordered HR to develop a program, the managers of both trained and the untrained (control) groups, and so on. Every evaluation is a political activity; the evaluator must be aware of the concerns of all the players and must respond diplomatically to them. The best time to do so is at the very beginning of the planning stage.

Who else may be involved? Perhaps customers will be interviewed, to determine the program's effectiveness. Are they accessible? Will they be good informants? Are there other, perhaps hidden, stakeholders? Is someone in upper management hoping that the program fails and that the failure will reflect on an enemy?

Who is the client? Oddly, this critical question does not always have a clear answer. The term *client* may refer to the person who has commissioned the evaluation—the one to whom the evaluator reports. But often there are others who may become involved with the evaluation and who may try to influence the process. Therefore, it is wise, as in the matter of stakeholders, to scan widely in trying to identify clients. All stakeholders and clients should, whenever this is possible, be briefed on the planned evaluation, and, as appropriate, their input should be sought and respected.

Identifying Purpose and Use. Lack of a clear, correct definition of its purpose is probably the most common reason why an evaluation runs aground. Usually the purpose of evaluation (formative or summative) is to provide information that will be used in making a decision. The evaluator should also recognize that the information obtained in the evaluation is likely to be only one of several inputs into the final decision. Additional inputs may have to do, for example, with the cost of the program or with downsizing of staff.

There are, of course, many other possible purposes for conducting an evaluation besides the purpose of determining the effectiveness of a training program. An evaluation may be part of a continuing system for monitoring, which guides and corrects a quality-control system. It may be used for sorting, grading, or rewarding, as in ranking the students in a class or determining the amount of the merit bonus for each employee. Its findings may serve as input for decisions about promotions, hirings, and dismissals. An evaluation may also be used for persuasive purposes by a marketing or advertising department. Whatever the uses to which evaluation data will be put, those purposes must be clarified, and the same preliminary steps described here should be carried out.

Identifying Objectives. In the process of defining the purposes of a proposed evaluation, it is also necessary to spell out the purposes of what is being evaluated. For example, if the evaluator does not know why a training program was installed, how can its effectiveness be measured? It should be obvious that the objectives of the evaluation should be well aligned with the objectives of the organization. When the client clearly knows the objectives of the organization, the objectives of the evaluation will have a straightforward explication. Similarly, if a proper needs assessment has been carried out before the program under examination was developed, then the needs assessment will dictate the objectives to be examined by the evaluation.

When goals are unclear, however, it becomes the evaluator's task to alert clients to this deficit. It is not uncommon for evaluation planning to stop at this point. In fact, the most valuable contribution an evaluator can make at that moment is to act as a catalyst for activities that will clarify organizational and program goals. Therefore, rather than bemoan the fact that they cannot get on with an evaluation, evaluators should recognize that this impasse is a possible and useful outcome of early planning and of the evaluability exercise. Early examination and discussion of what is being evaluated provide important information, which can be used later in making specific decisions about, for example, the methods that should be used in the evaluation.

Securing Collaboration. Many evaluations fail because of insufficient interest and cooperation, and so the development of collaboration—the preliminary enlistment of all interested parties—is critical. The parties will all be involved in various ways in later activities; therefore, if their commitment, cooperation, and contributions cannot be secured at the early stage, the evaluation probably should not be undertaken. Developing that commitment is a major goal of the evaluability exercise.

Assessing the Importance of the Evaluation. Because most clients operate in an atmosphere of rational management, they will assure the evaluator that evaluation information will be used. Too often, however, the evaluator learns later on that the information provided by the evaluation actually had no status or weight in decision making.

The evaluator should make every effort to determine how important evaluation information really is to the client. One clue to its importance is timing; another is the budget. When an evaluation is to be carried out at the last minute, and on a shoestring budget, the results are not likely to be taken very seriously. If an evaluation is planned so that its results will come in right at the decision-making moment, one can be sure that the data will have little impact.

Simulation activities can help in estimating the real importance of evaluation. Ask the client questions: Will the program be dropped if there is no increase in sales? if customers are dissatisfied? What are other signs that will influence the decision about the program? If the program works, but the licensing fee for its use is doubled, what will happen? Then the evaluator should focus on what the evidence must be in order for the evaluation to influence the decision. For example, how much higher will the sales of the trained group have to be in order for the program to be considered a success? What percent of customers must show dissatisfaction before the organization becomes genuinely concerned? Other useful types of probes involve considering worst-case scenarios—imagining, for example, that the evaluation data show that salespeople who took the training actually do much worse than those who did not: How will the organization respond? What will happen if the evaluation results are ambiguous? Will another evaluation be conducted? As these conversations with the client progress, the evaluator gets a clearer picture of the kinds of information (evidence) that will persuade the client, and the amount that will be needed.

Explaining the importance of the evaluation data has several benefits. It involves clients in thinking seriously about the evaluation (and provides them with a chance to supply helpful suggestions). It commits them to dealing seriously with the results. As just noted, it helps the evaluator determine what kinds of data should be sought, and in what amounts. Most important, it allows the fashioning of an evaluation that is likely to have some impact on decision making.

Becoming Familiar with the Program and the Players. As the evaluability exercise (planning) progresses, the evaluator should become increasingly familiar with the program to be evaluated, as well as with all the potential players in the evaluation. The evaluator should examine all relevant documents and should interview, probably informally, the relevant staff. The general principle is this: get to know what and who is being evaluated. This principle suggests the need for a qualitative and often informal approach to evaluation. Regardless of the particular method that will be represented by the final stages of the evaluation, at the planning stage it is best for the evaluator to take a stance like that of a reporter or an anthropologist: she should learn about the broader culture within which the evaluation will be done.

Considering Criteria and Standards. Because evaluation requires judgment, criteria or standards for making that judgment are always present in an evaluation. However, evaluations differ widely in how explicit those criteria and standards are. Is this a norm-referenced decision (based on comparison of something or somebody to others) or a criterion-referenced decision (based on comparison of something or somebody to a fixed standard)? To what extent can a quantitative standard be set? Quantitative criteria and standards are advisable because of their clarity; however, the evaluator should be sure that what truly matters in the evaluation can in fact be measured, and that the available instruments are valid for that task. Is it important to establish causality and statistical significance—for example, to show that one program is better than another at producing increased sales? The kinds of criteria and standards that the evaluator and the clients choose will be powerful drivers of the decision about the evaluation model and methods that will be needed.

Choosing Models and Methods. On the basis of all the preceding information and analysis, the evaluator must choose an evaluation model, or mix of models, and decide in general on the methods to be used. Then suggestions to clients and other participants can be made, to obtain feedback. Of interest at this time in the design process is the likely feasibility of a particular approach, given the time and funds available, the climate of the organization, and so on. Cultural differences in the acceptance of evaluation methods are real, and so the evaluator should be sure to seek the input of international decision makers and stakeholders.

The evaluation literature offers many different models (Smith and Geis, 1992; Worthen and Sanders, 1987). In practice, the evaluator, facing the constraints and complexities of the real situation, is usually led to design an amalgam of different approaches rather than select one model and follow it precisely. Usually the final model is the one that looks as if it will work.

Concluding the Early Stage. This description of the early stages has been necessarily linear. In fact, however, the various activities are likely to be revisited many times, and at each iteration there will be changes. For example, clients may begin to move toward different goals for the evaluation, or the preferred model for the evaluation may prove to be too costly, or it may become evident that several evaluations rather than a single one will be needed, or it may make sense to use a single major evaluation strategy and then modify it to suit those of a different culture. Like the product of any other kind of front-end activity, the plan that evolves from the early stage of evaluation will be the child of many parents and will have changed its shape many times during its evolution.

Reaching the Evaluability Decision. So much for the planning facet of the first stage. What about the evaluability question? Working through the planning steps, as just outlined, provides the critical information needed to answer that question. If the client cannot clearly be identified, if key participants refuse to cooperate, if the goals of the evaluation cannot be explicated or agreed on, if the timelines and budget are unacceptable, and if no combination of methods proves acceptable to clients from divergent cultures, then it is far better to abort the evaluation than to continue. Simply the observation that the necessary conditions for a successful evaluation are not available at this time in this organization should in itself be important and thought-provoking. If things have turned out well in planning, however, the evaluator will have assembled a group of involved and cooperative participants, will have focused the evaluation on identifiable and worthwhile goals, and will have prepared clients for the outcomes, and the clients themselves will be committed to paying attention to those outcomes. In short, the groundwork will have been laid—not just for an evaluation but for a successful one.

Middle Stage: Designing and Implementing

After planning is complete and the decision has been made to go forward with the evaluation, details of the evaluation must be fleshed out in a design, and then the design must be made a reality.

Designing the Evaluation. Regardless of which model of evaluation has been chosen, the evaluator must determine the data sources to be tapped, the instruments that will be required, the procedures to be followed, a budget, and timelines. If the evaluation has a quantitative component, it is always smart to consider what data relevant to the evaluation question(s) already exist in the organization. Evaluators are frequently surprised to learn how much information is routinely collected that may be of use to them. Examples of frequently used quantitative data sources are production records, sales figures, error rates, waste-volume figures, turnover rates, and revenue statements. Data sources for a qualitative evaluation include interviews of samples of all the identified stakeholders, observation of performances and interactions, and examination of pertinent documents.

Regardless of the method chosen, all evaluations require instruments, ranging from standardized, published tests to questionnaires created in house to lists of interview questions (interview protocols). In practice, evaluation instruments are rarely the purchased, standardized assessments; those are typically not specific enough to be useful. However, if instruments are acquired from outside the organization, it is essential that the evaluator know how to judge their quality. If instruments are to be developed, psychometric expertise may be required. The measurement of attitudes, aptitudes, or other constructs that do not have an obvious connection to observable job behaviors is most likely to require the help of external psychometricians.

Procedures for data collection, storage, analysis, and reporting must be determined. It is never a good idea to collect data without knowing how those data will be analyzed. Those who do so often face disaster when they realize at the analysis stage that they need information that they do not have, or that the information is not in a form that makes analysis feasible. Storage of the data must be planned, and confidentiality, when it has been promised, must be maintained. Allowing unauthorized access to evaluation data can precipitate a lawsuit. Software programs now facilitate the storage and analysis of qualitative and quantitative data (Miles and Huberman, 1994). The persons who will collect and analyze the data must be identified; their skills and available time must be commensurate with the task. Qualitative evaluations, in particular, require skilled data collectors. Because these data are often analyzed as they are collected, only people with interviewing skill, and who will be able to see the project through to its finish, should be data collectors.

At this stage of the design, a more detailed budget and specific timelines can be determined. The budget for an evaluation is going to be driven primarily by the questions asked. If funds are short, much useful information can be collected with careful sampling, especially via qualitative methods. It is not true that qualitative evaluation always takes more time and is therefore more expensive than quantitative evaluation. It typically takes far fewer subjects to reach qualitative conclusions than it does time to measure human variables with precision. Both designs require a time investment, and the evaluation plan should ensure that results will be available in time to be useful.

Preparing the Required Materials. If evaluation materials are purchased, they are typically easy to obtain. However, flawed administration of these instruments can destroy their validity, so the manual should be carefully followed, and the administrators should be trained, as necessary. As already mentioned, customized or original materials are frequently required, and HP technologists are now often asked to create them. There are many books available to guide the creation of questionnaires and survey instruments. Patton (1990), for example, provides excellent guidance for writing and asking interview questions. Performance tests and their associated rating scales require careful job/task analysis, but they typically do not require in-depth psychometric expertise (Shrock and Coscarelli, 1989). Cognitive, aptitude, or attitude measurements are the most difficult instruments to create; if psychometric expertise is not available in house, the evaluator should consider going outside for advice in these areas.

Conducting a Pilot Study. If the evaluation planned is more than an informal, formative one, the evaluator should consider conducting a pilot test of the instruments and their administration. Even an interview protocol benefits dramatically from a few pilot interviews. Pilot tests are cheap by comparison to invalid evaluation results, which are worse than nothing because they actively mislead the organization's decision making. The evaluation instruments, materials, and/or procedures should be revised on the basis of experience and data from pilot testing.

Implementing the Design. This would appear to be a straightforward step, given all the planning described so far. However, change is constant, and sometimes the needs for evaluation data will change right in the middle of an implemented design. This is less likely to happen, of course, if an evaluability analysis has been conducted at the start, and if all the necessary parties have been involved in the earlier stages; still, it does happen. It is a mistake to persist in an expensive evaluation when the results will not be used. Often, however, an evaluation itself reveals that the initial questions were naive, misdirected, or incomplete. The emergent design of a qualitative evaluation allows the focus to change, and a changed focus is not a weakness; a more controlled study might have to be scrapped altogether and redesigned. The evaluator should be prepared to shift the focus of an evaluation, as necessary, to meet the needs of the organization.

Informing Clients and Stakeholders. It is an error to assume that clients and stakeholders should not know the results of an evaluation until the final report is written. This notion is reasonable if evaluation is construed as a one-time megastudy, with a test of statistical significance at the end, but a more useful view of evaluation characterizes it as an ongoing process. Nothing is to be gained by surprising the client and the stakeholders. The clients in particular should be kept as informed as possible while the evaluation is proceeding. They should not be told things that are not yet known for certain, but they should always be told things that are.

Concluding Stage: Analysis and Reporting

Concluding stages of evaluation involve data analysis, formulation of results, decisions about what venues to use for reporting the findings, writing or using other methods of creating reports, and disseminating evaluation results.

Analyzing Data. The experience of analyzing evaluation data will differ according to the type of data collected and the model of evaluation chosen. Analysis of quantitative data typically goes quickly if a computer is doing the work. However, there are choices to be made. Quantitative data often can be analyzed in several ways (the term is *massaged*) and displayed in different ways. Desktop statistical-analysis packages have made once exotic quantitative analyses easily available and offer many options for data analysis and display.

Qualitative data are often thought to be time-consuming to analyze. However, this information is analyzed as it is collected; the themes and issues that constitute qualitative results are identified as the data are gathered. This model is characterized by its constant comparative method (Schwandt, 1997), which provides the rationale for focus shifts and for the inclusion of additional subjects. Data collection stops when no new results are turning up (that is, at the saturation point); therefore, data collection and data analysis end at the same time.

Considering the Ethical Implications of Results. There are few specific rules here, but ethics can often be confusing in evaluation work and even more so in work with diverse cultures. Evaluators often uncover information that can be highly damaging to individuals, as well as to programs. There are some important questions to ask: Is there enough evidence to support the accuracy of damaging information? Who needs to know it? Is the information central or peripheral in its overall importance? Will the havoc unleashed by the release of this information obscure more important findings of the evaluation? Can the sources of this information be identified? If so, were these sources promised confidentiality? These are some of the most troubling questions that an evaluation can raise. Every evaluator grappling with these questions must choose a course of action, proceed, and plan to lose sleep.

Reporting Results. Results of the evaluation should be reported to the agreed upon audiences in language and displays that they can understand. It is not unethical to create different reports for different audiences unless in doing so there is an attempt to deceive. Failure to report results in a lucid, illuminating way is a major reason why evaluation findings are not used. Evaluation findings have been reported with photo displays, videos, skits, and multimedia presentations, as well as through the more traditional media of written reports, case studies, graphs, and charts. The acceptance of particular media may vary by culture or subculture, and so the evaluator should be careful not to damage the credibility of the findings by choosing an inappropriate avenue for their dissemination.

The most common dissemination vehicle is the written report. If a report is not short, it probably will not be read. (The exception would be in a culture where short communications are considered trivial.) The maximum length, excluding appendices, is about thirty pages; the evaluator should try to do a good job in fifteen because long reports are another reason why evaluation findings are not used. The evaluator should resist the temptation to stuff every scrap of documentation into the appendices: if the report looks long, many potential readers will never open it to discover that the body of the report is actually very short. A written evaluation report should include at least an executive summary, a statement of purpose, a description of the intended audience, a description of the evaluand, focusing questions, a description of the methodology, a summary and interpretation of findings, and conclusions.

Follow-Up to Evaluation: Learning and Institutionalizing

Because evaluation is never finished, it is useful to consider what happens after findings are reported. This is a reflective time, when several issues should be entertained. What impact is the evaluation having? Follow-up interviews with stakeholders and clients can be very useful in this regard.

Is further evaluation of this evaluand necessary? If so, what form should it take, and with what timelines? Circumstances change, and the need for evaluation never ends, but there may be higher priorities for evaluation services. A follow-up evaluation of the same evaluand is usually less expensive because the instruments and much of the analytical work may already be in place. Much depends on how good the documentation of previous evaluations is—a point that should make clear one of the benefits of careful documentation. It is a plus if evaluation is institutionalized, and if the evaluation staff is relatively stable. As long as evaluators do not become biased about the evaluand (that is, as long as they do not "go native"), their collective memory becomes a valuable source of knowledge about the organization—its culture (or diverse cultures), its subcultures, and its issues.

What can the evaluator and the organization learn from a particular evaluation? It is to be hoped that those involved in the evaluation have learned more than just the findings about the evaluand, important as those may be. The evaluator and the organization should also have learned something about evaluation itself. For every evaluation, the evaluator should reflect on what went well and what did not go smoothly. Because evaluation cannot be reduced to a set of immutable principles, experience is essential to mastery. If an evaluation has been a success, and if the organization knows why, then the institutionalization of effective evaluation practices is enhanced. The more accepted evaluation is, the less expensive it is, because lack of cooperation, lack of access, and other forms of resistance entail serious costs.

CAVEATS

The number of ways in which evaluation can go wrong is probably almost infinite; the process is fraught with ethical, political, and technical questions. Nevertheless, a few common mistakes can be highlighted.

Getting the Timing Wrong

Good timing is essential to enhancing the use of evaluation results. Getting into a project too late and not finishing soon enough are major problems. Unless evaluation is well institutionalized in an organization, decision makers will not think to include an evaluator until the stage of formative evaluation, at the earliest, and by that point many decisions will already have been made. And, on the back end, evaluators must never be late. Unfortunately, it is not unusual for decision makers to want evaluation results sooner than the date to which they have agreed. Therefore, evaluators had best be early.

Choosing a Method the Client Does Not Value

If the evaluation is to have any credibility for the client, it is important that the method, the data sources, and the data type be ones that the client believes in. Cross-cultural issues abound here. Some people believe only numbers; others, who find numbers cold and sterile, want narratives and description. The evaluator should be certain that the client understands the chosen method. Perhaps the closest thing to a law in evaluation is the statement that if clients or stakeholders are unhappy with the results, their first move will be to criticize the method as invalid. Therefore, their buy-in is essential.

Using Poor Instruments

If the instruments used to gather the data are weak, it does not matter how good anything else is. It is crucial that evaluators know how to write questions, ask questions, observe accurately, and determine the psychometric quality and validity of instruments. If practitioners are unsure of their skills here, they should seek outside expertise.

Failing to Establish Rapport

Evaluators without good interpersonal skills have short careers. The cooperation of many others is required for the success of an evaluation, from the earliest goal-clarification stage through intermittent debriefings with clients to the final effort of disseminating the findings. An evaluator without "people skills" can easily surprise a client with the evaluation results. The surprise comes either from the evaluator's failure to discern the issues of importance to the client at the outset or from the evaluator's failure to keep the client informed as the evaluation progressed. Surprise is the enemy of evaluation use.

CONCLUSION

When evaluation is a successful part of HPT, its results make a difference; they are considered valid enough to inform the practice of improving human performance. There is also a sense that a team has produced the evaluation results, even if there is only one evaluator, because the client, the stakeholders, and the data sources have a sense of ownership of the product. Moreover, all who have a stake in the results feel that they have been heard, even if they do not agree with the results; in other words, organizational decisions are being driven by solid data, not by emotion and resistance. In addition, no one is surprised by the findings; evaluation is so well integrated into the HPT process that its results are accessible, and their dissemination is timely. Finally, evaluation is institutionalized: it comes to represent the indispensable flow of quality information that nourishes the learning organization and thereby improves human performance.

References

Coscarelli, W. C., Robins, D., Shrock, S. A., and Herbst, P. (forthcoming). The certification suite. *Performance Improvement.*

Dick, W., and King, D. (1994). Formative evaluation in the performance context. *Performance & Instruction* 33:9, 3–8.

Dionne, P. (1996). The evaluation of training activities: A complex issue involving different stakes. *Human Resource Development Quarterly* 7, 279–286.

Eyres, P. S. (1998). *The legal handbook for trainers, speakers, and consultants.* New York: McGraw-Hill.

Geis, G. L. (1989). The evaluator from parachuter to native. In S. Thiagarajan (ed.), *Performance technology 1989: Selected proceedings from the 27th NSPI conference.* Washington, DC: National Society for Performance Improvement.

Geis, G. L., and Smith, M. E. (1992). The function of evaluation. In H. D. Stolovitch and E. J. Keeps (eds.), *Handbook of Human Performance Technology: A comprehensive guide for analyzing and solving performance problems in organizations.* San Francisco: Jossey-Bass.

Guba, E. G., and Lincoln, Y. S. (1989). *Fourth-generation evaluation.* Thousand Oaks, CA: Sage.

Kaufman, R., Keller, J., and Watkins, R. (1996). What works and what doesn't: Evaluation beyond Kirkpatrick. *Performance & Instruction* 35:2, 8–12.

Kerlinger, F. N. (1986). *Foundations of behavioral research* (3rd ed.). Austin, TX: Holt, Rinehart and Winston.

Kirkpatrick, D. L. (1959). Techniques for evaluating training programs. *Journal of the American Society for Training and Development* 13:11, 3–9.

Kirkpatrick, D. L. (1994). *Evaluating training programs: The four levels.* San Francisco: Berrett-Koehler.

Lachenmaier, L. S., and Moor, W. C. (1997). Using business performance to evaluate multimedia training in manufacturing. *Performance Improvement* 36:7, 16–21.

Miles, M. B., and Huberman, A. M. (1994). *Qualitative data analysis* (2nd ed.). Thousand Oaks, CA: Sage.

Newstrom, J. W. (1995). Evaluating training programs: The four levels. *Human Resource Development Quarterly* 6, 317–320.

Patton, M. Q. (1990). *Qualitative evaluation and research methods* (2nd ed.). Thousand Oaks, CA: Sage.

Reynolds, A. (1993). *The trainer's dictionary.* Amherst, MA: Human Resources Development Press.

Robinson, D. G., and Robinson, J. C. (1989). *Training for impact: How to link training to business needs and measure the results.* San Francisco: Jossey-Bass.

Rutman, L. (1980). *Planning useful evaluations: Evaluability assessment.* Thousand Oaks, CA: Sage.

Schwandt, T. A. (1997). *Qualitative inquiry: A dictionary of terms.* Thousand Oaks, CA: Sage.

Scriven, M. (1967). The methodology of evaluation. In R. E. Stake (ed.), *Curriculum evaluation.* American Educational Research Association Monograph Series on Evaluation, no. 1. Skokie, IL: Rand McNally.

Shrock, S. A., and Coscarelli, W. C. (1989). *Criterion-referenced test development: Technical and legal guidelines for corporate training.* Washington, DC: International Society for Performance Improvement.

Smith, M. E., and Brandenburg, D. C. (1991). Summative evaluation. *Performance Improvement Quarterly* 4:2, 35–58.

Smith, M. E., and Geis, G. L. (1992). Planning an evaluation study. In H. D. Stolovitch and E. J. Keeps (eds.), *Handbook of Human Performance Technology: A comprehensive guide for analyzing and solving performance problems in organizations.* San Francisco: Jossey-Bass.

Smith, M. F. (1989). *Evaluability assessment: A practical approach.* Norwell, MA: Kluwer.

Stake, R. E. (1969). Generalizability of program evaluation: The need for limits. *Educational Product Report* 2:5, 39–40.

Stufflebeam, D. L., and Shinkfield, A. J. (1985). *Systematic evaluation.* Norwell, MA: Kluwer.

Tessmer, M. (1994). Formative evaluation alternatives. *Performance Improvement Quarterly* 7:1, 3–18.

Thiagarajan, S. (1991). Formative evaluation in performance technology. *Performance Improvement Quarterly* 4:2, 22–34.

Torraco, R. J. (1995). In action: Measuring return on investment. *Human Resource Development Quarterly* 6, 424–429.

Wholey, J. L. (1975). *Evaluation: Promise and performance.* Washington, DC: Urban Institute.

Worthen, B. R., and Sanders, J. R. (1987). *Educational evaluation: Alternative approaches and practical guidelines.* White Plains, NY: Longman.

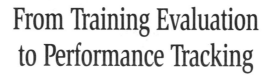

CHAPTER ELEVEN

From Training Evaluation to Performance Tracking

Ogden R. Lindsley

A s Human Performance Technology (HPT) shifts from training to performance improvement, measurement is forced to shift from training evaluation to performance tracking. For the past forty years (that is, since 1959), a paradigm of four levels—reaction, learning, behavior, and results—has ruled our thinking and practice in training evaluation (Kirkpatrick, 1994). Over the same period, out of every one hundred programs, one hundred have measured reaction, seventy have measured learning, fifty have measured job behavior, and only ten have measured business results (Phillips, 1994, p. 8). A *Training* magazine survey from 1996, however, reports that in the 1,400 companies surveyed, eighty-six out of one hundred courses measured reactions, fifty-one measured learning, fifty measured behavior, and forty-four measured results (Industry report, 1996, pp. 36–79). Therefore, this survey reports a big step forward in the measurement of long-neglected business results.

The terms *Standard Change Chart* and *Change Factor Fans,* used in this chapter, are copyrighted and are trademarks of Behavior Research Company for commercial use. Paper-version Standard Change Charts, overhead transparencies, computer templates, and on-site workshops are available from Behavior Research Company, P.O. Box 3351, Kansas City, KS 66103. (Fax: 913–362–5900.) Price lists can be found at *www.onlearn.com/brco.html.*

StatView, a trademark of Abacus Concepts, Inc., Berkeley, California, was used to make the figures that appear in this chapter. Zero Brothers Software offers an on-line course that teaches how to make Standard Change Charts with StatView. Information about Zero Brothers is available at *zerobros@aol.com.* Further information about StatView can be found at *www.sas.com.*

TRACKING IMPACT: RECENT MOVES

Now, at last, we are moving not only toward the measurement of business results but beyond—to the tracking of organizational impact. At many places, we see signs of this shift in the focus of evaluation. Performance tracking is on the move. Performance tracking promises to be fun and exciting and useful for a change. The following four recent examples should whet the reader's appetite for more.

MEASURIT's Tracking Training Impact

In MEASURIT's (1996) two-day seminar program, Tracking Training Impact, a five-level tracking model defines the assessment levels used to quantify training impact. At level 1, critical business issues and needs are assessed before there is any investment in training. This assessment identifies the most cost-effective solution to the presenting problem. All the remaining levels, up to and including level 5 (which assesses training's worth to the organization), are linked to the resolution of the business needs identified at level 1.

Esque and Patterson's *Getting Results*

For years we have needed collections of case studies to give us ideas on how we might track performance improvement in our projects. Of the twenty-two performance improvement case studies reported in Esque and Patterson's *Getting Results* (1998), seven (more than one-third) reported results that had an impact at the organizational level, and two of these reported impacts in terms of dollars in revenue. Twelve cases reported improved job performance. Three reported learning from training, and none reported learners' reactions to training.

Brethower and Smalley's *Performance-Based Instruction*

In their recently published book, Brethower and Smalley write, "Evaluation, from front-end through impact, is part of performance based instruction. In fact, it is the only form of instruction in which Level IV evaluation is routine" (1998, p. 196).

Spitzer's *Super-Evaluation*

Dean Spitzer, an IBM consultant and author of the best-selling management book *SuperMotivation,* is now presenting, at workshops and in consulting engagements, a novel approach to evaluation that he calls *Super-Evaluation* (1998). Evaluation, he says, is usually done entirely after the fact, and he suggests that the very first thing to be done in starting a project is to select the project's desired impact on the organization and use evaluation to mold the project to that desired outcome instead of simply using evaluation to assess consequences at the end. The decision about the desired impact, he says, should always come first, and the project should be designed to achieve that outcome. Thus, throughout the performance improvement project, the desired impact both guides the project and is itself continuously monitored.

MEASURING, MONITORING, AND TRACKING

Measuring, monitoring, and tracking must be clearly distinguished before the shift from conventional measuring to performance tracking can be seen clearly. *Measuring, monitoring,* and *tracking* must not be considered merely new words chosen to escape negative reactions to the word *evaluation;* these three terms must be clearly defined to make our evaluation alternatives clear.

All three are ways to put numbers on performance. These numbers let us see whether our project procedures are improving performance less and less or more and more. We can also use these numbers to see which one of our methods had the biggest and quickest effects on which one of our clients.

Measuring

Measuring is done before, occasionally during, and usually after the performance improvement project. It includes a set of actions to take and is always outside the system being measured. Measuring is what is taught in most conventional measurement and evaluation courses and workshops. Measuring is strong on the theoretical and statistical and weak on the practical. A measurement system is added to the performance being measured. Measuring is not continuous in real, calendar time.

Because measuring is not continuous but is usually done only a few times during a project, workers never adjust to it. Workers react to measuring negatively, as if it were a test. In their experience, tests have most often been followed by punishment rather than rewards.

Monitoring

Several years ago, I described the many differences between measuring and monitoring but did not separate monitoring into external monitoring and self-monitoring or tracking (Lindsley, 1997a). Most of the examples I listed under the rubric of monitoring would now be listed as tracking examples.

Monitoring systems are always outside the performance being improved. Monitoring differs from measuring by being continuous. It records all the time in which performance occurs. Monitoring requires an external recording system that is designed and added to the performance change system. Monitoring systems collect performance numbers as they happen so that corrections can be made in real time before the performance gets too far off course. Because monitoring systems are clearly outside the performing system, they are often suspect and reacted to negatively. Indeed, the word *monitor* itself has negative connotations from school days (hall monitor, playground monitor).

Tracking

Tracking occurs when a counter within the performing system records itself without interfering with the system's performance. Ideally, the performance itself leaves a track, like a rabbit in the snow: the performance records itself. Tracking gives the most accurate and most sensitive performance numbers. Tracking costs the least and disturbs performance the least. Tracking has face validity and is accepted by all workers and managers as an important indicator of performance improvement.

Tracking, like monitoring, continuously records performance, and so trends are clearly displayed. Clear trend displays make baselines unnecessary because jumps and turns in the trend line that have been produced by performance improvement methods are clearly seen. Baselines still add information about the trends before the performance improvement project, but they are no longer required to demonstrate results of the method.

KEEPING IT SIMPLE

A related shift has occurred, from academic and statistically sophisticated measurement to simple practical methods easy for workers to use on the shop floor. This shift away from the barren, hard-to-learn academic measures occurs even in level 1 participant reaction evaluations.

For example, the National Society for Performance and Instruction (NSPI), later the International Society for Performance Improvement (ISPI), used, for decades, a traditional standard nine-item session evaluation at its annual conferences, with a 5-point Likert scale. Participants circled a point for each item to record their reactions to the annual conference presentations. It was simple, it was standard, and it got done. The circled numbers on the ordinal Likert scales were averaged. (This bothered some of us purists because it was mathematically incorrect: medians would have been more accurate for the ordinal data.) The averaged results were interpreted by ISPI's program committee in making decisions about inviting presenters to return or to qualify to present different topics at the next year's conference. For the 1998 conference, however, ISPI changed its session evaluation form to a twenty-one-item checklist. The items on the checklist describe program committee interests directly. Simple totals of the number of checks to each of the twenty-one items give much more accurate information to the program committee than did the Likert scale averages of nine questions.

Using the old Likert scales, the ISPI program committee had to interpret when the overall average of the nine items was 4.67, to determine whether to invite a presenter to return to the convention. Now, when the committee reads that sixty-two out of sixty-eight participants checked the twentieth checklist item ("I believe this session should be presented next year in the Encore track that repeats the best sessions at this conference"), interpretation is unnecessary. Simple is better.

KISSING PERFORMANCE TRACKING HELLO

In aviation cadet training during World War II, I first heard that the KISS acronym means "*Keep it simple, stupid!*" But this shift to performance tracking involves more than just simplification; we must add four more features to simplicity. The acronym KISSING helps us remember all five of the features required to make performance tracking powerful: *Keep it simple, standard, impactful, natural,* and *graphic.*

S for Simple

Our performance tracking system should be so simple that if it has to be taught, it has to be taught only once. According to Donald A. Norman, head of the Appliance Design Center in the Consumer Products Group at Hewlett-Packard, the goal "is not to have zero training, but to have one-time training. If I don't quite understand a computer system immediately... and someone shows me, ... I never have to have it explained again" (Dickelman, 1998, p. 37).

Most of us have had to have conventional evaluation methods explained to us over and over and over again. By our new simplicity criterion, however, this is unacceptable. Job aids and checklists are simpler than flowcharts and rating scales. Recent books on HPT are full of checklists and case examples. Fuller (1997) features many realistic case studies, along with many assessment tools and checklists to simplify things for readers. Brethower and Smalley (1998) also include many examples, job aids, and checklists—even a computer disk, to make printing the checklists easy by eliminating the need to keyboard or photocopy.

Most of us spent hard years and hard cash in universities learning to write and talk in four- and five-syllable academic jargon. Academic talk is the hallmark of the learned professional specialist. With so much invested in our jargon, it is very hard for us to talk and write plain English to our clients and their workers. (For example, terminology from the field of behavior analysis had to be translated into plain English before Precision Teaching could become widespread; see Lindsley, 1991.) Mager (1986, p. 97) gives his manuscripts to two twelve-year-olds and asks them to draw a circle around any words they do not yet know; he reports that one-third of the circled words can be replaced by words that everyone knows. Mager's books are so beautifully clear that they are in great demand and have been easily translated into many foreign languages. Our information explosion has put even greater pressure on us to use short, clear, plain English words. The term *evaluation* has five syllables, whereas *tracking* has two; *sudden shift in level* has six syllables, whereas *jump* has one; *change in trend* has three syllables, whereas *turn* has one. In his *Super-Evaluation* presentations, Spitzer (1998) quotes Albert Einstein as follows: "Everything should be as simple as possible . . . but no simpler."

S for Standard

Every minute of every day our lives are governed and made easier by standards. Our buildings are made of beams of standard width and thickness. Our hats, dresses, trousers, shoes, and rings come in standard sizes. Everything we use— hand tools, furniture, utilities, appliances, vehicles, and computers—is designed, built, and used according to standards. Standards are vital to our society.

We use standard terms, methods, and analysis procedures in HPT. We use the standard seven, plus or minus two, in making our training lists and job aids (Miller, 1956). However, we do not use standard evaluation measures. Much has been written on the need for educational standards, but little real standardization has been done (Dean, 1994).

Imai (1997, p. xviii) tells how the Japanese *Gemba Kaizen* (workplace quality and production control) has three ground rules: housekeeping, elimination of waste, and standardization. Good housekeeping cuts the failure rate in half; standardization cuts that failure rate in half again, to one-quarter of the original failure rate.

The 5-point Likert scale came close to being a standard, and that is why it was used, but it produced very poor numbers that did little to improve performance. Percentage measures are also very popular and close to being a standard, but percentage measures are also very crude and weak performance measures. Percentage measures describe only the relationship between two things; they ignore the size of those two things. (We will return shortly to the dangers of using percentage measures.)

HINIBU and Ego Block Standard Measures. HINIBU stands for "Horrible If Not Invented By Us." It is a disease found in universities, small businesses, and even some large corporations. People infected with HINIBU cannot try anything new unless they have changed it enough to make it look as if they invented it in house. We all know that we should put our clients' corporate logos on the reports and materials we develop for them. However, we must be very careful not to let corporate personalization change the tracking system to the point that it is no longer standard.

Frequency: A Universal Standard. Without a doubt, the only possible across-the-board performance standard is frequency: How many of what thing happened in how much time? Each happening of everything in the world that happens can be counted. All counts cover a counting time. Every count divided by its counting time gives a frequency. Therefore, one thing's frequency can be used to compare it with the frequency of other things like it, or of things very different from it.

For example, the average six-year-old laughs three hundred times a day. Adults laugh between fifteen and one hundred times a day. Therefore, children laugh over three times more than adults. The normal blink rate for someone speaking on television is 31 to 50 blinks per minute (bpm). In the televised debates during the 1996 presidential campaign, Bill Clinton averaged 99 bpm, and Bob Dole averaged 147 bpm. Therefore, to judge on the basis of observed blinking, Clinton appeared twice as nervous, and Dole three times more nervous, than the most nervous of televised speakers.

We should almost always track quality by counting how many good things happened and how many bad things happened and then charting them separately. We should also use the natural counting times of our daily life and work. These times are number per minute, per hour, per day, per week, per month, per quarter, and per year. According to Skinner (1950), "Rate [frequency] is a universal datum." By this Skinner meant that everything in the universe has a frequency that can be counted and that occurs in time. Therefore, frequency provides a standard for comparison.

Frequency: A Dimension of Performance. Research has taken us beyond Skinner in demonstrating that frequency is a dimension of performance. This means that changing the frequency changes the performance.

Try this little experiment to convince yourself of this fact. Take a plain piece of paper and write down your starting time. Now write your signature as slowly as possible. Just barely move your pencil, writing letters as slowly as one or two a minute. Keep slowly writing your signature. After ten minutes, stop and look at your signature. What you wrote is your signature as you used to write it when you were in the third grade; it was in you all these years, stored at a very low frequency. Now write your current signature as many times as possible in one minute. Count up the number of letters written per minute in both conditions. Your third-grade signature should have been produced at the rate of 2 to 4 letters per minute; your current signature should have been produced at the rate of 150 to 220 letters per minute.

If you change the frequency of writing, you change the form of your signature. If the frequency of light waves is changed, the color of the light changes. If the frequency of sound waves changes, the tone of the sound changes. Just as frequency is a dimension of light and sound, frequency is also a dimension of performance. For a performance to be fully described, its frequency must be described.

This is why training people to high frequencies of performance makes them fluent. The form and control of the performance will change at high frequencies. Fluency produces more retention, more application, more stability, and more confidence (Binder, 1990, 1996). The guidelines and demands that fluency places on instructional design have been recently detailed (Lindsley, 1997b).

In short, what is standard is easier to do right. What is standard gets done. The best standard for performance is frequency.

I for Impactful

This chapter began with a description of a shift in focus for training evaluation, from a focus on the four levels of evaluation (Kirkpatrick, 1994) to a focus on evaluating the organizational impact of training. Four examples (MEASURIT, 1996; Esque and Patterson, 1998; Brethower and Smalley, 1998; Spitzer, 1998) illustrated this shift.

When we shift the focus to organizational impact, we must be careful to choose frequencies that we can use as guides to improve our project while we go along. The majority (forty-seven out of fifty-eight) of the projects included in three collections of impact projects (Phillips, 1994, 1997; Esque and Patterson, 1998) reported only before-and-after impact measures. Such measures justify a project to management, but they cannot guide performance improvers during the project. Only eleven of these fifty-eight projects (or just under one out of five) included continuous tracking data. Of these eleven, eight tracked months, one tracked quarters, and two tracked years. These times are not short enough to guide improvement accurately. Weekly frequencies are better, and daily frequencies are best for continuous feedback to guide workers. A daily chart appears in Esque and Patterson (1998), but it charts "cumulative percent of quota," which makes it impossible to reclaim the original frequencies for comparing or recharting.

Phillips (1994, 1997) advocates using return on investment (ROI) to measure organizational impact. The ROI percentage is equal to 100 times the quotient that is produced when net program benefits are divided by program costs. The suggested advantage of using ROI as a measure is that chief executives will have training impact reported to them in terms of the same financial figures that they have used for other investments. Because ROI usually cannot be computed until after a project is completed, however, it cannot guide the project en route. Therefore, it is an impact measure that seldom can be used for tracking.

In summary, only one-fifth of our published projects that measure impact track the impact continuously enough to guide project improvement. Of those that do, almost none track the weekly and daily frequencies that are most effectively used to improve projects.

N for Natural

The original, natural numbers that a performance system kicks out should not be transformed. This is the major strategic error made by most designers of management information systems: unable to leave nature alone, they "cook" the original numbers in attempts to focus attention on relationships between them. But, just as cooking vegetables causes them to lose much of their original flavor and texture, "cooking" original performance frequencies causes loss of the details and the sensitivity to change that are needed to guide performance improvement projects. Esque and Patterson (1998, p. 44) offer several examples of "cooked" data; a complete list would be very long.

The Dangers of Using Percentage Measures. Of the twenty-one data charts in Daniels (1989), nine measure percentages; of the seven performance data series in Daniels (1994), five measure percentages; nine of the twenty-two cases reported in Esque and Patterson (1998) measure percentages.

Percentage measures are often your client's favorite measures of performance. However, percentage measures are insensitive to changes in performance and are actually dangerous to use. Skinner was aware of the problems with percentage measures when he wrote, "Do not spend time on articles in which graphs show changes in the time, or number of errors to reach a criterion, or percent of correct choices made" (1969, p. 93). Holzschuh (1966) spent two years of full-time postdoctoral research comparing percentage measures and measures of how frequently students produced correct responses, to see how sensitive each measure was to changes in classroom curriculum. He concludes that percentage measures are "the worst thing that ever happened to education." One of my own most successful workshops (Lindsley, 1994) deals with the dangers of percentage measures and how to avoid them.

One common impact measure that a client may long have been recording is percentage or ratio of some standard, or percentage of a company aim or quota. When given percentages, we should try to locate the original numbers from which the percentages were calculated. The original, natural numbers are best for tracking performance improvement throughout the project. Because clients often love their percentages, we should not ask them to throw their percentages away. We should just locate the original numbers for tracking performance and then share both the originals and the percentages with our clients.

People think they understand and know how to use percentages, but they do not. In the mathematics section of standard achievement tests taken by both children and adults, eight out of ten of the errors are in calculating and interpreting percentages. Moreover, on a test of percentage problems, Parker and Leinhardt (1995) found that fewer than half of preservice teachers scored higher than 50 percent correct. Percentages are hard to grasp because they use language like *more than, less than, increased by,* and *decreased by,* which both hides the multiplication-related meanings of percentages and suggests a nonexistent symmetry. Because percentages are so hard to grasp, errors in calculating percentages also appear in many professional publications. For example, there is a percentage-calculation error in data reported by Esque and Patterson (1998), and there is another in Phillips (1994). (Try to find them!)

The Dangers of Averages. Shewhart, who originated Statistical Process Control (SPC) at Bell laboratories, writes, "It is well to keep in mind that numbers and order are the two aspects of original data that are amenable to mathematical analysis" ([1939] 1986, p. 90). If the traditional root-mean-square formula for the standard deviation is used to determine the upper and lower control limits, then the control charts are not sensitive to variations, because the order in the original data series is lost through the averaging process. The formula used to set SPC control limits, however, retains the order from the original data and is sensitive to variance outliers. Shewhart goes on to say, "It was the order that furnished the clue to the presence of assignable causes of variability that were later found and removed" (p. 90).

This means that original data should not be averaged; original frequencies should be kept intact. According to Shewhart ([1939] 1986), averaging destroys order, and order represents half the value of your data. This also means that graphs are necessary if the order in original data series is to be maintained, and that time-series graphs display changes more sensitively than do other types of graphs or tables.

G for Graphic

Is a picture worth a thousand words? Research has shown that charts have higher impact on readers than text-based pages do, that recall and comprehension are higher with charts, and that complex data relationships are more easily shown with charts. For example, Daniels (1994, p. 101) notes the ease with which employees can use graphic media for daily feedback, and Imai (1997, p. 249) reports the managerial power of companywide visual displays. He also describes (p. 114) the procedure known as *asaichi* (morning market), in which every morning, before work, factory rejects from the day before are displayed on a table, and countermeasures are adopted on the spot. This description matches Tosti's (1978) and Lindsley's (1995) ideas about telling workers what to do and what not to do just before their next chance to perform. Therefore, charts displaying the previous day's performance should be shared and discussed by the workers in a group at the start of each work day. Unfortunately, however, graphical power is not yet used by most human performance (HP) technologists. They visually display many flowcharts and diagrams of their procedures but almost no time-series data charts showing the effects of those procedures.

USING FILL-THE-FRAME CHARTS

Just as it is easy to lie with statistics (Huff, 1954), it is easy to lie with charts unless the charts themselves are standard. Most of us were taught to make charts by stretching our data to fill the frame of a chart. We made a rectangle with the number of what was being measured up the left side, and with the time over which it was measured across the bottom. No standards were given to us for what size the rectangle should be, what numbers should be used up the left side, or what units of time (minutes, days, weeks, months, or years) should be across the bottom. Most of us naturally draw a rectangle just big enough to contain our data points. Most of us also made the numbers add up on the left and across the bottom.

These fill-the-frame charts are what almost all computer graphing programs make for us. The user has no control over the exact size of the chart frame, and so the horizontal and vertical frame proportions cannot be set; the range of the data values controls the size of the horizontal and vertical sides of the frame. Fill-the-frame charts maximize the possibilities for seeing the details of data, but they also cause small changes in one chart to look just as big as large changes in another chart.

USING STANDARD CHANGE CHARTS

Ideally, performance improvement in industry should be tracked on standard charts, just as performance is tracked for students in Precision Teaching classrooms (see Linsley, 1997b). Facts that set the stage for designing standard change charts, as well as the features and benefits of the charts themselves, are described in the following sections.

Facts That Set the Stage

Five facts from three different sources set the stage for designing standard charts to track performance change:

1. Frequency can be used to track any and all performances (Skinner, 1950).

2. Every performance changes by multiplying or dividing (Meadows, Meadows, Randers, and Behrens, 1972).

3. Ratio charts are the best at showing rate of change and percentages (Schmid, 1954).

4. Standard chart slopes make reading change easy (Skinner, 1938).

5. Self-charting makes performance tracking affordable (Skinner, 1938).

In 1965, these five facts were combined in an effort to design a standard slope chart called the Standard Behavior Chart, named for what was charted on it (see Pennypacker, Koenig, and Lindsley, 1972). Although the chart was intended for use in an education context, it was not yet free of its developers' background in experimental psychology. Later on, it became clear that only the slope of the chart, and not its use, was standard; users began to chart many things other than behavior. After a name change, the Standard Behavior Chart became the Standard Celeration Chart (SCC), and the latter term is still its technical name, although in this chapter it will be referred to as the Standard Change Chart. Frequency measures are situated up the left side of the chart, and the standard slope represents change in frequency, or *celeration* (the term had to be coined). Upward slopes show acceleration, and downward slopes show deceleration.

Dimensions

In order for the full-size paper SCC to fit on slides, overhead screens, and standard-size notebook paper, its frame was made 8 inches wide and 5.3 inches high. So that most of a school semester could be fit onto one sheet, the horizontal time add scale covered 140 days, or twenty weeks. In order to include the full range of daily HP frequency, a vertical "multiply times 10" ($\times 10$) scale (base 10 log) showed a spread from one instance per day (.001 per minute) to 1,000,000 instances per day (1,000 per minute).

Slopes

The chart's proportions were also carefully selected so that a line drawn from the lower left corner to the upper right corner would indicate a doubling (times 2) in performance each week. This is an angle of 34 degrees. A line drawn from the upper left to the lower right corner of the frame shows a halving (a division by 2) of performance each week. The angles and meanings are symmetrical. Performance changing half as steep going only halfway up the chart in twenty weeks shows times 1.4 growth per week (an angle of 19 degrees). Performance changing twice as steep as times 2 would go all the way to the top of the chart in only ten weeks, multiplying times 4 each week (an angle of 53 degrees). Performance changing even steeper would go all the way up the chart in only five weeks, multiplying times 16 each week (an angle of 69 degrees).

If the proportions of these dimensions are kept standard, the SCC can be enlarged or reproduced to any size for presentation and publication without any change in the angle and meaning of the slopes and change factors. What *is* standard is the slopes and their meanings, not the physical size of the chart's frames.

These frame dimensions and change-factor angles are maintained for charts covering the various units of time: the daily, weekly, monthly, and yearly charts all have the same proportions and the same change-factor angles. This means that learning one set of change factors allows one to work with any and all units of time and all kinds of corporate organization. For example, the worker who has learned how to read her daily chart can easily read and understand her supervisor's weekly chart, her manager's monthly chart, and the yearly financial charts in the company annual report.

The factors related to decay in performance work in the same way except that they go down the chart rather than up. This symmetry makes it very easy to learn both growth and decay factors at once. These benchmark change factors are easily learned by adults in a one-day standard charting workshop. If the learners stand, hold their arms out at the correct angles, and repeat the particular factors as a leader calls them out at a pace of thirty per minute, they rapidly feel and learn the chart slopes; first-grade schoolchildren learn them in a few weeks of charting ten minutes per day.

Standard Self-Improvement Charts

Skinner (1938) taught his rats to produce their own standard performance frequencies on his cumulative response recorders. The standard slopes of these records displayed performance rate, or frequency. Following his lead, practitioners of Precision Teaching taught schoolchildren to chart their own daily performance on Standard Change Charts (see Duncan, 1971). The standard slopes of these charts displayed performance change, or weekly learning. Plotting hits and misses on their standard charts let the children track not only their own daily performance and accuracy but also their own weekly "hit" and "miss" learning (Pennypacker, Koenig, and Lindsley, 1972). "Hit" refers to a rate of correct performance; "miss" refers to a rate of incorrect performance. "Hit" learning is independent of "miss" learning. If a child's learning slope was shallow, the child changed something or asked another student for help. If nothing helped, the child called on the teacher for learning advice.

Standard Effectiveness Results

At the Morningside Academy (Seattle), and at Malcolm X College (Chicago), students chart their own performance and aim at doubling it each week. The results of these learning aims, combined with curricula designed to support such rapid learning, permit schools to give a money-back guarantee that students will gain two grade levels in their subject matter each year (Johnson and Layng, 1992).

Standard Efficiency Results

Standard Change Charts permit comparison of effects across departments and years. Workers do not have to stop and figure out each new chart. Precision Teachers have used the charts since 1970; therefore, in 1998, a practitioner of Precision Teaching or a child in a regular elementary classroom can instantly read a Standard Change Chart for a student who was in special education at a Montessori school in 1970.

SCCs save precious time because they can be read in one minute. Regular standard chart sharings are held every year at the annual conference of the Association for Behavior Analysis. For over ten years, each chart sharer was given two minutes at the overhead projector to present his or her chart. In 1998 the time was reduced to one minute, with no real loss in audience comprehension. One minute is enough time to read a chart because everyone in the room is familiar with the standard chart slopes and conventions.

Standard Statistical Results

SCCs make the upward bounces in data equal the downward bounces because frequencies bounce proportionally. Statisticians call this *normalizing the variance*. SCCs also make the total bounce the same size at low frequencies as at high frequencies. Statisticians call this *equalizing the variance*.

SCCs straighten out the concave upward performance change curves that are always seen with performance changes on add-scale charts. These straight lines make it easy to project and see where the performance will end up.

COMPARING STANDARD WITH FILL-THE-FRAME CHARTS

Many statisticians and managers of management information systems think, when they see a Standard Change Chart, that the SCC is merely a logarithmic chart of data. This is not true. To make the difference clear, I have prepared six standard charts, together with a fill-the-frame add chart and a fill the frame multiply (log 10) chart, of the same performance data time series. A comparison of these different chart views will show how Standard Change Charts make it easy to read changes from performance improvement charts.

The StatView statistical program (available for both Macintosh and PC environments) permits the exact chart frame size to be set and the axis type and ranges to be selected. This program also permits many different charts and views of a data set to be made, with no need to reenter the data. Therefore, a Standard Change Chart, a fill-the-frame add scale, and a fill-the-frame multiply scale chart for each data set can be made.

Figure 11.1 shows three charts of a subject named Dane learning SAFMEDS cards by practicing at least one minute each day. (The SAFMEDS acronym stands for "Say All Fast a Minute Each Day Shuffled." It was coined to ensure that learners would practice saying the whole stack of seventy to one hundred cards, practiced daily at fifty per minute, with the deck shuffled after each practice; see Graf, 1994.)

The top view of Figure 11.1 shows a Standard Change Chart with its Change Factor Fan of nine easy-to-recall change factors in the box to its right. To judge the amount of change in a plotted line of data, estimate the change factor by

Figure 11.1. Dane Learns Cards to Fluency on Daily Chart.

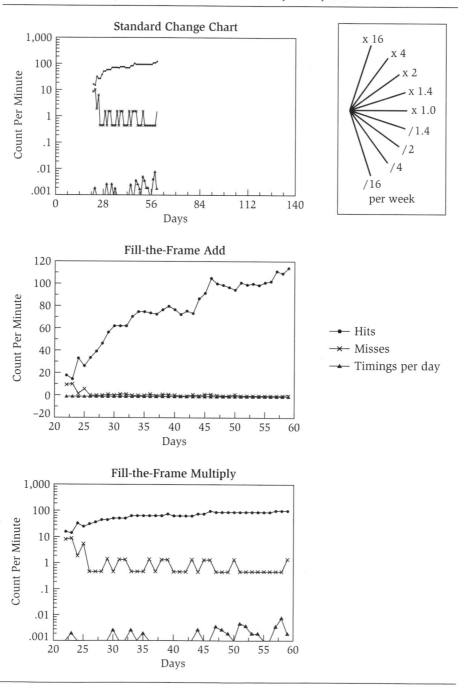

using the fan blades as guides. Note that Dane's hits accelerated at ×2 per week, up to about 80 per minute. Then his hits multiplied at less than ×1.4 per week, up to his fluency of over 110 per minute. Dane's misses divided at about 16 per week, going from 11 to 0 in one week. The misses then bounced from 1 to 0 per minute. On about fifteen days he practiced more than one one-minute timing each day in his attempts to get over 100 hits per minute. For a discussion of fluency and its advantages, see Binder (1990, 1996).

Look at the fill-the-frame add chart in the middle frame. The counts per minute can be read clearly, but the learning slope factors cannot be read unless they are calculated from the counts, because there is no Change Factor Fan, and the one at the top right applies only to Standard Change Charts. Looking at the fill-the-frame multiply chart in the bottom frame does not help, either.

Figure 11.2 shows three charts of a subject named Davis learning SAFMEDS cards, using the same cards and following the same instructions as Dane received. Note from the top Standard Change Chart that Davis's hits accelerated at a little less than ×1.4 per week for about seventy-five days. Then, for about twenty days, they leveled off at 25 to 28 per minute, with no acceleration (×1 per week). Note also that Davis's misses bounced along at 1 to 4 per minute: he practiced only one one-minute timing a day throughout.

Note that in a comparison of Dane's and Davis's fill-the-frame add charts, not much difference is seen unless the numbers on the charts' vertical axes are read. Their fill-the-frame multiply charts also do not look very different unless the axis numbers are read.

The three views shown in Figure 11.3 display the weekly frequency of shoes that conformed to specifications and shoes that had defects; the shoes were produced by the Wongpaitoon Footwear Company (WFC) in Thailand. At the start, the company was fifth in quality among twelve Reebok manufacturers in Thailand. After performance management, it was first in quality among thirty Reebok manufacturers worldwide (Sulzer-Azaroff and Harshbarger, 1995).

Note that the Change Factor Fan blades and values in the box in the upper right of Figure 11.3 are the same as the ones in Figures 11.1 and 11.2 except that the fan in Figure 11.3 says "per month" at the bottom, whereas in Figure 11.2 the fan says "per week" at the bottom. The angles and values of the blades are the same, but on the daily chart the change factors are given on a per-week basis, and on the weekly chart the change factors are given on a per-month basis.

Look at the Standard Change Chart in the top left frame, and see that there was no acceleration in shoes that met specifications. The number of defective shoes decelerated at a little less than "divide by 1.4" (/1.4) each month for about twenty weeks. Because the deceleration in defects had not leveled off, the program could have continued and achieved even higher levels of quality.

Figure 11.2. Davis Learns Cards, but Not to Fluency, on Daily Chart.

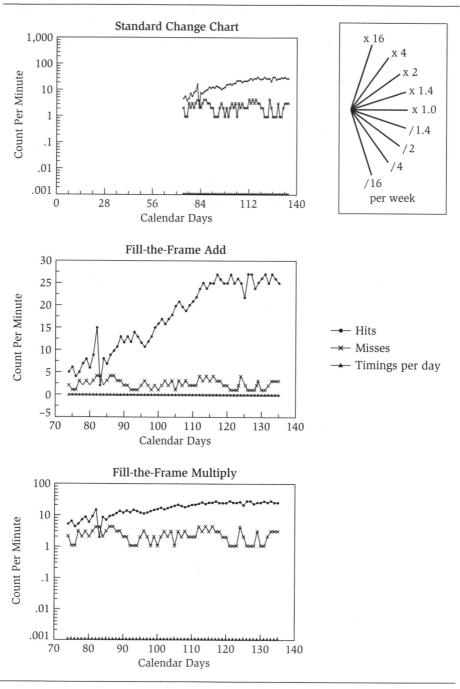

Figure 11.3. Quality in Reebok Plant on Weekly Chart.

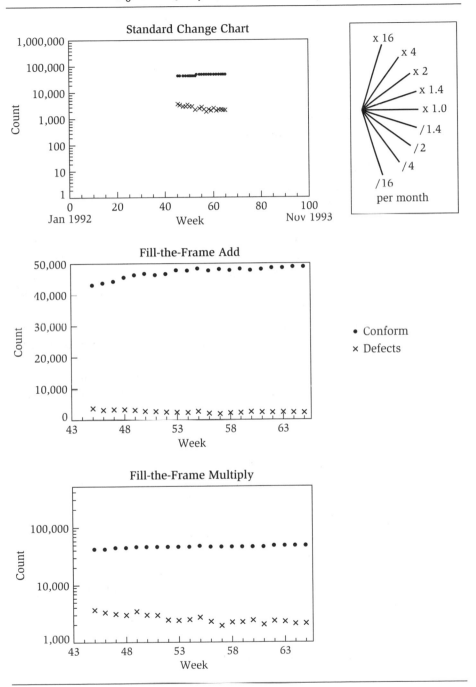

Looking only at the fill-the-frame add chart in the center of Figure 11.3 would be very reassuring because it looks as if 98 out of 100 shoes conformed to specifications. The quality goal would appear to have been reached, and performance improvement efforts might stop.

However, look back at the Standard Change Chart at the top, and see that the defects are still decelerating and are still at 2,000 per week. A projection of this deceleration suggests that if the program were continued, the defects would be down to 1,000 per week by November 1993 and maybe even down to 100 per week by November 1994. This forecasting is the great advantage of straight-line projection.

In Figure 11.4, we see three views of line assembly failures in parts per million (ppm) in the dip-soldering process at the Yokagawa Hewlett-Packard (YHP) plant. In five years, from August 1977 to July 1982, assembly failures were taken from 4,000 to 3 ppm (Imai, 1997, pp. 41–43).

Note that the Change Factor Fan blades in the upper right box are the same as those in Figures 11.1, 11.2, and 11.3 except here the change factors are per six-month periods. The charts shifted from daily to weekly to monthly data, with no new angles or factors to learn. Just remember that on the monthly chart, the change factors are for six-month periods.

The top view once again shows the failures on a Standard Change Chart. Note that the failures divide by about 4 every six months, up to sixty months, the start of 1980. Their deceleration line best fits the /4 blade on the Change Factor Fan. The failures were brought down to 40 ppm. During this first phase YHP improved working standards, collected and analyzed defect data, introduced process-control jigs, trained workers, encouraged quality-control circles, and reduced workers' careless mistakes. Jumps in deceleration are caused by the start of one of these actions.

Still in the top view, find the second phase in failure deceleration as the line turns from /4 up to /1.4 every six months, from the sixtieth month to the ninetieth month (in July 1982). In this second phase, YHP applied new technologies, revised engineering standards, improved PC board designs and production layout, and added just-in-time concepts. These procedures decreased YHP assembly line failures to only 3 ppm.

Looking at the fill-the-frame add chart in the center, note the decrease in failures up to about the sixtieth month, but the curve is concave upward and cannot be projected. The chart shows almost no decrease from the sixtieth to the ninetieth month. The add scale hides the valuable deceleration in failures during the second phase of the program. If the add scale were used to track improvement, it would look as if no further improvement could occur, and no further attempts to improve quality would be made.

The fill-the-frame multiply chart at the bottom of Figure 11.4 shows fair straight-line deceleration, but the upward turn at the sixtieth month is not as

Figure 11.4. Quality at Yokagawa Hewlett-Packard on Monthly Chart.

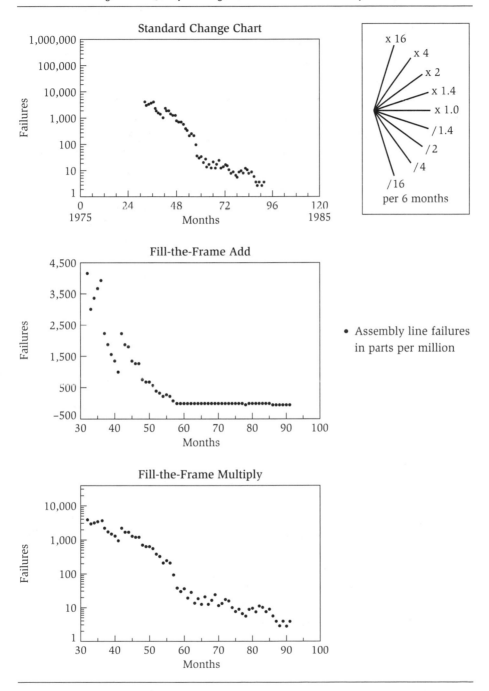

clear as in the Standard Change Chart at the top. Moreover, the deceleration factors cannot be easily read because no Change Factor Fan exists for a fill-the-frame chart.

By doing some simple arithmetic, compare the monthly failure reduction of /1.4 at the Wangpaitoon Footware Company (WFC) in Figure 11.3 with the six-monthly /4 assembly line failure at Yokagawa Hewlett-Packard (YHP) in Figure 11.4. The monthly /1.4 must be multiplied by itself six times to find out how big a division factor it would be if carried on for six months. This comes out to be /7.5 per six months. Divide WFC's /7.5 by YHP's /4 per 6 months and get 1.9. This means WFC's defect deceleration was 1.9 times more effective than the first phase of YHP's assembly line failure deceleration. Again, WFC may have stopped its quality effort too soon.

The three views shown in Figure 11.5 depict the number of formal internal complaints of sexual harassment at Healthcare, Inc., a large hospital chain (Hill and Phillips, 1997). A sexual harassment prevention workshop conducted during the month of October is indicated by the arrow on each chart view.

The standard Change Factor Fan for monthly charts is in the upper right box. The Standard Change Chart at the top shows the formal internal complaints multiplying by less than the ×1.4 fan blade and by more than the ×1.0 blade at an estimated factor of about ×1.1 every six months. After the workshop, the complaints decelerated at /2 with a slight upward turn at the end. The upward turn means the effect may have worn off in one year, and that another workshop probably should have been conducted. Further, the high turnover in healthcare staff gives another reason for repeating this workshop. Although not as steep as the /4 per six months at Yokagawa Hewlett-Packard shown in Figure 11.4, this harassment deceleration of /2 is half as big, and not bad for a single prevention workshop.

The deceleration in formal internal harassment complaints shown in the fill-the-frame add chart in the middle, and the fill-the-frame multiply chart at the bottom, show more detail and exaggerate the workshop effect but make it almost impossible to compute the change factors. The fill-the-frame charts also make it look as if the harassment deceleration was as steep as the assembly line failure deceleration in Figure 11.4.

The three views shown in Figure 11.6 depict the acceleration in employee suggestions implemented and those not implemented each year, along with the number of employees at Toyota. Over the course of thirty-five years, from 1951 to 1986, Toyota's implemented suggestions went from 181 per year to 2,542,762. The suggestions not implemented went from 608 to 105,948. The number of employees grew from 7,890 to 55,529.

The Change Factor Fan in the upper right box is now per five years for the yearly Standard Change Chart. The yearly Standard Change Chart in the upper

Figure 11.5. Sexual Harassment Prevention on Monthly Chart.

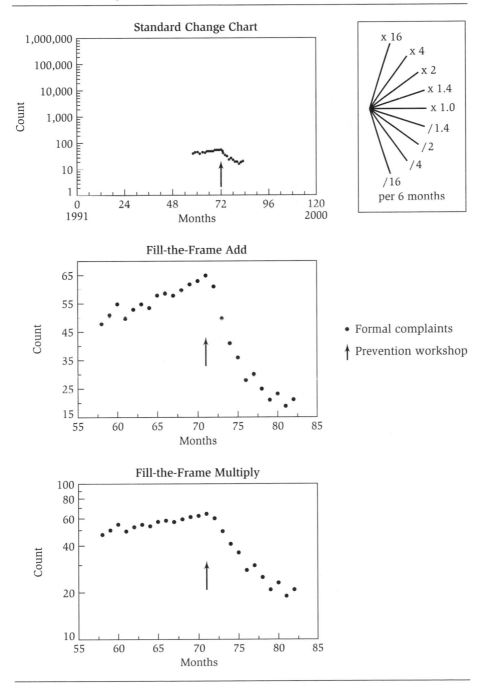

Figure 11.6. Toyota Employee Suggestions on Yearly Chart.

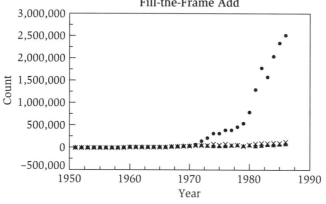

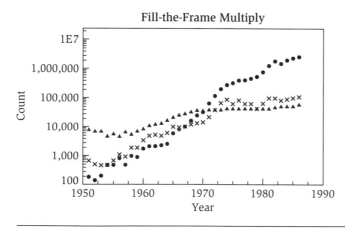

frame extends one hundred years, from 1950 to 2050. Note that the implemented suggestions have fairly consistently multiplied by 4 every five years. From 1951 to 1972, the suggestions not implemented multiplied at about the same factor as the implemented suggestions: by 4 every five years. Note also that the suggestions not implemented started out in the first few years above the implemented. Since 1972, the suggestions not implemented have been below the implemented suggestions and are multiplying at only about 1.1 every five years. This is the same factor as the recent employee growth.

As usual, the fill-the-frame add chart in the middle view gives us little information on the lower early values hidden by the increases since 1970. Also as usual, the fill-the-frame multiply chart in the bottom view shows an expanded view of what appears in the Standard Change Chart, but it does this at the expense of preventing familiar standard change factors, which immediately tell the size of the growth. It also gives no room for projecting the growth lines to future values.

TRACKING PERFORMANCE

Perhaps the most useful way to close this chapter is to offer a job aid (see Exhibit 11.1) to help in tracking performance. Remember the KISSING acronym when you are choosing what to count and chart for impact charts. Chart the daily or weekly impact of performance improvement procedures while using them, and improve procedures while working. Do not be trapped by procedural details chosen at the start of the project; instead, focus and refine your methods by tracking their results in action. A time-tested Precision Teaching slogan from the 1970s provides a fitting close: "Care enough to chart."

References

Binder, C. V. (1990, Sept.). Closing the confidence gap. *Training*, pp. 49–56.

Binder, C. V. (1996). Behavioral fluency: Evolution of a new paradigm. *Behavior Analyst* 19:2, 163–198.

Brethower, D., and Smalley, K. (1998). *Performance-based instruction: Linking training to business results.* San Francisco: Jossey-Bass.

Daniels, A. C. (1989). *Performance management: Improving quality and productivity through positive reinforcement* (3rd ed.). Tucker, GA: Performance Management Publication.

Daniels, A. C. (1994). *Bringing out the best in people.* New York: McGraw-Hill.

Exhibit 11.1. Performance-Tracking Job Aid.

Step	Action
1	Determine business issues and needs from focus groups.
2	Locate current business records of daily or weekly frequencies that would track these needs.
3	Reclaim original numbers if record is a percentage or "cooked" data.
4	Have workers tally at their workstations to create records for prime business needs not routinely recorded by your client.
5	Pinpoint a "quality pair"—something to do more often, and something to do less often—for each need. Pairs make for quality and accuracy.
6	Pinpoint accomplishment pairs that pass Gilbert's "Leave-It Test."[a]
7	Pinpoint behavior pairs that pass Lindsley's "Dead Man Test."[b]
8	Chart daily or weekly frequency pairs on Standard Change Charts.
9	Chart percentage records on add scales if business has recorded them.
10	For permanent storage, have numbers entered in a spreadsheet on a laptop by someone from the records office who attends chart-share meetings.
11	Post charts prominently in the workplace so that workers will see them in passing several times each day.
12	Post several copies of the same chart if team members use different locations (for example, one outside the men's room and another outside the women's room).
13	Have workers chart data, and have supervisors check charting accuracy.
14	Rotate charters, and guarantee that all will have a chance to chart and read charts.
15	Chart each frequency when it is reported, and share all charts (both frequencies and percentages) with workers and supervisors.
16	Share charts at the start of each day or week, rather than at the end.
17	Ask all workers for possible causes of all very good or bad days.
18	Act at once on employee suggestions to improve performance on the basis of charted good or bad days.
19	Mark change dates on charts with symbols for new procedures when they are begun.
20	Discuss changes in performance produced by procedural changes at the next morning's chart-share meeting.
21	Act today on new additions or corrections to the procedure decided on during the morning chart-share meeting.
22	Throughout the project, continue changing to improve.

[a]If you can leave it behind at the plant when you go home at the end of the day, it is an accomplishment. (For example, increased safety awareness is not an accomplishment. You take it with you when you go home at night.)

[b]If a dead man can do it, it is not a behavior. Do not waste time and money trying to produce it. (For example, accident-free days do not pass the "Dead Man Test." The dead never have accidents.)

Dean, P. J. (ed.). (1994). *Performance engineering at work.* Batavia, IL: International Board of Standards for Training, Performance, and Instruction.

Dickelman, G. J. (1998). Defending human attributes in the pursuit of performance-centered design: An interview with Donald A. Norman. *Performance Improvement* 37:4, 34–37.

Duncan, A. (1971). Precision Teaching in perspective: An interview with Ogden R. Lindsley. *Teaching Exceptional Children* 3:3, 114–119.

Esque, T. J., and Patterson, P. A. (eds.). (1998). *Getting results: Case studies in performance improvement.* Amherst, MA, and Washington, DC: Human Resources Development Press and International Society for Performance Improvement.

Fuller, J. (1997). *Managing performance improvement projects: Preparing, planning, and implementing.* San Francisco: Jossey-Bass/Pfeiffer.

Graf, S. A. (1994). *How to develop, produce, and use SAFMEDS in education and training.* Poland, OH: Zero Brothers Software.

Hill, D., and Phillips, J. J. (1997). Healthcare, Inc. In J. J. Phillips (ed.), *In action: Measuring return on investment* (2nd ed.). Alexandria, VA: American Society for Training and Development.

Holzschuh, R. D. (1966). *Superiority of rate correct over percent correct.* Unpublished manuscript, University of Kansas Medical Center.

Huff, D. (1954). *How to lie with statistics.* New York: Norton.

Imai, M. (1997). *Gemba Kaizen: A commonsense, low-cost approach to management.* New York: McGraw-Hill.

Industry Report. (1996). *Training* 33.10, 29.

Johnson, K. R., and Layng, T.V.J. (1992). Breaking the structuralist barrier: Literacy and numeracy with fluency. *American Psychologist* 47:11, 1475–1490.

Kirkpatrick, D. L. (1994). *Evaluating training programs: The four levels.* San Francisco: Berrett-Koehler.

Lindsley, O. R. (1991). From technical jargon to plain English for application. *Journal of Applied Behavior Analysis* 24, 449–458.

Lindsley, O. R. (1994). *Dangers of percent and how to avoid them* (Internal publication). Lawrence, KS: Behavior Research Company.

Lindsley, O. R. (1995). Do, don't, how; and did, didn't, why? *Performance & Instruction* 34:2, 23–27.

Lindsley, O. R. (1997a). Performance is easy to monitor and hard to measure. In R. Kaufman, S. Thiagarajan, and P. MacGillis (eds.), *The guidebook for performance improvement: Working with individuals and organizations.* San Francisco: Jossey-Bass/Pfeiffer.

Lindsley, O. R. (1997b). Precise instructional design: Guidelines from Precision Teaching. In C. R. Dills and A. J. Romiszowski (eds.), *Instructional development paradigms.* Englewood Cliffs, NJ: Educational Technology.

Mager, R. F. (1986). *The how to write a book book.* Carefree, AZ: Mager Associates.

Meadows, D. H., Meadows, D. L., Randers, J., and Behrens, W. W. (1972). *The limits to growth*. New York: Universe Books.

MEASURIT. (1996). *Tracking training impact*. Shawnee Mission, KS: MEASURIT.

Miller, G. A. (1956). The magical number seven plus or minus two: Some limits on our capacity for processing information. *Psychological Review* 63, 81–97.

Parker, M., and Leinhardt, G. (1995). Percent: A privileged proportion. *Review of Educational Research* 65:4, 421–481.

Pennypacker, H. S., Koenig, C. H., and Lindsley, O. R. (1972). *Handbook of the standard behavior chart*. Kansas City, KS: Precision Media.

Phillips, J. J. (ed.). (1994). *In action: Measuring return on investment*. Alexandria, VA: American Society for Training and Development.

Phillips, J. J. (ed.). (1997). *In action: Measuring return on investment* (2nd ed.). Alexandria, VA: American Society for Training and Development.

Schmid, C. F. (1954). *Handbook of graphic presentation*. New York: Ronald Press.

Shewhart, W. A. ([1939] 1986). *Statistical methods from the viewpoint of quality control*. New York: Dover.

Skinner, B. F. (1938). *The behavior of organisms*. Englewood Cliffs, NJ: Appleton-Century-Crofts.

Skinner, B. F. (1950, Nov. and Dec.). Lectures, Psychology 201a, Harvard University.

Skinner, B. F. (1969). *Contingencies of reinforcement: A theoretical analysis*. Englewood Cliffs, NJ: Appleton-Century-Crofts.

Spitzer, D. R. (1995). *SuperMotivation: A blueprint for energizing your organization from top to bottom*. New York: AMACOM.

Spitzer, D. R. (1998, May). *Super-Evaluation: A new paradigm for increasing the results you get from training*. Paper presented at meeting of the Kansas City chapter of the International Society for Performance Improvement.

Stolovitch, H. D., and, Keeps, E. J. (eds.). (1992). *Handbook of Human Performance Technology: A comprehensive guide for analyzing and solving performance problems in organizations*. San Francisco: Jossey-Bass.

Sulzer-Azaroff, B., and Harshbarger, D. (1995). Putting fear to flight. *Quality Progress* 28:12, 61–65.

Tosti, D. T. (1978). Formative feedback. *NSPI Journal* 19, 19–21.

CHAPTER TWELVE

Implementing Human Performance Technology in Organizations

Diane Dormant

Human Performance Technology (HPT) professionals implement a wide variety of interventions. Almost constantly, they try to get others to accept new and better ways of working. How can these professionals, who work in midlevel organizational roles, be successful? How can they get other people—over whom they have little or no authority—to accept new software, collaborative work groups, distance learning, just-in-time processes, virtual learning environments, and dozens of other improvements in the way they do their work? How can these professionals get more mileage out of their efforts, reduce their frustration, and increase their implementation success?

The answer to all these questions is to become effective as a change agent. Information on how to do this comes from basic sociological and educational research (for example, see Rogers, 1962; Havelock, 1973; Zaltman, Florio, and Sikorski, 1977), which has stood the test of time and has also been updated (Rogers, 1995; Havelock, 1995). Information also comes from contemporary practitioners of organizational change (see, for example, Conner, 1992; Hammer and Champy, 1993; Kotter, 1990, 1995; Morgan, 1988; Rummler and Brache, 1990; Schein, 1996). All these practitioners have had an impact in forming the position taken here, which is that success in the role of HPT professional (or change agent) depends, in any implementation plan, on understanding and accounting for four dimensions of the change situation:

1. The change itself
2. The users and their perspective on the change

3. The network of organizational people who can bring power and influence to bear on the change

4. Factors in the organizational system that may have an impact on the change and the change effort

In this chapter, these dimensions are discussed in some detail, and that discussion is followed by a brief examination of the HPT professional's role as change agent.

ASSESSING THE CHANGE

When people are confronted with changes that someone else wants them to accept, they take time to evaluate. For example, if a patient has a life-threatening heart valve defect, she will assess any proposed intervention with great care. If the doctor provides a clear explanation of the function of and procedure for installing a replacement valve, and if that procedure has a good prognosis, the patient is likely to think highly of submitting to the procedure. In fact, the patient's assessment could be made on the basis of five characteristics known to be important in gaining acceptance of an intervention:

1. The relative advantage of the proposed change
2. The simplicity of the proposed change
3. The compatibility of the proposed change with past practice
4. The adaptability of the proposed change to a specific situation
5. The social impact of the proposed change

On that basis, the patient's assessment could look like the one shown in Exhibit 12.1, where a total of twenty points or more indicates a very high rating.

Why did the targeted user give this intervention such a high rating? The answer is reflected in the comments that such a patient might make:

"If I don't get this new heart valve, I'm going to die" (relative advantage = 5).

"The way the doctor described the whole procedure, it seemed pretty straightforward" (simplicity = 4).

"The valve works like my own heart valve" (compatibility = 5).

"I wish I could try it a little bit, but this is an all-or-nothing-at-all situation" (adaptability = 1).

"What a joy it will be to be able to play with my children again" (social impact = 5).

Exhibit 12.1. Patient's Rating of a Medical Intervention.

The change: New heart valve
The user: Heart patient
The change agent: Cardiologist

Rating

5 Very positive	4 Positive	3 Neutral	2 Negative	1 Very negative

Relative advantage	5	
Simplicity	4	
Compatibility	5	
Adaptability	1	
Social impact	5	
Total	20	

Now consider another change, this one proposed at a multinational corporation. In this case, as the result of an executive mandate to cut costs, the director of corporate purchasing was going to introduce standardized purchasing procedures at all sites. In the past, individuals inside the company who were buyers for various goods and services had selected vendors independently, often because the vendors were local, personable, or likely to give the buyers informal benefits, such as golf trips or tickets to sporting events. The buyers' assessment of this proposed change might look like the one shown in Exhibit 12.2, where a total of ten points or fewer indicates a very low rating.

Why did the targeted users give this intervention such a low rating? The buyers' comments indicate why:

"I've developed my own approach, tailored to what I buy and the people I buy from. Corporate doesn't know as much as I do about how to buy in my area" (relative advantage = 2).

"These new procedures, with their statistics, strategic sourcing, and blood-thirsty negotiations, are so complicated and unpleasant that we're never going to get the things done that need to be done" (simplicity = 2).

"I've worked hard to develop vendor companies we can count on to work with us and give us what we need. Now we're going to throw all that out for a standard that fits no one" (compatibility = 2).

"Obviously, corporate thinks we should all do things the same way, whether we're trying to buy pencils, chemicals, lawyers, or real estate" (adaptability = 2).

Exhibit 12.2. Buyers' Rating of a New Purchasing Procedure.

The change: New purchasing procedures
The user: Buyers throughout the multinational company
The change agent: Corporate purchasing director

Rating

5 Very positive	4 Positive	3 Neutral	2 Negative	1 Very negative
	Relative advantage	2		
	Simplicity	2		
	Compatibility	2		
	Adaptability	2		
	Social impact	1		
	Total	9		

"My vendor network, which I spent about fifteen years building, is about to go down the tubes. Some of these people are my friends. How can I face them?" (social impact = 1).

Note that these ratings reflect the users' perceptions, not necessarily the realities (positive or negative) of the change. The five characteristics that we have been discussing are known to have a significant impact on users' perceptions of a proposed intervention, and their perceptions are known to have a significant impact on their acceptance of the intervention, regardless of how good it is (see Rogers, 1995, for a more detailed discussion of these characteristics). To understand targeted users' views of a proposed change, the change agent must gather firsthand data and then, on the basis of that information, plan to highlight the positives and offset the negatives.

Relative Advantage

People value interventions that are better than the alternatives, old or new. This point may seem obvious, but it is often overlooked. What are the advantages of the change to users? Are they aware of these advantages? The effective change agent needs to communicate any advantages to potential users in a clear and timely manner.

In the case involving the buyers, the new purchasing procedures were being proposed for two reasons: the company needed to achieve significant cost cutting throughout the organization, and the proposed procedures (developed by an external consulting group) had accumulated a track record of dramatic savings in dozens of companies. But these were benefits to the organization. The benefits to the users were not so immediately clear.

Historically, the company had provided lifelong employment, but global competition had recently led to restructuring and offers of early retirement. These developments had generated a sense of anxiety among all employees. In this climate, new procedures were likely to be seen as threatening. The implementation team—which had been created by the director of purchasing and included corporate purchasing people, an information specialist, and the training director—communicated early, through a much trusted top-level executive, that the new procedures were coming down the pike, and that those who adopted and learned them would keep their jobs and be given training and support throughout the transition period. It was also hinted that those who did not adapt to the new procedures would jeopardize their futures at the company.

Simplicity

People value interventions that are easy to understand. This ease of understanding must be from the user's perspective, not from the developer's or the HPT professional's. (For example, software is usually understandable to its developers, but the same software may not seem understandable to the administrative assistants who are expected to use it.) How a hard-to-understand intervention is introduced is critical to its positive reception. The effective change agent avoids unclear or misleading information, especially in the early stages.

In the case involving the buyers, the new purchasing procedures were complex. They involved data gathering and statistical analyses that had never been used in this company before. The buyers were going to go through a difficult learning phase in addition to radical changes in their day-in, day-out work. In a series of site meetings, the director of purchasing openly acknowledged the buyers' concerns and explained that a flexible schedule of training, as well as an on-site coach, would be available during the transition.

Compatibility

People value interventions that are compatible with past practice. The more easily the new system slips into the old one, the better. The effective change agent looks for ways in which the new is like the old—in tasks to be performed, work patterns, outputs—and then communicates these similarities.

In the case involving the buyers, many characteristics of the new purchasing procedures were different, but one thing remained the same: if at all possible, corporate wanted to maintain the organization's past commitment to a win-win relationship with its vendors. The implementation team turned again to the trusted top-level executive to send this message to the buyers. The team also scheduled a number of "vendor days" to describe the new procedures and affirm the company's long-standing policy of partnering with its valued vendors.

Adaptability

People value interventions that can be adapted to fit their specific situation. When adaptation by various groups of users is possible, that tends to offset the "not invented here" syndrome. The effective change agent accepts and even encourages modifications that will not destroy the critical functions or integrity of the intervention.

In the case involving the buyers, the implementation team offered opportunities for "local" adjustment. For example, purchases of chemicals could be handled somewhat differently from those of real estate; purchases made in Indonesia could be handled somewhat differently from those made in Germany.

Social Impact

People value interventions that have little or no impact on their relationship with other people. When everything else around them is changing, people need something stable to hang on to. Often they look for stability in their on-the-job relationships. The effective change agent identifies the intervention's impact, during training, start-up, or use, on the existing social system and plans support for those who may be stressed by the change.

In the case involving the buyers, the biggest social impact that the new purchasing procedures would have would be on the buyer-vendor relationship. Buyers who had bought from and socialized with the same vendors for years would now be putting everything up for competitive bids and, in the process, affecting many social relationships. The trusted top-level executive and the purchasing director acknowledged the pain inherent in the disruption of long-term relationships and enlisted the buyers in helping to design the details of the transition period.

OPTIMIZING STRENGTHS AND WEAKNESSES

It is not enough for an intervention to be good; it must also be perceived as good by its targeted users. As Conner (1992, p. 103) says, "Change management is perception management." Even when all the valued characteristics are present, users may not be able to see them unless they are helped to do so. The change agent needs to accentuate the positive and defuse the negative. Table 12.1 offers suggestions for optimization.

Table 12.1. Suggestions for Optimizing an Intervention.

Relative Advantage

Highlight any advantages for the user that exist.

For each disadvantage, offer a compensatory advantage.

Have cost-effectiveness figures, especially if the change costs more than the alternatives.

Emphasize aspects that provide quick or high payoff.

Simplicity

Identify relevant factors, advantages, and disadvantages.

Prepare a simply worded but comprehensive description of the change.

Make change visible via success stories, site visits, documents, and peer testimonials.

Relate complexities of use to training or job aids.

Acknowledge potential problem areas.

Compatibility

Identify aspects, procedures, results, and so on, that are similar to the way things have been done before.

Build on similarities.

Acknowledge potential problem areas.

Adaptability

Identify aspects that users are most likely to want to modify, whether or not modification is possible.

Highlight areas that can be modified without loss of effective functioning.

Acknowledge potential problem areas.

Social Impact

Identify relationships among key people and key groups.

Project how the change will affect these relationships.

Acknowledge and empathize.

Identify and communicate workable alternatives.

GUIDING USERS TO ACCEPT THE CHANGE

As already mentioned, one reason people do not accept a change is that they do not view it as positive. However, even when people do have a positive viewpoint, they may not move steadily and smoothly toward the desired outcome unless they are dealt with appropriately. Change agents can facilitate this process by doing several things:

1. As necessary, separating users into market segments, and planning for each group

2. Understanding resistance as a natural part of the change process, and taking it into consideration in planning

3. Recognizing the five developmental stages that people go through as they move toward acceptance of the change, and selecting strategies that match each stage

Segmenting the Users

To plan effectively, the change agent needs to target specific, relatively similar, users. This kind of targeting is much like market segmentation, in which groups with different needs and views receive different treatments. The indicators of when segmentation should be used include any attributes (such as sizable differences in education level, organizational status, or professional specialty) that are likely to result in radically different perspectives on or relationships to the change. For example, when a new information system is introduced, technology-oriented engineers are more likely to be positive about it than people-oriented salespeople. Therefore, a presentation to the engineers might emphasize the technical advantages, whereas a presentation to the salespeople might emphasize the database of past sales that will be available to them on their laptops just before they call on a customer. Prioritization of groups (on the basis of their impact on the change, the cost in resources, and so on) should reveal when customization is justified. The point is that, in dealings with significantly different groups, a "one size fits all" approach is likely to miss everyone.

Understanding Resistance

Perhaps the single most important skill that a change agent can have is the capacity to see the intervention from the viewpoint of its targets—those people who are being asked to accept, learn, and use the intervention in the workplace. The more convinced the members of the implementation team are that the intervention is wonderful, the more difficult they may find it to understand the targeted users' resistance, concerns, and anxieties. The ability to momentarily set aside one's own view to understand the users' view is the test of a world-class change agent.

There are literally dozens of possible reasons why even very reasonable people may not be inclined to cooperate the way we want them to, even when we think we have mutual interests. People do not cooperate because they have different priorities, or because they do not have the time and resources to do everything—including help us. They do not cooperate because of limitations in their own abilities, which make it difficult for them to comply with our requests. They resist because they have different assessments of how they might best help. They do not cooperate because they are simply unaware of what we really need. They resist because they do not trust us. Sometimes they help, but with less than enthusiasm, because they are angry with us. And, perhaps most important of all, they do not cooperate because they believe they have different stakes in actions than we do, and they fear that they will lose something they value in the process of cooperating with us (Kotter, 1985, pp. 63–64).

Whether resistance comes from regret about what one is losing or from other sources (see Table 12.2), it is based on underlying concerns that follow a pattern (Newlove and Hall, 1976). First, people have personal concerns that involve the intervention's impact on them: "Will I look stupid?" "Will I get fired?" If these personal concerns are responded to in ways that satisfy people, they move on to job concerns, which involve their use of the intervention: "How does it work?" "How do you use it?" If these job concerns are addressed, people finally move on to organizational concerns, which involve the intervention's impact on others and on the organization: "What will it do to our department?" "Will it really make the company more competitive?" (Note that, very often, the first message that targeted users receive about a proposed intervention is a message related to organizational benefits, not to their personal concerns.) This developmental progression of concerns is as natural as the seasons of the year. The effective change agent accepts it and makes appropriate plans.

Recognizing the Developmental Stages of Acceptance

As the evolving nature of users' concerns suggests, change is a process, not an event. Moreover, the process of the change's acceptance is accomplished in five stages:

1. Awareness
2. Curiosity
3. Visualization
4. Tryout
5. Use

Table 12.2. Reasons People Resist Change.

Personal Concerns

Less security, money, opportunity, challenge, status, autonomy, authority

Loss of contact with liked people

Dislike of or disrespect for sponsors

Dislike of the way change was presented

Job Concerns

Job harder to do right

Poor work arrangements

Too much to do already

More confusion

Bad timing

Organizational Concerns

Others' suffering

Decrease in departmental productivity

Decrease in profitability, competitiveness

Decrease in capacity to provide services

Disadvantages for the organization, society, the world

These stages are not absolute, discrete, always linear, or equal in length, but they are in general the probable, progressive stages that the targeted users of an intervention will go through as they make the change.

Each stage is different from the one before and builds on all those that have preceded it; each stage also lays the groundwork for those that follow. Different writers use different labels and numbers of stages. (For a comparison of how seven authors classify the stages of acceptance, see Zaltman, Florio, and Sikorski, 1977.) Table 12.3 presents these five stages, along with matching strategies recommended for the change agent (Dormant, 1986, 1992, 1997). At each stage, as potential users' needs and concerns are responded to, the users tend to move on to the next stage. When their needs and concerns are not responded to, however, they tend to dig in or regress. In the worst cases, they may even reject or sabotage the proposed change. This kind of negative response can happen at every stage, even the last one. It is never too late to resist, and so it is important to understand needs and concerns and make appropriate responses to them throughout the change process.

Stage 1: Awareness. At stage 1, *awareness,* people are relatively passive toward the intervention. They do not avoid information, but they do not look for it, either. If messages are positive, their interest increases. The way to persuade

Table 12.3. Stages and Strategies in Acceptance of Change.

Stage and Targeted Users' Reactions	Strategy
Awareness	**Advertise**
Passive awareness of the innovation	Being an ad agent—short and sweet
Little or no information about the innovation	Being credible and positive
Little or no opinion about the innovation	Appealing to needs
Curiosity	**Inform**
More active curiosity regarding the innovation	Identifying specific concerns
Expression of personal job concerns	Providing clear information
Questions about own work and the innovation	Emphasizing pluses, acknowledging negatives
Visualization	**Demonstrate**
Active visualization of the innovation	Giving images of success
Expression of work-related job concerns	Providing demonstrations
Questions about how the innovation works	Connecting with peer users
Tryout	**Train**
Active trying out of the innovation	Providing effective training
Opinions about the innovation	Providing job aids, checklists
Interest in learning how the innovation works	Promising technical follow-up
Use	**Support**
Active use of the innovation	Providing necessary technical help
Use of innovation on the job	Providing reinforcement
Detailed questions about use	Providing recognition

potential users at this or any other stage is to do the right thing at the right time (see Table 12.3). For example, stage 1 is not the time to load people down with information or catapult them into training—two common mistakes in implementation. The appropriate strategy is to introduce them to the change via a once-over-lightly advertising campaign, perhaps of the same weight as a television commercial. This is the time for flyers, posters, e-mail teasers, brief messages, and so forth—all with content aimed to connect with users' needs.

In the case involving the buyers, the trusted top-level executive wrote to all purchasing personnel worldwide. He announced the new purchasing procedures and acknowledged the challenge that they would bring to the buyers. He also noted that, in these competitive times, those who could get on board would be the ones most likely to survive and prosper.

Stage 2: Curiosity. If there has been a positive reaction to these stage 1 activities, people move on to stage 2, *curiosity.* They begin to have concerns about the intervention. What new demands will it make on them? How will it change their roles or rewards? They need relevant facts, and the appropriate strategy is to inform them. For example, they might be given a pamphlet called *Twenty Questions Users Most Frequently Ask,* a journal article on job satisfaction as it is related to a specific intervention, or some other credible presentation of relevant information. So long as the information they get responds to their needs, they are likely to remain positive toward the new system. In the case involving the buyers, a site on the World Wide Web was used to list common questions and concerns of purchasing personnel, give honest and informative answers, and elicit additional questions.

Stage 3: Visualization. If their concerns are satisfied, people move from a personal focus to a job focus at stage 3, *visualization.* Now they have concerns about how the intervention works. They think about procedural changes, and about problems with time and resources. If a user can see the intervention work in her mind's eye, she may remain positively disposed toward it. Again, this is not the time to teach users "how to"; it is the time to show them—to offer a demonstration or a successful implementation of the intervention, and the more the demonstration setting resembles their work situation, the better. It is also the time to connect targeted users with actual, successful users who are similar to them. With such experiences, targeted users can develop a "movie in the mind" of the intervention as a success in their own workplace.

In the case involving the buyers, at the annual global conference attended by purchasing representatives from all sites, one purchasing team made a presentation on actual use of the new procedures. This team was dealing with typical purchases, and its members were some of the best-known, respected buyers in the company. The team discussed not only its successes with the new procedures but also problems that had come up and how they had dealt with them.

Stage 4: Tryout. At stage 4, *tryout,* instead of asking, "How does it work?" people now ask, "Can I make it work?" They are ready to test the intervention for themselves. If they gain skills and confidence in handling and managing it, they will continue to be positive. Now, for the first time, they are ready for hands-on instruction, and the appropriate strategy is to train them or provide job aids (and these, of course, should be well-designed, job-related, performance-oriented, well-presented, reinforcing job aids).

In the case involving the buyers, most of the training was supplied by the experienced group of external consultants. They covered such topics as identification of qualified vendors, consolidation of purchases, solicitation of competitive bids, win-win negotiation, and vendor relationships. A highly flexible training schedule was announced on the Web site. Offerings were designed to be compatible with various sites, delivery systems, languages, and cultural characteristics.

Stage 5: Use. If people learn and are still positive, they move on to stage 5, *use*. Taking their new skills and knowledge back to the workplace, they are in the first, fumbling phase of on-the-job use. They may have problems and may need more help to master the intervention on the job and integrate it into their performance. At this stage, support consists of technical information and rewards. Technical information requires readily available technical expertise; rewards require the cooperation of users' bosses.

In the case involving the buyers, selected buyers who had expertise with the new procedures were assigned as coaches to all sites. Then, when a buyer with little negotiation experience went into a session with a vendor, an experienced coach was a member of the team. Rewards were provided through articles in the corporate newsletter and human-interest stories in local newspapers; in the case of one purchasing team, there was even a story (with pictures) in the business section of the *New York Times*.

Considering Cautions

Overall cautions to the change agent trying to facilitate users' passage through the acceptance stages include the following:

1. *Do not skip stages.* Even though the indicators of a stage may not be readily observable, the skillful change agent assumes that each stage will occur and plans appropriately.

2. *Do not hurry through the stages.* Although constraints on the situation may require more haste than one would wish, the pace should be kept as reasonable as possible.

CREATING A POWER NETWORK

Up to this point, we have discussed the relationship between the intervention and the users as if that were all there is to implementation. In reality, of course, implementation occurs in an organizational system that includes many people who may be affected by, or who may affect, the implementation effort. This section is about those people—key peers, sponsors, and bosses—and how to involve them as a power network for the change.

Influence of Key Peers

The influence of significant members of the peer group can affect how or if a person changes (Rogers, 1995). Within a relatively homogeneous user group, individual users accept change at different rates, and certain individuals have a sizable influence over other people's rate of change. Figure 12.1 shows that a few people accept early (innovators), a few people accept late (laggards), and most people accept in between (middle adopters). Because certain people in these subgroups can be important in helping or hindering a change effort, the effective change agent needs to identify and plan for them.

Innovators. According to Rogers (1995), "Venturesomeness is almost an obsession with innovators. This interest in new ideas leads them out of a local circle of peer networks and into more cosmopolite social relationships. . . . [Innovators desire] the rash, the daring, and the risky" (pp. 263–264). Such advance users of a new intervention sound desirable, but mavericks often lack credibility and followers. If, however, acceptable innovators can be identified— that is, innovators who have credibility with the user group—they can serve as models and perhaps can even demonstrate the intervention.

In the case involving the buyers, one who was extremely innovative, but also well respected throughout the purchasing department, was selected to head a demonstration team. His team was trained and applied the new proce-

Figure 12.1. Adoption Curve.

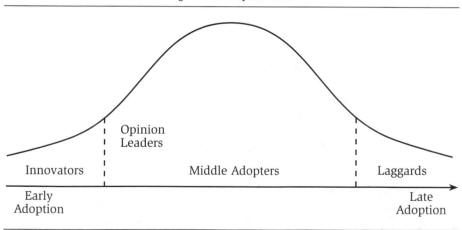

Source: Adapted from Rogers, 1995, p. 262.

dures first. Then, later on, they presented their experience at the annual purchasing conference.

Opinion Leaders. Most users fall into the large group of middle adopters, and among the earliest to accept change within this group are a few users who have special significance: the opinion leaders. Opinion leaders represent the norms of the group and are at the hub of the group's communication network. They are "certain influential people who are held in high esteem by the majority of their fellow men.... They watch the innovator to see how the idea works, and they watch the [laggard] ... to test the social risks of adopting the idea" (Havelock, 1973, p. 120). Once identified, they can provide information about the group and, if inclined to support the change, they can be of significant help. Note that a person who is an opinion leader for one intervention may not be for another. For example, users may be influenced by one person regarding a new computer and by another regarding a new retirement plan.

In the case involving the buyers, one or two at each site were identified as opinion leaders. Early in the change process, these buyers were interviewed about their concerns and their opinions about the change. Then, as each communication was sent out by the implementation team, they were contacted by a member of the team for their reactions and suggestions, which were incorporated into the specifics of the implementation plan.

Laggards. Laggards are the last to accept a change. It may seem best just to ignore them, but their negativity can be destructive. When they are identified and listened to, their need to criticize may be reduced. Besides, some of their observations may be valid and can serve as indicators of what is about to go wrong. The change agent can then suggest modifications to the intervention or prepare to deal with its weaknesses.

In the case involving the buyers, the most vocal laggards were readily identified. In order not to reinforce their self-importance, data were gathered informally. Some of their concerns, such as the issue of vendor relationships, were deemed important enough for the implementation team to address in its early communications to all the buyers; thus the complaints that the laggards might have made to others lost their impact.

Influence of Sponsors

Perhaps the most important person in a change effort is the sponsor of the change. Effective sponsors have the power and influence not only to envision and initiate an intervention but also to legitimize it and provide their continuing support. Generally speaking, the higher up in the organization a sponsor is, the better. (Therefore, sponsors rarely come from the user group.) However, to be cost-effective, "working" sponsorship, or cosponsorship, should also become a function of the lowest-ranking people with the authority to bring about the change.

In the case involving the buyers, the highest-ranking sponsor was the top-level executive who had sent out the initial announcement to all the purchasing people. However, because the buyers reported both to corporate purchasing and to site management, working sponsorship was necessary from both areas. The sponsorship of the corporate purchasing director was essential because he understood the new procedures and what the changeover would mean. He could also commit corporate resources for training, coaches, and other expenses. The sponsorship of the site presidents was essential because they could authorize time off in connection with the changeover and could commit resources for travel and other expenses incurred by the buyers during the transition. The site presidents also served as high-level spokespersons to vendors in the local community.

Defining Leadership. Sponsorship means not only the commitment of resources but also leadership, which no one describes more clearly and usefully than Kotter (1990). He discriminates between leadership and management in terms of goals: managers aim for predictable goals (for example, annual sales of $1 million, a reduction in production errors to .005 percent); leaders aim for change (for example, a restructured department, a learning organization). Of course, such different goals involve different tasks.

An implementation project does require both management and leadership, but there is a tendency to take care of the management tasks while ignoring the leadership tasks. Although sponsors are not the only project personnel who can provide leadership (see Gelinas and James, 1996), they are usually the best ones to clarify and communicate a vision to the users; align significant personnel; and, once users and others have begun moving in the desired direction, to motivate, inspire, and reward people, especially when the going gets rough. Of course, effective sponsors also commit the necessary resources to get the job done. The change agent's early identification and assessment of likely sponsors (see Exhibit 12.3) can literally save an implementation effort.

Facilitating Sponsorship. Even if sponsors have been identified and their abilities have been assessed, the change agent's work with them is not over. Throughout the project, sponsorship must be facilitated: the sponsors' strengths must be optimized, their weaknesses offset, and their leadership capacities developed. Moreover, because the sponsor tends to be a busy person who readily moves on to the next project, the expert change agent works to keep the sponsor aboard as long as the project needs a sponsor.

Exhibit 12.3. Sponsor Identification and Assessment.

To identify sponsors, ask these questions.

Who is the person most responsible for initiating the change? _____

Who is the highest-level person supportive of the change? _____

Who is the most committed supporter? _____

Which is the most supportive group? _____

To assess sponsors, rate each one on these questions.

Rate from 1 (absolutely NO) to 5 (absolutely YES), and then total.

1. Does X really believe the change will be useful?	1	2	3	4	5
2. Has X analyzed the situation?	1	2	3	4	5
3. Does X fully understand the change?	1	2	3	4	5
4. Does X fully understand the user group?	1	2	3	4	5
5. Does X empathize with what is asked of users?	1	2	3	4	5
6. Does X know what resources are needed?	1	2	3	4	5
7. Is X ready to commit time and effort?	1	2	3	4	5

Total _____

If total is 28 or above, the sponsor is probably a good one.

If total is below 21, the sponsor is probably weak and needs help.

If total is below 14, the project is probably in danger.

Influence of Bosses

One comment frequently made by people trying to gain acceptance for interventions is that top management wants the change, and end users are mandated to accept it, but middle management often has other priorities. As a result, bosses may refuse to give people time off for training or may even punish those who show enthusiasm for the change. Because the support of key bosses can help or hinder implementation, it is important to identify, enlist, and reward key bosses.

An organizational chart that accurately represents personnel relationships can clarify lines of authority and responsibility, the power structure of the organization, and the identities of the key bosses. In today's work world, however, organizational charts change so rapidly that it is often difficult to get consensus. Even so, it is worthwhile to know what various people think the authority relationships are. To whom do key people report? Who has sign-off authority? Whose endorsement is needed? The key issue is who controls rewards. Effective change agents identify all the people who connect the targeted users, sponsors, and implementers. Then, at each step of the way, everyone is kept informed or involved. In addition, if there are gaps in the implementation chain, the change agent acts to fill them in.

ALIGNING WITH THE ORGANIZATIONAL SYSTEM

Interventions, their targeted users, and the power network do not exist in isolation. They exist within an organizational system, which includes other factors that may be important to the change effort. Identifying these additional factors makes it possible to work around misalignments and take advantage of alignments. However, as Senge (1990, p. 7) emphasizes, such identification is not always easy, because organizational systems "are bound by invisible fabrics of interrelated actions. . . . Since we are part of that lacework ourselves, it's doubly hard to see the whole pattern of change. Instead, we tend to focus on snapshots of isolated parts of the system." To avoid this kind of myopia, effective HPT professionals must have general knowledge of the organizational factors for which they should be on the lookout. Among those factors recommended for attention are the organization's culture, its strategic direction, its technologies, and external factors.

Organizational Culture

Culture is the "pattern of basic assumptions—invented, discovered, or developed by a given group as it learns to cope with its problems. . . . [The assumptions are] taught to new members as the current way to perceive, think, and feel in relation to those problems" (Schein, 1985, p. 9). In the past, the established organization (for example, IBM, Apple Computer, McDonald's) had a singular, discernible culture, and that culture affected much that went on inside the organization, including its members' perceptions of proposed changes. Today, however, just as so much else has become unclear, so too has organizational culture. In fact, today's organization may be split into two cultures—one from the past, and one from the emergent future. Some members support the past, and others support the future, but even when top-level oratory is directed toward the future, the effective (and surviving) HPT professional is aware that organizations (like people) defend their values, beliefs, and habits (Argyris, 1987, 1990). Sometimes, even leaders who publicly work for a culture change may privately (often without their own awareness) undermine the change in order to preserve the existing culture. Effective change agents analyze and understand how the organizational culture, past or present, is likely to affect the change project.

In the case involving the buyers, the team responsible for introducing the new purchasing procedures knew that the long-term employees, who were used to lifelong employment and procedural independence, would offer the greatest resistance to the new standardized procedures, and so representatives of this group were interviewed for useful criticisms. (These interviews were also a means of defusing these criticisms, as we have seen.) Younger employees, who had come into the world of work during the current market conditions, were more supportive of the new procedures and could, in some cases, serve as demonstrators.

Strategic Direction

One of the strongest allies an HPT professional can have is the organization's strategic direction. A review of the organization's current strategy and initiatives can reveal useful ties between them and the intervention. Its alignment with current strategic initiatives can strengthen it; its misalignment with them may weaken it.

Common strategic initiatives involve cost-control measures, customer-focus methods, just-in-time procedures, shortened cycle times, diversity policies, globalization activities, standardized data systems, and empowerment programs. If a company is publicly committed to empowering its workforce, for example, then a change to promoting people on the basis of their seniority would be a change that is misaligned with the company's strategic initiative. By contrast, a change to flex-time, which allows employees to choose their hours, would be a change aligned with the strategic initiative.

An intervention directly aligned with strategic initiatives is a powerful tool for the HPT professional to use in enlisting management's support. The issue is not whether the particular strategy or initiative is a good one; rather, the issue is whether the particular strategy or initiative can strengthen the change effort. How much the change agent promotes the organizational strategy will depend in part on how much that strategy matters to the users and their management.

Technologies

The impact of technology drives not only today's interventions (for example, those involving information systems, purchasing procedures, sales databases, and manufacturing processes), but also much of today's implementation activity (for example, activity that involves the use of electronic mail, the World Wide Web, distance education, and interactive media). To make things more complex, technology in all areas is rapidly changing. The effective HPT professional assesses not only how existing technology may be aligned or misaligned with the change effort but also, as possible, identifies relevant technology that may be coming in the future.

External Factors

Factors that are external to the organization but part of the organizational system may involve stockholders, customers, competition, government regulations, workforce demographics, unions, pressure groups, vendors, and media representatives. The effective HPT professional assesses each of these factors for its potential impact on the change and the change effort.

Perhaps the single most important external factor today is globalization. Organizations that in the past dealt predominantly with one culture, one language, one government's regulations, and one nation's customers are now adjusting to multiple languages, cultures, governments, and markets. Companies, hospitals, and museums provide information and services in dozens of languages. Corporations expand to or partner with sites on every continent. They buy from vendors all over the world and have workforces with drastically different cultures and inconveniently different time zones. All these factors offer implementation challenges.

In the case involving the buyers, the team responsible for introducing the new purchasing policies to all sites worldwide had an early success in gaining the acceptance of buyers at the U.S.-based sites. However, when the team turned to the rest of the sites, a new set of problems was revealed. People in the United States had spoken out about what they disliked; at some of the sites elsewhere, a cultural value was to avoid all expressions of negativity, and so the team did not receive up-front critical information. It was also true that, outside the United States, some kinds of technology (such as e-mail) and related skills were lacking or different from what existed at the U.S. sites.

Among the problems facing global efforts is the fact that implementation costs tend to escalate across cultures. These include not only the expected costs of travel and personnel but also costs associated with delays (occasioned by slowed responses over distance and time zones), the lack of incentives and control with respect to distant sites, and the difficulty of developing functional global teams. One HPT professional who has experience in implementing changes both locally and globally recommends that resources and timelines be doubled or tripled for global sites.

ACTING AS A CHANGE AGENT

The job of getting other people to accept change is a hard one. It requires skill in a wide variety of areas: communication, training, organizational systems, team building, facilitation, project management, leadership, and, of course, change agentry. It is also a job that involves a lot of giving—listening, understanding, accepting, empathizing, informing, respecting, supporting—without much receiving in return. In fact, the more successful a change agent is, the more likely it is that he or she will be invisible. For all these reasons, people who are involved in series of implementation projects tend to burn out. What does a change agent need in order to survive and thrive?

Here are some recommendations for HPT professionals who are responsible for getting other people to accept change:

1. *Show respect.* Treat the targeted users and other stakeholders as you would like to be treated: with understanding, honesty, and respect.

2. *Create a team.* Work with an implementation team; only the simplest intervention can be handled by one person working alone.

3. *Get support.* Develop a relationship with at least one person outside the system with whom you can talk when things get rough.

4. *Be realistic.* Accept the realities and limitations of the project and of your role in it.

5. *Plan.* Develop an implementation plan that accounts for the four dimensions of the change situation—the change itself, the targeted users, the power network, and the organizational system.

The HPT professional may also choose to provide education on the change process itself to targeted users and others in the organization. The bigger and more disruptive the change, the more important such change education is likely to be. When people become aware that their discomfort, resistance, and anger are normal, and that change has predictable characteristics and stages, this awareness can lighten their load and facilitate their acceptance of the change. More than anyone else, Bridges (1980, 1991) focuses on the transition between the old and the new and gives such straightforward recommendations as "get someone to talk to," "arrange temporary structures," and "take care of yourself in little ways," along with more visionary suggestions, such as "explore the other side of change," "use this transition as the impetus to a new kind of learning," and "find out what is waiting in the wings of your life" (Bridges, 1980, pp. 78–81). Organizations that have the courage and vision to view change in this light also have the opportunity to become learning organizations that can cope with rapidly changing conditions. Individuals who have the courage and vision to view change in this light have the opportunity to become the flexible citizens most likely to survive and even thrive in the workforce and society of the twenty-first century. What nobler purpose could the HPT professional have than to offer workers and organizations the tools for survival?

References

Argyris, C. (1987). The case of the economic theory of the firm. *American Psychologist* 47:5, 456–463.

Argyris, C. (1990). *Overcoming organizational defenses.* Needham Heights, MA: Allyn & Bacon.

Bridges, W. (1980). *Transitions: Making sense out of life's changes.* Reading, MA: Addison-Wesley.

Bridges, W. (1991). *Managing transitions: Making the most of change.* Reading, MA: Addison-Wesley.

Conner, D. R. (1992). *Managing at the speed of change: How resilient managers succeed and prosper where others fail.* New York: Villard.

Dormant, D. (1986). The ABCD's of managing change. In M. Smith (ed.), *Introduction to performance technology.* Washington, DC: National Society for Performance and Instruction.

Dormant, D. (1992). Implementing human performance in organizations. In H. D. Stolovitch and E. J. Keeps (eds.), *Handbook of Human Performance Technology: A comprehensive guide for analyzing and solving performance problems in organizations.* San Francisco: Jossey-Bass.

Dormant, D. (1997). Planning change: Past, present, future. In R. Kaufman, S. Thiagarajan, and P. MacGillis (eds.), *The guidebook for performance improvement.* San Francisco: Jossey-Bass/Pfeiffer.

Gelinas, M. V., and James, R. G. (1996). *Developing the foundations for change.* Washington, DC: International Society for Performance Improvement.

Hammer, M., and Champy, J. (1993). *Reengineering the corporation: A manifesto for business revolution.* New York: HarperBusiness.

Havelock, R. G. (1973). *The change agent's guide to innovation in education.* Englewood Cliffs, NJ: Educational Technology.

Havelock, R. G. (1995). *The change agent's guide.* Englewood Cliffs, NJ: Educational Technology.

Kotter, J. P. (1985). *Power and influence: Beyond formal authority.* New York: Free Press.

Kotter, J. P. (1990). *A force for change: How leadership differs from management.* New York: Free Press.

Kotter, J. P. (1995). Leading change: Why transformation efforts fail. *Harvard Business Review* 73:2, 59–67.

Morgan, G. (1988). *Riding the waves of change.* San Francisco: Jossey-Bass.

Newlove, B. W., and Hall, G. E. (1976). *A manual for assessing open-ended statements of concern about an innovation.* Austin: University of Texas at Austin, Research and Development Center for Teacher Education.

Rogers, E. M. (1962). *Diffusion of innovations.* Old Tappan, NJ: Macmillan.

Rogers, E. M. (1995). *Diffusion of innovations* (4th ed.). New York: Free Press.

Rummler, G. A., and Brache, A. P. (1990). *Improving performance: How to manage the white space on the organization chart.* San Francisco: Jossey-Bass.

Schein, E. H. (1985). *Organizational culture and leadership: A dynamic view.* San Francisco: Jossey-Bass.

Schein, E. H. (1996). Kurt Lewin's change theory in the field and in the classroom: Notes toward a model of managed learning. *Systems Practice* 9:1, 27–47.

Senge, P. M. (1990). *The fifth discipline: The art and practice of the learning organization.* New York: Doubleday.

Zaltman, G., Florio, D., and Sikorski, L. (1977). *Dynamic educational change: Models, strategies, tactics, and management.* New York: Free Press.

CHAPTER THIRTEEN

The Language of Work

Danny G. Langdon

Applying Human Performance Technology (HPT) to workplace behavior requires systematic approaches to the analysis, improvement, and measurement of changes in the individual, in processes, in the work group, or in the whole organization. HPT is based on the presumption of a gap between actual performance and desired performance. In approaching an organizational culture, the performance consultant has as his or her primary tasks to identify this performance gap (via the diagnostic process) and then to determine the appropriate array of interventions (via the prescriptive tool) for filling the gap. HPT, as a product of the systematic design of instruction (called *instructional technology*), borrows from and builds on instructional technology.

Over the past two decades, this technology of human performance has developed through the writings of various theorists, whose works have been based on solving real-world problems. The foundations of the field have been refined as books have been published and practitioners have translated theory into action. These practitioners have also written for and made presentations to critiquing colleagues in professional-society conferences about what has and has not worked, refining their thoughts in new models that answer questions earlier models did not fully address.

For example, Mager and Pipe's (1997) important identification of the common practice of solving nontraining problems through training helped produce a conceptual framework that is well known to most training professionals today. The cue line "If you put a gun to their heads, would they be able to do it?" has helped thousands of trainers explain to managers why it would be inappropriate to train employees in, for example, how to smile, read documents, or answer phones. Similarly, Harless's (1969) equally important creation of the science of job aid development has saved training tens of millions of dollars while also improving the performance of hundreds of thousands of employees who now use job aids for a range of tasks (such as diagnosis, troubleshooting, and contract administration) that have little to do with training. In fact, the past decade's development of electronic support systems could not have occurred without the contribution of job aids theorists. Equally noteworthy was the contribution of Horn (1973) in the development of information mapping.

Another major and original pioneering step in the development of HPT occurred with the articulation of the theory of performance. Gilbert (1996) created a mental model of performance, exemplary performers, and potential for improved performance (PIP) that helped shape the work of many nascent performance consultants. Later, Rummler's Praxis Workshop, in the 1970s, presented a systematic approach to human performance analysis. With this he introduced the concept of deficits in an organization: deficits of knowledge (which training could solve), deficits of execution (which incentives, reengineered jobs, performance standards, or feedback could solve) or deficits of the individuals who were unable to intellectually, physically, or emotionally perform the job (which suggest the need to attend to selection in matching people with jobs). In his later work, joined by Brache (Rummler and Brache, 1995), Rummler expanded on the original elements by adding means for analyzing the performance situation. By examining current processes, the organization, and the performer, Rummler introduced a method of representing the understanding that people could have of business, and of their own performance in relation to the business. With this, performance began to take on clearer and more precise meaning. Consultants were able to apply Rummler's model to address performance problems that required a variety of interventions, of which training was becoming a smaller element.

Historic underpinnings provided by HPT pioneers like Mager, Gilbert, Harless, Rummler, and others helped to establish a strong message: filling the gap between what is and what ought to be is the primary task of the performance consultant. It was also established that this gap could and should be filled with the best and most appropriate interventions drawn from various disciplines. Hutchison and Stein (1996), as well and Langdon, Whiteside, and McKenna (1998), compiled lists and definitions of key interventions. The International Board of Standards for Training, Performance, and Instruction (Bratton, 1984) developed standards of competence that performance consultants could use, contrasting these standards with those used by training specialists and managers. Stolovitch and Keeps (1992) published the first edition of this volume, changing the practice of many neophyte performance consultants. Within the past five years, the American Society for Training and Development, on the basis of the thirty-five-year history of HPT, as developed by the International Society for Performance Improvement, has played a role in popularizing performance consulting throughout human resources and training. As never before, HPT is at the threshold of becoming a common means of dealing with performance in businesses. To make the most of this opportunity, HP technologists must be prepared with models that are genuinely performance-based. This will require some of the old paradigms to be rethought or used in other ways; Langdon and Whiteside (1997) suggest that this is true, for example, for the use of performance objectives.

Practitioners have continued to develop the principles of HPT through real-world applications, but one inadequacy in the technology remains: there is no commonly accepted way to capture (define) the performance problem. Mager and Pipe's previously noted cue line has not been extended into the broader issues of HPT. Similarly, Rummler's "white space on the organization chart" may easily become a black hole when necessary handoffs do not occur. The resulting gap between the management model (which provides brief, data-based information) and the HPT model (which accounts for human performance) has been illustrated in graphic ways. The traditional, management-based problem-solving model has not addressed the performance of people, but HPT models have not addressed management's need for detailed information that is both concise and based on data. Moreover, systems-oriented designers' need for thoroughness has often complicated the problem in ways that have obscured initial needs.

The inadequacy of the HPT model has been made all the more stark because a performance problem can occur simultaneously at multiple levels of an organization, not just at the trainer's usual levels of the individual or the group. Thus, although trainers often have been invited to work at these levels, other specialists are brought in to solve more general, organizational, and process-related problems. HPT is in need of a way to integrate and align performance at all levels of the business.

Training consultants tend to have a great deal of knowledge about individual performers, and they have an array of tools that they can use to complete their analysis of performance needs. However, when it comes to describing performance in a larger arena (business units or work groups) or a larger function (core processes, for example), training consultants have lacked appropriate tools. A job or task analysis may suffice for describing the gap between what is and what ought to be in terms of an individual or a group of individuals, but not necessarily for organizations and processes. Target-population analysis can provide additional insights. Data based on observations, employee surveys, or performance appraisals can offer (albeit subtly or indirectly) evidence of performance gaps. When the problem exists in a larger arena, however (the department, the process, or the whole organization), tools derived from instructional technology are often found to be inadequate.

What is needed is a new model for describing the gap between what exists and should exist. This model needs to meet three criteria:

1. It must combine, on the one hand, HPT's collective knowledge of people and the learning process, knowledge developed by researchers in behavioral and cognitive psychology, with, on the other, all that we know about performance from such specialty fields as organization development (OD), Total Quality Management (TQM), reengineering, ergonomics, and other areas.

2. It must extend beyond the individual to the whole organization in a systematic way that achieves alignment between human performance and total business performance.

3. It must completely and accurately capture the gap between actual and desired performance.

Without such a comprehensive model of performance across and within an entire organization, the potential benefits of HPT for the business world may be lost or minimal at best.

THE "LANGUAGE OF WORK" MODEL

The "Language of Work" model is a contemporary one that meets the criteria just outlined. It provides a coherent, concise diagnostic and prescriptive tool that describes the performance gap with precision. It can be used for performance analysis, intervention selection, and measurement. It is applicable to all levels of an organization and helps achieve overall work alignment. Most important, it can be used by the performance consultant and everyone else in the business organization.

The "Language of Work" model offers a view of work as a Human Performance (HP) system. As such, it characterizes the various dimensions of work (performance). These include behavior; requirements for organizational support; standards; and the environmental "noise" that often prevents the intended work outcomes of individuals, groups, processes, and organizations from being accomplished.

The performance utility of the model lies in its integration of all the components of performance, or *work*, as we will refer to performance from this point on.

The model is unique in that it offers a behavior-based language with which to define and discuss work with everyone in the organization. This is crucial to the possibility of doing performance analysis with others rather than on others. The model's definition of work is based on responses from hundreds of people in the business world (a sample including performance consultants) who were asked to define the term *work*. It was discovered that people in the workplace use the word *work* where performance consultants would use the word *performance*; thus, although each term is associated with a different group, the two can be considered synonymous. It was also discovered, however, that there is no common terminology for characterizing the composition of work, nor is there, in general, a complete and concise definition of what work is, and this discovery was the more crucial one in the development of the "Language of Work" model. Many people can identify, in one set of words or another, the work elements of inputs, process, and outputs, but other and equally important work elements are not identified by most workers, managers, executives—or, for that matter, by most performance consultants. Few people truly understand what work is from a *behavioral* point of view.

As a result, few people have the tools to improve their work. If there is no clear definition of what work is, then HP technologists cannot clearly describe the gap between what exists and what should exist, nor can they design and implement solutions that truly meet the needs that have been identified. Likewise, if there is no way to describe the actual situation and the desired situation in widely accepted terms, then people cannot make systematic, continuous improvement in their work. In short, if there is no clear definition of what work is, then the effective and efficient achievement of exemplary work is impossible. The "Language of Work" model provides performance consultants and those they assist with a much needed lingua franca that improves communication and performance across all levels and work environments.

At present, most people easily recognize that they are using a process: "Work is what I do." People also recognize that they are using certain material things (the inputs to their work) that they need to complete their work. People generally also recognize that they produce something (their outputs). It is surprising, however, that they often have difficulty defining exactly what those outputs are, and the higher up one goes in the organization, the truer this is. Inputs, process, and outputs—the components of the classic manufacturing model—represent barely half of work performance, however. The "Language of Work" model offers a way to characterize work performance more completely and consistently.

THE 6:4:4 MODEL

The "Language of Work" model can be best applied to work with the use of the 6:4:4 model, a construct that represents the six *elements* of a performance, the four *levels* of performance, and the four *parts* to a performance.

Six Elements of Work

In this model, what is known as the *Work Performance Proforma* provides the terms and the framework for systematically defining work behavior, work standards, work support, and work "noise." What objectives are to an instructional or training system, the Proforma is to performance. The term is adapted from the adjective pro forma, which refers (according to *Webster's*) to something "provided in advance to prescribe form or describe items" (the dictionary gives the example of a pro forma invoice); what is being described in this case is the composition of work.

The Proforma also helps set the context for how work is done at the levels of the individual, the work group, the business unit, and/or work processes. In so doing, the Proforma aids understanding and helps to achieve alignment of work with business objectives.

Over the past three decades, numerous attempts have been made to describe performance, although words other than those suggested here have been used (for example, *outcomes, accomplishments,* and so on). The principal models were devised by Gilbert, Harless, Tosti, Kaufman, Rummler, and Brethower (see Dean and Ripley, 1997).

In the "Language of Work" model, the Proforma is embodied in a paradigm that establishes work as being composed of the following six elements:

Inputs

Conditions

Process

Outputs

Consequences

Feedback

Each of these elements is defined in greater detail in Table 13.1; their interrelationships are illustrated in Figure 13.1.

To illustrate a typical Proforma, an individual produces certain outputs for a job, which are designed to achieve desirable consequences (results) for the business, the individual, and the work group. To produce these outputs and consequences, certain inputs will be needed, and these are used through a process for achieving the outputs. A part of this work includes adhering to certain conditions, which govern how the inputs are used and how the process will be utilized. As the work is done, certain feedback, given during processing, aids the worker in adjusting her work. After completion of the outputs, other feedback tells the worker that she has performed correctly or needs to make further adjustments. Thus the six-element Proforma can be used to describe the work of

Table 13.1. Six Work Elements Defined.

Element	Definition	Typical Sources
Inputs	Resources and requests available or needed to produce outputs; what must be present for something (outputs) to happen	• Client needs • People • Ideas • Equipment • Facilities • Funds • Information • Specific requests
Conditions	Existing factors that influence the use of inputs, processes, and feedback to produce outputs	• Rules • Policies • Environment
Process	The actions necessary for using the inputs to produce outputs, performed by someone or something under certain conditions	• Designing • Selling • Manufacturing • Servicing • Testing
Outputs	What is produced as a result of using inputs under certain conditions and through a process	• Services • Products • Knowledge • Facts
Consequences	The effects that an output has on a person, product, service, or situation	• Customer satisfaction • Needs met • Problem solved • Opportunity realized
Feedback	What completes the work cycle; response to outputs that confirms success or indicates adjustment is needed; response or aid to processing	• Client reactions • Information needs • Reinforcements

Figure 13.1. Interrelationships of the Six Elements of Work.

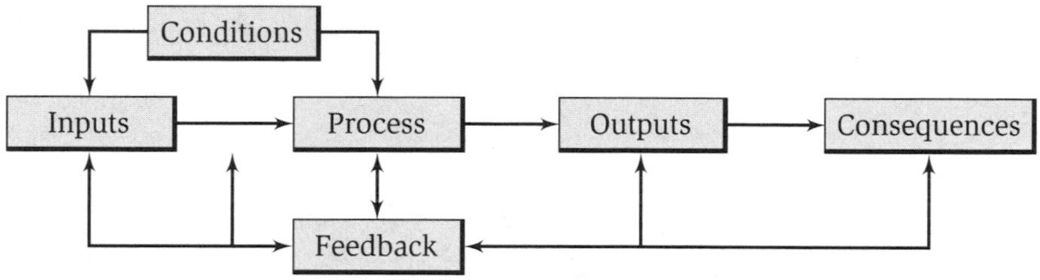

© 1994 Performance International.

the individual completely and concisely. Similarly, the same six elements can be used in any situation to define the work of the process (such as the consulting or the manufacturing process), the work group to which the individual belongs, or the entire business unit. Most important, however, when a common Proforma is used to describe work, all the work throughout the business can be aligned.

Four Levels of Performance

The work that requires definition may occur anywhere at any of the four levels of a business:

1. The level of the business unit
2. The level of processes
3. The level of the individual
4. The level of the work group

Is the performance need an individual worker's? a manager's? an executive's? a particular work group's? Is one of the core processes (such as marketing or manufacturing) not meeting performance expectations? Does the whole business require analysis for clarity about how work groups, processes, and individuals fit together in the achievement of business ends? Performance occurs at all four of these levels, and so a performance gap can exist anywhere. It is essential that the performance consultant have a way to get oriented to the level of the problem. Otherwise, he or she risks associating elements of behavior that do not belong with one another and therefore cannot be solved at a given level, or entirely missing important elements at a particular level. The "business sphere" depicted in Figure 13.2 can help with orientation to the proper level(s).

Figure 13.2. The Business Sphere and Levels of Performance.

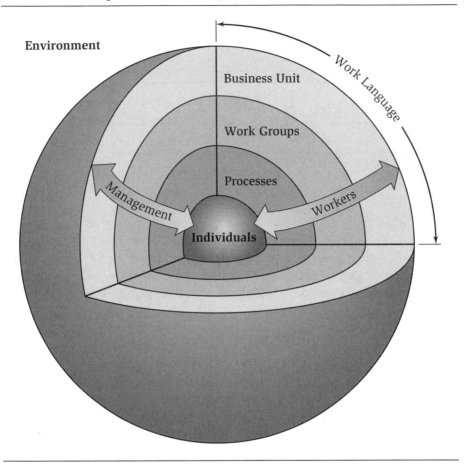

Any given business may establish its mission and define how it will achieve its desired ends, but in any business the four levels of work must be integrated and aligned. Suppose that a business has an exciting mission, a strong strategic plan, a good business plan, and the necessary financing. It is operational and has had some successes but is now aware that it must improve in several arenas. In a case like this one, a systems view of each level of the business's performance (that is, a view that encompasses each level both individually and in relation to the whole) can help in pinpointing needs. Ideally, the HP consultant would begin and continue with analysis and improvement in the sequence outlined in the paragraphs that follow:

1. The level of the *business unit* is the outermost, or most public, level. It is the level of work activity that encompasses the reason why the business (or organization) exists, meets its defined clients' needs, and acts in its competitive environment. All companies, businesses, and major organizations are themselves business units. Some organizations are composed of several smaller business units; others are made up of a single business unit. Each business unit has its own products or services. It has customers with whom it interacts and to whom it provides services. However, it also competes with other companies or business units.

2. The level of *processes* is where the core activities are carried out that produce the major outputs and consequences of the business unit through the action of one or more work groups. Processes do not depend on people and organization; rather, they specify the performance (outputs and consequences) desired for meeting clients' needs. Processes go by such names as *manufacturing, marketing, engineering, selling*; they are the "-ings" of business. As Hammer and Champy (1993) suggest, processes specify the start and finish points of work; thus a marketing process, for example, might be called the *concept-to-advertising process.*

3. The level of the *individual* includes particular workers, managers, and executives and encompasses the *jobs* of the people who make up the organization's work groups. Here, people who are performing their designated parts of a core process contribute to the work of others (that is, to work groups) for the benefit of the whole (that is, of the business unit). Just as work groups pass off work, so do individuals. Therefore, Rummler and Brache's (1995) notion of "managing the white space" of processes can be extended to facilitating the "white space" between individual work elements.

4. A business usually consists of two or more *work groups.* These are the administrative units formed to manage or facilitate work decisions, lines of authority, and reporting relationships, as well as to provide the legal and administrative support that employees require. Work groups either produce outputs directly for external or internal customers or provide support to those who have direct contact with clients.

From this perspective, a performance consultant can define, improve, and measure work at each of the four levels of a business. Furthermore, if the six elements of work are considered in connection with each level of the business, the levels can be brought into alignment so that work at one level supports work at all the others.

There is an optimal order in which the definition, alignment, and measurement of work should occur. Work within the business unit should be defined (and aligned) first. The consultant should then move on to core processes, to the individual jobs, and, finally, to the work groups. The reason for this sequence is that the goals of the business unit help define how work will be accomplished (through the processes) and by whom (the people in the individual jobs), as well as how it will be administered and organized for efficiency (through the formation of work groups).

Most current work by performance consultants does not deal with all four levels of a business. Instead, it generally focuses on the individual level or the level of the work groups, even though processes or an entire business unit will sometimes require analysis and improvement. It is rare, unfortunately, for a business unit to request the help of a performance consultant; nevertheless, HPT as a profession must be able to address needs at all four levels because each level influences and is influenced by all the others. Therefore, the performance model that should be used is one that takes account of these interrelationships.

Four Parts to Performance

In the business sphere, four parts of performance must be attended to. Figure 13.3 portrays them:

1. Behavior
2. Standards
3. Enablers (or support)
4. "Noise"

Figure 13.3. Parts of Work.

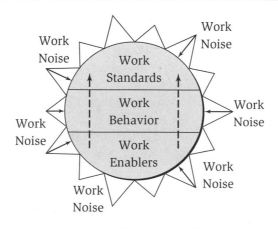

As already described, the *six elements* of work occur at all *four levels* of performance, but work must also be placed in its specific context so that it can be analyzed, measured, and supported. Proper alignment of the *four parts* of performance is also necessary so that each element supports others and no part prevents another from achieving its work with yet another.

Behavior. Behavior is the main part of work. At its simplest, behavior is a series of internal and external events that cause a desired conclusion to be reached. Behavior, for example, is the action of a fish when it swims.

We used to (and sometimes still do) think of behavior in terms of a stimulus triggering an associated response in a chain that leads to a desired set of consequences, and we usually think of behavior as occurring in an individual or in a group. As a result, we say that there is behavior at the levels of the individual and the work group. However, it is important to remember that behavior also occurs at the levels of the core processes and the business unit. A process is composed of a series of sequential events, each of which leads to the next (whether in a linear, branching, looping, or simultaneous fashion); and, likewise, the business unit is a dynamic organization in which various events lead to final outputs and consequences for the unit's clients. (As randomly arranged as the business unit may seem, it is in fact an organized set of events. It is not chaotic. If it were, improvement would be impossible.) Because behavior occurs at all four levels, behavior at any and all levels can be systematically analyzed and improved.

Standards. All successful work meets certain standards, whether implicit or explicit. Standards and behavior are not the same. We know that behavior, for example, is the action of a fish when it swims, but how fast should it swim? The speed prescribed for the fish's swimming is an instance of a standard applied to its behavior.

Standards define the costs, quantity, or quality of work to be performed. Theoretically, any work behavior could be carried out without regard to such standards. When standards are not clearly set and communicated, however, processes are inefficient, work groups must duplicate their efforts, and business units may go out of business.

Standards may be set for a variety of reasons and needs. These may include the requirements of regulatory agencies and the need to reach particular business goals. Standards may also give workers the incentive they need to reach production and service targets.

Understanding appropriate standards for individuals, processes, work groups, and business units gives performance consultants a direct way to achieve changes in work behavior. Standards can be set for all four levels of performance and for each of the six elements of work, and they can be set systematically, so as to avoid the vagueness that characterizes the setting of standards in many businesses.

Enablers. Work enablers, or support, are what it takes, according to Tosti and Jackson (1998), to make a "healthy organization." A fish, for example, no matter how fast it moves, needs clean, clear water in which to swim. A healthy organization is one that supports the work behavior that it wants to see occurring at all four levels of performance. An unhealthy organization either does not provide this support or provides it only marginally, and in a hit-or-miss fashion.

Some kind of support is required at every level of performance. Support for individual jobs may involve goals and objectives, assignments, equipment, an ergonomically sound workplace, performance reviews, schedules, computer hardware, and information on regulations. Support for work groups will include ethical models, mechanisms for conflict resolution, partnership arrangements, meetings, and so on. Support for the business unit may include a mission or vision statement, decision authority, centralization or decentralization of operations, and measures of success.

Just as work can be performed without reference to standards, so can work behavior occur without support, but the work will not be done as well as when the support is present, and at the highest appropriate level. This distinction between work behavior and work support helps performance consultants know what to change in order to achieve desired performance. Usually both work behavior and work support need to be altered (nevertheless, many single-shot consultants are prone to offer only support-based interventions).

"Noise." If a stream or a lake is polluted or overrun by motorboats, how will this interference from the human element affect a fish's ability to swim? Similarly, in business, how does the human element affect behavior? Does it help or hinder the attainment of standards? Does it negate the healthy enabling of work? "Noise" is best understood in terms of its negative impact on work. It is important, for instance, to eliminate the work "noise" that comes from managers who give assignments as orders, from executives who engage in demeaning or corrupt business practices, and from workers who reduce productivity by gossiping about other people and other work groups. "Noise" is a category that encompasses many of the problems that individuals and groups create as their attitudes, opinions, and habits affect the work of others.

The "Language of Work" model enables the performance consultant to work just as systematically with the problems and opportunities that result from "noise" as with problems involving behavior, standards, and support. By using this model, the consultant can identify what "noise" is present and determine how it can be minimized or eliminated at the levels of the individual, the work group, the core processes, and the business unit.

THE "LANGUAGE OF WORK" MODEL IN HPT

Work behavior, standards, support, and/or "noise" can be defined and described most completely and concisely with the six-element Proforma. Work behavior, standards, support, and/or "noise" exist at all four levels of performance. How can the "Language of Work" model serve as a vehicle for the HPT practitioner?

In general, the model can be used for performance analysis, intervention selection, and measurement. More specifically, it can help in providing a number of internal consulting services to an organization (job modeling, work-group alignment, process mapping, and reengineering, to mention only a few).

Performance Analysis

Both Brethower (1997) and Langdon and Whiteside (1997), "pathfinders" in the field of HPT, observe that today's business client requires "rapid" or "quick" analysis of the factors interfering with productivity. The term *rapid* does not imply that the analysis of work can be less than complete or accurate; rather, it suggests that the analysis must be done quickly so that the resulting recommendations can be implemented as soon as possible to bring about resulting improvements (changes, often in hard and soft technologies).

Over the past decade, as U.S. companies and the global marketplace have downsized and sought value-added services from suppliers and greater service to customers, increased accountability has been demanded of the performance consultant. Incomplete, inefficient, or unclear analyses are no longer tolerated. Business environments are changing so rapidly that decision makers must act quickly in order to survive and stay ahead of the competition. As a result of these increased demands, performance consultants must be quicker and more adept at performance analysis. They need models that are reliable and that do not require long ramp-up time or reams of edited copy for implementation. They require models that can involve the end user in the analysis so as to achieve efficiency, consensus, commitment, and sometimes, as an intervention, even some of the elementary orientation to the change itself. The "Language of Work" model, because it can be used at all the levels of performance, helps build widespread consensus and reduces the need to sell and influence that the more conventional approaches require. When the target population is involved in the analysis, a high degree of commitment to the suggested interventions is obtained.

Exhibit 13.1 summarizes the major elements of an analysis conducted with a major construction firm. Note that the six-element Proforma was used to capture the performance analysis requirements concerning a team of engineers who needed to structure and deliver (a process-level kind of work) an oral presentation in order to sell a potential client on a construction project. This method for analyzing the performance gap involved use of the categories "What Exists"

Exhibit 13.1. "Language of Work" Model Worksheet for Performance Analysis and Intervention Selection.

Request Title   Oral Presentation
Language of Work Proforma
Performance Analysis and Intervention Selection Worksheet
This is an analysis for a   ■ Process   ☐ Individual
                            ☐ Business Unit ☐ Work Group

	Inputs	Conditions	Process	Outputs	Consequences	Feedback
What exists	1. Marketing 2. Request for proposal (RFP) 3. Letter requesting presentation 4. Team	1. Accepted written proposal 2. AV services or capability 3. Company policies 4. Government rules 5. Presentation environment	Market VP 1. Analyze RFP 2. Analyze audience 3. Define content 4. Organize presentation team 5. Define visuals 6. Practice 7. Deliver	1. Oral presentation materials and audiovisual support 2. Project knowledge 3. Q&A 4. Project organization 5. Technical information	1. Winning new work based on presentation 2. A team image 3. Skilled presenters 4. Technical information presentation	1. Postpresentation review by customer 2. Practice review by team members
What should exist	1. Marketing 2. Request for proposal (RFP) 3. Letter requesting presentation 4. Team 5. Customer 6. Project manager 7. Project files	1. Accepted, with addendum, written proposal 2. AV services or capability 3. Company policies 4. Government rules 5. Presentation environment	1. Analyze RFP 2. Analyze audience 3. Define content 4. Define visuals 5. Organize presentation 6. Practice 7. Deliver	1. Oral presentation materials and audiovisual support 2. Project knowledge 3. Q&A 4. Project organization 5. Technical information 6. Project manager leadership 7. Benefits (selling points)	1. Winning new work based on presentation 2. A team image 3. Skilled presenters 4. Job-related technical information 5. Winning process for next presentation	1. Postpresentation review by customer 2. Practice review by team members 3. Proposal-writing team review 4. Production schedule 5. Project manager review 6. Self-review of presentation skills

Possible interventions						
Solutions						

and "What Should Exist." It included exemplary performers as well as observation, videotaping, interviews, and other analysis techniques. Normally, a document like the one shown in Exhibit 13.1 would be supported by descriptions of the more detailed analysis results for both "What Exists" and "What Should Exist." However, this summary alone is sufficient to demonstrate how the performance analysis can be portrayed clearly and concisely with the "Language of Work" model.

Note that in the "What Exists" category, the primary *outputs* are the presentation and its supporting audiovisual media (these would take the form of overhead projections, models, storyboards, and so forth). The *consequences* are a presentation that meets the perceived needs of the presenting company's client and wins work for the company. One example of the *inputs* is a letter requesting the presentation. The *conditions* include, as part of the presentation environment, the client requirements for the length and structure of the presentation. The *process* includes how the presentation is written, visualized, practiced, and implemented. *Feedback* includes practice reviews in a simulated setting. The "Language of Work" model's Proforma makes it possible to capture this information in a concise and easily understood framework. Note that the Proforma also specifies a clear "What Should Exist" analysis that can be easily compared to the "What Exists" state of work. When all its categories are taken together, the Proforma shows the performance gap. More detailed information (such as information about audience characteristics) can be attached for reference and used by the client as it is needed. Here, the concern is with capturing the performance (work behavior) data that constitute the performance gap. The result of this performance analysis is a clear and concise picture of what the current state of work is and how it differs from the desired state. On the basis of this demonstrated difference, the standards, necessary work support, and means for reducing "noise" can be specified.

Intervention Selection

Among performance consultants as a group, intervention selection is perhaps the least understood aspect of HPT. Nevertheless, because of intervention selection's position as the second most important aspect of HPT (after performance analysis), it is crucial that consultants approach the task systematically. The "Language of Work" model offers an organized means of selecting interventions.

We have already observed (see Exhibit 13.1) how the "Language of Work" model can be used to identify requirements for a change in performance and a desired change of state. The model would be used in the following way to select interventions:

1. *Identify where performance changes are needed.* The performance changes are noted for each work element through comparison of the "What Exists" in-

formation to the corresponding information in "What Should Exist." For example, in the Input column of Exhibit 13.1, four inputs are identified for "What Exists," but seven are identified for "What Should Exist."

2. *Identify the desired state of change.* The comparison just described shows that there are three new inputs for the presentation team (see the "What Should Exist" information in Exhibit 13.1). These new inputs need to be classified in terms of whether they will establish, improve, maintain, or extinguish performance. Because there are three new inputs, we can presume that these are to be established to achieve new performance. The four existing inputs need to be improved, maintained, or extinguished. Of these, one input is to be extinguished, one is to be improved, and the other two are to be maintained. The determination of what change is to occur is made by the performance consultant through testing, measurement, and observation.

3. *Suggest the intervention(s) most appropriate to the introduction of the identified change(s).* In this performance example, it is fairly simple to determine the needed interventions. Usually, a clear analysis makes the appropriate interventions self-evident. The key is an analysis that is concise and complete but without so much information that decision making is clouded. A job aid can also be created to help with systematic selection of the most suitable interventions.

Table 13.2 represents some of the interventions that were chosen for the presentation team whose situation is depicted in Exhibit 13.1. In the case of the presentation team, there are interventions that address all four of the primary states of change: establish, improve, maintain, and extinguish. It is useful for the performance consultant to begin by developing a list of the typical interventions that are effective in changing performance in each of the four performance states of change. (An example of a job aid of this kind appears in Table 13.3.) Then the

Table 13.2. Sample Performance Changes and Associated Interventions Selected.

If	Then...			
Performance state of change is...	Establish	Improve	Maintain	Extinguish
Sample intervention	Project team presentation package	Videotaping	Company presentation standards book	Reduction in role of marketing manager
Type of intervention	Job aid	Feedback	Performance standards	Decreased role or action

Table 13.3. Job Aid: Sample Interventions.

Improve Performance	Establish Performance
Action research	Employee selection
Business planning	Job aids
Coaching	Mentoring
Feedback	Modeling
Training	Training
Maintain Performance	**Extinguish Performance**
Compensation	Outplacement
Feedback	Upward evaluations
Performance standards	Decrease in role or action
Work schedules	Withholding of rewards

© 1997 Performance International.

consultant can assume a more detailed focus in order to determine which interventions are most effective in changing the six elements of performance when there is a particular need for a change in performance.

Measurement

In HPT, performance objectives or goals often form the basis for measuring performance changes. Analysis at the four levels of the organization is another approach that is often used. As an alternative, the "Language of Work" model provides a frame of reference to establish the purpose and content of measurement. In this way, it takes the mystery out of what things to measure, how, and in what order.

The "Language of Work" approach to measurement is based on the premise that the most important work elements, which should be measured first, are outputs and consequences. These represent the end results of a defined performance need. If, therefore, after measurement, either outputs or consequences fall short of the optimal level because of the interventions that have been used, it is then—and only then—appropriate to measure for cause. Measuring for cause implies measuring inputs, conditions, process, or feedback. The rationale for this approach is simple: Performance (at all four levels) is designed to achieve the goal, or end results; end results include outputs and consequences; therefore, it is appropriate to measure outputs and consequences first. If the desired outputs and/or consequences have not been attained, then it is appropriate to measure and search for the root cause in the inputs, conditions, process, and/or feedback that produced the outputs and consequences. Thus, in Exhibit 13.1, for example, it is important first to measure the actual presentation (the outputs) and whether the presentation resulted in the team's winning the new project (the consequences). If the construction job is not won, or if the presentation has been incomplete, the HP consultant can search inputs, conditions, process, and feedback for the root cause. Perhaps faulty information about the client's need has created an input problem. Perhaps the conditions of the presentation setting did not lend themselves to visual clarity. Perhaps the team did not listen well to questions from the client, or perhaps the team members responded poorly to feedback during the practice sessions. By measuring performance along this systematic path, the "Language of Work" model prevents speculation and instead guides measurement along a clear path of cause and effect.

SUMMARY

The "Language of Work" model is an integrated systems model specifically designed for use by performance consultants. It is unique in that it offers a common approach and language that can be used for performance analysis at any level of the organization. It allows the performance consultant to systematically identify specific standards that must be achieved, support that must be provided, and "noise" that must be eliminated or at least minimized. The model is easy to use, and it includes words—the language of work—that everyone in the organization can readily understand. Each element of the model's Proforma can be used to form a question: "What are your outputs as an organization?" or "What conditions govern your processes?" All the required data can be derived from the parties who are being affected, and the Proforma permits easy comparison of these data to similar data. With the Proforma, for example, one can compare current inputs with desired inputs and avoid confusing desired inputs with desired consequences. Apart from its uses for analysis, the "Language of Work" model can be used for measurement and intervention selection. It is a tool that can speed analysis, provide clarity about diagnosis at all levels of the business, and improve the quality of recommendations for intervention.

References

Bratton, B. (1984). Professional certification: Will it become a reality? *Performance Instruction* 23:1, 4–7.

Brethower, D. (1997). Rapid analysis: Matching solutions into changing situations. *Performance Improvement* 36:10, 16–21.

Dean, P. J., and Ripley, D. E. (1997). *Performance improvement pathfinders.* Washington, DC: International Society for Performance Improvement.

Gilbert, T. F. (1996). *Human competence: Engineering worthy performance.* Washington, DC: International Society for Performance Improvement.

Hammer, M., and Champy, J. (1993). *Reengineering the corporation.* New York: HarperCollins.

Harless, J. (1969). *Analysis of learning problems.* Springfield, VA: Guild V Publications.

Horn, R. (1973). *Information mapping workshop.* Framington, MA: Information Resources.

Hutchison, C. S., and Stein, F. S. (1996). Potential strategies and tactics for organizational performance improvement. *Performance Improvement* 35:3, 6–9.

Langdon, D. G., and Whiteside, K. (1997). The performance technologist's role in interventions: An interview with Joe Harless. *Performance Improvement* 36:10, 36–38.

Langdon, D. G., Whiteside, K., and McKenna, M. (1998). *The handbook of fifty performance improvement interventions.* San Francisco: Jossey-Bass.

Mager, R. F., and Pipe, P. (1997). *Analyzing performance problems.* Atlanta: Center for Effective Performance.

Rummler, G. A., and Brache, A. P. (1995). *Improving performance: How to manage the white space on the organization chart.* San Francisco: Jossey-Bass.

Stolovitch, H. D., and Keeps, E. J. (1992). *Handbook of Human Performance Technology: A comprehensive guide for analyzing and solving performance problems in organizations.* San Francisco: Jossey-Bass.

CHAPTER FOURTEEN

From Training to Performance

James Fuller

Making the transition from training to the use of Human Performance Technology (HPT) can be a complex task. Several issues present problems and potential barriers. For example, there is typically internal resistance to change, uncertainty regarding where and how to begin, and the question of what to do with the training department. These and many more issues must be addressed before a successful transition to HPT can be achieved. This chapter presents a practical and systematic approach for moving an organization from the typical focus on training as an activity to a broader focus on performance improvement.

STARTING WITH THE CURRENT SITUATION

When beginning the transition to HPT, start with the current situation and work toward overall implementation. Trying to convert an entire company at once will be too complex a task.

During the early stages of HPT adoption, it will be necessary to develop the capacity and capability to implement HPT projects. Creating a high level of excitement and then being unable to deliver results will cause clients to view the methodology as a failure (Kleiner, 1996). Moreover, for large-scale implementations, there may be significant resistance to adopting HPT all at once. Therefore, the plan should be to start small, build capability, and demonstrate results. Success is a powerful tool for decreasing resistance (Martin, 1995).

A quiet, grassroots approach has proved highly effective in large organizations (Ries and Trout, 1986; Fuller, 1996). Small, limited pilot projects use existing resources or limited hiring. Results are measured and used to demonstrate the efficacy of the methodology. This creates an openness to taking on larger and more visible projects until the practice is acknowledged as highly successful and vital to the future of the business.

VIEWING HPT AS AN ORGANIZATIONAL CHANGE ISSUE

HPT represents a significant change, and it eventually touches a wide range of personnel. People will no longer just go to training. The role of the manager in improving performance alters considerably. Different teams, groups, or departments will need to be involved in creating solutions that allow the removal of barriers to performance. To be successful, an organizational change this extensive requires a carefully planned approach (Conner, 1993).

The process of organizational change is a defined practice, and several key factors that must be addressed so that the probability of a successful transformation will be increased (Greenberg, 1994):

- The goal or end state must be well defined so that the people involved know where they are headed.
- There must exist a plan for implementing the change strategy.
- Strong sponsorship is required to initiate and sustain the change.
- Communication about the change must be clear and proactive.
- Some degree of resistance to change must be anticipated and resolved.

PLANNING THE IMPLEMENTATION

With all the various issues to consider in managing the change, it becomes evident that the transition to HPT requires some planning and attention to specific details. To take a haphazard approach to the transition from training to performance improvement is to invite resistance, delays, confusion, and perhaps the rejection of HPT entirely (Galpin, 1996). The phases of a planned approach are as follows:

1. *Preparing for HPT:* building the knowledge, skills, and processes that will allow early HPT practitioners to take an HPT approach to improving performance

2. *Demonstrating results:* beginning by implementing small projects that demonstrate HPT's impact on business needs in terms of cost, quality, quantity, and timeliness

3. *Building organizational awareness:* with results in hand, beginning to create awareness of HPT and its possibilities

4. *Addressing barriers to implementation:* as HPT is more broadly embraced, identifying and responding to any companywide issues with implementation

5. *Moving from a team effort to an organizationwide effort:* as the demand for HPT projects begins to outpace the HPT team, shifting the role of team members from implementers to mentors and facilitators of HPT's widespread adoption

PREPARING FOR HPT

The first phase of the transition to HPT involves preparation inside the training department. The initial HPT practitioners work quietly in the background. This work should be going on as HPT is promoted as the preferred method of improving performance. The risk is that, without adequate preparation, the promise of HPT will be greater than HPT's ability to deliver results. The initial implementation of a new process or approach must go well if the ability to promote the approach throughout the organization is not to be greatly limited (Kleiner, 1996).

There are several issues to address during the preparation stage. Who will act as the advocate or sponsor for developing HPT as a practice? Is there common understanding of what HPT is and is not? Which HPT model will be used? Who will actually do the early HPT projects? What capabilities will they need? What capabilities should the advocate for HPT be developing?

Building Strategic Support in the Organization

During this quiet stage of preparation, begin building strategic support inside the company. Successful organizational change requires strong sponsors (Conner, 1993), and so do performance improvement projects (Fuller, 1997). The objective at this early stage is not to attempt to win the whole company over; rather, it is to find one or two strategic managers who will support the implementation of a few HPT pilot projects so that results can be demonstrated.

The selection of sponsors is key. They should be high enough in the hierarchy to be seen as credible and powerful. However, going too high too early may cause problems. There may be enough enthusiasm about HPT's benefits to generate a directive to implement HPT more extensively than either HPT clients or practitioners would be ready for in the early stages. It is important to avoid being in the position of attempting to transform the entire company at once, with no demonstrated ability to do so. Typically, a sponsor who is a second- or third-level manager will be sufficient at the start.

Defining HPT for the Organization

In moving a team forward toward a goal, it is crucial that all the players on the team agree on what the goal is (Galpin, 1996). If the early HPT team cannot agree on a definition of HPT, the people outside that team probably will also not agree on one. An organizational change of this scope requires a clear, concise, easily understood definition of the goal state in order to be a success (Champy, 1995).

The definition selected may be an existing one that is simply adopted and used, or the HPT team may elect to create a new definition, one written specifically for its particular context, which takes account of unique language and unique cultural issues. Some HPT teams have created two definitions for managing the transition to HPT. The first is a detailed and lengthy description of what HPT is and is not. Generally, this longer definition is used only by the HPT team members, to keep themselves focused and aligned; the HPT team will have to take the time to read, understand, and continually refine this initial definition over time. The second definition will be used with people outside the HPT team; people outside will want a more concise and understandable explanation of HPT.

Sales experts have long promoted the use of the "thirty-second elevator pitch" to explain a product or a service to an uninformed customer (Ries and Trout, 1986): if the description of the product or service cannot be delivered during a thirty-second elevator ride, then the explanation is too elaborate and confusing, and the customer's attention and interest will not be captured. The same is true for HPT. When managers ask about "this HPT stuff," they are typically not looking for a thirty-minute presentation with charts and handouts. The explanation should include an easily understandable description that offers a general picture of HPT. It should cause the listener to want to find out more.

Selecting a Single HPT Model for the Organization

If creating a single definition of HPT is important, selecting a single model of HPT is crucial. The issue of HPT models is highly debated in the HPT field. There are some who argue that a rich collection of models allows for adaptability when in the face of different projects' needs; others believe that a single model allows continuous improvement of the model and its implementation. Both viewpoints have some validity. However, there are two overriding concerns with respect to models in the early stage of the transition to HPT: communication and consistency.

The selected HPT model will serve as a major communication vehicle for the HPT team and its efforts. Because models have a graphical appearance, people tend to remember and recognize them more readily than they would verbal descriptions or documents about HPT (Tufte, 1990). The existence of multiple models circulating throughout an organization does not lead to consistent, well-understood communication. Multiple models dilute brand-name recognition and logo identity, two major factors in establishing awareness (Beckwith, 1997). Another danger of providing multiple models is that individuals begin to gravitate toward and express preferences for specific ones, and some degree of "model battles" inevitably ensues, with people taking sides. Moreover, managers are constantly inundated with new books, methods, and models. Many proposed approaches to improving the organization's business have not worked, and so managers are often wary of new, enthusiastically touted approaches (Pascale, 1991). This wariness is heightened when there is disagreement on the implementation of a new approach. Managers have been known to postpone action on a proposal until there is a single model and consistent agreement on how the organization will use it (Champy, 1995). Therefore, circulating a number of models may delay the implementation of HPT. Avoid this scenario by doing the up-front work and selecting or creating a single model at the start. Additional models may be brought in to add nuance and depth after the HPT program is well established.

When selecting or creating an HPT model, be certain that it accurately conveys the HPT team's intended approach to performance improvement. The model must contain all the elements necessary to the achievement of a reliable and systematic approach to diagnosing the true causes of performance gaps. In general, the model should include elements referring to the following actions:

1. Beginning with the business need.
2. Determining the performance that will be necessary to the achievement of the business need.
3. Establishing the performance gap(s).
4. Determining the root cause(s) of the performance gap(s).
5. Selecting and implementing appropriate solutions that will remove root cause(s).
6. Measuring performance as a way of validating that the selected solution has achieved the business need.

Once the model has been selected or created, it should be tested with potential clients and HPT professionals as a way of discovering whether it can be easily understood. A model that clearly describes the HPT process is an important tool for recruiting and staffing the HPT team.

Dealing with Initial HPT Staffing Issues

It is not necessary to create a large staff of HPT professionals all at once. There is a significant advantage to starting small and building on success. It is difficult to find experienced HPT practitioners, and obtaining a qualified, experienced staff of them is almost impossible. Starting small and building gradually can extend the time available for locating or developing HPT staff. If the effort begins with a few simple resources, there may be no requirement to engage in a protracted discussion about funding. When HPT is being initiated in a large training department, there are typically one or two current staff members who can be redirected to the early HPT work, which may not require the acquisition of any additional resources.

Extreme care should be used in selecting the first few HPT practitioners. Their capabilities can greatly affect the success of the initial pilot projects. If there are no obvious, broadly experienced candidates for the initial HPT positions, then it will be necessary to develop HP technologists during this preparation stage of the transition. Desirable candidates from inside the organization typically have strong backgrounds in either systems thinking or people development. In making a choice between the two, select the candidates with backgrounds in systems thinking: experience indicates that skills in people development can be acquired faster than systems thinking can (Fuller, 1996). To locate potential candidates with strong systems thinking, turn to the quality or engineering functions. These candidates' skills in systems thinking, problem analysis, root-cause analysis, troubleshooting, and measurement can be rapidly applied to human performance systems.

Developing Initial HPT Skills

Stolovitch, Keeps, and Rodrigue (1995) have written a comprehensive article on the skill sets necessary for effective work as an HP technologist (see also Chapter Thirty-Two). They identify sixteen key areas in which a mature HP technologist must have skills. These include skills for conducting needs analyses, specifying performance improvement strategies, evaluating interventions, and managing performance improvement projects. However, this does not mean that HPT work must wait until all the HP technologists are fully developed in all sixteen areas. The article serves as a goal and direction setter for the development of HP professionals.

To prepare for early HPT projects, concentrate on building core abilities that will allow the HP technologists to implement the selected HPT model. This will generally mean focusing early development activities on the following areas:

- *The business:* Do the HP technologists understand what business the company is in, and can they construct a block diagram of its functions and processes?

- *The process:* Can the HP technologists implement the HPT process and systematically apply it to the elimination of barriers to performance?

- *Systems analysis:* Can the HP technologists conduct a root-cause analysis to identify the true causes of barriers to performance? If not, do they have access to resources that can help?

Developing the Skills of the HPT Advocate

If the transition to HPT is to be successful, it will require a strong advocate (Galpin, 1996). The advocate is responsible for maintaining a high level of awareness and excitement around the HPT process and projects. He or she relieves the developing HPT staff of responsibility for time-consuming program communications and presentations. Eventually the advocate will be in the position of attempting to convince potential project sponsors to let the team analyze performance needs before creating the solutions that seem obvious to the sponsor. To serve in this position, the advocate will require strengths in several areas:

- *Presentation:* As the success of HPT grows in the organization, the advocate will make presentations to highlight both the HPT process and the projects that have generated positive results. If the selected advocate has only average presentation skills, he or she should develop superior skills.

- *HPT fundamentals:* During presentations, questions will arise about the methodology and its relationship to other management approaches. The advocate should have a strong understanding of HPT fundamentals. A good starting point would be to read the present volume and the volume by Gilbert (1996).

- *Business and networking:* Because HPT affects multifunctional processes, the advocate should begin to develop an understanding of all the parts of the business and to initiate relationships with managers in various functions.

- *Sales:* To gain permission to use the HPT approach, the advocate should develop sales skills. Many an advocate has successfully asked somebody in the sales department for help; that approach is worth a try.

DEMONSTRATING RESULTS

Selecting Initial HPT Projects

In most companies, it is difficult to know where to start when there are so many obvious opportunities for improving performance. Selecting initial HPT projects is an important issue. In addition to improving performance, there are other purposes for the first projects. They provide an opportunity to demonstrate the effectiveness and efficiency of using HPT. The results of these projects will serve as future sales tools for promoting HPT. This will also probably be the first opportunity for the HP technologists to implement the HPT process and to practice their developing skills. The selection of the first projects must balance all three needs: achieving performance improvement, obtaining measurable results rapidly, and providing a somewhat safe learning project for the new HP technologists.

A training organization can serve as a ready-made lead generator for HPT projects. Managers have learned that they can bring performance problems to the training group and get solutions. Finding leads becomes a matter of reviewing the requests for help and then selecting a request that is well contained, appears to be neither too large nor too difficult, and has a manager/sponsor who is eager to get some rapid results.

Considering the Direct HPT Sales Approach and Why It Does Not Work

When a product or service—or a solution—is being sold, prospective customers typically seek assurance that it will work, meet their needs, and make them successful and happy (Beckwith, 1997). In the first stage of making the transition to HPT, there will be no evidence that HPT works in the organization, no success stories to show, no testimonials, and no financial analysis to show that taking this approach will make the project sponsor more successful. This describes the unenviable position of one attempting to sell a product that the customer can neither touch nor see, that comes with no assurances, that has no demonstrated success, and that the customer—who has not asked for it—only vaguely understands. This is not the optimal sales situation.

Unless one clearly has superior selling ability, taking a direct sales approach will typically not yield permission to use the HPT approach to performance improvement; the safe, established approach is training. Few managers have been punished or criticized for training their employees, even if it was not clear that the training was necessary. A positive response is more likely to come from a less direct sales approach to obtaining permission for proceeding with the first few projects.

Seeking Permission to Use HPT with a Training Request

When permission is being sought to proceed with HPT, there are alternatives to a confrontational sales approach. One alternative is not to ask ahead of time.

Why would this be acceptable? After all, when a manager requests a training course, it would be unusual to explain instructional design theory to ensure that she understands exactly how the training will be developed, so why should HPT be any different?

When the manager requests training and begins to explain the situation that has generated the request, simply agree to help with her problem. Of course, it will be necessary to obtain permission before engaging with the manager's team to conduct a performance analysis. However, rather than asking to do a "performance analysis" (which would be to use possibly confusing HPT jargon), ask if a staff member can talk with some members of the manager's team to understand what needs to be included and not included in the solution, and make a commitment to get back to them in a few days. The performance analysis will yield one of the following recommendations:

- The requested training is necessary, and it is clear exactly what should be included for success and efficiency (good news).

- It is clear exactly what needs to be in the training. There are also some nontraining issues that should be resolved if the training is to be effective (also good news).

- Training is not the solution; rather, there are some nontraining issues that can be addressed without taking people away from their jobs to attend training (still good news).

Capturing Early HPT Project Results

After completing the first HPT projects, it will be important to continue measuring the results of improved performance. As already mentioned, these measurements are important in making the transition to HPT. In fact, evaluation efforts are an integral part of HPT efforts: they begin at the start of performance analysis and continue throughout an HPT project.

One issue that has to do with the measurement of performance improvement projects' results is delay. It takes time to conduct a longitudinal before-and-after performance comparison, and this delay could significantly slow the HPT momentum that starts to build. The solution is to take a progressive evaluation strategy for the first few HPT projects.

Chances are that the first HPT project has been initiated by a training request. Start by capturing what would have been the costs of fulfilling the original training request. Include development, implementation costs, and attendee costs (time and travel). Compare these to the costs of the HPT project that was just implemented; the HPT costs will typically be lower. If so, you will have demonstrated bottom-line savings, referred to as *cost avoidance*. It is not the best kind of measure, but it is not a bad place to begin.

An intermediary measurement is "time on task" (Stolovitch, 1998). Many performance improvement projects seek to lower costs or to increase results by removing time-wasting activities. When that is the case, measure the percentage of time spent on desired tasks, both before the interventions are implemented and a couple of weeks after. Doing so will provide demonstrable, intermediary results while the data for the return-on-investment evaluation are being collected. Results for both cost avoidance and time on task can be effectively used to generate interest and confidence in the HPT method.

BUILDING ORGANIZATIONAL AWARENESS

With solid results in hand, move to the next phase in the transition process. The goal is to create awareness of HPT and its benefits. Once this awareness is present, managers with performance problems will come to the HPT team for assistance. Results can generate interest, but only if those results are well known.

Creating a Compelling HPT Presentation

The fastest and easiest way to generate awareness is to begin making presentations about HPT. This responsibility typically falls to the HPT advocate, but it can be assumed by any member of the HPT team. To prepare for this activity, generate a standard set of materials that will be used for every presentation. Consistency of the message is important, and confusion over HPT, the process, or the results will slow both interest and momentum.

In designing the presentation, it will be helpful to remember—and to mention in the presentation—that training will not solve all performance problems; Mager (1992) provides an excellent argument for this idea. Rummler and Brache (1995) offer a review of systems theory, as well as an exposition of their Human Performance System. The process for diagnosing and intervening in performance problems can be explained with the newly created or adopted HPT model. When it comes to project results, show clear links among business needs, required performance, the performance gap, root causes of the gap, selected performance solutions, and implementation results.

Getting Management's Attention

With practiced presentation in hand, you should begin building awareness of HPT's potential. The initial target audience is management. Managers typically are the ones who decide on performance improvement projects and who control the funding. They are the customers for HPT. This is where the earlier preparation in presentation and sales skills will begin to pay off. Show the process, demonstrate the benefits, address the questions, and invite managers to request assistance if they have performance improvement opportunities. Closing the sale during the presentation is typically difficult, however: there is too much new information to assimilate, and the managers will not be comfortable yet with a decision. They will need time to respond; an eager project sponsor will be much more helpful than one who has responded instantly to pressure and a hard sell.

With demonstrated results, it really is not difficult to get invited to a management meeting to talk about HPT. Call the leader of the meeting. Describe the $300,000 savings just achieved with HPT when the original request was for a training program, and offer to share how that leader's team may be able to achieve the same savings. If there are time-on-task results, describe the cost savings achieved, and ask if this team would be interested in accomplishing similar results. The leader will likely say yes; if he does not, call a different leader.

Telling the Rest of the Organization About HPT

The value of telling the management team about HPT is fairly obvious. What can easily be overlooked is the value of getting the HPT message out to individual contributors as well. As workplaces rapidly shift to self-directed learning environments, individual contributors can benefit greatly from an understanding of the HPT approach in taking advantage of their own performance improvement opportunities. As people become more sophisticated in their selection of performance improvement solutions, they will help to further the shift from training to a focus on performance.

HPT knowledgeable individuals can also help build momentum for the adoption of HPT. In one particular instance, an HPT advocate made a presentation to a group of shipping personnel during one of their lunch meetings. One month after the presentation, the training manager was speaking at the same meeting and was introducing the new training catalogue. One of the shipping employees stood up and asked what process had been used to determine which courses would be offered. He wanted to know whether the list of courses was based on analyzed performance needs or whether it was just one more collection of courses. The same afternoon, the training manager was on the phone to the HPT advocate to start the process of understanding and adopting HPT.

Identifying Opportunities for Showcasing Results

Familiarity with HPT and its results accelerates acceptance and enthusiasm. However, within a large or global company, it may require too much capacity to make personal presentations to the entire organization. Look for additional opportunities to spread the word about HPT successes. In most companies, there are typically a number of opportunities available:

- Showcase projects in the company newspaper. Try to get a success story in every issue.
- Create flashy case studies on successful projects, and place them in literature racks where people will see them.
- Put the case studies on the company's Web site.

- Send e-mail versions of the case studies to strategic managers.
- Make presentations at senior managers' staff meetings or at off-site meetings.
- Put the entire presentation, with commentary, on the Web.

ADDRESSING BARRIERS TO IMPLEMENTATION

With increased awareness come increased opportunities for performance improvement projects. The scope and impact of the projects will become larger over time. While moving from small to large projects, the HPT team will begin to experience new barriers to implementation. If these barriers are not anticipated and resolved, the entire transition to HPT may stall.

Dealing with Resistance from Other Training Managers

HPT radically changes how managers view and deal with performance improvement issues. In any large organization there are typically several training managers. They may be aligned to different business units, different geographies, or different functions, such as engineering, finance, and manufacturing. When there are multiple training managers, resistance to HPT may come from some or all of them.

The best way to understand their resistance is to see it through the lens of their personal Human Performance System (Rummler and Brache, 1995). Their job is to implement training. Their rewards and recognition are typically based on the extent of training offerings, on student evaluations, and on decreases over time in the cost of training. Having mastered these metrics, many training managers receive highly positive appraisals for their training efforts. If they are successful in their existing environment, HPT represents a risk to the currently stable environment. Resistance is natural.

To overcome their resistance, consider the following tactics:

- Send them copies of articles on the shift to HPT, as well as articles on the increased pressure to reduce training costs.
- Invite them to participate in researching HPT practices or developing HPT tools and processes.
- As a last resort, create pressure for change by selling the business-impact value of HPT to their managers.

Dealing with Organizational Turf Wars

When new HP technologists encounter performance improvement projects, they typically do not believe that the goals are achievable. Performance improvement solutions may include changes to compensation systems, for example, or may require changes to standardized documentation or manufacturing processes. The new HP technologists cannot see how they will be allowed to make changes in those areas. Their concerns are genuine: HP technologists typically do not have the authority to work in those areas. They do, however, have the ability to influence.

As HPT projects become larger, so do the scope and impact of the projects. More players are required to implement the necessary solutions. This is where relationship building and sponsorship development begin to provide value. If the current pay system is rewarding the wrong behavior, having an existing relationship with the compensation manager allows the HPT advocate to invite that manager to participate in the project and help guide the solution. The invitation is rarely denied when the advocate mentions, for example, that the project is for the senior vice president of sales and marketing. Turf wars are avoided through relationship building, early involvement in projects, and strong sponsorship (Robbins, 1997).

Finding Funding for HPT

Funding is an issue frequently raised during the transition to HPT. The question of who will pay for the HPT effort always seems to arise. If the HPT team is redirecting existing resources during the early stages of implementation, this is typically not a problem. However, if the early pilot projects require hiring new resources, then the financial sell can be more difficult.

As the demand for HPT and the size of the projects grow, funding will become an issue again. Management will need to decide how to finance the HPT effort. There are basically two choices. In one funding model, the company funds the HPT operation and provides guidance in setting priorities for projects; guaranteed funding may sound comforting and secure, but the demand for HPT assistance is typically underestimated by management and therefore underfunded. The other alternative is riskier but allows the HPT operation to scale its resources on the basis of demand. This model requires the HPT team to become self-funding. Like an internal consulting group, the HPT organization sells its services to functions and operations. This requires some marketing effort at first, but if results are established with positive bottom-line return on investment, internal customers will soon be demanding services. This alternative requires an HPT advocate (or perhaps a manager by this point) to maintain a strong awareness, marketing, and sales effort.

Determining What to Do
with Existing Training Departments

One great fear is that HPT will result in the demise of training departments. HPT is not antitraining. It simply requires a shift away from training as the focus and toward training as one of many solutions to performance problems. The transition to HPT will not make the training department obsolete. In fact, it may be busier and better funded than ever.

Managers have typically had only one resource available to them for improving performance: the training department. Because training cannot remove all performance barriers, however, sometimes performance has improved, but many times it has not. As a result, management historically has viewed training as a necessary cost and managed it as such. When HPT projects achieve performance results with measurable return on investment, management also begins to view these projects as an investment. Training is frequently identified as one of the solutions necessary for improving performance.

Because there will always be barriers to performance that are caused by lack of knowledge or skills, training will not disappear. The training department may be required to demonstrate that the training programs directly respond to and actually do solve business issues. This kind of accountability is very different from the demonstration of a high number of classes, high numbers of students, and high marks on student evaluations.

Dealing with HPT Staffing Issues

The most difficult barrier to growth and implementation of HPT may be staffing. It was probably difficult identifying and securing one or two HPT candidates during the early stages. During the significant growth stages, the issue is quite problematic. Many experienced HPT practitioners have found that they now prefer to consult. U.S. graduate universities are now producing fewer than four hundred graduates annually in instructional design and HPT (Ely and Minor, 1994), and they are in great demand. This raises the question of where to find HPT resources.

There are several alternatives. One is to vie for the few graduate students. Establishing a relationship with a university and becoming well known by the students before their graduation can make this easier. For long-range planning, identify internal candidates during the early stages of the HPT transition and start them on a graduate program well before they are needed, or identify internal professionals who are superior systems thinkers and run an internal development process. HPT resources will not present a problem if the staffing plan focuses at least one year ahead.

Addressing a Lack of Knowledge and Skills in Implementation

These staffing efforts may not yield perfect or experienced candidates. Even with a strong staffing plan, a focus on internal development may be required. This focus will help ensure that the performance consultants are able to achieve reliable results in the implementation of their HPT projects by running an effective performance analysis. There are some specific actions that can accelerate the development of internal HP technologists in this area:

- Identify external consultants who are willing to mentor HP technologists in addition to doing projects.
- Develop a recommended-reading list and HPT library.
- Attend local and international meetings of the International Society for Performance Improvement.
- Provide opportunities for functional cross-training.
- Offer courses on systems thinking, troubleshooting, quality tools, problem solving, and decision making.

Addressing a Lack of Familiarity with Noninstructional Solutions

HP technologists must become comfortable with and capable of conducting performance analyses. Once the barriers to performance are identified, HP technologists must also design solutions that will remove those barriers. Many of the necessary solutions will be noninstructional and will require expertise outside the HP technologists' experience.

Familiarity and expertise with different performance improvement solutions is the next development issue to address. Again, there are several alternatives that can be deployed:

- Develop focused expertise among members of the HPT team. One can focus on compensation, another on feedback systems, and so forth.
- Identify experts who can collaborate in the design and development of solutions in their areas of expertise.
- Increase the number of HPT candidates in the staffing plan who possess cross-functional experience.
- Identify external experts, and build a network of partners who can participate or advise on projects.

MOVING FROM A TEAM EFFORT TO AN ORGANIZATIONWIDE EFFORT

Success necessitates change, particularly in a large organization. As momentum and acceptance of HPT build, the requests for HP technologists will likely begin to exceed the capacity of the existing HPT department. HPT will have to shift from an HPT departmental service to a companywide methodology. The role of the HPT department will be to shift from the implementation of HPT to the leadership and development of HPT for the organization. It is important to prepare for these transitions before they are necessary.

Shifting the Roles of the Early HPT Practitioners

The role of HP technologists changes over time. At first, their responsibilities include helping to define HPT, selecting a model, and learning how to implement HPT. Then they are asked to run pilot projects. From there emerge larger and more complex performance improvement projects. Finally, the role becomes that of lead consultant: leading the assessments, managing the projects, and coordinating the activities of numerous people involved in performance improvement projects. Now comes the most difficult change of all: the HP professionals must stop doing what they do best. As the most experienced HPT practitioners, they must move from a role of implementing HPT to one of mentoring and developing new HP technologists. Knowledgeable HP technologists become the creators of HPT tools and processes for newer practitioners.

Creating a Manager of HPT for the Organization

Like the HP technologists, the HPT advocate will probably also experience a change of role. As the HPT department has grown over time, the advocate has probably become the HPT manager. Having a manager of HPT is a crucial first step toward the shift from an HPT services group to HPT as an organization-wide methodology. It may appear that HPT is becoming well established, but this is a vulnerable time. If others attempt HPT and fail, it will slow momentum and tarnish credibility. If other departments decide to change the model or the implementation, they will invite "model battle" and diminish management's confidence. This phase of the transition requires a strong, visible, and effective manager to lead the improvement and development of HPT tools and processes, as well as to provide leadership to developing HP technologists across the company.

SUMMARY

The transition from a focus on training to a focus on performance provides many challenges. However, it is achievable. It requires a carefully planned effort and considerable diligence. Ample effort and resources must be placed into the preparation stage or the effort will stall and may die. Nothing succeeds like success, so get early and tangible results. Make the results known, and continue to build up the HPT capabilities. Barriers to the transition will exist in the organization, but the HPT approach can identify and remove them.

References

Beckwith, H. (1997). *Selling the invisible: A field guide to modern marketing.* New York: Warner Books.

Champy, J. (1995). *Reengineering management.* New York: HarperCollins.

Conner, D. (1993). *Managing at the speed of change.* New York: Villard.

Ely, D. P., and Minor, B. B. (1994). *Education media and technology yearbook.* Englewood, CO: Libraries Unlimited.

Fuller, J. L. (1996). *Managing performance improvement projects: Preparing, planning, and implementing.* San Francisco: Jossey-Bass.

Fuller, J. L. (1997). Making the transition to a focus on performance. In J. Robinson and D. G. Robinson (eds.), *Moving from training to performance: A practical guide.* San Francisco: Berrett-Koehler.

Galpin, T. J. (1996). *The human side of change: A practical guide to organizational redesign.* San Francisco: Jossey-Bass.

Gilbert, T. F. (1996). *Human competence: Engineering worthy performance* (Tribute ed.). Washington, DC: International Society for Performance Improvement.

Greenberg, J. (ed.). (1994). *Organizational behavior: The state of the science.* Hillsdale, NJ: Erlbaum.

Kleiner, A. (1996). *The age of heretics: Heroes, outlaws, and the forerunners of corporate change.* New York: Doubleday.

Mager, R. F. (1992). *What every manager should know about training.* Atlanta: Center for Effective Performance.

Martin, J. (1995). *The great transition: Using the seven disciplines of enterprise engineering to align people, technology, and strategy.* New York: AMACOM.

Pascale, R. T. (1991). *Managing on the edge.* New York: Touchstone Books.

Ries, A., and Trout, J. (1986). *Marketing warfare.* New York: McGraw-Hill.

Robbins, S. P. (1997). *Essentials of organizational behavior* (5th ed.). Englewood Cliffs, NJ: Prentice Hall.

Rummler, G., and Brache, A. (1995). *Improving performance: How to manage the white space on the organization chart* (2nd ed.). San Francisco: Jossey-Bass.

Stolovitch, H. D. (1998, Mar.). *Calculating the return on investment in training: A critical analysis and a case study.* Paper presented at the meeting of the International Society for Performance Improvement, Chicago.

Stolovitch, H. D., Keeps, E. J., and Rodrigue, D. (1995). Skill sets for the human performance technologist. *Performance Improvement Quarterly* 8:2, 40–67.

Tufte, E. R. (1990). *Envisioning information.* Cheshire, CT: Graphics Press.

CHAPTER FIFTEEN

Human Performance Technology in Action

Roger M. Addison
Carol Haig

When a Human Performance Technology (HPT) consultant presents a solution to a human performance issue, especially a solution that is unfamiliar to the client, the consultant is challenged not only to establish personal credibility but also credibility for the intervention. These challenges can be more daunting than the process of developing and implementing the performance change itself.

The need to establish personal credibility is becoming even greater as opportunities for global work continue to expand and as more HPT consultants work in foreign countries and for international clients. Information presented at international training conferences, such as the conferences of the American Society for Training and Development (ASTD), the International Society for Performance Improvement (ISPI), the International Federation of Training and Development Organisations (IFTDO), in addition to the information presented at related industry-specific events, supports the trend of increasingly performance-focused multinational organizations.

Three themes expressed in recent conference literature show how interventions are selected and implemented worldwide:

1. Consultants applying HPT techniques in multinational settings must take a country's culture into account.

2. Developing countries are biased toward training as the solution to performance problems.

3. The interventions that are selected must factor in the country's ability to absorb new technology (Rosensweig, 1997).

According to Bassi, Cheney, and Van Buren (1997, p. 2), reporting in the journal *Training & Development*, "In a survey of training professionals at ASTD's 1996 International Conference, 86 percent 'strongly agreed' or 'agreed' that a shift from training to performance is a top trend." This report is corroborated by executives who ranked the shift to performance as the most probable trend for the following three years (American Society for Training and Development, 1998, p. 4).

Although the shift from training to performance is clearly gaining popularity among organizations, HPT is more than just another trend. HPT has staying power because it provides effective techniques that, used appropriately, enable consultants to present clients with the right solutions to the right problems at the right time. At the same time, HPT helps the consultants themselves establish the credibility that they need in order to become integral to the organization.

The core challenge of every HPT consultant is to sell the invisible: interventions can be documented on paper or on line, but clients cannot always see just what the HPT consultant helps them accomplish. This fact challenges HPT consultants to find ways to make not only results but also processes visible to clients, and very quickly.

This chapter opens with a description and discussion of the Performance Architecture Map, a model that makes HPT as a concept accessible to consultants and their clients. The model sets the context for the examples that follow, which describe the results that were achieved when HPT interventions were applied with consideration for organizational culture. Whenever it is possible to do so, the examples also show how the invisible was made visible to these organizations' managers. It is hoped that this chapter will serve consultants by helping them do the following things:

- Increase their confidence in HPT interventions and in the probability of their producing results

- Discover one model through which HPT will become clearer to them and their clients

- Identify HPT strategies that have demonstrated effectiveness at making line managers successful

- Acquire information for building trust and credibility with clients

THE PERFORMANCE ARCHITECTURE MAP

There are many definitions of *HPT,* but for the purposes of this chapter we will define it as a systematic set of methods, procedures, and strategies for solving problems, or realizing opportunities, that are related to the performance of people.

HPT can be applied to individuals, small groups, teams, and large organizations through the use of such interventions as training, communication, organizational development, work/job design, performance management, staffing, environmental engineering, ergonomics, motivation, rewards, and incentives. As a discipline, HPT treats the work, the worker, and the workplace as integral components of a systematic process that produces replicable and measurable results in a cost-effective manner.

Looking at the Model

The Performance Architecture Map (Figure 15.1) is one of many models that HPT consultants use to pinpoint the sites of performance issues in organizations. It is a navigational tool that can be used to identify the most likely causes of specific performance problems. It is useful to HPT consultants because it leads to quick and accurate diagnoses of performance issues and because it is a wonderful relationship builder. Clients easily accept this tool because the four quadrants make sense to them, and because they can use the terminology to discuss problems with consultants, bosses, and peers. They can look at this model, answer the questions, plot the results, and "see" where the issues lie. Thus clients can be the true owners and proponents of the diagnosis and the recommended interventions. HPT models like this one can help HPT consultants make the invisible become visible to their clients.

The Performance Architecture Map takes account of the usual dimensions of an organization's culture: vision, values, beliefs, and management practices. It then adds to these critical cultural elements the nature of staff and line relationships, issues of power and status, policies and procedures, communications, motivational systems, stories and legends, corporate identity, and the physical workspace (Addison and Johnson, 1997).

It is important that consultants acknowledge the critical role that the cultural dimension plays in the success of the performance improvement process. It is extremely difficult to perform a thorough analysis, recommend appropriate interventions, or measure results without factoring in the organization's norms and view of itself.

Understanding the Key Model Segments

There are four key segments in the Performance Architecture Map, which are read clockwise from the lower left quadrant:

1. Structure (the "what")
2. Motivation (the "why")
3. Environment (the "where")
4. Learning (the "how")

Performance Map™

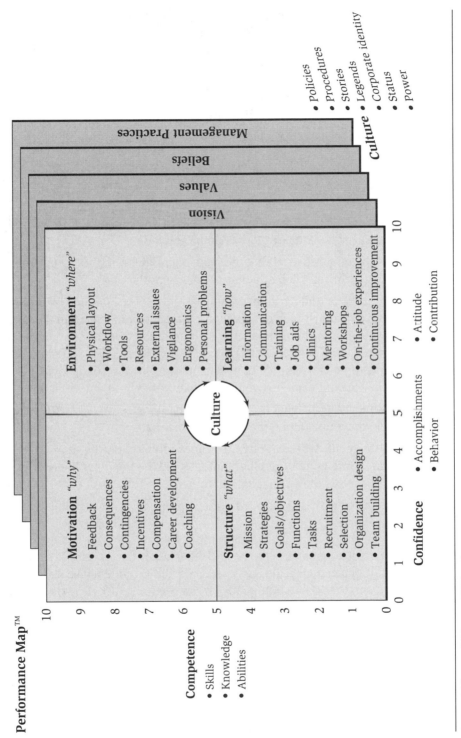

Figure 15.1. **Performance Architecture Map.**™

Performance Map™

Competence
- Skills
- Knowledge
- Abilities

Motivation *"why"*
- Feedback
- Consequences
- Contingencies
- Incentives
- Compensation
- Career development
- Coaching

Structure *"what"*
- Mission
- Strategies
- Goals/objectives
- Functions
- Tasks
- Recruitment
- Selection
- Organization design
- Team building

Environment *"where"*
- Physical layout
- Workflow
- Tools
- Resources
- External issues
- Vigilance
- Ergonomics
- Personal problems

Learning *"how"*
- Information
- Communication
- Training
- Job aids
- Clinics
- Mentoring
- Workshops
- On-the-job experiences
- Continuous improvement

Culture

Vision

Values

Beliefs

Management Practices

Culture
- Policies
- Procedures
- Stories
- Legends
- Corporate identity
- Status
- Power

Confidence
- Accomplishments
- Behavior
- Attitude
- Contribution

Source: Addison and Johnson, 1997, p. 4.

Structure is the foundation on which the organization stands. *Motivation* comprises the emotions, desires, and psychological needs that incite action. The *environment* is composed of the external and internal conditions that affect the growth and development of the organization. *Learning* increases employees' proficiency in given areas (Addison and Johnson, 1997).

Using the Map

The following six steps explain how to use the Performance Architecture Map:

1. Ask questions to determine the level of competence—the skills and knowledge—of the employee(s). Ask each respondent to rate the level of competence on a scale of 0 (low) to 10 (high). Sample questions: "What skills do your employees require to do the job?" "Can you tell me about what your employees do on the job?"

2. Mark the numeric level that the respondent gives on the Competence scale, which runs along the left-hand side of the map.

3. Ask questions to determine employees' level of confidence by probing for accomplishments, behavior, attitude, commitment, and contributions. With the respondent's help, rate the level of confidence on a scale of 0 (low) to 10 (high). Sample questions: "Can you tell me about the general attitude of your employees toward their jobs?" "What accomplishments would you like to see from your employees?"

4. Mark the numeric level that the respondent gives on the Confidence scale, which runs along the bottom of the map.

5. Mark the point where the two plot lines intersect on the map. The quadrant into which the plot point falls will be the most likely arena for a diagnosis of organizational problems.

6. Once the diagnosis is clear, use the map to determine possible interventions.

For example, if a manager tells the HPT consultant that an employee rates a seven on the Competence scale and a three on the Confidence scale, then the diagnosis falls in the Motivation quadrant (see Figure 15.2). The HPT consultant's next step will be to ask the manager questions about possible causes and interventions, using the sample list provided in the Motivation quadrant.

Selecting an Intervention

If there is a deficiency in the organization that falls into the Structural quadrant, possible interventions include developing goals, objectives, and a mission for the individual or the group. If the Motivation quadrant is selected, interventions include creation of incentive programs, a revised compensation package, or a

Performance Map™

Figure 15.2. Sample Performance Architecture Map.™

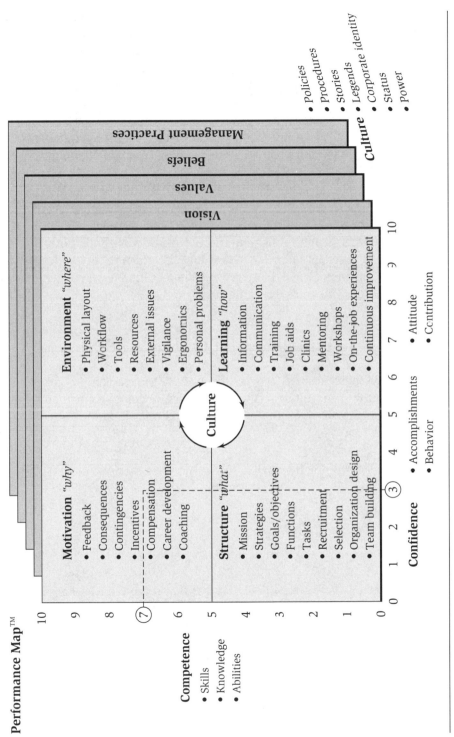

Source: Addison and Johnson, 1997, p. 4.

career path for each affected position. Interventions for issues that fall into the Environmental quadrant might include altering the physical workspace or the workflow; there may also be links to employees' personal problems. If the issue is based in the Learning quadrant, then a training intervention, a new job aid, or a mentoring program may be a viable intervention (Addison and Johnson, 1997, p. 5).

Once the HPT consultant has identified a specific quadrant as the site of a performance issue, it is also important to consider the other three quadrants. It is likely that these other areas will also influence the selection of an intervention.

Revisiting the Culture

At this point, it is essential to revisit the organization's culture. Any interventions recommended to the client must be aligned with the internal culture. Without such symmetry, the implementation is destined to fail. Both the HPT consultant and the client must understand how the organization works and how the selected intervention will be received. When culture is pitted against strategy, culture will win almost every time.

STRATEGIES THAT LEVERAGE HPT

There are five strategies that successfully bring HPT into action in organizations and help to grow a consulting relationship. These strategies are particularly useful in breaking down organizational "silos" and managing the "white space" (Rummler and Brache, 1995):

1. Aligning with the business
2. Networking
3. Building relationships
4. Growing clients to become HPT-aware
5. Leveraging training responsibility

For each strategy, there are particular tactics that serve the HPT consultant.

Aligning with the Business

HPT consultants have found success with the following five tactics for aligning HPT practice with the businesses it supports.

Learn the Client's Language. HPT consultants learn and use the technical terms specific to the industry, as well as the organizational "buzzwords du jour" when talking with clients or writing materials for them. They carefully avoid

HPT jargon and replace it with terminology from the client's world. For example, "needs analysis" is HPT jargon, but an HPT consultant working in the financial services industry, for example can discuss "performance audits" because an audit is meaningful in financial businesses.

Identify Senior Management Proponents. Once the HPT consultant has a program successfully implemented and a senior manager pleased with the results, that manager is a likely proponent for other interventions. The HPT consultant should ask for that support. Experience shows that these managers can become performance improvement partners, marketers, and even HPT evangelists.

Move from Support to Collaboration. As a consultant, become adept at building relationships with clients. Remember names, follow promotions, and offer services and ideas for new initiatives. When consultants build tight interpersonal relationships with clients and add value, the reward is being privy to advance information. A consultant who becomes part of the client's "inner circle" is able to spot performance improvement opportunities sooner and offer further HPT support, thus moving from support to collaboration.

Set Up Reliable Line Liaisons. When HPT consultants develop business friendships with line personnel, they receive current information. Their line allies test materials, suggest other resources, and market good HPT work. These vital contacts can be made at meetings and through collaboration on different projects. They can be enlisted for a new initiative. Successful HPT consultants stay in contact with their line liaisons.

Hire Line Employees with Parallel Skills. A talented salesperson with a flair for writing or presenting is a good prospect for an entry-level HPT position. If an HPT staff member is recruited from a pool of respected people within the client's organization, the HPT group's credibility will increase, and this development will make it easier to win the client's acceptance of HPT interventions.

Networking

Now that connections have been made through alignment with the businesses, the HPT consultant should take the next step and identify the resources needed to help the businesses improve its performance. Here are five effective tactics in this area.

Build Resources and Relationships. Consultants are valued for the specialists they know and the resources they can access. The broader their HPT networks are, and the more knowledgeable they are about business practices and clients' industries, the easier it is to give clients what they need. Many resources exist outside every organization. It is important to find them in order to help clients solve problems and meet their goals.

Get Involved Professionally. Active involvement in professional organizations and industry-specific groups helps HPT consultants learn more about the businesses they serve. Meeting with other members, finding out what they know, and making them professional resources adds value to the HPT consultant's skills.

Set Up Mutual Aid. Sometimes all a client needs is someone to do the legwork— locate the specialist, look at how another group solved a similar problem, or learn from a pilot project. HPT consultants often leverage their knowledge of various clients' activities by putting them in touch with each other to share information or explore interventions. A peer line manager can be more credible than a consultant, for example. The two managers can help each other and bring the HPT consultant in when they need particular expertise.

Let the Client Be a Marketer. Once credibility is established with a client, that client will sing the HPT consultant's praises to peers and superiors. Consultants can gain great mileage from creating innovative job aids, videotapes, training formats, and other developmental necessities that take on lives of their own— and often find their way to other managers who want to use them. One way to measure success is to track how quickly a new tool finds its way back to its creator and is presented as a great discovery.

Partner with Other Staff Groups. Some HPT consultants identify other departments that also support their clients. They meet with these groups, learn what the groups do, and discuss how, together, they can help their clients in common. For example, in one such alliance, the HPT consultants traded presentation skills for additional resources and were able to help each other and their clients. The HPT consultants made some good business contacts, and their clients received twice the expected service.

Building Relationships

As HPT consultants "work the room" (Roane, 1988) inside their organizations, they develop opportunities to address performance improvement issues. Here are four effective tactics for doing so.

Partner with Line Managers. Many managers will be excited to learn some HPT techniques. When an alert HPT consultant hears of a project in a client group, that consultant can offer to serve as a team member in exchange for the opportunity to learn more about the business. Line managers who are forward-thinking and like to try new things often welcome such "beta testing" opportunities. In exchange for valuable feedback, these managers have the first chance to use a new HPT product or service.

Help Managers Polish Their Presentation Skills. An HPT consultant can offer personal presentation coaching to client managers. Working privately with such managers can build rapport and help them be successful. One client, for example, was a good presenter and loved to instruct. With an HPT consultant's help, she further sharpened her presentation skills and went on to develop innovative customer service techniques that she now teaches her employees.

Showcase Client Managers. After strong, trusting partnerships have been developed with line managers, the HPT consultant can help them by showcasing them in special programs. In one such case, a client was a superb salesperson and a strong presenter. An HPT consultant convinced her to take the lead in a sales videotape and work with professional actors. She was grateful to be selected and gained new respect for HPT as a result. The two have become true partners. The client now approaches her HPT consultant with ideas, asks for solutions to HPT issues in her area, and has received editorial support on a series of professional articles she has written.

Give Clients Current Business Books. One of the easiest ways to be sure clients are current on the latest management theories and practices is to give them best-selling management books. Savvy performers want to read what is new in business. By giving them useful books to guide their thinking and enhance their knowledge, HPT consultants will please and impress their clients.

Growing Clients to Become HPT-Aware

When a client becomes a partner, the HPT consultant is in a position to grow that client's awareness of HPT. The true test of HPT-awareness transfer is when a consultant's own HPT words come back to him or her in conversation or by other means.

Get Clients to Give Presentations. One effective method of getting clients to become HPT-aware is to invite client-partners to speak at an HPT venue. The present authors used to coteach "Introduction to Human Performance Technology" at a local university. One of the guest speakers in this class was a line manager who used HPT tools and techniques to improve performance among his staff members. This speaker gave instant cachet to HPT. He leveraged his HPT "expert user" status to become a successful keynote speaker at an international conference, and he paid the ultimate compliment by using HPT language to describe what he had done.

Share HPT Tools and Models with Savvy Managers. Many managers have been shown how to use the Performance Architecture Map with great success. When they use this model to diagnose performance problems, they gain a degree of independence and control that increases their own self-esteem as well as the value of their HPT consultants.

Help Managers Design Special Off-Sites and Retreats. Innovative managers enjoy the process of inventing something new and exciting, teaching a new skill, or raising awareness. A consultant can offer HPT expertise to such clients, design one-of-a-kind activities to meet their needs and showcase them. For example, one HPT consultant designed a session for a senior manager who wanted to raise her transition team's awareness of its responsibilities during an acquisition. The manager and her HPT consultants created an amusing exercise called "Burgers and Banking," wherein a chain of diners merged with a bank, and the two businesses had to combine their operations, products, and services. The manager had fun leading the workshop, and the participants enjoyed themselves and got the message.

Leveraging Training Responsibility

An easy way to introduce HPT tools and techniques to an organization is through an existing training department's activities. Here are three key tactics for leveraging what is already in place.

Move Training Ownership to the Line. Managers are expected to coach their people on the job and to see that their employees acquire the skills and knowledge needed to do their jobs. What would happen if an HPT consultant developed programs and materials for them that the HPT department did not own? What if the group that controlled the content owned the materials? A purchasing course, for example, could belong to the purchasing department, interviewing skills to human resources, and selling skills to sales. Some HPT consultants have been able to transfer training ownership with great success. A consultant and a line manager agree to update or revamp materials as necessary: the consultant does the work, but the consultant does not own the product.

Train and Develop Line Trainers. When an HPT consultant must work with budgetary constraints, a small training staff, or more requests from clients than can be effectively handled, hiring subject matter experts (SMEs) as instructors can be an excellent solution. The HPT consultant develops the programs and trains the SMEs. The SMEs teach because they know the content best. This is an excellent strategy because it is easier to train an expert to instruct than it is to train an instructor to be a content expert.

Get Senior Managers to Teach. Consultants can innovate still more by using senior managers to teach formal classes and workshops. Many managers have strong presentation skills or have taught in the past and enjoy teaching. With help from a senior manager who is a proponent, an HPT consultant can create a culture change in support of manager-instructors.

SUCCESSFUL HPT IMPLEMENTATION: NINE CASES

When organizations are in pain, they call for help. Typically, organizations feel pain in work processes, in individual performance, or in every area. When a manager requests help, the consultant must find out where the intervention should be directed. It could be for a group of employees who all do the same job, or perhaps for a department or a division, or again the intervention may be part of a larger initiative that will affect the entire organization. A useful way to talk about this with clients is to refer to the needs of the *work* (processes), the *workers* (performers), and the *workplace* (organization).

As the Performance Architecture Map shows, it is important to identify the primary site of the performance improvement opportunity and then examine the other sites as well because an HPT intervention in a work process, for example, is likely to affect specific performers and, possibly, the whole organization. One trait of seasoned HPT consultants is that they never stop looking for opportunities to improve performance.

HPT lore suggests that 80 percent of the problems brought to HPT consultants are not related to training but rather to some other aspect of performance. Even if a training component is necessary, it is likely that it would be best first to address interventions in other quadrants of the Performance Architecture Map. The only times people need training are when they do not know how to do something or when something completely new has been added to their work responsibilities.

One useful way to identify an intervention that will be successful is to ask what changes have to take place in current performance. Is it necessary to *establish* performance (the performance is not yet present)? *improve* performance (the performance exists in the worker, in the work, or in the workplace but must be made better)? *maintain* performance (the performance exists and must continue at the current level)? *extinguish* performance (the performance exists and must be stopped)? (See Langdon, 1997.)

It will be useful to study the state of performance in each of the cases that follow. The cases come from both for-profit and not-for-profit organizations. The appropriate HPT interventions were successfully implemented with the strategies previously described in this chapter.

Creating a New Sales Culture

The training department of an energy services company was asked to develop its first sales training program. Fortunately, the HPT-savvy group realized the need for sales training originated not with the performers to be trained but with a change in the way the newly deregulated organization was doing business. The group recommended a sales performance audit to precede the training development. The audit identified all the components of a successful sales organization, such as incentives, tracking, sales management, and other tools and resources. Once the audit was completed, the company had a blueprint for creating its new sales culture. As the pieces were put in place, the training program was built and implemented successfully.

Two strategies brought success in this case. The first was the strategy of building relationships. The training manager in this case identified a proponent in senior management who would review the results of the sales performance audit. The senior manager, convinced that the missing components of the sales organization should be established, saw that they were established. The second strategy was that of leveraging training responsibility. This strategy took form when the senior manager demonstrated his commitment to the success of the training program by becoming the lead instructor and handpicking the other trainers.

Retraining Claims Processors

An insurance company's training department received a request to retrain two claims processors in one of the company's offices. The requesting line manager explained that these two employees had been on the job for some time and performed well but that recently their performance had deteriorated and they needed some refresher training.

As a seasoned HPT consultant, the training manager assumed that there was more to the story, and so she sent one of her HPT consultants to observe the two performers on the job. The HPT consultant entered a newly remodeled office, where the two employees in need of retraining had been placed in adjacent workstations. They were very pleased to be able, finally, to work next to each other because they were good friends.

The HPT consultant watched the two employees and observed that they talked to each other constantly. To partner with their manager in solving the problem, he shared the Performance Architecture Map. The manager identified the employees' declining performance on the grid. It did not take long to see the cause. To see if their performance would improve, the HPT consultant recommended that the employees be separated. Within a few days, the manager reported that their performance was back to the previous high levels.

By using the strategy of partnering with line managers, the HPT consultant shared responsibility for improving performance and provided a valuable tool for future use. In addition, he demonstrated another key principle of performance technology: observation uncovers a level of information that is rarely disclosed in conversation.

Simplifying a Ponderous Performance Review

The CEO of a high-tech firm was fanatical about developing his employees. To ensure their development, he insisted on the very best policies and procedures. He asked his human resources department to develop a leading-edge performance review program, with specific developmental plans provided, so that all employees would not only be fairly evaluated but would also be able to develop. The HR department responded by creating a state-of-the-art program. The cornerstones were two large manuals containing all the materials necessary for a successful performance review.

One year after its implementation, the program was considered a failure. No performance reviews had been completed. Managers complained that the process did not work. The CEO was distraught and still wanted his pet program to go forward. The HR department, looking for help, got in touch with an HPT consultant and were referred to an organization of consultants who specialized in redesigning information.

The consultants worked with the HR department to analyze the situation. They asked the HR manager to draw a flowchart of the steps in the failed performance review process. The steps themselves were clear and logical. When the consultants asked to see the other materials used in the program, they were given the two large manuals.

The consultants discovered that the manuals were complicated, poorly organized, not indexed, and intimidating. The required forms were also difficult to use. Managers disliked the amount of paper needed to complete a performance review and found the process too time-consuming. Upon closer examination, the consultants also saw that the manuals used HR jargon rather than the business terms more familiar to the managers.

The consultants proposed to simplify what was clearly a good system by changing the design of the materials rather than the design of the process. They replaced the two manuals with a simple job aid developed from the HR manager's flowchart. They redesigned the forms to include business language and clear formats, and they placed the most commonly used forms on the company's intranet for easy access.

The consultants recognized the importance of implementation, particularly the implementation of a redesigned program. They asked the CEO to reintroduce the program by advocating for it in a new introductory letter, to be followed by additional communication and by a special request for feedback on the program to be given directly to him.

The HR department had used the strategy of networking to find the needed expertise. The reimplementation was a success because the consultants used the strategy of aligning with the business.

Shrinking a Job Aid

The HR manager at a retail chain asked an HPT consultant to review some materials earmarked for store managers. The materials concerned what was then the new Family Leave Act. The HR manager knew from experience that HPT consultants had the writing and layout skills that are useful in simplifying complex communications. She envisioned a basic job aid that would allow managers to decide whether a situation was covered by the Family Leave Act and that would then guide them through a simple process for completing the paperwork.

The HR manager sent the consultant a thirty-six-page document that covered every conceivable situation an employee could face. It was filled with details, exceptions, and explanations and included a number of forms. Fortunately, the HPT consultant was both ignorant of the Family Leave Act and overwhelmed by its complexity. After eliminating detail and consolidating similar information, the consultant produced a six-page job aid that included a decision tree and an all-purpose form. The HR manager was delighted, and the store managers found the job aid easy to use.

This case demonstrates the value of being an HPT specialist rather than a subject matter expert. It also demonstrates the importance of coming through for clients when they request something outside a consultant's usual arena. The consultant in this case benefited from the strategy of growing clients to be HPT-aware. By educating the HR manager about the power of HPT, the consultant enabled the manager to successfully implement organizational practices in compliance with a new federal law. This case, like the case of the performance review, involved both the networking strategy and a solution that used redesigned information as well as a simplified process.

Helping a Dysfunctional Board Become Functional

Networking also paid off in the case of an HPT consultant who was referred to the board of a community organization that was in distress. The board members had been together for a year and were finding it increasingly difficult to work together as a team. Their trust in one other had deteriorated, and they were split into adversarial factions. The board asked the HPT consultant for assistance with team building.

Through a series of interviews and a one-day consultation, the HPT consultant determined that job descriptions, working agreements, targeted outcomes, and operational processes were all lacking. In short, there was total absence of all the structural underpinnings that are needed to conduct business; no amount of team-building activity would have been able to repair this situation.

The consultant named and described the missing elements, explained their importance, and suggested that the board determine how to put them in place. The board enthusiastically followed the consultant's recommendations and created its own structure for successful operation.

The HPT consultant had been able to zero in on the missing structure by using the strategy of aligning with the business. He also provided direction to a group of knowledgeable people who were then able, essentially, to "fix" themselves. This case illustrates an important skill for the HPT consultant: knowing when to stop. All clients have different needs, different levels of skill and knowledge, and varying degrees of interest in having an HPT consultant implement solutions. This case represents one of the best situations for an HPT consultant, when clients want to know what is wrong and are then willing and able to deal with the problem themselves.

Recovering Lost Millions

A very large nonprofit organization had lost control of the business operations that surrounded the variety of publications it distributed to its members. The organization did not even know how much it spent producing and mailing its publications. A group of HPT consultants who were working at this organization on another project became aware of this situation and brought it to the attention of their client. The result was a new project that reaped major rewards, both for the observant consultants and for their client.

Initially, the HPT consultants researched the number of different subjects covered in the publications and matched these subjects to members' interests. To the client's surprise, the subjects of most interest to members were represented by the fewest publications; and, conversely, the subjects of least interest were represented by many more publications. The HPT consultants recommended a realignment of the publications, and this recommendation resulted in considerable savings.

Even greater savings were realized, however, when the consultants took the next step: they requested samples of all the publications and the envelopes used to mail them. The majority of publications were produced on custom-size paper, costly in itself. To mail these publications, expensive custom-size envelopes were also required. The HPT consultants recommended that standard-size envelopes be selected first, and that the publications then be sized to fit the envelopes. This recommendation resulted in a return to standard-size paper and a consequent annual savings for the organization of $10 million.

In this case, the strategies included aligning with the business, networking, building relationships, and growing clients to become HPT-aware. As happened in this case, consultants often discover, in the course of an investigation, opportunities to improve an organization's performance. A seasoned HPT consultant will take the time to conduct a thorough investigation of all the organizational aspects that may be related to the stated problem, to help ensure that nothing has been overlooked.

Mentoring Unprepared Students

A large brokerage house was in the habit of forward-hiring new broker trainees and placing them in regional offices. The core training for these employees entailed a six-week school session that was offered once each quarter. In preparation for this school session, the new hires were to complete several self-study courses in order to acquire rudimentary knowledge.

On the first day of the school, the new hires were given a test to determine how much they had learned from the self-study courses. The test was widely discussed and feared because anyone who failed was eliminated from the school and usually from the company as well.

The new hires complained about the test, the manager of the school complained about the number of failures, and the regional office managers complained about their inability to adequately prepare their employees for the school. One of the company's regional staff development managers knew that the amount of guidance and support that the new hires received varied from office to office in her region. She suspected that those who passed the dreaded first test had more conscientious managers than those who failed. She proposed to her regional manager a study program for the new hires that would be the same for everyone and would prepare everyone equally for success in the school.

With endorsement and support from the line managers in her region, she and her staff created a mentored curriculum. It was managed locally and involved the broker trainees' immediate managers as mentors. Together, the managers and the broker trainees chose learning activities, tracked progress, and made sure that all the requirements were met before the start of the school.

As a result, the number of new hires who failed the first test decreased significantly, as did training costs and attrition. Other regional managers were impressed with the results and requested that the program be implemented in their areas. The strategies at work here were those of building relationships and leveraging training responsibility.

Working with Engineers in an Offshore Start-Up Plant

An HPT consulting firm had done successful work at an industrial chemical manufacturing plant in the United States. As a result, the manufacturer asked the consultants to develop a training program for engineers who were to start up and operate a plant that was being built in the People's Republic of China. The engineers at the manufacturer's U.S. plant were accustomed to maintaining their operations by making continuous modifications, but the manufacturer did not want to replicate these shortcuts in the China plant because of the high risk that the inexperienced engineers might make potentially catastrophic mistakes.

The consultants conducted a thorough job and task analysis, creating flowcharts so that they understood the work to be completed. They followed with a skills analysis for the Chinese engineers and had subject matter experts (SMEs) from the U.S. plant verify the accuracy of the task analysis.

Neither the consultants nor the SMEs from the United States spoke Chinese, and the Chinese engineers spoke limited English. The consultants recognized that, given the language differences and the need for accuracy and safety in the new plant, a guaranteed performance intervention was essential. They decided on job aids as the most effective method for meeting all the project's constraints.

The consultants hired a visiting Chinese professor from the University of California at Davis as an interpreter for the Chinese engineers who needed to be trained in the new operations. The deliverables were four binders that included detailed job aids and a guide to safe performance, in addition to a facilitator's guide for the SMEs from the United States. Three of the SMEs trained the Chinese engineers, who in turn were responsible for training those who assisted them in the new plant.

Now that all this careful, detailed work has been completed, the new plant operates at a higher level of production and quality than it was originally designed to do. Because of these outstanding results, when a second plant was built, this one in Malaysia, the same resources were used for performance guides. This plant, too, is exceeding its goals.

Networking was the strategy that made this project successful: the consulting firm was originally referred to the U.S. plant, and was offered the work for the new plant, because of its previous success. This case also illustrates how important it is for HPT consultants to have strong project management skills. It took more than a year for the five consultants and a large group of U.S. engineers to complete this project. The intricacies of the subject matter, the criticality of safety, and the language and cultural challenges all show how crucial the details of a project can be.

Reorganizing the Workspace of Crammed-In Employees

A government agency realized that its employees, working in crowded conditions, were not functioning as well as they otherwise could have, but the agency had no way to increase the size of the workspace. The agency engaged the services of a workspace redesign consultant to determine how best to reconfigure the limited space in order to reduce interference with the employees' work.

The workspace consultant knew that environment plays an important part in work productivity. She began with an analysis to uncover the concerns of managers and employees, observing and listening carefully to their answers when she asked, "What gets in the way of you doing your best work?" Her findings were as follows:

- Most employees had cluttered work surfaces because they did not have enough storage space.
- People with very different jobs were clustered together without regard for their differing workspace and privacy needs.
- Employees who needed to do critical thinking did not have adequate quiet space.
- Nearby common equipment was very noisy.
- Everyone complained about having too much work to do and felt very stressed.

To minimize these interferences, the consultant analyzed the physical space for its role both in supporting and interfering with the work being done. She then began a reorganization by moving those who required more concentration to quieter areas, separating them from noise and other distractions. This action enabled her to create a new circulation path, which redirected traffic through the entire space. It also reduced employees' travel time through the office and shielded their workspaces from the noisy equipment.

Next, to further minimize distractions, the consultant physically oriented people in their workspaces to be facing away from the busier areas. She added overhead shelves in each workspace so that employees could clear their cluttered work surfaces and work more easily and comfortably.

The result, besides happier employees, grateful managers, and higher-quality work completed more quickly, was improved overall departmental performance. Workers' complaints also diminished. Moreover, because the only addition was the overhead shelves, the reorganization costs were very low. The effective strategies in this case were networking, because the consultant had built a solid reputation that had earned her the referral, and building relationships, because effective solutions can grow only out of established relationships between consultants and clients.

CONCLUSION

In each of the cases discussed in this chapter, the consultants helped their clients be successful by using strategies that fit the situations and the organizational cultures. In each case, the best possible HPT intervention was the one most appropriate to the climate, the budget, and the time frame.

Relying on a Systematic Approach

The interventions were successful because the consultants relied on a systematic approach, using HPT models and tools to keep them focused on gathering all relevant information before making recommendations. In every case, the consultants leveraged strategies to involve clients, add value for the organization, and have a visible impact on the bottom line.

There are many frameworks from which performance can be improved in organizations. The Performance Architecture Map was chosen in this chapter because it illustrates the importance of using HPT models that fit the way in which managers describe their employees: according to competence and attitude. The map also successfully closes the language gap between HPT and business.

When performance models are used to involve the client and make analysis and solutions accessible, it is possible to shorten the client education process and create a working partnership more quickly. The more frequently consultants can put HPT performance tools into their clients' hands, the easier it is to turn the intervention or its results over to the client, and that is where ownership of the solution should rest—with the client.

Learning Lessons

There is enormous opportunity for learning as organizations are introduced to HPT tools and processes. A difficult lesson all HPT consultants eventually learn is that they can conduct a perfect analysis of the problem, get all the right client involvement, and recommend the most suitable intervention, but the intervention can still fail. It is devastating when that happens, but it is also imperative to conduct a postmortem assessment when it does.

For example, an HPT consultant was asked to analyze the training function at a large customer service telephone call center to determine what changes would benefit the training staff, the employees trained, and, ultimately, the customers served. The consultant used two HPT models to structure the analysis, worked with the client to identify appropriate contacts and resources inside the call center, and received enthusiastic approval for the analysis design. The consultant kept the client informed as data collection progressed, and the client encouraged the consultant to continue. At the end of the analysis, the HPT consultant produced a detailed report of findings and recommendations that touched the work, the workers, and the workplace. The client thanked the consultant profusely for all the work but never acted on the report or its recommendations. Some time later, the HPT consultant stepped back to examine the whole project. She determined that the work had been done well and that the findings were complete, but that the call center's culture was simply not ready to support the recommended steps.

Making a Call to Action

The preceding example reinforces the overarching principles of bringing HPT into action in organizations. At the very least, consultants should be sure to do the following things:

- *Anticipate and innovate.* The future belongs to those who anticipate and innovate (Barker, 1992). HPT consultants are on the cutting edge of change in organizations, and they must also be on the cutting edge of their own profession.

- *Enroll the clients.* The HPT processes placed in front of clients, and the results achieved through interventions, are in the client's domain and should be firmly rooted there. Clients should own their results.

- *Stay true to HPT.* HPT is not a fad. It is a research-based, systematic way of identifying and responding to issues of human performance in the workplace. Successful HPT consultants follow the documented principles that work, use models and tools that make sense, and make these principles, models, and tools accessible to their clients.

References

Addison, R., and Johnson, M. (1997). The building blocks of performance. *Business Executive* 11:68, 3–5.

American Society for Training and Development. (1998, May). *The 1997 national HRD executive summary: Trends in HRD.* 1997 third-quarter survey report. < http://www.astd.com >

Barker, J. (1992). *Future edge: Discovering the new paradigms of success.* New York: Morrow.

Bassi, L., Cheney, S., and Van Buren, M. (1997, Nov.). *Training industry trends.* < http//:www.astd.com >

Gilbert, T. F. (1996). *Human competence: Engineering worthy performance.* Amherst, MA, and Washington, DC: Human Resources Development Press and International Society for Performance Improvement.

Langdon, D. (1997). Selecting interventions. *Performance Improvement* 36:10, 11–15.

Roane, S. (1998). *How to work a room.* New York: Warner Books.

Rosensweig, F. (1997). Performance improvement in developing countries. In R. Kaufman, S. Thiagarajan, and P. MacGillis (eds.), *The guidebook for performance improvement: Working with individuals and organizations.* San Francisco: Jossey-Bass/Pfeiffer.

Rummler, G. A., and Brache, A. P. (1995). *Improving performance.* San Francisco: Jossey-Bass.

HUMAN PERFORMANCE INTERVENTIONS OF A NONINSTRUCTIONAL NATURE

Now that Parts One and Two of this handbook have established the fundamentals of Human Performance Technology (HPT) and the HPT general process model, the emphasis turns in Part Three to the design and creation of interventions for performance improvement. First, however, an explanation is in order for the title of Part Three.

As Rosenberg, Coscarelli, and Hutchison point out in Chapter Two, the relationship between instructional technology and HPT is a close one. Many HPT practitioners began their professional or academic careers in the instructional and training arenas, and a considerable number still spend a major portion of their time designing instructional interventions because HP technologists are frequently called on to improve performance through training. For these reasons, HP technologists are often associated with instruction, even though their vision and their range of actual practice are far wider in scope.

The fact is that most HP technologists view training as a last resort, to be employed only when no other means of achieving improved performance will work. Even when instruction is required, it is frequently only one among a number of interventions employed to address a problem or realize an opportunity. This is so because HP technologists are all too aware that instruction or training cannot solve problems when feedback or incentive systems are lacking, or when resources and organizational infrastructures are inadequate to support the desired level of performance; hence the title of Part Three, a title chosen to underscore the range of alternatives other than instruction that are available for achieving the desired results. Only through careful and judicious guidance of the client, however, can the HPT professional eventually succeed in shifting the focus away from the narrower confines of training and toward the broader issues involved in performance.

What are the noninstructional alternatives? The first two chapters of Part Three provide guidance for the design of strategies that affect whole organizations. Here, HPT practitioners operate on a large canvas as they seek to alter organizational structures or modify cultures to obtain the desired results in terms of human performance. The next four chapters focus on the creation of systems that help improve human performance through better selection of people, provide stronger motivation and better compensation for effective performance, and offer systematic feedback to guide behavior. The final three chapters deal with helping people perform better on the job through the design of effective job aids, performance support systems, and workplace environments that support creative thinking. These interventions are presented independently, but the reader should recognize that they are often employed in combination.

Although many more chapters could have been included in Part Three, the ones that follow are exceptional in representing the latest thinking of recognized specialists in each of the intervention areas. As a group, these chapters constitute an outstanding guide for those seeking to increase a repertoire of means other than instruction to improve human performance in organizational contexts anywhere in the world.

CHAPTER SIXTEEN

Designing Better Organizations with Human Performance Technology and Organization Development

Peter J. Dean

The purpose of this chapter is to show how Human Performance Technology (HPT) can incorporate its "twin separated at birth" (personal conversation with Allison Rossett, 1996), organization development (OD), to improve the design and functioning of organizations. And, if HPT and OD are twins separated at birth, then organizational design is a close relative. How HPT and OD came to take separate paths at birth is beyond the scope of this chapter, as is how organizational design came to be part of the family. The focus of this chapter is how these three fields can be integrated so that HPT and OD can help to improve organizational design efforts.

What connects some areas of the HPT literature (Gilbert, 1996; Dean, 1994, 1995; Dean and Ripley, 1997, 1998a, 1998b, 1998c) with some areas of the OD literature (Argyris, 1993; Cummings and Worley, 1993; Bunker and Alban, 1997; Rothwell, Sullivan, and McLean, 1995; Trist, 1981; Weisbord, 1992; Weisbord and Janoff, 1995; Dean, 1983; Dean, Blevins, and Snodgrass, 1997) is the goal of bringing about individual performance improvement, meaningful productivity, and organizational success. Selected research literature from the field of organizational design (Emery, 1993; Galbraith, 1995; Galbraith and Lawler, 1993; Kochan and Useem, 1992; Mohrman and Cummings, 1989; Nadler and Tushman, 1997; Oshry, 1996; Panza, 1990; Panza and James, forthcoming; Rummler, personal correspondence; Rummler and Brache, 1996; Senge, 1990; Senge and others, 1994; Tushman and O'Reilly, 1996; Tushman, O'Reilly, and Nadler, 1989; Weisbord, 1987; Dean, 1993; Dean, Dean, and Guman, 1992), which looks at change from an organizational viewpoint, resonates well with the goals of HPT and OD, which look at change from the standpoint of process and the individual.

This chapter can help HPT professionals become ambidextrous, as it were, with respect to their fund of knowledge about overall organizational performance improvement. By including concepts from OD and organizational design, HPT professionals can practice the craft of performance improvement with many more tools. Both HPT and OD should be used in designing work environments and organizations. What follows is a description of the three related fields of HPT, OD, and organization design, with attention to how they are unique and how they are similar.

ORGANIZATIONAL DESIGN

The organization is a sum-total system of formal arrangements that houses the interaction of the structure, processes, and systems of the enterprise. It is created and designed by managers to enhance the interface between humans and the work the enterprise sets out to accomplish. The design can either enhance or hinder accomplishment of the purposes of the enterprise.

The manager, as organizational designer, crafts these arrangements to bring about congruence and alignment among the enterprise's structure, processes, systems, work, people, and performance. In this way, organizational design (Dean, 1993; Nadler and Tushman, 1997) ties together the following organizational variables:

- *Strategic vision,* which involves the mental picture of what the organization has to do in order to survive in business
- *Structure,* which deals with how tasks are divided and coordinated by means of specialization and integration, decentralization and centralization, and formal patterns of relationships between groups and individuals (as, for example, when a department reports to a division)
- *Processes,* which define and measure sequences of steps, activities, and methods that produce a specified goal, result, consequence, or output for a particular internal or external customer or market
- *Systems,* which entail the procedures for budgeting, accounting, and training that make the organization run, as well as a particular set of procedures and rules, policies, devices, guides, and practices designed to control processes in a predictable way
- *Competence,* which concerns the way managers manage, the way employees are selected, placed, oriented, developed, and rewarded, and the skills of both managers and employees

- *Culture,* which involves the patterns of basic shared assumptions, beliefs, attitudes, expectations, and values as revealed in everyday work performance and practices, and which includes such formal aspects as policies, processes, and procedures, which influence those patterns, as well as the balance between suppliers of resources (labor, materials, tools, equipment, facilities) and the efficiency and effectiveness of organizational performance

- *Management and employees,* who work together for integration of goals, policies, procedures, standards, information and feedback systems, incentive systems, training, and budget

- *Value, quality, and impact* of products and services, as well as customers' *satisfaction* with them, which will ultimately lead to competitive advantage

By ambitiously attempting to create an enterprise that is aligned on all these variables, organizational designers hope to harness the individual value-added aspects of all the variables to compete more successfully in the global marketplace.

The Global Market, Change, and Organizational Design

The challenges of change in business today are often global in scale. Business forces, sociopolitical forces, and economic forces drive the need for organizational change in strategies, policies, structures, processes, systems, and tactics. Managerial discretion in the design, development, and deployment of organizational variables has become even more critical than in the past.

Writing on the inflexibility of organizations, Kochan and Useem (1992) suggest continuous, systemic organizational change that is integrated among these major variables. It must be oriented to the long term in order to provide a more suitable foundation for cooperation, learning, and innovation. These authors also suggest that learning and learning how to learn are the essential capacities for an organization in which improved organizational design is sought. Gilbert (1996) and Dean (1994) suggest that organizational design emerges from individuals' operating at different levels of vantage within an organization.

Galbraith and Lawler (1993) suggest that successful organizations will be those that are best able to design themselves to meet the new realities of business. Nadler and Tushman (1997) suggest that a truly high-performance work system would involve strategic organizational design pursued from the top down, a process that establishes an architectural frame for the total organization. In addition, operational designers would work from the bottom up, researching details, workflow, and the consistency of work.

Future success in the global marketplace will come from the shift toward a more open, flexible hierarchy with a participative learning system in which leaders and managers foster two-way communication, decentralized decision making, informal networks cross-cutting formal boundaries, and a common set of values (Kochan and Useem, 1992). It has also been suggested that all the organizational variables can be integrated within a self-designing learning organization (Mohrman and Cummings, 1989).

Whatever the suggestions for change on the basis of the field of variables within which an organizational designer may have to work, one idea becomes clear: whether the organization is a multinational corporation, a small business, or a religious organization, its design has effects on the performance of individuals. However, there exists a major misunderstanding in traditional managerial ranks about how to improve performance in people.

Management's Incorrect Inferences

The success of an organization depends on the ability of the performers in the organization to continue to perform well while dealing with change. According to Jitendra Vir Singh of the Wharton School at the University of Pennsylvania (personal correspondence, 1998), failure results from a fundamental attribution error in the everyday inferences about cause and effect that managers make about employees. This fundamental error predisposes individuals to overemphasize humans as the cause of problems and to underestimate the role that environmental variables play in causing resistance to plans for change. This results in managerial decision makers trying to "fix" individuals in the workplace rather than influencing workplace behavior by designing organizational contexts. This is the where knowledge of HPT enters the picture, for it deals with the interplay between the individual and the work environment.

HPT

HPT gives management the ability to manage organizational variables and their interfaces. For example, an HPT practitioner would work with processes for distributing information in order to communicate expectations for and feedback on performance. HPT also deals with resources for task support (such as tools, materials, equipment, supplies, and time to do the work), the nature of the physical work environment and the job design, and rewards, recognition, and incentives in the specific work operation. Therefore, decisions about the design of an organization have direct bearing on individual performance. The HPT professional does the following things (Dean, 1994):

- Focuses on the whole system to understand the complexity first
- Seeks to discover links between different structures, processes, and systems

- Uses both quantitative and qualitative methods, as needed
- Uses both analysis and synthesis, as needed
- Uses language to deliver information clearly and for joint understanding
- Uses observation, not hearsay, to collect facts
- Relies on direct, comparative, and economic measures
- Removes work that does not add value

The HPT professional attempts to align the person with a work-supporting system so that the entire organization, consisting of the variables already discussed, can work more efficiently and effectively. Therefore, organizational design and HPT are distinct and unique in their bases of application, and yet they seem to aid each other in improving the performance of the individuals and the overall performance of the organization. OD is likewise unique in its tools and methods, and yet it works to improve performance as well.

WHAT OD HAS TO OFFER

OD has traditionally focused on improving the human dynamics in the enterprise. OD encourages management to look at the informal operating patterns in the substructures, subprocesses, practices, and political arrangements of the organization. This effort directly engages the values, beliefs, and accepted norms of the organization. Like organizational design and HPT, OD is also a response to an expressed need for change. This change involves largely interpersonal issues and is intended to examine and alter the social processes of an enterprise's culture so that it can better adapt to new technologies, markets, challenges, and the rate of change itself with improved communications, decision making, and planning. Over the years, the field of OD has accumulated tools and methods that include the following:

- Sensitivity training (1940s)
- Conflict resolution and team building (1950s)
- Intergroup development and open systems planning (1960s)
- Sociotechnical systems analysis and measures of quality of work life (1970s)
- Organization transformation, Total Quality Management, and large-scale change (1980s)
- Reengineering, large-group intervention, transcultural planning, and transnational community building (1990s)

OD operates out of a set of core values, which include the following:

- Integration of individual and organizational needs
- Choice, freedom and responsibility
- Dignity, integrity, self-worth, and fundamental rights
- Cooperation and collaboration
- Authenticity and openness
- Effectiveness, efficiency, interdependence, and alignment
- A holistic, systemic vantage point and orientation toward stakeholders
- Participation, confrontation, and adaptability

OD has traditionally relied on the interpersonal strategy of normative reeducation, without giving attention to the economic, political, technological, legal, and ethical issues that affect the organization. Moreover, OD has largely not used evaluation or criterion-based measurement, yet it has used powerful interventions. Rothwell, Sullivan, and McLean (1995) suggest a number of OD intervention methods, described in the sections that follow.

Societal Interventions

These interventions are transcultural planning and community-building processes. They cut across beliefs, values, and national borders.

Total Organizational Interventions

These interventions include redesigning the strategic goals, objectives, and directions for improved long-term outcomes by using market trends and information collected from employees. Conflicts across groups or within subgroups of the organization are confronted and resolved. These interventions use communication audits, ethics audits, value system audits, and the like. Structural interventions can alter reporting relationships and the overall purpose of an organizational component. Process interventions are intended to improve the core processes and subprocesses of the work design or workflow of an organization, linking the people and the technology. Interventions aimed at large-scale systems change bring together as many individuals from the entire system as possible for a total-system overhaul; the technique most often used is the Future Search Conferences developed by Weisbord (1992).

Team and Group Interventions

The OD interventions used for teams, units, and cross-functional groups include the following:

- Conflict-resolution and third-party interventions, to reduce destructive conflict and improve relationships
- Diagnosis, survey feedback, and process consultation, to focus attention on how individuals and groups interact, on team building and the overall quality of work life, and on the assessment and clarifying of individual and group values
- Group, unit, and subunit goal setting, to improve current workflow and plan later workflows
- Open-systems mapping and planning, to improve inputs, outputs, and the transformation of processes and subprocesses for the purpose of reducing behavior that does not add value
- Quality circles and scheduling reviews, to optimize the productivity of teams, units, or subunits
- Job redesign and subprocess improvement, to better productivity, enrich job incumbents with greater individual responsibility, and allow for life-long career planning
- Group-process consultation, to improve subsystems and subfunctions, with this improvement to be reflected in development of subpolicies and procedure manuals
- Multiskill and cross-functional training, to provide individuals with the knowledge, skills, and attitudes necessary for them to do their jobs

Individual-Level Interventions

Interventions at the level of the individual include the following:

- Coaching and counseling, to establish helping relationships and address interpersonal problems
- Personal goal-setting meetings with the OD professional, the employee, and the supervisor
- Changes to the performance appraisal system, focusing on the methods of measurement and their consequences, and establishment of accurate job descriptions
- Individual training for knowledge, skills, and attitudes with immediate applicability to the job

COORDINATION OF HPT AND OD

Both HPT and OD are concerned with improving the effectiveness of the enterprise system and the effectiveness of the people who work in that system. With greater awareness of OD tools, the HPT professional can do a better job.

According to Toni Hupp, president of Organizations By Design of Warrenville, Illinois (personal correspondence, 1998), the HPT professional often has to correct the consequences of what has or has not been designed and must often enlist the help of an OD professional to help with the design, redesign, development, or rethinking of the work to achieve fit among the purpose, processes, and people of the organization. In this kind of collaboration, the HPT professional would work to correct the alignment or congruence of workflow through the different levels of the formal culture of the organization, whereas the OD professional would focus on the informal culture of the organization and the development of any potential among its people that is not being expressed in their performance (Emery, 1993). Many members of the International Society for Performance Improvement, Toni Hupp among them, have successfully coordinated the use of HPT, organizational design, and OD. Hupp, for example, does not attempt to create the perfect design but rather to create a self-adaptive system by aligning three fundamental areas:

1. *Environment (the external context) and strategic direction (the organization's responses, and its corresponding purpose and strategy)*. This area involves knowledge of organizational design.

2. *Work process and technology*. This area has to do with what it takes to produce the organization's products and services and measure the accomplishment of work. It involves the power of HPT.

3. *People, organizational structures, and HR systems*. This area has to do with how people are organized, how authority and responsibility are distributed, and how people are selected, developed, and rewarded. It coordinates knowledge of OD, organizational design, and HPT.

The self-adapting system thus created is designed to do several things:

- Be increasingly self-regulating and more responsive to its business context

- Deploy a work process that is fast, focused, and flexible

- Include people with the collective expertise to plan, coordinate, control, and troubleshoot their own start-to-finish work process

- Construct jobs that build contributors' ownership and commitment

Hupp relies on four key design principles:

- Thinking in wholes
- Creating self-regulating units

- Viewing people as a resource, not as a commodity
- "Walking the talk" (a concept sometimes also captured by the phrase "Be the change you want to see")

These four principles are described in the sections that follow.

Thinking in Wholes

The best design for a productive system is one in which each part of the system embodies the goals of the overall system. When there is joint optimization, the effectiveness of the whole is more powerful than the effectiveness of the parts.

Creating Self-Regulating Units

Units should be sufficiently self-regulating so that they can cope with problems and seize opportunities by rearranging their own resources. Here are some ways of allowing units to regulate themselves:

- Provide for internal coordination and control.
- Provide information and discretion directly to those who need it, when they need it.
- Provide "requisite variety": internal flexibility should be appropriate to environmental variability, and feedback systems should be as complex as the variances they need to control.
- Provide for redundancy of functions (via multiskilled contributors) rather than redundancy of parts (as would occur with staffing that supported narrowly conceived, specialized functions). Enhance capacity by enlarging roles, not by adding specialists.
- The design process should set minimal critical specifications: do not carve in stone what should be left to local discretion.

Viewing People as Resources

Jobs should meet the six psychological criteria set out by Emery (1993):

1. Elbow room (autonomy)
2. Learning (permission for individuals to set their own goals and get direct feedback)
3. Variety
4. Support and respect
5. Meaningfulness (permission for individuals to see the big picture and create something important)
6. A desirable future

Walking the Talk

The change process should demonstrate and reinforce the hoped-for outcomes. The design process is more about getting the system to see itself and adapt than about perfecting workflow and structure. The process should be participative, not representative; that is, it should be undertaken by the people who must make it work, not by a representative design team working in isolation. Moreover, the process is never finished: rather than being a transition from one stable state to another, it is a move from one period of transition to another.

Hupp offers three possible approaches to design:

1. Management can undertake it.
2. A design team can undertake it.
3. It can be undertaken by a critical mass of stakeholders working in large-scale organizational design conferences.

Design by Management. The advantages of this approach are that it offers speed and produces the design that management wants. (If managers have already decided what they want, the consultant should not try to manipulate the organization into reading the managers' minds and producing the design that the managers want.) The disadvantage is that it lacks input from knowledgeable sources and may also lack support from those who will be affected by the change.

Design by Design Team. The advantage of this approach is that it offers quality because the design is undertaken by people who are skilled in such work. It also offers some level of grassroots support, given the representative composition of the team. The disadvantage is that it lacks speed and may also lack widespread support because only a small group of employees will be involved (and that group will become isolated over time).

Design by Stakeholders. As already mentioned, in this approach the stakeholders would be working in the context of large-scale organizational design conferences. The general advantage of this approach is that if offers high-quality design, greater ownership, and speed. A general disadvantage is that this approach requires a large group of employees to be absent from their jobs while the conferences are going on. Another general disadvantage is that it requires careful planning: large "critical mass" groups are more difficult to facilitate than small design teams or management groups. Yet another general disadvantage involves management's readiness for the design: this process is a difficult one to stop, and if managers have second thoughts, their blunder is very public.

In addition to their general advantages and disadvantages, large-scale organizational design conferences entail some specific advantages. When work is designed for alignment with strategic direction, work processes, organizational structure, and jobs, the following benefits are gained:

- *Better coordination and information flow.* When work is organized around whole products or services, people who need to cooperate with each other are on the same team and are focused on a common goal. (In the past, work has typically been organized around functions, putting people who need to cooperate with each other in different work groups to pursue function-specific goals.)

- *Reduced costs and cycle time.* When workflow is streamlined, steps that do not add value are removed or minimized. This reduces costs, cycle time, and the opportunity for error. Moreover, when mature work teams plan and monitor their own work, fewer managers are needed. The managers who remain can focus on integrating efforts across teams and developing business strategy.

- *Improved responsiveness to customers.* When work is organized around products, services, or customer groups, employees get greater access to customers, become better at anticipating customers' needs, and provide better-informed and more responsive customer service.

- *More innovation.* When employees are given the opportunity and responsibility to improve their products, services, and processes, the distance between ideas and their implementation is reduced.

- *More value added through people.* When employees produce whole products or services rather than isolated fragments, they take more ownership of their jobs. Moreover, jobs that integrate thinking with doing result in greater job satisfaction. Finally, when managers focus on integrating instead of supervising, they concentrate on getting people to work together across boundaries, not on second-guessing individual efforts. This reorientation focuses them on adding value, not on micromanaging their subordinates' work.

- *More flexibility.* When the organization deploys a broadly skilled workforce, it gets more flexibility than when it deploys a narrowly skilled one.

Hupp recommends seven special precautions in the use of large-scale organizational design conferences:

1. At the front end, management needs to do the hard work of thinking through what will and will not be accepted.

2. Aligning the organization—that is, making it an open, learning organization in which the workers who perform the core process are invested with the authority and accountability to plan, make decisions, and seize the opportunities that are embedded in their processes—involves a fundamental power shift from hierarchical to participative power, and from expert diagnosis and prescription (doing things *to* the line organization) to the power of line contributors to examine and adapt their own system (doing things *through* the line organization).

3. Before the process begins, it should be confirmed that management is ready for the shift. Do managers intend to become strategic rather than tactical? integrators rather than empire builders? resource brokers rather than resource controllers?

4. Members of the planning or steering team for the conferences need to play the role of advocates for the process, not critics of it.

5. Change management means more than good public relations. It means engaging stakeholders in working through the real conflicts and polarities that underlie differences, not smoothing them over with insubstantial talk.

6. Facilitators of large-scale conferences need to make sure that enough time is allowed, and that forums are provided for handling conflict. They need to be skilled in building sustainable agreements among diverse stakeholders.

7. Sponsors, advocates, and consultants need to remember that the ultimate answers do not lie in the method of using large-scale conferences; that method is simply a tool. The system's stakeholders already have all the wisdom they need to find their answers. It is the job of sponsors, advocates, and consultants to get the stakeholders to discuss the right questions so that they can collectively uncover the truth that is already there, buried under the organizational clutter.

SUMMARY

This chapter has described organizational design, HPT, and OD and how they can work together to change the enterprise system. If the design of the organizational system is influenced, the way in which that system operates is also influenced, and the operation of that system has a direct influence over individual performers. Thus organizational designers directly influence the performance of individuals.

It has been said many times that the person most central to the destiny of a ship is not the captain, the engineer, the navigator, or the person at the wheel but rather the ship's designer, the person who sets in motion the processes in which everyone else will have a role. In the same way, the organizational designer must take advantage of all the available tools and technologies of HPT and OD to bring about desired and needed results. Collectively, these tools and technologies can help the organizational designer realize a vision for the organization.

Likewise, HPT professionals can take responsibility for using the principles of organizational design to link the value of HPT with OD, thereby helping companies organize themselves and deal with the complexities of large-scale organizational life. OD professionals can also use HPT models, methods, and measures to deal with the complexity of large organizations and with organizational design. The opportunity to coordinate the benefits of these three different fields is there for the taking.

References

Argyris, C. (1993). *Knowledge for action: A guide to overcoming barriers to organizational change.* San Francisco: Jossey-Bass.

Bunker, B. B., and Alban, B. T. (eds.). (1997). Large group interventions (Whole issue). *Journal of Applied Behavioral Science* 28:4.

Cummings, T. G., and Worley, C. G. (1993). *Organization development and change.* St. Paul, MN: West.

Dean, P. J. (1983). *Guidelines for the implementation of change by a change team.* Unpublished manuscript, University of Iowa.

Dean, P. J. (1993). *Reengineering the business enterprise by organizational redesign.* Unpublished manuscript, Pennsylvania State University.

Dean, P. J. (1994). *Performance engineering at work.* Barrington, IL: International Board of Standards for Training, Performance and Instruction.

Dean, P. J. (1995). Examining the practice of Human Performance Technology. *Performance Improvement Quarterly* 8:2, 68–94.

Dean, P. J., Blevins, S., and Snodgrass, P. J. (1997). Performance analysis: An HRD tool that drives change in organizations. In J. J. Phillips and E. F. Holton III (eds.), *In action: Leading organizational change.* Alexandria, VA: American Society for Training and Development.

Dean, P. J., Dean, M. R., and Guman, E. (1992). Identifying a range of performance improvement solutions: High yield training to systems redesign. *Performance Improvement Quarterly* 5:4, 16–31.

Dean, P. J., and Ripley, D. E. (1997). *Performance improvement pathfinders: Models for organizational learning systems.* Washington, DC: International Society for Performance Improvement.

Dean, P. J., and Ripley, D. E. (eds.). (1998a). *Performance improvement interventions: Methods for organizational learning.* Vol. 2: *Instructional design and training.* Washington, DC: International Society for Performance Improvement.

Dean, P. J., and Ripley, D. E. (eds.). (1998b). *Performance improvement interventions: Methods for organizational learning.* Vol. 3: *Performance technologies in the workplace.* Washington, DC: International Society for Performance Improvement.

Dean, P. J., and Ripley, D. E. (eds.). (1998c). *Performance improvement interventions: Methods for organizational learning.* Vol. 4: *Culture and systems change.* Washington, DC: International Society for Performance Improvement.

Emery, M. (ed.). (1993). *Participative design for participative democracy.* Center for Continuing Education, Australian National University.

Galbraith, J. R. (1995). *Designing organizations.* San Francisco: Jossey-Bass.

Galbraith, J. R., and Lawler, E. E. (1993). *Organizing for the future.* San Francisco: Jossey-Bass.

Gilbert, T. F. (1996). *Human competence: Engineering worthy performance.* Washington, DC: International Society for Performance Improvement.

Kochan, T. A., and Useem, M. (1992). *Transforming organizations.* New York: Oxford University Press.

Mohrman, S. A., and Cummings, T. G. (1989). *Self-designing organizations: Learning how to create high performance.* Reading, MA: Addison-Wesley.

Nadler, D. A., and Tushman, M. L. (1997). *Competing by design: The power of organizational architecture.* New York: Oxford University Press.

Oshry, B. (1996). *Seeing systems.* San Francisco: Berrett-Koehler.

Panza, C. M. (1990, Oct.). Picture this: The sequel. *Performance & Instruction,* pp. 12–18.

Panza, C. M., and James, R. I. (forthcoming). *Maps, maps, and more maps: Your mini-atlas to organization mapping.* Convent Station, NJ: CMP Associates.

Rothwell, W. J., Sullivan, R., and McLean, G. N. (1995). *Practicing organization development.* San Francisco: Jossey-Bass/Pfeiffer.

Rummler, G. A., and Brache, A. P. (1996). *Improving performance: How to manage the white space on the organization chart* (2nd ed.). San Francisco: Jossey-Bass.

Senge, P. M. (1990). *The fifth discipline: The art and practice of the learning organization.* New York: Doubleday.

Senge, P. M., and others. (1994). *The fifth discipline fieldbook: Strategies and tools for building a learning organization.* New York: Doubleday.

Trist, E. (1981, June). *The evolution of socio-technical systems: A conceptual framework and an action research program.* Occasional paper no. 2. Toronto: Ontario Quality of Working Life Center.

Tushman, M. L., and O'Reilly, C. (1996). Ambidextrous organizations: Managing evolutionary and revolutionary change. *California Management Review* 38:4, 8–30.

Tushman, M. L., O'Reilly, C., and Nadler, D. A. (1989). *The management of organizations: Strategies, tactics, analyses.* New York: HarperCollins.

Weisbord, M. R. (1987). *Productive workplaces: Organizing and managing for dignity, meaning, and community.* San Francisco: Jossey-Bass.

Weisbord, M. R. (1992). *Discovering common ground.* San Francisco: Berrett-Koehler.

Weisbord, M. R., and Janoff, S. (1995). *Future search.* San Francisco: Berrett-Koehler.

CHAPTER SEVENTEEN

Analyzing Corporate Culture

Claude S. Lineberry
J. Robert Carleton

When the previous version of this chapter was originally written, for the first edition of this volume (Lineberry and Carleton, 1992), there was still active debate about whether corporate culture even existed and, if it did, about whether it had a significant impact on organizational performance. Over the intervening years, that debate has been resolved: it is now generally agreed that all organizations, irrespective of size, have a culture, whose impact on organizational performance and results is enormous (Kotter and Heskett, 1992). The debate now focuses on how best to align the organization's strategy, culture, and supportive infrastructure to achieve and maintain competitive advantage in an increasingly turbulent global business environment. This question is given significant priority because of the exponential increase in mergers, acquisitions, and strategic alliances as a strategy for corporate growth and industry consolidation. This trend can be expected to continue into the next century.

The compatibility of cultures in mergers, acquisitions, and alliances is so crucial that it has given rise to a need to consider cultural due diligence (Carleton, 1997) as being at least as important as the traditional financial and legal due diligence that typically precede such deals. *Culture clash* is a term that continues to appear frequently in the world's financial and business press, usually in connection with explanations of why an intended merger, acquisition, or alliance failed or was abandoned at the last minute by one or both parties. Recent data show that some 55 to 77 percent of such deals do fail to deliver the organizational and/or financial results that were intended, and that more than 50 percent of those failures are attributable to serious cultural incompatibility (Healy, Krishna, and Ruback, 1992).

Corporate culture has been clearly established as a major driver of organizational performance and results, and of individual performance in organizations. Human Performance Technology (HPT), with its emphasis on analysis before intervention, represents a useful set of diagnostic models and methods for analyzing corporate culture. HPT can provide for a systemic and comprehensive view of corporate culture, whether in conjunction with a potential merger or acquisition or with an internal effort at culture change.

Increasingly, mergers and acquisitions are done on an international basis, in attempts to bring together two or more companies (Chrysler and Mercedes-Benz, Volkswagen and Rolls-Royce, British Petroleum and AMOCO) representing different national cultures. At a minimum, it can be said that as companies globalize the way in which they do business, operations in countries other than a company's home country are on the rise. In either case, the bringing together of two or more national cultures introduces an additional complexity that must be considered as part of an analysis of corporate culture.

This chapter will briefly define what corporate culture is, discuss the importance of aligning culture with the organization's strategy and infrastructure, present a model for analyzing or auditing a corporate culture at a level of detail that allows comparison with other corporate cultures, and reprise and update the major types of initiatives that facilitate change in an organization's culture.

DEFINING CORPORATE CULTURE

What is this thing that has so captured the attention of managers, consultants, and now Wall Street and the world's financial markets? It certainly is not new; corporate or organizational culture, by definition, has been around for as long as organizations have. Various definitions of organizational culture have been reported by Schein (1985), among them the following:

- The norms that evolve in working groups, such as the particular norm of "a fair day's work for a fair day's pay" that evolved in the Bank Wiring Room of the Hawthorne studies (Homans, 1950)

- The feeling or climate that is conveyed in an organization by the physical layout and the way members of that organization interact with customers or other outsiders (Tagiuri and Litwin, 1968)

- The dominant values espoused by an organization, such as product quality or price leadership (Deal and Kennedy, 1982)

- The philosophy that guides an organization's policy with respect to employees and/or customers (Ouchi, 1981; Pascale and Athos, 1981)

- The rules of the game for getting along in the organization; the "ropes" that a newcomer must learn to become an accepted member (Schein, 1968, 1978; Van Maanen, 1976, 1979; Ritti and Funkhouser, 1982)

All these definitions (and many others) touch on certain aspects of organizational culture, but none can be considered full and complete in itself. Schein (1985, p. 9) provides a fuller and more essential definition of the term: "a pattern of basic assumptions—invented, discovered or developed by a given group as it learns to cope with its problems of external adaptation and internal integration—that has worked well enough to be considered valid, and, therefore, to be taught to new members as the correct way to perceive, think and feel in relation to those problems." Or, in the tersely eloquent words of Burke and Litwin (1989), organizational culture is "the way we do things around here."

Many key organizational issues relating to effectiveness—quality, customer satisfaction, teamwork, innovation, decision making, and flexibility, to name a few—are primarily driven by the organization's culture. Therefore, an organization's culture is a critical aspect of the organization's survival and success, and so the ability to analyze, understand, and manage the culture is vital.

Whether we are dealing with an overall organizational culture or with a subculture, the concept of managing the culture may imply a much larger effort than is actually appropriate, and it may conjure up notions of total creation, replacement, or transplantation of a culture. What is meant, however, is some modification of an existing culture: a change in the values-beliefs-behaviors system. Change efforts may be relatively small, as when a particular behavior pattern is altered (so that, for example, the customer's name is now used in all telephone contacts), or relatively large, as when a new value is established in the culture (continuous improvement, for example, or customer focus). The scope of the effort and its focus emerge from a systematic, empirical analysis of the organization and its culture(s).

No matter what the scope and focus of the intended culture change, it is wise to keep in mind the caution offered by O'Toole (1985): anthropology indicates that a culture changes in one of two basic ways—through revolution or through evolution—and attempts at revolutionary culture change always fail; it is the shared experience and common history of a group over time that change the culture.

CREATING ORGANIZATIONAL ALIGNMENT

The term *organizational culture* typically does not refer to such things as the tasks people perform, the products and services they provide, or the procedures they follow. It refers primarily to a set of tendencies or behavior patterns that characterize the people in an organization.

Much of the literature on culture has focused on labeling types of culture. This literature often uses terms like *heroes, myths, legends, rites,* and *rituals* to describe the key components of an organization's culture. These terms and what they denote may prove interesting and informative, but they are only indicators or manifestations of culture; they do not adequately define it.

Culture is behavior. It is the way people in the organization tend to behave as they go about their work. There are at least two key characteristics of behavior patterns that are common to an organization's culture. First, they are groupwide: almost everyone in the group will exhibit the behavior pattern, which means that there are prevailing norms, expectations, and rewards that support specific behavior or punish different behavior. Second, they are values-driven: there is usually an underlying set of beliefs and assumptions that drive and support the behavior and represent the key values that are most important to the organization's culture.

Figure 17.1 shows a diagnostic template for organizational analysis and a framework for examining cultural behaviors, as well as the factors that influence or are influenced by them. The model describes directional factors, which flow from an organization's *vision*, its *mission*, and its *strategic goals* and *values*. It also shows conditional factors: the *external environment* and the *stakeholders*, both of which influence choices about the direction the organization will take. There are three interdependent, complementary paths for providing

Figure 17.1. Organizational Alignment Model.

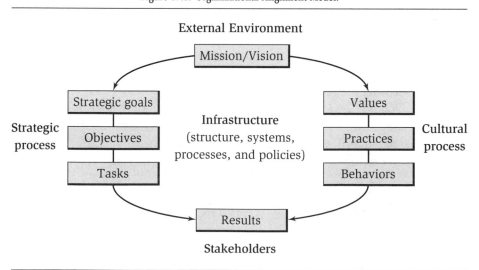

Source: Adapted from Tosti and Jackson, 1989; revised 1997. Used with permission.

direction—that is, for helping people move from a global, abstract statement or organizational mission and vision to specific, concrete organizational *results*.

The *strategic* process, at the left of the figure, focuses primarily on *what* has to be done: again, the broad *strategic goals* to be achieved in support of the mission and vision; the specific *objectives* that groups or individuals must accomplish to meet those goals; and the *tasks* that must be performed to meet specified objectives. The *cultural process*, at the right of the figure, focuses primarily on *how* things should be done: involved here are, again, the key *values* implied by the mission-vision statement; the specific *practices* that manifest those values; and the individual *behaviors* that will demonstrate or represent those values and practices to others inside and outside the organization.

The organization's *infrastructure*, at the center of the figure, consists of those organizational design and support components intended to support both the strategic process and the cultural process: the organizational *structure, systems, processes,* and *policies* that are intended to organize and facilitate the organization's performance.

There should be alignment of the three complementary, interdependent directional paths—the strategic process, the cultural process, and the infrastructure. For example, the key values held in the organization should be compatible with its strategic goals. There should also be alignment within each of the directional paths. For example, the practices of the organization's leaders and managers should be consistent with the espoused values of the organization.

To consider the factors that comprise and influence organizational culture, we must understand the directional and conditional factors that bear on the organization as a whole. The external environment is any condition or situation outside the organization that influences the organization's performance. It includes factors over which the organization has little or no control (such as the economy, governmental regulations, technology, competition, and the sociopolitical environment in which the organization operates). The mission and vision are statements of the intent and desired state of the organization, which serve to provide guidance for organizational purpose, which in turn is expressed in terms of what the organization is in business to do (its mission) and what the organization will look like when it is doing this correctly (its vision).

Strategic goals, values, and infrastructure, along with the mission-vision statement, provide direction for the organization: where it is going, and by what route. They define, in broad terms, how the organization intends to achieve its mission over time (its strategic goals) and how it intends to behave as it attempts to accomplish its mission and realize its vision (its values).

In addition, and in alignment with the strategic goals, the organization should define the values that it considers important:

"Customer focus: Placing the needs of the individual customer above personal or organizational need."

"Integrity: Conducting all customer interactions with unreserved honesty, candor, and openness."

Values statements such as these are aligned with the stated strategic goals and provide guidance for practices in the area of customer relations and for how people should behave in working with customers.

Objectives and practices are specifications of how the organization intends to achieve its strategic goals and demonstrate its values. Objectives specify the required results or achievements of individuals and groups in quantifiable, measurable terms, whereas practices specify what kind of performance will demonstrate and support the organization's values. At General Motors, for example, managers and supervisors are said to "walk their talk" when they demonstrate consistency between the stated values of the organization and their own performance.

Tasks and behaviors represent the execution of the organization's intentions on a day-to-day basis; they are the ultimate determinants of organizational performance. These elements show what really takes place in the organization on a continuing basis: what people do, and how they behave while doing it. Statements of mission, vision, strategy, and values are meaningful only insofar as they are translated into organizational performance at the level of task behavior.

Results are the outcomes produced by the organization as a function of the tasks and behaviors that are engaged in. These can be measured in a variety of ways, which include measures of productivity, customer satisfaction, profit, service quality, market share, and so forth.

Stakeholders are the individuals and groups significantly affected by the organization's performance and results: customers, employees, shareholders, suppliers, distributors, and possibly the general public. These groups have different relationships with the organization, as well as various expectations and perceptions of it, but all have an interest in its performance and results.

Organizational alignment occurs when the strategic process and the cultural process are mutually supportive and when there is a balance of emphasis on these two interdependent paths to the intended and desired organizational results. For example, the organization's strategic goals should be consistent with its values and should be perceived as such by the organization's people.

The impact of corporate culture on organizational performance and financial results is very real. Analysis and management of the corporate culture is key to business success and can no longer be seen as corporate "social work," to be looked after solely by the department of human resources. It is real business, as Kotter and Heskett (1992) demonstrate in their long-term study of a number of high-performing companies over a seventeen-year period. According to Kotter and Heskett, companies that actively managed their cultures in such a way that they were adaptive and flexible were able to outperform companies that had strong but rigid cultures; moreover, they outperformed them by an impressive margin (revenue increases of 682 percent versus 166 percent, share-price increases of 901 percent versus 74 percent and net-income increases of 756 percent versus 1 percent). Clearly, the activity of managing the corporate culture is a significant part of leading and managing the business.

ANALYZING AND AUDITING CORPORATE CULTURE

To manage, change or even understand a corporate culture, it is necessary to perform an analysis of that culture—that is, to do a cultural audit. An analytical model—that is, a model for performing a culture audit—is of particular value when an organization is considering a merger, acquisition, or alliance. The model presented in the sections that follow is based on extensive review of the current literature and on experience, gathered over the last fifteen years, with a number of projects in which there was an attempt to align, change, modify, and/or create a corporate culture and to deal with the "culture clash" that resulted from the absence of cultural due diligence before the merger, acquisition, or alliance took place. This model consists of twelve areas, or domains, for which organizational, operational, and behavioral data must be collected and analyzed:

1. Intended directions/results
2. Key measures
3. Key business drivers
4. Infrastructure
5. Organizational practices
6. Leadership/management practices
7. Supervisory practices
8. Work practices
9. Use of technology
10. Physical work environment
11. Perceptions and expectations
12. Cultural indicators and artifacts

The following sections describe these twelve domains of a culture audit.

Intended Direction or Results

What, from the top of the organization on down, does the company intend to accomplish? What is the business plan about? What are the strategic intent and the purpose of the organization? What results are expected from the business activity of the organization? Most important, how are these things talked about, described, and communicated?

This area alone can yield very telling data about "the way things are done." For example, most of the airline industry is very overt about the importance of customer service and satisfying customer needs. At the boardroom level, and generally at the senior executive level, this is clearly understood as an issue of competitive position and repeat business. Nevertheless, when one talks with the people on the plane, at the check-in counter, and in the airline's lounge, the definitions of customer service and customer satisfaction can take on some interesting nuances. On one major carrier, the cabin crew immediately announces that crew members' actual job is to ensure safety; the service-oriented aspects of their job clearly come second. In fact, when the "service" part of the flight commences, passengers are usually asked to stay in their seats and not get in the way. On another carrier, passengers are immediately encouraged to make their wishes known because the crew is there to make the flight as pleasant and comfortable for them as possible.

Asked about efforts to improve customer satisfaction, the first carrier's staff will talk about the money being spent on upgrading meals, decorating the aircraft, enlarging lounges, and attending to other physical aspects. The second carrier's staff will talk about passengers' experience and the airline's part in ensuring that customers are satisfied enough to choose the carrier again, with clear emphasis on the personal service that is being provided.

One staff focuses on equipment; the other, on attitude. Both are key components of customer satisfaction. Both are valid, but they are very different. A good case can be made for either approach, but one can also imagine the arguments that might ensue all the way through the ranks if these two carriers merged, even though both clearly value customer satisfaction and service as key elements of their business plans.

Key Measures

What does the company measure? Why? What happens as a result? The key measures say a lot about what drives the company, its executives, and its staff, particularly when the consequences for each measure are considered.

For example, one large retail company investigated why its initiative for enhancing customer service and employee retention was not producing results. A large part of the answer lay in this domain. When store managers' supervisors reviewed results with the store managers, the only real focus was inventory control, paperwork, and dollar volume received. Not only were these areas measured, success and failure in these areas had real consequences for both parties, whereas there was only a "nice job" comment for service and for improved retention of employees. Because the standard key measures kept all parties' hands very full, if not overloaded, there was no time to measure anything else. Especially in these times of lean staff, most people are extremely busy, particularly people in managerial and supervisory positions. The focus will always be on what they perceive as truly important, and the measurement of what is truly important will always take place in a context of perceived consequences for failure, and so both the measures and their consequences must be examined.

Key Business Drivers

What are the primary issues driving the business strategy? Is the focus on competitive edge? If so, how is that defined? As price differentiation? quality? market share? service? reliability? The answer will reveal how the company views its industry and thus its efforts in that industry. If one company defines success in terms of total market share, whereas another defines it as net profit margin, there is considerable room for disagreement about which actions are appropriate in correcting unacceptable results or deciding on suitable new-product offerings.

Infrastructure

How is the company organized? What is the nature of the reporting relationships? How are the staff systems related to the line systems? What is the nature of the relationships between and among groups and units? Are people expected to go directly to the people with whom they need to talk, or must proprieties be observed between different levels or functions? Are business units supposed to drive their business priorities first and foremost, responding to corporate, staff, or other unit needs as convenience permits? Or are they supposed to ensure that they are responsive to corporate needs and check with other units to ensure that there are no conflicts or unexpected impacts?

Organizational Practices

What formal and informal systems are in place? What part do they play in the daily life of doing the work? How much flexibility is allowed, at what levels, and in which systems? What is the relationship between political reality and business reality? How are budgets developed and managed? There may be significant disagreement, for example, over what are and what are not reasonable expenses, particularly when it comes to entertainment budgets, and these disagreements may result in dramatic upheavals.

Besides such formal systems as budgeting, this area includes how staff groups in such areas as legal, human resources, public relations, purchasing, and general services departments are accessed and used by line units and by one another. It is not unusual, for example, to find that a particular person or function is considered sacrosanct, regardless of the impact that this person or function may be having on important business issues. These people or functions are considered to be above the routines of getting the business of the company accomplished. In common parlance, these people or functions are referred to as political power bases, which are separate from or above the overall corporate structure.

Leadership and Management Practices

What is the balance between leadership approaches and management approaches with the staff? What basic value systems are in place with respect to employees? How are people treated, and why? How does the business plan get implemented through the management system? How are decisions made? Who is involved in what, and when?

There are distinct behavioral differences between management and leadership functions, and both are clearly important in running a successful business. The issue concerns which approach is predominant in each area or department of the company. This domain primarily involves the group in middle management but has an obvious impact on the following domain.

Supervisory Practices

What dynamics are at play in the immediate supervision of work performance? Supervisory practices have a major impact on employees' feelings about the company and the work they do. The nature of the interaction between the employee and the immediate supervisor is one of the primary climate-setters for the culture of the company. For example, supervisors in one company may be expected to be curt and aggressive about important issues, whereas that kind of brusque speech would be considered rude and abusive in another company.

Work Practices

How is the actual work performed? Is the emphasis on individual responsibility or group responsibility? What degree of control, if any, does the individual worker have on workflow, work quality, the rate at which work is performed, the tools that are used, and the supplies that are needed?

For example, two manufacturing companies may be making the same products, but one company allows any worker to stop the production line at any time he or she deems it necessary. This company views the individual worker as being in the best position to recognize a defective product. The other company does not allow unauthorized line stoppages. Instead, it has decided that only managers, who have knowledge of the overall production needs, can assess whether a stoppage is worth the lost production. Obviously, these are two very different ways of dealing with the same issue, yet each may be appropriate.

Use of Technology

This domain must be considered in relation both to internal systems and equipment and to the services and products that are provided to customers. How current is the technology that is being used? What are people accustomed to with respect to technological support and resources?

For example, conflicts and confusion may occur if a company that is firmly grounded in the use of e-mail merges with a company where individual computers are not generally available. Discussions about high-tech versus low-tech approaches to many aspects of running the business may quickly degenerate into name-calling sessions when "Luddites" and "techno-geeks" have different experiences and levels of comfort with a given technology.

Physical Work Environment

How do workplace settings differ? Open workspaces versus private offices, high-security areas versus an open-access approach, different kinds of buildings, furniture, grounds: all these factors may have a bearing on how people feel about work and about a company. Changes in these areas, particularly if they are perceived as arbitrary, may result in years of bad feeling. For example, two companies may have different approaches, but both approaches are based on valuing people and increasing productivity. The first company says, "We value people and know that an open office increases interactions and camaraderie and makes for happier and more productive workers." The second company says, "We value people, and private workspaces aid in the thought process, enabling greater focus and increased productivity."

Perceptions and Expectations

How do people expect things to happen? What do they believe is important? What do they think should be important, by contrast with what they perceive the company as finding important?

For example, to resolve a union-management schism at one plant in jeopardy of being closed, it was necessary to deal first with the conviction among the union ranks that management was a revolving door of short-timers who did not care about the plant or the community. This conviction was matched by management's equally strong belief that the employees and the unions did not care about the products, the competition, or the plant's profitability. Both statements were untrue, and yet both parties were so sure of their perceptions that they never discussed them with the other party. These strongly held beliefs (perceptions) were at the core of their inability to work together.

Cultural Indicators and Artifacts

How do people dress and address each other? What is the match between formal work hours and actual hours spent working? What company-sponsored activities exist, and what are they like? For example, some employees may perceive company picnics and social clubs as major tools for pulling people together and building a family atmosphere; other employees may perceive the picnics and clubs as instruments for imposing an unwelcome personal and familial atmosphere and may therefore resent them.

These twelve culture-audit domains account for the major components of corporate culture, but two areas commonly mentioned in discussions of corporate culture may appear to have been overlooked:

1. Values and beliefs

2. Myths, legends, and heroes

Actually, however, these areas are embedded in the twelve domains. With some digging into each domain, underlying values and beliefs can be uncovered, and this approach is far more effective than simply asking, "What are the values and beliefs around here?" That type of inquiry generally results in puzzled looks.

The same is true in the area of myths, legends, and heroes. These are simply the "story," or anecdotal versions, that give more direct and immediate meaning to the belief systems operating in the company. Myths, legends, and heroes will present themselves as the twelve culture-audit domains are examined, especially if techniques for gathering qualitative data are used. Indeed, when data are being accumulated on corporate culture, the most useful information does comes from qualitative processes, primarily interviews, focus groups, and observation. Information gathered in this manner is rich in anecdotes and examples of how the culture is acted out and talked about. Stories give personal meaning to the culture and provide examples and demonstrations that are easy for people in the target culture to relate to. It is these anecdotes and stories that enable those doing culture modification to engage in dialogue about work issues in a direct manner. A rich trove of stories and examples, derived directly from the target culture(s), makes these discussions much easier and makes their relevance to business needs and individual behavior much clearer.

Generic, off-the-shelf culture instruments are certainly appealing, given their relative ease of use and low cost, yet they are inherently more difficult to apply when an organization is undergoing culture change. To use these instruments, the change agents have to interpret the data for the people in the organization and translate the relevance of the data to the organization's current activity. These instruments generate no ready anecdotes or examples from the real-world situation that could help in understanding what has to change and why. It is far more problematic to modify a corporate culture in the absence of such qualitative data. The authors' own experience in designing and implementing projects for culture change and culture modification has led to the perception that the data from generic instruments, while possibly interesting and accurate, are rarely essential or even helpful to the change process. Perhaps they are better than nothing, however, for without good, deep qualitative data, the change process is much more troublesome from the design phase all the way through implementation.

Once there are sufficient data, the treatment of what has been gathered is the next step. The discussion of the twelve culture-audit domains offers examples of different approaches within each one. In those examples, there are no right or wrong ways of performing, just different ways that are potentially of equal validity in dealing with the same phenomena. Culture clash certainly can ensue from divergent ways of thinking, but it is highly unlikely that there will ever be two cultures that absolutely cannot be effectively merged. Most disagreements can be and have been successfully resolved. The issue is to recognize areas of disagreement, devise a plan, and manage according to that plan, just as companies do when there are divergent financial or information systems.

DEVISING INTERVENTIONS

If an intervention focusing on the organization's values is to be made, then one of the first considerations must be how the intervention will affect other organizational variables (such as structure and systems) and what will be required to align the intended culture change with the factors comprising the strategic process of the organization. O'Toole (1985) provides a checklist of general criteria for effective culture change, based on the experience of leading companies:

1. Culture change builds on the current culture and values of the organization.

2. It requires involvement and participation at all levels of the organization.

3. It is systemic, requiring consideration of all organizational components and variables.

4. It is planned and reflects a long-term commitment, as well as a continuous effort to inform and educate all the people in the organization about its rationale and process.

5. It is stakeholder-oriented, which is to say that it is clearly geared to respond to, or anticipate and react to, the organization's external environment.

6. It has the visible commitment and support of top management.

Given these organizational considerations, several types of interventions can be devised to effect change through some alteration of the organization's values.

Clarifying

Existing organizational values can be revisited, to provide reassurance that the values are valid and important to the organization. For example, when four divisions of a computer service company were merged to form one company, there was uncertainty about the values of urgency and personal responsibility that had driven practices and behavior in the separate divisions. This uncertainty was inhibiting the previous behavioral norms of risk taking, local-system development, and completion of tasks. Action was taken to clarify the existing values and to restate the managerial and organizational practices that supported them.

Emphasizing

At times, because of events in the organization's external environment, certain key values may take priority over others. For example, in the post-Lockerbie airline industry, and especially among international carriers, safety and security have received renewed emphasis as strategic goals and as cultural values. At one major international carrier, however, emphasis on the values of safety and security, which had been touchstones of the culture for many years, represented a potential conflict with the relatively new and also heavily stressed value of customer service. Some of the practices supporting safety and security were at odds with customer service–related practices (quick check-in, reduced waiting time, ease of baggage check-in, and so forth). The leaders of the airline had to recognize the potential conflict and confusion and very clearly emphasize that the long-standing values of safety and security would take absolute priority, given conditions in the industry. This decision did not signal abandonment of customer service as a strategic focus and value. Rather, it established a helpful priority in a potentially confusing situation.

Redefining

New practices can be introduced to support an existing value of the organization. For example, one of America's largest automobile manufacturers had a long-standing value of communication, but the practices supporting it focused more on the process and techniques of communication than on the willingness to communicate openly and honestly. The existing value was essentially redefined through the specification and introduction of several new practices that focused on this need and, ultimately, resulted in behaviors consistent with a new willingness to communicate openly and honestly.

Building

An espoused value that is primarily given lip service can be made a real value if it is identified and if practices are introduced to support it. In one international computer services organization, for example, there was a published and often stated value of making the customer the top priority, but there were no organizational practices that provided any support or direction for this value. No one challenged or disagreed with the value or its importance, but there was no agreed-upon support system of practices to make it real. After feasible practices that fleshed out the value were identified and introduced, the value of the customer as the top priority began to take on life and meaning in the organization, with the result that customers began to perceive a significant positive shift in the way the organization did business.

Creating

New values can be brought in, or existing values that are no longer relevant can be replaced. When an organization embarks on major culture change, it is often necessary to establish new values. In the American automotive industry, for example, foreign competition and domestic environmental concerns have resulted in a new strategic focus and in new values and practices. At one of the major automobile manufacturers, redefinition of the mission and vision and the creation of such values as competitiveness, continuous improvement, empowerment, and personal responsibility represent the initiation of a major long-term effort toward culture change.

SUMMARY

The focus on corporate culture, especially as a fundamental consideration in corporate mergers and acquisitions, will increase in the coming years. Moreover, globalization of companies will continue to increase as the market evolves more and more into a truly global one, and as companies are required to respond by doing business effectively across a variety of national cultures. The concepts and models of Human Performance Technology are the basis of the culture-audit model and techniques presented in this chapter. They have proved to be valuable in the analysis of a number of corporate cultures, some of which encompass several national cultures. The key, as with Human Performance Technology in general, is an emphasis on front-end analysis as a way of understanding what we would like to change.

References

Burke, W. W., and Litwin, G. (1989). A causal model of organizational performance. In J. W. Pfeiffer (ed.), *The 1989 annual: Developing human resources.* San Diego: University Associates.

Deal, T. E., and Kennedy, A. A. (1982). *Corporate cultures.* Reading, MA: Addison-Wesley.

Healy, P. M., Krishna, G. P., and Ruback, S. R. (1992). Does corporate performance improve after mergers? *Journal of Financial Economics* 31, 135–175.

Homans, G. (1950). *The human group.* Orlando, FL: Harcourt Brace.

Kotter, J. P., and Heskett, J. L. (1992). *Corporate culture and performance.* New York: Free Press.

Lineberry, C. S., and Carleton, J. R. (1992). Culture change. In H. D. Stolovitch and E. J. Keeps (eds.), *Handbook of Human Performance Technology: A comprehensive guide for analyzing and solving performance problems in organizations.* San Francisco: Jossey-Bass.

O'Toole, J. (1985). *Vanguard management: Redesigning the corporate future.* New York: Doubleday.

Ouchi, W. G. (1981). *Theory Z.* Reading, MA: Addison-Wesley.

Pascale, R. T., and Athos, A. G. (1981). *The art of Japanese management.* New York: Simon & Schuster.

Ritti, R. R., and Funkhouser, G. R. (1982). *The ropes to skip and the ropes to know.* Columbus, OH: Grid.

Schein, E. H. (1968). Organizational socialization and the profession of management. *Industrial Management Review* 9, 1–15.

Schein, E. H. (1978). *Career dynamics: Matching individual and organizational needs.* Reading, MA: Addison-Wesley.

Schein, E. H. (1985). *Organizational culture and leadership: A dynamic view.* San Francisco: Jossey-Bass.

Tagiuri, R., and Litwin, G. H. (1968). *Organizational climate: Exploration of a concept.* Boston: Division of Research, Harvard Graduate School of Business.

Tosti, D. T., and Jackson, S. F. (1989). *Organizational alignment.* Larkspur, CA: Vanguard Consulting Group.

Van Maanen, J. (1976). Breaking in: Socialization to work. In R. Dubin (ed.), *Handbook of work, organization, and society.* Skokie, IL: Rand McNally.

Van Maanen, J. (1979). The fact of fiction in organizational ethnography. *Administrative Science Quarterly* 24, 539–550.

CHAPTER EIGHTEEN

Human Resources Selection

Seth N. Leibler
Ann W. Parkman

Hiring highly qualified, reliable, productive people for the right jobs is a task that has long been clouded in mystery. People in all types of organizations around the world have been working for decades to perfect this daunting process, which has become one of the most difficult jobs in the business world today. Countless methods have been tried, and reams of paper have documented the extensive research done on the topic.

Yet, despite all the effort, human resources selection has still not been brought to the level of a science. The debate continues to rage over what truly is the most effective way to hire good people, and many think the methods available are about as reliable as the toss of a coin. Indeed, when it comes to hiring high-performing employees who contribute significant value during their tenure with an organization, the failure rate is high and demonstrates that human resources selection is rarely done well.

However, human resources selection is a process worthy of all the attention it receives and all the efforts to perfect it. Whether it is used to hire new employees, promote them, or reassign them, the selection process is critical to achieving the levels of workforce performance that organizations require. As the business world becomes increasingly global, ensuring that the selection process

The authors would like to thank Nancy Johnson Haines for her extraordinary contribution to this chapter.

is conducted systematically and consistently is truly a worldwide concern. Such factors as increased communication among customers and co-workers from different cultures, the necessity of working in international teams, and the growing dependence on knowledge workers have made choosing good employees more important than ever. Without the baseline talent and initiative that they provide, efforts to improve performance and achieve organizational goals are severely hampered.

In addition, errors in hiring at any level of the organization have serious long-term consequences for everyone involved. Supervisors must spend more time coaching the individual to raise performance to an acceptable level, and management must provide more training than anticipated, which will require additional time and expense. Other staff members must compensate for inadequate performance, and often the nonperforming individual is extremely dissatisfied in the work environment. Morale problems can also occur, and if the employee is ultimately fired, the organization may have to handle a lengthy appeal or grievance process and possibly even a legal challenge.

With these types of consequences at stake, it is very much in organizations' best interests to improve their processes for hiring talented, high-performing employees. However, creating a successful approach can be difficult. If not carefully executed, the human resources selection process can easily become highly subjective. Without explicit criteria and guidelines, people have a natural tendency to choose employees who are like themselves, without really considering the skills, knowledge, and other characteristics it takes to do a particular job effectively. In addition, it has become increasingly difficult to obtain an accurate picture of a candidate's qualifications, past performance, and desire to perform. Candidates are very well coached in the interviewing and selection process today. They often know what questions to expect, what types of answers prospective employers are seeking, and how to present themselves in ways that significantly increase their chances for success in being hired. Research also shows that more and more people are willing to lie to obtain employment. For example, one study found that 95 percent of college students surveyed were willing to make at least one false statement to a potential employer to win a job, and 41 percent had already done so (Frazee, 1996).

The challenges and potential consequences are serious indeed. But, even though it may not yet be possible to perfect the process of matching employees with the right jobs, it is possible to increase the frequency with which organizations succeed. The best way to accomplish that goal is to implement a consistent, objective, structured approach to the hiring process.

Although normally thought of as a responsibility solely for the human resources department, selecting high-performing employees is an area where Human Performance (HP) improvement professionals can add significant value. Since human resources selection is so crucial to maximizing workforce performance, participation in this essential process is a logical step for anyone with expertise in Human Performance Technology (HPT). The goal of HPT is to create a workforce that can perform at the high levels required in today's business world, and the selection process must serve as a fundamental element of the performance equation. Without a workforce capable of being trained to perform to expectations, the achievement of organizational goals becomes nearly impossible.

The systematic process that HPT provides for analyzing and improving performance serves as a highly effective approach to designing successful hiring procedures. By using HPT techniques to clearly define desired performance and thoroughly identify the skills, knowledge, and other characteristics necessary to achieve desired performance, organizations can create an objective, effective human resources selection process that minimizes errors and increases the chances of success.

This chapter provides guidelines for applying HPT to the selection process, both for new employees and for employees promoted or reassigned within an organization. Table 18.1 summarizes that process. Our discussion will be relevant to anyone with responsibility for hiring or promoting employees.

THE HPT HUMAN RESOURCES SELECTION PROCESS

With the use of HPT procedures, the selection process can be divided into four major tasks:

1. Describing the position to be filled in terms of specific functions that must be performed effectively

2. Specifying the skills, knowledge, and personal characteristics needed to achieve desired performance

3. Determining the selection criteria, including the characteristics an individual must possess when hired, not those that must be developed on the job through training or other means

4. Developing a systematic, objective procedure for assessing each candidate with respect to the selection criteria

Describing the Job

The starting point in successfully hiring, promoting, or reassigning employees is an accurate, complete description of the position to be filled. By identifying the tasks that must be performed in order for expectations to be met, one lays the foundation for determining the skills and characteristics that an employee must have to be successful. Such an analysis forms the basis of the human resources selection process.

Table 18.1. HPT Selection Process.

Steps in Selection Process	Conventional Practices	Critical Issues	HPT Contributions
Describing the position	1. Interview the person currently in the position, his or her supervisor, and others with similar jobs 2. Observe the person currently in the job 3. Review job descriptions 4. Derive performance objectives	Document all of the position's responsibilities, and account for special conditions Observe exemplary performers Use job descriptions only as supplemental information because they are often inaccurate Ensure that objectives describe performance and standards and that they outline the conditions under which the performance will occur and the standards will be applied	*Job analysis*, to identify tasks *Performance objectives*, to clearly define performance expectations
Specifying skills, knowledge, and personal characteristics required	1. Interview the person currently in the position, his or her supervisor, and others with similar jobs 2. Observe the person currently in the job 3. Talk with experts in the field	Be certain that the skills and knowledge being sought are based on tasks Ask probing questions to identify less tangible personal characteristics Clarify skills, knowledge, and characteristics to ensure that they are specific and measurable	*Goal analysis*, to make skills and characteristics explicit

Determining selection criteria	1. Use information gathered from job incumbents and supervisors or a skills hierarchy to give priority to the skills and characteristics perceived as most important 2. Use numerical weights to give priority to the skills and characteristics perceived as most important	Ensure that skills used as selection criteria will be relatively easy to find Include as selection criteria characteristics that are essential to the job and that are not likely to be developed by someone (for example, integrity)	*Skills hierarchies*, to determine which skills a person must have to enter the job
Designing and validating the assessment procedure	1. Interviews 2. Reference checks 3. Testing 4. Work sampling 5. Academic achievement	1. To reduce subjectivity, ensure that all interviews have the same structure 2. Focus interview questions around previous experiences that match job requirements 3. Gather validity data on tests to determine their effectiveness 4. Create environments for work sampling that closely model the job and that ensure that every candidate performs under the same conditions 5. Use academic achievement only as supplemental information 6. Collect data on the job success of people who were hired through the selection process, and revise the process, as necessary	*Job aids*, to ensure that all interviews are focused and follow the same structure *Potential problem analysis*, to identify possible difficulties with a candidate *Performance measurement*, using the specified objectives *Performance analysis*, to determine why objectives are not met

According to Werther and Davis (1996, pp. 119–120), "Knowledge about jobs and their requirements must be collected through a process known as job analysis. To match applicants to openings, Human Resources specialists must know what each job requires. Requirements must be specific enough to enable specialists to recruit those with the needed knowledge, skills and abilities. The analysis of the job should encompass all the important tasks the employee would perform, including activities and decisions. It should also take into account special conditions or constraints under which performance will occur. For example, if a new sales representative will have to generate leads by making unsolicited phone calls, or if a customer service representative will have to meet strict deadlines, those conditions will have a significant impact on the ability to perform proficiently.

In completing an analysis of the job, the primary sources of information will be the person currently in the job, the person who supervises that individual, and others with the same or similar jobs. The expectations of higher management should also be taken into account, and input should be gathered from people who will receive or use the work generated by the position. When a new position is being created, information from experts can also be beneficial.

When obtaining information from a person currently performing the job, the HPT professional should work with an exemplary performer and should use both observation and interviews. Because people often perform routine tasks almost unconsciously and have difficulty remembering every step they follow, observation is the only way to ensure that all the critical tasks are identified. Interviews supplement the observation process by uncovering such factors as the rationale for performing certain tasks, cues for when specific tasks should be performed, and the ways a performer knows a task has been successfully completed.

Additional sources of information are formal job descriptions or other written documentation about the job. These documents can sometimes be useful, but they should not be relied on too heavily. The descriptions are frequently out of date, overblown to justify salary levels, or devoid of critical nuances of the job that are too difficult to quantify. Their most valuable function is simply to help identify the questions that position supervisors or incumbents should be asked.

Once the job has been analyzed, the HPT procedure of deriving performance objectives from the job tasks can be applied. Performance objectives are statements that describe desired performance, outline the conditions under which the performance will take place, and identify the criteria that will be used to assess whether performance meets expectations. Here is an example:

Conditions: Employee is given a computer with word-processing software.

Performance: Employee is able to write a letter.

Criteria: All words are spelled correctly, with no grammatical or punctuation errors, and the addressee is neither demeaned nor insulted (Mager, 1997b).

Performance objectives play a critical role in the selection process because they define desired performance explicitly and provide an objective picture of performance expectations for the position to be filled. They serve as the foundation from which to derive the skills that will be necessary in order for a newly hired or newly promoted employee to meet those expectations.

Identifying Skills, Knowledge, and Personal Characteristics

Once the major tasks of a job have been described, the skills, knowledge, and other characteristics (such as personal attributes) needed to perform proficiently can be identified. At this point, all the skills and characteristics required to perform the job are specified. Those skills that the candidate must possess to enter the position will serve as the selection criteria and will be identified in the next step of the process.

A common error in carrying out this step is attempting to specify skills and knowledge without basing them on tasks. This error frequently results in broad criteria open to a wide range of interpretation. For example, if the skills and knowledge of an instructional designer were identified without consideration of the specific tasks the person would perform, the resulting specification might sound like this one: "Candidate should possess skills and knowledge in instructional design and development." This statement is very broad and could incorporate a wide range of skills and knowledge. It would be far more useful if the specification were based on specific skills in the area of instructional design because then it would focus the selection effort: "Candidate should be skilled in the design of computer-based training," for example.

The sources of information that were used in describing the tasks of the job will also be useful in defining the skills, knowledge, and personal attributes needed to do them well. Again, the primary sources of information will be interviews with supervisors, and interviews combined with observation of competent performers. Experts in the field may also be helpful. If a new job is being created, it may be necessary to talk with people in other companies who have similar jobs.

In many cases, the task of identifying skills and knowledge is fairly straightforward. The information can be obtained simply through direct questioning of knowledgeable people and observation of competent performers. However, identifying the required personal characteristics can be more complex. One must ask more probing questions and read between the lines to get a complete picture of these less tangible requirements. People often discuss characteristics in very vague language that can be interpreted to mean numerous things. For example, a supervisor might say that a customer service agent has to have a "can-do attitude" or that a sales agent must be "good with words." Such descriptions mean different things to different people. To break through this vague language and make personal characteristics explicit, a technique known as *goal analysis* is very helpful. Developed by Mager (1997a), it is a method for translating abstract language into measurable, observable performances.

Despite the effort required, clear identification of personal characteristics is worth the time invested. Such characteristics often determine the difference between a good candidate and a great one.

Deciding on Selection Criteria

Now that all the skills, knowledge, and other characteristics that an ideal performer would possess have been identified, the next logical step would appear to be finding a person who possesses them. In reality, however, it is highly unlikely that a single individual will meet all the criteria identified to perform the job as desired. Therefore, it is necessary to separate the criteria into two categories: those that are selection criteria, and those that can be met later through training or other means. Selection criteria are the skills and characteristics required of someone before he or she can enter the job, not those expected of a master performer. They serve as the basis of the hiring decision.

Emphasizing Skills, Characteristics, or Both. Traditionally in the hiring process, primary emphasis has been placed on determining whether a potential candidate has the skills required to perform the job. Characteristics were important, but they were often thought of as too difficult to assess and measure, as well as too difficult to control.

Characteristics can be defined as personal attributes, such as initiative, ability to handle difficult situations, self-confidence, willingness to learn, and so on. It is becoming more and more apparent that people are hired for their skills but are often fired because they lack these types of personal characteristics and are unable to function in the work environment and work well on teams. As organizations recognize this problem, many are shifting their focus from hiring for skills to hiring for characteristics.

One example is Crowe Chizek and Company, a midsized CPA and consulting firm based in the Midwest. In an attempt to improve its hiring process, the company identified underlying characteristics, as well as skills and knowledge, that influence employees' behavior and job performance. These characteristics included such factors as teamwork and cooperation, developing others, self-confidence, conceptual thinking, and commitment. The hiring process was designed around these and other requirements. Some of the characteristics are required for entry into any job, and others are used as differentiating factors (Holdeman, Aldridge, and Jackson, 1996).

Organizations that hire for characteristics are basing their selection process on the theory that if people possess certain basic qualities, they can be trained to do their jobs effectively and are more likely to succeed. This theory is highly complementary to the concept of HPT as a critical element in achieving desired workforce performance. Like any other approach to human resources selection, however, the validity of hiring for characteristics and training for skills is still being tested. It will undoubtedly be more effective for some organizations and certain types of positions but less effective for others.

The approach being recommended in this chapter is to use both skills and characteristics as selection criteria. To increase success in human resources selection, significant efforts should be made both to clearly define the characteristics an individual will require to succeed in a position and to accurately assess whether the candidate possesses them.

Identifying Skills That Will Serve as Selection Criteria. Information gathered earlier from supervisors and job incumbents will form the basis for deciding which skills will serve as selection criteria. If it is difficult to distinguish among those skills required upon entry and those that can be learned later, one can assign numerical weights to the skills according to their relative importance for entry into the job. Information on what weights to assign should be obtained from the position's supervisor, competent performers, or experts in the field. Experts can be particularly helpful when someone is being hired for a newly created position.

Another tool that can be used is a fundamental HPT technique known as a *skills hierarchy.* Often used by HPT practitioners to sequence instruction, a skills hierarchy maps out those skills that are prerequisites for performing certain tasks and those that must be learned before others can be learned. For example, tasks that a customer service representative might perform include describing products and handling complaints. Before those tasks can be performed, however, the representative must be able to interact tactfully with customers. Therefore, the ability to interact tactfully is a prerequisite to describing products and handling complaints.

Skills hierarchies provide information useful in determining whether the organization wants to expend the effort to train for certain skills or whether candidates should have them upon entering the job. For example, the company hiring a customer service representative may decide that it makes sense to train someone to handle complaints and describe products because these two areas depend on the mastery of information that is highly specific to the company. At the same time, the company may decide that it does not want to train someone to interact tactfully with customers. Therefore, the ability to interact tactfully with customers would become a selection criterion.

In deciding which skills will become selection criteria, it is important to take into account the feasibility of finding candidates who will have them. There are skills that many candidates can reasonably be expected to possess, skills that are less common but that can easily be learned on the job, and skills that are rarely found and that will require more expensive means (such as extensive training) to obtain. The skills best used as selection criteria are those that are commonly found, or that most people would possess if qualified for a particular position (for example, skills in word processing for a secretarial position), as well as skills that would be excessively time-consuming or expensive to train for (such as, for the position of medical technician, skills in interpreting medical terminology and abbreviations).

Skills less likely to serve as selection criteria are those that may not be commonly found but that can easily be learned on the job (such as skills in using an internal e-mail system). Highly complex skills that are very difficult to find may also have to be eliminated as selection criteria, even though they may be crucial to desired performance: they are typically crucial enough to justify the cost of training.

Identifying Characteristics That Will Serve as Selection Criteria. Determining which personal characteristics will serve as selection criteria is often more difficult than identifying which skills will fall into that category. Some characteristics, such as integrity, are so deeply inherent in an individual that their absence is not likely to be compensated for by anything the organization may do. Others (for example, a practical approach to problem solving) can be enhanced by the work environment and by appropriate supervisory guidance.

The best way to identify the characteristics that must be selection criteria is to clearly define them (using goal analysis; see Mager, 1977a) and to determine, on the basis of information from the position's supervisor and its incumbents, which characteristics are truly essential and whether they can be developed on the job. Any characteristics that are of high priority and unlikely to be developed on the job should be used as selection criteria.

Designing the Assessment Procedure

The assessment procedure is the method that will be used to evaluate whether a candidate possesses the identified selection criteria. Traditionally, the most common methods for assessing candidates have been interviews, reference checks, testing, and use of biographical data, academic records, and work samples. Most human resources departments still rely heavily on these methods, but advances in technology and changes in the way organizations staff their workforces have also brought some new techniques to the forefront. Today, methods such as hiring over the Internet, using teleconferenced interviews, and giving assignments that move from temporary to permanent status are being used to support, enhance, and even replace the methods typically thought of as critical to the hiring process.

Determining the Validity of the Assessment Procedure. There are pros and cons for most of the assessment procedures ever used or tested. The effectiveness of these procedures is determined by numerous factors, many of which vary greatly from organization to organization. Some companies may have great success with interviews and reference checks; others may find that interviews and reference checks are more effective when they are combined with testing. The variables are simply so numerous that no one can declare any one assessment procedure to be the method that every organization should use in hiring the best employees. In most cases, a combination of methods will get the best results.

When choosing assessment procedures, however, one should always include a plan for tracking and measuring their effectiveness. These data are essential in determining whether an organization is getting the greatest possible benefit from its hiring process. In the rush to fill open vacancies, many hiring officials lose sight of the necessity to collect data on the validity of their selection procedures. This information is critical because it enables the organization to assess which aspects of the hiring process are working and which are not. It is also important protection against lawsuits from rejected candidates.

To measure the effectiveness of assessment procedures, factors such as the employee's performance on the job, promotions, and amount of time with the company should be tracked. For each procedure used (such as interviews or reference checks), one should determine whether the skills and characteristics revealed by that procedure have proved to be present in the work performance of the person who has been hired. For example, if a hiring interview has indicated that a candidate possesses strong communication skills, one should examine whether communication is an area where that individual actually excels on the job. If a procedure consistently reveals certain skills and characteristics for which the employee does not meet expectations on the job, that procedure needs to be evaluated and improved.

Obtaining such information can be a time-consuming, difficult process, and it may not be practical to track every employee who has been hired. However, a representative sample should be tracked through observation of employees on the job and interviews with supervisors and colleagues. The time will be well spent because it will identify opportunities for improving the hiring process.

Using Common Methods. Many methods can be used to assess whether candidates possess the selection criteria that have been identified. Some of the most common are described in the sections that follow.

Interviewing. Of all the methods available, interviewing is the one most widely used and most closely associated with the hiring process. In nearly all organizations, the human resources selection process is built around this fundamental practice, which has been used for literally hundreds of years.

Interviews can be a useful technique for assessing the extent to which candidates meet selection criteria. They offer an opportunity to expand on what can be learned about an individual on paper, and to see candidates perform in something of a pressure situation. They are also useful for giving candidates information about the position, the organization, and the hiring process, thus allowing them a chance to assess their desire to accept a job should it be offered. This benefit of interviews should not be undervalued.

Yet, despite the popularity of the interview, research consistently shows that its reliability and validity as an assessment method are low. It is becoming more and more difficult to obtain a true assessment of an individual from an interview. Today's workforce is becoming better and better prepared to maneuver successfully through the hiring process, and the one element nearly everyone is prepared to handle is the interview. People know what types of questions are going to be asked, the types of answers being sought, and the importance of the impression they make in this small window of time.

In addition, interviews are often very unstructured, and human resources personnel fail to relate them to the selection criteria that have been identified. By their very nature, interviews are based on opinion and are therefore highly subjective.

There is research, however, that shows that paying more attention to the structure of the interview increases its effectiveness. Many organizations are now taking this approach and using what is known as a *behavioral interview*. This kind of interview attempts to analyze candidates' performance in situations similar to those that will be encountered in the position. Thus candidates are asked to describe situations they have faced in previous or current jobs and to tell about their methods of handling these situations. For example, an interviewer might say, "Tell me about a time you spoke with an irate customer" or "Describe a difficult people problem you have solved recently." To increase the validity of this technique, the situations asked about should be similar to those that will be faced on the job (Werther and Davis, 1996, p. 227). In some cases, organizations take this type of interview a step farther and ask candidates to work for a short period of time in a simulated job environment. Other techniques that have proved effective include ensuring that all candidates are asked identical questions and training interviewers to record responses systematically (Werther and Davis, 1996).

Regardless of the structure used for interviews, however, a downside is their cost (for example, organizations often have to fly candidates in for interviews), and a natural by-product of cost is a limit on the number of candidates who can be interviewed. For that reason, organizations often decline to interview candidates who may actually be highly qualified, a practice that further reduces the reliability of the interview process. Videoconferencing provides organizations with a way to reduce the costs of interviewing while also talking with more people. Nevertheless, because the hiring official and the candidate can see each other and answer each other's questions, the interview is much the same as a traditional one.

Recently, Dell Computer initiated this approach in a booth at a career search. Using what the company called *video-based interviewing,* Dell cut both its cycle time and its recruitment costs. Instead of sending a team of interviewers, Dell sent one, who screened résumés and faxed them to the Dell recruiters. Promising candidates were then invited for a video interview. Because of the convenience of the process, one recruiter interviewed someone who normally would have been passed over. This person turned out to be an excellent fit for a position that had been a difficult one to fill (Shadovitz, 1997). The equipment for videoconferencing can be expensive, but its costs are steadily dropping. Several businesses now offer videoconferencing facilities at reasonable prices.

Using HPT to Improve the Interview Process. HPT can be a valuable tool in improving the interview process. The same skills used by HP technologists to design the assessment procedures that determine whether trainees can perform to certain criteria can be used to shape interview questions and evaluate responses in a consistent, objective manner. HPT techniques can also be used to develop job aids to ensure that every candidate is asked the same interview questions and that responses are recorded in a consistent way.

Checking References. The reference check is another method for assessing whether a candidate meets the identified selection criteria, but its validity is questionable. Most candidates provide names of people who can be expected to provide positive information, and it has become rare to encounter anyone who will share negative experiences that an organization has had with an individual. Moreover, organizations often fear legal repercussions for providing negative information that results in rejection. Because there is uncertainty about what information may legally be disclosed, many organizations have been advised not to provide any negative feedback.

Recently, however, employers' opportunities to legally disclose negative information about former employees have increased; in fact, employers can now find themselves in legal difficulty for *not* disclosing certain information. In one such case, a former employee at an insurance company applied for a job at another insurance company. The first company had given the candidate a letter stating that he had lost his job in a restructuring. The candidate, hired by the second company, later shot and killed three of its workers and injured three others. The hiring company charged that the employee's former company had actually fired him for his violent tendencies and therefore had a duty to warn. The former employer settled the case out of court. There have also been other cases, in which less lethal behavior (theft or dishonesty) was not disclosed (Novack, 1995). Several states have now passed laws that protect employers who provide damaging but truthful responses to reference requests. The good news is that if a candidate is liable to be a danger to an organization's workforce or its customers, hiring officials are now far more likely to discover that information. The bad news is that it is still difficult to get former employers to disclose negative information about the more common types of performance problems. For most organizations, the safest rule about that type of information is not to disclose it without documented, irrefutable proof (Munk and Oliver, 1997).

Despite the legal obstacles, there are ways to make reference checks more reliable. Asking candidates for very specific types of references—for example, the name of the person who gave them their performance reviews—will reduce the chance of getting friends, relatives, or peers as references. Ensuring that the appropriate person (preferably a direct supervisor) is located will also help.

A second approach is to ensure that people checking references ask questions that elicit precise responses. One should ask specific questions about areas in which a candidate seems weak and pose open-ended questions that cannot be answered with "yes" or "no": "How have you approached solving difficult people problems?" A change in voice inflection, or any hesitancy to answer a blunt question, may also be an indication of problems (Werther and Davis, 1996).

Once a specific strategy has been developed for checking references, consider developing job aids to walk human resources personnel through the reference-checking process that has been designed. This will greatly increase the chances that the desired approach will be used.

Testing. Testing potential employees' intellectual abilities and job-related skills is a common way for organizations to assess candidates' qualifications. The tests given to potential employees are often standardized and adhere to the standards established by such organizations as the American Psychological Association, the American Educational Research Association, and the National Council on Measurement in Education. However, a recent trend in human resources selection has been to move away from standardized testing. Instead, organizations are using brainteasers, riddles, cognitive-reasoning scenarios, and a number of other "test questions" that, on the surface, appear to have little or nothing to do with a job. According to Munk and Oliver (1997), candidates are now being asked such questions as "How many golf balls fit into a swimming pool?" or "How many barbers are there in Chicago?" These types of questions are tied to the approach discussed earlier of hiring for characteristics. Although the questions have no direct relevance to the job, organizations are trying to measure such characteristics as intelligence, creative problem solving, willingness to learn, performance under pressure, and so on. Some skills, such as reasoning, problem solving, basic mathematics, and so on, can also be assessed.

For this type of testing in particular, and for any type of employment testing, it is critical to gather data on validity and reliability to demonstrate how the tests are related to selection criteria and performance on the job. Such data will help in evaluating the effectiveness of tests and will protect against potential legal difficulties. According to Eyres (1998, p. 164), "in order to meet long-standing and emerging legal requirements, [organizations] must develop, administer, and validate tests to ensure that they serve a business purpose and do not discriminate." If standardized tests are being used, it is also important to ensure that they were created for a target population with characteristics similar to those of the candidates being assessed.

Work Sampling. Work sampling is an assessment method that requires candidates to complete a task that they would normally be required to perform on the job. Such assessments can be highly valuable in predicting future performance. Work sampling ranges from quick, easy-to-complete exercises to elaborate job simulation. When used in its simplest and least expensive form, a candidate might be asked to complete a task (writing a press release, for example, or creating a spreadsheet). This type of work sampling is widely used.

The more complex version of work sampling requires employees to spend a period of time in a simulated job environment. Ranging in length from one day to months, these simulations require candidates to work in conditions very close to those of the job and to perform tasks that will be required. Their performance is observed and assessed.

Development Dimensions International (DDI) is a company that specializes in designing these types of assessments. One of the company's programs allows candidates to be "manager for a day." Candidates are placed in a simulated work environment, and their performance is videotaped and observed from television monitors. "We take all the crises a manager might experience in a year and cram them into a day," says DDI founder William Byham. Such assessments are costly, however. They run $3,000 and more for a full-day assessment of one candidate (Munk and Oliver, 1997).

When work sampling is used, HPT should also be used to create the environment in which the candidate will complete the assignment and be assessed. To be valid, work sampling must be conducted in consistent, objective environments. Every candidate must be given the same opportunity to succeed.

Checking Biographical Data. Biographical data are generally obtained from responses on application forms, from information on résumés, or from answers to questions in interviews. Questions may concern educational background, past experience, interests, and so on.

Biographical data have value to the extent that they can be verified, and they should always be checked. As mentioned earlier, it is not uncommon for candidates to lie about their backgrounds. Organizations must ensure, however, that there is a valid reason for requesting this type of information.

Considering Academic Achievement. Many hiring officials use academic achievement as an indicator of future performance, particularly for recent college graduates with little or no work experience. Academic achievement has actually proved ineffective as an indicator of future performance: "One of the reasons for disappointing results with grades as a predictor may be related to . . . variation in the quality of institutions and difficulty of subject matter" (Reilly and Chao, 1982, p. 1). Therefore, academic achievement should always be evaluated in light of other factors, such as improvement over the years, consistency, work while in college, and so on.

Making Temporary to Permanent Assignments. In recent years, organizations have begun using temporary employees to fill more and more of their employment needs. Growth in the temporary employment industry has been phenomenal, and "temp" workers have become a permanent fixture on the labor landscape. In addition to providing labor to help organizations through peak production times, or through gaps between the departure of existing employees and the hiring of new ones, temporary positions provide an excellent assessment tool for hiring. They give organizations an opportunity to observe the potential employee for an extended period of time in the actual position that would be occupied. Any missing skills can easily be identified, and the individual's personal characteristics can also be assessed.

One area in which organizations should exercise caution, however, is in the length of time an employee remains a temporary worker. If temporary employment exceeds a certain time limit (which can be as much as a year), the employee or the government can argue that the employment is not truly temporary. This opens the door to lawsuits for back benefits and any taxes that should have been paid by the employer. Courts, not wanting to provide a way for organizations to avoid paying taxes or providing health insurance and other benefits to employees, have been sympathetic to this argument.

Rehiring Former Employees. It is increasingly common to rehire employees who have left an organization either voluntarily or through downsizing. Organizations are now reversing the strategy of minimizing their workforces, and many are rehiring former employees to take advantage of the skills that were developed before the downsizing occurred.

Hiring former employees has its positive and negative aspects. The greatest benefit is that the organization knows how the employee performs because the employee has demonstrated his or her ability to meet performance expectations in the position previously held. There are significant risks, however. There is always the possibility that the employee harbors some resentment about his or her departure and could cause morale problems. Further, if the employee is being hired for a position different from the one held before, one cannot be certain that he or she will perform at the same level. Finally, if the employee left voluntarily and is hired back in a better position, or at a higher salary than before, other employees may feel slighted, and the company may be seen as rewarding those who leave.

LEGAL CONSIDERATIONS

Armed with selection criteria and assessment procedures, many employers have made the mistake of immediately initiating the selection process. Faced with a lawsuit months later, they have regretted their failure to seek legal counsel before forging ahead. As Arthur (1995, p. 53) warns, "If your company gets involved in a discrimination suit, ignorance of the law is not a defense!" Equal Employment Opportunity laws and guidelines basically state that all applicants must be given an equal chance to be considered for a position, and that selection criteria must be specifically related to a candidate's ability to do the job. The steps that organizations should take to protect themselves against lawsuits include the following basic ones:

- Avoiding certain types of questions on applications and in interviews. Topics to be avoided include the candidate's age, children, country of birth, immigration status, disabilities, physical characteristics (such as height or weight), lawsuits a candidate may have filed, maiden name of female candidates, AIDS or HIV status, and past injuries or accidents. If any questions related to these topics are asked, they must be directly related to a candidate's ability to perform the job.

- Checking employment practices for possible systemic discrimination. According to Arthur (1995, pp. 65–66), "businesses that do most of their recruiting by word of mouth might be charged with systemic discrimination if the word is being passed exclusively by a white male population to white male colleagues" (Arthur, 1995).

- Processing all applications in the same manner. Organizations should have an established procedure for accepting and processing applications and should avoid making any marks or notations about candidates directly on employment applications.

- Keeping extensive documentation of the hiring process.

- Making certain job requirements are related to the position and not arbitrarily set (Arthur, 1995).

Legal considerations in the area of hiring and selection are extensive and cannot be discussed adequately in this chapter; all organizations are advised to seek counsel from an attorney before implementing a human resources selection process.

THE CHALLENGE OF HIRING
FOR INTERNATIONAL ASSIGNMENTS

Among major corporations in virtually every industry, globalization has become a primary strategy. Organizations are seeking to expand their reach and increase sales by tapping large new markets overseas. This globalization strategy presents a unique challenge for human resources professionals. Hiring officials are now expected both to hire employees in their own countries who will be sent overseas and to find qualified native employees in other countries.

At the present time, it appears that organizations have much work to do before the international hiring process will be perfected. Failure rates in hiring for international assignments range from 20 to 40 percent, and the expense is substantial. A typical overseas assignment costs three to five times the expatriate's annual salary, according to a 1993 survey by the Washington, D.C.–based Employee Relocation Council (Solomon, 1996).

Succeeding at international hiring is not easy. To be successful, one must complete a thorough analysis of the job (as discussed earlier) and tailor the selection process. The type of position to be filled will be important in deciding whether to hire an employee who is a native of the country in question or to send an expatriate.

In many cases, it is most effective to hire employees who are natives of the country. According to Werther and Davis (1996, pp. 189–190), "Unlike relocated employees, foreign nationals are apt to be involved in the local community and understand local customs and business practices." These advantages should eliminate many of the problems that might confront an expatriate. In international hiring, it is best to rely on local hiring officials because they are much more able to determine whether an individual will meet the performance expectations that exist in the work environment at their offices.

For some positions, however, it is not feasible to hire someone who is a native of the country where the position is being filled. Many companies are starting new overseas operations, and employees require intimate knowledge of organizational procedures, goals, and operations. For these positions, or for positions in which employees may be sent overseas at a later time, the personal characteristics required for success are crucial; it should not be assumed that domestic employees who are exemplary performers will automatically excel overseas. Therefore, in addition to the skills needed, one should look for openness to new ideas, sensitivity to cultural differences, ability to adapt quickly to change, approachability, likability, and so on. Such characteristics will determine whether the individual will be accepted in the foreign work environment, and they will have a significant impact on the overall success of the assignment.

In all instances, international hiring should be handled with care. The most important rules are to create a systematic process for hiring, to track its effectiveness, and to assume that some time will be required to perfect it.

THE INTERNET AS A HIRING TOOL

As the popularity and accessibility of the Internet continues to explode, organizations and job seekers alike have begun using it as a hiring tool. Organizations are now posting their open positions on their Web sites, giving candidates the ability to peruse job opportunities twenty-four hours a day and to make their interest known immediately by e-mailing résumés.

Recruiting over the Internet has become popular because it has many advantages. The foremost advantage is the cost: posting job opportunities on a Web page is much less expensive than advertising. At some companies, Internet recruiting is even reducing the frequency with which they use headhunters. There are also numerous Internet job sites that work in much the same way as classified ads do but that offer advertising rates three to four times lower than those for print ads. Another advantage of recruiting over the Internet is the quality of the applicants organizations are finding: candidates show that they have some technical expertise simply by responding to an ad. Finally, companies can reach candidates who otherwise would have been extremely difficult to find, because the Internet eliminates geographical barriers and reaches a broader, more diverse audience.

So far, the Internet has been effective largely as a recruiting tool supplemented, after the initial screening process, by traditional methods of determining whether a candidate is suitable. In the future, however, the expanding capabilities of the World Wide Web will probably make it possible to complete more of the human resources selection process with this new technology.

CANDIDATES' IMPRESSIONS

Assessment is a two-way process. While managers are assessing the extent to which candidates meet a position's selection criteria, the candidates are gathering data about the organization and the available position. Candidates frequently share their perceptions with their peers, and negative impressions can reduce the pool of qualified candidates who might apply or accept employment with an organization. Positive impressions can do just the reverse, providing the organization with an edge over the organizations with which it competes for talent. Therefore, every communication with a candidate should reflect courtesy and efficiency of operation.

Open communication should be maintained with candidates throughout the selection process. They should know what to expect and the rationale for every step in the procedure. It is important to be precise, explicit, and clear about the selection criteria with the candidates and with those who will participate in assessing the candidates.

WAYS TO MINIMIZE SELECTION ERROR

The following recommendations are based on literature about the hiring process and on extensive experience in selecting high-performing employees.

1. Be prepared to devote significant time and resources to the hiring process. Unfortunately, there are no shortcuts to excellence in human resources selection. Hiring qualified, high-performing employees is crucial to the organization's success, and the costs of failure are enormous. The time devoted to designing an effective program is time well spent.

2. Use HPT techniques to maximize the likelihood of hiring employees who will meet or exceed expectations. Techniques used successfully by HPT practitioners for years are highly valuable in the selection process. These include the use of job analysis, to identify the tasks of a position and any special conditions; the use of performance objectives, to clearly define the desired performance; the use of skills hierarchies, to help determine which skills must serve as selection criteria; and the use of job aids, to ensure that a consistent, objective assessment process is being followed.

3. Rely on several assessment procedures rather than on just one. No one method is infallible. Using a variety of methods will provide more data and increase the chances of success.

4. Whenever it is reasonable to expect that candidates possess the skills and knowledge to complete a work sample, use this assessment method. Demonstration of competence in tasks critical to the job is a high indicator of future success.

5. Conduct structured, in-depth interviews. Structured interviews have a higher success rate than others. To achieve greater consistency and ensure that everyone follows the same process, write objectives for an interview that describe the desired outcomes, and create a job aid covering any specific questions or procedures that the interviewers should use.

6. Have several people (including the candidate's potential co-workers, if it is possible to include them) participate in the selection process. No matter how much quantifiable information has been gathered, the selection decision will ultimately reflect a judgment. One way of increasing the objectivity of this judgment is to include several others in the process.

7. Conduct a potential problem analysis on final candidates. A potential problem analysis is an attempt to anticipate any difficulties that might occur if a person were hired. For example, if a particular candidate were hired and later became a performance problem, what would the problem most likely be? How would the problem manifest itself? Why would it occur? How serious a problem would it be? Could the organization live with it, or would the problem have to solved? If it is determined that the problem would have to be solved, it may be necessary to gather more information on the likelihood of the problem's occurring.

8. Keep accurate records. Ensure that relevant data are collected and are used in assessing the validity, cost-effectiveness, and reliability of the selection process. Review these data periodically; this is the only objective way to improve the assessment process and document its relationship to the job requirements.

CONCLUSION

Developing an effective human resources selection process is a difficult task. There are many variables that have an impact on an organization's ability to hire high-performing employees, and there are many alternatives that can be used in the assessment process. Developing a strategy that works is a matter of analysis, design, and implementation of an objective hiring process, as well as of evaluation for its success or failure over time. HPT offers demonstrated, valuable tools that can be used to increase the organization's success in hiring highly qualified employees who contribute significant value. Given the critical role that human resources selection plays in the achievement of organizational goals, the time and resources applied to using HPT in improving the hiring process will be a wise investment.

References

Arthur, D. (1995). *Managing human resources in small and mid-sized companies* (2nd ed.). New York: AMACOM.

Eyres, P. (1988). *The legal handbook for trainers, speakers, and consultants.* New York: McGraw-Hill.

Frazee, V. (1996, Oct.) For your information: Students tell tales to win jobs. *Personnel Journal,* p. 26.

Holdeman, J., Aldridge, J., and Jackson, D. (1996, Aug.). How to hire Ms./Mr. Right. *Journal of Accountancy,* pp. 55–58.

Mager, R. F. (1997a). *Goal analysis* (3rd ed.). Atlanta: Center for Effective Performance.

Mager, R. F. (1997b). *Preparing instructional objectives* (3rd ed.). Atlanta: Center for Effective Performance.

Munk, N., and Oliver, S. (1997, Mar. 24). Think fast! *Forbes,* pp. 146–151.

Novack, J. (1995, Dec. 4). What if the guy shoots somebody? *Forbes,* p. 37.

Reilly, R. R., and Chao, G. T. (1982). Validity and fairness of some alternative employee selection procedures. *Personnel Psychology* 35, 1–62.

Shadovitz, D. J. (1997, Oct. 20). Interviewing from afar. *Human Resources Executive,* p. 47.

Solomon, C. M. (1996, Nov.). Failed assignments. *Personnel Journal,* pp. 79–85.

Werther, W. B., and Davis, K. (1996). *Human resources and personnel management* (5th ed.). New York: McGraw-Hill.

CHAPTER NINETEEN

Motivational Systems

John M. Keller

Charlie at age 15: "Why do I have to study this?"

Charlie at age 35: "Why do I have to lead this work team?"

Charlie at age 55: "Why have I spent most of my career working in this plant?"

Charlie appears to have had motivational problems all his life. He has been asking the "why" question for forty years or more but still does not seem to be getting answers. Many readers will believe that Charlie is somewhat pathetic. After all, it is our own responsibility to find out why we do the things we do, and to be responsible for our own motivation, is it not? To a degree it is. However, there are many situations in which one can dramatically improve a person's motivation by providing either answers to the "why" question or the stimuli and support for the person to create an answer.

Answers to the "why" question are one small but important part of a person's motivation. In fact, a traditional position has been that motivation is so complex and so unstable that it is not possible to understand or manage it in a systematic and predictable manner. Certainly, a person's motivation level can fluctuate frequently and unexpectedly, but there are also stable and predictable aspects of motivation. Furthermore, a human performance (HP) technologist can create environments that will have predictable and positive influences on people's motivation to learn, motivation to work, and motivation in general, which are major influences on performance. Moreover, as the world becomes more of a global community, there is an increasing need to understand and influence human motivation as a multinational influence on performance and achievement. This chapter provides an overview of major influences on motivation, as well as guidelines for designing motivational systems.

OVERVIEW

Role of Motivation

Motivation is one of three general influences on performance (see Figure 19.1). The other two are capability and opportunity. The amount and quality of a person's performance are determined by whether he or she has the following kinds of stimuli and support:

1. Internal motivation and motivational support from the environment
2. Knowledge and skills needed to do the job
3. Tools, resources, conducive working conditions, feedback, and other environmental factors that make it possible to do a job properly and well

Elements of all three of these factors must be present for people to have a positive level of performance. If any one of them is low or nonexistent, an individual is not likely to exert successful effort. Within this frame of reference, the focus of this chapter is on motivational factors that influence a person from both the inside and the outside—that is, the internal dimensions of personal motivation and the environmental influences that can be managed by an HP technologist.

Figure 19.1. Major Influences on Performance.

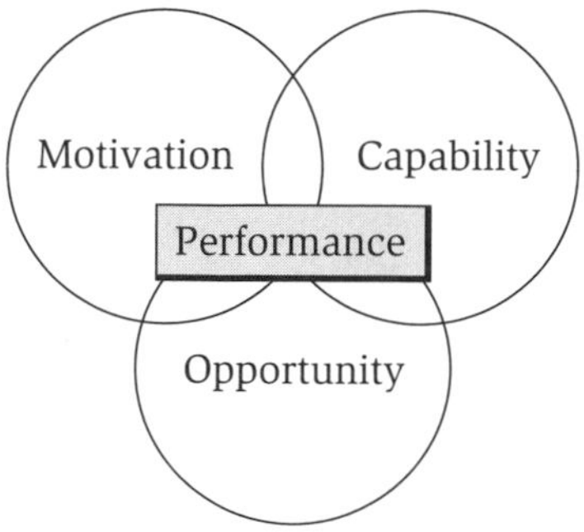

Characteristics of a Motivational System

A motivational system consists of people, with their internal motivational characteristics, and the environment, with its tactics and strategies that affect goal-directed effort and affect. One cannot understand a motivational system, however, nor the system itself be functional, unless one considers it in terms of how it is integrated into the larger system of influences on performance. Such a macro-level representation of an HP system must include both the internal, psychological factors and the external, environmental factors that influence performance. This statement assumes that an adequate explanation of human behavior cannot be based solely on behavioral observations or on inferences about human affect, attitudes, and cognition; rather, an adequate explanation must account for the influences and interactions of both. Figure 19.2 depicts a systems view of motivation and performance. The figure illustrates how antecedents and consequences influence performance, which itself occupies the central position in the figure. The figure is consistent with the assumption that capability, opportunity, and motivation all influence performance. The influence of capability is illustrated by the box labeled *Ability, knowledge, skill*. The box labeled *Learning and work design and management* represents opportunity.

Motivation is represented at several points. A person's initial motivation to pursue a goal is influenced by such personal characteristics as internal curiosity, motives, and expectations of success, and by environmental influences on the situation, such as job complexity, leadership style, and role match, illustrated by the box labeled *Motivational design and management*. After carrying out a performance, a person has a motivational, or affective, outcome in the form of

Figure 19.2. The Performance Factors Model.

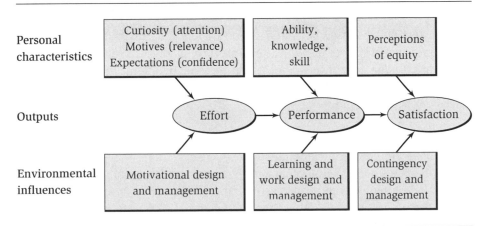

personal satisfaction or dissatisfaction, and this outcome will influence the person's desire to continue pursuing the same or similar goals. Satisfaction is influenced by the feedback and rewards obtained in relation to one's actual level of accomplishment (represented by the box labeled *Contingency design and management*) and by one's perception of equity in regard to the fairness of the consequences. There are also numerous feedback loops, illustrated in previous, more detailed, representations of the model (Keller, 1979, 1983), that explain these and other interactions. As previously presented and documented, the model was derived from the long tradition of research on holistic models of human performance (see, for example, Porter and Lawler, 1968; Vroom, 1964; Steers and Porter, 1983). This literature repeatedly illustrates how motivational influences must be considered in relation to other elements that influence one's capability and opportunity to perform well. Even though it is possible to focus on subsystems within this macrosystem, a complete performance support system will incorporate all these components.

In keeping with this tradition of research on human performance, other models also consider the influences of these three major factors and related subfactors on human behavior and its outcomes. For example, Gilbert (1978) lists environmental supports (opportunity) and a person's repertory of behavior (capacity) as two conditions for behavior to occur. He then discusses how information, instrumentation, and motivation have both environmental and personal components. To take another example, Rummler and Brache (1990) present six factors, in a closed-loop systems model, that affect human performance. Rummler and Brache do not include motivation as one of the factors, but they do indicate that it underlies all six: within them they have embedded motivational elements, together with elements of opportunity and capacity. Both of these well-known models emphasize some influences more than others, but neither provides detailed coverage of motivational elements.

Developmental Requirements

The HP technologist may be acting as an instructor, an instructional designer, or a performance system designer. Regardless of his or her specific role, the HP technologist must meet three requirements in applying the material in this chapter to the building of a motivational system that stimulates and sustains appropriate levels of motivation:

1. *The requirement to understand the components of human motivation.* This kind of understanding supports the selection process, so that it becomes possible to obtain people whose motivational profiles match the job requirements and the learning prerequisites. It also supports the process of identifying those motivational characteristics that can be modified by interventions and support systems.

2. *The requirement to map the relationships between motivational factors and other influences on performance.* This kind of mapping is represented in the Figure 19.2. The figure defines the intervention points where the performance technologist can introduce policies, strategies, and tactics that will influence motivation and performance.

3. *The requirement to use a problem-solving approach to creating an appropriate motivational environment.* This is a process of generating motivational interventions that are based on the identified needs of individuals or groups. It differs from prescriptive approaches, which attempt to predefine specific motivational conditions and solutions. By contrast, the problem-solving approach assumes that the levels of variation in the motivational dynamics of people and situations are usually complex and require the creation of unique solutions, or adaptations of given solutions. (Motivational systems or techniques that work in one setting normally have to be modified before they will succeed in a different culture or environment.)

This chapter contains a description of the major components of human motivation that must be considered in the process of either selecting appropriately motivated people or creating a motivating environment. It also describes a problem-solving approach to developing motivational conditions. This material incorporates the systems approach, typology, and problem-solving process used in previous work on the ARCS model (see Keller, 1987a, 1987b; Keller and Burkman, 1993) but extends them to the environment of performance improvement.

BASIC CONCEPTS AND TERMINOLOGY

Three assumptions underlie systematic motivational design.

1. *People's motivation can be influenced by external events.* This assumption may appear to be a truism, but it runs counter to the operating assumptions of many teachers, supervisors, and managers, who often assume that it is the individual's responsibility either to be internally motivated for training or work or to leave and do something else. These people believe that unless they have direct control over extrinsic rewards, such as financial incentives, they have no direct control over motivation. By contrast, it is easy to demonstrate that effective leaders can inspire motivation through positive modeling, attention to individual behavior, and motivating feedback, whereas ineffective teachers or managers can kill motivation by misuse of the same opportunities. To develop motivational systems, the HP technologist must assume that a person's motivation is influenced by others and is not purely a matter of the person's self-motivation or of the hiring manager's selecting the right person.

2. *Motivation of performance is a means, not an end.* The goal of a motivational system is to stimulate optimal levels of productivity, not to stimulate pleasure or entertainment for its own sake. Optimal motivation for productivity means that people, in a holistic sense, derive feelings of challenge, effectiveness, importance, and satisfaction while achieving at an acceptable level. It does not mean that people are driven to maximum levels of output without regard for their personal motivational requirements.

3. *Systematic design and implementation can predictably and measurably influence motivation.* This assumption directly supports the purpose of this chapter, which is to describe the components and operation of a motivational system.

COMPONENTS OF MOTIVATION

One requirement in developing a motivational system is to represent human motivation in a way that is both theoretically valid and useful for designing and evaluating motivational interventions. Four major categories (concepts), and a varying number of subordinate ones, can be used to represent the components of human motivation:

1. Attention
2. Relevance
3. Confidence
4. Satisfaction

Taken together, the four major categories of *attention, relevance, confidence,* and *satisfaction* constitute the foundations of the ARCS model (Keller, 1987a, 1987c; Keller and Burkman, 1993). These major categories remain constant; the subcategories always cover the primary motivational elements encompassed by each major category, but the wording and the number of the subcategories will vary with the circumstances.

The concern in this chapter is to illustrate how, in an HPT setting, various types of motivational issues can be addressed by the same process. The only differences are in the primary tactics that one might use to stimulate people's motivation to work as opposed to their motivation to learn. In other words, each of the four major categories contains core motivational elements that can be applied to all settings, as well as to individuals or to groups; their use depends on the results of an audience motivational analysis, which is conducted in the course of designing the motivational system. These four major categories provide the foundation for understanding how to build a system that stimulates and sustains the desired levels of motivation. In the problem-solving approach to developing motivational systems that is presented in this chapter, these four categories assist in analyzing motivational requirements and developing motivational interventions. The sections that follow give brief descriptions of the major categories and include tables containing sample subcategories and tactics.

Attention

People need and desire stimulation and variety, although in differing amounts. Sensory-deprivation experiments illustrate that when people do not receive stimulus inputs from the environment, they will begin to generate their own in the form of hallucinations. By contrast, too much stimulation leads to debilitating stress, which results in decreased in performance. However, the right amount of stimulation is not the same for everyone. Some people have high levels of sensation-seeking behavior; others prefer a more placid environment.

An appropriate level of stimulation can be achieved if the people who are selected are matched to the job, either upon selection or through job redesign. For example, a person who is overstressed may benefit from a shift to a more structured, routine work environment, whereas an understimulated person may be helped by more frequent breaks or opportunities to talk with co-workers. Programs for job enlargement or job enrichment can also add to the quantity and complexity of job requirements. The same principles apply in a classroom: sometimes it is best to simplify the environment if there are too many interesting distractions on the counters or walls, and it is important to vary the types of learning activities and assignments in order to sustain interest (see Table 19.1).

Table 19.1. Attention Categories and Tactics.

Attention Categories: Need for Stimulation and Variety	Attention Tactics for Motivation to Learn	Attention Tactics for Motivation to Work
Perceptual arousal Inquiry arousal Variety	Use novel approaches; inject personal or emotional material Ask questions; create paradox; stimulate inquiry Use variations in presentation style; use concrete examples and analogies; include human interest	Match people to jobs Provide stimulation Reduce stress Adapt tactics to situation

Relevance

A primary concern of people in settings where work or learning is expected is the "why" question. The perception of relevance depends on a match among people's motives and values, the job conditions or learning requirements, and the culture of the organization. A number of researchers—Murray, Maslow, Herzberg, and McClelland, for example—are known for their formulations of motives (see Hersey and Blanchard, 1988, for a review of classical motivational theories). Of these formulations, McClelland's (1976) is particularly useful in the design of motivational systems.

McClelland (1976) and others have shown that three basic needs—for achievement, affiliation, and power—are particularly useful in explaining differences in performance among people. High achievers like to have clearly defined goals, frequent indications of their progress toward the goals, personal responsibility for success, access to experts if they need help, and control over the resources necessary to accomplish a task. By contrast, people with a high need for affiliation enjoy opportunities to work in groups and to have close relationships with others; they do not like separation from others, and they tend to call on friends when they need help. A person with a high need for power enjoys having an influence on other people. In an immature person, this need can take the form of aggressive or disruptive self-serving behavior. (For example, high achievers are frequently promoted into jobs that demand a shift from personal achievement to the management of others, but unless these new managers are carefully selected and trained, they may be frustrated and ineffective.) In a mature person, the need for power can take the form of the satisfaction derived from stimulating and directing others' behavior, obtaining and providing resources, and successfully negotiating challenges, as necessary, to maintain morale and motivation. Differences in motivation are related to differences in learning style, which can be accommodated by a variety of motivational tactics (see Keller, 1987b; Keller and Burkman, 1993). An understanding of these differences can help the HP technologist match people to jobs or redesign jobs to match individuals (see Table 19.2).

Both in classrooms and in the workplace, competition and cooperation can be used to build relevance. Competition is a fact of life in most organizations, but it can be either productive or divisive. Pitting people against each other, and measuring their accomplishments only in terms of how they compare to each other, can create a vicious type of internal competition without mutual assistance or sharing of information. By contrast, motivation and performance may be increased when people work toward common goals in a cooperative environment while also receiving incentives for outstanding personal accomplishment.

Table 19.2. Relevance Categories and Tactics.

Relevance Categories: Desire to Satisfy Basic Motives	Relevance Tactics for Motivation to Learn	Relevance Tactics for Motivation to Work
Goal orientation Motive matching Familiarity	Develop goals with learners, demonstrate utility of the instruction Use authentic exercises; match individual and group activities to learning styles Use concrete examples and analogies to relate material to learners' lives.	Develop the perception of being best at something Set goals with employees Use competition based on standards defined by benchmarks or internal expectations Provide ways for employees to work cooperatively to achieve goals

Confidence

People have a desire to feel competent and in control of key aspects of their lives, and the perception of control is associated with healthier, more productive behavior. For example, people can tolerate higher levels of stress without ill effect if they believe that they have some measure of control over what happens to them. Furthermore, their self-esteem increases if they have opportunities to make decisions regarding the type of work they do or their approach to it. Consequently, a motivational system must make it possible for people to feel that they have some control over their roles and their work in the organization. Similarly, learners will be more intrinsically motivated if they know what outcomes are expected and have some discretion in deciding how to pursue those goals.

A common and frequently incorrect assumption is that experiences of success increase confidence, but success does not always have this result. It depends on a person's attributions regarding success. If people believe that they were successful in a given situation only because of luck or some other external influence, such as the goodwill of a manager, then their confidence is not likely to increase: next time, they may not be so lucky, or the manager may not be in a good mood. But if people believe that a success is due to their own efforts and abilities, then their confidence is indeed likely to increase. Therefore, HP technologists, whether working as teachers, as managers, or in some other role, should arrange feedback that attributes success to a person's hard work and personal ability—but one should not provide this type of feedback unless it is accurate, of course (see Table 19.3).

Table 19.3. Confidence Categories and Tactics.

Confidence Categories: Desire to Feel Competent and in Control	Confidence Tactics for Motivation to Learn	Confidence Tactics for Motivation to Work
Performance requirements Success opportunities Personal control	Explain learning requirements, criteria for success, and assessments Provide frequent and varied experiences that increase learning success Give learners opportunities to make decisions, and help them attribute success to personal ability and effort	Share control in areas where employees can be responsible for achieving goals Build your belief that you can lead your employees to success (self-fulfilling prophecy) Set challenging but achievable goals and quotas

Satisfaction

People have a desire to feel good about themselves and their accomplishments. These good feelings can come from obtaining extrinsic rewards in the form of material benefits. There are many types of incentive systems, and their effects can be complex (Keller, 1994), but monetary rewards are viewed as a measure of the value that an organization attaches to one's performance. Money is a scarce resource, however. Moreover, people expect differences in pay that are based on a variety of factors (seniority, status, education, performance), and so an organization has to limit its use of money as an incentive.

Fortunately, there are other powerful incentives that cost the organization very little and that should be part of any motivational system. People respond strongly to social reinforcement and other outcomes that reinforce intrinsic feelings of satisfaction. When other people, whether subordinates, peers, or superiors, offer positive recognition for one's efforts and accomplishments, it helps one feel valued and satisfied. This is especially true when the recognition comes from peers (because they are usually focusing more on their own challenges) and from superiors (because they often focus more on performance discrepancies than on accomplishments, or they simply do not realize the powerful benefits of positive feedback); see Table 19.4.

Table 19.4. Satisfaction Categories and Tactics.

Satisfaction Categories: Desire to Feel Good About Oneself	Satisfaction Tactics for Motivation to Learn	Satisfaction Tactics for Motivation to Work
Natural consequences Positive consequences Equity	Give learners opportunities to use new skills in natural, authentic settings to promote intrinsic satisfaction	Give employees feedback related to their personal growth and the meaningfulness of their accomplishments
	Use praise, positive feedback when appropriate, symbolic rewards, and incentives	Use symbolic rewards that are recognized and valued by others; provide motivational feedback; use incentives
	Use fair testing and grading practices, and be sure tests are authentic and matched to learning goals	Provide incentives and feedback consistently and fairly

VARIATIONS

The other approaches to motivational design include Wlodkowski's (1985), which is, like the ARCS model, a multifaceted approach. There are also numerous methods that focus on particular aspects of motivation or on specific motivational variables.

Wlodkowski considers the full range of motivational influences in developing motivational systems. His prescriptive approach defines conditions and associated solutions both for traditional schooling and for adult-learning situations. His model describes the primary motivational conditions that exist at the beginning of instruction, during instruction, and at the end of instruction. The model then describes the kinds of solutions that are appropriate to each of these situations. Wlodkowski's model does includes problem solving (with respect to identifying the specific tactics to be used with a given audience and situation), but the overall model is primarily prescriptive in nature, by contrast with the ARCS model, which emphasizes audience analysis and a problem-solving approach to motivational design.

Another category of motivational systems, this group more focused, are those that concentrate on incentives for stimulating and sustaining motivation and performance. In the workplace, there are three primary types of incentive systems (Belcher, 1987): pay for performance, pay for skills (or knowledge), and gainsharing. The pay-for-performance approach is probably the most difficult of the three to use effectively because it tends to be the one most misused; even in a school setting, such incentive systems as grades and tokens are difficult to use effectively as sustained influences on motivation (Stipek, 1998). The other two approaches are easier to use, but all three have to be monitored and adjusted if they are to remain consistent with expectations for job performance. Furthermore, they will not satisfy all the motivational requirements of the people in the workplace. Elements of intrinsic motivation (such as a feeling of being valued) are important if people are to be fully motivated to excel, as opposed to being motivated only to perform in a satisfactory manner.

Another approach to developing motivational systems is to build self-motivation in learners or workers. This is the theme of many self-help programs and workshops that help people develop high levels of goal orientation, self-confidence, and personal initiative. This approach is receiving more attention as learning occurs more frequently at the workstation, by means of electronic performance support systems and systems for distance learning (such as Web-based instruction). This is also an area in which one finds cultural differences in motivation. A traditional expectation in Japanese corporations, for example, is that employees will take responsibility for learning even when the material is abstract and theoretical, and for finding ways of applying their knowledge in practical ways (Keller and Taguchi, 1996). Self-motivation is desirable, of course, but performance interventions in which the relevance of instruction is both actual and apparent will be the most effective interventions.

Examples of systems based on one or two motivational factors can be found in research on the concepts of self-efficacy and need for achievement. It can also be found in the focus of constructivist designers (Duffy, Lowyck, and Jonassen, 1993), who give heavy emphasis to the concept of authenticity, which represents a form of relevance. All these systems are helpful in building approaches that strengthen a given feature of a person's internal motivation or that improve the environment. Nevertheless, these systems omit the other important motivational factors that are necessary in building a complete and balanced system.

EXAMPLES

There are many examples of motivational system planning. Keller (1994) identifies four current trends:

1. *Participative management.* This approach includes employees in problem solving, decision making, and teamwork. It has the motivational effect of helping employees feel valued and competent, and this effect

in turn increases their sense of their own relevance to organizational goals and achievements.

2. *Self-managed teams.* Use of this approach is on the increase. Employees working on self-managed teams are responsible for cross-training, joint decision making, peer evaluation, and cooperative teamwork. Self-managed teams were pioneered in manufacturing organizations (such as Volvo) but are now being used in such nonmanufacturing settings as the Federal Aviation Administration. This approach facilitates movement toward a learning organization, as described by Senge (1990).

3. *Use of managers as teachers.* This approach been a traditional expectation in Japan, where success as a manager depends partly on one's success as a teacher. It is now occurring more frequently in the United States. The concept supports such current trends as just-in-time training, decentralization of training and education, and development of a learning organization.

4. *Use of systems and techniques for rewarding employees.* This approach is not new; indeed, it is a continuing area of concern and has a long history. What is new are some of the programs that are now being used, such as pay for knowledge and pay for skills, in which employees receive raises upon the acquisition of knowledge or skills, as when a person working on a self-managed team learns a new job within the team's area of responsibility.

Each of these trends focuses on a specific type of motivational problem.

An even more recent trend is to engage in holistic motivational design that is integrated with other influences on performance, such as those illustrated by Figure 19.2 and by the models of Gilbert (1978) and Rummler and Brache (1990). Although the trend is recent, the concept is not a new one: in the 1950s and 1960s, many writers on organizational behavior were producing holistic models of the factors that influenced motivation and performance in organizations; Kurt Lewin's work on field theory was probably one of the strongest influences on this perspective. However, the recent rebirth of interest in holistic approaches, as represented in the HPT perspective, has brought these models to the forefront once again. Most of these models have elements in common, as is to be expected if they are indeed holistic models, but each model will have its distinctive emphasis and purpose and will be subject to its own validation studies.

BENEFITS

The primary benefit of viewing motivational problems from a holistic, systems perspective, as opposed to viewing them from a prescriptive or single-variable approach, is that viewing motivational problems holistically leads to integrated, systemic solutions. These solutions are usually multidimensional and are integrated with other factors that influence performance. They are multidimensional in that they include elements related to all the major influences on motivation.

Another benefit is that motivational tactics are included only on an as-needed basis, in the same sense that well-designed instruction includes only the content and skills identified through needs assessment and task analysis. This is important because incorporating too many (or too few) motivational tactics and interventions can have detrimental consequences. A challenge in motivational design is using the analysis and design processes to determine which motivational tactics will accomplish the motivational goals without taking too much time or being too expensive.

Two additional strengths of the holistic approach—as represented, for example, by the ARCS model—are its firm grounding in the research literature on human motivation and its ability to integrate successful practices within motivational categories (such as the ARCS categories of attention, relevance, confidence, and satisfaction). Thus the systematic motivational design process can be applied efficiently. Instead of focusing on isolated areas of motivational influence, such as reinforcement, feedback, or mentoring, the holistic approach (or use of the ARCS model) demonstrates how, from a systems perspective, all these influences are combined. This approach can then provide a frame of reference for focusing in more detail on special problem areas.

The systematic motivational design process has proved both practical and capable of broad application. The ARCS model, for example, has been validated in numerous contexts. At a junior high school in Japan, the ARCS model was integrated into an established comprehensive multiyear project for curriculum development (Suzuki and Keller, 1996; Keller, 1997). It has also been integrated into the instructional design process of the National Technical Education Group in Napierville, Illinois, where CD-ROM-based training is developed for new releases of most major software applications, and the U.S. Coast Guard is currently developing an even more comprehensive large-scale application of the ARCS model in its program for training and socializing recruits. Thus the ARCS model, which is being used in some twenty different countries, has withstood the test of cross-cultural application. Specific motivational tactics vary from culture to culture, but the overall framework of categories and design processes remains stable.

SPECIAL PRECAUTIONS

People complain that motivational programs eventually lose their impact because participants lose interest, or because organizations withdraw support. The problem may be adaptation.

Variation is an important component of motivation. People like variety. Commonplace events can become boring, both in the classroom and in the workplace. For example, there is often an initial benefit from paying bonuses for money-saving ideas, but after a time the suggestion boxes collect dust, and the motivational system has to be revamped to generate new interest. But high levels of motivation are more likely to be sustained over a longer period if managers provide appropriate styles of leadership, model the values and behaviors that they want others to exhibit, and provide training, incentives, and other interventions that are internally consistent. In other words, single-factor programs usually do not work by themselves; leaders must exhibit the same levels of intrinsic motivation that they are trying to stimulate and sustain in others.

STEPS IN DEVELOPMENT

This section discusses the ARCS model in detail and uses the model as an example in describing how to develop a holistic motivational system for workplace and classroom settings. The ARCS model contains an eight-step design process (see Figure 19.3). Steps 1 and 2, which belong to the analytical components of the process, produce information about the status quo and provide the basis for carrying out steps 3 and 4 (analyzing gaps in motivation and their causes). On the basis of these analyses, in step 5 one prepares objectives for the performance improvement project and specifies how they will be assessed. Then come two design steps. Step 6 consists of brainstorming for each motivational category, to generate a rich list of potential solutions. Step 7 is more critical and analytical; here, one selects those solutions that best fit the constraints of time, resources, and other factors. Step 8 includes both development and evaluation and resembles what is done in any other kind of development model.

Analysis

As is true of the development process for any kind of performance system, the development of a motivational system begins with the collecting of information (steps 1 and 2) and with its analysis (steps 3 and 4), to identify the motivational characteristics and gaps that will determine the objectives (step 5). In this process, there are two difficulties in determining the degree and nature of a motivational problem.

The first difficulty is that problems resulting in symptoms of demotivation may not be due to motivational causes. People can become demotivated as a consequence of what are in fact problems with capability or opportunity. For example, people who do not have and cannot get the skills required to perform satisfactorily will soon learn that they cannot succeed to a satisfactory degree. They will develop low expectations for success, or even feelings of helplessness, and

Figure 19.3. Steps in Motivational Design.

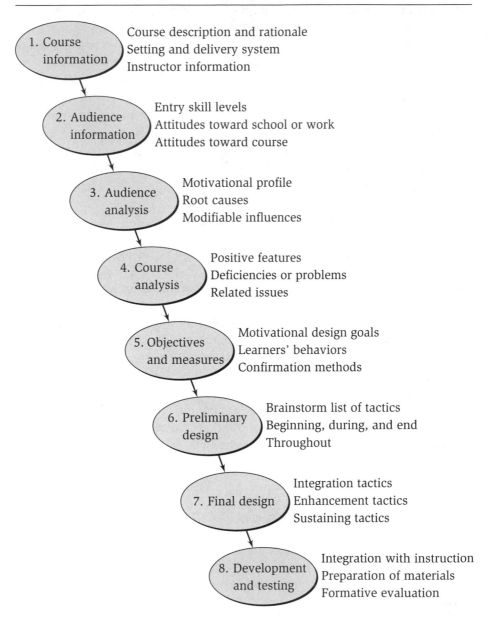

1. Course information — Course description and rationale / Setting and delivery system / Instructor information

2. Audience information — Entry skill levels / Attitudes toward school or work / Attitudes toward course

3. Audience analysis — Motivational profile / Root causes / Modifiable influences

4. Course analysis — Positive features / Deficiencies or problems / Related issues

5. Objectives and measures — Motivational design goals / Learners' behaviors / Confirmation methods

6. Preliminary design — Brainstorm list of tactics / Beginning, during, and end / Throughout

7. Final design — Integration tactics / Enhancement tactics / Sustaining tactics

8. Development and testing — Integration with instruction / Preparation of materials / Formative evaluation

will be demotivated, demonstrating lowered levels of effort and performance. A very similar situation will occur if there are inadequate resources or contradictory policies and procedures. The consequence will be demotivated employees, even though the root problem is lack of opportunity to perform at a high level. Consequently, in developing motivational systems it is critical to identify the root problem, regardless of the symptoms.

The second difficulty in identifying a motivational problem lies in the nature of motivation. By contrast with situations in which more is better, as in quality improvement, motivation follows a curvilinear relationship with performance. As motivation increases, performance increases, but only to an optimal point. Afterward, performance decreases as motivation increases to levels where excessive stress leads to performance decrements. There is always some level of tension, or stress, associated with motivation. On the rising side of the curve it is sometimes referred to as *facilitative stress;* on the downside, as *debilitating stress.*

Given that there is a motivational problem, one classifies it according to the four ARCS categories and determines whether the learners or employees are under- or overmotivated in each case. With respect to attention, people may be demotivated because they are bored and not paying attention to tasks, or because they are so overstimulated by the job opportunity or by requirements that they are trying to pay attention to too many things at once. In both cases, they are not focusing their attention on the critical tasks, but solutions differ according to whether the cause is under- or overstimulation.

With respect to relevance, people may have been placed in jobs in which they have no intrinsic interest, or jobs that hold no promise of advancement on their desired career paths. By contrast, the factor of relevance can be too salient when one's career path depends totally on one's success with a specific task in a current job; the high level of stress could easily cause one to make unnecessary mistakes.

Confidence can also be too high or too low. People who have the ability and skill to perform tasks, but who do not believe they do, lack persistence when the tasks become challenging. They will give up easily and inappropriately blame their failure on lack of ability rather than on lack of effort. People whose confidence is too high—that is, people who do not have as much skill or ability as they think they do—will be cocky about tasks. They will resist learning and typically will make mistakes without noticing or understanding that they have done so.

Dissatisfaction can result from expectations that were too negative or positive. For this reason, it is most appropriate to talk about satisfaction potential when doing audience analysis. When people are put into an undesired situation, their satisfaction potential is often low. This means that even if they have a positive experience that was not boring, was relevant, and was at an appropriate level of challenge, they may still harbor resentment because they did not choose the opportunity. By contrast, people who believe that a given job opportunity is going to be perfect—that it is exactly what they have wanted and will make them totally happy—are undoubtedly going to be disappointed with the reality of the situation.

There is no permanent motivational solution. This is a result of human physiology as well as of human psychology. If incoming stimuli in our environment are too regular and routine, we adapt; that is, we tune these stimuli out and may even fall asleep. If they are too irregular, however, we become stressed. Consequently, we need variation, but not too much of it, and there have to be variations in the patterns of variation. That is why novelty is sometimes useful purely for its motivational effect. It is also the reason why, during the phase of motivational analysis, one has to document patterns of leadership, working relationships, job complexity, and other factors that support continuing motivation.

In conducting motivational analysis, it is important to identify the nature of motivational gaps in these terms and to realize that the problems may be different in one subgroup or individual than in others. It is also important to identify the presence of any positive motivational factors. A motivational system has to be capable of solving motivational problems, but it also has to sustain desirable levels of motivation. The output of analysis indicates where there are motivational gaps to be closed and where satisfactory levels of motivation need to be sustained rather than changed.

Design

In motivational design, as in HPT in general, it is best to work on specifically defined problems. This needs to be stated because it can be more of a problem in motivational design than in some other performance areas. Often, people try to deal with the global issue of improving motivation by adopting a global solution. This can easily lead to faddish, expensive solutions, such as an elaborate new incentive system that is not targeted to the primary problems and does not succeed after the novelty wears off. Another frequently adopted global solution is to purchase a package of motivational tapes and self-study programs or a set of seminars. These may be stimulating for a while, but they typically do not address the specific problems in an organization. One of the benefits of the analysis process just described is that it helps one identify specific motivational problems, and this makes it easier to design a targeted set of solutions.

After choosing a specific problem to solve, the first task in step 6 (see Figure 19.3), the first of two design steps, is to brainstorm possible solutions. At this point, all potential solutions should be listed, regardless of their presumed feasibility. The goal, as in any other brainstorming process, is to produce as many ideas as possible. The second task is to define the ideal solution, regardless of constraints. The ideal solution might be constructed from several of the specific suggestions that were made during the brainstorming process, or it might emerge as a new idea from the stimulation provided by brainstorming. An important element at this point is not to worry about expense, organizational policies, or other constraints that might inhibit the discovery of an ideal solution.

Then, in step 7, one selects the most feasible tactics listed in step 6 and integrates them into a motivational system. The reason for making this a two-step process is that step 6 encourages one to envision, without restraint, all potential solutions, including those that might initially seem to be too grandiose or "ideal." By so doing, one is more likely to approximate an ideal than if one had narrowly focused from the beginning on the first possible solution. In step 7 of the process, the HP technologist creates the best possible solutions by combining ideas from step 6 and by applying several selection criteria.

These criteria (Keller, 1996) include expense, policy, acceptability, and proportionality. The cost of developing and implementing the motivational system must fall within acceptable budgetary limits. The motivational system must not violate policies regarding personnel assignment, management responsibility, or legal and union-related restrictions. Furthermore, the system must be acceptable to all the parties affected by it. For example, a change in leadership style may be a relatively inexpensive and highly effective solution, but if managers are unwilling to change their leadership styles, then the solution has to be rejected. Finally, the solution must be in proper proportion to the other activities of the organization, such as instructional content in training or task requirements in the workplace.

The motivational system, as indicated in the assumptions at the beginning of this chapter, is a means, not an end. It is there to support the organization by stimulating and sustaining individual development and productivity. Sometimes, however, the motivational system—which can range from a set of enhancements for a program of instruction or a major change in an organization's incentive structure—can become an end in itself. This happens when managers or HP technologists focus so much on how to sustain the motivational system (as often happens in token economies) or on how to tailor work to fit its reward structure that they become distracted from their primary jobs. People will focus on the reward structure, of course; therefore, rewards must be functionally related to the desired level of performance rather than to some level of performance that happens to be convenient. For example, education managers may be rewarded for the number of students in their education centers, but this kind of reward discourages these managers from developing alternative delivery systems that take training to the workplace but reduce class enrollments.

Development of the solutions, which also occurs as part of step 7, follows the same process that one would employ for any other area of application. The first activity is to prepare a plan of work for writing, developing media, doing developmental reviews, and preparing for implementation. As with any effective system development activity, it is important to have motivational tactics and strategies well integrated with other system components. For example, such tactics as icebreakers at the beginning of a training session can be a total waste of time if they do not meet specific needs of the audience and help prepare them for the topics and objectives of the course.

Implementation and Evaluation

Motivational systems are normally implemented as part of a package of HPT interventions and follow the schedule planned for the overall changes. This is easy to see when the motivational system consists of a set of motivational enhancements to a training course. But even when there is a major new motivational system, such as an incentive system, it is normally part of a more comprehensive package of changes in job definitions, performance appraisal procedures, and policy changes. In all of these implementation activities, it is important to observe whether the motivational elements are being implemented as designed and to document any variations. This information provides input to the evaluation.

Evaluating a motivational system is challenging for many of the same reasons that it is difficult to evaluate other performance improvement interventions. For example, it is seldom appropriate to create comparison groups by installing the system in one part of an organization but not in another. If a new system is being installed, or if changes are being made to an existing system, then it is possible to compare postintervention indicators with preintervention baseline measures. But when comparison cannot be based on changes in a group's performance, as when entirely new behaviors are being measured, results can be examined in light of predefined criteria.

In all of these situations, both global and specific measures can be used. Global measures include measures of absenteeism, grievances, and turnover. Specific measures include direct observation of leadership style, interviews with employees, surveys, and unobtrusive observation of conversations in lunchrooms and other settings, to assess employees' attitudes. The goal is to obtain measures that provide direct indicators of motivation, as evidenced by attitudes and level of effort, as opposed to indicators of performance in which motivational influences and consequences cannot be distinguished from other influences (see Keller, 1995).

SUMMARY

A person who wants to learn, work, or enjoy life will ask the "why" question, just as Charlie did at the beginning of this chapter. By contrast with Charlie, however, the motivated person will find answers to this question internally, will be given answers by others, or will seek answers from others.

However, the "why" question addresses only one aspect of motivation. A person who is motivated to work, for example, is one who finds sources of variety and curiosity in the job, regards the job as personally meaningful and as contributing to the fulfillment of important goals, finds challenges in work, has the confidence to be stimulated by these challenges, and gains feelings of satisfaction and respect in addition to extrinsic rewards.

This chapter has shown that it is possible to view motivation from a holistic perspective—as one of the factors that influence human performance and that can be positively influenced by the design of a motivational system. Motivation, far from being a nebulous, uncontrollable human characteristic, can be seen as a manageable part of a comprehensive approach to improving and sustaining desirable human performance.

References

Belcher, J. G. Jr. (1987). *Productivity plus: How today's best-run companies are gaining the competitive edge.* Houston: Gulf.

Duffy, T. M., Lowyck, J., and Jonassen, D. H. (1993). *Designing environments for constructivist learning.* New York: Springer-Verlag.

Gilbert, T. F. (1978). *Human competence: Engineering worthy performance.* New York: McGraw-Hill.

Hersey, P., and Blanchard, K. H. (1988). *Management of organizational behavior* (5th ed.). Englewood Cliffs, NJ: Prentice Hall.

Keller, J. M. (1979). Motivation and instructional design: A theoretical perspective. *Journal of Instructional Development* 2:4, 26–34.

Keller, J. M. (1983). Motivational design of instruction: A theoretical perspective. In C. M. Reigeluth (ed.), *Instructional design theories and models: An overview of their current status.* Hillsdale, NJ: Erlbaum.

Keller, J. M. (1987a). Development and use of the ARCS model of motivational design. *Journal of Instructional Development* 10:3, 2–10.

Keller, J. M. (1987b). Strategies for stimulating the motivation to learn. *Performance & Instruction* 26:8, 1–7.

Keller, J. M. (1987c). The systematic process of motivational design. *Performance & Instruction* 26:9, 1–8.

Keller, J. M. (1994). Trends and tactics in employee motivation. *HR Horizons* 115, 5–10.

Keller, J. M. (1995). *Development and validation of two measures of learner motivation.* Paper presented at the annual meeting of the Association for Educational Communications and Technology, Anaheim, CA.

Keller, J. M. (1996). *Motivation by design.* Tallahassee, FL: John Keller Associates.

Keller, J. M. (1997). Motivational design and multimedia: Beyond the novelty effect. *Strategic Human Resource Development Review* 1:1, 188–203.

Keller, J. M., and Burkman, E. (1993). Motivation. In M. Fleming (ed.), *Instructional message design* (2nd ed.). Englewood Cliffs, NJ: Educational Technology Press.

Keller, J. M., and Taguchi, M. (1996). Use of the systems approach to training design and delivery in Japanese corporations. *Performance Improvement Quarterly* 9:1, 62–76.

McClelland, D. C. (1976). *The achieving society.* New York: Irvington.

Porter, L. W., and Lawler, E. E. (1968). *Managerial attitudes and performance.* Burr Ridge, IL: Irwin.

Rummler, G. A., and Brache, A. P. (1990). *Improving performance: How to manage the white space on the organization chart.* San Francisco: Jossey-Bass.

Senge, P. M. (1990). *The fifth discipline.* New York: Doubleday.

Steers, R. M., and Porter, L. W. (1983). *Motivation and work behavior.* New York: McGraw-Hill.

Stipek, D. (1998). *Motivation to learn: From theory to practice* (3rd ed.). Needham Heights, MA: Allyn & Bacon.

Suzuki, K., and Keller, J. M. (1996, Aug.). *Applications of the ARCS model in computer-based instruction in Japan.* Paper presented at the annual meeting of the Japanese Educational Technology Association, Kanazawa, Japan.

Vroom, V. H. (1964). *Work and motivation.* New York: Wiley.

Wlodkowski, R. J. (1985). *Enhancing adult motivation to learn.* San Francisco: Jossey-Bass.

CHAPTER TWENTY

Feedback

Donald Tosti
Stephanie F. Jackson

In many situations where training is the primary intervention, much of the time that is invested in training would be better used in developing fluency of performance through feedback and practice. For example, many of the skills "taught" in leadership and management training, in sales training, or in training for communication already exist at some strength in the population. Training may be necessary to provide a framework for those skills, but an often neglected need is for sufficient practice, with feedback, to create the fluency and confidence to successfully apply those skills in the real world.

Feedback is information, about behavior or about its impact, that is "fed back" to an individual or a group, with the intention of influencing future performance. People do, of course, receive feedback as a direct consequence of performance itself, without intervention from others; if, for example, someone tries to tighten a loose screw with a screwdriver and the screw becomes still looser, that information will probably prompt the person to try turning the screwdriver the other way. The focus in this chapter, however, is on purposeful feedback provided by an individual or a system. Most people have experienced, either as givers or receivers, feedback that did not influence future performance or, worse, influenced it in undesirable ways. This chapter addresses those characteristics of feedback that increase its probability of having the intended effect on future performance.

According to the nature of the original performance, feedback may have either of two broad purposes:

1. To affect the quantity of performance (that is, to get people to continue doing something they are already doing, or to do more or less of it)

2. To affect the quality of performance (that is, to get people to change the way they do something)

Feedback directed at affecting the quantity of performance is *summative,* or evaluative, feedback; it "sums up" or evaluates performance. It might be expressed in terms like these: "Thanks for helping me get that report out; I really appreciate it. It'll make a big difference in preparing people for the budget review meeting next week." Summative feedback serves a motivational purpose; in the preceding example, its intent is to encourage the person to continue the behavior.

Feedback directed at affecting the quality of performance is *formative* (Tosti, 1978), or developmental, feedback; it attempts to change the "form" of the performance. It might be expressed in terms like these: "In our next report, try putting a brief summary of recommendations at the beginning. It will help us reach those people who are too busy to read the entire report." Formative feedback serves an advisory purpose.

CHARACTERISTICS OF FEEDBACK

Given these two purposes—affecting the quantity or quality of performance, or the "why" of feedback—we have a basis for examining the characteristics typically required to meet those purposes: the *who, what, where,* and *when* of feedback. A summary of these characteristics of feedback appears in Table 20.1.

Who

The critical *who* in feedback is the performer. Summative feedback should match the performer's motivational needs and expectations. (Formative feedback should also match the performer's results needs, but in this case needs are primarily related to levels of skill or ability.) For example, someone providing summative feedback might make identical statements to a novice and to an experienced performer, and the statements might be equally meaningful. Formative feedback, however, will usually need to be more detailed and specific if novices are to understand and act on it.

What

The *what* of feedback is the performance itself. Specificity about performance is one requirement of both summative and formative feedback. Feedback must clearly identify the performance to be strengthened or changed. An additional requirement of summative feedback is that receivers see it as commensurate with the value or effort of the performance. For example, most people do not

Table 20.1. Characteristics of Summative and Formative Feedback.

	Summative Feedback	Formative Feedback
Definition	Information that evaluates performance	Information that provides guidance about how to change performance
Why: The Purpose	To "motivate"; typically affects the quantity of performance	To "develop"; typically affects the quality or form of performance
Who: Performer Needs	Should fit motivational needs and expectations of performers: match their perceptions of what is appropriate reward or punishment	Should fit the developmental needs of performers: match their abilities, skills, and knowledge
What: Performance Needs	Should focus on the specific performance to be affected	Should focus on the specific performance to be affected
Where: Setting Needs	Can be given in either private or public settings; often has greater impact when given publicly	Usually best given in a private setting; may have diminished or unpredictable impact when given publicly
When: Timing Needs	Usually most effective when given soon after performance	Usually most effective when given soon before the next opportunity to perform

expect much feedback about a simple behavior like coming to work on time, although an occasional appreciative comment may help maintain the behavior. Most people do, however, want significant feedback when they have invested substantial effort in turning in an outstanding performance; in this case, a casual expression of appreciation may seem to undervalue the performance.

Where

A key issue concerning where to give feedback is privacy. Both summative and formative feedback can sometimes be effective whether given in public or private. However, summative feedback often has greater impact when given publicly. It may be seen as more meaningful and may be valued more highly.

Formative feedback, by contrast, may be less effective when given publicly. The performer may feel punished or demeaned by public advice or correction.

When

Perhaps the greatest single difference between summative and formative feedback lies in the issue of their timing. An often cited rule for feedback is to provide it immediately after performance. This was a basic principle underlying programmed instruction, for example, and the rule usually makes sense in the case of summative feedback. For example, a compliment right after you have done something is particularly meaningful; it may lose some impact if delayed. Formative feedback, however, is often more effective when it is delayed until the performer can act on it. Advice or correction that comes right after performance can be perceived as punishing criticism and may be forgotten if there is no opportunity to perform correctly in the near future.

POSITIVE AND NEGATIVE FORMS OF FEEDBACK

So far, summative and formative feedback have been described primarily in their positive forms—that is, as praise or recognition to encourage continued good performance, or as advice about how to improve performance. Both types of feedback also have negative forms, however. Table 20.2 summarizes the differences between the positive and negative forms of feedback and their typical impact on the performer.

Summative feedback can evaluate performance positively or negatively to influence its quantity. In its positive form, it serves to encourage continued performance; in its negative form, it serves to discourage continued performance. Similarly, formative feedback can provide advice on what to do to improve performance, or it can identify what was wrong with previous performance.

The negative form of summative feedback is sometimes both useful and necessary. It can be effective when the desired result is to stop behavior and there is no particular behavior to be substituted. For example, someone may be observed smoking near inflammable materials. It is important that the behavior stop immediately, but there is no special positive behavior to be substituted; the desired behavior is "not smoking."

Summative feedback in its negative form is less useful when there actually is a behavior to be substituted. For example, suppose a salesperson has just said, "You're wrong" to a customer. One might provide summative feedback in its negative form by saying something like this: "it's a mistake to tell customers they're wrong; don't do it again." That might stop the person from saying "You're wrong" again, but there is no reliable way to be sure about what the person will say the next time he or she perceives a customer to be wrong. In al-

Table 20.2. Summative and Formative Feedback: Positive and Negative Forms.

Positive and Negative Forms	Summative Feedback	Formative Feedback
Positive Form	Information evaluating performance as positive	Information about how to improve performance
	• Perceived as encouragement • Serves to maintain or increase performance	• Perceived as advice • Serves to change the quality or form of performance
Negative Form	Information evaluating performance as negative	Information about what is wrong with performance
	• Perceived as discouragement • Serves to decrease or eliminate performance; can result in unpredictable substitution	• Perceived as criticism • Serves to change the quality or form of performance by eliminating some aspect; can result in unpredictable change

most every situation of this type, it will be more useful to offer positive formative feedback on appropriate ways to respond.

The negative form of formative feedback—information about aspects of performance that were incorrect or inappropriate—can be useful in providing a contrast with correct performance, in offering clarification, or in highlighting aspects of performance that are causing serious problems. In most cases, however, positive advice about how to improve will be more useful than a description of what was done wrong.

PRINCIPLES OF DELIVERING FEEDBACK

A review of the preceding analysis suggests three general principles for effective feedback, whether formative or summative:

1. *Fit:* Effective feedback should fit the needs and expectations of the performer, as well as the nature of the performance itself.
2. *Focus:* Feedback should be specific, clearly focusing on the desired performance.
3. *Timing:* Feedback should be timed so that it is meaningful and useful to the performer.

FORMATIVE OR DEVELOPMENTAL FEEDBACK

This section deals in greater depth with these three principles as applied to formative feedback and offers specific guidelines for addressing the following three questions about feedback:

- Does it fit the performer and the situation?
- Is it focused on the desired performance?
- Is it timed so that it will be useful?

Does the Feedback Fit?

"Fitting" feedback means tailoring information to the performer's needs and providing it in amounts that the person can assimilate and respond to. There are three basic guidelines for fit:

1. *Use steps of appropriate size.* Be sure the requested change is within the performer's ability to understand and act on. In practice, this means asking for an initial level of improvement that can probably be made in one try, and it means providing information in amounts that the person can grasp in one session. Clearly, the situation will vary with the individual; what the novice sees as a big change may appear small to a skilled, experienced performer.

2. *Tailor information to the performer's needs.* People vary in the type and level of detail they need. Some may need only to be told what to change; others may need detailed information about why, how, where, or when.

3. *Use the language of the performer.* Use of this guideline may be especially crucial with novice performers. Terms and concepts that are familiar to an experienced person may sound like jargon to a novice. Even experienced people may not know certain terms, or they may have their own ways of describing performance.

Feedback can be offered at the level of direction, at the level of problem solving, or at the level of teaching. The following discussion provides a structure that can help in fitting feedback to the performer. The three levels are described in ascending order of complexity and detail.

Direction. Feedback at this level simply directs the performer's attention to things that need to be changed, or to simple suggestions for changing them. This level of feedback is best used when the change to be made is simple, or when the performer is experienced enough to perceive the change as relatively simple. Direction is appropriate when the performer says, "Just point me the right way; I can take it from there." When the need is for direction with a low level of guidance, *identify:* simply point out the needed change. When the need is for direction with a high level of guidance, *suggest:* offer a general idea about how to make the change.

Problem Solving. Feedback at this level involves a problem-solving interaction with a performer about what to change or how to change it. This level of feedback is best used when the change is relatively complex for the performer but does not require completely new ideas or skills. It is particularly useful when there are alternate ways to make improvements in performance. According to the situation, one might offer suggestions or serve primarily as a facilitator, helping the performer develop ways to make the change. Problem solving is appropriate when the performer says, "Help me figure out what to change, or how." When the need is for problem solving with a low level of guidance, *facilitate:* ask questions to help the performer develop solutions. When the need is for problem solving with a high level of guidance, *guide:* offer possible solutions and help the performer assess and refine them.

Teaching. Feedback at this level is appropriate when the desired change requires skills or knowledge that the performer does not have and cannot reasonably be expected to develop through a problem-solving discussion. It can range from demonstrating the performance and guiding the performer through practice to conducting formal training (or enrolling the performer in training). Teaching is appropriate when the performer says, "Show me what to do, or how to do it." When the need is for teaching with a low level of guidance, *demonstrate:* illustrate, or show the performer how to make the change. When the need is for teaching with a high level of guidance, *train:* conduct full training, with demonstration and practice.

Is the Feedback Focused?

Feedback should be unambiguous and free of extraneous information that might interfere with the message. It should clearly focus the performer on what needs to be done. There are five basic guidelines for focus:

1. *Concentrate on the behavior, not the person.* Be sure that feedback is phrased to avoid insults or unnecessary criticism. Feedback that is seen as a personal put-down is likely, at best, to distract the performer from what needs to be done. At worst, it may destroy the performer's confidence completely and make him or her to give up.

2. *Avoid mixed messages.* Do not mix praise with advice when it is possible to avoid doing so. Watch for the word *but* in feedback; it usually signals a mixed message. When performers receive positive evaluations that are combined with suggestions for improvement, the results are unpredictable. Some will hear only the positive evaluation and ignore the needed correction; others will hear only the correction and miss the reinforcement and confidence-building of the positive information. Some, of course, will hear and respond to both messages, but why depend on luck if one can exercise control over the communication?

3. *Avoid overload.* Try to stick to one subject or performance area at a time. Most people find it difficult to change in several areas simultaneously. Performers given feedback on multiple areas will usually have to select one or two to focus on, and those may not be the most important ones.

4. *Be specific.* Try to use concrete language. Describe exactly what needs to change—and how, as necessary. The performer needs to be able to translate the feedback into action. General phrases like "more forceful" or "better organized" may have to be supported by specific suggestions or examples.

5. *Check receptivity.* Make sure the performer is able to attend to the feedback. People who are distracted by other events are unlikely to benefit much from feedback. For example, someone who is preparing for a presentation may find it difficult to attend to feedback about coaching skills.

Is the Feedback Well Timed?

Whenever it is possible to do so, formative feedback should be given before a performance, when the performer has an opportunity to use it. Formative feedback given shortly after a performance is often seen as pointing out what the performer did wrong. It can be frustrating and feel punishing to have errors pointed out when there is nothing one can do about them. Moreover, the feedback may be forgotten by the time the situation comes up again.

For example, the managers of a telephone sales organization routinely gave salespeople feedback at the end of the day. This (relatively) immediate feedback had little effect on performance for at least two reasons. First, the employees were eager to go home and were not interested in listening to "critical" feedback at that time of day. Second, they could do nothing with the information at that time; by the next morning, when they were back on the phones, much of the formative feedback had been forgotten. The managers were then asked to hold their feedback sessions in the morning, before employees got to their phones. This arrangement gave salespeople immediate opportunities to use the information, and performance increased dramatically. This simple change in timing turned punishing criticism into helpful advice.

Usefulness is the key issue in timing feedback. As we shall see, immediacy can be helpful in increasing the impact (that is, the power to encourage) of summative feedback; formative feedback, however, is typically most useful when it is delayed until the person has another opportunity to perform. Thus there are two basic guidelines for timing formative feedback:

1. *Give feedback when the performer can use it.* Normally, formative feedback should be given before the person is going to perform again, not immediately after an error has been made. If the performance is going to be relatively simple, one may want to give feedback immediately before. If the performance is going to be complex, it is usually wise to give the feedback earlier, when the performer is making preparations.

2. *Give feedback often enough to prevent major errors.* This is particularly important with complex types of performance, in which certain kinds of behavior have the potential for serious consequences.

SUMMATIVE FEEDBACK

Summative, or evaluative, feedback can take different forms. Whatever form it takes, however, it must have two characteristics:

1. It must be linked to a specific behavior.
2. It must increase (or decrease) the likelihood that the behavior will be repeated.

The following discussion of guidelines focuses on positive, or motivational, summative feedback (that is, feedback related to rewards or recognition), which is given to increase or maintain the quantity of a particular kind of performance. As mentioned earlier, the negative form of summative feedback is less often useful and should be used sparingly.

Does the Feedback Fit?

"Fitting," in the context of positive summative feedback, means matching the reinforcement to both the person and the performance. For example, the chance to talk about one's work at a staff meeting may be a very rewarding opportunity for an outgoing employee but not for one who is shy; a short extra break might be appropriate for someone who has come in a little early to help you get out a report, but this reward would not fit the performance of someone who has put in many extra hours of personal time and effort over a long period.

Recognition comes in many forms. One of the simplest and most effective forms is verbal praise for a job well done (or significantly improved). For example, "Jo, all this week I've been admiring how efficiently you handle customer complaints" or "I really appreciate that you stayed to make sure we met that deadline."

It is important to recognize behavior that is not yet perfect. If only fully correct behavior and finished products are praised, people who are making good progress may become discouraged along the way. Providing motivational feedback for increments of achievement encourages people to attempt further achievement. After all, people act—or refrain from acting—partly because of the positive or negative consequences that result.

People often ask for other ways of providing motivational feedback besides direct praise. The following forms can be useful:

- *"Earshotting."* Tell someone else within the performer's hearing range about his or her fine performance; for example (near Marta's workstation so that she overhears), "Dennis, if you want some ideas about handling that kind of request, Marta would be the person to ask; she's really good at it."

- *"Bankshotting."* As in the bank shot in a game of pool, this is "bouncing" praise: get another person to express admiration to the performer of his or her performance ("Sheila, it was Fred who got the information on this order. Why don't you let him know you think it's a good job?").

Also effective, but used less frequently, are the following:

- *Formal recognition.* Acknowledge good performance formally and publicly. For example, mention it in a memo, put the performer's name on a plaque, or place an item in the company newsletter.

- *Preferred work assignments.* When someone is doing well or making good progress, give an assignment you know the person will enjoy: "Betty, those reports are excellent. You're doing them much more thoroughly. I know you enjoy organizing things. Why don't you take a break from what you're doing and take a look at my plans for rearranging our office? Tell me what you think about them."

- *Special rewards.* Add a special or personal touch for a fine (or much improved) job: "Peter, your installations have been trouble-free this month, and so much faster. How about celebrating a little and letting me treat you to lunch at that new restaurant?"

People tend to use the methods of reward or recognition that have worked for them in the past—and often, of course, these continue to work quite well. When people seem hard to motivate, however, one reason may be failure to use incentives that fit the performers. Here are two ways to find incentives that fit:

1. *Look for preferred activities.* Think about what the performer would probably do during a fifteen-minute break. Whatever the person would do is likely to be a preferred activity.
2. *Look for preferred work assignments.* What are the performer's favorite parts of the job? The things people do best are usually the things they like best.

Is the Feedback Focused?

Focusing summative feedback means clearly linking it to a specific performance: first, being specific about the performance; and, second, avoiding confusion by keeping rewards and recognition separated from negative information or punishment.

For example, if the principle is "be specific," a poor example of summative feedback would be "Good job for your first unit report." A fair example would be "Good report, Allen. You covered everything very well." Best would be "Allen, you did well on your first unit report. I especially like the way you tied it all together in the summary. I think everyone has profited by reading it." If the principle is "avoid mixed messages," a poor example of summative feedback would be "Paul, your report's good. But why don't you take a look at Jim's? He's got some good ways of illustrating a point." A fair example would be "Paul, you did a great job on your report. Why don't you review the one I got from Jim? It's also good, but it's different from yours; you and he should be producing consistent reports." Best would be "Paul, your report looks great. It's clear and concise." (Deal with desired improvements later, when Paul and Jim are getting ready to do the next reports.)

Is the Feedback Well Timed?

For optimum impact, motivational summative feedback should meet these two criteria:

1. It should occur soon after the work performance.
2. It should occur often enough to encourage continued good performance.

The sooner good performance is recognized, the greater the effect. Delays can reduce the impact; people may wonder why, if the work was genuinely good, it took so long to recognize it. Sometimes, of course, a delay is necessary; for example, praise for an accurate report will have to wait until the report can be reviewed and its accuracy has been determined.

Deciding how soon to give positive motivational feedback is easy: if it is possible to do so, one gives it as soon as one knows the work is good. Deciding how often is not so simple. Some people need recognition more often than others, and some kinds of performance may require recognition more often than others. Here are two useful guidelines:

1. If the performance is difficult, or if it is new to a person, provide motivational feedback more often.

2. If a person is performing well but seems to lack confidence, provide feedback more often.

When in doubt, it is safe to assume that most people feel they do not get enough recognition for what they do.

APPLICATIONS OF FEEDBACK: PRACTICAL ISSUES

The potential applications of feedback are virtually limitless. Space prohibits addressing them here in depth, but this section discusses selected issues and applications and provides suggestions for overcoming some of the real-world obstacles that people encounter in trying to apply the principles of feedback. There are situations, of course, in which it is difficult or perhaps impossible to adhere fully to the feedback guidelines outlined in this chapter. The more closely one can follow the guidelines, however, the more powerful the impact of the feedback will be.

What seems to pose the greatest difficulty for many people is the issue of timing and separating summative and formative feedback; many real-world situations do not lend themselves readily to separation of summative from formative feedback. This section presents some issues that have been raised and offers suggestions for dealing with them. Note, however, that not all suggestions will be appropriate to a particular situation.

In a situation where it feels comfortable to give summative feedback right after a performance, but uncomfortable to wait until later to give formative feedback (the discomfort arises because it does not seem fair or right to withhold information), the following suggestions may be useful:

- Let people know well in advance that you prefer to give advice at a later time, rather than right after a performance.
- Ask people to check with you for suggestions when they are ready to repeat the performance in question.
- Create a brief separation between summative and formative feedback. For example, give summative feedback, and then take a break; get a cup of coffee, and then open a discussion of "suggestions for next time."
- Give summative feedback, pause briefly, and then give formative feedback and create an opportunity to perform again (or at least to repeat those parts of the performance that need improvement).

If performance was so poor that there is little or no positive summative feedback that can be given right after the performance, the following suggestions may be useful:

- Acknowledge that the performance was not a success, and set up a later time to talk about how to improve it.
- Avoid punishing the person, and try to build confidence that he or she will be able to succeed the next time.
- If it is feasible to do so, and if the person will not be uncomfortable, consider creating an opportunity to perform again, this time with advice.

If time, distance, workload, or other factors make it difficult to provide two separate summative and formative feedback sessions, the following suggestions may be useful:

- Ask the person to take responsibility for calling or checking in to get advice when he or she is ready to perform again.
- If feedback is in written form, physically separate the summative and formative parts. Ask people to read only the summative feedback and to wait to read the formative feedback until they are ready to use it.

VALIDITY OF FEEDBACK

To be useful, feedback should be valid. One often neglected issue of concern in feedback systems is the validity of the source: if the source of the feedback has only limited opportunities to observe performance, then validity of the feedback comes into question. For example, performance appraisal systems often require managers to give feedback on things that they are seldom able to observe directly. The boss may have few opportunities to see employees managing their own teams, but she may nevertheless be expected to comment on their leadership performance. An old coach once said, "The only good advice comes from people who see you in the game." The "game" in which the boss sees people is often very different from the one peers or subordinates see.

One attempt to address this issue is the increasingly common use of "360-degree" feedback (see, for example, Jones and Bearly, 1996), in which people receive feedback from the boss, peers, and subordinates. This approach has the potential advantage of increasing the validity of the feedback, but it also has the potential disadvantage of creating confusion and serious information overload.

The authors' experience has been that multiple sources of feedback are most useful when the number of sources is limited, when they have different perspectives on the same "game," and when data from each source is provided separately and is clearly labeled. For example, comparing feedback from subordinates with feedback from peers can be very valuable. Some people will find congruity between peers' and subordinates' views, but others may not. Resolving that discrepancy can add significantly to the impact of feedback; people often gain powerful insights into their behavior when they ask, "What is this group seeing that the other group is not?" But adding a third source of feedback to the mix often creates overload, and combining feedback from very different sources reduces the validity of the composite feedback.

BASES OF COMPARISON FOR FEEDBACK

Feedback systems often provide information against a baseline, for comparison. Baselines can be of several types. There are norm-based feedback systems, in which people are compared to others (usually in terms of percentiles). There are standards-based feedback systems, in which people are judged against requirements. There are also feedback systems with personal baselines, in which one's own behaviors are compared to one's own personal average for that set of behaviors.

Normative comparisons, although quite common, have some serious disadvantages, in the authors' experience:

- Because norms are often built up over time or are based on people who are in a wide range of situations, it can be difficult to justify a norm as representing a meaningful baseline for a particular set of individuals at a given time and in a given situation.

- At the higher and lower levels, normative percentile data are notoriously unreliable; it often takes only a minuscule difference in absolute ratings to make a very large difference in one's percentile ranking.

- Normative/percentile feedback often has an emotional impact that detracts from the effectiveness of the feedback. People with very low scores are sometimes devastated by the data; those with very high scores sometimes decide that they have nothing left to accomplish.

- Particularly with normative feedback (although this phenomenon seems to hold true for all forms of feedback), the greater the gap between the performer's expectations and the reported data, the more likely the performer is to reject or deny the feedback, and the less likely to make changes in behavior.

Feedback using a standard as a baseline provides a very clear picture of the need for improvement, but it can be very hard to set standards legitimately for many behaviors. Standards work best for providing feedback about outputs or results. It is usually easier, for example, to justify the use of standards for measuring sales, revenue, or units than for evaluating such behaviors as establishing clear and realistic goals or encouraging people to take initiative.

Feedback using a personal average as a baseline cannot be used for evaluative purposes, but is very effective for developmental purposes. Because people are given information only about relative strengths and weaknesses, no person looks better or worse than others; people simply have different patterns of strengths and weaknesses. This kind of baseline reduces the emotional impact of feedback and improves people's ability to concentrate on the information. People are also quite willing to share such feedback with others and to learn from them.

SUMMARY

Feedback is a critical tool for maintaining or changing performance. However, it can serve two different and not always compatible functions. Summative (or evaluative, or motivational) feedback is typically most effective when it is given after a performance, to increase or decrease the likelihood that someone will continue an existing performance. Formative feedback is typically most effective when it is given before a performance, in the form of advice about how to change or improve the quality of the performance.

Fit, focus, and timing are important to the overall effectiveness of both forms of feedback.

Fit

Where fit is concerned, summative feedback should match the receiver's idea of appropriate recognition, and it should be appropriate to the perceived effort or importance of the performance. Formative feedback should match the receiver's ability to grasp and respond to it.

Focus

Where focus is concerned, both summative and formative feedback should be targeted to a specific performance and should not be mixed with other messages (in the case of summative feedback, with criticism or extraneous information; in the case of formative feedback, with praise for other work or with extraneous information).

Timing

Where timing is concerned, in summative feedback encouragement should come as soon as possible after the desired performance. In formative feedback, advice about improvement should precede the next opportunity to perform.

References

Jones, J. E., and Bearly, W. L. (1996). *360° feedback: Strategies, tactics, and techniques for developing leaders.* Amherst, MA: Human Resources Development Press.

Tosti, D. T. (1978, Oct.). Formative feedback. *NSPI Journal* 17:8, 19–21.

CHAPTER TWENTY-ONE

Designing Compensation Systems to Motivate Performance Improvement

Sivasailam Thiagarajan
Fred Estes
Frances N. Kemmerer

Human performance (HP) technologists have come a long way in designing interventions that help realize individual and organizational potential. The evolution of the field, from instructional design to total-systems design, represents a profound increase in both the scope and responsibility of practitioners. Although the bread-and-butter activity of most HP technologists will long remain the training of particular employees to function in specific ways, HP technologists are also being asked to devise recruitment and downsizing strategies, reorganize a variety of departments, redefine job roles, and refocus or help create compensation systems.

There are three very important overarching considerations that should be mentioned before we outline the structure of this chapter. First, an HP technologist operating alone will not, in practice, develop a comprehensive compensation system. Therefore, this chapter gives a high-level overview of compensation systems and the role in their development that an HP technologist can play in collaboration with compensation specialists, lawyers, economists, and other human resource professionals.

Second, early HP technologists, drawing on the work of behavioral psychologists, sometimes used the term *incentives* in the broad sense of all the rewards and remuneration given to an employee for the purpose of eliciting, improving, and maintaining work performance. Today, however, the term *incentives* refers, in standard business use, to such variable rewards as commissions, stock options, and bonuses, whereas the broader term for the total package received by an employee (including wages, salary, benefits, and variable rewards) is *compensation* (Wilson and Kanter, 1994). HP technologists will want to use the terminology of their business partners, of course, and in this chapter we use the term *compensation systems* in referring to the total package, but HP technologists should be aware of both senses of the term *incentives* because it is still sometimes used in the broad sense.

Third, the principles of psychology and economics are applicable to settings around the world. Nevertheless, in every situation faced by HP technologists working in global settings, the specific characteristics of the setting will dictate the principles to be applied, given the inevitable differences in laws, customs, cultures, and local economies. As a result, unless due consideration is given to the dimensions of two different settings, an intervention that worked brilliantly in the setting for which it was specifically designed may fail miserably in the second setting, not because a particular principle of psychology or economics is invalid but because the principle has not been applied appropriately to the second setting, or because the "packaging" of the intervention has fallen afoul of local customs and culture (Clark and Estes, 1998). Therefore, this chapter seeks to provide information that will be useful to an international audience and to global organizations.

Apart from these three overarching considerations, this chapter deals with compensation systems in general: with their role as formal organizational incentives, with what they can and cannot do, and with how they can be developed. The chapter begins with a concept analysis, the purpose of which is to identify the critical and variable attributes of compensation systems. The analysis is followed by discussions of the economic dimensions, benefits, limitations of compensation systems. Finally, the chapter presents an adaptation of the Human Performance Technology (HPT) process model for the development of compensation systems.

COMMON CHARACTERISTICS OF COMPENSATION SYSTEMS

An *incentive* is something that influences a person to act in certain ways. A *compensation system* is a collection of incentives and a set of procedures for using them. Organizations use compensation systems to support the motivation of their employees. All compensation systems, by definition, must be intentional, external, and standardized.

Earlier views of human resource management held that compensation motivated people. More contemporary thinking (see Pfeffer, 1998; Hertzberg, 1968; Lawler, 1990; Locke and Latham, 1990) holds that motivation is an internal attribute that is influenced by the design of an organization's performance system. This is not a technical quibble; the difference is fundamental to an HPT systems approach because, once a base level of adequacy has been reached, the intrinsic challenges and rewards of a job are much more powerful motivators than extrinsic reward systems are (Hertzberg, 1968).

Intentionality

Compensation systems are deliberately developed with the intention of influencing employees' performance. A compensation system must be aligned with business strategy, corporate culture, and the other elements of the performance system, such as performance management, assessment, communication, feedback, employee involvement, and education (McAdams, 1996). Powers (1992) discusses the value and necessity of this alignment. This is a top-down, systemic view of performance.

Externality

Consequences of work activities can be classified into four categories:

1. Those that are internal to the employee (a sense of accomplishment, a feeling of pride, increased self-confidence)
2. Those that are internal to the work group (approval of colleagues, enhancement of team spirit)
3. Those that are external and proceed from clients and customers (for example, letters from satisfied customers)
4. Those that are external and proceed from the organization (praise from supervisors, increases in salary)

Whether a compensation system involves the first three categories or not, it must always involve the fourth.

Standardization

Compensation systems should specify a standard procedure that identifies categories of employees, activities, incentives, and relationships among them. In a comprehensive compensation system, all employees are identified and classified into appropriate groups. This kind of classification permits appropriate matching among employee characteristics, incentives or rewards, and procedures for rewarding individuals or teams.

The compensation system also identifies target activities and accomplishments for each group of employees. This kind of targeting requires the organization to define its objectives clearly and to link them activities that contribute to their efficient achievement. Thus the compensation system must relate a set of incentives to diverse accomplishments and activities.

VARIABLE CHARACTERISTICS OF COMPENSATION SYSTEMS

Although all compensation systems must be intentional, external, and standardized, they may vary widely in their purposes, as well as in who is rewarded and why. The variable characteristics of compensation systems are presented in Table 21.1 (for a slightly different analysis of compensation dimensions and components, see Henderson and Risher, 1987).

Variations in Purpose

All compensation systems attempt to improve individual work activities and accomplishments, but different compensation systems may emphasize different specific purposes (Lawler, 1981). The three R's of compensation systems' purposes are *recruitment, retention,* and *results.*

Recruitment. This means encouraging competent people to work for the organization (for example, by wining and dining potential employees during recruitment interviews, and by outbidding the competition).

Retention. This means discouraging competent people from leaving the organization (for example, by giving employees annual pay raises and providing a comfortable working climate).

Results. This means encouraging competent people to accomplish more for the organization by linking their pay to productivity and by supplying the training and tools required for peak performance.

Variations in Performers

Compensation systems deal with a variety of job responsibilities and titles, ranging from custodian to CEO. Variations in how these employees are handled are described here.

Grouping of Performers. Some compensation systems divide the employees in each job category into various subgroups. For example, word-processor operators in an organization may fall into different subgroups according to their years of experience or their geographical locations. Other compensation systems, especially those in newly established organizations, may treat all employees basically the same.

Providing Individual Versus Group Incentives. Some incentives focus on rewarding individual productivity (for example, by recognizing the most valuable player). Others encourage group effort (for example, by giving a bonus to a team).

Variations in Performance

Compensation systems reward a variety of physical, verbal, intellectual, and interpersonal activities and accomplishments, which are essential components of the job function. Here are some alternative emphases in how they reward critical aspects of performance.

Maintenance Versus Improvement. Some compensation systems reward the employee for maintaining a certain level of performance (for example, by paying a regular monthly salary). Others focus on improvements in performance (for example, by paying special merit raises).

Potential Versus Actual Performance. Some compensation systems reward the potential for better performance (for example, by paying higher salaries to people with higher educational qualifications). Others pay for actual performance, irrespective of the labels attached to the performers.

Activity Versus Accomplishment. Some compensation systems reward people for their efforts (for example, by paying them by the hour). Others reward them for their accomplishments (for example, by paying them for the number of items produced).

Short-Term Versus Long-Term Accomplishment. Some compensation systems reward performers for short-term accomplishment. Others reinforce long-term impact. For example, a CEO may be rewarded for profits earned during the last quarter, the last year, or the last ten years.

Variations in Incentives

A variety of incentives are available for rewarding employees' performance. In general, these incentives may be classified into monetary and nonmonetary categories. Monetary incentives (see Table 21.1) include salaries, allowances, in-kind salary supplements, bonuses, and benefits. Nonmonetary incentives (see Table 21.2) include improved working conditions, tools and equipment, supervision, training, professional support, and career opportunities.

Most compensation systems use rewards to encourage desirable behaviors. Some also use negative incentives (punishments) to discourage undesirable behaviors. Examples of negative incentives include docking of pay for absence or lateness, fines for safety violations, suspension for policy violations, withholding of pay for resignation without adequate notice, written reprimands, censure, negative evaluations, and dismissal for continued inappropriate behavior.

Table 21.1. Types of Monetary Compensation.

Salary	*Deferred Income*
Base salary	Investment trust
Beginning salary	Pension plan
Holiday pay	Profit sharing
Market adjustment	Social security
Overtime pay	Stock option
Weekend pay	
	Loss-of-Job Coverage
Differential Pay	Guaranteed annual income
Merit pay	Outplacement assistance
Pay for knowledge	Severance pay
Pay for length of service	Unemployment insurance
Pay for performance	
	Other Perquisites
Allowances	Children's education
Clothing	Athletic leagues
Cost of living	Automobile
Entertainment	Cash and stock bonuses
Family	Club membership
Hardship	Commission
Housing	Company apartment
Relocation	Expense account
Training	Financial and postretirement counseling
Travel	Free or subsidized housing
	Free meals
Time Off with Pay	Gift
Disability payments	Legal service
Family-illness leave	Liability insurance
Jury duty	Loan
Maternity or paternity leave	Medical examinations
Military duty	Medical insurance
Personal leave	Parking
Sabbatical	Physical fitness program
Sick leave	Product samples
Vacation	Spousal travel benefits
	Survivor protection
	Tax services

Table 21.2. Types of Nonmonetary Compensation.

Working Conditions

Celebrations and rituals

Choice of project

Collegiality

Flexible calendar

Flexible schedule

Geographic location

Informality

Job enrichment

Nature of work

Organizational culture

Size of organization

Staff support

Type of community

Type of customer

Type of industry

Type of organization

Workload

Training

Mentoring

Off site training

On-the-job training

Professional conferences

Professional development

Training equipment

Training facilities

Training materials

Facilities, Equipment, and Materials

Access to supplies

Appropriate facilities

Cafeteria

Equipment-use training

Ergonomically designed furniture

Executive washroom

Job aids and documentation

Office size

Management

Access to information

Compatible values

Dynamic leadership

Freedom to innovate

Frequent feedback

Lunch with a manager

Participatory decision making

Participatory goal setting

Performance appraisal

Recognition by manager

Career Opportunities

Career counseling

Career ladder

Committee assignments

Entrepreneurial support

Job security

Job title

Membership in elite team

Opportunities for promotion

Patents

Professional growth opportunities

Royalties

Tenure

Variations in Timing

Some compensation systems immediately link the target activity or accomplishment with the reward. Others delay rewards. For example, a salesperson may be given a hefty commission immediately (as soon as the purchase order is signed), after a slight delay (when payment is received), or after a long delay (after the following Christmas). The frequency of rewards is closely related to the concept of immediacy. For example, bonus payments or outstanding-employee awards may be made weekly, monthly, quarterly, or yearly.

COMPREHENSIVENESS OF COMPENSATION SYSTEMS

The variable characteristics of compensation systems, taken together, contribute to their comprehensiveness. An extremely comprehensive system does the following things:

- Identifies several levels and categories of performers
- Specifies desired behaviors in detail, expected outcomes, and measurement strategies
- Provides a variety of incentives in different categories
- Prescribes detailed procedures for the distribution of incentives

A less comprehensive system merely identifies a few critical performers, performances, incentives, and procedures. The more comprehensive compensation system takes considerably more time, effort, and money to develop and implement but may not be as effective as a less comprehensive one. The cost-effectiveness of the system depends on its selection of the most appropriate variation on each theme to suit the situation.

Economists use the term *cost-effectiveness* to refer to the most productive use of the available resources for achieving a goal. The ABC's of cost-effectiveness are *adequacy, balance,* and *consistency;* that is, in order to be cost-effective, a compensation system must be adequate, balanced, and consistent (see Table 21.3).

A system that is adequate is one that can attract the candidates best matched to the requirements of positions. It also provides compensation sufficient to maintain the lifestyles associated with the occupations in question.

A system that is balanced is one that fairly matches compensation to level of contribution (Fay and Beatty, 1988). In a system that is horizontally balanced, people making equal contributions to the organization's overall goals receive equal compensation. In a situation that is vertically balanced, judgments about different individuals' and groups' different levels of contribution are made ac-

Table 21.3. ABC's of Cost-Effectiveness.

Adequacy
    Standard of living associated with the job
    Compensation associated with alternative jobs

Balance
    Horizontal (equal compensation for equals)
    Vertical (unequal compensation for unequals)

Consistency
    Between goal and means
    Between employees and compensation

cording to fair and objective criteria, with levels of education, experience, and scope of work perceived as fair bases of differential levels of compensation in different occupations. For example, technical training is considered more challenging than new-employee orientation and receives commensurately greater compensation.

A compensation system that is consistent is one whose parts are in uniform relationship. There are two relevant dimensions to consider. First, there must be consistency among the elements of the system; otherwise, the inconsistencies will yield counterproductive results, as when the commission structure leads the sales force to sell far more of certain products than the factory can possibly produce. Second, there must be consistency between types of compensation and types of employees, so that different individuals and groups receive the compensation they value and can use.

BENEFITS OF COMPENSATION SYSTEMS

Compensation systems are among the most potentially powerful HPT interventions. As already mentioned, their three major benefits are recruitment, retention, and increased productivity of competent individuals. Because salaries and benefits are the largest components of most organizations' budgets, it is both appropriate and necessary that HP technologists pay close attention to the effects of compensation packages on individual and group performance.

Humanists and behaviorists agree that one of the most fundamental laws of human performance is that individuals tend to repeat activities that are rewarding. Compensation systems attempt to apply this powerful principle to the workplace. When pay, benefits, and other rewards are associated with job-related accomplishments, the probability of appropriate behavior is increased.

Basic salary and benefits may be used to provide organizations with competitive advantage in attracting talented people and in preventing other organizations from luring away their best talent. Merit pay (Weinberg, 1987) and pay-for-performance schemes (McMorrow, 1987) encourage individuals and groups to demonstrate high levels of performance. Commissions and bonuses, which are directly associated with sales and other income-generating activities (Moynahan, 1991), relate corporate productivity and profits to the performance of individuals. Profit sharing and gainsharing (Schuster, 1986) link individual and group performance to the business goals of the organization. The addition of nonmonetary rewards and recognition enables organizations to leverage the impact of incentive budgets.

CAVEAT EMPTOR

Compensation systems are powerful tools, but they are not a panacea for organizational problems; they do not replace the intrinsic rewards of a job, nor do they replace other types of organizational reform or HPT. For instance, cases of the following types require other remedies.

1. *Managers want quick results.* In this case, managers are likely to be disappointed with the design of a new compensation system. More than most other HPT interventions, compensation systems are strategic long-term approaches. One-time bonuses and awards may reinforce some employees for some time, but the full impact of a comprehensive compensation system will not be realized in the short run.

2. *Managers are unwilling to upgrade equipment, tools, and work conditions.* In this case, a compensation system cannot compensate for lack of tools or equipment or for an inadequate environment. If job conditions are not conducive to productivity, then increases in salaries and bonuses will not yield greater productivity. In fact, environmental deficits may counteract the effects of increased salaries and may promote greater inefficiency.

3. *Managers are unwilling to disclose information to employees about salary scales and incentives.* A compensation system should be not only fair and balanced but also *visibly* fair and balanced. Unless information about compensation and incentives is shared, employees will have no clear indication of how fair the system is or of how their productivity is linked to specific rewards.

4. *Managers are unwilling or unable to specify the results and accomplishments they want.* In this case, improved compensation structures are meaningless and, by definition, arbitrary. As is true in any other type of HPT intervention, a job analysis should be carried out, and this analysis should clearly relate job responsibilities to desired organizational outcomes. Further, unless managers are

able to specify and set priorities for the responsibilities and accomplishments related to various tasks, it will be difficult to devise a rational system that matches rewards to the value of individual performance.

5. *HP technologists lack expertise or are unable to consult with competent professionals.* The design of a comprehensive compensation package requires expertise in the economic, labor, and legal domains (Balkin and Gomez-Mejia, 1987). For example, a pay-for-performance system may increase competition among individuals and teams. A certain level of healthy competition is appropriate in attempts to improve productivity, but too much competition may be counterproductive. When an HP technologist lacks expertise in certain fields or cannot access professional advice, it will be difficult for the HP technologist to design an efficient compensation system. It will be equally difficult for the HP technologist to sell the system to employees and managers once it is designed.

DEVELOPMENT OF A COMPENSATION SYSTEM

Entire books on compensation systems (for example, Wilson and Kanter, 1994), as well as portions of books on organizational improvement (for example, Boyett and Conn, 1988; Kilmann, 1984, 1989; Belcher, 1987), provide excellent guidelines for developing a compensation system. This section shows how the typical HPT process model—analysis, design, implementation, and evaluation—can be applied to the design and development of a compensation systems. (See Table 21.4, and note that evaluation activities, rather than being listed separately, are incorporated into all three phases of the model.)

The complexity of compensation systems, along with the need for them to be legally defensible, means that most compensation programs will be devised by compensation professionals, with input from employees, managers, and such other professionals as HP technologists, lawyers, and economists. The following description is intended to provide a high-level view in order to facilitate such participation.

Analysis

Begin with a Front-End Analysis. Analyze the budget for past years, and compute the historical base ratio of labor costs to profits. Identify external factors (such as competition) that will influence the compensation system. Collect data about employees' perceptions of an ideal compensation system and features of the actual system. In interviewing people, probe for the ideal state, in terms of recruitment, retention, and results. Collect data on the actual levels of competitive demand for the top candidates entering the workforce. Also collect data on retention and turnover rates in the industry, as well as data on the range of productivity among the best and worst performers in various job categories.

Table 21.4. Development Model for a Compensation System.

Analysis
    Front-end analysis
    Target-population analysis
    Systems analysis
    Job/task analysis
    Compensation analysis
    Specification of goals
    Review and revision of goals

Design
    Strategy-mix selection
    Specification of design elements
    Review and revision of the system
    Development of system specifications
    Documentation of the compensation system

Implementation
    Keeping employees informed
    Orienting employees to the compensation system
    Installing the system
    Making initial modifications to the system
    Continuously upgrading and updating the system

Establish a Compensation Task Force to Provide Inputs and Help Interpret Data.
Be sure to include decision makers, union members, and representative employees in this group. Ensure that members of the task force are familiar with the latest trends in the industry and with the mission and policies of the organization. To explain legal and tax implications, include outside consultants.

Analyze the Characteristics of the Target Population. Identify important characteristics of employees at all levels. Begin with general characteristics at each level, in terms of educational qualifications, technical qualifications, and experience. Interview representative employees in each job category for the type of compensation, benefits, and incentives they would like to receive and the disincentives they would like to avoid. Check for employees' perceptions of the total compensation available to them in other jobs or from other employers (economists call this *opportunity cost*). Through surveys and interviews, find out the differences in preferences among subgroups, such as between technical professionals and support staff. Collect information on job satisfaction and perceptions of job conditions. Identify conditions perceived as disincentives. Summarize the results of analysis of the target population by preparing a matrix of job categories and preferred types of compensation.

Conduct a Systems Analysis. Conduct a mega-analysis to identify the larger economic sector of which the particular organization is a part. Identify constraints and resources affecting the sector as a whole. Identify inputs, processes, outputs, and outcomes of subsystems. Summarize the results of the systems analysis by highlighting data critical to the design of the compensation system.

Conduct a Job/Task Analysis. Identify the various functions, tasks, and accomplishments related to different job categories. Observe employees, and interview them about their usual and unusual activities. Analyze this information to identify roles, responsibilities, functions, and accomplishments. Identify functional areas in the corporation. Subdivide each function into specific tasks and subtasks. Collect data on the inputs, processes, and outputs of each task. Identify links among employees at different organizational levels.

Conduct a Compensation Analysis. Identify and analyze the various incentives and disincentives that currently influence the performance of employees at different job levels. Review documents specifying the policies, regulations, and standard procedures that are related to different types of incentives. Prepare a balance sheet of monetary incentives (salaries, allowances, bonuses, and other benefits that can be converted directly into money) and nonmonetary incentives (recognition, rewards) for each job classification. Probe for disincentives associated with working conditions, physical facilities, workload, peer relationships, and other such factors. Survey employees for their perceptions of the adequacy, balance, and consistency of the current compensation system. Summarize the results of the compensation analysis by preparing a balance sheet of incentives and disincentives.

Conclude the Analysis Stage by Specifying Goals for the Compensation System. What is needed is not a single goal for the entire compensation system but rather a series of goals that take account of different needs among employees at different levels. Begin with a statement of the long-term goals. Then break this down into a series of short-term goals, to meet the needs in the organization. Specify goals for recruitment, retention, and results. Include all the different components of the total compensation system (monetary incentives, benefits, nonmonetary rewards and recognition, job conditions, opportunities for professional growth, and other such factors). Specify different goals for different types of employees.

Review and Revise Goals for the Compensation System. Obtain inputs and feedback from different experts and stakeholders. Begin by circulating the goals to the members of the task force. Have labor, tax, and legal experts review the goals. Check the goals against criteria for economic efficiency. Ask the reviewers to compare the different goals for internal consistency and to identify conflicting goals. Summarize the feedback, and use it to revise the goals.

Design

Select an Appropriate Mix of Compensation Strategies to Enable the Organization to Meet Its Goals. Redefine base salary levels for different jobs at each salary level. For each job, determine the appropriate split between fixed salary and variable incentives. Prescribe the types of compensation decisions to be made, as well as the basis for decisions at each level of the organization. Construct valid, reliable, objective, efficient instruments for measuring accomplishment in each job. Work out formulas for gainsharing or profit sharing. Identify nonmonetary incentives of different kinds, and specify how they are to be distributed. Also identify opportunities for professional development (such as training and promotion) and procedures for distributing them.

Specify Design Elements. During the initial design of the compensation system, provide the minimum amount of each type of compensation (salaries, for example, or rewards related to working conditions, status, feedback, opportunities for professional growth, and training support). What is missing in a compensation system becomes so salient to the employees that they will disregard the abundance of certain types of incentives if some other types are not available in minimally adequate quantities. The status of a job is related both to the level of responsibility and to the size of the paycheck. An impressive job title without increased responsibilities and salary will not be perceived as an incentive.

Compensation design is an exercise in efficient allocation of limited resources. An organization can afford to pay higher salaries if fewer people are hired. Therefore, consideration should be given to hiring people with lower qualifications at lower salaries and increasing their productivity with job aids, tools, and other HPT interventions.

Do not allow for automatic distribution of any benefit, bonus, or pay increase. Tie rewards to increases in performance or productivity.

Be sure that the compensation package does not interfere with employees' productivity. For example, bonus systems that pit employees against each other undermine the same cooperative team behavior that most astute managers say is essential to modern firms. Be careful in attempting to transfer compensation strategies from one organization to another: an incentive may produce dramatic results in one situation, but that does not mean it will produce similar results in a different situation.

What employers consider strong incentives, employees may perceive as weak. Conduct a reality check with representative employees on proposed incentives.

Be careful about any pay-for-performance system that requires competition among individuals or teams. Maintain an appropriate level of healthy competition, but avoid counterproductive, destructive competition.

Review and Revise the System Design. As before, solicit input from consultants, experts, and stakeholders. Collect data from representative employees at different levels, seeking information about their perceptions of the adequacy, balance, and consistency of the compensation system. Use the data to make suitable changes to the system.

Create System Specifications. Reexamine the compensation system to make sure it answers the following questions:

1. Whose performance is to be rewarded?
2. How does one job group differ from others?
3. What are the different conditions under which the same job is performed?
4. How is employee performance evaluated?
5. How frequently is employee performance evaluated?
6. What types of accomplishments are rewarded by the compensation system?
7. What is the relationship of different types of performance to organizational goals?
8. If there is no direct link between individual performance and organizational productivity, how can the two be related?
9. Who will evaluate performance?
10. Who is responsible for suggesting appropriate incentives?
11. What recourse does the employee have if he or she disagrees with a performance evaluation?

Document the Compensation System. Prepare procedural manuals that include job aids and decision tables. Create a computerized system for tracking compensation and incentives. Prepare training materials and administrative manuals for the implementation of the new system.

Implementation

Everyone, not just the members of the compensation task force, should be kept informed during the analysis and design phases of the new compensation system, and all the employees in the organization should be aware of the new system's features. Interim reports of progress and problems should also be made available to everybody in the organization. Before the implementation of the new system, all employees should attend brief orientation workshops.

The HP technologist should play a major role in installing the new system. Despite any number of systematic design efforts or any amount of evaluation, review, and revision, there are always new problems that turn up during the early stages of implementation.

The HP technologist should also assist the administrators in making appropriate modifications. After successful implementation, the HP technologist should continue to provide technical assistance and should encourage the local administrators to continuously upgrade and update the system.

CURRENT TRENDS AFFECTING COMPENSATION SYSTEMS

Given the rapid evolution of the compensation field, HP technologists have only recently incorporated compensation systems into their repertoire of interventions. This new interest is a welcome one because most other HPT interventions lose their impact unless appropriate adjustments to compensation systems are also undertaken. Indeed, manipulation of rewards has been a major component of HPT from its early days, and compensation packages represent the major type of formal reinforcement in the workplace. Again, however, the development of a compensation system is a complex activity that requires technical support from experts in economics, labor relations, and law.

The field of compensation design is undergoing interesting changes and influence from different trends. First, the workforce is changing significantly. More minorities, women, older people, and foreign-born employees are coming in, and the opportunity costs associated with different subgroups of employees are changing. For example, women do not play a secondary role and are not willing to work for lower incentives than men do. These factors are rapidly influencing the nature of compensation packages.

Second, affirmative action has become an accepted fact in the workplace, and most organizations have moved into valuing diversity. The new concept of comparable worth requires that people belonging to different subgroups receive equal pay, not only for the same work but also for comparable work. (The concept of comparable worth emerged, of course, because certain professions, such as nursing and teaching, were historically associated with women, and so pay scales in those professions were kept artificially low by comparison with pay scales in comparable professions traditionally dominated by men.)

Third, the nature of work is changing. With the move from a manufacturing-based industrial economy to a service- and information-based economy come new types of performance and accomplishment, which require new compensation systems. Highly skilled and highly mobile knowledge workers must be compensated in a way that is different from how lower-skilled, stable workers are compensated. Knowledge workers want a different mix of salary, benefits, and incentive packages. Their lives are complex, varied, and dynamic. They want flexible, cafeteria-style options that allow them to choose the total compensation package that best meets the needs of the moment, and they want to be able to change that package, as necessary. For higher-salaried knowledge workers and professionals, the tax implications of compensation have also become more important. Deferred compensation for executives and highly paid professionals has become a major area of innovation.

Fourth, few employees in the past, even among the executive ranks, owned more than a few token shares of the companies for which they worked; now the largest pool of capital in the world is represented by retirement funds, and employees already own a major stake in corporations. Employee stock-ownership plans (ESOPs) sometimes result in employees' owning 40 percent or more of the companies in which they work (Haasen and Shea, 1997), and the largest investors in many companies are the institutional investors (such as Merrill Lynch) of private retirement savings. Profit sharing has existed at progressive companies for years, but it is now coming to be widely recognized that distributing gains from growth is a good incentive for the people who produce those gains.

Fifth, global competition and freer international markets have meant increases in mergers, reengineering, downsizing, and bankruptcies around the world. Global companies move operations wherever conditions are most favorable for business. These trends are leading workers and governments to insist on greater portability of retirement and other benefits.

Sixth, an individual may join a global corporation right out of college, jump to a competitor after a few years, be merged into a third company, get fired in a downsizing, work in a temporary placement until starting a company that may in turn be bought by the individual's original employer, for which the individual may go back to work for a few years until "retiring" and becoming a consultant. These trends require new approaches to measuring accomplishments and designing compensation systems.

CONCLUSION

This chapter has applied the HPT perspective to compensation systems. It has identified the critical, variable, and economic characteristics of such systems, as well as their benefits and limitations. It has also described steps in the systematic development of a compensation package. Above all, it has stressed the importance of aligning the compensation system with business strategy and with other elements of the performance system.

If the chapter sometimes also appears to stress the complexity of the design process, that emphasis is intentional. Lawsuits, union protests, and other such consequences are liable to follow an amateurish attempt at creating a new compensation package. The task of designing a comprehensive system is far too complex to be attempted by an HP technologist alone. Therefore, at several points, this chapter reminds HP technologists of the contributions they can make in collaboration with compensation specialists, economists, lawyers, union leaders, labor specialists, and experts on affirmative action.

References

Balkin, D. B., and Gomez-Mejia, L. R. (eds.). (1987). *New perspectives on compensation.* Englewood Cliffs, NJ: Prentice Hall.

Belcher, J. G. Jr. (1987). *Productivity plus: How today's best-run companies are gaining the competitive edge.* Houston: Gulf.

Boyett, J. H., and Conn, H. P. (1988). *Maximum performance management.* Macomb, IL: Glenbridge.

Clark, R. E., and Estes, F. (1998). Technology or craft: What are we doing? *Educational Technology* 38:5, 5–11.

Fay, C. H., and Beatty, R. W. (eds.). (1998). *The compensation sourcebook.* Amherst, MA: Human Resources Development Press.

Haasen, A., and Shea, G. F. (1997). *A better place to work: A new sense of motivation leading to higher productivity.* New York: American Management Association.

Henderson, R. I., and Risher, H. W. (1987). Influencing organizational strategy through compensation leadership. In D. B. Balkin and L. R. Gomez-Mejia (eds.), *New perspectives on compensation.* Englewood Cliffs, NJ: Prentice Hall.

Hertzberg, F. (1968, Jan.–Feb.). One more time: How do you motivate employees? *Harvard Business Review,* pp. 53–62.

Kilmann, R. H. (1984). *Beyond the quick fix: Managing five tracks to organizational success.* San Francisco: Jossey-Bass.

Lawler, E. E. (1981). *Pay and organization development.* Reading, MA: Addison-Wesley.

Lawler, E. E. (1990). *Strategic pay: Aligning organizational strategies and pay systems.* San Francisco: Jossey-Bass.

Locke, E. A., and Latham, G. P. (1990). *A theory of goal setting and task performance.* Englewood Cliffs, NJ: Prentice Hall.

McAdams, J. L. (1996). *The reward plan advantage: A manager's guide to improving business performance through people.* San Francisco: Jossey-Bass.

McMorrow, J. (1987). Pay for performance—AT&T's plans. *Compensation and Benefits Management* 3:2, 52–55.

Moynahan, J. K. (1991). *The sales compensation handbook.* New York: AMACOM.

Pfeffer, J. (1998, May–June). Six dangerous myths about pay. *Harvard Business Review*, pp. 108–119.

Powers, B. (1992). Strategic alignment. In H. D. Stolovitch and E. J. Keeps (eds.), *Handbook of Human Performance Technology: A comprehensive guide for analyzing and solving performance problems in organizations*. San Francisco: Jossey-Bass.

Schuster, M. (1986). Gainsharing: The state of the art. *Compensation and Benefits Management* 2:4, 27–32.

Weinberg, I. (1987). Zero-based merit increases are a cost-effective way to reward achievers. *Journal of Compensation Benefits* 37:3, 346–347.

Wilson, T. B., and Kanter, R. M. (1994). *Innovative reward systems for the changing workplace*. New York: McGraw-Hill.

CHAPTER TWENTY-TWO

Job Aids

Paul H. Elliott

I magine yourself standing at your local ATM, ready to withdraw cash, but instead of being given the usual cues on the screen, you find that you are now required to attend a bank-sponsored training program so that you can learn how to select transactions by punching in the appropriate series of numerical commands from memory. Or imagine trying to leave an urgent message on a voice mail system that gives you no audio prompts; instead, you have to know all the appropriate numerical commands by heart. These two examples, extrapolated from everyday life, illustrate the need for job aids.

A job aid is a storage place, other than memory, for information that is used in performing a task. A job aid provides the performer with auditory or visual signals that offer directions for carrying out increments of a task. At work, a job aid may be a set of simple instructions for assembling a piece of equipment, or it may be a set of complex algorithms for analyzing a system.

BENEFITS OF JOB AIDS

Would you feel safe getting on an airplane if you knew that the crew had conducted the preflight routine entirely from memory? Would you be satisfied if the people installing a sprinkler system in your new office told you that they did not have to consult the postinstallation checklist because they had done identical installations hundreds of times before? In the workplace, there are many situations like these in which it would be unthinkable for employees to "wing it," no matter how experienced they might be.

Job aids reduce the need to recall information, and they minimize error. Thus they enable employees to perform tasks more accurately and to acquire new skills more quickly. Moreover, job aids are up to three times less time- and cost-intensive than formal training that has memory storage as its objective. If the task in question is highly likely to undergo a change, it is easier to revise a job aid than to develop a new training course.

Case Study 1

The electricity unit of a major midwestern utility company faced the challenge of preparing employees for a more competitive, deregulated market. The utility initiated several projects for improving internal processes, including those processes involved in customer service. One such initiative combined job roles: customer service workers would now have broader responsibilities instead of being specialists in one area. The aim was to provide a single point of contact for residential, commercial, and industrial customers.

The training department had to quickly design and develop cost-effective training in the marketing and technical areas for more than two hundred employees in the customer service department so that they could become competent in their new roles in a short time. Analysis clearly defined the necessary new work systems and new job roles, enabling the utility to ensure that employees received appropriate training. The training itself relied heavily on job aids. The steepness of the learning curve was reduced, training costs were cut, and the employees were able, in a brief span of time, to be productive and work safely.

Case Study 2

The Portland-based distribution center of a national retailer introduced a worksheet that allowed line employees to do in thirty seconds what their managers had taken an average of fifteen minutes every day to do. This change allowed a total annual savings of about $17,000. After this successful initiative, the retailer's Midwest and Utah distribution centers introduced similar job aids for specific tasks. These job aids reduced to ten minutes what had been an hour of intensive one-to-one training. The retailer's distribution center in northern California then introduced a job aid for the floor-ready auditing process, and that job aid has now been embraced as the standard for all the retailer's distribution facilities.

JOB AIDS AND HUMAN PERFORMANCE TECHNOLOGY

A human performance (HP) technologist does not start with the assumption that a job aid is inherently more valuable than any other kind of intervention. Job aids represent just one of the interventions at the HP technologist's disposal, and the need for a job aid must be established by analysis. Only after an HP technologist has discovered a performance problem, determined its cause, and estimated the potential value and cost of an intervention can he or she ascertain whether a job aid is needed.

ALTERNATIVES FOR STORING INFORMATION

When analysis reveals that deficient performance is due to lack of skills or knowledge, the HP technologist must decide which of several information-storage alternatives will be most effective in satisfying the need for information and correcting the problem:

- Developing a job aid only, and storing all information in some medium external to the performer

- Developing instruction only, and storing all information in the performer's long-term memory

- Developing a job aid in addition to supportive instruction, storing most information in a job aid, providing practice with using the job aid, and/or storing some information in the performer's long-term memory

- Developing instruction in addition to a prompting job aid, storing most information in the performer's long-term memory, and providing a summary job aid that cues recall of the information

These alternatives offer a range of choices for storing information, as seen in Figure 22.1.

Figure 22.1. Information-Storage Alternatives or Options.

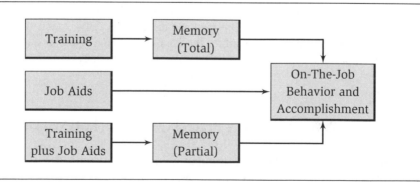

Each of these approaches offers advantages and disadvantages. For example, say that an HP technologist discovers during analysis that performance in the area of determining service installation dates with customers is deficient because the performers lack knowledge. After observing an employee who is accomplished in performing this task, the HP technologist produces a detailed description of what that employee has done. This description can be said to constitute the rules of performance for the task of determining an installation date.

If the HP technologist now elects to store these rules in performers' long-term memory, without use of a job aid, an instructional design and development process will be necessary. This process will lead to the following instructional module, with memory-storage events:

- Preview the task to be learned. Include the task's objectives and consequences.

- Prepare the learners. Define terms, and teach facilitating skills.

- Present the rules in small increments, using simple examples.

- Prompt the learners to state the rules, using more complex examples.

- Have learners perform the task without cues, and using still more complex examples.

- Have the learners practice applying the rules, in isolation, with close-approximation examples.

- Have the learners practice applying the rules as integrated with the task.

As an alternative, the HP technologist could elect to store the rules in a job aid, as depicted in the decision tree shown in Figure 22.2. Both alternatives are possible, as is a combination of the two.

In rare cases, regulations require that information be stored in long-term memory. Apart from such cases, however, this kind of storage offers the following advantages:

- Performers can access long-term memory and act more quickly than when they must access a job aid and respond to the information it contains. Speed usually means higher productivity.

- The performers' hands and eyes are unencumbered.

- If performers can respond quickly, without external aid, they are likely to be given more credit by other people (bosses, peers, customers), who often equate competence with speed and memory rather than with the quality of the performance alone.

Storing information in long-term memory involves the following disadvantages:

Figure 22.2. Decision Tree for Determining Installation Date.

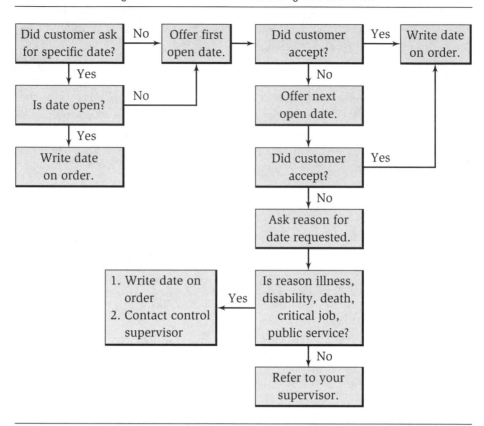

- Even with good teaching, loss of retention begins within seconds and can become serious within hours. When the interval between learning and on-the-job practice will be long, loss of retention often rules out any possibility of performance improvement.

- When activities are based on what is retained in memory, there is greater variability in performance.

- Such variables as noise, personal problems, and prior learning can hinder performers from accessing long-term memory.

- Instructional design and development, and production of instructional materials, take time and raise costs. Moreover, training for storage of information in long-term memory takes longer and raises the delivery costs, which typically exceed all other training costs combined.

- Retraining costs are higher when there is a change in the method of carrying out the task.

WHEN TO USE A JOB AID

If an HP technologist determines that storage of information in the performer's long-term memory is not the best alternative, then a job aid can be developed. Job aids are not limited to particular types of tasks; they have been developed for such linear tasks as equipment assembly and the filling out of forms, but they have also been developed for complex tasks like medical diagnosis, business negotiation, and the analysis of complex systems. The amount of information available in a job aid is not limited; a job aid can be a single sentence or many volumes.

The following tasks are ideal candidates for job aids:

- Tasks performed with relatively low frequency (say, once a year). A task performed once a day is performed with high frequency.

- Highly complex tasks. A task with many steps is more complex than a task with only a few. A task may be qualitatively complex if fine discrimination of stimuli is involved, or if it requires recognition of different stimuli belonging to the same class, or if it involves a series of binary discriminations, as in inspections or troubleshooting.

- Tasks with criteria that must be met if dire consequences (great financial loss, for example, or loss of life) are to be avoided.

- Tasks whose procedures are very likely to change in the future because of changes in technology, policy, or equipment. In such cases, other variables being equal, it is often not worth devoting time and other resources to the costly, time-consuming process of storing information in memory.

- Tasks that do not involve factors (such as strict time requirements) tending to rule out use of a job aid. For example, the responses of a pilot in flight must be immediate rather than guided by a job aid. Other inhibiting factors may exist in the performance environment. A sewer worker would find it difficult to consult a booklet in dark, wet conditions, and a surgeon would face the problem of how to render a job aid sterile. Social barriers may be another inhibiting factor in the use of job aids: as already mentioned, the approval of bosses, peers, and customers for the ability to produce information from memory may discourage performers from using job aids, no matter how complex the tasks.

DEVELOPMENT AND IMPLEMENTATION OF JOB AIDS

Any job aid that an HP technologist recommends must directly guide the task, address only the skills and knowledge that are relevant to the performance problem, and be cost-effective. The following tasks are involved in developing and implementing a job aid.

Task 1: Collecting Data

In this task, the HP technologist discovers the regulations, speed, physical conditions, social conditions, frequency, consequences, complexity, and change probability governing the performance of the task.

Task 2: Selecting the Correct Information-Storage Medium

This task entails choosing among the four alternatives already discussed: job aid only, storage of information only in performers' long-term memory, job aid plus supportive instruction, and instruction plus prompting job aids.

Task 3: Determining Whether Barriers to a Job Aid Can Be Overcome

Even though a barrier to a job aid may exist, sometimes the barrier can be minimized or outweighed by the potential benefits of the job aid. For example, if the use of a job aid is seen as liable to slow performance, a special job aid might be developed that prompts recall of information previously stored in the performer's memory. This kind of memory prompt could take the form of an outline, a key word, a flowchart, or a schematic drawing. The prompting job aid would be placed in the work environment in such a manner that consulting it would not slow performance unacceptably. Examples would be wall charts, laminated pocket cards, and stickers on machinery.

If a barrier to use of a job aid falls into the social category (that is, if the performer is embarrassed to use the job aid), the aid can be hidden from all but the user. Decision tables and key questions can be written on forms for interviewers, and stickers can be hidden inside the carrying cases of equipment.

The most difficult barrier to use of job aids is prejudice against them on the part of the performer and/or the performer's boss. In such cases, one or a combination of the following actions may help:

- Gain support by involving the boss in the analytical process before the job aids are produced.
- Conduct briefings for bosses on why job aids are developed and on their own role in the successful use of job aids.
- Carefully introduce the job aids to the performers in sessions that resemble training sessions, to instill confidence in the job aids.
- Call the job aids *training aids*.

Task 4: Determining Whether
Training Support Is Needed for the Job Aid

Rarely does an HP technologist prepare a job aid that can stand on its own, without some kind of formal introduction. Simply preparing a job aid and sending it out will meet with less success than introducing the aid in briefings or, more typically, building training seminars and courses around when and how to use the aid. This method is more expensive than just sending the job aid out, but the resulting greater probability of its use is generally worth the extra expense.

If the situation permits, self-instructional materials can be developed so that it becomes unnecessary to convene formal training sessions. These materials should include exercises that provide users with practice in using the job aid.

The combination of instruction and job aids can be particularly powerful and cost-effective when computer-assisted instruction and embedded job aids are possible; in this context, an obvious example of an embedded job aid is the help screen.

Task 5: Selecting the Format for the Job Aid

The HP technologist does not regard any given format for a job aid as inherently superior to any other. He or she matches the format to the characteristics of the task. For example, a task characterized by a linear sequence of steps would lend itself to a job aid with a "cookbook" format. Other common formats include worksheets, decision tables, algorithms, and checklists. Many job aids exhibit a combination of formats.

Task 6: Developing the Job Aid

The development of a job aid is an act of engineering rather than a creative act. The HP technologist builds the job aid according to specifications, guided by known rules for encouraging particular behavior and by theories of how humans seem to process information.

Each format has its own rules for writing and layout, but some generic rules apply to all job aids:

- Use specific, unambiguous language: "daily" and "turn until resistance is felt" rather than "often" and "a few turns."

- Use behavioral language: "push," "touch," "press," and "solder," for example, rather than "understand," "create," "satisfy," and "communicate."

- Write in short sentences. Use short words. Job aids should be readable.

- Organize steps into fifteen-second increments. To avoid loss of retention in short-term memory, allow for a step to be read and then performed rather than grouping steps.

- Put the stimulus first, followed by directions for the action to be taken in response to the stimulus. For example, "When you see a red light, apply the brakes" is better than "Apply the brakes when you see a red light."

- Use line drawings rather than photographs. Photographs show everything and may obscure the parts of the environment that the performer needs to attend to. Photographs are also more expensive to reproduce.

- Put drawings on the left and directions for action on the right. This layout imitates the performance situation: I see something, and then I do something. (This arrangement would be reversed, however, in a culture where words are read from right to left.)

- Avoid humor. Usually something funny is funny once, but the performer will use the job aid more than once. Humor may also distract the performer from the task.

Task 7: Editing the Job Aid

After developing the job aid, the HP technologist should submit it to three types of editing before it is tested.

- *Content editing.* Is the job aid technically correct? Is it complete? Does it omit extraneous information? Does it put the performer under stimulus control?

- *Structural editing.* Is the format of the job aid appropriate to the characteristics of the task? Is the information properly sequenced? Are the steps in small enough increments to minimize the need for retention? Is all the necessary information in one place? Are the drawings from the performer's perspective? Has critical information been highlighted? Are the steps numbered?

- *Language editing.* Does the text use the active voice? Do action statements begin with verbs? Are clear behavioral terms used? Are statements positive? Are pronoun references clear? Are sentences short? Are modifiers close to what they modify? (Of course, different rules might apply for languages other than English.)

Task 8: Testing the Job Aid

The HP technologist now needs to determine whether the desired performance will be produced as a result of the job aid's use. To find out, the HP technologist puts the job aid through a series of tryout/revision cycles. Tryouts (developmental tests) are carried out on a one-to-one basis with the employees for whom the job aid has been designed. As practicality permits, the tryouts are conducted in the actual environment where the job aid will be used.

According to circumstances and practicalities, the HP technologist then conducts a formal validation test of the job aid. The validation is carried out with a larger number of performers, and proper pretesting and controls are used. The HP technologist then conducts a follow-up evaluation that seeks answers to the following questions:

- Did the job aid solve or minimize the problem, or satisfy the information need, that was specified in the analysis?
- Does the value produced by the job aid exceed the cost of its development and implementation?

DELIVERY TECHNOLOGY FOR JOB AIDS

The characteristics of the task to be supported are what determine the choice between storing information in the performer's long-term memory and storing it in a job aid. The same rational approach should be used in selecting the delivery technology for a job aid. The goal should be to achieve the highest level of performance at the lowest cost.

The first thing to be examined is the nature of the task. One task characteristic that will affect the delivery technology for a job aid is how often the relevant information changes. When information changes frequently, electronic systems for performance support and document management take on added value. These systems permit someone to update the information once, at a central location, and then allow every user immediate access to the changed information.

Another task characteristic, dire consequences for errors, can drive the choice for an electronic job aid. For example, someone mixing hazardous materials in a chemical plant might use an electronic worksheet or an electronic system for performance support. The advantage over a paper worksheet would be the electronic job aid's ability to eliminate errors in calculation while providing written or audio warnings at key points in the mixing process.

Availability of the desired technology should also be considered. If the target audience has ready access to information technology or is already using computers in performing a task, then electronic performance support can be a cost-effective intervention. By contrast, it would not be cost-effective to replace airline seat-pocket cards with personal digital assistants.

The decision-making sequence is a critical factor in the selection of a delivery technology. The HP technologist needs first to decide whether the characteristics of the task justify the use of a job aid. Then, in view of the task characteristics, the availability of various delivery technologies, and cost considerations, the HP technologist selects the most appropriate delivery technology.

RESEARCH AND APPLICATIONS

Comparatively little formal research on job aids has been done by scholars or others in academic settings. Most of the evidence is anecdotal and comes from applications in industry and government. This is not surprising in that the purpose of a job aid is to directly affect on-the-job performance; most academic research concerns learning and, by inference, storage of information in memory.

In a review of the literature, Duncan (1986) reaches the following conclusions:

- Twenty years of data on the use of job aids in military and industrial settings show major payoffs in the form of improved performance and lower costs.
- There are many different definitions of job aids, and this diversity of definitions poses something of a dilemma.
- Most training models do not consider the use of job aids.
- Despite their major payoffs, job aids are a vastly underused tool.

In a review of studies conducted between 1958 and 1973 in the U.S. Air Force and the U.S. Navy, Rowan (1973) reaches the following conclusions:

- Job aids reduce training time.
- Job aids decrease dependence on highly skilled personnel.
- Job aids reduce the need for manpower.
- Job aids facilitate cross-training on systems.

Harless (1980) reports the following outcomes on the basis of case studies involving job aids:

- A one-week training course for an electronics manufacturer was reduced to one day with an accompanying eight-page job aid. Performance proficiency increased by 50 percent.
- A chemical company reduced the error rate in insecticide formulation from 10 percent to 1 percent by using a two-page job aid.
- A company found no significant difference in performance between an experienced group of technicians designated as experts and an inexperienced group of technicians who employed a job aid in troubleshooting a system.

SUMMARY

Job aids are but one of the interventions available to HP technologists and are subject to the same tests of relevance and cost-effectiveness as any other intervention. Job aids are storage places for information. They are employed in real time for guiding performance. They should provide stimuli and responses and reduce the need for the performer to recall information.

It is less expensive to develop a job aid than to store information in performers' long-term memory, and job aids often dramatically reduce formal training time. Because job aids can yield more accurate and reliable job performance, they force job aid developers and subject matter experts to define the desired performance. Disadvantages of job aids are that they may decrease the speed of performance, and it may not be possible or practical to use them in some cases. They may also cause bosses and others to give less credit to performers.

HP technologists do not have one favorite intervention. Nevertheless, the potential impact of job aids demands that their use be considered for every project in which analysis has revealed a need for information. Moreover, their use must be considered early in the development of training because the training design will take a very different direction if job aids are used.

Human performance technology itself is somewhat difficult to explain to clients; the potential benefits of this approach are not always immediately obvious. Clients want tangible solutions, often quickly, and many are impatient with talk of precise analysis and detailed design. If the use of a job aid is indicated, the client is given a tangible product with relative speed, and beneficial performance results are immediately obvious. It is difficult to beat an intervention that can be produced quickly and cheaply and has obvious benefits.

References

Duncan, C. (1986). *Introduction to performance technology.* Washington, DC: National Society for Performance Improvement.

Harless, J. H. (1980). *Job aids workshop.* Annapolis, MD: Human Performance Technologies.

Rowan, T. C. (1973, Mar.). *Improving DOD maintenance through better performance aids.* Springfield, VA: Advanced Research Projects Agency.

CHAPTER TWENTY-THREE

Performance Support Systems

Steven W. Villachica
Deborah L. Stone

Performance Support Systems (PSSs) are a new, rapidly evolving form of Human Performance Technology (HPT) that provide just-in-time, on-demand support for the performance of people and organizations. A PSS can facilitate a continuum of performance. At one end of this continuum lie procedural tasks that are performed in a simple stepwise manner, with little variation from one performance to the next. Because they require only near transfer, these tasks are often internalized; performers can complete them without having to concentrate on them, and performance that meets the relevant standard can occur quickly and automatically. Examples of procedural tasks include balancing a checkbook, completing college admissions forms, and placing orders, calculating bills, or counting inventory at a fast-food restaurant. A PSS used for such procedural tasks often streamlines or automates their performance.

At the other end of this continuum lie the complex cognitive tasks typically performed by knowledge workers. Execution of these tasks requires extensive use of performance domain–specific skills and knowledge, as well as their far

The authors would like to thank three people who generously provided insights, comments, and resources. Gloria Gery of Gery Associates revised a draft of this chapter and helped to formulate the section describing the integration of performance support components. Frieda Aboyoun of PricewaterhouseCoopers provided screen samples and information about the prototype of the Human Resources Benefits PSS. Steve Blumberg of *CBT Solutions* provided copies of invaluable reports and back issues.

transfer to the task at hand. Individuals performing such cognitive tasks must draw on multiple internal and external knowledge sources as they employ rich mental models and complex rules that enable them to solve problems in varying situations. Performers using a PSS for these kinds of tasks spend most of their time making decisions, monitoring progress, planning, and using rules of thumb. Building such expertise may take years; a PSS can either minimize or eliminate the time this process would otherwise take. A cognitive PSS may help a performer audit a securities firm, design a car, or create a performance intervention.

According to a recent survey (Kemske, 1997), the median age for a PSS application is a mere eighteen months. Hudzina, Rowley, and Wager (1996) observe that PSSs represent "one of the most dynamic areas in human performance systems. . . . One looking for guidance from the literature will find that writing in the field is diverse; it varies in scope and purpose" (pp. 36–37). Scales and Yang (1993), as well as Cole, Fisher, and Saltzman (1997), note that a standard definition of a PSS is lacking.

Given its newness, the field of PSSs is moving too fast for articles in the peer-reviewed professional literature to keep up, and so PSS research consists mostly of self-report surveys. Most articles are either opinion papers or case studies, and they vary widely in terms of quality and reported results. Authors often base their opinions solely on their own experiences, and secondary analyses of published data are nonexistent. Given this situation, we have based this chapter on the following sources:

- Our own experience creating PSS applications
- Our colleagues' comments
- An extensive search (using the key words *EPSS, PSS,* and *performance support*) of on-line databases and the World Wide Web
- A review of performance-related articles appearing in business publications

It is also important to note that most PSS articles describe efforts in the United States and Canada; only a handful originate elsewhere. Therefore, HPT practitioners outside North America should be aware that ethnic and cultural distinctions may limit the generalizability of these articles.

DESCRIPTION

In our conception, a PSS is an optimized body of coordinated on-line and off-line methods and resources that enable and maintain a person's or an organization's performance. The goal is to give performers what they need, when they need it, and in the form in which they need it so that they perform in a way that consistently meets organizational objectives. A PSS is an integrated intervention whose components are designed to work together to improve performance. A PSS consists of the people who use it, the processes it employs, and the devices it uses. Such a PSS systemically facilitates performance, often at multiple levels in an organization.

We use the five *I*'s to summarize the characteristics of a PSS:

- *Intuitiveness*: An electronic PSS has a consistent, predictable graphical user interface that employs rich metaphors and provides the guidance that performers need in order to be successful, even if they have minimal or no prior learning.

- *Integration:* PSS components are seamlessly integrated and designed expressly to work with each other (Rossett, 1991; Witt and Wager, 1994).

- *Immediacy:* A PSS offers on-demand access to tools, information, advice, training, communications, and other components.

- *Individualization:* PSSs support a range of expertise and individual differences in task-structuring support and learning. Consequently, PSSs can simultaneously meet the needs of novices, competent performers, and experts.

- *Interactivity:* Interactions between performers and a PSS resemble a dynamic dialogue (Gery, cited in Galagan, 1994).

BASIC CONCEPTS AND TERMINOLOGY

The development of any PSS depends on a sound, systematic "anatomy of performance," a framework that allows HPT practitioners to identify all the variables affecting performance and the interactions among them, to diagnose those variables that are not operating as expected, and to determine the mix of integrated interventions that will improve performance (Rummler and Brache, 1992). Consequently, PSSs encompass one of the widest possible ranges of HPT; in fact, a large-scale PSS may use most or all of the methods and interventions contained in this handbook. Table 23.1 illustrates the broad range of performance areas to which a PSS can be applied.

VARIATIONS

Different kinds of PSS applications vary in terms of how thoroughly they integrate different performance support components and the scale on which they operate.

Table 23.1. Performance Areas and Potential PSS Components.

Performance Area	Potential PSS Component
Performance specifications	Reference database specifying desired performance Software engineered to meet performance specifications
Task interference	On-demand access to job tools and information Computer interfaces that follow workflow Elimination or minimization of competing tasks through automation
Consequences	Facilitation of meaningful user goals Provision of timely consequences
Feedback	Reports and system messages describing user performance Design of information to ensure its relevance, accuracy, timeliness, specificity, constructiveness, and ease of understanding
Knowledge and skill	On-demand access to context-based instruction Information describing why desired performance is important Experts' mental models of job tasks embedded in the user interface
Individual capacity	Administration of job-selection tests

Integration of Performance Support Components

Assume that someone is using a PSS to perform a job-related task. In addition to the software application the performer uses, the PSS can contain different components that support learning, inputting, referencing, searching, retrieving, and navigating. These components can operate separately, be highly integrated, or function somewhere in between. As depicted in Figure 23.1, they can be arranged along a continuum that indicates their relative integration (Gloria Gery, personal correspondence). Less integrated forms of performance support appear on the left of the continuum; more integrated forms appear on the right. As a rule, less integrated forms require numerous breaks in context because the performer must interrupt any current task in order to receive support. More integrated forms require fewer breaks in context.

For example, the performer may be using a PSS that provides only external support. This support can appear either off line or on line, but using it requires the performer to completely shift from the task at hand in order to receive performance support. At point 1 on the continuum, the performer must stop what he or she is doing on the computer to consult an off-line, external resource, such as a colleague or a printed reference manual. This activity represents a significant

Figure 23.1. Continuum of Integration for Performance Support.

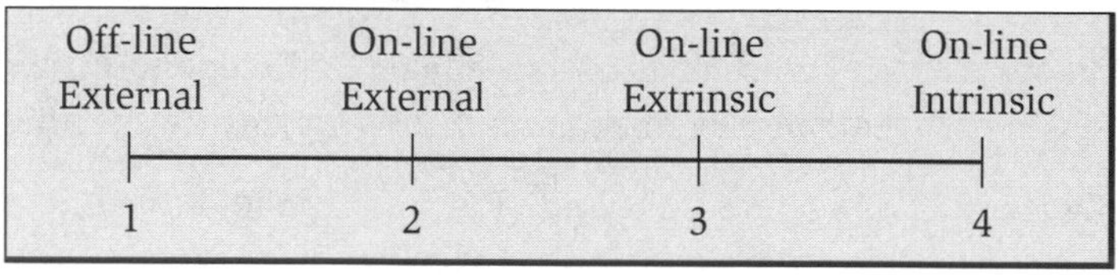

Off-line External	On-line External	On-line Extrinsic	On-line Intrinsic
1	2	3	4

break in the context of the task, and such interference may adversely affect performance effectiveness and efficiency. In addition, there is no context-sensitive access to these resources. The performer is fully responsible for integrating what he or she has accessed into the performance of the task.

A second form of performance support comes into play when a PSS is "bolted on" to the application the performer is using, as depicted at point 2. Such on-line external performance support usually occurs when the application is developed first and the support is developed afterward. In this situation, the performer must stop using the application and invoke a separate PSS that resides on the computer. This PSS may describe components of the application software, or it may provide knowledge resources about the task, the organization, or the performance domain. After accessing these resources, the performer must exit the PSS and transfer back to the software application. In other words, the performer is using either the application or its support at any given time, but never both at once. In this situation, the performer's focus must shift completely, from active doing to using performance support. In addition to searching for and retrieving any relevant information, the performer must also integrate what is accessed into the performance of the task. This action also represents a significant break in context, but it is not as large as at point 1. However, switching back and forth between the application and its support still produces a significant amount of interference and may diminish performance effectiveness and efficiency.

A different PSS may provide on-line extrinsic support to the performer, as shown at point 3. This type of performance support provides, within the application itself, mechanisms for invoking different types of support, including on-line "wizards" and "coaches," examples, on-line references, and practice activities. Typically, developers anticipate performance requirements and integrate context-sensitive support elements with the application itself. Either through hard links or rule-based access, the software presents filtered and relevant resources at the moment they are needed. The use of extrinsic support in the application results in far fewer breaks in context than at either point 1 or point 2. Less interference results in few opportunities for performance decrements and increases the probability of successful performance. Often this type of resource is called *just-in-time* or *context-sensitive* support.

Finally, the PSS may provide on-line intrinsic support to the performer, as shown at point 4. This type of performance support is fully integrated (or fused) with the application. According to Kemske (1997), 25 percent of PSS users report that their organizations employ intrinsic forms of performance support.

A low-end example of intrinsic support would be the tips provided by the help program of a computer's operating system: such tips take the form of short descriptions of toolbar buttons and other items as the cursor passes over them; the only break in context occurs with the eye movement required to read each object's description. A high-end example of intrinsic support would be a user interface that helps performers establish goals, structure work processes, access embedded knowledge, monitor their progress, and automate the performance of tasks. Another high-end example would be the alternative interface to a forms-based or command-based software system. This type of performance support appears as a "wizard" or "assistant" that enables novices to perform various tasks.

In general, intrinsic support is indistinguishable from the software application itself and does not require the performer to invoke it. In fact, intrinsic support *is* the application's user interface. A performance-centered interface can eliminate the need for application-specific training and can minimize or eliminate the need for prior knowledge about the task or performance domain. The use of high-end intrinsic support eliminates any contextual break from the performance of the task itself; performers simply feel as if they are always working in an ordinary way. The goal of intrinsic support is to guarantee performance; and, clearly, the greater the integration of various elements of performance support with the application, the fewer breaks in context, the less interference with performance, and the greater the potential improvement in performance efficiency and effectiveness.

Scale

PSSs vary in scale and can operate at the individual, group, or organizational level. Bill (1997) observes that early PSSs largely supported the work of autonomous individuals, involving "little or no communication with entities outside of the individual workstation" (p. 43). These early PSSs operated on a relatively small scale: the scale of individual tasks and jobs. Some authors, such as Raybould (1995c), Laffey (1995), Passmore and Lin (1997), and Bill (1997), have enlarged the scale of PSSs to include the organizational level, so that issues of knowledge management are addressed. These PSSs serve to diffuse the knowledge and best practices that experts would otherwise carry in their heads. In this capacity, a PSS can facilitate the creation, capture, dissemination, maintenance, and evolution of organizational knowledge. In the future, we expect to see sophisticated forms of PSSs that will facilitate performance at the business and industry levels.

EXAMPLES

A PSS for Securities Auditors

Figure 23.2 and Table 23.2 depict and describe examples of the CORNERSTONE Automated Examination Module (AEM), a large-scale PSS effort (for a detailed description, see Villachica and Stone, 1998a). The AEM is a "work organizer" for examiners who audit securities firms. Its user interface consists of a set of questions matching the mental model that experienced examiners use to conduct audits. The AEM also provides on-line access to procedures, standard spreadsheets, and forms that examiners use. The AEM uses examiners' responses to each question to create a first draft of the audit report. The AEM resides on the laptop computers that examiners carry to audits and replaces a paper-based process.

A PSS for Human Resources Benefits

Figure 23.3 and Table 23.3 depict and describe a prototype of the Human Resources Benefits PSS, which was proposed for use by PricewaterhouseCoopers customer service representatives and their clients (Gloria Gery, personal correspondence; Frieda Aboyoun, personal correspondence). The two sample screens present alternatives to a client who wants to withdraw funds from a 401(k) account. On the basis of the client's personal data, the system displays a summary called *Money Availability Options.* This summary clearly enumerates the client's available alternatives, with on-demand access to cell-specific layered explanations, definitions, and rules only a keystroke away. The screens can also be used directly by clients via an Internet application.

MAJOR BENEFITS

A PSS offers many of the same benefits as a job aid (see Chapter Twenty-Two, this volume). Besides promoting organizational learning and performance, a PSS offers two major advantages: reduced time to sustainable, near-expert performance and a high potential return on investment (ROI).

Reduced Time to Near-Expert Performance

Figure 23.4 compares traditional and PSS approaches to achieving and sustaining near-expert performance. At the left side of Figure 23.4, novices begin with traditional training (1). Because this training usually occurs away from the job site and employs massed practice, transfer of learning is low. Subsequent on-the-job training (either formal or informal) ultimately produces near-expert performance (2).

Figure 23.2. Sample Screens for CORNERSTONE PSS's Automated Examination Modules.

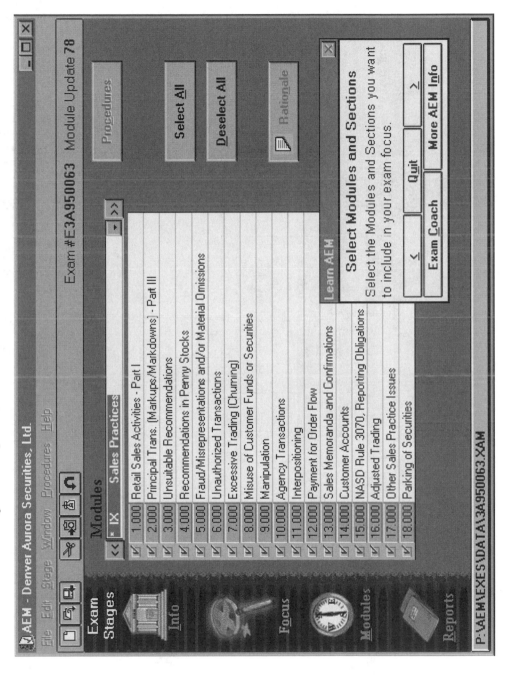

Figure 23.2. Sample Screens for CORNERSTONE PSS's Automated Examination Modules, cont'd.

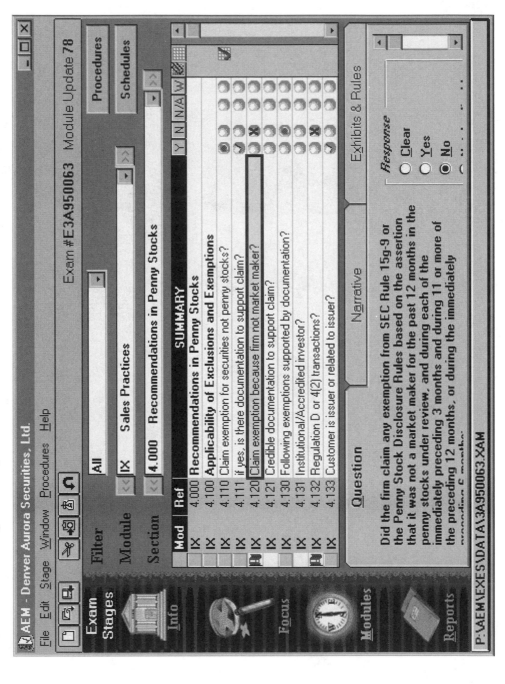

Table 23.2. Description of CORNERSTONE PSS.

CORNERSTONE PSS	Description
Project goal	Create one of the most comprehensive PSSs in existence by integrating on-line and off-line components to support a broad range of job performance.
Target audience	550 examiners of the National Association of Securities Dealers, Regulation Division. These individuals audit securities firms throughout the United States to ensure compliance with securities regulations and sales practices.
Components	Full-scale PSS composed of twenty-one components using ten media
Length of development effort	1.5 years
Impact data	*Performance results:* Reduced new employee ramp-up time from 2.5 to 1.5 years. Decreased the potential that regulatory violations might have harmed the investing public while novice examiners came up to speed. Provided experienced examiners with new opportunities for career advancement. Increased employee satisfaction. Eliminated the possibility that novice examiners might have relied on members of the securities firms they investigated to teach them about new products they encountered during exams. Increased consistency in exam performance and decreased unnecessary variation in exam processes by providing explicit learning about experts' decision processes. Supervisors, managers, and legal personnel returned fewer exam reports for rework. *Financial results:* Produced ROI of 42.3 percent, with payoff in 2.2 years. Reduced training delivery costs 43 percent by providing on-demand training.

Figure 23.3. Sample Screens for Prototype of Human Resources Benefits PSS.

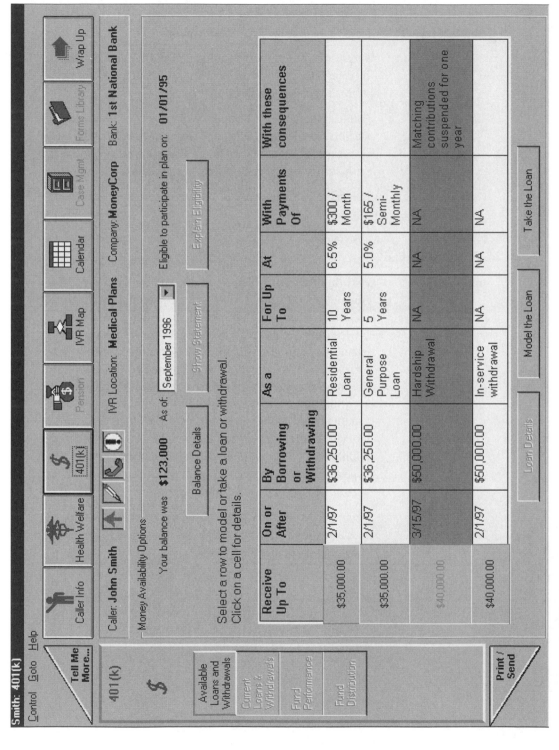

Figure 23.3. Sample Screens for Prototype of Human Resources Benefits PSS, cont'd.

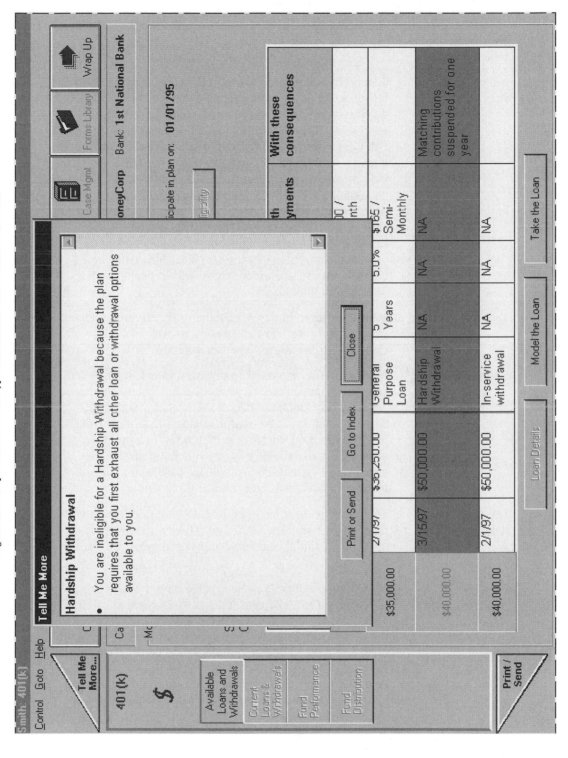

Table 23.3. Description of PSS for Human Resources Benefits.

Human Resources Benefits PSS	Description
Project goal	Support high business growth in benefits outsourcing business, including dramatic employee growth. Guarantee quality responses to inquiries and accurate transaction processing. Increase flexibility in work assignment among Call Center employees. Dramatically reduce training requirements. Maintain or increase business profitability. Provide on-demand access to employee-specific information and options under employee benefits plans. Support outsourcing of clients' and employee's direct interaction with their own data and benefits information via an intranet. Expedite employee enrollment or changes in benefit options and completion of various transactions (such as taking loans or distributions from defined benefit and defined contribution plans).
Target audience	More than seven hundred customer service representatives who currently work in Call Centers, as well as millions of client employees using corporate intranets.
Components	A powerful user interface, to organize knowledge and data and permit immediate job performance. Underlying logic would extract employee data from databases, and a rule-based system would be used to evaluate individual employee options on the basis of plan rules. In addition, a knowledge base would be linked to a given display via a rule-based system. The knowledge base would include plan rules, glossaries, and concept explanations.
Length of development effort	The prototype took one month to develop to support two tasks: (1) determining money availability options from a 401(k) plan and (2) modeling and selecting annual health care options.
Data on projected impact	*Performance results:* Projected reduction in training time of 30 percent to 50 percent. Estimated decrease in call handling time of 15 percent. Predicted 8 percent reduction in the number of customer service representatives who would otherwise have to be hired. Projected 16 percent increase in capacity to handle additional business. *Financial results:* Expected reductions in training time, call-handling time, and hiring would result in an estimated annual savings of $2.7 to $3 million.

New releases of software, or changes to policies and procedures, require additional learning, a situation that produces short-term drops in performance (3, 4). At the right side of Figure 23.4, near-expert performance quickly occurs and is facilitated by the highly modular advice of a PSS, as well as by the PSS's informational, instructional, and tool components (1). Because any necessary training occurs on the job, employs distributed practice, and provides various forms of feedback, transfer of learning is high. Novices can complete any initial training quickly (2). Like a well-designed job aid, a fully integrated PSS can also enable near-expert performance from the first day, with no training at all. As new releases or changes in policies and procedures are built into the PSS, few if any associated drops in performance appear (3, 4). Use of a PSS often makes it possible to obtain near-expert performance almost immediately and sustain it indefinitely.

High Potential ROI

The initial development costs of a PSS vary widely. Kemske (1997) estimates a median cost of $52,100 for development and delivery. Dublin (1993) reports that PSS development costs are between $100,000 and $1 million. In our experience, development costs have ranged from $100,000 to $6 million; the exact cost depends on the size and complexity of the project. Regardless of their initial costs, the PSSs we have created have paid for themselves between six and thirty months after their implementation.

Other favorable returns on investment arise from a variety of sources. For instance, American Express's Financial Advisors Division used a PSS to decrease novice training from twelve to two hours. This PSS also reduced the time required to perform a task involving bank authorization. Novices' task completion times dropped from 17.1 minutes to 3.9 minutes; experienced personnel's times fell from 4.8 to 3.2 minutes (Foster, 1997). Aetna Life and Casualty uses several PSSs, two of which facilitate computer troubleshooting and the interpretation of

Figure 23.4. Comparison of Traditional and PSS Job Preparation and Maintenance.

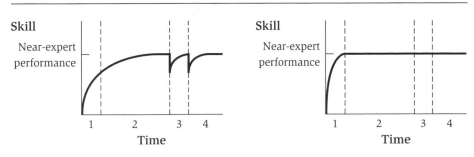

medical reports. The troubleshooting PSS has allowed Aetna to eliminate $3,000 per person in training costs. This PSS, developed internally at a cost of $20,000, had paid for itself within weeks. The PSS for interpreting medical reports was developed at a cost of $33,000 and saves $49,000 per year (Hequet, 1994). These favorable results came about because the objective of a PSS is to make people "smarter, faster, and more effective in the performance of existing jobs" (Berry, 1993, p. 299).

Raybould (1995b) cites broad strategic issues and cost factors for cost-justifying a PSS. Strategic issues include improved quality, increased retention of corporate knowledge, and improved responsiveness to business change. Cost factors include increased productivity, reduction in lost-opportunity costs, reduced support costs, and reduced training costs. Brown (1996) provides a broader model for justifying PSSs, beginning with descriptions of business and performer needs and with discussions of current business trends on which a PSS can capitalize.

SPECIAL PRECAUTIONS

HPT practitioners who are contemplating the use of a PSS should recognize that a PSS is not a panacea that can magically close any performance gap. They should also be aware of several cautionary circumstances:

1. The PSS approach, because of its relative newness, offers no common vocabulary; there is no dictionary that translates PSS-related terms for HPT practitioners and others who have widely differing backgrounds. These differences in background lead to a variety of experiential "silos," with widespread lack of communication, continuous reinvention of the wheel, and absence of the progress that could otherwise be achieved.

2. The PSS approach may lead to the deskilling of the workforce—the elimination of human expertise and, potentially, of jobs (Clark, 1992, 1995; Longman, 1997). Sherry and Wilson (1996) disagree with this point, but it may be moot: the same PSS that automates or eliminates the intermediary or "middleman" jobs may also create other value-added jobs. Ultimately, the deskilling issue may be resolved in the future, when enough data may exist to conduct empirical analyses.

3. Cognitive, organizational, and logistic constraints are required in the provision of appropriate "granules" of on-the-job training (Clark, 1992).

4. Clark (1992), having reviewed the literature on learner control over the interface, notes that it benefits experienced learners more than novices. She cites evidence showing that automated performance tools do not always improve performance, and she describes the increased degree of complexity inherent in creating a PSS.

Success Factors

Horn (cited in Foster, 1997) observes that a large number of PSSs remain in pilot mode, with full-scale development never realized. Scales and Yang (1993) contend that successful PSS efforts depend on the experience of the project manager. This is a perception that characterizes our own experience; indeed, the project manager for a PSS must employ strategies and tools that are far more complex than those typically used by HP technologists. Scales and Yang also cite total implementation costs and organizational readiness for accepting the technology as factors in the success of a PSS.

To ensure favorable development and implementation costs, Clark (1992) suggests basing the PSS on favorable and clear ROI. A PSS that does not account for ROI will tend to address trivial performance gaps that will never have an impact on the organization (if such a PSS is ever completed at all). Without a focus on the bottom line, PSS efforts may wander, quickly exceeding budget while missing project milestones. ROI also provides important guidance in determining the critical success factors that the project must meet, and it sets the baseline against which subsequent summative evaluations are measured.

As Gery (1991) notes, "No matter what technologies you are using or what activity you are trying to support, the main issues in system development are always more organizational than technical" (p. 231). Organizational readiness is a critical issue in creating a successful PSS. Dorsey, Goodrum, and Schwen (1993) contend that managers "are the keystone to a successful change process" (p. 29). A successful, large-scale PSS must have powerful organizational sponsors who are capable of mandating change and forming the multidisciplinary teams that will develop the PSS. The creators of a successful PSS use a variety of organizational development strategies that generate ongoing user support.

Competence

Because of their relative complexity, the development and implementation of a PSS require a cadre of people who possess diverse expertise. According to Marquardt (1996), human resources development professionals should know how to take the following actions:

- Identify the benefits of a PSS
- Analyze opportunities for using it
- Design PSS information structures, navigational strategies, and interfaces
- Develop or incorporate embedded tools
- Foresee how the PSS will interact with the organization's work practices

Creating a PSS requires the integration of a variety of personnel and the roles they play. Stevens and Stevens (1995) suggest that skills are needed in understanding and assessing performance needs as well as in human-computer interface design, team leadership, and microcomputer application design. Gery (1991) describes sixteen roles that individuals can play in the creation of a PSS, regardless of whether the team consists of three people or thirty; Brown (1996) lists nine roles.

STEPS IN DEVELOPMENT

Even though PSS development is a variant of the standard development models for instructional systems design, Milheim (1997) has noted an apparent dearth of detailed strategies for designing and developing PSSs, but these strategies do exist. Development models for software products offer detailed strategies that can be applied to PSS creation. Villachica and Stone (1998b), for example, describe a development method based on successful software engineering practices, particularly Rapid Application Development, or RAD (Martin, 1991). Adapted to the creation of PSSs and other interventions, this RAD methodology employs such strategies as collaborative analysis and design, prototyping, usability tests, small project teams using powerful tools, and strict processes for setting priorities to ensure that high-quality work is delivered on time and within budget. Similar strategies appear in various other sources (see, for example, Witt and Wager, 1994; Nieveen, Akker, and Plomp, 1994; Law, Okey, and Carter, 1995; Collis and Verwijs, 1995).

Analysis

During the analysis phase, HPT practitioners creating a PSS often employ both detailed feasibility analysis and cognitive task analysis. Various authors (Gery, 1991; Carr, 1992; Ladd, 1993; Cognitive Technologies, 1995; Thomas, Baron, and Schmidt, 1995; Raybould, 1995a; Brown, 1996; Reeves, 1996) provide criteria for determining the feasibility of a PSS. In this group, Raybould provides the most detailed job aid describing when a PSS may be appropriate. It is important to note, however, that these feasibility analyses do not adequately stress the issue of organizational feasibility. To state the issue simply, a large-scale PSS usually will not be implemented unless there exist organizational sponsorship and readiness.

To specify the standards that expert-level performance should meet, PSS developers often conduct cognitive task analyses, collecting data from a range of performers, including novices, competent performers, and experts. These analyses focus on workflow and potential process improvement (Witt and Wager, 1994). Cognitive task analysis also focuses on making rules and relationships explicit.

Design/Production

The PSS should adopt a design that (as the saying goes) leads, follows, or gets out of the way. Novices, cross-trainees, or other casual performers are concurrently building two skill sets—one for the performance domain, and the other for the PSS itself. Because these individuals do not necessarily benefit from user control over the interface, the interface should gently lead them through the appropriate activities, providing the scaffolding necessary for performance that meets the relevant standard. When performers are competent, however, and still tuning their skills, the interface should quietly follow, interrupting only when called on or when the performer makes an error. For experts and other seasoned veterans, the user interface should be transparent and unobtrusive, matching the mental models and procedures that these people use on the job. In sum, the user interface should help all performers reflect on their performance and restructure it, as appropriate.

Dorsey, Goodrum, and Schwen (1993) argue that a PSS must be more than just a pretty interface. The user interface and other PSS functions must match performers' actual tasks. Common violations of these design precepts, according to Dickelman (1995), include the use of layers upon layers of menus, hidden shortcuts that use obscure commands or strange key combinations, cryptic field labels, and on-line help documents the size of *War and Peace.*

Reaching these design goals requires the use of performance-centered design (Gery, 1995, 1997a, 1998; Raybould, 1995c) so as to integrate the knowledge, data, and tools required for success in performing a task and to provide task-structuring support that helps performers create the required deliverables. Performance-centered design exists to support the potential first-day performance of novice and expert performers alike (Gery, 1995). Designers provide this support by ensuring that all PSS activities occur within the performance zone, a hypothetical space in which the PSS accurately represents business processes, matches the preferences and personal styles of the people using it, and provides only absolutely necessary information (Dickelman, 1996; Cole, Fisher, and Saltzman, 1997; Dickelman, cited in Kemske, 1997).

The HPT practitioner designing a PSS for international, transnational, or cross-cultural use must account for the greater diversity of the people who will use the system. For example, a graphical user interface, an instructional case study, or the physical depiction of a person may be appropriate to one group of people but inappropriate or even offensive to another. Moreover, the overall design architecture of the PSS must be appropriate to the entire range of people who will use it, but it should still allow for local customization. Because of the greater complexity and risk inherent in the design process, the HPT practitioner designing a PSS should conduct usability tests as early as possible, using representative members of the entire target audience.

Implementation

PSS implementation must be an ongoing concern, from initial project planning through maintenance. One reason why RAD-based development strategies are successful is that they provide for continuous change management. These strategies should be combined with marketing and organizational change efforts that run through the development and shelf life of a PSS. In addition, the implementation of any international, transnational, or cross-cultural PSS must also allow sufficient time for any necessary translation, local customization, and testing.

Evaluation

According to Kemske (1997), who reports a dearth of PSS evaluation, only 31 percent of survey respondents said they had evaluated a PSS for its effectiveness, only 10 percent of that group had evaluated a PSS for improved job performance, and only 5 percent had evaluated a PSS for ROI. (It should be noted that lack of evaluation in this area is probably no worse than the lack of evaluation in other areas of performance improvement intervention, including training.) Despite the dearth of data, however, 87 percent of these respondents said that end users believed their PSSs were important. Kemske concludes that PSS evaluation "will need to become more sophisticated and widespread" (p. 13). Gery (1997b) and Dorsey, Goodrum, and Schwen (1993) provide comprehensive lists of potential measures for use in a PSS evaluation.

A LOOK TOWARD THE FUTURE

Kemske (1997) asks whether PSSs are "real, or . . . just another trend" (p. 6). A review of the literature reveals that PSSs are definitely real. For example, Caudron (1996) attributes today's greater leaps in employee performance to PSSs. In a similar vein, Milheim (1997) notes that "with the increasing prevalence of personal computers on employee desktops, . . . [PSSs] may soon begin to alter significantly the manner in which employees generally function and are trained" (p. 103). We believe that PSSs will move out of their current "niche" status to grow in importance for HPT practitioners. Given the increasing appearance of PSSs on the job, HPT practitioners may well conclude that their primary role, rather than to create isolated performance interventions, is to create systems that support workplace and organizational performance.

Estimating what will happen over the next ten years is risky, of course. We agree with Rosenberg (1995), who says that HPT and PSSs have the same future, one of direct integration into key organizational processes, and that, as a measure of their success, both HPT and PSSs eventually will "disappear as separate processes and tools, and be absorbed directly into the business mainstream" (p. 98).

The reader interested in pursuing further advice, both worthwhile and amusing, may want to attend conferences of the International Society for Performance Improvement, consult Cjelli (1992), Gery (1996), and Dublin (1998), and access the following on-line resources:

www.cbtsolutions.com

www.epss.com

www.ispi.org

www.hingh.com

www.performance support.com

www.tgx.com/enhance

References

Berry, W. E. (1993). HRIS can improve performance, empower, and motivate "knowledge workers." *Employment Relations Today* 20:3, 297–303.

Bill, D. T. (1997, May–June). EPSS and the learning organization. *CBT Solutions,* pp. 42–47.

Brown, L. A. (1996). *Designing and developing electronic performance support systems.* Boston: Digital Press.

Carr, C. (1992). PSS! Help when you need it. *Training & Development* 46:6, 30–38.

Caudron, S. (1996). Wake up to new learning. *Training & Development* 50:5, 30–35.

Cjelli, D. (1992). How to avoid subsequent-system stress with performance support systems. *Performance & Instruction* 31:10, 29–31.

Clark, R. C. (1992). EPSS—look before you leap: Some cautions about applications of electronic performance support systems. *Performance & Instruction* 31:5, 22–25.

Clark, R. C. (1995). Twenty-first-century human performance. *Training* 32:6, 85–90.

Cognitive Technologies. (1995). *Is an EPSS appropriate for your application?* < http://www.clark.net/pub/kmcgraw/EPSSselect.html >

Cole, K., Fisher, O., and Saltzman, P. (1997). Just-in-time knowledge delivery: A case study of an award-winning support system demonstrates the vital characteristics and primary design goals for generating peak performance. *Communications of the ACM* 40:7, 49–53.

Collis, B. A., and Verwijs, C. (1995). A human approach to electronic performance and learning support systems: Hybrid EPSSs. *Educational Technology* 34:1, 5–21.

Dickelman, G. J. (1995). Things that help us perform: Commentary on ideas from Donald A. Norman. *Performance Improvement Quarterly* 8:1, 23–30.

Dickelman, G. J. (1996, Sept.–Oct.). Gershom's law: Principles for the design of performance support systems intended for use by human beings. *CBT Solutions,* pp. 26–30.

Dorsey, L. T., Goodrum, D. A., and Schwen, W. M. (1993). Just-in-time performance support: A test of concept. *Educational Technology* 33:11, 21–29.

Dublin, L. E. (1993). Learn while you work. *Computerworld* 27:35, 81–82.

Dublin, L. E. (1998). *Ten laws for successfully using performance technology.* < http://www.dublingroup.com/dgpages/10laws.htm >

Foster, E. (1997). Training when you need it. *Infoworld* 19:8, 51–52.

Galagan, P. A. (1994). Performance support systems: A conversation with Gloria Gery. *Technical and Skills Training* 5:3, 6–10.

Gery, G. (1991). *Electronic performance support systems: How and why to remake the workplace through the strategic application of technology.* Tolland, MA: Gery Performance Press.

Gery, G. (1995). Attributes and behaviors of performance-centered systems. *Performance Improvement Quarterly* 8:1, 47–93.

Gery, G. (1996). *The EPSS top ten lists.* < http://www.cbtsolutions.com/html/9701_ger.htm >

Gery, G. (1997a). Granting three wishes through performance-centered design. *Communications of the ACM* 40:7, 54–59.

Gery, G. (1997b, May). Why don't we weigh them? *CBT Solutions,* p. 66.

Gery, G. (1998). *Traditional vs. performance-centered design.* < http://www.epss.com/lb/artonlin/articles/ggl.htm >

Hequet, M. (1994). Should every worker have a line in the information stream? *Training* 31:5, 99–102.

Hudzina, M., Rowley, K., and Wager, W. (1996). Electronic performance support technology: Defining the domain. *Performance Improvement Quarterly* 9:1, 36–48.

Kemske, F. (1997). *1997 electronic performance support systems report.* Hingham, MA: SB Communications.

Ladd, C. (1993). Should performance support be in your computer? *Training & Development* 47:8, 22–26.

Laffey, J. (1995). Dynamism in electronic performance support systems. *Performance Improvement Quarterly* 8:1, 31–45.

Law, M. P., Okey, J. R., and Carter, B. J. (1995). *Developing electronic performance support systems for professionals.* Paper presented at the annual convention of the Association for Educational Communications and Technology, Anaheim, CA. (ED 383 317)

Longman, P. J. (1997). The janitor stole my job: New software is expanding competition for white-collar jobs. *U.S. News & World Report* 123:21, 50–52.

Marquardt, M. J. (1996). Cyberlearning: New possibilities for HRD. *Training & Development* 50:11, 56–57.

Martin, J. (1991). *Rapid application development.* Old Tappan, NJ: Macmillan.

Milheim, W. (1997). Instructional design issues for electronic performance support systems. *British Journal of Educational Technology* 28:2, 103–110.

Nieveen, N., Akker, J.V.D., and Plomp, T. (1994). *Exploration of computer-assisted curriculum development.* Paper presented at the annual meeting of the American Educational Research Association, New Orleans. (ED 374 775)

Passmore, D. L., and Lin, V. (1997). *Definition of EPSS.* < http://milkman.cac.psu.edu/ ~ cx118/epss/epss.html >

Raybould, B. (1995a). *Job aid: When to use an EPSS.*
< http://www.astd.org/library/epss.htm >

Raybould, B. (1995b). Making a case for EPSS. *Innovations in Education and Training International* 32:1, 65–69.

Raybould, B. (1995c). Performance support engineering: An emerging development methodology for enabling organizational learning. *Performance Improvement Quarterly* 8:1, 7–22.

Reeves, T. (1996). *Do you need an EPSS?* < http://itech1.coe.uga.edu/EPSS/Need.html >

Rosenberg, M. J. (1995). Performance technology, performance support, and the future of training: A commentary. *Performance Improvement Quarterly* 8:1, 94–99.

Rossett, A. (1991). Electronic job aids. *Data Training* 10:7, 24–29.

Rummler, G. A., and Brache, A. P. (1992). Transforming organizations through Human Performance Technology. In H. D. Stolovitch and E. J. Keeps (eds.), *Handbook of Human Performance Technology: A comprehensive guide for analyzing and solving performance problems in organizations.* San Francisco: Jossey-Bass.

Scales, G. R., and Yang, C. (1993). *Perspectives on electronic performance support systems.* Paper presented at the conference of the Eastern Educational Research Association, Clearwater, FL. (ED 354 883)

Sherry, L., and Wilson, B. (1996). Supporting human performance across disciplines: A converging of roles and tools. *Performance Improvement Quarterly* 9:4, 19–36.

Stevens, G. H., and Stevens, E. F. (1995). Designing EPSS tools: Talent requirements. *Performance & Instruction* 34:2, 9–11.

Thomas, B. E., Baron, J. P., and Schmidt, W. T. (1995). *Evaluating a performance support environment for knowledge workers.*
< http//:www.cecer.army.mil/kws/tho_know.thm >

Villachica, S. W., and Stone, D. L. (1998a). CORNERSTONE: A case study of a large-scale performance support system. In P. J. Dean and D. E. Ripley (eds.), *Performance improvement interventions: Performance technologies in the workplace.* Washington, DC: International Society for Performance Improvement.

Villachica, S. W., and Stone, D. L. (1998b). Rapid application development for performance technology: Five strategies to deliver better interventions in less time. In P. J. Dean and D. E. Ripley (eds.), *Performance improvement interventions: Performance technologies in the workplace.* Washington, DC: International Society for Performance Improvement.

Witt, C. L., and Wager, W. (1994). A comparison of instructional systems design and electronic performance support systems design. *Educational Technology* 34:6, 20–24.

CHAPTER TWENTY-FOUR

Workplace Design
for Creative Thinking

Lynn Kearny
Phyl Smith

Human performance technologists have an investment in helping people perform at their best. People's performance starts with their invisible thinking and becomes their visible action. When their thinking is impaired, the value of their performance will likely be impaired as well. Even when performers understand their work goals, job design, priorities, and products, their physical work environment can easily block their best performance (Smith and Kearny, 1994).

We have all experienced this situation, but the impacts of our physical work environments on our thinking and our performance tend to be ignored. Because both thinking and most environmental interference are invisible, this connection is easy to overlook. People consistently say, "I can't think in this place" and "I'll have to take this work home to get anything done."

The authors gathered information about customs and trends in international work environments from colleagues in the Environmental Design Research Association. Information and observations about North American and northern European work environments were provided, respectively, by Francis Duffy of London and by Andreas van Wagenberg of Eindhoven University, The Netherlands. Information about eastern European work environments was provided by Lubomir Popov of the University of Wisconsin–Milwaukee. Information about work environments in India was provided by Vikas Narayan of New Delhi.

THE SITUATION

The need for good physical ergonomics, or body-to-equipment design, has long been recognized by industrial engineers who have needed to design blue-collar work environments for safe, improved manual labor. In recent years, physical ergonomics has also been recognized as a serious business issue in white-collar work environments (see, for example, Becker and Steele, 1994; Ostrom, 1994) primarily because of the physical injuries that employees have suffered from ill-fitting furniture and equipment.

However, even though our human bodies may now fit well in ergonomically correct desk chairs, our human minds are still forced to function in workplaces full of distractions that constantly interfere with thinking. Today, when optimizing employees' thinking is seen as a competitive imperative, organizations are beginning to pay attention to the importance of cognitive ergonomics (that is, the invisible fit between thinking and the sensory environment of sights, sounds, sensations, smell, temperature, and the like).

It does not take an architect, an interior designer, or a senior manager with a huge budget to make a meaningful difference in people's ability to think and perform well. This chapter describes how Human Performance Technology (HPT) professionals can help organizations optimize their workers' intelligence by using the design of the work environment to support effective thinking, both individually and collaboratively, especially among knowledge workers.

Rapid Change

Organizations are changing rapidly under the pressure to do more with less and still move faster than the competition. Organizations are casting about for ways of coping with all this change, through process reengineering, organizational redesign, training in creativity and innovation, and work teams used for every conceivable purpose. Survivors of downsizing are struggling with increased workloads, more responsibilities, and broader spans of control. People are being forced to learn how to adapt to constant change, and to do so under a continuing barrage of interruptions and new demands. Their physical work environment may well be adding to these interferences with their thinking.

Intellectual Capital

Creative thinking and the resulting innovations in applying creativity are now seen as the next dominant global economic focus that will grow out of the Information Age. Only organizations that recognize and develop creative approaches to their markets will survive all the new pressures. Therefore, the most valuable asset for organizations will be their intellectual capital. Productive thinking is the resource that organizations will use to convert technological complexity and fast-moving market changes into competitive products and services. Most organizations' investments in intellectual capital will be worth three times as much as their investments in machinery and equipment (Stewart, 1997).

Every day, organizations and business publications are engaged in discussing the issues of creativity, innovation, and intellectual capital, but very little attention is being paid to one key concern: How can workplaces be made to stop interfering with their people's productive thinking, especially when productive means *creative?*

Creativity

How can we address the elusive subject of creative thinking, and how can we establish that the workplace has any effect on it? Csikszentmihalyi (1996) identifies creative people as having the following characteristics:

- They have choice.
- They have easy access to knowledge.
- They pay full attention to knowledge.
- They enjoy complexity and are equally able to use both flexible, idea-generating (divergent) thinking and focused, problem-solving (convergent) thinking.
- They alternate between imagination and reality, and they pay attention to the connections between the two.
- They do not feel the need to invest attention in monitoring threats to their egos.

What is interesting about this list is that it is not concerned only with personal characteristics. Many of the items represent circumstances external to the person (for instance, having choice, having easy access to information, and being able to focus without distraction). Clearly, some of these circumstances can be provided—or impeded—by the way the workplace is set up. Creativity is limited or enhanced according to the constraints built into the workplace, and according to whether these constraints allow individuals the flexibility to provide themselves with the external circumstances—the environment—they need.

THE PROBLEM

Organizations use performance improvement techniques, from training and technology to teamwork and communication, with the goal of improving their people's ability to think and act productively. What organizations must start doing now is to use their next most important resource, the work environment, to support this crucial goal.

Organizations waste money when they place people in a work environment that interferes with their productivity. Not only is people's thinking hampered, the organization's everyday operations are also slowed. Most organizations are unaware of the resulting financial losses, and so no one is accounting for them on balance sheets or income statements, and yet workplace interference with performance continues to drain people's energy and focus, year after year, like an invisible tax. How does this happen?

Performance

Every workplace is full of sensory stimuli. Sounds hit our ears, and movements catch our eyes. Some stimuli are work-related; others are not. Our invisible mental work, thinking, begins with the reception and processing of the available sensory stimuli. These are our first steps toward visible action: our performance. Our next step is to decide whether we will invest any of our very limited attention in a particular stimulus. Do we hold on to this information, or do we ignore it? We also have to use our attention to search for the book or paper we need, a work surface to spread our materials on, or a place to store a project not currently being worked on. Another hook for our attention is our need to keep finding the person with whom we must interact and the place where we can sit for a quiet discussion. People find all these different kinds of demands on attention distracting, time-wasting, annoying, and stressful—in short, problematic. Because distracted, stressed people are not as productive as focused people, the organization also suffers (Smith and Kearny, 1994).

Paying attention means using what cognitive scientists call *working memory*, or short-term memory, which is the part of memory of which we are most aware while we are working. Working memory is our information processor. We invest our attention in a piece of information, think about it, and determine what action to take.

Miller and Simon have established the limits of working memory at seven plus or minus two small bits of information, or five large and complex "chunks" of information (Miller, 1956). The size of a chunk seems to be influenced by our level of expertise. When we have to think about more chunks than our capacity allows, we lose our effectiveness as thinkers, and the quality of our decisions drops dramatically (Simon, 1979). When we are presented with some of the distracting stimuli already described, we may well push aside work-related chunks of information and shift our attention to the distractions. Afterward, we must take time to find our lost train of thought and become focused on it again. Frequent interruptions, and our adaptations to them, drain the energy we should be investing in our work. Csikszentmihalyi (1996) believes that we are all very much alike in our mental capacity for processing information;

our greatest difference, in terms of our creative use of mental energy, lies in how much uncommitted attention each has for dealing with new information, given that there are limits to how much one person can attend to at any one time, and given that survival takes precedence.

Performance Variables

In analyzing a workspace to improve productivity, an HP technologist should focus on three performance variables:

1. Routine versus complex work

2. Screening behavior

3. The need for protection or stimulation

Routine Versus Complex Work. Routine work is defined as tasks that are familiar to the performer and that have well-known steps with well-defined outcomes. Many clerical and manufacturing tasks quickly become routine. The more routine a task is, the less attention is needed for doing it, and the less likely the worker is to be seriously interrupted by random distractions.

Complex work is defined as tasks that may be unfamiliar to the performer, who may have to figure out what steps to take in order to accomplish these tasks. Complex tasks usually involve finding and integrating new information, as in researching and writing a report, or conducting a front-end analysis. The more complex the task is, the more the performer may need to be protected from distractions.

Screening Behavior. Even with no conscious awareness of this performance factor, people can instantly recognize their own particular screening tendencies, as well as those of their co-workers (Mehrabian, 1976). In the authors' experience, screening behavior is probably the most important performance variable in the workplace. People with high screening abilities are generally able to ignore or screen out such sensory stimuli as sounds and sights that do not contribute to the task at hand. For example, a high screener can usually be comfortable writing a report at an open work table in a noisy reception area.

People with low screening abilities have more difficulty ignoring random sights and sounds. They tend to react quickly to each stimulus and allow their thinking to be interrupted by it. Low screeners are easily distracted and often try to work alone, in closed conference rooms or in quiet areas at home.

The Need for Protection or Stimulation. People can become bored and prone to committing errors while performing routine work because it requires less attention than they have available, and so they are more likely to welcome distractions or even search for them, either where they are working or elsewhere (for example, by listening to a radio while processing forms). The stimulation helps them "stay with" the task (Steele, 1973; Goodrich, 1986).

However, when an employee is trying to integrate a great deal of information and many constraints into a new configuration, with an unclear goal and no clear procedures, his or her capacity for attention is already at its limit. People who screen poorly find that an overheard conversation in the neighboring cubicle demands their attention and reduces their productivity.

It is easy to understand why people have difficulty getting their daily work done, not to mention being creative and working well with others, if we picture the distractions created by the typical crowded, noisy, cluttered work environment. There is little storage, work surfaces are buried in materials, and there is no place to meet for a quiet discussion, much less a confidential one. It is also easy to identify the sources of the heavy stress that develops for many people as they try to work in this kind of environment. The bottom line is that interferences from the workplace waste people's valuable time and cost organizations large amounts of time and money.

Impact on Performance

Organizations invest their resources in recruiting intelligent, experienced people, modeling competence, training, and providing their people with current information. Using people to produce useful ideas and innovations requires them to think in complex ways—that is, in ways that are particularly exploratory and creative.

Creative thinking is of two major types. In *divergent* thinking, the thinker is searching widely for new information and new approaches to the expansion of existing knowledge. In *convergent* thinking, the thinker is focusing on how best to combine the most useful elements of newly collected data with information already in the thinker's possession, so as to produce an effective new solution. We are constantly cycling back and forth between divergent and convergent thinking. To think well, we need workspaces that support each kind of thinking.

For example, we start thinking divergently when we are asked to develop a new marketing campaign. We gather information about possible target markets, demographics, and customer preferences from all our resources—the Internet, competitors' materials, and our team members. While working divergently with our team members to explore and generate ideas, we need a work area where we can all gather comfortably, post ideas and information for easy viewing, and see each other as we discuss our issues.

Our next step is to think convergently, so as to integrate our new material with what we already know about the organization's goals and constraints. The more complex, ill-defined, and unfamiliar our task is (and note that creativity and innovation by definition involve the unfamiliar and the ill defined), the more we need protection from distractions while trying to do work that requires focusing and integration. If we do not have adequate work surfaces on which to lay out all our work, or if we do not have enough protection from visual and auditory distractions, we will not be able to stay focused on our task, and we will have trouble producing coherent, well-integrated ideas.

Once our target market and general approach have been selected, we may need to think divergently again. We may seek input from other team members, do some benchmarking, and conduct Internet research to find effective approaches to marketing tasks. Then we shift back to convergent thinking as we integrate what we have learned and flesh out the marketing plan.

Teamwork and Collaboration

Organizations often mistakenly think of their people's work as either all collaborative teamwork or all individual work. This view can result in the design of work areas for either one type of activity or the other. In reality, people often perform both types of work and need different workspace supports for each type. Even with teamwork, not everything is accomplished in a group setting. A large proportion of team members' total time is spent on individual team-directed tasks. These may involve researching, developing ideas from the group into more specific proposals, writing reports, or communicating and negotiating with other groups.

If team members frequently need to work face to face, their work areas either should be very close together or should be in a common area with seating, work surfaces, electronic connections for data access and conference calling, enough privacy for confidentiality, and storage space for materials. Similarly, if a group is assigned to a common work area as its primary workspace, each member should also have some type of individual space to use. Each person must have adequate personal work surfaces, storage, and protection from noise and other distractions to support productive focusing on separate tasks.

An exception to these requirements might occur in an organization with an effective electronic infrastructure containing groupware tools to foster communication, idea generation, and dialogue. Such a system may require that employees meet face to face only when initiating projects and on other occasions, as necessary. Generally, however, physical proximity is an important factor in successful collaboration.

Ergonomics

Why not just require people to toughen up, ignore the distractions, and adapt to whatever workspaces they are given? Indeed, workplaces are often designed on the assumption that people will adapt their natural mental and physical processes to their particular environments.

This assumption ignores the fact that people's constant adapting of their natural behavior demands their energy and drains the supply they need for work.

Some degree of easy adaptation may be part of a usefully flexible attitude, but too much forced adaptation can create ongoing stress that culminates in illness and absence. The least stressful work behavior is the most natural. When organizations understand and incorporate both physical and cognitive ergonomic supports in workplaces, they will no longer be paying for interference from nonproductive sources of stress.

Physical Ergonomics. If an individual were to be asked, today, "What gets in the way of your working most easily?" the answer would most likely involve the physical, active part of performance. Good physical ergonomics has become a workplace requirement. Because physical actions are easily visible, organizations have learned how repeated unnatural movements can strain and injure people's muscles and impede their performance. A related common source of injury is adaptive behavior: people's often unconscious response to ill-fitting chairs, as well as to poorly placed work surfaces and equipment. Adaptation creates physical stress and leads to joint or back problems, which can be a basis for legal action. To prevent physical interference with performance, organizations now realize they must support individuals' different sizes and natural movements. They require furniture and equipment manufacturers to make products that are adjustable. Many organizations also train their people to take responsibility for their own ergonomic comfort and safety.

Cognitive Ergonomics. Just as the body must be supported in a physical work environment, so must the brain be supported in a mental work environment. Without an understanding of how the mostly invisible sensory environment affects people's ability to think, organizations continue to allow poor cognitive ergonomics to obstruct overall cognitive performance. Settings in which this is allowed to occur routinely force people to think less efficiently and less creatively.

Let us now examine a method for developing a workplace that supports thinking instead of interfering with it. The steps in this kind of development are *analysis, design and production, implementation,* and *evaluation.*

ANALYSIS

Establish Value

How can the HP professional estimate the costs of a workplace that interferes with performance, as well as the potential benefits of overcoming these interferences? Three methods can provide an effective way of examining these financial impacts when hard data are not available:

1. In the *work group member estimate method,* if the six members of a work group estimate that workplace interference is causing each of them to waste approximately an hour a day, then the group's weekly loss is thirty hours. An average wage of $25 per hour plus a 30 percent load equals $32.50 per hour. Thirty hours a week at $32.50 per hour equals $975 per week, or $50,700 per year (Smith and Kearny, 1994).

2. In the *Demarco and Lister* method, the amount of time in which people are present but not producing (because of one kind of interruption or another) is called *body time.* Body time is separated from the amount of time in which people are steadily producing, which is called *brain time.* When brain time is reasonably high (approximately 40 percent of total paid time), the work environment is supporting performance; anything less indicates that people are being subjected to excessive distractions and are producing at a reduced level. To estimate the cost of the distractions, whatever value the organization usually assigns to people's paid work time is assigned to any body time that exceeds 60 percent of total paid time (Demarco and Lister, 1987).

3. The *BOSTI study method* (Brill, 1985) was a seven-year, seventy-office study undertaken by the Buffalo Organization for Social and Technological Innovation (BOSTI) to measure the effect of the physical environment on productivity. This method showed that work environments correctly designed to meet the needs of their occupants at all levels can increase their job performance by 5 percent to 15 percent of their annual salaries with payoff of the investment in two years.

Note that all three of these methods deal only with loss of time and productivity, as calculated on the basis of salary costs. But what is the best way to estimate the cost of lost opportunities when an organization is unable to innovate quickly enough or respond creatively enough because its people are too distracted to think well or are too hampered by the environment to work well in teams? If the organization is currently assigning value to the cost of lost opportunities, its own figures should be folded into any cost-benefit estimates that involve improvements to the work environment.

Identify Variables

Several key variables should be included:

- How the workplace affects teamwork and collaboration
- How the workplace affects individual work
- How the workplace affects both team and individual creativity
- How the workplace affects growth of the organization's intellectual capital
- How the workplace can be used to support people's optimal performance

The people actually doing the work are the best sources of information. The more they are involved in the environmental change process, the more favorable the results will be.

Ask Questions

Educate First. It is essential to develop a common language to be used by everyone, across all departments: management, facility management, organization development, human resources, technology, engineering, and finance. All the organization's people, as participants in a cross-functional collaborative team planning how their workplace can support creative performance, must be able to use the same concepts, understandings, and words when talking about work, thinking, performance, and work environments. This approach also helps people acknowledge the interdependence of different styles and needs. Using uniform terminology does not require training; terms and concepts can be introduced and explained by the HP professional during data-collection meetings, described next.

Gather Data. After clearly identifying how the organization functions, the HP professional should get oriented by wandering around and quietly observing what is happening. Notes should be made on these observations, and they should be clarified as necessary during subsequent interviews.

Groups and individuals should be interviewed directly, but distribution of questionnaires should be avoided because they are potentially confusing and frequently superficial; missing information often minimizes their usefulness. Personal interviews offer an immediate opportunity not only for clarifying specific points but also for expanding crucial information. Providing people the opportunity to participate freely, face to face, can create the essential sense of significance that is basic to the acceptance of change.

It is useful to interview small groups (under eight people) first and then follow up by interviewing the individual group members to discover valuable additional information. Two wise, timesaving moves are to quickly define the common-language concepts and terms while asking questions and to present the earlier observations and ask for a group's feedback in order to check the accuracy of these impressions. Exhibit 24.1 presents some sample questions for a workplace-analysis interview.

During the life of the project, an alert HP technologist will look for ways to improve performance still more. Asking people about what gets in the way of their doing their best work can sometimes produce answers that are related more to the design of their jobs than to their workspaces. The HP technologist must be sure to separate these two issues at the time of the interview so that the specific data for workspace support and interference will be accurate. However, it can be valuable to clarify work goals, priorities, and products later in the same interview. Then, as necessary, work processes as well as workspaces can be improved.

Exhibit 24.1. Sample Questions for Workplace-Analysis Interview.

I. What work do you do?

II. Is your work more routine or more complex? How do you do it?
What do you need in order to do it?

III. Is it easy or hard for you to screen out distractions?
Would you say that you tend to be a high screener or a low screener?

IV. What gets in the way of your doing work most easily?

V. What environmental supports do you need?
  a. When performing routine work?
  b. If performing complex creative work?
    1. When thinking divergently to collect new information, what resources or support do you need for stimulation?
    2. When thinking convergently to combine new information with old, what resources or support do you need for focusing?
    3. When collaborating in teamwork, what support do you need for working divergently? convergently?
    4. When working individually on complex creative work, what are your strongest skills? What gets in the way of your using them most easily? What can best support you in using them?
    5. What most motivates you?

VI. How much time in an average day do you think you may waste because of what gets in your way? To what extent is stress a factor?

VII. What are your performance-support priorities?

DESIGN AND PRODUCTION

In the analysis phase, the HP technologist has gathered data identifying ways in which the workplace hampers productivity, especially creative thinking. The job in this phase is to design solutions for any problems that have been identified. Solutions will be most effective if the performers participate in a feedback process during the design phase.

At this stage, the HP technologist will have engaged in some divergent thinking while collecting information and will have discovered some solutions for providing support. Convergent thinking can now be used to produce new ideas for a valuable new product: a performance-based workplace.

The role of creative performance in establishing corporate position and profit is obvious. No matter what kind of workplace people are using to accomplish their work, from traditional settings to settings for telecommuting, their thinking processes and their needs do not change. Csikszentmihalyi (1996) provides some valuable input for this phase:

- Creativity motivators include the sense of freedom, autonomy, challenge, and internal rewards.

- Too many demands on attention and time are obstacles to creativity.

- The greatest need is for the ability to manage the quality of working time.

- The best work environment is a dynamic one that can be manipulated to enhance creativity.

Using a common language to talk about the workplace and performance, the HP technologist can now collaborate with the people involved to plan a performance-based workplace that will provide various levels of stimuli to support people's different thinking needs. Figures 24.1 and 24.2 show floor plans for a performance-based workplace (these are only examples, of course, and should not be used as templates for a workplace design). A performance-based workplace should take account of the specific needs of the group in question; a "one size fits all" approach should not be used.

Each of these two sample workplaces includes a higher-stimulus "idea" area, to support collaborative, idea-generating divergent thinking by supporting both casual and planned interactions and discussions among individuals and team members. These higher-stimulus areas provide the following elements:

- Changing displays of idea-generating materials, to make tacit information explicit

- Technological tools for accessing information resources

- White boards, pinboard areas, layout surfaces, stools, chairs, and coffee

Each of the sample workplaces also includes a lower-stimulus "focusing" area, to support problem-solving, convergent thinking by providing the following elements:

- Individual and teamwork areas that are protected from the interference of visual and auditory distractions

- Easy-to-move furnishings and equipment for teams' flexible use in support of their work

- Accommodations for people's differing needs with respect to personal territory

People should be helped to understand how to use a performance-based workplace. For example, they can be encouraged to view it as a participatory, self-organizing tool, a place in which they are expected to challenge conventional ideas and one another and to assume responsibility for developing self-management skills in performance. They can accomplish these goals by taking the following actions:

- Identifying and making explicit what gets in the way of their best performance, and eliminating or reducing these interferences

- Determining the stimulation levels they require in support of their different modes of creative thinking

- Choosing different levels of stimulation in support of the diverse phases of their thinking while collaborating with co-workers

Figure 24.1. Sample 1: Floor Plan for a Performance-Based Workplace.

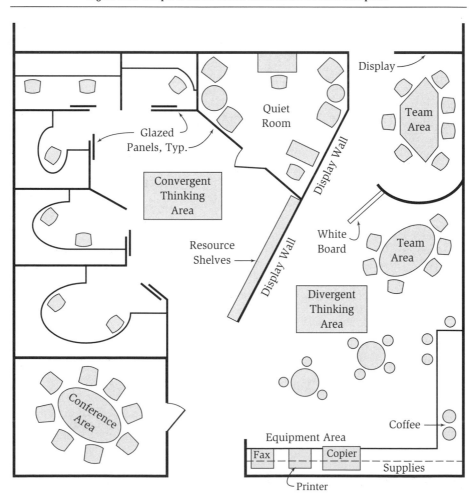

Note: The abbreviation *TYP* stands for *typical;* this standard abbreviation used in architecture and design indicates that the description of one particular feature (dimensions, materials, location, installation, and so forth), usually on a drawing or in a list, applies to all other similar features used in the same project.

These actions will go far in creating and maintaining a flexible work environment for everyone. These actions will also be supported as people decide what their mutual goals are, evaluate their decisions, resolve their conflicts, and divert their egos into finding as much reward in choice and in the ability to control their performance as they previously may have found in the status symbol of a workspace that was assigned according to their hierarchical positions in the organization. As these actions are taken and supported, people will increase their ability to add useful knowledge to the organization's fund of intellectual capital.

The performance-based workplace is also an ideal solution for people working in alternative, out-of-the-office ways (teaming, "hot-desking," telecommuting, and so on) that do not require individual workspaces. When these freewheeling

Figure 24.2. Sample 2: Floor Plan for a Performance-Based Workplace.

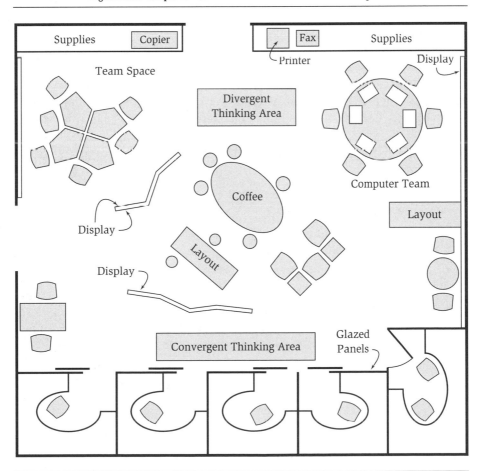

people periodically schedule work time in the home office, they must to be able to use it in the most productive way possible. Will they be exchanging new information and ideas from the field with other people? If so, they will need to use a higher-stimulus "idea" area. Will they be formulating individual reports on their recent work in the field? If so, they will need a lower-stimulus "focusing" area. When the home office base offers a choice of stimulation levels, they can be responsible for selecting the one most supportive of performance.

IMPLEMENTATION

Implementation does not wait until analysis and design have been completed; it begins while a common language is being developed at the data-gathering phase, and it continues throughout data analysis and design. As people begin to understand the influence of the workplace on work, thinking, and productivity, they implement small-scale changes themselves each day.

A large-scale workspace change often occurs in several stages, according to its complexity and the number of people involved. This kind of change is politically and mechanically complex, and it requires collaboration with a number of partners: organizational leaders, facilities managers or property managers, the relevant departmental managers, the performers themselves, and consulting specialists. Several suggestions can be offered for the implementation phase:

- Collect data and develop broad criteria that define a performance-based workplace.

- Use a feedback process with all performers to check accuracy of the data and secure their buy-in.

- Estimate the costs of lost time, as well as other costs, that are being imposed by the existing workplace.

- Secure management's approval for redesigning the workplace in order to build the organization's competitiveness.

- Find a facilities manager who is knowledgeable about cognitive ergonomics, or educate one, or recommend a workplace designer who is trained in performance-based workplace design.

- Leverage this person's expertise to design a flexible, performance-based workplace on the basis of the criteria established by analysis.

EVALUATION

After the new design has been in place for three to six months, it will be time to evaluate the changes. The following questions can be posed to performers:

- How do you as an individual use the workplace differently from the ways you used it before?
- How have the changes affected your ability to do your job? Is it easier or harder to do a good job?
- How have the changes affected the way you feel about doing your work?
- Are you getting more work done now? Are you getting less done?
- Is there still anything that gets in your way?
- How have the changes affected your work with your team?
- Is it easier or harder for your team to do a good job?
- What ideas do you have for making your workplace even more supportive?

The following questions can be posed to management:

- What changes are you seeing in overall performance?
- How are teams working together now, by comparison with how they worked before?
- What changes are you seeing in the quality of ideas, decisions, and information being produced?
- What changes have you noticed in the number of complaints and the level of absenteeism?
- What, if anything, is still missing?

COGNITIVE ERGONOMICS: BENEFITS AND PRECAUTIONS

The key tool for creating intellectual capital is the human mind and its thinking processes. A workplace that offers appropriate physical and sensory support for thinking has enormous potential to help organizations challenge their assumptions about the work they need to accomplish and the changes they need to make in order to optimize their workers' creative thinking. A few forward-looking organizations are just beginning to redesign their workplaces to these ends (see "Blueprints for Business," 1997). Such organizations, concerned about increasing their intellectual capital, encourage creative thinking by recognizing the need for and providing high-quality cognitive ergonomics in the workplace.

Nevertheless, many facilities groups and many designers are not knowledgeable about cognitive ergonomics. The facilities and property management functions have traditionally been isolated; they seldom have a direct connection with the strategic direction of the company. These functions are typically perceived as cost centers to be minimized, and the measure of their performance is their ability to lower the square-footage cost of the workplace. Because these functions have not been seen as rich resources for improving the organization's overall performance, they have not been asked to take responsibility for affecting the performance of the people they serve.

This situation is changing somewhat in organizations that are asking facilities to create work areas that will increase interaction among workers, house teams in group areas that will enhance teamwork, or provide areas for convergent thinking. Most facilities managers, however, still see their role as one of aggressively cutting costs. As a result, facilities groups often participate, unintentionally, in marginalizing their own function and have become a major target for outsourcing.

But there is an attendant opportunity: surviving facilities groups are often looking for a chance to become strategic partners with business leaders. These groups can be partners for the HP technologist as well but may be unaware of the potential that they hold in their own hands. To work with these partners, the HP technologists may need to help them recognize and understand certain issues: complex versus routine work, limited capacity for attention, screening behavior, and the environmental supports needed to promote effective thinking.

AN INTERNATIONAL PERSPECTIVE ON WORK ENVIRONMENTS

North America

North America, constantly experimenting, is seen as having the world's most influential workplace designers, and perhaps the most submissive end users of workspaces. Here, strong developers build for efficiency and maximum profit, with the goal of accommodating large workforces. Building cost per person is low. Less attention is paid to the human quality of the work environment. Workspaces tend to be uniform in color and spatial arrangements. Workers seem to accept wide-open floor plans, cubicles, and workstations far away from windows. The value of disciplined work is very important in this culture.

Northern Europe

Workplaces in the United Kingdom, Scandinavia, Germany, Belgium, The Netherlands, and Luxembourg reflect a different set of values. Rather than the corporation dictating how the worker works, or the developer calling the shots, it is the user who is influential. There is much less belief in the organization as a corporate or powerful entity and much more belief in the importance of the individual as the core of society. Organizational goals are concerned with efficiency from the top down, and with effectiveness from the bottom up. Concerns focus on the best uses of time and on the need to stay in touch with the outside world.

The typical building is complex, expensive, thin rather than deep, and of low density. It has many cores rather than a single core, is inefficient rather than efficient, is environmentally sensitive, has many amenities, and is designed so that individuals have more control over their own environments. European offices tend to be alike and not reflective of hierarchy. There are often rows of glazed-glass-enclosed individual offices, with group work arranged outside. European offices also tend to be more informal, less controlled, and more accidental. Northern European countries place greater importance on the quality of the office environment and have generated "workers' councils." These groups have the statutory right to negotiate for the quality of life for office workers, who in turn are able to insist on those things that make them feel better (for example, having a direct view of the outdoors, being in a room by oneself, having a door that can be shut and a window that can be opened).

Alternative office-layout concepts are a hot topic, and facilities managers are expected to create solutions that meet the needs of different teams. Sometimes layouts are open, and sometimes they are more closed. A frequent layout uses small, one-person rooms with windows, for concentration and brainstorming. Working from home is increasingly popular, and there is a continuing need to educate people about working in these new ways.

Eastern Europe

Workers performing routine tasks are usually placed in desk-to-desk arrangements in big groups, in tight environments. Creative workers are often assigned closed-door offices for two, and these are usually about two hundred square feet in size; departmental managers, full professors, and political functionaries usually have offices of this type. Professionals who need to do considerable reading are also accommodated in offices that accommodate no more than two.

Given the shortage of space, people are allowed to work at home, reporting to the office at certain times for coordination of duties. There, a person may have a "hot desk" (usually in a room cluttered with other desks). In some organizations, people have only conference rooms, used on a permanent weekly schedule by different groups.

Some work requires teams of five to ten people (occasionally twelve to fourteen) to work together. If there are more than seven or eight people in one room, smaller informal groups may emerge, breaking down the collegial team spirit and causing potential conflicts.

India

The typical Indian workplace can best be described as an open office with permanently allocated seating spaces. Senior bosses have enclosed cabins at the ends, with windows. Junior staff members are placed in the middle, sometimes with no access to a window. These workplaces are all increasingly dependent on technology; personal computers, e-mail, and the Internet are now very much a part of the Indian work culture.

SUMMARY

HP technologists miss an important opportunity if they redesign goals, motivation systems, jobs, and work processes without paying attention to the pervasive negative impact of work environments on performance. Redesigning people's work environments to provide optimum support for their best performance is basic to the effective practice of Human Performance Technology.

References

Becker, F., and Steele, F. (1994). *Workplace by design: Mapping the high-performance workscape.* San Francisco: Jossey-Bass.

Blueprints for Business. (1997, Nov. 3). *Business Week,* pp. 112–132.

Brill, M. (1985). U*sing office design to increase productivity.* Buffalo, NY: Buffalo Organization for Social and Technological Innovation.

Csikszentmihalyi, M. (1996). *Creativity: Flow and the psychology of discovery and invention.* New York: HarperCollins.

Demarco, T., and Lister, T. (1987). *Peopleware.* New York: Dorset House.

Goodrich, R. (1986). The perceived office: The office environment as experienced by its users. In J. Wineman (ed.), *Behavioral issues in office design.* New York: Van Nostrand Reinhold.

Mehrabian, A. (1976). *Public places and private spaces.* New York: Basic Books.

Miller, G. A. (1956). The magical number of seven, plus or minus two: Some limits on our capacity for processing information. *Psychological Review* 63:2, 81–89.

Ostrom, L. (1994). *Creating the ergonomically sound workplace.* San Francisco: Jossey-Bass.

Simon, H. A. (1979). *Models of thought.* New Haven: Yale University Press.

Smith, P., and Kearny, L. (1994). *Creating workplaces where people can think.* San Francisco: Jossey-Bass.

Steele, F. (1973). *Physical settings and organization development.* Reading, MA: Addison-Wesley.

Stewart, T. (1997). *Intellectual capital: The new wealth of organizations.* New York: Currency.

HUMAN PERFORMANCE INTERVENTIONS OF AN INSTRUCTIONAL NATURE

The recommended first step in designing a human performance (HP) improvement intervention is analysis, to help determine the nature of the performance gap. If the root causes are environmental or motivational in nature, then the direction that the HP project takes is toward the design of interventions of a noninstructional nature. If the performance gap is partly due to lack of skills or knowledge on the part of performers, then the HP practitioner turns to instruction or training as a means of achieving the desired results.

Part Four focuses on instructional approaches to achieving performance improvement in organizational, educational, and work settings. The seven chapters comprising this part describe a variety of instructional vehicles and provide basic guidelines for their design and use, but the central concern is still what occurs after the instructional event has taken place.

Learning from instruction is often a very costly means of achieving desired outcomes, and so the chapters in Part Four treat instruction strictly from a performance perspective. Moreover, instruction is only as effective as its implementation and support systems, and its value depends on the degree to which on-the-job conditions foster and reinforce its transfer and use. These two themes underlie all seven chapters, which constitute a unique group in that their treatment of the topics is so thoroughly oriented toward performance.

The first two chapters deal with live instruction, which is generally associated with immediate, synchronous settings. Both present comprehensive descriptions of group-based instruction and offer guidelines for employing this form of instruction to obtain the highest degree of transfer to the work setting. Many of the small-group activities discussed in the second of these two chapters will also be applicable to noninstructional contexts and needs.

The third chapter of Part Four focuses on mentoring systems, which often include instruction. They go far beyond instruction, however, to build lasting relationships with major performance implications.

The next two chapters deal with multimedia learning systems—an area of great interest to organizations and educational systems throughout the world, given the apparently almost universal belief that great learning efficiencies can be achieved through multimedia technologies. Each of these two chapters focuses on a specific theme. The first addresses issues of learning effectiveness through design principles. The second centers attention on the hardware, software, and communications technology involved in multimedia learning. Both deliver a consistent message and a set of cautions for HPT practitioners seeking to achieve on-the-job performance through multimedia.

The sixth chapter describes an instructional system that makes use of available resources. It deals with structured on-the-job training systems, which use an organization's personnel in carefully designed ways to create competent performance right in the workplace. The emphasis on use of existing resources in a structured manner to achieve large performance gains is a particularly powerful message to organizations and countries where funds to improve performance are limited.

The final chapter of Part Four describes instructional systems that offer a potential increase in learning opportunities. Distributed learning systems are no longer the exclusive domain of university or state education departments. They are now increasingly used by large corporations and business consortia to deliver instruction to worksites. Their demonstrated ability to improve performance is the theme of this chapter.

As before, the authors of the chapters in this part of the handbook are all recognized experts on the topics about which they have written. They are also devoted to making the instructional vehicles with which they deal take a strong performance orientation.

Readers of Part Four will find the overall approach to instruction handled in a manner rarely found elsewhere. This is the best slice of information currently available, but readers should expect radical changes and innovations in this arena over the next few decades. Although the instructional interventions presented here do not constitute an exhaustive or exclusive list, they are a good representation of the effective strategies that can be applied to virtually any context in the world.

CHAPTER TWENTY-FIVE

Live Classroom Instruction

Stephen L. Yelon

Human performance (HP) technologists travel many paths to solve performance problems. Those called *instructional designers* specialize in creating instructional solutions. They produce self-instruction, tutorials, simulations, on-the-job training, and classroom instruction (Mager, 1997). Trainers or instructors are the professionals who deliver the instruction. Thus classroom instruction is one type of solution for performance problems. Classroom instruction can be a powerful means to produce enhanced job performance.

WHAT IS CLASSROOM INSTRUCTION?

The purpose of classroom instruction is to teach workers the knowledge they require to perform on the job. There are three distinguishing attributes of classroom instruction:

1. A live instructor

2. A group of students

3. A location separated from the workplace

Group teaching by a live instructor differentiates classroom instruction from individualized instruction, self-instruction, and tutorials; separation from the workplace distinguishes classroom instruction from on-the-job training.

485

Most of us can picture ordinary classroom instruction. With interactive video used for global training, however, face-to-face live instruction has taken on new meaning. In synchronous virtual classrooms, instructors can "face" students in remote locations. In one typical configuration, an instructor can see and hear all the students on video monitors in her room while at the same time students can see the instructor and other students on monitors in their locations.

WHEN SHOULD CLASSROOM INSTRUCTION BE USED?

Classroom instruction has been and still is the most predominant form of instruction. Students, instructors, and employers expect and are accustomed to classroom instruction. Classroom instruction also has the economical potential of affecting many students at once (Gage and Berliner, 1991), yet it is understandable that some instructional designers may wish to avoid classroom instruction because of the expense and the inconvenience of developing instruction, providing trainers, producing materials, removing people from their work, and scheduling and arranging classrooms and equipment. Designers may also wish to avoid the negative images of a teacher presenting from a lectern and writing on a chalkboard. Well-meaning practitioners do not want to resurrect the feelings of embarrassment and boredom associated with meaningless lectures or with tests on isolated facts and useless skills.

Designers should not select classroom instruction by force of habit or circumstance, nor should they avoid it. Well-designed classroom instruction is a legitimate, creative, and rewarding choice for some performance problems. As such, designers may carefully choose classroom instruction as the best intervention for a particular type of performance problem. As shown in Figure 25.1, the thoughtful HP technologist first decides if instruction is the general solution to a performance problem and then decides if classroom instruction is the specific solution.

Is Instruction the Solution?

Designers choose instruction as a remedy when they observe three conditions (Mager and Pipe, 1997):

1. People lacking the skills or knowledge to do a job well

2. People needing to learn the required skill or knowledge

3. Job aids cannot provide the support or the learning necessary to perform the necessary task

In this chapter, we will use the Unique Products Corporation (UPC) as a recurring example of what goes into the design of classroom instruction. UPC creates

Figure 25.1. Deciding to Use Classroom Instruction.

Start with a performance problem

Is the solution instruction? See **Checklist 1**

No → Use alternate performance intervention → Exit

Yes ↓

Is classroom instuction possible? See **Checklist 2**

No → Use alternate instructional intervention → Exit

Yes ↓

Is classroom instuction preferable? See **Checklist 3**

No → Use alternate instructional intervention → Exit

Yes ↓

Plan to use classroom instruction for the appropriate instructional element.

↓

Exit

Checklist 1: When all yes, proceed
1. Workers lack worthwhile skill or knowledge?
2. Workers must learn skill or knowledge?
3. Learning too complex for job aid?

Checklist 2: When any yes, proceed for that element
1. Can each worker practice the performance in the classroom?
   a. Is practice realistic?
   b. Is moderate simulation good preparation for other practice?
   c. Does part practice enable more efficient outside complete practice?
2. Can instructors explain skill in the classroom?
3. Can instructors orient in the classroom?
4. Can instructors motivate in the classroom?

Checklist 3: When most yes, proceed. Compared to alternative instructional approaches, is classroom instruction likely to be more
1. effective?
   a. providing realistic practice?
   b. providing supervision and support?
2. accommodating of workers' differences?
3. flexible?
   a. providing momentary changes needed during the course?
4. affordable?
   a. providing a reasonable staff-to-participant ratio?
   b. accommodating all learners?
   c. providing efficient learning for all?
   d. avoiding costly and disruptive errors?
5. convenient in fitting time constraints?
6. agreeable to clients?

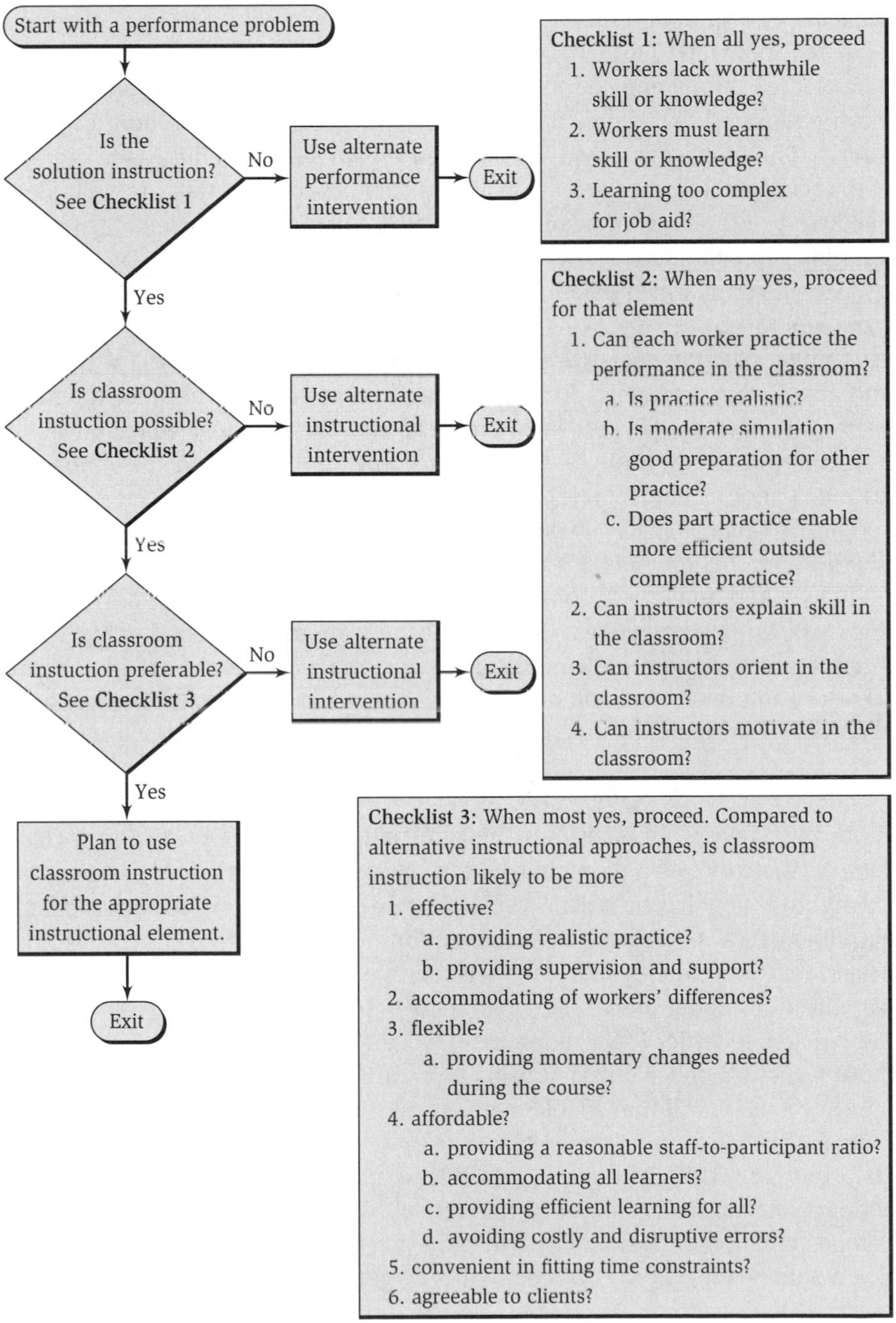

custom publications. Because each publication is unique, work demands vary. UPC managers conduct frequent meetings to gain agreement on publication processes, designs, and treatments.

When some top UPC managers became dissatisfied with the number of products created during one quarter, HP technologists at UPC investigated the situation and found that the managers were conducting the production meetings poorly. The managers talked too much in meetings, ignored ideas in conflict with their own, tolerated debate on routine items, permitted staff to repeat ideas needlessly, allowed team members to interrupt, let members evaluate and dismiss ideas prematurely, allowed some to dominate meetings, postponed timely decisions, summarized incompletely, ended without agreement, and allowed members to agree to decisions simply as a way to escape from meetings. Consequently, team members were unclear about decisions; they duplicated work and acted inappropriately. Some staff members were angry because the managers were not listening to them in the meetings. They complained continuously and did what they thought was best for the products, and the managers arranged additional meetings to handle unresolved problems.

The HP technologists concluded that if the managers could manage to conduct the production meetings more efficiently, they would be able to increase the speed and quality of production. The managers had to learn how to conduct task-oriented meetings. Because the steps involved in conducting a productive meeting were too complex for the managers to learn on the job and were beyond what a job aid alone could remedy, the HP technologists chose classroom instruction as the intervention for this performance problem.

Is Classroom Instruction Possible?

A designer chooses a specific form of instruction, such as self-instruction or classroom instruction, as a possible solution. Designers know that if practice in a classroom is possible, instructors can also probably administer other instructional activities (such as explanations, orientation, and motivation) in a classroom. Therefore, to decide if classroom instruction is a potential solution, designers ask questions about practice. Can students practice the skill in a classroom? Is the practice realistic? If not, does the practice nevertheless prepare learners for more realistic practice outside the classroom? If realistic practice is possible for part of the task, will that enable more efficient learning from complete practice outside the classroom (Yelon, 1992a)?

In this case, UPC instructors were able to arrange for individuals to practice conducting realistic meetings in a classroom. They were also able to explain and demonstrate in the classroom how to run a meeting. If they had found that practice was impossible in the classroom, they might have arranged to have students practice on the job.

Designers also consider logistical possibilities when selecting kinds of class-room instruction (such as laboratory instruction or live interactive video). De-signers may decide, for example, that it is possible to use live interactive video in the presence of six conditions:

1. A large number of learners at distant locations who need instruction.

2. Insurmountable obstacles (travel difficulties, bad weather, high costs, time away from work) to using a training center.

3. Staffing problems (for example, too few qualified instructors to make travel to the learners' locations efficient).

4. Availability of video equipment and technical support.

5. Ample development time (that is, double the normal time) to create highly structured lectures (Boettcher, 1997; Galindo, 1997).

6. A reasonable chance of success, given the ability to focus on learning over technology, advise students to be proactive, exploit the strength of video and graphics, collaborate with a support team, train everyone (in-cluding qualified facilitators) on site, plan for activity, provide for other means of communication (such as phone or e-mail), and present well-coordinated if not perfectly delivered lessons (Boettcher, 1997; Filipczak, 1997; Fredollino and Galindo, 1994; Predko, Spurgin, Galindo, and Gizinski, 1993).

Is Classroom Instruction Preferable?

If instructors can teach a desired performance in a classroom, then designers will ask if it should be in a classroom. Which form of instruction will generate realistic conditions for practice and best provide the needed supervision, feed-back, and support for learners? Which can handle a wide range of differences among learners? Which is most flexible in meeting the needs of individuals and the problems of the group? Which is most responsive to changing circumstances during instruction? Which is available when needed? Which fits the time con-straints? Which is most affordable? Which has the most cost-effective staff-to-participant ratio? Which can accommodate all the learners needing instruction? Which helps students learn most efficiently? In which approach are response errors least costly and least disruptive? Which is most agreeable to clients?

AT UPC, the staff found that, for this task, classroom instruction had more advantages than on-the-job training, tutorials, or self-instruction. Trainers could provide the most carefully sequenced and realistic practice conditions and the most flexible peer and staff supervision. Staff could provide tutorial help, man-agers could share useful individual experiences, and class simulations could ad-dress the unique problems shared by this group. A few instructors could teach all thirty managers at the same time, with only a few weeks of preparation.

Managers and supervisors readily accepted classroom instruction as long as it was timely, lectures were short, practice was plentiful, and trainers followed up with supervision on the job.

In summary, performance technologists decide to use classroom instruction by asking if the general solution to a performance problem is instruction, and if the specific solution is classroom instruction. To be chosen, classroom instruction must be possible and preferable.

ROLE OF CLASSROOM INSTRUCTION IN HPT

Does it seem contradictory that instructors teach in a room separate from a job site to help workers learn skills to use at that job site? This apparent contradiction is an illusion; well-designed classroom instruction is not an isolated intervention. It is part of a comprehensive, coordinated, and continuous system for performance change, one that includes instruction inside and outside the classroom, as well as intervention before and after formal instruction (Alderman, 1988; Beaudin, 1987; Broad, 1997). Classroom instruction includes preclass intervention, instruction in the classroom, instruction out of the classroom, and postclass intervention. Each phase has its own purpose.

Preclass Intervention

Before instruction begins, HP technologists engage workers and their supervisors to obtain information to make classroom instruction meaningful, transferable, and understandable. They assess and account for prerequisite ideas and skills and relate desired performance to participants' needs in a comfortable, nonthreatening manner. They encourage participants to prepare for instruction and remove barriers to transfer.

Instruction in the Classroom

Instructors combine instruction in and out of class so that students can learn the desired performance. The following eight elements of classroom instruction help produce retention and transfer (Gagné, Briggs, and Wager, 1992):

1. Motivation to learn the performance
2. Orientation to establish mental readiness to learn
3. Acquisition of knowledge
4. Successful application of knowledge through practice
5. Continuous improvement through feedback and revision
6. Integration of each performance with others learned
7. Motivation to use the performance
8. Evaluation of job readiness

Instruction Outside the Classroom

To supply the same eight elements, instructional technologists arrange experiences outside the classroom. There, designers emphasize any functions that are impossible inside the four walls of a classroom.

Postclass Intervention

After formal instruction is complete, instructional technologists maintain contact with workers and their supervisors to facilitate the transfer of learning (Alderman, 1988; Beaudin, 1987, Broad, 1997). In postclass intervention, instructional designers ensure that the former students stay interested in using the desired performance, perfect their skills, and remove barriers to their use.

Before training, the UPC designers gathered information about performance in meetings. They talked to managers and their supervisors to assess their prerequisites and to get meaningful instructional examples. To build motivation, designers also described the new performance to be learned and how performance would increase meetings' productivity. To reduce participants' anxiety, designers explained that learning would be quick and painless. In addition, to encourage students to prepare for instruction, designers asked them to choose their next series of meetings as course projects. They discussed ways to eliminate or work around possible roadblocks to using new meeting skills on the job.

To supplement classroom instruction, the UPC instructors arranged for managers to conduct real meetings under supervision. After class, instructors accompanied supervisors to observe managers conducting real meetings. After each observation, using a job aid, instructors led a discussion with managers and their supervisors about the managers' strengths and weaknesses. In addition, instructors asked managers and supervisors if anything was interfering with their use of the meeting skills they had learned. When the group discovered barriers, they explored ways to remove them.

Classroom instruction is part of a comprehensive approach to performance improvement. Designers must plan classroom instruction to render workers able and willing to perform and to arrange job conditions so that workers can use and want to use what they are learning.

MODELS OF CLASSROOM INSTRUCTION

According to their views of learning and of the task that learners must acquire, designers may employ various instructional models for classroom instruction. In *direct instruction* models (Gunter, Estes, and Schwab, 1995; Joyce and Weil, 1996), students learn specific skills and knowledge by means of instructor-controlled orientation, explanations, demonstrations, questioning, guided and independent practice, and feedback. *Nondirective instruction* models allow students to control the process of learning so that they can develop into confident, self-directed individuals. The premise of these models is that students can direct themselves (Joyce and Weil, 1996). The instructor attempts to understand the students' circumstances and helps them define, pursue, and evaluate their own objectives.

Whereas direct instruction emphasizes supplying students with information, *inductive thinking* models emphasize having students supply their own insights (Gunter, Estes, and Schwab, 1995; Joyce and Weil, 1996). Students learn thinking and problem solving by participating in carefully sequenced activities, using data to discover ideas. For example, to discover categories, teachers give data to students and direct them to list the data, group the data, and then label the groups. In further contrast to models focused on individual learners, *cooperative learning* models have students working in pairs or in larger groups, with consultation from a teacher (Gunter, Estes, and Schwab, 1995; Johnson and Johnson, 1990; Joyce and Weil, 1996; Aronson, Blaney, Sikes, and Snapp, 1978). The goal is to acquire knowledge by working in groups to answer questions, accomplish tasks, or investigate problems.

Situated in a different type of classroom, such as a laboratory or studio, the *cognitive apprenticeship* model (Rogoff, 1990; Schön, 1987) has students learn professional ways of thinking and acting. Students and teachers work side by side in the lab or studio, doing relatively realistic tasks. Students use the instructor as a model and as a coach. Along with performing the tasks, students must justify and evaluate their work.

There are many functional, research-based models for classroom instruction, which designers may apply as a whole or may use in combination. The choice depends on the objective, the time constraints, the students' ability and willingness to use the model, and the competence of the staff in implementing the model.

To promote learning the steps to start a meeting, a UPC instructor may directly explain, provide a reading, a video, a role-playing exercise, a guest interview, or a panel. The teacher may direct students to answer questions based on the explanation individually, then in pairs, and then with the whole group. Alternatively, using an inductive approach, the instructor may present a meeting situation and have students define the problem and seek the solution by themselves or in cooperation with other students. An instructor may guide students by sequencing activities or by listening and clarifying the students' analyses of their progress.

ELEMENTS OF CLASSROOM INSTRUCTION

Regardless of the specific model a classroom instructor chooses, instruction must foster each of the eight instructional elements already described. The instructor or the learner may supply the instructional elements directly or inductively, to individuals or to groups, in an ordinary classroom or in a special laboratory. Note that in Table 25.1 the name of each functional element and the resulting learner performance are grouped sequentially into categories of instructional introduction, core, and conclusion.

Table 25.1. Basic Elements of Classroom Instruction.

I. An instructional introduction contains elements to produce the following:
  A. Motivation to learn: Students know why they should learn to achieve the objective, where the performance is used, and the consequence of use.
  B. Orientation to instruction
    1. Objective: Students know what they will learn to do and how they will be evaluated.
    2. Overview: Students know the main parts of the performance, how the parts are related to each other, and where this performance fits into their jobs.
    3. Review of past: Students recall knowledge that they must keep in mind to learn this new performance.
    4. Agenda: Students know the order of the activities in this segment and why these activities were selected.
II. An instructional core contains elements to produce the following:
  A. Acquisition of essential knowledge for performance.
    1. Information: Students can recall and explain essential information needed to perform (that is, the situation in which the performance is needed, the steps to take when performing, the required feelings and attitudes while performing, and the facts, concepts, and principles needed to take each step properly).
    2. Demonstration: Students know and recognize the application of the essential knowledge.
  B. Application of essential knowledge, including practice, feedback, and revision: Students know how well they can apply their conception of the performance. Students know what they do well, what they do poorly, and what they should do to improve. Students know when more practice is needed and what sort of practice to pursue.
III. An instructional conclusion contains elements to produce the following:
  A. Integration of learning.
    1. Summary of main ideas: Students recall the main parts of the performance and the relationship of the parts.
    2. Objectives integrated with other segments: Students are aware of what they have learned to do, know how this performance relates to other objectives learned or to be learned, and where this performance fits into their work.
  B. Motivation to use the learning: Students know why they have learned this performance and why they should use it on the job.
  C. Evaluation of job readiness: Students know how well they have learned and how well they are prepared for on-the-job performance.

Introductory Elements

An introduction encourages and directs students. An introduction promotes motivation to learn and helps establish expectations about desired performance. It helps organize conceptions of the structure of the content, brings to mind needed prior knowledge, and establishes a justifiable agenda for the instructional events. The introduction may include the instructor's assertions or questions, just as it may include photos, videos, student discussions, and simulation activities.

Core Elements

The core prepares students for the most realistic practice possible. Students test their knowledge and attend to criticism and suggestions for improvement, supplied naturally or by instructors or peers. To be prepared to practice, students observe a demonstration of the performance. To observe that demonstration perceptively, students learn needed facts as well as concepts and principles from materials, activities, fellow students, or instructors.

Concluding Elements

Instructors design a conclusion to motivate and enable learners to recall and use what they are learning. Instructors or students may summarize the main ideas and relate the new skill to the situation of use and to other job skills. Instructors ask students to recall the makeup of the performance they are learning. Instructors or students state why the skill is important to use. To reinforce the skill, and to instill confidence, instructors provide a test, a last "supervised practice" to assess what students have learned.

To begin the UPC unit called "Starting Productive Meetings," an instructor conducted a discussion titled "How Can You Start a Meeting So Your Discussion Will Stay on Track?" Then the instructor stated, "You will conduct meetings for your final evaluation according to the Meeting Performance Qualities Checklist. Section 3 of the checklist refers to starting a meeting." The instructor continued, "A good start consists of four main steps: introducing the meeting to provide context and motivation; specifying ground rules to promote efficient progress; stating, clarifying, and verifying the problem to provide a focus; and explaining the format for responding, to help organize contributions."

The instructor reviewed the previous unit: "What are examples of ground rules, problem statements, and response formats that you learned as part of the general framework of this course?" The instructor added, "First you will hear a short lecture about starting a meeting. Then you will see a demonstration. Finally, you will plan, practice, and get feedback on the start of your meetings."

Then, according to the agenda, other instructors explained and demonstrated the steps for the start of a meeting and supervised practice. To finish, an instructor asked students to summarize the steps to start a meeting. She used a diagram to show where the start fits among all the steps in preparing and conducting a meeting, and she had the students suggest ways to perform under the constraints of the job. She added, "You have learned to start a meeting using four systematic steps. Why use each of the four steps?" For the final activity, the instructor asked each student to perform the start of a meeting before trying it with staff.

WHAT IS GOOD CLASSROOM INSTRUCTION?

To be effective in creating classroom instruction, designers base their judgments on instructional principles—general statements implying ways to teach so that students are likely to be motivated, pay attention, comprehend, learn, recall, and transfer what they are learning to the job. Instructional principles may apply to all elements of instruction or just to one. For example, all aspects of instruction, as well as preinstructional and postinstructional interventions, should be meaningful to learners. In contrast, the principle of active, objective-oriented practice applies only to practice. Further, some principles, such as consistency, refer to the relationship of all instructional elements.

To be effective in producing successful job performance, designers apply many instructional principles derived from many sources. Instructional principles come from learning theories, instructional theories, research reports on teaching, practical experiences, and systematic observations (Brophy and Good, 1986; Clark, 1994; Gagné, 1985; Gagné, Briggs, and Wager, 1992; Driscoll, 1994; Keller, 1992; Peterson, 1988; Reigeluth, 1983; Yelon, 1996). Table 25.2 lists eleven general principles that imply how to be effective in all types of instruction, including classroom instruction (note that the term *instruction* can refer to any classroom or "homework" arrangements—instructors' statements and actions, learners' interactions, class activities, materials used—that are intended to produce learning). This list is one expression of these ideas; other designers have similar general suggestions, although they use somewhat different terminology.

These principles should be employed in designing classroom instruction within a comprehensive approach to performance change. The principles provide general guidelines that designers can apply in many ways as they create instructional solutions. Designers continue the development process by empirically testing their principle-based solutions.

However, in this time of global training, it is important to note that, although general instructional principles may seem universally valid, some principles and procedures may not be appropriate across national or organizational groups; the norms for the people of a particular country or in a particular profession may prohibit the application of some principles and procedures (Morical and

Table 25.2. Principles for Observing, Planning, or Evaluating Instruction.

1. *Meaningfulness:* To produce interest in learning to perform, instruction fosters connections between the performance and learners' needs.

2. *Prerequisites:* To promote readiness to learn and ease of comprehension, instruction detects, accounts for, and builds on what learners know about the performance.

3. *Open communication:* To guide learning, instruction provides all the information needed to achieve greater skill and knowledge.

4. *Essential content:* To ease understanding and to speed learning, instruction includes clear, organized, vital content needed to achieve the performance.

5. *Functional aids:* To ease and speed learning, and to foster transfer, instruction includes learning aids and potential job aids.

6. *Novelty:* To gain, maintain, and guide learners' attention, instructional stimuli are varied.

7. *Modeling:* To promote effective practice, instruction includes a full demonstration of the desired performance.

8. *Active, objective-oriented practice:* To promote the acquisition and transfer of performance, instruction includes practice of the performance required, in the final course assessment and in the workplace.

9. *Pleasant conditions:* To foster interest in learning and transfer of the performance, instruction associates pleasant feelings with performance and instruction.

10. *Pleasant consequences:* To encourage performance improvement after practice, instruction provides complete feedback, praise, and remediation.

11. *Integration and consistency of instructional system elements:* To promote transfer efficiently, and to reach performance improvement goals, instruction coordinates:

    a. Major instructional system components (real-world goals, objectives, content, methods, and evaluations)

    b. Resources (such as participants, staff, and environment)

    c. Instructional operations with work operations and other performance interventions

Note: Instruction may refer to any classroom or "homework" arrangement to produce learning, including instructor statements and actions, student interaction, class activities, or materials use.

Source: Adapted with permission from Yelon, 1996. Copyright by Longman USA 1996.

Tsai, 1992). For example, people in some cultures may want to hear a lecture given by a noted authority instead of engaging in an activity in which they are called on to derive their own ideas or talk about their problems, whereas in other cultures people may prefer to work on team projects and may not wish to listen to someone telling them how to act. To avoid "culturally crippled training," each principle and procedure should be tested for its appropriateness to each circumstance (Filipczak, 1997). If there is any doubt about what would be appropriate to a particular set of circumstances, a resource for cross-cultural training (such as the Center for Intercultural Relations, at Andrews University) can be consulted. At any rate, there may be merit in diplomatically introducing new, purposeful instructional strategies and persuading the group to increase its tolerance; a group of learners may be willing to accept instruction that is not absolutely culturally sound if there would otherwise be no instruction at all (Filipczak, 1997). The eleven principles listed in Table 25.2 are described in the sections that follow.

Principle 1: Meaningfulness

When learners can associate a new skill or a new idea with their personal experience, their interests, their values, or their aspirations, the subject is meaningful. Learners are more likely to want to attend to and pursue meaningful subjects. To motivate students to learn a new performance, instructional designers create activities so that the students will perceive the relationship of the performance to their experiences, interests, values, and aspirations (Keller, 1992; Rogers, 1983). Using information about a learner's past performances, present tasks, and work goals, designers develop statements, events, interactions and activities that will result in students' relating the performance to be learned to their work. Students are more likely to become interested in learning a skill that will help them avoid past problems, contribute to present interests, correlate with present values, and fulfill occupational goals. Students are also likely to stay interested enough to want to use the knowledge on the job. Therefore, it is crucial for designers of global instruction to know their students.

Designers strive to produce meaningful instruction before, during, and after formal classroom instruction. Before instruction begins, designers observe and question potential learners and their supervisors to discover aspirations. During these early discussions, designers explain both that students will better accomplish their purposes by learning certain skills and ideas and that supervisors expect and approve of this change in performance. At this stage, designers may ask potential students to commit themselves to try the desired skill. In addition, designers may ask students to bring to class some relevant job-related case, question, or problem.

Designers strive for meaningfulness throughout instruction, both inside and outside the classroom. Some instructors tell learners when the skill is useful and what they will gain by its use; other instructors ask students to supply that information. Role players, acting out or describing cases drawn from earlier interviews and observations, may show the consequences of using or not using the skill. Sometimes instructional information and examples provide solutions to students' typical work problems. Instructors refer to the learners' culture in case histories, analogies, and examples (Morical and Tsai, 1992). At other times students present their individual problems and derive specific solutions. Instruction is also directly linked to students' jobs by way of realistic demonstrations and practice. After formal instruction, designers promote the application of the newly acquired skills by communicating with graduates to remind them to use what they have learned.

For example, before instruction the UPC designers asked the managers, "How have you been running your meetings? What do you want to accomplish in your meetings? Why do you think your meetings are not as productive as you would like? How would you like to improve your meetings?" During instruction, instructors showed managers the uses and rewards of effective meeting procedures (such as problem posting) by describing cases drawn from interviews and observations.

Instructors called on the managers to present their meeting-problem scenarios, and instructors posed questions about typical problems that occur in UPC meetings: "What might you do when a minority of your group members do not agree with the majority? when someone in your group gets very angry? when someone in your group dominates the meeting?" Instructors showed managers a well-run, typical product development meeting and asked managers to write out meeting plans that incorporated their new skills.

Outside the classroom, instructors joined small teams of managers to observe them leading real meetings. Instructors also talked to supervisors about encouraging, enforcing, and rewarding what workers have learned about conducting meetings.

Principle 2: Prerequisites

Learners have the cognitive prerequisites for a task when they have mastered the essential contributing knowledge and skill. This means that they can readily understand the next level of skill without special preparation. Thus, in order for participants to be ready to learn a desired performance, the designers must determine and build on what the participants already know (Driscoll, 1994). To know what to look for in learners' repertoires, designers determine the knowledge and skill embedded in the desired performance and then assess the learners' knowledge and skill (Gagné, 1985). When designers take learners' prior knowledge into account, the learners are more likely to comprehend what happens in the classroom (Bloom, 1984). In this situation, learners can build on what they know and can avoid the frustration of falling behind.

Designers can assess participants' ideas and skills formally or informally, by questioning and/or observing, before a course, at the start of a course, or at the start of each segment of a course. Then designers can use such strategies as individualized instruction, grouping, or whole-class review of essential prior knowledge to enable learners to connect prior knowledge to new ideas (Yelon, 1996).

Designers must be sensitive to the feelings of the learners while taking account of prerequisites. The learners may feel threatened by a questions about their competence, by assignments involving remedial instruction, or by comments about adjusting vocabulary for those who are uninformed.

During instruction, designers should arrange for learners to link new information to old by using activities that require them to make connections between what they know and what they are learning, or by asking them to reflect on how the new ideas relate to the old ones. Other aspects of students' prior knowledge that designers must take into account are job experience, personal interests, career goals, cultural subgroup membership, and teamwork habits.

In the case of UPC, the designers informally questioned managers during a lunch before the course: "What ground rules do you use for your meetings? In what way did you state a problem in a recent meeting? What do you do if a team member suggests an idea that you do not agree with?" Designers also observed managers conducting their meetings. Early in each course, instructors asked students to perform a specific skill as they would on the job. Instructors assigned readings to individuals according to their backgrounds, created groups of beginning and advanced students, and reviewed basics with the whole class.

Principle 3: Open Communication

To be able to focus their attention, learners must know what they are to learn, how instruction will progress, and how they will be evaluated. To provide that knowledge, designers create statements, activities, or opportunities for peer interaction that will ensure that students have the information they need to achieve greater skill (Ausubel, 1980; Mager, 1997; Driscoll, 1994; Yelon, 1992c).

At the beginning of a course, instructors may tell the students exactly what to expect on the test, or they may ask the students to derive appropriate assessments that match how they will be required to perform on the job. Instructors may explain (or require students to explore) how they need each piece of course content to meet course requirements, how they may link course activities with requirements and content, and how to learn to perform. Instructors may use universally understood visual models (Morical and Tsai, 1992; Yelon and Reznich, 1992).

Instructors and peers continuously answer questions and give an accurate assessment of progress, in person or through individual e-mail or chat rooms. At the end of each segment of a course, instructors or students summarize, integrate, and synthesize the content, to highlight the major ideas and to show

how to put new skills to use on the job, without interference. Throughout instruction, instructors discover which instructional methods are working well and which methods they must change.

At UPC, when the course began, the instructors said to the managers, "At the end of the course you will be asked to conduct a full meeting according to a version of the checklist in front of you, as amended by what we all decide during the course. After the course your supervisor will observe you conducting meetings according to the derived list of qualities of an effective meeting performance."

Later on in the course, the instructors said, "This draft list of qualities contains the main ideas of the course. It shows the steps of conducting a meeting, including preparation, beginning, gathering information, summarizing, achieving consensus, and concluding. Each step is a unit in the course. Note also the skills associated with each step. You will learn each of these skills as we deal with its appropriate step. Each practice exercise in each unit is a skill that you will use in your meetings, so attend carefully to the demonstrations."

Principle 4: Essential Content

Instructional time is a precious resource. There is always more content to learn than there is time to learn it. Accordingly, instructional designers want students to learn efficiently. One approach to efficiency is to select and give priority to essential content—that is, the content that students need in order to learn to perform. Designers choose skills that are likely to produce results, and ideas that give a functional framework for thinking. Designers check to ensure that learners in a particular culture will understand the framework (Morical and Tsai, 1992). Designers want instructors to add to efficiency by being organized, clear, concrete, and well paced. Designers choose activities in which students will produce mainly pertinent information, with little extraneous content. Designers want instructors who are coaching and counseling students to help them focus on critical content.

By analyzing the tasks to be learned, designers derive and select only key information appropriate to the type of knowledge (Gagné, 1985; Chilcoat, 1989). For facts, designers consider as essential content an organized, well-supported, illustrated body of factual propositions. For concepts, designers choose definitions and examples of the category. For principles, designers choose statements of a relationship between variables and evidence for that predictable relationship. If instructors are to explain skills, designers choose the ordered, simplified steps of the skill (Clark, 1994; Merrill, 1983).

In presentations, discussions, activities, and materials, designers organize and sequence the essential content to promote complete, accurate recall (Clark, 1986). They organize the content into modules that are easily adapted to different cultures (Morical and Tsai, 1992). Instructors begin to communicate essential ideas by using the most concrete experiences needed by the group (Dale,

1969). They move from real action to simulations and then on to video, still pictures with audio, and descriptions in words. With direct instruction and text materials, instructors may explain each technique, show an example of the technique, and then reexplain the technique. Designers sequence ideas so that they build on each other, moving from obvious to subtle, from concrete to abstract, or from main to supporting ideas. Further, when instructors are explaining, debriefing an activity, summarizing a discussion, or helping students express themselves, they reduce the essential knowledge down to a form that will be simple and easy to recall; they choose the best and the fewest words to make a point, they express content in words that participants understand, and they choose examples that embody the idea (Yelon and Massa, 1987). Instructors continue to make the organization of content apparent by using transitions, summaries, outlines, charts, diagrams, and task descriptions, or by asking students to create these items. In addition, instructors associate related ideas by explaining common properties.

When instructors explain essential information, they pace the presentation to help students comprehend, and they check comprehension (Clark, 1986). They group and emphasize ideas to reduce the amount of information students will acquire at once. They present a moderate number of ideas in one session, provide new information in small doses at a reasonable pace, use simple sentences, and repeat important ideas. Instructors modulate their voices and visually highlight ideas to accentuate important points; they make few parenthetical remarks, avoid audible pauses, and use good pausing and phrasing to deemphasize unimportant details (Chilcoat, 1989).

At UPC, the instructors began the course on effective meetings concretely, by having relatively inexperienced managers observe and participate in an excellent meeting. Then managers viewed videotapes and heard descriptions of meeting incidents.

For the unit on preparing for meetings, instructors presented the steps for preparation in the order in which the steps are used (for example, determining the meeting's purpose, creating discussion questions, and creating posting formats). For each major subskill, such as the skill of writing a good question, they described the substeps; for necessary concepts, such as the concept of the well-stated question and its qualities, they arranged for students to acquire definitions and examples. They grouped major course contents, and they divided twelve meeting techniques into two categories: responses to normal interactions, and responses to emotional interactions.

Principle 5: Functional Aids

Learners understand and recall information more quickly, more completely, and more accurately when they can use mechanisms that simplify and organize complex content and connect new ideas to old ones. Therefore, to ease learning and speed instruction, designers build (or have students build) learning aids (Clark, 1986; Yelon, 1984).

Instructors present (or have students make) diagrams and charts, using universal symbols during an overview, to show the structure of a course. During acquisition and application of essential content, learners may create or use supplied mnemonics to recall a list of ideas or steps. They may use diagrams, decision trees, or drawings to comprehend the path to take in a task. They may use checklists to summarize the qualities of an acceptable performance. They may also view highlighted examples on slides, transparencies, or videotapes that use arrows, colors, stars, and subtitles to focus attention.

The UPC instructors began the course by showing a diagram of all the steps of an effective meeting. When stating the course requirements, the instructors asked the students to relate each objective to the diagram and to the detailed checklist used to assess meeting behavior. As instructors presented content, they asked students to create mnemonics to aid their recall of the effective techniques associated with each step. They also asked students to fill in a decision aid so as to understand which meeting technique to use for which situation, and they encouraged students to use this aid on the job. The designers also inserted subtitles during parts of the "excellent meeting" videotape, to highlight each incidence of a manager's demonstrating an effective technique.

Principle 6: Novelty

People must attend to ideas and experiences if they are to learn. People pay close attention when there is a change in what they see, hear, or feel. Therefore, to gain, direct, and keep attention, instructional designers periodically vary aspects of instruction (Keller, 1992).

Designers may vary the format, content, and style of materials to direct the learner's eye. Designers may also program a variety of activities into a course: individual work, group work, pair discussions, use of Internet chat rooms and e-mail, Web searches, library work, problem solving, readings, videos, directed activity, questions, puzzles, games, discussions, simulations, explanations, demonstrations, examples, practice, and feedback. Instructors may vary what they do, what they say, and how they say it. They change volume, tone, or pace when they want to gain and direct attention to important points. They gesture and move, and they continue to make changes in order to maintain attention for the duration of a lesson. Instructors use culturally appropriate humorous stories, incongruous events, and novel experiences to arouse attention and promote retention in memory (Dowling, 1995).

The UPC instructors annotated examples of a good meeting plan. They wrote useful new terms (such as *response format*) on a chalkboard. They highlighted the important steps in the meeting diagram. When explaining how important it is to post responses, they said directly, "The structure of a question will strongly influence the answers you get." By showing a satirical videotape of a terrible meeting, instructors explained how to get active participation in a meeting. They arranged the schedule to include variety: a lively lecture on how to use a meeting procedure, a videotaped example of the procedure, a live demonstration of the procedure, a role-playing simulation for practice, and a discussion to review the practice.

Principle 7: Modeling

Learners can gain the most from practice if, along with acquiring information about how to perform, they observe a complete demonstration of the desired task. Learners gain the most from a complete demonstration of a skill if they pay attention, perceive all the steps, and commit the steps to memory before practice. Thus, in the interest of completeness, instructors may use a four-step demonstration (Maddocks and Yelon, 1986; Yelon, 1996) that captures attention, focuses on each step's qualities, and calls for a mental image of the skill:

1. Tell students they will have to perform what they observe.
2. Tell students what to observe in the demonstration.
3. State each step, and then perform it.
4. Ask students to commit the steps to memory before practice.

If students control the process, they can be taught to follow the steps to produce a complete demonstration: students can ask someone to demonstrate what they must learn to perform, ask the demonstrator what to observe in the demonstration, ask the demonstrator to state each step and then perform it, and commit the steps to memory before practice. In addition, instructors should demonstrate so that students see the action from the performer's angle and are close enough to see it clearly. Instructors may also assign names to the steps, for ease of recall.

The instructor acts as a model of professional demeanor by behaving enthusiastically and professionally in all contacts with participants (Bandura, 1986). Instructors should follow ethical principles for instruction: benefiting students, doing no harm, protecting students from misuse of the instructor's power, and acting objectively and fairly.

To start a demonstration of how to post contributions in a meeting, a UPC instructor said, "You will have to post in practice, on the test, and on the job. Watch and listen for these steps during the demonstration of posting. In step 1, listen. In step 2, reduce the contribution. In step 3, verify the contribution. In step 4, write the contribution on the flipchart in the response format." As she demonstrated step 3, the instructor said, "Now I will verify the reduced contribution." Then the instructor turned to a role-playing group member and said, "John, are you saying that we should use a box format on this page of the publication?" Finally the instructor said to the students, "Before you practice, state the steps for posting to each other."

Principle 8: Active, Objective-Oriented Practice

All students must test the performance they are to learn, and all must learn the performance that the company requires on the job. Practice is a trial run at application, to improve skilled performance. To be sure that students have learned a desired skill, designers of classroom instruction build in active practice of the skills required in the real world (Gropper, 1983; Gagné, 1985; Driscoll, 1994). For each individual skill and for each team skill, designers arrange for each individual or team to practice the whole skill, as well as the subskills and contributing knowledge. Instructors may also require students to learn to identify appropriate situations for the skill's use.

All other instructional elements revolve around practice (Yelon and Berge, 1992). Information and demonstration are to prepare learners to act, and feedback and remediation are to prepare learners for more practice. Instructors should brief students before practice, and they should follow practice with debriefing.

Designers consider many aspects of practice. Practice may take place in or out of class. Instructors commonly move from basic to advanced practice. In some cases, instructors ask students to perform a skill repeatedly, in order to produce automaticity of performance (Salisbury, Jacobs, and Dempsey, 1987); in other cases, instructors give students permission to adapt performance while remaining true to a principle (Yelon and Desmedt, 1988; Yelon, Desmedt, and Williamson, 1988).

Instructors clearly specify and guide practice with brief, precise instructions about performance qualities. Instructors also attend to practice and coach students. Students must have time to practice on their own. To promote retention and reduce fatigue and error, as well as to increase fluency, speed, and automaticity of performance, instructors schedule short practice sessions over time. In order for students to remain alert and interested, practice must also vary in style and content (Keller, 1992).

Each practice set must be challenging and must go beyond the learners' previous level of competence (Keller, 1992). Instructors encourage participants to provide their own feedback, just as they would on the job. Practice includes mental exercise when physical resources are unavailable, or when students are tired. When actual practice is inconvenient or inappropriate, instructors teach students how to relax and visualize performing correctly.

The UPC instructors arranged for each manager to practice all the skills in running a realistic meeting according to the checklist of meeting behaviors. The practice proceeded in progressive order, culminating in the conducting of a whole meeting. Accordingly, during the individual units, instructors also asked managers to practice such relevant content as recalling the order and timing of steps to take in a meeting, or recognizing a good question.

Principle 9: Pleasant Conditions

When students learn in a comfortable setting, they associate their good feelings with the subject and the process. From then on, students enjoy the subject. To relate agreeable feelings with a desired performance, instructional designers continuously arrange pleasant instructional conditions (Keller, 1992).

Before instruction, the UPC designers conducted friendly interviews, spending time talking about job-related items and general topics. When planning the course, designers asked students for their choices of pace, sequence, topics, degree of detail, and level of mastery of the course (Clark, 1986). In the classroom, designers attended to appearance, location, and level of comfort. They also attended to psychological comfort by respecting and supporting students.

To be pleasant, the instruction need not be "edutainment," nor does it require slick presentations in fancy training centers. Instruction may be engaging and pleasurable even under some physically uncomfortable circumstances. When instruction is respectful, relevant, active, and well paced, when students have their desired degree of personal control and choice, when they sense caring staff who respect their differences and believe in their potential success, when the program's values match or diplomatically extend their own values and expectations, when the course celebrates small successes, and when there is an air of good humor, students will feel good about the course and the subject matter.

The UPC instructors worked with managers as colleagues attempting to create an acceptable product and reputation. They also arranged a comfortable classroom.

Principle 10: Pleasant Consequences

To learn from practice, students must know how well they did. To be willing to perform again, students must feel confident. Thus, following practice, instructors or peers inform and encourage the learners through complete feedback (Cameron and Pierce, 1994; Chance, 1992). Whenever possible, designers rely on natural consequences of performance to inform students.

When giving feedback, instructors or trained peers use checklists to be objective. When commenting on an inadequate performance, they refer only to the performance and its consequences and refrain from commenting on personality. They state what was right and wrong, what students should have done, and what to do to improve. To enhance confidence, they encourage students by emphasizing the positive qualities of performance, and they point out positive consequences of a proper performance (Chance, 1992; Cameron and Pierce, 1994). Whenever possible, instructors ask students to review their own performance first, to encourage self-evaluation.

During practice in leading meetings, the UPC managers got the normal reactions of anger when they interrupted team members or did not post what they had said. After practice, managers used a checklist to review their own performance. Instructors provided feedback, too. They sometimes said, for example, "You interrupted team members three times and did not post what they said. What were the consequences of leading a meeting in that way? How can you avoid those consequences?" Other times they said, "Good job. Your performance on the checkpoints for opening the meeting focused your staff's attention. However, you didn't acknowledge all responses. In the next practice, follow the checkpoints that call for repeating and posting all responses. Also keep up the good opening."

Principle 11: Integration and Consistency of Instructional System Elements

The outcomes of a course of instruction depend on the proper interaction of all its elements (see Figure 25.2). To foster improved workplace performance through classroom instruction, HP technologists use systems thinking. For the course to achieve its purpose, designers must coordinate all its elements with the elements of the system of which it is a part (Cruz, 1997).

To ensure that learners gain functional skill and knowledge, instructional designers create classroom instruction through the coordinated functioning of five elements (Cohen, 1987; Freiberg and Driscoll, 1996; Neidermeyer and Yelon, 1981; Tyler, 1950; Yelon and Berge, 1988; Cruz, 1997; Shambaugh and Magliaro, 1997):

1. Real-world performance
2. Objectives
3. Content
4. Methods
5. Evaluations

When designers create a match among practice, tests, objectives, and real-world performance, students will learn the desired job skill and be more likely to transfer what they have learned to the workplace and achieve the results desired by the organization.

For learners to use at work what they are learning in class, they must want to use the skill, must be aware of situations for its use, must be adaptable enough to change their approach when things change in the workplace, and must be supported both physically and psychologically in the work environment (Ford and Weissbein, 1997; Yelon, 1992b; Yelon, Reznich, and Sleight, 1997). To secure the necessary physical and psychological support, instructional designers coordinate instruction with the operations of the workplace and with other perfor-

Figure 25.2. Integration of System Elements.

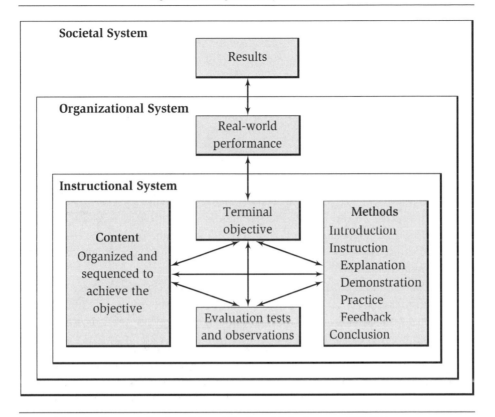

mance interventions. For example, when workers must report to supervisors, designers may use a number of strategies to involve supervisors in the course design, in order to ensure that supervisors support the use of the new skill and that the workers perceive that support (Broad, 1997; Foxon, 1997).

The objective of the UPC course on effective meetings was for managers to conduct an effective and efficient meeting, just as they would on the job. Designers derived the course content from the steps for conducting a meeting. The instruction showed why students needed this process, demonstrated how to conduct an effective meeting, and provided opportunities for practice in conducting an effective meeting. The test at the end of the course assessed how well managers now conducted meetings.

Supervisors were in on the process of course development, and the managers were aware that their supervisors expected them to use the new skills. Instructors asked the managers to prepare and conduct real meetings as part of the course, and the instructors observed and evaluated meeting performance after the course. After the class was over, instructors provided a meeting-agenda checklist, a meeting-procedure decision aid, and a checklist for meeting performance. The designers had also established a reward system for those who conducted excellent meetings.

CHOICE OF METHODS FOR CLASSROOM INSTRUCTION

Counter to common stereotypes, the lecture format is not the only classroom method. An instructor may use a wide array of instructional methods in the classroom, including platform methods, small-group methods, and self-instruction (Gage and Berliner, 1991). Platform methods include live lectures, live interactive video, conventional video, and film. Small-group methods include dyads, simulations, and discussions. Self-instructional methods include the use of textbooks, programmed instruction, interactive video, and Web-based and computer-assisted instruction.

It is tempting and sometimes necessary for instructional designers to select a method on the basis of only one criterion, such as the designer's philosophy, the instructor's skills, or the convenience of the method itself. For example, some designers, irrespective of the situation, choose "teacher-proof" materials and methods because they want uniform instruction; others use the lecture format only rarely because their philosophy guides them toward learner involvement (Eitington, 1989); still others select the lecture format because they themselves are skilled at presenting information in this way.

However, in choosing methods for classroom instruction, designers should consider more than one variable; instruction should involve the previously discussed elements and principles of instruction, and it should take account of the available resources. The first thing to be evaluated is the degree to which the prospective method applies the relevant instructional principles. Designers should also choose methods with an eye to the best fit in terms of constraints involving the staff, the participants, and the instructional environment. Designers check their choices by means of empirical testing.

In sum, instructional designers weigh methods for each instructional element according to instructional principles and the available resources. They add precision to the chosen methods by checking their plans with all concerned and by testing their plans, as resources allow.

Choosing a Method of Conveying Information About Starting a Meeting

At UPC, the instructional designers began by considering three methods for conveying this kind of information:

1. Delivery of a lecture on the qualities of each step in starting a meeting, with the use of video or live illustrations accompanied, as appropriate, by overhead transparencies

2. Demonstration of starting a meeting, with learners asked to rate the demonstrated performance according to a checklist

3. Learners' self-instruction, carried out by their reading a text, which would include descriptions of starting a meeting and transcripts of actual meetings, and by their viewing videotaped examples of good meetings

All three methods contained the essential content: the steps and their qualities. All three also openly defined these qualities via a checklist, linked examples to definitions, and included concrete illustrations (in this regard, the live examples and videotapes afforded the most vivid presentation of the material). All were meaningful and used examples taken from the students' job context. The checklist and transparencies were useful aids. Each method had built-in variation (here, the demonstration had the most). All seemed pleasant, but learners would have the most control in the self-instructional method and the least control in the lecture. With all three methods, the information conveyed was consistent with other elements in the whole course and in the job.

The three methods seemed equally good until the designers asked which of the three the instructional staff was most able to administer, and which of the three it most preferred. The answer was that the instructional staff would be equally adept at administering all three methods but preferred the two in which instructors would be active. The designers then asked which method fit the learners' level of knowledge and experience, which fit the learners' culture, and which method the learners preferred. They found that all three methods fit the learners' prerequisites and experience. The norms for this group also indicated that these learners liked to participate and had little patience for long presentations.

Next, the designers asked which method best fit the instructional environment. In this area, they took account of the following factors:

- A budget adequate for paying two instructors and buying supplies

- The availability of three instructors

- The fact that the thirty learners could not be away from their jobs for longer than three days

- The absence of any self-instructional materials and prepared videos

- The fact that all the necessary video equipment was available

- The availability of about one month for planning

- The availability of one large room that could hold twenty-five learners and one small room that could hold ten

Given the size of the available rooms, the designers decided to offer the course twice, to fifteen managers at a time. They chose the short-lecture format because it would take the least amount of time and would therefore allow for more practice within the three-day span of the learners' availability. They vowed to keep the lecture short and to the point. They also decided to videotape an entire real meeting, to illustrate each point in the lecture: they would have had to prepare similar examples for parts of a meeting in any case, they would have to spend time rehearsing the examples if they were performed live, they wanted a predictably short time for illustrating each point in the lecture, they had ample video equipment, and they had enough time in the planning month to make the tapes.

Choosing a Method of Providing Practice in Conducting Meetings

UPC designers provided practice in conducting parts of a meeting early in the course. To add meaning, challenge, and consistency, they employed real tasks and had colleagues act as team members. To promote flexible use of meeting procedures, instructors gave managers permission to produce variations on the procedures. They arranged for each of the fifteen managers in each course to practice often, dividing the group approximately in half and giving each manager five to ten minutes to perform and five to ten minutes to get feedback. The total time for all the presentations, practice of tasks, and a shortened role-played version of a whole meeting was about two days, spread over four afternoons.

Between the four initial afternoon sessions and the two final afternoon sessions, the managers performed and videotaped two whole practice meetings with their real teams. Between meetings, they used the checklist to analyze the videotapes with a supervisor and one of the two instructors (the instructors encouraged the managers to provide feedback as well). The managers selected portions of the videotaped meetings to show at a half-day group debriefing session. After the debriefing, the managers performed two more practice meetings and debriefed again.

In the last session, the managers evaluated their personal strengths and weaknesses and made plans for remediation of their weaknesses. The designers arranged for continued, intermittent, supervised practice and coaching of selected subskills and adherence to the performance checklist.

DELIVERY AND MANAGEMENT
OF CLASSROOM INSTRUCTION

Instructors carefully attend to instructional delivery and management, as well as to design; see Table 25.3 for a list of some instructional management and delivery tasks.

Table 25.3. Examples of Instructional Delivery and Management Tasks.

Delivery

Present lectures
Facilitate groups
Administer self-instruction
Implement activities
Follow customized procedures
Deal with difficult students
Answer questions
Conduct briefings
Administer practice
Conduct debriefings
Give feedback
Administer remediation
Administer tests and projects
Score and give feedback on tests and projects

Management

Recruit, select, and inform students
Decide on number of students
Fill out proper forms for training
Create schedules for all instructional elements
Account for possible interferences
Allow time for students to work, think, and rest
Plan a comfortable environment
Choose and control rooms, facilities, furniture, and air temperature
Secure and maintain materials, supplies, equipment, and staff
Evaluate, analyze, and certify workers
Assess the course
Thank instructors
Report results
Remedy flaws

Instructional Principles Applied
to Delivery of Classroom Instruction

To present content clearly through oral instruction, instructors apply the principles of essential content and novelty. They use the best words, and as few of them as possible, to make their points. They avoid making parenthetical remarks, and they use good phrasing. They accentuate important points by raising their voices, by saying that the point is important, and by highlighting the point on a visual aid. They pace the presentation by using simple sentences and by presenting only a few ideas in one session.

At UPC, for example, in the explanation of starting a meeting, an instructor talked only about essential content, making its organization apparent by using transitions and summaries between steps, by explaining each step, by showing an example of that step, and then by explaining the step again:

> So far, as you see on our diagram [*pause*], we've talked about and illustrated two of the four steps in a meeting's start. [*Pause.*] What were those? [*Pause; discuss and post.*] We've talked about introducing the meeting [*pause*] and stating the ground rules. What were those? [*Pause; discuss and post.*] Now comes a very important step [*pause*]: state the problem or question. [*Pause.*] Note how stating the problem is highlighted on the diagram. [*Pause.*] Here's how we state the problem. [*Pause.*] And here's an example on video. [*Pause.*] So, the way to state a problem is . . . [*Pause.*] What questions do you have about the way to state the problem or question?

In applying instructional principles to delivery, instructors are continuously ready to adjust their platform delivery skills, their facilitative skills, and their preclass and postclass intervention skills according to methodological constraints and instructional principles. For example, instructors using live interactive video are able to include discussions and exercises in lectures but report that they do not get a personal sense of their students, nor do their students get a personal sense of them (Galindo, 1997). The instructors feel less spontaneous because they cannot focus and then quickly refocus on individual students and events. Their humor falls flat. They cannot move close to the learners, hear what they are saying inside conversations, or perceive subtle clues to how they are feeling. Some instructors compensate for these shortcomings by making an early trip or two to the students' location and employing the help of facilitators thereafter.

Instructional Principles Applied to Management of Classroom Instruction

Instructional technologists also apply instructional principles to the management of classroom instruction. For example, the UPC designers, applying novelty, varied the type and duration of activity with the following schedule:

1. Minilecture and demonstration: twenty-five minutes
2. Pair practice in analyzing the start of a videotaped meeting: twenty minutes
3. Individual planning for the start of the learner's own meeting: twenty minutes
4. Break: ten minutes
5. Practice in presenting the start of the learner's own meeting; debriefing others: one hour

In addition, using the principle of pleasant conditions, they regulated the room temperature, reduced interruptions by isolating the classroom, and arranged the room so that everyone could see and contribute.

Concerned and Competent Staff

To ensure that instructors will act in a flexible, creative, supportive, and enthusiastic manner, designers select concerned and competent staff to deliver and manage instruction. An instructor can have a strong positive influence on performance by delivering instruction according to plan and by providing an intelligent and supportive human presence (Brophy and Good, 1986; Clark, 1989). In general, to produce effective instruction, competent instructors must have many positive characteristics (Maddocks and Yelon, 1986):

- *Concern for the subject, their students, and their instruction.* Competent instructors know and believe in their subject matter (Shulman, 1987). They can translate the subject matter into terms that learners understand, readjust the level of content to the level of their students, present the same idea in various ways, create credible concrete examples and analogies, break down the steps of a performance, point out the pitfalls in a performance, extract the essential content for a performance, structure and organize content, and model the desired performance. They can diagnose mistakes from an answer or from a performance and can devise remediation on the spot. They feel that what they are teaching is important for learners to master.

- *Knowledge of their students.* Competent instructors are aware of the general characteristics of their students, but they also investigate the specifics for each group they teach. They ascertain their motives and concerns. They discover their jobs and their work environment.

- *Self-knowledge.* Competent instructors know themselves. They have healthy personalities and have good interpersonal skills. Accordingly, they are supportive, enthusiastic, self-assured, and flexible in dealing with students.

- *Excellent instructional planning and delivery skills.* Competent instructors know how to apply the principles of design in a flexible manner. They do not adopt methods without assessing them (or, as necessary, revising them). They are good presenters, facilitators and tutors. They know how to handle groups of people and how to coach individuals.

In sum, to ensure the most effective classroom instruction, designers apply instructional principles to its delivery and management, and they select instructors who know and believe in their subject matter, who know their students and themselves, and who have excellent instructional planning, development, and delivery skills.

CONCLUSION

Instructional technologists develop classroom instruction in a heuristic, creative, and flexible manner, basing their decisions on instructional principles and resources. They choose instruction because it is the best intervention for a performance problem. After choosing an instructional remedy, they generate goals, objectives, and content. Using the derived goals, objectives, and content, designers plan a general but consistent instructional program that includes real-world performance, objectives, contents, methods, and tests. As part of the general plan, designers propose preclass and postclass interventions, as well as instruction inside and outside the classroom. They decide if classroom instruction is a possible and desirable choice for each instructional element. They then select and customize methods for each element according to instructional principles and resources. Finally, they create, test, and correct instructional materials progressively. In this way, instructional designers develop classroom instruction, one among many instructional interventions, to produce enhanced job performance. This sort of classroom instruction is a legitimate performance intervention, a carefully orchestrated blend of many instructional methods, and an integral part of a comprehensive performance plan.

References

Alderman, F. L. (1988, Apr.) *A guide to implementing effective transfer of training strategies.* Paper presented at the annual conference of the National Society for Performance Improvement, Denver.

Aronson, E., Blaney, S., Sikes, J., and Snapp, M. (1978). *The jigsaw classroom.* Thousand Oaks, CA: Sage.

Ausubel, D. (1980). Schemata, cognitive structure and advance organizers: A reply to Anderson, Spiro, and Anderson. *American Educational Research Journal* 17:3, 400–404.

Bandura, A. (1986). *Social foundation of thought and action: A social cognitive theory.* Englewood Cliffs, NJ: Prentice Hall.

Beaudin, B. P. (1987). Enhancing the transfer of job-related learning from the learning environment to the workplace. *Performance & Instruction* 26:9–10, 19–21.

Bloom, B. S. (1984). The 2 sigma problem: The search for methods of group instruction as good as one-to-one tutoring. *Educational Researcher* 14:6, 4–16.

Boettcher, J. B. (1997, Aug.). Video instruction at a distance. *Syllabus,* pp. 46–47.

Broad, M. L. (1997). Overview of transfer of training from learning to performance. *Performance Improvement Quarterly* 10:2, 7–21.

Brophy, J., and Good, T. L. (1986). Teacher behavior and student achievement. In M. C. Wittrock (ed.), *Handbook of research on teaching* (3rd ed.). Old Tappan, NJ: Macmillan.

Cameron, J., and Pierce, W. D. (1994). Reinforcement, reward, and intrinsic motivation: A meta-analysis. *Review of Educational Research* 64:3, 363–424.

Chance, P. (1992, Nov.). The rewards of learning. *Phi Delta Kappan,* pp. 200–207.

Chilcoat, G. W. (1989). Instructional behaviors for clearer presentations in the classroom. *Instructional Science* 18:4, 289–314.

Clark, C. M. (1989, Oct.). *The good teacher.* Lecture presented at conference of the Norwegian Research Council for Science and the Humanities, Trondheim, Norway.

Clark, R. C. (1986). Defining the "D" in ISD. Part 1: Task-general instructional methods. *Performance & Instruction* 25:1, 17–20.

Clark, R. C. (1994). *Developing technical training.* Phoenix, AZ: Performance Technology Press.

Cohen, S. A. (1987). Instructional alignment: Searching for a magic bullet. *Educational Researcher* 16:8, 16–20.

Cruz, B. J. (1997). Measuring the transfer of training. *Performance Improvement Quarterly* 10:2, 83–97.

Dale, E. (1969). *Audiovisual methods in teaching* (3rd ed.). Hinsdale, IL: Dryden Press.

Dowling, E. (1995). *The standup trainer.* Coralles, NM: Creative Training Techniques Press.

Driscoll, M. P. (1994). *Psychology of learning for instruction.* Needham Heights, MA: Allyn & Bacon.

Filipczak, B. (1997, Jan.). Think locally, train globally. *Training,* pp. 41–46.

Ford, J. K., and Weissbein, D. A. (1997). Transfer of training: An updated review and analysis. *Performance Improvement Quarterly* 10:2, 22–41.

Foxon, M. (1997). The influence of motivation to transfer, action planning, and manager support on the transfer process. *Performance Improvement Quarterly* 10:2, 42–63.

Fredollino, P. P., and Galindo, J. P. (1994, Oct.). *Some reality issues in delivering professional degree programs using interactive instructional television: Perspectives of faculty and students.* Paper presented at meeting of the Quality in Off-Campus Credit Programs, Orlando, FL.

Freiberg, J. H., and Driscoll, A. (1996). *Universal teaching strategies* (2nd ed.). Needham Heights, MA: Allyn & Bacon.

Gage, N. L., and Berliner, D. C. (1991). *Educational psychology* (5th ed.). Boston: Houghton Mifflin.

Gagné, R. M. (1985). *The conditions of learning and theory of instruction.* Austin, TX: Holt, Rinehart and Winston.

Gagné, R. M., Briggs, L. J., and Wager, W. W. (1992). *Principles of instructional design* (4th ed.). Orlando, FL: Harcourt Brace.

Galindo, J. (1997). *Instructors' early perceptions of interactive instructional television.* Practicum paper, Michigan State University.

Gunter, M. A., Estes, T. H., and Schwab, J. (1995). *Instruction: A models approach* (2nd ed.). Needham Heights, MA: Allyn & Bacon.

Johnson, D. W., and Johnson, R. T. (1990). *Cooperation and competition: Theory and research.* Edina, MN: Interaction.

Joyce, B., and Weil, M. (1996). *Models of teaching* (5th ed.). Needham Heights, MA: Allyn & Bacon.

Keller, J. M. (1992). Motivational systems. In H. D. Stolovitch and E. J. Keeps (eds.), *Handbook of Human Performance Technology: A comprehensive guide for analyzing and solving performance problems in organizations.* San Francisco: Jossey-Bass.

Maddocks, M., and Yelon, S. L. (1986). Identifying trainer competencies. *Performance & Instruction* 25:9, 9–12.

Mager, R. F. (1997). *Making instruction work* (2nd ed.). Atlanta: Center for Effective Performance.

Mager, R. F., and Pipe, P. (1997). *Analyzing performance problems* (3rd ed.). Atlanta: Center for Effective Performance.

Merrill, M. D. (1983). Component display theory. In C. M. Reigeluth (ed.), *Instructional design theories and models: An overview of their current status.* Hillsdale, NJ: Erlbaum.

Morical, K., and Tsai, B. (1992). Adapting training for other cultures. *Training & Development* 46:4, 65–68.

Neidermeyer, F. C., and Yelon, S. L. (1981). L.A. aligns instruction with essential skills. *Educational Leadership* 38:8, 618–620.

Peterson, L. J. (1988). 13 powerful principles for training success. *Performance & Instruction* 27:2, 47–55.

Predko, J. E., Spurgin, M. E., Galindo, J. P., and Gizinski, S. (1993, Oct.). *Collaborative implementation of new technologies: Lessons learned from administrators, faculty, and students.* Paper presented at meeting of the Quality in Off-Campus Credit Programs, Charleston, SC.

Reigeluth, C. M. (ed.). (1983). *Instructional design theories and models: An overview of their current status.* Hillsdale, NJ: Erlbaum.

Rogers, C. R. (1983). *Freedom to learn for the 80s.* Columbus, OH: Merrill.

Rogoff, B. (1990). *Apprenticeship in thinking: Cognitive development in social context.* New York: Oxford University Press.

Salisbury, D. F., Jacobs, J. W., and Dempsey, J. V. (1987, Apr.). *Automaticity training: Implications for education and technology.* Paper presented at annual meeting of the American Educational Research Association, Washington, DC.

Schön, D. A. (1987). *Educating the reflective practitioner.* San Francisco: Jossey-Bass.

Shambaugh, N. R., and Magliaro, S. G. (1997). *Mastering the possibilities: A process approach to instructional design.* Needham Heights, MA: Allyn & Bacon.

Shulman, L. S. (1987). Knowledge and teaching: Foundations of the new reform. *Harvard Educational Review* 57:1, 1–21.

Tyler, R. W. (1950). *Basic principles of curriculum and instruction.* Chicago: University of Chicago Press.

Yelon, S. L. (1984). How to use and create criterion checklists. *Performance & Instruction* 23:3, 1–4.

Yelon, S. L. (1992a). An algorithm for incorporating practice in and around a lecture. *Performance & Instruction* 31:9, 22–26.

Yelon, S. L. (1992b). MASS: A model for producing transfer. *Performance Improvement Quarterly* 5:2, 13–23.

Yelon, S. L. (1992c). Writing and using instructional objectives. In L. J. Briggs, K. L. Gustafson, and M. H. Tillman (eds.), *Instructional design: Principles and applications.* Englewood Cliffs, NJ: Educational Technology Publications.

Yelon, S. L. (1996). *Powerful principles of instruction.* Reading, MA: Addison-Wesley.

Yelon, S. L., and Berge, Z. L. (1988). The secret of instructional design. *Performance & Instruction* 27:1, 11–13.

Yelon, S. L., and Berge, Z. L. (1992). Practice-centered training. *Performance & Instruction* 31:8, 8–12.

Yelon, S. L., and Desmedt, J. (1988). Improving professional judgment and performance: Training for open job skills. *Performance & Instruction* 27:2, 34–46.

Yelon, S. L., Desmedt, J., and Williamson, J. (1988). Integrating principle-based rules into skill instruction. *Performance & Instruction* 27:10, 33–38.

Yelon, S. L., and Massa, M. (1987). Heuristics for creating examples. *Performance & Instruction* 26:8, 13–17.

Yelon, S. L., and Reznich, C. (1992). Visible models of course organization. *Performance & Instruction* 31:8, 7–11.

Yelon, S. L., Reznich, C., and Sleight, D. (1997). Medical fellows tell stories of application: A grounded theory on the dynamics of transfer. *Performance Improvement Quarterly* 10:2, 134–155.

CHAPTER TWENTY-SIX

Team Activities for Learning and Performance

Sivasailam Thiagarajan

This chapter begins with two major themes:

1. Team activities can increase the effectiveness of Human Performance Technology (HPT) interventions.

2. Team activities can improve the efficiency of the HPT development procedure.

To demonstrate these themes, various examples are presented in the first section of this chapter. The second section is a concept analysis whose purpose is to identify critical and variable features of team activities and explore different types of these activities. The sections that follow the first two discuss the benefits and limitations of team activities and provide guidelines for adapting the standard HPT process model to the development of team activities. The final section of the chapter explores facilitation techniques, especially those intended for use with international and intercultural groups.

TEAM ACTIVITIES AS A REINFORCEMENT OF HPT INTERVENTIONS

The following five vignettes describe how team techniques added value to a team-building strategy, a wellness program, a personnel selection process, an incentive system, and an instructional module featuring practice and feedback.

Elephant Grope

A high-tech corporation was suffering heavily from turf battles among its various divisions. To reduce the damage, the organization decided to intervene with a team-building strategy, with the goal of encouraging employees to create common guidelines.

The team-building strategy was strengthened by a team activity called Elephant Grope. Participants were organized into homogeneous teams of engineers, managers, accountants, sales staff, and support staff. In the first phase, each homogeneous team came up with its own set of guidelines for improving interdepartmental collaboration. In the second phase, each homogeneous team presented its guidelines to the other teams. Teams took turns critiquing the guidelines from their respective points of view. In the third phase, each team retired to its own corner and revised the guidelines on the basis of other teams' input, but without compromising its core values. In the fourth phase, each team presented its revised guidelines, this time with no critique. In the fifth phase, the teams were reorganized in such a way that each one included an engineer, a manager, an accountant, a salesperson, and a member of the support staff. These heterogeneous teams, drawing on varied vantage points, now developed eclectic sets of guidelines. In the sixth phase, each team presented its composite guidelines. In the seventh and final phase, with contributions from all the teams, the facilitator prepared a common list on a flip chart.

Buddy System

Sensible exercising contributes to the physical wellness of employees and increases their productivity, but most exercise programs suffer from a major problem: they are usually solitary and boring. Recognizing this problem, a manufacturer began designing fitness equipment that required two people to participate simultaneously. The partners did not have to be matched in strength and endurance; the equipment could be adjusted for individual differences.

The simple addition of a partner to the program added immensely to its motivational strength. Whether because misery loves company or because of mutual support or peer pressure, this team activity enabled people to endure the boredom of the exercise regimen.

Cross-Cultural Role-Playing Exercise

A multinational corporation received a large contract for a construction project in West Africa. To increase the productivity of the project team, the corporation decided to invest significant time and resources in personnel selection (a frequently used HPT intervention). An initial pool of potential technical advisers was identified through telephone interviews, after résumés had been reviewed. The final selection was conducted at the corporate headquarters and involved a lengthy role-playing activity that featured several critical confrontations between host-country counterparts and the technical advisers. Three experienced field hands played the roles of the African team members, standardizing their behavior to reflect the local cultural values, beliefs, and preferences in such areas as work ethics, interpersonal relationships, perceptions of time, collaboration, and individualism. At the conclusion of the team activity, the corporate role players rated the performance of each potential candidate on such factors as tolerance of ambiguity, perceptual acuity, emotional resilience, and openness to new ways of doing things. The final selection of technical advisers was based on a number of factors (including technical competence), with the candidates' performance in the cross-cultural role-playing activity given significant weight.

Team Poker

The manager of a fast-food restaurant had problems because workers were arriving late. To reduce tardiness, she created an incentive system. Every time a worker arrived on time, he or she received a fifty-cent bonus for that day. This arrangement cost the restaurant about $1,200 a month and was effective—for a couple of months, after which the workers reverted to their tardy arrivals.

The manager then added a team activity to the incentive system. She randomly organized the workers into teams of five people. Every day that all the members of a team arrived on time, she gave that team a playing card from a shuffled deck of cards. Every other Friday, the teams created the most powerful poker hands they could from the cards collected over the previous two weeks. The team with the best hand received a bonus of $500, to be divided among the members. The minor addition of a team activity to the incentive system reduced the system's cost and increased its effectiveness.

Monkey Business

A training workshop on presentation skills included a module on how to tell jokes. A team activity called Monkey Business was used to strengthen this instructional intervention. The session began with a demonstration of the six critical principles of telling jokes (for example, "Never forget the punch line" and "Adapt the joke to make it relevant to the current audience"). Participants were then divided into six teams of five members each, each team was given a printed copy of a different joke, and team members helped one another practice presenting the team's joke.

After ten minutes, members of the first team were sent individually to present the joke to the other five teams. Each member of the audience wrote down two specific suggestions on how the presenter could improve his or her skills. The same procedure was repeated with the other teams, each of which took a turn making its presentation. At the end of these sessions, each participant had presented a joke and had critically evaluated the five other people's presentation of a joke. Thus the team activity provided the critical instructional elements of practice and feedback.

TEAM ACTIVITIES AS A REINFORCEMENT OF HPT PROCEDURES

Just as team activities can be integrated with different HPT interventions to reduce costs and increase benefits, team activities can also improve the efficiency of the HPT process. The activities can be used at all stages, from front-end analysis to final implementation. The four examples that follow show how these activities can be used to support needs analysis, strategy selection, job aid design, and formative evaluation.

Hello

Systematic analysis of the needs and characteristics of the target audience of performers is a crucial activity in the initial stages of designing and developing any HPT intervention. This activity often requires significant resources. Unfortunately, it also very often lacks face validity for the impatient client.

A game called Hello has been used successfully to conduct instant analysis at the start of a workshop. Before the workshop, the trainer makes a list of crucial questions. For example, the list may include questions about the participants' perceived needs, their job experiences, their expectations for the workshop, and their attitudes toward the topic of the workshop. At the start of the workshop, the participants are divided into as many teams as there are questions, and each team is given a different question. Each team then spends three minutes devising a strategy for collecting relevant data. The next three minutes are spent on actual data collection. This phase is followed by a three-minute period in which each team tabulates its data and produces a summary report on a blank transparency. In the final three minutes, each team reports the outcome of its investigation. The result of this activity for the trainer is useful data; for the participants, the result is an opportunity to get to know one another.

Two-by-Two

In the initial stages of the HPT process, selecting suitable interventions, strategies, or media is crucial. To enable a multidisciplinary group of HP technologists and clients to reliably complete this task, a modified version of the Delphi technique can be used.

For example, a group of seven people recently evaluated ten different strategies for solving the parking problem in a congested shopping mall. In this case, a game called Two-by-Two was used. This is an activity for comparing the different costs and benefits of alternative solutions.

Each member of the group was given a form containing a list of alternative solutions and was asked to evaluate the cost of each solution on a scale of 1 to 5 (with 5 being the most expensive solution and 1 the least expensive). The filled-in forms were then collected from the participants and replaced with blank ones. Participants now evaluated the same list of solutions for effectiveness, again on a scale of 1 to 5. Meanwhile, the facilitator was quickly computing the mean and the standard deviation from the earlier cost ratings. After the effectiveness ratings were collected, the participants were given the mean and the standard deviation of the cost ratings. The participants discussed major discrepancies and rerated the alternatives, using the same cost scale and taking account of data and opinions from other team members.

This procedure—alternately rating solutions in terms of cost and effectiveness, receiving feedback, and discussing discrepancies—continued for several rounds until the variance was reduced. The facilitator then prepared a two-by-two matrix of high and low cost and high and low effectiveness, placing each solution in one of the four quadrants. After an appropriate amount of discussion, the participants selected the best of the low-cost, high-effectiveness alternatives.

Tutorial Recording Exercise

Most computer-related procedures are presented in the form of procedural checklists. The usual approach for creating such a job aid is to conduct a task analysis, design a prototype version of the job aid, try it out on representative users, and fix any problems.

A team activity called Tutorial Recording combines elements of task analysis, design, and developmental testing and revision. There are three people on the team: a subject matter expert, a job aid designer, and a representative end user. During this team activity the subject matter expert, in tutorial mode, teaches the procedure to the end user. All the necessary computer equipment is provided so that there is hands-on practice for the end user. The tutorial session is also recorded on audiotape or videotape.

Meanwhile, the job aid designer is observing the tutorial session and taking notes. He or she is also using another computer that runs a special program for rapidly producing a procedural checklist. While the subject matter expert walks the end user through the procedure, the job aid designer is preparing a checklist that is based on this tutorial session. Throughout the session, the end user is encouraged to ask questions, the subject matter expert repeats and rephrases his or her instructions, and the job aid designer makes changes, as appropriate, in the checklist.

At the end of the tutorial session, the job aid designer questions the end user about the experience of carrying out the complex procedure and dealing with confusing decisions. The designer then presents the checklist to both the subject matter expert and the end user. On the basis of technical feedback from the subject matter expert and suggestions from the end user, the checklist is immediately revised.

The first end user is now replaced by a fresh one. During the second tutorial session, the new end user attempts to complete the procedure by following the checklist. Only when he or she is stumped does the subject matter expert supply additional information, which is immediately incorporated into this job aid. After two or three tutorial sessions of this kind, a useful version of the procedural checklist is produced.

Good News, Bad News

A crucial component of the HPT process is the formative evaluation that collects data for the improvement of products and procedures. A team activity called Good News, Bad News is useful in collecting such data from focus groups.

This activity was recently used by a designer of ergonomic keyboards. Before the team activity, a focus group of twenty-four representative users was given the new keyboard. The group was divided into six teams of four members each. For each of three dimensions—the layout of the keyboard, the touch and feel of the keyboard and tactile feedback from the keyboard, and the flexibility of the keyboard (that is, its ability to be switched from a QWERTY layout to a Dvorak layout)—two teams were assigned. Of the two teams assigned to the each dimension, one was assigned to reporting good news and the other to reporting bad news.

After having used the keyboard for a week, the users were all reassembled. The members of each team were asked to compare notes and prepare a case that would establish the keyboard as superior or inferior on the specific dimension that had been assigned.

After fifteen minutes of preparation time, each team for each dimension was given five minutes to make its case. Thus, at the end of the first team's presentation, the opposing team (assigned to the same dimension) took its turn. This procedure was continued until all three pairs of teams had presented their cases. The entire session was taped. The evaluator then briefly reviewed the comments and asked the teams to suggest modifications that would retain the strengths of the keyboard while reducing its weaknesses.

FACTORS THAT INCREASE THE USE OF TEAM ACTIVITIES

In 1977, I conducted an informal survey of several randomly selected trainers, asking them whether they did or did not use training games, simulations, role playing, and other such methods. The results indicated that a mere 2 percent used team activities. The same survey was repeated in 1997, when a mere 2 percent reported *not* using such activities. Obviously, this was a sloppy bit of research, but the fact remains that more and more trainers, instructional designers, and HP technologists are using interactive experiential approaches. Several trends seem to be contributing to this accelerating use of team activities. A few of them are discussed in the sections that follow.

Learning Organization

Senge (1990) brought about a dramatic shift in professional thought by pointing out that learning disabilities are fatal to organizations. His conceptual framework integrates five disciplines. In a subsequent book, Senge and others (1994) provided operational strategies and tools for building a learning organization. All five disciplines in this framework, especially those of team learning and shared vision, require team activities for learning and implementation.

Teamwork

During the past decade, traditional hierarchical bureaucracies have been replaced by team-based organizations. As a result, performance improvement efforts are undertaken in small groups, and this trend increases the demand for team interventions. If, moreover, employees are going to work in teams, then it makes sense to train them in teams.

Self-Help Groups

People have discovered the advantages of receiving and giving training and therapy through mutual sharing of experiences, insights, and skills, without the need for a subject matter expert. Innovative team techniques help these self-help groups.

Large-Scale Participation

McLagan and Nel (1995) point out that there is a global trend for everyone to get involved in how their managers are making decisions in their workplaces and in how politicians are making decisions in local and national government. Such involvement makes not only moral sense but also business sense. New team techniques are developing that involve masses of people in real-time strategic changes (Jacobs, 1994).

International and Intercultural Interaction

New possibilities for travel and communication technologies have made distance insignificant. Around the world, through the Internet and videoconferencing, virtual teams interact instantaneously. The "hard" skills of technology and the "soft" skills of cross-cultural communication have to be learned and used in team settings.

Computerization

Ten years ago, team approaches like simulation gaming were constrained by the state of the art in communication and computing technologies. Now, on everyone's desktop, we have computer power capable of providing interactive, high-fidelity, virtual-reality simulations in any complex area. For example, a mere $100 buys a driver-education software program, complete with a steering wheel.

Virtual Participation

As Schank (1997) points out, effective learning and innovative performance are hampered by fear and intolerance of failure. Becker (1998) explains that the major disadvantage of team activities is the fear of losing face in front of others. An unobtrusive but powerful benefit of the computer revolution is the enabling of interaction by introverts. You can fail with dignity in computer simulations of interpersonal confrontations. In Internet chat rooms, for example, you can reveal your ignorance in total anonymity.

Greater Availability of Resources

How-to books on team activities have proliferated over the past few years. For example, *Games Trainers Play* (Scannel and Newstrom, 1985) has had several sequels. Pfeiffer's annual collection of team activities used to be the only one; now it is split into two volumes and joined by yearbooks and annual publications from major publishers that feature team activities. An Indiana University graduate student recently counted 3,947 published icebreakers in books and magazines, and the number is constantly increasing. Jossey-Bass/Pfeiffer has begun publishing a newsletter on team activities and distributing a catalogue devoted exclusively to games and activities.

Multiple Intelligences

Recent research on the nature of intelligence has deposed traditional IQ measures as the sole indicators of effective performance. Newer frameworks of intelligence, including Gardner's (1983) multiple intelligences, Sternberg's (1996) successful intelligence, and Goleman's (1995) emotional intelligence, emphasize interpersonal skills. This shift has enormous implications for the use of team activities in a variety of HPT interventions, including instruction, personnel selection, and workflow redesign.

Cognitive Science

Cognitive methods for training and performance improvement strongly support team activities. Clark (1998) identifies learning in a team setting as a feature of cognitive apprenticeship. Team learning enables peer tutoring and forces articulation of ideas that ensure effective elaborative rehearsal.

Changing Nature of the Target Population

Prensky (1998) points out that new employees who were born after 1970 and raised on video games are different from those for whom traditional HPT interventions have been designed. The Nintendo generation prefers, among other things, play to work, payoffs to patience, and active learning to the passive variety. These newcomers have shorter attention spans and greater ability to interact in an asynchronous mode. All these characteristics favor team activities.

WHAT ARE TEAM ACTIVITIES?

Unfortunately, the term *team activities* is an ambiguous one. However, alternative terms, such as *instructional games, simulations,* or *experiential learning,* identify only a subset of the domain and confuse the issue. Here are the critical attributes of team activities, as the term is used in this chapter:

- Team activities involve more than one person. It is possible to conduct a team activity with only two people, but it usually involves more.
- Team activities require active participation. All members of the group respond actively rather than listening passively.
- Participation in a team activity is interdependent, not independent. The action of one person elicits reactions from others, and so team activities involve interaction.
- Team activities achieve specific outcomes. They increase the effectiveness and efficiency of human performance in measurable terms.
- Team activities are structured. They have rules for taking turns, making moves, and receiving consequences.

VARIATIONS ON TEAM ACTIVITIES

Within this definitional framework, there is a wide range of variation, briefly discussed in the sections that follow.

Group Membership

All team activities involve more than one person, but the exact number can vary between two and fifteen. There are conflicting research findings about the optimum size for a small group. The optimum size depends on the type of activity and its purpose. As long as each member of a group can interact with every other member, team activities can be effectively undertaken.

Types of Members

Arguments and empirical data have been advanced in support of homogeneous and heterogeneous groups, in terms of ability, personality, cultural characteristics, expertise, experience, job level, and other such factors. The appropriate mix of membership characteristics depends on the type and purpose of the activity. Sometimes a group may change from homogeneous to heterogeneous composition during the same activity.

Virtual Membership

Innovative use of computers has enabled the creation of virtual participants similar to the imaginary friends of childhood. It is now possible for anyone to participate in a team activity, interacting with (or acting against) any number of virtual partners (or opponents) who represent any combination of cultural and personality variables.

Active Participation

The frequency, nature, and distribution of active participation may vary from one activity to another. The usual type of participation involves discussion within the group. However, with computer networks and teleconferencing, team activities can reach beyond face-to-face interaction. These electronic technologies permit wider geographical dispersion of a team.

Interaction

According to the nature of the activity and its purpose, different members of the team may have different responsibilities and opportunities for interaction. For example, members of a team may be assigned different roles (such as those of leader, moderator, reporter, or monitor).

Competition

A major continuum in team activities is that of competition-cooperation. Much has been written about the evils of competition (Kohn, 1986) and its inevitability (Olson, 1990). There are no simple prescriptions for the optimum level of competition in an activity. The nature of the task determines the location of the activity along the competition-cooperation dimension.

Structure

Team activities have rules that control structure and sequence. The nature, number, and complexity of these rules may vary from one activity to another. Rules can be imposed formally and rigidly or informally and flexibly. For example, in most brainstorming sessions, the rules are few, simple, and rarely enforced. However, in a computer simulation, the rules may be many and complex and are rigidly and reliably implemented by the software program.

Playfulness

People generalize the playfulness of games to all team activities. However, any team activity (including a game) can be undertaken in either a serious or a playful mode. People who refuse to play a decision-making game will show no hesitation to participate in the same activity when it is called a "modified Delphi technique for iterative processing of divergent inputs."

TYPES OF TEAM ACTIVITIES

Team activities have been classified into a number of traditional categories. Although there is overlap among these categories, they provide a convenient scheme.

Games

Technically, a game has four critical characteristics: conflict, control, closure, and contrivance (Stolovitch and Thiagarajan, 1980). The conflict in a game is usually competition among players or teams. However, any obstacle to achieving a predefined goal constitutes conflict. The control element is provided by the rules of the game, which specify who gets a turn, how he or she makes a move, and what the consequences are. A special rule for ending the game provides closure. Finally, contrivance in games prohibits the most efficient solution to the problem (for example, a basketball player's simply clutching the ball and running with it).

Simulation games have the additional characteristic of correspondence between aspects of the game and of the real world (Greenblat, 1988). For example, the artifacts and procedures used in a war game correspond to those in a real war (except for the killing and destruction). In some simulation games, the correspondence between the game and reality is not direct. For example, in an instructional simulation game called Ghetto, a throw of the dice represents a chance event, going around the board represents surviving a year, and poker chips represent a combination of time, money, and credibility.

Role-Playing Exercise

This activity involves participants' acting out characters assigned to them in a scenario (Wohlking and Gill, 1980). In this framework, participants perform spontaneously, without the constraints of specific lines or rules. Role playing is for practice and instruction in interpersonal skills. However, it can also be used to support other HPT interventions. For example, managers can be asked to play the role of newly hired employees and thereby come up with a list of the characteristics that would be desirable in an incentive system.

Team-Building Exercises

These activities focus on trust, collaboration, openness, and other interpersonal factors (Reddy and Jamison, 1988; Phillips and Elledge, 1989). For example, in a typical outdoor experiential exercise, participants choose partners and climb trees, using a series of ladders, platforms, and cables, to a level that challenges them. This activity provides physical and mental challenges and a context for gaining insights into taking acceptable risks, setting personal goals, handling fear and stress confidently, and trusting other people. Team-building activities are frequently used to strengthen culture-change interventions.

Group Discussions

These activities are used for joint decision making and creative problem solving. In a specialized format called Groupprograms (Thiagarajan, 1978), the behavior of the members of a group is controlled by audiotape recordings and printed materials. A booklet provides participants with topics for discussion. The roles of a moderator and of a note taker are assigned through an audio tape recording that refers each participant to a page reference that identifies the role he or she is to assume. Feedback on the appropriateness of the group's conclusions is provided by model responses or by a process checklist.

Computerized Activities

These activities are structured by computer software-hardware combinations. For example, a team of executives is provided with individual keypads, and choices are projected on a large screen. Each participant selects an alternative through the individual keypad. The computer processes the choices and provides statistical feedback. Several creativity packages (Mattimore, 1990) are also being used in more and more team settings. These packages systematically walk a team through the various steps of the creativity process.

ADVANTAGES OF TEAM ACTIVITIES

Twelker (1975), having examined the research evidence on simulations and gaming, concluded nearly a quarter of a century ago that if we do not quite know what we are doing, we are nevertheless having a lot of fun. Not much has changed since then to revise Twelker's conclusion. Part of the reason for the paucity of empirical data is our tendency to ask the wrong questions, which follow the pattern "Which is better: X or Y?" If we go beyond such trivial questions, we find, in classic texts on small-group psychology, useful prescriptions for effective use of team activities. Anecdotal data from practitioners suggest several apparent benefits of team activities.

Motivational Benefits

For most people, team activities are more fun than noninteractive approaches. In one study, for example, most subjects, asked to compare an individual interview with a focus group, claimed that the focus group was less intense, less anxiety-provoking, and less boring (Templeton, 1987). Further probing revealed that this enhanced motivation for team activities was due partly to coaction (the effect of two or more people working in one another's presence) and partly to social reinforcement. Team activities enable participants to receive praise from their peers.

Organizational Benefits

From the organizational point of view, here are some benefits of using small group activities:

- Team activities appear to increase the probability that a task will be completed, apparently because of checks and balances within the team and because of participants' mutual learning from one another.

- Activities appear to increase team cohesion. When such activities are used appropriately, team members tend to help each other confront external forces. Over time, this tendency results in increased camaraderie among team members.

- Team activities frequently build cooperation and trust, whereas individual competition often results in people's enhancing their own productivity by reducing other people's productivity, withholding information, and carrying out other subtle forms of sabotage. Team activities encourage people to collaborate in achieving the best outcome for the group.

- Team activities frequently reduce resistance to change. Involving groups of employees in exploring different concerns about a change, and in collaborating on the creation of a work plan, appears to give employees ownership of the change. Data from change efforts indicate that the earlier the stakeholders become involved in a change, the easier the change is to implement.

- Team activities encourage employee participation. There is very little incentive for individual employees to come up with suggestions for productivity improvement in most organizations. The use of team activities appears to decentralize productivity improvement and involves more employees at more levels of the corporation.

- Team activities encourage creative problem solving. Groups consistently outperform individuals in developing creative solutions to technical problems. This phenomenon appears to be due to the alternative viewpoints found on a team and to members' freedom to build on one another's ideas.

- Team activities appear to facilitate multicultural interaction. The trust and collaboration derived from these activities seemingly make it easier for multicultural team members to accept different values and beliefs and to provide open feedback to one another.

Instructional Benefits

From the instructional point of view, here are some benefits of using team activities:

- Team activities appear to facilitate holistic learning. Most traditional training techniques impose a linear structure on what is being taught. The use of a simulation game, in which several players interact with each other simultaneously, enables us to present different variables at the same time (Duke, 1974).

- Team activities tend to facilitate transfer of training. Simulation games and role playing bring the training event close to the job situation. It is obviously easier to apply interpersonal skills learned in an interpersonal setting than it is to apply those learned in any other setting (van Ments, 1983).

- Team activities appear to force learners to respond actively. The learner in self-instructional mode, even if he or she is required to respond to questions, may find it possible to skip the process of active response. In an instructional game, however, it will be difficult for a learner to bypass active responding. The scoring system and peer pressure strongly encourage the learner to respond.

- Team activities can make drill and practice more interesting. All technical skills require repeated practice, with feedback, for fluency. In self-instructional mode, drill and practice may become boring. Team games remove the tedium by providing company to share and ease the misery.

- Team activities frequently enhance instructional feedback. Along with practice, feedback is a critical requirement for effective learning. In most team activities, learners receive frequent feedback from their peers. This feedback often comes in a specific form and is operationalized into score points.

DISADVANTAGES OF TEAM ACTIVITIES

Team activities are not a panacea. The empirical literature is replete with data that highlight the limitations, dangers, and inefficiencies of these activities when they are used inappropriately. For example, Hackman (1990), in his survey of groups that work and those that do not, stresses the complex interactions involved in team activities. Even writers of practical manuals emphasize that behind every benefit lurks a potential cost. The following paradoxes of experiential learning packages (Thiagarajan, 1980) also apply to other types of team activities:

- They provide greater confidence in what has been learned, but learners seem to lack a sense of learning.

- They are easier to remember, but participants may remember the wrong things.

- They facilitate transfer of skills, but they provide fewer skills to transfer.

- They are very effective for affective learning, but this raises a number of ethical issues.

- They make some facilitators popular but other facilitators unpopular.

The following additional disadvantages are also frequently reported by practitioners:

- Team activities reinforce mediocrity. Peer pressure and potential embarrassment may force peak performers to reduce their productivity to the average level of the team. In addition, team activities require participants to spend time and energy attending to interpersonal variables. In situations where individual technical expertise is to be used, team activities may be inappropriate.

- Team activities distract participants. In a problem-solving situation, a few vociferous members of the team may divert the others from a logical solution through tangential discussions. In an instructional intervention, participants may pay more attention to winning than to the instructional content.

- Team activities spread ignorance and prejudice. If the members of a group have above-average levels of information and knowledge, the likely result of a team activity is increased understanding. However, if the initial level of knowledge in a group is below average, a highly probable outcome is an increase in ignorance and prejudice. Team activities, therefore, should not be used in situations where ignorance prevails.

- Team activities make people anxious. Not everyone has the interpersonal skills required for participation in team activities. Peer pressure can make shy people intensely anxious. As Becker (1998) points out, losing face in a team activity decreases learning, creates long-term negative attitudes, and increases withdrawal, antagonism, and sabotage. In the absence of a sensitive facilitator, a team may traumatize its introverted members.

- Team activities are perceived to be inefficient. Most task-oriented, pragmatic professionals do not want to waste time on these activities. Such perceptions are reinforced by typical committee work. Team activities have an image problem in most corporations.

WHEN TO USE (OR AVOID) TEAM ACTIVITIES

As is true of any other kind of HPT intervention, team activities should be selected (or avoided) on the basis of systematic front-end, target-population, and task analyses. Team activities are likely to fail miserably in the following situations:

- When management is unwilling to wait for the intervention to have an impact
- When top management does not want to share power and decision-making authority
- When management wants team building as a one-shot affair
- When corporate reward systems reinforce individual achievement to the detriment of teamwork
- When most tasks are not interdependent
- When communication channels do not function effectively
- When management does not want to face the reality of its own weakness
- When management does not want input from workers because it has predefined all the problems and all the solutions

Appropriate use of team activities is likely to produce cost-effective results in the following situations:

- When management recognizes that teamwork and employee participation are necessary for improving productivity
- When projects are complex and interdisciplinary
- When the organization is young and its operating procedures are fluid
- When team members have been dissatisfied with one another
- When employees have been complaining about confusing goals, values, mission statements, and beliefs
- When people have been complaining that others are encroaching on their turf
- When people have been unable to clearly specify their roles and responsibilities
- When managers are frequently surprised by bad news
- When there have been frequent clashes between supervisors and workers

DEVELOPMENT OF TEAM ACTIVITIES

The HPT process of analysis, design, evaluation, and implementation is readily applicable to the development of team activities. Guidelines for adapting this process to the development of team activities are presented in the sections that follow.

Analysis

During front-end analysis, several symptoms suggest the suitability of team activities. These include an increasing number of interpersonal clashes and complaints about low morale and motivation. During target-population analysis, information about the preferences and skills of potential participants in team settings should be collected through the use of questions such as the following:

- What is the range of interpersonal skills among members of the target population?

- What misconceptions about team activities do they have?

- What existing habits are likely to interfere with the effective use of team activities?

- What types of team activities have they already used? With what degree of success?

- What are the preferred types of team activities?

- What is the preferred size for a team?

- What types of members are preferred for a team?

- What tools and equipment (such as networked computers) can participants use to facilitate their team interactions?

The organizational system should also be analyzed to identify factors that can facilitate or inhibit the effectiveness of team activities. Here are some sample questions to be asked during this analysis:

- What is the organization's perception of team activities? Do the cultural values reward independent achievement in preference to team-based collaboration?

- How do the standard operating procedures of the organization affect team activities?

- Does the organization use multifunctional teams?

- How efficient does management perceive team activities to be?

- Do managers believe in specialized job responsibilities or in cross-functional responsibilities?

- How are physical facilities organized? Do rooms and furniture lend themselves to teamwork? How must the physical environment be modified to facilitate team activities?

In addition to the usual task-analysis information needs, here are some questions for the development of team activity:

- What jobs and functions require interpersonal interaction?
- Who receives the outputs of particular jobs?
- What are the advantages and disadvantages of putting several independent performers together on a team?
- Does this job, task, or subtask require individual activity, or can it benefit from teamwork?
- Is this job or task dull, boring, and repetitious? Can the presence of other workers make it less tedious?

Design

The design phase in HPT begins with the specification of outcomes and a blueprint for the selected intervention. The team activity should be attached to a selected HPT intervention so that it does not become an end in itself. Here are some guidelines for creating effective team activities:

- Practice what is being preached. Use team activities for designing team activities. In addition to experts in the selected intervention, the design group should include representatives of the target population.
- Design the activity for maximum flexibility. For example, if an activity has been designed to require exactly fourteen people interacting for exactly forty-five minutes and assuming exactly three roles, its rigidity may impede its ability to be effective. Alternative approaches to team activities should be provided.
- Try to achieve a balance between personal and task needs. For example, an instructional game in which winning depends exclusively on mastery of skills is no more interesting than a criterion test. If winning depends entirely on chance, however, there is no need to master the skills. What is needed is an optimum balance between chance elements and instructional elements.
- Permit local "finish." The initial task in a team activity should be to modify methods and materials to suit local needs, preferences, constraints, and resources. This provides ownership to participants.
- Highlight the productivity of the team activity. Unless tangible products or specific learning gains are made salient, participants may complain about excessive process and little product.

Evaluation

Team activities, like other types of HPT interventions, should undergo developmental testing and revision. Here are some guidelines to add to the standard formative procedures:

- Evaluate and revise a team activity in stages. Begin with a self-review and revision by the designer. Check the design against data from different analyses (performance analysis, learner analysis, system analysis, task analysis). Make appropriate changes so as to improve the alignment of the design with the analysis.

- Anticipate the reactions of different participants. At the self-review stage, arrange for role playing of the various cultural and professional subgroups that will be involved in the team strategy. Using appropriate exaggeration, react to materials and tasks. Revise elements that are likely to be culturally offensive or confusing to different subgroups.

- Conduct an expert review and revision. Have subject matter experts check the appropriateness, accuracy, and adequacy of the intervention. In addition, have experts from the target population react to the blueprint. Solicit feedback from experts in the specific type of team activity.

- Test components of the activity on individuals. Check for clarity of directions, and revise the package to improve its user-friendliness.

- Conduct team testing as early as possible. Gather a group of articulate participants to collect feedback. During later stages of group testing, use more representative participants. Collect data through observation during the activity and during the debriefing at the end.

- Conduct a field test in which the intervention is implemented by a facilitator other than the designer. The focus of this test should be the usability of the package by an external facilitator. Observe the facilitator during the activity, without intervening. Make appropriate changes to the facilitator's manual.

Implementation

With a dynamic corporate culture and a flexible design, the implementation of team activities can be relatively easy. Here are some guidelines for the implementation stage:

- As early as possible, obtain management's commitment to the use of team activities. Do not surprise decision makers with a team package when they are expecting a strategy that emphasizes independent work.

- From the initial stages on, keep facilitators and members of the target population informed about the project's progress. Actively seek their input at various stages.

- Conduct a force-field analysis of factors that facilitate and inhibit team strategies. For example, conflict between the work ethic and the implied playfulness of the activity could be a major inhibitor. In this situation, reduce playfulness to increase acceptance.

- Anticipate complaints of inefficiency. Develop logical arguments and collect data to highlight the efficiency of the team activity by comparison with independent activity. Include in the list of benefits such intangibles as ownership and motivation. If it is not possible to collect efficiency data from within the organization, use success stories from similar organizations in the same industry.

- Implement the team activities gradually. Begin with the most flexible component that is likely to have the most visible impact. Add the other components later.

FACILITATION OF TEAM ACTIVITIES

Once an activity has been developed, it has to be conducted with members of the appropriate team. The relationship between development and facilitation of team activities is analogous to the relationship between development and delivery of instruction. Facilitation, according to Schwarz (1994), is "a process in which a person who is acceptable to all members of the group, [is] substantively neutral, and has no decision-making authority intervenes to help a group improve the way it identifies and solves problems and makes decisions, in order to increase the group's effectiveness." This definition identifies the ideal context for facilitation and focuses on team performance rather than on team learning.

Most HPT practitioners already have many of the characteristics of an effective facilitator, but it is still worthwhile to examine the desirable characteristics for a facilitator, as presented in the literature (Bacon, 1996; Hunter, Bailey, and Taylor, 1995; Kaner, 1996; Schwarz, 1994; Weaver and Farrell, 1997). Table 26.1 contains a list of these characteristics.

Facilitation can take place in a variety of situations. These situations can be conveniently classified according to the type of task (say, preparing a mission statement) to be accomplished by the team, or the type of event (say, a new-product launch) in which the team participates. Table 26.2 provides a list of task-related facilitation activities, with each activity accompanied by an illustrative question; training is subsumed under the category of facilitated activities.

Table 26.3 provides a list of events. The facilitator of an event, lest he or she be relegated to the function of a recreation director, should question clients and representatives of teams about the primary purpose of the event and should try to convert it to a task-oriented activity with specified objectives.

AN OVERVIEW OF THE FACILITATION PROCESS

A comprehensive discussion of the facilitation process is beyond the scope of this chapter, but the following section provides an overview of the process at three levels of detail (see Tables 26.4, 26.5, and 26.6):

1. The *mega* level, which affords a big-picture view of the facilitation process, from the initial contact with a client to the long-term follow up after the project

2. The *macro* level, which involves the details of an actual intervention, from the opening of a session to the debriefing of participants

3. The *micro* level, which involves the types of specific competence related to specific tactics in a facilitated activity

INTERNATIONAL AND INTERCULTURAL FACILITATION

With more corporations becoming global and more HPT practitioners consulting around the world, a frequently asked question is "Will this team activity work in country X or with culture Y?" The answer is yes. Participants from different cultures are open to team activities that are appropriately positioned and

Table 26.1. Desirable Characteristics of Facilitators.

Ability to blend intuitive and rational approaches	Intrapersonal intelligence
Ability to blend qualitative and quantitative approaches	Long-term focus
	Neutrality
	Objectivity
Ability to improvise	Open-mindedness
Accountability	Playfulness
Assertiveness	Preference for diversity
Balance	Process expertise
Confidence	Realism
Consistency between word and deed	Respect
Continuous learning	Self-esteem
Creativity	Self-sufficiency
Efficiency	Sense of humor
Emotional detachment	Service
Emotional resiliency	Simplicity
Empathic listening skills	Sincerity
Enthusiasm	Technical expertise
Flexibility	Tolerance for ambiguity
Impartiality	Tolerance for lack of closure
Inclusiveness	Trust
Innovativeness	Truthfulness
Integrity	Versatility
Interpersonal intelligence	Willingness to share responsibility

Table 26.2. Task-Oriented Facilitation Activities.

Action planning
How do we achieve our mission?

Change management
How can we ensure the smooth implementation of the new system?

Consensus building
On what do we agree about critical issues in our workplace?

Creative problem solving
How do we reduce the impact of the shippers' strike?

Culture development
What stories, songs, and symbols reflect our culture?

Focus-group data collection
How do you make a decision about your computer purchase?

Decision making
Which of these strategies should we implement?

Design
What should our training device look like?

Detective problem solving
What is the root cause for the decline in shipments to eastern Europe?

Environmental analysis
What factors influence the growth of our industry?

Future scanning
What economic changes in the next decade are likely to affect our organization?

Future search
How can we get everyone in our community to help improve our school system?

Large-group, real-time, total-systems change planning
How can all of us decide on our priority goals for next year?

Mission statement
What is the mission of our organization?

Organizational transformation
How can we transform our company into a green organization?

Philosophy retreat
What is the purpose of our organization?

Policy formulation
How should we handle conflicts of interest among our top managers?

Presentation planning
How should we present the new policy at the next board meeting?

Process improvement
How can we reduce the cycle time for processing customer orders?

Product improvement
How can we improve the flight simulator?

Project management planning
What delays should we expect during the project, and how should we deal with them?

Quality improvement
How can we reduce waste in our assembly line?

Strategic planning
What should be our priority area for the next ten years?

Systematic problem solving
How do we reduce turnover among our salespeople?

Team building
How can we increase the level of trust in our team?

Therapy
How can we help the team members reduce their mutual distrust?

TQM
How can we delight our customers?

Training
How can we encourage idea sharing among employees in different plants?

effectively debriefed. When team activities are used for instructional purposes, people in most cultures will accept them if the facilitator is skilled and flexible.

An important factor in the successful use of a team activity is the context. If the instruction is timely, if the learning objectives are based on observable and meaningful behavior, and if the activity is set in a proper business framework, then people will learn, and their learning will be transferred to the workplace.

Perhaps the reason why the transferability of team activities across cultures is questioned at all has to do with the notion that these activities are recent

Table 26.3. Events for Conversion to Task-Oriented Activities.

Annual meeting	Monthly meeting
Annual retreat	Open house
Board meeting	Progress review
Closure ceremony	Sales conference
Company picnic	Sendoff party
Founders' day	Stockholders' meeting
Inauguration	Victory celebration
Job fair	Visitors' day
Kickoff	Weekly meeting

Table 26.4. Mega Model of the Facilitation Process.

Make initial contact	Talk to the contact client
	Determine who the client is
	Identify need
	Diagnose need
	Analyze context
Plan for facilitation	Assemble planning group
	Meet with members of the group
	Contract with the client
	Specify details
Conduct premeeting discussions	Identify cofacilitators
	Train cofacilitators
Present contract to the full group	Discuss ground rules
	Revise ground rules
Conduct facilitated activity	Open the session
	Conduct different activities
	Conclude the sessions
Complete facilitated activity	Present report and recommendations
	Conduct immediate follow-up
	Conduct long-term follow-up

Table 26.5. Macro Model of a Facilitation Intervention.

Open the session	Welcome the participants Introduce yourself Introduce the topic Explain the format
Set the agenda	Review the agenda Modify the agenda
Establish ground rules	Discuss ground rules Modify ground rules
Collect data	Encourage discussion Include everyone
Formulate the problem	Redefine the problem
Collect ideas	Discuss ideas Identify alternatives Evaluate alternatives
Reach an agreement	Strive for consensus Reach closure
Debrief the participants	Share insights Plan next steps

Table 26.6. Micro Model of Facilitation Tactics.

Adjourning	Framing	Opening
Answering questions	Funneling	Organizing
Arranging the room	Gatekeeping	Orienting
Asking questions	Giving feedback	Paraphrasing
Briefing	Handling complaints	Presenting information
Bringing closure	Handling emotions	Preventing closure
Celebrating	Increasing playfulness	Questioning answers
Challenging	Increasing seriousness	Rearranging furniture
Checking for consensus	Increasing the level of	Receiving feedback
Closing	competition	Recording
Coaching	Increasing the level of	Redirecting questions
Cofacilitating	cooperation	Regrouping
Communicating nonverbally	Interpreting	Resolving conflicts
Confronting	Interrupting	Respecting
Contributing	Intervening	Rewarding
Converging	Letting go	Setting climate
Debriefing	Linking	Slowing down
Diverging	Listening	Speaking
Encouraging	Loosening the structure	Speeding up
Establishing ground rules	Maintaining silence	Stacking
Evaluating	Mind mapping	Stimulating
Focusing on commonality	Mirroring	Summarizing
Focusing on diversity	Modeling	Sympathizing
Focusing on the group	Monitoring	Taking charge
Focusing on the individual	Motivating	Tightening
Focusing on the process	Negotiating	Tracking
Focusing on the results	Observing	Transitioning

inventions of the West, and particularly of the United States. The reality, however, is that team activities have been around for a long time, all around the world. To combat the epidemic misconception that team activities will not work in other cultures, the following cautionary tactics are suggested:

- Don't believe the experts. When well-meaning people warn you against the use of team activities in a specific country, you need to probe for the basis of their data. Eventually you may discover that their cautionary advice is less about the participants' potential reactions to team activities than about the advisers' own projections.

- Don't believe your contact client. Just as the fish is the creature that is the least aware of water, citizens of a country or members of a culture are perhaps the least knowledgeable about local values and preferences. Your informant from a different country (for example, the president of a corporation) is also likely to be of a generation and from a social class that are different from the generation and social class of your target population.

- Don't believe in stereotypes. All generalizations about a country or a culture are only probabilistic approximations. It is possible that the specific group you are facilitating is a biased sample of the general population. Moreover, professional values may reduce the saliency of cultural values. As a Japanese photographer put it, "I share more values and beliefs with a photographer from the U.S. than with a manager in Japan."

I am not trying to suggest that there are no significant differences in the way participants from different countries or cultures react to team activities. Actually, each group and each individual will react differently to team activities. The secret of successful facilitation with any group is to adjust the activity before, during, and after its implementation so that the activity becomes transparent and the outcome becomes salient.

Here are some guidelines for facilitating groups in a flexible fashion:

- Identify the values and preferences that are likely to influence the team activity. For example, a group in India might feel uncomfortable about physical contact, disclosure of personal emotions, and excessive celebrations of small successes; so would a group of engineers in the United States.

- Identify characteristics of the team activity that are likely to clash with these values and preferences.

- Make adjustments to the activity, or plan strategies for persuading the participants to tolerate their initial discomfort.

- Introduce the activity. Monitor the team, and make real-time adjustments to make the activity transparent.

- At the conclusion of the activity, debrief the team to discover strategies for modifying the activity for more effective use with similar groups in the future.

CONCLUSION

Ordinary people working in teams can achieve extraordinary things. Team activities support the fundamental HPT tenet that we should always be accountable for the ultimate target group. The successful design and use of these activities will also require increased commitment to the idea that involving the target group in every stage of Human Performance Technology is essential, ethical, and effective.

References

Bacon, T. R. (1996). *High-impact facilitation.* Durango, CO: International Learning Works.

Becker, R. (1998, Feb.). Taking the misery out of experiential training. *Training* 35:2, 78–88.

Clark, R. C. (1998). *Building expertise.* Washington, DC: International Society for Performance Improvement.

Duke, R. D. (1974). *Gaming: The future's language.* New York: Halsted Press.

Gardner, H. (1983). *Frames of mind: The theory of multiple intelligences.* New York: Basic Books.

Goleman, D. (1995). *Emotional intelligence.* New York: Bantam.

Greenblat, C. S. (1988). *Designing games and simulations: An illustrated handbook.* Thousand Oaks, CA: Sage.

Hackman, J. R. (ed.). (1990). *Groups that work (and those that don't): Creating conditions for effective teamwork.* San Francisco: Jossey-Bass.

Hunter, C., Bailey, A., and Taylor, B. (1995). *The art of facilitation: How to create group synergy.* Tucson, AZ: Fisher Books.

Jacobs, R. W. (1994). *Real-time strategic change: How to involve an entire organization in fast and far-reaching change.* San Francisco: Berrett-Koehler.

Kaner, S. (1996). *Facilitator's guide to participatory decision-making.* Gabriola Island, BC, Canada: New Society.

Kohn, A. (1986). *No contest: The case against competition.* Boston: Houghton Mifflin.

Mattimore, B. W. (1990). Mind blasters. *Success* 37:5, 46–47.

McLagan, P., and Nel, C. (1995). *The age of participation: New governance for the workplace and the world.* San Francisco: Berrett-Koehler.

Olson, H. A. (1990). *The new way to compete: How to discover your personal competitive style and make it work for you.* San Francisco: New Lexington Press.

Phillips, S. L., and Elledge, R. L. (1989). *The team-building sourcebook.* San Francisco: Jossey-Bass/Pfeiffer.

Prensky, M. (1998, Jan.). Twitch speed. *Across the Board,* pp. 14–19.

Reddy, W. B., and Jamison, K. (eds.). (1988). Team building: Blueprints for productivity and satisfaction. San Francisco: Jossey-Bass/Pfeiffer.

Scannel, E. E., and Newstrom, J. W. (1985). *Games trainers play.* New York: McGraw-Hill.

Schank, R. (1997). *Virtual learning: A revolutionary approach to building a highly skilled workforce.* New York: McGraw-Hill.

Schwarz, R. M. (1994). *The skilled facilitator: Practical wisdom for developing effective groups.* San Francisco: Jossey-Bass.

Senge, P. M. (1990). *The fifth discipline: The art and practice of the learning organization.* New York: Doubleday.

Senge, P. M., and others. (1994). *The fifth discipline fieldbook.* New York: Doubleday.

Sternberg, R. J. (1996). *Successful intelligence: How practical and creative intelligence determine success in life.* New York: Simon & Schuster.

Stolovitch, H., and Thiagarajan, S. (1980). *Frame games.* Englewood Cliffs, NJ: Educational Technology Publications.

Templeton, J. F. (1987). *Focus groups: A guide for marketing and advertising professionals.* Chicago: Probus.

Thiagarajan, S. (1978). *Grouprograms.* Englewood Cliffs, NJ: Educational Technology Publications.

Thiagarajan, S. (1980). *Experiential learning packages.* Englewood Cliffs, NJ: Educational Technology Publications.

Twelker, P. A. (1975). Examining the research evidence on simulation/gaming. *Improving Human Performance Quarterly* 4:3, 96–104.

van Ments, M. (1983). The effective use of role-play: A handbook for teachers and trainers. East Brunswick, NJ: Nichols.

Weaver, R. B., and Farrell, J. D. (1997). *Managers as facilitators.* San Francisco: Berrett-Koehler.

Wohlking, W., and Gill, P. (1980). *Role playing.* Englewood Cliffs, NJ: Educational Technology Publications.

CHAPTER TWENTY-SEVEN

Performance Improvement with Mentoring

Margo Murray

Ask ten successful people in as many different careers or occupations to describe the factors contributing to their success, and nine of them will probably say, "Early in my career, I was fortunate to have a mentor." Most mentoring experiences are described in positive terms by both protégés and their mentors. Occasionally, we do hear and read about experiences that were unpleasant or destructive for the protégés, as well as about some that were less than rewarding for the mentors. Those negative experiences are most often reported after the experience of a mentoring relationship that was informal and usually had developed by happenstance, and in which there had been no specific discussion or mutual agreement about the expectations of either partner.

These unhappy outcomes can be avoided if the mentoring process is facilitated. Organizations in both the public and the private sector are planning more carefully and designing processes to guide participants toward clarifying their expectations of each other at the beginning of their relationships.

More and more managers and leaders are turning to mentoring as a strategy for improving human performance in leaner, flatter organizations. Now that technology has leveled the playing field for many businesses, an exceptionally competent workforce is seen as the most promising competitive advantage. The wide range of entry-level knowledge and skills among workers make classroom instruction both ineffective and inefficient. Limited time for the myriad tasks in every worker's job makes it essential that each learning experience be focused on specific individual needs and skill gaps.

Some organizations are now describing themselves as "learning organizations" with the same fervor that many expressed when describing themselves as "total-quality organizations." The criteria for attaining the stature of learning organization are even fuzzier than for becoming a total-quality organization. For many products and services there are quality measures that can be communicated clearly enough to performers, vendors, and customers for the relevant goals to be achieved, but I have yet to hear any proponent of the "learning organization" goal describe performance indicators in such a way that an observer would say that the description was accurate. A facilitated mentoring process, however, integrated into the culture of the organization and aligned with other Human Performance (HP) improvement processes, can create a continuous learning climate and allow a company to earn the status of learning organization.

Myths still abound in descriptions of mentoring processes. To clarify the foundation for the discussion and examples used in this chapter, let us begin with some basic concepts and definitions of terms. (Later in the chapter, when specific examples of particular organizations' mentoring processes are being related, the terms used will be those of the individuals involved.)

PROCESS, ROLES, AND TASKS OF MENTORING

The term *mentoring* is often used incorrectly to describe what someone does. It is useful to distinguish the mentoring process from the role of mentor and from the tasks that a mentor performs.

In current best practice with facilitated mentoring, the term *mentoring* describes the process that is implemented to deliberately pair two people who have unequal levels of a relevant set of skills and experiences. The objective of this process is to transfer knowledge and experience of these skills from the person who has more of them to the person who has fewer.

The role of *mentor* is taken on by someone who is willing to help someone else learn and grow by interacting with this person to transfer skills and experience. Mentors may perform several tasks in the process of their interactions with their protégés. These include but are not limited to tutoring, coaching, listening, counseling, teaching, modeling, giving feedback, demonstrating, giving information, facilitating desired performance, and guiding. Table 27.1 shows examples of the types of skills that are being transferred today with facilitated mentoring processes in some well-known organizations. The following examples are intended to clarify what mentors may do in carrying out their roles with their protégés.

Tutoring

A recent graduate and newly hired engineer in petroleum exploration brings state-of-the-art technical knowledge in petrochemical engineering, and particularly in computer modeling. She is paired with a mentor who is a highly skilled

Table 27.1. Skills Transferred Through Mentoring.

Job Title	Growth Objective from Mentoring
Capital projects accountant	Acquire experience in trade relations, purchasing skills
Commodity manager	Improve people skills; increase exposure and awareness to upper management's activities; develop courage
Copy center manager	Develop presentation skills, using multilingual capabilities
Electrical design engineer	Gain experience to develop finance and business proposals
International trade specialist	Increase drive; improve time management
Market development manager	Strengthen sales skills; improve balance between assertiveness and flexibility
Personnel relations manager	Improve skills with cost impact of personnel decisions; improve compensation and benefits skills
Project coordinator	Learn more about the structure of the organization; develop skills in project management
Quality program manager	Develop task-oriented approach to total-quality management
Technical services center representative	Learn how to set priorities for career goals; articulate and quantify smaller steps toward long-term goals
Territory representative	Develop more effective skills in handling visits to customers
Warehouse supervisor	Learn company policies and procedures

and experienced engineer. He tutors her in communicating and negotiating effectively with contractors who design equipment.

Coaching

A sales representative in a sports apparel distribution firm has set an objective to strengthen her sales skills in order to improve sales results in her territory. Her mentor agrees to accompany her on sales calls to observe and coach her while she is interacting with customers. Coaching is done just before the task is to be performed and is carried out through subtle, timely interventions during the sales call itself.

Listening

A personnel relations manager feels drained by constant complaints about company policies and procedures. He wants his mentor just to listen to him ventilate his own frustration with the policies, which he must interpret, but which he sees no way to change at this time.

Counseling

A recent college graduate is hired by a small public accounting firm. This junior employee is immediately given a series of short-term auditing, tax planning, and consulting assignments with clients, and for each one she reports to a different manager. Her mentor counsels her on career paths in the firm, helping her explore all her options and select an area of specialization before she becomes a senior employee.

Teaching

An electrical design engineer in an aerospace company sets a long-term career goal of becoming a general manager. His mentor agrees to teach him how to develop financial analyses and business proposals.

Modeling

A commodities manager has an objective of gaining exposure to and awareness of upper management's activities. She asks her mentor to allow her to observe him modeling appropriate behavior at business-related social events with higher-level executives.

Giving Feedback

A territory representative knows every feature and benefit of the product being sold. His goal is to develop his skills in effective handling of visits to customers. The action plan agreed to with the mentor includes having the mentor observe several customer visits and give feedback on the quality of interaction with the customers.

Demonstrating

The manager of a copy center has a long-term career goal of working in public relations, which will require good presentation skills. Her mentor invites her to a meeting of a professional society to watch him demonstrate how to make an effective presentation. After the event, they discuss strengths and areas for improvement in the mentor's presentation.

Guiding

A technical services center representative has a development objective of learning how to set priorities for his career goals and of articulating and quantifying the smaller steps that will be needed in achieving his long-term goals. His mentor takes on the role and task of guiding the protégé in the process of determining the investment he is willing to make in his own career development.

Giving Information

A warehouse supervisor aspires to be the manager of her building. Her mentor provides information on company policies and procedures that managers must follow and interpret to their subordinates.

Facilitating Desired Performance

An experienced project coordinator recognizes that he puts some people off with his abrupt way of demanding progress reports. His mentor agrees to facilitate the development of his project management skills and to focus on the project coordinator's style of communication and interaction with members of the project teams.

One additional point may help to distinguish mentoring from on-the-job training: most on-the-job training is conducted by the immediate supervisor of the function or group. It is sometimes delegated to a team leader or to the lead performer, but in either case the objective is to produce or refine the skills needed for performance in the current job.

EVOLUTION OF THE MENTORING CONCEPT

The principles and practices of modeling and mentoring have been key elements in the arts, the crafts, and commerce since ancient times. In arts or crafts guilds, a young person was apprenticed to a master who was considered to be excellent in the trade or profession (Murray and Owen, 1991). The master taught, coached, and guided the development of the relevant skills. To become a master, the apprentice had his skills judged on the basis of a work sample (a painting, a horseshoe). The term *masterpiece* originated from this practice.

The skills required of a new master are as different from those required of a blacksmith's apprentice as a high-tech clean room is from a blacksmith shop, and yet the one-to-one process by which the skills are learned is very much the same. Mastering an art, craft, or profession certainly increases one's marketability in diverse workplaces. Flexibility is essential when workplaces include people from dozens of different cultures. This flexibility can be strengthened by enabling the transfer of the requisite skills and experiences in a facilitated mentoring process.

MENTORING MYTHS

Myths about mentoring continue to proliferate in all types of publications. Many of these popular myths are readily dispelled with data from actual experience; some indicate pitfalls that must be recognized, avoided, and thereby prevented from jeopardizing the success of a desired program. Here are a few typical myths:

- Women, in order to tap in to power, must seek men as mentors.
- Imitating a role model whose performance and behavior are not always admirable or relevant limits one's growth.
- One-to-one mentoring relationships cannot succeed because mentors will not give the time.
- Structuring or formalizing a mentoring relationship will take the magic out of it.

Traditionally, mentors have been thought of as older, long-service people who select their own protégés and take them firmly in hand to guide their lifetime career development—and the lucky protégés then live happily ever after. When we read the dark side of the stories, we get the impression that mentors use protégés for work projects, take credit for their work, and sometimes even abuse the mentoring relationship and the mentoring partner, refusing to let go when the protégé has outgrown the relationship. Or mentors complain that neophytes attach themselves to their coattails and expect to be carried along to success, without having to make much of a personal effort. But these kinds of relationships, whether positive or negative, are what could be defined as a role-modeling or sponsorial relationships (Murray and Owen, 1991). Someone who strives to emulate a successful person (one who may not even be aware of the imitator's positive regard) is not in an actual mentoring relationship. Nor are the fortunate few who have sponsors to recommend them for advantageous appointments or other benefits.

VALUE ADDED THROUGH MENTORING

Mentoring processes are currently designed and implemented to support a wide range of business imperatives. For example, a rapidly growing financial institution has implemented a mentoring process, recognizing that leadership will be the key to superior returns for all stakeholders. A nuclear power regulatory agency has established a mentoring process with emphasis on increasing cross-cultural awareness and the valuing of diversity among its employees. A technical services consulting firm expects to expedite the transfer of professional and technical skills and to reduce excessive turnover of highly educated and skilled people.

Career Development and Succession Planning

Implementing a mentoring process that targets career development and succession planning may seem questionable at first glance, in light of the decreasing number of opportunities for promotion in leaner, flatter organizations. A closer look reveals that when there is less room at the top, there is little or no margin for error in promoting people.

In a recent study of the drivers for implementing mentoring processes for 636 pairs of employees (Murray, 1997), 42 percent of the reporting organizations had put their facilitated mentoring processes in place to support career development of employees. A significant number (30 percent) of the mentoring relationships had been created for the purpose of transferring technical skills. Only 4 percent of the mentoring relationships were reported to have been established with the purpose of planning for succession or facilitating executive or management development, and this finding may be an indication of leaner, flatter organizations with few opportunities for advancement. Other drivers of mentoring processes were diversity (12 percent), multiskilling and flexibility (9 percent), gender diversity (3 percent), and employee morale (less than 1 percent).

Cross-Cultural Awareness and Valuing of Diversity

Multinational firms and organizations are now hiring employees of both genders with widely differing ages, educational backgrounds, cultural experiences, physical abilities, and ethnic backgrounds. Where sensitivity to these differences is lacking, communication may break down, and the impact on business results can be severe. Even unintentional offenses may result in legal action or loss of customers. One very common problem is substandard performance from employees, which results from misunderstandings about assignments when there are differences of language or communication style.

For decades, organizations in the United States have been trying, with mixed results, to take collective approaches to these issues. The popular "social responsibility" training of the 1960s, the seminars on race relations of the 1970s, the T-groups of the 1980s, and the diversity workshops of the 1990s have failed, for the most part, or fallen short of the desired outcomes. The expressed goals of these approaches were to have people in organizations value the differences between themselves and others and realize that there is strength in the availability of multiple ways to solve problems and seize opportunities. But preaching at groups of people that they "really oughta wanna" like people who are different from themselves has not worked, and informal mentoring relationships have actually exacerbated the problem because many self-appointed mentors have proceeded to clone themselves in their protégés. When people who are different in education, age, culture, gender, or some other respect have been deliberately paired, however, the result has often been that both partners actually do come to respect and value these differences; it is easier to see the strength that derives from diversity when one is working on a one-to-one basis with another person, and with an agreed-upon goal.

The same organizations that were previously described as having reported on the drivers for their mentoring processes (Murray, 1997) were also asked to identify the gender of each partner in the 636 pairs of employees. Almost half the pairs (43 percent) consisted of a male mentor with a male protégé. Recall that 3 percent of the pairs that had been matched for the express purpose of increasing the valuing of gender diversity; of that number as well, over half consisted of two same-gender employees.

Transfer of Professional or Technical Skills

As already mentioned, rapid changes in technology have leveled the playing field for many businesses and made traditional training in group courses or classes less effective and certainly more inefficient. When extant knowledge and skills vary widely, group training that is aimed at the average learner probably hits the mark for only about 15 percent of the trainees, with the other 85 percent forced to sit through nice-to-know or irrelevant content. When training is focused on specific deficiencies in technical or professional skills, however, the motivation to learn is much higher, and the process is more efficient.

Mentoring processes are often designed to match technicians or professionals up with peers, in order to facilitate two-way transfer of skills. This broader skills base makes each of the participants more flexible and more readily assignable to a different function in the organization. Obviously, this practice increases their value to the organization, as well as their ability to sustain their motivation for peak performance.

USES OF MENTORING IN VARIOUS ENTERPRISES

The types of organizations that have implemented facilitated mentoring processes run the gamut from aerospace companies to universities, and the types of added business value they seek vary just as widely. The following examples illustrate the uses of facilitated mentoring in different kinds of enterprises.

Aerospace

With the draw down in defense spending, many companies that historically depended on government contracts for a major source of their business have found they now have to become more competitive for the fewer contracts available. Some have lost points on proposals because they did not have enough minority or female executives or subcontractors. In these cases, mentoring processes have been established to expedite the development of minority and female executive candidates. In addition, some larger corporations have taken on the role of mentor to small businesses operated by women and minorities, and this practice has gained them points in the competitive bidding process.

Banking Industry

When one rapidly growing bank established an aggressive marketing strategy, one result was a change in the set of core skills required of the bank's officers and managers. New managers, who had experience and skills in marketing and sales, were recruited from financial institutions (such as brokerage firms), from sales jobs in real estate, and from management positions in retail merchandising. The gaps in their experience and skills were in banking services and products. A development map was designed for the purpose of involving mentors who could coach the new managers on specific skills and help put their existing skills in the context of retail banking.

Community Foundations

Even before federal laws were passed to limit the time that welfare benefits would be provided to families, some community foundations saw a need to help people develop job-seeking and job-keeping skills. A community group in a midwestern city obtained foundation funding to pilot a mentoring process for women on welfare. The targeted women were matched with successful (that is, employed) female mentors. Formal training sessions were scheduled for the mentors and the mentees (the group's term), with topics that ranged from budgeting for home expenses to resisting an aggressive door-to-door salesperson. The mentees reported success in obtaining jobs, going back to school, and ending abusive personal relationships.

Computer Industry: Manufacturing, Sales, and Service

One company, to improve its business results in this highly competitive industry, used reengineering to create a strategy of selling solutions to customers. Before, there had been specialists in hardware, software, and customer services, and a mentoring process now matched these specialists up across functions to enable two-way transfer of skills. On eleven essential job skills, people were able to achieve a measurable increase of 61 percent in their levels of skill (Duncan, 1995) in addition to demonstrating gains in nine of eleven career-effectiveness skills that were measured with an assessment instrument.

Financial Services

A bank's credit card division was experiencing unacceptably high turnover among customer service representatives. Quality and productivity were also below standard. A comprehensive job and task analysis revealed that all new hires were scheduled for twenty days of training in a lockstep format that was led and paced by the trainer. Analysis of the target population showed that many of the new hires had extensive experience in customer service, some had strong computer skills, and a few had actual knowledge of credit card products. The training format was revised to be learner-oriented, with a combination of trainer modeling, self-study with print materials and computer help screens, and coaching with a mentor. Areas for mentored coaching included defusing the anger of customers who questioned their bills, navigating through complicated computer screens of customer history, and planning job performance with supervisors. Within six months the average training time had dropped to fourteen days, retention of desired employees increased, and the quality of service improved.

Health Care Product Distribution

In a company that distributed health care products, a mentoring process was implemented to improve retention of warehouse workers and improve communication across functions. The results in the first year were that 18 percent of the warehouse workers were promoted or made lateral moves into other functions in the company.

Highway Engineering Industry

An agency with an aging workforce in the managerial and higher-level administrative ranks wondered why it was losing bright young engineers after four years on the job. The formal training ran about twenty-seven months, so these losses meant a high cost to the agency. The newer engineers saw that the older, more senior people tended to promote the careers of people who were very much like themselves in terms of education, gender, and ethnicity. The message sent to those outside that group was that there would be no promotional opportunities for them, and so they left. A decision was made to implement a mentoring process that would make developmental experiences available to everyone on an equitable basis.

Information Systems

A supplier of large-scale information systems had an average sales cycle of nine months. Because it was thought that the company's experienced salespeople would not be willing to coach new salespeople, for fear of creating new internal competitors, an orientation workshop for these prospective mentors communicated the benefits that they would obtain from taking on this added role. After the mentoring program was established, one of the new mentors happily told the others that his protégée had closed her first big deal in just three weeks.

UNIQUE BENEFITS OF MENTORING: PERCEPTIONS AND REALITY

Since 1971 I have conducted workshops and collaborated with clients on implementing mentoring processes in this country and in Argentina, Australia, Egypt, Finland, India, Ireland, Taiwan, the Netherlands, Sweden, and Venezuela. In the assessment phase of this work, I ask clients to identify the expected benefits for mentors, protégés, and the organization. At the beginning, it is essential to dispel the prevailing myths about mentoring and to clarify whether expectations can become reality. This process also captures baseline data for later evaluation of benefits. Moreover, unless a clear link can be made between mentoring and the organization's goals, needs, and opportunities, it is highly unlikely that the mentoring process will survive. The following summaries cite only a few examples of the many benefits reported by participants in mentoring programs in a range of organizations and countries.

Benefits for Protégés

In addition to a number of more personal benefits reported by protégés—the availability of a "sounding board," new avenues for information, new friendships, fun, the feeling that the organization cares, a feeling of being welcome, greater feelings of loyalty, the opportunity to receive honest feedback, being believed in by another person—the following benefits have been identified through analysis of development plans, checkpoint surveys, and self-reports of participants.

Greater Comprehension of Business Objectives. Increased organizational awareness and a clearer understanding of corporate culture and goals are often cited as gains by participants in mentoring processes. Further exploration has revealed that mentors are much more likely than line supervisors to provide information on the mission, goals, and future direction of the organization. Some protégés also describe a deeper sense of accountability, as well as a feeling that their contributions matter.

More Focused Development. When learning activities are focused on specific diagnosed needs, skill development is far more effective and efficient. Learning from a mentor's experience avoids costly and demotivating trial and error. One protégé in a small engineering firm said, "In one hour of coaching with my mentor, I solved some problems I had been struggling with for four months."

Increased Sense of Safety While Learning. Fear is a fierce obstacle to learning. Few of us would tell our bosses about all our weaknesses or lack of experience. Mentors provide a safe environments in which to practice skills. One protégé reported, "I found it was OK to be wrong, learn from my mistakes, and ask stupid questions. I could be real."

Higher Productivity and Evaluations. These increases may be partly attributable to protégés' improved skills in planning, negotiation, and feedback, improvements that show up when they are interacting with their supervisors. Another variable is the well-known Hawthorne effect: perhaps any extra attention improves performance.

More Possibilities for Advancement. Advancement can be accelerated by a guided career path, without the need for time-consuming, irrelevant assignments. With clarity of direction, people are more likely to develop the skills necessary for taking on greater responsibility. Even when there are few opportunities for promotion, people become more competitive for every opportunity when they have more competence, more confidence, and more visibility. For example, one country's department of justice perceived that women were not competing successfully for management positions. Development plans for employees included a combination of individual coaching with mentors and group training in areas of common need. After twelve months, three of the mentored women had taken up extra tertiary studies, two had been transferred to more challenging positions, one had been promoted to middle management, and one had been reclassified to a higher grade.

Greater Political Awareness. Participants have reported gaining greater insight into the maze of politics in their organizations. This increase in insight has made them feel more confident and powerful because the mentoring process accelerated their acceptance as insiders.

More Career Resiliency. When changes in markets, products, services, or the economy cause some functions or entire jobs to disappear, people with broad experience and multiple skills will land on their feet in different functions or new organizations. Directed learning activities shorten the time necessary for gaining the experience that will be needed for effective work in a different function.

Increased Visibility. Given the hectic pace of their demanding jobs, line managers are perhaps understandably lax about giving their subordinates the individual visibility and exposure that may be beneficial. One participant reported, "In the mentoring process I feel noticed and visible; it has expanded my network base immensely."

Greater Teamwork Skills. Learning to work closely with another person tends to make it easier to be a contributing member or a leader of a team.

Benefits for Mentors

One of the greatest challenges for an HP technologist in implementing and sustaining a mentoring process is the task of recruiting good mentors. For example, shy people may be reluctant to volunteer as mentors and yet may readily agree to serve when invited to do so. Even more of a challenge is knowing how to reward mentors appropriately so that they will maintain their motivation to keep agreements with their partners. Fortunately, a facilitated program can offer mentors some key personal and professional benefits.

Enhanced Influence in the Organization. Mentors are respected for the value they add in the development of future leaders of the organization. Through their protégés, mentors extend their influence on the mission and direction of the organization.

Attention to Developmental Needs. The mentor's skills in coaching, performance planning, and feedback are honed by working with protégés at varied levels of skill and experiences. Protégés often teach their mentors new skills as well.

Professional Assistance on Work Projects. A protégé may have a technical skill relevant to a project the mentor wants to have done. When a task can be taken as a learning experience by the protégé, additional work is accomplished for the mentor. Such tasks must be relevant to the development objectives of the protégé, however.

Maintenance of Motivation. A protégé's fresh viewpoint can spark the mentor's enthusiasm and motivation. Renewed enthusiasm is an antidote to burnout.

Access to New Perspectives on the Organization. Often managers and executives are shielded from problems at the operating levels when there is fear that the messenger will be shot. Problems and issues are discussed more openly, however, when there is a bond of trust with a mentor. Once again, the protégé's fresh point of view is a contribution in itself.

Opportunity to Have Ideas Challenged. Experienced, competent people may become complacent about the decisions they make and the strategies they use, and for a subordinate to challenge these decisions and strategies can be a career-limiting move. Working with a protégé who asks why something is done a particular way, however, may cause a mentor to reexamine habitual approaches and find that they are outdated or ineffective. Many mentors urge their partners to challenge their thinking, and they apparently enjoy this intellectual exercise more than they enjoy hearing "Yes, boss."

Benefits for the Organization

In lean times, or whenever organizations are trying to do more with less in order to stay competitive, no program will be supported unless it contributes to the overall results that are desired. Organizations are now evaluating the impact of facilitated mentoring on business results as well as on the skills and experience of mentors and their protégés. Here are some areas where positive outcomes have been reported.

Productivity. Improved performance and productivity are reported by both mentors and protégés. Protégés' skills are strengthened, and they are able to work more effectively and efficiently. Developmental projects carried out by protégés often assist mentors with their work.

Development of Skills. Most mentors report that coaching of protégés is done on their own time, at no out-of-pocket cost to the organization. When mentoring is used as an alternative training strategy, employees become competent faster and at lower cost than in classroom training. Training that is individually based and self-paced is "just in time" training.

Costs. A municipal court system reported savings of over $6,000 when a protégée working with a mentor to prepare for the job of electronic recording monitor discovered that she did not like or want the job (Capaul, 1996). Terminating the six-week training process after a few short meetings with the mentor saved not only the instructional cost but also the self-esteem and job satisfaction of the protégée, who avoided a wrong career move.

Recruitment. Prospective employees are attracted to a firm that offers facilitated growth and development. A recruiter told me he had interviewed more than one hundred business school graduates for management trainee positions in a large paper-pulp manufacturing company. He was surprised to hear two-thirds of them ask if the company had a mentoring process.

Retention. Managers in a large consulting firm estimated that it costs $140,000 to replace a lost professional in their organization. The best and brightest people stay with a company that cares about their development—and, with better career counseling, sometimes the people who should leave do leave, and sooner.

Organizational Image. Public recognition that an organization provides a caring, developmental environment that includes a mentoring process can enhance the corporate image.

Strategic Goals. Organizational results are better when everyone knows the targets. Sharing mentors' experiences helps others avoid making the same mistakes. More competent and confident employees produce better results, creating a competitive edge. During a time of rapid change in one company, a participant commented, "This process gave us an element of stability, and it gave me an anchor in a time of chaos."

Benefits for Supervisors

Coordinators of facilitated mentoring programs may be surprised to find that the supervisors of protégés also recognize that they, too, can benefit directly from having their people work with mentors. This is a sensitive area, and it is a potential pitfall if it is not managed well. It is essential that all managers and supervisors of prospective protégés be briefed on what the mentoring process is and is not, and on the roles and responsibilities of all participants; otherwise, the supervisors may easily resent and feel threatened by a third person who is involved with a subordinate. Satisfied supervisors have offered comments like these:

"It gave me another resource for supporting employee development."

"I'm stretched pretty thin with day-to-day operations and have little time for people's career development. This helped."

"I was promoted to this job on the basis of my technical expertise and have had no training in career development."

"My employee got better at performance planning and communicating with me. That helped both of us."

PITFALLS AND PREVENTIVE ACTIONS

When potential pitfalls are articulated, they can be tackled proactively with one or more problem-solving strategies and prevented from jeopardizing the success of the new program. Table 27.2 lists possible pitfalls of a facilitated mentoring program, along with strategies that may prevent them.

One pitfall in any mentoring process, whether pairings are facilitated or informal, is that the mentor may take on an advocacy role for the protégé, but organizational policies can restrict the extent of this advocacy. In one federal agency, for example, all promotions are decided by a board or panel of administrators. The guidelines for the mentoring process explicitly prohibit any mentor from serving on the promotions board when that mentor's protégé is a candidate for promotion. A more likely situation is that the protégé will expect the mentor to take on the advocacy role. When no policies constrain such advocacy, the mentor must describe exactly how his or her support for the protégé may be demonstrated.

SYSTEMATIC DESIGN

Analysis

Some organizations want to have a mentoring process in place just to say that they have one, whether or not it fills an assessed need. To avoid offending such clients and losing business, I use the term *readiness assessment* in referring to this phase of the front-end work. Its purpose is still to determine the needs, goals, and opportunities that the organization is facing as it considers a facilitated mentoring process. The data gathered in the readiness assessment also enable the design of relevant briefings and orientations for participants in the mentoring process.

This readiness assessment includes scanning the work environment for commitment to and support of mentoring, as well as for any indicators of resistance or objections to the proposed process. Top managers, administrators, decision makers, and opinion setters are interviewed in one-to-one sessions. The objective is to get the widest possible range of opinions and expectations. Data are also elicited on goals, needs, and opportunities that may not be supported by a mentoring process.

Design/Production

One of the critical success factors for mentoring is the design of the mentoring process. It should be designed to fit the unique environment and culture of the organization and the targeted participants. As with any other kind of performance

Table 27.2. Pitfalls and Prevention Strategies.

Pitfall	Solution
Objection that the approach has been tried before	Clarify exactly what the facilitated mentoring process is; get people who are pro and con involved in development; show that mentoring is what competitors are doing
Inadequate resources	Show proof it reduces training costs; relate benefits to organization goals and objectives; present a success case (best practice, benchmarking); show cost avoidance with better retention of staff
Protégés' unwillingness to risk being open	Have mentoring pair sign a confidentiality agreement; establish level of disclosure on both sides
Perception of program as exclusive, only for certain people	Clearly define the business case for the process; establish clear, thorough communication as to what mentoring is and is not; align the mentoring process as one human resource strategy; offer resources used in the process to others
Lack of mentors	Get supervisors and managers to nominate mentors; show how program can benefit mentors; have prospective protégés nominate several choices as mentors; tie mentoring to key areas for results and reviews
Geographic obstacles to best pairings	Leverage technology (e-mail, fax, and telephone); establish a budget for travel; schedule coaching sessions during other meetings, vacations
"Tall poppy" or "heir apparent" syndrome	Use briefings to communicate goals, objectives; design for open entry and exit and for individual applications; get all stakeholders involved in the process
Conflict between mentor and protégé's supervisor	Clearly define roles and responsibilities; emphasize benefits to both protégé and supervisor; communicate rewards for supervisor
Flagging commitment of mentors	Use formal evaluation and credit; lunch with a "big cheese" (an executive with status); team performance bonus
Perception of program as a "flavor of the month" or "magic bullet"	Link mentoring to organizational goals; make mentoring a consistent part of management responsibility; include regular reviews and publicized successes; get high-level support for a minimum of three years; show how mentoring is aligned with other HPT strategies; provide feedback on results, success stories

improvement intervention, it is essential to conduct a pilot test of the design and implementation process to ensure that the desired outcomes are likely to be achieved. Good instructional design strategies are vital to selecting and/or producing the resources that will be needed by the participants. For example, a mentor matched with a protégé on the basis of the protégé's job-specific skill deficiency may lack the requisite skills in coaching and feedback; therefore, it may become necessary to design skill practice to fill these gaps.

Implementation

Any instructional intervention must have an implementation plan. A critical success factor for a mentoring process is a communication plan that ensures that everyone who needs to know something about the mentoring process gets the information in a timely manner. A well-designed mentoring process has a coordination team to administer it and ensure that it is sustained as a viable strategy for improving human performance and results.

Evaluation

An evaluation process for the mentoring process itself must be planned at the beginning. Key baseline data must be captured before information about the proposed process begins to contaminate it (Murray and Owen, 1991). The evaluation plan must be crafted to capture only the data that one intends to use. Therefore, the first question should be "What will we do with the data?" Some of the most useful kinds of data are those that are needed in order to do the following things:

- Report the impact of the mentoring process on the organization's business results
- Continuously improve the design of the process
- Determine whether the mentoring pairs are meeting developmental objectives in the transfer of skills

In addition, mentors' effectiveness must be evaluated by mentors and protégés jointly agreeing on what constitutes progress in the transfer of skills, the sharing of information, and the honoring of agreements about time and focus.

CONCLUSION

Beneficial results of mentoring processes are not accidental. The key to ensuring the desired results and to securing the mentoring process itself is to use all the best HPT practices in planning, design, implementation, and evaluation. The mentoring process must be closely linked to the mission, goals, and priority strategies of the organization. Stand-alone programs are extremely vulnerable to economic downturns, budget cuts, and changes of affection. Only integrated, facilitated processes that are linked to current and future mission and business imperatives can be expected to stand the buffeting of the winds of change.

References

Duncan, M. (1995, Jan.). Mentoring applied: IBM. *Manager's Mentor,* pp. 1–3.

Murray, M. (1997). *Facilitated mentoring processes drivers.* Oakland, CA: MMHA The Managers' Mentors.

Murray, M., and Owen, M. (1991). *Beyond the myths and magic of mentoring: How to facilitate an effective mentoring program.* San Francisco: Jossey-Bass.

CHAPTER TWENTY-EIGHT

Multimedia Learning Systems: Design Principles

Ruth Colvin Clark
Preston Zuckerman

*S*hockwave, DVD, streaming video, applets—the technological jargon and the capabilities behind it are changing so fast that, as one technophile put it, "If you haven't been programming for the World Wide Web in the last month, you're already outdated." What this means for instructional designers is that it is rapidly becoming very easy to provide learners with information in a rich and diverse mix of representations, including audio, text, video, color, and still or animated graphics. Computer technology has been evolving rapidly; the human brain, however, as the product of millions of years of evolution, has not been changing rapidly, and it can be overloaded by the sensory output that technology is capable of delivering. Human learning remains as it has been for thousands of years: dependent on a memory system with processing limitations.

These limitations require the human learner to devote many years of discipline-specific experience to the achievement of high levels of expertise. More than twenty years of cognitive research by experts in diverse disciplines show that approximately ten years' discipline-specific sustained experience is required for the achievement of mastery-level performance in that discipline (Ericsson, 1990). For example, it is estimated that the average chess player has about fifty thousand play patterns stored in long-term memory, and that it takes about ten years of regular practice to build these patterns (Simon and Gilmartin, 1973).

This chapter examines the role of design principles, as applied to instruction delivered via computer technology, in building this kind of expertise. In this context, the chapter also examines the role of the performance improvement specialist, whose job is to help relative novices move toward a state of greater expertise, and who must provide this help in a cost-effective manner.

INSTRUCTIONAL METHODS
VERSUS INSTRUCTIONAL MEDIA

This chapter, in its previously published version (Clark, 1992), summarized the media-comparison research addressing the question of which media are best for learning. Hundreds of media-comparison studies have been conducted over the past fifty years. In these studies, instructional methods (illustrations, practice exercises, examples, and the like) were held constant, but instruction was delivered via diverse media (video, classroom techniques, computers). The studies have all yielded the same conclusion: no significant differences in learning outcomes were shown (Clark, 1990; Clark, 1983); only when instructional methods were varied did significantly different learning outcomes result. For example, if the computer version of instruction has used an interactive simulation, and if the classroom version has used a receptive lecture, then differences in learning outcomes did occur because the instructional methods, not the media, are what caused the learning. An instructional method is any technique that is used with the intended result of transferring knowledge and skills and that serves to help learners process information in a cognitive mode. For example, such methods as using animation, chunking information, showing pictures, and providing simulations, practice, and demonstrations are what cause learning, and these methods can be employed with a variety of media.

After the first version of this chapter appeared (Clark, 1992), the methods-versus-media issue was addressed once again. In an update of his earlier research (Clark, 1983), R. E. Clark restates his original position—that instructional methods, not media, are what influence learning: "If learning occurs as a result of exposure to any media, the learning is caused by the instructional method embedded in the media presentation. . . . Media influence cost or speed (efficiency) of learning, but methods are causal in learning" (Clark, 1994, p. 26). The consensus of researchers is that, instead of asking which instructional medium is best, it would be more productive to ask how cognitive processes are affected by the instructional methods carried by various media (Mayer, 1997).

That is the question on which this chapter will focus. We agree that instructional methods, not the media per se, are what cause learning. However, not all media are equally effective in delivering all instructional methods. For example, an instructional simulation of any complexity is difficult to deliver via any medium other than the computer. Further, some kinds of practice, such as role playing, are difficult to deliver outside the classroom. Thus, although it is not literally the computer or the instructor that causes learning, it is the computer's or the instructor's ability to carry unique methods that makes the learning of some knowledge and skills easier via the computer or in the classroom. The performance improvement professional's job is to capitalize on each medium's ability to foster learning and build expertise.

Computer technology encompasses some of the most versatile media. It can deliver a broad range of instructional methods, using such diverse modalities as audio, text, color, and video. With the advent of Web-based systems of delivery, computer technology may now also become the most ubiquitous delivery system, available to anyone with a computer and a modem.

An understanding of how specific methods may serve critical cognitive processes is essential to the most effective use of those instructional methods. Thus the instructional designer needs to match a diverse complement of instructional methods to the specific cognitive requirements of learning. In this chapter, we will summarize the research on the human cognitive processes involved in learning, and we will consider computer-based examples of instructional methods that have been shown to facilitate those processes.

WHAT'S NEW?

Since the first version of this chapter appeared (Clark, 1992), the most salient changes have been advances in the technological ability to distribute, via the Internet, a broad range of instructional methods ubiquitously, to virtually any computer anywhere in the world. Less well known is the new cognitive research in several arenas: the instructional methods used for managing cognitive load, the improvement of retrieval from long-term memory, and the building of metacognitive skills. Moreover, the evolution of constructivist models of learning has swung the pendulum toward the active role of the learner in the instructional process. The budding interest in "situated learning environments" (Clark, 1992) has blossomed, and this approach is illustrated by the many computer-delivered training programs that now provide real-world examples. In this chapter, which concerns design principles for multimedia approaches, we will keep the original focus on the instructional methods that augment human cognitive processing, but we will add the updated research, as well as more recent examples of multimedia instruction.

To illustrate the interaction between instructional environments and cognitive processes, we will use a taxonomy of instructional environments. The taxonomy includes four instructional architectures—the frameworks for training design that work best with different levels of expertise and different performance outcomes—

based on specific philosophical assumptions about the learning process and the outcomes of learning. We will define and illustrate the four architectures and indicate how each one interacts with human cognitive processes. Finally, we have added a discussion of metacognition, which takes on increasing importance in the hypermedia instructional environments characteristic of Web-based training.

THREE VARIABLES OF LEARNING

Research over the past twenty-five years has found, somewhat unhappily, that very few instructional methods are universally applicable to all learners and all performance goals. Instructional design would be much more straightforward if universally applicable methods could be prescribed. But we must always take account of three major variables that interact in the learning process: the experience of the learner, the performance outcomes, and the instructional strategies.

Variable 1: Experience of the Learner

We know that when we provide learners with instruction, what they perceive is a function not only of what we provide but also of their current mental models. Figure 28.1 represents the same sensory input—a cat—in two very different ways, according to two different viewers' prior mental models of the animal. We know that visual perception is influenced by the prior experience of the viewer, and so is learning. Therefore, some instructional methods that are effective with novices in a discipline are ineffective with journeymen or experts in the discipline, and vice versa. Indeed, one of the challenges for any instructor is a diverse population of learners who have a wide range of relevant expertise. Computer technology is a particularly convenient delivery medium for providing different instructional methods that can accommodate these differences in learners. As we progress through our discussion of instructional methods, we will make a distinction between those methods that are more appropriate for relative novices and those that are better for learners who have some knowledge of and experience with the skills being built.

Variable 2: Performance Outcomes

We can classify performance outcomes into two major categories: those that involve informing, and those that involve performing. In other words, the goal may be primarily to build awareness (information), or it may be primarily to build new or changed behavior (performance). These goals are not mutually exclusive, but planning for an instructional design should begin with a consideration of the primary goals of the instructional intervention. A briefing is one common method of communicating information (informing); a desired outcome that involves new or changed behavior is better served by some form of training

Figure 28.1. Two Views of a Cat.

that requires practice and feedback (performing). We will see that some instructional architectures better serve the informing goal, and others better serve the performing goal.

If the goal of instruction is for the learner to perform, then two subcategories of performance come into play: *procedural performance* and *principled performance*. Procedural tasks are accomplished in more or less the same way each time they are attempted (for example, accessing e-mail). By contrast, principled tasks require judgment because there is no single approach that can be used with every situation in which principled performance is called for; thus the effective sales representative adjusts the sales approach to the customer, the customer's requirements, the products, and the sales representative's own relationship with the customer. Principled tasks are usually found in situations where there are so many environmental variables that it would be impossible or impractical to provide a procedure suited to each one. We will see that some instructional architectures more effectively support procedural performance, and others more effectively build principled performance.

Variable 3: Instructional Strategies

From ancient times, discussions of how humans perceive reality, and of what reality actually is, have reflected different philosophical positions. Not surprisingly, then, the predominant approaches to instruction today fall at various points along a continuum that runs from the primacy of the external instructional interface to the primacy of learners' own role in building their unique mental models (Reynolds, Sinatra, and Jetton, 1996), and this continuum itself has philosophical underpinnings. These are reflected in the continuum that runs from rationalism at one extreme to empiricism at the other. Along this underlying continuum, the rationalist view is that external reality is nonexistent, or at least not susceptible to direct experience, because ideas are mental artifacts unique to each individual. The empiricist view is that the outside world is relatively independent of human mental processes and is the source of all knowledge. Each of the four instructional architectures, or strategies, that we will discuss in the next section uses different instructional methods, which affect novice and experienced learners differently and which support different performance outcomes.

FOUR INSTRUCTIONAL ARCHITECTURES

Although there are few "pure" types of instruction, the following taxonomy is offered to illustrate the predominant assumptions about human learning and to help the instructional designer consider different ways to use technology for learning. The four instructional architectures (strategies) that we will be discussing in this section are as follows (Clark, 1998):

1. Receptive instruction
2. Directive instruction
3. Guided discovery
4. Exploration

Receptive Instruction

A metaphor for this strategy would cast the learner as a sponge and the instructional medium as a vessel pouring out knowledge. Examples of this type of instruction include college lectures, corporate briefings, and linear video programs. For the most part, this strategy requires minimum interaction between the learner and the instructional medium. Figure 28.2 shows a screen from a computer-based training program that describes the features and benefits of a new satellite-based, handheld global telephone system. This program, delivered on CD-ROM, uses animated sequences, voice, and music to give the learner an overview of the system.

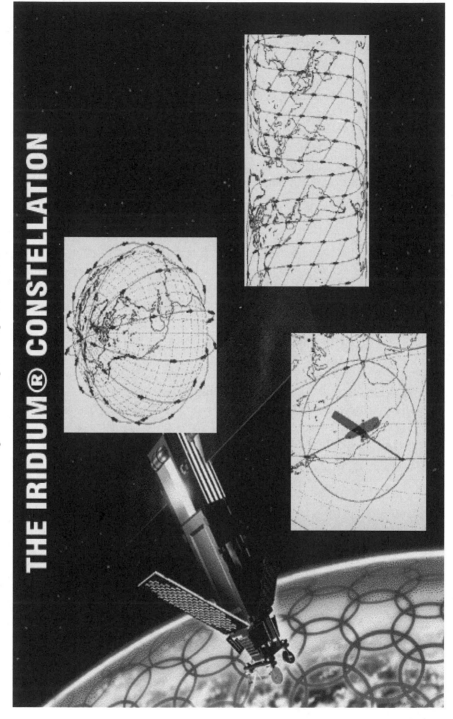

Figure 28.2. Example of Receptive Instruction.

Directive Instruction

The directive architecture of instruction dominated much business and industrial training from the post–World War II era through the 1960s. An exemplar of this type of training was programmed instruction, which originally was delivered in textual form via programmed books and was later the method of choice in much of the early computer-based training. In directive instruction, the learner responds to instructional stimuli whose goal is to build specific associations that form the basis of skills to be applied on the job. The instruction chunks the knowledge and skills into small learning segments that are sequenced in the requisite order. Frequent opportunities are provided for learners' responses. Response errors are immediately remediated via corrective feedback. The learning assumptions are behavioral, based on a stimulus-response model of learning. The role of instruction is to provide an effective series of stimuli to which the learner responds correctly, thus building a complex repertoire of skills. For example, Figure 28.3 illustrates a screen from a computer-based training program designed to teach procedures for using a new computerized telephone system. This screen provides feedback on the learner's accomplishment, informs her that the call has reached its natural conclusion, and cues her to close the call and hang up. The instruction is delivered via CD-ROM and by means of both visual and auditory modalities.

Guided Discovery

A shift away from the empiricist and toward the rationalist end of the continuum was stimulated by a cognitive focus on the mental events involved in learning. From this shift, several new instructional strategies evolved that generally gave learners greater control over selecting the content, sequence, or methods of instruction. These strategies also took account of the importance of the learner's mental models in the instructional process. The goal of this architecture is to help learners acquire mental models similar to those of experts in a discipline.

One common form of guided discovery provides learners with problems as the basis for learning. The problems are adapted from actual work settings. Learners are given some flexibility in solving these problems, with instruction support (sometimes called *scaffolding*) available to assist the learning. The instruction plays the role of coach and facilitator, to help learners, who often work in teams, obtain the knowledge and skills they need to solve the problems. Errors in problem solving are seen as opportunities for learning and are not discouraged. An important element of these programs is the use of an instructional environment that is "situated" in real-world types of settings and problems so that new knowledge and skills are readily transferable to the job.

Figure 28.3. Example of Directive Instruction.

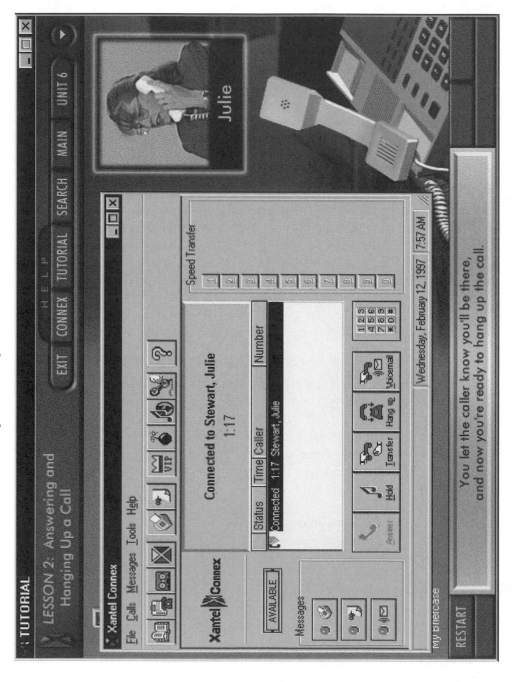

Figure 28.4 shows a screen taken from a program designed to train experienced purchasing agents in strategies for cost management and analysis. Note that learners are "situated" behind their desks. After an orientation from the "boss," they are immersed in several problems presented on their laptop computers. A number of resources are available. These including spreadsheets, calculators, Web sites, reference manuals, and conferences with suppliers.

Exploration

The architecture of exploration is based on what is termed a *constructivist* philosophy of learning. The constructivists place great emphasis on the unique nature of each learner's mental models. Constructivism assumes that learners build their own knowledge, and that this is a unique process for each learner. Some constructivists suggest that it is impossible to try to build consistent knowledge and skills in any group of learners because variance in learners' mental models and goals will influence the final result. At an extreme, the constructivists suggest that traditional instructional design models based on job analysis and learning objectives are meaningless because learning outcomes are so learner-dependent.

The architecture of exploration gives maximum control to the learners, who are provided a rich, networked database of information, examples, demonstrations, simulations, and exercises. From this database they can select whatever is appropriate to their current needs and preferences. There is little interest in imposing prespecified knowledge and skills because this is assumed (by the extreme constructivists, at least) to be impossible. Instead, it is left to the learner to construct a unique mental model.

An example of the architecture of exploration is illustrated by Figure 28.5, which shows a screen from a tutorial intended to help experienced programmers learn to program with Microsoft Visual Basic 5.0. Learners can choose from any section of the course, work through labs, study examples, and find references on the World Wide Web. The Web, with its emphasis on hypermedia design, has made this form of instruction common.

ASSUMPTIONS ABOUT LEARNING: FROM EMPIRICIST TO RATIONALIST

We have already discussed the continuum that runs from empiricism to rationalism with respect to assumptions about learning. Which of the four architectures reflects the most empiricist assumptions, and which the most rationalist? With their heavy reliance on external input, the architectures of receptive and directive instruction fall on the empiricist end of the continuum; both view the learner as a relatively passive agent, either absorbing new knowledge or building

Figure 28.4. Example of Guided Discovery.

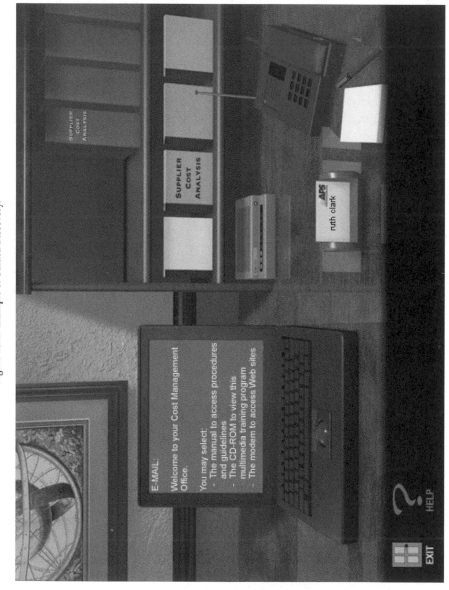

Figure 28.5. Example of Exploration.

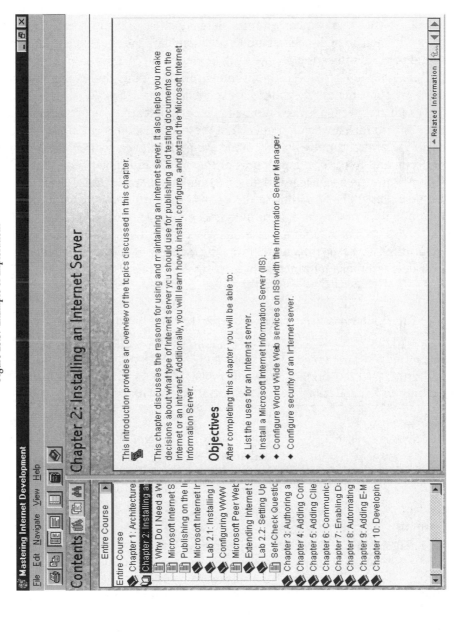

new connections via carefully programmed sequences of stimuli. The architecture of exploration is the most rationalist of the four in its comparative deemphasis on building a mental model common to the learner population. The architecture of guided discovery falls in the middle, recognizing the interaction of the external environment with the mental models of the learners; the goal is for all learners to build mental models that emulate those of expert performers in a domain. Further, the architecture of guided discovery recognizes the importance of the instructional environment in providing job-realistic problem-solving opportunities that compress experience.

Which architecture is best? No one approach to learning is universally effective. The optimal application of each of these architectures is a function of the expertise of the learning audience and the performance goals: to inform or to perform, and to perform procedures or to perform principled tasks. Table 28.1 summarizes the major features and recommended applications of each of the architectures; the information in the various columns will become clear as we continue with our discussion of human cognitive learning processes, and we will revisit each of the four architectures to examine the differences among them in terms of how they interact with those processes. We shall start with a brief overview of human information processing as it relates to learning.

Table 28.1. Instructional Architectures and Support for Human Cognitive Learning Processes.

Architecture	Load Control in Working Memory	Encoding into Long-Term Memory via Rehearsal	Retrieval from Long-Term Memory (Transfer)	Metacognitive Skills
Receptive	Low	Low	Low	Calls on
Directive	High	High if interactions are elaborative	High if principle of identical elements is used	Compensates for
Guided discovery	Moderate	High	High	Calls on; can build
Exploration	Up to learner; small chunks in the design will help learner	Up to learner; potentially high if elaborative interactions are present and used	High if principle of identical elements or analogical transfer principles are used	Calls on

Source: Paas and Van Merrienboer, 1994.

OVERVIEW OF HUMAN INFORMATION PROCESSING

As mentioned earlier, instructional methods are what cause learning, as a result of how effectively they support the human memory systems and the processes that move information through them. The models of memory and information processing are best thought of as metaphors that provide a basis for understanding how learning occurs.

Three Kinds of Memory

It is currently accepted that information from the environment is processed through three distinct memory systems: sensory memory, working (or short-term) memory (WM), and long-term memory (LTM). Table 28.2 summarizes the major features of these memory systems.

Modes of Processing in the Memory Systems

Learning for performance goals occurs when information from the environment enters the senses and is ultimately stored in LTM in such a way that it can be retrieved when it is relevant to the job. In this process, environmental input is stored briefly in sensory memory. A portion of it is then encoded into WM, which is the center of all conscious thought. Because of its limited capacity, WM can manage only a limited amount of information at any one time. The information, once in WM, is either rehearsed or lost. There are two types of rehearsal: maintenance rehearsal, in which information is repeated over and over; and elaborative rehearsal, in which new information is associated with prior knowledge. Elaborative rehearsal is more effective than maintenance rehearsal for encoding new knowledge into LTM.

Table 28.2. Features of Human Memory Systems.

Memory System	Features
Sensory memory	Holds large amounts of sensory data (visual or auditory) for a brief time (2–5 seconds)
Working memory	Has a limited capacity of seven (plus or minus two) chunks Information decays rapidly without rehearsal Is the center of conscious processing or thought
Long-term memory	Permanent memory Has a very large capacity Memory structures called *schemata* are the basis for problem solving and inferences

Source: Paas and Van Merrienboer, 1994.

Over time, complex memory structures called *schemata* are built in LTM. Schemata form the basis for the mental models that help humans interpret experience, solve problems, and make inferences. To be useful, the new knowledge encoded into LTM must be brought back into WM when it is needed. This process is called *retrieval.* When there is failure of retrieval, transfer of learning to the job does not occur: the new knowledge may be present in LTM, as evidenced by testing that follows training, but failure to retrieve it precludes its application to the job.

The cognitive processes and the memories do not work independently of one another. In particular, the schemata that are already in LTM have a great impact on what is selected for attention, on the capacity of WM, and on the encoding of new knowledge into LTM. This is the psychological basis for the differences in learning between novices and experts: novices, with a less elaborate structure of schemata, require instructional methods that are different from those required by experts.

Metacognition and Self-Regulated Learning

The cognitive processes just outlined are monitored and adjusted by the "operating system" of information processing that is called *metacognition.* The processes of metacognition are instrumental in the setting of learning goals, the selection of effective learning techniques, the monitoring of progress toward goals, and the adjustment of strategies, as necessary. In secondary schools, for example, metacognitive support is provided externally for learners through explicit objectives, assignments, and quizzes. At the university level, by contrast, it is more typical to find a diminished level of metacognitive support whereby learners are left to their own devices to set learning goals, complete assignments, and get extra help.

INSTRUCTIONAL METHODS, INSTRUCTIONAL ARCHITECTURES, AND COGNITIVE PROCESSES

An instructional method, as already defined, is a technique for facilitating or augmenting a cognitive process that results in the transfer of knowledge or skills into LTM. Instructional methods (and, at a higher level, the instructional architectures) can do the following things:

1. Help manage cognitive load in WM
2. Focus learners' attention on relevant parts of instruction
3. Encourage the encoding of new knowledge into existing LTM schemata
4. Support the transfer of new knowledge to the job via retrieval from LTM, even long after training
5. Provide external metacognitive support, or call on learners' metacognitive skills

This chapter cannot discuss the hundreds of instructional methods, or even the four architectures, in terms of how they interface with all the major cognitive processes just summarized. Instead, to illustrate types of interactions, we will focus on how the instructional architectures interact cognitively to do the following things:

1. Manage cognitive load in WM

2. Support the transfer of new knowledge via the encouragement of information retrieval from LTM

3. Compensate for or call on metacognitive skills

For a more comprehensive discussion of how instructional methods interact with all the major cognitive processes, the reader is referred to Clark (1998).

MANAGEMENT OF COGNITIVE LOAD

The previously published version of this chapter (Clark, 1992) described in detail the research that defined the major features of WM. To summarize, the major features of WM are as follows:

- Information in WM is perishable. It decays rapidly without rehearsal.

- The storage capacity of WM is small: seven (plus or minus two) chunks of information. Chunk size, however, is a function of experience; that is, because experts form larger chunks than novices do, experts apparently have greater WM storage capacity.

- In WM, cognitive load has a negative impact on processing. Experiments have indicated that even small amounts of data stored in WM have a slowing effect on processing in WM. Therefore, if learners are overloaded, the rehearsal process that requires WM capacity will be disrupted, and learning will be impeded.

The encoding of information into LTM depends on the appropriate rehearsal of new information in WM. But this rehearsal can take place only when WM has capacity that can be dedicated to this rehearsal. When WM is fully loaded by new information, there is limited capacity for rehearsal, learning will be blocked, and the learner's attempts to process new information will lead to frustration. We call this phenomenon *cognitive overload*. One goal of good instructional design is to manage cognitive load so that learners have WM capacity that can be devoted to the rehearsals that result in learning (Clark and Taylor, 1994).

Instructional Methods and Cognitive Load

In the previously published version of this chapter (Clark, 1992), three load-management methods were described:

1. Designing of screens that display (for example, via cue cards) the factual or procedural information that is required during instruction

2. Drill and practice to build automaticity

3. External devices for memory support, such as job aids to supplement WM

Cognitive Load and the Four Architectures

How do the four architectures compare with respect to their load-management qualities? Which architectures impose the greatest cognitive load, and which the least?

The greatest risk of cognitive overload is imposed by the architecture of receptive instruction because there is typically little external provision for the learner's processing in the form of interactive practice. Therefore, the learner does not have a structured external opportunity to clear his or her working memory. In addition, there may be few options for the learner's control over the rate of the information's delivery. According to the amount, the complexity, and the organization of information, the novice learner is at risk for cognitive overload.

By contrast, the architecture of directive learning makes many provisions for management of cognitive load. This behaviorally based architecture breaks content into small steps, provides for the learner's frequent responses (with corrective feedback), and tends to use a simple-to-complex prerequisite approach to the sequencing of new information and skills. Thus working memory is supported by the chunking of content, by frequent clearing via interactions that stimulate rehearsal, and by a controlled sequence of information, from less complex to more complex. For this reason, the architecture of directive learning is very effective in teaching procedural skills to novices.

The architecture of guided discovery imposes moderate amounts of cognitive load. By immersing the learner in problem solving, it uses a more global organizational strategy whereby the learner may face a number of conceptual issues at once. Load control must be managed through selection of the cases or problems to be solved (for example, a series ranging from more to fewer constraints) and by the provision of scaffolding (by which various types of support guide the new learner). Load management in this architecture is a major challenge to the instructional designer.

Finally, the architecture of exploration leaves load management up to the learner, who is free to select from a rich environment of alternatives those that are appropriate to him or to her. The instructional design should allow the learner to select from a prescribed sequence or, alternatively, to branch out, in network fashion, to related topics and information. Successful learning will depend on learners' having enough schemata to find their way through available resources and select what they need. It will also depend on the learners' strong metacognitive skills so that they can make appropriate load management decisions (for example, choosing to do practice exercises when these are necessary).

TRANSFER OF KNOWLEDGE: METHODS ENCOURAGING RETRIEVAL FROM LTM

In many cases, a learner acquires new knowledge and skills, as demonstrated by the results of on an end-of-class test. The knowledge and skills are retrieved from LTM in the instructional setting, but they do not go on to be applied to the job. In other words, they are not transferred. The reasons include (among many others) the organization's failure to support the application of the new skills; in this chapter, however, we are focusing on the psychological basis of failure to transfer new knowledge or skills to the job.

The term *inert knowledge* refers to new knowledge and skills that are encoded into LTM but are not transferred at a later time when they could be useful. For example, a math student gets an A on exponential notation, but next semester, in her astronomy class, she fails to apply her notational skills, even though they would simplify her computations. What could the math instruction have done to increase the probability of transfer?

Behavioral theories of transfer are based on the principle of identical elements, as proposed by Thorndyke (1932). He suggests that transfer occurs to the extent that elements in the transfer environment are similar to those that were present at the time of learning. This principle is the basis for high-fidelity simulations that teach the use of new computer software; to maximize transfer, the training environment works to emulate the real-world look and feel as closely as possible.

High-fidelity simulation works well for transfer of procedural tasks that are completed more or less the same way each time. However, it falls short when the goal is to build principled skills, which require adjustment to each situation. The behavioral guidelines for transfer effectively serve training for procedures, and so effective computer-based training must closely emulate the actual system to which the procedures are to be transferred. For more complex tasks involving problem solving and judgment, however, Thorndyke's principle of identical elements has proved insufficient. Cognitive theories of transfer, expanding the behavioral focus on matching the training to the job environment, embrace the concept of analogical transfer.

Analogical transfer proposes that learners solve problems by building a robust schema in LTM, a schema that is based not on surface features but on the deep structure of problems. For example, novice and experienced physicists were given 120 physics problems to categorize. The novices tended to form such categories as "pulley problems," "motion problems," and the like; their categories were based on surface features of the problems. The experts, by contrast, tended to group the problems on the basis of their underlying principles, such as angular motion, the second law of thermodynamics, and the like (Chi, Feltovich, and Glaser, 1981). Indeed, one feature of expertise in a complex domain is the ability to see beneath the "cover story" and into the deep structure and to apply the appropriate principles. Experts solve new problems by making analogies that are based on an extensive database of solution principles that have formed schemata over years of experience.

How can instructional designers encourage analogical problem solving? How can expertise be accelerated? Cognitive instructional research has yielded some answers. In one study, for example, Gick and Holyoak (1983) looked for conditions that would help learners transfer knowledge from a story involving a many-sided attack on a fortress to a problem in which rays were required to converge on a tumor from different directions so as not to harm healthy tissue. They found that the best approach was to provide the learners with several stories, each of which was different on the surface but all of which used the principle of convergence as the basis for the solution. Thus, in addition to the story about the fortress, a story involving firefighters was told, in which a burning oil rig was put out by many small hoses positioned around the circumference of the fire. Rehearsal was stimulated when the learners were asked to represent the commonalities in these two stories with a diagram. Later, by comparison with a group that been exposed only to the story about the fortress, more of the learners who had been exposed to the two stories were able to solve the tumor problem. The key was to provide multiple examples with diverse external features but a common deep structure, and to focus learners' attention on the deep structure through an assigned rehearsal.

Researchers have found that giving learners some worked examples to study, along with assigned problems to solve, increases learning by comparison to giving learners only problems that they have to work themselves (Paas, 1992). These results are explained in terms of the reduction in cognitive load that is provided by the worked examples, which free WM to learn the principles behind the problems. The same experimenters (Paas and Van Merrienboer, 1994) also conducted a further study in which subjects were given a number of problems, which they worked out themselves or which were worked out for them. Both low-variable and high-variable problems were used. The results are summarized in Table 28.3. Notice that, as before, worked problems yielded better results than did assigned problems. The high-variable problems also yielded better transfer of learning on problems that were somewhat different from those studied (that is, problems involving far-transfer learning).

Table 28.3. Learning Outcomes with High- and Low-Variable Worked Examples.

Outcomes	Conventional (Students Work All Problems)		Worked (Students Study Worked Problems)	
Problem types	Low-variable	High-variable	Low-variable	High-variable
Time in training	1,230 seconds	1,406 seconds	561 seconds	625 seconds
Perceived mental effort of student (1–5 scale)	4.2	4.5	3.2	3.3
Percentage correct (test)	28.9	27.8	47.8	62.2

Source: Paas and Van Merrienboer, 1994.

It is our conclusion that providing learners with diverse examples, along with some relevant rehearsal activity, helps build a robust schema. A robust schema increases the probability that knowledge will be transferred to new problems that, on the surface, may appear different from earlier problems but that actually have a similar deep structure.

Transfer and the Four Architectures

Directive Learning and Simulation Fidelity. For training of procedural skills, the directive approach works well if the instructional interface incorporates key elements of the work environment. Thus the learner practices in a simulated environment, with features similar to those of the job. How realistic do simulations need to be? From a cost-benefit perspective, this is an important issue because high-fidelity simulations, especially for the operation of complex equipment, are expensive to build. Unfortunately, the relationship between fidelity and learning is not straightforward. Cox, Wood, Boren, and Thrope (1965) conducted a study in which a ninety-step procedure was practiced at three levels of fidelity:

1. On the real equipment, at a cost of $11,000

2. On a high-fidelity mockup of the real equipment, at a cost of $1,000

3. On a cardboard mockup with photographs, at a cost of less than $10

These three treatments yielded no significant differences in final performance.

One issue to be considered is which elements of the job environment need to be simulated accurately, and which do not. Before a simulated learning environment is designed, it is recommended that some research be done to distinguish the key job-relevant cues that must be simulated in order for accurate skill building and transfer of learning to occur.

Guided Discovery and Cognitive Apprenticeships. One exemplar of the architecture of guided discovery is the cognitive apprenticeship. Typically, the learner begins instruction in a job-realistic environment (for example, the learner may be sitting at a desk). The learner is then presented with a problem in the form of a case study. Assistance is available through coaching, reference manuals, Web sites, and expert problem solvers, among other options. Unlike what occurs in directive learning, feedback typically is neither immediate nor in the form of "Incorrect—try again." Instead, the learner takes actions to solve the problem and is able to view naturalistic consequences of his or her choices. For example, in Figure 28.6, the learner has asked a customer some inappropriate questions about marital status in a simulated loan interview, and a bank lawyer is now providing feedback about the guidelines for fair lending. At the end of the week of simulation training, the learner earns a commission on all appropriate loans that have been made and receives a performance appraisal from the boss.

We propose that the cognitive apprenticeship promotes high levels of transfer for principle-based tasks, as a result of a "situated" environment mirroring that of the job, and as a result of the learner's exposure to varied-context examples and cases from which schemata are built. The following are some key features of computer-driven cognitive apprenticeships:

- *"Situated" learning:* The learner is situated both physically and psychologically in an environment reminiscent of the job environment.

- *Problem-based learning:* The learner is immersed in a series of varied-context work problems and has a variety of resources for help.

- *Scaffolding:* The learner is provided with sources of assistance so that, with reasonable effort, he or she can succeed in solving the problems.

- *Time compression:* As the learner faces a number of problems during the simulation, his or her experience is compressed (see Gabrys, Weiner, and Lesgold, 1993, who report on Air Force technicians in a cognitive apprenticeship who gained two years' competence in twenty-five hours of training).

- *Action-based errors and feedback:* Learning is achieved through making and correcting errors, and instead of receiving immediate instructional feedback ("correct" or "incorrect"), the learner takes actions and observes their realistic consequences.

- *Ability to save and replay:* The learner can rework a specific problem, trying different approaches and improving efficiency and effectiveness.

Figure 28.6. Feedback in a Cognitive Apprenticeship.

The current climate is enthusiastic about cognitive apprenticeships, but they are not to be tackled lightly. Few have been rigorously evaluated, and their design is complex and expensive to produce. A recent review by Anderson, Reder, and Simon (1996) suggests that the benefits of this instructional model have been overstated in the literature; they suggest that transfer of knowledge results from a combination of varied-context problems and abstract instruction. Responses to this review, as well as rebuttals (Greeno, 1997; Anderson, Reder, and Simon, 1997), point to the still unsettled status of these instructional environments.

METACOGNITION, LEARNER CONTROL, AND INTERACTIVE MULTIMEDIA

The previously published version of this chapter did not discuss metacognitive skills. However, with the advent of the Internet and exploratory architectures, which allow learners much flexibility in accessing information, a discussion of metacognitive skills is warranted.

An individual with good metacognitive skills is able to set appropriate learning goals, select effective learning strategies, monitor his or her own progress, and adjust learning strategies, as necessary. Individuals of equal intelligence learn more effectively as a result of better metacognitive skills. They are self-regulated learners.

A major distinction among the four architectures is the amount of control that each gives learners in making instructional decisions for themselves. In the architecture of exploration, learner control is maximized. In keeping with the constructivist perspective that learners must actively build their own mental models, training in the exploratory architecture is provided as a richly networked source of guidelines, examples, simulations, references, illustrations, and practices to be accessed as they are needed. At the opposite end of the continuum, the architecture of receptive instruction typically allows minimal learner control and provides information in a sequence and at a rate that have been preengineered into the instruction. By contrast, the architecture of directive instruction may offer the learner limited control over which lessons to take and the pace at which to take them, but it typically lays out a recommended plan of instruction that incorporates a prescribed sequence of rule, example, and practice with corrective feedback. The architecture of guided discovery offers the learner control over actions to take and resources to access, although scaffolding that is provided early in the instruction may impose some limits.

In general, research indicates that high levels of learner control are ineffective for novice learners (Williams, 1993; Lee and Lee, 1991). Because novices do not have enough schemata to make good selections for themselves, the exploratory architecture is not recommended for them. In general, high control for novices should be provided for pacing through a program and for previewing or reviewing materials, but otherwise novices are better off in a more directive architecture, especially when strong logical content prerequisites are built into the lessons.

In addition to the learners' level of experience, the probable level of their metacognitive skills should also be considered. Learners with high self-regulatory abilities are able to make good learning decisions for themselves and will manage effectively in conditions of high learner control. Thus the architecture of exploration calls on the learner's good metacognitive skills, whereas the architecture of directive instruction compensates for their absence.

SUMMARY

Our goal in this chapter has been to illustrate the interaction between the instructional environment and human cognitive processes, an interaction that must be considered in the design of effective computer-mediated instruction. We have updated the media-versus-methods research described in the previously published version of this chapter. We have also used four architectures of instruction to represent four predominant approaches to instructional design, each one based on different assumptions about the role of instruction in causing people to learn. We have described the human cognitive processes that underlie learning, and we have illustrated the interactions between the four architectures and those cognitive processes.

References

Anderson, J. R., Reder, L. M., and Simon, H. A. (1996). Situated learning and education. *Educational Researcher* 25:4, 5–11.

Anderson, J. R., Reder, L. M., and Simon, H. A. (1997). Situated versus cognitive perspectives: Form versus substance. *Educational Researcher* 26:1, 18–21.

Chi, M.T.H., Feltovich, P. J., and Glaser, R. (1981). Categorization and representation of physics problems by experts and novices. *Cognitive Science* 5, 121–125.

Clark, R. C. (1990). Instructional methods vs. instructional media. *Bulletin of the American Society for Information Science* 16:6, 16–19.

Clark, R. C. (1992). Computer-mediated instruction. In H. D. Stolovitch and E. J. Keeps (eds.), *Handbook of Human Performance Technology: A comprehensive guide for analyzing and solving performance problems in organizations.* San Francisco: Jossey-Bass.

Clark, R. C. (1998). *Building expertise: Cognitive methods for training and performance support.* Washington, DC: International Society for Performance Improvement.

Clark, R. C., and Taylor, D. (1994). The causes and cures of learner overload. *Training* 31:7, 40.

Clark, R. E. (1983). Reconsidering research on learning from media. *Review of Educational Research* 53:4, 445–459.

Clark, R. E. (1994). Media will never influence learning. *Educational Technology Research and Development* 42:2, 21–29.

Cox, J. A., Wood, R. D. Jr., Boren, L. M., and Thrope, H. W. (1965). *Functional and appearance fidelity of training devices for fixed procedures tasks.* HUMRRO Technical Report no. 65-4. Alexandria, VA: Human Resources Research Office.

Ericsson, K. A. (1990). Theoretical issues in the study of exceptional performance. In K. J. Gilhooley and others (eds.), *Lines of thinking: Reflections on the psychology of thought.* Hillsdale, NJ: Erlbaum.

Gabrys, G., Weiner, A., and Lesgold, A. (1993). Learning by problem solving in a coached apprenticeship system. In M. Rabinowitz (ed.), *Cognitive science foundations of instruction.* Hillsdale, NJ: Erlbaum.

Gick, M. L., and Holyoak, K. J. (1983). Schema induction and analogical transfer. *Cognitive Psychology* 15, 1–38.

Greeno, J. G. (1997). On claims that answer the wrong questions. *Educational Researcher* 26:1, 5–17.

Lee, S. S., and Lee, Y.H.K. (1991). Effects of learner control versus program control strategies on computer-aided learning of chemistry problems: For acquisition or review? *Journal of Educational Psychology* 83:4, 491–498.

Mayer, R. E. (1997). Multimedia learning: Are we asking the right questions? *Educational Psychologist* 32:1, 1–19.

Paas, F.G.W.C. (1992). Training strategies for attaining transfer of problem-solving skill in statistics: A cognitive-load approach. *Journal of Educational Psychology* 84, 429–434.

Paas, F.G.W.C., and Van Merrienboer, J.J.G. (1994). Variability of worked examples and transfer of geometrical problem-solving skills: A cognitive-load approach. *Journal of Educational Psychology* 86:19, 122–123.

Reynolds, R. E., Sinatra, G. M., and Jetton, T. L. (1996). Views of knowledge acquisition and representation: A continuum from experience centered to mind centered. *Educational Psychologist* 31:2, 93–104.

Simon, H. A., and Gilmartin, K. (1973). A simulation memory for chess positions. *Cognitive Psychology* 5, 29–46.

Thorndyke, E. L. (1932). *The fundamentals of learning.* New York: Teachers College, Columbia University.

Williams, M. (1993). A comprehensive review of learner control: The role of learner characteristics. In M. R. Simonson (ed.), *Proceedings of the annual conference of the Association for Educational Communications and Technology.* New Orleans: Association for Educational Communications and Technology.

CHAPTER TWENTY-NINE

Multimedia Learning Systems: Technology

Diane M. Gayeski

The term *multimedia* describes the integration of multiple information-presentation modalities (text, audio, pictures, graphics, motion video, and animation) through the use of microprocessor-based digital technologies. Put in simpler terms, it has to do with the capability of a properly configured computer to present a variety of stimuli within one self-contained program. The term *interactive multimedia* refers to digital programs that allow users to control the rate and sequence of presentations. In some cases, the term also refers to the ability of a program to offer customized feedback based on the user's input.

Many people tend to define *multimedia programs* as "CD-ROMs" or "Web pages," but the term is more comprehensive. It describes a set of rapidly developing technologies and applications that includes CD-ROMs, digital video (or versatile) discs (DVDs), Internet and intranet Web pages, on-line discussion groups and knowledge bases, and live collaboration through computer networks. These technologies are increasingly important for organizational learning and performance improvement because, for the first time, both live and "prerecorded" information in a variety of formats can be presented by one common and widely available device: the personal computer. Moreover, in addition to their presentation capabilities, multimedia programs go beyond their traditional print, audio, and video ancestors because of the power of the computer to request, process, and respond to the user's input, to perform calculations and powerful searches, and to record data. An interactive multimedia program is truly a two-way interaction: both the program and the user provide information. It is the marriage of preplanned and/or preproduced media with the idiosyncratic presentation of those media elements. As described in Chapter Twenty-Eight, design issues for multimedia programs are critical and complex because the instructional techniques have a more significant impact on the success of a multimedia intervention than the instructional technologies do. With some applications, users—not just designers—actually add to and create the learning environment.

This immediate and collaborative approach to learning is congruent with the styles and needs of contemporary organizations and with the approach of human performance technology (HPT). In many subject areas, "canned" courses with long lead times for design and production are no longer very effective because of the rapid changes in content. Moreover, the ability to gather classes of students together in one place for lectures is limited by time, money, and people's willingness to travel, not to mention by their personal scheduling difficulties. Perhaps most important, management philosophies are turning away from top-down provision of information or indoctrination and toward a much more collaborative and multimodal approach that empowers employees to generate and share new ways for improving organizational performance.

This chapter provides an overview of the current and emerging multimedia technologies, formats, and applications that support organizational learning. In keeping with HPT principles, however, we need to remember that improved performance and organizational learning can be achieved by many different means, only some of which are traditional instruction. Today's multimedia applications range from drill-and-practice exercises through interactive tutorials to "knowledge capture" and collaboration software. Examples of these applications are presented, along with a theoretical basis for understanding why interactive multimedia programs provide unique tools for achieving goals. Both the pitfalls and the promises of these new technologies are discussed. Finally, the chapter presents some resources for readers who wish to follow the ever-changing landscape of hardware, software, and applications.

BASIC CONCEPTS AND TERMINOLOGY

Microprocessors and digital media files are the technological basis of multimedia systems. We generally consider the microcomputer to be an integral element of an interactive media systems. In fact, however, other types of microprocessor-based hardware can provide the "brains" that run and manage multimedia presentations. For example, there are stand-alone interactive media-control units that employ microprocessors but are not otherwise full-fledged computers. These include DVD playback units, CD-i (compact disc interactive) units, and analog videodiscs (these contain chips that decode programming controls and support both the selection of content from a menu and the ability of the program to respond to the user's questions). The various modalities incorporated into multimedia programs are stored in digital form, which allows them to be displayed and controlled by a microprocessor. These media can also be seamlessly integrated; for example, an audio file can play while a picture with a text overlay is being displayed.

Interactivity is probably the essential component of a multimedia learning system. Multimedia programs can be interactive in many ways. Simple systems allow the user to regulate his or her own rate of progress through a relatively linear sequence of information (sometimes this functionality is called *page turning*), and tutorials consist of question-answer-feedback sequences. Programs with more sophisticated formats modify themselves on the basis of having developed a "model" of the student. Newer technologies actually support live interaction over the Internet, with subject matter experts and other learners (Fenrich, 1997; Gayeski, 1998). To a large extent, the amount and type of interactivity will depend on the design of the program. Many programs do not exploit the power of the computer to actually record and process the user's input; instead, they limit themselves to simple mouse clicks on menu items. In terms of technology, the interactivity of these programs depends on the user interface (keyboard, touch screen, joystick or other simulation controller, simple remote-control keypad) and on the ability of the system to store the user's input (on a floppy disk, on the personal computer's hard drive, or on a network).

The ability of a multimedia program to present different stimuli and feedback according to the user's input is called *branching.* The term *single branching* refers to a program's having only two different presentation paths, which are based on the user's responses. Single branching is typically found in question-and-answer sequences in which the learner gets one type of feedback if his or her response is correct and another type of feedback for any incorrect response. The term *multiple branching* refers to a more complex pattern of feedback, in which the user may be taken to any of a number of sections of a program on the basis of his or her responses. For example, if the user's answer to a question is incorrect but also embodies a common misconception, tailored feedback will address that particular confusion rather than just telling the user, "Wrong; try again." If a response is correct but misspelled, specific feedback on the misspelling will again be provided. With the use of microprocessors, digital media, and various techniques for receiving users' input and displaying appropriately branched presentations, it is possible to achieve many different types of applications to support learning and performance.

VARIABLES AND VARIATIONS

There are many variables involved in multimedia applications and technologies, and more variations on them are being developed every day. Many people stereotype multimedia training as being about long and complex CD-ROM-based tutorials. Actually, however, there is a whole range of techniques that can be used to support conventional training, replace conventional classroom training with some sort of programmed learning resource, or eliminate the need for training altogether by way of electronic performance support or on-line collaboration.

Learning Resource or Complete Course?

Multimedia programs are perhaps most commonly used as a learning resource rather than as a means of providing a complete course. For example, computer-based presentation slides that support conventional classroom presentations are very commonly used. One advantage of using computer-generated slides is that handouts can be automatically created from them. Moreover, these slide shows are easily converted to a format that allows them to be posted on a Web site or an intranet for later review. This kind of application can be expanded if the presentation is combined with audio, digital video, or animation clips, or if the program is able to launch other computer applications automatically. A workshop on financial analysis, for instance, could use digital slides and might also include buttons on which the presenter could click to automatically launch a spreadsheet program.

Another way to use multimedia technologies as a learning resource is to incorporate short multimedia exercises or tests into conventional training. For example, some corporations provide introductory readings and a pretest over the Internet before participants are sent to a classroom training course. This procedure is intended to ensure that they all have the prerequisite knowledge. Given the rich mix of information available on the World Wide Web, many training programs also incorporate research sources that are posted on public Web sites.

As organizations become more familiar with multimedia technologies in the context of their traditional training services, many of them decide to use these technologies to offer complete courses. The obvious advantage of these self-contained courses is that they can eliminate travel, make training available on demand, and incorporate engaging elements of visual content and interactivity. In addition, organizations typically find that training time is compressed by 20 to 40 percent, with no resulting loss of the training's effectiveness. Many case studies have reported more effective learning and greater consistency with these courses by comparison with traditional classroom learning. For example, Union Pacific Railroad reported having been able, by using computer-based training (CBT), to implement new company processes a year earlier than would have been possible with conventional classroom training, and the U.S. Air Force found that the ability of learners to diagnose and repair aircraft systems correctly the first time was increased by more than 80 percent, an improvement that represented a savings of millions of dollars (Allen, 1996). However, it is important to note that multimedia training courses are time-consuming to produce; a typical development time would be three hundred to six hundred hours to create one hour of training (Fenrich, 1997; Gayeski, 1997).

On-Line or Off-Line Storage and Delivery?

Another variable involved in multimedia programs is whether they will be stored and transmitted locally or broadcast via the Internet or an intranet. Off-line multimedia programs are generally delivered via floppy disk or CD-ROM and are then accessed locally on a personal computer. However, the emerging trend is to store and deliver training and performance support on a private or public network.

The advantage of delivering multimedia information off line is that the media elements are generally available more quickly because the user does not have to wait for graphics, audio, or video to be downloaded through a network. It is now technically possible to deliver video clips over the Internet, but the download time is generally too slow for this option to be practical. Material is also more secure when it exists only on individual computers rather than on an Internet site that might be vulnerable to unauthorized access. The material is also accessible when the user is off line, as when he or she is working on an airplane or in a hotel room.

The advantage of delivering multimedia information on line is that duplication and shipping costs are eliminated, and information can be updated frequently through the use of free or inexpensive network technologies. Many organizations find that the content of courseware needs to be updated often, and it is difficult to manage new versions if they are shipped on floppy disks or CD-ROMs. Furthermore, on-line information that uses World Wide Web formats (sometimes called *Web-based training*) can incorporate links to other Web sites, e-mail addresses, and even on-line collaboration (Hall, 1997).

Collaborative or "Canned" Courseware?

A stereotype sometimes held about multimedia programs is that they are typically "canned" courseware with which learners interact. It does often consist of static content that has been developed by a team of designers and producers on the basis of input from one or two subject matter experts. This is changing rapidly, however, for two reasons: first, multimedia programs are moving onto the Internet and onto intranets; and, second, there is a shift from content-driven training to collaborative communication. It is now possible for groups of learners and experts to interact on line via typed text, graphics, audio, and even video images. This allows training to be offered to dispersed learners, with no sacrifice of spontaneity or interaction with other people.

Other approaches to collaborative learning include threaded discussion groups and knowledge databases. Using these technologies, learners can read and post material that is organized according to topic. Lotus Notes is one example of a software tool that allows users to collaborate by sending e-mail, by posting, editing, and commenting on documents, and by organizing knowledge according to topic folders.

Synchronous or Asynchronous Multimedia Programs?

Another variable of multimedia programs is whether they are synchronous (with all participants in a given course or experience interacting together at the same time) or asynchronous (with participation occurring individually, at different times). Traditionally, multimedia training programs have been designed and deployed as asynchronous media because organizations find it difficult or impossible to get learners together in time and space. Examples of this modality are CD-ROMs or Web sites that are used by learners whenever they have the need and the time. As already mentioned, most of these programs are of the "canned" variety; increasingly, however, learning programs are relying on the contributions of experts and learners, and these contributions can be sent via e-mail or posted to a threaded discussion group on a Web site.

A growing category of multimedia instruction uses synchronous communication over the Internet. Several new software tools allow an instructor or facilitator to lead sessions in a "live Internet broadcast." Instructors and learners employ standard Web browsers (such as Netscape Communicator or Internet Explorer) to call up a private Web site that can display text, graphics, and even video windows showing other learners or prerecorded content. Not only does this technology allow instantaneous and very inexpensive collaboration among participants, it also shortens the time needed to design and deliver the instruction because, basically, a content expert or trainer can lead a session "live," using a few simple presentation graphics or examples. These "live" courses do allow the learners to be dispersed, but they still all have to be available at the same time, and this is a problem, especially when there is an international audience, with members in different time zones.

Local or Remote Storage?

Multimedia programs can be stored on a variety of devices. Early interactive video systems had two forms of storage: one form for the video portion (typically videotape or videodisc), and one for the computer programming, text, and graphics (typically a floppy disk). Many CBT programs that do not contain video or audio are stored on conventional diskettes or are delivered on a set of diskettes that the user installs on the hard drive of a personal computer. Most current multimedia programs are stored on CD-ROM because of the large storage capacity of this medium and because a CD-ROM cannot be inadvertently erased. DVDs look like conventional CD-ROMs but have even more capacity and can therefore store long movies or a great number of video clips and computer animations; obviously, this greater capacity can support very rich instructional programming.

An interactive media program can also be stored on a server and delivered over the World Wide Web (a server, of course, is a computer that is connected to the Internet, or to a local network, and that allows other computers to access content on it). When the program is stored on a server that allows access to anybody on the Internet, the program is said to be stored on a public Web site. Access to a server can be limited to an internal audience only, however, and when the program is stored in World Wide Web format, but with access limited to an in-company audience, it is said to be stored on an intranet. Company intranets as well as the Internet are being used to deploy programs for in-house training, for free public information and education, and for fee-based instruction. For example, Sun Microsystems, the California-based company with offices all over the world, has instituted Sun University, which delivers courses through the company's intranet as well as through conventional classes. All the courses are listed on the World Wide Web. Prospective students can find an appropriate course, register, have their managers notified of their registration, enable precourse materials to be sent to them, have the appropriate account billed for the course, and even access follow-up material—all from one convenient Web page (Deloro, 1997).

MULTIMEDIA TECHNOLOGIES FOR INSTRUCTION AND PERFORMANCE SUPPORT

Numerous combinations of hardware, software, program goals, and design strategies are available under the umbrella of multimedia technologies, and they offer rich but sometimes confusing sets of options. As we have seen, multimedia programs may vary on many dimensions, and the various applications can effectively address different kinds of performance problems and situations. Although multimedia programs can be used to deliver conventional instruction, they are also a powerful tool for performance support, feedback, testing and assessment, collaboration, and incentives. The following examples of multimedia technology show just a sample of the myriad applications, simple and complex, that can be used to improve individual and group performance in the workplace.

Interactive Presentation Graphics

Perhaps the simplest and most common way to use multimedia programs as a learning tool is to use them in the form of presentation-support tools. Instead of static overheads or slides, classroom instructors can use computer-generated graphics to enhance lectures and discussions. Generally, these graphics are shown by a projector linked to a computer. Another common device is a liquid crystal display (LCD) panel that is linked to a computer and placed on the stage of a conventional overhead projector. One obvious advantage of this technology is that it eliminates the expense of producing color overheads and slides. Moreover, the presenter can easily make changes to customize a presentation for a particular audience. The concurrent creation of handouts and speaker notes from a computer-generated slide presentation is extremely simple.

Beyond just showing static slides, multimedia presentations can also show video clips, audio clips, 3-D graphics, and simulations. For example, a facilitator leading a discussion about business decisions can use a spreadsheet model to let the audience see how various financial elements interact with each other. Instructors can also create links to their presentation slides, links that actually launch other pieces of software. For example, a bulleted list of various tax software programs can be created and projected, and when the instructor clicks on the name of a particular program, it automatically executes and is ready for the instructor to demonstrate to the class.

Use of a Web Site

A Web site is a relatively inexpensive and easy-to-use addition to conventional instruction and other performance improvement interventions. For example, many college professors now maintain Web sites on which they post syllabi, readings, assignment specifications, exercises, and class lists. Instead of having students go to the library to access readings on reserve, instructors can provide many of these materials on a Web site. Instructors can also post schedule changes class notes and can even maintain password-protected areas where students can view their own grades and get private feedback on assignments. Similar Web sites are used by corporate trainers and by consultants who are mentoring their clients.

Use of a Web Tour

Most people are aware of the vast resources that are now available for free on the World Wide web. Instead of recreating instructional and resource materials from scratch, it is possible for HP technologists to identify reliable and appropriate source materials on the Web. A tour of these materials can then be created through the development of a Web page that incorporates links to other sites, along with commentary on those sites. For example, a Web tour on self-directed learning was developed by the present author to accompany a short, publicly available workshop for human resources professionals. This Web page guided participants on a tour of a dozen Web sites put up by professional organizations, universities, and private corporations that had posted research and demonstrations on self-directed learning. One site, which included an on-line assessment of learning styles, actually provided immediate scoring and advice to the user on selecting his or her most effective learning strategies.

Multimedia Tutorials

Multimedia tutorials are interactive lessons that provide users with instruction, testing, and immediate feedback on their continuing progress in mastering a body of content. Although these tutorials are difficult and time-consuming to develop, they are at least as effective as conventional training. They also save time and travel expenses. Topics for multimedia tutorials range from technical skills (for example, how to make a pizza) to interpersonal or "soft" skills (for example, how to use effective leadership behavior). These tutorials generally include rich graphics, audio, and video and are delivered via CD-ROM. It is also possible for tutorial programs to record learners' responses and scores on final tests and to archive the scores in a central database for inclusion in personnel files and for analysis by training departments.

On-Line Communities of Practice

As organizations become aware of the need to manage and enhance the collective knowledge of their employees, many are providing tools for collaboration, to be used by colleagues who share similar interests or challenges. These tools include electronic databases, e-mail lists, and mailing-list manager programs. (The latter are often called *list serves,* a term derived from LISTSERV, the name of a popular program of this type; a list serve helps an on-line group of people collaborate via e-mail that is sent to all members.) People using these tools are often called *communities of practice.* A community of practice may be a relatively stable group of people in a particular company, or it may transcend organizational and even national boundaries. For example, TRDEV-L, the very successful list serve for professionals in training and development, has several thousand members around the world who respond regularly to one another's questions and comments about their profession.

Digital Job Aids

When individuals are required to use information that does not have to be recalled from memory, the creation of multimedia digital job aids is often appropriate. For example, many corporations are now putting their policy manuals on their intranets. Instead of trying to get employees to learn the policies by heart, and instead of constantly updating print-based policy manuals, these organizations provide constantly updated and easily searchable policy documents that can be accessed from a desktop computer.

Other kinds of decision-making tools can also be created with ease. If sales representatives, for example, are occasionally required to calculate complicated discounts or payback analyses, a simple digital job aid or spreadsheet template can be created so that a computer does the calculations for them. When the British firm Thames Water introduced a computerized system for customer information and billing, the firm also developed what it called its Preference-Based Performance Support (PSS) system, to provide specific help screens and full-screen references for some thousand users. The PSS system runs on the Thames Water mainframe, alongside the firm's customer information system, and it has so increased efficiency for users that Thames Water is introducing similar PSS projects for a number of its other systems.

Simulations

In many situations, an individual requires exposure to situations that are dangerous, costly, or crucial to the protection of his or her reputation. Here, multimedia simulations can offer practice with those situations and allow learners to explore the effects of various choices. For example, a new consultant can learn negotiation skills by interacting with a simulated client rather than risking the loss of an important contract. Operators in nuclear power plants can practice various routine and emergency procedures without taking equipment off line or risking potential disasters. Medical personnel can practice diagnosis and alternative treatments, even using medical equipment hooked up to mannequins or to virtual-reality representations of patients, to practice such procedures as endoscopy.

Virtual Worlds

A quickly emerging technology in multimedia is called *virtual reality* or *virtual worlds.* A virtual-reality application uses computer-generated 3-D models of actual or imaginary spaces with which a user can interact. The users can "travel around" a virtual scene by means of a mouse, a joystick, or even various types of gear worn on the body, such as data gloves. Virtual-reality applications can support vicarious travel around a new city, a museum, or a campus. On a smaller scale, users can walk around a room before it is actually constructed, to assess the design. Another application uses a Web site that allows employees to explore various meeting rooms that are available in a company, in order to select the most appropriate space for a presentation. The employees can observe the sight lines from various seats and can even practice with the various lighting and audiovisual controls available in different rooms.

BENEFITS OF MULTIMEDIA APPLICATIONS

Multimedia programs do not represent only a single technology but rather a whole spectrum of applications presented through digital media. Today it is not necessary to choose between a CD-ROM and a live chat room for coaching on the Web. Instead, it is possible to mix and match technologies and strategies. For example, some training programs on CD-ROM now have links to Web sites, to allow the training material to be constantly updated and to enable the exchange of e-mail among learners. Many on-line training programs incorporate electronic performance support tools, such as spreadsheet templates, that can be downloaded to the user's hard drive. A few of the benefits that can be achieved with multimedia tools for learning and performance support are discussed in the following sections.

Individualized Learning and Obtaining Information on Demand

Digital media can provide text, audio, video, and animation to encode information that learners can explore at their own pace. Intranets enable users to access continuously updated policies and productivity tools as the need arises. Because intranets and CD-ROMs are inexpensive, information can be made available to a much wider audience than was previously possible. Because electronic text can be easily searched, it is possible to gain efficient access to the information needed to accomplish a particular task.

Standardizing

Multimedia materials for training and performance support can be carefully designed and tested and then disseminated in a standardized form, literally throughout the world.

Record Keeping

Multimedia programs can pose questions, solicit learners' responses, and then record those responses. Responses can be summarized, and individual scores can be saved in personnel files.

Collaborating

On-line systems allow users to interact with fellow learners and content experts. This functionality enhances individuals' ability to put concepts into action and to update material.

Rapid Updating

Materials posted on Internet and intranet sites can be easily updated without the cost of reproduction and distribution. Users can be sure that they are working with the most current versions of policies, tools, and information.

Desktop Learning

Multimedia programs can be displayed on most conventional home and office computers and even on laptop models. This capability makes it easier to access materials in a wide variety of settings than when one must locate a VCR or even carry manuals and books around. Ernst and Young, for example, has instituted a system called Learning Environment to Accelerate Performance (LEAP), which allows its workforce, 80 to 90 percent of whom work on the road, to access databases and instructional programs (Alexson, 1997). With a system like this one, information can be made available as soon as the time is ripe for learning, and this capability reduces the kinds of performance problems that occur when individuals are ready to learn but have to wait until formal classes are offered.

SPECIAL PRECAUTIONS

These new media are not without disadvantages, of course. Although computers are hardly uncommon in today's offices, multimedia software and hardware are still not quite standardized, and hardware is in a constant state of flux because of rapid improvements in technology. There are still risks in terms of the reliability of the technology, and certain ethical and legal issues need to be considered.

Leading Edge or Bleeding Edge?

Most organizations naturally want to buy and use the most current technology available; even the latest system is outdated within a year. However, it is always a close call to know whether one is buying leading-edge or bleeding-edge technology. The term *bleeding edge* alludes to the fact that some systems, too new to have been well tested or to have strong support, may not gain widespread acceptance in the marketplace and are therefore risky propositions: the time and money that have to be invested may not pay off in the long run. Many an organization has invested time and money in a new system, only to find that soon thereafter the hardware is taken off the market and is no longer supported by its vendors.

In considering multimedia and the stability of the system, it is important to remember that the software is more of a factor than the hardware is. Organizations often try to use the most current authoring tools and operating systems but find that they have not been well tested and are still full of bugs. As difficult as it is to design and produce sound multimedia instruction, many developers find that they spend even more time fighting hardware and software problems for which there are no clear solutions. Because of the rapid changes in technology, organizations also have often found that their investments are obsolete within relatively few years. This is why some of the payback calculations for multimedia have not held true. It is more than just a matter of the technology not being the most current or powerful. The problem is that older technologies are often "dereleased" (that is, they are no longer being made) and cannot be repaired.

Change in Organizational Culture

When organizations institute multimedia for learning, they often replace classroom training or other face-to-face interactions. This change can also change the organizational culture, inadvertently and for the worse. There are financial benefits from reducing training time and travel expenses, but the by-products of training sessions can be even more important than the training itself is. It can be difficult to enculturate new people into an organization simply by having them interact with multimedia training without actually visiting other company sites and spending time with colleagues. Some people feel that these technologies depersonalize the organization and can make communication too rigid and one-way. Changes to the corporate culture can also be quite positive, however. For example, Hewlett-Packard's system, Connex, helps employees identify in-house experts who can become mentors, and intranet knowledge-sharing programs can also allow employees from all over the world to share best practices and work in virtual teams (Cohen, 1998).

Intellectual Property and Copyright Issues

Because multimedia programs make it possible to easily store and modify the ideas and work of others, this mode of training opens questions about intellectual property and copyright issues. Is it legitimate to hire a trainer to develop a multimedia course in her area of expertise and then lay her off but continue to use her work? Is it reasonable to ask excellent performers to share their secrets with others in the company who may be competing for similar positions in the future? Is it ethical to copy material from another Web site, modify it a bit, and call it one's own? These questions are still being discussed and reviewed in the courts, and many situations are still unclear.

Privacy and Security Issues

Because many multimedia systems store such user data as test scores and responses to questions, they bring up issues of individual privacy and security. Is it possible for others to gain access to personal files and even change them? Who should have the right to review learners' responses to training materials? Now that many training courses are offered on the Internet or on intranets, is it possible for competitors to pry into sensitive or proprietary content?

Learning Styles and Disabilities

Multimedia systems are touted as being more flexible than conventional classroom training in addressing individual learning styles and needs. The fact is, however, that most of them require excellent reading skills and at least some dexterity with a mouse and keyboard. It is very difficult to make a multimedia program as responsive to learning styles as a classroom program can be, and learners who need social interaction are often disadvantaged by individualized types of instruction. Moreover, many individuals with even slight learning or sensory disabilities cannot adequately make use of multimedia instruction, and organizations that do not offer alternative instruction may be liable to lawsuits.

Resources Needed for Development and Management

Making the transition to multimedia learning and performance support, even in a modest fashion, requires new and different resources for development and management. Even if an organization buys off-the-shelf CD-ROMs, it can find itself bogged down by calls from users whose systems are not working properly and who need help in configuring their computers and software. Many course-ware topics require frequent updating or customization, and responding to this need takes equipment and authoring skills on the part of an in-house specialist. If design and development are to be done in house, a new range of skills in these areas, ranging from flowcharting through computer authoring to video and graphics production and editing, will be required. In-house training departments often do not know how to write good requests for proposal for multimedia programs, and they lack the experience to evaluate and manage vendors because they are so unfamiliar with the terminology and the requirements of these projects.

STEPS IN DEVELOPMENT

The steps in developing a multimedia program for learning and performance support are generally similar to those for other types of media. The most significant change is that a multimedia program entails, in most cases, the development of several versions with built-in testing, rather than the development of a single version that every learner sees.

Identification of Performance Gaps, Causes, and Solutions

Before a program is conceived, it is essential to identify one or more specific performance gaps and to determine their causes. For example, if performance is inadequate, is it because knowledge is lacking (a situation that could be remedied by instruction) or because incentives to perform are lacking (a situation that could be alleviated by some sort of system for feedback and collaboration)? If it is not necessary to memorize material, electronic performance support or on-line manuals should be considered instead of conventional instruction. If individuals understand content but are having difficulty applying it, then discussion groups or on-line forums might help that situation.

Selection of the Development Team

Because the development of most multimedia programs involves a range of technical and creative skills, development is typically accomplished by a team. The organization must choose how to staff its internal departments, and it must decide whether computer programming and technical support should reside in the information systems department, the training department, or both. A multimedia program is often developed by a team made up of members from many different organizations. A typical team might include an in-house project manager, interactive designers and evaluators hired as consultants, production vendors, and computer specialists who manage an intranet server or duplicate and distribute CD-ROMs.

Selection of Mode of Interactivity

On the basis of the needs analysis and overall recommendations, the designer, often along with the development team, selects the appropriate mode of interactivity. As the examples in this chapter have shown, the mode of interactivity can range from a simple program for presentation support to a complex virtual-reality simulation. A "canned" package can be used, or an on-line discussion group and knowledge database may be selected. The choice depends both on the analysis of the performance gap and on the available project resources.

Rapid Prototype Development

A more contemporary approach than fully scripting a program before it is produced is to develop one or more rapid prototypes of an interactive intervention. Rapid prototyping makes it possible to design, develop, and test an application iteratively; it is then possible to get feedback on design approaches before too much time or money has been invested. Interface designs, program analogies and metaphors, and explanations of content, while still in a rough stage, can all be tried out with representative learners. Even advanced interactive programming can be "faked" for the purpose of getting user input at the early stages. On the basis of assessments of these prototypes, a full-scale design can be created, and an accurate budget and time frame for completing the final program can be provided. It is advisable to have highly trained and experienced designers develop and test the prototypes; less skilled (and less costly) program developers can then flesh the prototypes out with all the content because the major design decisions already will have been made.

Design of Questions and Interactivity

Even before all the content has been scripted and flowcharted, it is generally necessary to design test questions and other mechanisms for gaining user interactivity. These questions should not be a mere afterthought; in fact, they provide the entire basis for interactivity and feedback. Even in programs for which there is no testing, other means for gaining interactivity (such as encouraging e-mail collaboration) should be developed.

Design of Content

Once the major decisions have been made about the nature of the application and its interactivity, the actual content must be developed and organized. In most interactive programs, it is a challenge not just to write text and decide which video or graphics should be seen but also to decide how the content should be indexed and accessed.

Acquisition and Development of Media and Content Assets

Because users expect a rich visual and even auditory experience, it is important to make information appealing and instructionally effective. Multimedia programs can contain literally hundreds and even thousands of individual graphics, audio and video clips, and animations. Developers need to decide whether these should be licensed from other sources, adapted from existing in-house resources, or created from scratch.

Alpha and Beta Tests

Once program content is complete, it is submitted to various levels of testing. Alpha testing is the first stage at which members of the development team try out the entire program for consistency, completeness, and robustness (checking for "bugs" or "crashes"). Beta testing occurs when in-house testing and revisions are complete and the program is ready for a selected group of actual users. These testers understand that the program is still in a somewhat imperfect form and that their job is to review it for content, usability, and soundness. Sometimes developers use a group of long-standing customers or experienced employees as beta testers.

Management of Records, Content, and Equipment

Once the program is complete, resources still need to be dedicated to the updating of content and to the management of any records (such as test scores or on-line registrations) that the program generates. Developers are also often responsible for multimedia learning labs or other dedicated equipment, such as the servers used by their programs. All will need maintenance and updating.

SUMMARY

Multimedia learning and performance systems are currently the technology that most trainers and performance technologists are looking to as a replacement for more conventional media (such as videotapes and slide programs) and even for in-person training. The challenge is not to pour old wine into new bottles but to use the power of these new media to "rewire" our systems for learning and performance. Multimedia learning and performance systems allow us to change not just our technology of learning but also our philosophy of learning, from a top-down, "indoctrination" mode to a new model of collaboration and just-in-time performance support (Gayeski, 1997).

It is important to remember that multimedia can and should be used for a wide variety of interventions, not just for training. As HP technologists, we recognize that imparting new skills and concepts is only one possible solution to a performance gap. Collaboration systems, for example, can provide ongoing feedback and coaching. Computerized job aids and other electronic systems can be used to support decision making by eliminating the need to memorize new information. On-line testing is used in employee selection and in counseling for career development. Creative applications, such as interactive games and contests, can even provide new systems for incentives and motivation.

It is also crucial to recognize that multimedia systems should be seen not as a replacement for but as an addition to other media and formats for learning. Interactive media, by allowing learners to master prerequisite content before a live course, or to continue learning collaboratively after a class is over, can make traditional training even more effective.

The key to effective use of multimedia is the strategic selection of the proper design modality. The latest hardware and special effects are only tools, and they may be expensive and challenging ones to use. A hopeful sign in this complex industry is that the biggest growth in multimedia is in on-line systems that are standardized, easy to develop and modify, widely accessible, and driven by their immediacy and the importance of their content. Human Performance Technology provides a critical set of application and assessment criteria that can help all of us make better use of the wonderful multimedia communication tools that are available now and those that are still to come.

References

Alexson, M. (1997, Dec.). Anytime, anywhere learning. *New Media,* pp. 36–42.

Allen, R. (1996, May). The ROI of CBT. *CD-ROM Professional,* pp. 17–21.

Cohen, S. (1998, Jan.). Knowledge management's killer app. *Training & Development,* pp. 50–57.

Deloro, J. (1997, Aug.). Web school. *Interactivity,* pp. 19–21.

Fenrich, P. (1997). *Practical guidelines for creating instructional multimedia applications.* Orlando, FL: Harcourt Brace.

Gayeski, D. (1997). Rewiring your organization's learning and communication system. *Performance Improvement* 36:3, 36–39.

Gayeski, D. (1998). *Designing and managing computer-mediated learning: An interactive toolkit.* Ithaca, NY: OmniCom.

Hall, B. (1997). *Web-based training cookbook.* New York: Wiley.

CHAPTER THIRTY

Structured On-the-Job Training

Ronald L. Jacobs

In spite of recent advances, information about on-the-job training (OJT) remains somewhat contradictory. On the one hand, annual surveys of training methods used in organizations fail to mention OJT altogether, continuing to suggest that the classroom program is the most frequently used training method (for example, "1997 industry report: What employers teach," 1997). On the other hand, a growing body of research has shown that employees receive substantially more training through OJT than through classroom programs (Brown and Reich, 1997; Eck, 1993; Holzer, 1990). Furthermore, OJT has been reported as the most frequently used training method across most jobs and job levels, including skilled and semiskilled industrial, sales, and supervisory-managerial positions (Utgaard and Davis, 1970; Churchill, Ford, and Walker, 1985; Kirkpatrick, 1985).

Perhaps the contradictory information about OJT demonstrates the adage that truth depends on the perspective of the respondent. If those who manage corporate training centers are asked what training methods they use, their response is likely to be "Classroom training." If the same question is posed to those who perform on the front lines of organizations, their response is likely to be "OJT." This reality has prompted more and more Human Performance (HP) technologists and managers to recognize the importance of on-the-job training in organizations (Jacobs and Jones, 1995).

In general, OJT involves having a novice employee accompany an experienced employee, either a peer or a supervisor, to learn specific information in the actual work setting. The experienced employee demonstrates and discusses the information associated with a task and then provides opportunities for feedback and practice. The process is repeated until the task has been learned. Although OJT has always existed in organizations, recent developments have sought to make this training method more reliable and predictable through the use of a systematic planning process.

The focus of this chapter is structured OJT. When used wisely and appropriately, structured OJT can be at least as effective as many off-the-job training methods. HP technologists often believe, mistakenly, that OJT is by its nature exclusively unstructured, although this view is far less prevalent now than ever before. However, there is a continuing need for updated information about this training method, particularly in view of its increased use in organizations.

This chapter seeks to update what is known about structured on-the-job training. It is organized to define structured OJT in depth from a systems perspective, to discuss structured OJT case studies, to summarize structured OJT research with emphasis on cost-benefit analysis studies, and to discuss issues related to structured OJT.

DEFINITION OF STRUCTURED OJT

OJT is similar to other forms of training in that it can be divided into two forms: unstructured and structured. Unfortunately, most instances of OJT are unstructured, or informal, which means that they occur with no planning or involvement by management. Unstructured OJT occurs when trainees acquire task knowledge and skills through any or all of the following means:

- Impromptu explanations or demonstrations by others
- Self-initiated trial-and-error efforts
- Self-motivated reading, investigating, or questioning
- Imitation of others' behavior

Unstructured OJT has been called many things over the years: *follow-Joe (or follow-Jane) training, sink-or-swim training, sit-by-Nellie training,* and *learning the ropes,* to give just a few of its names. Anyone of working age has been subjected to this type of training at some point in his or her career and knows the range of frustrations it can cause. Moreover, unstructured OJT carries with it a number of organizational issues:

- The desired level of competence is rarely if ever achieved; even when it is, all trainees rarely achieve the same level of competence.

- The training content is often inaccurate or incomplete, or else it represents an accumulation of bad habits, misinformation, and possibly unsafe shortcuts on which employees have come to rely over time.

- Experienced employees are seldom able to communicate what they know in a way that others can understand.

- Experienced employees use different methods each time they conduct the training, and the methods are not equally effective.

- Many employees fear that sharing their knowledge and skills will reduce their own status as experts and possibly even threaten their job security.

As far as can be determined, Jacobs and McGiffin (1987) made the first reference in the Human Performance Technology (HPT) literature to structured on-the-job training. However, the roots of contemporary structured OJT are clearly linked to the innovative efforts undertaken during World War II as part of the government-sponsored Training Within Industry (TWI) project (Dooley, 1945). In the TWI project, OJT was used as the cornerstone approach to help industry partners deliver various kinds of technical training by various means, including job instruction training, job relations training, and job methods training. Today, organizations refer to their structured OJT programs in a number of different ways: *task training, buddy training, job coaching,* and *skills training,* among other names. Absent from the literature only a few years ago, structured OJT is now generally recognized, under one or another name, as a form of training.

OJT assumes that the trainee is altogether lacking competence to perform the task in question, and that task information is best presented or facilitated by a trainer. Thus OJT is distinct from other ways of gaining or imparting task information on the job (see Table 30.1). Specifically, structured OJT is defined as the planned process of developing task-level expertise by having an experienced employee train a novice employee at or near the actual work setting (Jacobs and Jones, 1995). This definition makes three points clear:

1. Structured OJT, like other structured training approaches, requires a substantial investment of time and effort before it can be used.

2. The training occurs for the purpose of passing along discrete sets of tasks. (Structured OJT is commonly misunderstood as involving the preparation of trainees to perform entire jobs, not small parts of jobs.)

3. As shown in Table 30.1, structured OJT is identified as one of three basic ways in which individuals learn task information on the job. The approach of *self-directed discovery* assumes that the trainee, with no trainer available, will be able to learn the task from information available in the work setting. Either this information is put there intentionally or it is a natural part of the work environment. The unstructured form of self-directed discovery can be character-

Table 30.1. Ways of Acquiring Task-Level Information on the Job.

	Self-Directed Discovery	Coaching	On-the-Job Training
Unstructured	Employee learns by doing, with limited information intentionally placed in the work setting to guide learning. Employee must figure out each part of the task without assistance. False assumptions and errors are the result.	Employee learns by working alongside or nearby an experienced employee who seldom knows exactly how or when to intervene as the task is performed.	Employee is trained by an experienced employee whose experience as a trainer is likely to be limited and whose task expertise may also be questionable. Training content, methods, and outcomes very across employees.
Structured	Employee learns while doing, using the information engineered into work setting to guide learning. Employee can trust the system to help make the learning easier and reduce frustration.	Employee learns by working alongside or nearby an experienced employee who uses systematic knowledge of the task to know when and how to intervene. Training outcomes are relatively predictable.	Employee is trained by an experienced employee who has expertise in training and in the task to be learned. Training content, methods, and outcomes are consistent across employees.

ized as learning by doing or through trial and error. The structured form of self-directed discovery relies on job aids, electronic performance support systems, and self-paced training materials. *Coaching* is often confused with OJT because a trainer is present, but coaching assumes that the trainee can already perform some if not all of the task. In general, the trainer's role in coaching is to point out specific ways of improving performance on tasks that have already been learned. When coaching sessions are unstructured, the trainee works alongside others, who (it is hoped) will somehow know when and how to intervene. Structured coaching may stand alone or be part of structured OJT, when additional corrections and remediations may be required.

Structured OJT as a System

Some have suggested that OJT be viewed simply as an interaction between two employees in the work setting. This perspective seems wholly inadequate, however, given the increasing demand that training programs be held accountable for their contributions. Jacobs and Jones (1995) suggest that structured OJT is best viewed as a type of system within the larger organizational system (see Figure 30.1). Structured OJT can be developed and improved more effectively when a systems perspective is used, it is argued, than when any other kind of perspective is used (Jacobs, 1989). Indeed, structured OJT represents the interaction of several components—the training inputs, the training process, the training outcomes, and the organizational context—that are essential to the success of any training system.

Training Inputs. The training inputs of structured OJT are as follows:

- *The novice employee.* The novice employee lacks the competence required to perform as expected on the job. He or she should possess the underlying desire to learn and the prerequisites needed to learn the specific content in question.
- *The experienced employee.* The experienced employee acts as the trainer. In addition to possessing a combination of abilities in the specific training content, the trainer should have training ability.
- *The training location.* This is where the structured OJT will occur, and so the atmosphere should be conducive to training and learning. The training location should contain the resources required for training, and the delivery of the training should involve no more than minimal conflict with normal production and service delivery.
- *The learning task.* More than most other training approaches, structured OJT focuses exclusively on discrete units of work, or job tasks. The task should be selected for its suitability to the approach of structured OJT. It should be analyzed into its component parts, related to training objectives, and combined with other information into a training module.

Figure 30.1. Structured OJT as a System.

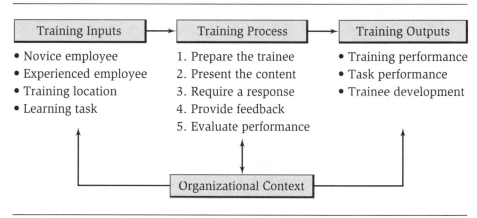

Source: Copyright © Ronald L. Jacobs, 1995. Used with permission.

Training Process. In this component of structured OJT, the trainer delivers the content to the trainee, or at least the trainer facilitates the delivery of the content. Thus the actions of the trainer before, during, and after training are of interest here. The training process includes the trainer's actions as he or she prepares for the training, uses the training module, and ensures that the trainee has learned.

Training Outputs. The training outputs come about through the combination of training inputs during the training process. The training outputs include the trainee's ability to perform the task to the level defined by the training objectives and to the level required by the job requirements. In a broader sense, the training outputs also include the trainee's ability to achieve his or her own development goals. It is the achievement of the training objectives, which are based on the needs of the organization and of individuals, that drives the training in the first place.

Organizational Context. Structured OJT, as a system, exists within the larger organizational context, which represents, in effect, another system unto itself. The organizational context, perhaps more than any of the other components, determines the ultimate success of structured OJT because its influence is so pervasive. Indeed, a number of issues are directly connected to the organizational context:

- The business priorities of the organization
- The nature of the continuous improvement efforts

- Management's overall perception of training as an avenue to improved organizational performance
- Contractual agreements between management and employees
- The alignment between organizational goals and training goals, which allows and encourages experienced employees to function as trainers
- The extent to which the culture of the organization encourages employees to share job-related information

Structured OJT Process

Figure 30.2 presents the structured OJT process, which is used to design, deliver, and evaluate structured OJT (Jacobs and Jones, 1995). The structured OJT process should be considered a subset of the larger performance improvement process. As such, the structured OJT process becomes useful only when the existing or anticipated performance problem is caused by lack of knowledge or skill. The six steps of the process are summarized in the sections that follow.

Determining Whether to Use Structured OJT. The first step of the process is to determine whether it is in fact appropriate to use structured OJT for the situation in question. To perform this step, one needs to know the features of structured OJT and the specific selection criteria. The following selection criteria are critical:

Figure 30.2. Structured OJT Process.

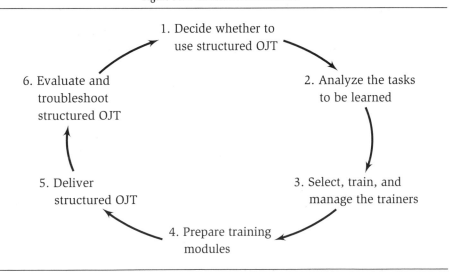

1. Decide whether to use structured OJT

2. Analyze the tasks to be learned

3. Select, train, and manage the trainers

4. Prepare training modules

5. Deliver structured OJT

6. Evaluate and troubleshoot structured OJT

Source: Copyright © Ronald L. Jacobs, 1995. Used with permission.

- *Nature of the task:* Immediacy of doing the task, frequency of the task, difficulty of the task, and consequences of error
- *Available resources:* Experienced employees to serve as trainers, time for training during the work day, proper equipment, tools, data
- *Constraints in the work setting:* Demands to find a proper training location, undue work distractions
- *Financial considerations:* Number of trainees requiring training, predicted financial benefits
- *Individual differences:* Mastery of training prerequisites, trainee preferences

Analyzing the Tasks to Be Learned. The discrete job tasks or units of work should be analyzed to derive the training content and training objectives. Analyzing a task also reveals the pattern of the work behavior involved in doing the task; that is, although tasks may differ in content, their performance follows relatively consistent patterns (observing procedures, troubleshooting, making decisions, inspecting, revising or adjusting, planning, comprehending, and so on). Knowledge of these behavioral patterns assists in determining how best to document the work and how to present the information to trainees later on, as part of the training.

Selecting, Training, and Managing the Trainers. Structured OJT is effective only when there are experienced and knowledgeable employees to serve as trainers. Trainers should have adequate competence both in the work being presented in training and in presentation of information to others. Thus, in many organizations, the development of trainers is often an extensive process in itself. The following characteristics of prospective trainers constitute criteria that are critical to trainer selection:

- Possession of adequate task-specific knowledge and skills
- Attendance at specialized training related to the task
- Overall willingness to share information with others
- Respect of peer employees and managers
- Interpersonal skills that are already developed
- Ability to read and write task-specific information
- Overall concern for improving the organization
- Consistency of training with job expectations

Preparing the Training Modules. The training content and other important information about the task should be assembled into a structured OJT module.

The module guides the trainer while he or she delivers the training, and the trainee uses it as a reference during the training. Module components include the following elements:

- Title of the task
- Rationale statement
- Training objectives
- Training prerequisites
- Training content or work documentation
- Performance tests and documentation forms
- Additional information or resources that go with the training content

Delivering the Structured OJT. Before delivering the structured OJT, the trainer should get ready to train. The trainer then delivers, or facilitates the delivery of, the training content. Delivery is guided by five training events:

1. Preparation of the trainee
2. Presentation of the training
3. Requirement for a response
4. Provision of feedback
5. Evaluation of performance

As shown in Table 30.2, how these training events are used depends on the type of training involved (managerial training, technical training, or training for awareness); that is, the same basic training events are used for each type of training, but the details within the steps differ to accommodate the nature of the training. In general, managerial training gives the trainee the ability to plan, direct, or facilitate the work of others. Technical training gives the trainee the ability to manipulate objects, equipment, tools, data, or other resources. Training for awareness informs the trainee of certain ideas, processes, or policies, or it motivates the trainee to accept some planned change activity in the organization.

Evaluating and Troubleshooting the Structured OJT. The various steps of the process and the outcomes of the structured OJT should be evaluated and, as necessary, undergo improvement. Logically, the evaluation should focus primarily on the results of the training, which will include the trainee's outcomes, the organization's outcomes, and any unanticipated effects of the training.

Table 30.2. Structured OJT Training Events and Types of Training.

Managerial Training	Technical Training	Training for Awareness
1. Prepare the trainee	1. Prepare the trainee	1. Prepare the trainee
a. Explain the purpose and rationale of the training	a. Explain the purpose and rationale of training	a. Explain the purpose and rationale of training
b. Determine whether the trainee has the prerequisites	b. Determine whether trainee has the prerequisites	b. Determine whether trainee has the prerequisites
c. Explain general safety and quality requirements	c. Explain general safety and quality requirements	c. Explain general safety and quality requirements
d. Explain how training will be done	d. Explain how training will be done	d. Explain how training will be done
e. Respond to questions about the training	e. Respond to questions about the training	e. Respond to questions about the training
2. Present the training	2. Present the training	2. Present the training
a. Position the trainee	a. Position the trainee	a. Position the trainee
b. Present an overview of the model or process	b. Present an overview of the operation, equipment, and workflow	b. Present an overview of the topic or issue
c. Present examples of the model or process in use	c. Describe and show each behavior	*Inform*
d. Explain the parts of the model or process	d. Explain specific safety and quality points	c. Explain the parts of the topic or issue
e. Demonstrate techniques by applying the model or process	e. Summarize the entire task	d. Present examples of the topic or issue
f. Summarize the entire task		*Motivate*
		e. Describe the present and desired conditions
		f. Describe implications for individuals and organization
		g. Discuss commitment behaviors

Table 30.2. Structured OJT Training Events and Types of Training, cont'd.

Managerial Training	Technical Training	Training for Awareness

3. Require a response
  a. Ask the trainee to explain the purpose and rationale
  b. Ask the trainee to describe the model or process
  c. Ask the trainee for examples of the model or process
  d. Ask the trainee to explain the parts of the model or process
  e. Ask the trainee to demonstrate techniques
  f. Ask the trainee to summarize the task
	3. Require a response
	  a. Ask the trainee to explain the purpose and rationale
	  b. Ask the trainee to present an overview
	  c. Ask the trainee to explain safety and quality requirements
	  d. Ask the trainee to describe and show each behavior
	  e. Ask the trainee to explain specific safety and quality requirements
	  f. Ask the trainee to summarize the entire task
		3. Require a response
		  a. Ask the trainee to explain the purpose and rationale
		  b. Ask the trainee to present an overview
		Inform
		  c. Ask the trainee to explain parts of the topic or issue
		  d. Ask the trainee for examples
		Motivate
		  e. Ask the trainee to describe present and desired conditions
		  f. Ask the trainee to discuss implications for self and others
		  g. Ask the trainee to describe commitment behaviors

4. Provide feedback
  a. Inform the trainee about the correctness of the responses
  b. Provide coaching and guidance
  c. Point out embedded cues in the task setting
	4. Provide feedback
	  a. Inform the trainee about the correctness of the responses
	  b. Provide coaching and guidance
	  c. Point out embedded cues in the task setting
		4. Provide feedback
		  a. Inform the trainee about the correctness of the responses
		  b. Provide coaching and guidance
		  c. Point out embedded cues in the task setting

5. Evaluate performance
  a. Evaluate the trainee's self-report
  b. Evaluate performance test results
  c. Document the trainee's performance
	5. Evaluate performance
	  a. Evaluate the trainee's self-report
	  b. Evaluate performance test results
	  c. Document the trainee's performance
		5. Evaluate performance
		  a. Evaluate the trainee's self-report
		  b. Evaluate performance test results
		  c. Document the trainee's performance

Source: Copyright © Ronald L. Jacobs, 1995. Used with permission.

STRUCTURED OJT CASE STUDIES

A relatively comprehensive set of case studies related to structured OJT is beginning to emerge. Until now, an information base of this kind has not been available. These case studies are important because they describe the range of structured OJT's current use and, to some extent, insights into its potential future use. Table 30.3 summarizes selected case studies related to structured OJT and shows that structured OJT, to present the three major types of training, has been used in at least four different ways:

1. As a single training program
2. As a series of related training programs
3. As a training program related to a work process (by contrast with a job)
4. As a training program combined with other training approaches

Possibly the most common way of using structured OJT is as a single training program that addresses a specific task or set of work-related information. Here, the structured OJT modules are used strategically by the organization; that is, trainees receive the training program precisely when they need to learn the particular information. For example, structured OJT is used in a large hospital to help newly promoted supervisors in the housekeeping area become more aware of the organization's mission and vision statements. The structured OJT is delivered by experienced supervisors and managers from the same area. The same training content is also presented in a hospitalwide classroom program, but that program is only offered twice a year, a schedule that makes it difficult to provide the information to individuals on an as-needed basis. Indeed, the structured OJT version of the content has allowed a more immediate context for this information, requiring the new supervisors to go out and identify how the mission and vision statements are (and are not) reflected in their own work area, and this activity has encouraged discussions about how to improve some aspects of the housekeeping department.

Structured OJT has also been used to present a series of training programs related to the same job. Here, several structured OJT modules are developed, each module addressing a specific task or set of work-related information. When the module is completed, the results of the training achieve a larger outcome than any one of the modules could have achieved alone. Together, the modules can be viewed as similar to a training curriculum. Trainees often progress through the modules in a specified sequence. For example, a large retail organization undergoing rapid expansion uses structured OJT to develop promising frontline employees as future first-level managers. Certain store managers have been designated to function as trainers, and they travel periodically to the various stores

Table 30.3. Selected Case Studies Related to Structured OJT.

Use of Structured OJT	Managerial Training	Technical Training	Training for Awareness
As a single training program	Front-line employees learn to conduct team meetings in an industrial supply company Shift managers learn to plan employees' work schedules in a fast-food restaurant Production employees learn to document workflows in a large electric utility	Operators learn to perform critical tasks in a truck assembly plant Customer service reps learn to perform data-entry tasks in a regional insurance company Counter employees learn to make desserts in a regional ice cream restaurant	Newly promoted supervisors become aware of mission and vision statements in a large hospital Employees become aware of changes in a profit-sharing plan in an industrial supply company
As a series of related training programs	Front-line employees learn to perform supervisory tasks in a retail organization Shift managers learn to perform customer service tasks in a national motel chain	Personal advisers learn to develop financial plans for customers in a regional bank Lab technicians learn eighteen quality-control tests in an oil refining company	Front-line employees become aware of ten concepts related to implementing self-directed work groups in a manufacturing company
As training related to a work process	First-line supervisors learn to troubleshoot workflow problems in an auto supply company	Customer service reps learn to perform tasks from nearby functions, based on customer service workflows, in a producer of nutritional supplements	New hires become aware of the assembly stations in their workflow in an electronic components manufacturer Operators become aware of a new production process in an auto supplier plant
In combination with other training approaches	Cabin attendant trainees learn service delivery tasks through classroom training and structured OJT in an international airline	Bank tellers learn to perform advanced operations through classroom, simulation, and structured OJT in the work setting in a regional bank system	Newly hired production employees become aware of safety and quality requirements through classroom and structured OJT in a truck assembly plant

Source: Copyright © Ronald L. Jacobs, 1995. Used with permission.

within their sale regions to provide an integrated series of training modules on such management topics as store security, recruitment and selection of employees, store layout and display, and performance management.

Increasingly, structured OJT is being used to present training related to work within a work process (as opposed to a job). Often, the tasks related to a process are performed within two or more adjoining work areas, as is commonly found in many manufacturing and customer service organizations. Here, employees can receive cross-training on the critical tasks that should be shared within a process. For example, the customer service division of a multinational producer of nutritional supplements has been reorganized according to workflow instead of separate functions. As a result, structured OJT has been used to cross-train employees, as appropriate, on tasks that are identified as customer service workflows rather than as jobs. Thus employees understand better how their own work relates to that of their colleagues, such as the individuals in the pricing department and the contracts department, who also have the opportunity to improve customer service when specific types of inquiries are made.

Finally, structured OJT has been used in follow-up training, or in combination with off-the-job training programs. Such combinations recognize that classroom programs may be better than structured OJT at achieving some kinds of training objectives, whereas structured OJT may be better at achieving others. For example, a large midwestern bank has developed a program for newly hired tellers that combines training in a classroom, training in a teller-simulation room in the training center, and structured OJT in the workplace. The classroom component is used to introduce various bank-specific information, general banking concepts, and industry standards. The simulation component provides trainees with training on teller tasks (entering a deposit, withdrawing from an account, entering a payment, cashing a check, and so on) in a low-pressure environment. The structured OJT component builds on the simulation by certifying mastery of the initial tasks and introducing more advanced tasks, which in turn must be mastered before the newly hired teller is placed in a bank office.

STRUCTURED OJT RESEARCH

In the past decade, there has been a marked increase in research on structured OJT. In general, the research can be divided into two basic themes that have importance for HPT. The research comprising the first theme describes the nature of structured OJT as it appears in various organizations, as well as the requirements for its use. The research comprising the second describes the financial benefits derived from using structured OJT as compared to other training approaches. Although this chapter is not intended to be a comprehensive review of the OJT literature, the following sections describes some of the prominent literature comprising these two themes.

Nature of Structured OJT

The research related to the nature of structured OJT suggests that organizations consider this training approach to be an important part of their training efforts. For instance, Rothwell and Kazanas (1990) conducted an exploratory study with 127 organizations to understand the nature of these structured OJT programs and the organizations' commitment to preparing their employees to deliver the programs. In general, the results showed that supervisors still deliver most structured OJT programs, especially in organizations in the manufacturing sector, and that most of the organizations are doing a substantial amount of in-house training on topics in structured OJT (for example, developing materials and delivering the training). This is to say that organizations seem to recognize the need to prepare the employees who will deliver structured OJT to others, realizing that the training will not be as effective without this investment.

DeJong (1993) and DeJong and Versloot (1994) provide several in-depth case study analyses of structured OJT's use in the Netherlands. These case studies provide helpful insights into the actual composition of structured OJT programs in those organizations and into how the programs compare across organizations. Although the methodology inhibits generalizing beyond these settings, the studies suggest that workplace learning in the form of structured OJT is highly valued across the organizations for its inherent effectiveness, that trainers are selected from among the most capable employees, that training documents are developed to accompany the training, and that the training is taken seriously by trainers and trainees alike. Another impression from the case studies is that these organizations have accepted structured OJT as a continuous organizational activity.

Yang and McLean (1996) surveyed experts to identify the kinds of competence needed by trainers in structured OJT. The rationale of this study was that if structured OJT was to be effective, then more efforts should be made to develop those individuals (often rare in organizations) who would deliver the training. The authors identified two sets of competence for structured OJT, one set deemed important by training professionals and the other deemed important by line employees who had already had extensive experience with structured OJT. There were differences between the two sets, but there was also enough overlap that it was possible to begin describing a core set of competence for trainers.

Finally, in a survey of 118 organizations that was conducted on behalf of the Singapore Productivity Standards Board, Jacobs and Osman-Gani (1998) found that OJT in some form was one of the most frequently used training methods in that country. The results also showed that the two major reasons for using structured OJT were changes in the work and turnover. By comparison with unstructured OJT, structured OJT was reported to help employees work more independently and to reduce absenteeism. The two major problems with using structured OJT were difficulty in documenting the work and the time constraints that structured OJT imposed on the workday. Even though the study was conducted among Singapore organizations, the results are similar to findings for U.S. organizations (Rothwell and Kazanas, 1990).

Financial Benefits

Several studies have investigated the financial benefits of structured OJT by comparison with other training approaches. Two basic questions have been addressed by this research: (1) What are the financial benefits of increasing the efficiency of training? (2) What are the financial benefits of increasing the effectiveness of training? For the first question, Jacobs and McGiffin (1987) showed that structured OJT was able to reduce the training time for new lab technicians from twelve weeks to three, and that there was a savings in wages and benefits of about $10,000 for the initial group of trainees. Jacobs, Jones, and Neil (1992) and Jacobs (1994) have also reported a series of cost-benefit analysis studies in a manufacturing company. The studies generally showed structured OJT to be four to five times more efficient than unstructured OJT in terms of the time required to achieve the training objectives. Moreover, this research showed that, in terms of the value of employees' performance outcomes, structured OJT provided the organization twice the financial benefits of unstructured OJT.

Interestingly, however, a study by Jacobs and Hruby-Moore (1998) of a failed program for structured OJT shows that the forecast benefits of structured OJT will not actually occur unless there are efforts to ensure management's commitment and the provision of adequate time and other resources for the training.

In terms of training effectiveness, few studies have examined financial gains derived from structured OJT, but Jacobs (1994) reports that when new employees learned certain tasks through structured OJT, the quality of their work was higher than when they learned the tasks through unstructured OJT. Specifically, the results showed that when employees learned tasks through structured OJT, the cost of rework was reduced by at least two-thirds.

On the basis of the literature, one can conclude that structured OJT is being adopted in many organizations, in the United States and elsewhere, and that these organizations recognize the need to invest organizational resources in ensuring that this training approach is properly implemented.

FUTURE ISSUES FOR STRUCTURED OJT

In this area, three issues related to structured OJT seem to be at the forefront:

1. How to address cross-cultural issues related to structured OJT
2. How to view structured OJT in the broader context of employee development
3. How to make the best use of technology in implementing structured OJT

Cross-Cultural Issues and Structured OJT

There is evidence that structured OJT is increasingly used in organizations on a global basis, which is good. Indeed, in many countries, structured OJT seems to be the most logical training approach, given that access to HPT professionals and training resources may be relatively limited in those organizations. However, it should be noted that present conceptualizations of structured OJT were derived by HPT researchers and practitioners working in U.S. organizations and undoubtedly relying on assumptions derived from North American culture. Although organizations involved in the global economy face many of the same issues, there are cultural factors, grounded in national identity, language, and history, that influence organizational effectiveness in spite of the similarity of the issues (Hofstede, 1990).

Indeed, cross-cultural issues have grown in importance as more and more organizations have crossed national boundaries in search of new labor pools and markets for their products and services. In doing so, organizations have invariably discovered that certain management approaches, which may have worked well at home, are not necessarily transferable to another culture, nor can the same rate of success be achieved with them unless they undergo some degree of adaptation (Osman-Gani and Jacobs, 1996). Unfortunately, there is little cross-cultural information related to structured OJT that can guide practice. For instance, no information exists on using structured OJT in, say, Korean organizations, where, mainly because of differing cultural assumptions about individual role and status, relationships between managers and employees are known to differ markedly from the corresponding relationships in U.S. organizations. Given the underlying interpersonal basis of OJT, these cultural differences are likely to make a difference in the training's effectiveness. Researchers are just now beginning to address some of these issues. Jacobs (1996), for example, proposes a framework for identifying cross-cultural research questions related to structured OJT, questions based on structured OJT's inputs, process, outputs, and organizational context.

Employee Development and Structured OJT

More and more organizations are viewing structured OJT from the broader perspective of employee development (Jones and Jacobs, 1997). Indeed, research has shown that employee development programs, as a means of responding to constant change, can provide valuable outcomes to organizations when employees are encouraged to participate in training and education programs to achieve individual and organizational goals. In this sense, structured OJT should be viewed as one of several means available for achieving goals related to employee development.

However, recent perspectives on employee development seem to stress the importance of structured OJT, primarily because of its emphasis on the task level. Jacobs (1997) has proposed that organizations should consider a taxonomy of employee development outcomes, ranging from the novice to the specialist to the advanced specialist, the expert, and the master, as a means of differentiating levels of competence. The taxonomy suggests that employee development, instead of being seen in terms of employees' upward progress on job ladders, should be seen in terms of progress on task ladders; that is, goals for employee development should logically coincide with smaller units of work, such as tasks, since the boundaries of jobs are becoming less and less distinct. The concept of the task ladder embodies the recognition that for certain units of work (for example, the task of troubleshooting problems with customer service) there are different expectations for entry-level and senior-level customer service representative (CSRs). Entry-level CSRs require a structured development experience, which may include initial training, coaching, and feedback, to help them acquire the basic range of customer service problems. Senior-level CSRs, however, should be able to solve a wider range and more complex set of problems. Therefore, senior-level CSRs require a structured development experience that goes beyond what is available to an entry-level CSR. Historically, structured OJT has been used to present information to entry-level employees, and yet the question remains: Might structured OJT, as now defined, be equally suitable for presenting more complex job information?

Structured OJT and Technology

Until recently, technology has had little influence on structured OJT. Indeed, it may seem contradictory to mention technology in the same breath as structured OJT, which calls for close contact between trainers and trainees. However, beyond changing the underlying character of structured OJT, technology could be used in at least two ways. First, technology could be used to help document the work of training, an issue of importance to many organizations (Jacobs and Osman-Gani, 1998). Invariably, when work is documented on paper, the information tends to become obsolete in one or more respects, given continuous efforts toward improvement, but handheld information devices and network links could reduce reliance on paper documents, allowing training revisions to be posted immediately, and across various organizational locations. Devices like these could also easily store a virtual library of updated work documents and information about an employee's progress in training. Second, technology could be used as part of a virtual structured OJT session, whereby the trainer and the trainee may be in different locations but can interact by way of an Internet or intranet connection. In this situation, training might take place in conjunction with a computer-based task.

Arguably, most of the technological advances that would be related to structured OJT could actually be implemented at the present time. However, deciding whether in fact to use technology seems the greatest issue to be considered. After all, technology is merely a tool for helping to achieve a goal; its use is not the goal itself. Therefore, any use of technology would at least have to be scrutinized from a financial perspective, to determine whether the cost of this investment would make sense.

CONCLUSION

Structured OJT is being used with increasing frequency in organizations. Certainly, structured OJT should not be the solution selected to address all performance problems caused by lack of knowledge or skill. Nevertheless, there is compelling evidence to suggest that structured OJT, used appropriately, can help individuals achieve training objectives faster, and to a higher standard, than other training methods can. To achieve these outcomes, organizations must recognize the need to invest resources in this training approach, which historically, in most instances, has been unstructured. How to achieve the desired training outcomes, all the while conducting training in actual work settings, remains the challenge in many organizations.

References

Brown, C., and Reich, M. (1997). Developing skills and pay through career ladders: Lessons from Japanese and U.S. companies. *California Management Review* 39:2, 124–142.

Churchill, G. A., Ford, N. M., and Walker, O. C. (1985). *Sales force management: Planning, implementation, and control.* Burr Ridge, IL: Irwin.

DeJong, J. A. (1993). Structured on-the-job training at Hoogovens Ijmuiden. *Journal of European Industrial Training* 17:2, 8–13.

DeJong, J. A., and Versloot, A. M. (1994). Structuring on-the-job training. In A. Brooks and K. Watkins (eds.), *Proceedings of the annual conference of the Academy of Human Resource Development—1994.* Baton Rouge, LA: Academy of Human Resource Development.

Dooley, C. R. (1945). *The Training Within Industry report (1940–1945): A record of the development of management techniques for improvement of supervision—their use and the results.* Washington, DC: Training Within Industry Service, Bureau of Training, War Manpower Commission.

Eck, A. (1993). Job-related education and training: Their impact on earnings. *Monthly Labor Review* 116:10, 21–38.

Hofstede, G. (1990). *Culture's consequences: International differences in work-related values.* Thousand Oaks, CA: Sage.

Holzer, H. H. (1990). The determinants of employee productivity and earnings. *Industrial Relations* 29:3, 403–422.

Jacobs, R. L. (1989). Systems theory applied to human resource development. In D. Gradous (ed.), *Systems theory applied to human resource development.* Alexandria, VA: American Society for Training and Development.

Jacobs, R. L. (1994). Comparing the training efficiency and product quality of unstructured and structured OJT. In J. Phillips (ed.), *The return on investment in human resource development: Cases on the economic benefits of HRD.* Alexandria, VA: American Society for Training and Development.

Jacobs, R. L. (1996). A framework for studying structured on-the-job training from a cross-cultural perspective. In D. N. Lascu, E. Kaynak, and Z. U. Ahmed (eds.), *Proceedings of the International Management Development Association—1996.* Hummelstown, PA: International Management Development Association.

Jacobs, R. L. (1997). A taxonomy of employee development: Toward an organizational culture of expertise. In R. Torraco (ed.), *Proceedings of the annual conference of the Academy of Human Resource Development—1997.* Baton Rouge, LA: Academy of Human Resource Development.

Jacobs, R. L., and Hruby-Moore, M. (1998). A cost benefit analysis study which resulted in unfavorable financial outcomes: Learning from failure. *Performance Improvement Quarterly* 11:2, 93–100.

Jacobs, R. L., and Jones, M. J. (1995). *Structured on-the-job training: Unleashing employee expertise in the workplace.* San Francisco: Berrett-Koehler.

Jacobs, R. L., Jones, M. J., and Neil, S. (1992). A case study in forecasting the financial benefits of unstructured and structured on-the-job training. *Human Resource Development Quarterly* 3:2, 133–139.

Jacobs, R. L., and McGiffin, T. (1987). A human performance system using a structured on-the-job training approach. *Performance & Instruction* 25:7, 8–11.

Jacobs, R. L., and Osman-Gani, A. A. (1998). Structured on-the-job training: Status, impacts, and implementation issues in Singapore organizations. In R. Torraco (ed.), *Proceedings of the annual conference of the Academy of Human Resource Development—1998.* Baton Rouge, LA: Academy of Human Resource Development.

Jones, M. J., and Jacobs, R. L. (1997). Developing frontline employees: New challenges for achieving organizational effectiveness. In R. Kaufman, S. Thiagarajan, and P. MacGillis (eds.), *The guidebook for performance improvement: Working with individuals and organizations.* San Francisco: Jossey-Bass/Pfeiffer.

Kirkpatrick, D. (1985). Effective supervisory training and development. Part 2: In-house approaches and techniques. *Personnel* 62:1, 52–56.

1997 industry report: What employers teach. (1997, Oct.). *Training,* p. 56.

Osman-Gani, A. A., and Jacobs, R. L. (1996). Differences in perceptions of human resource development across countries: An exploratory study of managers in a multinational enterprise. *Journal of Transnational Management Development* 2:3, 21–36.

Rothwell, W., and Kazanas, H. (1990). Structured on-the-job training (SOJT) as perceived by HRD professionals. *Performance Improvement Quarterly* 3:3, 12–26.

Utgaard, S. B., and Davis, R. V. (1970). The most frequently used training techniques. *Training and Development Journal* 24:2, 40–43.

Yang, J. C., and McLean, G. (1996). Structured on-the-job training competencies. In E. Holton (ed.), *Proceedings of the annual conference of the Academy of Human Resource Development—1996.* Baton Rouge LA: Academy of Human Resource Development.

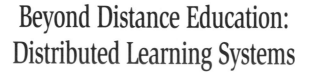

CHAPTER THIRTY-ONE

Beyond Distance Education: Distributed Learning Systems

Ellen D. Wagner

Distance learning seems to have finally come of age. After almost two decades of being positioned as "almost as good" as face-to-face, instructor-led instruction, the professional literature provides ample empirical evidence supporting the important role played by well-designed and well-implemented distance learning initiatives.

Even as distance learning courses and programs have become ubiquitous features on the teaching and learning landscape, the discipline of distance learning is experiencing a significant expansion of its methodological underpinnings. Distributed learning represents a methodologically distinct variation on distance learning that responds to calls for supporting needs of individuals on terms that they are increasingly defining for themselves.

At first glance, the difference between these two terms may appear to be one of semantics. However, there are operational distinctions between distance learning and distributed learning that affect how performance improvement interventions are positioned and implemented. Both distributed learning's "just in time, just for me" orientation and distance learning's "extended classroom" approach of meeting the performance improvement needs of geographically dispersed learners require design and development consideration to leverage the unique strengths of each approach in practice. The following discussion describes some of the similarities and differences between these two closely related yet operationally distinct performance improvement methodologies. This discussion helps set the stage for subsequent descriptions of factors to be considered in developing both distance and distributed learning interventions.

ATTRIBUTES OF DISTANCE LEARNING

Distance learning (also called *distance education, distance education and training,* and *teletraining,* depending on the application environment) involves the transmission of educational, instructional, or training programming to two or more people at two or more locations separated by space or in time. It has evolved in large part as a response to demands for improving information-access equity, with particular attention paid to improving proximity of instructional resources via telecommunications technology.

Correspondence-related variations on distance learning have been a component of continuing and extended studies programs in the United States since 1892 (Pittman, 1990), but technology-mediated distance learning has grown logarithmically since the late 1980s (Moore, 1990). Until that time, technology-mediated distance learning had been far more commonplace outside the United States. "Electronic" distance learning programs, beginning with radio broadcasting, made their first appearance in the early 1930s. Countries such as Australia and Canada used electronic distance learning to provide rural and minority students with access to educational resources that would otherwise have been out of reach. Other countries have applied distance learning methods in more strategic, less marginalized ways; for example, during the 1930s Joseph Stalin chose distance learning as a way of increasing the number of technicians and technologists in Soviet society. Distance learning has been used in Africa, on a scale that is proportionally far greater than what has been seen in Europe or North America, for purposes of adult education, health education, and political education (Perraton, 1982).

Table 31.1 displays the names, dates of establishment, and number of enrollments of national "open universities" as of 1992, giving some idea of the scope of distance learning's influence on a global scale. In reviewing these numbers, Brown and Brown (1994) suggested that if the number of learners receiving distance learning programming in elementary, secondary, training, and noncredit areas had been included in these estimates, the number of participants in distance learning efforts would probably have been quadrupled. If one were to adjust these figures to account for the explosive growth in distance learning courses and programs since 1992, it is very likely that these numbers could be increased tenfold beyond that.

In his classic treatise on the topic, Keegan (1990) suggests that distance learning exhibits the following attributes:

Table 31.1. Major Open Universities of the World as of 1992.

Institution	Date Established	Enrollment
University of South Africa	1951	50,000
Open University, U.K.	1969	50,000
Universidad Nacional, Spain	1972	83,000
Femuniversitat, Germany	1974	37,000
Open University of Israel	1974	12,000
Allama Iqbal Open University, Pakistan	1974	150,000
Athabasca University, Canada	1975	10,000
University Nacional Abierta, Venezuela	1977	29,000
University Est a Distancia, Costa Rica	1977	11,000
Sukhothai Thammathirat OU, Thailand	1978	200,000
Central Radio and TV University, China	1978	1,000,000
Open University of Sri Lanka	1981	18,000
Open Universiteit, Netherlands	1981	33,000
Korean Air and Correspondence University	1982	300,000
University of the Air of Japan	1983	22,000
Universitas Terbuka, Indonesia	1984	70,000
Indira Gandhi National Open University, India	1986	30,000
National Open University of Taiwan	1986	48,000
Al-Quds Open University, Jordan	1986	Not available
Universidade Aberta, Portugal	1988	3,800
Open University of Bangladesh	1991	Not available
Open University of Poland	Proposed	Not applicable
Open University of France	Proposed	Not applicable

Source: Brown and Brown, 1994.

- There is limited regular contact between instructor(s) and learner(s). Unlike traditional classroom sessions, where students and instructors meet in person on a daily or weekly basis, distant students and instructors may meet face to face only once or twice while a course is in session, if they ever meet in person at all.

- Various media (print, audio, video, or computer) are used to transmit course content. One distance learning scenario may audio record lectures and distribute the tapes to be reviewed prior to an interactive session conducted via audiographic teleconferencing (a technology that transmits audio and still graphics over a standard voice-grade telephone line). Another may provide text-based case study exercises supplemented by on-line computer-based activities to be completed at a later time. Both scenarios may use satellite-distributed programming to provide direction to the total learning experience.

- There is some provision for two-way communication in the instructional process. Telecommunications technologies typically provide an interactive link through which discussion and dialogue are maintained among geographically dispersed course participants. However, written correspondence serves as the primary means of interaction in nontechnological, self-paced distance learning implementations.

- People tend to receive instruction individually or in small groups rather than in large groups. Instead of meeting with others at a centralized location, a learner may complete a course at a workstation, at home, in the office, or at some other location where he or she may be the only course participant at that particular site. A small number of individuals may convene with one another at one site, to be connected with small groups or with individuals located at other locations. Individual learners and small groups of learners participating in a common distance learning experience collectively constitute a *learning cohort* that functions as a single entity, in much the same way that participants in traditional classrooms operate as a single entity.

Implicit in this description is the notion that distance learners are found in locations that are distinct and apart from the institutions and organizations offering instruction. In its simplest sense, distance learning offers an alternative to site-based classroom instruction by extending the reach of the classroom instructor via technology.

Technology is particularly significant in distance learning settings because it fosters interaction (or, at a minimum, the perception of interaction) between the instructor and the learners, among learners, and between learners and the content they are expected to learn (Moore, 1989). Distance learning practitioners view this interactivity as the single most significant attribute that defines the contemporary distance learning experience. The two-way technologies provide vehicles for real-time exchanges of audio, video, text, and graphical information. It is this two-way, real-time exchange capacity that serves as one of distance learning's primary identifying characteristics (Wagner, 1994).

Technologies most often associated with distance learning include print, audioconferencing, audiographic teleconferencing, interactive compressed-video teleconferencing, computer-mediated conferencing, and video teleconferencing using satellite, broadcast, coaxial cable, and fiber optic transmission media. These technologies facilitate the interactive exchange of information that helps replicate the communication dynamics typically encountered in conventional classroom settings.

Distance learning courses and programs tend to be utilized in environments where all classes, site-based and distant, are scheduled according to a master calendar. Classes tend to begin and end on a fixed schedule and tend to be managed by an instructor. Distant learners are often supported by facilitators who minister to the needs of students at fixed (albeit distant) instructional sites or centers. Distance learning experiences tend to employ a cohort-group model to motivate and retain participants. In distance learning settings, interactions are employed with the intent of establishing a "social presence" marked by intimacy among participants and immediacy of responses between the instructor and the learners (Gunawardena, 1995). In distance learning settings, concern for the interactions between teachers and students, among students, and between students and content reflect a concern for message-transmission fidelity between sender(s) and receiver(s).

ATTRIBUTES OF DISTRIBUTED LEARNING

Distributed learning differs from distance learning in that it tends to focus on the needs of individuals looking for immediate access to information, performance support tools, and instructional opportunities. This contrasts with distance learning's orientation, which is focused on extending the classroom via technology. Distributed learning also tends to maximize connections between and among learners and resources, regardless of their relative physical locations. In other words, in a distributed learning setting a learner may be physically at a centralized site, whereas the resources that are needed may be at some physical distance from that centralized location. Another scenario may be that the learner is far from the resources, and both learner and resources are at sites that are distant from the primary organizational location. What is most relevant here is that the physical locations of learners and learning resources are irrelevant; what is relevant is the connection that exists between and among learners and resources.

As is true in distance learning, technological developments and strategies for technology use actively shape distributed learning experiences. However, some differences between the two approaches are worth noting. Whereas distance learning is influenced by technologies that enable conferencing, distributed learning is influenced by the interactive connectivity linking learners with learning resources. The technology deployment in distance learning has been affected by deregulation and competition in the cable television and telephone industries. Distributed learning has been jump-started by developments in the computer hardware, software, and networking industries. Whereas distance learning has employed several modalities (audio, text, video) for connecting people, distributed learning technologies converge audio, video, and data-transmission media into a single integrated digital "pipeline."

Technological Influences on Developments in Distributed Learning

To better understand the expansion from the cohort-oriented, classroom extension model of distance learning to include the individualized, "anytime, anywhere" model of distributed learning, it is worth taking a closer look at specific technological developments that have influenced both models:

- *Accelerated desktop computer processing speed.* The processing power of today's desktop computers rivals that of large mainframe computers of a decade ago. These increases in desktop-accessible speed and power greatly increase the ability of individuals to generate creative computing solutions to meet their own needs, on their own terms. This means that powerful, customizable computer-based performance improvement solutions are within reach of the majority of computer users.

- *Platform-independent data-transmission protocols.* In the not-too-distant past, the selection of an operating system defined how and with whom one could exchange data files. Given the tremendous developments in networking protocols, it is now possible for UNIX users to share data with Microsoft Windows 95 users, who can in turn share that information with Macintosh OS users, who can in their turn share information with OS/2 users. This means that concerns of networking can be focused less on the tools of communications networking than on the intent of interpersonal networking.

- *Improved browser technology, and such features as Java-enabled client-server interactivity.* Readily accessible "new media," such as on-line multimedia and hypermedia, offer computer users at all levels of proficiency a gateway to an array of full-motion, fully animated, interactive, responsive information resources. Features like "streaming" audio and video transmit digital bits representing sounds, pictures, and motion in real time as a Web page loads on a user's computer, allowing Web sites to offer real-time multimedia programming comparable to that available on a CD-ROM (as long as sufficient bandwidth is available for transmission). There is every indication that in the next few years, on-line multimedia will be the rule rather than the exception for learning facilitation and professional development. For example, a recent survey using the HotBot search engine shows that the number of Web pages containing streaming media content increased more than 275 percent between September 1997 and January 1998. This represents an increase from approximately 100,000 pages containing streaming media functionality to more than 280,000, with the number of pages increasing monthly at logarithmic rates (Guglielmo, 1998).

- *Content objects and knowledge-content distributors.* A content object is a modular data unit that encapsulates information to describe and present a concept, a skill operation, or a procedure. Employing a categorization schema called a *meta–data structure* defines an object's descriptive attributes (that is, whether it is text, animation, audio, or video information; the size and type of the file; the topic being presented in the object; the performance that the object is intended to elicit; and so on). The meta–data structure makes it possible to combine powerful database capabilities with on-line search and file-retrieval capabilities so that specific content objects can be identified, located, and retrieved. Known as *knowledge-content distributors,* or KCDs (Masie, 1998), these content-object/ meta–data structure tools operate as "wholesalers" of on-line and digital learning content from multiple vendors, providing user organizations with the ability to mix and match learning products. In practical terms, this means that users can select and compile the precise content objects that they specify.

• *Improved backend database technologies.* Combined with the browser and interactive features already noted, programs employing full-scale database backends make it possible for even small businesses to leverage the power of real-time on-line transactional processing. They also make it possible to offer adaptive, fully individualized professional development resources that respond to a user's profiled needs and interests by establishing search-and-sort protocols that access only the information that is relevant according to that user's profile.

• *The ubiquitous availability of commercial Internet service providers (ISPs).* Many people forget that the *.com* designation for commercial Internet users has been available only since the privatization of the National Science Foundation's NSF-Net in the mid-1990s. Until that time, most Internet users were affiliated with government and government-sponsored research organizations, educational institutions, and branches of the military. Burgeoning numbers of commercial Internet service providers and the competition among them have dramatically affected the access to service, types of service, costs for service, and provision of user support that Internet users have come to expect.

• *Improved access to the bandwidth needed for large-file transmission.* Because of complaints from those who bemoan the delays they encounter downloading large graphical files over the "World Wide Wait," and because of consumer demands for more bandwidth, Internet service providers are escalating plans for upgrading network and modem capabilities. Asynchronous digital subscriber line (ADSL) service, offering transmission speeds up to thirty times faster than what is available over standard (twisted copper pair) voice-grade telephone lines, is starting to emerge in selected markets. Transmission speeds more than a thousand times faster than those currently available are very likely to be offered in the next few years.

Influences from Human Performance Technology on Distributed Learning

Evolving technology has certainly exerted its influence on the emergence of both distance and distributed learning, but the most important variables influencing the initiation of a distant or distributed learning experience come from a need to bring about individual and/or organizational performance improvement in the workplace. Today's economy and business environments operate by new rules, shaped by an organization's ability to adapt and respond to change. This in turn depends in large part on that organization's employees' ability to think critically, solve problems, and anticipate new possibilities (Carnevale, 1991; Rothwell, 1996). The growing workplace demand for information, instruction, and training resources that are available when and where support is needed is tacit acknowledgment of the need for more individualized performance support. Increasingly, learning resources can be accessed on line; the presence of a growing on-line learning and performance support marketplace is shifting the balance of power from providers to consumers. It is easy to understand why there is growing impatience with traditional methods of designing, delivering, and managing learning experiences that are increasingly out of touch in a "wired world."

Training continues to play an important role in supporting the ongoing development of employee knowledge and skills. As a case in point, the American Society for Training and Development's 1998 State of the Industry Report indicates that more than 81 percent of all training continues to be delivered in classroom settings by instructors or trainers (Bassi and Van Buren, 1998). Even so, there is growing recognition that training may be insufficient for the kinds of continuous, individualized performance improvement that are enabled through distributed learning:

- Training usually is not proactively developed to meet a company's strategic business needs. Rather, it is implemented to react to a performance deficiency. Distributed learning provides a means of proactively pursuing information and performance support resources when and where those resources are needed.
- Training is often designed as something "done to" learners. Specific outcomes need to be achieved, and learners are expected to conform to a path dictated by the designer of the learning experience, the instructor for the learning experience, or both. Typically, training is not designed to be flexible enough to meet an individual's learning needs, and typically it is not available at the time it may be needed by any given individual. Distributed learning provides a means of responding to an individual's self-determined need for improvement wherever there is access to Internet or network connections.
- For those who want to apply what they have just learned, returning to work from the training setting can be disheartening. The crises of the moment often interfere with the best intentions. Goals set after completion of a training experience get set aside to deal with the details of day-to-day business operations, and often the goals are never implemented. Distributed learning helps bring training and information resources directly to the desktop. It makes it easy to track down resources needed to make decisions. It can even help locate resources, both on line and off line, that are available at times and in formats that meet the individual's needs.

CHALLENGES IN DESIGNING DISTANCE AND DISTRIBUTED LEARNING SYSTEMS

Even though the rationale for initiating a distance or distributed learning (D&DL) implementation may be compelling, there are several other considerations that need to be factored into one's thinking before one embarks on a particular design path:

- The courses that designers are expected to develop for distance and distributed learning contexts may or may not look like courses as we have always known them. This is especially true in the "lifelong learning" market represented by postbaccalaureate adult learners staying abreast of rapidly changing developments in their chosen disciplines. It is also true of training and performance support efforts that focus on updating knowledge and skills of individuals working in rapidly changing industries. This is an important point that should be included as part of the expectation setting that should be undertaken when constructing a D&DL design.

- A basic goal of any learning design is to establish parameters within which the outcomes of the particular design intervention can be achieved. When the design is for a familiar venue, such as a classroom, it is well to bear in mind that the audience will tend to have expectations of what is likely (or not likely) to occur. Distance and distributed learning audiences may not have the same degree of experience with these two modes as they do with classroom-based experiences. They may not understand the challenges or the opportunities, or even the differences, that D&DL experiences offer. Actively setting expectations around what is likely to be encountered during the D&DL experience is an important component of learner motivation.

- The demand for traditional course offerings (for example, a five-day, site-based, instructor-led course offered at a centralized training center) may wane in an era of alternative means for accessing content when and where it is needed. Even so, there are times when getting groups of people together in face-to-face instructional settings is an essential part of the total learning experience. It is important to balance the things that distributed and distance learning can do very well with the things that can be done even better in other presentation modalities. It is also important to remember that distance learning's unique attributes make it appropriate for certain tasks for which distributed learning may not be as appropriate, and that distributed learning may be better than distance learning for achieving certain learning outcomes.

- Distance learning experiences may serve as a surrogate for the training experiences with which most of us are familiar, but distributed learning experiences represent a completely new approach for supporting informational, instructional, and performance support needs of individuals. Some training professionals (Filipczak, 1996; Cohen, 1997) have even suggested that (distributed) training offered via the Web is more similar to a performance support system than it is to our expectations of training. The logical extension of this discussion seems to suggest that the value of a distributed learning experience is somehow suspect because it is not the same as (classroom-oriented, instructor-led) training. It may be more productive to consider what the outcome of a learning experience is supposed to be, and then to select an instructional approach that accommodates the necessary conditions and constraints of the learning task, than to debate the value of any particular approach out of context.

- The strategies used for constructing instructional designs must increasingly account for learner-determined and learner-navigated paths while also continuing to maintain instructor-directed and domain-dependent learning parameters. In other words, distributed learning strategies must account for individual users' desire to move about in the on-line experience on terms they define for themselves. At the same time, sponsors of the learning experience need assurances that the topics that each learner must master are going to be mastered, regardless of the path that the user takes as she or he moves about. This means that design strategies need to include significantly more flexibility for individualized learner control and learning management than has typically been found in more behaviorally oriented models of teaching and learning.

CONSIDERATIONS IN DESIGNING LEARNER-CENTERED INSTRUCTION

Whether one is working in a context of distance or distributed learning, developing learner-centered designs involves a significant philosophical and methodological shift from behavioral to cognitive perspectives, and from objectivist to constructivist perspectives. Wagner (1990) notes that in most traditional learning contexts, instructional design activities tend to focus on the arrangement of contingencies to elicit specific responses. The seemingly algorithmic nature of the process of design ("First you state your goal, then you define your objectives . . . ") almost suggests a stimulus-response relationship (" . . . and then your student will perform certain tasks with 80 percent accuracy, 90 percent of the time"). Even in cases where designs are developed to accommodate cognitive tasks (such as knowing, remembering, thinking creatively, and solving problems), designs tend to reflect an objectivist rather than a constructivist orientation (Wagner and McCombs, 1995).

Duffy and Jonassen (1992) note that objectivist perspectives have shaped instructional design practice since it first emerged. Objectivism suggests the following propositions:

- The world is completely and correctly structured in terms of entities, properties, and relationships.
- Meaning exists in the world outside the realm of human experience.
- People have different understandings of meaning, which are based on their different experiences, but these are only partial understandings.
- The goal of complete and correct understanding is to get people to know, without bias from their prior experiences, the entities, attributes, and relations that exist.

Duffy and Jonassen (1992) suggest that constructivism provides an alternative basis for conceptualizing instructional experiences, whereby there are many ways in which to structure the world. This further suggests that there are many meanings or perspectives for an event or concept. Consequently, there is not a single correct meaning or understanding for which learners must strive.

A constructivist perspective makes perfect sense from a theoretical position, but the notion of "self-determined correct answers" can easily strike fear in the heart of a Human Performance (HP) technologist responsible for demonstrating that learners are achieving "world-class standards," or that they have achieved specific performance-based outcomes. In order to counter such concerns, constructivists emphasize situating new (cognitive) experiences in the context of authentic (learning) activities (Brown, Collins, and Duglid, 1989). Learners are given an opportunity to draw on their own experiences, interpretations, and situational relevancies to tailor their instruction to fit their realities for a given situation. This provides an alternative to the prevailing approach guiding the design of instruction, whereby learners are provided with a plan of action, and success is simply a matter of following that plan.

Distance and distributed learning both provide a unique design and implementation context in which to infuse learner-centered principles. In D&DL settings, where learners are not in physical proximity to their instructors, and where technology mediates the learning experience, there is a perception that learners may need to work more independently than in traditional settings (Kember, 1995). This is even more pronounced in distributed learning settings, where learners must establish their own paths for achieving performance outcomes. There is a general perception that successful learners tend to demonstrate a high degree of self-efficacy and are willing to take on challenging tasks on the basis of their previous experiences of success. There is also the belief that successful students are intrinsically motivated to succeed, and that they tend to believe that the control they exercise over events in their lives is internally mediated (Riddle, 1994).

Ironically, evidence from psychological and educational literature indicates that all learners benefit from instruction in which they are motivated, feel that they exercise control over their learning experience, are respected, and are accountable for their own learning outcomes. However, there continues to be the perception that these variables, although essential components of distant and distributed education learning experiences, may not be as important in traditional training and instructional settings. There is also the perception that, as "alternatives" to traditional instruction, distance and distributed learning experiences use instructional designs, models, and techniques that are oriented toward the needs of individuals more than may be typically encountered in traditional group settings.

STAGES IN DEVELOPING DISTANCE AND DISTRIBUTED LEARNING SYSTEMS

Designers working in distance and distributed learning environments will need to approach their endeavors with all these circumstances and constraints in mind. However, even though it is important to respond to the demands of a specific distance or distributed learning endeavor, designers must focus on the core activities associated with the actual construction of performance improvement interventions. These include the time-honored activities associated with instructional system design: assessment, design, development and evaluation.

Assessment

Assessment encompasses a broad range of activities used to establish the parameters within which a D&DL experience needs to be developed. Assessment includes determining the domain of the content to be included in the experience, and it often results in the establishment of content benchmarks (that is, clearly articulated measures defining a topic's conceptual range and learner mastery of content included in that range). Assessment identifies and describes the performance that results from an expressed or observed need, and it targets the essential tasks that need to be addressed. Assessment also considers the needs and interests of a broad array of stakeholders. This group includes but is not limited to the following:

- Learners for whom a learning experience is intended
- Instructors or facilitators responsible for monitoring learners' progress
- Managers of the performance improvement endeavor to which the learning experience belongs
- Experts (with their expectations) from the market in which "high-performing graduates" must demonstrate their skill and content mastery

In concrete, pragmatic terms, assessment takes a close look at the attributes of the audience for which instruction is intended, to ensure that such design elements as treatment, tone, and mode of presentation are appropriately selected. Assessment also considers the context in which a course will be implemented, points out the need for technical support, as appropriate, and ensures that resource scheduling has been addressed. Assessment activities determine whether either distance or distributed learning is the most appropriate means of instructional delivery for the targeted audiences.

Some of the techniques used for conducting assessments include site visits, observations, analysis of extant documents, reviews of annual reports, surveys, reviews of literature, industry summaries, interviews, questionnaires, and such focus group activities as user requirement workshops, where individuals representing targeted groups articulate learning needs and delivery preferences. Other rich sources of assessment data include summaries from other relevant course evaluations, instructor evaluations, and program evaluations. Recommendations for future research, or summaries of "next steps" from evaluation reports, also provide information that can be useful in compiling the data from which to begin constructing a learning design.

The technologies needed to implement a proposed course present designers who are working in distance and distributed learning contexts with a broad array of challenges. In many cases, technology questions are posed from the perspective of an organization's staff in information technology or management information systems staff. Course designers need to be aware of the impact that a proposed design may have on a variety of stakeholders, including designers and developers, administrators and managers, and support staff in addition to the learners. Examples of questions that D&DL stakeholders should be able to answer before embarking on a D&DL endeavor are listed in Table 31.2.

Design

Design activities typically involve reviewing information collected during the assessment stage and then constructing a proposal for meeting as many of the needs outlined by the assessment as possible. The intended audiences are identified. Learning objectives and performance objectives are articulated. Performance standards are established. Primary and secondary resources for supporting the delivery of the learning experience are identified. Instructional strategies and tactics are specified. Media needed to support the delivery of a course are specified. The end result of a D&DL course design effort is a design blueprint that describes in great detail all the elements of a course that must be in place for the course to be successful. Table 31.3 offers a sample planning checklist for course design and development, highlighting sample questions to be asked in developing a D&DL design blueprint.

Regardless of the specific responses to these and other questions, there are key elements common to effective and implementable course designs, whether the designs have been crafted for a distributed learning experience, a distance learning experience, or a face-to-face, instructor-led experience. These are outlined in the sections that follow.

Clearly Articulated Objectives or Alternatives. Regardless of one's (objectivist or constructivist) orientation, learners need to know what is expected by others or what they should expect from themselves to be successful in a given learning task. From an objectivist perspective, learners should be able to articulate what

Table 31.2. Sample Assessment-Stage Questions from Stakeholders.

Designer, Developer	Administrator, Manager	Support Staff	User
What kind of bandwidth is available for delivery?	What are the costs associated with this design?	What bandwidth is required for distribution?	What are the connectivity options?
What is the delivery environment?	What kind of program maintenance is available?	What kinds of computers do learners need?	What kind of system will I need to access information?
What is the timeline for development?	What is the equipment replacement schedule?	What operating systems are involved?	How much of this is actually going to be implemented on line?
What resources are available for development?	What staff is required for implementation?	What are the connectivity options?	How much will be through other media? How much will be face to face?
What effects are to be achieved?	What is the ROI?	What are the server requirements?	
What outcomes are to be achieved?	What are the economies of scale?	What kinds of plug ins will be needed?	How will this improve my learning?
For whom is this really intended?	What is the impact on achievement?	How will network traffic be managed?	How will this help me do my job better?
Who needs to be involved in the decisions?	What is the impact on efficiency?	Who will monitor interactive chat areas and on-line questions?	How will this improve my access to learning resources?
Who needs to approve this design?			How easy is this for me to use?

Table 31.3. Course Design and Development Planning Checklist.

Questions	Priority		Action/Owner
❏ What are the outcomes or goals for your D&DL course? Is it tied to a more comprehensive curriculum? Is it linked to other course design and development efforts?	❏ High ❏ Mid ❏ Low		
❏ Who are the stakeholders for this course? (This includes learners, managers, funders, marketers, and any other group that may be affected by this effort.)	❏ High ❏ Mid ❏ Low		
❏ Do you have, or can you make a successful case for, a development budget appropriate for your project? To whom is the funding request to be made?	❏ High ❏ Mid ❏ Low		
❏ Is a stand-alone, networked, or speaker-supported approach more appropriate for your needs?	❏ High ❏ Mid ❏ Low		
❏ D&DL designs involve many technology requirements. Can those technology requirements be met in this design?	❏ High ❏ Mid ❏ Low		
❏ Are you willing and able to take ownership of the project, including implementation, support, and updates?	❏ High ❏ Mid ❏ Low		
❏ Have you determined your return on investment (ROI)? What economies of scale do D&DL provide?	❏ High ❏ Mid ❏ Low		
❏ Cost benefits frequently go beyond ROI. What additional benefits might accrue from this project? How can you demonstrate this?	❏ High ❏ Mid ❏ Low		
❏ What staff resources will be needed to deploy this course?	❏ High ❏ Mid ❏ Low		
❏ Does the content for this course change frequently, or is it reasonably static?	❏ High ❏ Mid ❏ Low		
❏ How many learners are you planning to teach? Where are they? How will they interact with you? What kinds of support will they need in order to perform appropriately?	❏ High ❏ Mid ❏ Low		
❏ How will you account for the human interactions that users need to experience? What kinds of outcomes do you hope these interactions will achieve?	❏ High ❏ Mid ❏ Low		

they expect do as a result of an instructional or performance improvement intervention. From this perspective, performance objectives should be employed and should be stated with action words. Designers should consider the conditions under which an expected performance is to be offered, and they should consider what measures will be employed to demonstrate that an objective has actually been achieved.

From a constructivist perspective, learners need to be able to index new ideas (for example, in the realms of information, skills, and abilities) to their own personal experience because the experience in which an idea is embedded is critical to an individual's understanding of and ability to use that idea. The constructivist approach suggests that one should not focus on transmitting the "action plans" typically embodied in performance objectives but instead should focus on developing learners' skills so that they can construct their own action plans in response to situational demands and opportunities (Duffy and Jonassen, 1992). This calls for situating new learning in the context of authentic experiences (that is, experiences that are likely to be encountered, and in which the new knowledge will be used). It is important to show learners how to construct plausible interpretations of what is being learned so that they attain a measure of comfort in generating alternative or original (situationally contingent) learning plans for themselves. This approach suggests that, although all such interpretations are not equal, it cannot be presumed that there is a single right response or course of action.

Instructional Strategies. Instructional strategies help define the approach to be used in ensuring that content is presented in ways appropriate to the achievement of the intended outcomes. Examples of instructional strategies include interaction techniques, learning activities, and attentional and mnemonic devices. Instructional strategies also address learning styles and cognitive strategies likely to be employed by learners so that designs can complement the natural abilities that learners bring to the tasks in question.

Content Selection, Treatment, and Presentation. What needs to be said? How much information is enough? How can one tell if there is too much information for a given learning task? How should content be presented? What style of presentation should be used? What tone should be used? What level of vocabulary is most appropriate? Are the examples clear and relevant? Are they appropriate for all prospective members of a learning cohort?

Capabilities and Limitations of Development. Is it essential to develop one's own customized teaching and learning solution, or can off-the-shelf courseware be used? Are the designer and the developer of the D&DL experience also the teacher and the technology support staff? How much time is available for design and development? What kind of budget exists to support the course design and development efforts? Will there be support for course maintenance?

Technologies. What tools offer the best coverage for course distribution? How can the maximum transmission fidelity be achieved? What kinds of investment and support will be necessary to ensure seamless, transparent, and reliable transmission service?

Interaction. As Wagner (1997) notes, very few topics in the world of distance learning have generated as much discussion and debate as the construct of interactivity. Discussions of interaction in distance learning implementations have typically focused on Moore's (1989) "teacher-with-learner, learner-with-learner, learner-with-content" schema (see, for example, Cyrs, 1997). This interaction schema implies the purpose, intent, and/or intended outcome of an interaction by indicating who or what is to be involved in a transaction. However, the explicit description of an interaction's purpose, intent, and outcome is still left to the imagination.

The earlier emphasis on the agents of an interaction set the stage for a more meaningful discussion of the outcomes enabled by a variety of types of interactions that are implemented in distance and distributed learning designs. Wagner (1997) has identified categories of interactions that focus on achieving specific performance outcomes in distance and distributed learning settings:

- *Interaction for participation* provides learners with a means of engaging with one another. Participative interaction ranges from using names of participants in discussions to articulating one's interest in assuming leadership responsibilities in a learning cohort.

- *Interaction for communication* offers the ability to share information and opinions, or to have an intentional influence on the opinions or beliefs of others.

- *Interaction for feedback* refers to any information that allows learners to judge the quality of their performance. From a behaviorist perspective, feedback provides reinforcement, which is intended to correct and direct performance. Cognitivists suggest that feedback provides learners with information about the correctness of a response so that they can either determine that a response is right or wrong or correct an incorrect response so that long-term retention of correct information is enabled.

- *Interaction for elaboration* involves coming up with alternative examples to explain a new idea, or developing alternative explanations for why an idea may be framed in a particular way. It makes new information more meaningful for learners. When a bit of information associated with a given idea is expanded or even manipulated, it becomes easier to recognize all the various conceptual "hooks," or points of conceptual similarity, that may be associated with that information.

- *Interaction for learner control and self-regulation* provides learners with the information needed to manage the depth of study, range of content covered, type of alternative media needed for information presentations, and time actually spent on a specific learning task (Kinzie, 1990).

- *Interaction for motivation* suggests that curiosity, creativity, and higher-order thinking are stimulated by relevant, authentic learning tasks of optimal difficulty and novelty for each student.

- *Interaction for negotiation* involves the willingness of another individual to engage in a dialogue, to come to consensus, or to agree to conform to the terms of an agreement.

- *Interaction for team building* is necessary to ensure that individual members of a team actively support the goals of the group. Interactions facilitate such desirable behaviors as recognition and acceptance of individual differences, expression of respect for the team as well as for its members, effective listening, a shared sense of responsibility. and confirmation of expectations within the group.

- *Interaction for discovery* refers to the cross-fertilization of ideas that occurs when people share their perspectives with one another in the pursuit of defining new constructs, concepts, and procedures.

- *Interaction for exploration* provides a vehicle for defining the scope, depth, and breadth of a new idea. Just as it is important to recognize a new idea, it is also important to distinguish a new idea from existing ideas and to determine the parameters within which a new idea will retain its unique identity.

- *Interaction for clarification* relates to finding one's way through a sea of performance expectations that may or may not be clearly articulated.

Development

D&DL courseware development involves the actual production of the interventions called for by a specific design. A designer may or may not be directly involved in constructing the interventions that are called for, but it is imperative that a designer be familiar enough with the interventions being proposed to understand the constraints that may be encountered in development.

An effective course design needs to specify how the following activities will be accommodated:

- *Creative design.* An appealing visual appearance requires the input and participation of professional artists. If an intervention is not presented in an engaging, motivating way, even the most effective instructional design in the world may not be able to capture the interest or participation of its intended audience.

- *Interaction and interface design.* The less ambiguous the intent of the functional directions on a Web page or a computer-based training screen, the more likely users will be to engage in activities presented by means of that Web page or screen. A well-designed user interface reduces the need for adjunctive training in using an on-line application. It can even increase the accuracy of users' responses because users can concentrate on the critical learning task instead of deciphering hard-to-read or hard-to-understand directions.

- *Subject matter expertise.* The credibility of a learning intervention is directly proportional to the accuracy of the information it presents. Subject matter experts play an essential role in conceptualizing, shaping, and reviewing the information presented in a learning design.

- *Content creation.* Information presented to learners must be configured in such a way that they can use it effectively. This means using a writing style and treatments that offer the most appropriate perspectives for the audience and for the medium that has been selected for transmission. This also means selecting or creating graphics, illustrations, and tables that exemplify key points or summarize information in meaningful ways. In any kind of mediated instruction, it is crucial to involve the producers and developers of those media in the process of content creation because their input has a direct impact on the physical appearance of the content in the presentation. This step may involve video screenwriters, directors, producers, and editors. It may also involve computer programmers and coders, database analysts and programmers, and quality-assurance or testing personnel.

- *Programming.* Programming requirements will vary from application to application and from development environment to development environment. The requirements may include but not be limited to database development, HTML programming, CGI and C++ coding, and Java scripting (in any of its current iterations). Programmers will be able to work most successfully when there is, at a minimum, a clearly articulated set of functional and technical specifications for the application under construction that guide the programmer's efforts.

- *Systems operation.* Well-written and well-produced resources cannot have the impact they deserve if there are difficulties in getting the programming distributed to the right audience. Steps must be taken to ensure that signals are broadcast, that servers are operational, that networks are appropriately configured, that end users' machines have the appropriate capacity, and that the appropriate browsers have been installed.

Another way to consider development requirements is to review the kinds of activities typically involved in development and to determine how many of these activities need to be included in any one particular development effort. These activities include but are not limited to the following:

Technical writing

Storyboarding and scripting

Coding and scripting

Authoring

Video and audio recording

Video and audio digitizing

Postproduction editing

Graphic design

Desktop publishing

Editing

Usability testing

Pilot testing

Alpha and beta reviews

Bug testing

Related review and revision efforts

Evaluation

Evaluation is the process of interpreting information to make effective decisions. Evaluations help people make judgments about value, quality, and importance. Here are some typical evaluation questions:

Did the learners learn anything?

Can the learners do what the design indicated they should be able to do?

How is this learning to be demonstrated?

Was this course worth the effort?

Would we offer it again?

Designers should keep in mind that the fruits of an evaluation, in the simplest state, may consist of nothing more than the ability to use the results of one experience as the rationale to undertake another, similar experience. But evaluation methodologies can also provide a highly rigorous means of quantifying impact, effects, and results. From the perspective of a course design, the evaluation of learners (for example, testing and performance appraisal) should determine whether the course objectives have been achieved.

In making a decision about implementing a distance or distributed learning intervention, it is also useful to think in terms of the benefits to be accrued from the implementation. These benefits may include the following:

• *Reduction of turnover.* In a situation where turnover is high because of a perceived lack of opportunity, interactive technology-based training can offer employees opportunities for skill development that open up new avenues of growth in the organization. The cost savings can be calculated if the full measure of hiring, training, outfitting, and supporting replacement personnel can be accurately calculated.

- *Improved morale.* Organizations where morale is low because of a perception that employees are not highly valued can correct that perception by an investment in interactive technology. This investment can be correctly seen as an investment in the employees themselves.

- *Increased use of training and support programs.* By making an investment in interactive technology-based training and support, an organization signals the importance and value it places on these things. This, in turn, can motivate employees to avail themselves of these resources, thereby enhancing their own value to the organization.

- *Competitive advantage through use of leading-edge interventions.* Until interactive technology is the norm, those organizations that adopt it for employee development will be recognized as leading-edge organizations. This perception is often accompanied by the belief that these organizations provide leading-edge products and services to their customers and to the marketplace (Derryberry and Wagner, 1997).

SUMMARY

This chapter has presented a brief overview of issues to be addressed in considering the addition of distance learning and distributed learning to an organization's repertoire of performance improvement skills. Distance learning and distributed learning offer two related yet distinct methods for responding to the learning and performance support needs of individuals. Neither approach is necessarily intended as a replacement for classroom instruction; rather, they offer two distinct alternative means of improving access to learning opportunities and resources. As with any other kind of technology-based solution for performance support, there will be a strong tendency for either distance or distributed learning to be oversold as the best of all possible solutions. The likelihood of successfully implementing either of these two approaches is greatly enhanced when the methods of Human Performance Technology are employed.

References

Bassi, L., and Van Buren, M. E. (1998). The 1998 ASTD State of the Industry Report. *Training and Development* 52:1, 22–43.

Brown, F. B, and Brown, Y. (1994). Distance education around the world. In B. Willis (ed.), *Distance education strategies and tools.* Englewood Cliffs, NJ: Educational Technology Publications.

Brown, J. S., Collins, A., and Duglid, P. (1989). Situated cognition and the culture of learning. *Educational Researcher* 19:1, 32–42.

Carnevale, A. P. (1991). *America and the new economy.* San Francisco: Jossey-Bass.

Cohen, S. (1997). A guide to multimedia in the next millennium. *Training and Development* 51:8, 33–43.

Cyrs, T. E. (ed.). (1997). *Teaching and learning at a distance: What it takes to effectively design, deliver, and evaluate programs.* San Francisco: Jossey-Bass.

Derryberry, A. P., and Wagner, E. D. (1997). An expanded approach to ROI. *Technical and Skills Training* 8:4, 14–19.

Duffy, T. M., and Jonassen, D. H. (1992). *Constructivism and the technology of instruction: A conversation.* Hillsdale, NJ: Erlbaum.

Filipczak, B. (1996). Training on intranets: The hope and the hype. *Training* 33:9, 24–32.

Guglielmo, C. (1998). Audio gives the Web an earful. *Interactive Week* 5:5, 43.

Gunawardena, C. (1995). Social presence theory and implications for interaction and collaborative learning in computer conferencing. *International Journal of Educational Telecommunications* 1:2–3, 147–166.

Keegan, D. (1990). *The foundations of distance education.* London: Croom Helm.

Kember, D. (1995). *Open learning courses for adults: A model of student progress.* Englewood Cliffs, NJ: Educational Technology Publications.

Kinzie, M. B. (1990). Requirements and benefits of effective interactive instruction: Learner control, self-regulation and continuing motivation. *Educational Technology Research and Development* 38:1, 5–21.

Masie, E. (1998, Apr. 27). Emerging acronyms spell market change. *Computer Reseller News,* p. 59.

Moore, M. G. (1989, Apr.). *Three modes of interaction.* Presentation at the annual meeting of the National University Continuing Education Association, Salt Lake City, UT.

Moore, M. G. (ed.). (1990). *Contemporary issues in American distance education.* New York: Pergamon Press.

Perraton, H. (1982). Distance teaching north and south. In J. Daniel, M. Stroud, and J. Thompson (eds.), *Learning at a distance: A world perspective.* Edmonton, Alberta, Canada: Athabasca University/International Council for Correspondence Education.

Pittman, V. (1990). Correspondence study in the American university: An historiographic perspective. In M. G. Moore (ed.), *Contemporary issues in American distance education.* New York: Pergamon Press.

Riddle, J. F. (1994). *Factors contributing to achievement and course satisfaction of distance education students.* Doctoral dissertation, University of Northern Colorado.

Rothwell, W. J. (1996). *Beyond training and development: State of the art strategies for enhancing human performance.* New York: American Management Association.

Wagner, E. D. (1990). Instructional design: Contingency management for distance education. In M. G. Moore (ed.), *Contemporary issues in American distance education.* New York: Pergamon Press.

Wagner, E. D. (1994). In support of a functional definition of interaction. *American Journal of Distance Education* 8:2, 6–29.

Wagner, E. D. (1997). Interactivity: From agents to outcomes. In T. E. Cyrs (ed.), *Teaching and learning at a distance: What it takes to effectively design, deliver, and evaluate programs.* San Francisco: Jossey-Bass.

Wagner, E. D., and McCombs, B. L. (1995). Learner-centered psychological principles in practice: Designs for distance education. *Educational Technology* 35:2, 32–25.

PART FIVE

THE PROFESSIONAL PRACTICE OF HUMAN PERFORMANCE TECHNOLOGY

A s should be eminently clear by now, Human Performance Technology (HPT) is, more than anything else, a field of professional practice with global application. It is a relatively young but growing field. Because it is still coalescing into a profession, many HPT-related issues remain largely untreated. These have to do with the conduct, practice, and professional growth of Human Performance (HP) technologists.

Practitioners come to this field from a disparate variety of disciplines, and as HPT professionals they must possess not only technical abilities and competence in practice but also broader competence in business. Many, however, entered the field with academic or corporate backgrounds but virtually no formal preparation for dealing professionally with clients, either as internal consultants or as external consultants.

The eight chapters in Part Five deal with various facets of HPT professional practice. The first of these chapters delves deeply into the skill sets, characteristics, and values required of the HP technologist. It draws on observation, documented practice, writings, research, knowledgeable client informants, and experienced HPT practitioners to provide basic and advanced professional criteria for current and future practice.

The second chapter of Part Five discusses issues related to the standards and ethics for an eventual HPT profession. Although the chapter does not specify what these standards or ethics should be, it offers a basis for their creation, along with a model for ethical decision making.

In the third chapter, two very experienced authors draw on their extensive knowledge of performance consulting and on an in-depth survey that they conducted to define and describe what the job of the HP consultant is. The chapter creates a clear and comprehensive portrait of what it means to be a performance consultant.

The fourth chapter presents an irreverent, highly detailed, informative examination of what it takes to survive and even thrive in the Mad Hatter world of HPT. It draws on the authors' considerable experience and on the experience of twenty recognized HPT practitioner-leaders. The chapter includes a self-assessment tool and a list of suggested readings.

A key role of the HP consultant is to influence others to act, and that is the topic of the fifth chapter in Part Five. The chapter analyzes three sets of influencing behaviors and illustrates how HPT can be used to examine complex, covert performances and then affect their direction.

HPT is not only a professional field of practice but also a business, and HPT practitioners must think and act the way businesspeople do if they hope to build credibility with organizational clients and survive in practice. The sixth chapter of Part Five provides information for neophyte and seasoned practitioners alike on how to treat HPT as a business, use the language of business decision makers, and sell HPT's credibility in business environments.

The final two chapters of Part Five deal with two fundamental issues for professional HPT practice. The first of these two chapters, written by a legal specialist, concentrates on the legal implications and ramifications of HPT activities and interventions. The second, written by a recognized authority on return on investment (ROI) in performance improvement projects, presents a convincing rationale, strong research support, and a demonstrated model for presenting ROI evidence to clients.

The reader turning to Part Five may be tempted to dip into particular chapters of current personal interest, but all eight chapters, read all the way through, will make the reader a better-rounded practitioner; nowhere else is such a range of HPT-related professional issues gathered together. Collectively the fourteen authors who produced these eight chapters form an outstanding team of skilled, practicing professionals. They have all documented the evidence of their successes, and all, through their many publications, have repeatedly contributed to the advancement of HPT practice.

CHAPTER THIRTY-TWO

Skill Sets, Characteristics, and Values for the Human Performance Technologist

Harold D. Stolovitch
Erica J. Keeps
Daniel Rodrigue

The purpose of this chapter is to suggest sets of skills, characteristics, and values necessary for the practice of Human Performance Technology (HPT) today and in the future. To do this, the chapter examines the nature of HPT, particularly as it relates to and compares with other apparently similar fields. As it unfolds, the chapter discriminates between Human Performance (HP) technologists and the other professionals who populate the crowded world of business consulting. It also raises some fundamental questions: Are HP technologists treading on other professionals' turf? If not, how does one characterize HPT's uniqueness, as well as its value to organizations? Is HPT a profession per se? If so, who should identify the required skill sets for this profession? Certainly, as HPT's span of practice expands across the globe, and as its practitioners intervene in ever more diverse areas, a critical question to ask is whether one should reasonably expect any single HP technologist to possess complete working knowledge of all the potential tools that can be applied in the field. In addition, there are many who would like to have HPT become officially recognized as a profession. Should there be a set of professional standards, or should there be some kind of a certification process? Should it be national or international in nature? Finally, the chapter asks how HP technologists should be educated and kept current in this constantly expanding field.

One of the best ways to recognize and define a professional field is by observing what its practitioners do. From this observation, we can then deduce an initial skill set, key characteristics, and values required to perform professionally. As an

651

example, physicians are clearly involved with health. They examine the human body and, on the basis of learned theory and practice, diagnose problems or malfunctions and recommend therapy based on clearly defined standards. Similarly, musicians deal with music. Their work consists of analyzing a composition, practicing it on their instruments, and then performing it for an audience. In each of these examples, by studying what the practitioner does, we can begin to logically derive the skill sets, characteristics, and values each lives by.

What of HPT? Mager (1992b) suggests that because HPT is concerned with human performance, HP technologists should be observed doing whatever it is they do with respect to matters of human performance. By clearly defining the object or focus of their work, we can begin to identify the skills required to perform as a professional. We can also deduce what type of person best fits the practice requirements. However, we must start by defining what we mean by HPT.

WHAT IS HPT, AND WHAT DOES IT MEAN OPERATIONALLY?

The literature provides numerous but related definitions of HPT. Hutchison (1989, p. 6) cites the National Society for Performance and Instruction's definition: "HPT is a set of methods and processes for solving problems or realizing opportunities related to the performance of people. It may be applied to the performance of single individuals or large organizations. It is characterized by the following features: it is systematic; it views performance in terms of inputs, processes, outputs, and feedback; it is data-based; its methods are derived from experimentation and research; it is operational; it attempts to define its results in measurable terms and its methods in ways that allow others to reliably apply them." Svenson and Wallace (1989, p. 1) reduce this long statement to a more succinct form, defining HPT as "a powerful collection of theory and methods that enables systematic maximization of any organization's performance." Gilbert (1992, p. xiv) adds that "our focus is on human accomplishment, the valuable output of behavior." This is in keeping with Nichols's comments (1977) in characterizing performance as "the outcomes of behavior. Behavior is individual activity whereas the outcomes of behavior are the ways in which the behaving individual's environment is somehow different as a result of his or her behavior."

This leads us to conclude that the HP technologist's activities are focused on improving performance. In operational terms, this suggests that he or she must be able to define the desired level of valued performance, the current state, accurately measure the distance between these two, and propose, design, or perhaps even help implement cost-effective interventions to close the gap. The preceding sentence describes somewhat concisely the HPT process and presents a first cut at the basic skills required of an HP technologist. As a starting point, when we observe HP technologists, this is in fact what we see them doing. They identify, systematically observe, and quantify inadequate performance. They then recommend and help design and implement appropriate means of achieving desired goals for human performance. These can be viewed as the basic technical or intervention skills of HP technologists. In addition and as a complement to intervention abilities, we also observe skilled practitioners constantly talking and working with people. This means that they must also possess what are called "people" skills: communication, leadership, management, teamwork, and interpersonal skills.

We have noted that professions can be recognized or defined through observation of the behavior of their practitioners. However, this is only a starting point. Delving more deeply into a field, one begins to find writings and artifacts produced by its adherents, historians, and scholars. One also finds that, from modest beginnings, most professions grow in diversity as the vision and range of practice develop. As an example, the medical profession was originally populated in large part by general practitioners trying to address all health problems. Over time, it has expanded to include dozens if not hundreds of specialties. The same principle applies to the field of HPT. From a core of activities centered on performance analysis and, essentially, instructional interventions, it has grown in scope and scale to encompass a broad range of problems and activities; one need only scan the pages of this volume to observe the extent of HPT's territory. It is therefore not surprising that we find HP technologists working in areas that seem to overlap with those of other disciplines (for example, organizational development and ergonomics). It is also not especially remarkable to see HP technologists beginning to specialize by organizational context, organizational level, or form of intervention. The analogy with medicine continues to hold true.

Physicians may differ by specialty. Nevertheless, they all remain physicians. Something binds them together. They all share a similar form of initial training. They also learn and apply similar general principles and techniques. This common, unique approach shared by all practitioners of medicine facilitates the communication of ideas and experiences. In addition, all obtain excellent basic skills and knowledge for dealing with the various human systems. Their shared background allows them to recognize potential illnesses in areas other than their own specialties and to refer patients to other practitioners or to seek diagnostic and treatment advice from colleagues.

The field of HPT is evolving rapidly. It has certainly reached the point where no one practitioner can master every aspect of it. Specialization has set in. At the same time, it is also obvious that there are deep common threads among its varied practitioners. Common models and a common vocabulary are required for HP technologists to communicate and function effectively together. There is a need for all HP technologists to possess a common, solid, shared, general foundation. What is it? Where does it come from? How does it affect the definition of skill sets for HP technologists?

ORIGINS AND UNDERLYING ASSUMPTIONS OF HPT

To understand the current skill set of HP technologists, it is useful to begin with a brief retrospective. HPT "is a relatively new field that has emerged from the coalescing of principles derived from the carefully documented practice of thoughtful behavioral psychologists, instructional technologists, training designers, organizational developers, and various human resource specialists" (Stolovitch and Keeps, 1992b, p. 3). HPT's roots lie in behaviorism and in Skinner's work, which demonstrated how "small-step instruction, coupled with extensive feedback, could significantly enhance learning" (Skinner, cited in Rosenberg, Coscarelli, and Hutchison, 1992, p. 16). Skinner's behavioral cause-and-effect discoveries led to a series of developments, from the teaching machine of the 1950s to the design process for programmed instruction of the early 1960s and onward to the computer-assisted instruction of the 1960s and 1970s (Deutsch, 1992). This heritage helps explain why current HP technologists, searching to uncover the root causes of performance inadequacy, focus so strongly on the identification and analysis of stimuli within a system that may trigger certain responses and the consequences they engender (Stolovitch and Keeps, 1998).

As research and theory have evolved in related fields, they have affected practitioners dedicated to improving human performance. Specifically, Rosenberg, Coscarelli, and Hutchison (1992) have identified a number of disciplines as exerting major influence on today's HPT practice. A partial list includes the following disciplines:

- Systems theory
- Learning psychology
- Instructional systems design
- Cognitive engineering
- Information technology
- Ergonomics and human factors engineering
- Psychometrics
- Feedback systems
- Organizational development

This list allows us to gain insight into where many of HPT's current practitioners acquired their background knowledge. In addition, a number of practitioners came into the HPT field with previous experience as instructional technology managers, course designers, and training specialists, and the skills acquired in these positions have markedly influenced their vision of organizations. Many HP technologists also migrated into the field from instruction and are now working in the much broader domain of performance (Robinson and Robinson, 1998).

To define a set of skills for HPT requires an understanding of what has gone into the development of its current practitioners. So far we have addressed observation of what practitioners do and information about the knowledge and experience base they possess. Before we can deal with skill sets, however, we need to examine one more element: the underlying assumptions and view of the field that guide HP technologists' actions.

First, in terms of ends, HP technologists do not view their field as a traditional scientific discipline, such as physics or psychology. For them, HPT is not primarily focused on creating new knowledge or establishing universal truths; rather, they see it is an applied field of practice, one that seeks "results from the utilization of meanings from the fundamental disciplines" (Phenix, 1964). For HP technologists, HPT is structured primarily by real-world problems of human performance, and this fact explains why the field characterizes itself as an applied field of practice and not as a discipline. Foshay and Moller (1992, p. 702) capture its essence by stating that it "draws from any discipline that has prescriptive power in solving any human performance problem. It also may draw from other applied fields, when they contribute technologies of use in solving human performance problems." This is a field of application that exploits scientific knowledge and method to very practical ends.

Second, with respect to means, HP technologists view the field as a performance science because of its methodology. It contains the three elements, described by Gilbert and Gilbert (1989, p. 7), that are needed to define such a science:

1. It possesses its own subject matter: human accomplishments.

2. It is able to apply strict measures: the potential for improved performance as well as human accomplishment.

3. It offers prediction and control—in this case, of human behavior and its outcomes.

As Gilbert and Gilbert point out, science is "a little methodology and a few good tricks, rigorously and systematically applied." This statement is a good summary of the practice of HPT.

Third, HPT as a field of applied science builds its theoretical base on the following major underlying assumptions (Geis, cited in Stolovitch and Keeps, 1992a, pp. 5–6):

Human performance is lawful and can be predicted and controlled. Knowledge of human behavior is limited, and thus HPT must rely on practical experience as well as scientific research. HPT draws from many research bases while generating its own. HPT is the product of a number of knowledge sources: cybernetics, behavioral psychology, communications theory, information theory, systems theory, management science, and, more recently, the cognitive sciences. HPT is neither committed to any particular delivery system nor confined to any specific population and subject area. It can address any human performance, but it is commonly applied within organizational and work settings. HPT is empirical. It requires systematic verification of the results of both its analysis and intervention efforts. HPT is evolving. Based on guiding principles, it nevertheless allows enormous scope for innovation and creativity. Although HPT cannot pretend to have a firm theoretical foundation of its own, the theory- and experience-based principles that guide it are molded by empirical data that accumulate as a result of documented, systematic practice. In many ways, HPT shares attributes with other applied fields (management, organizational development, medicine, psychiatry).

In summary, HP technologists see their field as intended to deal with practical human performance matters in a scientific manner, and as based on a broad set of respectable theoretical and empirical foundations. Before we can define the unique skills necessary to the practice of HPT, however, we must discriminate between HPT and other applied fields of practice that appear, at first glance, to operate from similar perspectives.

WHAT MAKES HPT UNIQUE?

HP technologists claim four unique strengths for solving human performance problems, and they assert that each of these separately distinguishes them from professionals working in other, apparently similar fields of practice:

1. HPT is able to combine and integrate multiple interventions and technologies for improving human performance. The HP technologist views human and organizational systems as complex. Rarely does a single intervention have a lasting effect. A host of variables generally influences performance outcomes. This means that a basket of interventions as diverse as redesign of the environment, change of incentives, upgrading of skills, and creation of job aids may be required for a relatively straightforward performance gap (Stolovitch and Keeps, 1998). As Rosenberg, Coscarelli, and Hutchison (1992, p. 25) assert, "the usefulness [of HPT] lies in the assumption that combinations of interventions, taken from a variety of fields, provide greater value when applied to a performance problem/opportunity than any specific intervention does when used alone." Other specialized professionals, such as specialists in organizational de-

velopment, tend not to possess the range and repertoire to integrate multiple disciplines and technologies in the design of their interventions. HP technologists, by contrast, as a normal part of their activities, proactively seek to identify and integrate ideas from a variety of sources and disciplines. The combination and integration process per se is viewed as greatly enhancing the value of what they do.

2. No other professional discipline dealing with organizations is capable of bringing to bear as broad a range of skills as HPT does on the analysis and solution of human performance problems (Foshay and Moller, 1992). The variety of disciplines from which HPT derives its theoretical base allows it to apply a vast array of analytical and interventionist procedures to specific situations. This is particularly true "in the perspective of the models used to diagnose performance problems, to select appropriate interventions, and to measure the results" (Foshay and Moller, 1992, p. 702). Other types of practitioners tend to have narrower views or more limited sets of capabilities. The HP technologist is able to conduct highly refined performance analyses, create a wide variety of instructional and noninstructional interventions, and design scientifically crafted implementation, evaluation, and long-term monitoring systems to ensure desired performance.

3. HP technologists have a unique weltanschauung, or view of the world. The conceptual approach and framework of HPT allow practitioners to characterize in precise terms the nature of performance gaps, their causes, and the variables affecting performance, as well as to specify appropriate remedial actions. HP technologists view organizations as adaptive systems. They can focus their work on "three levels of performance variables that ultimately determine the performance of organizations and individuals: the organization, process, and job/performer levels" (Rummler and Brache, 1996, p. 35). Few other fields of practice are equipped to analyze performance problems from a perspective of such multiple levels. HP technologists are steeped in systems thinking and have no difficulty maintaining an organic view of human and organizational behavior (Dean and Ripley, 1997).

4. The systematic process and well-defined procedures of HPT are rigorously applied by its practitioners to transform viewpoint into action. This process includes activities in five clearly defined phases: defining the problem or opportunity, conducting the analysis, designing and developing the intervention, implementing and maintaining the intervention, and evaluating the intervention. It is through this kind of rigorous application that HP technologists have built their reputation. This does not imply that other specialized fields of practice do not use strict, systematic processes as they apply their own tools and techniques to a problem. However, this fourth HPT strength sends a clear signal that the application of this process is a fundamental part of the HP technologist's profession.

Despite HPT's claims to uniqueness, there is still some confusion about the differences between HP technologists and other professional specialists. It is obvious that there is some overlap between HPT and other fields that deal with organizations and work performance, but there are also defining boundaries. With which other specialists are we concerned?

Instructional Technologists

Job description: Instructional technologists analyze performance deficiencies from the perspective of skills or knowledge that are lacking. They then design, develop, test, and deliver learning materials, programs, or systems whose aim is to eliminate identified skill and/or knowledge gaps.

Goal: Improvement of skills and/or knowledge.

Target: Individual learners or learner groups.

Activities: Analysis and design of instructional products or systems.

Deliverables: Instructional products, services, and systems.

Environment: Classroom, laboratory, job site.

Professional vision: The professional vision of the instructional technologist is that of a specialist in the design of learning systems.

Similarities: Instructional technologists and HP technologists take a systems approach, conduct systematic analyses, have common antecedents (systems, communications, psychology), focus on the causes of performance deficiencies, and anticipate the obstacles that inhibit the introduction of innovations.

Differences: The work of HP technologists is more directly linked to business results. Measurement and marketing issues have greater importance. HPT generally views instruction as an intervention of last resort. HPT focuses on the alignment of people, programs, policies, and work systems. HPT's repertoire of interventions includes but also extends far beyond instruction (Rossett, 1992b, Robinson and Robinson, 1998); therefore, it is normal practice for the HP technologist to conduct a front-end analysis in order to determine what the problem is and whether instructional interventions are really required. With respect to improving human performance, "most practitioners tend to indicate that instructional technology is a subset of performance technology" (Hutchison, 1990). This distinction between instructional technology (IT) and HPT is an interesting one. Hutchison also points out that 83 percent of all HPT interventions are still largely related to IT-type tactics. The obvious conclusion is that a strong relationship between these two fields continues to exist, although more divergent forms of HPT interventions, such as organizational design, strategic alignment, culture change, and work redesign, appear to be increasing in salience and frequency (Fuller, 1997; Stolovitch and Keeps, 1992b).

Human Resource Management Professionals

Job description: "The goal of human resource management is to enhance the productive contribution of employees to the organization" (Werther, Davis, and Lee-Gosselin, 1990, p. 10). The human resource department has two broad functions: to meet the organization's needs in terms of human resources (recruitment, personnel selection, personnel evaluation, industrial relations, forecasting future personnel needs), and to respond to employees' needs (for example, with competitive salary scales, monetary and nonmonetary incentives, and pension plans). These two functions are accomplished with a focus on social goals, organizational goals, functional goals, and employees' personal goals. Human resource management specialists are generally staff personnel. They advise or counsel line managers. They normally have no direct decision power or influence on personnel behavior and performance. Generally speaking, employee performance is under the direct responsibility of line managers (Werther, Davis, and Lee-Gosselin, 1990, p. 18). As human resource departments grow in size and complexity, human resource management personnel tend to become specialists in specific areas, such as salary or compensation analysis, human resource development, labor management, and human resource planning, to name only a few.

Goal: Enhancement of the productive contributions of employees to the organization.

Target: The whole organization.

Activities: Companywide compensation and incentive analysis, job definitions, recruitment, employer-employee relations, employment equity, human resource planning, human resource development, and all other aspects related to personnel management.

Deliverables: Salary scales, incentive plans, pension plans, safety procedures, job advertisements, appraisal systems, equity policies, harassment policies, and other products and services related to the overall management of employees throughout the organization.

Environment: The entire organization.

Professional vision: The vision of human resource management professionals is both a generalist one (in that these professionals attend to all organizational aspects of employee management and employee relations) and a specialist one (in that they address specific aspects of human resource management).

Similarities: Human resource management professionals and HP technologists take a systems approach, rely on analysis, have a number of common antecedents (systems, communications, psychology), and understand the need to establish suitable job incentives.

Differences: The primary focus of HP technologists is to attain specific outcomes for human performance. Human resource management professionals, except for those who specialize strictly in performance improvement, are involved in a broad range of personnel and human interventions that are not necessarily linked to specific instances of desired performance. Human resource management professionals' priorities lie in the creation of systems for managing and compensating people. They tend to engage in broad-brush, general activities for all employee groups. When asked by line managers to intervene in specific deficiency areas, they generally bring in other specialists (such as HP technologists).

Training Specialists

Job description: Training specialists implement solutions or interventions that have been designed by IT or HPT practitioners. Their main objective is to build skills and knowledge: "The training and development specialist designs, develops, conducts, and/or evaluates learning experiences" (Longanbach, 1994).

Goal: Development of individual and/or group skills and knowledge.

Activities: Course preparation and delivery, coaching and follow-up of learners (individuals and groups).

Deliverables: Instruction and skill transfer.

Environment: Worksite or classroom.

Professional vision: These professionals specialize in helping workers acquire skills and knowledge and transfer these to the job.

Similarities: Training specialists and HP technologists alike are focused on improving human performance on the job.

Differences: Training is a narrow and specific subset of HPT. It addresses only one of the causes of performance deficiencies. The training specialist focuses on improvement in skills and knowledge, but this is generally not enough to create lasting change in performance if the environment is insufficiently supportive, if workers have been poorly selected, or if obstacles to motivation or incentives are inhibiting transfer (Ford and Weissbein, 1997).

Organizational Development (OD) Specialists

Job description: "OD [specialists aim] at changing attitudes, perceptions and people's behavior in order to increase organizational effectiveness. OD is a systematic, planned set of efforts, used at every level of an organization to resolve human problems that seem to paralyze employee efficiency at different levels of the organization. These problems may result from any of the following: poor cooperation or communication, attitudes, confidence level, and poor interpersonal communication. Theory and practice of OD are based on the assumption that employees are interested to improve themselves and want to be a part of work groups. It is therefore important for management to develop abilities and competencies which will enhance or stimulate the employees to improve their own behavior" (Beckhard, cited in Bergeron, 1989, p. 237).

Goal: Improved business results.

Activities: Participation in a wide range of activities, including work-climate diagnosis, group decision making, creation of questionnaires for attitude and climate surveys, training activities generally focused on communication and interpersonal dynamics, introduction of means for enhancing communication among groups, group facilitation, facilitation of teams seeking structural changes, conducting of communication-network studies to determine information flows and breakdowns, designing of employee career plans, conducting of individual behavioral counseling sessions, identification and planning of objectives (integration of personal goals into the objectives of the organization), and assistance in diagnosing and determining management-style profiles (French and Bell, cited in Bergeron, 1989, p. 237).

Deliverables: Products and services emanating from the OD specialist's activities.

Environment: The whole organization or specific subsets of it.

Professional vision: In general terms, the professional vision of an OD specialist is that of an organizational communications specialist and facilitator.

Similarities: Both HPT and OD attend to the array of variables that affect human performance. Both analyze systems to determine root causes of performance deficiency, to design interventions, to help implement these, and to monitor the results. Both also draw from similar theoretical sources (for example, psychology and organizational behavior). HPT recognizes that enhanced communication is a key element of improved human performance, which is also a central theme of OD.

Differences: OD usually begins at the macro level and is often initiated by requests from upper management (French and Bell, cited in Bergeron, 1989, p. 237). Historically speaking, HP technologists have been called in to work at specific points in an organization, and frequently with lower-level management. This is changing, however; as Silber (1992) reports, a number of HP consultants have begun to consult at the macro level. HP technologists are usually directly involved in solving targeted "lack of performance" problems in business units, and their findings may (but usually do not) trigger work on attitudes or on overall company communications or morale problems. OD and HPT practitioners may both participate in similar kinds of activities at some point in their interventions, but their starting points are different. HP interventions that address the cultural level of organizations are a recent addition to the HPT repertoire (Silber, 1992). The key distinction is that OD specialists tend to focus on communication and attitude issues, helping managers and workers make decisions on how to work better and support their implementation efforts, whereas HP technologists are more likely to be hard-core problem solvers, frequently engaging in technical as well as management issues, generally creating interventions, and then helping with their implementation. HP technologists have a strong affinity with measurement and hard data. Style is also a discriminator; as Bollen and Vanasse (1994) suggest, the area of consultation is perhaps where the greatest differences are to be found between OD and HPT. For example, in the world of HPT, the customer typically asks for a solution from the expert; in OD, the customer is made part of the solution process by becoming an involved participant. OD interventions tend to be more consultant-centered (in the sense of facilitation) than HP interventions, which are more product-oriented.

Industrial Engineers

Job description: Industrial engineers analyze, design, organize, control, and supervise production processes, which include man-machine interfaces. The optimization of this interface is one of their key objectives.

Goal: Production output.

Activities: Analysis, diagnosis, and solution of production problems.

Deliverables: Operations procedures lists, operations manuals, safety procedures, proposals to replace equipment and machinery, workflow designs, and systems within the operating facility.

Environment: Generally speaking, the plant and its associated environments.

Professional vision: The professional vision of an industrial engineer is that of a production specialist.

Similarities: Both the industrial engineer and the HP technologist have the objectives of increasing performance and optimizing the man-machine interface.

Differences: Industrial engineers operate within a narrower set of environments than HP technologists do. Industrial engineers have more specialized training and experience for solving specific production problems. Generally, they do not deal with the human side of the interface (that is, the motivational, feedback, or communications systems in organizations).

Business Consultants and Change Agent Specialists

Job description: Business consultants come in many varieties. Typically, they specialize in management-type consulting: strategic planning, and analysis of congruence among the various organizational functions (financial systems, human resources, production systems, marketing, sales). Change agents are typically called in to help and counsel management before or in the midst of periods of major upheaval (downsizing, reengineering, restructuring, mergers).

Goal: Business results.

Activities: According to the nature of the specialty, these specialists generally work with the highest levels of management to create macro shifts in the operation of a company.

Deliverables: Generally, a plan and a timetable for its implementation.

Environment: Usually the entire organization or major functions and processes within it.

Professional vision: The professional vision of a business consultant or change agent is that of a high-level specialist.

Similarities: Business consultants and change agents may get involved in analysis and design activities similar to those of HP technologists when dealing with areas that directly affect human performance. Like HP technologists, business consultants and change agents target improved organizational results and generally deal with specific, concrete measures.

Differences: HP technologists are usually called in when there is a specific issue linked to human behavior and results. Rarely will an HP technologist work, for example, on the restructuring of a company's financial systems, even though what the HP technologist does may have a strong impact on the company's overall financial performance.

OBSERVATIONS: PULLING IT ALL TOGETHER

Several observations emerge from this brief, superficial description of these applied fields of practice, their goals and activities, and their similarities to and differences from HPT. First, all are concerned with organizational performance, but each from a specific vantage point. If, at the outset, deficiencies in skills and knowledge are the obvious reason for the gap between desired and actual performance, then the instructional technologist is well qualified to step in. Similarly, if a diagnosis demonstrates that company morale is a key cause of poor performance, then the services of an OD specialist will be sought. Performance problems with clear-cut causes naturally lead to the selection of the most appropriate professional.

When situations are fuzzier, however, organizations are uncertain about who should be called. One tendency is to turn to the most familiar person. Another is to select whoever is able to diagnose complex sets of interrelated issues, determine the types of interventions that should be implemented, and say which combination will deliver the optimal effect. This leads us to a second observation: the range and process of HPT makes HP technologists very attractive for a wide spectrum of performance issues. HP technologists seek to improve human performance, regardless of the cause of the deficiency, and their ability to analyze all types of performance subsystems and their interrelationships positions them as a unique resource for identifying causes of performance deficiency. Other professionals are less well equipped to handle HPT's technical and managerial range across levels and environments. However, once the causes of a performance deficiency have been isolated, the HP technologist may then have to turn to other specialists for the development of suitable interventions.

A third observation underscoring the uniqueness of the HP technologist is that he or she maintains a conscious, directed focus on human performance and on the range of methods and tools that have been developed to deal with it. The HP consultant's work is solely focused on the performance that emanates from the human actors in the organizations and on all the factors that affect it. This does not mean that the HP technologist works in isolated fashion, or alone. Because HPT professionals operate across a wide territory, they can definitely benefit from learning techniques and work skills that have proved effective for other types of specialists. As Bollen and Vanasse (1994, p. 149) strongly suggest, HPT practitioners, "with a knowledge of both IT and OD principles and techniques, will be equipped with a more complete set of tools for designing, recommending, and implementing the most effective intervention." Moreover, the HP technologist's learning to work in teams with these other professionals can only lead to more effective outcomes.

A fourth observation is that, because of HP technologists' focus, skills and knowledge, and constant involvement in real-life human performance situations, they are perhaps best equipped to carry out initial diagnoses. In this sense, HPT professionals can play the role, so to speak, of *general performance practitioners*. As Rummler and Brache (1992) point out, they pinpoint the source of poor performance (for example, an inadequate motivational system, inadequate or incomplete work processes, individual job performers' lack of skills) and then suggest as well as facilitate the implementation of cost-effective interventions, using the most appropriate specialists. Thus this ability to be a general performance practitioner is another special characteristic of the HP technologist; it underscores Rummler's observation, in Chapter Three of this volume, about the uniqueness of the HPT field as the only technology that "endeavors to bring such a holistic framework or anatomy to issues of human performance."

THE HP PROFESSIONAL'S SKILL SET

All the foregoing material on HPT activities, working principles, and underlying assumptions leads us to a definition of the skills necessary to the performance of an HP technologist's work.

Basic Skills Required by All HP Technologists

All HP technologists must be able to perform essential activities required by the five major phases of the HPT systematic process. The "family link" among all HP technologists is the general HPT model and framework. It provides a common professional language, and it imposes a systematic, scientific approach on all HP practitioners. Application of the HPT process is the core. HP practitioners need not be expert in every individual step, but all HP practitioners should be able, with a high degree of skill and confidence, to conduct appropriate performance analyses, design and develop interventions, and establish operational plans for implementing, monitoring, and evaluating interventions.

When we use the term *skill*, we mean a practical ability and dexterity, or a proficiency. We have grouped the basic skills for accomplishing HPT tasks into two broad categories, each of which can be further broken down into two subsets. Category 1 comprises technical skills. These include skills in analysis and observation, design skills (creativity, logical thinking, media/technology knowledge), and evaluation skills. Category 2 deals with "people" skills and includes management skills (organizational and project management), communication, and interpersonal skills.

Category 1: Technical Skills

Analysis and Observation. The first phase of the HPT process requires strong analytical and observation skills. HP technologists must be able to examine a situation, dissect it into various elements, and determine and explain the relationships between them. They must be able to observe and then discern which elements of a job-related task, process, or situation have an impact on performance. A primary skill required of HP professionals is to be able to discriminate between exemplary and average performance, given that the purpose is to improve current performance levels. Directly linked to this is the ability to recognize, observe, and dissect the behavior of top performers so that they can be emulated later on by others (Gilbert, 1992, p. xiv).

Design. The second and third phases of the process (design and development) require another set of skills that include the ability to design, orchestrate, and logically sequence a series of activities (for example, instructions, job aids, and incentive or feedback programs) that will solve the problem or improve performance. Design skills also require knowledge of the most appropriate medium and/or technology to be used for the situation. Not all interventions include technological devices, but when they do, the choice has a direct impact on the speed of the intervention's development and implementation, as well as on its budget. HP technologists should be able to recommend a range of implementation alternatives, each potentially different in terms of cost, speed, and overall impact on performance. However, all alternatives should be powerful enough to solve the performance deficiency.

Evaluation. Evaluation to improve or verify the effects of an intervention is a crucial part of the HP technologist's job. It is essential that the HP technologist have the skills to develop an evaluation strategy and build a means of measuring results. The needed skills may include those necessary for measuring return on investment (Phillips, 1997), collecting suitable data, analyzing data, reporting on how well an intervention is working, and using evaluation information to improve results.

Category 2: "People" Skills

Management Skills. The final phases (implementation and maintenance, evaluation) require strong managerial skills. To implement a solution or a set of solutions successfully, an HP technologist must ensure that the intervention plan is implemented as designed and that corrective actions are applied at appropriate moments. Project management skills include the ability to properly identify project subtasks and milestones (Greer, 1998). The HP technologist needs to know when it is appropriate to call meetings and must be able to assign, in collaboration with the client, "the right resources (e.g., skilled people, money), in correct quantity, at the right time and at the right locations" (Jackson and Addison, 1992, p. 76).

Communication and Interpersonal Skills. In all phases of the work, the HPT professional must be able to communicate effectively, both orally and in writing. HP technologists continually communicate with clients, colleagues, clients' employees, and all other persons potentially affected by the scope of the work. All HPT professionals need skills in clear, precise, simple, straightforward communication. Similarly, interpersonal skills are essential to the success of any project that involves a number of individuals. The HP technologist must become a person with whom others want to do business: "People buy from people they like" (Murphy, 1987, p. 7). The HP technologist frequently has to persuade and influence others to accept new ideas or innovative approaches. Interpersonal skills are crucial to the success of a project, allowing ideas to flourish among all affected subsystems and parties. Poor interpersonal skills can impede the acceptance of even the best ideas.

Review of the Literature on Skills

The literature does not offer much in the way of formally documented skill requirements for HP technologists. However, it does contain many references to the types of competence required by instructional technologists, whose specialty is closely associated with HPT (it is also useful to remember that the majority of interventions designed by HP practitioners are still largely instructional in nature). As a first step toward deducing a set of basic HPT skills from this material, we consulted a list of sixteen areas of competence established for professionals in instructional technology and training (Bratton, 1984). These established areas of competence have gone through many iterations of testing and revision since their first publication, and they offer an excellent foundation for laying out a basic HPT-specific skill set. They were clustered according to the same subgroups of skills that have just been presented, and they were then refined and restated in light of the broader scope of current HPT practice. Table 32.1 presents the results of this process and acts as a starting point for naming, at a relatively high level, the basic skill requirements for HPT.

In the absence of rigorous scientific studies aimed at determining the specific skills required to perform the work of an HPT specialist, there is general consensus among those authors and investigators who have done some research on the subject (Gilbert, 1996; Hutchison, 1990; Robinson and Robinson, 1998; Rummler and Brache, 1996; Silber, 1992). Table 32.1 reflects and summarizes that research rather well and lists what the literature gives as the desired skills, areas of competence, and activities of HP professionals. Further to this point, in addition to the broad skill categories listed in Table 32.1, 118 areas of specific skills and knowledge considered important for HPT professionals were presented at the 1990 conference of the International Society for Performance Improvement (ISPI). Hutchison (1990, p. 2) lists the key ones as "analysis; integration and synthesis; salesmanship and marketing; negotiation and conflict management; communication; presentation and facilitation; change management; project management; planning (strategic, tactical and contingency); research; theory building and model building; implementation; evaluation and measurement." In one form or another, many of these also appear in Table 32.1.

Spitzer (1988) asked fifty-nine respondents to rate seventeen areas of competence felt to be "extremely important," "important," or "not important" to the work of an instructional or HP technologist. The analysis-related areas of competence, including needs assessment, performance analysis, and task analysis, were judged extremely important by all respondents, as were instructional design, oral and written communication, project management, teamwork, understanding the dynamics of the organization, and consulting skills. Once again, these findings track closely with the content of Table 32.1.

Table 32.1. HPT Skills.

Basic Skill Groups	HPT Skill Requirements

Analysis and observation	1. Determine projects appropriate for HPT.
	  a. Analyze information regarding a situation and decide if it is an HP problem.
	  b. Determine if the situation is suitable for HPT analysis and intervention.

Analysis	2. Conduct needs assessments/front-end analysis.
	  a. Develop needs assessments/front-end analysis, including selection of procedures and instruments.
	  b. Conduct needs assessment/front-end analysis, including worth analysis, and interpret results to suggest appropriate actions or interventions.
	  c. Determine the appropriateness, completeness, and accuracy of any given needs assessment/front-end analysis plans and results.

Analysis and observation	3. Assess performer characteristics.
	  a. Discriminate and select among entry skills assessment, prerequisite assessment, and aptitude assessment.
	  b. Discriminate exemplary performers from average and deficient performers.
	  c. Observe exemplary performers to determine the activities, job steps, procedures they do that the average or deficient performers do not do. Note the relevant expert characteristics and methods of working/thinking.
	  d. Determine the appropriateness, comprehensiveness, and adequacy of a given assessment of worker/job situation characteristics.

Analysis	4. Analyze the structural characteristics of jobs, tasks, and content.
	  a. Select and apply procedures for analyzing the structural characteristics of a job, a task, or content that are appropriate for that job, task, or content.
	  b. State a rationale for the selection.

Analysis and communication	5. Write statements of HPT intervention outcomes.
	  a. Discriminate objectives, stated in performance terms, from HPT intervention goals, instructional goals, organizational goals, learner/worker activities, instructors' or other people's activities, and objectives written in other styles.
	  b. State outcomes in performance terms that convey the intent of the HPT intervention.
	  c. Evaluate the accuracy, comprehensiveness, and appropriateness of statements of worker outcomes in terms of the job, task, or content analysis and judgment/opinion of the client, subject matter expert, or other relevant stakeholders.

Table 32.1. HPT Skills, cont'd.

Basic Skill Groups	HPT Skill Requirements
Analysis and observation	6. Analyze the characteristics of a setting (learning/working environment). a. Analyze setting characteristics to determine relevant resources and constraints. b. Evaluate the accuracy, comprehensiveness, and appropriateness of a setting analysis.
Design and communication	7. Sequence performance intervention outcomes. a. Select a procedure for sequencing performance outcomes appropriate for a given situation. b. Sequence the outcomes and state a rationale for the sequence.
Design	8. Specify performance improvement strategies by selecting strategies appropriate for the setting, the characteristics of the performers, the resources and constraints, the desired outcomes, and other relevant factors.
Design and communication	9. Sequence performance improvement activities. a. Specify a sequence of performance improvement activities appropriate for the achievement of specified outcomes. b. State a rationale for the sequence.
Design, evaluation, and management	10. Determine the resources (media, technologies, equipment, money, people) appropriate for the performance improvement activities, and create all components. a. Develop resource specifications for each specified HPT intervention strategy and performance outcome. b. Evaluate existing HPT interventions to determine appropriateness with respect to specified performance outcomes. c. Adapt existing HPT interventions. d. Prepare the specifications for the production of materials and/or systems where required (storyboards, job aids, procedure manuals, electronic performance support tools). e. Organize, supervise, and monitor development and production of systems and materials. f. Create interventions ready for testing.
Evaluation and management	11. Evaluate HPT interventions. a. Plan a formative evaluation (trials with subjects, expert review, analysis of implementation considerations). b. Develop a range of information-gathering techniques (questionnaires, interviews, performance tests, simulations, structured observations, return-on-investment simulations).

Table 32.1. HPT Skills, cont'd.

Basic Skill Groups	HPT Skill Requirements
	c. Conduct trials. d. Analyze data. e. Generate specifications for revision on the basis of evaluation feedback. f. Evaluate the appropriateness, comprehensiveness, and adequacy of formative evaluation plans, information-gathering techniques, and revision specifications.
Design and evaluation	12. Create HPT interventions and implementation. a. Determine the components of each HPT intervention. b. State the rationale for each HPT intervention. c. Evaluate the appropriateness, comprehensiveness, and adequacy of each HPT intervention. d. Create an implementation plan for each HPT intervention, as well as for the entire HPT intervention system. e. Design means for evaluating HPT interventions once implemented. f. Design means for monitoring and maintaining the effects of HPT interventions.
Management	13. Plan, manage, and monitor HPT projects. a. Create an HPT project plan (including timelines, budgets, staffing) appropriate for the nature of the project and the setting. b. Manage and monitor an HPT project.
Communication	14. Communicate effectively in visual, oral, and written form. a. Create error-free communications that result in specified performance improvement. b. Create reports that are meaningful and informative to the client organization and project team. c. Create audit trails that document all aspects of an HPT project. d. Create communications that are free of bias.
Communication and interpersonal skills	15. Demonstrate appropriate interpersonal, group-process, and consulting behaviors. a. Select appropriate interpersonal behaviors with individuals and groups, and state a rationale for selecting the behaviors for each situation. b. Demonstrate appropriate group-process behaviors with individuals and groups, and state a rationale for selecting the behaviors for each situation. c. Demonstrate appropriate consulting behaviors with individuals and groups, and state a rationale for selecting the behaviors for each situation. d. Evaluate the appropriateness of interpersonal, group-process, and consulting behaviors in given situations.

Table 32.1. HPT Skills, cont'd.

Basic Skill Groups	HPT Skill Requirements
Communication	16. Promote HPT as a major approach to achieving desired HP results in organizations. a. Select appropriate strategies for promoting HPT in specific organizational settings. b. State a rationale for selecting each strategy. c. Create opportunities for promoting HPT. d. Implement appropriate promotion strategies for each opportunity.

Source: Stolovitch, H. E., Keeps, E. J., and Rodrigue, D. (1995). Skills sets for the human performance technologist. *Performance Improvement Quarterly* 8:2, 40–67. Copyright 1995 by the Learning Systems Institute, Florida State University, Suite 4600 University Center, Bldg. C, Tallahassee, Florida 32306-2540. Reprinted by permission from *Performance Improvement Quarterly.*

Ray and Sword (1993, p. 33) examine the HP technologist as a reengineering specialist. They group the required skills and knowledge areas into eight major categories of competence:

1. Strategic planning and visioning

2. Process reengineering

3. Planning information technology

4. Knowledge of the company's operations and industry

5. Facilitation of group process and organizational change

6. Project planning and program management

7. Data collection, analysis, and interpretation

8. Solution design, prototyping, and building

With the exception of skills in planning information technology, Table 32.1 again appears to cover all the relevant areas; "reengineering process," a term coined by Hammer and Champy (1994), has a meaning of its own, but the skills that are relevant to this area can largely be subsumed under the rubric of performance analysis and HPT intervention design.

Patterson (1985), after an extensive survey involving IT managers who were concerned with human performance problems, concludes that important capabilities included design, communication, and organization. He also stresses the "essential" need for analysis skills.

Rosenberg (1994, p. 25), writing of what is needed in order to move from a training paradigm to HPT, lists the essential skills as "analysis, project management, evaluation and systems integration, applied to solving human performance problems or realizing performance improvement opportunities."

Duncan and Powers (1992, p. 86) stress the need for HP practitioners to present themselves in "full dress" when they meet clients: "The more the consultant fits in with the group, the more quickly [he or she] will be accepted by the target audience. . . . 'Full dress' includes one's knowledge, preparation, and application skills." To extend this analogy, we might view the sixteen skills listed in Table 32.1 as the HP professional's "basic wardrobe," on which he or she may draw at the appropriate time.

Other Useful Skills

Many other skills, abilities, and characteristics have also been found useful to HPT practice and have been documented in various books, reports and articles. According to the sources listed here, HP technologists need to be able to do the following things:

- Duncan and Powers (1992)

  Create consensus

  Listen attentively and objectively

  Orchestrate effective and efficient meetings

  Give and receive feedback constructively

  Present a nonthreatening image

  Nurture relationships between internal and external consultants

  Demonstrate business knowledge and perspective

- Spitzer (1992)

  Facilitate and lead teams

  Negotiate effectively

  Recognize when to purchase an already prepared intervention

- Jewell and Jewell (1992)

  Involve the customer's managers in HPT interventions

- Bellman (1998)

  Give clients the data they need to recognize the HP technologists's accomplishments

  Lay the groundwork for a long-term partnership

  Tell the truth

  Take risks

  Establish partnerships focused on the work that needs to be done

- Steininger (1990)

  Share recognition with others

  Give authority with responsibility

  Take charge, make tough calls, and let everyone know why they were made

Be visible or invisible as the situation demands

Demonstrate, teach, tutor, and mentor

Provide psychological support to team members and clients

Demonstrate an "all for one, one for all" attitude

- Sink (1992)

  Provide clear explanations of what an HP technologist does and how it is done

- Hutchison and others (1988)

  Demonstrate the eleven traits most highly correlated with leadership (intelligence, ability to get along with others, technical competence, motivation of self and others, emotional stability, self-control, planning and organizational skills, strong desire to achieve tasks, ability to make use of group processes, ability to be effective and efficient, ability to be decisive)

- Elliott (1998)

  Align the purpose of the project with the organization's business goals

- Tosti and Jackson (1992)

  Demonstrate skills in leadership, teamwork, and partnering

- Zigon (1987)

  Market ideas and HPT

- Gayeski (1993b)

  Eliminate what is unnecessary

- Westgaard (1992)

  Demonstrate ethical behavior

  Perform only to professional standards

- Gilbert (1996)

  Focus on accomplishments rather than on human behavior

- Rummler and Brache (1996)

  Integrate treatments into existing programs

  Package treatments into soundly conceived and effectively administered programs

- Geis and Smith (1992)

  Establish who the clients are

  Integrate broad and disparate sets of data

- Pipe (1992)

  Demonstrate creativity through nonhabitual thought and lateral thinking

- Carr (1992)

  Stop digging when the most fundamental practical cause of a performance deficiency has been reached

- Davidove (1991)

  Identify results valued by the client

  Create client self-sufficiency

  Create audit trails

- Robb (1998)

  Keep the goal always in sight

  Improve processes and human performance in support of the client's business goals

Which Are the Most Important Skills?

Are all the skills that have been listed here of equal importance? Certainly, all are useful to the professional HPT practitioner. However, experienced professionals tend to focus on some of these as being more crucial than others. The suggestions in the paragraphs that follow have been synthesized from the writings of established HPT professionals.

The most important general skill the HPT practitioner must possess is the ability to keep a steady focus on the client's need. The practitioner must engineer solution systems that get the job done (Gilbert, 1992). The HP technologist must not lose sight of the primary mission, which is to determine the intervention, or the set of interventions and conditions, that will allow or induce people to perform optimally and eliminate performance deficiencies (Spitzer, 1992; Stolovitch and Keeps, 1998). It is easy for an HP technologist, especially when he or she lacks experience, to get carried away by the enthusiasms and constraints of the client organization. Separating needs from wants or whims while keeping a steady eye on the valued outcomes will be essential to success.

HP practitioners must be more "cause-conscious than solution-oriented" (Stolovitch and Keeps, 1992b, p. 8). They must be able "to quickly and accurately identify and understand the issues affecting performance" (Rummler and Brache, 1992, p. 39). As Spitzer (1988) emphasizes, analytical skills are the key to successful HPT practice.

HP technologists must maintain a systems view of organizations. Whatever the specific problem or opportunity, HP technologists must "adopt a holistic viewpoint toward performance problems, which means that they examine any given problem within the broader context of the [system] and subsystem[s] in which it is situated" (Stolovitch and Keeps, 1992b, p. 5). One must always be careful, when introducing change in one area, of the potential effects on other, related areas. The HPT three-level framework (organization, process, and job/performer) proposed by Rummler and Brache (1996) is useful in helping the HPT practitioner adopt and maintain a systems view.

According to Duncan and Powers (1992, p. 90), "the HP technologist must know how and when to involve others." The practice of HPT naturally includes many players. The HPT practitioner must be able to obtain support from authority figures, draw together opposing views, and seek out skilled and knowledgeable individuals to make specific contributions to the success of a project. A key part of involving others is being able to recognize one's own limitations and finding the right persons to be involved at the right moment. Skilled HPT professionals frequently work in teams, drawing strength from the diverse abilities they can bring to bear on a problem or opportunity.

For Rossett (1992a, p. 103) a crucial skill is to conduct "systematic analyses" because the "output of each analysis activity serves as the input for subsequent efforts and decisions." This means that HPT practitioners must be rigorous in applying established analytical methodologies. The more systematically and prudently the information is gathered, the more probable it is that the design and implementation of the intervention will be successful. And, even though analysis is an important and serious business, verifying one's own perceptions is at least equally important because the information that HPT practitioners collect may be incorrectly interpreted (Rossett, 1992a, p. 100). Particularly for external HPT consultants, perception of a situation becomes interpretation of reality. Double- or triple-checking one's perceptions and interpretations against those of others who are more familiar with the context is of foremost importance.

Sorting out priorities, in terms of what is important for the overall success of an organization, is an essential skill for HPT practitioners: "The most successful performance interventions are aligned with business results needs [and are] focused in key result areas . . . [and] on improving systems, not just on attacking symptoms" (Spitzer, 1992, p. 117). The intervention must have an impact on the client's business to be considered successful.

An ounce of sound design is worth pounds of the most exotic and up-to-date media technology production: "Most research over the last two decades shows little difference in learning between programs with high production values and those that are much more simply but soundly designed" (Gayeski, 1992, p. 442). The able practitioner is not distracted by the latest technological fad; technology choices are selected on the basis of cost-effectiveness and efficiency.

In summary, experienced HPT professionals focus on the key skills that make the difference: the ability to analyze, design, communicate, think systemically, work systematically, influence, work in teams, and focus on critical performance and results.

Preliminary Conclusions About Basic HPT Skills

As we have seen, there is considerable consistency among authors on what constitute the basic or essential skills for HPT professionals. Nevertheless, as Hutchison (1990, p. 5) says, there is still a need to clarify and refine these areas of competence, as well as standards for HP technologists. There is also a need to specify the degree of expertise or mastery that HPT professionals require in the various skills. The question of standards has not yet been adequately addressed by the HPT community and is beyond the scope of this present chapter, but aspects of this topic will emerge later, as we examine the issues of standards and certification.

CHARACTERISTICS OF THE OUTSTANDING HPT PROFESSIONAL

HPT is concerned with exemplary performance as a means of determining the potential for improved performance (Gilbert, 1996, p. xvi). Exemplary performers possess a combination of skills and characteristics that permit them to attain outstanding accomplishments. Up to this point, we have focused our attention on basic HPT skills, but does any single practitioner exhibit all of them?

Sink (1992, pp. 566–567) suggests that six characteristics set the outstanding HPT professional apart:

1. They are driven by results. "Outstanding HPT practitioners are results-oriented. They solve human performance problems." They "do not become so intrigued with the processes and procedures of HPT that they lose sight of the true problem and the desired results."

2. They are investigative. They know what to look for and how to find it. They possess the art of being able to ask "the critical few questions."

3. They know how to set and maintain standards. From "the start of an intervention, the experienced HPT professional sets expectations for standards of quality . . . [and] institutes quality checks at all key points in a project."

4. They are cooperative and collaborative. Successful HPT practitioners "display and encourage collaboration" with clients, subordinates, peers, and other professionals.

5. They are flexible but still maintain key principles. Talented HPT practitioners easily adapt to new contexts and shifting priorities. They deal with sudden constraints or increased scope. However, they also consistently apply their systematic processes and stay with what is best for the client and for the ultimate success of the project.

6. They are willing and able to add value. "Successful HPT professionals go beyond doing a good job." The exemplary HPT practitioner constantly seeks to give the client more than improved performance. Frequently, this effort takes the form of educating clients on HPT principles, providing them with new resources, or introducing them to technologies that will have an impact beyond the current project.

In brief, the outstanding HPT performer not only has mastered the skills of the field but also has developed a set of professional characteristics that greatly enhance his or her effectiveness.

CURRENT PRACTICE AND PRACTITIONERS

As already mentioned, many current HPT practitioners came from the field of instructional technology and training. Their basic skill sets have been influenced by their own initial training and experience, which was largely centered on learning issues. Over time, they have adopted a much broader view of human performance and a more businesslike approach to "worthy accomplishments" (Gilbert, 1996). It is not surprising that graduate students interested in HPT are now being asked to possess deeper business knowledge and are being taught consulting and management skills, in addition to developing their capacity to evaluate the impact of a broad array of interventions (Rosenberg, cited in Rossett, 1990). Therefore, current practitioners also need to develop their business and management skills in order to grow, and all the more so as an increasing number of individuals, among them some with M.B.A. degrees, come into the field with a variety of backgrounds (Robinson and Robinson, 1995, p. 12).

Again, however, what are the limits? Can anyone possess all the skills that HPT seems to be encompassing? Can anyone be proficient in every skill and characteristic mentioned so far? Is it necessary for one individual to master them all? Obviously, the answer to all these questions is no, but HPT has the scope to accommodate a variety of specialists as well as generalists. There is now a place in the HPT community for expertise clusters to form.

This is a positive development for HPT. It should encourage people to acquire some specialization as part of a personal inventory of skills. It should also lead to cooperation and sharing within the HPT community. Some universities are sending the message out to their HPT students. Medsker and Fry (1992, p. 54), for example, describe their program at Marymount University as follows: "Recognizing that no performance technologist can be an expert in every intervention, . . . [we] acquaint students with the variety available and . . . build proficiency in some." This statement also underscores the importance of what binds all HP technologists together: the ability to conduct "the critical diagnosis and bring in a team of specialists to design and implement a broad set of treatments" (Rummler and Brache, 1992, p. 44). This ability to act as the chief diagnostician is in itself one of the defining skills of the HPT professional. Mager (1992a, p. 743) eloquently sums up how one should view the ever-growing array of skills that are emerging as relevant to HPT: "Though it can easily be verified that the world of music is huge, one need learn only a minuscule fraction of what is knowable to become a very competent musician.... Therefore, the recognition of the fact that there is much one could know about HPT should not deter one from a decision to become worthy in the field."

THE FUTURE OF HPT AND SKILLS REQUIREMENTS

The role of the HPT practitioner is evolving at a rapid pace. This trend will continue and even accelerate as clients continue to ask HP technologists to intervene in more and more varied situations. As the role of the HPT practitioner expands, the direction it appears to be taking is mostly toward consultation (Sink, 1992; Robinson and Robinson, 1995). What new skills will the HPT consultant of the future require?

In order to discern specific future skills requirements, we briefly look ahead to identify major trends evolving in the workplace and the challenges associated with them. Brandenburg and Binder (1992) present four such major trends:

1. The increase in international competition, with the accompanying emphasis on productivity and quality

2. The growing diversity of the workforce, with its impact on entry-level skills, personal values, and learning needs

3. The accelerating turnover of knowledge, especially in the scientific and engineering worlds

4. The rapid advances in information technology

All these trends demand greater and more cost-effective investment in human resource development. In a similar vein, Sink (1992, p. 573) notes, "Future trends in HPT closely parallel trends in business and society. Increased automation in the practice of HPT is already being emphasized in most organizations." Viewing these trends from the perspective of 1999—the step up to the next millennium—one sees an even greater need for both knowledge and wisdom in using technology to achieve desirable human performance results.

As a direct consequence, "in work environments that change ever more rapidly, one important need may be to learn while working.... Workers will use on-the-job information systems to access policies, procedures, and data as needed—a sort of 'just in time' training. The technologies to do the above are currently available . . . [and] the challenge will be to integrate tools into existing organizational structures and reward systems" (Brandenburg and Binder, 1992, p. 658). What is and will be the impact on HP consultants? The same authors note that HP consultants will need to be keenly aware of and knowledgeable about the characteristics of these future systems, in which there will be more interactivity between users via the World Wide Web, organizational intranets, electronic conferencing of every variety, systems that will use multiple technologies, a multiplicity of communication protocols, and the increasing use of digital technologies. They see the HP technologist as occupying a crucial role as instigator, coordinator, and manager of change for improved individual and organizational performance (p. 669), and they cite the following as key skills for the twenty-first century:

- Recognizing and exploiting the potential of HPT as an integrator of technologies and methods from other fields
- Mastering front-end analysis methods that incorporate a systems view of organizations
- Obtaining management's support to do front-end analysis
- Dealing with an expanded range of interventions and methods
- Forging alliances and working relationships with specialists in other fields, and with other approaches to human performance
- Anticipating and assessing the mutual impacts of multiple technologies
- Even more than in current practice, designing and implementing systems for measurement and continuous improvement in order to achieve optimized integrated solutions

Brethower (1993, p. 18) believes that the future will require HP technologists "who have the special knowledge and skills needed to conduct performance-based, learn-as-you-earn, workplace development projects." Brethower also cites small organizations as the probable preferred workplaces for most HPT practitioners because these continue to employ most of the workforce.

Gayeski (1991a, p. 47) notes the same trend, saying that "more of us will be working for small companies in the next decade". She also foresees that the "performance technologist must learn to develop electronic job aids, expert systems, and interactive multi-media training and performance support systems," and she emphasizes that "more than ever, we will be change agents, helping our clients adapt to the challenging times that face us." She believes that mastery of several technologies (desktop media-development systems, expert and mentoring systems, electronic performance support tools) will be of major importance to the profession.

Laiken (1993, pp. 35–36) suggests other areas where HP technologists are likely to spend more time:

- Helping to develop organizational vision, philosophy, mission statements, and strategic goals
- Assessing organizations' overall learning needs and the development of educational interventions (at macro levels)
- Working on team development
- Using a performance management cycle (for example, negotiating performance expectations, setting behavioral objectives, discussing and updating performance development plans) at all levels of the organization
- Coaching managerial personnel

Many HPT professionals have already begun to perform what appear to be future tasks, whose frequency and intensity will probably increase over time, as will the pressure to produce more complex, integrated intervention systems for improving performance and business results (Stolovitch and Keeps, 1998). Time will also be a constantly decreasing commodity as cycle times continue to shrink. One conclusion that can be drawn from the various futuristic views is that the execution of multiple new tasks will require additional and complementary skills: more skills in technology, in organizational behavior, and certainly in business as it is conducted in internationally competitive markets. This will force HPT practitioners to work smarter, not harder—to achieve results in less time.

In view of the many major challenges that will confront the field, one additional and absolutely essential skill, needed today but sure to be needed even more in the future, is delegation. Gayeski (1991b, p. 40) highlights this idea: "We'll need to learn to share our skills with subject-matter experts and part-time instructional developers so that some of the work can be shared by them."

DEVELOPMENT AND DEFINITION OF SKILLS FOR HPT PRACTITIONERS

As the field evolves, and as the number of individuals calling themselves HP technologists increases, a logical question arises: How are skills developed in the field, and who has the authority to define the required skill sets?

Currently, the primary means for developing HPT skills is through practice and experience. At this point, there are few HPT practitioners with more than twenty-five years of direct experience in the field. Most acquired their entry-level skills in related fields like IT, behavioral psychology, and management. They then went on to accept new challenges and expand their repertoires of competence. We must remember that HTP is a new domain, one that parallels the fast-paced evolution of what has been the impact of technology on the industrial world over the last thirty-five years. We sometimes forget that programmed instruction, one of the major roots of HPT, did not become well known until the 1960s (Deutsch, 1992), and that HPT as a distinct field only made its appearance in the late 1970s (Dean and Ripley, 1997).

The individuals who defined the original scope and purpose of HPT, pioneered its first interventions, and were responsible for creating HPT as an applied field of science certainly have something to say about the required skills. As a first source of direction regarding HPT practitioners' skills, one should review the publications of such HPT pioneers as Thomas F. Gilbert, Robert F. Mager, Joe Harless, Roger Kaufman, Geary Rummler, and Donald Tosti. Their writings on the field's theoretical underpinnings, as well as on its practical applications, have become, over time, the foundation of the current HPT framework and a primary source of inspiration.

Clients are another source of skill identification and development. They are the ones experiencing performance deficiencies and calling for help. They often intuitively know what kind of individual they want to be dealing with and what sort of help they need. Without pinpointing specific skills, they are looking for someone who first of all will listen and who then will be able to analyze the situation and recommend a viable, cost-effective solution (Robinson and Robinson, 1995). Clients also buy from people they like. Because they are constantly conducting business transactions, they are sensitive to the "people" skills exhibited by individual HP practitioners (Bellman, 1998). "The powerful analytical abilities typically possessed by performance technologists need to be supplemented by the necessary human skills to gain acceptance of ideas not yet largely understood" (Murphy, 1987, p. 6)—and this statement is as true today as it was twelve years ago. The field has everything to gain by being alert and attentive to customers' comments because these communicate, in many ways, the behavior that clients want us to exhibit. The major skills they look for are those that offer results; therefore, HP technologists should constantly be honing those skills.

The evolution of ideas in the management sciences is yet another source of skill identification. Concepts and processes related to change agentry, sociotechnical systems, culture change, total-quality management, and process reengineering, for example, have an enormous impact on organizational—and, consequently, human—performance. As clients ask HP technologists to become involved in projects related to these concepts, or as work on performance problems and opportunities intersects with initiatives related to these concepts, the skills required to deal with them naturally emerge. HP consultants are constantly being stretched by the introduction of new ideas from other fields.

The community of HPT practitioners is itself another and major source of skill development and identification. Books written by HPT professionals and scholars are becoming more frequent. These generally present clearly defined models, detailed examples of performance problems and solutions, analytical procedures, and documented HP cases. Professional workshops on specific skills and issues abound. Publications and conferences sponsored by ISPI, for example, provide excellent forums for the exchange of innovative thinking and skill requirements among HPT experts and practitioners. The sharing of ideas and experiences with newly discovered skills, or with techniques that practitioners have found particularly helpful in their day-to-day practice, creates a rich professional network that is a stimulating resource for learning and skills acquisition.

PROFESSIONAL STANDARDS FOR HPT PRACTITIONERS?

It is evident that, even though they are not organized in any systematic way, there are many sources of skill development and identification for HPT practitioners. Individuals enter the field through many doors. They practice, gain experience, read, attend workshops and conferences, are perhaps mentored, and eventually view themselves as HPT professionals. No formal mechanisms exist, however, for officially defining skill sets and means of developing competence in HPT; there is no certification or sanctioning of practitioners. Should there be? Is there a need to create professional standards for the HPT community?

As already mentioned, the medical profession has clearly defined sets of standards for general practitioners and specialists. These declare who may practice, and to what extent. The standards allow all practitioners to communicate easily and rapidly among themselves, sharing a fixed, common terminology, common tools, and sets of standardized approaches. One practitioner can easily transmit and receive information from another. Many other domains, such as painting and sculpture, remain relatively untouched by general standards, even though all artists know how to prepare their colors and present their work; there are no set, clearly defined standards governing these arts. Much is left to imagination and creativity, and yet artists still communicate with their clients and among themselves, even though their communications may not be as rapid and precise as those of physicians.

What about the field of HPT? Is there a need for a common set of recognized standards, and for certification of professional HP technologists? Is it better to allow each individual practitioner the liberty to practice as he or she feels is most effective?

Over the past fifteen years, there have been numerous arguments for and against HPT certification. Although no official set of professional standards yet exists, the American Society for Training and Development (ASTD) and ISPI are discussing operational procedures to create them by the year 2000. The field currently operates as a free-market enterprise, with both the advantages and the difficulties of that status.

The advantages are creativity and the natural law of supply and demand. It is the customer, as the user of HPT services, who defines competence and value.

On the negative side, the field continues to suffer from lack of credibility with higher management, a condition particularly felt by internal HP consultants. Moreover, without recognized professional work standards and a certification process, the field is vulnerable to charlatans, and it remains vague and difficult to explain to those who are not part of the practicing HPT community. The field possesses no specific mechanism for defining required skills and knowledge, and it offers no clear, standard means of preparing individuals who are eager to enter the field.

As the reader will have noted, quite convincing arguments have been made on both sides of this question, but this chapter does not take sides; we believe that those who seriously call themselves professional HP technologists will ultimately make the decision. What this chapter presents instead is a brief summary of the arguments for and against standards and a certification process.

Arguments in Favor of Standards

A key problem caused by the current lack of standards in the field is the lack of credibility given to HP specialists by higher management and other colleagues: "Our interventions should be creative and expansive, but currently our profession lacks the appropriate theoretical base, identity, and reporting structure within our organizations" (Gayeski, 1993a, p. 36). This concern has been expressed by a number of other practitioners, who feel that the certification process embodies professionalism, competence, prestige, and self-improvement. They have argued that certified or sanctioned standards are an opportunity to take the following actions:

- Show that an individual's knowledge and skills surpass the minimum required for practice

- Validate an individual's qualifications, knowledge, and practice on the basis of predetermined standards

- Officially recognize the achievements a professional has made in his or her area of practice

- Provide a benefit to the professional, the profession, and the public being served

Arguments Against Standards

Others have argued that official standards and certification could stifle creativity in the field. Boothe (1984, p. 20) summarizes his arguments with an emotional plea: "Let's retain the freedom to explore, discover, compete, grow, and even fail now and then." Reasons advanced against official standards and certification are as follows:

- No one has yet defined the problem (the true need for certification).
- The few professions that have experienced this kind of regulation are those that serve the masses with a definable service.
- Certification would mean the HPT profession's telling the user group what it ought to want.
- The best that certification could guarantee is mediocrity.
- Certification is solely in the interest of the universities and, as such, could dampen growth and the search for excellence among those practitioners who are not university-sanctioned.
- The focus of the field's energies would be on certification rather than on competence.
- The mission statement of ISPI, which HP technologists view as their professional society, implies a quest, whereas a certification system implies arrival at a destination.

PREPARATION AND TRAINING OF THE HPT PRACTITIONER

For individuals discovering HPT and deciding to become HPT professionals, what preparation and training will be appropriate? What knowledge and abilities should prospective HP technologists possess before entering the job market? Where will they acquire these? This section presents suggestions for the type of curriculum offerings that university faculties can provide to prepare students for the workplace. It also suggests other potential training alternatives.

Members of the academic community who have made HPT a focus of study, representatives of business organizations, and HPT professionals have been communicating about ways to improve the preparation and training of future HPT practitioners. The consensus among these various groups is that there is a strong need to provide students with practical skills. University faculty members active in HPT are open to this idea and have begun to take concrete steps. The question, however, is where to begin.

Patterson (1985) conducted a study on the preparation of instructional technologists in universities. What he found holds some relevance for the field of HPT because it is largely in IT departments that HPT is taught. The study focused on the skills that government agencies and business organizations require of instructional technologists. The survey included a fifty-item questionnaire and a number of interviews. It was sent to ASTD members occupying a major role in instructional product and/or program development. Forty participants representing four major workplace categories were selected. Ten were in manufacturing, ten in service industries, ten in medicine, and ten in government and social agencies. Major questions focused on requirements for competence and business knowledge among instructional technologists, as well as on the levels (depth) of competence required.

The study concluded with a number of useful suggestions for university preparation of instructional technologists. It recommended (Patterson, 1985, p. 38) that academic programs preparing individuals as program and product development specialists provide each learner with the following kinds of preparation:

1. A strong foundation of studies in the behavioral sciences (theories of learning and instruction, models of communication, a variety of instructional development models and the theory and practice of front-end analysis and evaluation of results).

2. Multiple experiences and study in the design and production of training programs requiring design, analysis, instructional media production (or selection), formative evaluation, product/program revision and final program evaluation.

3. The opportunity for acquiring effective communication skills including writing, organizing messages during the phases of program/product development, and executing presentations using a wide variety of appropriate audiovisual media.

4. Assurances that emerging instructional media technologies will not be preselected or overemphasized as the final solution to an instructional problem.

5. Opportunity for study and experience in the area in which the individual wishes to pursue a career.

6. Knowledge and skills in the management of the formal and informal organizational processes in program/product development (for example, project management skills, strategic planning, budgeting and resource allocation, personnel selection and supervision, cost-benefit analysis of project results).

7. Practical experience in [human] performance technology in which . . . learners' behaviors and performance as . . . pre-professional developer[s] are clearly evaluated in the context of the problem to be solved and the goals of the organization. It is essential that specialists entering training and HRD possess the analytical skills to identify the problems that are appropriate for their respective capabilities and to be able to judge the cost-benefit of solving the designated problems.

Although it focused on instructional technologists, the Patterson study provides an excellent starting point for considering the formal preparation of HP technologists. Many of the skills and kinds of competence identified as desirable by the respondents are applicable to HPT. The strong emphasis on practical experiences and analytical skills resonates strongly with the HPT field.

Since the Patterson study appeared, several universities have implemented some of its recommendations. A few, like San Diego State University and the Université de Montréal, have gone beyond these recommendations and now incorporate an HPT perspective, offering courses that deal specifically with HPT skills and issues. Medsker and Fry's description (1992, p. 53) of the master's degree program at Marymount University, a program launched within the Human Resources Development program, offers a picture of a program with a strong HPT orientation, a skills-centered curriculum, and competence-based courses: "Students demonstrate mastery primarily through hands-on projects that require application of course principles to work-related situations." The overall program has been logically designed with a sequence of courses that students are encouraged to follow, and the program attempts to develop specific practical expertise.

The involvement of universities in the preparation of HP technologists is essential to the building of credibility for the field. If the programs that universities provide also produce graduates who can demonstrate practical skills in analysis, design of a small range of interventions, and evaluation, in addition to basic knowledge of business practices and organizational dynamics, then credibility for the field will be enhanced even more.

Rossett (1990) proposes another interesting approach to the preparation of HP technologists. She, too, sees the university as an important source of competent HPT practitioners. However, instead of focusing on HPT program outputs (that is, program graduates), she suggests that attention be placed on inputs (that is, students who are entering HPT programs). Basically, her idea calls for establishing specific requirements for entry into a graduate HPT program; the students who are selected should already possess some of the skills or knowledge considered necessary for work in the field. For example, individuals with majors in organizational behavior, information systems, or industrial psychology, or people who are otherwise likely to possess some of the relevant skills (second-career individuals or reentering women) would be likely candidates. An alternative for attaining the same objective would be to specify prerequisite skills and establish acceptable routes to acquiring them. This alternative could include identification of courses in business, economics, psychology, and other relevant areas.

A very appropriate means of preparing HPT practitioners is to introduce HPT to current IT students. Rossett (1990, p. 49) suggests that IT courses be given an HPT flavor, and she provides suggestions for infusing HPT perspectives. She particularly stresses the importance of providing at least one course that deals with analysis and strategic thinking beyond the traditional instructional boundaries.

Two programs currently in the process of developing HP professionals in a university environment have demonstrated attractiveness in terms of enrollment, as well as success through students' accomplishments. Boise State University currently offers a distance-based master's degree program in Human Performance Technology. Along with high enrollments, the program has seen its graduates successfully find HPT work in large organizations. The University of Southern California has also launched a well-attended doctoral program with the appealing designation of Human Performance at Work. Both programs focus on producing high-level specialists in HPT.

Although universities are gradually moving to implement programs of relevance for the preparation of HPT practitioners, day-to-day experience and the performance of on-the-job activities still remain the most effective ways of learning and developing HPT skills. Carroll (1992, p. 335) says, "People learn by doing; they try to act in order to understand," adding that "integration [of learning] can occur only through meaningful action." If beginning practitioners are to demonstrate basic HP skills when they leave university programs, and before they present themselves to prospective employers, they will need guided practice and feedback on these skills.

This idea suggests that some form of mentoring from members of the HPT community would be invaluable. HPT as a field can only benefit by producing better practitioners through cooperation between universities and practitioners, and the production of more skilled practitioners will only enhance the credibility of the field. It may even be beneficial to require that the master's degree student who wishes to become an HPT practitioner work under the supervision of an experienced HPT mentor for a number of months and demonstrate competence in the basic skills. As a result, universities could produce higher-caliber students and build their reputation in the business world (as sources of students and contracts), experienced practitioners could benefit from low- or no-cost assistance for a number of months (as happens in law, accounting, and medicine) and have the opportunity to judge for themselves the value of potential future hires, and students could have opportunities to practice and develop competence, gain experience (and more substance for their résumés), explore the field in a hands-on way, and approach the job market with greater confidence. As Gilley and Eggland (1989) mention, mentoring programs "are more career-oriented" in their focus than simple on-the-job training, and the use of mentors would fit well with the development of HPT professionals.

In short, many avenues exist for the preparation of future HP technologists. The number of practitioners, university programs with HPT content, and local chapters of ISPI are all increasing. This trend in itself suggests that more opportunities to learn, practice, and gain experiences are becoming available. This augurs well for future HPT practitioners.

HOW SHOULD WE KEEP OURSELVES CURRENT?

All groups that view themselves as professional provide means for practitioners to keep current with changes and developments in their fields. Generally, members are offered a variety of developmental opportunities, such as books and journals, local professional events, regional or national conferences, workshops, meetings and committee work. All of these have one major purpose: to sustain competence and keep professional practitioners current on important issues.

The HPT field is relatively well organized in this respect. ISPI offers HP practitioners two journals, sponsored books and occasional publications, international and local conferences, and HPT institutes. The rapid growth the field has been experiencing over the last fifteen years has been paralleled by a marked increase in publications and events directly aimed at HPT practitioners.

Coleman (1992) cites five major means for HPT practitioners to keep abreast of the field's continuous expansion: joining (professional societies such as ISPI), reading, attending (conferences, workshops, and institutes), networking, and sharing. He suggests that each practitioner create an individual professional development program that includes plans for each of the five activity areas and that these plans match the individual's present areas of expertise and new interests with the available time and resources and with the level of effort that the individual wants to make.

Of all the ways in which HPT practitioners can keep themselves current, participation in professional organizations is one of the best. Participation, besides offering the chance to learn from the activities of the organization, provides opportunities for networking. Duncan and Powers (1992, p. 88) make a strong case for developing oneself in this manner, stating that "networking can supplement or take the place of a mentor. A strong network gives the HP consultant referent and expertise power and validates the kind of work that he or she is doing." This point of view, upheld by many in the field, suggests that participation in professional events should begin very early in the HPT practitioner's career. Students desiring to enter the field should be encouraged to join local professional groups, such as ISPI chapters, and to become involved in their activities.

VALUES FOR HPT PROFESSIONALS

HPT is spreading geographically at an astounding pace. For example, the number of local ISPI chapters throughout the world has multiplied fivefold in the past ten years. Organizations like the International Federation of Training and Development Organizations (IFTDO) have made HPT a central focus of interest, as has ASTD with its increased emphasis on "performance improvement." Nevertheless, when there is activity, success, or growth without a firm set of values, a field can be endangered during its fragile state of expansion.

Although HPT struggles to define basic and advanced skill sets and has addressed, directly and indirectly, the desirable characteristics of HPT professionals, it has remained silent with respect to values. In closing this chapter, we propose, on the basis of our close association with the HPT community, our own practice, and our study of the professional literature, a first-draft set of HPT practitioner values. These are certainly incomplete, but they have guided our professional activities over the past twenty years and have helped us weather many professionally challenging adventures. These twelve value statements are presented in the first person plural, to emphasize their credolike quality.

1. Our clients are, or become, professional partners and friends. They are as delighted to work with us as we are to work with them. HPT is a field of practice that focuses on *human* performance. To achieve success requires a harmonious, collaborative relationship between HPT specialists and clients. The achievement of desirable behavior and accomplishments changes results, on the basis of open communication and complicity of action and spirit. This enhances the probability of long-term relationships and success.

2. We are fully committed to our clients' best interests. We address their needs with the most cost-effective solutions. This value emphasizes the service nature of HPT professionals. It commits us to meeting needs rather than wants. It gives performance consulting precedence over order taking and implies the precedence of prudent thought over enthusiasm for a currently popular intervention.

3. We provide value to our clients that is greater than the cost of our services. HPT is concerned with cost-effectiveness. Accomplishments resulting from HPT interventions must far outweigh the costs of their attainment. Commitment to this value should result in data-based decision making, tracking of results, and demonstrated worth to the client.

4. We perform our services in partnership with our clients and in a non-threatening manner. Collaboration is key to our success. Although HPT possesses its own jargon, tools, and viewpoints, these must be melded with those of the client's system through mutuality. To accomplish this requires partnership and an environment of relaxed sharing. The purpose of our involvement in a project is to contribute our specialized capability, but in ways that the client system can easily assimilate and leverage with internal capabilities.

5. We apply only the highest standards of ethical and professional conduct in our work. Key to credibility and trust is the client's confidence that we conduct ourselves ethically and according to a high standard of performance. Although HPT has not defined a code of ethics or a set of standards, models of appropriate conduct do exist in related fields and can serve as guidelines for us.

Although it may sound old-fashioned to say so at the dawn of the twenty-first century, honorable conduct is still appropriate in our practice.

6. Our professional practice is based on the scientific principles of HPT and its respected precedents. What distinguishes our work from that of many other organizational consulting fields is its firm adherence to what science has discovered about human behavior and performance. We are committed to applying scientific, documented knowledge to the production of valued accomplishments, and we are committed to supporting and contributing to the expansion of the scientific knowledge base of human performance. When a client comes to us not just with a problem but also with the belief that a particular type of solution will effect a miracle cure, we must approach this enthusiasms with openness to listening but skepticism about the potentially miraculous results. It is our duty to separate enthusiasm from data-based fact and guide the client toward interventions with the highest probability of success, even if they are distant from those initially envisioned.

7. We develop and support people in their personal and professional growth. The field of HPT is about human behavior and accomplishment. Personally and through interactions with others, we constantly seek to improve knowledge and performance capability. By our example, we demonstrate what the field stands for.

8. Our aim is to build maximum client self-sufficiency, not consultant dependency. Despite the temptation of becoming a permanent fixture in client organizations, we must seek to transfer performance capability to those we serve. The ability to accomplish this is a major contribution HPT makes to clients.

9. We encourage and support our clients in their own professional growth. The most desirable form of conduct in HPT practice is partnership and client support. As an added value, we contribute to growing client capability. This results in both successful projects and enhanced client/personal accomplishment potential.

10. We accept responsibility. We allow ourselves to accept congratulations for our successes because we are prepared to live with the consequences of our failures. We are dedicated to applying scientific principles to the achievement of human accomplishments, but not all of our efforts are successful. Accepting failure professionally, along with its consequences, painful as they may be, is necessary. Our ability to accept responsibility for our failures is a precondition of our right to receive the benefits of successful practice.

11. We welcome challenges that allow us to stretch and expand our competence. HPT is a rapidly developing field, and we must continuously expand our knowledge and skills if we are to meet the new conditions of the constantly evolving work environment. Rather than back away from new challenges, we should seek them out as a means of professional growth.

12. We treat commitments, promises, and professional relationships as sacred trusts. We apply our skills to the changing of human behavior and to the fostering of human accomplishments. The work is generally performed within tight time and budgeting constraints, and clients' expectations of us are often high. This is a challenge that requires dedication and focus. Keeping our commitments—written or oral, formal or casual—is indispensable to our professional credibility.

In summary, skills without values decrease the professional nature of the role the HPT practitioner can play in organizations. The set of values proposed above represents one point of view; ultimately, the HPT community as a whole must create its own value set. This will require severe testing in the fires of many cultures and contexts before a universally accepted HPT value system can be forged.

CONCLUSION

HPT addresses some key societal and organizational concerns. Governments, social agencies, nonprofit organizations, and for-profit businesses all require optimal use of their resources. Of all their resources, humans are generally the most costly—and the most valuable (Stewart, 1997; Edvinsson and Malone, 1997). Gains or losses of human productivity have direct and significant impacts on the bottom line. HPT offers systemic and systematic means to analyze and intervene in work-related human performance situations. Its complete focus on improving human performance, along with its strong record of success, makes it a unique, viable, and valuable field of practice.

To work as an HP technologist requires mastery of HPT's basic processes and skills. This means that HP practitioners must demonstrate strong technical competence that includes analytical, design, and evaluation skills. They must also exhibit "people" skills and communication competence, which includes managerial, organizational, and interpersonal skills. Practitioners who are recognized as experts in the field distinguish themselves by their mastery of both types of skills, their constant focus on end results, and their continued striving to learn and improve their capabilities. They also achieve recognition through their adherence to strict, high standards of work and conduct.

Today's HP technologists include a variety of former educators, behavioral psychologists, training specialists and managers, instructional technologists, and management professionals who gravitated toward the world of HPT and gained skills through practice and experience. As the field evolves, specific university programs are emerging that teach HPT concepts and processes and provide opportunities to develop practical skills. As the field solidifies, HPT practitioners are gaining more business skills and starting to work at higher levels in organizations. They are also reaching out to practice in areas generally associated with other professionals, such as specialists in organizational development and human resources. Over time, the limits of the field will have to be more clearly demarcated. For now, however, HPT's focus on improving human performance, its skills in diagnosing performance gaps, and its skills in designing effective interventions make it increasingly attractive to organizations.

The future appears promising for HP technologists. Organizational demands to improve performance demonstrate the need for professionals with the skills, characteristics, and values to make it happen. As Carr (1994, p. 6) has pointed out, "we help organizations take a variety of steps that make better performance easier for their performers." The opportunities are there. To seize them requires that HPT practitioners acquire a wide range of skills that help organizations achieve their goals. The greater our skills, the greater our acceptance by the business and educational communities. We must accumulate and document success stories for HPT, to demonstrate that we add value. We must analyze our successes, to identify the skills and personal characteristics that made them happen. We must report on the required skill sets, characteristics, and values so that universities, mentors, and internship programs can integrate these and in turn ensure that students acquire them. As the role of the HP practitioner expands toward that of an overall organizational performance consultant, operating in a global context, current HP technologists should also verify their own skill sets, personal characteristics, and professional values in order to meet the new and exciting challenges.

References

Bergeron, P. G. (1989). *La gestion moderne: Théorie et cas* [Modern management: Theory and cases] (2nd rev. ed.). Boucherville, Quebec, Canada: Gaëtan Morin.

Bollen, J., and Vanasse, S. (1994). *Implementing performance technology: Where organization development and instructional technology principles meet.* Paper presented at the annual conference of the National Society for Performance and Instruction, San Francisco.

Boothe, B. (1984). Certification—beyond reason. Please don't certify me, doctor, I'm on a roll. *Performance & Instruction* 23:1, 21–22.

Brandenburg, D. C., and Binder, C. (1992). Emerging trends in human performance interventions. In H. D. Stolovitch and E. J. Keeps (eds.), *Handbook of Human Performance Technology: A comprehensive guide for analyzing and solving performance problems in organizations.* San Francisco: Jossey-Bass.

Bratton, B. (1984). Professional certification: Will it become a reality? *Performance & Instruction* 23:1, 4–7.

Brethower, K. S. (1993). Strategic improvement of workplace competence: Breaking out of the incompetence trap. *Performance Improvement Quarterly* 6:2, 17–28.

Carr, C. (1992). How performance happens (and how to help it happen better). Part 12: Ten keys to successful performance facilitation. *Performance & Instruction* 31:1, 36–40.

Carr, C. (1994). What do instructional technology and Human Performance Technology really do? *Performance & Instruction* 33:1, 4–6.

Carroll, J. M. (1992). Minimalist documentation. In H. D. Stolovitch and E. J. Keeps (eds.), *Handbook of Human Performance Technology: A comprehensive guide for analyzing and solving performance problems in organizations.* San Francisco: Jossey-Bass.

Coleman, M. E. (1992). Developing skills and enhancing professional competence. In H. D. Stolovitch and E. J. Keeps (eds.), *Handbook of Human Performance Technology: A comprehensive guide for analyzing and solving performance problems in organizations.* San Francisco: Jossey-Bass.

Davidove, E. (1991). The most important lesson I've learned as a consultant about the systems approach to instructional design. *Performance & Instruction* 31:10, 11–13.

Dean, P. J., and Ripley, D. E. (1997). *Performance improvement pathfinders: Models for organizational learning systems.* Washington, DC: International Society for Performance Improvement.

Deutsch, W. (1992). Teaching machines, programming, computers, and instructional technology: The roots of performance technology. *Performance & Instruction* 31:2, 14–20.

Duncan, J. B., and Powers, E. S. (1992). The politics of intervening in organizations. In H. D. Stolovitch and E. J. Keeps (eds.), *Handbook of Human Performance Technology: A comprehensive guide for analyzing and solving performance problems in organizations.* San Francisco: Jossey-Bass.

Elliott, P. (1998). Assessment phase: Building models and defining gaps. In D. G. Robinson and J. C. Robinson (eds.), *Moving from training to performance: A practical guidebook.* San Francisco: Berrett-Koehler.

Ford, J. K., and Weissbein, D. A. (1997). Transfer of training: An updated review and analysis. *Performance Improvement Quarterly* 10:2, 22–41.

Foshay, W. R., and Moller, L. (1992). Advancing the field through research. In H. D. Stolovitch and E. J. Keeps (eds.), *Handbook of Human Performance Technology: A comprehensive guide for analyzing and solving performance problems in organizations.* San Francisco: Jossey-Bass.

Fuller, J. (1997). *Managing performance improvement projects.* San Francisco: Jossey-Bass/Pfeiffer.

Gayeski, D. M. (1991a). Futures for performance technologists. Part 2: PT in emerging organizations. *Performance & Instruction* 30:2, 45–47.

Gayeski, D. M. (1991b). Futures for performance technologists. Part 3: Tools and technologies. *Performance & Instruction* 30:3, 35–40.

Gayeski, D. M. (1992). Video-based instruction. In H. D. Stolovitch and E. J. Keeps (eds.), *Handbook of Human Performance Technology: A comprehensive guide for analyzing and solving performance problems in organizations.* San Francisco: Jossey-Bass.

Gayeski, D. M. (1993a). Re-framing the practice of training, PT, and corporate communication. Part 1: Communication is what we do. *Performance & Instruction* 32:7, 36–38.

Gayeski, D. M. (1993b). Re-framing the practice of training, PT, and corporate communication. Part 4: Reduce (not just produce) information. *Performance & Instruction* 32:10, 37–40.

Geis, G. L., and Smith, M. E. (1992). The function of evaluation. In H. D. Stolovitch and E. J. Keeps (eds.), *Handbook of Human Performance Technology: A comprehensive guide for analyzing and solving performance problems in organizations.* San Francisco: Jossey-Bass.

Gilbert, M. B., and Gilbert, T. F. (1989). Performance engineering: Making human productivity a science. *Performance & Instruction* 28:1, 3–9.

Gilbert, T. F. (1992). Foreword. In H. D. Stolovitch and E. J. Keeps (eds.), *Handbook of Human Performance Technology: A comprehensive guide for analyzing and solving performance problems in organizations.* San Francisco: Jossey-Bass.

Gilbert, T. F. (1996). *Human competence: Engineering worthy performance* (3rd ed.). Washington, DC: International Society for Performance Improvement.

Gilley, J. W., and Eggland, S. A. (1989). *Principles of human resource development.* Reading, MA: Addison-Wesley.

Greer, M. (1998). *The project manager's partner: A step-by-step guide to project management.* Amherst, MA: Human Resources Development Press.

Hammer, M., and Champy, J. (1994). *Reengineering the corporation: A manifesto for business revolution.* New York: HarperCollins.

Hutchison, C. S. (1989). Moving from instructional technologist to performance technologist. *Performance & Instruction* 28:9, 5–8.

Hutchison, C. S. (1990). What's a nice P.T. like you doing? *Performance & Instruction* 29:9, 1–5.

Hutchison, C. S., and others. (1988). Leadership skills. *Performance & Instruction* 27:8, 2–5.

Jackson, S. F., and Addison, R. M. (1992). Planning and managing projects. In H. D. Stolovitch and E. J. Keeps (eds.), *Handbook of Human Performance Technology: A comprehensive guide for analyzing and solving performance problems in organizations.* San Francisco: Jossey-Bass.

Jewell, S. F., and Jewell, D. O. (1992). Organization design. In H. D. Stolovitch and E. J. Keeps (eds.), *Handbook of Human Performance Technology: A comprehensive guide for analyzing and solving performance problems in organizations.* San Francisco: Jossey-Bass.

Laiken, M. (1993). From trainer to consultant in 5 (not so easy!) steps. *Performance & Instruction* 32:10, 32–36.

Longanbach, P. (1994). *Roles and competencies of the HRD professional in a high-performance organization.* Paper presented to Skill Builder Systems, Washington, DC.

Mager, R. F. (1992a). Afterword. In H. D. Stolovitch and E. J. Keeps (eds.), *Handbook of Human Performance Technology: A comprehensive guide for analyzing and solving performance problems in organizations.* San Francisco: Jossey-Bass.

Mager, R. F. (1992b). The "T" in "PT" has got to go. *Performance & Instruction* 31:2, 57–58.

Medsker, K., and Fry, J. (1992). Toward a performance technology curriculum. *Performance & Instruction* 31:2, 53–56.

Murphy, S. E. (1987). Selling your wares: The missing PT competency. *Performance & Instruction* 26:7, 5–8.

Nichols, F. W. (1977). Concerning performance and performance standards: An opinion. *NSPI Journal* 16:1, 14–17.

Patterson, A. C. (1985). Preparing educational technologists. *Training and Development Journal* 39:12, 38–39.

Phenix, P. H. (1964). *Realms of meaning.* New York: McGraw-Hill.

Phillips, J. J. (1997). *Return on investment in training and performance improvement programs.* Houston: Gulf.

Pipe, P. (1992). Ergonomic performance aids. In H. D. Stolovitch and E. J. Keeps (eds.), *Handbook of Human Performance Technology: A comprehensive guide for analyzing and solving performance problems in organizations.* San Francisco: Jossey-Bass.

Ray, J. A., and Sword, S. M. (1993). Reengineering and human performance. *Performance & Instruction* 32:7, 29–35.

Robb, J. (1998). The job of the performance consultant. In D. G. Robinson and J. C. Robinson (eds.), *Moving from training to performance: A practical guidebook.* San Francisco: Berrett-Koehler.

Robinson, D. G., and Robinson, J. C. (1995). *Performance consulting: Moving beyond training.* San Francisco: Berrett-Koehler.

Robinson, D. G., and Robinson, J. C. (1998). *Moving from training to performance: A practical guidebook.* San Francisco: Berrett-Koehler.

Rosenberg, M. J. (1994, Apr.). *From training to performance.* Presentation at a conference of the National Society for Performance and Instruction, San Francisco.

Rosenberg, M. J., Coscarelli, W. C., and Hutchison, C. S. (1992). The origins and evolution of the field. In H. D. Stolovitch and E. J. Keeps (eds.), *Handbook of Human Performance Technology: A comprehensive guide for analyzing and solving performance problems in organizations.* San Francisco: Jossey-Bass.

Rossett, A. (1990). Performance technology and academic programs in instructional design and technology: Must we change? *Educational Technology* 30:8, 48–51.

Rossett, A. (1992a). Analysis of human performance problems. In H. D. Stolovitch and E. J. Keeps (eds.), *Handbook of Human Performance Technology: A comprehensive guide for analyzing and solving performance problems in organizations.* San Francisco: Jossey-Bass.

Rossett, A. (1992b). Performance technology for instructional technologists: Comparisons and possibilities. *Performance & Instruction* 31:10, 6–10.

Rummler, G. A., and Brache, A. P. (1992). Transforming organizations through Human Performance Technology. In H. D. Stolovitch and E. J. Keeps (eds.), *Handbook of Human Performance Technology: A comprehensive guide for analyzing and solving performance problems in organizations.* San Francisco: Jossey-Bass.

Rummler, G. A., and Brache, A. P. (1996). *Improving performance: Managing the white space in the organization chart* (2nd ed.). San Francisco: Jossey-Bass.

Silber, K. H. (1992). Intervening at different levels in organizations. In H. D. Stolovitch and E. J. Keeps (eds.), *Handbook of Human Performance Technology: A comprehensive guide for analyzing and solving performance problems in organizations.* San Francisco: Jossey-Bass.

Sink, D. L. (1992). Success strategies for the human performance technologist. In H. D. Stolovitch and E. J. Keeps (eds.), *Handbook of Human Performance Technology: A comprehensive guide for analyzing and solving performance problems in organizations.* San Francisco: Jossey-Bass.

Spitzer, D. R. (1988). Instructional/performance technology competencies. *Performance & Instruction* 27:7, 11–13.

Spitzer, D. R. (1992). The design and development of effective interventions. In H. D. Stolovitch and E. J. Keeps (eds.), *Handbook of Human Performance Technology: A comprehensive guide for analyzing and solving performance problems in organizations.* San Francisco: Jossey-Bass.

Steininger, T. (1990). Leaders: The good, the bad and the ugly. *Performance & Instruction* 29:7, 3–3.

Stolovitch, H. D., and Keeps, E. J. (eds.). (1992a). *Handbook of Human Performance Technology: A comprehensive guide for analyzing and solving performance problems in organizations.* San Francisco: Jossey-Bass.

Stolovitch, H. D., and Keeps, E. J. (1992b). What is Human Performance Technology? In H. D. Stolovitch and E. J. Keeps (eds.), *Handbook of Human Performance Technology: A comprehensive guide for analyzing and solving performance problems in organizations.* San Francisco: Jossey-Bass.

Stolovitch, H. D., and Keeps, E. J. (1998). Implementation phase and performance improvement interventions. In D. G. Robinson and J. C. Robinson (eds.), *Moving from training to performance: A practical guidebook.* San Francisco: Berrett-Koehler.

Svenson, R., and Wallace, K. (1989). Performance technology: A strategic management tool. *Performance & Instruction* 28:8, 1–7.

Tosti, D., and Jackson, S. F. (1992). Influencing others to act. In H. D. Stolovitch and E. J. Keeps (eds.), *Handbook of Human Performance Technology: A comprehensive guide for analyzing and solving performance problems in organizations.* San Francisco: Jossey-Bass.

Werther, W. B. Jr., Davis, K., and Lee-Gosselin, H. (1990). *La gestion des ressources humaines* [Human resources management] (2nd ed.). Montreal, Quebec, Canada: McGraw-Hill.

Westgaard, O. (1992). Standards and ethics for practitioners. In H. D. Stolovitch and E. J. Keeps (eds.), *Handbook of Human Performance Technology: A comprehensive guide for analyzing and solving performance problems in organizations.* San Francisco: Jossey-Bass.

Zigon, J. (1987). Marketing, not selling, performance technology to top management. *Performance & Instruction* 26:7, 9–15.

CHAPTER THIRTY-THREE

The Relevance of Standards and Ethics for the Human Performance Technology Profession

Peter J. Dean

The field of Human Performance Technology (HPT) is affected by standards and ethics even if the majority of practitioners are not aware of them. This is not to say that most practitioners are unethical, but only that they do not usually think about professional issues or their behavior in this context.

Standards are performances that can be measured and evaluated. Standards are often used in professional fields for licensing. Ethics are value-based assumptions and moral claims that have an impact on behavior (Dean, 1992, 1993, 1994). The HPT professional deals with many organizational issues (Dean and Ripley, 1997, 1998a, 1998b, 1998c) that involve values, standards, or ethics. These include the following (Cavanagh, Moberg, and Velasquez, 1981, p. 368):

- Employee rights (due process, privacy)
- Sexual harassment
- Whistleblowing
- Misuse of power
- Discouragement of intrinsic motivation
- Selection and placement
- Corporate culture
- Corporate social responsibility
- Agreed-on incentive systems versus actual systems

- Terminations
- Organizational structure, design, and politics
- Performance appraisals
- Drug testing and physical exams
- Diversity and discrimination
- Planning, policy, and control
- Government relations
- Safety and health issues
- Technical development
- Foreign payments
- Environmental protection
- Product safety and reliability
- Quality management
- Purchasing (gifts, bribes)
- Automation and robotics

STANDARDS FOR PROFESSIONS

Professions have standards to guide practice. Professions are characterized by roles, a common language, common functions, specialized preparation before practice, organizations of members, and, ultimately, by their consistent products. As a profession matures, it also includes a means of self-monitoring—a means of ensuring that its practitioners uphold professional standards and do not perform below a minimum level of competence. These standards evolve for the purpose of maintaining and increasing the credibility and accountability of those in the profession.

Recent years have seen changes in the way HPT is viewed by leaders in business and industry. More and more people are entering the HPT profession, some through in-house transfers and some through the path of career change. University curricula are also changing to reflect acceptance of HPT. This influx brings with it new and creative energy that will enhance the profession. It also brings some who are not prepared for the rigor that the role of HPT professional demands. HPT professionals require a vision within the framework of standards. Areas of performance competence and standards are essential in holding us all accountable and in ensuring that the needs of organizations and clients are being served.

To date, the only group thinking about standards for the HPT profession has been the International Board of Standards for Training, Performance and Instruction (IBSTPI) (International Board of Standards for Training, Performance and Instruction, 1988), which started as a joint task force of the International Society for Performance Improvement (ISPI) and the Association of Educational Communications and Technology (AECT). This group of academics and internal and external consultants has developed standards for instructional design, instruction, and the management of training, but standards for HPT have not yet been attempted. Whether IBSTPI (currently composed mostly of instructional designers associated with AECT) or another task force completes the HPT standards, based on core areas of competence for HPT professionals, the group working on it must be open to all views.

Some standards are obvious, falling under general criteria of "goodness." Many of the current admonitions for or against behavior fall into this category, as seen below. McLagan (1989), for example, indicates that Human Performance (HP) professionals should be aware of key standards of ethical behavior that touch on the following issues:

- Confidentiality
- Inappropriate requests
- Intellectual property
- Truth in claims
- Organizational versus individual needs
- Customer and user participation
- Conflicts of interest
- Personal biases
- Individual and population differences
- Appropriate interventions
- Consequences of interventions
- Fair pricing
- Use of power

Similarly, Westgaard's "credo" for HPT professionals (1988) lists what professional HP technologists should not do:

- Violate professional, academic, or business ethics by being less than honest in billing or by submitting low proposal bids and higher final bills
- Promise that solutions will work when the opposite may be true
- Make false claims concerning return on investment

- Use client information for personal gain
- Falsify data
- Compromise HPT for the sake of personal or political gain by providing interventions that are acceptable to the client but incorrect for the context
- Take credit for the work of another
- Make false claims about any other professional's behavior or potential accomplishments

To sum up so far, these organizational issues (Cavanagh, Moberg, and Velasquez, 1981), key standards (McLagan, 1989), and "don'ts" for HPT professionals (Westgaard, 1988) are starting points, or ethical objectives, from which a profession can begin setting standards.

Measurement of Standards

These ethical objectives may not be as difficult to measure as one might expect. A good measurement is objective-based; that is, it measures the extent to which training, management, or program objectives have been met (Mager and Pipe, 1984). The specific objectives in a competence-based professional development management system provide the criteria against which to measure accomplishments— a means of identifying which behaviors have met or exceeded the criteria, and which have not.

With the ultimate goal of creating standards, one approach to measurement, suggested by Erickson's work (1990), involves distilling performance goals into areas of competence that are addressed in training and, three to six months after training, asking trainees to describe how they would handle particular situations. The situations to which Erickson refers all involve job-related skills, but the ethical objectives being discussed here could just as easily be reinforced (Trevino, Sutton, and Woodman, 1985), especially in the decision-making realm (Trevino, 1986). Successful measurement paves the way for certification.

Certification

According to Gilley, Geis, and Seyfer (1987, p. 7), "Professional certification has been a primary issue . . . for professional societies. Consequently there has been much activity related to developing certification, credentialing, or licensing for practitioners in the field of human performance technology." As already mentioned, actual standards and measurements of those standards have not yet emerged from any HPT group, and so certification has not received much attention. No matter what one thinks about the issue of certification, however, it appears that a number of the organizations claiming to speak for the professions of training and human performance improvement have embarked on a quest that involves not just the question of whether to use certification but also the question of how to go about doing so. This external pressure for quality is consistent with the continued evolution of a profession. It is safe to say that HPT professionals will only be hearing more about this issue in the future. Because the establishment of a certification program is likely to affect all members of our profession, it is essential that we become informed about the pros and cons of certification, as well as about the standards that are very likely to serve as measures of competence.

Enhancement of Professional Credibility

One of the first things that defines a profession is the language with which its members describe what they do. This common language enables practitioners to communicate with each other about their roles and functions with some degree of understanding. This precision allows clearer communication about the field and thereby increases the degree of professional unity. It also allows the layperson to gain a better understanding of the roles, functions, and processes involved in the field and the theories that underlie them. Together, these go a long way toward enhancing professional credibility.

In establishing HPT standards, along with measures of competence, a common language must be used to describe HPT roles and functions. If the standards are to have an ethical base, then the underpinnings of ethics in the profession must be understood in addition to a language of ethics (Dean, 1993).

ETHICS OF PROFESSIONALS

Professionals representing HPT must do so from an ethical base; that is, when official standards are published, the HPT professional must endeavor to bring those standards into practice. Moreover, whether they want to be or not, HPT professionals are uniquely positioned to influence ethical awareness in the workplace. Clients place their trust in the hands of HPT professionals. With that trust, responsibility and duty become part of the task of helping improve individual and organizational performance. Understanding the basic underpinnings of ethical theory and empirical research in ethics will give professionals a grounding in the ethical implications of their interventions as they practice their craft.

One ethical question involved in the choice of a performance improvement intervention is whether it is the right one to address the performance problem or opportunity. Careful assessment and analysis of needs is the first step in identifying performance problems or opportunities. In addition to assuming responsibility for being able to apply the systems and strategies of assessment and analysis (Harless, 1973; Gilbert, 1978; Mager and Pipe, 1984; Kaufman, 1986; Rossett, 1987; Rummler and Brache, 1990; Dean and Ripley, 1997, 1998a, 1998b,

1998c; Stolovitch and Keeps, 1992), the practitioner has a fiduciary duty to be sure that the process of performance improvement being used contributes to the "organization's change goals" (Bednar, 1988, p. 31). This is to say that the practitioner must be sure that changes likely to be brought about by the intervention will be aligned with the goals of the organization.

Corporate Codes of Ethics

Traditionally, organizations establish corporate credos, codes of ethics, and ethical programs (Murphy, 1989). A credo is a statement that declares the organization's values by providing a general set of beliefs and principles. According to Sturdivant and Wortzel (1990, p. 128), "Most managers report today that the credo has a powerful influence on their decision making. It stands for day to day values."

Ethical codes are behavioral guidelines. They reflect and support the ethical values of the organization, clarify expectations, and recognize specific ethical issues. As Sturdivant and Wortzel (1990, p. 129) report, "Ninety percent of Fortune 500 firms and nearly half of smaller firms have ethical codes or codes of conduct that provide specific guidance to employees in functional business areas."

Codes of ethics are developed for a variety of reasons: to demonstrate commitment by the CEO, maintain public trust and credibility, encourage managerial professionalism, protect against improper employee conduct, define ethical conduct in light of new laws or social standards, or reflect changing corporate structure and culture (Berenbeim, 1987, p. 14). Most codes of ethics address three issues:

1. Being a good employee of the organization
2. Not doing anything (that is, taking unlawful or improper actions) that might harm the organization
3. Being good to the customer

Codes of ethics may also address other issues, in keeping with the needs of the organization (Robin, Giallourakis, David, and Moritz, 1989, pp. 66–73):

- Exhibiting standards of personal integrity and professional conduct
- Prohibiting racial, ethnic, religious, or sexual harassment
- Reporting questionable, unethical, or illegal activities to managers
- Seeking opportunities to participate in community services and political activities
- Conserving resources and protecting the quality of the environment in areas where the company operates

Although codes do establish expectations, researchers agree that, used in isolation, they have a limited effect on the promotion of an ethical environment (Berenbeim, 1987; Dean, 1992; Robin, Giallourakis, David, and Moritz, 1989).

Ethics Programs

An ethics program must be applied in conjunction with a corporate credo and an ethical code. Ethics programs most often consist of training events and communications. Some organizations use training to explain the meaning of the credo and ethical guidelines and to discuss the problems of applying those standards (Andrews, 1989, p. 102).

Ethics programs sensitize employees to ethical issues, broaden awareness of codes of ethics' directives, and emphasize the organization's commitment to its ethical principles (Berenbeim, 1987). In fact, ethical training should not be discounted, for it may be a key to establishing consistent business ethics. Training "makes ethical analysis an integral part of the company's decision-making process" (Dean, 1992, p. 288).

An organizational survey by Perry, Bennett, and Edwards (1990, p. 8) indicates that the following materials and formats are the ones most commonly used in ethics training:

- Codes of ethics (79 percent of respondents)
- Lectures (63 percent)
- Workshops and seminars (53 percent)
- Case studies (46 percent)
- Films and discussion (41 percent)

Case studies and discussions have been found most effective; "they give participants a sense of how to analyze and resolve ethical problems in a way that is consistent with the company's code or standards of corporate conduct" (Berenbeim, 1987, p. 18). Moreover, when case studies are combined with the Critical Incident Technique, participants in training actually generate information related to their organization that they can draw on later as they make decisions (Dean, 1992, p. 287).

HPT and Corporate Clients

As corporations and other groups increase their concern with ethics, HPT professionals ought to be able to help organizations, as well as their own professional associations, recognize that the ethical climate in an organization is one of the environmental factors affecting performance and productivity. For instance, the motivation of employees can be negatively influenced by the following factors:

- Inconsistent application of policies
- Lack of concern for the rights or safety of the individual
- Failure of the organization to comply with the law
- Misrepresentations to suppliers or clients

Likewise, withholding information or establishing unrealistic expectations in an attempt to gain control or power are unethical acts that damage performance output (Dean, 1993).

Another important service expected of performance improvement professionals is help in recognizing how a solution implemented at one level will affect the organization as a whole. This area of service is one of the HPT professional's ethical responsibilities. Shifting viewpoints from one level to another can increase individual decision makers' awareness of the impact that their decisions are having on their organization.

A LANGUAGE FOR THE TWO SIDES OF ETHICS

Normative ethical theories have been suggested for centuries, beginning with the pre-Socratics of the sixth century B.C., who proposed that there are various ways to classify decisions. There are two basic approaches: consequentialism (which involves results or ends) and intentionality (which involves rules or means). Each of these first principles represents a vantage point with respect to the purposes and processes of ethical decision making (Dean, 1993).

Results: Consequentialism, Utilitarianism, or Ends

Consequentialism examines the net benefit produced for all stakeholders, but primarily those stakeholders who hold stock in a company. It evaluates an action in terms of the efficiency and effectiveness of its consequences (Arthur Andersen and Co., 1992). Thus the rightness or wrongness of an action is determined by its consequences; people's rights, duties, sense of justice, and values are not of primary concern (Bentham, [1789] 1979; Mill, [1863] 1957; Sidgwick, [1874] 1966). "The end justifies the means" is an expressions used to encapsulate consequentialism.

Consequentialism suggests that planning, calculation, decision making, and evaluation can encourage creativity, innovation, productivity, and entrepreneurship. It should result in the best possible consequences for the organization's goals. These consequences maximize the satisfaction of the organization's constituencies (usually the owners).

One question that a consequentialist asks is "Which action will produce the greatest good?" To answer this question, he or she must also ask which action produces the greatest good *for whom*. In terms of how the latter half of this question is answered, consequentialism can be divided into two areas: utilitarianism and egoism (Dean, 1993).

Utilitarianism, as Dean (1993) and Ferrell and Fraedrich (1991) suggest, examines consequences to others. Business is most comfortable with utilitarian theory, which traces its roots to Adam Smith ([1776] 1937), author of *The Wealth of Nations* and father of modern economics. Although Smith wrote about utilitarianism, most businesspeople do not realize that he also wrote persuasively about duty and justice in *The Theory of Moral Sentiment,* seventeen years before *The Wealth of Nations* was published. Utilitarian theory was further defined by the research of Jeremy Bentham ([1789] 1979) and John Stuart Mill ([1863] 1957). These two men used utilitarian standards to evaluate and criticize the social and political systems of their time. As a result, utilitarianism is commonly associated with social improvement (Shaw and Barry, 1989).

There are a variety of factors, in addition to social improvement and avoidance of harm, that make utilitarianism attractive to business and industry today:

- It provides a basis for formulating and testing policies.
- It provides an objective way of resolving conflicts of self-interest.
- It recognizes the four primary stakeholders: owners, employees, customers, and society.
- It provides the latitude in moral decision making that organizations seem to need (Dean, 1993; Shaw and Barry, 1989).

Since the 1700s, Bentham has been well known for his "greatest happiness" principle: his concept of the greatest good for the greatest number of people is based on the outcome that produces the most happiness for all persons. According to Brady (1990, p. 39), "the reason Bentham was so interested in this principle is that it provided the rationale for advocating reform of laws and institutions that protected only the traditionally preferred classes of citizens, while dealing harshly with others. Tradition, he felt, often discriminated, but the greatest happiness principle did not; it gave equal weight to every individual." An additional appeal of utilitarianism is its emphasis on efficiency, which "is a means to higher profits and to lower prices, and the struggle to be maximally profitable seeks to obtain maximum production from limited economic resources" (Beauchamp and Bowie, 1988, p. 26). Each of the following areas of activity is an example of utilitarianism in business and industry today because each determines the worth of an action by evaluating the consequences for all the people affected by it (Brady, 1990, p. 21):

- Cost-benefit analysis
- Study of environmental impacts

- Majority rule
- Product comparison for consumer information
- Tax law
- Consumer behavior in the free market

Consequentialism has some obvious drawbacks. It becomes easy to overlook the ethics of the means (the behavior) that are used to achieve the actual ends (the accomplishment). In addition, the long-term consequences are often not taken into account. This could create an effect whereby the pursuit of short-term profits leads to long-term destruction of the resource base. Bok (1980) suggests that decision makers should periodically assess managerial strategies to be sure that all of the organization's constituencies are being considered, not just the owners.

Rules: Intentionality, Deontology, or Means

Intentionality is referred to as *deontology* by ethicists. It is defined as a moral philosophy that "focuses on the rights of individuals and on the intentions associated with a particular behavior" (Ferrell and Fraedrich, 1991, p. 45). A deontologist believes that the moral rightness or wrongness of an action takes precedence over and, for the most part, can be judged independently of the consequences (Baron, 1991; Wagner, 1991). Whereas the consequentialist conducts an ends analysis to determine ethical alternatives, the deontologist is more concerned with a means evaluation. In deontology, what matters is the nature of the act in question, not just its results (Shaw and Barry, 1989). Such actions as keeping a personal promise, abiding by the terms of a contract, repaying a debt, and ensuring fairness of distribution are considered "right," regardless of their consequences (Beauchamp and Bowie, 1988).

Deontology emphasizes the importance of duty and motives in making and acting on ethical decisions (Beauchamp and Bowie, 1988). Our behavior is important because it binds us to (or prohibits us from) an action (Wagner, 1991). It provides a standard of behavior through rules. The following are some common deontological practices in business and industry (Brady, 1990, p. 22):

- Distributing benefits and profits equitably
- Upholding constitutional rights
- Making decisions that are based on doctrines or codes
- Specifying hours of operation
- Wearing uniforms

Deontological practices and standards "attempt to generate a total set of expectations that seem to preserve important relations and values" (Brady, 1990, p. 22).

Establishing standards of intentionality, however, does not guarantee ethical outcomes. What it does do is provide the individual with a set of guidelines to follow in ethical decision making (Dean, 1993).

Many ethical theories have been developed from the vantage point of deontology, the most prominent of which is reason-based ethics, as explained by Immanuel Kant ([1785] 1965). Kant pursued moral principles that do not rest on consequences and that define actions as inherently right or wrong, apart from circumstantial factors. In accordance with deontological theory, Kant believed that moral rules were a result of reason alone, and that reason guides our moral beliefs (Shaw and Barry, 1989). His idea of pure reason recognizes the "possibility of discovering and knowing moral laws or principles without necessarily liking them or experiencing them, but just by recognizing their authenticity" (Brady, 1990, p. 49). For example, the statement "Lying is wrong" may be morally right whether a person likes it or not; in other words, it is unconditionally necessary to tell the truth, regardless of the consequences: telling the truth inherently possesses ethical worth. Kant's categorical imperative is composed of three basic principles:

1. *Universality.* An action is morally right for a person in a certain situation if and only if the person's reason for carrying out the action is a reason that he or she would be willing to have every person act on, in any similar situation (Velasquez, 1992, p. 80). One technique commonly associated with this principle is to ask oneself, "Would I feel comfortable discussing this action on *60 Minutes* or in front of my grandmother?"

2. *Reversibility.* The person's reasons for acting must be reasons that he or she would be willing to have all others use, even as a basis of how others treated him or her (Velasquez, 1992, p. 81). This golden rule of ethics requires one to ask oneself, in assessing an action, "How would I like it if I were treated this way?" If one would wish the same action to be taken with respect to oneself, then the action meets the requirements of the reversibility principle.

3. *Respect for persons.* "Rational creatures should always treat other rational creatures as ends in themselves and never as only a means to an end" (Shaw and Barry, 1989, p. 64). In attempting to meet this requirement, a person must do two things: respect the freedom of others by treating them only as they have consented to be treated, and develop each person's capacity to choose freely among alternatives (Velasquez, 1992, p. 81). Kant's contention is that all human beings possess inherent worth and should be treated with the moral dignity to which they are entitled (Shaw and Barry, 1989). From the perspective of deontology, people act according to such moral duties and rights of the individual. This principle of respect for a person's rights has become a theory of its own.

These two vantage points—consequentialism and intentionality—involve us in continuously examining our own sense of right and wrong and revising it, as appropriate. With just a basic understanding of each vantage point, performance improvement professionals can help their clients view their problems through a wider-angle lens.

A Seven-Step Process for Ethical Decision Making

There are many different models for ethical decision making in the literature. Most, however, contain the basic processes represented in Werhane's seven-step process (1992) for ethical decision making. Werhane's model is particularly appropriate for performance improvement professionals because it can be used as an ethical analysis embedded in a needs assessment. The process can provide an entry point for a needs assessment and can reveal aspects of the problem up front. This may even help make the needs assessment more effective and efficient. The seven steps are as follows:

1. *Identify the relevant facts.* Key factors that shape the situation and influence ethical issues must be identified.

2. *Define the ethical issues.* All issues related to the situation must be identified, and the ethical issues must be separated from the nonethical issues. Issues may be identified at all levels of the organization.

3. *Identify the primary stakeholders.* Those individuals and groups who are involved in the situation that will be affected by a decision are the primary stakeholders. A decision's impact on them must be considered.

4. *Determine the possible alternatives.* All alternative interventions need to be identified.

5. *List the ethical implications of each of the alternatives.* Each alternative needs to be evaluated according to the impact on the stakeholders and according to the two ethical theories already described.

6. *List the practical constraints.* Any factors that might limit the implementation of an alternative or render it too difficult or risky must be identified.

7. *Determine what actions should be taken.* After the information gathered in the previous six steps has been weighed, an alternative and a strategy for its implementation must be selected.

SUMMARY

HPT professionals have a responsibility to represent the latest research and standards of the HPT profession. Moreover, they are uniquely positioned to facilitate the value of ethical standards throughout the workplace. This idea has been considered under the assumption that professions have standards and that professionals have ethics. The language used in the field of ethics has also been considered. Concern for the ethical performance of HPT professionals should be embedded in the standards of HPT.

The importance of standards and ethics across national boundaries is beyond the scope of this chapter. However, Tom Donaldson and Tom Dunfee of the Wharton Ethics Program represent one resource for further investigation. Donaldson and Dunfee (personal communication, 1998) focus on international business ethics as a key factor in the longevity of a thriving global economy. They also caution (Donaldson and Dunfee, 1995), with an eye to potential clashes in value systems and cultural norms, that without ethical standards (or *hypernorms,* as they call them) business performance will suffer in global and transnational organizations. The work of Donaldson and Dunfee, together with a consideration of standards and ethical first principles, as outlined in this chapter, can serve as a foundation for embedding ethics in the standards for HPT professionals working internationally.

References

Andrews, K. B. (1989). Ethics in practice. *Harvard Business Review* 67:5, 99–104.

Arthur Andersen and Co. (1992). *Ethics for managers: Instructor's guide.* St. Charles, IL: Arthur Andersen and Co.

Baron, D. (1991). *Business and its environment.* Englewood Cliffs, NJ: Prentice Hall.

Beauchamp, T. L., and Bowie, N. E. (1988). *Ethical theory and business* (3rd ed.). Englewood Cliffs, NJ: Prentice Hall.

Bednar, A. (1988). Needs assessment as a change strategy: A case study. *Performance Improvement Quarterly* 1:2, 31–39.

Bentham, J. (1979). *An introduction to the principle of morals and legislation.* London: Athlone. (Originally published 1789.)

Berenbeim, R. E. (1987). *Corporate ethics.* Research report no. 900. New York: Conference Board.

Bok, S. (1980). Whistleblowing and professional responsibilities. In D. Callahan and S. Bok (eds.), *Ethics teaching in higher education.* New York: Plenum.

Brady, F. N. (1990). *Ethical managing: Rules and results.* Old Tappan, NJ: Macmillan.

Cavanagh, G. F., Moberg, D. J., and Velasquez, M. (1981). The ethics of organizational politics. *Academy of Management Review* 66, 363–374.

Dean, P. J. (1992). Making codes of ethics 'real.' *Journal of Business Ethics* 11:4, 285–291.

Dean, P. J. (1993). A selected review of the underpinnings of ethics for Human Performance Technology professionals. Parts 1 and 2. *Performance Improvement Quarterly* 6:4, 3–49.

Dean, P. J. (1994, Feb.). Some basics about ethics. *Performance & Instruction*, pp. 36–45, 49, 87–96.

Dean, P. J., and Ripley, D. E. (eds.). (1997). *Performance improvement pathfinders: Models for organizational learning systems.* Washington, DC: International Society for Performance Improvement.

Dean, P. J., and Ripley, D. E. (eds.). (1998a). *Performance improvement interventions: Methods for organizational learning.* Vol. 2: *Instructional design and training.* Washington, DC: International Society for Performance Improvement.

Dean, P. J., and Ripley, D. E. (eds.). (1998b). *Performance improvement interventions: Methods for organizational learning.* Vol. 3: *Performance technologies in the workplace.* Washington, DC: International Society for Performance Improvement.

Dean, P. J., and Ripley, D. E. (eds.). (1998c). *Performance improvement interventions: Methods for organizational learning.* Vol. 4: *Culture and systems change.* Washington, DC: International Society for Performance Improvement.

Donaldson, T., and Dunfee, T. (1995). Toward a unified conception of business ethics: Integrative social contract theory. *Academy of Management Review* 19, 252–284.

Erickson, P. R. (1990, Jan.). Evaluating training results. *Training and Development Journal*, pp. 57–59.

Ferrell, O. C., and Fraedrich, J. (1991). *Business ethics: Ethical decision making and cases.* Boston: Houghton Mifflin.

Gilbert, T. F. (1978). *Human competence: Engineering worthy performance.* New York: McGraw-Hill.

Gilley, J., Geis, C., and Seyfer, C. (1987, Feb.). Let's talk certification: Questions and answers for the profession about the profession. *Performance & Instruction*, pp. 7–17.

Harless, J. (1973). An analysis of front-end analysis. *Improving Human Performance* 12:4, 7–13.

International Board of Standards for Training, Performance and Instruction. (1988). *The standards: Professional reference guide to the competencies—the standards for instructors, instructional designers, and training managers.* Western Springs, IL: International Board of Standards for Training, Performance and Instruction.

Kant, I. (1965). *The metaphysical elements of justice.* (Trans. J. Ladd). New York: Library of Liberal Arts. (Originally published 1785.)

Kaufman, R. (1986). Obtaining functional results: Relating needs assessment, needs analysis, and objectives. *Educational Technology* 26:1, 24–26.

Mager, R. F., and Pipe, P. (1984). *Analyzing performance problem* (2nd ed.). Belmont, CA: Pitman Management and Training.

McLagan, P. W. (1989). The concept of responsibility: Some implications for organizational behavior and development. *Journal of Management Studies* 20:4, 411–423.

Mill, J. S. (1957). *Utilitarianism.* New York: Bobbs-Merrill. (Originally published 1863.)

Murphy, P. E. (1989, Winter). Creating ethical corporate structures. *Sloan Management Review*, pp. 81–87.

Perry, D., Bennett, K., and Edwards, G. (1990). *Ethics policies and programs.* Washington, DC: Ethics Resource Center.

Robin, D., Giallourakis, M., David, F. R., and Moritz, T. E. (1989). A different look at codes of ethics. *Business Horizons* 32, 66–73.

Rossett, A. (1987). *Training needs assessment.* Englewood Cliffs, NJ: Educational Technology Publications.

Rummler, G. A., and Brache, A. P. (1990). *Improving performance: How to manage the white space on the organization chart.* San Francisco: Jossey-Bass.

Shaw, W., and Barry, V. (1989). *Moral issues in business* (4th ed.). Belmont, CA: Wadsworth.

Sidgwick, H. (1966). *The methods of ethics.* New York: Dover. (Originally published 1874.)

Smith, A. (1937). *The wealth of nations.* New York: Modern Library. (Originally published 1776.)

Stolovitch, H. D., and Keeps, E. J. (eds.). (1992). *Handbook of Human Performance Technology: A comprehensive guide for analyzing and solving performance problems in organizations.* San Francisco: Jossey-Bass.

Sturdivant, F. D., and Wortzel, H. V. (1990). *Business and society: A managerial approach* (4th ed.). Burr Ridge, IL: Irwin.

Trevino, L. K. (1986). Ethical decision making in organizations: A person-situation interactionist model. *Academy of Management Review* 11:3, 106–617.

Trevino, L. K., Sutton, C. D., and Woodman, R. W. (1985, Aug.). *Effects of reinforcement contingencies and cognitive moral development on ethical decision-making behavior: An experiment.* Paper presented at the annual meeting of the Academy of Management, San Diego.

Velasquez, M. G. (1992). *Business ethics: Concepts and cases* (3rd ed.). Englewood Cliffs, NJ: Prentice Hall.

Wagner, M. F. (1991). *An historical introduction to moral philosophy.* Englewood Cliffs, NJ: Prentice Hall.

Werhane, P. H. (1992, July). *Corporate moral and social responsibility.* Paper presented at workshop on ethics practice and teaching, Colorado Springs, CO.

Westgaard, O. (1988). *A credo for performance technologists.* Western Springs, IL: International Board of Standards for Training, Performance and Instruction.

CHAPTER THIRTY-FOUR

Performance Consultant: The Job

James C. Robinson
Dana Gaines Robinson

In the 1980s, the job of performance consultant did not exist. This job was created in the early 1990s in a few organizations that required a role that partnered with line management and had a strong focus on performance improvement. With some early successes in these innovative organizations, the job became the topic of several articles and of the book *Performance Consulting: Moving Beyond Training* (Robinson and Robinson, 1995). Now, in the late 1990s, "performance consultant" is a job title in numerous organizations and is certainly a role in many others.

WHY THE JOB EXISTS

What forces have contributed to the demand for performance consultants? There appear to be several.

First, the globalization of business and the intense competitive pressures that it produces have resulted in a focus on people as the greatest competitive edge for organizations. Products and services can be replicated, but the collective intelligence of employees is unique to an organization. In this rapidly changing global economy, those organizations that can optimize their intellectual capital and human potential will be most successful.

Second, as leaders in today's organizations strive to maximize the capability of their employees, they have been substantially increasing the investment made in training and development. For example, over $55 billion is spent each year in developing the workforce in industrial and service organizations in the United States ("Industry Report," 1997).

Third, with these huge investments in the development of people have come increased expectations of business and industry leaders for the training and development departments in their organizations. Unfortunately, research clearly indicates that the amount of skill transfer from training efforts usually is no more than 10 percent to 20 percent (Baldwin and Ford, 1988), and so there is a need for most training and development functions to reengineer. Those functions that are most successful in this transition process base their restructuring on the concepts and techniques of Human Performance Technology (HPT). They also add two major components that result in the creation of the performance consultant's job: partnerships with business leaders, and links to business needs.

Partnerships with Business Leaders

To be truly effective, some people in the performance department must develop a partnership with the leaders of the business units or lines of businesses that are being supported. Because human performance improvement requires the allocation of significant resources beyond training, business leaders need to be guided in making some difficult decisions and allocating resources so that performance change will result. Such guidance can occur only where relationships are founded on mutual trust, rapport, and credibility. This becomes a major job output for a performance consultant and requires demonstrating in-depth knowledge of the "business of the business" and discussing with the leader (referred to as a *client* in this chapter) the business strategies, measures, challenges, and threats that are having an impact on that business unit. In addition, the performance consultant must leverage this relationship so that opportunities for working together are identified proactively, not just reactively. Successful performance consultants are both tenacious and skillful in building these types of partnerships.

Links to Business Needs

In today's world, business leaders want assurance that the efforts of performance departments will truly contribute to the effectiveness of the organization. Therefore, the performance consultant's work begins with clarification of current and future business goals of the organization. Once a business goal is defined, performance consultants work with their clients to discover what people must do more, better, or differently if the business goal is to be achieved. In this manner, the performance requirements, which are defined, are specifically linked to the business goals of the organization. This specific link between performance and business goals has great appeal to business leaders and is critical to effective performance improvement.

PHASES OF THE HUMAN PERFORMANCE IMPROVEMENT PROCESS

To understand the job of the performance consultant, it is important to acknowledge the six phases of the Human Performance Improvement (HPI) process that performance consultants use as they complete their work. The performance consultant is directly accountable for activities in some of these phases and is indirectly involved in activities for all the phases. A major role for the performance consultant is to be accountable for the client relationship throughout the entire HPI process.

Partnership Phase

Activities in this phase result in the formation and growth of strong partnerships with clients. We define *clients* as those individuals in an organization who are accountable for achieving the business goals of a business unit, a department, or the entire enterprise. As discussed earlier, these partnerships are critical to the HPI process in that trust and credibility are required if the performance consultant is to influence a client to take all the actions needed to enhance performance. The key concept regarding this phase is that these partnerships are ongoing and independent of any project, work, or intervention.

Entry Phase

The activities in this phase alert the performance department that there is an opportunity to work on a specific situation. This can be a performance problem, where current performance is substandard, or it can be a performance opportunity, where the organization wishes to enhance performance. Entry can occur in two ways. *Reactive entry* results when someone calls with a request for assistance; typically, this request comes in the form of a request for a solution, such as delivery of a training program or facilitation of a team-building session. *Proactive entry* occurs when, through discussions with clients about their business needs and strategies, the performance consultant determines that a performance need exists for which support would be helpful. Proactive entry has no preconceived solution attached; rather, it is the business need that becomes the focus. One goal of performance consultants is to shift the balance of how entry occurs so that an increasing proportion of work is identified proactively. This can occur only if the partnership with clients is strong.

Assessment Phase

The activities here are those associated with front-end analysis. They include the identification of performance requirements, presented in the form of a performance model and/or competence model. This phase also includes gap and cause analyses, which identify the specific gaps between desired performance (future state) and actual performance (current state) and the reasons for these gaps. This phase concludes when decisions are made with the client about the interventions that will be undertaken to change current performance into desired performance.

Design Phase

In this phase, the interventions are designed, developed, and piloted to ensure their effectiveness. Typically, three categories of interventions are used:

1. Learning interventions
2. Work-environment interventions
3. Client interventions

The learning interventions include developing the instructional strategy, piloting the learning process, and finalizing the learning materials. The work-environment interventions include making changes to the systems and processes that are having an impact on the performers. The client interventions include such actions as the client's communicating the business case for, and the importance of, the intervention to the target population. Clients must also actively remove obstacles and provide the resources that are required.

Implementation Phase

In this phase, the various interventions designed to change performance are implemented. An important element of this phase is clients' communication of their expectations for performance change and the benefits of the performance change, both to the organization and to the performers.

Measurement Phase

The activities of this phase actually begin with the assessment phase because measurement is really a front-end process. Baseline data are obtained during the assessment phase and are used in assessing the results of learning, work-environment, and client interventions. Measurement will identify the degree of performance change and the operational impact that has occurred. These results are shared with the client and can reveal the need for additional actions.

JOB OUTPUTS FOR THE POSITION
OF PERFORMANCE CONSULTANT

Over an eighteen-month period prior to this writing, Partners in Change, Inc., conducted research regarding the job of performance consultant. Information was obtained from a total of twenty-two organizations that employ people in the job of performance consultant. All the organizations were for-profit businesses in the United States and Canada. Added to this database was our work experience with dozens of organizations that were making the transition to a performance focus and were therefore redeploying people into the performance consultant job. From all these data, strong patterns are beginning to emerge regarding what performance consultants do, how they are measured, and how they are selected. This chapter summarizes the information we have obtained.

One interesting finding is that the job title "performance consultant" is one most frequently used, but other titles, including the ones listed here, are also used to describe the same position:

- HR consultant
- Learning consultant
- Learning and performance adviser
- Learning services consultant
- Manager of performance strategies
- Organization development consultant
- Performance improvement consultant
- Relationship manager
- Training and performance consultant

Therefore, it is not possible to discuss this job only by referencing the job title. It becomes critical to identify the outputs for which someone in the position is responsible. In this chapter, we will use the title "performance consultant" when referring to the job.

Our research and work experience indicate that the position of performance consultant is most frequently accountable for all or a combination of the following five job outputs:

1. Form and grow partnerships with sustained clients
2. Identify and qualify opportunities for performance improvement
3. Conduct performance assessments, including gap and cause analysis
4. Manage multiple performance-change interventions
5. Measure the results of performance improvement interventions

These outputs require the performance consultant to be involved at some level in all six phases of the HPI process. The performance consultant has primary accountability for the partnership and entry phases and significant accountability for the assessment and measurement phases (where accountability may be shared with a performance analyst). For both the design and implementation phases, accountability for the actual design and implementation of interventions is managed by other individuals (such as an instructional designer or a human resources specialist). However, the performance consultant often works as a macro–project leader, ensuring that all interventions are being implemented in a manner that contributes to the performance and operational changes desired by the client. Let us look at each of these outputs in more detail.

Form and Grow Partnerships with Sustained Clients

As already noted, this is a critical accountability for the performance consultant. We personally do not know of a successful performance consultant who has not formed strong, ongoing relationships with clients.

There are actually two types of clients with whom performance consultants work. *Sustained clients* are individuals who have accountability for achievement of business goals in the organization and require a partnership with a performance consultant independent of any project or intervention. These are long-term, ongoing relationships. *Project clients* are the individuals who have accountability for achievement of business goals for the specific intervention being undertaken; these partnerships are transactional in nature. To make the process of working with clients more complex, there can be client teams for a specific project—in other words, several individuals who share accountability for the business need being focused on.

What all clients have in common is the power to resource the actions needed to enhance the performance required by their specific business goals. Clients can change the work processes, modify job assignments, and provide necessary skills to people so they can perform as required. They can enhance systems, focusing on both the tangible systems (equipment, facilities, materials) and the intangible systems (policies, norms, compensation).

What sets sustained clients apart is that they are individuals with a very wide scope of responsibility who have ultimate accountability for a broad range of business goals. Forming relationships with these individuals becomes the glue to making the entire process work. We have found that performance consultants generally form sustained partnerships with people whose position titles are "president," "vice president," or "director"—clearly, those whose job it is to lead the organization. As one performance consultant told us, "You form these relationships with the top of the house."

Forming partnerships has both a strategic and a tactical element. The strategic element deals with the identification of the clients with whom a sustained partnership must be formed; then performance consultants must be assigned the responsibility of partnering with these clients. Our research at Partners in Change, Inc., indicates that a performance consultant is most often dedicated to one or more lines of business and forms an ongoing partnership with ten individuals, on the average (the range is from three to forty), within those lines of business. The key here is to ensure that all those who qualify as sustained clients are supported by a performance consultant—that no client slips through the cracks.

Our research also indicates that the amount of time a performance consultant dedicates to forming and building partnerships ranges from a low of 2 percent to a high of 75 percent; the median percentage is 20 percent—the equivalent of one day a week. The tactical aspect of forming and growing these partnerships requires the implementation of best practices, such as the ones described in the paragraphs that follow.

Demonstrate Knowledge of the "Business of the Business." This involves a keen understanding of the business goals and strategies and the external environment in which the business unit operates. It also involves knowledge of the current performance of the business unit as compared to goals and objectives. It requires staying in touch with what is happening in various sites, plants, and units. The performance consultant must feel comfortable in any discussion with business unit leaders involving current hard measures of results, the performer group's effectiveness, and/or competitive pressures. The performance consultant is expected to participate in this type of discussion, raising questions that promote insight into the performer group's readiness to support the business goals.

Serve on Task Forces with the Client Organization to Address Business Issues. Here, clients observe performance consultants providing input and adding value in interventions other than those managed by the performance department. The performance consultant's participation in a task force often enhances results for the task force because of the performance consultant's questions and perspective regarding required human performance and the factors that affect it.

Coach the Client. Effective performance consultants become guides and coaches to their clients on the performance implications of business issues. They also provide observations regarding clients' own performance and its impact on others. Clients report that they value this type of input from performance consultants because, as one client said, "It makes me pause and think in ways I have not done before."

Operate as a Single Point of Contact for the Client and Others in the Client's Organization. Line managers often complain that they must answer the same question from a variety of individuals (training managers, human resources managers, organization development consultants, quality consultants), each of whom has an interest in human performance. They also grow confused in determining who should be called for a specific need. Clients would much rather have one person in the human performance area with whom they can partner for all performance needs. Our research at Partners in Change, Inc., indicates that very innovative organizations are currently moving toward establishment of relationship managers or business advisers—people who are the single point of contact for the business unit. These individuals then bring in other human performance specialists, such as human resources specialists, instructional designers, and quality specialists, to join the project team for specific interventions.

Proactively Identify Opportunities for Performance Interventions. Here, the performance consultant initiates discussions with clients to discuss business goals and strategies. These may be planned meetings or portions of staff meetings. In these discussions, the consultant raises questions regarding any changes in human performance that may be required. Projects are identified that will engage the performance consultant and others, and that might not have been identified but for the conversation that the consultant initiated.

The effectiveness with which a performance consultant forms and builds partnerships with clients is measured in many ways. Here are some examples of these measurements:

- Results of a client satisfaction survey administered one or more times a year

- The frequency with which clients publicly acknowledge the quality of the partnership and the service being provided by the performance department

- The number of times the client suggests that colleagues call the performance consultant for support (the number of referrals made)

- The number of interventions being implemented or already implemented for the client and the client's organization

- The client's acknowledgment that the performance consultant is knowledgeable about the client's business issues, ratios, and financial reports and about their implications for the client's organization

- The types and numbers of meetings to which the performance consultant is invited by the client (for example, being asked to attend meetings that deal with business strategy and/or significant business problems)

The critical need to form strong partnership with clients cannot be overstated. Our research at Partners in Change, Inc., indicates that when performance improvement interventions fail, lack of a strong client-consultant partnership is the most frequent cause.

Identify and Qualify Opportunities
for Performance Improvement

This output corresponds to the entry phase of the HPI process. As already indicated, opportunities can be generated through either a proactive or a reactive approach. The proactive approach is initiated through planned meetings in which the performance consultant discusses business goals and strategies with each client with whom a partnership has been established. When it is apparent that a business goal will require performers to do something more, better, or differently, the performance consultant discusses the future performance that will be required of the performer group. Many times clients have not identified the required performance. Clients have often reengineered the process but have not defined the best practices required of the performers who are expected to operate within that process. This being the case, the performance consultant identifies the need to clearly define the required human performance, any performance gaps, and the causes of those gaps. The situation has now moved to the assessment phase of the work.

Needs are also identified reactively when a client calls to request solutions, often in the form of learning activities, from the performance department. In these situations, the performance consultant needs to discuss with the client what the performers must do more, better, or differently to achieve the goals that the client has in mind. Again, this discussion often leads to the need to conduct a performance assessment.

Each of these discussions requires a high degree of skill on the part of the performance consultant to "ask the right questions right." When conducting a proactive discussion, the consultant begins with questions about the business need and then moves to questions about performance requirements. In this discussion, there may or may not be a conversation about the learning or work-environment needs of the group that must perform differently.

For the management of a request that has been obtained reactively, the process is reversed. The conversation generally begins at the solution level because the request has been obtained in that manner ("I would like to build the decision-making skills of my managers"). The performance consultant's questions help the client focus on the performance needs and the business goals to which decision-making skills are linked. This can be a most challenging conversation as the consultant "pushes back" in response to the client's perceived solution.

In each type of conversation, the performance consultant is asking questions to determine which of the following criteria are true for the specific situation (when all the criteria are affirmed, it is clear that the situation has a high probability of achieving a successful outcome):

1. The performance consultant has direct access to the true client for the situation. In other words, the consultant can meet face to face with the owner of the business/performance needs to which the intervention is linked.

2. There is a business need that is of interest and concern to the client.

3. The client is seeking performance change or improvement for a group of people (not just for one or two people).

4. The client is willing to share accountability for producing the desired change—that is, the client will be an active player in the process.

5. The client will provide the performance consultant with time and with access both to the appropriate people and to documents, so that the consultant can obtain the required information before taking action to change the situation.

When any one of these criteria is not in place, the probability of performance improvement is minimal. In the entry phase of the HPI Process, a performance consultant is determining which criteria are and are not present. When a criterion is missing (for example, the client is unwilling to be actively involved in the process of producing change or will not provide time to obtain important information), the consultant discusses the limitations and risks of moving forward. Again, the need to have a strong relationship becomes clear; a strong relationship facilitates the ability to have candid, even difficult discussions in an open manner.

The time required to conduct proactive and reactive conversations with clients is included in the 20 percent of time a performance consultant devotes to building and forming partnerships. It should also be apparent that the results of either of these conversations will be enhanced immensely when the performance consultant and the client have a strong working partnership. The relationship is the vehicle for trust, rapport, mutual respect, and credibility.

Conduct Performance Assessments

These activities correspond to the assessment phase of the HIP process. Many people ask about the difference between needs assessment for training and for performance improvement. The major difference is that needs assessment for performance improvement focuses on the necessary on-the-job performance and identifies all causes of the performance gap, including learning issues, work-environment barriers, and management/client issues. Needs assessment for training focuses on deficiencies in skill and knowledge but not in performance. The following are examples of outputs for this phase:

- *Performance models* that identify the best practices needed to achieve the job outputs for a specific position
- *Competence models* that identify the skills, knowledge, and attributes required for an individual to be successful in a given job area
- *Process models* that include descriptions of effective flows of work and/or information, resulting in specific outputs
- *Gap analysis,* to determine the distance between desired performance (future state) and actual performance (current state)
- *Cause analysis,* which identifies the reasons for performance gaps (inclusive of deficits in skill and/or knowledge)
- *Data-reporting meetings,* in which the performance consultant and other project team members report on the results of the assessment and engage the client in determining which interventions will be required

We are learning that in some organizations performance consultants are expected to produce these outputs; in other organizations, a performance analyst has ultimate accountability for the assessments. However, even when there is a performance analyst on staff, the performance consultant is usually an active member of the project team and will conduct interviews, participate in the model-forming meetings, and so on.

In order to produce this output, performance consultants need to evidence strong capability in each of the following best practices:

- Forming data-collection strategies and determining which methods and sources of information will be optimal for the type of information required
- Creating data-collection instruments, including interview guides, behavioral observation checklists, and questionnaires
- Collecting data through such methods as one-to-one interviews, focus-group interviews, and questionnaires
- Analyzing raw data to identify patterns and themes
- Organizing findings into user-friendly reports that facilitate insight and discussion

Probably the most important best practice for a performance consultant in this phase is to facilitate meetings with clients in which findings are reviewed and discussed. Too frequently these meetings are managed in presentation mode, with the client permitted to be passive. The challenge is to actively engage the client in a meaningful discussion about what the findings mean and about their implications for achievement of the performance and business goals.

It is vital that the consultant let the data speak, raising insights in the minds of the clients through a questioning process—not an easy task!

Our research at Partners in Change, Inc., indicates that time spent in the output of performance assessment ranges from a low of 5 percent to a high of 87 percent. The lower percentages relate to those situations where the performance consultant is a member of a project team, or where analysis has been handed off to another person (for example, a performance analyst). The median proportion of time spent by performance consultants overall to produce this output is 27 percent.

How does someone measure the effectiveness of a performance assessment? We have found that the overriding measure is the degree to which clients will commit themselves to action and then take the actions identified by the assessment information. If an assessment concludes and no action is taken, then the assessment is really a research study; it is not being used to drive business decisions. Another criterion for the success of an assessment is that three types of interventions are at least discussed and potentially identified: client interventions, learning interventions, and work-environment interventions. The following criteria are also used to measure this output:

- Client feedback indicating satisfaction with the quality of the work and the manner in which it was accomplished

- Number of assessment contracts entered into each year (clients request services that they deem valuable)

- Models for performance or competence are validated when found to be effective through actual use on the job

Manage Multiple Performance Change Interventions

This output corresponds to the design and implementation phases of the HPI process. Most often, design and development of interventions are handed off to individuals who have expertise in the relevant specific areas. For example, design and delivery of learning interventions are often managed by instructional designers and/or instructional technologists. Interventions designed to address obstacles in the work environment may be the responsibility of multiple internal organizational specialists from a variety of functions (marketing, engineering, human resources, information technology). The performance consultant often plays the following roles in the design and implementation phases:

- The performance consultant provides continuity in the HPI process by clarifying the big picture of the entire intervention for the implementation team, as well as specific details regarding the performance assessment and the client's expectations for the project.

- The performance consultant acts as a liaison between the client and the implementation team, a role that involves informal updating of the client on the progress, challenges, and issues of the implementation team. It also involves providing the implementation team with information about the client's expectations and the client's support. This informal communication does not replace the formal project updates that the implementation team should be providing to the client, but it is an ongoing information stream that is valued by the client and the implementation team alike.

- The performance consultant brokers specific interventions to outside resources when the organization does not have the internal capability or resources to design and implement those activities. In these cases, the performance consultant often forms a contract with an outside supplier and is a key contact as the supplier designs and develops the interventions. Again, the outside supplier will make formal project updates face to face with the client. We have found that some organizations require performance consultants to spend some of their time staying current with supplier options. These organizations operate under the axiom that an unknown option is no option—the performance consultants are held accountable for knowing the options.

Our research at Partners in Change, Inc., on the time spent by performance consultants for this output ranges from a low of 5 percent to a high of 80 percent. The median time spent by performance consultants to complete this output is 25 percent. Again, it is important to stress that this time is being spent in managing, not in doing the project work. In some organizations, especially those reporting the higher percentages of time, the performance consultant is still involved in "doing" activities, such as actually designing the training or facilitating sessions; we have learned that approximately one-third of the organizations that employ performance consultants have them wear this dual hat. For two-thirds of the organizations that we have researched or worked with, the performance consultant is freed of any accountability for design and delivery.

We believe that as performance departments become more sophisticated, fewer organizations will have performance consultants both consult and provide solutions. We make this observation for two reasons. First, intervention specialists, either internal or external, are becoming more readily available. As clients become familiar with the work of these specialists, clients will feel more comfortable relying on them to perform the work rather than on performance consultants. Second, the percentage of time that performance consultants devote to the partnership phase will continually increase. Stronger relationships with clients result in more client requests for performance consultants to be engaged in strategic business initiatives and planning, independent of performance improvement projects. This leaves little time to actively conduct the work involved in interventions.

On the output of managing multiple interventions, a performance consultant's success can be measured in the following ways, among others:

- Projects' intended goals are achieved.

- Projects are completed on time and within budget.

- There is positive feedback from clients regarding the projects' effectiveness and timeliness.

- It is affirmed that the performance consultant operates in a self-managed manner, taking the initiative, as necessary, to complete work and updating the client, as appropriate.

Measure Results of Performance Improvement Interventions

This output corresponds with the measurement phase of the HPI process but includes activities from the assessment, design, and implementation phases. It also involves working with the implementation teams as they develop and implement the various learning and work-environment interventions. It goes without saying, of course, that it also involves working closely with the client.

We want to clarify what we mean by the term *measurement*. We are referring to the formation and use of reliable data-collection instruments to determine the degree of performance change that has occurred and what, if any, impact there has been on the operational indicators associated with the project. This is more than an informal conversation with the client, in which it is generally agreed that everything is working well enough; it requires the use of multiple sources of information, comparison of postintervention results with the baseline data obtained at the time of the assessment, and sharing of information with the client. The following outputs are included in this phase:

- A measurement plan that describes the purposes of the measurement efforts, the data sources and data-collection methodologies, and their reporting formats

- Identification of data sources that can provide reliable information regarding performance change, the effectiveness of the interventions, and their impact on job outputs

- Selection and design of appropriate data-collection tools, including interview guides, questionnaires, observation checklists, and documentation templates

- Collection of data in a manner that demonstrates rigor in such areas as sample size and objectivity of observations

- Analysis of data to determine data patterns, degree of change in key areas, and conclusions that actually describe the amount and direction of change resulting from the interventions

- A report to the client, in objective format, of data results, patterns, and conclusions (almost always presented in a meeting, to ensure mutual understanding and engage the client in discussion about further interventions and actions that may be required)

A key to success in this phase is the clarity with which the client, in the entry phase, has understood the importance and benefits of measuring the degree of change and its impact on performance and business needs. The effective performance consultant positions measurement as an activity that will do the following things:

- Document results that have actually occurred because of the intervention, thus providing an objective, reliable report about the value of the intervention

- Provide the client with information about what is working, what is not working, and why (the latter category of information gives the client information for taking additional actions that will continuously improve this specific intervention)

- Identify the overall success of the intervention, as well as the tools and actions that contributed to its success (so that, in the future, if a similar type of need is identified, it will be evident whether these tools should be used again or whether they will require some rework)

Many of the best practices associated with measurement are the same as those required for assessment. What is vital is that performance results be linked to the operational measures, and that the reasons be identified for any lack of results. The performance consultant also needs to include the various intervention teams and specialists in the design and planning of the measurement plan. It is important that results of individual interventions be affirmed in addition to results of the total intervention (for example, the effectiveness of a revised information system would have to be determined, as would the skills acquisition and effectiveness of coaches).

Our research at Partners in Change, Inc., indicates that only half of performance departments are systematically measuring performance change, work-environment change, and operational results. The reasons given for why resources are not expended for measurement include the fact that clients do not ask for this service. We believe that the same could be said for assessment, partnering, and many of the other outputs associated with a performance department. Initially, clients rarely do ask for these services, but they come to want them once they have experienced the value derived from them; as already noted, options that are unknown are not options. What we need are measurement systems that provide reliable information in a user-friendly, cost-efficient manner. Therefore, the challenge rests with those of us in the profession to build this type of process and form the required tools.

We have identified the following indicators for measuring the quality of a performance consultant's work in designing and implementing an impact-measurement project:

- The project has been carried out on time and within budget.
- The client is using the results to take actions that continuously improve the process of performance change with respect to the specific intervention.
- The data-collection process and instruments are reliable and free of bias.
- The client and others involved in the intervention provide positive feedback on the quality of the measurement and the information that has been provided.

PRINCIPLES GUIDING THE WORK OF PERFORMANCE CONSULTANTS

We have learned, in reflecting on the job of performance consultant and considering the five job outputs they are expected to produce, that there are principles guiding the day-to-day work of performance consultants. Each of these principles is demonstrated through multiple practices. The more these principles are in evidence, the greater the success of the performance consultant.

1. Performance consultants must be knowledgeable about the "business of the businesses" they support.

2. The most successful partnerships between performance consultants and their clients are collaborative in nature. In some instances, we all will work as experts or as "pairs of hands," but the overriding majority of our work must be completed in partnership and collaboration with our clients. The forming of strong, ongoing relationships with clients is a particular challenge to external consultants, who many times offer their services on a transactional basis and who often lack the internal networks to stay current on the "business of the business."

3. Performance consultants accept joint accountability with their clients for producing performance change. It is through the synergy of collaboration that this type of change occurs.

4. Work is done to identify and align the business needs, the performance needs, the needs of the work environment, and the learning needs before any intervention is designed or implemented. Performance consul-

tants spend a large portion of their time working on the front end of the HPI process.

5. The role of the performance consultant is to influence; the role of the client is to decide. An analogy would be a car trip in which we, as consultants, occupy the passenger seat and guide the trip while the client sits behind the wheel and steers, ultimately making the final decisions about the route, the destination, and whether we will travel together at all.

CLOSING REMARKS

We hope that this chapter has provided an in-depth view of what performance consultants do and how they work. Clearly, the job is a dynamic one, with its shape and form changing as the needs of clients and organizations change. What is known is that the job requires a great deal of both technical and relationship competence. There is also a need to feel comfortable working with ambiguity; indeed, the performance consultant often wants to create ambiguity where there has been structure (for example, when a client calls with a request for training, and the performance consultant wants to raise questions that cause the client to pause and reconsider the need for training). Once the client is less certain about what actions are needed, the performance consultant and the client may have a better opportunity to work together toward improved performance.

What is also certain is that the demand for performance consultants will grow. Many of the specialist roles associated with our profession (for example, the roles of designer and facilitator) can and will be outsourced, but there is little evidence that relationships with clients can be successfully outsourced. The internal practitioner is the individual who is in the best position to work synergistically with clients to identify and address performance goals that support business needs. The job is challenging, and there will be some disappointments for those who move into the role of performance consultant, but many rewards await as well.

References

Baldwin, T. T., and Ford, J. K. (1988). Transfer of training: A review and directions for future research. *Personnel Psychology* 41:1, 63–105.

"Industry Report 1997." (1997, Oct.). *Training,* p. 36.

Robinson, D. G., and Robinson, J. C. (1995). *Performance consulting: Moving beyond training.* San Francisco: Berrett-Koehler.

CHAPTER THIRTY-FIVE

Survival Tactics in Human Performance Technology Projects

Miki M. Lane
Gina Walker
Michael J. Peters

*M*ore, better, faster, for less. More, better, faster for less. More, better, faster for less.... Like a slave galley's drum, the words beat a tempo from the top of Anne Espi's throbbing head to the bottom of her swollen feet. For the past six months, the words had been her mantra as she struggled to bring her Human Performance Technology (HPT) project to a successful conclusion: *More, better, faster, for less.* For the past six months, Anne's family had considered her existence a rumor while her colleagues fretted for her sanity. *More, better, faster, for less.* And now the project was completed. The learners had learned, their performance had improved. But at what cost to the HPT consultant—personally, professionally, and financially? What does success mean if, in the process, the HPT consultant dies or feels like dying?

HPT practitioners, like the fictional Anne Espi, enter the business world eager to do well and to do good, only to discover themselves lost in the wilderness, their HPT training and tools woefully inadequate to the task, despite the fact that there was once a time when the profession's only tool was a penknife known as programmed instruction. Systems, processes, and media were added later on to the survival kit. Now that kit has been expanded to include a more comprehensive package of performance processes and interventions, but it is still not enough.

It is not just that HPT skills are not always valued or valuable; without them, the HPT professional is not even in the game. The tools must be constantly modified and adapted to meet the reality of the ever-shifting performance jungle.

Other knowledge and skill sets must be added—customer service, project management, financial and business acumen, knowledge of technology, political astuteness, marketing, sales—all of them critical to ensuring that practitioners stay warm and well fed during the process of plying the HPT craft. Most important, however, is the ability to apply these tools while facing the unknown challenges lurking in the uncharted territory of each new project.

This chapter deals with detecting these hidden perils to the success of projects. It differs from other chapters in this volume, where the reader will find well-researched and firmly demonstrated concepts and principles of HPT. This chapter focuses instead on a less formal body of knowledge addressing the implicit dangers of HPT projects. It represents the years of experience of its authors and their colleagues, who have trekked through the wilderness, slugged it out in the trenches, and acquired a trick or two for doing what it takes to survive and even succeed while carrying out this hazardous undertaking.

The content of this chapter draws on the responses of twenty experienced, successful HPT consultants to the questionnaire presented in Exhibit 35.1. We will refer to the accumulated wisdom of these experts as we provide examples, advice, and tips throughout the chapter.

This chapter is divided into two main parts. The first deals with bad things that happen to well-intentioned HPT professionals. It describes a host of problem situations, all too common, and offers some immediate tips for prevention and survival. The second section focuses on defining one's own personal survival and success. It offers some upbeat thoughts on how to recognize and acknowledge accomplishments. Here the reader will also find a self-assessment tool on readiness to face the realities of the organizational jungle. The chapter concludes, as one might expect, with final words of encouragement and advice.

WHEN BAD THINGS HAPPEN TO GOOD PEOPLE: WHAT CAN GO WRONG, AND WHY IT DOES

There is much danger along the HPT trail. Grizzly-bear customers terrify the eager-to-please HPT practitioner, eat the supplies, and threaten the project with budget starvation. The rapidly setting sun of schedules leaves the HPT consultant in a constant state of foreboding. The HPT process maps have no resemblance to the twisting, tortuous project paths on which consultants find themselves. The HPT scouting team constantly argues about which way is north. In short, a multitude of bad things happen to the good people who strike out on the HPT trail.

Almost every HPT professional who has survived HPT project chaos possesses a repertoire of war stories about projects from hell. Listening to them, one begins to question whether any project ever goes right. The answer is both

---

Exhibit 35.1. Questionnaire on Survival and Success Factors in HPT Projects.

Thank you for agreeing to participate in this survey. As one of the leaders in the field, your input will be very beneficial to helping others involved in HPT projects succeed in their endeavors.

Following is a list of questions that we will be asking you in our phone call. These questions are only meant as discussion points, and the conversation may lead to mutually agreed upon additional questions. We anticipate that the call should be about 20 minutes.

1. How do you measure success or failure in your HPT projects?
2. How would you measure customer satisfaction in your HPT projects?
3. How do you measure career/business success?
4. How do you measure personal success?
5. What do you do to strike a balance between your personal and professional life?
6. What kinds of things can go wrong in an HPT project?
7. How do you overcome problems that might arise in your HPT projects?
8. Can you cite an example of an HPT project that had some problems but ended up being successful? What made it successful?
9. Can you cite an example of an HPT project that was not successful? What happened? Why?
10. What are your fears when you start a new project, and how do you combat those fears?
11. Based on your experience, what concrete suggestions would you offer to:
   - People just starting out as either internal or external HPT professionals?
   - Internal training specialists wanting to move to HPT projects?
   - Experienced HPT professionals?

---

yes and no. Human performance is, after all, about humans. Inevitably, the HPT professional will encounter various aspects of the comedy and tragedy that characterize the human drama. We cannot change the nature of the human condition, but we can learn to recognize its appearance in HPT projects. What follows are descriptions of some very human factors that frequently have an impact on project success. These descriptions also include suggestions for what the HPT consultant can do about these human factors.

Contentious Customers: Love, Hate, and Power

Customers come in a wide variety of sizes, shapes, and personalities. Despite surface differences, there are many similarities. All have performance improvement needs; otherwise, they would not be calling for help. All are under pressure to perform. All require an attentive ear and frequent reassurance. Some bring their performance problems and ask for solutions; others bring prospective solutions and ask for assistance in producing them. All are looking for help—fast, cheap, effective help.

These obvious needs are not the whole picture. The experts surveyed for this chapter suggest that understanding the following aspects of client behavior will help us navigate through the choppy waters of many HPT projects:

Priorities Shift. Often the assumptions of the initial proposal will disappear; the top priority is now at the bottom, and the initial plans are now directed toward the wrong problem. Clients march to their own orders, not to the consultant's. Be prepared to react—by changing the *what, why, how,* and *how much* of the project—or find another project.

Trust Is Fleeting. Clients frequently have hidden agendas—organizational, personal, or both. Like an iceberg, these agendas may be only partly visible. Battles for power and position may underlie a request for performance improvement, and the assistance of HPT professionals is often used to serve the requirements of these hidden agendas. In many ways, HPT consultants are pawns in someone else's chess game. And understanding of this reality, both in concept and in practice, should guide the selection of the results to be achieved and the services to be rendered. It should also guide the marketing and relationship-building strategies. Even if clients do not have hidden agendas, many key players believe that they are present and act accordingly. Suspicions about the most innocent acts are common.

The Dog Ate My Homework. Clients rarely understand the implications of their failure to meet their own requirements. They may also be loath to pay the consequences (in time, money, or results) of that failure.

Clients Are the Center of Their Universe. Few clients really understand what the HPT consultant is trying to achieve. They view things from their own familiar perspectives. In any given organization, for example, marketing professionals typically believe that perception is reality, whereas engineers tend to hold the opinion that reality is perception. Meanwhile, salespeople and customer service representatives know the two are not the same but may try to convince customers otherwise. From their vantage point, HPT professionals try to reconcile the differences between perception and reality. It can be a difficult road.

All these aspects of behavior can give rise to a variety of situations that make clients appear contentious. Each situation engenders a form of resistance that may test the HPT practitioner's mettle. A client's resistance may also increase as problems become more discernible and as rational solutions begin to present themselves. If solutions are new and different, they may be perceived as threatening. If they are familiar and well tested, however, they may be viewed as unimaginative. Only the best HPT marketers can sell solutions as being both tried and true and boldly creative. The following example is a case in point; look for evidence of resistance in this true and very typical story.

"So Much to Do, So Little Time!"

As an internal HPT consultant in a large pharmaceuticals firm, Verna has been called in to the drug testing division to help the management team (one vice president and four assistant vice presidents) develop individual and divisional objectives for the upcoming fiscal year. Given the culture of the organization, all the members of the management team have either doctorates or medical degrees. They are usually out of town overseeing their respective research projects.

Verna schedules an initial meeting with the vice president to discuss the project and review the previous year's objectives. At the meeting she learns that the team has recently consulted with another professional, this one external, to address the same issue. Apparently there were some problems with the external consultant, and nothing of substance was accomplished. After briefly reviewing the previous year's objectives, Verna discovers that they have not been stated in performance terms and are based mainly on activities rather than on results. She schedules a meeting with the entire team to discuss her findings and ways in which she and the team can work together to formalize the upcoming year's objectives.

The meeting, scheduled to last from 9:00 to 10:30 A.M., begins half an hour late. The vice president then proceeds to spend the first forty-five minutes of the meeting discussing team business. Verna is left with fifteen minutes for her one-hour presentation. She uses this quarter-hour to discuss objectives and to schedule two types of subsequent activities. One is a three-hour group training session on objectives. The other consists of meetings with individual team members to work on their specific objectives.

When Verna arrives to conduct the three-hour training program on objectives, the vice president informs her that she has only one hour to work with the group. She mentally restructures the session and manages to deliver it within the allotted hour. The group has many questions, but they are cut short by the vice president. Verna arranges a follow-up meeting to discuss the group's revised objectives.

The vice president calls Verna to cancel this session. In doing so, he states that the group has learned a great deal from the previous session and that the revised objectives are right on target. He thanks Verna for her excellent consulting work.

Two weeks later, Verna has the opportunity to review the group's revised objectives. She notes that, although there is definite improvement, they clearly still require additional work.

Scenarios such as this one are played out all too frequently on the HPT stage. At times, overcoming resistance is easy and spontaneous. At other times, it requires a cool head and thoughtful inquiry. What can the HPT consultant do? Here are some expert tips on dealing with clients' resistance:

1. Recognize that resistance will occur, and identify it as soon as it is displayed. Expect it and prepare for it.

2. Accept as normal those client behaviors that short-circuit the HPT consultant's best efforts and plans. In fact, worry if they do not occur. Surface acquiescence may mask deeply rooted opposition.

3. Help clients acknowledge their resistance. Point out what is happening— how certain decisions will have a negative impact on desired results. Encourage clients to acknowledge that their behaviors are a form of resistance, and help them identify why the resistance is occurring.

4. Do not take clients' resistance personally. Knowing that clients, however unwittingly, may act to obstruct a project's success should result in a certain detachment on the part of the HPT consultant, which can provide a basis for guiding clients toward more productive behaviors and outcomes.

The following suggestions from our twenty HPT experts are aimed at keeping contentious clients on track:

1. Plan carefully. Prepare yourself with information and a strong suit of armor. Planning provides the best means of avoiding potential pitfalls, power plays, resistance, and sudden twists and turns.

2. Set up a problem-solving process early in the relationship, even at the initial meeting.

3. Establish indicators of success and progress milestones early. Return frequently to these, as well as to the documented objectives of the project. Keep the client's eye on the targeted accomplishments.

4. Stop your activities if the client seems to withdraw from the project. Do not proceed without the client's commitment.

5. Identify the key motivators of the client team members, and continually stress these motivators.

6. Do your homework on the business context of the project. Relate business goals and characteristics to the current project.

7. Keep the perspective that the HPT practitioner's job is to make the client look good.

8. Maintain clear, concise, results-oriented communication with the client. This is of particular significance in international projects, where perceptions and language play critical roles.

9. Remember that process is as important as outcome, especially in cross-cultural projects. Build trusting relationships that facilitate problem solving.

The HPT practitioner should expect every client to become contentious at some point. The consultant's survival depends on his or her being prepared for these moments, dealing with clients diplomatically and firmly, and then wisely guiding contention back to cooperation.

Budget Battles: When Dollars Don't Make Sense

Every HPT professional should become immediately suspicious upon hearing that money "is not a problem." Money is *always* a problem; for example, the rule for home renovation is that it always takes three times as long and costs twice as much as the best estimate. Without clearly defined budgets based on sound, proper calculations of personnel and direct costs, and without firm controls, HPT projects are soon headed toward the reefs.

As arrogant as this may sound, few clients understand what it takes to carry out an HPT project. What HPT professionals do is change behavior to attain desired accomplishments. This effort is not easy, and it is seldom cheap. It takes time and resources to create interventions that will efficiently and effectively achieve results. The projects that pose the most dangerous threats to the HPT practitioner are those characterized by the following situations:

- No formal budget has been created; the budget is informal and open-ended. Beware. One day, someone in authority will demand an accounting. When there are no concrete, implementable products in evidence, reactions to expenditures on analysis and design are usually negative and angry.

- A large overall dollar amount has been earmarked, but the scale of the project really requires additional funds. Many external HPT consultants are particularly vulnerable on this score. A contract for several hundred thousand dollars is hard to resist, and yet the number one killer of small consulting firms is the underbudgeting of projects. If the dollars (no matter how many) do not make sense, major disaster may be looming.

- The scope of the project has not been clearly defined; only the overall budget is clear. But all projects change in scope, usually through the addition of unforeseen components (for example, new target audiences, more content, multiple variations, extra travel, and more expensive media). What might have appeared feasible under the initial budget is now impossible without more funding. Despite their own increased or enlarged demands, client organizations seldom understand why more money is required, and they frequently resist requests for increased funding.

Any of these situations can turn an exciting HPT project into a financial nightmare. What can be done? Right at the outset, HPT practitioners must emphasize value rather than cost and must educate clients about the potential for return on investment (ROI) in HPT projects. Stewart (1997), Edvinsson and Malone (1997), and Phillips (1997) have demonstrated, very forcefully, the high yield from investment in human capital. Robinson (1990), Phillips (1997), Stolovitch and Maurice (1998), and Swanson (see Chapter Thirty-Nine, this volume) have shown that human performance (HP) projects frequently provide ROI ratios of 10:1 and higher. The HPT practitioner must learn to demonstrate how appropriate budgeting can result in high returns, thereby countering clients' incredulity at what it really costs to bring about performance improvement. Cutting corners may save pennies but can result in huge dollar losses. The following true case demonstrates this principle clearly.

"I Can Get It Cheaper . . ."

The airline was excited that it was at long last updating its ticketing software. Under the new system, tremendous increases in efficiency would be realized, especially at ticket counters and boarding gates. The updated system, radically different from the previous one, required retraining of ticket counter and gate personnel. The airline called for proposals to develop the training. The two finalists were an HPT firm and a traditional training firm. The HPT proposal recommended a variety of interventions, including environmental redesign, job aids, a simulation database, on-site support, and several others, in addition to the training of supervisors and staff. Although the airline viewed the proposed approach as comprehensive, it also considered its budget prohibitive—twice the amount of the training firm's budget. Result: the training company was hired. Its development budget was immediately reduced because the new system had encountered serious cost overruns. Training time was also cut from eight to four hours per person, to reduce training delivery expenses. When the new system went live, many of the personnel, despite the training, were incapable of dealing with the endless streams of passengers. The resulting chaos, which caused delays, angry battles with passengers, extreme bad will all around, and ridicule in the press, led to an estimated $100 million loss for the company. (The "good news," of course, was that the company had saved two hundred thousand dollars in training and its implementation.)

A simple moral emerges from this case: clients cannot have "good," "cheap," *and* "fast"; they get only two of these at a time. If the purpose is to achieve the desired results within a reasonable period of time, it will cost the client in time and resources. "Chainsaw" cost cutting, without commensurate changes in deadlines, activities, or results, is a clear signal for the HPT professional to run for cover.

Here are some tips, based on responses to the questionnaire in Exhibit 35.1, from experienced HPT practitioners:

1. Before you write a proposal, make sure that the client has budget approval.

2. Copyright the proposal. Include a confidentiality clause. Some clients use proposals to shop around for lower quotes.

3. Educate clients on the costs involved in HPT projects. They rarely understand what it takes to effect significant change.

4. Specify the project's scope in your proposal, even if it is an assumed one. Get agreement on the assumptions, and control the project so that it remains aligned with the agreement.

5. Add a contingency clause to the budget, asking for a range of from 15 percent to 30 percent of the budget for unforeseen events, changes, and delays. This adjustment permits slight but not major changes in the project's scope. (Some consultants add a 50 percent contingency.)

6. Do homework on what other HPT professionals charge for similar work, and verify work ratios (for example, number of work hours per deliverable hour; percentage of time/budget allocated to project management).

7. Maintain meticulous logs of work hours and records of expenses. This keeps the client informed, educates clients for future projects, and helps in estimating future work.

8. Keep the client's expectations realistic. If the budget is fixed, reduce the scope. If the scope is fixed, increase the budget, or have the client do more with internal resources.

There are also ways to manage budgets efficiently and keep costs in line. The following are additional tips derived from responses to the questionnaire in Exhibit 35.1:

1. Manage the client's expectations at each phase of the project. Focus on the feasible.

2. Manage the client's obligations to the project. Establish timetables for project meetings and reviews. Clarify resource requirements far enough in advance to avoid costly delays.

3. Manage changes in scope. Because even minor adjustments can have major budgetary implications, inform the client about the change-of-scope cost and corresponding rationale. Obtain written approval for increases in the budget before proceeding.

4. Manage the client's understanding of the HPT process. Lay it out clearly. Provide a strong rationale for each step. Explain costs and benefits in a way that is meaningful to the client.

5. Manage the client's communications with superiors, customers, and other stakeholders. Help keep the content of these communications realistic so that impossible (and expensive) promises are not made.

6. Do not reinvent the HPT wheel. Use models, templates, and technology to reduce activities and costs.

In summary, manage the project closely—its budgets, timelines, resources, deliverables, and events. Enhance the probability of your survival by partnering with the client to create viable budgets and reasonable deliverables.

Schedule Skirmishes: Black Holes in the Space-Time Continuum

In HPT projects, as in nature, time can warp activities and results. In recent years, the external pressures of competition and the nanosecond life span of products and technology have drastically reduced the amount of time available to complete an HPT project. The advent of personal computers, faxes, overnight shipping, and e-mail has further encouraged the compression of project timelines. Projects that used to take six to nine months to complete are now due in two or three months or even less time.

The situation is worsened by two factors: human performance requirements are generally thought of late in a major organizational change event, and clients do not realize how long it actually takes to accomplish performance goals. Although it has been almost everyone's experience that things always take longer than anyone imagines, very few people seem to apply this knowledge to new ventures. Why are schedules usually off, and usually right from the start?

Vision Without a Plan. Many clients are "big picture" thinkers, as are some HPT consultants. The vision of what can be achieved may blind us to the mundane activities required to get there. Implicit tasks, not always accounted for in the scheduling process, include negotiating resources; taking account of vacations, illnesses, major organizational events, the inaccessibility of key subject matter experts (SMEs), and team formation; resolving conflicts with other scheduled activities; finding test subjects; and conducting other routine project management tasks. When these tasks are not planned for, the result is disappointment and frustration as the minutiae accumulate and add to the project's time requirements. An incomplete plan will soon deviate from set timelines.

Expansion of the Project's Scope. Like the universe, HPT projects are constantly expanding. As a project progresses, new ideas occur: Perhaps other populations can benefit from this work. Why not include more products? Can't the entire global community be involved? Different versions using a variety of media could be produced. Each bright idea, from the addition of one more reviewer to the change in definition of a key concept, alters the scope—and warps the timeline.

Competing Client Priorities. Clients do not revolve around the HPT project; the project revolves around them. Clients and SMEs have other commitments and priorities, which can wreak havoc with a timeline. Wait for approval, and the project comes to a halt; move ahead, and the result may be wasted effort and rework.

The Invisible SME. The unavailability of SMEs is one of the biggest destroyers of timelines. Knowledgeable people who can provide content and access to resources are frequently in high demand among others besides HPT consultants. Scheduling adequate time for these individuals' input or review is often a major headache and a serious disturber of the disturber.

The Black Hole of Review. Almost all respondents to the questionnaire shown in Exhibit 35.1 cited this as a major contributor to schedule delays. HPT deliverables, created in a frenzy of activity, are submitted for review and disappear from sight. Reviewers, overwhelmed by the demands of travel and other commitments, do provide feedback, but often too little, and often too late. To proceed without proper buy-in and go-ahead is dangerous; to delay is threatening to the project's success.

The Wishful Schedule. Too often, schedules reflect wishes and not reality. Even experienced HPT consultants guess wrongly about how long a task will take. Many have a tendency to think heroically—"It should take me only two days to do this"—forgetting that it took many more days the last time. Experienced professionals also create timelines that are based on how long it may take them to do something, without considering that others with less experience may require additional time.

The Law of Cumulative Delays. Consultants and clients are often equally guilty here. A delay in the analysis report or in the production of prototype material may mean that an SME or reviewer, having made a commitment to a date that is now past, is no longer available. Delays in the client's or organization's completion of tasks can disrupt the workflow of the HPT consultant and the project team. Delays are unavoidable, of course; the goal is to minimize them so that they do not become fatal. The following survival tips are meant to ensure continued life and health for projects and HPT consultants alike:

- Create time-and-action calendars and RASCI matrices (see Exhibit 35.2). A RASCI matrix shows all the players involved in a project, as well as the tasks to be performed. *R* stands for responsibility for the performance of a task. *A* stands for approval authority. *S* stands for support, *C* for consultation, and *I* for informing those who must be kept informed. If anticipated time requirements (in hours or days for each task) are included, people can plan their time accordingly. As this chapter has already emphasized several times, planning is important. HPT projects generally involve a number of people (clients, intervention developers, SMEs, line managers, reviewers, target population representatives, desktop publishers, union officials), and each individual requires clear guidelines for when he or she must do something, what the task requirement is, and how long it will take. It is also useful for everyone involved to know the overall timeline, what others have to do, and their specific deadlines. Many planning systems exist, but we have found two tools to be the most useful: the RASCI matrix (see Exhibit 35.2) and the simple Gantt chart. Most HPT practitioners are familiar with Gantt charting; Exhibit 35.3 presents a sample Gantt chart. It lists tasks and timelines in weeks. The numbers in parentheses represent projected person-days for the task, and anticipated and actual times can easily be tracked. There are also software packages that incorporate Gantt charts, as well as other planning systems. The Gantt chart and the RASCI matrix form the basis for generating individual time-and-action calendars. These can be adjusted weekly, according to the project's progress.

- Hold a kickoff meeting with all the involved parties. A kickoff meeting, where expectations can be set, the process to be followed can be reviewed, and roles and responsibilities can be agreed on, is key to building a project team. The presence of an organizational sponsor can add luster to the event. The consequences of not meeting milestones and deadlines should be reinforced at this meeting. Follow-up minutes or a memo will reinforce the importance of this event.

- Provide weekly updates on the project's progress. Use a standard template to document progress, and communicate it to the project team. Add congratulatory notes for on-time, high-quality accomplishments. Raise red flags where delays are occurring, and suggest corrective actions. As we HPT professionals are constantly telling our clients, clear expectations and timely feedback improve performance.

- Help clients understand the consequences of scheduling delays. The experienced HPT consultant anticipates timeline problems. Clients are not always aware of the consequences of their actions. As soon as a scheduling delay that is due to a client's or client organization's activities rears its head, signal it to the client, along with possible consequences. An ounce of proactive problem solving is worth pounds of reactive schedule scrambling. A simple ABC mnemonic for schedule management is *anticipate, bargain, communicate.*

Exhibit 35.2. Sample RASCI Matrix.

Activity	Client	HPT Consultant	Development Team (2)	Customer Service Representatives (4)	Field Managers (2)	Desktop Publishers	Graphic Designer	Union
				Participants				
Analyze mandate for client services	A / 2	C / 4	R / 20	C / 10	C / 10			I
Develop new mandate	S / 2	S / 2	R / 16	C / 4	C / 4			I
Verify new mandate	A / 2	I	R / 16	C / 4	C / 4			C / 2
Analyze total inventory of client service tasks	C / 4	C / 8	R / 24	C / 36	C / 10			I
Create new task inventory		S / 2	R / 24	C / 10	C / 8	S / 8		C / 3
Evaluate new task inventory	A / 2	C / 2	R / 16	C / 16	C / 8			C / 2
Review staffing and staff organization		C / 4	R / 16	C / 4				I
Develop staffing strategy and organization	A/C / 4	S / 2	R / 24	C / 8	C / 4	S / 16	S / 8	I
Verify staffing strategy and organization	A / 4	S / 2	R / 24	C / 8	C / 4			I

Note: Numbers in cells represent estimated number of hours to complete activity.

Exhibit 35.3. Sample Gantt Chart.

Activity	Timeline (Weeks)											
	1	2	3	4	5	6	7	8	9	10	11	12
1. Analyze task interferences (12)	├──┤											
2. Create task elimination/ redeployment list (8)			├┤									
3. Eliminate/redeploy tasks (6)				├──┤								
4. Evaluate task elimination/ redeployment results (8)						├────┤						
5. Analyze job (9)	├─┤											
6. Create new job description (8)		├─┤										
7. Implement new job description (7)				├┤								
8. Evaluate impact of new job description (8)					├────┤							

Process Perversions: Creating Chaos out of Order

Examine any HPT process model. It is orderly and aesthetically pleasing. Unfortunately, real-life HPT projects are not. The process model is the map; the project is the reality of the trip.

HPT is about changing organizations. The model says that rational managers rationally make rational decisions about their businesses. There is an expectation that orderly change will occur, and that gains from improvement will be realized. HPT models neatly lay out what must be done to create the necessary performance improvement (also known as *change*)—and all this in spite of past experience to the contrary.

The logical flow of analysis, design, development, implementation, and evaluation is easily disrupted by the daily drama of human events, as the following case illustrates.

"We are Certifiable . . ."

A CEO announced with pride that senior management was committed to the certification of sales representatives. To encourage increased professionalism in sales, and to show the market that this company was and would be a leader in technology, all the company's sales reps were to become certified in four key areas over the next twelve months. Press releases and fanfare accompanied the announcement.

In the trenches, sales managers huddled over the implications of this widely touted initiative. Senior management's directive was simple and straightforward: Determine the certification requirements; train; test; report the results to the CEO. The HPT consulting team was to make it happen—analyze, design, develop, and so forth.

It would be impossible for the near future, however, to arrange a kickoff meeting with the sales managers who were assigned to the project. Worse, the end of the quarter was in sight, and sales figures were down. Still worse, it was rumored that a number of high-producing sales representatives were upset over the announcement and threatening to leave. Just to complicate matters, a preliminary estimate of the time that would be needed for certification training in the four key areas showed that the minimum would be twenty days per sales rep, and, given pressure from the market, managers were already resisting the idea of release time for training. Moreover, a recently published research study circulating through the sales force suggested low to negative correlations between sales and certification of sales reps.

The client responsible for the project was uncertain whether the organizational climate was ideal for interviewing and talking with sales personnel. Couldn't the HPT team just pull stuff together? Couldn't they begin by building a test bank with multiple-choice questions? Whatever happened, this client said, some kind of concrete progress, complete with numbers, had to be generated within three months.

The path of HP analysis, intervention design, and implementation is seldom smooth, and the expression "You can't make an omelet without breaking eggs" applies well to HPT projects. Performance improvement means no more doing it the old way. Therefore, unless everyone is convinced that the new way will be better, in all likelihood there will be project slowdowns, blocks, and, in extreme cases, sabotage (Rogers, 1995).

Despite the maelstrom that is reality, however, some HPT consultants insist on attempting to make the HPT process model work by the book. Step by step, they move against the current, performing each task in sequence according to a prespecified, unalterable plan. Admirable as this tenacity may seem, it serves no purpose if the process is right but the product and the outcome are wrong. The HPT process and its models are meant to serve as guidelines; they were never meant to be rigidly applied. They suggest the right road to follow, but the sage advice of experienced travelers has always been to exercise "intelligent flexibility." Successful attainment of the desired outcome often lies in applying the spirit of the process with integrity.

How does one survive and thrive on chaos? Once again, our twenty questionnaire respondents offer their counsel:

- Know your client organization. HPT projects do not take place in a vacuum. Wise HPT professionals take systems theory to heart, along with the law of maximization—that is, you cannot maximize a subsystem and the whole system simultaneously, and so, in practical terms, the creation of a perfect project will not bring about the result of a perfect whole organization. Optimization is necessary: doing the best you can in the overall organization while disrupting other affected subsystems as little as possible. This requires careful study of the larger organization and the influences and events that affect it. If the HPT professional understands the client organization, there is greater probability that a workable (if not the best) set of improvement interventions will be created.

- Know your client's sacred cows, and then, as Kriegel and Brandt (1996) suggest in *Sacred Cows Make the Best Burgers,* eliminate those that are counterproductive. Specific groups and persons may be "protected species"; certain terms, values, and practices may be venerated; particular kinds of behavior may be frowned on. If the HPT professional is ignorant of these usually implicit (because no one ever mentions them) customs, objects of veneration, or taboos, the performance improvement project may be quickly derailed, and the practitioner may be left bruised as well as stymied over what went wrong. To become aware of sacred cows and factor them in, create trusting relationships with members of the client organization. Ask people to list what they think an outsider might miss. If in doubt, question and verify before you act. The HPT process is easily undone by unconscious faux pas.

- Do not go it alone. Performance improvement projects almost always require a team effort. The relationship of the HPT consultant and client should be a partnership (Bellman, 1998). Explain the HPT process clearly, without jargon, to the client and other stakeholders. Justify what the process demands. Build buy-in to the process. When obstacles appear, solicit input. Fresh perspectives can lead to breakthrough problem solving when the HPT process appears to be in jeopardy, as the following case illustrates.

Access Denied

Irma was fuming. How could she possibly design appropriate interventions if she could not speak to members of the target audience for her analysis? It wasn't fair!

Once again, her friend Fatima kindly explained that in this country women could not interview men privately; it was not done.

"But how will I uncover their real perceptions, with examples of how things are currently done?" Irma wanted to know. "I need details. I understand the language. A written survey won't do it for me! I have to probe."

"What if you trained my brother Hamid to conduct the interviews?" Fatima offered. "You already have your interview protocols prepared. He studied sociology and has a good sense of organizations from his work as a manager. We'll have him record the interviews, with permission, and you can listen and transcribe. If you have more questions, he can go back and ask them."

• Build a strong supportive network of colleagues. Besides the client and the team, other HPT professionals can be of immense assistance. With access to the Internet and e-mail, a performance consultant can have a worldwide support system.

• Adopt the client's point of view without losing the HPT perspective. Organizations create environments, adopt ways of viewing the world, and build processes that, over time, become institutionalized. These are no longer consciously thought about; they just are. To an outsider, they may appear illogical and outdated and may create barriers to efficient performance consulting. Examples given in the questionnaire responses include the following institutionalized barriers:

• Rigid hierarchies that force specific chains of communication

• Absence of confidentiality (bosses always have the right to know everything)

• Committee-based decision making, with no decision if one committee member cannot decide

• Refusal to accept an intervention because "that has never been done here"

• Rules about processes (for example, "No evaluation permitted") that conflict with HPT

Any or all of these barriers can disrupt or bog down the work of the HPT consultant; head-on confrontation rarely succeeds. In these cases, viewing the world through the client's and the organization's eyes can help the HPT practitioner understand what is happening and why the HPT process is creating problems. From this vantage point, mutually acceptable solutions may emerge, as in the following case.

Alpha-Beta Soup

Jorge had been arguing with his client for nearly two weeks, explaining the need to do "real learner" tryouts; testing the new course on managers, experts, and trainers would simply make no sense.

"But we always hold alpha and beta tests," the client protested. "During the beta test, we always bring in managers, subject matter experts, and trainers. If they approve the course, we can implement it."

But these managers, experts, and trainers were not the intended audience. As passionately as Jorge argued, however, his client remained adamant.

"It has always been done this way," the client declared. "It is part of our process. The beta test must be carried out with this knowledgeable group in order for the course to be accepted."

Impasse?

Jorge, in some despair, turned to his client and asked, "Would it be acceptable for me to conduct some informal, small-scale testing of the modules—with,

say, two to four people—before the beta test, just to see how real learners perform with them? Nothing major. I just want to see how the materials fly before
you beta test."

"No problem," the client replied. "You want a few of the workers to practice
with the modules before the beta test? I'll call some of my supervisors. I'm sure
we can round up some people for you. Just as long as I get my beta test!"

Slight repositioning and an acceptance of the client's perspective may be all
it takes to continue toward the goal.

Inaccessible Expertise: Stalking the Elusive SME

Virtually every HPT project requires the input of SMEs in order to succeed. HPT
professionals rarely know enough about context and content to operate on their
own, and there is seldom enough documentation, if it exists at all, to satisfy
project requirements. According to the nature of the project, SMEs may be
needed to describe the organization and how it functions, explain processes and
outputs, or provide technical content.

But true SMEs are as rare and elusive as many endangered species. Hunting
them down and capturing them to get all the right information is one of the
most exasperating and difficult tasks of the HPT consultant. Moreover, caution
is required even when the client provides SMEs. Are they the right ones? Is what
they have to say current enough and credible enough for the HPT consultant to
rely on? Will the SMEs be available in a crunch? Many other questions also arise
in dealings with SMEs: Will they agree with each other? Is there one SME who
has ultimate subject matter authority? Do the SMEs understand the needs of
HPT? Can they think the way novices do? Are they comprehensible?

The HPT consultant must be aware that SMEs do not usually see themselves
as being paid to act as SMEs for HPT projects; their priorities are generally elsewhere, and the HPT project is often viewed as a nuisance—a drain on precious,
overcommitted time. When it comes to WIIFM—"What's in it for me?"—most
SMEs attribute low personal value to HPT-type projects. They perceive their own
rewards as deriving from their "real" work, where they are recognized for their
knowledge and skills by those whom they value, and the organization usually
agrees with them.

It is dangerous to depend on a single SME, who may suddenly go into hid-
ing or be captured by "more important priorities." Sometimes the best SME is
a team of SMEs. A team does increase the "herding cats" problem for an HPT
consultant, but this arrangement offers several advantages: diversity of expertise, more access to expertise, validation when there is uncertainty about content, and additional reviewers when these are necessary.

Another SME danger involves what SMEs know and what they believe others should know. Most expertise is acquired through trial and error and through

practice; it is rarely communicated in words. For example, if you ask a friend to explain how she maintains her balance on a bicycle, she will not be able to give you an explanation, even though she never falls off her bike. Experts cannot always articulate what they know how to do. As a result, they frequently create explanations that are incomplete or even inaccurate. Observation and verification are needed to validate the input of SMEs. SMEs also often believe that neophyte performers need to know "everything"; as a general rule, however, SMEs omit information that is important for novice performers but include information that is irrelevant. Paradoxical formulations are also not unusual with SMEs.

Finally, SMEs may be so elusive that they do not even exist. Sometimes, strange as it sounds, no one really knows the subject, and the HPT consultant is suddenly thrust into the uncomfortable role of winging it, as in this anecdote from an actual project.

Can It Be Done?

Val was getting really concerned. Her job was to prepare usable documentation and job aids for new accounting and payroll personnel on the legacy systems that had evolved over the past eighteen years. She had been given several SMEs, but each time she had consulted with them, she had come away with little of substance. Yes, they did use the legacy systems to do their own jobs, but they could never answer the hard-core questions she asked. Worse, they argued among themselves, and no consensus was forthcoming.

Val had to complete the segment on payables reports. In desperation, she spent two days exploring and experimenting, and she prepared eight different sample reports. Now she faced the SMEs and presented her samples. She asked if the reports had been accurately produced and if the procedures were correct.

Several minutes of silence ensued as the SMEs pored over the documents. And then there was pandemonium.

"How did you create these reports?"

"These reports are *great!*"

"Can you show us how to do them?"

Here, as taken from the questionnaire responses, are some sage tips for dealing with SMEs.

• Beware of clients bearing gifts. It may sound like a gift from the universe when a client says, "I'm giving you Bob as your SME. He's not busy, so you can have him on this project." Be cautious: true SMEs are in such high demand that one who is not busy may not be worth having. He or she may lead you in the wrong direction, with concomitant loss of your time and credibility. Be appreciative of the offer, but check out the SME's qualifications and work style. An elusive SME who knows something is still better than an accessible, incompetent one.

• Check for the completeness of the SME's knowledge. Some SMEs are great but narrow in the scope of their knowledge. They may represent the whole from a biased, partial perspective. Verify not only the depth of the SME's knowledge but also its breadth with respect to the project. As necessary, obtain complete subject matter expertise from several sources.

- Check the SME's credibility and reputation. The HTP project depends on the credibility of its content. If the SME is not credible or not respected, chances are that reviewers, implementers, and perhaps even the targeted performers will view the project outputs with suspicion. Check out the SME's "believability index." If it is low, determine who is believed and respected, and get those people's fingerprints on the gun.

- Have the SMEs speak with one voice. There is a saying that with two SMEs you get at least three opinions. When you are working with a team of SMEs, create a procedure for reaching consensus, or have the client designate an SME spokesperson who resolves differences, approves revisions, and accepts responsibility for content.

- Hold an SME kickoff meeting. Face to face or by phone, long or short, the SME kickoff meeting is necessary for establishing contact information and ground rules, which will involve accessibility, review-cycle time, methods for reaching consensus, and decisions on who speaks for the SME team with the voice of final authority. Setting the ground rules early, explaining the implications of delinquent behavior, and building commitment to the project will reduce the SME-related hazards over the life of the project and improve your chances of success.

- Prune SME content with the shears of necessity. SMEs generally include more information than performers will need in order to achieve appropriate levels of mastery. Do all twenty-seven of the variations that one might encounter have to be included? Can they be appended somewhere? The true story that follows is an example of SME overkill.

Natural Gas

For twenty minutes, Carlos explained the workings of gas lamps to eighteen trainee field service reps. He took a lamp apart. He showed them different types of gas lamps. He explained the principles of the gas lamp. Finally, he distributed job aids in the form of worksheets and directed the trainees, working in pairs, to disassemble a lamp and perform an intricately prescribed set of procedures on it before replacing its glass globe. Using the job aids, the nine pairs of trainees worked on the assigned task. After another twenty minutes, all had managed to accomplish it. At the end of the training session, Carlos called for questions.

"Carlos, how often will we get to do this in the field?"

"Not often," replied Carlos. "In my thirty-two years with the gas company, I never had to do it. Once, though, I did see a long winding driveway lined with dozens of gas lamps leading to a mansion. It was a spectacular sight!"

"Where was that?" one of the trainees asked.

"On a vacation I took in Venezuela."

- Focus on the performance objectives. Constantly verify whether the content provided by SMEs is necessary and/or sufficient for the desired performance levels to be met.

- Use SMEs and others to help gather documentation. An SME's inaccessibility may leave the HPT consultant with little recourse other than finding answers in documents. The more that has been collected, the more independent the consultant can become. When the SME's accessibility is a critical factor, use the SME to verify and edit rather than generate material.

- With SMEs, make the most of media. Record SMEs' demonstrations and explanations on audiotape or videotape. The HPT consultant does not even need to be present if structured questions or guidelines are used. The consultant can then review the tapes and return to the SMEs with further questions, as necessary.

- Get the materials that SMEs use in presentations. Most SMEs have to give presentations at various times. Ask for copies of their presentation materials. They provide content and clues about what the SMEs consider important. Also get copies of articles and presentations that SMEs have found useful, and ask the SMEs to highlight critical information if they have time.

- Observe exemplary performers in the presence of an SME. Ask the SME to provide commentary, pointing out what is happening and why. Explanations and descriptions of real-life events clarify performance issues and tend to focus on subtleties that make the difference between ordinary and extraordinary performance.

- Have SMEs review only clean drafts of project work. The job of the SME is to provide and validate content. Sloppy drafts, with errors in grammar and spelling, distract from the main task. Not only may the SME feel obliged to engage in editing, he or she may question your credibility if the presentation of your work is inadequate. Make your drafts clean enough to keep the SME focused on content.

- Manage SMEs and their time efficiently. Assume that SMEs have other priorities besides your project. Minimize their time on the project. Provide time-and-action calendars for them. Make efficient use of their face-to-face time with project team members. Provide specific directions and job aids to facilitate their tasks (writing cases, creating lists of procedures, writing solutions, reviewing documents).

In summary, SMEs are crucial to most HPT projects. They are elusive, their knowledge is often incomplete, and they are frequently impatient because of the pressure of other work. Effective management of SMEs, their activities, and their inputs and outputs can make the difference between success and failure for an HPT project.

DEFINITIONS OF PERSONAL AND PROJECT SUCCESS

Up to this point, this chapter has focused on what can go wrong in HPT endeavors, on the consequences of these events, and on what the HPT professional can do to maintain sanity, survive, and even achieve success. The chapter now turns to the fundamental question of what success is in HPT practice.

A reasonable definition of personal success is "project success." After all, if the project achieves its desired goals, hasn't the HPT consultant also achieved his or hers? The achievement of project goals, however, is in the eye of the beholder.

Success for the Client

The client generally has some specific agenda with respect to the HPT project: to attain organizational objectives, to contain the project's budget, to please the boss, to move up a rung on the ladder of career success, to gain credibility, to obtain more knowledge about HPT, to create fundamental change. If the project succeeds but the client is dissatisfied about not having accomplished some targeted personal goal, then the overall success of the project may be diminished.

Success for the Targeted Performers

The client may be delighted with the project's results, but the targeted performers may be left dissatisfied. Short-term gains in productivity that come at the cost of long-term resentment may be too expensive. Impressive, immediate results can turn into a slow, lengthy hemorrhage that costs a company dearly. For example, quick gains through the reductions in labor costs that have resulted from downsizing have often led to a company's inability to meet demand in a fast-turnaround market. HPT is based on the goal of improving performance in a way that is valued by everyone affected by the change.

Success for the Consultant

The operation was successful, but the doctor died; this twist on an old saw is not unheard of. It can come about from burnout (giving so much that the price of the project's success is the consultant's exhaustion), life imbalance (the work went well, but the consultant's family deserted), financial ruin (all the eggs were in one basket, and all other business has dried up), or loss of integrity (everybody is happy, but a lot of principles had to be abandoned). Success is relative and often confusing.

Success in General

The HPT consultant must decide and define what constitutes success, not just for the client and other stakeholders but for himself or herself personally. Methods of measuring success must be created and implemented, sometimes in spite of the client's lack of interest in collecting evaluative data. True personal success in HPT projects comes from knowing what success means for everyone involved and obtaining evidence that the project is indeed a success.

Here, taken from the questionnaires, are some brief tips on success:

1. Get all the key players to articulate up front what success will look like.
2. Focus on concrete indicators of success—indicators that are directly tied to key business needs.
3. Get the stakeholder team to propose meaningful measures of success along with a means of collecting data.
4. Build into any set of success measures those measures that involve good project management.

In assessing success, the consultant should also consider less formal but equally important indicators. These include unsolicited compliments about project processes and results, interest on the part of individuals and groups that did not participate in the project, subtle internal changes triggered by the project, and requests for repeat business. Over the longer term, the success of the project, of the HPT consultant, and of the stakeholders is reflected in evidence that the project's solution has become part of the organization's culture, in changes in clients' vocabulary and perspective, and in indications that high returns have been realized on the resources invested in the project. Here are some ways of obtaining this kind of information:

1. Identify external, objective reviewers who can validate the project's results.
2. Push for transfer and payoff evaluation data.
3. Conduct a project-review meeting with the client to gather evidence of accomplishments.

An important aspect of customer satisfaction is leveraging it when it has been attained. This not only validates the project's success but also enhances the results of this success for everyone, including the HPT consultant. Here are some tips for leveraging satisfaction:

1. Obtain referrals from clients, or ask if they will serve as references.
2. Encourage clients to publicize the projects' successes in newsletters and other promotional material.
3. Invite satisfied clients to new-client meetings, where they can share their successes; testimonials from credible sources are a convincing

way to obtain a new client's buy-in, third-party endorsements are powerful destroyers of barriers with new and inexperienced clients, and this sort of invitation reflects well on the satisfied client and creates a strong ally for the future.

Career and Business Success: Where to Go from Here?

Whether they work internally or externally, HPT professionals should always be seeking to enhance their career and business success. What success means varies with the individual. For one, it may involve the impact on corporate needs and culture of the work that has been accomplished. For another, it may be the ability to pick and choose desirable projects. For still another, it may be money, clients' respect, or invitations to partner with exciting clients.

Recognition from professional peers and respected organizations can also enhance one's sense of success. This kind of recognition may take the form of professional-society awards, positive feedback from colleagues about the quality of one's work, publication in journals, opportunities for service, and election to office in HPT professional organizations. Success may also be measured in terms of professional growth, which can take the form of pushing beyond the normal scope of professional work, adding new areas of competence, or mentoring HPT interns and graduate students.

Here are some tips for enhancing personal career and business success:

1. Write articles for clients' newsletters.
2. Submit articles to professional journals.
3. Give presentations at professional conferences.
4. Participate in professional-society committees.
5. Contact the editor of the business section of the local newspaper to report on HPT successes.
6. Guest lecture at universities, or mentor a student intern.

On the specific issue of business success, we offer three pieces of advice gained from our accumulated years of practice:

1. *Take the cash, and let the credit go.* The HPT consultant serves the client organization in achieving the results it seeks. For this work the consultant is paid. Making the client and the client organization look good is wise business practice. Let them receive the public accolades.

2. *You can't sell price, and you can't buy time.* Clients and their organizations seldom understand why HPT projects have to cost as much as they do. Any price is too high. Therefore go for value. Present a worth analysis, with estimates of potential ROI. Show how the costs of the project pale in comparison

with its benefits. Worth is value compared to cost. Sell value. At the same time, establish realistic timelines for the project's and your own personal success. Clients rarely accept how long it takes to complete HPT projects, and they will push to cut timelines. But HPT consultants must never sell themselves short. Time cannot be bought back.

3. *Once integrity is lost, you can't buy it back.* Know when to walk. Some projects are political, idiosyncratic, unrealistic, or unethical. They require the HPT consultant to make compromises that debilitate and corrupt. A professional sells two commodities: competence and integrity. If the project calls for competence beyond the scope of the HPT consultant, or if it may jeopardize his or her professional or personal integrity, then the consequences should be carefully weighed. No sum of money is worth the loss of integrity. Selling one's integrity is a bad business proposition, at any price.

HPT projects have a way of becoming all-consuming. In their desire to serve clients well, HPT consultants run the risk of serving themselves poorly. Sixty-, seventy-, and even eighty-hour work weeks can become a way of life in today's high-pressure environment. Over the long term, this kind of schedule is a prescription for disaster. Here are some tips on how to get a life—and keep it:

• Serve, but do not be a servant. As consultants, HPT professionals do work whose very nature is service. HPT professionals have a process but no content. They use HPT to achieve the performance improvement desired by the client and the organization. Internal or external, the HPT consultant is responsible for making it happen in a way that meets the client's expectations and shows the client off to best advantage, but good will and professional ethics and behavior can become a noose with which a demanding client can strangle the consultant. Therefore, serve generously while maintaining reason and balance. Establish limits and processes for decision making and problem solving. Serve, but as a partner in the performance improvement venture.

• Come to terms with FUD: fear, uncertainty, and doubt. The question "Can it be done?" arises at some point in nearly every project. Fear, uncertainty, and doubt are normal signposts. Acknowledge them, put them in their place, trust the process, and proceed.

• Take a long view of short-term crises. Nobody ever died from an HPT project. Crisis, disaster, and surges of adrenaline can overwhelm perspective and balance. The truth is that most HPT projects end successfully, although never perfectly. Step back from the crisis of the moment to regain perspective.

• Make personal life a priority. Schedule personal time as if it were part of a project. No HPT project is more valuable than your personal and family time. Therefore, make official projects of vacations, time with your family and friends, and relaxation time. Write them into your calendar, and make them immovable. Make your work projects accommodate your personal time rather than the other way around. In the long run, this healthy attitude will contribute to more effective and efficient work results.

• Calculate what your financial requirements are, and work to meet them. Making money costs time, and taking time costs money. HPT consultants only earn when they work, so strike a balance between taking time and making money.

CONCLUSION

This chapter was written for practicing HPT professionals by practicing HPT professionals, with input from twenty additional senior, very successful HPT professionals. Its purpose was to provide advice derived from years of practice and to share an array of tactics for surviving and succeeding in the HPT consulting business. In conclusion, we offer an HPT survival self-assessment (see Exhibit 35.4). Take the assessment, and ponder the results. This is not a scientific instrument; rather, it is intended to stimulate your thinking and perhaps trigger some changes that will contribute positively to your consulting work and your personal life. We also offer the following list of suggested readings, which may help you improve your chances of survival and success. Live long and prosper in the exciting HPT universe!

Exhibit 35.4. Self-Assessment of Business Survival Skills.

Complete each of the following sentences with the phrase that best represents your typical response.

1. When evaluating a project, I consider it to be a success if:
    a. the client is happy
    b. it meets client objectives as well as time and budget requirements
    c. it meets not only client requirements but also HPT professional standards

2. When assessing client satisfaction, I:
    a. accept client comments as the major indicators
    b. probe the client to identify possible differences in our perceptions
    c. use bottom-line indicators, such as the request for repeat business and unsolicited referrals

3. I consider an intervention to be effective if:
    a. the performer enjoys and values what has been created
    b. the performer applies what has been created to the job
    c. application of what has been created translates into improved bottom-line results

Exhibit 35.4. Self-Assessment of Business Survival Skills, cont'd.

4. When reflecting on how I am viewed by my fellow practitioners, I would say that I:
   a. maintain a low professional profile, with few of my colleagues aware of my work
   b. enjoy a positive reputation for producing high-quality work
   c. project the image of a contributer to the field, receiving requests to participate in the professional community (to write articles, serve on professional committees)

5. In terms of selecting project work, I:
   a. reject projects that require me to go beyond my experience and current skill level
   b. accept projects that push me beyond my normal scope of activities
   c. seek out projects that offer opportunities for expanding my repertoire of professional skills

6. In defining personal success, I focus on the achievement of:
   a. financial awards
   b. professional accomplishments
   c. a balanced integration of high professional achievement and a personally rewarding lifestyle

7. In dealing with the challenge of achieving balance in my life, I find it:
   a. easy to leave work at work
   b. difficult to leave work at work
   c. almost impossible to draw the line between work and personal life

To score yourself:

- If you chose 4 or more "a's" as a response to the questions, you are probably a cautious type and have taken few personal or professional risks. You need to acquire a few survival skills to be able to handle the tougher challenges that lie in wait for you.

- If you chose 4 or more "b's", you have attained a degree of survival savvy that will serve you well in your future forays into the unknown. You still have a distance to go, though, if you want to master the wilds.

- If you chose 4 or more "c's", consider yourself in the ranks of the expert practitioners whom we surveyed in researching this chapter. You are in the company of the greats.

Suggested Readings

Bell, C. R., and Nadler, L. (eds.) (1979). *The client-consultant handbook.* Houston: Gulf.

Bellman, G. (1990). *The consultant's calling: Bringing who you are to what you do.* San Francisco: Jossey-Bass.

Bermont, H. (1983). *Psychological strategies for success in consulting.* Washington, DC: Consultant's Library.

Block, P. (1981). *Flawless consulting: A guide to getting your expertise used.* Austin, TX: Learning Concepts.

Cockman, P., Evans, B., and Reynolds, P. (1992). *Client-centered consulting: A practical guide for internal advisors and trainers.* New York: McGraw-Hill.

Cohen, W. A. (1985). *How to make it big as a consultant.* New York: AMACOM.

Coscarelli, W. C. (1995). "Flawless consulting" for the external consultant. In G. L. Anglin (ed.), *Instructional technology: Past, present and future.* Englewood, CO: Libraries Unlimited.

Dougherty, A. M. (1990). *Consultation: Practice and perspectives.* Pacific Grove, CA: Brooks/Cole.

Gallessich, J. (1982). *The profession and practice of consultation.* San Francisco: Jossey-Bass.

Garratt, S. (1991). *How to be a consultant.* Aldershot, Hampshire, England: Gower.

Gebelein, S. H. (1989). Profile of an internal consultant: Roles and skills for building client confidence. *Training and Development Journal* 3, 52–58.

Gilley, J. W., and Coffern, A. J. (1994). *Internal consulting for HRD professionals: Techniques and strategies for improving organizational performance.* Burr Ridge, IL: Irwin.

Golembiewski, T. (ed.). (1992). *The handbook of organizational consultation.* New York: Dekker.

Greenbaum, T. L. (1990). *The consultant's manual: A complete guide to building a successful consulting practice.* New York: Wiley.

Hansen, J. C., Himes, B. S., and Meier, S. (1990). *Consultation: Concepts and practices.* Englewood Cliffs, NJ: Prentice Hall.

Holtz, H. (1983). *How to succeed as an independent consultant.* New York: Wiley.

Keeps, E. J., and Stolovitch, H. D. (1992). *Consulting—stepping out: A guidebook to transform internal specialists into external consultants.* Montreal, Canada: Erica J. Keeps and Harold D. Stolovitch.

Kelley, R. E. (1986). *Consulting: The complete guide to a profitable career.* New York: Scribner.

Kubr, M. (1993). *How to select and use consultants: A client's guide.* Management Development Series, no. 31. Geneva, Switzerland: International Labor Office.

Lippitt, G. L., and Lippitt, R. (1978). *The consulting process in action.* San Francisco: Jossey-Bass/Pfeiffer.

Margerison, C. J. (1988). *Managerial consulting skills: A practical guide.* Aldershot, Hampshire, England: Gower.

Markham, C. (1993). *The top consultant: Developing your skills for greater effectiveness.* London: Kogan Page.

Metzgar, R. O. (1993). *Developing a consulting practice.* Thousand Oaks, CA: Sage.

Nelson, B., and Economy, P. (1997). *Consulting for dummies.* Chicago: IDG.

Pinto, J. K., and Slevin, D. P. (1987). Project success: Definitions and measurement techniques. *Project Management Journal 2,* 67–75.

Robinson, D., and Robinson, J. C. (1995). *Performance consulting.* San Francisco: Berrett-Koehler.

Stolovitch, H. D., Keeps, E. J., and Rodrigue, D. (1995). Skill sets for the human performance technologist. *Performance Improvement Quarterly* 8:2, 40–67.

Tovar, M., Gagnon, F., and Schmid, R. (1997). Development of a consultation profile perceived as successful by Human Performance Technology consultants. *Performance Improvement Quarterly* 10:3, 67–83.

Weinberg, G. M. (1986). *The secrets of consulting.* New York: Dorset.

Weiss, A. (1992). *Million dollar consulting: The professional's guide to growing a practice.* New York: McGraw-Hill.

References

Bellman, G. (1998). Partnership phase: Forming partnerships. In D. G. Robinson and J. C. Robinson (eds.), *Moving from training to performance: A practical guidebook.* San Francisco: Berrett-Koehler.

Edvinsson, L., and Malone, M. S. (1997). *Intellectual capital: Realizing your company's true value by finding its hidden brainpower.* New York: HarperBusiness.

Kriegel, R., and Brandt, D. (1996). *Sacred cows make the best burgers.* New York: Warner Books.

Phillips, J. J. (1997). *Return on investment in training and performance improvement programs.* Houston: Gulf.

Robinson, D. G. (1990). *Training for impact: How to link training to business needs and measure the results.* San Francisco: Jossey-Bass.

Rogers, E. M. (1995). *Diffusion of innovations* (4th ed.). New York: Free Press.

Stewart, T. A. (1997). *Intellectual capital: The new wealth of organizations.* New York: Doubleday.

Stolovitch, H. D., and Maurice, J.-G. (1998). Calculating the return on investment in training: A critical analysis and a case study. *Performance Improvement* 37:8, 9–20.

CHAPTER THIRTY-SIX

Influencing Others to Act

Donald Tosti
Stephanie F. Jackson

There are two primary ways to get things done: do them yourself, or get others to do them with you or for you. The first approach offers near-complete control but severely limits how much you can accomplish. The second approach requires giving up some control but offers virtually unlimited scope for accomplishment. This chapter focuses on the second approach to getting things done—influencing others—and has two purposes:

1. To analyze three sets of "influencing" behaviors: leadership, teamwork, and partnering

2. To illustrate the application of Human Performance Technology (HPT) to the analysis of complex and heavily covert performances

Leadership, teamwork, and partnering have been analyzed, discussed, and described in many ways: in terms of personality traits, skill requirements, impact on others, stylistic preferences, or some combination of these. HPT takes a functional, or performance-based, approach to this analysis and description. Instead of asking what good leaders, team members, and partners are like, HPT asks what purposes they accomplish and how. The functional approach has two significant benefits:

1. It is results-oriented. It emphasizes the results expected of good leaders, team members, and partners rather than emphasizing the people themselves or the subject matter.

2. It provides a useful framework for reconciling apparently contradictory phenomena. For example, Winston Churchill and Mohandas Gandhi were both acknowledged leaders but with very different traits, behaviors, and styles. Making sense of the wide differences among leaders is facilitated by scrutiny of their actions in light of the purposes or functions those actions serve. Examining complex performances in this way makes it clear that very different behaviors may accomplish the same purposes with different populations, environments, or conditions.

Influence behaviors are critical both to the effectiveness of organizations and to the effective execution of HPT projects. An authoritarian, bureaucratic approach to organizational performance can be effective, but it works best in stable, homogeneous environments against competition that takes a similar approach. An authoritarian approach is, in effect, an attempt to approximate the "do it yourself" approach to performance at the organizational level—and the conditions that once made it workable no longer exist. The need to work across geographic and cultural boundaries and adapt to rapidly changing conditions requires both the effective use of influence and a clear understanding of purposes and functions.

Similarly, HPT practitioners are seldom if ever able to dictate (as opposed to influence) the activities of others. Effective practice of the HPT craft can require working as a member of a project team, working in close partnership with client personnel or other HPT teams, or leading other practitioners' efforts.

An additional reason for examining these performance areas is their complexity. They are heavily covert, "alternate route" performances. Some behavior is not directly observable, and there may be many different ways to accomplish the same, or very similar, tasks. In the past, this fact apparently caused some HPT practitioners to avoid these performance areas or to view them as "arts" that were not amenable to the precise behavioral analysis that has characterized many HPT efforts. Microanalysis of complex behaviors like leadership is in fact impractical, and precision of measurement is difficult. Nevertheless, the difficulty of obtaining *perfect* precision does not mean that we should not try to achieve *greater* precision.

INFLUENTIAL BEHAVIORS: SIMILARITIES AND DIFFERENCES AMONG LEADERS, TEAM MEMBERS, AND PARTNERS

The phenomena of leadership, teamwork, and partnering are interrelated. Many of the skills and behaviors of a good leader are also useful to good team members and partners. The following differences lie in the role of the influencer and in the primary purposes for which those skills and behaviors are used:

- Leadership involves influencing the performance of individuals or groups from a position of authority.
- Teamwork involves influencing the performance of a group from the position of a working member.
- Partnering involves influencing the performance of two distinct groups from a position inside one of the groups.

Figure 36.1 briefly summarizes the relationships among leadership, teamwork, and partnering. Subsequent discussions of each phenomenon offer greater detail. Because space prevents a full discussion of all three areas, we decided that this chapter will emphasize leadership and partnering.

The figure assumes that leaders can be effective whether or not they are also strong team members or partners. (Writings about Gandhi and Churchill suggest that the former had some ability to work as a team member; the latter, little or none at all.) Team members can be more effective if they are also able to perform leadership functions, but good teamwork does not require it. Similarly, partners can act more effectively by adding leadership and teamwork functions to their capabilities.

FUNCTIONS OF LEADERSHIP

Organizations and groups of people are complex systems for getting work done. The functions of leadership, then, are to see that the key needs of the system—that is, people's key work-related needs—are met so that they can produce optimum

Figure 36.1. Key Functions of Leaders, Team Members, and Partners.

	Core Functions	Supporting Functions	
Leader	Direction Motivation Guidance		
Team Member	Support Shared participation Trust	Direction Motivation Guidance	
Partner	Respect Shared risk Openness	Support Shared participation Trust	Direction Motivation Guidance

results. There are three basic needs common to such diverse groups as a tribe of hunter-gatherers, a basketball team, the executive committee of a corporation, and a mob storming the Bastille:

1. *The need for a common direction.* Examples would be "bring in the harvest," "make the goal," and "free the prisoners."

2. *The need for motivation.* This is the need for a reason to work with others toward a common direction. Without motivation, individuals may fall away from the group or may focus on meeting their own needs at the expense of the group's. The executive committee will be ineffective if its members are concerned solely with their own personal advancement; the tribe of hunter-gatherers may starve if individuals eat all the berries they find without saving or sharing.

3. *The need for some kind of guidance.* Both the group and the individuals in the group need to know whether they are on track and what they can do if they are not. The mob storming the Bastille will be helped by knowing where the gates are left unguarded; the basketball player will be helped by advice on how to get into the open to receive a pass.

The discussion of these three functions is grounded in years of psychological research and theory. Basic to all living organisms are the needs for a signal to act, for some kind of reward or reason for taking action, and for ongoing feedback to adjust or guide behavior. The same functions have parallels in systems theory. For example, an analogy could be drawn between the leader of a group and the driver of an automobile: the driver provides direction (knowledge of where he is going), provides motivation by operating the gas pedal, and provides guidance by using the steering wheel. The behaviors of a group leader and a driver are very different, but the functions they perform are the same.

When one person provides some or all three of these functions—direction, motivation, and guidance—in a group or organization, that person is usually called a *leader.* Thus the fundamental functions of leadership and its associated results are as follows:

- *Direction:* People's activities and behaviors are focused on desired common outcomes.

- *Motivation:* People invest appropriate effort in working constructively to accomplish the desired outcomes.

- *Guidance:* People receive and act on information that improves their ability to accomplish the desired outcomes.

Although this functional description of leadership differs from descriptions found in much literature on the subject, it is not incompatible with those descriptions; the greatest difference lies in the use of functions or purposes to organize the description. Bennis and Nanus (1985), for example, describe leadership in terms of four "strategies," five key leadership skills, and their effect (empowerment) on followers, but most if not all of the content of that description is encompassed within the three functions described here.

The functional view assumes that leadership is not inherent in the individual; it is neither a set of traits nor something people are born with. Rather, leadership is something one provides to a group to meet certain needs. It is defined by the relationship between the leader and the group, and it encompasses both the leader's behavior and its effect on the group.

In executing leadership functions to improve the performance of individuals or a group, there are two generic strategies a leader can adopt:

1. Take what exists, and make it work to its fullest capacity.
2. Change what exists to make it work better.

The first strategy represents the "master mechanic" approach. Mechanics do not redesign a car; they tune it, clean it, and supply it with the best parts and fuel to make it work to its fullest potential. The second strategy represents the "master inventor" approach. Inventors dispense with the existing order and design something new. The inventor approach is clearly riskier, but sometimes it is well worth the risk. In HPT terms, the difference between these two strategies is analogous to the difference between solving performance problems and identifying new opportunities to improve performance.

Both strategies are legitimate in particular circumstances, and they are not incompatible. For example, in the process of making something work better, people often find ways to change it. In the process of trying to redesign something, people may find a way to make the original item work better. A leader may operate in either or both of these modes.

Other writers (Burns, 1978; Zaleznik, 1977) have made the same distinction between leadership strategies. Burns, for example, labels these two approaches *transactional* and *transformative* leadership. He describes the transactional approach (improve what you have) as characteristic of management, and the transformative approach (change it) as the key to leadership. We prefer to avoid this kind of leader-manager distinction, for two reasons. First, it suggests that leadership consists primarily in changing what exists, a definition that limits the applicability of the concept. Second, the creation of a sharp contrast between leaders and managers may suggest that one cannot be both, and it often leads people to consider one better than the other. Bennis (1990), for example, takes the leader-manager separation to an extreme in an article that extols the virtues of leaders and leadership behavior, in part by denigrating managers and management behavior.

An HPT approach should begin with the assumption that, given the right circumstances and support, people can often learn to exhibit the behavior of leadership, management, or both. To do otherwise is to place unnecessary and usually inappropriate limits on people and their capacity to perform. Kotter (1990) and Georgiades and Macdonell (1998) take approaches to leadership and the leader-manager distinction that are more compatible with HPT.

Whether one takes a transformative or transactional approach to leadership, the need to perform the functions of direction, motivation, and guidance does not change. The difference lies primarily in the form of behavior used to accomplish each function.

The lists in Tables 36.1 and 36.2 show examples of how the behavior of a leader would differ from transformative to transactional mode. Nothing about these lists suggests a need to distinguish between different types of people. It is quite possible for one person to perform both kinds of actions—simultaneously, in some cases. For example, leaders (or managers) could readily communicate high expectations (transformative leadership) while setting objectives (transactional leadership).

The practices of successful leaders are often called *competencies* because they represent the skills and knowledge required for getting results through leadership. We prefer to avoid this term, however, and simply refer to leadership *practices*. Our reason for this preference is that the term *competency* tends to focus people exclusively on the use of skill development to ensure good leadership, but our experience is that successful leaders do not necessarily have greater skills than others; rather they use leadership practices with greater ease and frequency. The issue is not so much one of knowing what to do and how to do it as one of practicing and developing confidence in a variety of situations so that the behavior of leadership becomes comfortable and habitual.

For example, one key leadership practice is keeping people informed of the "big picture." Most people in a leadership position know how to do that. The most effective leaders are those who have incorporated this behavior into a near-automatic repertoire so that they not only review the big picture at formal

Table 36.1. Transactional Versus Transformative Leadership Strategies.

Leadership Function	Leadership Strategies	
	Transactional Emphasis	Transformative Emphasis
Direction	Goals and objectives	Vision and values
Motivation	Recognition and rewards	Expectations
Guidance	Feedback	Modeling

Table 36.2. Sample Transactional and Transformative Leadership Practices.

Behaviors Emphasized by Transactional Leadership	Behaviors Emphasized by Transformative Leadership
Setting clear, measurable objectives	Communicating high expectations
Meeting performance standards	Living up to potential
Establishing procedures and systems to guide and support the work	Establishing principles to guide priorities and decision making
Dealing with existing systems in a practical, realistic way	Looking for opportunities to do things better
Getting the work done	Getting ready for the future
Making use of knowledge based on experience	Taking new and different perspectives
Taking action	Communicating a picture of the future

meetings but also make regular reference to it in daily interactions, and in a variety of ways. In leadership as in many other kinds of complex performance, skills and knowledge are necessary but not sufficient; fluency of behavior is often what differentiates the best from the rest.

FUNCTIONS OF TEAMWORK

In analyzing teamwork, a key issue is identifying what it takes to effectively exert influence as a member of a team when one is not the designated leader and when one has no direct authority over other people. Reports of studies (for example, Potter-Brotman, 1988) to identify the practices distinguishing highly effective influencers indicate that effective influence practices are clustered under three major functional areas:

- Providing support through clarity so that people have consistent expectations about the process and structure of the working relationship
- Building and maintaining trust so that people are willing to consider and act on one's information, judgments, and commitments
- Encouraging shared participation so that all members of the team contribute effectively and efficiently to the outcome and feel that they have had an impact

Table 36.3 gives examples of behavioral practices that contribute to each of these functions.

Table 36.3. Sample Teamwork Practices.

Support	Trust	Shared participation
Clarifying team members' roles	Providing information accurately and openly, without hidden agendas	Contributing one's own ideas and suggestions
Confirming the nature of team and individual commitments	Talking about groups or individuals only in ways in which one would be willing to talk to them face to face	Asking others for their opinions, information, or suggestions
Linking people's efforts to the group's overall mission	Informing others as soon as it appears that one may not be able to meet a commitment	Encouraging the group to review alternatives and reach consensus

FUNCTIONS OF PARTNERING

Leadership and teamwork have to do with the functions that the leader performs for the team, and with the functions that team members perform within the team. Partnering addresses the relationship between teams, a relationship in which differing goals, expectations, or working methods are often a significant issue. Partnering occurs when separate groups or teams, with different interests, must work together for specific purposes. It is a way of working interdependently with other groups or organizations to gain maximum benefits for both.

Although the relationship in both partnering and teamwork is an interdependent one, there are differences between partnering and teamwork that go beyond the complexity added by the need to work across groups. For example, a work team typically has one common overriding mission, but in a partnering relationship the missions of the groups may be quite different. Members of a team should have few if any conflicting goals; in a partnering relationship, the parties often have a number of goals that are at least potentially in conflict.

A prerequisite for a partnering relationship is the establishment of mutual goals so that both teams have a clear reason for working together and have agreement on their joint purposes. Given these mutual goals, effective partnering involves accomplishing three major functions:

- Maintaining a spirit of openness so that people freely share information that the other group needs and raise and address potential conflicts that, left unaddressed, could interfere with the effectiveness of the partnership

- Demonstrating respect for others so that different ideas are considered fairly and differences between teams do not easily become sources of conflict or suspicion

- Ensuring shared risk and responsibility so that people contribute fully to the effort rather than wasting time trying to ensure that they are not blamed for problems

Avoiding a destructive "us versus them" mentality requires both parties to a potential partnering relationship to have mutual goals or interests, as well as clear agreement on what those mutual interests are. For example, the vendor-purchaser relationship can become adversarial when the vendor focuses on the goal of selling the most product for the highest price or the least effort. The purchaser is then encouraged to look at getting as much as he can from the vendor at the lowest possible price.

In practice, it is in both parties' mutual interest to have a product or service that functions effectively and to see that the other party is given fair financial treatment. Purchasers who treat a vendor well will ensure themselves a healthy, cooperative supplier who can perform well for them and will be likely to put out extra effort. Vendors who treat a purchaser well also help to ensure themselves a loyal, supportive customer.

This may sound simple and logical, but much actual behavior in customer-supplier relationships, as in other kinds of partnerships, is adversarial. This kind of relationship comes about when the parties choose to focus on areas in which their goals are not congruent, to the detriment of areas in which they actually do have mutual interests. The partnering functions help those in partnering relationships emphasize their areas of mutual interest and avoid adversarial behavior. Table 36.4 provides examples of practices that contribute to the accomplishment of each of the partnering functions.

Table 36.4. Sample Partnering Practices.

Openness	Respect	Shared Risk and Responsibility
Raising difficult issues for resolution rather than holding back	Asking for reasons when others behave differently from one's expectations, rather than assuming the worst about them	Looking for ways to solve problems jointly with partners rather than determining which partner is at fault
Freely sharing information that others need or can use		
Responding nondefensively when others raise problems or question one's point of view	Acting as if one expects others to do their best	Contributing effort to as many aspects of the partnership as feasible rather than trying to carve out one's own piece of the effort
	Conforming to others' traditions when it is feasible and appropriate to do so	
		Accepting responsibility

Until recent years, partnering had not received as much attention as leadership and teamwork, but it is becoming more and more crucial in our highly competitive global environment. "Indeed," according to Kantor (1997), "the concept of partnering is being widely embraced by both business-to-business and consumer-marketing companies. Jack Welch, legendary CEO of General Electric, coined the term boundaryless organization to highlight the value of collaboration inside and outside the company."

PURPOSES OF FUNCTIONAL ANALYSIS

One of the long-standing difficulties that performance analysts and others have encountered in working with complex phenomena like influence lies in the wide variety of situations that people can encounter, and in the correspondingly wide range of behaviors that might be useful or appropriate in those situations. Our functional analysis of leadership, teamwork, and partnering has yielded a comparatively small number of functions, or purposes. The power of those functions lies in their provision of a simple framework within which to make sense of the enormous number of individual skills and behaviors that a leader, a team member, or a partner might exhibit. In reducing that complexity to a few key functions, we do not mean to deny the richness and complexity of leadership, teamwork, or partnering but rather to provide a practical framework for making the most effective use of them.

In what follows, we focus in greater depth on the process of performance-based functional analysis, using leadership as an example. We have chosen leadership in part because it is considered a particularly difficult area. Bennis and Nanus (1985, p. 4), in their book on leadership, have this to say on the topic:

> Decades of academic analysis have given us more than 350 definitions of leadership. Literally thousands of empirical investigations of leaders have been conducted in the last seventy-five years alone, but no clear and unequivocal understanding exists as to what distinguishes leaders from nonleaders, and perhaps more important, what distinguishes effective leaders from ineffective leaders.

PROCESS OF FUNCTIONAL ANALYSIS

When might one want to do a functional analysis, and why? It is particularly useful in planning large-scale organizational change or in analyzing complex, alternate-method performances. Functional analysis can provide a framework for coherently organizing a wide range of situations and behaviors in a way that helps to do the following things:

- Present information clearly to others
- Effectively organize and focus training, feedback, and other interventions
- Structure the search for alternate or additional behaviors during an analysis
- Provide a clear focus for large, complex efforts
- Provide a structure for organizing large amounts of data
- Clarify the relationship between existing or desired behaviors and outcomes

Another way in which functional analysis has been helpful is worth mentioning at greater length. It has proved useful, in work across cultural boundaries, at providing focus to issues and gaining initial agreement on purposes, an agreement that then serves to facilitate subsequent discussions and decisions. The following case illustrates the use of a functional approach in a situation requiring the effective use of influence across different national and organizational cultures.

> A software company was formed by a consortium of international airlines to develop a computer reservation system. Managers of the company came from the owning airlines, which represented nine countries. Within a short time, the company found itself far behind schedule and far ahead of budget. The diversity of corporate and national cultures led to difficulties with openness and communication, and these problems threatened the organization's ability to make effective decisions and take advantage of its developing technology. Managers reported that communication with their colleagues tended to range from nonexistent to dysfunctional.
>
> The company undertook an effort to build a common "leadership culture," which was based strongly on partnering functions. Managers across the organization participated in agreeing on a set of business values or principles (that is, functions), which were crucial to effective cooperation. They also participated in fleshing out those functions, in terms of behavioral practices. Next came a series of working sessions that openly addressed the existing differences in culture, as well as strategies for having the agreed-upon principles and practices form the basis of a common organizational culture to which all could commit themselves.

In this case, because the members of the organization began with broad statements of values or purposes, they were able to establish common ground, and from this basis it became easier to resolve troublesome differences in practices. A few years after this effort, the company participated in a survey of organizational cultures and was found to have the most open culture of all those studied. This software company is now profitable and growing rapidly.

Four basic questions comprise the functional approach to analyzing, describing, and changing complex behaviors:

1. What functions or purposes do we want to accomplish?
2. What behaviors will help us accomplish those functions?
3. How are we doing now?
4. How can we improve?

The first two questions represent a broad approach to task analysis—to organizing and describing performance. The full set of questions represents an approach to performance change and/or performance improvement. The remainder of this chapter addresses each of these questions in more detail.

Our intent is not to suggest that traditional approaches to task analysis or performance problem solving are wrong, or that the functional approach described here is better in any absolute sense. In fact, the four questions are compatible with task analysis and performance problem solving. In addressing large-scale, complex performance change situations, however, it has been useful to ask these questions in this form, for the following reasons:

- The questions, asked in this form, have been effective in communicating with managers and others who do not have HPT backgrounds.

- They help to keep the focus on results, accomplishments, and outcomes.

- They encompass situations in which change is desirable (to prepare for future needs, or to take advantage of opportunities), as well as situations in which there is clearly an existing performance problem.

- They are flexible enough to efficiently encompass types of performance that are large and complex, that include alternate ways to be successful, and that include much covert behavior.

What Functions or Purposes Do We Want to Accomplish?

HPT traditionally has been a results-oriented discipline, although in practice we sometimes get bogged down in the details of behavior analysis or subtechnologies, losing sight of our purposes. Emphasizing our purposes helps us keep them as guiding principles. The question then becomes, Where do those purposes come from? Who decides, and how? In theory, there are two approaches to making this decision:

1. Someone decides what functions should be accomplished, on the basis of knowledge, experience, theory, personal beliefs, logical analysis, and so on.

2. Functions are derived empirically from an analysis of relevant data.

In practice, a combination of both approaches is usually desirable and is almost always used, whether or not it is explicitly identified as such. When top managers in an organization "arbitrarily" decide what functions will be expected of customer service, they are not creating those functions out of thin air. They are working from some kind of database, whether it is derived from reading, informal observation of customer service, customer surveys, or simply years of experience in the organization. When people conduct studies to gather data for the purpose of defining the requirements of customer service, decisions about what data to look for are not made randomly. They are driven by preexisting ideas about the probable functions of customer service, whether or not those functions have been made explicit.

The functions of leadership described earlier—providing direction, motivation, and guidance—were derived from just such a combination of approaches: from both research and theoretical literature on leadership and performance systems, from empirical studies, and from logical analysis of what purposes leaders should be expected to serve for followers. For those who prefer to see their purposes expressed in more results-oriented terms, an effective leader's team would have the following characteristics:

- It would know where it is going. It would be able to describe its mission and goals. It would spend the bulk of its time on tasks and behaviors directly related to achieving those goals *(direction)*.

- It would have reasons for going in that direction. It would find its work, as well as its goals and tasks, rewarding. It would generally prefer team goal–oriented behavior, at least in the work setting, to non-goal-oriented behavior *(motivation)*.

- It would know how it is doing and what to change. It would receive information about its progress and how to improve. It would be able to act on that information *(guidance)*.

The deriving of a set of functions for highly complex performance is seldom if ever based solely on completely reliable hard data. Therefore, how can one know which are the right functions? There may be no such thing as right functions, but there are criteria for determining whether one has a good or useful set of functions:

1. They appear comprehensive and capable of incorporating existing data.
2. They are useful in communicating to others. They make sense and are interpreted consistently by most people.
3. They are predictive. They can be used to generate examples of behavior that will contribute to the function with an acceptable degree of success.

Our own experience so far is that the functional analysis of leadership performance meets these criteria. Here are two more practical guidelines for choosing a usable set of functions:

1. Use a relatively small number of categories—perhaps three to five—but not so few that they are too inclusive and offer no possibility of discrimination.

2. Try to minimize overlap between functional categories. Make the functions distinctive.

What Behaviors Will Help Us Accomplish Those Functions?

Given a broad functional description of performance, how does one move to the specific behaviors that will embody the functions in question? Again, the best approach seems to be a mix of armchair analysis and data collection. It may be true that all leaders perform the functions of providing direction, motivation, and guidance, but it is also true that leadership behavior varies widely and that there are many ways to perform those functions. Thus, while the functions of leadership may be common to all or most leaders, the specific behaviors used to accomplish those functions will vary according to the strengths and preferences of the leader, the needs and expectations of the followers, and the environmental situation at the time. Here is one approach to identifying the leadership behaviors appropriate to a given organizational situation:

- Conduct preliminary interviews to get an overall picture of the organization, its situation, and its people.

- Generate behavioral practices that represent the functions of leadership and appear potentially relevant to the organization and its people.

- Test those practices through a variety of data-collection methods, to determine their relevance.

Behavioral practices are simply broad statements of behavior that might be executed in a variety of specific ways. For example, a practice might be "behaving as though you expect others to do things right." This practice can contribute to providing motivation through setting high expectations and is likely to be rewarding to people. More specific behaviors that might be encompassed by this practice are as follows:

- Giving instructions at a level of detail appropriate to the individual, and avoiding too-detailed instructions that imply low expectations

- Expressing confidence in individuals when assigning them tasks or responsibilities

- Allowing people to decide when they need help, or when progress should be checked, rather than imposing progress checks
- Complimenting success in language that indicates that it was expected, rather than expressing surprise at success

This second level of detail is usually unnecessary—as well as costly and time-consuming to deal with—when initial data are being gathered. It is more useful later on, if training or other interventions focusing on specific behaviors are required.

Table 36.5 shows sample practices relevant to leadership functions. They were chosen to provide examples of different functions and of both the transformative and transactional approaches. The table could be expanded to occupy many pages.

The "best" practices for a given organization will be worded in language that is meaningful to the people who will see them and that describes behavior that is currently a high priority for the organization. Some practices are likely to be identified as high priorities in most situations because they contribute heavily to

Table 36.5. Sample Leadership Behaviors.

	Direction	Motivation	Guidance
Transactional	Effectively translates company strategy into projects and/or job assignments.	Lets people know that their efforts are important	Is readily accessible to people seeking guidance
	Makes sure people are clear about what is expected of them	Makes a point of telling others about the good work done by the team	Gives feedback by focusing more on how to avoid problems in the future than on assigning blame
Transformative	Keeps people informed of the big picture	Behaves as if others are expected to do things well	Acts in a way that is consistent with the stated values and principles of the group
	Anticipates what the future may hold and how the team can take advantage of it	Links individual and team efforts to the overall success of the organization	Consistently asks, "What can we learn?" when things do not go as expected

accomplishing more than one function. For example, Bennis and Nanus (1985) cite listening as a key leadership skill, and practices associated with effective listening can clearly be useful in determining how best to provide people with direction, motivation, and guidance.

In fact, the particular skill of listening offers an illustration of the potential value of a functional approach to performance. Listening has been cited in many studies as a key distinguishing feature of effective managers and leaders. Knowing this is of some use to potential leaders—but knowing the functions of leadership provides additional useful information about what to listen for, and about how to use the information that is gained.

How Are We Doing Now? How Can We Improve?

Questions about how the organization is doing and how it can improve are related to solving performance problems. When desired functions and behavioral practices have been established, the next step is to test them against reality in the organization. To what extent do people currently have clear direction, for example? Do they know the organization's mission and how their jobs are related to it? Do they have a clear picture of what the organization and their jobs should be like in order to achieve the leader's vision? To what extent does the leader's behavior support the organization's direction? To what extent do organizational influences (such as information and reward systems, training, and other factors) support the direction?

SUMMARY AND CONCLUSIONS

This chapter set out to illustrate the application of a performance-based functional approach to the analysis of a set of complex performances—leadership, teamwork, and partnering—that are particularly relevant to HPT practitioners. A broader purpose of this chapter has been to make the point that HPT is independent of the nature of the performance it addresses.

In the past, applications of HPT have often emphasized areas that are currently fashionable or that lend themselves fairly readily to clean, precise analysis. The penchant for precision and measurability, which has been fundamental to HPT and has served it well, has sometimes led people to avoid complex areas in which precision is difficult to achieve, and yet these are just the areas in which HPT may have the most to offer. Complete precision may not be possible and, given the nature of leadership and other complex alternate-route performances, may not even be desirable. However, to the extent that HPT can bring a focus to purpose, and greater precision to complex and difficult areas of performance, it will provide an important service. Among the most critical of these areas in the coming years will be influence-related performance. In the near term, partnering may be the most significant of these performances, given the increasing globalization and the increasing use of strategic alliances across organizations.

References

Bennis, W. (1990). Managing the dream: Leadership in the twenty-first century. *Training* 27:5, 43–48.

Bennis, W., and Nanus, B. (1985). *Leaders: The strategies for taking charge.* New York: HarperCollins.

Burns, J. M. (1978). *Leadership.* New York: HarperCollins.

Georgiades, N., and Macdonell, R. (1998). *Leadership for competitive advantage.* New York: Wiley.

Kantor, R. M. (1997). The power of partnering. *Sales & Marketing Management* TK:TK, TK–TK.

Kotter, J. P. (1990). What leaders really do. *Harvard Business Review* 68:3, 103–111.

Potter-Brotman, J. (1998). How to keep ideas moving. *Training and Development Journal* 42:5, 32–34.

Zaleznik, A. (1977). Managers and leaders: Are they different? *Harvard Business Review* 55:3, 67–78.

CHAPTER THIRTY-SEVEN

The Business of Human Performance Technology

Darryl L. Sink

In today's work environment, many people feel they have to achieve maximum performance to compete. It is no wonder, then, that university programs in Human Performance Technology (HPT) attract such bright students. Not only can they study the latest techniques and technologies to do better themselves, but after earning their credentials they can help others as well—and get paid for it. What could be more ideal?

Once they get their degrees and look for work opportunities, however, the reality can be disillusioning. Even when businesses or nonprofit groups are able to see their productivity or profit problems, they may not realize that HPT can help to solve them. Becoming an HPT professional quickly leads to the realization that an HPT practice, whatever else it may be, also has to be a business.

This chapter focuses on the business factors crucial to HPT professionals. The first section argues for mastering and applying business values in serving clients rather than slipping into the comfortable but narrow role of an instructional designer, trainer, or human resources specialist. The second section discusses the critical difference between the broad view of HPT as a business and the niche nature of most HPT consulting. The third and final section focuses on real-world issues that challenge the launching and sustained success of an HPT enterprise and shows how business and HPT are inextricably intertwined because such business matters as marketing an HPT practice, monitoring its cash flow, and even obtaining start-up capital take as much time as improving performance.

THE NEED FOR A BUSINESS PERSPECTIVE IN HPT

To assume a business perspective is to view clients' needs in terms of business problems that HPT professionals can solve and opportunities that HPT professionals can capitalize on, thereby improving the financial performance of clients' organizations. Business-minded decision makers tend to be concerned about issues like these:

- Reducing high rates of turnover
- Decreasing the warranty costs associated with products
- Maintaining quality and profitability during rapid growth
- Expanding markets to gain market share
- Regaining customers lost to competitors
- Increasing shareholders' equity and profits
- Increasing employees' productivity with minimal capital investment

If these issues seem alien to the HPT realm, HPT practitioners must also realize that their own pet issues sound equally foreign and irrelevant to decision makers in business. In order to be heard and taken seriously, however, HPT experts must learn how to relate to business-minded decision makers' issues, as well as to the context in which these issues arise.

Given HPT's roots in training, instructional design, human resources, and industrial psychology, newly minted HPT specialists tend not to feel particularly comfortable with such a strong business orientation; most have not been trained to worry about how their work can help companies save money and become more profitable. After having spent a few years in the work force, however, most HPT practitioners have learned to expand somewhat from their roots in training and education. They have discovered how to implement and recommend a variety of nontraining interventions that can supplement or even replace training, and they have learned to use the whole range of HPT solutions as means of improving performance. But they need to go still farther: the effective application of HPT requires a total business perspective. Understanding both why we need this change and what its benefits can be is the first step toward realizing the full potential of HPT.

The business concept of profit can illustrate how to begin making this change. Here is what an early pioneer in systematic management practices has to say about profit, with respect to both for-profit and not-for-profit enterprises (Allen, 1989, p. 7–3):

> The purpose of most business enterprises is stated as profit, a term which is often misunderstood. We can clarify it for ourselves and for others if we recognize that a business enterprise exists to provide goods or services of such value that customers or clients are willing to buy them at a price greater than the cost of production. This difference is used to pay for growth, improvement and rewards. We call it profit. Thus, profit is really a measure of how well we serve our customers.
>
> If you manage a profit-making unit, the purpose will relate to profitability or contribution to profit. If your unit is not-for-profit, the purpose may be to heal the sick, aid the poor and oppressed, ensure safety and security, and so forth.

The HPT professional who works in a for-profit enterprise probably already sees how the concept of profit is relevant to a discussion about taking a business perspective. HPT professionals who work in not-for-profit organizations or departments (for example, in government and education) may well understand profit in terms of Allen's view of it, as money left over for growth, improvements, and rewards; indeed, the nonprofit organizations must have a profit to grow, implement better services, and attract and keep qualified people. Allen's clarification captures the crucial value of profit to the institutions that do society's work, whether those institutions are private or public nonprofit enterprises. An HPT practitioner has to feel comfortable in a decision maker's cost-conscious environment. The first step in effectively delivering HPT services to these institutions is to accept the importance of concepts like profit to the people one wants to serve—and to interact with them in a style that clearly and consistently shows that one understands their concerns and is on their side.

Mastering Business Talk

As HPT professionals shift focus from training to improving performance and realizing valued business results, they must know how to earn the organizational decision maker's confidence in their business sense, as a way of encouraging the client to listen to what they have to offer. Here are three areas in which HPT professionals can and should augment their business knowledge:

1. *The basics.* Those who have not had at least one course in the fundamentals of accounting, marketing, business management, and business finances need to remedy this deficiency. Local colleges generally offer introductory courses.

2. *Knowledge of sales processes, personnel selection, and budget management.* Workshops, seminars, mentoring arrangements, or conferences typically teach these areas better than formal college courses do. Learning experiences and readings that stress a disciplined approach will provide a stronger foundation than the latest best-selling business book will.

3. *Knowledge and understanding of current business issues.* This kind of information makes the HPT professional more aware of clients' problems, as well as of the total value of HPT products and services. It also raises the HPT professional's level of comfort with business discussions. *Fortune, Fast Company, Business Week,* and the *Wall Street Journal* (in addition to their Web sites) are excellent sources of information about current business issues.

Understanding the Client's Business Needs

Business needs are problems or opportunities that usually involve one or more of the following four issues:

1. Financial losses or gains (potential or actual)
2. Losses or gains (potential or actual) in the organization's customer base
3. Losses or gains in productivity
4. Job satisfaction

Business problems are concerned with the existing state of things; opportunities tend to be related to changes in technology, processes, tools, customer needs, and competitors. Table 37.1 lists areas that represent typical business problems and opportunities.

Table 37.1. Typical Business Problems and Opportunities.

Business Problems	Business Opportunities
Customer dissatisfaction with products, services, operations	Better productivity tools
High turnover rates (financial loss)	Better processes and controls
Rework due to errors, high damage rates, or high warranty costs (loss of revenue or potential loss of revenue)	Growth, including rapid growth
	Merger
	Change in regulations
Costs of manufacturing or service (not competitive, or unprofitable)	Major demographic shift in market served
Loss or potential loss due to security-safety issues	New machinery, or new equipment for testing and measurement
Overcompensation for some, under-compensation for others	Meeting demands
Too much time to get products from concept to market	Lower costs, more powerful computing and communications

HPT practitioners seeking to assist clients with these issues face a threefold challenge:

1. It is often difficult to get to the level of an organization where business issues can be accurately and clearly articulated.

2. The people with whom the HPT professional interacts may have prematurely picked a solution that is inappropriate, grossly inadequate in terms of its scope and depth, or much more extensive than necessary.

3. Reaching the person or group empowered to make decisions about resource allocation can be difficult.

Nevertheless, understanding business needs and staying focused on them is crucial to helping clients achieve the desired business results. Some clients understand what it means to target business needs (that is, problems and opportunities), and some do not. To illustrate this point, here is the transcript of a phone conversation that an HPT consultant had with a prospective client from a fast-growing software company:

CLIENT: We hear you do course design.

CONSULTANT: Yes, that's true.

CLIENT: We have six courses we want developed for our sales force. Each one should be two days long. We need the courses in three months. Can you meet with me?

And here is the transcript of a second prospective client's telephone request. This client called from a fast-growing company that manufactures filtration systems for large machinery:

CLIENT: I was searching the Internet for a company that can help us. We've been growing 20 percent every year for eight years, mostly through acquisitions. One company we recently acquired on the East Coast makes tubing and has technology very compatible with what we need to build our filtration systems. The problem is, the company is small, with only a few people that know the technology, and we've already added seventy people to the plant over the last four months. We're not sure what we need, but we know we have to document the technical knowledge these few people have and find ways to transfer it to other people in a way that will allow us to continue growing. By the way, the company has another plant in the Midwest, and our solutions need to work there, too. We want it done right. Do you do things like needs analysis, job aids, and consulting? What else can you tell me about your services that might be related to my needs?

The first prospective client was not thinking about needs; he had a solution in search of implementation. The second described a problem and expressed the willingness to explore whatever solutions the HPT consultant could recommend, and that orientation made the consultant's job more straightforward. Thinking of products and services in terms of problem solving is an important mind-set for successful selling (Rackham, 1996), but the second caller realized that it is also important for successful buying. She had both a problem and an opportunity to help her company grow, and she wanted the HPT consultant to help her figure things out and develop solutions.

The moral of the story for HPT professionals is to focus on the business need even if the person or group requesting services does not have that focus at the outset. This focus is especially important because the eventual solution will probably involve many more people than the initial caller. In general, HPT practitioners prove their value by looking beyond the obvious and doing what can be done to ensure long-term solutions.

Reaching Decision Makers

How can the HPT professional reach decision makers and gain the necessary approval, money, people, and other resources for implementing HPT services, products, and tools? By and large, the process for reaching decision makers is the same for internal HPT consultants as for external consultants, but the constraints are different. Therefore, the material that follows, based loosely on the research and writings of Rackham (1989), focuses mainly on the process by which an external HPT consultant can reach decision makers. Differences are noted, as necessary, for the process to be followed by internal HPT professionals. Rackham's research is particularly important to HPT businesses because it deals with major sales as opposed to small sales; almost all HPT interventions fall into the category of major sales because they usually cost a considerable amount of money. Rackham also discusses what happens when there is no defined purchasing channel for a company's products, services, or tools, as is frequently the case for HPT products and services. For gaining entry and moving through to decision makers, Rackham suggests paying close attention to three focal points:

1. The *receptivity* of those who are responsive to the HPT consultant's concern about the organization's business needs but who have no particular needs themselves

2. The *dissatisfaction* of those whose unmet needs are causing them to be unhappy with the current state of things

3. Access to the *power* that resides in the hands of the organization's decision makers

Receptivity. The HPT consultant needs to find individuals, groups, or committees who recognize that his or her message offers a high payoff. These people are most likely only to listen and provide information about the people who have needs; no more than that can be expected from this group.

Dissatisfaction. Dissatisfied individuals, groups, or departments are the ones most likely to perceive problems in areas where the HPT professional can help. Here is where the consultant must become highly investigative, asking questions that uncover performance gaps. Doing so helps clients discover how dissatisfied they have become with the current situation and how the HPT expert's products, services, and tools may be able to solve their problems. These people may also be decision makers, but often they are not. They are essential, however, to the consultant's ability to identify and gain access to the decision makers.

Power. The people with power—decision makers—are the individuals, committees, or boards most likely to approve, block, or influence action. The consultant need not become discouraged if she or he cannot gain access to the decision-making group and instead has to let those with the need present their case up the chain. The HPT professional can guide the sponsors in preparing for such a presentation, mostly by helping them realize that the decision makers will be less interested in descriptions of the need and its solution than in statements about the implications of the need and its solution. The consultant can also educate the sponsors about how to present the solution effectively. How much money can be saved or made, how productivity can be increased, how costs can be reduced if rates of turnover are lowered—these are the kinds of points that will motivate those with authority to act.

Internal HPT units have to modify this process. They already have the access that external HPT consultants lack, but in reaching the client the internal HPT specialist will still need to start with those willing to provide information, move on to those who have reasons for change, and then progress to those who have the power to ordain change. Internal HPT personnel should be careful to spend the necessary time doing their homework before meeting with decision makers. HPT staff members must be sure that all the problems and alternative solutions have been identified and that their implications have been analyzed before the internal HPT representative comes face to face with the people in charge.

From inside or outside, however, selling the business of HPT may start at any stage in the overall process just described. For example, as already mentioned, the people with the need may also be the decision makers, and they may control their own budgets. In general, however, for successful entry into a new area or group within a company, the path described here should be followed. For external HPT consultants, moreover, success requires a sponsor who can help, advise, and, as necessary, act as an advocate in places to which the external expert cannot gain access. Having more than one sponsor may be a good idea as well, not only for moving the process ahead but also for ensuring that the external consultant's relationship with the organization continues in the event that the original sponsor loses access. Groups, departments, and committees can also become sponsors, a possibility important to external and internal HPT consultants alike, especially if they are trying to penetrate new divisions or areas that could benefit from HPT products and services.

THE BUSINESS OF HPT VERSUS HPT BUSINESSES

The business of HPT and an HPT business are not the same. The business of HPT is to study and use Human Performance Technology in achieving worthwhile accomplishments that the client considers valuable; it is comprehensive and almost without boundaries. An HPT business, by contrast, necessarily concentrates its efforts on a few specialties.

The Business of HPT

The business of HPT is to research, study, and discover information that has practical usefulness, as opposed to theoretical elegance. It involves front-end analysis techniques and processes for figuring things out (for example, the root causes of a human performance problem, or what will be needed to maximize human performance when a new technology or system is introduced into the organization). HPT professionals analyze problems and opportunities and then select appropriate interventions, develop them, and implement them. The range of HPT interventions is almost limitless (see, for example, Hutchison and Stein, 1997); the following list includes some of the major categories:

- Establishment and communication of standards and expectations
- Organizational development
- Feedback systems
- Rewards and incentive programs
- Streamlining of procedures
- Establishment of policies for better decision making
- Provision of tools and job aids
- Training
- Knowledge management
- Improvement of work environments
- Ergonomics

HPT Businesses

In order to determine needs for improved performance and make recommendations, every HPT business provides some kind of analysis that is based on perceived core areas of competence. Nevertheless, few if any HPT businesses, whether they are internal or external to organizations, seek to provide the full range of products and services that would span the many techniques and interventions offered by the whole field of HPT.

Some businesses concentrate on analysis itself, recommending solutions and referring customers to others who have specialized expertise (they may coordinate this effort, however, or assist in project management). Other businesses offer analysis along with products and services that are related to one or two of the intervention categories, but they also refer customers to other entities for interventions that do not fall within their own range of expertise or within their own business focus. Still other HPT businesses concentrate on managing the entire process, from analysis through implementation.

The Importance of a Business Focus

The business of HPT encourages, if not demands, a comprehensive approach to any human performance problem or opportunity. At the same time, HPT practitioners running HPT businesses are coached by business consultants to focus on their own core areas of competence and stick to what they know best. Because its resources are limited, an HPT business must avoid overcommitting itself and focus on what will be most beneficial to the organizations it serves.

Be comprehensive, be focused—this is an apparent contradiction. One way around it is suggested by Allen (1989), who recommends the writing of commitment statements in at least five areas, as raw material for a statement of key objectives or a mission statement. The overall purpose of this effort is to focus the HPT business so that its goals, strategies, and resources are all aligned with the purpose of realizing identified accomplishments, whether profits or something else.

Exhibit 37.1 comprises eight mission statements. They come from internal HPT units, external HPT businesses (small, large, and international), and independent HPT consultants. Two are for internal units that sell externally, to generate additional revenue. The different statements are distinguished by the particular work context of the HPT business and the nature of the products and services it provides.

CONSIDERATIONS IN STARTING
AND RUNNING HPT BUSINESSES

Internal HPT Businesses

Whether a company is creating an internal HPT business entity from scratch or making the transition to HPT from an existing operation (such as a training unit), starting and maintaining the entity require strong marketing skills and a systematic approach to business management. Some internal HPT businesses

Exhibit 37.1. Sample Mission Statements.

1. Small HPT Business—External

The key objective of the management team of this small business is to manage a highly capable, responsive, value-added consulting and training organization so that it contributes to the growth and profitability of the business while maintaining the high integrity that the company has established.

We will accomplish this by marketing, selling, and delivering consulting, custom design and development services, training, and support tools using the technologies of documentation design, instructional design, and performance improvement to meet the identified needs of government and *Fortune* 500 companies.

This company will operate primarily in the continental United States. Our business will concentrate its sales and marketing efforts in the Midwest and the West. We will continue to focus on our existing clients while marketing to attract new clients.

We will encourage our people to participate in decisions. We will help them to develop their skills and abilities and will recognize and reward them for their contribution.

2. Small HPT Business—External

To provide consulting and products to create a culture of work in organizations where employees understand their jobs, learn how to improve them, and know how to maintain quality and make contributions to the business as a whole

3. Large Corporation, HPT Business—Internal

Employee professional development is responsible for establishing and managing an employee education curriculum for generic professional development skills, workstation application skills, and related services aligned with our company's business needs. We accomplish this by using a highly leveraged strategy of external suppliers.

4. Large Corporation, HPT Business—Internal

To provide and evangelize educational opportunities for all company employees [This HPT business is an internal entity in a large corporation that is a part of an internal corporate university.]

5. Large Corporation, HPT Business—Internal (doing business internally and externally)

Vision: To be the recognized leader in performance enhancement

Mission: To enhance the individual, team, and organizational success of our company and our clients

We are committed to results, not efforts—to demonstrating effectiveness in addition to efficiency, and to delivering total solutions rather than part of an answer. We

Exhibit 37.1. Sample Mission Statements, cont'd.

understand that to achieve this we will need to partner not only with our clients but also with other professionals in our firm. Our role, as part of the overall human resource development capability, requires coordination with all others in our firm who are responsible for ensuring that our people have the ability to serve our clients in a superior manner.

6. Large Corporation, HPT Business—Internal

Purpose: We exist to help America's field employees be successful in the performance of their jobs and reach their business goals. We provide distinctive educational expertise, products, and services through direct channels and indirect/partner channels [the businesses].

Mission: We enable learning to occur and be applied at the most beneficial times and places. We do this by providing performance support resources of unique and distinctive value. We ensure that solutions are applied by coordinating implementation, establishing measures, and developing support plans.

Vision: Continuous Learning anytime, anyplace; performance in the workplace; power in the marketplace

7. Large Corporation, HPT Business—Internal and External

Vision and Mission: Our vision is to help transform organizations through human performance improvement. Our mission is to apply the industry's best intellectual capital in performance and competency management to help organizations solve complex problems, implement strategies, and distinguish themselves in their marketplaces.

8. Medium-Size International Corporation, HPT Business—External

Vision: To be the leading provider of high-quality, technology-based business skills training and development services and products

Mission: To help our clients improve their overall business performance and long-term success by increasing the business skills, knowledge, and competence of their executives, middle managers, and professionals

provide products and services to the parent organization; their budgets are simply part of the parent organization's budget. This is often the arrangement in not-for-profit educational or government organizations, but it also exists in many large corporations. Other HPT departments are partially funded and have fixed budgets but also charge internal clients on a cost-recovery basis for some products and services. For example, an internal HPT business may charge for training classes, especially those provided by external vendors, but not for consultant services. This arrangement occurs in both not-for-profit and for-profit organizations.

Still other HPT departments are expected to recover costs for all their services and products. In most cases, internal departments are not permitted to sell externally, but where they are permitted to do so, they usually are required to make a profit. These entities truly have to function as separate businesses, competing both with other internal services and with external suppliers. Yet other HPT departments sell their products and services both internally, on a cost-recovery basis, and externally, for profit.

These, like those that must recover all their costs, are true for-profit businesses and serve as profit centers for the large corporations that they represent. They market and sell internally and externally in addition to producing and delivering their products and services. They resemble external HPT businesses but have the advantages—and, to a lesser extent, some of the potential liabilities—of being part of a large corporation. One advantage that they have over an external business is better access to external and internal clients and decision makers. One disadvantage has to do with the perceptions of external clients: when the HPT business is part of a company selling something other than HPT products and services (computers, for example), it is a bit more difficult to convince external customers that the entity's core business is indeed HPT.

The challenges can be great when it comes to the quarterly financial reporting of the larger organization. For example, in one quarter an HPT group may bring in revenue that exceeds expectations, but it will not count against the next quarter. Thus the group can be held separately accountable for each quarter's revenue. Independent HPT firms typically do not face this problem to a significant extent, because their income can be less rigorously tied to quarterly financial reporting.

Among other important issues are internal marketing and sales calls, which must occur if the HPT unit is to gain and retain the mind share of decision makers, and the balancing of staffing needs. It may be harder for an internal HPT unit to ramp up for increases in business: the time needed to secure permission to recruit qualified people and then to interview, hire, and place them may be as long as six months. Generally, this is not such a difficult issue for external HPT businesses, in which there is usually a flatter organizational hierarchy, with few decision makers outside the operational scope of the organization.

External HPT Businesses

HPT external businesses require start-up capital, just as internal HPT entities do, but they do not have the support of a parent company. In general, a start-up company that offers consulting, learning products, and intellectual tools can look to four main sources of capital:

1. Self-financing (owner-funded start-up or purchase of an existing firm)
2. Clients (sponsors, contractors)
3. Investors (partners, venture capitalists)
4. Loans

Self-Financing. Individual consultants who successfully start HPT businesses through self-funding usually begin with a contract in hand; some who have left the corporate world turn right around and sell their services back to their previous employers. This approach has one inherent danger: when the project or consulting engagement is over, the HPT firm may find itself without another contract.

To avoid the ups and downs of living from one project to another, an entrepreneur must engage in marketing and pursue sales at the same time that project work is under way. Fortunately, there are opportunities to spread the word about the company's products and services without incurring excessive expenses. These include speaking at conferences, conducting workshops, writing articles, and networking.

If a firm is lucky enough to have its own capital or is able to borrow the money, it can buy an existing company for its clients and contracts. Several companies specialize in the sale of training- and HPT-related businesses.

Financing Through Clients. Another viable strategy for starting a business is to partner with a client to develop a product that, in generic form, may have value to other clients. A product is usually very expensive for an individual or a small businesses to create, and so it represents a major financial commitment. Many a large, product-driven HPT business originally developed its product through an agreement with a client whereby the HPT firm would own a generic version that it would then be able to sell.

Financing Through Investors. Yet another way to obtain capital is to approach either a limited number of individuals (often called "angels") or venture capitalists for start-up funding. In either situation, the investors' main objective is to realize a good return, after a certain period, on what they have invested. Investors will usually have questions like these:

> When can I reasonably expect to recover my investment? (Usually three to five years out.)
>
> How much will I get in return for my investment? (A lump-sum payout equal to an annual minimum return of 25 percent.)
>
> How will I get my return? (Cashout, market value of stock issued through an initial public offering.)

The investors' confidence that these objectives will be met—and therefore their willingness to invest in the start-up—will be a function of their confidence in the start-up's management team (that is, its experience and skills), the uniqueness of the HPT product or service, the product's or service's protection from copying, the size of the market for the product or service, and the competitive environment. All these concerns are best addressed in the start-up's business plan, as documented and presented by the start-up's founder.

Financing Through Loans. Still another way to secure capital is through borrowing—directly from a bank via a Small Business Agency–backed loan, or from an existing HPT firm's current owners if they are willing to take a note in lieu of a portion of the proceeds from selling the business. In any instance of "debt equity," the lenders expect to be paid back, over a period of time, from the net positive cash flow of the business. Lenders' confidence, and therefore their willingness to be sources of funding, will be determined by the same factors that influence venture capitalists.

Other Considerations

Would-be HPT entrepreneurs need to be aware of other issues before taking the plunge.

Handling Initial Costs. The size and geographic proximity of the targeted market are important practical considerations in starting an HPT business because the cost of successfully selling a product or service is inversely correlated to the size of the market and directly correlated to the distance of the major market from the business's place of operation. Thus the initial cost of sales may exceed the relatively scarce cash reserves available for carrying the business until revenue starts coming in. A number of potentially great HPT products or services never make it beyond the introductory phase because their start-up companies are undercapitalized.

Staffing. It is often difficult to find and hire good, trustworthy associates with diverse, wide sets of skills. The very small staff of a start-up external HPT business must be able to work harmoniously in filling the wide range of functions (from delivering training to copying, collating, and shipping manuals) needed to operate and grow the business and must also be comfortable working for a young business with an uncertain future.

Leaving the Business. One issue that is often neglected when an HPT business is started is how the founders will get out of the business, but this issue is likely to have an influence on how the business is defined and run. Will it be a product-driven company, a consulting practice, or both? Decisions must be made about going it alone or partnering with others, and about asset sales versus a stock sale (Yegge, 1996). An internal HPT business should also think about how it can survive after the entrepreneurial leader who started it gets promoted, changes jobs, or retires. If the internal HPT entity primarily revolves around one individual, it will probably be lost when that individual leaves.

Coping with Cash Flow Issues in the Small HPT Business. One crucial quality sets the small, independent HPT business apart: its vulnerability to periods of negative cash flow (where expenses exceed revenues). In a small, independent enterprise, cash is king; the firm that is out of cash is out of business. In these companies, money for the budget almost always has to be generated from earnings, and so a small external HPT business must be ready to make rapid decisions about how it will operate through periods of reduced cash receipts.

An HPT business within a larger organization, by contrast, usually has substantial cash reserves. Unless these businesses are corporate profit centers, their managers vie for resources by justifying the budgeted expenses on the basis of the value of the services provided to the organization, not by generating actual income; their main task is to draw the desired results out of the resources that have been allotted.

Conditions of positive cash flow, however, can reveal some advantages that small businesses have over large HPT corporations or departments. For example, if business has been considerably better than expected, the small HPT entity can usually respond more quickly to the advantages offered by the unanticipated revenue. It can build new products, upgrade its infrastructure, or add professional staff without lengthy budget cycles, justifications, and missed schedules.

Drucker (1985) describes ways for entrepreneurs to take advantage of unexpected success, unexpected failure, and many other changes. Resnick (1992) offers a more complete picture than space allows here of the differences between running a small and a large business. Bangs (1992) and Goldstein (1992) describe approaches that small businesses can use in monitoring, controlling, and reacting to changes in cash flow.

Running the HPT Business as a Business. An HPT entity, whether for profit or not for profit, internal or external, international or local, must identify and solve its clients' business problems, but it also needs to run itself in a businesslike way and use HPT to improve its own performance. The technical and management activities of the HPT business must be addressed in a balanced, organized manner. A partial list of these types of functions appears in Table 37.2. For a more complete treatment of management work and technical work in business, see Allen (1989) and Drucker (1974).

Growing the HPT Business. If the HPT business is providing products and services of the highest quality and value to its targeted market, and if there is a desire to grow the business, then three factors become important:

1. The business must maintain the high quality of its products and services.

2. It must find ways to market and sell its products and services.

3. It must efficiently manage its own operations so that it can profitably continue to market, sell, and deliver its products and services.

Table 37.2. Technical and Management Activities of the HPT Business.

Management Work	Technical Work
Forecasting	Doing marketing research
Developing objectives and strategies	Advertising
Scheduling	Selling
Budgeting	Providing sales service
Developing policies and procedures	Designing products
Developing an organizational structure	Manufacturing products
Delegating	Consulting
Building relationships	Addressing financial issues
Communicating	Attending to legal issues
Motivating	Purchasing
Selecting people	Overseeing personnel
Developing people	Controlling financial resources
Developing standards	Overseeing medical compensation
Measuring performance	Managing information services
Evaluating performance	Evaluating personnel
Correcting performance	Managing projects

An excellent book on the strategic necessity and value of addressing the business of the business, and not just the product or service, is Gerber (1985).

Marketing and Sales. The marketing and sale of HPT products and services can take many forms, ranging from individual networking to expensive television advertisements. The following approaches to marketing are some of the most common:

- Using direct mail
- Telemarketing
- Giving speeches
- Exhibiting at trade shows or conducting product showcases
- Publishing books, articles, and newsletters
- Listing the firm on the World Wide Web

All can be used individually or in combination to generate successful leads. All require time, effort, and money. All are appropriate, according to the audience being targeted, the marketing budget, and the nature of the products and services. Schrello (1994) is an excellent resource in these areas.

Because marketing and sales go together, salespeople are a must for growing an external HPT business. According to the HPT products and services and the marketing effort, it will take, on the average, one experienced salesperson to generate approximately $1 million in annual revenue. It will also take the salesperson about eighteen to twenty-four months with the HPT business to reach the that revenue mark. Thus the small HPT firm takes a large risk by hiring a sales force to grow the business, and yet the size of the sales force is the critical element in growing from a small to a large HPT business. In the majority of cases, growth occurs through the addition of more salespeople because HPT businesses have very few channels for sales and distribution. There are no wholesale or retail outlets for HPT products and services, and so most companies create their own sales and distribution channels by hiring sales representatives.

Management. Skills in personnel selection, project management, customer service, tool selection for employees, employee development counseling, and providing inducements to worthwhile accomplishment are all part and parcel of HPT practice. Thus HPT professionals can take advantage of their HPT expertise as they run their own organizations, for effective HPT practice goes beyond simply providing a product or a service to a client. It also means seeking ways to serve the client's best business interests. This objective will mean applying business principles and practices to the HPT unit itself, to ensure that the unit practices what it preaches. No matter how large or small the enterprise, it will face universal issues, but the smaller the organization, the more pivotal any one of these issues can be in determining its future and even its survival.

SUMMARY

The successful HPT provider uses his or her academic background as an expert on performance but also makes a commitment to the business community—to its language, its values, its goals, and its practices. Making this commitment means taking the initiative on behalf of the targeted clients' institutions: scrutinizing them with the broadest possible view of their needs and of the HPT tools available for them and their personnel to improve performance, and finding ways to get done what they need to have done. It means having the restraint to define how much the HPT unit can do, the discipline to do it well, and the knowledge to point the client to resources for other solutions beyond the HPT unit's scope. It means learning to talk and work with the client's people, making the contacts and gleaning the information to define problems with precision, and then making a persuasive case to those in a position to take action.

The HPT professional who gains satisfaction from the mastery of Human Performance Technology will always find opportunities in this intriguing field. But the HPT entrepreneur—the person driven to launch and lead a successful enterprise, internal or external—must soon realize that such an ambition requires mastery of business as well.

References

Allen, L. A. (1989). *Behavioral interviewing workshop.* Mountain View, CA: Louis A. Allen Associates.

Bangs, D. H. (1992). *Financial troubleshooting.* City, TK: Upstart Publishing.

Drucker, P. F. (1974). *Management: Tasks, responsibilities, practices.* New York: HarperCollins.

Drucker, P. F. (1985). *Innovation and entrepreneurship.* New York: HarperCollins.

Gerber, M. (1985). *The e-myth: Why management doesn't work and what to do about it.* New York: Ballinger.

Goldstein, H. A. (1992). *Up your cash flow.* Los Angeles: Granville.

Hutchison, C. S., and Stein, F. S. (1997). A whole new world of interventions. *Performance Improvement* 36:10, 28–35.

Rackham, N. (1989). *Major account sales strategy.* New York: McGraw-Hill.

Rackham, N. (1996). *SPIN selling.* New York: McGraw-Hill.

Resnick, P. (1992). *The small business bible.* New York: Wiley.

Schrello, D. M. (1994). *How to market training & information.* Long Beach, CA: Schrello Direct Marketing.

Yegge, W. M. (1996). *A basic guide to buying and selling a company.* New York: Wiley.

CHAPTER THIRTY-EIGHT

Legal Implications of Human Performance Technology

Patricia S. Eyres

During the last decade, every industry has faced concerns about legal pitfalls in managing the workplace. Pick up a daily newspaper, and you are apt to see headlines announcing the latest sizable jury verdict against an employer. Turn on an evening news broadcast, and hear about penalties against employers for violations of workplace health and safety legislation. Open a professional or trade journal and locate articles, practice tips, and even editorials devoted to issues involving liability and litigation. Talk to any Human Performance (HP) technologist, and you will discover that managers are focusing increasing time and resources on the myriad regulations and legal precedents now governing their industries.

In the work environments of the 1990s, HP technologists have become acutely aware of the wave of litigation flooding employers, a large percentage of it brought by prospective, former, and existing employees. The increasing number of statutes, administrative regulations, and judicial precedents has spawned publications devoted exclusively to assisting managers who must keep abreast of the legal standards to which they are held accountable.

Much of the litigation in recent years has strongly affected the workplace. One of the leading sources of concern has been compliance with antidiscrimination statutes. Hiring and selection criteria, performance appraisal/feedback systems, testing and evaluation, training interventions, and placement are all sources of substantial liability because of increasing governmental and judicial scrutiny. As a result of the increased attention to liability issues, employers are becoming more savvy about the impact of Human Performance Technology (HPT) interventions on their workplaces, especially as those interventions affect the well-being and productivity of their workforces.

Minimizing the risk of litigation is crucial to business success in today's legal climate. In addition to the whopping fees for attorneys, investigators, and expert witnesses, there is a hidden cost to litigation: managerial time lost to giving testimony, staff time lost to compiling defense data, and administrative and managerial time lost to combing the files for production in court, in addition to reduced executive and managerial productivity and diminished morale among the remaining population of workers.

Performance-based training and documentation or certification of training programs are extremely useful in preventing liabilities because the criteria focus specifically on job-related skills. This kind of system serves three functions: first, it increases the likelihood that employees will learn proper ways of handling hazardous situations on the job; second, it facilitates consistency in training; and, third, it minimizes the possibility of designing subjective and discriminatory program content.

There are literally hundreds of federal and state statutes regulating the content of training programs, from environmental regulations to health and safety codes. Greater awareness of legislative enactments and judicial precedents, as well as better understanding of administrative regulations, will help minimize liabilities. How-to training for those responsible for the design and implementation of legally defensible training programs is also a must. It is here that trainers and HP technologists can add the greatest value to organizations by recognizing the need for compliance training, recommending implementation to management through systematic analysis of training needs, and then designing effective programs to meet those needs.

In every legal context, training programs are examined to determine whether they are performance-based and linked to expected job outcomes:

- In the regulatory arena, the Occupational Safety and Health Act (OSHA) views the hazard communication standard as performance-based. Inspectors examine hazard communication programs from the perspective of whether the curriculum, methodology, and evaluation mechanism were designed to allow employees to perform safely in the work environment.

- In the civil courtroom, an injured party may allege that training was deficient because the company knew or reasonably should have known what training would be necessary to prevent injury but failed to deliver the appropriate level of instruction. The jury will be asked to determine whether the human error was foreseeable and whether training met the requirements for allowing employees to perform safely in the work environment.

- In a civil rights/discrimination lawsuit, the aggrieved party may allege that she was excluded from opportunities for training for reasons that were not reasonably job-related. The trier of fact, usually a jury, will focus on whether the selection process was based on skills and qualifications reasonably related to anticipated job performance.

- In a discrimination claim involving a lack of objective performance standards or an improperly designed test instrument, once again the jury will look directly at the analysis of objective job-related performance standards and whether they could be consistently applied.

- When nontraditional training (for example, "New Age" or adventure training) has been adopted, the determination may involve whether the objectives of the program were reasonably necessary for the development of a job-related performance skill. If not, the court may conclude that the objectives did not justify the intrusion into religious freedom and privacy or the physical and emotional risk.

In each instance, the focus is on the link between job performance and training. Indeed, by focusing on performance-based technologies to design and deliver training, the HP technologist provides the basis for a solid defense against any claims of wrongdoing. This is because HPT employs a systematic approach to analyzing, improving, and managing performance in the workplace through the use of appropriate and varied interventions.

Certainly, heightened sensitivity to liability issues has benefited HP technologists by providing opportunities for interventions designed to avoid legal pitfalls. Organizations are supplementing their supervisory training programs with courses on such diverse topics as complying with the requirements of the Equal Employment Opportunity Commission (EEOC), avoiding sexual harassment, conducting nondiscriminatory preemployment interviews, and enforcing legally defensible performance appraisals. In addition, employers who provide products and services to the government are devoting management training hours to the nuances of the Drug Free Workplace Act, the Family and Medical Leave Act, and other regulations.

Employers in many industries are also implementing more stringent safety-awareness programs in response to increased regulatory scrutiny under OSHA and industry-specific health and safety statutes. The health care industry in particular is focusing more attention on statutory and common law requirements for HIV/AIDS training, especially as this kind of training affects safety procedures designed to protect health care workers from on-the-job exposure to HIV-contaminated waste.

A positive outgrowth of these legal concerns is greater respect for the important role of HPT and recognition that appropriate interventions are instrumental in reducing potential liabilities. However, HP technologists must also be sensitive to how their own conduct can result in liability for themselves and their clients or employers. In their enthusiasm to develop interventions that are appropriate from a technical point of view, instructional designers and HP technologists make myriad choices about methods for effectively achieving desired outcomes, and these in turn positively influence performance. Many times these choices are based on reasonable criteria and are supported by appropriate data. Even the most thorough research and data collection, followed by methodical development of technical interventions, may be subject to legal scrutiny. HPT is certainly not immune to the legal challenges inherent in the management and development of people.

In turn, HP technologists and their colleagues in human resources and training must be sensitive to the legal ramifications of training methods and technical interventions. The discipline is constantly challenged to deliver high-quality programs and interventions while minimizing the exposure of the organization and individuals to lawsuits.

The technologically complex work environments of the next century will create even greater potential for HP problems in the workplace. As organizations attract a workforce with increased ethnic and gender diversity, they will face expanded legal challenges as they seek to design, deliver, and select legally defensible HP programs. Similarly, as businesses seek new methods of competing and excelling in a global marketplace, they will adopt innovative methods for training and developing employees and executives alike.

In addition to workplace diversification, rapidly developing technology will challenge traditional assumptions about the selection of trainees for training in advanced skills and management. Instructional design specialists must be alert to situations in which language barriers or cultural differences in approaching the learning process may impede skills-based training programs. Congress, state legislatures, and the courts are poised to impose more stringent controls on how employees are trained and evaluated. Employers will need to document their selection criteria carefully to avoid claims that they have violated Equal Employment Opportunity guidelines. Time-honored methods of testing and evaluation will be subject to increasing scrutiny by regulatory agencies and, ultimately, by the courts.

The area of copyright violations creates perhaps the greatest legal challenge in a global economy. The U.S. Copyright Act provides the most comprehensive regulatory standards for protection of intellectual property rights, but international treaties and regulations are focusing increasing attention on penalties for pirating words, research, and the multimedia materials that are being created all around the world.

HOW TO STAY OUT OF TROUBLE WHEN EVALUATING EMPLOYEES' PERFORMANCE

HP technologists are frequently required to evaluate employees, to determine whether they have learned the content of a training intervention, can apply that information to job tasks, or can perform the necessary tasks to succeed on the job. Some evaluation methods, such as scored tests, are objective. Other appraisal tools are inherently subjective and require the HP technologist to assess employees' abilities by means of observation and subjective criteria.

Evaluation and testing serve the necessary function of weeding out those who do not demonstrate an ability to perform on the job; thus a participant in training who has been improperly excluded from a job assignment or advancement opportunity because of a performance evaluation may lose tangible employment opportunities. Unfortunately, however, subjectivity breeds complaints of discrimination.

It is both practical and legally defensible to appraise employees' performance with reference to a set of standards that mirror the training objectives. Therefore, it is necessary to develop specific and measurable learning outcomes or performance expectations for all participants in training courses. Indeed, comprehensive performance criteria are an essential factor in avoiding discriminatory performance reviews. The evaluation of performance requires the articulation of the essential learning outcomes and of the standards by which performance will be evaluated. This process accomplishes several important functions:

- It establishes an objective set of measurable standards that can be quantified.
- It forces a precise focus on the knowledge, education, skills, or experience required for satisfactory performance after training.
- It requires accurate assessment, in objective rather than subjective terms, of the specific physical and/or mental functions of the job.
- It promotes consistency in standards for all participants.
- It promotes consistency in comparing an employee's performance with acceptable performance criteria because every employee is judged against the same objective criteria.
- It increases the likelihood of placing or keeping an individual who, after training, can perform to the requirements of the job.
- It facilitates good documentation of the essential learning objectives and of the skills and/or knowledge required.

Objective Performance Standards

Standards-based appraisals are an especially effective way to support and document decisions to hold employees back, refuse to permit them to work without direct supervision, or promote one employee over another. Every intervention should have measurable performance standards. These standards should mirror what is expected of an employee who completes a training workshop.

Standards should apply to specific, significant tasks. If the employee's expected skill or knowledge is expressed in vague, general language, it will be difficult and perhaps impossible to write clear, meaningful standards for evaluation. Wherever possible, tasks should be described in concrete terms that delineate the specific actions that the employee takes, and these task descriptions should reflect a fully acceptable or satisfactory level of performance. Standards should be attainable, should reflect what is expected of a fully trained and competent employee, and must be high enough for work units to accomplish their objectives.

To be most effective, the HP technologist should express standards precisely. The more precise they are, the easier it will be to evaluate performance and give employees guidance on expectations. Vague or general words or phrases, such as *reasonable, seldom,* or *rapidly,* should be replaced with more precise terms whenever possible. The performance appraisal process should be structured to ensure consistent application and avoid unfounded charges of discrimination. It is always difficult, for example, to deliver bad news or to criticize likable people whose performance is unacceptable, and so managers, supervisors, and even trainers, to avoid discomfort, turn to euphemisms like "The chemistry just isn't right" or "You're just not suited for this type of work" or "You really would be happier doing something different." When the precise bases for establishing inadequate performance are not documented, however, an unhappy employee may assert that the reason given for his or her discharge, demotion, or discipline was a pretext for discrimination, the jury will often agree. Trainers or evaluators can take several concrete steps to ensure consistency, objectivity, accuracy, and fairness throughout the performance appraisal process:

- Do not avoid poor performance ratings for fear of charges of discrimination. Instead, address performance issues consistently for all employees, on a timely basis.

- Be accurate and objective in performance ratings. Rate good performance as well as poor performance. Rate performance for all participants, including those who excel. This serves as comprehensive documentation.

- Address performance problems immediately, during training or in an on-the-job intervention, as necessary. Failure to identify poor performance in a timely manner allows the problem to continue. The obvious problem is that the employee is not made aware of the performance deficiency and therefore cannot correct it.

- Keep complete and accurate records of all evaluations and the specific, objective bases for them.

Legal Challenges to Testing

Legal challenges to employment tests have generally centered on arguments that the tests had adverse or differential effects on minorities and were not demonstrably valid predictors of job performance. In 1971, the U.S. Supreme Court ruled that even if an employer did not intend to discriminate by the use of a test, any test that had an adverse effect on women or minority groups would have to be validated as a job-related test if the employer wished to avoid being charged with and perhaps found guilty of illegal discrimination.

After an effort of more than six years, the EEOC, the Civil Rights Commission, and the U.S. Departments of Labor and Justice jointly adopted, in 1978, the Uniform Guidelines on Employee Selection Procedures. The Uniform Guidelines apply to all employers who are subject to federal discrimination laws, and they apply without exception to any and all selection procedures, from scored paper-and-pencil tests to unscored application forms.

The Uniform Guidelines and the seminal U.S. Supreme Court cases of *Griggs* v. *Duke Power Co.* and *Albemarle Paper Co.* v. *Moody* form the foundation for lawsuits involving tests used as tools in selection and performance assessment. Essentially, these cases involved a three-step inquiry for determine whether a test has created a discriminatory adverse impact on an identifiable protected group (such as women, people with disabilities, or racial minorities):

1. The complaining party bears the initial burden of showing that the test has excluded protected individuals at a significantly higher rate than it has excluded others. This charge is difficult to prove but its demonstration is usually accomplished through statistical evidence. (If the person challenging the test does not meet this burden of proof, then the court never reaches the question of the test's validity.)

2. When the evidence shows a statistical disparity suggesting that identifiable protected groups do appear to have been disproportionately excluded, the burden shifts to the employer or trainer/test designer to validate the test—that is, to show the test is job-related. If the employer, when challenged, fails to establish that the test is job-related, the court may order the employer to discontinue using the test and may also award damages to the complaining party. In order to show the test's job-relatedness, the employer must show that the test is "demonstrably a reasonable measure of job performance" (*Griggs* v. *Duke Power Co.*) or "bears a demonstrable relationship to successful performance on the job for which it is used" (*Walls* v. *Mississippi State Dept. of Public Welfare*). It is this issue on which the Uniform Guidelines attempt to shed some light.

3. If the employer does establish the test's job-relatedness, the challenging party may then attempt to rebut the employer's proof by showing that the particular test is not required by business necessity because an alternative selection or evaluation device meets the objectives and does so with less adverse impact on protected groups.

According to Title VII of the U.S. Civil Rights Act of 1964, it is not illegal for an employer to administer a professionally developed tests of ability or to act on the basis of the test results as long as the administration of the test and the actions taken on the basis of the results are not designed, intended, or used for discriminatory purposes. Therefore, workplace tests should be race- and gender-neutral predictors of job performance. Furthermore, they should be prepared by experts and be validated according to the standards set forth in the Uniform Guidelines.

If a test designer bypasses professionally developed tests in favor of those developed in house, the employer may face charges of discrimination, because "homegrown" tests are more difficult to validate than professionally researched tests are. If an in-house test is challenged by an employee, the organization may be required to stop using it until it has been properly validated. Moreover, court may order the placement or promotion of employees who have been adversely affected by an unvalidated test.

Several types of disabilities covered under the Americans With Disabilities Act are affected by tests. These include learning disabilities, such as dyslexia and attention deficit disorder, which have an impact on the ability to perform effectively in a timed testing situation, and sensory impairments (primarily of sight and hearing), which affect the ability to read test questions and hear the instructions. Difficulties with motor coordination and dexterity affect the ability to sit, use a writing implement, or respond on a computer-based test, and some medical conditions, such as diabetes, epilepsy, asthma, and conditions triggered by environ mental conditions, may cause a person to require breaks during a long testing situation.

SEXUAL HARASSMENT: A FORM OF SEX DISCRIMINATION

The effects of sexual harassment on the performance of workers are profound. Sexual harassment is now an international concern, with the passage of significant new legislation in 1998 in western Europe and Canada. These new standards match U.S. regulations in many respects. The recent European legislation made sexual harassment both a civil and a criminal liability.

Accordingly, HP technologists must be aware of the legal ramifications of this conduct, both in order to aid their employers or clients in its detection and avoidance and in order to ensure that their own programs are free from this form of sex discrimination. People—men as well as women—who have been sexually harassed are often embarrassed or humiliated. Many believe that they will not be able to stop the harassment by direct action, and they often go to great lengths to deal with it indirectly. Typical responses include asking for a job transfer or resigning from a job, withdrawing and becoming emotionally distant, or becoming angry and hostile. Such indirect behavior can create a great deal of stress and anxiety, which is often as negative as the effects of the harassment itself.

It is not only the person who is sexually harassed who is affected. Sexual harassment creates a hostile, intimidating environment that makes good performance and teamwork difficult if not impossible. Why do people who have been sexually harassed often hesitate to come forward? People who have been sexually harassed have many reasons for remaining silent. They are often embarrassed to be targets of sexually oriented behavior. Some feel intimidated and fearful that direct confrontation may result in loss of their jobs. Some fear that they will be ridiculed or accused of having encouraged the harassers, or they may doubt that their complaints will be taken seriously.

Sexual harassment is a type of unlawful sex discrimination, under federal law and under the laws of most states. The EEOC, the federal agency that enforces the federal antidiscrimination laws, has defined sexual harassment as unwelcome sexual advances, requests for sexual favors, and other verbal conduct of a sexual nature when

1. submission to such conduct is made either explicitly or implicitly a term or condition of an individual's employment,
2. submission to or rejection of such conduct is used as the basis for employment decisions affecting such individuals, or
3. such conduct has the purpose or effect of unreasonably interfering with an individual's work performance or creating an intimidating, hostile or offensive working environment.

There are two basic types of sexual harassment. The first is quid pro quo or conditional harassment. This is the most easily understood type of sexual harassment. It occurs when an employment benefit is conditioned—for example, on sexual favors: "Sleep with me, and your future in this job is assured." It also occurs when an employment detriment is suffered or threatened as a result of refusal to engage in sexual conduct: "I'm the one who writes your performance appraisal."

The second form is sexual harassment that involves a hostile working environment. It includes jokes, insults, cartoons, comments of a sexual nature, innuendo, leering, and repeated use of terms of affection. It may also include more subtle conduct, such as compliments, touching, requests for dates, or any sexually suggestive behavior that may not be easily recognizable but is perceived negatively. Unlawful conduct can occur on or off the worksite. Often, this kind of conduct occurs at parties and social functions where drinking has occurred.

Sexual harassment may exist where the work environment is so sexually charged by consensual relationships that a nonparticipant asserts the existence of a hostile environment. Two recent cases involved alleged job detriment to nonparticipating employees who complained about consensual activity by others.

Most cases of harassment involve males' harassment of females, but harassment also includes female-to-male, male-to-male, and female-to-female conduct.

Only "unwelcome" conduct is unlawful, but the target's voluntary participation does not necessarily mean that the conduct is welcome. Cases frequently arise in which it is alleged that the female plaintiff joined in and told off-color jokes herself, but she testifies that she participated only because she was embarrassed and felt that her participation was necessary in order for her to be accepted.

For whose conduct is an employer, as employer, legally responsible?

- *Managers and supervisors.* Legally, supervisors and managers are employers. The employer is liable regardless of whether the specific acts complained of were authorized or forbidden by the employer, and regardless of whether the employer knew or should have known of the conduct. Therefore, the sole existence of the employer's policy against sexual harassment will not be a shield against liability.

- *Co-workers.* Employers are liable for the conduct of the complainant's co-workers if a manager knew or should have known of the conduct but failed to take immediate and appropriate corrective action.

- *Clients, customers, vendors, and the public.* Employers must also take action if an employee is subject to harassment by clients or customers, vendors, or members of the public.

An employer must take steps to ensure that all employees are aware of the prohibition against sexual harassment and of what this prohibition means. The courts have clearly mandated that immediate and appropriate corrective action be taken whenever a complaint is made. If a manager becomes aware of conduct of a sexually harassing nature, however, he or she must act even if no complaint has been made.

When there is an unlawfully hostile work environment, it is offensive, intimidating, or abusive because of sexually explicit or demeaning behavior. The harassers may be supervisors, co-workers, or even third parties, such as trainers, consultants, and other who interact with employees in the work or training environment. The unwelcome behavior may include physical touching or gestures, offensive jokes or remarks, sexual innuendo, the display of explicit pictures or cartoons, and graphic e-mail or voice mail messages.

In a significant training-related case, *Hartman* v. *Pena,* the Federal Aviation Administration retained an external organization to design and deliver a series of workshops on diversity and sexual harassment. Each set of trainees attended three complete days of training. One controversial exercise required male participants to walk down a "gauntlet" of female colleagues, during which the male employees were pinched, patted, and groped. In a later complaint by eleven male controllers, the court in Chicago decided in favor of the complainants and, in keeping with other cases throughout the country, held that a single incident of unwelcome and offensive touching will generally be sufficient to establish the claim of a hostile work environment.

Another example from the training/HP arena is *Trent* v. *Valley Electric Association, Inc.,* which involved both sexual harassment and retaliation claims. The employee, a meter reader for a rural public utility company, was required to attend a safety program conducted by a contract trainer. She was the only female present. She complained that the presenter had used foul language and made a series of sexually offensive references, including a description of the sexual experiences of linemen at a Nevada brothel. When she protested to her company's general manager, saying she was not "one of the boys," he replied that "for some purposes" she was. The general manager did complain in writing to the contract trainer's organization, but he also fired the complaining employee. The court of appeal allowed her to proceed with a claim of retaliation and discrimination.

Similarly, in *Stacks* v. *Southwestern Bell Yellow Pages,* the court found sex discrimination and a hostile training environment. This finding was based on a supervisor's comment that women in sales were the worst thing that had ever happened to the company, as well as on evidence that he had permitted strippers to perform and sexual videotapes to be shown at sales meetings and in training. The defendant argued that the incidents at these mandatory training sessions were "isolated," but the court disagreed and sent the case to a jury, asking that the jurors consider appropriate relief for the employee.

Technology has created even more creative methods of unlawful sexual harassment, including faxes, e-mail messages, and multimedia displays. For example, Chevron Corporation incurred liability of $2.2 million for a series of sexually explicit jokes and graphics that were transmitted to the electronic mailboxes of employees who did not welcome the content. The legal standards are the same: if the content is of a sexual nature, is unwanted or unwelcome, and creates a hostile, offensive, or intimidating work environment, then the material must be removed. This is true even if the visual material (as in the rare case) is serious art rather than sexual cartoons.

Significant liabilities for sexual harassment often arise more from the employer's response to a complaint than from the sexual behavior that triggers a protest. In *Weeks* v. *Baker & MacKenzie,* for example, the jury initially awarded over $6 million in punitive damages to a secretary who had been subjected to a sexually hostile environment for fewer than seventy days; the employer, over a period of several years, had ignored a series of similar complaints about the same offender. In upholding more than $3 million of the original award, the trial judge found that the employer had failed to meet its legal obligation to take immediate and appropriate corrective action to stop the offending behavior, and that, if the employer had done so, new employees such as the plaintiff in the case would not have confronted a legally hostile work environment. In another high-profile case, *McKenzie* v. *Miller Brewing Co.*, a manager who was terminated for sexual harassment (for discussing a risqué episode of *Seinfeld*) convinced a jury to award $26 million for wrongful termination. The basis for the ruling was that the employer, which took immediate action without conducting an appropriate and complete internal investigation, had failed to meet its obligation to balance the rights of the accused with those of the accuser. The common thread in these two cases is the employer's failure to conduct an appropriate—and legally required—investigation.

COPYRIGHT LAW: RISKS, RIGHTS, AND RESPONSIBILITIES

Whether through handouts, audiovisual aids, multimedia presentations, audiorecordings and videotapes, or on-line interactive tools, HP technologists use a variety of formats to express ideas and exchange information. Those who are most successful draw on a wide variety of materials to research, design, and deliver effective presentations. Presenters—stand-up trainers and speakers—inform, instruct, persuade, and entertain. Consultants and HP technologists also develop tools and instruments for skill development and performance improvement. Instructional designers create processes, develop instructional technologies, and package materials for use as job aids.

Copyright is a legal device that gives the creator of a work that conveys information or ideas the right to control how the work is used. The Federal Copyright Act of 1976 grants authors a wide range of intangible, exclusive rights over their work. These include the right to make copies of a protected work, the right to sell or otherwise distribute the work publicly or privately, the right to create derivative work (that is, to prepare new work based on the protected work or to create adaptations of the original or derivative work), the right to display work in public, and the right to perform, act out, or recite the work before a public audience.

HP technologists must obtain written permission to use a copyrighted work when they take an author's words or the particular sequence of words that comprise the author's expression, when the work is not in the public domain, and when the intended use of the work goes beyond the bounds of fair use. (Under the "fair use" privilege, creators of new work are permitted to make limited use of a prior author's work without asking for written permission. All authors and other copyright holders are deemed to give their automatic consent to the fair use of their work by others, as long as proper acknowledgment is given and full citation to the copyrighted material is set forth.)

Copyright violations occur with any use of written, audiorecorded, videotaped, or electronically stored materials when the copyright holder has not given express permission for this use. If the materials have been registered with the U.S. Copyright Office, the copyright holder may bring an infringement action against unauthorized users. Penalties for copyright infringement can be severe and may include actual damages or special statutory damages under the Copyright Act, as well as a court order that the infringer immediately stop using, publishing, selling, or displaying the copyrighted materials. The following discussion summarizes the major copyright issues that affect HP technologists in the United States and elsewhere (as when copyrighted intellectual property is transmitted or shared on the Internet).

Reproduction of Passages, Sequences of Words, or Other Creative Expressions

The Copyright Act gives the copyright holder the exclusive right to reproduce, and to authorize others to reproduce, the copyrighted work. It is the author's creative expression that is protected, rather than the ideas and facts encompassed in the expression. The owner secures a copyright from the moment the work is fixed in tangible form, regardless of whether the work is officially published, and independent of its registration with the U.S. Copyright Office (by officially registering the work, the copyright owner secures additional rights to pursue damages in an infringement action). Thus even unpublished handout materials are subject to protection.

To avoid copyright violations, the HP technologist should carefully observe all the formalities of obtaining permission to use protected materials. These formalities include four specific steps:

1. While researching and preparing materials, keep careful records of all sources, as well as complete identification of copyright holders.

2. Seek permission of the copyright holder to copy, reprint, incorporate, or compile any portion of the protected work into new training materials or HPT instruments.

3. Once permission has been obtained, add a statement to all copies that the work is reprinted with the express permission of the copyright holder.

4. If the copyright holder cannot be located or has expressly denied permission to use the material, the HP technologist may not do more than cite the original source.

Use of Training Instruments or HPT Materials

Training instruments and HPT materials include questionnaires, exercises, games, tests, checklists, forms, and related instructional aids. All tangible training tools, instruments, or related materials, including those in electronic format, are subject to protection under the Copyright Act.

An HP technologist may step over the legal line by assuming that materials not derived directly from published books or magazines can be freely used. It cannot be assumed, however, that the doctrine of fair use will shield the user from charges of copyright infringement simply because the material has been employed for educational purposes. Fair use is the primary exception to the author's exclusive right of reproduction, but it applies only in narrowly defined circumstances. In most situations involving internal corporate training or commercially presented workshops, this doctrine does not apply.

Another misconception is that an exercise, game, role play, case study, or simulation created by another person may be used freely as long as tangible copies are not distributed. Thus, instead of making copies, misinformed trainers use overhead transparencies to display the instrument, or they post it on the wall, or they read the instructions aloud to a group of trainees. But all these activities violate the copyright holder's exclusive rights to display, use, and perform protected work.

Violation Such as Faxing, Digital Copying, or Electronic Transmitting of Copyrighted Materials

An HP technologist can also violate the Copyright Act through fax or on-line transmissions of unauthorized copies of copyrighted materials, even when they are not incorporated into other training materials. These violations frequently occur in collaborative work on research projects or in course development. Direct copying of materials from the Internet or downloading of files and attachment of those files to other documents are common forms of copyright infringement.

The U.S. Copyright Act has not completely caught up with the increasing technological ease of capturing and manipulating resources on the Internet, but it is clear that creators of intellectual property can and must take steps to protect their valuable electronic resources from copyright infringement. HP technologists can expect to see legislators and regulators actively expanding and enforcing rights in the near future.

Unauthorized Use or Violation of an Existing License Agreement

In these cases, infringement occurs in two contexts: use without any authorization at all, and use that exceeds the bounds of the permission granted. The latter situation is often considered both infringement and breach of contract. A license agreement from a copyright owner is a contract. As such, it is subject to the same enforcement rights as any other commercial agreement. Under state laws, breach of contract may incur a wide range of damages in civil court lawsuits. These claims may be raised concurrently in infringement actions in federal or state trial courts.

Copyright Protection for the HPT Professional

HP technologists must also be aware of their own right to protect their valuable work from unauthorized use by others. Those who create materials for use in their own businesses or for sale to others should be vigilant about registering their work for appropriate copyright protection and should be prepared to enforce their right to stop an infringer. (They should also be prepared to negotiate reasonable licensing fees when authorizing use by others, however, and they should understand the ramifications of giving or withholding permission to colleagues who ask to reprint their work products.) One useful approach is for HP technologists to use a checklist for obtaining, enforcing, and documenting protection of their intellectual property.

In cases where there has been infringement of the HP technologist's work, the HP technologist who holds the copyright in the work can file his or her own lawsuit, seeking damages in addition to any others (such as criminal penalties) that a court may impose. The HP technologist can also file suit to stop further unauthorized use of the copyrighted material for commercial or private gain. For more information about these issues, see Eyres (1998).

HAZARD COMMUNICATION AND TRAINING

Perhaps the costliest area of liability in the HP context arises when employers are required to communicate information to employees about hazardous conditions in the workplace but fail to do so adequately. Employers in manufacturing and other high-risk industries are well aware of federal and many state statutes mandating employees' right to know of and understand hazardous conditions on the job.

The most comprehensive legislation is the expanded OSHA hazard communication standard, which requires employers to inform and train all workers who may be exposed to hazardous chemicals under normal operating conditions or in foreseeable emergencies. Failure to comply can be very expensive. From 1992 through 1998 alone, the Occupational Safety and Health Administration issued penalties in excess of $1 million each in more than ten separate cases. For example, McCrory Corporation was fined more than $3.1 million after a 1991 fire at one of the firm's New York department stores. The penalty included $49,000 each for six locked doors and $49,000 each for the store's fifty-eight employees, who had not been trained in emergency evacuation procedures. In 1994, Triangle Pacific Corporation was charged with forty-six serious, willful, repeated violations at its manufacturing plant in Nashua, New Hampshire. The charges include failure to develop a training program for employees who were required to perform machine setup and maintenance failure to provide training about blood-borne pathogens for employees who were responsible for performing first aid. Likewise, Taraco Environmental Service and Excavation, an installer and remover of underground storage tanks, was charged with willful violations in 1995 after investigation of an explosion that injured four employees. Among the charges was the company's failure to provide adequate training for employees.

Other claims in other cases have cited negligent selection of curriculum designers, instructors, or training vendors. The employer's liability may be based on a broad statute such as OSHA, on an industry-specific measure, or on a judicially imposed precedent. The government itself may become a claimant when it promulgates statutes specifying the required scope and content of training and when the trainer or employer fails to comply with those statutes. The employer's duty is based on the "standard of care" for trainers, HP technologists, or curriculum designers in the employer's particular industry. A minimum or threshold standard of care may be established by federal or state statutes, but in particular industries, such as hazardous waste control or nuclear power, the standard of care may be more stringent than the statutes themselves. In these cases, or when there is no governmental regulation, the standard of care may be imposed by judicial precedent, by the employer's own safety policies, or by a combination of these elements. Where OSHA is concerned, employers must also provide information and training to workers whenever a new hazard is introduced into the workplace. Further, employees who are transferred to new work areas must be informed of hazards and given any relevant training upon being assigned. New employees must be notified about hazards and trained before they start work areas where they may be exposed to hazards.

Industries that were not heavily regulated in the past are now facing statutorily imposed standards for training workers. In Florida and Washington State, for example, there are significant new requirements for training health care employees in universal precautions and other safe work practices when those employees are exposed to the occupational hazard of blood-borne diseases. Likewise, employers in all industries that provide products or services to the government must now implement sweeping training programs on the dangers of substance abuse on and off the job. For additional examples of specific new training requirements, see Eyres (1998).

Thus an employer's duty to train may be based on a statute that prescribes a level and type of training to be conducted, and the statute itself imposes a standard of care. This means that if an accident occurs and an injury results, the claimant may be able to contend that the employer failed to comply with the applicable standard of care because no training was conducted at all, as if often the case in work environments where skilled labor is in short supply and workers are transferred to new areas without first undergoing training. A variation on this situation was seen in the case of a California employer who was subject to criminal prosecution under a state code when an employee who could not speak English was initially trained in his primary language but was paired on the job with a supervisor who spoke only English. The employee was injured when he failed to use equipment properly after being transferred to a new assignment. In view of this kind of liability, special attention should be given to employees who rotate from one work area to another or who perform functions that take them to many parts of the facility. Employers and the departments responsible for designing training programs must ensure that each element of training prescribed by the relevant statute is provided.

Even when the prescribed training is provided, the employer may still breach the standard of care if the training is inadequate. Statutes themselves set forth only a minimum standard of care. If employers in the same or similar industries provide a greater level of training, use significantly different training methods, or offer more substantial performance improvement interventions, then compliance with the bare minimum may not be sufficient protection from exposure to lawsuits.

Most legislation, even when it is industry-specific, does not prescribe the training methods to be used, but training is most often found to be inadequate when trainees do not learn or apply the training content. Thus, even if the trainer covers each element of training set forth in the statute, the training may be found inadequate if the methods or techniques used do not result in employees' practical understanding or ability to apply the information on the job. For instance, in a recent case in Iowa that involved a chemical spill, the injured plaintiff alleged that workers had been inadequately trained to clean the spill because the employer had conducted classroom training, with explanations on spill-cleaning procedures, but had failed to provide on-the-job instruction or simulated exercises and was therefore negligent. Accordingly, evidence of an employer's fulfillment of the threshold duty or standard of care imposed by statute (for example, evidence concerning the substance, scope, and timing of mandated training) may be bolstered by evidence that appropriate training techniques and instructional design principles have been used.

Instructional design specialists can limit their exposure to liability by setting specific, measurable training objectives that mirror the tasks that employees will be expected to perform. Then curriculum designers or HP technologists must implement training techniques that convey the appropriate information. Finally, they must evaluate each trainee's performance on the measurable job-related objectives. Each stage should be appropriately documented so that examination of the training circumstances, which may come months or even years after the training has occurred, will yield pertinent information about the nature, scope, and effectiveness of the training.

In noncriminal actions, typically alleging personal injury or property damage, the standard of care for trainers and their employers is not limited to the training mandates prescribed by statute. Common law may supply an additional civil remedy. This kind of remedy arises most often in actions asserting that the employer or trainer either (1) negligently failed to train or omitted important information from the training program or (2) provided inadequate training. In the first instance, the existence of a statute that mandates training may set the threshold standard of care, or the claimant may prove that, despite the minimum requirements of a statute, additional training was required under the circumstances. For example, most statutes do not impose a duty to pair employees with supervisors who speak the same language, but because training often occurs on the job, particularly in high-risk work environments, an employer's failure to ensure on-the-job training appropriate to a worker's needs and linguistic background may result in substantial liability for the employer if that employee is injured on the job. Common law liability is created by judicial precedent. These decisions are generally binding on future cases in the same jurisdiction and are often persuasive as well in jurisdictions that have no contrary precedents. For example, in a California case, Brown-Forman Distillers Corporation was found liable for failing to train employees on the law as it related to regulatory requirements in the alcoholic beverage industry. When the distiller's employees broke the law by moving competitors' displays in retail stores and an employee was discharged for blowing the whistle, the court concluded that the company should have trained its employees on the law.

Employers may not escape liability for damages resulting from complete failure to train, or from inadequate training, by asserting that they released control over training content to instructors (either internal or external consultants) or to an external vendor. In most states, when an employer mandates or sponsors the training program, the principle of agency will apply; the instructor or vendor acts on behalf of the employer. Moreover, under most statutory schemes, the duty to train cannot be delegated. Further, in most states common law as it relates to negligence imposes a duty on the employer to conduct an appropriate investigation before retaining an instructor, consultant, or vendor, particularly where hazard communication and training are concerned. Therefore, HP technologists and organizational development specialists have the additional responsibility of carefully selecting instructors and vendors, to avoid claims of negligence in selection. Sometimes the applicable statutes specify instructors' qualifications; some industries require certification. In the absence of legislative guidance, expert testimony on the appropriate standard of care would be placed in evidence in a court of law. To minimize liability, the safety records of external vendors should be examined, and the investigation process should be carefully documented. In addition, references should be contacted for every instructor or vendor. Finally, representatives from the employer's training or human resources department should monitor the scope, content, and delivery of training to ensure that the necessary substantive topics are covered effectively.

CONCLUSION

No industry or workplace is immune to costly lawsuits. Therefore, HP professionals, design experts, and instructional media professionals must be knowledgeable about statutory requirements in their industries. They must also be sensitive to restrictions on the scope and content of training programs and other human performance interventions, to avoid infringing on employees' rights to be free of religious infringement, employment discrimination, or invasions of their privacy rights.

In the final decade of this century, and beyond the year 2000, human performance improvement will be a major force in business organizations. HP specialists must forge a partnership with management to make sure that workplaces are in compliance with the myriad regulations governing employees in the public and private sectors. HP professionals cannot afford to be an independent source of legal liability for organizations or for themselves. Rather, HPT can and should make the difference in ensuring the productivity and creativity that will be needed in meeting the challenges that the next century will bring.

Reference

Eyres, P. (1998). *The legal handbook for trainers, speakers, and consultants: The essential guide to keeping your company and clients out of court.* New York: McGraw-Hill.

CHAPTER THIRTY-NINE

Demonstrating Return on Investment in Performance Improvement Projects

Richard A. Swanson

Performance improvement professionals, like other decision makers in organizations, must work up budgets, justify their own salaries, and propose strategies, projects, and programs to top management, and yet a recent study of professional practices reports that only 3 percent of the development programs in organizations are evaluated in terms of financial results. This is true even though the research clearly demonstrates that the ratio of return on investment (ROI) for interventions focused on performance improvement is 8:1 in a year or less. To help fill this gap, case studies of actual financial results, as well as practical tools for calculating the financial return on performance improvement investments, are presented in this chapter.

STATUS OF FINANCIAL ANALYSIS IN THE PROFESSION

Our inability to change the popular but mistaken perception that Human Performance Technology (HPT) costs organizations more than it returns in benefits has been the Achilles' heel of our profession since its inception. Organizations are more than economic entities, but they still are economic entities. Any organization that remains alive will ultimately judge each of its components from an ROI perspective and will do so with or without valid data (Becker, 1993; Dean and Ripley, 1997; Edvinsson and Malone, 1997; Ulrich, 1997).

A performance improvement intervention tends to be presented and understood in the following four ways (Swanson, 1995):

1. As a major business process—something that an organization must do to succeed

2. As a value-added activity—something that is potentially worth doing

3. As an optional activity—something that is nice to do

4. As a waste of business resources—something that has costs exceeding its benefits

The dominant views of HPT and human resource development (HRD) interventions are that they are optional activities or have costs greater than their benefits. The simple idea that improvement interventions are not a good investment is popular and entrenched; Krugman (1994), an economist, informs us of the dangers of pop economics and of the fact that simple ideas (right or wrong) have staying power.

In terms of actual evaluation of development programs in the field, a recent study reports that "three percent are evaluated for financial impact" (Bassi, Benson, and Cheney, 1996, p. 11). The irony is that this is the highest level of the profession's most widely endorsed evaluation scheme: the flawed, functionally impotent four-level evaluation model developed by Kirkpatrick (Alliger and Janak, 1989; Holton, 1996). Sadly, even Kirkpatrick's recent best-selling book (Kirkpatrick, 1994) is devoid of any elementary economic theory or principle-referenced processes or tools.

Framework for ROI Thinking

Economic thinking related to human systems, capacity, expertise, and effort is disjointed, but history fairly consistently validates the notion that there is much to be gained from being purposeful in managing these domains. Throughout history, ideological responses to the possibility of capturing the spoils of human expertise have ranged from communes to slavery to meritocracies. Whatever the ideology, there is the recognition that there is such a thing as human capital, and that knowledge and expertise have high worth. The importance of increasing one's expertise is confirmed in the societal correlation of educational level with economic success.

Even so, most firms are ambivalent about investments in the development of their personnel and the systems in which they function. Organizations can get to performance and ROI in ways other than offering development programs. For example, they can outsource expertise, or they can establish the expectation that employees will manage the development of their own expertise. Neither of these two options requires an organization to make direct financial outlays for performance improvement interventions.

For the performance improvement and HRD professions, the Training Within Industry project (Dooley, 1945) was a watershed. This 1940–1945 massive national performance improvement effort clearly and consistently demonstrated the economic impact of interventions focused on developing human resources and the required conditions for achieving financial benefits.

In the 1960s and 1970s a renaissance in the profession provided the incentive to think more about performance improvement interventions as an investment. The literature increasingly reported ROI methods and studies of programs' costs and benefits (Cullen, Sawzin, Sisson, and Swanson, 1976, 1978; Gilbert, 1978; Meissner, 1964; Swanson and Sawzin, unpublished industrial research project, 1975). In the 1980s this trend toward financial analysis continued, with a greater focus on costs and on the human resource management perspective versus performance improvement (Cascio, 1987; Flamholtz, 1985; Head, 1985; Kearsley, 1982; Spencer, 1986). These companywide financial analysis methods take an accounting perspective rather than a performance improvement perspective.

Until the 1980s, follow-up financial analysis methods did not address the decision-making dilemmas faced by organizations at the up-front investment-decision stage of their organizational planning. Difficult as it may seem, any organization can conduct an after-the-fact cost-benefit analysis. What was needed was a method for forecasting those costs and benefits at the point when the investment decisions would be made. The forecasting financial benefits (FFB) method was designed to fill this gap (Swanson, Lewis, and Boyer, 1982; Swanson and Geroy, 1983; Swanson and Gradous, 1988). The FFB method is best suited to short-term interventions purposefully connected to performance deficiencies. The problem with this forecasting method is that it is not as easily applied to large-scale change and to interventions loosely connected to specified performance requirements.

Basic ROI Method

The basic ROI method has proved to be a helpful tool in overcoming the difficult and often resisted problem of talking about performance improvement efforts in terms of dollars and cents. The model and the method for analyzing actual and forecast financial benefits are relatively simple and straightforward. They both have three main components:

1. The performance value resulting from the program
2. The cost of the program
3. The benefit resulting from the program

The basic ROI model is as follows:

$$\text{Performance Value} - \text{Cost} = \text{Benefit}$$

The ROI analysis method is an expansion of the three model components into three separate worksheets. Readers wishing to receive detailed instruction on the model should consult Swanson and Gradous (1988).

The following three topics have been used in this chapter to present core ROI case studies from the literature:

1. Classic ROI case studies

2. Case studies of demonstrating ROI to clients before a decision to invest in performance improvement

3. Case studies of new ROI theories and tools

CLASSIC ROI CASE STUDIES

There is a substantial cache of economic research surrounding Human Performance Technology, training, organization development, human resource development, and performance improvement interventions. Unfortunately, it spread throughout the literature and generally is not in the hands of practitioners. Readers wishing to receive detailed instruction on financial analysis methods should see Mosier (1990). Five early ROI classics provide excellent examples. In chronological order, each is briefly abstracted here.

1. Dooley (1945), a 330-page report of a massive five-year nationwide effort, is not a research report, but data worth noting, on the financial results of sample Training Within Industry (TWI) programs, are sprinkled throughout. The refrain of TWI personnel was "Will it fix a production problem?" If not, they did not support the program. When they did support a program, they were able to track the results. The case study of optical lens grinding establishes a value of $15 for the high-quality completion of a grinding task (pp. 271–292). At the time, this amount was quite significant and was multiplied by the large number of new workers needed to grind lenses. In another report, HPT methods at one arsenal are determined to have brought about a savings of more than $1 million.

2. Meissner (1964), a study of a "simple" work behavior—bagging groceries—compares bagging with training to bagging with no training. The underlying premise is that there is a right or optimal way of doing any work and that expertise has financial consequences. In this study, a major paper manufacturer conducted twenty in-store experiments to determine the cost-effectiveness of a training program in "bagsmanship." The dependent variable was bag cost. The study concludes that there was an ROI ratio of 8:1 on the training investment if stores paid for the training materials and an ROI ratio of 11:1 if the bag supplier paid for the training materials. An additional assumption is that

attention to preventing damaged goods and to improving customer relations will increase ROI.

3. Thomas, Moxham, and Jones (1969) compares the cost-effectiveness of two alternative forms of general training for machine operators in a clothing plant. (The operators are designated as either "new" or "old.") The analysis was based on a comparison of the performance of 139 old and 92 new operators over a four-year period. The dependent variables were performance levels, retention, and length of the training period. It was found that the average performance level of the new operators was raised by as much as 30 percent during the first year after innovative training and then leveled off. The ratio of benefits to costs over the four-year period was 8:1.

4. Swanson and Sawzin (1975), an unpublished industrial training research project that was later reported in the literature as Cullen, Sawzin, Sisson, and Swanson (1976), is a controlled experimental study comparing structured on-the-job training (OJT) to unstructured OJT training for two groups of twenty semiskilled extrusion molder operators. The dependent variable was expertise in producing high-quality plastic pipe. The study concludes that the time an operator required to reach competence under unstructured OJT was significantly higher ($p < .005$) than under the structured OJT method (16.3 versus 4.55 hours). Workers who received structured OJT also produced significantly less waste ($p < .01$) and solved significantly more production problems ($p < .025$). The financial break-even point for the development and delivery costs of structured OJT (by comparison with the absence of costs for development and delivery in unstructured OJT) came at ten trainees; therefore, every trainee beyond the tenth represented additional return on the existing investment in training. Extrapolation of these data to the actual number of employees who would require training yielded an ROI ratio of 10:1 over a two-month period.

5. Rosentreter (1979) reported on a financial analysis of an adult education program offered to company managers through a community college. The program focused on communication skills for goal setting. Thirty-four of sixty-eight managers attended this fifteen-hour training. The dependent variables were employee turnover, employees' punctuality, and grievances. Results in all three domains were compared for employees reporting to the trained managers and employees reporting to untrained managers. There was no significant difference in punctuality and numbers of grievances between the experimental and control groups, but there was a significant difference in turnover, and that turnover was financially analyzed. In view of the financial consequences of reduced turnover, there was an ROI ratio of 9:1 for the training.

The results of these classic studies are quite consistent. They demonstrate that interventions embedded in a purposeful performance improvement framework yield very high returns on investment: ROI ratios of 8:1 or more in a year or less. By contrast, there is no evidence that unfocused and unsystematic interventions yield positive returns or returns that exceed their costs.

CASE STUDIES OF DEMONSTRATING ROI TO CLIENTS BEFORE AN INVESTMENT DECISION

There are many studies in the realm of forecasting the financial benefits of performance improvement investments. These studies are also dispersed throughout the literature. As before, five studies, presented here in chronological order, are briefly abstracted.

1. Geroy and Swanson (1984) forecast the financial benefits of a geometric dimension and tolerancing performance improvement program for 136 corporate employees. Using the FFB method, managers forecast ROI ratios of 7:1, 11:1, 11:1, and 22:1. All agreed that the training would be a sound investment for the corporation. The follow-up financial analysis of actual performance of two trained workers yielded a ROI ratio of 27:1 for one and 159:1 for the other. This ideal situation had relevant, low-cost training ($80.50 per employee) and high-gain application opportunities in the workplace. In this study, the benefits derived from just two employees more than paid for training all 136 employees.

2. Swanson and Gradous (1988) puts forth the theory and practice of forecasting financial benefits. Also included in this volume are eight cases and supporting data from actual organizations. The ROI ratios of all these cases met or exceeded 8:1.

3. Swanson and Sleezer (1989), a study of a health maintenance organization, reports the forecast and actual performance values, costs, and benefits from a complex companywide organizational development (OD) intervention that was combined with an aggressive marketing campaign. The dependent variable was members. The forecasting phase of the study yielded underestimates, as shown by the actual data, but led to valid investment decisions, which had been the purpose of the forecasting method. Therefore, this phase further validated the FFB method. With respect to the total actual performance value resulting from the performance improvement effort, two top executives were called on to estimate the relative contributions of the marketing and OD components to the total $12.5 million gain. One executive estimated the OD performance value contribution resulting from the $44,590 OD investment as $5,040,000 (an ROI ratio of 11:1), and the other estimated it to be $7,452,000 (an ROI ratio of 16.4:1).

4. In Jacobs, Jones, and Neil (1992), the originator of the term *structured on-the-job training* reports, along with his coauthors, on a study that compared the

forecast financial benefits of unstructured and structured forms of OJT. The setting was a large truck-assembly plant, and the focus was on three production tasks. The results showed the forecast structured OJT performance value to be twice what the performance value was for unstructured OJT at the end of an equivalent evaluation period. From an ROI perspective, the forecast $39.04 average training cost per worker on task 1 resulted in an added average performance gain of $16,065 over the unstructured OJT option. This resulted in a forecast ROI ratio of 411:1 for the training investment. The forecast $195.20 average training cost per worker on task 2 resulted in an added average performance gain of $3,174.75 over the unstructured OJT option. This resulted in a forecast ROI ratio of 16:1 for the training investment. The forecast $139.40 average training cost per worker on task 3 resulted in a added average performance gain of $8,889.30 over the unstructured OJT option. This resulted in a forecast ROI ratio of 63:1 for the training investment.

5. Clements and Josiam (1995) applied the FFB method to an actual small hotel franchise. The dependent variable was front-desk transactions. They compared the forecast performance values, training costs, and benefits of unstructured buddy-system training to those of a structured self-tutorial package. The forecast $81,000 performance gain from the structured training over the unstructured option represents an ROI ratio of 8.7:1 in three months.

These studies clearly demonstrate that the results of performance improvement interventions focused on human development can be forecast in terms of their worthiness as financial investments. The research further provides evidence that interventions that are focused on appropriate dependent performance variables and that are systematically executed will financially forecast and actually produce ROI ratios of 8:1 or more.

CASE STUDIES OF NEW ROI THEORIES AND TOOLS

There is a substantial array of new related economic research studies. In chronological order, five studies are briefly abstracted here.

1. D'Aveni and Ravensscraft (1994) studied vertical integration, cost structure, and performance at the line-of-business level. They conclude that vertical integration results in overall lowered costs in spite of the additional bureaucratic costs. Vertical integration cost reductions "may arise from transaction-related costs, shared common costs, and enhanced productivity" (p. 1193). When an organization alters its structure (for example, its vertical integration), the effect on performance improvement functions is fundamental. The ability of HPT to be central to the organization is dependent on its ability to respond systemically

(bureaucratically) and to demonstrate its economic contributions (improvements in transaction-related costs, shared common costs, and enhanced productivity). The structural impact on performance improvement processes and functions has to do with alignment with the business unit versus having a function and programs that transcend subunits. Opinions sway over time, but the economics of these organization strategies for the profession should be studied.

2. Romanelli and Tushman (1994) report that "small change in strategies, structures, and power distributions did not accumulate to produce fundamental transformations" (p. 1141). Their view of revolutionary change largely discounts most performance improvement transformational theories and practices of working from the bottom up or from the middle out. They further conclude that the popular cascading model of change within a framework of interdependent relationships actually resists change and prevents small changes in organizational subunits from taking hold. This and other, similar studies challenge the viability of traditional interventions to be a major contributor to the long-term economic vitality of an organization and deserve additional research. The results of this line of research would ultimately challenge and refine the mission of the performance improvement professions and how they position themselves in the organization.

3. Hendricks and Singhal (1995), in a study sponsored by the U.S. Department of Labor, hypothesize the effectiveness of total-quality management (TQM) on firms' performance. TQM companies showed significant gains in the dependent variables of operating income and sales growth, capital expenditures, employment growth, and total assets by comparison with a control group of firms. There were no significant differences in cost control. This study of companywide implementation of an intensive personnel development intervention and the use of standard economic performance data over time, as compared to a control group of firms, casts a large economic-analysis net. Comparisons of the economic performance of multiple firms that invest in their human resources and those that do not need to be studied by the profession. Such studies would serve to elucidate the economic contribution of human capital to an organization.

4. Lyau and Pucel (1995) examined labor productivity returns from investments in a manufacturing industry and its 237 large and medium-sized firms. Two labor productivity–related dependent variables (sales per worker and direct costs of training) and two training investment–related dependent variables (total training costs and direct costs of training) were studied. A significant relationship between investments in training and labor productivity, as measured by value added per worker, was found. This is defined as the dollar value of products sold, minus the cost of the materials in those products, divided by the number of workers. On the average, firms increasing their training expenditure by 10 percent could expect an increase in labor productivity of 1 to 1.2 percent. Studies that lead to core generalizations about the return on companywide ex-

penditures are needed to advance the status of the development of human resources in the operational budgeting process.

5. In this study, Swanson and Mattson (1997) describe the development and validation of the Critical Outcome Technique, which represents a unique development in post hoc program evaluation. Until now, the primary avenue of being able to predictably demonstrate the financial results of interventions has been through a systematic development process including up-front performance analysis and systematic follow-up evaluation. The Critical Outcome Technique is conceptually similar to the famed Critical Incident Technique in that it functions within the milieu of an ongoing organization while yielding critical outcome data. The five steps are outcome verification, outcome inquiry, outcome verification and attribution, outcome valuation, and outcome report (see Swanson, 1996; Mattson, Quartanna, and Swanson, 1998). Metaphorically, the Critical Outcome Technique is a "strategy for finding the needle [financial performance] in the haystack [the organization]" and could be an appropriate and powerful tool for validating the financial impact of certain performance improvement interventions.

Each of these studies offers a challenge and an opportunity in the financial analysis of intervention benefits. Each is also deserving of further investigation. Economics is purported to be one of the foundational theories of the performance improvement discipline. Therefore, it is crucial that we continually update our knowledge of the economic theories and practices relevant to the profession.

ROI PRACTICES

The promise of HPT is that verifiable positive effects will result from a scientific and systemic approach to performance improvement. Other fields pursuing similar goals have been criticized for not meeting their own criteria and for discrepancies between their espoused values and their values in practice in the intrinsically difficult balance of organizational elements (Rummler and Brache, 1995). They often get lost in their rhetoric and process skills. HPT is vulnerable to the same criticisms. ROI practices are a means of economically connecting the performance goals of efficiency and effectiveness with selected interventions and performance results. There are a number of ways of keeping score in organizations. Almost all organizations have at least one way to keep financial score. Some keep only financial score. Beyond the HPT rhetoric, it is fairly clear that the profession has hardly ever kept financial score.

ROI Prediction as an Element of Front-End Analysis

The ROI of the performance improvement process is an integral part of the up-front analysis phase. The up-front analysis peels back the context and culls out the important organizational, group, and individual performances. It is easy to see that getting a handle on the important performances is the heart of performance analysis. ROI, as a component of performance analysis, is crucial to obtaining management support for programs designed to improve performance.

With respect to ROI connecting performance analysis and organizational strategic decision making, there are four issues to be highlighted:

1. Needs versus wants

2. Costs versus benefits

3. Individual versus group performance

4. Financial versus nonficial goals

Needs Versus Wants. The logic of sound performance analysis is that decision makers do not always know that they need, that what decision makers want is not necessarily what they need, and that the trick is for decision makers to end up wanting what they need. Identifying wants is inherently easy by comparison with identifying needs, or performance requirements. Pursuing performance requirements through a systematic performance improvement process will consistently lead to improved performance. Pursuing perceptions of wants will not consistently lead to improved performance.

Costs Versus Benefits. The cost-only perspective culminates in a clear objective to lower costs. Cost burden, or overhead, is grudgingly supported by organizations, and they go to enormous lengths to reduce costs that they believe have no added value. A hypothetical situation could involve one firm viewing employees' furniture as a major cost item, with management going to great lengths to get the lowest price on employees' chairs; the financial goal is to cut costs. By contrast, another firm reviews the research on ergonomic chairs and their contribution to employees' time on task, performance, and reduced medical claims. This firm's managers make a decision to invest in rather expensive ergonomic chairs, with the expectation of financial gain. Their goal is to get a good return on investment. Performance improvement through HPT has historically been viewed from a cost-only perspective and has been grudgingly supported by management. ROI is crucial to changing the cost-only perspective into an investment perspective.

Individual Versus Group Performance. The ROI methods that are used must acknowledge and accommodate both individual and group or system performance. Procedural work that is attributable to individual workers is on the decline. Knowledge work and system work is on the increase. It is common for individuals to participate in development programs with the expectation that the resulting workplace decisions and actions will affect group or system performance rather than individual performance.

Financial Goals Versus Nonfinancial Goals. Not all human-focused programs are directly linked to the attainment of organizational financial goals. They are referred to as performance *drivers,* not performance *outcomes* (Swanson and Holton, forthcoming). Many are supported by decision makers to perpetuate tradition and culture, to comply minimally with regulations, or to accommodate a decision maker's whim. Many are believed to be connected to performance, and it is believed that, given time, they will ultimately result in better performance. In all these instances, ROI is of little or no value unless top decision makers in the organization are willing to place a financial value on the existence of the performance driver itself.

Categories and Dimensions of Performance

The financial analysis method being presented here requires that a unit of performance be selected as the focal point of the forecast. Some clearly definable performance outcome is always present in any task or work group. If a performance outcome cannot be identified, perhaps the intervention should not be implemented at all. Given the variety of organizations and their missions and goals, along with the levels at which interventions can be applied, there is almost no limit to the specific units of work performance or outcomes that could be used. Everything from items produced to annual profit, time to complete a project, and loyal customers will show up on the list. All these situation-specific units of work performance can be initially identified as performance outcomes or performance drivers.

Performance drivers are the units of core output of the system or process being affected by the intervention. They can be counted or assessed in terms of the time taken to produce them. Thus the units are named and then expressed in terms of quantity or time. Performance drivers can also be thought of as quality features that are believed to have a direct impact on performance outcomes. The assumption is that, over time, improvements in performance drivers will result in improvements in performance outcomes.

The familiar "quantity" dimension is the number of things or tasks produced in a fixed period of time. The time interval is most likely already specified in the work system. It could be as short-term and concrete as having fifty computers assembled and packaged per eight-hour day. A longer-term example would be having twelve active accounts at the end of a twelve-month period.

The "quality features" or performance driver dimension is more elusive. Performance drivers are the characteristics of the products and services produced, or the means of producing them, that meet agreed-upon specifications. Product and/or service quality features include design, procurement, manufacturing, marketing, sales, service, customer education, and ultimate disposition (Tribus, 1985). The means of production can be thought of as the performance variables: mission/goal, systems design, capacity, motivation, and expertise (Swanson, 1996).

The ultimate issue in the area of performance drivers is whether the organization is able to wait for the quantity and time effects. If not, the organizational decision makers are responsible for saying, "I think that if this happens it is worth so much money" (for example, every dissatisfied customer costs us $200 in profit per year).

HOW TO DETERMINE ROI

The second major purpose of this chapter is to provide a means of learning about and producing forecasts and actual financial ROI data for performance improvement programs. The selected performance improvement ROI method is a practical step-by-step method for making accurate decisions based on the financial value of improved performance projections for a program, the cost of implementing a program, and the return on the program investment (Swanson and Gradous, 1988; Swanson and Holton, forthcoming).

As noted earlier, the model and the method for determining the return on investment of a performance improvement effort are relatively simple and straightforward. The three components of the ROI model are converted into a method with the expansion of the three components into three separate worksheets. In this section, each worksheet is presented along with a brief description. In addition, an example of the ROI method is applied to a performance improvement case.

Performance-Time Graph

The performance-time graph helps one visualize the ROI method in a performance improvement framework (Figure 39.1). The vertical performance-unit axis registers performance levels at both the beginning and the end of the program for each option being considered. The horizontal axis is the length of time to reach the performance goal for each option being considered. Figure 39.1 compares two options and a performance level greater than zero. Option 2, a structured intervention (systematically designed and delivered), is visually compared to option 1, an unstructured intervention (trial and error/on-the-job training). According to this figure, the structured option results in the individual or work group performance goal being reached in a much shorter time than under the unstructured option. In this instance, the added "performance wedge" between option 2 and option 1 is the added value resulting from the program. If the unstructured option has no direct costs and the structured option (option 2) has costs, these costs are subtracted from the performance values to determine the financial benefits.

Figure 39.1. Performance-Time Graph.

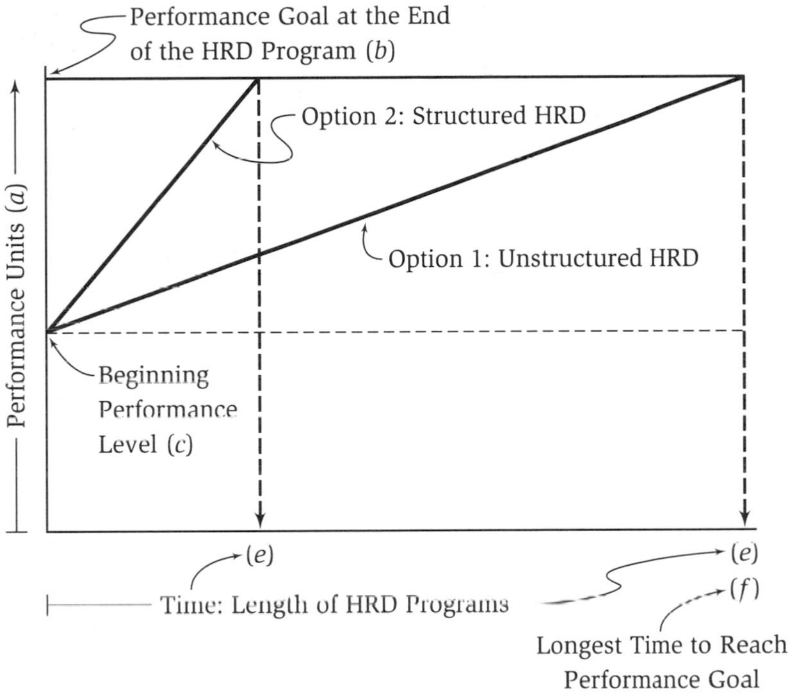

Source: Swanson and Gradous, 1988, p. 50.

Performance Value Analysis

The performance value is the financial worth of the number of performance units that result from an intervention. The performance value is calculated by multiplying the total number of units expected to result from the program by the dollar value of one unit. Exhibit 39.1 shows the worksheet for this analysis.

Cost Analysis

A program cost is any expenditure that the organization chooses to attribute to the program. What is an intervention cost in one organization may not necessarily be a program cost in another. The important condition to be met is that the forecaster account for costs in the same manner as the organization accounts for costs and that these practices remain constant from forecast to forecast. To ensure this, the ROI method allows forecasters to customize the Cost Analysis Worksheet (Exhibit 39.2) to include the terminology and categories of the organization.

Exhibit 39.1. Performance Value Worksheet.

Note that performance units and time units for all options *must remain consistent* throughout the forecast.

Program _____ Analyst _____ Date _____

Option name	1	2
Data required for calculations:		
(a) What unit of work performance are you measuring?	_____ unit name	_____ unit name
(b) What is the performance goal per worker/work group at the end of the HRD program?	___/___ no. units / time	___/___ no. units / time
(c) What is the performance per worker/work group at the beginning of the HRD program?	___/___ no. units / time	___/___ no. units / time
(d) What dollar value is assigned to each performance unit?	$ _____ /unit	$ _____ /unit
(e) What is the development time required to reach the expected performance level?	___ ___ no. time	___ ___ no. time
(f) What is the evaluation period? (Enter the longest time (e) of all options being considered.)	___ ___ no. time	___ ___ no. time
(g) How many workers/work groups will participate in the HRD program?	___ no. workers/groups	___ no. workers/groups

Calculations to determine net performance value:

	Option 1	Option 2
(h) Will worker/work group produce usuable units during the HRD program? If no, enter -0-. If yes, enter known performance rate or calculate average performance rate. [(b + c)/2]	no. _____ units	no. _____ units
(i) What total units per worker/work group will be produced during the development time? (h × e)	_____ no. of units	_____ no. of units
(j) How many units will be produced per worker/work group during the evaluation period? {[(f − e) × b] + i}	_____ no. of units	_____ no. of units
(k) What will be the value of the worker's/work group's performance during the evaluation period? (j × d)	$ _____	$ _____
(l) What is the performance value gain per worker/work group? [k − (c × d × f)]	$ _____	$ _____
(m) What is the total performance value gain for all workers/work groups? (l × g)	$ _____ (Option 1)	$ _____ (Option 2)

Source: Swanson and Gradous, 1988, pp. 34–35.

Exhibit 39.2. Cost Analysis Worksheet.

Program _____ Analyst _____ Date _____

	Option name	1 _____	2 _____
Analysis:			
	Needs assessment	_____	_____
	Work analysis	_____	_____
	Proposal to management	_____	_____
	Other _____	_____	_____
	Other _____	_____	_____
Design:			
	General HRD program design	_____	_____
	Specific HRD program design	_____	_____
	Other _____	_____	_____
	Other _____	_____	_____
Development:			
	Draft and prototype	_____	_____
	Pilot test and revise	_____	_____
	Production and duplication	_____	_____
	Other _____	_____	_____
	Other _____	_____	_____
Implement:			
	Program management	_____	_____
	Program delivery	_____	_____
	Participant costs	_____	_____
	Other _____	_____	_____
	Other _____	_____	_____
Evaluation:			
Program evaluation and report		_____	_____
Performance follow-up		_____	_____
	Other _____	_____	_____
	Other _____	_____	_____
Total HRD program costs		$ _____	$ _____
		(Option 1)	(Option 2)

Source: Swanson and Gradous, 1988, p. 97.

Benefit Analysis

The benefit computation is a simple subtraction activity recorded on the Benefit Analysis Worksheet (Exhibit 39.3). The costs are subtracted from the performance values to obtain the benefits. Any reasonable option should forecast a positive benefit. The optimal financial benefit is the highest one.

Exhibit 39.3. Benefit Analysis Worksheet.

Program _____	Analyst _____	Date _____
Option	1 _____	2 _____
Performance Value	$ _____	$ _____
Minus Cost	_____	_____
Benefit	$ _____	$ _____

Note: Circle your choice of option.

Source: Swanson and Gradous, 1988, p. 126.

ROI CASE STUDY FOR COACHING INTERVENTION

The following case study serves as one illustration of the ROI method. Most interventions address multiple performance variables, but this case focuses on the need for expertise among workers and supervisors and on a change in the job requirements among supervisors. The case presents the original situation and critique, along with the forecasts of the performance values, costs, and benefits.

The manager of a government auditing and collection agency regularly put groups of new recruits through a 240-hour training course before sending them off to work in the field, but the course was just the beginning of their training. On average, an additional fifteen months of on-the-job experience were required for the new staff to become competent.

Believing that the time to reach full competence could be shortened, the internal performance consultant gathered a committee of eight experts to discuss the situation and devise a plan for accelerating learning on the job. Their strategy was simple: teach the experienced staff how to be more effective coaches of the new staff, and provide the incentive for them to follow through.

After exploring several alternative packages for developing coaching skills in supervisors, the committee settled on the option of asking the National Association of Auditors (NAA) to conduct a four-day training program. This option was then compared to the current, more leisurely method of bringing the workers to full competence. Ten experienced staff, who now would be expected to coach one new worker each as part of their supervisory responsibilities, were to be trained.

The committee asked the performance consultant to forecast the ROI of the project and to include the committee's work in the project's costs. Establishing the unit of performance as "a collection" and the dollar worth of each collection per hour, with a performance standard of $175 worth of collections per hour, required a consensus decision on the part of several top managers.

Prediction of the Coaching Program's Performance Value

Forecasting the new performance value in this case presents an obstacle worth noting. The unit of performance was rather arbitrarily determined. An auditor-collector works with a number of clients who have extremely diverse characteristics. Thus one client's work could take many days to process, whereas another's could be processed in a few hours. Clients' personalities and the variety of their economic endeavors confound the issue of finding an appropriate unit of performance. Finally, however, the dollar amount collected was established as the primary performance unit for purposes of the forecast. Past records of exemplary, average, and below-average performers provided the basis for setting an average of $175 in identified collections per hour as the primary performance goal of the development program. This average figure accommodated all the types and sizes of clients that any one auditor-collector could be expected to work with over a period of time.

Clearly, one could be genuinely concerned that this unit of performance, set for purposes of the forecast, not be carried into the trainees' workplace as the single measure of performance quality. The measure does have great utility in forecasting, but it may also distort performance in the workplace over time. Finding a single simple measure of performance for a previously undefined job has the potential of intoxicating managers with ideas of control. Such quantity-only goals could end up encouraging dishonesty and the leveraging of "profitable" clients and could result in generally poor customer service in the workplace. The Performance Value Worksheet for the coaching skills program is shown in Exhibit 39.4.

In-Depth Cost Analysis of the Coaching Case

The Cost Analysis Worksheet for the coaching skills program is shown in Exhibit 39.5. The performance consultant forecast the costs of the program to the nearest dollar, as shown in the exhibit.

Analysis. The expenses of the committee would primarily fall within this phase. A check of wage classifications and rates showed that, on average, each committee member's salary amounted to $15 per hour. With benefits added, the cost of each member's time was calculated to be about $20.60 per hour. The committee planned to meet about five times for four hours each time. Committee time for the project would total $3,296: $20.60 per hour × 4 hours × 5 meetings × 8 members. No food or travel costs for committee members would be charged to the program.

Two of the committee members planned to prepare for the work of the committee by meeting with a class at a local college to study effective coaching. Eight hours of class time and a tuition fee of $175 for each totaled about $680: ($20.60 per hour × 8 hours × 2 members) + ($175 tuition fee × 2 members).

Writing the performance improvement proposal to the director of the agency was to be done in committee sessions, but typing the proposal would require the skills of a secretary. Secretarial time was valued at $10.60 per hour, with benefits included. Five hours would be needed to type, duplicate, and distribute the proposal to management. Total secretarial and duplication costs were forecast to be $70: ($10.60 per hour × 5 hours) ($17 duplication cost).

Design. The major expense of this phase would be incurred in changing some of the language of the presenter's script and the case studies and altering other small procedural details of the NAA's usual coaching skills program. Two people working about ten hours would be needed to customize the program, and this would cost $412: $20.60 per hour × 10 hours × 2 staff.

Development. The major expense for this phase would be for typing and duplicating a customized coaching manual for each of the ten coaches at a cost of $20 per manual. The forecast total for this phase was $280: ($20 per manual × 10 coaches) + ($20 per manual for 4 extra manuals).

About four hours of the HRD manager's time would be needed to telephone each of the ten participants to prepare them to attend the session. The telephone time would be used to discuss any concerns that the manager-coaches might have. This time was forecast to cost about $82: $20.60 per hour × 4 hours.

Implementation. The HRD manager planned to spend one half-day briefing the ten coaches before turning them over to the NAA trainer. This half-day would be followed by three days of customized training. After the training, the performance consultant again planned to spend one half-day with the participating coaches, this time in a debriefing session. (The cost of the coaches' lost productivity for four days and the performance consultant's time for one day would be included in the cost forecast. The NAA trainer's time would be included in the fee to be paid to the NAA for the entire course.) The performance consultant's time for one day of meeting with the coaches was expected to cost about $164: $20.60 per hour × 8 hours.

The performance consultant believed that the coaches' productivity would drop about 50 percent during the four days of training. The drop was not forecast at

Exhibit 39.4. Performance Value Worksheet for the Coaching Skills Program.

Note that performance units and time units for all options *must remain consistent* throughout the forecast.

Program ___Coaching Skills___   Analyst ___C. Sleezer___   Date ___3/1/88___

	Option name	1 Unstructured	2 NAA Course
Data required for calculations:			
(a)	What unit of work performance are you measuring?		
(b)	What is the performance goal per worker/work group at the end of the HRD program?	$\dfrac{175}{\text{no.}}$ $\dfrac{\$}{\text{units}}$ / $\dfrac{Hr.}{\text{time}}$ (Dollar ($) unit name)	$\dfrac{175}{\text{no.}}$ $\dfrac{\$}{\text{units}}$ / $\dfrac{Hr.}{\text{time}}$ (Dollar ($) unit name)
(c)	What is the performance per worker/work group at the beginning of the HRD program?	$\dfrac{0}{\text{no.}}$ $\dfrac{\$}{\text{units}}$ / $\dfrac{Hr.}{\text{time}}$	$\dfrac{0}{\text{no.}}$ $\dfrac{\$}{\text{units}}$ / $\dfrac{Hr.}{\text{time}}$
(d)	What dollar value is assigned to each performance unit?	$ __1__ /unit	$ __1__ /unit
(e)	What is the development time required to reach the expected performance level?	$\dfrac{2625}{\text{no.}}$ $\dfrac{Hrs.}{\text{time}}$	$\dfrac{2250}{\text{no.}}$ $\dfrac{Hrs.}{\text{time}}$
(f)	What is the evaluation period? (Enter the longest time (e) of all options being considered.)	$\dfrac{2625}{\text{no.}}$ $\dfrac{Hrs.}{\text{time}}$	$\dfrac{2625}{\text{no.}}$ $\dfrac{Hrs.}{\text{time}}$
(g)	How many workers/work groups will participate in the HRD program?	$\dfrac{10}{\text{no.}}$ (workers)/groups	$\dfrac{10}{\text{no.}}$ (workers)/groups

Calculations to determine net performance value:

	87	$	units	87	$	units
	no.			no.		
(h) Will worker/work group produce usable units during the HRD program? If no, enter -0-. If yes, enter known performance rate or calculate average performance rate. $[(b + c)/2]$				195,750		
(i) What total units per worker/work group will be produced during the development time? $(h \times e)$	228,375 no. of units			261,375 no. of units		
(j) How many units will be produced per worker/work group during the evaluation period? $\{[(f - e) \times b] + i\}$	228,375 no. of units			261,375 no. of units		
(k) What will be the value of the worker's/work group's performance during the evaluation period? $(j \times d)$		$ 228,375			$ 261,375	
(l) What is the performance value gain per worker/work group? $[k - (c \times d \times f)]$		$ 228,375			$ 261,375	
(m) What is the total performance value gain for all workers/work groups? $(l \times g)$		$ 2,283,750 (Option 1)			$ 2,613,750 (Option 2)	

Source: Swanson and Gradous, 1988, pp. 84–85.

Exhibit 39.5. Cost Analysis Worksheet for Coaching Skills Program.

Program _Coaching Skills_   Analyst _C. Sleezer_   Date _3/1/88_

Option name	1 _Unstructured_	2 _NAA Course_
Analysis:		
Needs assessment		3,296
Work analysis		
Proposal to management		70
Other _(tuition and time)_		680
Other		
Design:		
General HRD program design		
Specific HRD program design		412
Other		
Other		
Development:		
Draft and prototype		
Pilot test and revise		
Production and duplication		280
Other _(HRD manager)_		82
Other		
Implement:		
Program management		
Program delivery		3,000
Participant costs		38,400
Other _(HRD manager)_		164
Other		
Evaluation:		
Program evaluation and report		989
Performance follow-up		
Other _(secretarial)_		42
Other		
Total HRD program costs	$	$ _47,415_
	(Option 1)	(Option 2)

Source: Swanson and Gradous, 1988, p. 110..

$240 per hour (the full rate) because the coaches would presumably have projects in motion, and problems with these projects could be handled by a phone call or two, as needed, during the four days they would be off the job. One committee member who was planning to attend the training as a coach verified this presumption. The lost productivity would amount to $38,400: $120 per hour × 8 hours × 4 days × 10 coaches.

A call to the NAA established that the fee to be paid to it as compensation for the use of one trainer for three days and for the original course content would be roughly $1,000 per day, for a total of $3,000. No travel or food expenses were expected or forecast.

Evaluation. The HRD manager believed that two government evaluators would spend three days in monitoring the training, evaluating the results, and reporting to the agency director. Their time for evaluation and reporting would amount to just under $989: $20.60 per hour × 8 hours × 3 days × 2 trainers.

Typing, and distributing the evaluation report were expected to take three hours of secretarial time, or about $32: $10.60 per hour × 3 hours. Duplicating the report was expected to cost another $10.

Cost Analysis Decisions

Perhaps not perfectly obvious are two decisions, made to ensure that costs were not unnecessarily overstated. The first decision was not to estimate the cost of the meeting room where the program would be delivered. It was the site for all regular meetings of the collection staff, and no differentiation was made among the variety of activities held there. The second, more crucial decision was to charge to the program 50 percent of the coaches' lost productivity during their time in the program. The coaches' salaries while in training were easily covered by the 50 percent of their productivity not charged to the program. Charging for time lost and productivity lost would have overstated the cost of the program.

Benefit Analysis Decisions

Exhibit 39.6 presents the benefit analysis for the existing (that is, unstructured) program and the proposed NAA program. From a strictly financial perspective, the structured program would appear to be by far the more desirable, with $2,566,335 in benefits versus only $2,283,750 for the existing program. Although other decision criteria would also need to be applied before a program choice could be recommended to decision makers, in this instance the only serious consideration was the up-front cost of the program with the higher benefit. The agency was on a fixed budget and would have to appeal to a special government agency to fund this effort. Nevertheless, the new coaching program was supported by the decision makers because of its forecast benefit.

Exhibit 39.6. Benefit Analysis Worksheet for the Unstructured and NAA Programs.

Program _Coaching Skills_   Analyst _C. Sleezer_   Date _3/1/88_

	Option	1 _Unstructured_	2 _NAA Course_
Performance Value		$ 2,283,750	$ 2,613,750
Minus Cost		0	47,415
Benefit		$ 2,283,750	$ (2,566,335)

Note: Circle your choice of option.

Source: Swanson and Gradous, 1988, p. 145.

FINANCIAL ANALYSIS AS AN ELEMENT OF DECISION MAKING AND ACCOUNTABILITY

It is important to note that criteria other than ROI are being used to gain support for performance improvement programs. Financial benefit is only one criterion for choosing a particular program or program option. There are five other useful criteria to use in comparing and choosing among options:

1. Appropriateness of the program to the organizational culture and tradition

2. Availability of the program

3. Perceived quality of the program design

4. Cost of the program

5. Expected financial benefit to the organization

These nonfinancial criteria cannot be ignored. Organizations are not totally rational and certainly are not totally directed by economics. For example, a program forecasting high financial benefit that would fly in the face of the organizational culture and tradition will most likely never get off the ground.

The forecast should be presented to organizational decision makers as a part of the proposal resulting from the needs assessment. At a minimum, the proposal must contain four major elements:

1. Performance need

2. Program goal

3. Program options

4. Program recommendation

The ROI forecast would be included as a part of the program recommendation. The recommended presentation strategies are as follows:

- Address each of the four proposal elements.

- Use the ROI method.

- In making a written proposal, use concise sentences and paragraphs.

- When appearing in person, present your information in the same order as your on-paper proposal and at a pace preferred by your audience.

- Use one or two visuals, such as the performance-time graph or the forecasting figures, to illustrate the benefit expected to result from the program.

- In your written proposal include the visuals cited above and consider adding other easily understood graphic information.

CONCLUSION

When ROI data are presented with assurance, the odds are increased that HPT's contributions to the improvement of the organization will be accepted and realized. This conclusion proceeds from the following three observations:

1. Systematically designed and implemented performance efforts based on sound up-front analysis yield ROI ratios of 8:1 or greater in a year or less.

2. Professionals have tools available to assess the actual ROI on sound performance improvement efforts.

3. Professionals have tools available to forecast the ROI for sound performance improvement efforts.

References

Alliger, G., and Janak, E. (1989). Kirkpatrick's levels of training criteria: Thirty years later. *Personnel Psychology* 42:2, 331–342.

Bassi, L., Benson, G., and Cheney, S. (1996). The top ten trends. In American Society for Training and Development (ed.), *Trends: Position yourself for the future.* Alexandria, VA: ASTD Press.

Becker, G. S. (1993). *Human capital: A theoretical and empirical analysis with special reference to education* (3rd ed.). Chicago: University of Chicago Press.

Cascio, W. F. (1987). *Costing human resources: The financial impact of behavior in organizations.* Boston: PAWS-Kent.

Clements, J. C., and Josiam, B. M. (1995). Training: Quantifying the financial benefits. *International Journal of Contemporary Hospitality Management* 7:1, 10–15.

Cullen, G., Sawzin, S., Sisson, G. R., and Swanson, R. A. (1976). Training: What's it worth? *Training and Development Journal* 30:8, 12–20.

Cullen, G., Sawzin, S., Sisson, G. R., and Swanson, R. A. (1978). Cost effectiveness: A model for assessing the training investment. *Training and Development Journal* 32:1, 24–29.

D'Aveni, R. A., and Ravensscraft, D. J. (1994). Economies of integration versus bureaucracy costs: Does vertical integration improve performance? *Academy of Management Journal* 37:5, 1167–1206.

Dean, P. J., and Ripley, D. E. (1997). *Performance improvement pathfinders.* Washington, DC: International Society for Performance Improvement.

Dooley, C. R. (1945). *The Training Within Industry report (1940–1945): A record of the development of management techniques for improvement of supervision—their use and the results.* Washington, DC: Training Within Industry Service, Bureau of Training, War Manpower Commission.

Edvinsson, L., and Malone, M. (1997). *Intellectual capital.* New York: HarperBusiness.

Flamholtz, E. G. (1985). *Human resource accounting.* San Francisco: Jossey-Bass.

Geroy, G. D., and Swanson, R. A. (1984). Forecasting training costs and benefits in industry. *Journal of Epsilon Pi Tau* 10:2, 15–19.

Gilbert, T. E. (1978). *Human competence: Engineering worthy performance.* New York: McGraw-Hill.

Head, G. E. (1985). *Training cost analysis.* Washington, DC: Marlin Press.

Hendricks, K. B., and Singhal, V. R. (1995). *Does implementing an effective TQM program actually improve operating performance? Empirical evidence from firms that have won quality awards.* Williamsburg, VA: School of Business, College of William and Mary.

Holton, E. F. (1996). The flawed four-level evaluation model. *Human Resource Development Quarterly* 7:1, 5–21.

Jacobs, R., Jones, M., and Neil, S. (1992). A case study in forecasting the financial benefits of unstructured and structured on-the-job training. *Human Resource Development Quarterly* 3:2, 133–139.

Kearsley, G. (1982). *Costs, benefits, and productivity in training systems.* Reading, MA: Addison-Wesley.

Kirkpatrick, D. L. (1994). *Evaluating training programs: The four levels.* San Francisco: Berrett-Koehler.

Krugman, P. (1994). *Peddling prosperity.* New York: Norton.

Lyau, N. M., and Pucel, D. J. (1995). Economic return on training at the organization level. *Performance Improvement Quarterly* 8:3, 68–79.

Mattson, B. W., Quartanna, L. J., and Swanson, R. A. (1998). Assessing the business results of management development using the critical outcome technique at

CIGNA Corporation. In R. Torraco (ed.), *Proceedings of the annual conference of the Academy of Human Resource Development—1998*. Baton Rouge, LA: Academy of Human Resource Development.

Meissner, F. (1964). Measuring quantitatively the effect of personnel training. *Training Directors Journal* 18:3, 230–236.

Mosier, N. (1990). Financial analysis methods and their application to employee training. *Human Resource Development Quarterly* 1:1, 45–71.

Romanelli, E., and Tushman, M. L. (1994). Organizational transformation as punctuated equilibrium: An empirical test. *Academy of Management Journal* 37:5, 1141–1166.

Rosentreter, G. E. (1979). Economic evaluation of a training program. In R. O. Peterson (ed.), *Studies in training and development: Research papers from the 1978 ASTD national conference*. Alexandria, VA: ASTD Press.

Rummler, G. A., and Brache, A. P. (1995). *Improving performance: How to manage the white space on the organization chart* (2nd ed.). San Francisco: Jossey-Bass.

Spencer, L. M. Jr. (1986). *Calculating human resource costs and benefits*. New York: Wiley.

Swanson, R. A. (1995). Human resource development: Performance is the key. *Human Resource Development Quarterly* 6:2, 207–213.

Swanson, R. A. (1996). *Analysis for improving performance*. San Francisco: Berrett-Koehler.

Swanson, R. A., and Geroy, G. (1983, Aug.). *Economics of training*. Paper presented to the International Federation of Training and Development Organizations, Amsterdam.

Swanson, R. A., and Gradous, D. B. (1988). *Forecasting financial benefits of human resource development*. San Francisco: Jossey-Bass.

Swanson, R. A., and Holton, R. A. (forthcoming). *Results: How to measure performance, learning, and satisfaction outcomes*. San Francisco: Berrett-Koehler.

Swanson, R. A., Lewis, D. R., and Boyer, C. M. (1982). *Industrial training and economic evaluation: Program development and evaluation in the private sector*. Oslo, Norway: Norwegian National Academy of Banking.

Swanson, R. A., and Mattson, B. W. (1997). Development and validation of the critical outcome technique. In R. Torraco (ed.), *Proceedings of the annual conference of the Academy of Human Resource Development—1996*. Baton Rouge, LA: Academy of Human Resource Development.

Swanson, R. A., and Sleezer, C. M. (1989). Determining financial benefits of an organization development program. *Performance Improvement Quarterly* 2:1, 55–65.

Thomas, B., Moxham, J., and Jones, J.G.G. (1969). A cost benefit analysis of industrial training. *British Journal of Industrial Relations* 7:2, 231–264.

Tribus, M. (1985). *Becoming competitive by building the quality company*. Kingsport, TN: American Quality and Productivity Institute.

Ulrich, D. (1997). *Human resource champions: The next agenda for adding value and delivering results*. Boston: Harvard Business School Press.

PART SIX

THE FUTURE OF HUMAN PERFORMANCE TECHNOLOGY

The past thirty-five to forty years have seen Human Performance Technology (HPT) evolve to the point where it is finally emerging as a recognized, important field of professional practice and academic interest. The future appears to hold even greater promise. The final part of this handbook engages in some crystal ball gazing.

The first two of this part's five chapters examine emerging trends in noninstructional and instructional interventions, respectively. They discuss what HP technologists should be tracking to stay current with developments.

The third of these chapters is concerned with research in the field. Professional practice is frequently ahead of the fundamental underpinnings of HPT research; for many areas of practice, solid research is lacking. The authors of this chapter, while acknowledging this deficit, present excellent recommendations for an HPT research agenda, offering considerations with respect to both methods and content. With HPT's growing presence in academic programs, this chapter should be of particular interest to academic readers and others seeking to build the field's research base.

The fourth chapter of Part Six examines HPT practice in the context of the global business environment. It offers an in-depth view of HPT in diverse national and cultural settings and gives a glimpse of the directions that may be taken by further writings on this subject of growing interest.

The fifth and concluding chapter of Part Six is a thoughtful examination of new frontiers for HPT. Using the metaphor of a tree, the author revisits the roots of the field and then traces its development outward, sketching the likely challenges and opportunities for the field's multibranched future.

Part One of this handbook opened a wide sphere of discussion by examining the fundamentals of the HPT field; Part Six closes that circle. The authors of the chapters in Part Six are scholars, researchers, writers, thinkers, and practitioners. Their vision is that of seasoned professionals exploring contemporary issues and events that suggest the future of their field.

Because HPT is a world within worlds, it must respond to changes in its larger environment. Thus the future of HPT will be linked to broader futures, such as those that develop from changes in the world of work, in workers, and in how workers view their jobs. HPT is not a closed system, not a collection of known techniques to be mastered; it will evolve through successive iterative cycles like those that characterize the HPT general process. And so HP technologists will continue to explore, learn, grow, and move into the future, toward the opening of new vistas, new challenges, and new realities for the field.

CHAPTER FORTY

Emerging Trends in Human Performance Interventions

Dale C. Brandenburg
Carl V. Binder

The field of Human Performance Technology (HPT), devoted to the systematic and cost-effective support and improvement of human performance, intersects with many other disciplines and technologies. HPT brings a particular set of assumptions and perspectives to improving human productivity, but it is also a cross-disciplinary melting pot of methods, tools, and theoretical perspectives borrowed from other bodies of knowledge and practice. This chapter discusses general trends in HPT and in several intersecting fields. It also describes specific developments and applications and suggests directions for the future.

To set the stage for the discussion to come, it may be instructive to look at a set of predictions from a gathering of human resources experts. The following list of consensus statements was generated from a futures group meeting at the 1996 Human Resource Institute conference (Groe, Pyle, and Jamrog, 1996, pp. 59–60):

- Technology in the form of computer and telecommunication devices will be omnipresent.

- Big companies (as we know them today) will not exist. Virtual companies and multiple company alliances will result in a more amorphous global business environment. Office complexes will disappear, and the "village society" will reemerge. Everyone, in one way or another, will become an independent contractor.

- The lines between work, workplace, home, family, and leisure will continue to blur. This development will lead to philosophical questions: What is life? What is work?

- The worldwide business economy will be dramatically more competitive. As a result of the emergence of boundaryless markets, it will be more difficult for a company to differentiate its products and services.

- The new world of boundaryless companies and workers will result in less control by companies.

- Global economies will require leaders to think beyond local markets and understand the conditions that drive the international system.

- Global communication mechanisms, such as the Internet, will have a profound impact on how we engage in commerce.

- The evolution of true worldwide telecommuting will be a reality.

- A high percentage of the workforce will consist of transportable professionals, specialists, and executives engaging in "free agency."

- New investment markets will emerge, especially in those developing countries that consume more goods and services. A shift in the worldwide professional and skilled workforce may lead to issues of a "human resources trade balance."

Two themes from this list seem central to any discussion of trends in human performance improvement: changes in organizational structure and process, and changes in information technology. Throughout this chapter, we will see how these two streams of evolution intertwine and reflect each other in various contexts.

Technology in general, and specifically information technology, has continued to expand its role in the overall world economy (Organisation for Economic Co-operation and Development, 1996b). Although most studies of the organizational impact of technology have concentrated on the manufacturing sector, the trend in service industries is also large and growing. Those concerned about performance improvement in organizations can now benefit from an increasingly powerful technology toolbox. In fact, our technologies for creating environments for learning and performance support are changing more rapidly than our ability to decide how and when to apply these technologies efficiently and effectively. Knowing when and how to use specific technologies and develop specific applications could be considered the special niche of the HPT field.

In this chapter, we will revisit and update some topics that we have covered before (Brandenburg and Binder, 1992) while examining additional categories of trends and issues. The chapter concludes with a summary and discussion of implications for the future of HPT.

THE TREND OF MERGING LEARNING AND WORK

Distinctions among education, training, and on-the-job performance support continue to blur. The need for flexibility in the workplace, new models for organizing work, and a focus on core competencies has led a growing number of organizations to demand that employees manage their own development (Cappelli and others, 1997) rather than attend prescribed "one size fits all" training programs. Human resources development (HRD) organizations in larger companies are reducing staff and outsourcing many human resources functions, including training. Other forces affecting the conditions and requirements for individual learning include shorter product-cycle times, less employee travel, less time away from work, and the increasing demand for upgrading of skills. Work environments are changing ever more rapidly, and workers increasingly must learn while working. These forces lead naturally to increased use of technology (Bassi, Benson, and Cheney, 1996) for more efficient use of resources and greater speed in their deployment.

Companies concerned about productivity and cost reduction are now routinely using technologies to support rapid communication and assimilation of information, areas previously considered to be esoteric. These technologies include the Internet, intranets, electronic performance support, videoconferencing, satellite broadcast, technologies for collaboration and communication, and other forms of distance learning and remote access. Many decisions to use such technologies are based on considerations of cost savings (such as for travel, lodging, facilities, and instructors), but it is not yet clear that these technologies are being used in more effective ways. An important role for HPT in this context is to provide methods for performance needs analysis, design, and systematic implementation planning as a way of ensuring that the new technologies produce performance results that are at least as good as those produced by the methods and technologies they replace.

More organizations are making the conceptual shift from the development of instructional programs to the development of total performance systems. This shift corresponds to the trend toward renaming training departments—now being called departments for "performance improvement," "performance development," and the like—and integrating training into management groups that also control such performance variables as job design, field coaching, knowledge management, and compensation. The newer approach, in line with the tenets of HPT, considers the overall performance environment, which includes the following elements (Silber, 1990, p. 19):

- Information provided to workers (such as information about desired results, or information in the form of feedback and job aids)

- The design of work processes and tools (ergonomics, computer screen design, interactive computer interfaces, workflow controls, appropriate support tools, performance supports, on-line job aids)

- External incentives (such as money) and internal motivations (job satisfaction, empowerment, and structure)

- Training or other forms of skill improvement

As the pace of technological change continues to accelerate, many more jobs will require constant adaptation to new information and task requirements. As a result, at multiple levels, the operational distinction between learning and work will continue to disappear. Centralized training departments will have to do more with less staff, move instruction closer to worksites (and especially to personal workstations), and deliver learning in more flexible environments. Training as a distinct activity will no longer be the primary learning vehicle for many types of jobs. In this environment, three strategies with overlapping definitions will become more widespread: just-in-time (JIT) training, one-stop resources, and virtual colleges with various types of resources for performance support.

1. *JIT training.* Workers will use on-the-job information systems to access policies, procedures, and data on an as-needed basis. They will also engage in brief segments of technology-mediated or one-to-one coached learning on the job. JIT training (or, perhaps better, JIT learning) may be viewed as the obtaining of an appropriate amount of knowledge or skill either just before or during the time the knowledge or skill is needed. This arrangement presumes that instruction is already developed but packaged in usable chunks ("objects") and distributed when called for, or that it is uniquely created, by means of an expert system or through the efforts of an experienced co-worker, for selection of only those components that are needed. The concept of JIT training suggests not only that the training or learning is delivered on a timely basis but also that it matches the scope of the performance requirements, with enough time and content but nothing in excess. The challenge—potentially met through implementation of the HPT principles of systematic needs analysis and performance-based design—is to ensure both the training's relevance and its effectiveness.

2. *One-stop resources.* These resources exist in a wide variety of situations, although the root of the strategy is a customer-focused marketing concept: to provide convenience and save time by offering everything for a given type of customer from a single source. For example, the U.S. Department of Labor has created one-stop resources to provide comprehensive job-related information for dislocated workers, career guidance, and job placement services to its tar-

get population. As another example, the Detroit Empowerment Zone, in order to spur economic development in depressed areas of the city, established a "one-stop capital shop" for accessing comprehensive information about public and private sources of business capital, entrepreneurial education and counseling, technical assistance for small companies, and grant information for minority- and women-owned businesses.

For employees in a typical service business, the one-stop concept is embodied by workstations that provide immediate access to customers' accounts as well as to the latest technical reference materials and internal management documents so that employees can get immediate answers to technical or procedural questions. With the advent of widespread access to the Internet and its related technologies, "storefront" Web sites often provide access to combinations of other Web sites, repositories, and databases useful to particular types of workers (for example, sales representatives). These one-stop information resources may include on-line references and job aids as well as decision support, filtered newsfeeds, technology-mediated learning programs, schedules and registration for conventional training programs, collaboration systems, and other resources.

3. *Virtual colleges.* In today's environment, there is no compelling reason to believe that all performance improvement tools and resources should be housed in a single organization's physical space or information system. More and more virtual organizations or colleges are emerging to leverage a broader array of available resources, primarily through various forms of brokering. Electronic forms of the virtual college or resource organization exist in three categories: private ventures, public/private partnerships, or wholly public entities.

An example of a private venture, and the one that probably offers the most comprehensive set of services, is the Talent Alliance *(www.talentalliance.org)*, a membership entity that bills itself on its home page as a "virtual organization of experts—high tech, high talent." Major organizations like AT&T, DuPont, GTE, Johnson & Johnson, TRW, and United Parcel Service, are current members. The Talent Alliance's services include training, career counseling, job/talent matching, a futures forum, and research on industry trends. All contact and participation takes place on line.

An example of a public/private partnership is the National Technological University, which forms alliances between companies and university schools of engineering to sponsor degree-granting programs as well as short courses. Most of the programs are delivered via distance learning.

An example of a wholly public entity is the Michigan Virtual Auto College, established in 1996 to meet the coming need for more than one hundred thousand automotive workers by the year 2003. Major funding for its current operations is derived from the state government, and the state's three major research universities head its board of directors. Its long-range plan is to deliver training over the Internet, using community colleges and other public organizations as virtual training sites.

JIT training, one-stop resources, and virtual colleges are not necessarily mutually distinguishable. What they have in common is the need, across multiple boundaries, for integration among functions, organizations, disciplines, and technologies. Consequently, as is true in nearly all border-spanning efforts, systematic implementation and maintenance planning are essential. Certain conditions, including those that follow, are necessary to the development and implementation of such systems:

- Alignment of tasks with organizational structure and responsibilities
- Greater integration of knowledge and experience across disciplines
- Methods for reliably calculating development time and costs
- Clear system design and development methodologies
- New definitions of subject matter expertise
- Organizational reward systems consistent with necessary organizational changes

Alignment is a critical prerequisite, as it is in any other type of systems-based approach to organizations. The following organizational components are among those that need to be aligned (Bassi, Benson, and Cheney, 1996, p. 38):

- Strategies, vision, mission, and goals
- Beliefs and values
- Management practices (leadership styles, decision making, communication)
- Work practices and processes (jobs, tasks, skills, knowledge, abilities)
- Human resource systems (employee selection, training, development, compensation)
- Systems involving technology, measurement, and communication

The greater the desired integration among organizations, functions, and resources, the greater the need for alignment, and the more complex it will be.

As a discipline, or family of disciplines, HPT can provide the essential glue for efforts aimed at improving performance where learning is merging with work. Application of mature HPT methodologies for alignment, analysis, design, development, implementation, and continuous improvement of performance systems can make the difference between success and failure.

FLUID ORGANIZATIONAL STRUCTURES AND METHODS

According to Cappelli (1997, p. 11), the past ten years of organizational research and history seem to point toward a "revolution in the way work is organized and managed." The same period has also seen a questioning of the role of human resource systems in the changing work paradigm. Cappelli urges the design of new human resource systems that take the following issues into account:

- Work organization
- The collapse of promotion ladders
- Flatter organizational structures
- Employment security
- Job tenure

These issues in turn have significant implications for the changing work paradigm and lead to the following contradictory trends:

- The paradox of teamwork with reduced job tenure
- The frustration of upward mobility without a promotion ladder
- The paradox of declining employee commitment and work-related attitudes with no apparent decline in employee performance
- Lifestyle concerns associated with uncertain job prospects
- Unstable employment patterns
- The future of unions

Thus the workforce is pushed to operate more as an external than as the internal entity it has traditionally been considered to be, and this trend in turn leads to a more market-driven approach to human resources. A market-driven approach would imply that departments of human resources will have to demonstrate return on investment, and this development in turn would lead to increased use of and demand for HPT principles and tools. Such a value-added perspective in human resources would achieve a more relevant customer focus.

A rethinking of the human resources function will also have implications for HRD functions. McLagan (1996, p. 63) claims that administrative functions need to be moved to "specialist suppliers, technology, and other organizational functions." More managerial responsibilities must be moved to the line, to teams, and to employees themselves. Given what the future probably holds in store, we are more likely to see more changes than stability in the traditional functions of human resources and organizational development. The expressed need for specialists naturally leads to more opportunities for performance technologists to have significant roles in nontraditional organizations.

New Organizations

Operational models for the HRD function in organizations are changing rapidly, with increasing fluidity in organizational structures and processes and with reduced workforce stability. These trends are leading to new models of organizations and even of economic value. This state of flux and the growth of the knowledge-driven economy have led directly to changes in organizational structures and human resources–related activities. The emergence of virtual companies, strategic partnering, and telecommuting, along with the integration of multiple technologies and entrepreneurial ventures, has had a significant impact on the Western industrialized countries so that these economies "are increasingly based on knowledge and information. Knowledge is now the recognized driver of productivity and economic growth, leading to a new focus on the role of information, technology and learning in economic performance. It has brought about calls for emphasis on research and innovation, training, and flexible structures of work" (Organisation for Economic Co-operation and Development, 1996a, p. 6).

According to economist Paul Romer (cited in Kurtzman, 1997) this state of affairs has significant implications for how companies organize themselves to participate in the new world economy. According to Romer, no one has figured out what the optimal institutions and structures will be.

Methods of Change

How companies organize and reorganize themselves to face today's and tomorrow's business opportunities has long been of concern to HPT. The contributions of HPT to the organizational aspects of human resources are linked primarily to the methods used for organizational development, redevelopment, and change management. Two general methods will be considered here: process improvement (or *reengineering*, as it has more recently been called), and organizational learning.

Hammer (Hammer and Champy, 1993) is popularly credited with inventing the concept and practice of process reengineering, but HPT professionals are more likely to cite Rummler (Rummler and Brache, 1995) as the true pioneer in this field. The concept of reengineering has become synonymous with downsizing or "rightsizing." There is little doubt that, over the past ten years, reengineering has not only been applied but also misapplied, and to such an extent that one must question its future. Bushko, Lee, and Raynor (1996) report less application of reengineering. They cite a study, performed by the Mercer consulting firm of New York, wherein no correlation was found between reengineering and business success. According to a recent lead story in one industry trade magazine ("Reexamining reengineering," 1996) 65 percent of surveyed companies reported that reengineering had not been successful, with one reported problem being that many companies were cutting too much and losing highly skilled employees, whom they were then were forced to rehire as consultants. According to the layperson's interpretation, *reengineering* is a nasty word that means massive disruption, with little return on investment. What has apparently been forgotten is a *systems approach* to organizational transformation. A systemic process would include more positive human resources practices, such as reskilling, revising incentive and reward systems, and using new performance measurements as well as new and more appropriate organizational structures. However, given the likely future context of work and the ongoing need for adaptation to today's process-driven culture, there will continue to be a significant need to develop and modify work processes. This likelihood would argue for a more humane approach to managing change—an approach to which HPT is well suited.

Applications of the concept of the learning organization, originally championed by Senge (1990), appear to offer a significant contrast to applications of reengineering in that reengineering proposes quick fixes, whereas adoption of the principles of the learning organization will require a longer and more evolutionary process. The learning organization's major concepts—personal mastery, mental models, shared vision, team learning, and the fifth discipline of systems thinking—are very consistent with the "human" aspect of HPT. This approach to organizational development connects the needs and skills of individuals to the goals of organizational performance. Organizations are viewed as patterns of interaction rather than as physical entities. According to Senge (1990, p. 32), the architects of learning organizations "must develop and improve the infrastructural mechanisms so that people have the resources they need: time, management support, money, information, ready contact with colleagues, and more."

Organizations like the Ford Motor Company have adopted a massive process to train more than thirty thousand managers and engineers in the principles of the learning organization over the next few years; in a different cultural environment, Intel Corporation is undertaking a similar effort. Many other executives and managers have also been enlisted by Senge to spread the word on, and the success of, this "movement." But some still question the relationship between the adoption of these principles and bottom-line business success. The benefits of these principles have been demonstrated (Senge and others, 1994), but their long-term implementation cycles, coupled with the concomitant impatience for results, can wreak havoc with the adoption process.

Both of these general methodologies have faltered in specific cases, often because of incomplete strategies for implementation. The subject of implementation has recently attracted more attention from HPT leaders. The analysis and evaluation tools of HPT continue to receive considerable attention in HPT publications, but some leaders (for example, Joe Harless, as cited in Langdon and Whiteside, 1997) are now speaking out in favor of filling the gaps. More implementation concepts, reflecting complex interactions among new technologies and systems, need to be created, tested, and validated in deployment settings. This effort could take the form of multiple strategies yielding an integrated set of solutions (Brethower, 1997). To date, the preferred method is to apply and extend the methods proposed by Rummler and Brache (1995) for process reengineering. A critical need in this area, with respect to the theme of this chapter, concerns implementation when there are multiple technologies in the workplace.

Implementation and Integration of Multiple Technologies

The growth of technology in general, together with the incorporation of performance technology in the workplace, requires systems thinking and leads to the necessity of integrating separate technologies. People who have led the successful deployment of new technology, integrating it smoothly into the work environment with existing technology, generally agree on the fundamental concepts related to the human components of this implementation (Ralls, 1994). Three common lessons have been derived:

1. Involve workers in technology design and implementation.
2. Train workers to use the technology.
3. Give workers control over the technology.

Although these procedures appear simple enough, they are not commonly applied; deploying technology for technology's sake continues to be the mantra of numerous companies. It is not hard to find managers who point to factory warehouses and aisles littered with hardware too complex and too unreliable to serve their needs.

For example, in a survey of 364 users and vendors of advanced manufacturing technology (AMT), 57 percent of the respondents stated that a purchased AMT system had failed to meet business expectations, and 49 percent reported that their implementation schedules had been lengthened by as much as 50 percent (Uzmeri and Sanderson, 1990). These results are consistent with a number of other surveys showing that complex systems fail to achieve their intended aims. These findings are not surprising, given that implementing some of the massive new systems for information technology—systems designed to yield enterprise-and companywide control of electronic information, including the areas of personnel systems, electronic commerce for order and invoice processing, inventory control, process control, supplier and vendor communications, and anything else that can be converted to electronic format—not only can take years but also combines business process reengineering with information technology reengineering. This kind of implementation requires massive training efforts, with cross-disciplinary task forces across the entire enterprise. The implementation strategy is the key to success for an intervention of this kind.

The continued development of technology will place greater and more complex demands on performance technologists. Indeed, hardware- and software-based performance technologies (such as multimedia training and tools), teleconferencing, and Internet-based and Web-based tools already challenge the ability of any one person to understand and use them appropriately, to say nothing of integrating them with other technologies and systems already in the workplace. Optimization in the deployment of integrated technologies will become a critical objective for many performance interventions.

The successful transfer and integration of technology will be critically dependent on the specialists and generalists who perform the actual implementation. Furthermore, policies and procedures for working across unit and departmental lines will take on increasing importance in the development and deployment of technology. Implementation systems that take account of workers' participation, organizational and individual incentives, physical and emotional resources, skills, and organizational culture need to be woven into a core of simultaneous and aligned activities. The task may appear daunting, but its execution is within the reach of HPT.

The successful integration of multiple technologies clearly depends on the creation of implementation strategies and on the resulting infrastructure. This creation process poses significant challenges to HPT professionals. The tools and methods of HPT can assist in the effective integration or linking of various technologies with various organizational models, and while doing so they will measure the accomplishments that these technologies are intended to enhance. The cost-effectiveness of HPT might very well be assessed on the basis of how well performance technology itself can be integrated with other technologies for improving the performance of individuals, work groups, and entire organizations.

KNOWLEDGE MANAGEMENT

The phrase *knowledge management* has come into vogue over the last several years and has become one of those vague but powerful business mantras repeated often and everywhere. In the simplest terms, it refers to strategies and processes for using knowledge to enhance competitive advantage or support professional communities. Many consulting firms and software developers have jumped on a bandwagon driven by ideas like these:

- People and what they know are essential to organizations.

- Intangibles (such as conceptual models, processes and procedures, formulas, diagnostic algorithms or guidelines, and operational know-how) are marketable, competitive assets.

- Organizational agility demands that individual performers, groups, and organizations as a whole continue to learn in order to remain competitive.

- Organizations can strategically manage the accumulation and sharing of knowledge at a departmental or companywide level in order to improve performance and must implement processes and tools for doing so.

Prominent writers on the learning organization and organizational process improvement (for example, Senge, 1990; Ulrich and Lake, 1990) have influenced both the philosophy and the implementation of knowledge management. Growing numbers of organizations now include functions with titles like "knowledge manager" and "chief knowledge officer." At the end of the 1990s, knowledge management has become a hot investment area in high technology and a growing practice in virtually every significant consulting firm.

Definition of Knowledge

The idea that knowledge is of a higher order than information, which in turn is more refined than data, has become lore among current writers, consultants, and managers. Information is thought to be structured data, whereas knowledge is understood to be actionable information, or know-how. From the perspective of HPT, we might define the term *knowledge* as information accessed or learned and applied in support of human performance; HPT practitioners and theorists have been using similar definitions for years (see, for example, Gilbert, 1978).

Knowledge Management and Information Technology

Even before the emergence of the craze for knowledge management, software tools of various types were applied to support knowledge and its application to organizations. Computer-based training systems, on-line documentation, expert systems, and various types of electronic performance support systems were among the earliest knowledge software. These were simply job aids or efforts to automate learning processes (as, for example, in the case of programmed instruction).

Developments in technologies related to databases, data analysis and extraction, and computer communications have brought another generation of tools and have emerged in parallel with the terminology of knowledge management. For the most part, those involved with adapting these technologies to the support of performance are either information technologists or business managers, not HPT practitioners. Consequently, they may often benefit by working with

HPT practitioners, as we have suggested in the past (Binder, 1989; Brandenburg and Binder, 1992).

The advent of inexpensive storage capacity was another enabling factor for knowledge management. When storage technology became powerful and flexible enough to enable the archiving and retrieval of virtually unlimited data of all kinds (including text, video, audio, and "unstructured" documents and graphics), and when storage capacity was no longer a limiting factor, enterprisewide or companywide knowledge management became a possibility.

However, technology enthusiasts have often made naïve assumptions about what technology per se could accomplish. A common belief (whether implicit or stated explicitly) is that technology can transform large amounts of unstructured data and information into knowledge through various forms of automatic indexing, "fuzzy logic," sentence parsing, case-based reasoning, agents, "wizards," or other forms of computer intelligence. These things may be possible someday, broadly speaking, but the reality of today is that this approach is profoundly limited. Human preprocessing of information, in one form or other, will be needed for the foreseeable future if the desired result is to support efficient and effective performance.

Various types of computer-based communication and collaboration technology have contributed immensely to the evolution of knowledge management; for example, an early form of collaboration technology was e-mail, with the ability to attach documents. As databases were combined with communication channels like electronic bulletin boards, group access to collaborative repositories of information arrived. Nevertheless, because of "push" advertising and news services (whereby information arrives automatically in one's e-mail box), bulk e-mailing, and the explosive growth of Web technology, the threat of information overload, and of performance decline rather than performance improvement, is growing faster than the ability of most organizations or individuals to manage it.

Management of Knowledge Management

As the possibilities for access to and communication of information have grown, organizations have begun to face new problems that require new organizational solutions. In many quarters, the "informated" organization envisioned by Zuboff (1988) has evolved into a balkanized network of on-line communities and information sources. Many *Fortune* 500 corporations have hundreds and even thousands of intranet sites, and some of our most advanced organizations are strangling on their own technology. Just as between 70 and 80 percent of all first-time reengineering projects fail (Hammer and Champy, 1993), most so-called knowledge management efforts experience limited success.

Management of any asset or resource, whether financial, physical, or human, demands standardized policies, procedures, and processes. In the area of knowledge management, while technology standards (file formats, communication protocols, HTML syntax, and so on) have been evolving to support the technology itself, other types of standards have been lagging behind. A glaring example can be found in the design and function of intranet sites used by organizations to share internal information. In many of the most technologically advanced companies, hundreds of employees have learned the basics of site design, and department-level access to this kind of technology gives rise to many sites or databases every week. Typically, each cluster of sites is organized differently, uses different tools, and provides content that may be partly or wholly redundant with what is available elsewhere. Often the creators and managers of these sites are competing with others for the attention of employees and customers rather than collaborating to support efficient and effective performance across the enterprise. The very fact that these sites exist is information that is often passed more by word of mouth or by e-mail than by a single, effective user interface that offers a guide to all the information needed to support performance.

The emergence of organizational titles like "chief knowledge officer," or "CKO," reflects a growing understanding at the top of most organizations that there is a problem. Raising the CKO function to the level of senior management is a move toward alignment, integration, and strategic intent, but CKOs and their ilk often come from the area of information technology and may lack in-depth understanding of human performance. This is an area where HPT can add significant value—for example, by starting with performance requirements in the design of knowledge management systems and the selection and structuring of content.

The difference between useful knowledge and neutral or unhelpful "knowledge" is that the former is presented in a way that supports important job functions. In other words, implicit in the alignment process that should occur at the onset of a knowledge management project is front-end performance analysis. A corollary of this point, which runs counter to some efforts to produce knowledge repositories across the enterprise, is that knowledge management is most powerful when it addresses a particular performance domain or set of accomplishments (for example, sales and marketing, operations, or customer service) or when it supports domain-specific standards within a larger framework.

Nevertheless, the knowledge required for performance in most of today's organizations is likely to come from multiple sources or functions within the organization. For example, effective management of sales knowledge requires a focus on what sales representatives do and produce, but the sources of the necessary knowledge may include people in corporate marketing, product management, customer service, research and development, and other areas. In this context, HPT can contribute by introducing processes and tools for front-end performance analysis, aimed at identifying the content and structure that will best support performance, and ideally working with information systems specialists to identify software performance requirements as well.

New Organizational Processes and Functions

Knowledge management requires new cross-functional communication processes for sharing information. These will often involve task forces or collaborative work groups that are assigned various tasks. Knowledge management can leverage models for document management and include workflow planning and automation, editing and approval cycles, and efforts to capture content as early in the process as possible. Especially in organizations (for example, high-tech marketing companies) where individuals change jobs quite frequently, establishing standard processes and models is the only alternative to chaos and information overload. These processes and standards are difficult to establish and maintain, but they will be of increasing strategic importance.

At many levels, new and increasingly sophisticated processes for knowledge management require people to impose intelligence on information. Humans can add value to ongoing knowledge management processes in a number of ways, including those that follow:

- By defining knowledge classification schemes, key words, and index terms to support tagging of documents and other "knowledge objects," individual interest profiling, and access

- By tagging, screening, and structuring information as it enters the system (captured from end users or from within centralized departments or groups)

- By defining logical and page templates, and information or document structures, on the basis of users' performance requirements

- By monitoring and maintaining various types of standards

- By transforming information into knowledge through the creation of documents, the extraction of relevant information from existing documents, and the combining of information with other sources

Most of these activities fall within the core areas of competence of HPT practitioners and are likely to define the emergence of new job functions (knowledge manager, specialized on-line librarian). The best organizations will leverage these new functions so that the value they add to the information dramatically increases the relevance and usability of knowledge for large numbers of end users. It will be important to cost-justify these job functions by estimating not only the amount of time and effort they will save across an entire group of performers but also the productivity or effectiveness they will add.

Standards for Knowledge Architectures

The term *knowledge architecture* is another that has emerged and is being used in various ways. We define the term *knowledge architecture* as a content framework specifying the structure of knowledge for a given performance domain and including at least the following features:

- *Standard terminology:* Labels for categories, key words, and defined topics or subtopics of information (for example, *market trends* as a standard term in a sales knowledge system)

- *Standard sequences:* Predictable sequences of topics, based on logical and prerequisite relationships (for example, *technical background* before *product information*)

- *Standard information templates or structures:* Logical and page formats that present information to support performance (for example, tables that list features as solutions to specific customer problems)

- *Standard links:* Defined links between categories of information to support understanding, cross-referencing, and performance that requires cognitive associations (for example, links between market segments and customer needs)

This type of content framework is only now beginning to emerge in the knowledge management marketplace. Some of the earlier technologies have focused on filtering news feeds, for example, by assigning classificatory language and allowing users to use that language to define their interests. An emerging alternative to the standard search engine is the predefined hierarchy of links or menu items—a rudimentary content architecture. As companies continue to refine their systems, such schemes will become more prevalent as a means of imposing consistency on how knowledge is chunked, labeled, stored, and accessed.

Integration of Knowledge Management with Training

In the best case, knowledge management (which is usually focused on access and communication tools) must come together with learning methods and processes. Currently, it is common for training organizations to be completely disconnected from those creating on-line reference systems, intranets, and electronic collaboration tools. The ideal is to use the same knowledge architecture for both training and knowledge management when the knowledge architecture is intended to support the same performers. Even traditional training (for example, classroom workshops) can be integrated with on-line knowledge management systems by designing the use of those systems into prestudy and classroom activities and follow-up support. Technology-enabled learning management systems (for example, LearningSpace from IBM/Lotus, as well as various forms of Internet-based learning) are collaborative environments that can be seamlessly integrated with intranets and Web sites. Extension of knowledge management to support field coaching and on-the-job training is an obvious direction for integrating these processes. Such integration will require cross-functional alignment and collaboration.

Maintenance

As with other organizational processes that involve flows and repositories of information, maintenance and updating will be crucial to the long-term success of knowledge management systems. Knowledge management is inherently focused on maintaining up-to-date information for users, and when information falls out of date, users will quickly abandon the system as unreliable. Instead, they will make phone calls or send e-mails to individuals whom they consider to be experts (thus increasing the costs that knowledge management was intended to reduce).

Knowledge architecture defines topics and subtopics of needed knowledge, organizes and sequences that knowledge, and presents it to users with value-added filtering and tagging. It provides a strong foundation for knowledge maintenance as well. When chunks of knowledge are tagged with predefined topical key words, for example, it is much easier for those responsible for maintenance and updating to identify and revise those chunks, as necessary.

Knowledge management, at the time of this writing, is still more promise than reality but is vigorously emerging in most large organizations. HP technologists may bring important areas of competence to the general managers and information technologists now mainly responsible for knowledge management.

SMALL COMPANIES AND PERFORMANCE TECHNOLOGY

Rapid growth in small business is expanding opportunities for HPT applications outside major corporations. Although this discussion uses examples primarily from the manufacturing sector (because of the availability and organization of resource material), parallel examples can be drawn, and arguments made, for other economic sectors.

Petzinger (1998, p. 1) describes the current state of affairs: "Megamergers and consolidations are all sideshows compared with restructuring of the economy into ever-smaller pieces. Like dandelions gone to seed major companies have released millions of experienced workers to the wind, and they're thriving in small niches. . . . In manufacturing, new economies of locality are beginning to conquer old economies of scale. . . . As information technology advances, pundits warn of small business 'disintermediation,' wiping out middlemen. They're wrong. Technology creates far more opportunities than it eliminates."

One national trade group of small-business owners recently reported that the intention to hire more people is the highest it has been in fourteen years (National

Federation of Independent Business Education Foundation, 1998). Changes in the manufacturing sector illustrate this trend. A major shift has occurred in the size of manufacturing firms since the middle of the 1970s. From 1980 to 1990, the number of manufacturing firms grew from 319,000 to 378,000, and 98 percent of these firms employ five hundred or fewer workers (Modernization Forum, 1993).

However, the growing role of small firms in American manufacturing has not generally enhanced national economic competitiveness. The overall rate of growth in productivity has slowed since 1970, but it has slowed twice as fast in small firms, from a 3.4 percent change in value added per work hour in 1947–1967 to a 1.3 percent change in 1967–1987 (Luria, 1993). This decline in productivity has brought with it a widening wage gap and has therefore decreased earning power for the average worker.

Needs Facing Small Manufacturers

Numerous studies conducted over the past 15 years have examined the needs of smaller manufacturers (Manufacturing Studies Board, 1986; Organisation for Economic Co-operation and Development, 1993; National Research Council, 1993; Shapira, 1990). These studies show remarkable similarity in their findings; therefore, only results from the Organisation for Economic Co-operation and Development (1993) are listed here, for illustrative purposes. That study showed that smaller manufacturers have needs related to the following areas:

- Capital
- Prediction of demand
- Apparent costs of developing innovations
- Adaptation of marketing functions
- Costs of monitoring future applications
- Finding technological information
- Employee skills
- Government regulations

In order to meet these needs, companies have to adopt a systems approach. The components of the solutions that are found will probably comprise those proposed by the Modernization Forum (1993):

- Deployment of new technology
- Market diversification
- Improvements in the processes used for organizing work
- Skill development for managers and frontline workers alike

- Access to financial resources
- Interfirm cooperation
- Advanced practices of business management

To implement solutions of this type, small companies require access to experts and resources that lie outside their typical purview. Many of these issues deal with human resources, but significant expertise in this area is rarely found in companies with fewer than two hundred employees. Therefore, few smaller companies take a total systems approach to performance improvement or modernization.

Most studies indicate that some form of external assistance is needed, either through direct interventions or through incentives. A range of solutions is likely to be involved, from free market to direct government intervention, and may involve assistance through the following channels:

- Major customers (but relationships with major customers are most often adversarial)
- Equipment vendors (but selling is of paramount importance to them)
- Universities (but they are more interested in research than in small applied projects)
- The federal government (but, generally speaking, the government historically has been against establishing an "industrial policy," the establishment of the Manufacturing Extension Partnership notwithstanding)
- Trade associations (but they are generally more interested in legislative agendas than in direct assistance to members)
- Peer networks of companies (but trust has to be established among members before benefits of any scale can be achieved)

Regardless of these deficiencies, each channel offers opportunities for HPT practitioners who are able to devise means of participating in the small-company market.

Application of HPT's Tenets

To date HPT has not played a direct role in the types of assistance just outlined. However, the solution components cited by the Modernization Forum (1993) and listed earlier correspond significantly with the tenets of HPT. Moreover, many tools and techniques have been developed and validated for accelerating the deployment of technology in smaller companies, and these show promise.

One is called High Integration of Technology, Organization, and People, or HI-TOP, an analysis technique developed by Majchrzak, Fleischer, and Roitman

(1991). HI-TOP proposes to eliminate the independent, asynchronous planning generally followed in the deployment of new advanced manufacturing technology. A HI-TOP analysis has three goals:

1. To indicate what people and organizational capabilities are needed for a particular technology plan

2. To determine whether the appropriate people and organizational capabilities are likely to be in place

3. To suggest changes in the technology plans, the organization, and people if the necessary capabilities are missing

The process is designed to reduce surprises and smoothly implement the needed changes in technology, the organization, and people.

Another technique, this one focusing on the process of how new technology should be launched in a manufacturing setting, is described by Beal (1994). His time-based approach starts with the initial systems requirements, before the machinery is ordered, and moves through the process of building and testing machine components, ending with the actual launch of "job one" on the shop floor. His model takes the best-practice transfer-of-training guide offered by Broad and Newstrom (1992) and translates it for this application. The result has been a niche business of working with smaller machine-tool builders in order to build customers' (machine purchasers') requirements into the training and organizational elements before, during, and after the machine has been constructed.

The Role of the HPT Professional as an Intermediary

It is less likely that an HPT professional would work with a single small company than with a group of companies. This goal would most easily be accomplished if relationships were established with third-party or intermediary organizations. Such relationships can be built with organizations that are sensitive to and have significant knowledge of the needs of small companies. Therefore, an environment driven by the demand side rather than the supply side is likely to offer the best opportunities for the enterprising HPT practitioner.

Intermediary organizations take many forms (for example, local business associations, economic development agencies, and, to some extent, community colleges). The intermediary organizations that are most successful in achieving firm-level improvements and modernization forge new relationships in a region and facilitate intrafirm and interfirm learning that reduces the costs and risks associated with the deployment of new forms of organizational behavior (Flynn and Forrant, 1995). In a sense, they create the social infrastructure required to build trust and cooperation among firms. Notable examples are the Westside Industrial Retention and Expansion Network (WIRE-Net), in Cleveland, Ohio, which has more than three hundred member companies that participate in a wide range of business assistance and training programs; the Berkshire Plastics Network (Bosworth, 1997), based in Springfield, Massachusetts, which established an apprentice program to attract skilled workers; and the Labor-Management Council for Economic Renewal of Taylor, Michigan, comprising forty-two United Auto Workers–represented manufacturing companies that meet regularly to share information and learn about strategies for implementing new work practices to improve competitiveness.

HPT professionals could serve as specialized consultants and as network brokers acting to facilitate the initiation and maintenance of improvements and organizational change activities. This would be a relatively new role for an HPT professional, but it is one that will probably be important if HPT is to have long-term influence on the growth and survival of small companies. In general, according to Bosworth (1997, p. 1), these cooperatives or networks "demand a fundamentally new partnership between the public labor market agencies and the internal human resource development systems of employers. But developing true partnerships with individual firms, one-by-one, is an impossible task. The experiences of a few . . . projects suggest the need for new mechanisms to foster interfirm cooperation that will support the pursuit of joint solutions to common human resource development problems." One option would include the delivery of cost-effective workshops and other methods of technology transfer. This market is open to many independent HPT professionals who can package and market their tools and methods in public or third-party-sponsored workshops.

In light of the preceding discussion, what opportunities exist for performance technology? There exist opportunities for theoretical contributions from research studies, application studies leading to tool development and testing, consulting activities, and commercial sales and product development—all geared to the mutual benefit of performance technologists and their customers in this market. To enter this market, the performance technologist is likely to work with an intermediary organization rather than to attempt direct one-to-one ventures.

SUMMARY

As organizational structures undergo rapid change in the dynamic context of the global economy, technologies available for supporting and improving human performance are also emerging at an accelerated rate. Future trends in HPT will be tightly linked to interactions between these two types of changes, and to the changes that emerge from that interaction itself.

Given increasing demands to integrate learning with work, the means of delivering performance improvement and training to workers will continue to evolve, as will the organizations that support these means. Technology-enabled learning and performance support will be the standard rather than the exception in many environments, as will a shift from training to on-the-job coaching. Various forms of JIT learning, one-stop resources, and virtual HRD organizations will evolve to support performance in organizations undergoing constant change and employee turnover. The need for greater integration of technologies and processes, more systematic and broader alignment of goals and plans, and ongoing implementation planning will also accelerate in response to these trends. HPT professionals are uniquely qualified to support these changes.

Knowledge management will become a strategic activity in most large organizations, and the most successful efforts will combine the use of appropriate technology, performance-based analysis and implementation, and the application of human intermediaries to add value in the knowledge management process. As the global economy shifts human resources from larger companies to smaller ones, there will be greater opportunities for HPT in smaller organizations. The challenge will be to leverage existing and emerging public and private collaborations and intermediary organizations to provide HPT methods and processes to smaller companies in ways that are cost-effective and practical for this growing market.

References

Bassi, L., Benson, G., and Cheney, S. (1996). The top ten trends. *Training and Development* 50:11, 28–42.

Beal, P. (1994, Sept.). *Should equipment builders provide training?* Presentation at the national technical and skills conference of the American Society for Training and Development, Philadelphia, PA.

Binder, C. (1989). Hypertext design issues. *Performance Improvement Quarterly* 2:3, 16–33.

Bosworth, B. (1997). *Interfirm cooperation for work force development.* Chapel Hill, NC: Regional Technology Strategies.

Brandenburg, D. C., and Binder, C. (1992). Emerging trends in human performance interventions. In H. D. Stolovitch and E. J. Keeps (eds.), *Handbook of Human Performance Technology: A comprehensive guide for analyzing and solving performance problems in organizations.* San Francisco: Jossey-Bass.

Brethower, D. M. (1997). Rapid analysis: Matching solutions to changing situations. *Performance Improvement* 36:10, 16–21.

Broad, M., and Newstrom, J. (1992). *Transfer of training.* Reading, MA: Addison-Wesley.

Bushko, D., Lee, W., and Raynor, M. (1996). Issues and trends: New opportunities, new challenges. *Journal of Management Consulting* 9:2, 37–46.

Cappelli, P. (1997, July–Aug.). Rethinking the nature of work: A look at the research evidence. *Compensation & Benefits Review* 29, 4–50.

Cappelli, P., and others. (1997). *Change at work.* New York: Oxford University Press.

Flynn, E., and Forrant, R. (1995). *Facilitating firm-level change: The role of intermediary organizations in the manufacturing modernization process.* Boston: Jobs for the Future.

Gilbert, T. F. (1978). *Human competence: Engineering worthy performance.* New York: McGraw-Hill.

Groe, G. M., Pyle, W., and Jamrog, J. J. (1996). Information technology and HR. *Human Resource Planning* 35:2, 57–69.

Hammer, M., and Champy, J. (1993). *Reengineering the corporation: A manifesto for business revolution.* New York: HarperBusiness.

Kurtzman, J. (1997). An interview with Paul M. Romer. *Strategy & Business* 6, 78–88.

Langdon, D. G., and Whiteside, K. S. (1997). The performance technologist's role in interventions: An interview with Joe Harless. *Performance Improvement* 36:10, 36–38.

Luria, D. (1993, Mar.). *A high-road policy for U.S. manufacturing.* Address to the semiannual executive board meeting of the Manufacturing Extension Partnership, Ann Arbor, MI.

Majchrzak, A., Fleischer, M., and Roitman, D. (1991). *Reference manual for performing HI-TOP (High Integration of Technology, Organization, and People) analysis.* Ann Arbor, MI: Industrial Technology Institute.

Manufacturing Studies Board. (1986). *Human resource practices for implementing advanced manufacturing technologies.* Washington, DC: National Academy Press.

McLagan, P. (1996). Creating the future of HRD: Great ideas revisited. *Training and Development* 50:1, 60–65.

Modernization Forum. (1993). *Skills for industrial modernization.* Dearborn, MI: Modernization Forum.

National Federation of Independent Business Education Foundation. (1998). *Small-business economic trends.* Washington, DC: National Federation of Independent Business Education Foundation.

National Research Council. (1993). *Learning to change: Opportunities to improve the performance of smaller manufacturers.* Washington, DC: National Academy Press.

Organisation for Economic Co-operation and Development. (1993). *Small and medium-sized enterprises: Technology and competitiveness.* Paris: Commission of the European Communities.

Organisation for Economic Co-operation and Development. (1996a). The knowledge-driven economy. *OECD Observer* 200, 4–9.

Organisation for Economic Co-operation and Development. (1996b). *Technology and industrial performance: Technology diffusion, productivity, employment and skills, international competitiveness.* Paris: Organisation for Economic Co-operation and Development.

Petzinger, T. Jr. (1998, Jan. 9). The front lines: Small business. *Wall Street Journal*, p. 2–1.

Ralls, S. (1994). *Integrating technology with workers in the new American workplace.* Washington, DC: Office of the American Workplace, U.S. Department of Labor.

Reexamining reengineering. (1996, June 5). *Chemical Week* 158:22, 29–32.

Rummler, G. A., and Brache, A. P. (1995). *Improving performance: How to manage the white space on the organization chart* (2nd ed.). San Francisco: Jossey-Bass.

Senge, P. M. (1990). *The fifth discipline: The art and practice of the learning organization.* New York: Doubleday.

Senge, P. M., and others. (1994). *The fifth discipline fieldbook.* New York: Doubleday.

Shapira, P. (1990). *Modernizing manufacturing: New policies to build industrial extension services.* Washington, DC: Economic Policy Institute.

Silber, K. H. (1990, Aug.). How technology is changing training. *Data Training,* pp. 18–23.

Ulrich, D., and Lake, D. (1990). *Organizational capability: Competing from the inside out.* New York: Wiley.

Uzmeri, V., and Sanderson, S. (1990, Aug.). Buying advanced manufacturing technology. *Manufacturing Engineering,* pp. 11–15.

Zuboff, S. (1988). *In the age of the smart machine: The future of work and power.* New York: Basic Books.

CHAPTER FORTY-ONE

Emerging Trends in Instructional Interventions

Laura R. Winer
Nick Rushby
Jesús Vázquez-Abad

"Would you tell me, please, which way I ought to go from here?"
"That depends a good deal on where you want to get to," said the Cat.
"I don't much care where—" said Alice.
"Then it doesn't matter which way you go," said the Cat.
"—so long as I get somewhere," Alice added as an explanation.
"Oh, you're sure to do that," said the Cat, "if you only walk long enough."
—Lewis Carroll, *Alice in Wonderland*

The Cheshire Cat was right—if you do not care where you want to get to, it does not matter which way you go. However, unlike Alice, Human Performance Technology (HPT) professionals do care about their own destinations and those of the people for whom they design and develop instructional interventions. As we leave the 1990s and the twentieth century, we must reflect on the past, examine the present, and plan for the future. Without careful thought about where we are now and where we want to go, it would be too easy to wander aimlessly down paths that may not take us to the most desirable destinations. To respect that the term *technology* in the phrase *Human Performance Technology* refers to the application of knowledge, it is incumbent upon us to examine the objectives of instructional interventions, how and when they are used and could be used and by whom, what we now know about how people learn, and what means are or will soon be available to us for communicating with and among learners.

WHERE ARE WE NOW?

Despite the hype, classrooms are still where it is at, and in many important ways the situation has not changed significantly in the 1990s as compared to the 1980s (Vázquez-Abad and Winer, 1992). According to Bassi and Van Buren (1998), reporting on an American Society for Training and Development (ASTD) survey of private sector U.S. organizations with more than fifty employees, over 80 percent of all training time is still classroom-based and instructor-led. Data from the U.S. Office of Technology confirm the continuing popularity of classroom-based lectures or labs (Rae, 1994). Computer-based training was reported to be used by 44 percent of the companies, and other forms of intervention (such as videoconferencing and computer conferencing) were used by 11 percent and fewer. The most widespread training technology, with 100 percent of companies reporting its use, is job aids. The acceptance of this form of on-the-job training (OJT) supports the growing trend toward integrating learning and work, with less focus on passing a course and more on performance. The figures referring to the number of companies that make use of different technologies do not, however, account for how the vast majority of employees spend their training time.

As just described, most training time is spent in classrooms. Self-paced learning methods and use of training technologies account for just 13 percent of training time in U.S. companies (Bassi and Van Buren, 1998). Data from Japan, a country where there is a strong commitment to training, indicate that there is more classroom training in proportion to OJT than previously suggested in the literature there, and that a variety of training techniques are used in classroom training (Keller and Taguchi, 1996). The use of off-the-job training seems to be related to the focus of the training. For employee self-development, off-the-job training is more common, whereas for training directly related to the employee's current job, on-the-job training use is much stronger.

The message that people are the most important asset is having an impact, and firms are expressing increasing interest in knowledge management and intellectual capital (Bassi, Cheney, and Van Buren, 1997). Two trends relate directly to instructional interventions. The first is the growing shift toward companies' defining themselves as learning organizations, in which training is integral to work rather than separate from it. The second is the development of a concept known as *learning technologies*, or "the use of electronic technologies to deliver information and facilitate the development of skills and knowledge" (Bassi, Cheney, and Van Buren, p. 48), thus combining presentation methods and distribution methods.

ASTD created a benchmarking forum in 1991 to facilitate comparative analysis and identification of successful practices in training and performance improvement. The data, drawn from fifty-five large multinational companies, allowed the forum to provide a picture of the practices in place in companies that are positioned as worldwide leaders in training, learning, and performance improvement. Results of the 1997 benchmarking forum indicate five main findings (Bassi and Cheney, 1997):

1. Outsourcing is on the upswing

2. Training departments in large corporations are becoming more centralized

3. Classroom training remains the dominant delivery approach

4. Training delivery is using a variety of learning technologies, including the Internet

5. More companies are performing more detailed and systematic evaluations

Lloyd, Rushby, Vincent, and Megarry (1994) offer the following predictions for the twenty-first century:

- Organizations will have to cope with more varied and faster-changing customer needs, shorter product life cycles, and more competition from more countries.

- Changing patterns of demand will lead manufacturing companies to take on the characteristics of service companies, and vice versa, as well as to the reorganization of companies of all sizes.

- Increased use of new technologies will change the way companies organize and manage their activities and will redefine the skills they need.

- Technological changes will tend to result in much more knowledge-intensive processes, significant increases in productivity, and profound changes in occupational structures.

- Increasing numbers of businesses in developed economies will transfer manufacturing and assembly operations to developing economies, where labor and social costs are lower. This means that businesses in developed economies will have to focus on the value-adding, knowledge-based functions of research and development, marketing and distribution, and design and management in order to stay competitive.

- The onus will be on all organizations to get closer to their customers, provide superior customer service, and constantly improve all aspects of their effectiveness and efficiency. Crucial to their success will be the quantity and, most important, the quality of their workforces.

It is already apparent that, because of significant demographic changes and the changing skill requirements brought about by the introduction of new technologies, employers need to be increasingly innovative in human resources planning and development. In a time of uncertainty, the only organizations to prosper will be those that can learn from their mistakes (and their successes) and adapt to changing circumstances. Being a learning organization means more than providing opportunities for employees to learn (in their own time and on company time, at work and at home, according to their preferred learning styles); it must pervade the organizational ethos. According to Burke (1995), organizations developed as repressive institutions, but the learning organization must embrace effective instructional interventions for its members so that they can develop their competence and thus (by a process of aggregation) enable their organizations to build their core capabilities. These organizations will behave like strongly motivated learners, engaging in a continual cycle of review (What are our core capabilities, and what do we need them to be?), identification of learning needs, determination of the learning interventions required, and evaluation of the outcomes.

Trends noted in the field of human resources development (HRD) and in the training industry lead to a number of conclusions about what the learning needs are. Employees need to be more knowledgeable to start with, and they need to upgrade their knowledge and skills on an ongoing basis. Organizational restructuring and increased demands for individual productivity mean that formal courses are harder to justify. Time compression, rather than price resistance, is a major constraint. This means that instructional interventions must be more flexible so that learning can fit more seamlessly with other activities. Individuals must take more responsibility for their learning. More education and training are needed, at reduced costs (both direct and indirect). Productivity is now seen in terms of value added, and this fuels the demand for just-in-time training.

OVERVIEW OF RECENT DEVELOPMENTS

It seems that we have been traveling forever along a path toward a promised land where technology provides an effective and affordable means of supporting training. Since the earliest days, almost ninety years ago (we refer here to the aspirations expressed by Thorndike in 1912), the vision has remained just that—a vision. In part this is due to our continually rising expectations. In a world where the rate of change in technology is rapidly accelerating, we forget that technology's effective application often lags behind, particularly in fields as conservative as education and training. Generations of technology now come and go, on a scale of time that is measured in months, but training and, to an even greater degree, education operate on a scale of time that is much longer. Innovation comes slowly in instructional technology (IT).

Quantitative change is relatively easy to predict. For example, it was obvious some years ago that the power of desktop computer systems would increase exponentially, that the volume of data that could be stored and the speed at which the data could be accessed would also increase, and that the quality of graphics would improve to match and exceed that of broadcast television (the standard by which instructional graphics are measured). Nevertheless, the dropping costs of technology are continually being matched by increases in functionality. Developers, not unreasonably, use this enhanced functionality to improve the quality of their instructional materials so that the real cost of providing technology-based instruction remains almost constantly at a level where careful cost justifications are always required.

Predicting qualitative change is more difficult. Some innovations change the rules so that predictions of rates of change become invalid. The use of the Internet (together with intranets and extranets) in training is a major qualitative change that is affecting not only how we do training but also the costs of training, and it is enabling us to do radically different things. The long-predicted explosion of growth is closer, but it has not yet been reached. For the discerning instructional technologist, however, recent developments in technology have enabled some highly cost-effective instructional applications.

Evolution of Distance Learning

Distance learning strategies have been practiced in educational and training situations in the past. The present availability of information and communication technologies has enhanced the place of distance learning as a credible, efficient, appealing (and sometimes preferred) means of providing instruction.

The two established instructional techniques of audioconferencing and videoconferencing have been joined by hybrid technologies of computer conferencing, which enable small groups of participants to see each other (if still with poor resolution) and share information on their computer screens. These systems overcome a major disadvantage of business television because they provide a return path for the learners to share their thoughts and questions with others in the learning group. We are witnessing how Internet-based technologies are expanding access to instruction as well as the scale of instruction.

Traditional distance learning is defined as instruction in which the learner and tutor are separated by time and/or space; interaction is one to one, either asynchronous (by mail) or synchronous (by telephone). The new communication technologies are adding other means (e-mail, chats) for asynchronous and synchronous learner-tutor interactions and opening up the possibility of rich group interactions among learners, with or without the intervention of tutors. Interactive Distance Learning (IDL) offers a bridge between the classroom and single-user CD-ROM ("Training that proves a point," 1997). Many business television networks in the United States and Europe are evolving into systems that rely on a satellite-delivered transmission from a trainer in a central studio to multiple receiver sites. Feedback is handled either via keypads (over phone lines) or via the Internet. IDL is live, supports live interaction, enables groups to work together, and is not carved in stone (or pressed on disc).

One of the main players in IDL, Convergent Media Systems, has developed the Convergent Automated Presentation System (CAPS), which incorporates camera, graphics, script, and text control systems as well as keypad-based feedback. Numerous corporations with widely distributed staff who require ongoing updates are using IDL systems to provide more consistent training at significantly reduced costs, and with measurably improved performance. Organizations like BMW North America, Bell Atlantic, New England Mutual Life, RE/MAX, Unisys, and the Ford Motor Company have all found IDL technology beneficial. An important impact of the IDL training itself derives from the fact that travel costs and time out of the office are financially negligible and so training can be scheduled in smaller chunks (for example, two hours of training every day for a week versus two solid days of training).

The Consortium for Affordable and Accessible Distance Education is a collection of educational institutions, national and international government and quasi–government agencies, foundations, and private corporations that are developing and demonstrating a high-performance electronic communications infrastructure. The consortium's activities are detailed by Ljutic (1996), who also reports on an initiative by Community Telecentres, which was developed to support teleworking, teletraining, public administration, telemedicine, and other activities in small and medium-sized enterprises in less developed countries.

As another example of innovation, the TeleScopia Project, described by Collis, Vingerhoets, and Moonen (1997), was a one-year undertaking of the Commission of the European Community involving a consortium of thirteen project partners in eight countries under the direction of Deutsche Telekom. The project united telecommunications providers, course providers, and researchers with access to the most powerful telematics channels feasible for training delivery.

A number of issues are raised by global training via videoconferencing, and these issues come together around the concept of interactivity (Filipczak, 1997). International participants do not all necessarily perceive interactivity the same way. For example, the more American-style "edutainment" may not go over well: it may be acceptable in American courses to give game show–type prizes, but this practice may be too frivolous for some European audiences. Contact with other cultures can be seen as a positive secondary effect of videoconferencing, especially for the multinational company with a global corporate culture in which it wants its employees to be comfortable. Logistical factors, such as limited bandwidth and access time, must be taken into account, and language issues must also be considered. For example, English is often the de facto business language, but this does not mean that all participants will have sufficient language skills to participate spontaneously in discussions. A combination of asynchronous text-based communication with live videoconferencing may be appropriate. Moreover, even providing closed captioning in English may greatly improve comprehension because many people understand what they read better than what they hear (especially when accents are unfamiliar). Combining videoconferencing with on-site training can also help to create a dynamic bond, and it varies the originating site so that each group can host the others.

As a final example of distance learning, Volunteers in Technical Assistance *(http://vita.org/)* has been experimenting with using low Earth-orbit satellites for shortwave communications in Africa as a way to overcome problems posed by poor telephone connections. Some African countries are subject to ongoing political unrest or instability, however, and so long-term projects in those countries may be risky investments.

Impact of the Internet

The Internet is often considered to be an essentially new system for the delivery of information. As such, its potential is enormous: massive data banks that are distributed all over the world, together with powerful search mechanisms, links among different kinds and formats of information, and a global transparent interconnection, are all combined to provide access to previously unimaginable quantities of information. Nevertheless, we should not forget that in 1997 there were only approximately fifty-seven million people worldwide with access to the Internet, fourteen million of whom had e-mail access only. This represents less than 2 percent of the world population; even in the United States, less than 16 percent of the population aged fifteen and older has access (Doyle, 1997). Still, as a repository of information, the Internet has especially appealing features. If it is true that any kind of information, even if often not validated, can be offered by anyone with access to a server, then this also makes for a very flexible, versatile, and dynamic information bank. The advent of so-called push technology, whereby information is automatically sought on one's behalf around the world, filtered, and offered according to a user-determined profile, makes this an even more powerful information assistant for workers whose knowledge must be continually updated.

Internet technology has had a significant impact on the way in which instructional materials are delivered to learners. More important, it has changed the nature of the interaction between learner and tutor and among learners themselves. An ongoing criticism of technology-based instruction has been that it is often isolated instruction—the learner cannot easily benefit from interactions with other learners in the same or different courses. By contrast, the Internet provides a potential profusion of interactions; the problem now is to filter and structure those that are of greatest benefit.

The Internet is used for more than "surfing"; witness the popularity of chat rooms and discussion groups. These can be used to simulate the classroom at the same time as other pressures are taking training out of the classroom. Many groups are also working on structures to support peer interaction. For instance, San Francisco State University has a program in multimedia studies *(http://msp.sfsu.edu)*. DigitalThink *(http://www.digitalthink.com)* offers training with bulletin boards and live chat sessions. Virtual-U *(http://virtual-u.cs.sfu.ca/vuweb/)* is an on-line software system that allows universities and organizations to offer their courses on-line.

UOL Publishing has adopted a "traditional" model of Internet-based instructional delivery and management that can trace its ancestry to the large-scale network-based computer-based training (CBT) solutions of the 1970s and 1980s. UOL has teamed up with a number of course providers who make their instructional materials available through the UOL Web site *(http://www.uol.com)* to a potentially worldwide audience of learners. The learners pay to access the materials, take assessment tests, and be managed through their courses. The Web site also hosts other courses for specific organizations. Access to those courses is restricted to these organizations' employees. UOL also provides a managed service for its clients, who are (for now) predominantly in North America and Britain. A more recent player in the United Kingdom is Solstra, developed by British Telecom and FutureMedia, which is targeted at organizations wanting to leverage their existing CBT materials, and which in time may develop into a publicly available value-added service.

Oracle Education, second behind IBM in supplying IT training, formed a new unit in 1996 to deliver training via the Internet. Oracle Learning Architecture, or OLA *(http://ola.us.oracle.com/html/maola.html)* currently has more than three hundred training courses on line. More important, it has formed an alliance with some thirty-five partners to establish standards, a common platform, and new distribution means. OLA is also working on the idea of reusable content objects, which will enable the realization of an on-line modular curriculum, a concept that hinges on the existence of common standards for developing and displaying content. The Internet, providing a powerful combination of anarchic and standards-based development, may well be what allows this curriculum to come about.

Transcend Technologies, based in the United Kingdom, has developed a niche business that combines Web-based assessment and training in safety-critical areas in the transportation, oil and gas, and nuclear industries. In all these industries it is essential that management have the assurance that its highly distributed workforce is competent to undertake safety-critical tasks. The penalties (in terms of money as well as injury and mortality) for not having this assurance far outweigh the costs of effective assessment and training. Internet technology ensures that all the staff who are involved can get access to the system, wherever they are in the world, and the centralized record-keeping and management system ensures that assessment and training are always current.

If the individualized instruction offered by traditional CBT is a cost-effective alternative to traditional lectures, then until recently there has been no effective alternative to the interpersonal interactions that form an essential aspect of the learning community. Isolated learning in front of a computer screen is a very sterile experience by comparison with the rich interaction of a college or residential training center. A number of institutions, however, have taken advantage of computer-mediated conferencing to enhance their provision of distance learning.

In one of the most surprising such instances, the Southampton Institute (in the United Kingdom) captured the high ground of the distance M.B.A. degree with a part-time course offered through the Internet that combined the instruction of specialist tutors from around the world with the best library and learning support available at the time. The initial course was greatly oversubscribed, and new courses were started every few months instead of annually. The fees were kept at a level comparable with those of other distance M.B.A. programs, but the operating costs were a fraction of those incurred by competitors.

By contrast, the UK Open University has taken a more conservative path, carefully reconnoitered by research but marked by significant numbers of participants (Thomas, Carswell, Price, and Petre, 1998). The Open University has built on the existing tutorial structures and complemented them with computer-mediated conferencing and electronic submission of assignments.

The Internet and intranets can also be used to support more traditional approaches to instruction. Witness software like Symposium *(http://www.centra.com)*, which delivers live instructor-led training and self paced learning via Internet or corporate intranets (Cohen, 1997b).

As companies have developed intranets to support their enterprises, the human resources (HR) function has examined how that technology can be used to support training. An intranet provides a greater degree of privacy from the outside world than does the public Internet, and total separation is better than restricted access via systems of passwords. PA Computing Group's Management Centre, in the United Kingdom, is a provider of management development that uses an extranet (that is, an intranet accessible, with certain controls, from other organizations). In this case, there is little tutorial delivery via the extranet. Instead, the extranet is used to prepare organizational delegates for intensive residential courses and to support their learning after the formal courses end.

From these examples it is only a short step to the concept of the virtual class, eloquently described by Tiffin and Rajasingham (1995). The virtual class employs a flexible learning paradigm, which recognizes that people do not learn from books alone but need to interact with other people, and particularly people with similar learning interests. The virtual class provides a technology-mediated environment where people can meet, talk, access, work with a wide range of resources, and learn. In so doing, it starts to move us away from the shackles of learning in a fixed place at a prescribed time. The virtual class sounds like something from a work of science fiction, and yet the reality of Tiffin and Rajasingham's vision—the Global Virtual University—is scheduled to open its virtual doors to its first postgraduate students in 1999 and to be in full operation by the year 2000.

Reconceptualization of Training as Learner-Centered

Training is being reconceptualized in terms of more flexibility. This model has the learner, as the central decision maker, choosing among a range of options for content, location, method and time of delivery, instructional approach, and learner support. The key aspects of training are evolving, from being fixed to being flexible and subject to control by the learner (Collis, Vingerhoets, and Moonen, 1997).

This perspective, which can be characterized as emphasizing learning versus teaching, is also known as *learner-centeredness*. While much of the development work came from distance education, the assumptions that the students are adults, self-motivated, accountable for their own learning, and should be respected, as well as that they exercise control over their learning outcomes, also apply to most employees who are in training programs or engaged in other forms of on-the-job learning. The implications of these principles are wide-reaching, for they affect all aspects of the instructional development (ID) process. As reported in Wagner and McCombs (1995), the Midcontinent Regional Education Laboratory has developed a set of twelve psychological principles for learner-centered training:

1. Learning is a natural process of pursuing meaningful goals. It is active, volitional, and internally mediated.

2. The learner's goal is to create meaningful and coherent representations of knowledge.

3. The learner constructs knowledge by linking new information with existing and future-oriented knowledge in uniquely meaningful ways.

4. Metacognitive skills (that is, the ability to monitor one's cognitive actions) are important in learning.

5. Motivational and affective variables influence the quantity and quality of learning.

6. Individuals are naturally curious, their curiosity can be thwarted by negative emotions.

7. Authentic learning tasks of appropriate difficulty and novelty stimulate motivation.

8. The state of the individual's physical, intellectual, emotional, and social development will have an impact on the learning process.

9. Social interaction in flexible, diverse, and adaptive instructional settings facilitates learning.

10. Social acceptance contributes to increased self-esteem and learning.

11. As a function of environment and heredity, learners have different abilities, as well as different preferences for modes of learning and learning strategies.

12. Individuals construct reality and interpret their life experiences through cognitive filters consisting of personal beliefs, thoughts, and understanding based on prior learning.

In order for these concepts of learner-centered instruction to be operationalized, seven dimensions must be organized so as to accommodate the learner's choices:

1. The social organization of the instruction may be individually oriented, or it may be class- or group-oriented.

2. The content, its sequence, and the learning activities should offer a range of possibilities.

3. There should be a range of learning materials (for example, CBT materials, video-library resources, multimedia databases) to provide the learner with options.

4. The learner should be able to choose the kind and timing of any interaction with the instructor and other learners.

5. The technical platforms of the instruction should be varied.

6. The language of learning materials and of learning interactions should be a matter of choice.

7. The learner should be able to select a format of distance learning, face-to-face interaction, or a mix.

Whereas flexibility on many of these dimensions may previously have been seen as desirable but impractical, new technology makes it possible.

A learner-centered approach changes the role of both trainers and trainees. As one example, some learners may not be at ease in a learning environment where they suddenly must exert control over things that were previously presented as givens. This is a cultural issue, both in terms of organizational culture and in terms of the wider culture to which learner-employees belong; for example, "employees in Japan accept the expectation for self-directed learning, a concept promoted by the adult education literature of the U.S., but not widely accepted in the context of corporate training" (Keller and Taguchi, 1996, p. 63).

Alternative Structures

Informal Training. Formal training is what happens in courses and is usually highly structured. Informal learning is self-motivated, self-directed, and purposeful. It often takes place in the course of doing work. Informal or incidental learning, which according to some estimates accounts for 90 percent of workplace learning (Watkins, in Sorohan, 1993), cannot be structured or designed, but it can be enhanced and supported. Organizations should encourage employees to be proactive in their learning, to engage in critical reflection (that is, to question tacit assumptions), and to think creatively (that is, to reframe problems).

The U.S. Bureau of Labor Statistics has reported that employees in the United States spend an average of 70 percent of their total training time in informal activities (Benson, 1997). Employees in larger corporations tend to receive more formal training than their counterparts in smaller companies do, but no such relationship exists for informal training. The two most commonly reported areas of informal training are computer-related training and production-construction training. The 1995 U.S. Bureau of Labor Statistics (BLS) survey on employer-provided training (Benson, 1997) showed that 57 percent of computer-related training was informal, whereas 81 percent of production-construction training was informal. These findings are largely consistent with previous studies, with one notable exception: in the BLS Survey, 84 percent of employees reported receiving formal training, and 96 percent reported receiving informal training, figures significantly higher than previous studies had indicated. The BLS survey attempted to estimate the costs associated with informal training. The data indicate that the wage-and-salary cost of informal training is $48.4 billion per year, almost as high as the $55.3 billion (in direct training costs plus participants' wages and salaries) estimated by the American Society for Training and Development as the cost of formal training (Bassi and Van Buren, 1998). Seen in this light, the support given to "accidental trainers" (Blumfield, 1997) is more than a "nice to have" element.

On-the-fly training is widespread; witness the American Dialect Society's honoring of *alpha geek* (the term connotes the most computer-savvy person in a workplace) as one of the most original terms of 1996 (Blumfield, 1997); as alpha geeks are identified by their peers, they quickly become "accidental trainers." Referring questioners to formal learning may be the most appropriate response to many informal requests, especially with the increase of modular training, which allows users to find out exactly and only what they want to know. However, learning from peers is a popular option even among those who consider themselves self-directed learners. This tendency to consult peers for help can be supported so that users may consult "knowledgeable strangers" rather than "ignorant friends." For example, PhelpS (McCalla and others, 1997) is a computer-based system designed to identify fellow workers who are both knowledgeable about a specific task and available at the moment when help is needed.

One advantage of informal training is that trainers and trainees are more apt to speak the same language than when trainers come from outside the employee group. Therefore, it is useful to provide guidelines for the "accidental trainers" of the world on they can best help those who come to them. Four simple tips can be useful:

1. Sketch out the big picture so that the user can see the forest and not just the trees.

2. Don't touch someone else's mouse or keyboard; doing so invades personal space and may communicate impatience.

3. Build on the learner's experience, whether it is computer-based or of other types.

4. Find out how the learner wants to learn: By reading? By being told what to do? By observing?

Learning Through Electronic Performance Support Systems and On-the-Job Training. The fundamental goal of an Electronic Performance Support System (EPSS) is to provide assistance in learning and in performing some set of tasks. The main characteristics of an EPSS are a reduced need (or no need) for training, integration of software into performance, and a change in focus from knowing to performing (Cole, Fischer, and Saltzman, 1997). An EPSS can be used in initial training and may lower the level of the required mastery required because of the existence of on-the-job help. Even with a lower initial level of required mastery, frequently encountered tasks will often be handled better because of the existence of a familiar support system.

Users' expectations are less and less those associated with a "captive market" and large-scale training systems; even among novice users, expectations are becoming more aligned with shallow learning curves and high performance (Gery, 1997). Training, documentation, and support are coming to be viewed as able to compensate for poor design. Because users come and go, novices must be considered a permanent public and must be accommodated without frustrating the experts. The benefits of an EPSS include enhanced productivity, reduced training costs, increased worker autonomy, increased quality because of uniform work practices, and knowledge capitalization. An EPSS adapts to the individual learner's pace. The learning context matches the operational context and offers an engaging learning mode in which the learner must actively seek information (Desmarais, Leclair, Fiset, and Talbi, 1997).

There is, of course, a very ill-defined dividing line between an EPSS (which focuses on performance but includes some implicit teaching) and a CBT system (which focuses on training and thus improves performance). According to Gustafson and Branch (1997, p. 79), "one of the profound changes will be a move away from the notion that education or training occurs in one environment, and performance occurs in another. . . . In what promises to be an increasingly complex and dynamic world, information in the next decade will be far too abundant, and some of it much too transitory, to warrant formal instruction. . . . Embedded instruction, expert systems to guide performance, microworlds, and an increased emphasis on learning how to learn and apply knowledge, will call for new design and development procedures that will be somewhat different from those depicted by current ID models."

Factors contributing to the success of an EPSS are both technical and organizational and include the number of users, the availability of domain experts and EPSS implementation specialists, and the appropriateness of the tasks themselves to this type of support. Many skills are required for the successful completion of an EPSS (Benko and Webster, 1997). These include skills in instructional analysis and design, technical analysis, on-line writing, programming, and graphic art, in addition to subject matter expertise. Even more so than with conventional training, it is preferable to integrate EPSS development with application development. A strategy for performing cost-benefit analysis is outlined in Desmarais, Leclair, Fiset, and Talbi (1997).

Many EPSS projects are being developed by large corporations, which perceive that one advantage of an EPSS is its ability to ensure employees access to the same information wherever they are. Specific data about particular EPSS developments are often difficult to obtain because an EPSS is often considered a competitive advantage and, as such, is subject to strict confidentiality regulations. However, a few examples are public knowledge. American Express (*http://www.epss.com*, with case studies available at *http://www.epss.com/lb/lb_index.htm*) credits its EPSS with a significant reduction in training time (from twelve hours to two), an increase in productivity (with requests taking an average of four minutes rather than seventeen to process), and a reduction in data-entry errors (from 20 percent down to 2 percent). A large Canadian utility company experienced positive results in a trial of an EPSS for customer service representatives (Desmarais, Leclair, Fiset, and Talbi, 1997). In Korea, there are examples of EPSS use in shipbuilding, telecommunications, finance, and engineering. The National University of Singapore is involved in interactive multimedia and in the development of projects in artificial intelligence, case-based reasoning, and intelligent information retrieval. In Scandinavia, EPSS applications are found in the fishing, shipping, oil, and engineering industries.

More explicit forms of on-the-job training include self-study, computer-based education programs, professional coaching, and project teams; a 1991 Ernst & Young study (Rae, 1994) estimates that 90 percent of learning was accounted for by these means. There are six basic approaches to on-the-job training (Rae, 1994):

1. *GAFO (Go Away and Find Out):* This approach prevents learners from becoming trainer-dependent, but it must be used in a deliberate way, as the first step in guided self-learning; otherwise, it is likely to result in wasted time for all con-

cerned. It can be especially useful in the orientation of new employees to help them meet people, find their way around the organization, and obtain information.

2. *Nellie and Fred:* This approach can be described as "training by exposure" (that is, sitting by Nellie or Fred—or the local alpha geek). For this approach to be successful, Nellie or Fred must be efficient and effective at the task but also must have been taught how to instruct, must be given the necessary resources and allowed sufficient time to prepare and perform the training, and must not be expected to maintain the usual level of productive output while training someone else.

3. *One-to-one instruction:* This form of training may occur on the job or simply at the job. It is usually a variation on "tell, show, and do," although it can be supplemented with text-based, conventional video, CBT, or interactive video materials.

4. *Coaching:* This is a form of one-to-one instruction in which a manager or supervisor works with his or her own employees to systematically develop their abilities and skills by using tasks at work in a planned progression. It includes formal appraisal of the employee by the coach.

5. *Delegation:* If delegation is used in a structured and controlled manner, it can be an effective and efficient way to have employees learn while doing. It is important that the tasks delegated and the people selected to perform them be chosen thoughtfully and that constructive feedback be given to the chosen employees.

6. *Mentoring:* This approach involves the development of an employee through the use of an experienced person as a mentor. It can be directive (as in work with a personal trainer), nondirective (with the onus for progress on the learner rather than on the mentor), or supportive (when a position between directive and nondirective mentoring is assumed).

The term *desktop learning* refers to the use of desktop computers to improve skills and knowledge (Keegan and Rose, 1997). It can be delivered via CD-ROMs or over the Internet. For example, Apple University has developed two CDs for use by Apple managers anywhere in the world. The CDs were developed largely as a response to reductions in resources: fewer trainers and fewer dollars for travel, together with an increase in the pace of business, which made the scheduling of training difficult. The CDs combine narrated text and video. They also provide reference materials (for example, lists of interview questions). The advantages are clear: learning can take place anytime, anywhere; learners' exposure to embarrassment is limited because they are working alone; content is delivered in a consistent fashion; and learners can go at their own pace—often more quickly than they could in a classroom situation. In the case of Apple, although the learners appreciated these factors, it is interesting to note that they missed the classroom interaction.

Learning in Communities of Practice. The term *communities of practice* was coined by Lave and Wenger (1991). The new book by Wenger (1998) expands on previous work to present a theory of learning based on the assumption that engagement in social practice is the fundamental process by which we learn. Communities of practice are found in all aspects of life. They include both explicit and implicit structures and practice. Because communities of practice are based on joint learning, rather than on tasks with formal beginnings and endings, they tend to emerge and linger rather than sharply form and disband. Current research on learning supports the power of communities of practice (Sorohan, 1993):

1. We learn best when we direct our own learning.

2. We learn from each other.

3. We learn most effectively in context.

4. We continuously create knowledge, and so we need to learn how to capture and share it.

5. We learn unconsciously, and so we need to learn how to recognize and question tacit assumptions.

The Institute for Research on Learning (IRL), based in Palo Alto, California *(http://www.irl.org)*, is dedicated to searching for new models of successful learning. A basic assumption is that learning is fundamentally situated in social, physical, and temporal settings. It is not a transfer of knowledge but rather a process of building understanding. In this spirit, one can identify "communities of practice," or a "naturally occurring and evolving collection of people who together engage in particular kinds of activity, and who come to develop and share ways of doing things—ways of talking, beliefs, values, and practices—as a result of their joint involvement in that activity" (Linde, cited in Galagan, 1993). Traditional formal instructional interventions deal with teaching explicit knowledge to individuals; communities of practice deal with tacit knowledge for both individuals and groups. Communities of practice can play a key role in educating an organization's employees, but this does not mean that they should necessarily be "managed" in a formal sense. By contrast with designed organizations (teams, committees, and task forces), communities of practice tend to be emergent, informal organizations that are not explicitly designed. Communities of practice cannot be mandated, but they can and should be supported; new technologies can play an important role in supporting and linking communities of practice. According to Ralph Volpe, manager of Xerox Corporation's Education and Learning Unit, in Rochester, New York, "If you can recognize and leverage the idea of naturally existing communities of practice, training gets better because you're not fighting human nature" (quoted in Stamps, 1997, p. 42.)

The knowledge that is resident in communities of practice cannot simply be catalogued as a skill set and then implemented in a knowledge base. Often the strength of such communities is that they support the development and diffusion of tacit or implicit knowledge (Stamps, 1997). Examples of communities of practice in action can be found in such diverse organizations as workshops to create world-class flutes, where the creators rely on comments like "It doesn't look right" to adjust the instruments, and Xerox, where some employees feel different grades of copier toner to decide which ones will work best with which kinds of paper.

A more formalized approach to creating communities of practice was adopted by Xerox in conjunction with researchers at the Palo Alto–based IRL. Xerox, in response to long-standing complaints from customers about being bounced around when seeking help for their problems, wanted to merge three separate customer service departments into one. The training implications alone were significant: the estimates was for fifty-two weeks of classroom training for each person. The Xerox/IRL project proposed creating groups of six or seven employees, who would come from the departments involved in customer service, and letting them work together to serve customers and to teach and learn from each other at the same time. The pilot project was enthusiastically received by the employees, but the project did not survive past the pilot phase (Stamps, 1997). This experience highlights the link between innovative training practices and business practices. Approaching training in this way had important implications for the way the company worked: this kind of learning model logically entails a model of work that may not be implementable for a number of reasons. Those reasons may be financial, cultural (with respect to the organization or the community at large), or political (this kind of change may imply significant power shifts within an organization, and these may leave certain sectors, especially the training function, feeling quite threatened).

The Internet and corporate intranets are being heralded as ways of willing into existence numerous communities of practice that will be able to exploit collaborative groupware (computer and network applications that are designed to support work by groups or teams). However, the technology is not enough. Work issues in common and people's will to teach and learn from others are what drive the creation of communities of practice. This is not to deny the role that technology can and does play in facilitating collaboration, but many argue that face-to-face collaboration is necessary for true collaboration. Work by Chomienne, Vázquez-Abad, and Winer (1998) has shown that collaboration can occur without face-to-face interaction in defined learning tasks, but it remains to be seen whether this will hold true for the more amorphous learning goals of communities of practice. For example, skeptics point to the accelerating rise in business travel despite the development of videoconferencing and the Internet (Stamps, 1997).

Learning Sciences

Collaborative Learning. In industry, much of the impetus for collaborative learning comes out of work done in computer-supported collaborative work (the terms *collaborative* and *cooperative* are often used interchangeably; in the interests of clarity, we will use the term *collaborative*). See McConnell (1994) as a starting point for exploring references and resources in this area, or visit the Web site of the Forum for Computer Supported Collaborative Working *(http://www.csc.liv.ac.uk/ ~ team-it/index.html)*. With the development of groupware, an obvious next step is to explore computer and network applications that support group or team learning.

Collaborative learning is an area that has been explored in education for some time. Several elements are essential to collaborative learning (Johnson and Johnson, 1994; Salomon, 1992):

- Face-to-face interaction
- Positive interdependence
- Individual accountability
- Cooperative social skills
- Group processing

The results of research on collaborative learning in educational settings, although generally positive, are inconclusive for cognitive results, but significant effects have been found in affective areas. Slavin (1983) has concluded that the effects of collaborative learning are primarily motivational in nature because working with others toward a group goal creates peer support for individual learning, which in turn increases both individual motivation to achieve and the motivation to help others. Likewise, according to Abrami and others (1995, p. 196), "there is little doubt that cooperative learning produces superior results when the objective is the promotion of positive attitudes and feelings toward learning, classmates, and self." Given the importance of affect and motivation in training as well as in education, the positive effects in these areas alone warrant serious consideration for the inclusion of collaborative learning in settings for training. The push toward more collaborative work also means that employees who have often worked alone will now have to learn how to work with others. Learning together how to work together seems an obvious route because team learning increases the correspondence between the training environment and the work situation.

It is clear that collaborative learning requires new skills of tutors and learners alike. For example, new skills are required of the participants in a computer conference. If these skills were of little or no advantage outside the conference, then it could be argued that the opportunity cost of holding the conference was too high. However, it is increasingly apparent that these are now actual "life skills" for effective managers and that they will be required for the learners' survival and success beyond the learning experience itself.

If a computer conference is used, frequent access to it should be encouraged when participants are only reading material posted by others (this practice is known as *lurking*). A more positive form of lurking is for the learner to reply to each message, indicating that it has been read, even though a substantive comment is not forthcoming ("I've read what you said, and I may comment later when I have something to say"). A busy conference creates its own synergy, whereas one with infrequent interactions may wither. Axelrod (1990) points to the need for frequent interactions to keep cooperative groups functioning effectively.

There is still no substantial body of research on the topic, but the work that has been done indicates that computer conferencing offers a uniquely democratic forum for the discussion of issues in education, training, and development. Diffident participants can contribute without having to interrupt or talk over others, and everyone has the same access (subject, of course, to the availability of the necessary equipment). Furthermore, visual cues that may be used in assuming or ascribing status and power are missing. Boshier (1990) describes the computer conference as an ideal discourse—people are free of coercion or distorting self-perceptions, are open to other perspectives and points of view, and are accepting of others as equal participants. There are important forces here for equal opportunity.

Two of the most common tutor roles in computer-mediated communication are those involved in acting as a help line and those involved in serving as a moderator. The tutor acting as a help line fields questions and problems from individuals. Whenever an issue is likely to be of general interest, the tutor posts it (possibly removing the questioner's name or other identifying information from the message) where other members of the group can read it and comment. In the role of moderator, the tutor both facilitates and acts in a directive capacity. This role includes helping small groups of learners identify common professional interests. It also includes helping them identify a tangible objective and then ensuring that the group members work effectively on the tasks that they have set themselves. The tutor does this either directly, as a project manager for the group, or indirectly, by ensuring that an effective project management function exists in the group. The skill of the facilitator/moderator serves to maximize the positive aspects of the experience while minimizing the negative features.

The training literature includes few examples of collaborative learning in which the objective was not to train for team performance. However, one report on training naval air traffic controllers (Holubec, Johnson, and Johnson, 1993) found that, by comparison with the traditional instructional methods of the U.S.

Navy, collaborative learning techniques improved higher-order reasoning skills and resulted in no failures among the trainees. Because technical training programs often attract students who have not performed well in traditional academic environments, making alternative collaborative learning available to this population could yield even higher payoffs than would be found for groups of academic high achievers.

Some early work on applying network-based collaboration to training fell prey to technical problems, and these made it difficult to evaluate the true potential of groupware (Schrum and Lamb, 1997). However, a number of trials at the U.S. Air Force Academy showed that the use of an electronic network did enable and support collaborative and group activities, and Hewlett-Packard uses its intranet to conduct postclass discussions among groups of trainees (Cohen, 1997a).

Using the Constructivist Approach. For instructional interventions to be most effective, their designers must have the most up-to-date knowledge possible about how people learn. People have learned, of course, even with interventions that were developed under now outdated understandings of human learning, but it is reasonable to expect that the efficacy of instructional interventions can be improved by a deeper, more nuanced understanding of the nature of human learning.

Constructivism is a learning theory that, although not totally new (witness the work of Ausubel, Bruner, Piaget, and Vygotsky, among others), is currently receiving much attention. It represents a significant break with the behaviorist and cognitivist traditions that have dominated the twentieth century (Ertmer and Newby, 1993). Its most profound divergence from those traditions is that it views learning and understanding as functions of the individual's creation of meaning from his or her own experience and prior knowledge.

Knowledge cannot simply be imprinted onto an individual's mind; rather, each individual constructs meaning in interaction with the specific environment. Because that environment often includes other people, the process of constructing meaning is frequently a social one, carried out in intimate interaction with others. Interaction with people, objects, and concepts shapes both what we learn and our understanding of it (Scribner and Sachs, cited in Sorohan, 1993). The importance of the environment in creating understanding logically implies that learning is best situated in a meaningful context.

Constructivist approaches emphasize several elements:

- Situating tasks in real-world contexts
- Modeling and coaching
- Encouraging collaborative learning, so that learners are afforded access to multiple perspectives

- Encouraging learners to negotiate social situations
- Encouraging learners to engage in reflective awareness
- Guiding learners in the process of constructing knowledge

The constructivist approach to learning is anchored in the concepts of flexible learning situations and learners' control over their own learning choices (Cooper, 1993; Jonassen, Campbell, and Davidson, 1994). Two factors that must be considered in the design of an instructional intervention are the learner's level of expertise and the requirements of the learning task in terms of cognitive processing.

In examining the contributions of learning theories to instructional design, it is important to practice a kind of systematic eclecticism, choosing the approach that will be most appropriate to the specific context. The behaviorist approach of practice-reinforcement-feedback enlarges learning and memory. The cognitivist approach adds purpose and understanding. The constructivist approach develops adaptive learners who function well in changing, nonoptimal environments that require interaction for the solution of ill-defined problems.

Considering Affect and Motivation. According to Roger Schank, founder of the Institute for Learning Sciences *(http://www.ils.nwu.edu)* at Northwestern University, "Motivation is the single biggest problem in education for children or adults. Nobody learns anything he or she doesn't want to learn. To keep something in your head, you have to be engaged psychologically" (cited in Beach, 1993, p. 42). Traditionally, instructors have dealt with motivation in the implementation phase of instructional interventions. However, the increasing reliance on mediated instruction means that issues related to affect and motivation must also be dealt with systematically during the analysis, design, and development phases of interventions. Work by Main (1993) has examined how Keller's model (1983) for the motivational design of instruction can be integrated into a standard model for instructional systems design. Combining ARCS (attention, relevance, confidence, and satisfaction) with ADDIE (analysis, design, development, implementation, and evaluation) leads to new sets of questions to be asked. For example, the issue of relevance in the analysis phase requires an understanding of the relationship between the professional (and personal) goals of the learner and the instructional intervention. Attention-getting strategies and activities need to come to the fore in the design phase. The conjunction of the emotional and cognitive aspects of learning also poses a challenge to HRD professionals. This challenge may be experienced in terms of how the learning process is affected by the attitudes of mature workers who have been sent for retraining because their jobs are being phased out, for example, or by the attitudes of managers who have been sent to mandatory training for interpersonal skills.

Experiential and Discovery Learning. Roger Schank's Institute for Learning Sciences has recently been a vocal proponent of learning by doing, with the doing ideally taking place on the job. From this perspective, instruction should be provided on request, and preferably in the form of stories from experts (when the job is computer-mediated, the experts' stories can be accessed from within the system). Schank's theory promotes learning through exploration and reflection on errors and unexpected outcomes.

Action learning, or the practice of giving teams of learners real business problems to solve, is the favored strategy for executive education (Sorohan, 1993). At General Electric, for example, executives travel around the world to research global issues facing the company, but before they go, they work with university professors to hone their organizational, research, and decision-making skills. Upon returning, they share their findings with senior management.

The term *functional context training* is a term used to denote instruction that is integrated into the job environment. For example, a literacy program for automobile assemblers would integrate instruction in reading and writing instruction with the manuals and equipment used on the job (Sorohan, 1993).

EMERGING TRENDS

Flexibility

The concept of flexibility is multidimensional. It is in this broad area that new information and communication technologies—that is, computer hardware and software—have the most important impact on instructional interventions.

The concept of learning technologies, introduced earlier, is key to much of the flexibility that we can now offer or envision for the future. Learning technologies enhance the flexibility of learning options via electronic means.

Briefly, flexibility can be analyzed on five dimensions:

1. Time
2. Content
3. Entry requirements
4. Instructional approach and resources
5. Course delivery and logistics

It is important to distinguish between enriching the communication aspects of a course experience and making the course design more flexible. The following issues, among others, are raised in the context of flexibility:

- Instructors must respond to learners and to the learning context rather than simply planning and delivering instruction.

- Learners must be more self-directed and more self-motivated and must engage in more solitary study, less face-to-face group interaction, and less in-person peer-to-peer communication.

- Companies and other organizations will have more difficulty planning the financial and time costs of training and controlling the quality of training courses.

- The goal of flexibility for learners may be seen as unmanageable, unacceptable, unaffordable, or unrealistic.

There is still a wide gap between the vast majority of training practices and our knowledge about how people really learn. For example, proponents of communities of practice may appear to be preaching revolution, but an examination of the training profession's history reveals that some of today's perceived challenges from inside the training community have actually been issued before (Stamps, 1997)—in the form, for instance, of the idea that expertise is often resident within groups of adult learners (Malcolm Knowles), or the notion that the best way to find out what to teach is to observe master performers (Thomas Gilbert), or the belief that training should be lean and elegant rather than filled with "nice to know" material (Robert Mager).

We are witnessing a blurring of the traditional boundaries between training and working. The learning environment is being redefined. On-the-job, just-in-time training is replacing just-in-case, classroom-based training. Just-in-time learning is being called a "paradigm shift for the year 2000" by major international corporations (Collis, Vingerhoets, and Moonen, 1997). In this form of flexible training, defined as access to integrated learning materials, information banks, communication channels, and tools, the learner can call up whatever amount and type of learning material is most necessary and most useful at the most opportune time.

The logical extension of using just-in-time training is to use just the right amount of training. This extension proceeds from the modularizing of training and the development of "infonuggets," "granularized content," "chunks," and "reusable content-units" (Gordon, 1997). The concept of using just the right amount of training is to using an EPSS in that it provides in-context support to perform a task. The content is granularized, or broken into chunks, to enable people to get a quick piece of information or a brief tutorial; for example, workers at a Boeing aircraft factory consult brief videos for illustrations of specific tasks involved in building airplanes.

The modularizing of courses also facilitates their flexible on-line delivery. For example, Learn It Online *(http://learnitonline.com)* offers CBT tutorials on Microsoft Windows 95, Netscape Navigator, and Microsoft Office for an annual subscription fee; the courses can be accessed in any order.

A fully modularized curriculum would require standardized architecture and a common interface. Without prerequisites and structure, tasks like navigating and selecting chunks can be extremely inefficient; likewise, access to and manipulation of "infonuggets" would have to be very well organized. It is also important to identify what can be broken into chunks without the risk of destroying the whole: there is a significant difference between designing coherent instruction that can be divided up into chunks and creating an incoherent "whole" out of discrete and possibly mismatched parts.

Cultural Issues

According to Liang and Schwen (1997, p. 43), the "cultural context [of an instructional intervention] is defined as the specific context in which [an] ID project is carried out under . . . [the] traditions, values, beliefs, and influences" of the particular society. The cultural contexts in which instructional interventions are developed can vary significantly. Interventions may be transported across cultural boundaries or introduced into one national culture that is incorrectly viewed as homogenous. In either case, there are many different instructional paradigms. Dills and Romiszowski (1997) have compiled a volume that describes a plurality of paradigms for instructional design, delivery, and evaluation. Many of them are culture-specific, and instructional technologists would do well to be aware of the circumstances in which they can be effective—or disastrous.

The Technology Push

One development that should have significance for the long term is the trend toward mobile information technology and mobile learning. In mobile learning, information technology is used to reach people who need or prefer to have their learning linked to their day-to-day work or leisure activities. This is one more way in which true flexibility is achieved so that people can learn where they want or need to learn instead of gathering at designated centers of learning (Rushby, 1998).

Computers used for work can support learning when they are programmed to "push" the worker to take a learning break at regular intervals. One example of this technology is KnowDev, developed by Innovative Technology Products *(http://www.ikp.net/home.html)*.

New technology can also help less developed countries leapfrog over gaps in development gaps. For example, the Africa Growth Network (AGN) uses satellite technology, the Internet, CD-ROMs and the One Touch audience response system to provide education, training, and communication solutions to corporations and individuals anywhere in southern Africa ("AGN spans Africa's skills gap," 1997).

Telelearning is the use of multimedia learning environments that are housed in powerful desktop computers linked by the Information Highway. A multimedia learning environment may include any combination of text, graphics, photographs, audio, video, animations, and music. The Canadian TeleLearning Network of Centres of Excellence, or TL-NCE *(http://www.telelearn.ca)*, is leading a national initiative to create new learning strategies that will integrate effective pedagogies with new technology. TL-NCE aims to research, develop, and demonstrate new learning models, using technology to improve and extend educational opportunities that support the development of a knowledge-based economy and a learning society in Canada. Leading-edge companies and organizations are well on their way to deploying interactive systems for workforce training. The research projects of this network are oriented toward developing methods and tools that will facilitate the design, development, and delivery of learning systems at a distance and the integration of knowledge-processing components with multimedia learning resources.

Technology must be selected and applied in support of knowledge management. The activities of knowledge management can be characterized as either codifying (that is, documenting and appropriating) knowledge or disseminating knowledge within and throughout an organization. Interactive software, e-mail, and Internet technologies, in stripped-down form or with all the bells and whistles, can now facilitate, support, and enable activities that were once impossible to imagine, or at least to implement. For example, common databases of solutions to common problems and directories of internal and external expertise can be means by which employees can share a wealth of knowledge. The facilitation of human exchanges is one of the most significant impacts of the new technologies; witness the shift toward talking about "information and communication technologies" rather than simply "computers." These technologies have a unique role to play. Web sites, chat rooms, and e-mail can facilitate communication and knowledge sharing among employees. Interactive software and on-line forums can allow more than one person to work on a problem at a time. Computer conferencing can create virtual meeting spaces for people in different geographic locations.

CONCLUSION

What is emerging most clearly from the technological explosion is, ironically enough, a refocusing on people. The learner, once a relatively passive body in a classroom, is evolving into a much more active performer on the job, choosing the learning tools and the learning path in the quest for value-added performance.

As time goes on, and as a reflection of what we are coming to understand about how people learn best and about how best to use instruction in the improvement of human performance, instructional interventions will take place less often in classrooms and will become more integrated into work. Factor in the contributions made by informal learning, and the norm for the next century—a norm outside of which no organization will survive—emerges as the worker who is a continuous seeker of information, constantly constructing and perfecting skills in a highly networked, perpetually communicating world.

References

Abrami, P. C., and others. (1995). *Classroom connections: Understanding and using cooperative learning.* Orlando, FL: Harcourt Brace.

AGN spans Africa's skills gap. (1997). *AV Magazine,* p. 23.

Axelrod, R. (1990). *The evolution of cooperation.* Harmondsworth, England: Penguin.

Bassi, L. J., and Cheney, S. (1997). Benchmarking the best. *Training & Development* 51:11, 60–64.

Bassi, L. J., Cheney, S., and Van Buren, M. (1997). Training industry trends, 1997. *Training & Development* 51:11, 46–59.

Bassi, L. J., and Van Buren, M. E. (1998). The 1998 ASTD state of the industry report. *Training & Development* 52:1, 21–43.

Beach, B. K. (1993). Learning with Roger Schank. *Training & Development* 47:10, 39–44.

Benko, S., and Webster, S. (1997). Preparing for EPSS projects. *Communications of the ACM* 40:7, 60–63.

Benson, G. (1997). Informal training takes off. *Training & Development* 51:5, 93–94

Blumfield, M. (1997). The accidental trainer. *Training* 34:9, 42–52.

Boshier, R. (1990). Socio-psychological factors in electronic networking. *International Journal of Lifelong Education* 9:1, 49–64.

Burke, J. (1995). *Connections.* Boston: Little, Brown.

Chomienne, M., Vázquez-Abad, J., and Winer, L. R. (1998). *Design, development and pilot test of a distributed collaborative science learning laboratory.* Presentation to EdMedia 98, Freibourg, Germany.

Cohen, S. (1997a). Intranets uncovered. *Training & Development* 51:2, 48–50.

Cohen, S. (1997b). New learning tools. *Training & Development* 51:9, 60.

Cole, K., Fischer, O., and Saltzman, P. (1997). Just-in-time knowledge delivery. *Communications of the ACM* 40:7, 49–53.

Collis, B., Vingerhoets, J., and Moonen, J. (1997). Flexibility as a key construct in European training: Experiences from the TeleScopia Project. *British Journal of Educational Technology* 28:3, 199–217.

Cooper, P. A. (1993). Paradigm shifts in designed instruction: From behaviorism to cognitivism to constructivism. *Educational Technology* 33:5, 12–19.

Desmarais, M. C., Leclair, R., Fiset, J.-Y., and Talbi, H. (1997). Cost-justifying Electronic Performance Support Systems. *Communications of the ACM* 40:7, 39–48.

Dills, C. R., and Romiszowski, A. J. (1997). *Instructional development paradigms.* Englewood Cliffs, NJ: Educational Technology Publications.

Doyle, R. (1997). By the numbers: Access to the Internet. *Scientific American* 277:1, 26.

Ertmer, P., and Newby, T. J. (1993). Behaviorism, cognitivism, constructivism: Comparing critical features from an instructional design perspective. *Performance Improvement Quarterly* 6:4, 50–72.

Filipczak, B. (1997). Think locally, train globally. *Training* 34:1, 41–48.

Galagan, P. A. (1993). Helping groups learn. *Training & Development* 47:10, 57–61.

Gery, G. (1997). Granting three wishes through performance centered design. *Communications of the ACM* 40:7, 54–59.

Gordon, J. (1997). Infonuggets: The bite-sized future of corporate training? *Training* 34:7, 26–33.

Gustafson, K. L., and Branch, R. M. (1997). *Survey of instructional development models* (3rd ed.). Syracuse, NY: ERIC Clearinghouse on Information and Technology.

Holubec, E., Johnson, D. W., and Johnson, R. T. (1993). Impact of cooperative learning on naval air traffic controller training. *Journal of Social Psychology* 133:3, 337–346.

Johnson, D., and Johnson, R. (1994). *Learning together and alone: Cooperative, competitive and individualistic learning* (4th ed.). Needham Heights, MA: Allyn & Bacon.

Jonassen, D. H., Campbell, J. P., and Davidson, M. E. (1994). Learning with media: Restructuring the debate. *Educational Technology Research and Development* 42:2, 31–40.

Keegan, L., and Rose, S. (1997). The good news about desktop learning. *Training & Development* 51:6, 24–27.

Keller, J. M. (1983). Motivational design of instruction. In C. M. Reigeluth (ed.), *Instructional design theories and models.* Hillsdale, NJ: Erlbaum.

Keller, J. M., and Taguchi, M. (1996). Use of the systems approach to training design and delivery in Japanese corporations. *Performance Improvement Quarterly* 9:1, 62–76.

Lave, J., and Wenger, E. (1991). *Situated learning: Legitimate peripheral participation.* New York: Cambridge University Press.

Liang, C. C., and Schwen, T. (1997). A framework for instructional development in corporate education. *Educational Technology* 37:4, 42–45.

Ljutic, A. (1996). Learning to telecommunicate: Distance learning projects in less-developed countries. *Learning and Leading with Technology* 23:8, 65–67.

Lloyd, C., Rushby, N., Vincent, G., and Megarry, J. (1994). *Converging technologies and learning needs.* Sheffield, England: Department of Employment.

Main, R. G. (1993). Integrating motivation into the instructional design process. *Educational Technology* 33:12, 37–41.

McCalla, G. I., and others. (1997). A peer help system for workplace training. In B. du Boulay and R. Mizoguchi (eds.), *Proceedings of the eighth world conference on artificial intelligence in education.* Amsterdam: IOS Press.

McConnell, D. (1994). *Implementing computer-supported collaborative learning.* London: Kogan Page.

Rae, L. (1994). Training 101. *Training & Development* 48:4, 19–25.

Rushby, N. (1998). Where are the desks for the virtual class? *SIGCUE Outlook* 26:2, 33–36.

Salomon, G. (1992). What does the design of effective CSCL require and how do we study its effects? *SIGCUE Outlook* 21:3, 62–68.

Schrum, L., and Lamb, T. A. (1997). Computer networks as instructional and collaborative distance learning environments. *Educational Technology* 37:4, 26–31.

Slavin, R. E. (1983). When does cooperative learning increase student achievement? *Psychological Bulletin* 94, 429–445.

Sorohan, E. G. (1993). We do; therefore we learn. *Training & Development* 47:10, 47–55.

Stamps, D. (1997). Communities of practice. *Training* 34:2, 34–42.

Thomas, P., Carswell, L., Price, B., and Petre, M. (1998). A holistic approach to supporting distance learning using the Internet: Transformation, not translation. *British Journal of Educational Technology* 29:2, 149–162.

Thorndike, E. L. (1912). *Education.* New York: Macmillan.

Tiffin, J., and Rajasingham, L. (1995). *In search of the virtual class: Education in an information society.* London: Routledge.

Training that proves a point. (1997). *AV Magazine,* pp. 31–32.

Vázquez-Abad, J., and Winer, L. R. (1992). Emerging trends in instructional interventions. In H. D. Stolovitch and E. J. Keeps (eds.), *Handbook of Human Performance Technology: A comprehensive guide for analyzing and solving performance problems in organizations.* San Francisco: Jossey-Bass.

Wagner, E. D., and McCombs, B. L. (1995). Learner-centered psychological principles in practice: Designs for distance education. *Educational Technology* 35:2, 32–35.

Wenger, E. (1998). *Communities of practice: Learning, meaning, and identity.* New York: Cambridge University Press.

CHAPTER FORTY-TWO

Research in Human Performance Technology

Wellesley R. Foshay
Leslie Moller
Thomas M. Schwen
Howard K. Kalman
Debra S. Haney

Human Performance Technology (HPT) is a new field, invented by thoughtful practitioners grappling with human performance problems in real-world settings. As a consequence, practice, it seems, has usually outrun theory; growth in the field's knowledge base seems most often to follow from reflection on experience rather than to develop through any kind of systematic experimentation process.

One could conclude from this observation that HPT is inherently atheoretical. There is no need, however, to be so pessimistic. HPT is an applied field of practice, not a discipline. Consequently, HPT theory develops through the synthesis of models from contributing disciplines and cognate fields of practice. As theory is developed, it is validated through systematic application in real-world settings; conventional experimentation is feasible only in a few circumstances. Therefore, research is possible in HPT, but it is likely to employ a variety of alternative paradigms. This approach is consistent with current thinking on research methods in a variety of related fields of practice in the social sciences.

This approach also means that development of HPT theory is a shared opportunity for practitioners and academic researchers. Practitioners often are the first to identify issues and problems in need of improved solutions. By contrast, academic researchers are often in an excellent position to synthesize trends and discover new ways to derive new models and technologies for HPT from the contributing disciplines. At the same time, they rely on constant feedback from practitioners to test and refine their work.

895

This chapter explains the implications for theory of asserting that HPT is a field of practice but not a discipline. It then goes on to examine the three major sources of theory for HPT, with attention to their models of human performance and their research questions. Finally, it draws what we hope are some useful conclusions about HPT research methods.

HPT AS A FIELD OF PRACTICE

The distinction between a fundamental discipline and an applied field of practice is central to an understanding of how theory develops. Phenix (1964, p. 273) characterizes disciplines as fundamental because they are "concerned with the deliberate and direct pursuit of one of the six possible kinds of meaning" that he outlines. In other words, the disciplines are structured primarily by their rules of inquiry, or by how they seek to establish truth. By contrast, Phenix (p. 273) characterizes fields like education as derivative, or applied, because they "result from the utilization of meanings from the fundamental disciplines in the solution of problems arising out of biological and social exigencies." In other words, the applied fields are structured primarily by the real-world problems they address, and they are not particularly concerned with the logical purity of their epistemology.

In this context, it seems clear that HPT is an applied field and not a discipline. It is structured primarily by the real-world problem of human performance in the workplace. It may draw from any discipline that has prescriptive power for solving any human performance problem. It also may draw from other applied fields when they contribute technologies of use in solving human performance problems. Thus Brethower (1995) argues that the uniqueness of the field lies in the range of the technologies it can use to ensure high performance with respect to current and strategic business needs.

Gayeski (1995) uses the image of a tree in characterizing the relationship of HPT to other applied fields and fundamental disciplines. In this schema, the disciplinary roots of HPT are communications, systems theory, and applied psychology. The bodies of prescriptive theory constitute the trunk of the tree. From the forces of greatest influence within HPT—instructional design (ID, which includes programmed instruction), organizational design (OD), information science (IS), and HPT's own framework for problem analysis, coordinated intervention, and measured outcomes—come a broad range of "branch" interventions. The most significant of these are instructional and learning systems, performance support systems, workplace design, incentive systems, and organizational design and development. Thus the process of theory development in HPT occurs at two levels—that of the trunk and that of the branches—and both are grounded in the root disciplines. The process includes considerable "horizontal" (cross-field) generalization of concepts, principles and models, as well as the "vertical" application of disciplines to corresponding prescriptive theory and interventions. This kind of cross-fertilization is characteristic of theory development in all fields and disciplines.

We will now examine in more detail how the process of theory development works in the field of HPT. Our discussion spans the four bodies of prescriptive theory just mentioned—ID, IS, OD, and HPT's own framework for analysis, prescription, and measured outcomes—although limitations of space preclude a full discussion of each. Because HPT's own theory is well treated elsewhere in this volume, and because good references are available for the contributions of ID, the most space will go to a discussion of opportunities for development of HPT theory through application of OD and IS. In the near term, it can be argued, these two areas are likely to lead to the most rapid growth in HPT theory.

OPPORTUNITIES FOR BUILDING HPT THEORY
FROM INSTRUCTIONAL DESIGN

Training was the first widely used HPT intervention and is the most familiar way of correcting a gap in knowledge or skill among performers. ID grew up as an application of general systems theory, learning theory (based on behavioral and cognitive psychology), and communication theory. Its focus is on the systematic design, development, and assessment of training. The core processes of ID are as follows:

- Identification of the gap in knowledge and skill in a target population of performers (that is, needs assessment)

- Analysis of the structure and content of the tasks and knowledge that will be required to fill the gap (that is, task or content analysis)

- Design and development of instructional strategies that will teach the tasks and knowledge to the target population

- Implementation of the strategies and evaluation of the outcomes

- Revision on the basis of the evaluation

ID has contributed to HPT theory in three ways:

1. ID serves as the basis for a family of instructional and learning interventions.

2. The five-phase systematic process, as just outlined, for problem analysis, intervention, and evaluation was the precedent for the HPT framework.

3. ID participates in a grand convergence, now under way, of roles and tools across fields. The roots of ID in behaviorist learning theory are now being subsumed by cognitive learning theory and constructivist epistemology. This change has broad implications for the way in which HPT addresses questions of knowledge management in organizations through both IS and ID.

OPPORTUNITIES FOR BUILDING HPT THEORY FROM OD

OD is concerned with planned systemic change and organizational problem solving to improve organizational psychological well-being and effectiveness. OD's foundation is interdisciplinary, embedded in applied behavioral science and systems theory, as is HPT. Whereas HPT tends to focus on organizational and individual processes, OD efforts tend to focus on three components:

1. *Organizational culture.* Values, attitudes, and beliefs influence individual and group behavior, learning, and goal achievement. An organization's culture—its personality and soul—is transmitted through symbolic rituals, ceremonies, business vision, strategy and goals, and day-to-day communication. Company X is open to divergent ideas and tolerant of failure; Company Y is conservative, paternalistic, and fearful of litigation. Each company's culture influences its workers' behavior and performance.

2. *Organizational structure.* The way in which work is organized and controlled, as well as reporting relationships, job tasks, the physical work environment, and the human-technical interface (that is, the sociotechnical systems) set the boundaries and patterns for social interaction, a key factor in knowledge transfer and organizational learning.

3. *Organizational processes.* Processes are how the organization gets its work done to create added value for its customers. Broken processes are at the root of human error, lengthy cycle times, waste, and poor quality. Process improvement is of particular interest to HPT and OD practitioners and researchers. Reengineering redefines how work is done, but it also forces changes in the structural and cultural components of the organization.

OD efforts usually focus first on the team/group and/or the organizational level, whereas HPT efforts tend first to focus on the group and/or individual level. OD interventions tend to focus on radical change in group norms and in group/team structure and function, whereas HPT interventions also include incremental change of processes. OD and HPT have many similarities in the areas of contracting with clients, diagnosing problems, designing interventions, and implementing solutions. OD relies on an action research model, as does HPT.

OD and HPT practitioners alike prefer to act as process consultants, helping clients take responsibility for and ownership of problems so that clients' be commitment will be strong enough for the implementation to be successful. OD interventions include processes (reengineering, job redesign), human resources management (quality circles, team building, reward and recognition programs), and strategy (for example, organizational visioning).

OD and HPT roles and goals converge at the point where processes and interventions improve individual and group intellectual abilities or result in individual or organizational learning. OD interventions often involve experiential learning methods (T-groups, adventure education, role playing, simulations) that stimulate self-awareness, reflection, and personal learning about one's behavior in groups. HPT practitioners diagnose performance problems by using models such as those drawn from Rummler and Brache (1990), Rossett (1987, 1996), and Gilbert (1996). However, OD models—such as McKinsey's 7S framework (Peters and Waterman, 1982, pp. 9–11), Beer's social systems model, Weisbord's (1976) "six box" model, and many others—also provide similar systemic conceptualizations useful for diagnosis and intervention design. The OD perspective can be of use in generating research questions for HPT. Table 42.1 shows a modified version of the McKinsey 7S framework. It can serve as a means of organizing HPT opportunities for research and incorporates a few representative research questions.

OPPORTUNITIES FOR BUILDING HPT THEORY FROM INFORMATION SCIENCE

HPT has long recognized the importance of providing timely and relevant information about job performance. Intervention strategies as simple as a job aid on a reference card or as complex as an Electronic Performance Support System are based on this principle. HPT recognizes that providing the right information, in the right form, when and where it is required will often be much more advantageous than training as a way of closing gaps in knowledge. HPT also recognizes that much training for skills can be eliminated through proper design of job tasks and work environments. These principles, particularly when they are applied to data retrieval and to work done on computers, define a common ground between HPT and information science.

IS is an interdisciplinary applied field, with many contributing and cognate fields. Three branches of IS support HPT:

- Information technology (the study of computer-based information storage and communication devices)

Table 42.1. OD Systems Perspective for HPT Research, Using McKinsey's 7S Framework.

Organizational Component	Application Opportunity	Conceptual Learning Opportunity
Culture	What HPT interventions can best reinforce cultural values or accelerate transformation?	How do HPT interventions contribute to organizational cultural renewal?
	How can rituals, ceremonies, events, and communications be used to improve performance?	Why do symbols, rituals, ceremonies, and impression management affect intrinsic motivation and performance?
Structure	What structural components interfere with performance?	How does "meaningfulness" of work tasks contribute to personal satisfaction, motivation, and performance?
	What is the best balance between fitting people to tasks and fitting tasks to people?	Why do alternative physical environments affect performance?
Processes	How can work processes best be analyzed to reduce human error and improve performance?	How do alternative work-process configurations affect individual and group performance?
		What is involved in unlearning old behaviors?
Strategy	How can performance improvement efforts best be aligned with organizational initiatives and priorities?	What are the critical factors that enable performance improvement efforts to align with organizational initiatives and priorities?
	How can HPT interventions best contribute to generating organizational learning?	Why are integrated solutions difficult to implement?
	How can positive performance change be sustained?	
People	What are the most efficient individual and group diagnostic tools and interventions to improve competence, skills, and performance?	How do confidence and over-confidence affect autonomous work teams' performance?
	How can the time for developing novices into intermediate and expert performers be reduced?	

Source: Peters and Waterman, 1982, pp. 9–11.

- Information systems (the study of operations and procedures focused on information)

- Information management (the study of information to support decision making)

Information technology has traditionally focused on the quantity of information (the number of bytes processed) rather than on its quality (how the information can be used). As technology has grown in sophistication over the last ten years, however, attention has shifted from data and information to knowledge management and its organizational context.

Data, information, and knowledge all exist on the same continuum, from the perspective of information technology, with one end static and less valuable and the other dynamic and more valuable. Organizational knowledge is dynamic, changes over time, and frequently becomes obsolete.

Managing knowledge is an activity based in the phases of the knowledge life cycle (creation, identification, capture, classification, codification, storage, maintenance, and sharing). Each phase provides opportunities for applied and conceptual HPT research questions of relevance to researchers and practitioners alike. Examples are shown in Table 42.2.

OPPORTUNITIES FOR BUILDING HPT'S OWN THEORY

What gives HPT the power to deal with the real-world complexity of organizational and individual performance is HPT's approach to the analysis of human performance problems and its prescription of interventions. Thus the HPT framework integrates problem analyses and interventions from the fields of ID, OD, and IS.

Brethower (1995) characterizes the theoretical structure of HPT as derived from principles of general systems theory and psychology. By applying general systems theory, Brethower says (p. 24), HPT analyzes organizational and individual performance in terms of a framework that has seven basic categories of variables:

1. Mission (a performance system's major purpose or reason for being)

2. Inputs (information, technology, people, money, or materials that initiate or are resources for a work process)

3. Processing system (a system that processes inputs, generating at least one output valued by an external receiver)

4. Internal feedback (information—about the performance of individuals, work groups, or processes—that is used to guide performance)

Table 42.2. The Knowledge Life Cycle as a Basis for HPT Research Questions.

Phase	Application Opportunity	Conceptual Learning Opportunity
Creation	How can employees be trained to look for opportunities in which their knowledge can benefit others?	What is the relationship between individual creativity and productivity?
Identification	How does the organization identify the company expert in a particular procedure or operation?	What factors make someone an expert?
Capture	How can the organization best get information out of people's heads, where it resides as tacit knowledge, and into an organizational repository accessible to all, where it becomes explicit knowledge?	How can knowledge systems be constructed to support knowledge identification and conversion?
Classification	What is the best approach to classifying the organization's knowledge?	What intellectual strategies are best suited to organizing task-relevant knowledge?
Codification	How can the organization make organizational knowledge easy to understand and use?	How should content be codified so as to facilitate its use?
Storage	How can the organization best facilitate the decision making process in which a community of practice decides where and how knowledge will be stored?	What is the relationship between organizational structure and knowledge-repository choices?
Maintenance	How are changes in a work procedure best monitored to ensure that the knowledge base is current?	What is the relationship among knowledge creation, knowledge decay, and organizational factors?
Sharing	How can organizational structure and processes best support information sharing?	How do media and methods of communication affect information sharing?

5. Outputs (information, money, material, or added value that is produced by a work task or process)

6. Receiving system (a set of systems that are closely linked to a processing system and that receive its outputs)

7. External feedback (information—from customers and other external sources—that is used to guide performance)

He goes on to cite five basic principles from psychology as the prescriptive basis for the design of effective interventions. He states them in the language of behavioral psychology, but comparable terminology exists in a cognitive framework. These principles are universal (p. 30):

1. Behavior is a function of interactions between the person and the environment.

2. Behavior is influenced by the situation in which it occurs.

3. Conceptual learning requires direct interaction, with multiple examples and nonexamples.

4. Performance will continue if and only if it leads to something valued by the performer.

5. Intelligent performance requires feedback.

The process by which this analytical framework and these prescriptive principles is applied is very similar to the five-step process used in ID. The principal difference is that the analysis of performance problems and the design of interventions will take account not just of knowledge and skills (as ID does, too) but also of a wide range of additional factors that may be causing—or that could correct—performance problems. Brethower (1995) gives examples of how the seven categories of variables can be used to generate models of organizational and individual performance, both good and bad. He also gives examples of how interventions can be generated through application of the five basic psychological principles.

This framework also allows for the generation of useful HPT research questions. For example, at every stage of the analysis and intervention process, one could ask the following questions:

- In each category of variables, which specific ones are of greatest use with a given kind of organizational or performance problem?

- For each of these specific variables, what is the best measure, both for initial problem analysis and for measurement of intervention effects?

- What recurring patterns of variables allow us to characterize organizational and individual performance patterns by type?

- What patterns of interactions occur within these types, and how are they explained through application of the five basic psychological principles? What power to predict organizational or individual performance do these patterns give us?

- For each type of performance pattern, what interventions successfully apply the five basic psychological principles?

It is instructive to examine the interventions described elsewhere in this book and to characterize each in terms of these five research questions. With this framework, HPT theory can develop through the refinement of these interventions and the development of new ones.

CONTEMPORARY ISSUES FOR HPT, WITH OPPORTUNITIES FOR RESEARCH

Unprecedented rapid change, unpredictable and random events in the external environment, and increasing demands for improved productivity have caused organizations to rethink their purposes and societal contributions. Organizations are now scrambling to try every program and succumbing to every management fad that seems to offer them the promise of remaining competitive. Four emerging innovations can be identified as significantly influencing senior executives and as having importance for HPT practitioners and researchers:

1. Strategy design
2. Change management
3. Organizational learning
4. Knowledge management

These four innovations create opportunities for organizations to define and redefine their fundamental purposes and to rethink organizational structure, processes, and values. An HPT framework based on the bodies of theory described in this chapter can be invaluable in this process. The synergies among HPT, IS, and OD have particularly great potential. Indeed, HPT, IS, and OD share highly correlated conceptual agendas. For example, whereas OD tends to focus on organization-level interventions and HPT tends to focus on individual-level interventions (see Figure 42.1), these two different perspectives are nevertheless related and open up various classes of interventions that could bring value to individual and organizational performance. Research is needed to investigate opportunities for integrating HPT, IS, and OD, and especially to identify the critical success factors for implementing effective integrated solutions. The agendas of these three fields overlap to such a degree that field designations will not be useful in discriminating between and among categories of research questions, but the particular level at which an intervention is undertaken does seem to entail a powerful way of eliciting questions of common interest that are narrow enough in scope to be manageable.

Strategy Design

The survival of organizational HPT and OD units will depend on their leaders' focusing on appropriate value-adding tasks. Rigid, crumbling hierarchical structures and the command-and-control management style are being replaced by autonomous, self-directed, cross-functional work teams. Industrial Age work processes are being redesigned to eliminate work activities that do not add value. In this climate, opportunities abound for HPT, IS, and OD to be involved in interventions.

Change Management

As a result of technical innovation, government deregulation, global competition, the opening of new markets, and stagnant growth in existing markets, organizations are engaging in a process of change that would have been unimaginable a few years ago. They are acquiring new kinds of understanding about their external environments and internal processes. They are learning to manage this new understanding in a dynamic and flexible fashion so as to allow for rapid response and improved performance throughout the organization.

An engineering model of change management assumes that all the systemic effects on the organization have been considered and can be controlled, but organizations are rarely capable of proactively changing before they have to. Although a number of practices have emerged to manage the implementation of change, management of organizational change is nevertheless an illusion. Change is not a linear process; it is neither predictable nor under our control. Misguided quick fixes (downsizing, outsourcing, restructuring, reengineering) have destroyed employees' trust and loyalty and permanently changed the leader-employee relationship; well-managed change can be expected to reduce employees' uncertainty, fear of change, pain, and natural resistance to change.

Figure 42.1. Levels and Focus of Interventions in OD and HPT.

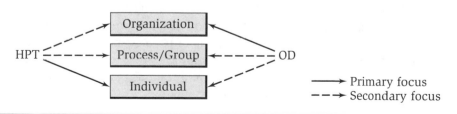

Encouragement of Organizational Learning

Sophisticated HPT practitioners recognize that most learning takes place in the natural work environment, on the job, and through social interaction (coaching) and work team collaboration rather than in the classroom. Day-to-day problem solving involves research, dialogue, and identifying and resolving "undiscussables." Team members learn together and create meaning. When people share what they have learned from experience and reflection, the organization is able to grow continuously and improve its performance. The challenge for HPT practitioners is to create, coordinate, and sustain learning as part of daily activities rather than as short, isolated training events. The "training solution" alone is insufficient and inadequate to create the conditions for organizational learning in the natural workplace environment.

Knowledge Management

The current merging of computer and telecommunications technologies and the emergence of powerful software tools are creating profound changes in how organizations communicate and use information to generate new knowledge and make decisions. Organizational knowledge is increasingly warehoused in data repositories that are easily accessed and updated through an organizational intranet. At the same time, however, individuals are becoming less productive as they attempt to cope with the overload of information and data. Moreover, despite these sophisticated data-repository systems, loss of organizational knowledge through employee attrition, job rotation, or lack of discipline (such as the failure to document learning from projects) has serious implications for organizational survival.

The ability to improve performance now depends on the ability to convert tacit knowledge to explicit knowledge. HPT professionals are now reducing novices' learning curves and simplifying and improving decision making by building Electronic Performance Support Systems that mimic an expert's mental model. Thus they are capturing experts' tacit knowledge by developing expert systems.

RESEARCH OPPORTUNITIES PRESENTED BY THE FOUR INNOVATIONS

Combining the four innovations (strategy design, change management, organizational learning, and knowledge management) and the three levels of intervention (the level of the organization, of the group or process, and of the individual) enables us to build a framework for categorizing HPT research opportunities (see Table 42.3). The table lists representative questions that will be of interest to sophisticated practitioners and researchers alike.

Table 42.3. Framework for Research Based on Four Innovations and Three Levels of Intervention.

Innovation	Organization Level	Group/Process Level	Individual Level
Strategy design	How does the organization ensure that all business units are working toward a common vision and goals?	What core knowledge is required to achieve organizational goals? How can the organization best gather strategic intelligence about competitors and the external environment and use that information to advantage?	What core areas of competence are required to achieve organizational goals? How can acquiring the necessary competence best be facilitated?
Change management	How should work be organized to maintain effectiveness and achieve change goals? Is the concept of the change integrated across the organization?	How can business processes be made more reliable in a period of transition? What critical knowledge is necessary to inform group decision-making processes?	How does the sense of urgency (or lack of urgency) influence individual performance? Do the individuals in key units have the skills to support change?
Organizational learning	Is the organization poised to use its collective knowledge toward regeneration?	How can learning best be transferred among employees? Are the appropriate internal and external information resources locally available to problem-solving efforts?	Are the leaders of the organization skilled in recognizing, creating, and preserving organizational learning?
Knowledge management	How can the organization best use its knowledge for competitive advantage?	How can the organization's information best be captured, warehoused, and made available to appropriate work groups or processes?	How can employees' knowledge best be discovered, generated, organized, and applied so that individuals can perform at high levels?

Because the foundations of OD, IS, and HPT include similar as well as different perspectives from which to analyze and implement solutions, no one of these three perspectives would provide a complete interventional architecture, and the questions listed in the table do not belong exclusively to any one of the three. Thus a reading of the table from left to right suggests that OD, IS, and HPT contribute to diagnoses and interventions at varying degrees of depth along a continuum.

Questions like the ones in Table 42.3 are as important to practitioners as to researchers, but researchers in particular will have to be nimble so as to collect the data that are associated with volatile phenomena. To avoid doing harm, they will also need to be sensitive to interactions between the inquiry process and the intervention (complexity and risk increase, of course, as one escalates from individual- to organizational-level interventions). At any rate, sophisticated practice and research questions overlap to such a degree in HPT that they are nearly indistinguishable. Therefore, researchers and practitioners would best serve the field and benefit each other through greater collaboration.

METHODS FOR HPT RESEARCH

Effective investigation of the research questions discussed in this chapter demands the careful selection and combination of research methods. Almost all the relevant research in HPT is action research conducted by HPT practitioners in functioning organizations. In HPT, as in ID, OD, and IT, some research questions require the quantitative methods of natural science; others require qualitative methods.

Quantitative Methods

The foundation of HPT is the study of individual (and, by extension, group) performance under various antecedent and subsequent events. Binder (1995) points out that although this formulation, called *functional behavior analysis,* is rooted in behavioral psychology, similar methods are found in cognitive psychology and are even consistent with moderate constructivist epistemology. Binder demonstrates that foundational HPT models like Gilbert's (1996) are direct extrapolations of the principle of functional behavioral analysis. This observation has three important implications for HPT research methods:

1. The effectiveness of any HPT intervention must ultimately be judged by cumulative changes in individual behavior, as measured before and after the intervention. Binder points out that this imperative for measured results allows us to validate our prescriptive principles, provide our clients mechanisms for accountability, and support individual and group decision making.

2. The reproducibility of any intervention is the basis on which any pre-scriptive principle of HPT is judged. It would be naïve, however, to believe that a given instance of changed performance is necessarily the result of a simple cause-and-effect relationship. A suitable criterion of an intervention's repro-ducibility would involve patterns of probability for particular instances of changed performance to occur under particular patterns, varying and complex, of conditions and consequences.

3. The measures and methods to be used in this kind of HPT research are quantitative. Qualitative methods are important in describing and understanding the principles that underlie the complex behaviors studied by researchers and practitioners, but Binder's point is well taken: the prescriptive principles for the HPT interventions that result from those studies must ultimately be tested quan-titatively. Thus, it might also be argued (probably not without some disagree-ment with Binder), HPT research can benefit from qualitative as well as quantitative methods at different stages in the process of theory development.

Quantitative methods do not necessarily imply statistical inference. Binder ar-gues that because the principle of functional behavioral analysis requires the unit of measurement to be individual behavioral events, statistical testing of hy-potheses in large groups is probably not a useful method for HPT research, given that such generalities mask the interactions of effects that are basic to functional analysis. It is interesting to note that cognitive psychologists, such as Scandura (1977), have long made a similar argument. Although it would be inappropriate to rule out the methods of statistical inference entirely, their utility is limited.

According to Binder, the essential problem in HPT, as in any other kind of re-search enterprise, is measurement. For HPT, Binder (1995, p. 108) suggests the following kinds of measures:

- Measures of quality (counting according to type or category): number of correct versus incorrect answers, or number of acceptable versus unac-ceptable units; number of different classes or categories, as defined by objective criteria; number of units completed within a specified time limit

- Measures of quantity (counting according to amount produced): number; volume; market value (in units of currency)

- Measures of cost (counting according to dollars or time spent): costs for labor; material and environmental costs; costs of management

Qualitative Methods

Qualitative research is an umbrella term that is used to cover a range of meth-ods. On the surface, the assumptions of quantitative and qualitative research may appear to be incompatible, but qualitative methods can be seen as com-plementary to the functional analysis–based quantitative approach described in the previous section. Specifically, the emphasis on context in the qualitative paradigm is at least somewhat comparable to the perspective of functional analysis. Furthermore, for many qualitative techniques the essential unit of analysis is individual behavior (with groups represented as a collection of individual behaviors), the context of which is described in depth and from multiple viewpoints. Thus, while there are important differences for HPT between the qualitative and the quantitative approaches (particularly in the study of groups), one way to use qualitative methods is as a means of generating theory, which can then be further tested by quantitative means as well as by further qualitative study. The specific qualitative methods most useful to HPT include observation (which can take place anywhere on a continuum running from the perspective of a participant observer to that of an observer participant), interviews, and case studies.

Observation. In participant observation, the researcher becomes, to varying degrees, involved in the actual situation and develops in-depth relationships with the study group while still retaining the separation of researcher from actors. This involvement leads the researcher to understand and gain insights into the culture, context, and feelings of the group, and it makes the attachment of meaning to the observed phenomena much more authentic.

Participant observation is not, as the name may inaccurately suggest, an inactive stance; on the contrary, the participant observer becomes an actor in the situation and may engage in activities like those of the other participants. The participant observer constantly interacts with the other participants—through the observation itself, of course, but also through active listening and conversation. At the same time, however, the participant observer is directed by the need to probe deeper, looking for an understanding of the group's membership, identity, behavior, rules, processes, values and mores, and relationships to the physical world or structure. In keeping with the method of participant observation, the researcher is constantly interpreting information and revising propositions or research questions. Furthermore, the researcher may be looking for contrasting situations and/or outside factors, any of which may shed light on or influence the situation.

Participant observation is a time-consuming, skilled process that requires good observational and interpersonal skills along with an adherence to method. This method may have a certain appeal to many in our field because of its perceived "people" orientation and because its requirements seem less constricting and less rigorous than those for quantitative methods. This perception is erroneous, however. Indeed, many a study has failed when a researcher untrained in this method has produced work that suffered from his or her preconceived ideas or from conclusions based on insufficient information.

Nonparticipant observation is a less obtrusive method for conducting research. It tends to focus on very specific information or behaviors. The objective of nonparticipant observation is to identify and record behaviors associated with the purpose of the particular study. In nonparticipant observation, the researcher does not participate as a member of the group; rather, he or she must either be identified as an observer (and must minimize his or her interactions with the group) or choose methods (such as video or audiorecording) that allow for minimal interactions with the situation. This method is often used in combination with others.

Nonparticipant observation, as compared with participant observation, has both advantages and disadvantages. On the positive side, according to Borg and Gall (1989, p. 396), "the main advantages of nonparticipant observation are that it is less likely to be obtrusive than participant observation and less likely to be distorted by the emotional involvement of the observer." On the negative side, nonparticipant observation minimizes the opportunity to gather some kinds of information (such as about attitudes or perceptions) that are not easily acquired on the basis of observation alone.

Interviews. Interviewing is another major qualitative method. It is used to understand how insiders view a situation and includes questioning about the interview subject's thought process.

An interview may be structured or unstructured, according to how predetermined or standardized its focus is. It allows the researcher to describe the subject's perception of a situation, its structure, and its dimensions. It also allows the researcher who has observed a behavior or a set of behaviors to probe more deeply into understanding the cognitive process, or thinking, of a subject, and it provides an opportunity for more reflective thought on the part of the subject (for example, away from his or her normal job situation). Work behavior is often more complex than what can simply be observed, and interviews provide opportunities to follow up or get additional background information that can help make sense of a situation.

Case Studies. The case study is another useful qualitative approach. In this approach, the researcher locates and closely examines a situation or environment believed to be prototypical of other workplaces, or one that is uniquely of interest because of some phenomenon. Thus the case study becomes an example of a type of HPT problem. The case study should provide a description rich enough to allow the reader to feel that he or she is present, but the information drawn from a case study is not directly generalizable to other situations because no two environments are ever the same.

HPT practitioners may confuse case studies with accounts of interventions, which are common in professional journals, but a proper case study involves significant examination of the case and uses several methods for gathering data (such as participant observation, document analysis, and interviews). Research using less than exhaustive information collection and analysis will lead to shallow understanding, which can be even more detrimental than no research at all because the richness of the cultural context is missed, and adequate analysis and interpretation are precluded.

Borg and Gall (1989) describe five kinds of case studies:

1. *Historical case studies* use interviews and document analysis to describe how an organization has developed over a period of time. For example, a researcher may want to examine why or how certain values or work practices exist today; knowledge of the origin and history of the relevant issues may affect decisions about how to construct changes.

2. *Observational case studies* examine the ongoing interactions of an organization or a part of the organization. This is a long-term approach to understanding the day-to-day interactional dynamics of a group of people and how they cope with certain issues that confront them. For example, observational case studies might examine how communication patterns change or interpersonal relationships develop, or what the impact on performance might be when an organization moves the basis of its operations to information technology.

3. *Oral histories* are first-person narrative accounts by individuals describing past events. For example, through one person's experience, an HPT researcher might investigate how downsizing has affected motivation. Several oral histories combined can provide new insight into ways of accomplishing the goal of downsizing without reducing productivity.

4. *Situation analyses* are case histories that look at particular events from all major points of view. This approach provides a very comprehensive understanding of these events. A situation analysis is similar to a well-constructed needs assessment. In a needs assessment, it is not unusual to encounter different perceptions of a problem; the best understanding is usually based on all the different points of view.

5. *Clinical case studies* help in understanding a specific type of individual of interest. Using observation, interviews, and quantitative testing devices, the researcher investigates the individual and identifies possible performance improvement strategies for him or her. For example, one might study how the productivity of nontraditional workers is improved when they are provided with a certain type of mentoring. Another common application of the clinical case study is in cognitive task analysis and software development, where the method is usually called a *think-aloud protocol.*

With any of the qualitative methods discussed here, the challenge for HPT researchers is clearly to select the one or the ones that will offer the best fit with the particular research objective. The ultimate goal of a qualitative research method is to provide an understanding of a phenomenon by examining all the elements and their related effects. According to Borg and Gall (1989, p. 385), "This emphasis on studying the whole setting in order to understand reality is perhaps the most important characteristic of the qualitative research paradigm and results in much investigation being aimed at an understanding of the social, cultural and historical setting in which the investigation occurs."

The advantage of a qualitative or naturalistic method is its ability to ascribe meaning to a situation by studying things in context rather than in artificial isolation, as happens in controlled experiments. Sherman and Webb (1988) list four characteristics of qualitative research methods that are of importance to HPT research:

1. Events can be understood adequately only if they are seen in context; therefore, qualitative researchers immerse themselves in the setting.

2. The contexts of inquiry are not contrived; they are natural. Nothing is predefined or taken for granted.

3. The qualitative researcher wants those who are studied to speak for themselves, to offer their own perspectives in words and action. Therefore, qualitative research is an interactive process in which the persons studied teach the researcher about their lives.

4. Qualitative researchers attend to experience as a whole, not in terms of separate variables. The aim of qualitative research is to understand experience as being unified.

These characteristics are also consistent with the values of qualitative research as described by Borg and Gall (1989), and they are the characteristics that seem most relevant to HPT. Specifically, Borg and Gall (1989) list the following values:

- *Phenomenology:* The researcher must develop the perspectives of the group being studied (that is, the researcher must develop an "insider's" viewpoint; we would add that the researcher must do so from multiple perspectives).

- *Holism:* The researcher must attempt to perceive the big picture or the total situation rather than focusing on a few elements in a complex situation, as is the usual procedure in quantitative research.

- *Nonjudgmental orientation:* Judgments, hypotheses, or preconceptions may distort what the researcher sees; therefore, the emphasis is on recording the total situation in qualitative terms without superimposing one's own value system.

- *Contextualization:* All information must be considered only in the context of the environment in which it was gathered.

CONCLUSION

This chapter has suggested that research in HPT should draw on the prescriptive theory of its cognate applied fields and on the principles of its underlying disciplines: instructional design, organizational development, information science, and the HPT analytical framework itself. We have argued for a balance between quantitative research (based on functional behavior analysis) and qualitative research (using a range of naturalistic methods), with qualitative research informing quantitative research.

HPT research is of necessity action research, and so there will be few occasions for research to be conducted on the basis of the experimental paradigm or statistical inference. This view is consistent with much current thinking in HPT's related fields.

Well-designed quantitative research and well-documented naturalistic inquiries are available but still, unfortunately, rare in the literature of HPT. The need is great and must be met if the field is to advance theoretically.

The research paradigm is feasible even for busy practitioners. Indeed, this chapter has pointed to some common strategic business challenges that are creating unprecedented opportunities for HPT interventions that use action research. If only we will take the time to reflect systematically on our experience, it will be possible for us to expand the empirical base of the field.

References

Beer, M. (1980). *Organizational change and development: A systems view.* Glenview, IL: Scott, Foresman.

Binder, C. (1995). Promoting HPT innovation: A return to our natural science roots. *Performance Improvement Quarterly* 8:2, 95–113.

Borg, W., and Gall, M. (1989). *Educational research* (5th ed.). White Plains, NY: Longman.

Brethower, D. M. (1995). Specifying a Human Performance Technology knowledge base. *Performance Improvement Quarterly* 8:2, 17–39.

Gayeski, D. M. (1995). Changing roles and professional challenges for Human Performance Technology. *Performance Improvement Quarterly* 8:2, 6–16.

Gilbert, T. (1996). *Human competence: Engineering worthy performance.* Amherst, MA: Human Resources Development Press.

Peters, T. J., and Waterman, R. H. Jr. (1982). *In search of excellence: Lessons from America's best-run companies.* New York: Warner Books.

Phenix, P. H. (1964). *Realms of meaning.* New York: McGraw-Hill.

Rossett, A. (1987). *Training needs assessment.* Englewood Cliffs, NJ: Educational Technology Publications.

Rossett, A. (1996). Training and organization development: Separated at birth? *Training* 33:4, 53–59.

Rummler, G. A., and Brache, A. P. (1990). *Improving performance: How to manage the white space on the organization chart.* San Francisco: Jossey-Bass.

Scandura, J. M. (1977). *Problem solving: A structural/process approach with instructional implications.* Orlando, FL: Academic Press.

Sherman, R., and Webb, R. (1988). *Qualitative research in education: Focus and methods.* Bristol, PA: Falmer Press.

Weisbord, M. (1976). Organizational diagnosis: Six places to look for trouble with our without a theory. *Group and Organization Studies* 1:4, 430–447.

CHAPTER FORTY-THREE

Practicing Human Performance Technology in a Global Business Environment

Alicia M. Rojas
Dawn E. Zintel

Rapid advances in information technology, automation, and telecommunications are making the world smaller every day. Such technology permits managers, customers, suppliers, and employees around the world to hold videoconferences and teleconferences, facilitating instant communication and decision making. Cable television programs are broadcast worldwide via satellite. The use of mobile phones and pagers is increasing throughout the world. The fax machine makes information accessible anywhere at the push of a button. History is being made with the advent of the Internet, which facilitates information flow in real time. For example, the exchange of products and services via the World Wide Web is changing the way we conduct business.

Major companies are also being forced to "go global," as their governments' commitment to an open-market policy and to free trade among regional countries has increased local competition. Harris and Moran (1996) list a number of global environmental forces affecting organizations:

- Global sourcing
- New and evolving markets
- Economies of scale
- Movement toward homogeneous demand
- Lower transportation costs
- Government tariffs and taxes

- Telecommunications and other global technological phenomena
- Homogeneous technical standards
- Competition from nondomestic organizations
- Risk from volatile exchange rates
- Customers who are themselves becoming more global

What is the impact of this trend toward globalization? Increasingly, customers are requiring products and services that are sensitive to their cultures in all respects, from design to utilization (Elashmawi and Harris, 1993). Companies around the world, as well as such international organizations as UNESCO, Organization of American States, Food and Agriculture Organization, and the World Bank, have seen the economic impact and have learned that they must take cultural variables into consideration. For example, in November 1977, a major Argentine newspaper reported that an American company, Dunkin' Donuts, had found an alternative to closing its struggling stores in Argentina; the company decided to fill its doughnuts with a type of marmalade, *dulce de leche,* which most Argentines enjoy. It is part of their cultural tradition. The company's stores in Argentina became successful and profitable, and, as a surprising consequence of that decision, the company now plans to introduce this product into the U.S. market.

The need for attention to cultural details is not new. In the mid-1970s, one of the authors developed a customer service training program for the Royal Bank of Canada, which had thirty-five thousand employees worldwide at that time. The course would be taught in Venezuela, so the materials were translated into Spanish. After the first class, the training department learned that students were unhappy with the course. It turned out that the translator had used Colombian Spanish and that the Venezuelans had taken exception to this.

The error lay in the notion that one can generalize from a particular region or language to the world at large. Global corporations such as IKEA (Sweden), Siemens (Germany), Toyota (Japan), Toshiba (Japan), Procter & Gamble (USA), General Motors (United States), and Heineken (the Netherlands) have learned that culture makes a difference. They all tailor their products, services, and advertising to their diverse international markets. Another example is Electrolux, the European appliance manufacturer; in order to meet the widely varying needs of its customers across Europe, Electrolux has 120 refrigerator designs with 1,500 variations (Brake, Walker, and Walker, 1995).

In addition to global environmental forces that influence technical, social, political, economic, and cultural systems in every country, immigration is changing the demographics of most countries. In 1993, *Time* magazine reported the following developments; one out of four babies born in Brussels was Arab; whole parts of the Paraguayan capital of Asunción were Korean; there were forty thousand "Canadian" residents in Hong Kong, many of whom spoke Cantonese as a first language; and almost half of the world's Mormons lived outside the United States (Iyer, 1993).

Because of this globalization, HP technologists throughout the world must learn how to deal with multicultural labor forces and customers, as well as all of the intercultural issues associated with them. Globalization has become a business reality, but many organizations and individuals are not well prepared for the challenge of being influenced by the forces of the global environment or by cultural variables. Therefore the future role for Human Performance Technology (HPT) practitioners is to help these organizations discover new ways of doing business in a global context. In order to do so, however, HPT professionals themselves must learn how to work successfully in the global environment.

In this chapter, we present basic information on the criteria for success in working globally and provide tools to help HPT professionals prepare to do so. First, however, we explore definitions of culture and examine its different components.

CULTURE AND CULTURAL VARIABLES

What is culture? Elashmawi and Harris (1993) note that various cultural groups have different answers for this question. Most Asians and Arabs define culture with such words as *food, clothes, art,* and *religion.* Most Westerners focus on words such as *values, beliefs,* and *behavior,* although Europeans also often describe cultures with such words as *art, music,* and *food.* What one knows about people in other cultures is often the obvious (for example, their dress, languages, foods, behavior, customs, and rituals). Some authors, such as Hofstede (1997), call these cultural elements "practices."

A review of the literature provides insight into how culture is perceived and therefore defined. Brislin (1993, p. 4) writes that "culture consists of ideals, values, and assumptions about life that are widely shared among people and that guide specific behaviors. Assumptions and ideals are not immediately obvious. Rather they are stored in people's minds and consequently are hard for outsiders to see." Trompenaars and Hampden-Turner (1998, p. 6) offer this perspective: "Culture is the way in which a group of people solves problems and reconciles dilemmas." They go on to explain that the problems can be placed in three categories: "those which arise from our relationships with other people; those which come from the passage of time; and those which relate to the environment" (p. 8). Another definition is "the fundamental values, beliefs, attitudes, and patterns of thinking that are embedded in a society's or region's view of how the world works and of how individuals and groups can and should operate in that world" (Brake, Walker, and Walker, 1995, p. 261). Indeed, various authors have defined culture in different ways, highlighting a range of cultural variables and value orientations, as is summarized in Table 43.1.

Table 43.1. Culture and Cultural Variables.

Hofstede (1997)	Harris and Moran (1996)	O'Hara and Johansen (1994)	Brake, Walker, and Walker (1995)	Trompenaars and Hampden-Turner (1998)	Deresky (1994)	Elashmawi and Harris (1993)
Culture	Cultural Variable	Cultural Variable	Cultural Variable	Value Orientation	Culture	Culture
Power distance	Sense of self and space	Language	Environment	Relationships with people:	National variables:	Language
Avoidance of uncertainty	Communication and language	Context (space, emotions, other reactions to communication)	Time	Universalism versus particularism	Economic systems	Nonverbal communication
Individualism versus collectivism	Dress and appearance	Time	Action	Neutrality versus emotionalism	Legal systems	Space and time orientation
Masculinity versus femininity	Food and eating habits	Equality or power	Communication	Individualism versus communitarianism	Political systems	Religion and belief systems
	Time and time consciousness	Information flow	Space	Specific versus diffuse bonds	Physical systems	Pattern of thinking
	Relationships		Power	Achievement versus ascription	Technological know-how systems	Self-image
	Values and norms		Individualism	Relationships with time: Synchronic versus sequential	Sociocultural variables:	Set of values
	Beliefs and attitudes		Competitiveness	Relationships with nature: Inner-directed versus outer-directed	Religion	Material culture
	Mental process and learning		Structure		Education	Aesthetics
	Work habits and practices		Thinking		Language	
					Variables that perpetuate the following factors:	
					Cultural variables (values, norms, beliefs)	
					Attitudes (work, time, materialism, individualism, change)	
					Individual and group employee behavior (motivation, productivity, commitment, ethics)	

Although there is more to learn about values and culture than can be captured in this brief chapter, one cultural variable that is critically important is communication. By studying just this one variable, we can learn much about how cultures differ. Hall (1990) and other intercultural experts distinguish between high-context and low-context cultures in the context of communication. People in a high-context culture use a minimum of words, are indirect, and are not explicit. They are looking for meaning and understanding in what is not said, and they rely on body language and nonverbal communication. By contrast, people in a low-context culture use explicit words to "spell it all out." The emphasis is on sending and receiving information accurately and directly by means of words. Table 43.2 identifies the main characteristics of low-and high-context cultures.

The terms *low-context* and *high-context* are the end points on a continuum. Cultures tend to fall between the two extremes. Figure 43.1 shows where some countries are on the continuum.

Table 43.2. Low- and High-Context Characteristics.

Low-Context Characteristics	High-Context Characteristics
Truth-seeking	Harmony-seeking
Explicit	Implicit
Logical or objective	Intuitive or subjective
Analytical or quantitative	Holistic
Highly verbal	Highly nonverbal
Innovative	Traditional
Pragmatic or results-oriented	Structured or process-oriented
Egalitarian	Hierarchical

Figure 43.1. Continuum of Cultural Context and Its Effects on Communication.

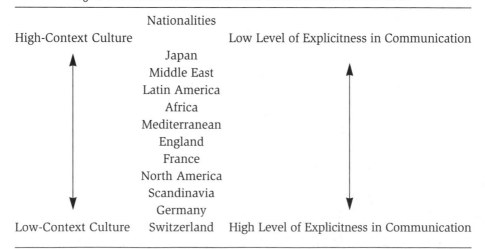

	Nationalities	
High-Context Culture		Low Level of Explicitness in Communication
	Japan	
	Middle East	
	Latin America	
	Africa	
	Mediterranean	
	England	
	France	
	North America	
	Scandinavia	
	Germany	
Low-Context Culture	Switzerland	High Level of Explicitness in Communication

How might the concept of low- and high-context cultures affect the HP technologist's work? In Table 43.3, Carey (1998) summarizes how cultures on opposite ends of the continuum differ with respect to social patterns, communication styles, decision-making processes, and management principles.

Hofstede (1997) describes five levels of culture:

1. The national (country) level
2. The regional, ethnic, religious, and linguistic-affiliation levels within each country
3. The level of gender
4. The generational level
5. The social level (and, for those who are employed, an organizational or corporate level according to the way employees have been socialized by their work organizations)

Table 43.3. Comparison of Cultural Conditions.

	Low-Context Culture	High-Context Culture (polychronic)
Social patterns	Informal, outgoing, and casual behavior	Formal and reserved behavior, codes of conduct
	Quick familiarity, individual focus	Lengthy relationships, group focus
	Gifts as tokens, given in single gesture	Gifts as symbols, given repeatedly to build trust
	Emotional sensitivity not valued	Emotional sensitivity highly valued
	Time viewed as sequential and rigorous	Time viewed as random and elastic
Communication styles	Efficient, direct, and straight-forward approach	Use of small talk to build trust
	Tendency to get down to business	Time taken for relationships
	Expectations of candor and conflict	Consensus and harmony demanded
	Value placed on collective brainstorming	Independent reflection valued
	Value placed on constructive criticism	Saving face valued
	Tendency to listen and ask for information	Tendency to listen to and answer questions
	Request for feedback from subordinates	Instructions given to subordinates

Table 43.3. Comparison of Cultural Conditions, cont'd.

	Low-Context Culture	High-Context Culture (polychronic)
Decision-making processes	Attempts to be objective, logical	Attempt to be subjective, personal
	Emphasis on facts and measurement	Intuition and insight valued
	Tendency to take risks	Risk avoidance
	Linear thought	Circuitious thought
	Cost-benefit analysis	Face-saving analysis
	Value placed on inductive reasoning	Value placed on deductive reasoning
	Distrust of complexity	Distrust of simplicity
	Attempts to simplify	Complexity valued
	Experiments with reality	Reliance on prior, logical arguments
Management principles	Task-related activities	People-related activities
	Egalitarian structure	Hierarchical structure
	Emphasis on high achievement	Emphasis on high process
	Single focus	Multiple focus
	Emphasis on profit, task, and results	Emphasis on relationships and harmony
	Narrow concentration	Concurrent concentration
	View of failure as impersonal; quick recovery	View of failure as personal; career stigma
	Strict agenda; tendency to budget time	Floating agenda; tendency to allow time
	Strict deadlines	Flexible deadlines
	Integration of roles, rank, and status	Separation of roles, rank, and status

Source: Carey, 1998. © 1998 International Society for Performance Improvement. Reprinted with the permission of the International Society for Performance Improvement.

Hofstede (p. 8) states that "the core of culture is formed by values," and he points out that values are broad tendencies to prefer certain states of affairs over others. They are acquired in early childhood and established by age ten. Consequently, they are difficult to change. Most people may not even be aware of the values they have. Values become invisible. Therefore, they cannot be discussed or directly observed; they can only be inferred from the way people act under various conditions.

If one studies the differences in values between generations, one may find that the values underlying culture are prioritized differently over time. Although the rankings may shift, the core cultural values tend to remain the same over time. A clear example of this appears in Elashmawi and Harris (1993), a study of the differences in values between generations of Japanese workers in a business setting. Those older than thirty-five had traditional values, as well as traditional priorities for their values: group harmony, group achievement, group consensus, relationship, seniority, family security, and cooperation. In contrast, the younger generation (twenty-five to thirty-five years old) valued the following things in the following order: freedom, relationship, family security, equality, self-reliance, privacy, and group harmony. As this list shows, they continued to share certain core values of Japanese culture: relationship, family security, and group harmony. When working with the Japanese, the HP technologist can be more effective by recognizing the impact of those values on the business process and on personal interactions. Value orientations represent the "preferred" way of thinking or acting by the majority of a specific population. This is of critical importance to HPT.

The HP technologist should also be aware of gender-related differences within a culture. For example, one of our U.S. colleagues, Kathy Indermill, recently developed a course on self-governance for nongovernmental organizations (community organizations dealing with such issues as family planning and irrigation projects). The course was pilot-tested in Nepal with prominent, well educated, and well-traveled representatives of organizations from Nepal, Sri Lanka, Bangladesh, the Philippines, and India. There were fifty men and three women in the class. Indermill learned, first, that women would have to be specifically invited to these events or they would not attend and, second, that the women who did attend would have to be called on in class to give their opinions because their male counterparts would not give them an opportunity to participate. This situation is representative of gender roles in countries where women have different rights from those that women enjoy in Western countries. Asked how the men had responded to a young American woman leading the class, Indermill said that they were very respectful and attentive to anyone from the United States, regardless of the person's age or gender. Had the self-governance class been taught in Italy, where seniority and age are critical to the success of team-building efforts, this event might have been received very differently.

It is not always easy to define *culture* or to distinguish between a culture's values and practices. Based on our research, beliefs, and experience, we have presented our concept of the relationships among values, culture, and practices in Figure 43.2. As the figure shows, we feel that values define the culture. In turn, the culture and its value orientations determine cultural practices.

Figure 43.2. Relationships Among Values, Cultures, and Practices.

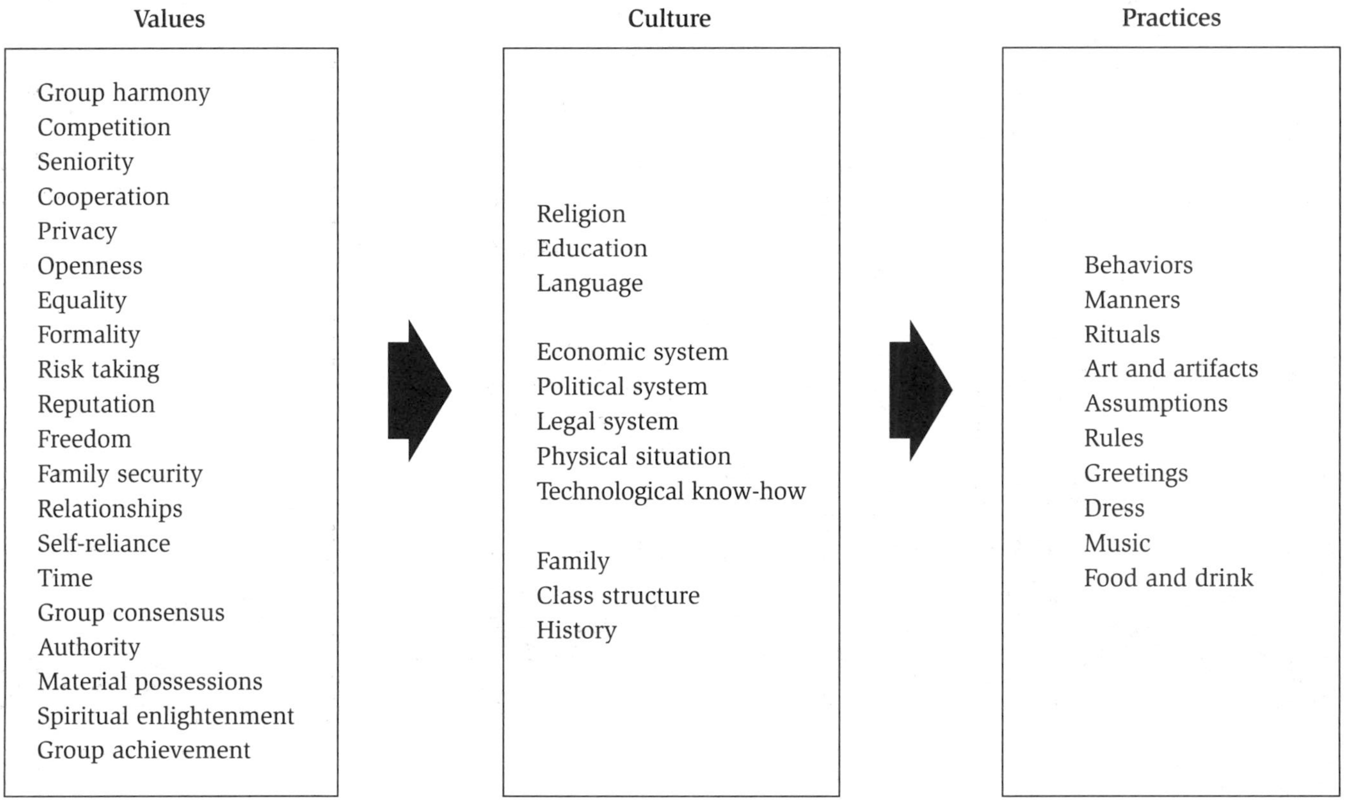

Values	Culture	Practices
Group harmony	Religion	Behaviors
Competition	Education	Manners
Seniority	Language	Rituals
Cooperation		Art and artifacts
Privacy	Economic system	Assumptions
Openness	Political system	Rules
Equality	Legal system	Greetings
Formality	Physical situation	Dress
Risk taking	Technological know-how	Music
Reputation		Food and drink
Freedom	Family	
Family security	Class structure	
Relationships	History	
Self-reliance		
Time		
Group consensus		
Authority		
Material possessions		
Spiritual enlightenment		
Group achievement		

CORE AREAS OF COMPETENCE FOR SUCCESSFUL GLOBAL WORK

What does an HP technologist need in order to work successfully in a multicultural, global business environment? On the basis of our experience and our synthesis of the extensive literature on this topic, we have identified two important attributes:

1. A global mind-set
2. Awareness (including self-awareness and cultural awareness)

Global Mind-Set

Rhinesmith (1993) believes that functioning successfully in a culturally diverse work environment, at home or abroad, requires the development of a certain mind-set and a particular set of skills. For Rhinesmith (p. 24), a mind-set is a "way of being" and a "predisposition to see the world in a particular way that sets boundaries and provides explanations for why things are the way they are, while at the same time establishing guidance for the ways in which we should behave." In other words, a mind-set is a "filter through which we look at the world." He adds that people with a global mind-set tend to approach the world in six specific ways:

1. They look for the bigger, broader picture, especially the context.
2. They accept life as a balance of contradictory forces that are to be appreciated, pondered, and managed.
3. They trust process rather than structure to deal with the unexpected.
4. They value diversity, multicultural teamwork, and play as the basic forum within which they accomplish their personal, professional, and organizational objectives.
5. They flow with changes as opportunities and are comfortable with surprises and ambiguity.
6. They seek to be open to themselves and others by rethinking boundaries, finding new meanings, and changing their direction and behavior.

In other words, being open, flexible, and willing to adapt to differences is essential to working in a global environment.

Awareness

HPT professionals need to understand that the field of HPT evolved in North America, western Europe, and the United Kingdom. People from other cultures may not easily accept concepts such as "measurable objectives," "objective data analysis," "quantifiable results," and "feedback." For example, Americans are accustomed to obtaining feedback on their products or performance as a way to collect data that will help them improve; for Germans, asking for feedback is like admitting failure. The American notion of an "excellent performer" may be completely rejected by someone in another culture. Even more enlightening to many American HPT practitioners is the discovery that Americans have a lot to learn about consensus building and problem solving; many other cultures have centuries' more experience than we do in coming to terms with very complex issues, which may be influenced by regional, religious, and linguistic factors (to name only a few such influences).

The constant challenge for HPT professionals is to assess their own cultural assumptions, business practices, biases, and stereotypes and then to question whether these will be accepted in another country or in a multicultural situation. It is important to look for differences as well as similarities and not to assume anything. For example, when two thousand managers in twenty-five countries were asked to identify the variables needed for successful competition in business, their responses were diverse. Japanese managers identified product development, management, and product quality as the major variables. German managers thought that workforce skills, problem solving, and management were most important. American managers identified a different set of factors: customer service, product quality, and technology (Kanter, 1989). Imagine the difficulty one would face if one tried to instill in the German managers the Japanese principles for successful competition.

Working with people from cultures different from one's own, whether in one's own country or another, means delving deeper into the rationales for cultural practices. Why do people act the way they do? What is important to them? How are they used to performing? Developing cultural awareness is not easy. The following information about culture and cultural variables will help HP technologists who are going to be working in other countries or with multicultural groups in their own country.

MODEL FOR SUCCESSFUL APPLICATION OF HPT IN A GLOBAL ENVIRONMENT

When do we consider cultural variables in HPT projects? How do we know that we have the appropriate mind-set, and how does the HP technologist apply the global mind-set? As we have seen, global forces (such as new and evolving markets, economies of scale, movement toward homogeneous demand, and international business transactions) are influencing industries, governments, and educational systems. These forces strongly affect the design and implementation of HPT methodologies. Cultural and organizational variables must also be considered in HPT projects, because these variables determine the inputs, processes, results, and feedback system. Figure 43.3 reflects these relationships between the critical components that global HP technologists must integrate into their own practices.

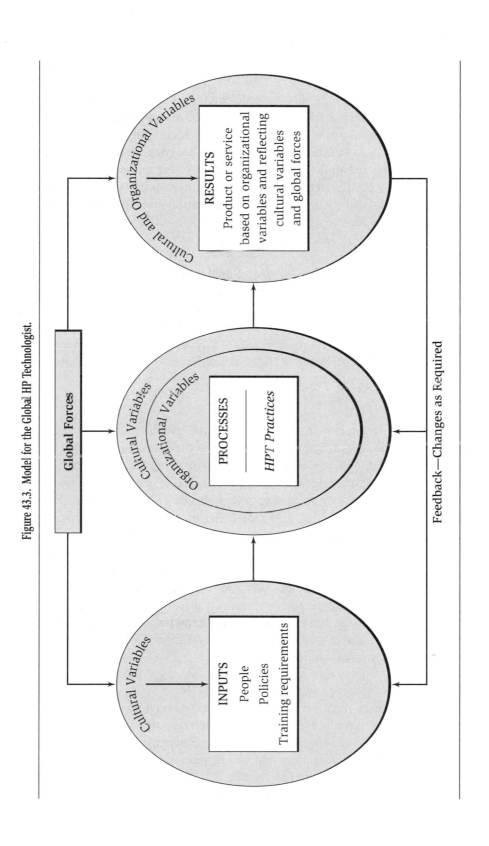

Figure 43.3. Model for the Global HP Technologist.

Inputs

In the implementation of an HPT methodology, global forces and cultural variables will heavily influence the inputs, whether those are people, policies, training requirements, the education and training of audiences, employees, or customer requirements. Thus the results of an audience analysis for a training program should include some data on the cultural traits of the audience members. Are they bilingual? Are they engineers? Are all of them men? What are their nationalities? What are their primary communication styles? What are their instructional traditions?

Processes

HPT processes are molded by organizational variables that require, for example, performance improvement programs, new compensation programs, and advanced communication systems. These organizational variables are modified by the culture of employees and customers. For example, if human resources policies are imposed across countries, they may not be accepted by all employees. The wise HP technologist is prepared for the cultural nuances that may influence the implementation of new systems, policies, or procedures.

Results

The results of the implementation process are HPT products and services, which should combine organizational and cultural factors. It is important to create a balance among employees' and customers' values, cultures, and practices, always within the framework of environmental forces. For example, companies such as Toshiba (Japan) and Procter & Gamble (United States) are making use of cultural differences so that they may better understand their customers and thus improve their products and services. This is how those companies aim to gain a competitive advantage. Just as companies should be responsive to their external clients, they must also be responsive to their internal clients. For example, when Coca-Cola of Ghana began to distribute boxed lunches to its employees, the employees became restless and dissatisfied. The company then learned that it is a long-standing tradition in Ghana for women to prepare lunch for their families. The company discontinued distribution of the boxed lunches, and employees' morale improved.

Feedback System

Once HPT products and services have been implemented and evaluated, there is a feedback system in place. Some changes may be considered as a result. Occasionally, changes are observed in both the organization and the culture. For example, Wal-Mart in Argentina adapted its management practices to its employees' cultural characteristics. As a result, the company reported a better working environment and achieved its business goals.

JOB AID TO GUIDE GLOBAL HP TECHNOLOGISTS

When you are ready to implement an HPT project, follow the steps we list here. This will enable you to identify the critical success factors.

Before the HPT Project Begins

1. Determine your level of cultural awareness by filling out the survey in Exhibit 43.1. Rate yourself on each of the ten dimensions.

Exhibit 43.1. Awareness Survey.

Identify where you are on the continuum in terms of the criteria for success that have been identified for global HPT practitioners.
(1 = not aware or capable; 5 = fully aware or capable)

1. **Self-awareness**
   Degree to which you know and understand what factors about your own culture are an integral part of your thinking, values, and behavior on an ongoing basis

   | 1 | 3 | 5 |

2. **Cultural sensitivity**
   Degree to which you know and understand cultural influences on your behavior and are able to establish personal relationships

   | 1 | 3 | 5 |

3. **Nonjudgmentalism**
   Degree to which you are able to grasp what another culture considers important, as well as how organizations and individuals function in that culture; ability to examine unfamiliar perspectives, values, and behaviors in the context of the surrounding culture

   | 1 | 3 | 5 |

4. **Flexibility**
   Ability to tolerate and handle changes, surprises, and high levels of ambiguity and to adjust to how people prefer to learn in another culture

   | 1 | 3 | 5 |

5. **Cross-cultural communication**
   Awareness of verbal and nonverbal differences in communication between you and people in another culture

   | 1 | 3 | 5 |

Exhibit 43.1. Awareness Survey, cont'd.

6. **Business awareness**
   Awareness of the social, political, economic, and cultural assumptions and contexts in which the local organizations operate, and of which models, theories, concepts, standard business practices, and materials are inappropriate for the culture

   1   3   5

7. **Social awareness**
   Awareness of customs, traditions (including holidays), and cultural taboos so that you can operate effectively within an organization as well as in the country

   1   3   5

8. **Skill in empathically gathering information**
   Ability to listen actively to the other culture, use observation skills to learn and understand, be descriptive rather than judgmental about events, ask questions appropriately, and avoid questions that are too personal, embarrassing, or probing for the culture

   1   3   5

9. **Skill in gathering data without distorting filters**
   Ability to collect and validate data in a different culture where the possibility of error is magnified; ability to be sure that data are not filtered in such a way that your own cultural biases affect accuracy of interpretation or blend two or more cultural perspectives and interpret them in a way that transcends any single one of them

   1   3   5

10. **Process orientation**
    Ability to learn how to deal with the unexpected through exploration and trial and error, instead of relying on rules and structure

    1   3   5

Source: Rhinesmith, 1993; Marquardt and Engle, 1993; Harris and Moran, 1996.

2. Identify the activities (attending courses, researching topics in libraries, consulting the Internet or friends) that will help you raise any self-rating lower than 4.

3. If you travel to other locations, either domestic or abroad, be sure to gather factual background information on the history, the demographics, the politics, the economics, the social systems, and the religion of the place. Collect information about the people (including customs, traditions, beliefs, values, and cultural taboos). Identify the current economic, social, and cultural problems faced by the people you will work with at the new location. Also collect information on local practices and business procedures. For example, learn about the main colloquialisms of the language, greeting protocols, food preferences, fashions, the organizational and managerial hierarchy, and the way gender differences are expressed.

While the HPT Project Is in Development

1. Identify the main cultural variables that may affect your work and your relationship with the people in the other location (domestic or foreign) by using the checklist shown in Exhibit 43.2.

Exhibit 43.2. Checklist for Cultural Analysis.

Cultural Variable	Value Orientation
Environment	Control ❑ People can dominate or change the environment to fit their needs. Harmony ❑ People should live in harmony with the world surrounding them. Constraint ❑ People believe that they are constrained by the world around them. They believe in fate and luck.
Time	Single focus ❑ Schedule- and deadline-driven; concentrate on one task at a time Multiple focus ❑ Emphasize relationships, not deadlines; can do multiple tasks at a time Fixed ❑ Punctuality important Fluid ❑ Punctuality loosely defined

Exhibit 43.2. Checklist for Cultural Analysis, cont'd.

Cultural Variable	Value Orientation
Time (cont'd.)	**Past** ❑ Time rooted in fixed notions of the past; continuance of traditions important **Present** ❑ Short-term focus with immediate results; historical origins of issues ignored **Future** ❑ More interested in long-term results; willingness to forgo short-term successes
Action	**Doing** ❑ Goal- and achievement-oriented; task-focused; productivity important; propensity for action as a way of solving problems **Being** ❑ Stress personal relations in the process of accomplishing tasks; a more reflective and theoretical orientation to tasks
Communication	**High-context** ❑ Rules for speaking and behaving are implicit in the context; shared experience makes things understood without the need to state them explicity. **Low-context** ❑ Stress exchange of information and facts; meaning expressed explicitly, usually in words. **Direct** ❑ Prefer explicit one- and two-way conversation; deal with conflict **Indirect** ❑ Prefer implicit communication and avoid conflict **Expressive** ❑ Personal and emotional style; subjectivity inherent; relationships stressed **Instrumental** ❑ Unemotional and impersonal; high degree of objectivity; task achievement stressed **Formal** ❑ Important to follow protocol and social customs **Informal** ❑ Casual; lacking in ceremony; do not follow protocol
Space	**Private** ❑ Use of space individually oriented; prefer distance between individuals **Public** ❑ Use of space group-oriented; prefer close proximity

Exhibit 43.2. Checklist for Cultural Analysis, cont'd.

Cultural Variable	Value Orientation
Power	**Hierarchy** ❑ Formal, vertical perception of authority between individuals and groups **Equality** ❑ Horizontal or informal perception of authority; minimization of levels of power
Individualism	**Individualistic** ❑ The self or "I" more important than the group; value independence **Collectivist** ❑ Group interests take precedence over individual interests; identity based on social network; loyalty highly valued **Universalistic** ❑ Abstract rules more important than relationships; societal obligations emphasized **Particularistic** ❑ Relationships more important than abstract rules; changing circumstances and personal obligations given more weight
Competitiveness	**Competitive** ❑ Stress on achievement, assertiveness, material success **Cooperative** ❑ Quality of life, interdependence, relationships stressed
Structure	**Order** ❑ High need for predictability and rules. Conflict is threatening. **Flexibility** ❑ Tolerance of unpredictable situations and ambiguity. Dissent is accepted.
Thinking	**Inductive** ❑ Reasoning based on experience and experimentation **Deductive** ❑ Reasoning based on theory and logic **Linear** ❑ Preference for analytical thinking that breaks problems into chunks **Systematic** ❑ Preference for holistic thinking that focuses on the big picture and the interrelationships between components

Source: Brake, T., Walker, D. M., and Walker, T. (1994). *Doing business internationally: The guide to cross-cultural success.* New York: McGraw-Hill. Used with permission of The McGraw-Hill Companies.

2. If you do not have enough information on the cultures you are working with, use the many resources available at libraries, professional associations, and universities, or check the World Wide Web for resources. Learn from other people who have lived with or worked with the cultural groups involved in your project.

3. After completing your cultural analysis, apply what you have learned to your project. Be sure that you have considered all the cultural variables and value orientations pertaining to your project.

CONCLUSION

Whether you are an independent contractor working from your home, a manager at a large transnational corporation, or an employee at a small business anywhere in the world, you will be influenced by global issues. The world economy is changing so dramatically that you do not even have to travel to another country to deal with a diversity of people and organizations.

According to Hofstede (1997), *culture* is the way in which each person thinks, feels, and acts. As we have shown, there are many factors to consider when categorizing cultural differences. The literature and our own professional experience indicate that culture affects the way people negotiate, manage, educate, and train diverse labor forces; design and implement marketing campaigns; compete at national and international levels; implement various types of human resources practices; communicate; and make decisions.

The literature on working in a global business environment offers extensive and rich examples of cultural differences. Because there are no clear-cut rules about how to act in each cross-cultural situation you will encounter in your work, you can seek guidelines for appropriate conduct from published models, cultural information, and varied published cases and examples.

You will need to be culturally prepared and to accept diversity of thinking, acting, and feeling. It does not matter where you work; in your country or abroad, you will be part of a diverse working team. You will need to learn the complexities of communicating with diverse cultures and with both genders. You will have to be aware of the complexities of your own culture, and if you have an assignment abroad you will also need to recognize the complexities of the culture you are visiting.

You will need to act in a professional manner, remembering that your own entire culture is being judged according to your behavior and attitudes. You will need to accept the challenges of intercultural experiences, too, because they will help you grow, both personally and professionally.

You will need to assume personal responsibility for learning about intercultural differences, and you will have to be open to finding them in people and situations, whether these differences appear in terms of cultural practices, values, or beliefs.

Most of all, you will need to apply HPT principles, concepts, models, and techniques, taking into account the different forces that influence them in our global environment. The world is changing rapidly. As an HP technologist, your place is in the forefront—you must think globally and act locally.

References

Brake, T., Walker, D. M., and Walker, T. (1995). *Doing business internationally: The guide to cross-cultural success.* Burr Ridge, IL: Irwin.

Brislin, R. (1993). *Understanding culture's influence on behavior.* Orlando, FL: Harcourt Brace.

Carey, C. E. (1998). GlobaLinks revisited: Cross-cultural conditions affecting HPT. *Performance Improvement* 37:2, 8–13.

Deresky, H. (1994). *International management.* New York: HarperCollins.

Elashmawi, F., and Harris, P. R. (1993). *Multicultural management: New skills for global success.* Houston: Gulf.

Hall, E. T. (1990). *The silent language.* New York: Doubleday.

Harris, P. R., and Moran, R. T. (1996). *Managing cultural differences* (4th ed.). Houston: Gulf.

Hofstede, G. (1997). *Cultures and organizations: Software of the mind.* New York: McGraw-Hill.

Iyer, P. (1993, Fall). The global village finally arrives. *Time,* pp. 86–87.

Kanter, R. M. (1989). *When giants learn to dance.* New York: Simon & Schuster.

Marquardt, M., and Engle, D. W. (1993). *Global human resource development.* Englewood Cliffs, NJ: Prentice Hall.

O'Hara, M., and Johansen, R. (1994). *Globalwork: Bridging distance, culture, and time.* San Francisco: Jossey-Bass.

Rhinesmith, S. H. (1993). *A manager's guide to globalization: Six keys to success in a changing world.* Alexandria, VA, and Burr Ridge, IL: ASTD/Irwin.

Trompenaars, A., and Hampden-Turner, C. (1998). *Riding the waves of culture: Understanding diversity in global business* (2nd ed.). New York: McGraw-Hill.

CHAPTER FORTY-FOUR

Frontiers for Human Performance Technology in Contemporary Organizations

Diane M. Gayeski

The seed that grew into the set of ideas and practices now known as Human Performance Technology (HPT) was planted and nurtured in the era and location that perhaps best exemplify the American dream. The rich medium of HPT's development was a mixture of scientific research, enthusiasm for economic prosperity, and marketing for new ideas and products, a mixture that was an outgrowth of World War II. HPT has gone through various stages of evolution—as "programmed instruction," "instructional systems design," and, finally, what is sometimes called "performance consulting" (Robinson and Robinson, 1995).

These stages of evolution may appear to represent separate theoretical bases and professional practices, but I see the field as a more integrated, evolving whole. One way to visualize HPT is to see it as a tree (see Figure 44.1), one with roots and a trunk whose concentric rings show its development, a tree with branches that evoke how these ideas have reached up and out to make useful contributions while gaining sustenance in the real world. The tree's roots are in applied psychology, communications, and systems theory. As the tree grew, its core ring of programmed instruction was in turn surrounded by ever more expanding methods, which include instructional systems design and educational technology, workplace information systems, organizational systems design, and the more encompassing umbrella of integrated performance solutions. Finally, the work that is done to provide useful contributions to society is represented by specialties and sometimes by organizational departments called "training/learning systems" or "work design" or "performance support" or "feedback and incentive systems" or "organizational communication" or "organizational design and development."

Over the past six decades, the concept of HPT has been extended to the global level and has been modified to fit with professional practice in a variety of organizational settings. Researchers and practitioners have developed and validated models, theories, and practices that enable professionals to engineer excellent performance and accomplishment in the workplace. Literally thousands of magazine and journal articles and conference presentations have shown how better individual and group performance can follow from thorough needs analysis, from the identification of performance gaps, from the application of integrated instructional, environmental, and motivational interventions, and from rigorous evaluation.

Figure 44.1. HPT as a Tree.

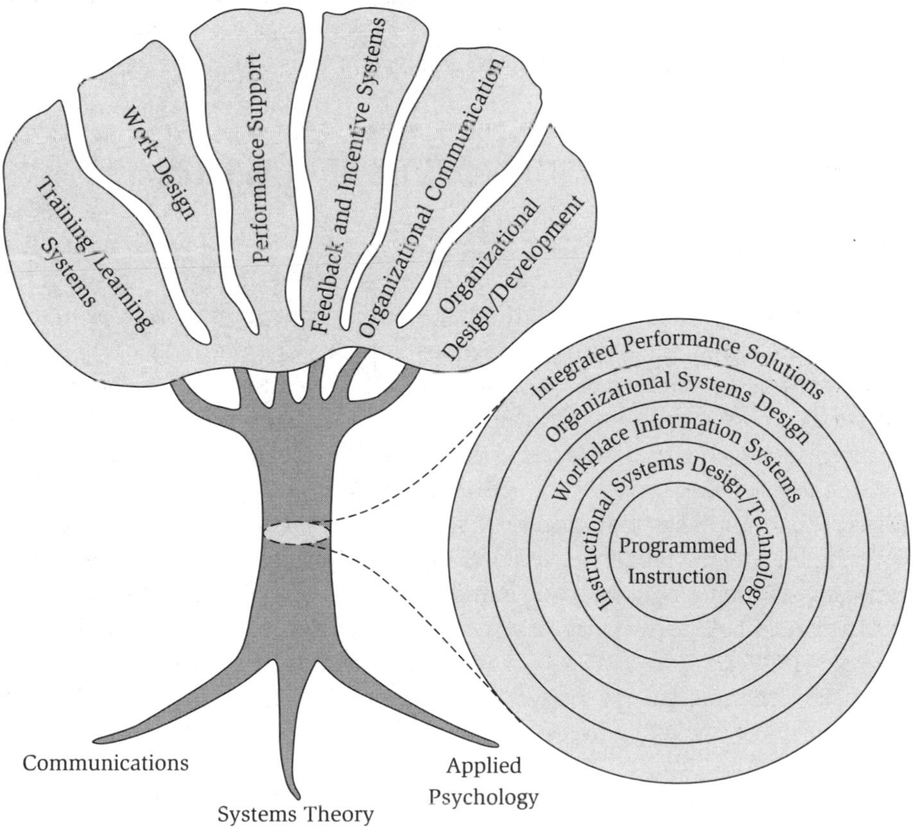

More than ten thousand individuals around the world are now members of the International Society for Performance Improvement, a professional organization that has as its mission the development of the theory and practice of HPT. Moreover, related professional societies, such as the American Society for Training and Development and the Society for Applied Learning Technologies, have also embraced missions that are broader than these societies' traditional orientations toward training and technology. They, too, are moving closer to an emphasis on organizational performance.

Nevertheless, despite this dedication of resources, and despite the apparent proof of the validity of HPT models, the term *Human Performance Technology* is virtually unknown outside HPT's professional circles. Why have these ideas and terms not become as widely accepted as other business initiatives such as total quality management and business process reengineering? (If we're so smart, why aren't we rich?) What is the future for HPT, and how can the profession create the research, practice, models, and publicity necessary to make a larger impact on the way that organizations function? What should be the agenda for research and development in HPT over the next ten years, and how may HPT practitioners be required to refocus our strategies and tactics?

THE CHANGING NATURE OF THE HPT ENVIRONMENT

Over the past decades, there have been major changes in the organizations that drive economies, as well as in the management theories and practices that influence how organizations are led. Most nations have moved from primarily agricultural and manufacturing economies, which were internally oriented, to economies that are international and primarily driven by service- and knowledge-based corporations. Leadership has moved from a command-and-control focus to approaches that emphasize employees' involvement and motivation.

For the most part, workers are no longer considered "hands" who contribute physical labor to tasks that have been specified for them. Today, most workers contribute primarily problem-solving skills and behaviors and are required to invent new solutions. It is interesting to reflect on the historical assumptions of HPT and to ponder how new models of organization may challenge those assumptions. Nickols (1990, pp. 190–191, 196) claims that the body of knowledge known as HPT is directly traceable to the work of Frederick Taylor, and he argues that the techniques that worked in bygone eras are inappropriate today:

> Taylor believed that studying work and improving on it entailed a science that far transcends the individual worker's knowledge of skill, task, or job and that the work of studying the work of others requires special skills and knowledge. . . .

For almost 100 years, from the time Taylor began his studies at Midvale in 1876 until Drucker's *Age of Discontinuity* (1969), the focus of most managers and industrial engineers was understandably the overt, physical behavior of the worker. . . . But in 1969, Drucker pointed out a profound shift in the nature of work itself. It had been shifting from a materials base to an information or knowledge base. . . .

So in 1974 I left the Navy, became a consultant, and set out to solve the problem of making knowledge work productive. I do not, now, think it can be done—not in the conventional sense, anyway. I certainly do not think that human performance technology is the answer. In fact, I think it has reached the end of the road. The more than 100 years of relying on external agents to improve the performance and productivity of other people is over. The target has changed. To make knowledge work productive requires nothing less than the complete reengineering of the configurations of social, technical, financial, and political factors we call organizations, specifically, those portions of organizations to which I refer as *work* and *work control systems.*

If some researchers and practitioners, like Nickols, feel that HPT has reached the end of its usefulness because of the dramatic changes in the nature of work, others argue that the same changes in today's economies and organizations make the future of HPT very bright. Along with the shift from manual to mental work and the changes in management styles, the last decade has also seen the weakening of many large corporations.

Worldwide, the rise of small, entrepreneurial, and "virtual" organizations is occurring, as is much more self-employment. Technologies now allow small enterprises and individuals to work from remote locations and homes with customers and partners around the world. Regions and cities in different parts of the world are promoting economic prosperity by providing state-of-the-art communications infrastructures and government policies that support telecommuting and small, home-based workplaces with highly automated facilities. In Ireland, for example, several communities are vying to attract highly skilled independent workers by underwriting the installation of high-speed telephone and data wiring. Northern Italy has experienced tremendous economic growth through small, high-tech factories that can supply customized clothing and leather goods to major markets on every continent.

These changes in the scale of production and distribution worldwide mean greater competition for organizations. Now, companies compete at the global level rather than just at the local or even the national level. Many enterprises are lean, flexible groups of dozens of partners, not thousands of employees. The pressure for greater efficiency and enhanced performance may mean that there will be renewed interest in the contributions of HPT (Brethower, 1997, p. 8): "The future of human performance technology (HPT), and those who practice it effectively, is bright because of changes occurring in the marketplace. . . . Its emphasis on performance improvement works very well in relatively small, well-focused organizations. For more than 25 years, HPT has focused on providing the knowledge and performance support necessary for value-adding human performance. The future for HPT will be very bright if we can take advantage of the opportunities before us."

It is clear that new forms of organization provide both challenges and opportunities for the practice of HPT. There is still a good deal of work that is done in a preconfigured and standardized manner by large groups of employees. In these situations, classic models of finding exemplary performers, identifying performance gaps among the majority of performers, and then closing those gaps through major interventions such as training or incentive systems will continue to be useful. But it is also clear that these situations are diminishing in number. Many HPT practitioners find that the most significant performance gaps exist only at the level of an individual performer, or that these gaps change almost on a daily basis as the content and methods of work change. Many training developers have observed that by the time a course or even an electronic performance support tool has been developed, it is obsolete.

Another challenge that HPT practitioners face is the nature of their own work situations. Many training and human resources departments have been downsized or eliminated. Much of the work in HPT is now being done by outside contractors. Thus HPT practitioners' ability to get to know an organization's goals and culture is often limited, as is their long-term influence and ability to initiate systemic changes. It is often unclear who the major client or sponsor is and who has the authority to make the sometimes sweeping changes in the learning, incentive, selection, and work environment that HPT models lead us to prescribe.

The character and expectations of the workforce are changing. No longer is there a relatively homogeneous and stable base of employees in most organizations. Rather, these organizations now have a diverse and constantly migrating collection of performers who influence most of their products and processes. These people may not be together in a physical sense, and they may report to different managers. Many of them may be external contractors who work for a vendor or for themselves. Although journalistic articles and studies observe that training and incentive systems are very important considerations to the new "knowledge worker," it is also true that more of these individuals come to the workplace with extensive education and with a much more independent attitude. Organizations are faced with the dilemma of wondering how much training to provide to employees who are likely to take their valuable, expensive new knowledge to the competition. Now that so much work is performed by "temps" and outside contractors, there is also often the question of how much support and learning opportunity should be provided to them.

HPT must also evolve to incorporate globalization and accommodation of diverse national, regional, and even corporate cultures. As Carey (1998, p. 9) points out, "the disciplines covered within HPT are based on Western values and American culture." Not all individuals or cultures have the same standards for "high performance," and so different sets of behaviors and drivers need to be considered. Intercultural competence means more than being able to carry out routine social and business interactions smoothly. Not every culture values individual achievement over group cohesion, nor does every culture value punctuality, conformity, or profit over stability. Many of the assumptions and interventions developed within the framework of HPT must be challenged if practitioners are to work effectively in an increasingly diverse economy.

All the factors discussed here pose important challenges to HPT practitioners. Many of the assumptions of HPT models of practice no longer hold. Our professional relationships with project sponsors, the intended recipients of interventions, and the organizational homes for HPT are clearly changing, and HPT professionals must adapt their practices and expectations to these new realities.

WHERE HPT IS (AND SHOULD BE) PRACTICED

HPT, although it embraces many types of theories and tools, has grown from a base of practice in human resources and training (Dean, 1995). Most HPT practitioners work in corporate departments or in consulting companies that are or at least were identified with training. Many professionals have been able to successfully expand their roles beyond training and thus have increased their influence and business:

> When Tom LaBonte came to PNC Bank Corp. in Pittsburgh back in February 1994, he found a training and development department that designed and delivered courses in a traditional, if decentralized and unfocused, fashion. Today, senior vice president LaBonte presides over 165 people, most of whom are performance consultants charged with improving the $71 billion bank's business results [Henricks, 1997, p. 32].

Despite numerous success stories like this one, many training and human resources professionals have found it very difficult to make the transition from their traditional roles to the more comprehensive HPT roles. This does not seem to be a "training" problem. Many practitioners know about HPT principles and want to put HPT theories and models into practice, but they cannot. In an article reviewing the preparation and subsequent professional practice of Human Performance (HP) technologists, Rossett and Czech (1995, p. 128) report that most well-educated and confident graduates of master's degree programs in this area were basically unable to use the full range of skills and interventions that they had learned: "While respondents were generally confident of their skills regarding PT [performance technology], particularly their ability to make a case for needs assessment, they recognize limits to their influence." Similarly, Dean (1995, p. 68) reports that "the conditions that must exist for organizations to benefit from all HPT can offer them are lacking. First, few individuals have the knowledge and skill necessary to implement the methods, measures, and models of HPT, and second, those who do seldom have the opportunity and authority to apply HPT where it will most benefit the organization."

These authors and others argue that traditional notions of training and human resources limit the effectiveness of HPT practitioners. Often they are pigeonholed into employment situations where managers and clients expect traditional "courses on demand." Moreover, practitioners typically do not have the kind of influence necessary for questioning and changing the behavior and systems of higher-level managers. It is much more politically sensitive and time-consuming to raise questions about management practices, incentive systems, and job descriptions than it is to develop a video or put on a course. Many HPT professionals simply do not have the organizational clout to survive the process and outcomes of a genuinely candid and comprehensive performance intervention. Most research in this area shows that it is necessary to obtain personal authority or an organizational champion for HPT efforts.

These situations and perspectives lead us to question where HPT's most appropriate organizational homes may be. Some HPT professionals and departments have moved out of human resources staff functions and have become attached to various line organizations. There are HPT consulting companies that now mainly work for clients who are line managers (such as plant managers or vice presidents of operations) rather than being contracted by training departments. Overall, this development points to the necessity for questioning where an HPT professional can really make a significant contribution to an organization. It appears that the HPT practitioner's role needs to be one with power, authority, and status. This description, unfortunately, does not characterize the current job situations of most professionals who aspire to apply HPT.

ROLES, SKILLS, AND ATTITUDES OF HPT PROFESSIONALS

What are the various performance factors that affect the ability of HPT practitioners to achieve excellent performance themselves? What knowledge, skills, attitudes, and working conditions can help us close the gap between the potential of HPT and the current state of anticipation that characterizes the field?

Stolovitch, Keeps, and Rodrigue (1995, p. 44) have identified a comprehensive list of skill sets for the HP technologists, which they categorize as "technical skills" (analysis, observation, and design skills) or "people skills" (management and communication skills). On the basis of a synthesis of numerous studies and their own experiences, these authors state that the following skills and behaviors are the most important:

- A steady focus on the client's need
- Analytical skills and a focus on the causes of gaps rather than a focus on the solution
- A holistic view of performance problems
- The ability to work effectively with others
- Rigorous application of established methods
- The ability to question and rethink one's own interpretations and assumptions
- The ability to sort out priorities
- An orientation toward sound design rather than technological fads

These observations are echoed by many individual case studies. Tom LaBonte, the senior vice president at PNC Bank who successfully made the transition from traditional training to performance consulting, states that a performance consultant should understand senior management's goals and makes them his own: "He sits in their meetings, he has a very good understanding of where they are going and their requirements, and focuses our resources on improving those results" (Henricks, 1997, p. 33).

The attention to results is imperative in the contemporary business climate. No longer is training considered a frill. There are no dollars or hours to be wasted. Mass-oriented interventions, such as courses, work designs, and job aids designed for large numbers of users, are largely being replaced by shorter, faster, more customized solutions. Even those who are pessimistic about the relevance of HPT's traditional orientations do see a significant role for experienced professionals in this area (Nickols, 1990, p. 196): "There are few, if any, prefigured work routines facing the knowledge worker. Most work for knowledge workers requires them to configure their response to or action in a given situation. . . . Consequently, the emphasis of power and authority in our organizations must shift from ensuring compliance to seeking contribution. . . . The one remaining trick in the performance technologist's bag is helping knowledge workers create better methods and better tools. In the information age, this means better hardware and better software."

How can one develop more appropriate skills, attitudes, and job descriptions? The response to closing skill gaps is education and practice. Although there are some workshops and institutes on HPT, there are still relatively few college curricula in this area. Moreover, there are few documented models to follow, nor are there many role models in organizations for novices to emulate. One way of moving the typical attitudes and orientations of traditional training and human resources professionals away from a service-oriented, reactive stance and toward a more consultative, proactive stance involves incentives. HPT professionals should be compensated for solutions and return on investment rather than for the volume of their training materials, the number of bodies in classroom seats, or the speed and consistency of their responses. Professional organizations in HPT should continue to reinforce and reward documented and innovative solutions that are effective and efficient rather than rewarding technical achievement or the spending of large amounts of money and time.

Perhaps the consideration should be whether HPT is a job or a profession rather than a set of skills. The profession currently operates under the assumption that HPT represents a full-time job filled by a specialist, but perhaps these skills should be infused into the workplace, to become an element of every manager's professional toolkit. Instead of teaching HPT in colleges of education, perhaps it would be better to teach it in business schools along with financial analysis and marketing. After all, is it not the job of managers to improve their units' performance?

Another concern is that the broad range of knowledge encompassed by HPT appears to be almost unattainable by any one individual. Hutchison and Stein (1997) present a long list of specialties that, they argue, belong to HPT. They recommend (p. 28) that an individual HP technologist be an "expert in 15 to 25 or more tactics across 10 or more . . . strategy areas" and "have working knowledge of 45 to 75 or more tactics across 15 or more strategies." They acknowledge that after publishing an initial article along these lines they received several phone calls from people who challenged their numbers as being too high to achieve. They stand by these numbers, however, claiming that they and many of their colleagues have significantly exceeded this level of expertise. In any case, the long list of interventions and organizational roles belonging to HPT can seem overwhelming and overstated. This kind of concern was raised by the assistant training manager in an aircraft facility who posted the following message to an on-line discussion group called TRDEV-L *(http://train.ed.psu.edu/TRDEV-L):*

> OK, so how do you differentiate a HPT person from a general business consultant? Or is it the point that trainers want to become MBA's or whatever and conduct the larger intervention? Why is it not enough for trainers to identify that this is not a training problem and leave it up to the suits to define and fix it. It is after all what they are there to do. . . . I'm not quite sold on HPT. It seems to be a larger domain than any one person can handle (even with much smaller exam-

ples). Cross-functional teams made up of trainers, OD people, and management/ engineers would seem to be more useful. Anyway you cut it, it still comes up with individuals specializing in training, OD etc. Perhaps it WOULD help to be able to understand how the different roles interact. That I can buy into.

HOW CAN HPT BE TRULY "VALUE-ADDED"?

HPT's success hinges on HP technologists' ability to learn and address what is important to organizations today and what will matter in the future. From the preceding discussion, it is clear that what is valued has already changed. Developing solutions that generate homogeneous, reproducible performance and output is becoming less important than the ability to quickly synthesize rapid and individual solutions to ephemeral and unique performance gaps. In many situations, the function of the HPT practitioner will be more to consult with managers than to be a staff producer of programs and other types of interventions. Henricks (1997, p. 33) quotes a successful performance consultant who describes an unusual method of measuring her success in building strategic relationships: "It's measured in how many meetings did I conduct with line managers to help them decide on ways to approach their performance problems."

It would seem difficult to question the significance of an HPT professional's ability to synthesize many theories and tactics and be effective in helping managers achieve peak performance. However, another barrier faces HPT practitioners: they are not the only ones who have recognized the limitations of conventional methods of performance improvement. Other professions and departments are moving beyond their traditional roles. Some claim to have the same set of skills and solutions as HPT. The HPT practitioner's educational preparation and initial practical experience were typically in training, but HPT has now expanded to encompass other interventions, such as incentive systems, ergonomics, and even high-tech information systems. It should come as no surprise, then, that specialists in human resources, engineering, communications, and information systems are also broadening their horizons and skills and are also interested in becoming more strategically involved in creating comprehensive business solutions.

Therefore, one challenge that HPT faces is to define its turf. Not everyone will become the chief adviser to management, the most sought-after consultant, the "chief learning officer," or the leader of the largest and most powerful department. Clearly, HPT must define its boundaries, distinguish itself from other specialties, and not overpromise what individuals or interventions can actually deliver. As individual practitioners and the field grow, it is important for HP technologists to broaden their horizons and yet respect the complexity and depth of other practitioners and fields. HPT professionals must embrace team-work and be flexible and collaborative as they participate in achieving the goal of excellent performance.

CONSIDERATIONS IN BUILDING OUR FUTURE TOGETHER

The frontiers of HPT are open, there to be explored and enjoyed, but one must strike a balance between relying on demonstrated methods and recognizing when old assumptions no longer hold. Two activities are necessary to the suc-cessful implementation of HPT:

1. Being effective in explaining what HPT is to those decision makers who are receptive to hearing about—and able to sponsor—methods, even long and costly ones, that are likely to have major payoffs in sustained performance improvement.

2. Overcoming the political obstacle of people (whether they are clients and sponsors or professionals in departments of training and human resources) who want to maintain the status quo or who are looking for a quick fix rather than for the possibility of uncovering the more deeply rooted problems that are im-peding performance.

There are two major barriers to the adoption of HPT:

1. HPT practitioners' typical roles in organizations make it more likely for them to be engaged by middle-level managers, who generally do not have the incentives or the authority to engage in long-term, multidisciplinary interven-tions. These clients and sponsors often view human resources professionals and HP technologists as "producers" who provide short-term, well-defined services (such as "delivering" courses) rather than as advisers or analysts. Often such clients, when they engage HPT practitioners, are primarily interested in docu-menting that they have somehow addressed a problem; sponsoring a course or commissioning a CD-ROM is a nonthreatening, possibly interesting way to show management that one has completed this kind of objective. If the intervention does not improve performance, then the human resources and training staffs can always be blamed.

2. Human resources professionals and HPT practitioners are generally not trained in techniques of negotiation or consultation. They also tend to be people who are service-oriented and nurturing rather than competitive and challeng-ing. These factors lead HPT practitioners to be more interested in completing the tasks given them than in charting new territory with clients or sponsors who have not, after all, come to their doors asking for help. It is also possible that

people who choose these professions tend to be more risk-averse. In today's competitive environment, many people are worried about compromising their careers by going outside the traditional boundaries of their roles.

Given the environmental challenges and opportunities identified here, it is clear that practitioners must jump from trying to plan the future to engaging in actively designing it. Incremental approaches and short-term objectives are more relevant when the territory is already known and defined. HPT is not a well-defined territory, either in terms of its practice or in terms of the larger picture of the organizations, communities, and economies in which it is practiced. Rather, HPT practitioners are charting new frontiers and designing innovative approaches—they are inventing the future of this field.

If HPT professionals do have (or wish to create) a field, they must consider two areas: (1) professional identity, and (2) a common language and set of practices based on identified theory. Many would argue that these already exist. However, analysis of numerous articles and presentations yields as many definitions and responses as there are individual researchers and practitioners.

First, what do HPT practitioners call themselves, and is this important? It is not important to have a name for the field or to have job titles if one takes the position that HPT is a set of skills that can (and should be) practiced by any competent managers. It is important if HPT wishes to carve out an identity that is different from "management" or "human resources" or "organizational development." To quote again from an electronic posting to TRDEV-L, here is a discussion group member recounting the challenges of his own effort to find a name for his department:

> Several weeks ago, I asked the list members to share names of their departments, especially those involved in moving from training to performance improvement [PI]. We are in the process of moving to PI and wanted to change the name of our office to reflect the new focus.
>
> I did receive several comments wanting to know why it was necessary to change the name of the "Training Office" to something new. I guess my answer is that you consider a change when you find that you are doing more than just training. We train trainers and medical professionals in developing countries. In the past we have focused almost entirely on training. As we move into PI, we find ourselves considering many other factors (other than training) which impact job performance. To help communicate this broader perspective to our internal staff and trainers around the world, we felt it was important that we change the name of our office.
>
> To the question of changing our job titles, that is still up for discussion. As none of our staff has the name "trainer" in her/his title, we didn't feel it was essential to change these at this time. Our trainers in the field, however, will continue to be referred to as trainers. Over time we may consider a change, but not at this time.

The member goes on to thank everyone who sent him suggestions, appends a "brief summary" of what was offered (no fewer than eleven departmental names and an even dozen job titles), and adds:

> Several folks asked why training is becoming a four letter word. I am not sure that is the case. I also don't think we need to change just to keep up with buzz words. However, when what we do expands beyond training, then we need to consider how those with the organization perceive our role and function when we still say we are the training office.
>
> So what did we name our office? After considering the nature of what we do and our target audience (and your suggestions) we are leaning toward the "Learning and Performance Support" Office. We feel our primary focus is still on learning interventions but that we are expanding to support other performance improvement interventions.

Along with considering at least some standardization in titles for the HPT field, the profession needs to consider some further standardization of its language. Most professionals and academic fields are characterized by sets of terms that have consistent meanings. This is not, unfortunately, the case with HPT, as Brethower (1997, p. 9) points out: "Performance technologists have many common words, but few common meanings. For example, front-end analysis means different things to different people, as do, I'm [loath] to admit, performance and improvement. . . . Consequently, we can't even talk about work in meaningful ways. . . . It would also help if human performance technologists were to get better at converting the language of fads into HPT language and showing how HPT does, in systematic and reproducible ways, what the fads only promise."

As HPT practitioners collaboratively design their futures, they need to be adept at applying their own models and tactics to themselves. What are the major performance gaps in HPT professionals' ability to perform up to the level of their abilities and aspirations? Why is it that the term *Human Performance Technology* is not well recognized among executives? One answer is that articles about HPT are not appearing in newspapers and business journals. HPT advocates should read (and publish in) mainstream publications that can influence their most appropriate advocates.

Where can one scan the trends? The futurists of HPT should make it a practice to talk to college students and members of "Generation X." They should be just as aware of what is keeping the CEO up at night as they are of the issues in their own specialties. HPT practitioners should spend time learning new languages, studying finance, and contributing to the betterment of their communities, not just learning the latest computer platform or application.

The frontiers of HPT—the greatest areas of opportunity—may be in the cottage industries of rural North America and Europe, or in the new independent industries in Poland and China. For example, one of my own colleagues has left his role as a researcher and speaker in multimedia to become the personal adviser to the king of a small African country. Perhaps HPT practitioners should pay less attention to turf than to performance. It may not matter what one is called, to whom one reports, or what department is listed today on one's business cards. HPT practitioners need to become "integrating generalists" (Hutchison and Stein, 1997) or "Renaissance Communicators" (Gayeski, 1993) who are dedicated to improving the conditions of individual work, organizations, and societies at large.

References

Brethower, D. M. (1997). The future is bright for Human Performance Technology. *Performance Improvement* 36:9, 8–11.

Carey, C. E. (1998). GlobaLinks revisited: Cross-cultural conditions affecting HPT. *Performance Improvement* 37:2, 8–13.

Dean, P. (1995). Examining the practice of Human Performance Technology. *Performance Improvement Quarterly* 8:2, 68–94.

Gayeski, D. (1993). *Corporate communications management: The Renaissance Communicator in information-age organizations.* Woburn, MA: Focal Press.

Henricks, M. (1997, Oct.). From trainer to consultant. *Inside Technology Training,* pp. 32–34.

Hutchison, C. S., and Stein, F. S. (1997). A whole new world of interventions: The performance technologist as integrating generalist. *Performance Improvement* 36:10, 28–35.

Nickols, F. W. (1990). Human Performance Technology: The end of an era. *Human Resources Development Quarterly* 1:2, 187–197.

Robinson, D. G., and Robinson, J. (1995). *Performance consulting: Moving beyond training.* San Francisco: Berrett-Koehler.

Rossett, A., and Czech, C. (1995). They really wanna, but . . . : The aftermath of professional preparation in performance technology. *Performance Improvement Quarterly* 8:4, 115–132.

Stolovitch, H., Keeps, E., and Rodrigue, D. (1995). Skill sets for the human performance technologist. *Performance Improvement Quarterly* 8:2, 40–67.

Afterword to
the Second Edition

Roger Kaufman

The forty-four chapters of the second edition of the *Handbook of Performance Technology* document a number of relentless shifts in our field. These include the shift from training to performance improvement; from the focus on means to a primary concern with ends and consequences; from the preoccupation with individual performance to an integrated concern with individual, organizational, and societal consequences; from the notion of time spent to the idea of value added; and from the focus on improvement in the United States to a focus on worldwide improvement. Collected in one volume, these writings by notable practitioners and theoreticians have shown the concepts and tools that we will need in widening our horizons and moving away from a narrow focus on individual performers and toward a focus on literally adding value to the entire world. Our field has also moved from a singular focus on questions of how to improve performance to questions of what will improve performance, as well as to a concern for why performance should be improved at all.

These shifts have not been casual, nor do they represent a passing fad. "Quick fixes" have repeatedly appealed to our organizational instincts, and one great solution after another has first captured our hearts and then, after disappointing us, swiftly receded into the dark recesses of our libraries and office shelves. One panacea after another has had its run, only to be put aside for something newer and more attractive. It is not through this endless array of fleeting enthusiasms that we will build genuine and enduring performance improvement.

There are scientific as well as pragmatic underpinnings for the ethical and responsible transformation of our field from questions of "how" to questions of "what" and "why." We must be professionally responsible in what we use, do, produce, and deliver, and we must prudently monitor the external consequences of our actions. The future of human performance technology (HPT) will not be about instantaneous solutions that please our clients at the expense of usefulness, impact, and valued societal payoffs. The future of HPT will be about integrating "how, "what," and "why" into a seamlessly coherent unity—an elegant construct of science, technology, and ethical practice.

LEARNING FROM YESTERDAY

Our field was originally focused on the design and delivery of learning (and occasionally of improved performance). Our delivery methods and means, with their ties to human testing and assessment, media, programmed instruction, and, over the last twenty years, computer technology, were tangible, acceptable, and conventional (or became so relatively quickly). They represented a fixation on quick results and a concern with how would-be performance improvement specialists could deliver something concrete—immediately.

Our "how to do its" provided us with a sense of confidence. We were able to deliver interventions to an audience of clients who grew up believing that the solution to almost every performance problem was a combination of training and direct contact with workers, aimed at getting them to perform. The emphasis was on individual performance improvement. The processes and tools were logical and ostensibly credible—they had face validity.

These enterprises and tools attracted a lot of attention. Important professional organizations—for example, the National Society for Programmed Instruction, as it was called, and the American Society for Training and Development—became U.S. forums for the newest in training and individual performance improvement methods and techniques. Nevertheless, apart from our delivering activities and programs that seemed useful to clients, improved organizational performance never seemed to be a result of our efforts.

ADDING "WHAT" TO THE
PERFORMANCE IMPROVEMENT AGENDA

Overall, our "how to do its" lacked focus and a coherent purpose. It was interesting and usually exciting to present a popular training program, but what did it accomplish? Assessment of value added was not part of the conventional agenda.

When Robert P. Mager's work on preparing performance objectives began to gain deserved attention, an argument began to gain credence: if we are going to improve performance, we should define what improved performance will look like, and it should be measured. So-called behavioral objectives were commonly adopted and used (even though many people wanted to write objectives that were not quite measurable and that stated desired directions for change but not firm criteria for measuring results). Many talked about measurable objectives, but relatively few really took them seriously enough to prepare verifiable standards of performance. Few argued against the usefulness and wisdom of clearly stating where we were headed and how we would know we had arrived, but verbal acceptance of this idea was not accompanied by its widespread application.

At approximately the same time that measurable objectives were attracting serious attention, Thomas F. Gilbert was telling people in our field that there was a very important difference between behavior and accomplishment, although the two were strongly tied. The difference appeared at first to be subtle, but the implications were profound. It is one thing to behave; it is another to have behavior actually accomplish required results.

Intertwined in the discourse on performance and accountability for results was yet another, related concept: needs assessment. Intrigued by the vital difference between ends and means (although they, too, were related), I began work on defining *need* as the gap between current and required results. In 1969, when I coauthored a first article on the topic, there were many who perceived the distinction between needs and wants as trivial. Later, often with my colleagues and students, I developed approaches to needs assessment that allowed us to identify gaps in results and set priorities on the basis of what it would cost to meet needs by comparison with what it would cost to ignore them. Our definitions of *need* and *needs assessment* depended on the understanding that results and performance, as defined by both Mager and Gilbert, had to be clearly respected.

These basic approaches and tools defined a new and additional area of concern for performance technologists: the linking of "how to's" with pragmatic and justifiable purposes. This was an additional stepping-stone for the field's migration from questions of how to questions of what, although the element of "why" was still lacking. The justification for our desire to initiate any intervention, for training or anything else, was not fully articulated—perhaps because justifying this desire was not an element of either the conventional wisdom or the traditional tools of our discipline. Most of the standard approaches, as Harless (1975) so clearly defined them in connection with the four elements of performance engineering, were still stalled in the default mode of training and individual performance improvement. Adding the element of "what" to our field established a necessary link between the element of "how" and our purpose. Still missing from HPT as its evolution unfolded, however, were two questions that we were not asking: (1) If individual performance improvement is the solution, what is the problem? and (2) What is the problem if the organization is the solution?

ASKING "WHY": VALUE ADDED TO EXTERNAL CLIENTS AND SOCIETY

As the chapters in this handbook show, we are now either asking or beginning to ask the right questions. We have learned how to engineer human performance improvement. We understand the politics of the environment as well as group and cultural dynamics. We realize that we now have an international stage, and that we can manage change in a realistic and humane manner. We have the tools we require for delivering our services well into the future. But if we are to make a serious contribution to our clients and their organizations, both public and private, our accomplishments must also be concerned with external clients and with society. If the organization is the solution, what, indeed, is the problem? An organization is a means to societal ends. The learning organization, tools and processes like reengineering and quality management—these are only means of adding value to external clients and to society. Incorporating a concern for social responsibility into our professional activities is no longer merely an option; it has become a necessity.

One emerging construct for defining the focus of an organization is the construct of an ideal vision. An ideal vision formulates, in terms of performance, the kind of world we want to create for the future. It is focused on results and value added rather than on means, resources, activities, or solutions. Many view this kind of focus, and the very notion of an ideal vision, as impractical and irrelevant to the "real world." We must remember, however, that everything belonging to earlier phases of HPT (for example, programmed instruction, measurable objectives, and needs assessment) was at one time viewed in the same way.

An organization's definition of its ideal vision is an essential ingredient of its mission: what part of its ideal vision does the organization commit itself to delivering and moving ever closer toward? The ideal vision helps to establish the organization's strategic alignment as well. If an organization does not intend to add value to external clients and society, then what is its mission, and how long can the organization expect to last if it does not contribute to external clients and to society?

CREATING THE FUTURE

Our future clearly lies in the integration of "how" with "what" and "why." We will build on what we know and on what we can deliver. Our horizons will extend from the here and now to the creation of a useful future. We will see the concepts and tools of performance improvement expand from individual performance to include organizational contributions, and we will see both of these integrated with external and societal value added. Our basic tools will be expanded to integrate three levels of results—outcomes, outputs, and products—and our planning will focus on three levels: megaplanning, macroplanning, and microplanning, as shown in the following table, which depicts relationships among levels of planning, levels of results, and primary clients for each level of planning and each level of results:

The Relationships Among Levels of Planning, Levels of Results, and Primary Clients for Each.

Level of Planning	Level of Results	Primary Clients
Megaplanning	Outcomes	External clients and society
Macroplanning	Outputs	Internal clients and the organization
Microplanning	Products	Individuals or small groups

To guide strategic thinking in the integration of the "how," "what," and "why" elements, I suggest the use of six critical success factors:

1. Moving out of today's comfort zones to the largest frame of reference for thinking, planning, action, and delivery of continuous improvement

2. Focusing on ends rather than means

3. Aligning all three levels of planning and results

4. Starting all performance improvement with an ideal vision—a vision of the kind of world we want to create for the future—as the basis for the organization's planning, activity, and accomplishments

5. Preparing objectives, at all levels, that state both where we are headed and how we will know we have arrived

6. Defining the term *need* as the gap between current and desired or required results

As we advance in the direction of adding value to society, the contributions that we can and do make will become more and more clear, and our psychological and economic rewards will accurately reflect our contributions.

Reference

Harless, J. H. (1975). *An ounce of analysis is worth a pound of cure.* Newnan, GA: Harless Performance Guild.

Suggested Readings

Barker, J. A. (1992). *Future edge: Discovering the new paradigms of success.* New York: Morrow.

Block, P. (1993). *Stewardship.* San Francisco: Berrett-Koehler.

Conner, D. R. (1992). *Managing at the speed of change.* New York: Random House.

Conner, D. R. (1998). *Leading at the edge of chaos: How to create the nimble organization.* New York: Wiley.

Drucker, P. F. (1973). *Management: Tasks, responsibilities, practices.* New York: HarperCollins.

Drucker, P. F. (1993). *Post-capitalist society.* New York: HarperBusiness.

Drucker, P. F. (1994, Nov.). The age of social transformation. *Atlantic Monthly,* pp. 53–80.

Gilbert, T. F. (1978). *Human competence: Engineering worthy performance.* New York: McGraw-Hill.

Gilbert, T. F., and Gilbert, M. B. (1989, Jan.). Performance engineering: Making human productivity a science. *Performance & Instruction,* pp. 3–9.

Hammer, M., and Stanton, S. A. (1995). *The reengineering revolution: A handbook.* New York: HarperCollins.

Handy, C. (1995–1996). *Beyond certainty: The changing worlds of organisations.* London: Arrow.

Kaufman, R. (1992). *Strategic planning plus: An organizational guide* (rev. ed.). Thousand Oaks, CA: Sage.

Kaufman, R. (1997, Sept.). A new reality for organizational success: Two bottom lines. *Performance Improvement,* p. 3.

Kaufman, R. (1998). *Strategic thinking.* Washington, DC, and Arlington, VA: International Society for Performance Improvement and American Society for Training and Development.

Kaufman, R., and Keller, J. (1994, Winter). Levels of evaluation: Beyond Kirkpatrick. *Human Resources Quarterly,* pp. 371–380.

Kaufman, R., Rojas, A. M., and Mayer, H. (1993). *Needs assessment: A user's guide.* Englewood Cliffs, NJ: Educational Technology Publications.

Kaufman, R., and Swart, W. (1995, May–June). Beyond conventional benchmarking: Integrating ideal visions, strategic planning, reengineering, and quality management. *Educational Technology,* pp. 11–14.

Kaufman, R., Thiagarajan, S., and MacGillis, P. (eds.). (1997). *The guidebook for performance improvement: Working with individuals and organizations.* San Francisco: Jossey-Bass/Pfeiffer.

Kaufman, R., and Watkins, R. (1996, Spring). Costs-consequences analysis. *HRD Quarterly,* pp. 87–100.

Kaufman, R., Watkins, R., and Stith, M. (1998, Summer). The changing organizational mind. *Performance Improvement Quarterly,* pp. 32–44.

Kirkpatrick, D. L. (1994) *Evaluating training programs: The four levels.* San Francisco: Berrett-Koehler.

Mager, R. F. (1997). *Preparing instructional objectives* (3rd ed.). Atlanta: Center for Performance Improvement.

Marshall, R., and Tucker, M. (1992). *Thinking for a living: Education and the wealth of nations.* New York: Basic Books.

Martin, R. (1993, Nov.–Dec.). Changing the mind of the corporation. *Harvard Business Review,* pp. 81–94.

Naisbitt, J., and Aburdene, P. (1990). *Megatrends 2000: Ten new directions for the 1990s.* New York: Morrow.

Osborne, D., and Gaebler, T. (1992). *Reinventing government: How the entrepreneurial spirit is transforming the public sector.* Reading, MA: Addison-Wesley.

Popcorn, F. (1991). *The Popcorn report.* New York: Doubleday.

Rummler, G. A., and Brache, A. P. (1990). *Improving performance: How to manage the white space on the organization chart.* San Francisco: Jossey-Bass.

Senge, P. M. (1990). *The fifth discipline: The art and practice of the learning organization.* New York: Doubleday.

Toffler, A. (1990). *Powershift: Knowledge, wealth, and violence at the edge of the twenty-first century.* New York: Bantam.

Triner, D., Greenberry, A., and Watkins, R. (1996, Nov.–Dec.). Training needs assessment: A contradiction in terms? *Educational Technology* 36:6, 51–55.

Witkin, B. R., and Altschuld, J. W. (1995). *Planning and conducting needs assessments: A practical guide.* Thousand Oaks, CA: Sage.

Zemke, R., and Kramlinger, T. (1982). *Figuring things out: A trainer's guide to needs and task analysis.* Reading, MA: Addison-Wesley.

THE EDITORS

HAROLD D. STOLOVITCH is president of Harold D. Stolovitch & Associates (HSA) Ltd., specialists in the application of Instructional Technology and Human Performance Technology to business, industry, government, and the military. HSA, founded in 1981, has offices in Montreal, Vancouver, Los Angeles, and San Francisco. Its clients include more than one hundred leading companies and government organizations in North America, Europe, and Asia.

Stolovitch received his B.Ed. degree (1961) from McGill University, Montreal, and his M.S. (1975) and Ph.D. (1976) degrees in instructional systems technology from Indiana University, Bloomington. He has been a major contributor to the research and writing that have defined Human Performance Technology over the past forty years. He has authored more than one hundred books, papers, articles, and chapters on various aspects of instructional and performance technology. His books include *Audiovisual Training Modules* (1978), *Instructional Simulation-Gaming* (1978, coauthored with S. Thiagarajan), *Frame Games* (1980, coauthored with S. Thiagarajan), and *Introduction à la technologie de l'instruction* [Introduction to instructional technology] (1983, coauthored with G. LaRocque). With E. J. Keeps, he coauthored a chapter in the 1998 book *Moving from Training to Performance: A Practical Guidebook*, edited by D. Robinson and J. Robinson. Stolovitch has also produced numerous games, simulations, and other interactive resources for addressing personnel selection, proficiency maintenance, and training needs. He is former editor of the *Performance Improvement Journal* and is now a contributing editor of that journal and of the *Performance Improvement Quarterly*.

Stolovitch retired in 1997 as full professor and program head of Instructional Systems Technology at the Université de Montréal, Quebec. He was a distinguished visiting scholar at the University of Southern California's School of Education in 1989–1990 and 1996–1997 and is currently a clinical professor of Human Performance Technology at that institution.

Harold Stolovitch is a frequent presenter and keynote speaker at major conferences on human performance and instructional technology throughout the world. He is past president of the International Society for Performance Improvement (ISPI) and has received numerous academic and professional awards and honors, among them ISPI's Member for Life designation.

ERICA J. KEEPS is executive vice president of Harold D. Stolovitch & Associates Ltd., where she also serves as a principal consultant and as chief operating and financial officer. She received her B.A. degree (1968) in sociology from the University of Michigan and her M.Ed. degree (1977) in educational psychology from Wayne State University.

Keeps has been a consultant to business and industry, manager of corporate training at J. L. Hudson Co., and training administration manager at Allied Supermarkets. In 1978 she founded Performance Strategies, Inc., a Human Performance Technology consulting firm. For more than thirty years she has been a practitioner of Instructional Technology and Human Performance Technology.

Keeps has a number of publications to her credit, including articles in *Performance Improvement Journal,* the *Performance Improvement Quarterly, Journal of Organizational Behavior Management,* and *Human Resource Development Quarterly.* She has also designed and supervised the development of numerous instructional materials and diverse systems for improving human performance, and she has provided staff development for training managers, instructional designers, human performance engineers, and consultants in addition to managing a variety of large-scale projects and conferences.

Keeps is a former member of ISPI's executive board and is past president of the Michigan chapter of ISPI. Among her numerous professional honors are ISPI's 1993 Distinguished Service Award and honorary life memberships in the Detroit and Montreal chapters of ISPI.

Stolovitch and Keeps were the editors of the first edition of the *Handbook of Human Performance Technology: A Comprehensive Guide for Analyzing and Solving Performance Problems in Organizations* (1992).

THE CONTRIBUTORS

ROGER M. ADDISON is a performance architect, a faculty member of the ISPI Institute, and a past president of ISPI. He received his B.S. degree (1970) in psychology from Eastern New Mexico University and his M.Ed. (1975) and Ed.D. (1978) degrees in educational psychology from Baylor University. His experience with performance improvement systems has included work as a contractor and consultant in organizational culture change, performance analysis, program design, implementation, evaluation, and continuous improvement. He was named ISPI's Member of the Year in 1987 and in 1998 received ISPIs highest award, Life Member. In 1989 he also received ISPI's Outstanding Product Award.

CARL V. BINDER, founder of two existing Human Performance Technology consulting firms, is a frequent writer and speaker on instructional effectiveness and performance improvement. He has worked to commercialize the fruits of basic research for more than twenty-five years and currently consults with Fortune 500 corporations and educational agencies while being involved with several entrepreneurial ventures. He studied with B. F. Skinner while a graduate student at Harvard University and conducted seminal research during the 1970s on behavioral fluency. Binder invented the Product Knowledge Architecture, a domain-specific content framework for knowledge management in sales and marketing organizations.

DALE C. BRANDENBURG, research professor and director of workplace education at Wayne State University, currently manages two multimillion dollar projects in workplace education, one funded by the U.S. Department of Education and one as part of Detroit's Empowerment Zone. He received his B.S. degree (1966) in mathematics and his M.A. degree (1968) in behavioral psychology, both from Michigan State University, and his Ph.D. degree (1972) in educational measurement and statistics from the University of Iowa. He specializes in needs assessment, technical training strategy, and the impacts of technology deployment on workforce issues. Brandenburg has published many works in the human performance and training areas. His most recent book, *The Workplace Literacy Primer* (coauthored with W. J. Rothwell), uses a Human Performance Technology approach to examining and developing literacy interventions.

DALE M. BRETHOWER, a licensed clinical psychologist, is professor of psychology at Western Michigan University. He teaches in a master's program in industrial/organizational psychology and in a doctoral program in applied behavior analysis. He earned an A.B. degree in psychology from the University of Kansas (1958), an A.M. degree in experimental psychology from Harvard University (1961), and a Ph.D. degree in educational psychology from the University of Michigan (1970). Slated to be the 1999–2000 president of ISPI, he has served on ISPI's board of directors. Brethower serves as an editor for the *Performance Improvement Quarterly,* the *Journal of Organizational Behavior Management,* and the *Journal of Applied Behavior Analysis.* He has authored or coauthored ten books and more than fifty published papers. For more than thirty years, Brethower has served as a consultant to more than sixty organizations in the public and private sectors. He received a Lifetime Achievement Award from the Organizational Behavior Management Network of the Association for Behavior Analysis.

J. ROBERT CARLETON is a senior partner and cofounder of Vector Group, Inc., and a past president of the International Board of Standards for Training, Performance, and Instruction. He has served as manager of research and evaluation for Southland Corporation, director of training and organizational development for Alameda County (California), and performance officer for the Bank of America. He has been instrumental in the development of the model, process, and techniques for Cultural Due Diligence as a consideration in corporate mergers and alliances.

RICHARD E. CLARK is professor of educational psychology and technology at the University of Southern California, where he directs doctoral and master's programs in human performance at work. He is also president of Atlantic Training Inc., a corporation that offers university-certified workshops in human performance improvement. He received his B.A. degree (1964) in history and political science from Western Michigan University, his M.A. degree (1964) in mass communication from the University of Pennsylvania, and his Ed.D degree (1970) in instructional systems technology from Indiana University. He is the author of more than one hundred published articles, monographs, and book chapters on training, technology, knowledge work, motivation, and ways to solve human performance problems.

RUTH COLVIN CLARK is an instructional psychologist specializing in cognitive instructional methods applied to design of classroom and multimedia training. Having served as a training manager for five years, she is now president of Clark Training & Consulting. For more than ten years, she has offered award-winning seminars in design of classroom and multimedia training, cognitive methods of instruction, and needs assessment. In addition to work in the design and presentation of seminars, her consulting work involves cognitive task analysis of knowledge workers. Her books include *Developing Technical Training* and *Building Expertise: Cognitive Methods for Training & Performance Improvement*. She was the 1996–1997 president of ISPI, where, in collaboration with the board of directors and many members, she initiated the highly successful Institute for Performance Technology.

WILLIAM C. COSCARELLI is professor of curriculum and instruction, with a specialization in instructional design, at Southern Illinois University, Carbondale. He received his B.S. degree (1972) from Purdue University and his Ph.D. degree (1977) in instructional systems technology from Indiana University. He is coauthor of *The Guided Design Guidebook* (1986, written with G. White) and *Criterion-Referenced Test Development: Technical and Legal Guidelines for Corporate Training and Certification* (1989, coauthored with S. Shrock) and author of the *Manual for the Decision-Making Inventory* (1984). He has served as an editor of the *Performance Improvement Quarterly* and is a past president of ISPI.

PETER J. DEAN is a senior fellow (from 1997 to 2000) in the ethics program of the Wharton School's Department of Legal Studies at the University of Pennsylvania. He is also a tenured associate professor and curriculum editor in the physician executive M.B.A. program at the College of Business, University of Tennessee. Previously, he was assistant professor of management and organization and assistant professor of instructional systems design at Smeal College of Business Administration, Pennsylvania State University. He received his Ph.D. from the University of Iowa in 1986. His industry experience includes employment with Rockwell International Corporation and consulting on management, organization, and performance issues with Fortune 50 companies. He is the editor of the *Performance Improvement Quarterly*.

DIANE DORMANT, adjunct faculty member in the Department of Instructional Systems Technology at Indiana University, is a consultant, a writer, and a teacher. Through Dormant & Associates, Inc., she and her colleagues provide support services for change implementation and offer analysis-and-planning procedures through the Change Mapping Workshop. She received a B.A. degree in English and an M.A. degree in psychology from the University of Houston, as well as a Ph.D. degree in instructional systems technology from Indiana University. She is a past president of ISPI.

PAUL H. ELLIOTT is president of Human Performance Technologies, LLC, of Annapolis, Maryland. Elliott's expertise is in the analysis of human performance, the design of interventions that optimize human performance in support of business goals, and strategies for transitioning from training to performance models. He assists organizations in performance analysis, instructional design, product and process launch support, the design of advanced training systems, and the design and implementation of integrated performance interventions. He received his B.A. degree (1970) from Rutgers University, his M.S. degree (1972) in instructional technology from Syracuse University, and his Ph.D. degree (1975) in educational psychology from the University of Illinois. In 1996 he served as executive in residence for ASTD, where his focus was on the paradigm shift from training to performance.

FRED ESTES is an education and development program manager for the Hewlett-Packard Company and an adjunct professor in the performance technology program at the University of Southern California. In addition to teaching and managing educational programs, he has worked in expert systems software product design and development and has owned his own performance consulting company. His research interests are in the development of expertise, cognitive task analysis, learning, and performance improvement. He has recently published works (coauthored with Richard E. Clark) about cognitive task analysis and the development of technology. He received his B.A. degree (1972) in English from Hamilton College, his M.A.T. degree (1974) in English teaching from Colgate University, his M.A. degree (1979) in educational administration and policy analysis from Stanford University, and his Ed.D. degree (1996) from the University of Southern California.

PATRICIA S. EYRES is a California attorney with extensive civil litigation experience. As president of Litigation Management & Training Services, Inc., she consults with business owners and government agencies on timely legal issues affecting the workplace. In the variety of training programs she conducts to sensitize managers and human performance technologists to legal liabilities arising in the workplace, she presents methods for preventing costly lawsuits and minimizing disruption from unavoidable claims. She received her B.A. degree (1974) in political science from Stanford University and her J.D. degree (1977) from Loyola University School of Law, Los Angeles.

WELLESLEY R. (ROB) FOSHAY is vice president for instructional design and cognitive learning at TRO Learning, Inc., makers of PLATO, a computer-based resource. In his twenty-five years of being active in ISPI, Foshay has served a term on ISPI's board of directors and in 1995 received ISPI's Distinguished Service Award. He is a frequent presenter at ISPI conferences, has contributed chapters to ISPI books on performance technology, and has published frequently in its journals. He was a founding member of the International Board of Standards for Training, Performance, and Instruction and a coauthor of the Instructional Designer Competencies. In addition to these organizational affiliations, Foshay has served on many national and local committees and task forces. He received his doctorate in instructional design from Indiana University. He has contributed more than forty articles to research journals and books on a wide variety of topics in training and education and currently serves on the editorial boards of two research journals.

JAMES FULLER is the principal consultant for Redwood Mountain Consulting. He is responsible for assisting client organizations with the strategic implementation of performance consulting. Previously, he was director of performance technology at Hewlett-Packard, where he worked for eighteen years. Fuller created Hewlett-Packard's performance consulting group, led the development of performance technology practices, and developed the company's performance improvement consultants. He held management positions in R&D, manufacturing, marketing, sales, support, and education. Fuller received his M.S. degree in instructional and performance technology from Boise State University and is currently pursuing an Ed.D. degree in performance technology at the University of Southern California. He is the author of *Managing Performance Improvement Projects* and *From Training to Performance Improvement*.

DIANE M. GAYESKI is a founding partner of OmniCom Associates in Ithaca, New York, and is a professor at the Roy H. Park School of Communications at Ithaca College. Since 1975, she has been involved in R&D, consulting, teaching, and writing about new design and management models and technologies for communication and performance improvement. She earned a Ph.D. degree (1979) in educational technology from the University of Maryland. Gayeski has written eight books and numerous articles, has led more than two hundred consulting and research projects, and is a frequent presenter at conferences and executive briefings.

GEORGE L. GEIS was professor emeritus of higher education at the Ontario Institute for Studies in Education, University of Toronto. For more than forty years, he taught and spoke about Human Performance Technology, carrying out research and publishing articles in the field. The author of more than one hundred articles and book chapters, he consulted widely with business and not-for-profit organizations. He held several offices in ISPI, received ISPI's Distinguished Service Award, and was an Honorary ISPI Member for Life. George Geis passed away as this book was going to press.

THOMAS F. GILBERT was president of the Performance Engineering Group, a company he founded in 1978. He received both his B.S. degree (1947) and his M.S. degree (1948) in psychology from the University of South Carolina and his Ph.D. degree (1951) in psychology from the University of Tennessee. He taught psychology from 1951 to 1961 at Emory University, the University of Georgia, Harvard University, and the University of Alabama. As a resident consultant at Bell Laboratories in 1956, he introduced the concept and term *programmed instruction*. He was the founder of TOR Education (1961) and Praxis Corporation (1964) and the author of many papers and books, including *Human Competence,* which was selected Management Book of the Year by the U.S. Civil Service Commission. He was a National Science Foundation Postdoctoral Fellow (1956) and was the first Honorary ISPI Member for Life (1962). He was also a recipient of the Association of Behavior Analysis Lifetime Achievement Award and of ISPI's Distinguished Professional Achievement Award.

MICHAEL GREER, a consultant and administrator of workshops in project management, is the author of *The Project Manager's Partner* (1966), as well as related courseware and mentoring guidelines. Greer also wrote *ID Project Management: Tools and Techniques for Instructional Designers and Developers* (1992). For many years, Greer managed teams of contractors as they worked side by side with new product developers to create training and performance improvement systems for major corporations. In his role as consultant and project management (PM) workshop administrator, Greer has helped many organizations redesign their PM practices. His primary mission is to demystify PM and make it accessible to new and part-time project managers. In recent years, he has provided PM-related tools, articles, and links to Web sites through his own Web site, "Michael Greer's Project Management Resources" *(http://MichaelGreer.home.mindspring.com).*

CAROL HAIG is the founder of Carol Haig & Associates, a performance improvement consultancy based in northern California. With more than twenty-five years of experience working in corporations, Haig is a skilled project manager who has designed and developed materials and programs that measurably affect business results. She received her B.S. degree (1968) in secondary English education from the State University College of New York at Plattsburgh and her M.S. degree (1971), also in secondary English education, from the State University College of New York at Buffalo.

DEBRA S. HANEY is president of Performance Knowledge, Inc., a consulting organization specializing in knowledge management, performance technology, and training. Her company works with Fortune 500 companies. Her recent work has been in the cultural, organizational, strategic, and leadership factors involved in knowledge management. She received a B.S.B.A. degree in marketing and a B.F.A. degree in visual design (1986) from Northern Arizona University and her M.S. degree (1993) in instructional systems technology from Indiana University. She is currently a doctoral candidate at Indiana University.

CATHLEEN SMITH HUTCHISON is managing partner of Metamorphosis Consulting Group, a full-service change management consulting network. She has more than twenty years of experience in organizational development, instructional design and development, and Human Performance Technology. She specializes in managing corporate change, including such change components as culture change, reengineering, team building, coaching, and strategic planning. Hutchison has consulted in North America, Europe, Africa, and the Middle East, working with all levels of organizations in a variety of industries. She has published numerous articles and coauthored the first and second volumes of *Instructor Competencies: The Standards.* She is a longtime member of ISPI and a past vice president, as well as a founding director of the International Board of Standards for Training, Performance, and Instruction.

STEPHANIE F. JACKSON is a principal of Vanguard Consulting, Inc. Previously, she was manager of a custom training and development group for the Forum Corporation, vice president of Operants, Inc., and consultant with Harless Performance Guild. She has designed, developed, and managed performance improvement projects in a wide range of settings, working with such varied groups as physicians, upper-level managers, engineers, plant workers, salespeople, and prison inmates. She received her B.A. degree in English (1960) from Cornell University and her M.A. degree (1964) from Western State College. She is a past president of ISPI and has been awarded life membership in the society.

RONALD L. JACOBS is professor and section head of workforce education and lifelong learning at Ohio State University. He received his B.F.A degree (1973) in film arts and English from Ohio University, his M.S. degree (1975) in educational technology from the University of Toledo, and his Ph.D. degree (1980) in instructional systems technology from Indiana University. He is engaged in research and practice on structured on-the-job training and employee development, with an emphasis on the financial impacts of these interventions.

HOWARD K. KALMAN is a Ph.D. candidate in instructional systems technology at Indiana University. His specialization includes strategic alignment and transformation of the training function and needs and task analysis. He has more than eight years of experience in designing, developing, and managing technical training programs for Fortune 500 firms. He received his B.S. degree (1980) in communications from Ohio University and his M.S. degree (1986) in instructional systems technology from Indiana University.

ROGER KAUFMAN is professor and director of the Office for Needs Assessment and Planning at Florida State University. He is also research professor of engineering management at Old Dominion University. Kaufman has previously held senior positions in the private and public sector and consults with major organizations worldwide. He earned his Ph.D. at New York University and is a fellow of the American Psychological Association, a fellow of the American Academy of School Psychology, and diplomat of the American Board of Professional Psychology. He has published thirty-three books and 178 articles in Human Performance Technology and related fields. A past president of ISPI, Kaufman has been awarded ISPI's highest honor, Member for Life, and is also a recipient of the Thomas F. Gilbert Professional Achievement Award.

LYNN KEARNY is a human performance consultant specializing in improving human performance through work system analysis and development. An award-winning instructional designer, she has developed training programs, job aids, feedback systems, and other performance system enhancements for private and public institutions for more than twenty years. Her specialties include facilitation and graphic recording for visioning, strategic planning groups and problem-solving groups, and visual communications. For six years she has been collaborating with Phyl Smith to build Human Performance Technology practitioners' awareness of workplace design as a powerful performance system intervention. Her three published books are on visual communication, facilitation, and workplace design.

JOHN M. KELLER is professor of instructional systems and educational psychology at Florida State University. He earned his Ph.D. degree in instructional systems design and organizational behavior at Indiana University. Since then, he has amassed more than twenty years of experience working with education, government, and corporate organizations in the United States and abroad on problems in the area of performance improvement and training. He has made major contributions to the development methods for motivational design of instruction and measures of learner motivation. He is perhaps best known as the creator of the ARCS model of motivational design. He has contributed to the design of performance improvement and systematic training design processes for several major corporations and government agencies, including Citibank, IBM, Samsung, and the Federal Aviation Administration.

FRANCES N. KEMMERER is assistant professor of educational administration and policy studies and institutional coordinator for the USAID-funded Improving the Efficiency of Educational Systems Project at the State University of New York, Albany. Her special fields are educational finance and the economics of education. She received her B.A. degree (1963) in religion and her M.A.T. degree (1968) in philosophy from Manhattanville College, as well as her Ph.D. degree (1981) in education from the University of Chicago. She has published the results of her domestic and international research in numerous government reports and journal articles.

Miki M. Lane is a senior partner in MVM: The Communications Group, a consulting firm providing performance improvement solutions to businesses, industries, governments, and nonprofit organizations throughout North America and abroad. Prior to becoming a full-time consultant, he was an assistant professor and director of the Educational Media Center at McGill University. He is currently an adjunct professor at that university. He earned his A.B. degree (1967) in paleontology at the University of California at Berkeley and both his M.A. degree (1971) in instructional product development and his Ph.D. (1977) degree in education at the University of California at Los Angeles. He has held numerous positions in ISPI and is a frequent presenter at the society's annual conferences.

Danny G. Langdon is an expert in work systems, instructional design, and performance improvement systems. He is principal consultant of his own firm, Performance International, in Santa Monica, California. The firm specializes in the Language of Work approach to business improvement through job modeling, process mapping, work group alignment, and reengineering. He is the author of six books in the field of instructional and performance technology, ten book chapters, and many articles. He is a past president of ISPI and has received three international awards from ISPI for innovative contributions to the field of performance technology. Among other positions over the past thirty years, Langdon has been the director of corporate training for the Morrison Knudsen corporation and director of performance improvement for International Technology.

Seth N. Leibler is president and CEO of the Center for Effective Performance, an Atlanta-based company that supports organizations throughout the world in engineering job performance to meet management's standards. He has been in the business of improving human performance for thirty years, as both an executive within organizations and a consultant. For eight years, Leibler managed the Center for Professional Development and Training at the Centers for Disease Control. He has a doctorate in educational psychology and is coauthor (with A. Parkman) of a chapter on personnel selection that was published in the *Guidebook for Performance Improvement* and in *Introduction to Performance Technology*. He has also published extensively on different aspects of performance technology, especially in *Workforce Training News,* and he is a contributing editor to *Corporate University Review.* Leibler is a past president of ISPI.

Ogden R. Lindsley, professor emeritus at Kansas University, is founder and president of Behavior Research Company, which has been providing performance tracking and change charting materials and systems to schools and corporations since 1960. He earned his Ph.D. degree (1957) in psychology at Harvard University under B. F. Skinner's direction. He founded the first human operant laboratory, coined the term *behavior therapy,* and developed Precision Teaching and Standard Change Charting. He is a past president of the Association for Behavior Analysis and in 1998 received ISPI's Thomas F. Gilbert Distinguished Professional Achievement Award.

CLAUDE S. LINEBERRY is cofounder and senior partner of Vector Group, Inc., where he consults with a number of global companies around the world on their organizational effectiveness. He received his B.A. degree (1962) from the University of Alabama and his M.A. degree (1968) in psychology from the University of Connecticut. A past president of ISPI, he received the organization's Honorary Member for Life award in 1997.

ROBERT F. MAGER is president of Mager Associates, Inc., a firm in Carefree, Arizona, that offers services ranging from performance problem solving to instructional development and implementation. He received both his B.A. degree (1948) and his M.A. degree (1950) in experimental psychology from Ohio University and his Ph.D. degree (1954) in experimental psychology from the State University of Iowa. He is the author of nine books, of which six (one coauthored) are widely used and known as the Mager Six-Pack. In addition to books and papers, he has produced films and workshops on aspects of Human Performance Technology.

LESLIE MOLLER is an assistant professor of instructional systems at Pennsylvania State University. Previously, Moller worked for more than fifteen years as a corporate and consulting instructional designer. He received his Ph.D. degree (1933) in instructional research and development from Purdue University. He is a former associate editor of *Performance & Instruction* and is currently a contributing editor of the *Performance Improvement Quarterly.*

MARGO MURRAY is president and chief operating officer of MMHA, The Managers' Mentors, Inc., an international consulting firm founded in 1974. She earned a B.S. degree (1963) at Sacramento State College and an M.B.A. degree (1977) at John F. Kennedy University. Murray was elected to membership in Beta Gamma Sigma, National Honor Society in Business. She has a unique combination of experience in line and staff management, academic work in business and behavioral sciences, and expertise in structuring and managing human performance systems. Her innovations include application of a criterion-referenced approach to management skill development and creation of a facilitated mentoring process. She is the author of *Beyond the Myths and Magic of Mentoring: How to Facilitate an Effective Mentoring Program,* which includes twenty years of research and client experiences with her Facilitated Mentoring Model. Her custom-designed programs and published articles have won professional awards and White House recognition for excellence.

ANN W. PARKMAN is cofounder, executive vice president, and managing partner of the Center for Effective Performance. She has more than twenty years of experience working with private and public organizations in improving human performance. Her published writings include chapters in the *Guidebook for Performance Improvement, Introduction to Performance Technology,* and *Getting Results: Case Studies in Performance Improvement,* as well as articles in *Workforce Training News.* She is also a contributing editor to *Corporate University Review.* During the six years in which she was director of the Instructional System Division of the Centers for Disease Control, the division was selected four times by ISPI as Outstanding Training Organization and received six awards for the quality of its work. Parkman is the 1998–1999 president of ISPI and is a past president of the Atlanta chapter of ISPI.

MICHAEL J. PETERS is president of MJP & Associates, Inc., and a senior associate at Harold D. Stolovitch Associates Ltd. Peters received his B.A. degree (1974) in education from the University of Michigan and his master's degree (1979) in instructional design from Wayne State University. In his twenty-two years in the education and training field, he has been a teacher, instructional designer, developer, project manager and performance technology consultant. He specializes in analysis of human performance problems and the design of instructional systems. Peters has applied performance technology principles to a wide range of industries and business functions.

ESTHER SAFIR POWERS is president and CEO of E. Powers & Associates, an Atlanta-based consulting firm that helps people lead, energize, and grow their organizations. She has a varied and extensive background that includes more than twenty-five years of experience in both education and industry. She received her B.A. degree (1969) in music from McGill University and both her M.A. degree (1982) in education and her Ph.D. degree (1985) in instructional technology from Georgia State University. She is a past president of ISPI.

DANA GAINES ROBINSON is president of Partners in Change, Inc., a consulting firm that assists human resources and human resources development functions in transitioning from a traditional focus to a function that partners with management to change performance. She has a bachelor's degree in sociology from the University of California at Berkeley and a master's degree in psychoeducational process from Temple University. With J. Robinson, she is coauthor of *Training for Impact: How to Link Training to Business Needs and Measure the Results, Performance Consulting: Moving Beyond Training* (recipient of the 1996 Society for Human Resource Management Book Award), and *Moving from Training to Performance: A Practical Guidebook.*

JAMES C. ROBINSON is chairman of Partners in Change, Inc., a consulting firm that assists human resources and human resources development functions in transitioning from a traditional focus to a function that partners with management to change performance. He has a master's degree in adult education from Syracuse University and another master's degree from the University of Wisconsin. With D. Robinson, he is coauthor of *Training for Impact: How to Link Training to Business Needs and Measure the Results, Performance Consulting: Moving Beyond Training* (recipient of the 1996 Society for Human Resource Management Book Award), and *Moving from Training to Performance: A Practical Guidebook.*

DANIEL RODRIGUE is a marketing specialist and performance technologist. He has worked for IBM Canada Ltd. in different marketing positions for more than fifteen years and has served as a mathematics teacher in the public education system and as a human performance consultant in the railroad industry. He received his B.Ed. degree (1974) from McGill University and his M.Ed. degree (1994) from the Université de Montréal.

ALICIA M. ROJAS is president of Rojas International, a consulting firm specializing in quality improvement, strategic planning, needs assessment, and multicultural issues in Human Performance Technology. She has consulted for business and industry, education, government, and international organizations in the United States, Latin America, the Caribbean, and Africa. She has authored several articles and books and frequently presents papers, seminars, and workshops at professional conferences and meetings. Rojas earned her Ph.D. degree (1984) from Florida State University. She is an active member of ISPI, where she served as director of the 1996–1997 and 1997–1998 boards and participated in several committees.

MARC J. ROSENBERG is a senior consultant with the OmniTech Consulting Group, Inc., a custom marketing, management, and corporate learning consulting firm serving Fortune 1000 and other companies worldwide. Rosenberg specializes in corporate learning consulting, including strategy development, E&T/business alignment, needs assessment, performance improvement, evaluation and curriculum design, knowledge management, and technologies for multimedia, Internet, intranet, and performance support. He has earned degrees in marketing communications and educational communications, in addition to a Ph.D. degree (1977) in instructional design from Kent State University. While at AT&T, he developed the company's education and training strategy and directed major corporate initiatives. A founding member of the editorial board of the *Performance Improvement Quarterly,* he has authored more than thirty articles in the field. He is a past president of ISPI.

ALLISON ROSSETT, professor of educational technology at San Diego State University, is a consultant in performance and training systems. A graduate of the

University of Massachusetts, she is the author of *Training Needs Assessment, A Handbook of Job Aids,* and *First Things Fast: A Handbook for Performance Analysis,* two of which won awards. Rossett has presented keynote speeches in the United States and abroad.

GEARY A. RUMMLER is vice chairman of the Rummler-Brache Group, a research and consulting firm specializing in the design and development of performance systems for business and government in the United States and abroad. He received his B.B.A. degree (1969), his M.B.A. degree (1960), and his Ph.D. degree (1970) in education from the University of Michigan. He is coauthor of *Training: Handbook for Professionals* (1988, with G. S. Odiorne) and *Improving Performance: Managing the White Space on the Organization Chart* (1990, with A. P. Brache). He has published a variety of books and articles that have appeared in numerous professional and management journals and handbooks. In 1986 he became the seventh inductee into the HRD Hall of Fame.

NICK RUSHBY has worked in technology-based learning since 1971. At present, he develops training for IT systems, reviews training materials and training strategies, and uses mobile solutions for assessing competence in the workplace and for delivering performance support systems. His current research interests are in virtual organizations for learning. The author and editor of a number of books and papers on technology-based training, he currently edits the *British Journal of Educational Technology.*

THOMAS M. SCHWEN is chair of the Indiana University instructional systems technology department and is a Human Performance Technology consultant for several Fortune 500 firms. He has managed millon-dollar contracts for a wide range of projects, working for both educational and business organizations. For twenty-three years Schwen was associate dean for learning resources at Indiana University. He received his B.S. degree (1964) in history and English from Mankato State University and his Ed.D. degree (1970) in instructional systems technology from Indiana University.

SHARON A. SHROCK is professor of instructional development and technology at Southern Illinois University at Carbondale, where she teaches graduate courses in evaluation and advanced research methods and coordinates graduate programs in instructional design and technology. She consults with a number of global corporations in developing criterion-referenced assessment systems. She received both her B.S. degree (1971) in education and economics and her Ph.D. degree (1979) in instructional systems technology from Indiana University. She is coauthor (with W. Coscarelli) of *Criterion-Referenced Test Development: Technical and Legal Guidelines for Corporate Training and Certification* and has served as a senior adviser to ISPI.

DARRYL L. SINK is president of Darryl L. Sink & Associates, Inc., a firm in Monterey, California, specializing in Human Performance Technology consulting and custom training development. His firm was twice awarded ISPI's Outstanding Instructional Product of the Year award. He has personally completed more than 350 projects in his career. Sink received his B.S. degree in education and his M.S. and Ed.D degrees in instructional systems technology from Indiana University. He served as ISPI's vice president for finance from 1993 to 1995 and received ISPI's Professional Service Award in 1997.

PHYL SMITH is founder of Working Spaces, San Francisco, a consulting firm specializing in the use of participatory behavior-based design to enhance human performance. Her firm has designed more than one hundred corporate, academic, and manufacturing projects. Advocating cross-discipline responsibility, she collaborated with L. Kearny in writing *Creating Workplaces Where People Can Think* (1994). The book aims to educate human resource professionals about work environment interferences with performance. She is a frequent conference presenter and consults with companies on using their workplace to support their reorganization plans. She chairs the Work Environments Section of the Environmental Design Research Association. Smith has a B.S. degree from the University of Texas.

DEAN R. SPITZER is senior performance consultant with IBM Corporation. A pioneer in the field of Human Performance Technology, he has had leadership positions in business, government, and academia. He received his B.A. degree (1970) from Antioch College, his M.A. degree (1972) from Northwestern University, and his Ph.D. degree (1974) from the University of Southern California. Spitzer has authored more than 130 publications, including *Super Motivation: A Blueprint for Energizing Your Organization From Top to Bottom,* which received the 1996 Outstanding Communication Award from ISPI. He is a contributing editor of *Educational Technology* and has served as associate editor and contributing editor of *Performance & Instruction.*

DEBORAH L. STONE, president of DLS Group, Inc., completed her graduate work in instructional technology at San Francisco State University and serves on the advisory board of the University of Colorado's Graduate Division of Instructional Technology. She has received seventeen professional awards for her work in instructional design, technology-based training, and performance support systems. A frequently published author and international presenter, she was ISPI's 1991–1993 vice president for technology applications.

RICHARD A. SWANSON is professor and director of the Human Resource Development Research Center at the University of Minnesota and senior partner of Swanson & Associates, Inc. He has consulted extensively with organizations in the United States and abroad. He received his B.A. degree (1964) and M.A. degree (1965) from the College of New Jersey and his Ed.D. degree (1968) from the University of Illinois. His book *Analysis for Improving Performance* received awards from ISPI and the Society for Human Resource Management. Swanson has more than two hundred publications on the subjects of performance and the development of human resources. His most recent book is *Results: How to Evaluate Performance, Learning, and Perceptions in Organizations.* He has served as editor of the *Performance Improvement Journal,* was the founding editor of *Human Resource Development Quarterly,* and has served as president of the Academy of Human Resource Development.

SIVASAILAM ("THIAGI") THIAGARAJAN is president of Workshops by Thiagi, a firm in Bloomington, Indiana, specializing in the design and delivery of training workshops. He is an adjunct professor of instructional systems technology at Indiana University and vice president of the Institute for International Research, Inc. He received his B.S. degree (1960) in physics from the University of Madras and his Ph.D. degree (1971) in instructional systems technology from Indiana University. He is the author of twelve books and more than 150 articles on different aspects of Human Performance Technology.

DONALD T. TOSTI is a principal of Vanguard Consulting, Inc., which specializes in the application of Human Performance Technology to large-scale organizational change and cultural alignment. His most recent efforts have focused on customer retention and the alignment of organizational behavior with a company's brand or with its promise to its customers. He received his B.S. degree in engineering and his M.S. and Ph.D. degrees in psychology from the University of New Mexico. He has authored or coauthored many publications in the areas of leadership, management, and organizational and behavioral change and is a frequent presenter at professional society meetings. He has served ISPI as treasurer and as vice president for research and is a Member for Life of the society.

JESÚS VÁZQUEZ-ABAD is associate professor of science education at the Université de Montréal. He is also a principal investigator in the Canadian Government's TeleLearning Network of Centres of Excellence, where he works on developing ID principles for distance collaborative science learning laboratories. He has been a faculty member at the Universidad Nacional Autónoma de México (UNAM) and at Concordia University. He received his B.Sc. degree (1978) in physics from UNAM, his M.A. degree (1980) in educational technology from Concordia University, and his Ph.D. degree (1987) in educational technology from the Université de Montréal.

STEVEN W. VILLACHICA is a senior instructional designer for DLS Group, Inc., and specializes in creating performance support systems. He is currently completing his doctoral work in educational technology at the University of Northern Colorado. Villachica has been a member of ISPI for the last nine years and has twice won the society's Outstanding Systematic Approach award. He has also served ISPI as a 1998 co-CrackerBarrel Chair, as a regional consultant, and as a member of the nominations committee. In addition, he is a former chapter president and a former vice president of technology for the Front Range Chapter.

ELLEN D. WAGNER is vice president for consulting services at Informania, Inc., an international performance improvement consulting firm based in San Francisco. She supervises all design and development services involved in Informania's customized performance systems developments. Wagner also directs Informania's assessment, testing, and evaluation operations. She earned her B.A. and M.S. degrees from the University of Wisconsin–Madison and her Ph.D. degree in educational psychology from the University of Colorado–Boulder. Before joining Informania, she served as chair of the educational technology department and director of the Western Institute for Distance Education at the University of Northern Colorado. She is also a former project director with the Western Cooperative for Educational Telecommunications, Western Interstate Commission for Higher Education.

GINA WALKER, regional director for Harold D. Stolovitch & Associates Ltd and president-elect of the Montreal chapter of ISPI, has also taught at Concordia University, where she served as director of the M.A. program in educational technology. She worked for fourteen years in human resource management at the Royal Bank of Canada, where she received a special award for her role in helping the organization achieve a major culture shift. Walker received her B.A. degree (1974) in psychology from Lafayette College and her M.A. (1977) and Ph.D. (1994) degrees in educational technology from Concordia University. She has presented at professional conferences, served on professional task forces, and authored a number of publications.

LAURA R. WINER is a research associate at the Université de Montréal, working on a project for the Canadian Government's TeleLearning Network of Centres of Excellence. The intention of the project is to develop instructional design principles for collaborative distance education and training. She is involved in numerous research and consulting projects related to implementing new technologies in education and training. She received her B.A. degree (1978) in English literature and her M.A. (1981) and Ph.D. (1986) degrees in educational technology from Concordia University.

STEPHEN L. YELON is professor of educational psychology at Michigan State University, where he teaches master's and doctoral students about instructional design. He consults with educators and trainers about all aspects of instructional design and conducts research on the nature of transfer. A frequent contributor to ISPI journals, he is the author of *Powerful Principles of Instruction* (1996).

DAWN E. ZINTEL is president of The Training Alliance, Inc., which provides performance technology expertise primarily to high-tech companies in California. Her workshop "Going Global: Designing Training for Multicultural Learners" has been offered at several ISPI international conferences and is based on a series of articles that were researched and written for ISPI publications. She received her B.A. degree (1970) in geography and her M.A. degree (1981) in educational technology from Concordia University and has Class I and II diplomas in education from McGill University.

PRESTON ZUCKERMAN is founder and president of Learning-Edge, a company that produces technology-delivered instruction. Learning-Edge provides state-of-the-art multimedia/Internet solutions to address each client's particular needs. Founded in 1988, the company has been a leader in the training and communication fields for many years. Learning-Edge has received several prestigious awards. In sixteen years directing the training and publications departments at Four-Phase Systems (now known as Motorola Computer Group) and at ITT Corporation, Zuckerman successfully introduced criterion-referenced, self-paced, and media-based instruction into both organizations.

International Society for Performance Improvement

The International Society for Performance Improvement (ISPI) is the leading international association dedicated to improving productivity and performance in the workplace. Founded in 1962, ISPI represents more than ten thousand members throughout the United States, Canada, and in nearly forty other countries. Monthly meetings of over sixty different chapters provide professional development, services, and information exchange.

ISPI's vision is to be the preferred source of information, education, and advocacy for improving workplace performance through the application of Human Performance Technology (HPT)—a process of selection, analysis, design, development, implementation, and evaluation of programs to most cost-effectively influence human behavior and accomplishment. The Society's mission is to improve the performance of organizations in systematic and reproducible ways through the application of HPT. Assembling an annual conference and other educational events, producing several periodicals, and publishing dozens of books and resources, including the *Handbook for Human Performance Technology,* are some of the ways ISPI works toward achieving this mission.

ISPI members include performance technologists, training directors, human resource managers, instructional designers, human factors practitioners, and organizational development consultants. ISPI members work in more than three thousand organizations, including Fortune 500 companies, governmental agencies, military, academic institutions, consulting businesses, and other organizations.

ISPI makes a difference to people by helping them grow into skilled professionals who use integrated and systematic approaches to add value to their organizations and to the profession. Whether designing training programs, building selection or incentive systems, assisting organizations in their own redesign, or performing myriad other interventions, ISPI members produce results.

ISPI makes a difference to organizations by increasing professional competence and confidence. ISPI members help organizations anticipate opportunities and challenges and develop powerful solutions that contribute to productivity and satisfaction.

ISPI makes a difference to the field of performance technology by expanding the boundaries of what the industry knows about defining, teaching, supporting, and maintaining skilled human performance. By supporting research and development, providing information on a variety of technologies, and facilitating membership interaction, ISPI members use approaches and systems that ensure improved productivity.

For additional information, please contact

ISPI

International Society for Performance Improvement
1300 L Street, N. W., Suite 1250
Washington, D.C. 20005
Telephone: (202)408–7969
Fax: (202)408–7972
Website: www.ispi.org
E-mail: info@ispi.org

NAME INDEX

SUBJECT INDEX